FOURTH EDITION

A HISTORY OF WORLD SOCIETIES

Volume II
Since 1500

John P. McKay

*University of Illinois at
Urbana-Champaign*

Bennett D. Hill

Georgetown University

John Buckler

*University of Illinois at
Urbana-Champaign*

HOUGHTON MIFFLIN COMPANY

Boston   Toronto
Geneva, Illinois   Palo Alto
Princeton, New Jersey

Senior Sponsoring Editor: Patricia A. Coryell
Senior Associate Editor: Jeffrey Greene
Manufacturing Manager: Florence Cadran
Marketing Manager: Clint Crockett

Printed in the U.S.A.
Library of Congress Catalog Card Number: 95-77000
ISBN Student Text: 0-395-75379-1
ISBN Examination Copy: 0-395-76584-6
123456789-VH-99   98 97 96 95

John P. McKay Born in St. Louis, Missouri, John P. McKay received his B.A. from Wesleyan University (1961), his M.A. from the Fletcher School of Law and Diplomacy (1962), and his Ph.D. from the University of California, Berkeley (1968). He began teaching history at the University of Illinois in 1966 and became a professor there in 1976. John won the Herbert Baxter Adams Prize for his book *Pioneers for Profit: Foreign Entrepreneurship and Russian Industrialization, 1885–1913* (1970). He has also written *Tramways and Trolleys: The Rise of Urban Mass Transit in Europe* (1976) and has translated Jules Michelet's *The People* (1973). His research has been supported by fellowships from the Ford Foundation, the Guggenheim Foundation, the National Endowment for the Humanities, and IREX. His articles and reviews have appeared in numerous journals, including *The American Historical Review, Business History Review, The Journal of Economic History,* and *Slavic Review.* He edits *Industrial Development and the Social Fabric: An International Series of Historical Monographs.*

Bennett D. Hill A native of Philadelphia, Bennett D. Hill earned an A.B. at Princeton (1956) and advanced degrees from Harvard (A.M., 1958) and Princeton (Ph.D., 1963). He taught history at the University of Illinois at Urbana, where he was department chairman from 1978 to 1981. He has published *English Cistercian Monasteries and Their Patrons in the Twelfth Century* (1968) and *Church and State in the Middle Ages* (1970); and articles in *Analecta Cisterciensia, The New Catholic Encyclopaedia, The American Benedictine Review,* and *The Dictionary of the Middle Ages.* His reviews have appeared in *The American Historical Review, Speculum, The Historian, The Catholic Historical Review,* and *Library Journal.* He has been a fellow of the American Council of Learned Societies and has served on committees for the National Endowment for the Humanities. Now a Benedictine monk of St. Anselm's Abbey, Washington, D.C., he is also a Visiting Professor at Georgetown University.

John Buckler Born in Louisville, Kentucky, John Buckler received his B.A. (*summa cum laude*) from the University of Louisville in 1967. Harvard University awarded him the Ph.D. in 1973. From 1984 to 1986 he was an Alexander von Humboldt Fellow at the Institut für Alte Geschichte, University of Munich. He has lectured at the Fondation Hardt at the University of Geneva, and has participated in numerous international conferences. He is currently the professor of Greek history at the University of Illinois. In 1980 Harvard University Press published his *The Theban Hegemony, 371–362 B.C.* He has also published *Philip II and the Sacred War* (Leiden 1989), and co-edited *BOIOTIKA: Vorträge vom 5. International Böotien-Kolloquium* (Munich 1989). He has assisted the National Endowment for the Humanities, and reviews articles for journals in the United States and Europe. He has published substantially on Plutarch in *Aufstieg und Niedergang der römischen Welt* (Berlin, New York. 1992). His articles have appeared in journals both here and abroad, including the *American Journal of History, Classical Philology, Rheinisches Museum für Philologie, Classical Quarterly, Wiener Studien, Symbolae Osloenses,* and many others.

Contents in Brief

❊ ❊ ❊ ❊ ❊ ❊ ❊ ❊

Contents

Maps

Timelines/Genealogies

The comparative timeline, *A History of World Societies: A Brief Overview,* begins on page 1232.

Listening to the Past

Preface

A History of World Societies has grown out of our desire to infuse new life into the study of world civilization. We know full well that historians are using imaginative questions and innovative research to open up vast new areas of historical interest and knowledge. We recognize that these advances have dramatically affected economic, intellectual, and, especially, social history, and that new research and fresh interpretations are revitalizing the study of traditional, mainstream political, diplomatic, and religious developments. Despite history's vitality as a discipline, however, it seems to us that both the broad public and the intelligentsia have been losing interest in the past.

It is our conviction, based on considerable experience in introducing large numbers of students to the broad sweep of civilization, that a book reflecting current trends can excite readers and inspire a renewed interest in history and the human experience. Our strategy has been twofold.

First, we have made social history the core element of our work. We not only incorporate recent research by social historians but also seek to re-create the life of ordinary people in appealing human terms. A strong social element seems especially appropriate in a world history, for identification with ordinary people of the past allows today's reader to reach an empathetic understanding of different cultures and civilizations. At the same time we have been mindful of the need to give great economic, political, intellectual, and cultural developments the attention they deserve. We want to give individual students and instructors a balanced, integrated perspective so that they can pursue on their own or in the classroom those themes and questions that they find particularly exciting and significant.

Second, we have made every effort to strike an effective global balance. We are acutely aware of the great drama of our times—the passing of the era of Western dominance and the simultaneous rise of Asian and African peoples in world affairs. Increasingly, the whole world interacts, and to understand that interaction and what it means for today's citizens, we must study the whole world's history. Thus we have adopted a comprehensive yet manageable global perspective. We study all geographical areas and the world's main civilizations, conscious of their separate identities and unique contributions. We also stress the links between civilizations, for it is these links that have been transforming multicentered world history into the complex interactive process of different continents, peoples, and cultures that we see today.

CHANGES IN THE FOURTH EDITION

In preparing the fourth edition, we worked hard to keep *A History of World Societies* up-to-date and to strengthen our distinctive yet balanced approach. Six goals shaped our plan for this new edition.

More Concise Treatment of Western History

To achieve the optimal length, we shortened the text by approximately 10 percent overall. We accomplished this reduction primarily through cuts in Western-oriented material while adding important new information to our non-Western coverage. Thus the proportion of non-Western material has grown, but the overall length of the book has decreased. For this edition, two chapters on Rome were combined into one (Chapter 7), three chapters on medieval Europe were combined into two (Chapters 12 and 13), and three chapters on nineteenth-century Europe were combined into two (Chapters 25 and 26).

Updated Approach to Social History

In a thorough revision of our coverage of social developments we give greater attention to cultural and intellectual life and somewhat less to quantitative and demographic aspects. Increased emphasis on culture and attitudes invigorates our social history core and accurately reflects current scholarship and changing interests within the historical profession. Accordingly, this edition has expanded discussions of religious life, including the spread of Buddhism in ancient India (Chapter 3); popular religion in Mesopotamia (Chapter 1), in classical Greece (Chapter 5), in Aztec and Inca society (Chapter 14), and in revolutionary France (Chapter 23); the evolution of Jewish religion (Chapter 2), of Eastern monasticism (Chapter 8), and of Calvin's Geneva (Chapter 15); and the resurgence of Christianity (Chapter 31) and of Islam (Chapter 34) in the twentieth century.

Consistently greater attention to popular culture includes new sections on the experiences of Jews under Islam and Christianity (Chapter 9); on the cult of the royal mummies in Inca society (Chapter 14); on troubadour poets and recreation in the Middle Ages (Chapters 12 and 13); on community values in eighteenth-century Europe (Chapter 19); on Chinese attitudes toward wealth and consumption (Chapter 22); and on the counterculture in the 1960s (Chapter 33). New material on health and health care features recent research on medieval European practices and early hospitals (Chapter 12), on eighteenth-century practitioners in Europe (Chapter 19) and the Ottoman Empire (Chapter 21), and on declining birthrates in Asia and Latin America (Chapter 36).

Interactions between cultures are also highlighted: the relations between Egyptians and Nubians (Chapter 1), pagans and Christians (Chapter 7), Muslims and Jews (Chapter 9), European educated elites and popular classes (Chapters 18 and 19), Europeans and Africans in the slave trade (Chapter 20), Chinese and foreigners in the eighteenth century (Chapter 22), and rich and poor nations since 1945 (Chapter 36).

We also carefully revised sections on the life of the people to set social developments consistently in their broad historical context.

Incorporation of Recent Scholarship

We carefully revised every chapter to reflect recent scholarship. Because we are committed to a balanced approach, we once again incorporated important new findings on political, economic, and intellectual developments. Revisions of this nature include material on the Babylonian Captivity (Chapter 2), the spread of Buddhism in India (Chapter 3), living patterns in neolithic China (Chapter 4), democratic ideology in Athens and the political background of Plato and Aristotle's thought (Chapter 5), and Roman commerce and frontier relations between Romans and Germans (Chapter 7). Similar revisions in Chapter 8 through 17 incorporate new material on Islamic education in world perspective (Chapter 9), African geography (Chapter 10), the origins of European feudalism (Chapter 12), the Aztec practice of human sacrifice (Chapter 14), the political uses of pornography in early modern Europe (Chapter 15), and Louis XIV's relations with the nobility (Chapter 17).

There is important new material reflecting recent scholarship on the cultural impact of the Enlightenment (Chapters 18 and 19); the Swahili states and transatlantic slave trade (Chapter 20); the institutions of the Mughal state under Akbar (Chapter 21); Chinese foreign policy under the Qing (Chapter 22); banks in continental industrialization and the early labor movement (Chapter 24); the role of class conflict in nineteenth-century domestic politics, imperialism, and the origins of World War I (Chapters 26, 27, and 29); educational reforms and political culture in republican France (Chapter 26); the idea of race in the United States (Chapter 28); Nietzsche and his influence (Chapter 31); the Nazi state and the origins of Italian fascism (Chapter 32); and the growing diversity of life in the Third World (Chapter 35). Recent developments in Europe and the Western Hemisphere (Chapter 33) and in Asia and Africa, especially in China and South Africa (Chapter 34), are examined from an updated post–cold war perspective.

In short, recent research keeps the broad sweep of our history fresh and up-to-date.

Integrated Treatment of Women and Gender

We broadened our treatment of women's history and gender issues and integrated it into the main narrative rather than reserving it for separate sections. This approach reflects current scholarly thinking. Our updated discussion of Hellenistic women is integrated in the central narrative (Chapter 5). Gender roles and attitudes toward divorce are considered in the context of early Islam (Chapter 9). New material on European women in agriculture and commerce during the Middle Ages (Chapters 12 and 13), on gender roles in Aztec society (Chapter 14) and in early European arts and letters (Chapter 16), on women in the Ottoman Empire (Chapter 21), and on Japanese women in agriculture and family relations (Chapter 22) are appropriately positioned. Elite women and peasant women in village communities are reconsidered in the context of the Enlightenment (Chapters 18 and 19) and the French Revolution (Chapter 23). Women in twentieth-century European dictatorships are compared systematically (Chapter 32), and the place of women in Third World economic development and population growth is stressed (Chapter 35).

New "Problems of Historical Interpretation"

The addition of more "problems of historical interpretation" in the third edition was well received, so we increased their number in the fourth. We believe that the problematic element helps students develop the critical-thinking skills that are among the most precious benefits of studying history. New examples of this more open-ended, interpretive approach include the debate over the origins of Rome (Chapter 7), the impact of the Renaissance on the lives of ordinary and elite women (Chapter 15), the motives and legacy of Christopher Columbus (Chapter 16), popular reading habits in eighteenth-century Europe and their significance (Chapter 19), the question of racial identity in the United States and how it developed (Chapter 28), European social tensions and the origins of World War I (Chapter 29), the nature of twentieth-century dictatorships (Chapter 32), the validity of *Third World* as an analytical concept (Chapter 35), and prospects for the United Nations and world government (Chapter 36).

Revised Full-Color Art and Map Programs

Because the past can speak in pictures as well as in words, artwork remains an integral part of our book, and the illustrative component of our work was carefully revised. We added many new illustrations—our art program includes nearly two hundred color reproductions—letting great art and important events come alive. As in earlier editions, all illustrations were carefully selected to complement the text, and all carry captions that enhance their value. The use of full color throughout this edition clarifies the maps and graphs and enriches the textual material. The maps and their captions have been updated.

DISTINCTIVE FEATURES

Distinctive features, both new and revised, will promote historical understanding.

New Primary-Source Chapter Feature

One of our goals is to show how historians sift through and evaluate evidence—to suggest how historians actually work and think. We want to encourage students to think critically and to realize that history is neither a list of cut-and-dried facts nor a senseless jumble of conflicting opinions. To help students come to this realization, at the end of each chapter in the fourth edition we added a two-page passage from a primary source. This important new feature, entitled "Listening to the Past," extends and illuminates a major historical issue considered in the chapter. For example, in Chapter 3, a selection from the *Mahabharta* tells an ancient Indian creation story; and in Chapter 6, a selection from *Plutarch's Lives* recounts the sacrifice of a famous queen for her people. Chapter 12 presents a mind-opening Arab account of the First Crusade, and the German traveler Olearius provides a fascinating and influential picture of the Russian state and society in Chapter 17. A report on discussions with Africans concerning the abolition of the slave trade is found in Chapter 20, and a Jesuit priest's report on a trip to the Mughal court of Akbar is featured in Chapter 21. Writer Stephan Zweig probes the sexuality of young men and women in nineteenth-century Vienna in Chapter 26, and a reporter witnesses the bloody climax to Gandhi's civil disobedience in Chapter 30. A Jewish doctor who survived Auschwitz describes the horror of the Nazi death camps in Chapter 32, and poor rural women in today's Third World tell their stories in Chapter 35.

Each "Listening to the Past" section opens with a problem-setting introduction and closes with "Questions for Analysis" that invite students to evaluate the evidence as historians would. Drawn from writings addressing a variety of social, cultural, political, and intellectual issues, these sources promote active involvement and critical interpretation. Selected for their interest and importance and carefully fitted into their historical context, these sources do indeed allow students to listen to the past and to observe how history has been shaped by individual men and women, some of them great aristocrats, others ordinary folk.

Improved Chapter Features

Distinctive features from earlier editions have been retained but improved. To help guide students toward historical understanding, we again pose specific questions at the beginning of each chapter. These questions are answered in the course of each chapter, and each chapter ends with a concise summary. We re-examined and revised the questions and summaries to maximize their usefulness.

Once again in the narrative itself we quote extensively from a wide variety of primary sources, demonstrating in our use of these quotations how historians evaluate evidence. Thus the examination of primary sources is not only highlighted in the "Listening to the Past" material but is an integral part of the narrative as well. We believe that such extensive quotation from primary sources will help students learn to interpret and think critically.

Each chapter again contains an annotated listing of suggestions for further reading. Brief descriptions of each work will help readers know where to turn to continue thinking and learning about specific topics. These bibliographies have been revised and updated.

Revised Timelines

The chapter timelines that appeared in earlier editions are substantially improved, and the comparative timelines that were dispersed throughout the third edition have been brought together in an ap-

pendix at the end of the book. Comprehensive and easy to locate, this useful timeline will allow students to compare simultaneous political, economic, social, cultural, intellectual, and scientific developments over the centuries.

Flexible Format

World history courses differ widely in chronological structure from one campus to another. To accommodate the various divisions of historical time into intervals that fit a two-quarter, three-quarter, or two-semester period, *A History of World Societies* is published in three versions that embrace the complete work:

- One-volume hardcover edition: *A History of World Societies*
- Two-volume paperback edition: *A History of World Societies*, Volume 1, *To 1715* (Chapters 1–17), and Volume 2, *Since 1500* (Chapters 16–36)
- Three-volume paperback edition: *A History of World Societies*, Volume A, *From Antiquity Through the Middle Ages* (Chapters 1–14), Volume B, *From 1100 Through the French Revolution* (Chapters 13–23), and Volume C, *From the French Revolution to the Present* (Chapters 23–36)

Overlapping chapters in the two-volume and three-volume editions facilitate matching the appropriate volume with the opening and closing dates of a specific course.

ANCILLARIES

Our learning and teaching ancillaries enhance the usefulness of the textbook:

- *Study Guide*
- *Computerized Study Guide*
- *Instructor's Resource Manual*
- *Test Items*
- *Computerized Test Items*
- *Map Transparencies*

The excellent *Study Guide* has been thoroughly revised by Professor James Schmiechen of Central Michigan University. Professor Schmiechen has been a tower of strength ever since he critiqued our initial prospectus, and he has continued to give us many valuable suggestions as well as his warmly appreciated support. His *Study Guide* contains learning objectives, chapter summaries, chapter outlines, review questions, extensive multiple-choice exercises, self-check lists of important concepts and events, and a variety of study aids and suggestions. The fourth edition also retains the study-review exercises on the interpretation of visual sources and major political ideas as well as suggested issues for discussion and essay, chronology reviews, and sections on studying effectively. The sections on studying take the student through reading and studying activities like underlining, summarizing, identifying main points, classifying information according to sequence, and making historical comparisons. To enable both students and instructors to use the *Study Guide* with the greatest possible flexibility, the guide is available in two volumes, with considerable overlapping of chapters. Instructors and students who use only Volumes A and B of the textbook have all the pertinent study materials in a single volume: *Study Guide,* Volume 1 (Chapters 1–23). Those who use only Volumes B and C of the textbook also have all the necessary materials in one volume: *Study Guide*, Volume 2 (Chapters 13–36). The multiple-choice sections of the *Study Guide* are available in a *Computerized Study Guide*, a tutorial version that tells students not only which response is correct but also why each of the other choices is wrong; it also provides the number of the textbook page where each question is discussed. These "rejoinders" to the multiple-choice questions also appear in printed form at the end of the *Study Guide.* The *Computerized Study Guide* is available for IBM® computers.

The *Instructor's Resource Manual*, prepared by Professor John Marshall Carter, contains instructional objectives, annotated chapter outlines, suggestions for lectures and discussion, paper and class activity topics, primary-source exercises, map activities, and lists of audio-visual resources. The accompanying *Test Items*, by Professor Charles Crouch of Georgia Southern University, offer identification, multiple-choice, map, and essay questions for a total of approximately 2,000 test items. These test items are available to adopters in both IBM® and Macintosh versions, both of which include editing capabilities.

In addition, a set of full-color *Map Transparencies* of all the maps in the textbook is available on adoption.

Acknowledgments

It is a pleasure to thank the many instructors who have read and critiqued the manuscript through its development.

Eva Baham
Southern University

Lester Bilsky
University of Arkansas, Little Rock

Kenneth Capalbo
Quincy University

Donald Clark
Trinity University

Frank Coppa
St. John's University

Francis Danquah
Southern University

Gloria-Thomas Emeagwali
Central Connecticut State University

Fuabeh Fonge
North Carolina Agricultural and Technical State University

Bruce Garver
University of Nebraska, Omaha

Ruth Hertzberg
Shippensburg University

Ahmed Ibriham
University of South Carolina

Michelle Scott James
MiraCosta College

Delmarie Klobe
Kapiolani Community College

David Kopf
University of Minnesota

Jim Norris
University of Arkansas, Monticello

Evelyn Rawski
University of Pittsburgh

Edward Reynolds
University of California, San Diego

Cynthia Talbott
University of Northern Arizona

Colonel Steven Wager
United States Military Academy, West Point

Mary Watrous
Washington State University

Colonel James Scott Wheeler
United States Military Academy, West Point

Barbara Woods
South Carolina State University

It is also a pleasure to thank our editors at Houghton Mifflin for their effort and support over many years. To Elizabeth Welch, Senior Basic Book Editor, we owe a special debt of gratitude and admiration. To Jean Woy, Editor-in-Chief for History and Political Science, to Sean Wakely, Senior Sponsoring Editor, and to Jeff Greene, Senior Associate Editor, we express our sincere appreciation. And we thank most warmly Jan Fitter, Leslie Anderson Olney, and Carole Frohlich for their contributions in development, production, and art and photo research.

Many of our colleagues at the University of Illinois continued to provide information and stimulation for our book, often without even knowing it. N. Frederick Nash, Rare Book Librarian, made many helpful suggestions for illustrations, and the World Heritage Museum at the university allowed us complete access to its sizable holdings. James Dengate supplied information on objects from the museum's collection, and Caroline Buckler took many excellent photographs of the museum's objects. Such wide-ranging expertise was a great asset for which we are very appreciative. Bennett Hill wishes to express his sincere appreciation to Ramón de la Fuente for his patience, encouragement, and research assistance in the preparation of the fourth edition.

Each of us has benefited from the generous criticism of his co-authors, although each of us assumes responsibility for what he has written. John Buckler is the author of Chapters 1–7 and 11; Bennett Hill continues the narrative in Chapters 8–10, 12–16, 20–22, and 28; and John McKay is the author of Chapters 17–19, 23–27, and 29–36. Finally, we continue to welcome the many comments and suggestions that have come from our readers, for they have helped us greatly in this ongoing endeavor.

J.P.M.   B.D.H.   J.B.

Introduction

The Origins of Modern World Societies

The origins of modern societies lie in the ancient and medieval past. Scholars trace the roots of world civilizations to the ancient Middle East, India, and China. Geographical factors, especially four great rivers, conditioned the development of those civilizations.

Early Egyptian society relied on the 4,000-mile-long Nile River. To the east, successive civilizations flourished in Mesopotamia, the area between the Tigris and the Euphrates Rivers. The Indus River in northwestern India, which flows about 1,980 miles before reaching the ocean, nourished ancient Indian civilization. In China the Yellow River, 2,700 miles long, facilitated the birth of Chinese civilization. These rivers helped enrich the soil, allowing steadily expanding amounts of land to be cultivated and increasing the production of food. Increased food production led to population growth and wealth, ingredients essential to the evolution of sophisticated social structures. The achievements of each society became the legacies that later cultures absorbed and used.

History, the study of change over time, reveals that each age reinterprets the cultural legacy of its predecessors in an effort to meet its own needs. The modern world exists as the product of all that has gone before.

THE ANCIENT WORLD

The modern world inherited numerous cultural elements from the ancient world. Into the West came the beliefs of the Hebrews (Jewish forebears) in one God and in themselves as a chosen people with whom God had made a covenant. The book known as the Old Testament or Hebrew Bible embodies Hebraic law, history, and culture. Greek architectural, philosophical, and scientific ideas have exercised a profound influence on Western thought. Rome gave the West the Latin language and Roman law. Latin became the instrument of oral and written communication for over a thousand years; Roman concepts of law and government molded Western ideas of political organization. Christianity, the spiritual faith and ecclesiastical organization that derived from the teachings of a Palestinian Jew, Jesus of Nazareth (ca 3 B.C.–A.D. 29), also shaped Western religious, social, and moral values and systems.

The ancient Eastern world witnessed the appearance of religions and philosophies that continue to influence modern societies. In South Asia before 250 B.C., Indians developed ideas about the nature of life and the afterlife that affected all later generations. From India, Buddhism spread to China and other parts of Asia. Hinduism, a collection of religious beliefs that encompasses a sacred division of society, emerged to become the dominant feature of India's cultural heritage. In China mastery of the land and the evolution of a systematic method of agriculture that would support a large population led to a sophisticated intellectual life. The period before A.D. 200 witnessed the birth of three powerful forms of Chinese thought: Confucianism, Daoism (also written as Taoism), and Legalism.

The Hebrews

The Hebrews probably originated in northern Mesopotamia. Nomads who tended flocks of sheep, they were forced by drought to follow their patriarch Abraham into the Nile Delta in Egypt. The Egyptians enslaved them and put them to work on various agricultural and building projects. In the crucial event in early Jewish history, the lawgiver Moses, in response to God's command, led the Hebrews out of Egypt into the promised land (Palestine) in the thirteenth century B.C. At that time, the Hebrews consisted of twelve disunited tribes made up of families. They all believed themselves descendants of a common ancestor, Abraham. The family was their primary social institution, and most families engaged in agricultural or pastoral pursuits. Under the pressure of a series of wars for the control of Palestine, the twelve independent Hebrew tribes were united into a centralized political force under one king. Kings Saul, David, and especially Solomon (ca 965–925 B.C.) built the Hebrew nation with its religious center at Jerusalem, the symbol of Jewish unity.

The Hebrews developed their religious ideas in scriptures, or sacred writings, known as the Old Testament. During their migrations, the Jews had come in contact with many peoples, such as the Mesopotamians and the Egyptians, who had many gods. The Jews, however, were monotheistic: they believed that their God was the one and only God, that he had created all things, that his presence filled the universe, and that he took a strong personal interest in the individual. During the Exodus from Egypt, God had made a covenant with the Jews. He promised to protect them as his chosen people and to give them land. In return, they were to worship only him and to obey the Ten Commandments that he had given Moses. The Ten Commandments constituted an ethical code of be-

havior, forbidding the Jews to steal, lie, murder, and commit adultery. The covenant was to prove a constant force in Jewish life. The Old Testament also contains detailed legal proscriptions, books of history, concepts of social and familial structure, wisdom literature, and prophecies of a messiah to come. Parts of the Old Testament show the Hebraic debt to other cultures. For example, the Book of Proverbs reflects strong Egyptian influences. The Jews developed an emotionally satisfying religion whose ideals shaped not only later faiths, such as Christianity and Islam, but also the modern world.

The Greeks

Ancient Middle Eastern peoples like the Hebrews interpreted the origins, nature, and end of humankind in religious terms. The Greeks brought reason to bear on these issues. In the fifth century B.C., small independent city-states dotted the Greek peninsula. Athens created an especially brilliant culture that greatly influenced Western civilization. Athens developed a magnificent architecture whose grace, beauty, and quiet intensity still speak to humankind. In their comedies and tragedies, the Athenians Aeschylus, Sophocles, and Euripedes were the first playwrights to treat eternal problems of the human condition. Athens also experimented with the political system that we call democracy. All free adult males participated directly in the making of laws and in the government of the city-state, or *polis,* in which they lived. Since a large part of the population—women and slaves—was not allowed to share in the activity of the Assembly, and since aristocrats held most important offices in the polis, we must not confuse Athenian democracy with modern democratic practices. The modern form of democracy, moreover, is indirect rather than direct: citizens express their views and wishes through elected representatives. Nevertheless, in their noble experiment in which the people were the government, and in their view that the state exists for the good of the citizen, Athenians created a powerful political ideal.

Classical Greece in the fifth and fourth centuries B.C. also witnessed an incredible flowering of philosophical ideas. Though not the first people to speculate about the nature of humankind and the universe, the Greeks were first to consider these questions in rational instead of religious terms.

Hippocrates, the "father of medicine," taught that natural means—not magical or religious ones—could be found to fight disease. He based his opinions on observation and experimentation. He also insisted that medicine was a branch of knowledge separate from philosophy. This distinction between natural science and philosophy was supported by the Sophists, who traveled the Greek world teaching young men that human beings were the proper subject for study. They laid great emphasis on logic and the meaning of words and criticized traditional beliefs, religion, and even the law of the polis.

Building on the approach of the Sophists, Socrates (ca 470–399 B.C.) spent his life questioning and investigating. Socrates held that human beings and their environments represent the essential subject for philosophical inquiry. He taught that excellence could be learned and that by seeking excellence through knowledge, human beings could find the highest good and ultimately true happiness. Socrates' pupil Plato (427–347 B.C.) continued his teacher's work. Plato wrote down his own thoughts, which survive in the form of dialogues. He founded a school, the Academy, where he developed the theory that visible, tangible things are unreal and temporary copies of "ideas" or "forms" that are constant and indestructible. In *The Republic,* the first literary description of a utopian society, Plato discusses the nature of justice in the ideal state. In *The Symposium,* he treats the nature and end of love.

Aristotle (384–322 B.C.), Plato's student, continued the philosophical tradition in the next generation. The range of his subjects of investigation is vast. He explores the nature of government in *Politics,* ideas of matter and motion in *Physics* and *Metaphysics,* outer space in *On the Heavens,* conduct in the *Nichomachean Ethics,* and language and literature in *Rhetoric.* In all his works, Aristotle emphasizes the importance of the direct observation of nature; he insists that theory must follow fact. Led by thinkers such as Aristotle, the Greeks originated medicine, science, philosophy, and other branches of knowledge.

These intellectual advances took place against a background of constant warfare. A long and bitter struggle between the cities of Athens and Sparta, the Peloponnesian War (459–404 B.C.), ended in Athens's defeat. Shortly afterward, Sparta, Athens, and Thebes contested for hegemony in Greece, but no single polis was strong enough to dominate the others. Taking advantage of the situation, Philip II (r. 359–336 B.C.) of Macedon, a small kingdom comprising part of modern Greece and Yugoslavia, defeated a combined Theban-Athenian army in 338 B.C. Unable to resolve their domestic quarrels, the Greeks lost their freedom to the Macedonian invader.

In 323 B.C. Philip's son, Alexander of Macedonia, died at the ripe age of thirty-two. But during the twelve years of his reign, Alexander had conquered territory stretching from Macedonia across the Middle East into Asia as far as India. Because none of the generals who succeeded him could hold together such a vast empire, it disintegrated into separate kingdoms.

Scholars label the period from approximately 800 B.C. to 323 B.C., in which the polis predominated, the Hellenic Age. The period from 323 B.C. to the collapse of Egypt at the hands of Rome in 30 B.C.—characterized by independent kingdoms—is commonly called the Hellenistic Age. The Hellenistic period witnessed two significant developments: the diffusion of Greek culture through Asia Minor and the further advance of science, medicine, and philosophy.

Rome

Situated near the center of the boot-shaped peninsula of Italy, the city of Rome conquered all of what it considered the civilized world. Rome's great achievement rested in its ability not only to conquer peoples but to absorb them into the Roman way of life. Rome created an empire that embraced the entire Mediterranean basin. To the Middle Ages and the modern world it bequeathed three great legacies: Roman law, the Latin language, and flexible administrative practices.

Scholars customarily divide Roman history into two periods: the republic (ca 509–31 B.C.), during which Rome grew from a small city-state to an empire; and the empire, the period when the old republican constitution gave way to a constitutional monarchy. Between 509 and 290 B.C. Rome subdued all of Italy, and between 282 and 146 B.C. Rome slowly acquired an overseas empire.

The dominant feature of the social history of the early republic was the clash between patrician aristocrats and plebeian commoners. Whereas the Greeks speculated about the ideal state, the pragmatic Romans developed methods of governing themselves and the peoples they conquered. Their special genius lay in government and law. Because the Romans continually faced concrete challenges, change was a constant feature of their political life. The Roman Senate was the most important institution of the republic. Composed of aristocratic elders, it initially served to advise the other governing group, the magistrates. But as the Senate's prestige increased, its advice came to have the force of law. Roman law—the *ius civile,* or "civil law"—consisted of statutes, customs, and forms of procedure. The goal of the ius civile was to protect citizens' lives, property, and reputations. As Rome expanded, first throughout Italy and then around the Mediterranean basin, legal devices had to be found to deal with disputes among foreigners or between foreigners and Romans. Sometimes, Roman magistrates adopted parts of other (foreign) legal systems. On other occasions, they used the law of equity: with no precedent to guide them, they made decisions on the basis of what seemed fair to all parties. Thus with flexibility the keynote in dealing with specific cases and circumstances, a new body of law—the *ius gentium,* or "law of the peoples"—evolved. This law was applicable to both Romans and foreigners.

The Roman conquest of the Hellenistic East led to the wholesale confiscation of Greek sculpture and paintings to adorn Roman temples. Greek literary and historical classics were translated into Latin. Greek philosophy was studied in the Roman schools. Greek plays were adapted to the Roman stage. Educated people learned Greek as a matter of course. Rome assimilated the Greek achievement, and Hellenism became an enduring feature of Roman life.

With territorial conquests Rome also acquired serious problems, which surfaced by the late second century B.C. Characteristically, the Romans responded practically, with a system of provincial administration that placed at the head of local governments appointed state officials, who were formally incorporated into the republic's constitution. The Romans devised an efficient system of tax collection as well.

Overseas warfare required huge armies for long periods of time. A few officers gained fabulous wealth, but most soldiers did not and returned home to find their farms in ruins. Wealthy men with cash to invest bought up these small farms, creating for themselves vast estates called *lati-fundia*. Roman law forbade landless men to serve in the army, so most veterans migrated to Rome seeking work. Victorious armies, however, had already sent tens of thousands of slaves to Rome, and veterans could not compete in the labor market with slaves. A huge unemployed urban proletariat resulted. Its demands for work and political reform were bitterly resisted by the aristocratic Senate, and civil war was the result in the first century B.C.

The reign of Augustus (31 B.C.–A.D. 14) marked the end of the republic and the beginning of the empire. By fashioning a means of cooperation in government among the people, magistrates, Senate, and army, Augustus established a constitutional monarchy that replaced the republic. His own power derived from the various magistracies he held and the power granted him by the Senate. As commander of the Roman army, he held the title *imperator,* which later came to mean "emperor" in the modern sense. Augustus ended domestic turmoil and secured the provinces. He founded new colonies, mainly in the western Mediterranean basin, which promoted the spread of Greco-Roman culture and the Latin language to the West. Colonists with latifundia exercised authority in the regions as representatives of Rome. (Later, after the empire disintegrated, they would continue to exercise local power.) Augustus extended Roman citizenship to all freemen. A system of Roman roads and sea lanes united the empire. For two hundred years the Mediterranean world experienced the *pax Romana*—a period of peace, order, harmony, and flourishing culture.

In the third century A.D. this harmony ended. Rival generals backed by their troops contested the imperial throne. In the disorder caused by the civil war that ensued, the frontiers were left unmanned, and Germanic invaders poured across the borders. Throughout the empire, civil war and barbarian invasions devastated towns and farms, causing severe economic depression. The emperors Diocletian (r. A.D. 285–305) and Constantine (r. A.D. 306–337) tried to halt the general disintegration by reorganizing the empire, expanding the state bureaucracy, and imposing heavier taxation. For administrative purposes, Diocletian divided the empire into a western half and an eastern half. Constantine established the new capital city of Constantinople at Byzantium. The two parts of the empire drifted further apart in the fourth century, when the division became permanent. Diocletian made an unrealistic attempt to curb inflation by arbitrarily freezing wages, and prices failed. In the early fifth century the borders collapsed entirely, and various Germanic tribes overran the western provinces. In 410 and again in 455, Rome itself was sacked by the barbarians.

After the Roman Empire's decline the rich legacy of Greco-Roman culture was absorbed by the medieval world and ultimately the modern world. The Latin language remained the basic medium of communication among educated people for the next thousand years; for almost two thousand years, Latin literature formed the core of all Western education. Roman roads, buildings, and aqueducts remained in use. Roman law left its mark on the legal and political systems of most European countries. Rome had preserved the best of ancient cultures for later times.

Roman military expansion to the east coincided with Chinese expansion to the west. The remarkable result was a period when the major civilizations of the ancient world were in touch with one another. In spite of constant warfare between the Roman emperors and the Persian kings in western Asia, important commercial contacts by land and maritime routes developed, linking the Roman world, China, and India. Over the famous Silk Road, named for the shipments of silk that passed from China through Parthia to the Roman Empire, were transported luxury goods as well as ideas, artistic inspiration, and religious lore. Established in the second century A.D., this web of communication linking East and West was never entirely broken.

Christianity

The ancient Western world also left behind a powerful religious legacy: Christianity. Christianity derives from the life, teachings, death, and resurrection of a Palestinian Jew, Jesus of Nazareth (ca 3 B.C.–A.D. 29). Thoroughly Jewish in his teaching, Jesus preached the coming of the kingdom of God, a "kingdom not of this world" but one of eternal peace and happiness. He urged his followers and listeners to reform their lives according to the commandments, especially the one stating, "You shall love the Lord your God with your whole heart, your whole mind, and your whole soul, and your neighbor as yourself." The heart of Christian teaching is love of God and love of neighbor.

Some Jews believed that Jesus was their long-awaited messiah. Others viewed Jesus as a threat to their ancient traditions and thus hated and feared him. Though Jesus did not preach rebellion against the Roman governors, the Roman prefect of Judaea, Pontius Pilate, feared that the popular agitation surrounding Jesus could lead to revolt against Rome. So when Jewish leaders handed Jesus over to the Roman authorities, to avert violence Pilate sentenced him to death by crucifixion—the usual method for common criminals. Jesus' followers maintained that he rose from the dead three days later.

Those followers might have remained a small Jewish sect but for the preaching of a Hellenized Jew, Paul of Tarsus (ca A.D. 5–67), who traveled between and wrote letters to the Christian communities at Corinth, Ephesus, Thessalonica, and other cities. As the Roman Empire declined, Christianity spread throughout the Roman world. Because it welcomed people of all social classes, offered a message of divine forgiveness and salvation, and taught that every individual has a role to play in the building of the kingdom of God, thereby fostering a deep sense of community in many of its followers, Christianity won thousands of adherents. Roman efforts to crush Christianity failed. The emperor Constantine legalized Christianity, and in 392 the emperor Theodosius made it the state religion of the empire. Carried by settlers, missionaries, and merchants to Gaul, Spain, North Africa, and Britain, Christianity became a fundamental element of Western civilization.

India

The vast subcontinent of India, protected from outsiders by the towering Himalayan Mountains to the north and by oceans on its other borders, witnessed the development of several early civilizations, primarily in the richly cultivated Indus Valley. Only in the northwest—the area between modern Afghanistan and Pakistan—was India accessible to invasion. Through this region, by way of the Khyber Pass, the Aryans, a nomadic Indo-European people, penetrated India around 1500 B.C. By 500 B.C. the Aryans ruled a number of large kingdoms in which cities were the centers of culture. The period of Aryan rule saw the evolution of a caste system designed to distinguish Aryan from non-Aryan and to denote birth or descent. The four groups, or castes, that emerged—the *Brahman* (priests), the *Kshatriya* (warriors), the *Vaishya* (peasants), and the *Shudra* (serfs)—became the permanent classes of Indian society. Persons without a place in this division or who lost their caste status because of some violation of ritual were *outcastes.*

Through the Khyber Pass in 1513 B.C. the Persian King Darius I entered India and conquered the Indus Valley. The Persians introduced techniques for political administration and for coin minting, and they brought India into commercial and cultural contact with the sophisticated ancient Middle East. From the Persians the Indians adopted the Aramaic language and script and adapted that script to their needs and languages. In 326 B.C. the Macedonian king Alexander the Great invaded the subcontinent, but his conquests had no lasting effect. Under Ashoka (r. 269–232 B.C.), ancient India's greatest ruler, India enjoyed a high degree of peace and stability then from 180 B.C. to A.D. 200 suffered repeated foreign invasions.

India's most enduring legacies are the three great religions that flowered in the sixth and fifth centuries B.C.: Hinduism, Jainism, and Buddhism. One of the modern world's largest religions, Hinduism holds that the Vedas—hymns in praise of the Aryan gods—are sacred revelations and that these revelations prescribe the caste system. Religiously and philosophically diverse, Hinduism assures believers that there are many legitimate ways to worship Brahma, the supreme principle of life. India's best-loved hymn, the Bhagavad Gita, guides Hindus in a pattern of life in the world and of release from it.

Jainism derives from the great thinker Vardhamana Mahavira (ca 540–468 B.C.), who held that only an ascetic life leads to bliss and that all life is too sacred to be destroyed. Nonviolence is a cardinal principle of Jainism. Thus a Jain who wishes to do the least violence to life turns to vegetarianism.

Mahavira's contemporary, Siddhartha Gautama (ca 563–483 B.C.), better known as the Buddha, was so deeply distressed by human suffering that he abandoned his Hindu beliefs in a search for ultimate enlightenment. Meditation alone, he maintained, brought that total enlightenment in which everything is understood. Buddha developed the "Eightfold Path," a series of steps of meditation that could lead to *nirvana,* a state of happiness attained by the extinction of self and human desires. Buddha opposed all religious dogmatism and insisted that anyone, regardless of sex or class, could achieve enlightenment. He attracted many followers, and although Buddhism split into two branches after his death, Buddhist teachings spread throughout India to China, Japan, Korea, and Vietnam. Buddhism remains one of the great Asian religions and in recent times has attracted adherents in the West.

China

Whereas Indian mystics discussed the goals and meaning of life in theological terms, Chinese thinkers were more secular than religious in outlook. Interested primarily in social and economic problems, they sought universal rules of human conduct. Ancient China witnessed the development of Confucianism, Daoism, and Legalism— philosophies that profoundly influenced subsequent Chinese society and culture.

Kong Fu Zi (551–479 B.C.), known in the West as Confucius, was interested in orderly and stable human relationships, and his thought focused on the proper duties and behavior of the individual in society. Confucius considered the family the basic unit within society. Within the family male was superior to female, age to youth. If order is to exist in society, he taught, order must begin in the family. Only gentlemanly conduct, which involved a virtuous and ethical life, would lead to well-run government and peaceful conditions in society at large. Self-discipline, courtesy to others, punctiliousness in service to the state, justice to the people—these are the obligations and behavior expected of the Confucian gentlemen. Confucius minimized the importance of class distinctions and taught that even men of humble birth, through education and self-discipline, could achieve a high level of conduct. The fundamental ingredient in the evolution of the Chinese civil service, Confucianism continued to shape Chinese government up to the twentieth century.

Daoism treated the problems of government very differently. A school of thought ascribed to Lao Zi, of whom little is known, Daoism maintained that people would find true happiness only if they abandoned the world and reverted to nature. Daoists insisted that the best government was the least active government. Public works and government services require higher taxes, which lead to unhappiness and popular resistance. According to the Daoists, the people should be materially satisfied and kept uneducated. A philosophy of consolation, Daoism enjoyed popularity with Chinese rulers and their governing ministers.

Legalism is the name given to a number of related political theories originating in the third century B.C. The founders of Legalism proposed pragmatic solutions to the problems of government, exalted the power of the state, and favored an authoritarian ruler who would root out dissent. Though Legalism proposed an effective, though harsh, solution to the problems of Chinese society, it was too narrow in conception to compete successfully with Confucianism and Daoism.

In 256 B.C. the leader of the state of Qin deposed the ruling king and within thirty-five years won control of China. The new dynasty was called *Qin,* from which the Western term "China" derives. Under the Qin Dynasty and its successor, the Han, China achieved a high degree of political and social stability and economic prosperity. Though sometimes threatened by internal disorder and foreign invasion, China's cultural heritage remained strong. By the end of the Han Dynasty (ca A.D. 200), writing, Confucianism, and the strong political organization of a vast region had left an enduring mark on the Chinese people.

THE MIDDLE AGES IN EUROPE (CA 400–1400)

Fourteenth-century European writers coined the term "Middle Ages," meaning a middle period of Gothic barbarism between two ages of enormous cultural brilliance—the Roman world of the first and second centuries, and their own age, the fourteenth century, which these writers thought had recaptured the true spirit of classical antiquity. Recent scholars have demonstrated that the thousand-year period between roughly the fourth and fourteenth centuries witnessed incredible developments: social, political, intellectual, economic, and religious. The men and women of the Middle Ages built on their cultural heritage and made phenomenal advances in their own right.

The Early Middle Ages

The time period that historians mark off as the early Middle Ages, extending from about the fifth to the tenth century, saw the emergence of a distinctly Western society and culture. The geographical center of that society shifted northward from the Mediterranean basin to western Europe. Whereas a rich urban life and flourishing trade had characterized the ancient world, the Germanic invasions led to the decline of cities and the destruction of commerce. Early medieval society was rural and local. Latifundia, or large farms, were the characteristic social unit.

Several ingredients went into the making of European culture. First, Europe became Christian. Christian missionary activity led to the slow, imperfect Christianization of the Germanic peoples who had overrun the Roman Empire. Christianity introduced these peoples to a universal code of morality and behavior and served as the integrating principle of medieval society. Christian writers played a powerful role in the conservation of Greco-Roman thought. They used Latin as their medium of communication, thereby preserving it. They copied and transmitted classical texts. Writers such as Saint Augustine of Hippo (354–430) used Roman rhetoric and Roman history to defend Christian theology. In so doing, they assimilated classical culture with Christian teaching.

Second, as the Germanic tribes overran the Roman Empire, they intermarried with the old Gallo-Roman aristocracy. The elite class that emerged held the dominant political, social, and economic power in early—and later—medieval Europe. Germanic custom and tradition, such as ideals of military prowess and bravery in battle, became part of the mental furniture of Europeans.

Third, in the eighth century the Carolingian Dynasty, named after its most illustrious member, Charles the Great, or Charlemagne (r. 768–814), gradually acquired a broad hegemony over much of modern France, Germany, and the northern Italy. Charlemagne's coronation by the pope at Rome in a ceremony filled with Latin anthems represented a fusion of classical, Christian, and Germanic elements. This Germanic warrior-king supported Christian missionary efforts and encouraged both classical and Christian scholarship. For the first time since the decay of the Roman Empire, western Europe achieved a degree of political unity. Similarly, the culture of Carolingian Europe blended Germanic, Christian, and Greco-Roman elements.

Its enormous size proved to be the undoing of the Carolingian Empire, and Charlemagne's descendants could not govern it. Attacks by Viking (early Scandinavian), Muslim, and Magyar (early

Hungarian) marauders led to the collapse of centralized power. Real authority passed into the hands of local strongmen. Scholars describe the society that emerged as feudal and manorial. A small group of military leaders held public political power. They gave such protection as they could to the people living on their estates. They held courts, coined money, and negotiated with outside powers. The manor or local estate was the basic community unit. Serfs on the manor engaged in agriculture, the dominant form of economic activity throughout Europe. Since no feudal lord could exercise authority or provide peace over a very wide area, political instability, violence, and chronic disorder characterized Western society.

The Central and Later Middle Ages

By the beginning of the eleventh century, the European world was showing distinct signs of recovery, vitality, and creativity. Over the next two centuries, that recovery and creativity manifested itself in every facet of culture—economic, social, political, intellectual, and artistic. A greater degree of peace paved the way for these achievements.

The Viking and Magyar invasions gradually ended. Warring knights supported ecclesiastical pressure against violence, and disorder declined. Improvements in farming technology, such as the use of the horse collar and wind and water mills, led to an agricultural revolution. Farmland was better used and new land brought under cultivation. Agricultural productivity increased tremendously, leading to considerable population growth.

Increased population contributed to some remarkable economic and social developments. One sign of the recovery of Europe and of the vitality of the central Middle Ages was the rise of towns and the growth of a new commercial class. Surplus population and the search for new economic opportunities led to the expansion of old towns such as London and Cologne and the foundation of completely new ones such as Munich and Berlin. A new artisan and merchant class, frequently called the "middle class," appeared. Medieval sociology recognized only three classes: the clergy, who prayed; the nobility, who fought; and the peasantry, who tilled the land. The middle class—engaging in manufacturing and trade, seeking freedom from the jurisdiction of feudal lords, and pursuing wealth with a fiercely competitive spirit—

fit none of the standard categories. Townspeople were a radical force for change.

The twelfth and thirteenth centuries witnessed an enormous increase in the volume of local and international trade. For example, Italian merchants traveled to regional fairs in France and Flanders to exchange silk from China and slaves from the Crimea for English woolens, French wines, and Flemish textiles. Strongly capitalistic, merchants adopted new business techniques to make more money. These developments added up to what scholars have termed a commercial revolution, a major turning point in the economic and social life of the West: the transformation of Europe from a rural and agrarian society into an urban and industrial one.

The central Middle Ages saw the birth of the modern centralized state. Rome had bequeathed to Western civilization the concepts of the state and the law, but for centuries after the disintegration of the Roman Empire the state as a reality did not exist. Beginning in the twelfth century, kings worked to establish means of communication with all their peoples, to weaken the influence of feudal lords and thus to strengthen their own authority, and to build efficient bureaucracies. Drawing on the Roman ius civile, kings created courts of law, which served not only to punish criminals and reduce violence but also to increase royal income. The law courts thus strengthened royal influence. People began to extend their primary loyalty to the king rather than to the Christian church or the local feudal lord. By the end of thirteenth century, the kings of France and England had achieved a high degree of unity and laid the foundations of modern centralized states. In Italy, Germany, and Spain, strong independent local authorities continued to predominate.

In the realm of government and law, the Middle Ages made other powerful contributions to the modern world. The use of law to weaken feudal barons and to strengthen royal authority worked to increase respect for the law itself. After a bitter dispute with his barons, King John of England (r. 1199–1216) was forced to sign the document known as Magna Carta. Magna Carta contains the principle that there is an authority higher than the king to which even he is responsible: the law. The idea of the "rule of law" became embedded in the Western political consciousness. English kings after John recognized this common law, a law that judges applied throughout the country. Exercise of common law often involved juries of local people to answer questions of fact. The common law and jury system of the Middle Ages have become integral features of Anglo-American jurisprudence. In the fourteenth century, kings also summoned meetings of the leading classes in their kingdoms, and thus were born representative assemblies, most notably the English Parliament.

In their work of consolidation and centralization, kings increasingly used the knowledge of university-trained officials. Universities emerged in western Europe in the thirteenth century. Medieval universities were educational guilds that produced educated and trained officials for the new bureaucratic states. The universities at Bologna in Italy and Montpellier in France, for example, were centers for the study of Roman law. After Aristotle's works had been translated from Arabic into Latin, Paris became the leading university for the study of philosophy and theology. Medieval Scholastics (as philosophers and theologians were called because they belonged to schools) such as Thomas Aquinas (1225–1274) sought to harmonize Greek philosophy with Christian teaching. They wanted to use reason to deepen the understanding of what was believed on faith. Medieval universities developed the basic structures familiar to modern students: colleges, universities, examinations, and degrees. Colleges and universities represent a major legacy of the Middle Ages to the modern world.

Under the leadership of the Christian church, Christian ideals permeated medieval culture. The village priest blessed the fields before the spring planting and the fall harvesting. Guilds of merchants sought the protection of patron saints. University lectures and meetings of parliaments began with prayers. Kings relied on the services of bishops and abbots to do the work of the government. At the center not only of the religious life of the community but also of the social, political, and often economic life was the parish church. The twelfth and thirteenth centuries witnessed a remarkable outburst of Christian piety, as the Crusades (or "holy wars" waged against the Muslims for control of Jerusalem) and Gothic cathedrals reveal. More stone was quarried for churches in medieval France than had been mined in ancient Egypt, where the Great Pyramid alone consumed 40.5 million cubic feet of stone. Churches and cathedrals were visible manifestations of community civic pride. But ideals can rarely be achieved. As centuries passed, abuses in the church multiplied; so did cries for reform.

The high level of energy and creativity that characterized the twelfth and thirteenth centuries could not be sustained. In the fourteenth century, every conceivable disaster struck western Europe. Drought or excessive rain destroyed harvests, causing widespread famine. The bubonic plague (or Black Death) swept across the continent, taking a terrible toll on men, women, and children. England and France became deadlocked in a long and bitter struggle now known as the Hundred Years' War (1337–1453). Schism in the Catholic church resulted in the simultaneous claim by two popes of jurisdiction. Many parts of Europe experienced a resurgence of feudal violence and petty warfare. Out of this misery, disorder, and confusion, a new society gradually emerged.

THE ISLAMIC WORLD (CA 600–1400)

One of the most important developments in world history—one whose consequences redound to our own day—was the rise and remarkable expansion of faith of Islam in the early Middle Ages. Inspired by Muhammad (ca 570–632), a devout merchant of Mecca in present-day Saudi Arabia, Islam united many pagan tribes of Arabia before Muhammad's death. Within two centuries his followers controlled Syria, Palestine, Egypt, Iraq, Iran, northern India, Spain, and southern France, and his beliefs were carried eastward across central Asia to the borders of China. In the ninth, tenth, and eleventh centuries the Muslims created a brilliant civilization centered at Baghdad in Iraq.

Muhammad believed that God sent him messages or revelations. These were later collected and published as the Qur'an, from an Arabic word meaning "reading" or "recitation." On the basis of God's revelations to him, Muhammad preached a strictly monotheistic faith based on the principle of the absolute unity and omnipotence of God. Since God is all-powerful, believers must submit to him. *Islam* means "submission to God," and the community of Muslims consists of those who have submitted to God by accepting the final revelation of his message as set forth by Muhammad. (Earlier revelations of God, held by Muslims to be the same God worshiped by Jews and Christians, had come from the prophets Abraham, Moses, and Jesus, whose work Muslims believe Muhammad completed.)

Driven by the religious zeal of the *jihad,* the obligation to expand their faith, Muslims carried their religion to the east and west by military conquest. Their own economic needs, the political weaknesses of their enemies, a strong military organization, and the practice of establishing army camps in newly conquered territories account for their rapid expansion.

The assassination of one of the caliphs, or successors of Muhammad, led to a division within the Islamic community. When the caliph Ali (r. 656–661) was murdered, his followers claimed that because he was related by blood to Muhammad, and because Muhammad had designated him leader of the community prayer, he had been Muhammad's prescribed successor. These supporters of Ali were called *Shi'-ites,* or *Shi'a,* partisans of Ali; they claimed to possess special divine knowledge that Muhammad had given his heirs. Other Muslims adhered to traditional beliefs and practices of the community based on precedents set by Muhammad. They were called *Sunnis,* a term derived from the Arabic *Sunna,* a collection of Muhammad's sayings and conduct in particular situations. This schism within Islam continues today. Sufism, an ascetic movement within Islam that sought a direct and mystical union with God, drew many followers from all classes.

Long-distance trade and commerce, which permitted further expansion of the Muslim faith, played a prominent role in the Islamic world, in contrast to the limited position it held in the heavily agricultural medieval West. The Black and Caspian Seas, the Volga River giving access deep into Russia, the Arabian Sea and the Indian Ocean, and to a lesser extent the Mediterranean Sea—these were the great commercial waterways of the Islamic world. Goods circulated freely over them. Muslim commercial tools such as the bill of exchange, the check, and the joint stock company were borrowed by Westerners. Many economic practices that modern students consider basic to capitalism were used by Muslim merchants and businessmen long before they became common in the West.

Long-distance trade brought the wealth that supported a gracious and sophisticated culture in the cities of the Muslim world. Baghdad in Iraq and Córdoba in Spain, whose streets were thronged with a kaleidoscope of races, creeds, customs, and cultures and whose many shops offered goods from all over the world, stand out as superb examples of cosmopolitan Muslim civilization. Baghdad and Córdoba were also great intellectual centers where Muslim scholars made advances in mathematics, medicine, and philosophy. The Arabs translated many ancient Greek texts by writers such as Plato and Aristotle. When, beginning in the ninth century, those texts were translated from Arabic into Latin, they came to play an important part in the formation of medieval European scientific, medical, and philosophical thought. Modern scholars consider Muslim civilization in the period from about 900 to 1200 among the most brilliant in the world's history.

TRADITION AND CHANGE IN ASIA (CA 320–1400)

Between about 320 and 1400 the various societies of Asia continued to evolve their own distinct social, political, and religious institutions. But also in these years momentous changes swept across Asia. Arab conquerors and their Muslim faith reached the Indian subcontinent. The Turks, moving westward from the Chinese border, converted to Islam. China, under the Tang and Song Dynasties, experienced a golden age. Japan emerged into the light of written history. These centuries witnessed cultural developments that have molded and influenced later Asian societies.

India

Under the Gupta kings, who ruled from around 320 to 500, India enjoyed a great cultural flowering. Interest in Sanskrit literature—the literature of the Aryans—led to the preservation of much Sanskrit poetry. A distinctly Indian drama appeared, and India's greatest poet, Kalidasa (ca 380–450), like Shakespeare, blended poetry and drama. Mathematicians arrived at the concept of zero, essential for higher mathematics, and scientific thinkers wrestled with the concept of gravitation.

The Gupta kings succeeded in uniting much of the subcontinent. They also succeeded in repulsing an invasion by the Huns, but the effort exhausted the dynasty. After 600 India reverted to the pattern of strong local kingdoms in frequent conflict. Then, between 600 and 1400, India suffered repeated invasion as waves of Arabs, Turks, and Mongols swept down through the northwest corridor. By around 1400 India was as politically splintered as it had been before Gupta rule. The most lasting impact of the invaders was the victory of Islam over Hinduism and Buddhism in the Indus Valley (modern Pakistan). Elsewhere Hinduism resisted Islam.

One other development had a lasting effect on Indian society: the proliferation and hardening of the caste system. Early Indian society had been divided into four major groups. After the fall of the Guptas, further subdivisions arose, reflecting differences of profession, trade, tribal or racial affiliation, religious belief, even place of residence. By 800 India had more than three thousand castes, each with its own rules and governing body. As India was politically divided, so castes served to fragment it socially.

China

Scholars consider the period between 580 and 1400, which saw the rule of Tang and Song Dynasties, as China's golden age. In religion, political administration, agricultural productivity, and art, Chinese society attained a remarkable level of achievement.

Merchants and travelers from India introduced Buddhism to China. Scholars, rulers, the middle classes, and the poor all found appealing concepts in Buddhist teachings, and the new faith won many adherents. China distilled Buddhism to meet its own needs, and Buddhism gained a place next to Confucianism in Chinese life.

The Tang Dynasty, which some historians consider the greatest in Chinese history, built a state bureaucracy unequaled until recent times for its political sophistication. Tang emperors subdivided the imperial administration into departments of military organization, maintenance and supply of the army, foreign affairs, justice, education, finance, building, and transportation. To staff this vast administration, an imperial civil service developed in which education, talent, and merit could lead to high office, wealth, and prestige. So effective was the Tang civil service and so deeply rooted did it become in Chinese society that it lasted until the twentieth century.

Under the Song Dynasty (960–1279), greatly expanded agricultural productivity, combined with advances in the technology of coal and iron and efficient water transport, supported a population of 100 million. (By contrast, Europe did not reach this figure before the late eighteenth century.) Greater urbanization followed in China. Political stability and economic growth fostered technological innovation, the greatest being the invention of printing. Tang craftsmen invented the art of carving words and pictures into wooden blocks, inking the blocks, and then pressing them onto paper. The invention of movable type followed in the eleventh century. As would happen in Europe in the fifteenth century, the invention of printing lowered the price and increased the availability of books and contributed to the spread of literacy. Printing led to the use of paper money, replacing the bulky copper coinage, and to developments in banking. The highly creative Tang and Song periods also witnessed the invention of gunpowder, originally used for fireworks, and the abacus, which permitted the quick computation of complicated sums. In the creation of a large collection of fine poetry and prose, and in the manufacture of porcelain of superb quality and delicate balance, the Tang and Song periods revealed an extraordinary literary and artistic flowering.

Between 1127 and 1279 the Song emperors built a large merchant fleet. Trade expanded as Japan and Korea eagerly imported Chinese silks and porcelains. The Muslims shipped Chinese goods across the Indian Ocean to East African and Middle Eastern markets. Southern China participated in a commercial network that stretched from Japan to the Mediterranean. The Mongol conquest of China (ca 1279) under Jenghiz Khan and his grandson Kublai Khan ended a glorious era in Chinese history and brought the country under foreign rule. In 1368 Hong Wu, the first emperor of the Ming Dynasty, restored Chinese rule.

Japan

The chain of islands that constitutes Japan entered the light of written history only in sporadic references in Chinese writings, the most reliable set down in A.D. 297. Because the land of Japan is rugged, lacking navigable waterways, and because only perhaps 20 percent of it is arable, political unification by land proved difficult until modern times. The Inland Sea served both as the readiest means of communication and as a rich source of food; the Japanese have traditionally been fisherman and mariners.

Early Japan was divided into numerous political units, each under the control of a particular *clan*, a large group of families claiming descent from a common ancestor and worshiping a common deity. In the third century A.D. the Yamato clan gained control of the fertile area south of modern Kyoto near Osaka Bay and subordinated many other clans to it. The Yamato chieftain proclaimed himself emperor and assigned specific duties and functions to subordinate chieftains. The Yamato established their chief shrine in the eastern part (where the sun-goddess could catch the first rays of the rising sun) of Honshu, the largest of Japan's four main islands. Around this shrine local clan cults sprang up, giving rise to a native religion that the Japanese called *Shinto,* the "Way of the Gods." Shinto became a unifying force and protector of the nation.

Through Korea two significant Chinese influences entered Japan and profoundly influenced Japanese culture: the Chinese system of writing and record keeping, and Buddhism. Under Prince Shotoku (574–622), talented young Japanese were sent to Tang China to learn Chinese methods of administration and Chinese Buddhism. They returned to Japan to share and enforce what they had learned. The Nara era of Japanese history (710–794), so called from Japan's first capital city north of modern Osaka, was characterized by the steady importation of Chinese ideas and methods. Buddhist monasteries became both religious and political centers, supporting Yamato rule.

In response to the attempt of a Buddhist monk at Nara to usurp the throne, in 770 the imperial family removed the capital to Heian (modern Kyoto), where it remained until 1867. A strong reaction against Buddhism and Chinese influences followed, symbolized by the severance of relations with China in 838. The eclipse of Chinese influences liberated Japanese artistic and cultural forces. A new Japanese style of art and architecture appeared. In writing, Japanese scholars modified the Chinese script. They produced two *syllabaries,* sets of phonetic signs that stand for syllables instead of whole words or letters. Unshackled from Chinese forms, Japanese writers created their own literary styles and modes of expression. The writing of history and poetry flowered, and the Japanese produced their first novel, *The Tale of Genji,* a classic of court life by the court lady Murasaki Shikibu (978–ca 1016).

The later Heian period witnessed the breakdown of central authority as aristocrats struggled to free themselves from imperial control. In 1156 civil war among the leaders of the great clans erupted. By 1192 the Minamato clan had defeated all opposition. Its leader Yoritomo (1147–1199) became *shogun,* or general-in-chief. Thus began the Kamakura Shogunate, which lasted until 1333.

In addition to the powerful shogun, a dominant figure in the new society was the *samurai,* the warrior who by the twelfth century exercised civil, judicial, and military power over the peasants who worked the land. The samurai held his land in exchange for his promise to fight for a stronger lord. In a violent society strikingly similar to that of western Europe in the early Middle Ages, the Japanese samurai, like the French knight, constituted the ruling class at the local level. Civil war among the emperor, the leading families, and the samurai erupted again in 1331. In 1338 one of the most important military leaders, Ashikaga Takauji, defeated the emperor and established the Ashikaga Shogunate, which lasted until 1573. Meanwhile, the samurai remained the significant social figure.

AFRICA AND THE AMERICAS BEFORE EUROPEAN INTRUSION (CA 400–1500)

Between approximately 400 and 1500, Africa and the Americas witnessed the development of highly sophisticated civilizations alongside more simply organized societies. Only recently have Asians, Europeans, and Americans learned very much about Africa and the Americas before the arrival of Columbus. The more that scholars learn about these early civilizations, the more they appreciate their richness, diversity, and dynamism.

Early African Societies

Africa, the world's second largest continent (after Asia), covers 20 percent of the earth's land surface. Africa is diverse in both topography and peoples. Five geographical zones divide the continent, and geography has shaped the economic development of the peoples of Africa. The native Berbers of North Africa have intermingled with Phoenicians, Greeks, Italians, Muslim Arabs, and Spanish Jews, who over the centuries settled there. Egyptians are a cultural rather than a racial group, and black Africans live south of the 3.5 million-square-mile desert, the Sahara.

A settled method of agriculture, expanding west from southern Palestine, reached the Nile Delta in about the fifth millennium before Christ. From the Nile Valley settled agriculture moved west across the southern edge of the Sahara and arrived in the central and western Sudan by the first century B.C. The village was the basic social unit, comprising families and clans affiliated by blood kinship. Extended families made up villages that collectively formed small kingdoms. The arrival of the camel around A.D. 200 spurred the development of long-distance trade, which in turn fostered the expanded control of small kingdoms over sizable territories.

Between 200 and 700, a network of caravan routes running south from the Mediterranean coast across the terrible Sahara to the Sudan developed. Arab-Berber merchants exchanged manufactured goods for African gold, ivory, gum, and slaves from the West African savanna. This trade stimulated the mining of gold in parts of present-day Senegal, Nigeria, and Ghana, as well as the search for slaves for the Middle Eastern and European markets. In addition, the trans-Saharan trade encouraged the growth of urban centers in West Africa. Sizable concentrations of people grew at Jenne, Gao, Timbuktu, and Kumbi, each a center of the export-import trade and each ruled by black merchant dynasties. These cities played a dynamic role in the commercial life of West Africa and became centers of intellectual creativity. Perhaps the most far-reaching consequence of the trans-Saharan trade was the introduction of Islam to West Africa. Conversion led to the involvement of Muslims in African governments, bringing efficient techniques of statecraft and advanced scientific knowledge and engineering skills. Between the ninth and fifteenth centuries, Islam greatly accelerated the development of the African kingdoms.

The period from 800 to 1450 witnessed the flowering of several powerful African states. In the western Sudan, the large empires of Ghana (ca 900–1100) and Mali (ca 1200–1450) arose. Each had an elaborate royal court, massive state bureaucracy, sizable army, sophisticated judicial system, and strong gold industry. Indeed, the fame of Ghana rested on gold, and when the fabulously rich Mali king Mansa Musa (r. ca 1312–1337), a devout Muslim, made a pilgrimage to Mecca, his entourage included one hundred elephants, each carrying one hundred pounds of gold.

Meanwhile, the East African coast gave rise to powerful city-states such as Kilwa, Mombasa and Mogadishu, which maintained a rich maritime trade with India, China, and the Muslim cities of the Middle East; like the western Sudan, the East African cities were much affected by Muslim influences. In southern Africa the empire of Great Zimbabwe, built on the gold trade with the east coast, flourished between the eleventh and fifteenth centuries.

The Geography and Peoples of the Americas

Across the Atlantic, several great Amerindian cultures flourished between 400 and 1500. The Americas, named for the Florentine explorer Amerigo Vespucci (1451–1512), who in 1502 sailed down the eastern coast of South America to Brazil, extend 11,000 miles from the Bering Strait to the tip of South America. Like Africa, Mexico and South America are highly varied geographically. Mexico is dominated by high plateaus bounded by coastal plains; thickly jungled lowlands run along the Caribbean coast of Central America, whose western uplands have a more temperate climate and fertile agricultural lands. South America contains the high Andes Mountains, plains around the continent's periphery, and tropical rain forests.

Asian peoples crossing the Bering Sea from Russian Siberia some twenty-thousand years ago migrated southward, and by 2300 B.C. settled in central Mexico and the area of modern Peru. They raised corn, beans, squash, and, in Peru, white potatoes. Careful cultivation of the land produced bumper crops, which contributed to a high fertility rate and in turn to a population boom. Amerindian civilizations used their large labor forces to construct religious and political buildings and standing armies.

Population growth facilitated the growth of successive Mesoamerican (the area of present-day Mexico and Central America) civilizations: the Olmec, Teotihuacán, and Toltec. Each of these societies was based on an agricultural economy, and each contained ceremonial centers to which pilgrims thronged. Each civilization collapsed before successive waves of new invaders, who absorbed the cultural legacy of their predecessors.

The last peoples to arrive in central Mexico were the Aztecs, who—building on Toltec antecedents—created the last unified civilization before the arrival of Europeans. Aztec society included a strong mercantile class, a nobility of soldiers and imperial officials, and a large population of agricultural and manual workers—all presided over by the fabulously rich court of the emperor. The Aztecs controlled a large confederation of city-states by sacrificing to their gods prisoners seized in battle and by demanding from subject states an annual tribute of people to be sacrificed. The sophistication of Aztec cities astounded the Spanish, who subsequently conquered them. The capital city of Tenochitilán numbered perhaps 250,000 people, who thronged the flower-decked public squares and marketplaces where all varieties of goods were available. Aqueducts reflecting sophisticated engineering skills supplied the city with fresh water. In sculpture, architecture, and engineering, the Aztecs created a remarkably dynamic civilization.

So too did the Maya of Central America. They invented an original system of writing and a calendar considered more accurate than the European Gregorian calendar, and they attained a level of mathematical knowledge not equaled by Europeans for centuries. Recent decipherment of Maya hieroglyphics reveals that their stele are actually historical documents providing a wealth of information about the Maya royal dynasties. The Maya proved themselves masters of abstract knowledge and of the recording of history.

Like the Aztecs, the Incas of Peru were a small militaristic group who vanquished surrounding peoples and established a strong empire. Whereas the Aztecs controlled subject peoples through terror, the Incas governed by cultural unification. They imposed their language and religion on newly conquered peoples, whom they transferred to areas that had long been under Inca rule. A remarkable system of roads, bridges, and tunnels linked the Inca Empire. Highly gifted organizers, the Incas created a state that was virtually unique for its time in assuming responsibility for the social welfare of all its people.

EARLY MODERN EUROPE
(CA 1400–1600)

The early modern period was a time of great change in European society. Men and women of the Renaissance and the Reformation laid the foundations of a new Europe, but Europe still remained very different from its modern contemporary incarnation. The industrial and the French revolutions, the growth of nationalism, and the profound secularization of culture occurred in the eighteenth and nineteenth centuries; these forces unleashed what we mean when we speak of the "modern world." Even so, by late-twentieth-century standards, fifteenth- and sixteenth-century Europe remained—in its class structure, economic life, technology, and methods of communication—closer to imperial Rome than to present-day Europe and America.[1] Our emphasis, therefore, rests on *early* modern Europe. The Renaissance, the Reformation, and the expansion of Europe overseas drastically altered European attitudes, values, and lifestyles. Overseas expansion eventually led to the imposition of European lifestyles, religions, and patterns of government and commercial exchange on African, South American, and Asian peoples.

The Renaissance

While war, famine, disease, and death swept across northern Europe in the fourteenth century, a new culture was emerging in Italy. Italian society underwent great changes. In the fifteenth century, these phenomena spread beyond Italy and gradually influenced northern Europe. These cultural changes have collectively been called the Renaissance. The Italian Renaissance evolved in two broad and overlapping stages. In the first period, from approximately 1050 to 1300, a new economy emerged, based on Venetian and Florentine banking and cloth manufacturing. At the end of the thirteenth century, Florentine bankers gained control of papal banking. From their position as tax collectors for the papacy, Florentine mercantile families began to dominate. The wealth so produced brought into existence a new urban and aristocratic class.

In the industrial cities of Venice and Florence, members of this new aristocratic class governed as oligarchs. They maintained the façade of republican government: in theory, political power resided in the people and was exercised by their chosen representatives, but in reality, the oligarchs ruled. In cities with strong agricultural bases, such as Verona, Mantua, and Ferrara, despots predominated. In the fifteenth century, political power and elite culture

[1]Eugene F. Rice, *The Foundations of Early Modern Europe, 1460–1559* (New York: Norton, 1970), p. x.

were centered at the princely courts of oligarchs and despots. At his court the Renaissance prince displayed his patronage of the arts and learning.

The second stage of the Italian Renaissance, which lasted from about 1300 to 1600, was characterized by extraordinary intellectual and artistic energy. Scholars commonly use the French term *renaissance* ("rebirth") to describe the cultural achievements of the fourteenth through sixteenth centuries. As an intellectual movement the Renaissance possessed certain hallmarks that held profound significance for the evolution of the modern world.

Fourteenth- and fifteenth-century Italians had the self-conscious awareness that they were living in new times. They believed that theirs was a golden age of creativity, an age of rebirth of classical antiquity. They identified with early Greek and Roman philosophers and artists, copied the lifestyles of the ancients, and expressed contempt for the medieval past. The Renaissance manifested a new attitude toward individuals, toward learning, and toward the world in general.

Individualism stressed personality, uniqueness, genius, the fullest possible development of human potential. Artist, athlete, sculptor, scholar, whatever—a person's potential should be stretched until fully realized. The thirst for fame—the burning quest for glory—was a central component of Renaissance individualism.

Closely connected with individualism was a deep interest in the Latin classics. This feature of the Renaissance became known as the "new learning," or "humanism." The terms *humanism* and *humanist* derive from the Latin *humanitas,* which refers to the literary culture needed by anyone who would be considered educated or civilized. Humanists studied the Latin classics to discover past insights into human nature.

A new secular spirit constitutes another basic feature of the Italian Renaissance. Secularism is a basic concern with the things of this world rather than with otherworldly matters. Medieval people certainly pursued financial profits ruthlessly, but in the Middle Ages, the dominant ideals focused on life after death. Renaissance men and women had deep spiritual concerns, but the fourteenth and fifteenth centuries witnessed the slow and steady growth of secularism in Italy. Economic changes, preoccupation with moneymaking, and the rising prosperity of the Italian cities precipitated a fundamental change in the attitudes and values of the urban aristocracy and middle classes.

The age also saw profound changes that have enormously influenced the modern West. The invention of the printing press in the mid-fifteenth century revolutionized communication. Printing made government propaganda possible, bridged the gap between the oral and written cultures, and stimulated the literacy of laypeople. Whereas women in the Middle Ages often had great responsibilities, in the Renaissance their purpose came to be merely decorative—to grace the courts of princes and aristocrats. As servants and slaves, black people entered Europe during the Renaissance in sizable numbers for the first time since the collapse of the Roman Empire. In northern Europe urban merchants and rural gentry allied with rising monarchies. With the newly levied taxes paid by business people, kings provided a greater degree of domestic peace and order. In Spain, France, and England, rulers also emphasized royal dignity and authority; they used the tough ideas of the Italian political theorist Machiavelli to ensure the preservation or continuation of their governments. Feudal monarchies gradually evolved in the direction of nation-states.

As the intellectual features of the Renaissance spread outside Italy, they affected the culture of all Europe. A secular attitude toward life is a dominant feature of modern Western societies. Its germ was planted in the attitudes and approaches of the Italian humanists. Those humanists studied classical literature to understand human nature and to strengthen their interest in the world around them. A strong belief in the complete realization of individual potential has become an abiding component of the Western world-view.

The Reformation

The idea of religious reform is as old as Christianity itself. Jesus had preached the coming of the kingdom of God through the reform of the individual, and over the centuries his cry has been repeated. The need for the reform of the individual Christian and of the institutional church is central to the Christian faith. Christian humanists of the fifteenth and sixteenth centuries urged the reform of the church on the pattern of the early Christian communities.

In 1517 Martin Luther (1483–1546), a professor of Scripture at a minor German university, launched an attack on certain church practices. Asked to recant, Luther rejected church authority itself. The newly invented printing press swept Luther's prolific ideas across Germany and the rest of Europe. He and other reformers soon won the support of northern German princes who embraced Luther's reforming or "Protestant" ideas. Some of the princes coveted church lands and revenues. Others resented the authority of the strongly Catholic Holy Roman emperor Charles V. By accepting Luther's religious ideas—and thereby denying orthodox Catholic doctrine—the princes also rejected the emperor's political authority. In a world that insisted on the necessity of religious unity for political order and social stability, the adoption of the new faith implied political opposition. In England, largely because the papacy would not approve his request for a divorce, King Henry VII (r. 1509–1547) broke with Rome and established the Anglican church. Kings and princes, political and economic issues, played the decisive role in the advance of the Reformation.

In the first half of the sixteenth century, perhaps a fourth of the population of western Europe accepted some version of Protestantism. Besides northern Germany, all of Scandinavia, England, Scotland, and the cities of Geneva and Zurich in Switzerland and Strasbourg in Germany rejected the religious authority of the Roman church and adopted new faiths. The number of Protestant sects proliferated, but the core of Protestant doctrine remained. First, Protestants believe that salvation comes by faith alone, not from faith and good works, as Catholic teaching asserts. Second, author-

ity in the Christian church resides in the Scriptures, not in tradition or papal authority (which all Protestants rejected). The church itself consists of the community of all believers; medieval churchmen had tended to identify the church with the clergy.

In the later sixteenth century, the Roman church worked to clean up its house. The Council of Trent, meeting intermittently from 1545 to 1563, suppressed pluralism and the sale of church offices, redefined doctrine, made provision for the education of all the clergy, and laid the basis for general spiritual renewal. New religious orders, such as the Society of Jesus (or Jesuits), sought to reconvert Protestants. A new church department, the Holy Office, tried to impose doctrinal uniformity everywhere.

The break with Rome and the rise of Lutheran, Anglican, Calvinist, and other faiths shattered the unity of Europe as an organic Christian society. Nevertheless, religious belief remained exceedingly strong. In fact, the strength of religious convictions caused political fragmentation. In the later sixteenth and throughout most of the seventeenth centuries, religion and religious issues continued to play a major role in the lives of individuals and in the policies and actions of governments. Religion, whether Protestant or Catholic, decisively influenced the evolution of national states. Though most reformers rejected religious toleration, they helped pave the way for the toleration and pluralism that characterize the modern world.

BENNETT D. HILL

16

The Age of European Expansion and Religious Wars

A detail from an early 17th-century Flemish painting depiction maps, illustrated travel books, a globe, a compass, and an astrolabe. *(Source: Reproduced by courtesy of the Trustees, The National Gallery, London)*

Between 1450 and 1650 two developments dramatically altered the world: Europeans' overseas expansion and the reformations of the Christian church. Europeans carried their cultures to other parts of the globe. Overseas expansion brought them into confrontation with ancient civilizations in Africa, Asia, and the Americas. These confrontations led first to conquest, then to exploitation, and finally to profound social changes in both Europe and the conquered territories. Likewise, the Renaissance and the religious reformations drastically changed intellectual, political, religious, and social life in Europe. War and religious issues dominated the politics of European states. Although religion was commonly used to rationalize international conflict, wars were fought for power and territory.

- Why, in the sixteenth and seventeenth centuries, did a relatively small number of people living on the edge of the Eurasian landmass gain control of the major sea lanes of the world and establish political and economic hegemony on distant continents?

- How were a few Spaniards, fighting far from home, able to overcome the powerful Aztec and Inca Empires in America?

- What effect did overseas expansion have on Europe and on conquered societies?

- What were the causes and consequences of the religious wars in France, the Netherlands, and Germany?

- How did the religious crises of this period affect the status of women?

- How and why did African slave labor become the dominant form of labor organization in the New World?

- What religious and intellectual developments led to the growth of skepticism?

- What literary masterpieces of the English-speaking world did this period produce?

This chapter addresses these questions.

❊ DISCOVERY, RECONNAISSANCE, AND EXPANSION

Historians of Europe have called the period from 1450 to 1650 the "Age of Discovery," "Age of Reconnaissance," and "Age of Expansion." All three labels are appropriate. "Age of Discovery" refers to the era's phenomenal advances in geographical knowledge and technology, often achieved through trial and error. In 1350 it took as long to sail from the eastern end of the Mediterranean to the western end as it had taken a thousand years earlier. Even in the fifteenth century, Europeans knew little more about the earth's surface than the Romans had known. By 1650, however, Europeans had made an extensive reconnaissance—or preliminary exploration—and had sketched fairly accurately the physical outline of the whole earth. Much of the geographical information they had gathered was tentative and not fully understood—hence the appropriateness of "Age of Reconnaissance."

The designation "Age of Expansion" refers to the migration of Europeans to other parts of the world. This colonization resulted in political control of much of South and North America; coastal regions of Africa, India, China, and Japan; and many Pacific islands. Political hegemony was accompanied by economic exploitation, religious domination, and the introduction of European patterns of social and intellectual life. The sixteenth-century expansion of European society launched a new age in world history. None of the three "Age" labels reflects the experiences of non-European peoples. Africans, Asians, and native Americans had known the geographies of their regions for centuries. They made no "discoveries" and undertook no reconnaissance, and they experienced "expansion" only as forced slave laborers.

Overseas Exploration and Conquest

The outward expansion of Europe began with the Viking voyages across the Atlantic in the ninth and tenth centuries. Under Eric the Red and Leif Ericson, the Vikings discovered Greenland and the eastern coast of North America. They made permanent settlements in, and a legal imprint on, Iceland, Ireland, England, Normandy, and Sicily. The Crusades of the eleventh through thirteenth centuries were another phase in Europe's attempt to explore and exploit peoples on the periphery of the continent. But the lack of a strong territorial base, superior Muslim military strength, and sheer misrule combined to make the Crusader kingdoms short-lived. In the mid-fifteenth century, Europe seemed ill prepared for further international

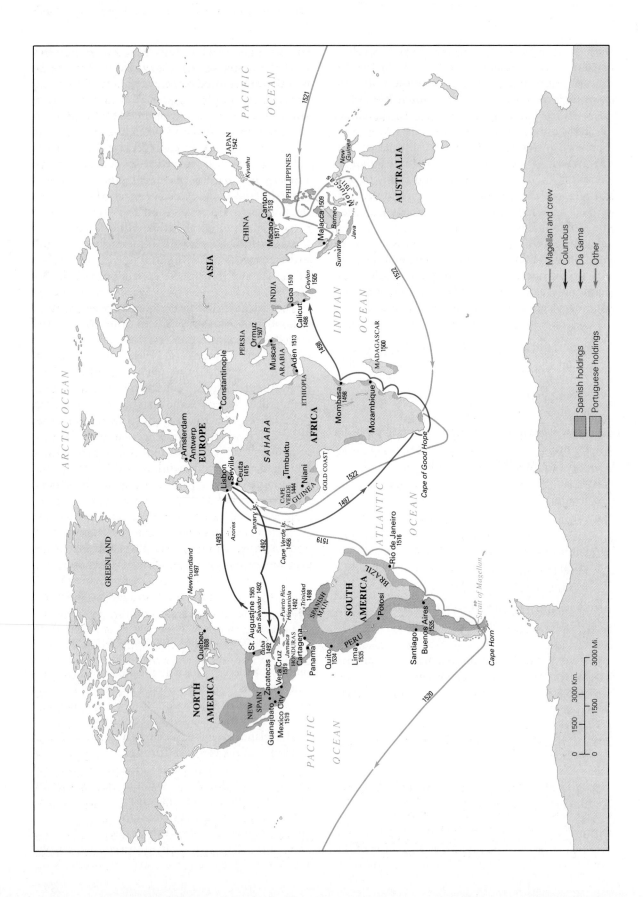

ventures. By 1450 a grave new threat had appeared in the East: the Ottoman Turks.

Combining excellent military strategy with efficient administration of their conquered territories, the Turks had subdued most of Asia Minor and begun to settle on the western side of the Bosporus. The Muslim Ottoman Turks under Sultan Mohammed II (r. 1451–1481) captured Constantinople in 1453, pressed northwest into the Balkans, and by the early sixteenth century controlled the eastern Mediterranean. The Turkish menace badly frightened Europeans. In France in the fifteenth and sixteenth centuries, twice as many books were printed about the Turkish threat as about the American discoveries. Yet the fifteenth and sixteenth centuries witnessed a fantastic continuation, on a global scale, of European expansion.

Political centralization in Spain, France, and England helps to explain those countries' outward push. In the fifteenth century, Isabella and Ferdinand had consolidated their several kingdoms to achieve a more united Spain. The Catholic rulers revamped the Spanish bureaucracy and humbled dissident elements, notably the Muslims and the Jews. The Spanish monarchy was stronger than ever before and in a position to support foreign ventures; it could bear the costs and dangers of exploration. But Portugal, situated on the extreme southwestern edge of the European continent, got the start on the rest of Europe. Still insignificant as a European land power despite its recently secured frontiers, Portugal sought greatness in the unknown world overseas.

Portugal's taking of Ceuta, an Arab city in northern Morocco, in 1415 marked the beginning of European exploration and control of overseas territory (Map 16.1). The objectives of Portuguese policy included the historic Iberian crusade to Christianize Muslims and the search for gold, for an overseas route to the spice markets of India, and for the mythical Christian ruler of Ethiopia, Prester John.

In the early phases of Portuguese exploration, Prince Henry (1394–1460), called "the Naviga-

MAP 16.1 Overseas Exploration and Conquest in the Fifteenth and Sixteenth Centuries The voyages of discovery marked another phase in the centuries-old migrations of European peoples. Consider the major contemporary significance of each of the three voyages depicted on this map.

tor" because of the annual expeditions he sent down the western coast of Africa, played the leading role. In the fifteenth century, most of the gold that reached Europe came from the Sudan in West Africa and from the Akan peoples living near the area of present-day Ghana. Muslim caravans brought the gold from the African cities of Niani and Timbuktu and carried it north across the Sahara to Mediterranean ports. Then the Portuguese muscled in on this commerce in gold. Prince Henry's carefully planned expeditions succeeded in reaching Guinea, and under King John II (r. 1481–1495) the Portuguese established trading posts and forts on the Guinea coast and penetrated into the continent all the way to Timbuktu (see Map 16.1). Portuguese ships transported gold to Lisbon, and by 1500 Portugal controlled the flow of gold to Europe. The golden century of Portuguese prosperity had begun.

The spices Europeans wanted, however, came from South Asia and the Moluccan islands, not from African kingdoms. Thus the Portuguese pushed farther south down the west coast of Africa. In 1487 Bartholomew Diaz rounded the Cape of Good Hope at the southern tip, but storms and a threatened mutiny forced him to turn back. On a second expedition (1497–1499), the Portuguese mariner Vasco da Gama reached India and returned to Lisbon loaded with samples of Indian wares. King Manuel (r. 1495–1521) promptly dispatched thirteen ships under the command of Pedro Alvares Cabral, assisted by Diaz, to set up trading posts in India. On April 22, 1500, the coast of Brazil in South America was sighted and claimed for the crown of Portugal. Cabral then proceeded south and east around the Cape of Good Hope and reached India. Half of the fleet was lost on the return voyage, but the six spice-laden vessels that dropped anchor in Lisbon harbor in July 1501 more than paid for the entire expedition. Thereafter, convoys were sent out every March. Lisbon became the entrance port for Asian goods into Europe—but not without a fight.

For centuries the Muslims had controlled the rich spice trade of the Indian Ocean, and they did not surrender it willingly. Portuguese commercial activities were accompanied by the destruction or seizure of strategic Muslim coastal forts, which later served Portugal as both trading posts and military bases. Alfonso de Albuquerque, whom the Portuguese crown appointed as governor of India

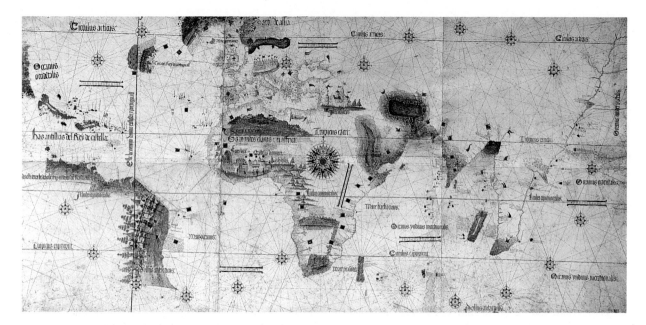

✦ **The Cantino Map**   This map (1502) is named for the agent secretly commissioned to design it in Lisbon for the duke of Ferrara, an avid Italian map collector. It reveals such good knowledge of the African continent, of the islands of the West Indies, and of the shoreline of present-day Venezuela, Guiana, and Brazil in South America that modern scholars suspect there may have been clandestine voyages to the Americas shortly after Columbus's. *(Source: Biblioteca Estense Universitaria, Modena)*

(1509–1515), decided that these bases and not inland territories should control the Indian Ocean. Accordingly, his cannon blasted open the ports of Calicut, Ormuz, Goa, and Malacca, the vital centers of Arab domination of south Asian spice trade (see Map 16.1). This bombardment laid the foundation for Portuguese imperialism in the sixteenth and seventeenth centuries—a strange way to bring Christianity to "those who were in darkness." As one scholar wrote about the opening of China to the West, "while Buddha came to China on white elephants, Christ was borne on cannon balls."[1]

In March 1493, between the voyages of Diaz and da Gama, Spanish ships entered Lisbon harbor bearing a triumphant Italian explorer in the service of the Spanish monarchy. Christopher Columbus (1451–1506), a Genoese mariner, had secured Spanish support for an expedition to the East (see Listening to the Past). He sailed from Palos, Spain, to the Canary Islands and crossed the Atlantic to the Bahamas, landing in October 1492 on an island that he named San Salvador and believed to be the coast of India.

Technological Stimuli to Exploration

Technological developments were the key to Europe's remarkable outreach. By 1350 cannon made of iron or bronze and able to fire iron or stone balls had been fully developed in western Europe. This artillery emitted frightening noises and great flashes of fire and could batter down fortresses and even city walls. Sultan Mohammed II's siege of Constantinople in 1453 provides a classic illustration of the effectiveness of cannon fire.

Constantinople had very strong walled fortifications. The sultan secured the services of a Western technician, who built fifty-six small cannon and a gigantic gun that could hurl stone balls weighing about eight hundred pounds. The gun had to be moved by several hundred oxen and could be loaded and fired only by about a hundred men working together. Reloading took two hours. This awkward but powerful weapon breached the walls of Constantinople before it cracked on the second day of the bombardment. Lesser cannon finished the job.

Although early cannon posed serious technical difficulties for land warfare, they could be used at sea. The mounting of cannon on ships and improved techniques of shipbuilding gave impetus to European expansion. Since ancient times, most seagoing vessels had been narrow, open boats called *galleys,* propelled largely by oarsmen: slaves or convicts who had been sentenced to the galleys manned the oars of the cargo and war ships that sailed the Mediterranean (both types of ship carried soldiers for defense). Well suited to the calm and thoroughly explored waters of the Mediterranean, galleys could not withstand the rough winds and uncharted shoals of the Atlantic. The need for sturdier craft, as well as population losses caused by the Black Death, forced the development of a new style of ship that did not require soldiers for defense or a large crew of oarsmen.

In the course of the fifteenth century, the Portuguese developed the *caravel,* a small, light, three-masted sailing ship. Though somewhat slower than the galley, the caravel held more cargo and was highly maneuverable. When fitted with cannon, it could dominate larger vessels, such as the round ships commonly used in commerce. The substitution of windpower for manpower, and artillery fire for soldiers, signaled a great technological advance and gave Europeans navigational and fighting ascendancy over the rest of the world.[2]

Other fifteenth-century developments in navigation helped make possible the conquest of the Atlantic. The magnetic compass enabled sailors to determine their direction and position at sea. The astrolabe, an instrument developed by Muslim navigators in the twelfth century and used to determine the altitude of the sun and other celestial bodies, permitted mariners to plot their latitude, or position north or south of the equator. Steadily improved maps and sea charts provided information about distances, sea depths, and geography.

The Explorers' Motives

The expansion of Europe was not motivated by demographic pressures. The Black Death had caused serious population losses from which Europe had not recovered in 1500. Few Europeans emigrated to North or South America in the sixteenth century. Half of those who did sail to begin a new life in America died en route; half of those who reached what they regarded as the New World eventually returned to their homeland. Why, then, did explorers brave the Atlantic and Pacific Oceans, risking their lives to discover new continents and spread European culture?

The reasons are varied and complex. People of the sixteenth century were still basically medieval: their attitudes and values were shaped by religion and expressed in religious terms. In the late fifteenth century, crusading fervor remained a basic part of the Portuguese and Spanish national ideal. The desire to Christianize Muslims and pagan peoples played a central role in European expansion. Queen Isabella of Spain, for example, showed a fanatical zeal for converting the Muslims to Christianity and concentrated her efforts on the Muslims in Granada. But after the abortive crusading attempts of the thirteenth century, Isabella and other rulers realized full well that they lacked the material resources to mount the full-scale assault on Islam necessary for victory. Crusading impulses thus shifted from the Muslims to the pagan peoples of Africa and the Americas.

Moreover, after the *reconquista*—the Christian reconquest of Muslim areas—enterprising young men of the Spanish upper classes found economic and political opportunities severely limited. As a study of the Castilian city Ciudad Real shows, the traditional aristocracy controlled the best agricultural land and monopolized urban administrative posts. Great merchants and a few nobles (surprisingly, since Spanish law forbade noble participation in commercial ventures) dominated the textile and leather-glove manufacturing industries. Thus many ambitious men emigrated to the Americas to seek their fortunes.[3]

Government sponsorship and encouragement of exploration also help to account for the results of the various voyages. Individual mariners and explorers could not afford the massive sums needed to explore mysterious oceans and to control remote continents. The strong financial support of Prince Henry the Navigator led to Portugal's phenomenal success in the spice trade. Even the grudging and modest assistance of Isabella and Ferdinand eventually brought untold riches—and complicated problems—to Spain. The Dutch in the seventeenth century, through such government-sponsored trading companies as the Dutch East India Company, reaped enormous wealth, and although the Netherlands was a small country in size, it dominated the European economy in 1650.

Scholars have frequently described the European discoveries as a manifestation of Renaissance curiosity about the physical universe—the desire to know more about the geography and peoples of the world. There is truth to this explanation. Cosmography, natural history, and geography aroused enormous interest among educated people in the fifteenth and sixteenth centuries. Just as science fiction and speculation about life on other planets excite readers today, quasi-scientific literature about Africa, Asia, and the Americas captured the imaginations of Europeans. Oviedo's *General History of the Indies* (1547), a detailed eyewitness account of plants, animals, and peoples, was widely read.

Spices were another important incentive to voyages of discovery. Introduced into western Europe by the Crusaders in the twelfth century, nutmeg, mace, ginger, cinnamon, and pepper added flavor and variety to the monotonous diet of Europeans. Spices were also used in the preparation of medicinal drugs and incense for religious ceremonies. In the late thirteenth century, the Venetian Marco Polo (1254?–1324?), the greatest of medieval travelers, had visited the court of the Chinese emperor. The widely publicized account of his travels in the *Book of Various Experiences* stimulated the trade in spices between Asia and Italy. The Venetians came to hold a monopoly of trade in western Europe.

Spices were grown in India and China, shipped across the Indian Ocean to ports on the Persian Gulf, and then transported by Arabs across the Arabian Desert to Mediterranean ports. But the rise of the Ming Dynasty in China in the late fourteenth century resulted in the expulsion of foreigners. And the steady penetration of the Ottoman Turks into the eastern Mediterranean and of Muslims across North Africa forced Europeans to seek a new route to the Asian spice markets.

The basic reason for European exploration and expansion, however, was the quest for material profit. Mariners and explorers frankly admitted this. As Bartholomew Diaz put it, his motives were "to serve God and His Majesty, to give light to those who were in darkness and to grow rich as all men desire to do." When Vasco da Gama reached the port of Calicut, India, in 1498, a native asked what the Portuguese wanted. Da Gama replied, "Christians and spices."[4] The bluntest of the Spanish conquistadors, Hernando Cortés, announced as he prepared to conquer Mexico, "I have come to win gold, not to plow the fields like a peasant."[5]

A sixteenth-century diplomat, Ogier Gheselin de Busbecq, summed up explorers' paradoxical attitude: in expeditions to the Indies and the Antipodes, he said, "religion supplies the pretext and gold the motive."[6]

The Problem of Christopher Columbus

The year 1992, which marked the quincentenary of Columbus's first voyages to the Americas, spawned an enormous amount of discussion about the significance of his voyages. Journalists, scholars, amateurs, and polemicists debated Columbus's accomplishments and failures. Until the 1980s most writers generally would have agreed with the Harvard historian Samuel Eliot Morison in his 1942 biography of Columbus:

The whole history of the Americas stems from the Four Voyages of Columbus; and as the Greek city-states looked back to the deathless gods as their founders, so today a score of independent nations and dominions unite in homage to Columbus, the stout-hearted son of Genoa, who carried Christian civilization across the Ocean Sea.[7]

In 1942, we must remember, the Western Powers believed they were engaged in a life-and-death struggle to defend "Christian civilization" against the evil forces of fascism. As the five hundredth anniversary of his famous voyage approached, however, Columbus underwent severe criticism.

Critics charged that he enslaved and sometimes killed the Indians and was a cruel and ineffective governor of Spain's Caribbean colony. Moreover, they said, he did not discover a previously unknown continent: Africans and other Europeans had been to the Western Hemisphere before him. And not only did he not discover a "new" continent, he not not realize what he had found. In short, according to his harshest critics, he was a fool who didn't know what was going on around him. Some claim that he was the originator of European exploitation of the non-European world and destroyed the paradise that had been the New World.[8]

Because those judgments rest on social and ethical standards that did not exist in Columbus's world, responsible scholars consider them ahistorical. Instead, using the evidence of his journal (sea log) and letters, let us ask three basic questions: (1) What kind of man was Columbus, and what forces or influences shaped him? (2) In sailing westward from Europe, what were his goals? (3) Did he achieve his goals, and what did he make of his discoveries?

Pepper Harvest To break the monotony of their bland diet, Europeans had a passion for pepper, which—along with cinnamon, cloves, nutmeg, and ginger—was the main object of the Asian trade. Since one kilo of pepper cost 2 grams of silver at the place of production in the East Indies and from 10 to 14 grams of silver in Alexandria, 14 to 18 grams in Venice, and 20 to 30 grams at the markets of northern Europe, we can appreciate the fifteenth-century expression "As dear as pepper." Here natives fill vats, and the dealer tastes a peppercorn for pungency. (*Source: Bibliothèque Nationale, Paris*)

The central feature in the character of Christopher Columbus is that he was a deeply religious man. He began the *Journal* of his voyage to the Americas, written as a letter to Ferdinand and Isabella of Spain, with this recollection:

On 2 January in the year 1492, when your Highnesses had concluded their war with the Moors who reigned in Europe, I saw your Highnesses' banners victoriously raised on the towers of the Alhambra, the citadel of the city, and the Moorish king come out of the city gates and kiss the hands of your Highnesses and the prince, My Lord. And later in that same month, on the grounds of information I had given your Highnesses concerning the lands of India . . . your Highnesses decided to send me, Christopher Columbus, to see these parts of India and the princes and peoples of those lands and consider the best means for their conversion.[9]

He had witnessed the Spanish reconquest of Granada and shared fully in the religious and nationalistic fervor surrounding that event. Just seven months separated Isabella and Ferdinand's entry into Granada on January 6 and Columbus's departure westward on August 3, 1492. In his mind, the two events were clearly linked. Long after Europeans knew something of Columbus's discoveries in the Caribbean, they considered the restoration of Muslim Granada to Christian hands as Ferdinand and Isabella's greatest achievements; for the conquest, in 1494 the Spanish pope Alexander VI (r. 1492–1503) rewarded them with the title of "Most Catholic Kings." Like the Spanish rulers and most Europeans of his age, Columbus understood Christianity as a missionary religion that should be carried to places and peoples where it did not exist. Although Columbus's character certainly included material and secular qualities, first and foremost, as he wrote in 1498, he believed he was a divine agent:

God made me the messenger of the new heaven and the new earth of which he spoke in the Apocalypse of St. John after having spoken of it through the mouth of the prophet Isaiah; and he showed me the post where to find it.[10]

A second and fundamental facet of Columbus the man is that he was very knowledgeable about the sea. He was familiar with fifteenth-century Portuguese navigational aids such as portolans—written descriptions of routes showing bays, coves, capes, ports, and the distances between these places—and the magnetic compass. He had spent years consulting geographers, mapmakers, and navigators. And, as he implies in his *Journal,* he had acquired not only theoretical but practical experience:

I have spent twenty-three years at sea and have not left it for any length of time worth mentioning, and I have seen everything from east to west [meaning he had been to England] and I have been to Guinea" [North and West Africa].[11]

Some of Columbus's calculations, such as his measurement of the distance from Portugal to Japan as 2,760 miles (it is actually 12,000), proved inaccurate. But his successful thirty-three-day voyage to the Caribbean owed a great deal to his seamanship and his knowledge and skillful use of instruments.

What was the object of his first voyage? What did Columbus set out to do? He gives the answer in the very title of the expedition, "The Enterprise of the Indies." He wanted to find a direct ocean route to Asia, which would provide the opportunity for a greatly expanded trade, a trade in which the European economy, and especially Spain, would participate. Two scholars have recently written, "If Columbus had not sailed westward in search of Asia, someone else would have done so. The time was right for such a bold undertaking."[12] Someone else might have done so, but the fact remains that Columbus, displaying a characteristic Renaissance curiosity and restless drive, actually accepted the challenge.

How did Columbus interpret what he had found, and did he think he had achieved what he set out to do? His mind had been formed by the Bible and the geographical writings of classical authors, as were the minds of most educated people of his time. Thus, as people in every age have often done, Columbus ignored the evidence of his eyes; he described what he saw in the Caribbean as an idyllic paradise, a peaceful garden of Eden. When accounts of his travels were published, Europeans' immediate fascination with this image of the New World meant that Columbus's propaganda created an instant myth. But when he sensed that he had not found the spice markets and bazaars of Asia,

his goal changed from establishing trade with the (East) Indians and Chinese to establishing the kind of trade the Portuguese were then conducting with Africa and with Cape Verde and other islands in the Atlantic (see Map 16.1). That meant setting up some form of government in the Caribbean islands, even though Columbus had little interest in, or capacity for, governing. In 1496, he forcibly subjugated the island of Hispaniola, enslaved the Indians, and laid the basis for a system of land grants tied to the Indians' labor service. Borrowing practices and institutions from reconquest Spain and the Canary Islands, Columbus laid the foundation for Spanish imperial administration. In all of this, Columbus was very much a man of his times. He never understood, however, that the scale of his discoveries created problems of trade, settlers, relations with the Indians, and, above all, government bureaucracy.[13]

The Conquest of Aztec Mexico and Inca Peru

Technological development also helps to explain the Spanish conquest of Aztec Mexico and Inca Peru.

The strange end of the Aztec nation remains one of the most fascinating events in the annals of human societies. The Spanish adventurer Hernando Cortés (1485–1547) landed at Vera Cruz in February 1519. In November he entered Tenochtitlán (Mexico City) and soon had the emperor Montezuma II (r. 1502–1520) in custody. In less than two years Cortés destroyed the monarchy, gained complete control of the Mexican capital, and extended his jurisdiction over much of the Aztec Empire. Why did a strong people defending its own territory succumb so quickly to a handful of Spaniards fighting in dangerous and completely unfamiliar circumstances? How indeed, since Montezuma's scouts sent him detailed reports of the Spaniards' movements? The answers to these questions lie in the fact that at the time of the Spanish arrival the Aztec and Inca Empires faced grave internal difficulties brought on by their religious ideologies; by the Spaniards' boldness, timing, and technology; and by Aztec and Incan psychology and attitudes toward war.

The Spaniards arrived in late summer, when the Aztecs were preoccupied with harvesting their crops and not thinking of war. From the Spaniards' perspective, their timing was ideal. A series of natural phenomena, signs, and portents seemed to augur disaster for the Aztecs. A comet was seen in daytime, a column of fire had appeared every midnight for a year, and two temples were suddenly destroyed, one by lightning unaccompanied by thunder. These and other apparently inexplicable events seemed to presage the return of the Aztec god Quetzalcoatl and had an unnerving effect on the Aztecs. They looked on the Europeans riding "wild beasts" as extraterrestrial forces coming to establish a new social order. Defeatism swept the nation and paralyzed its will.

The Aztec state religion, the sacred cult of Huitzilopochtli, necessitated constant warfare against neighboring peoples to secure captives for religious sacrifice and laborers for agricultural and infrastructural work. Lacking an effective method of governing subject peoples, the Aztecs controlled thirty-eight provinces in central Mexico through terror. When Cortés landed, the provinces were being crushed under a cycle of imperial oppression: increases in tribute provoked revolt, which led to reconquest, retribution, and demands for higher tribute, which in turn sparked greater resentment and fresh revolt. When the Spaniards appeared, the Totonacs greeted them as liberators, and other subject peoples joined them against the Aztecs. Even before the coming of the Spaniards, Montezuma's attempts to resolve the problem of constant warfare by freezing social positions—thereby ending the social mobility that war provided—aroused the resentment of his elite, mercantile, and lowborn classes. Montezuma faced terrible external and internal difficulties.[14]

Montezuma refrained from attacking the Spaniards as they advanced toward his capital and welcomed Cortés and his men into Tenochtitlán. Historians have often condemned the Aztec ruler for vacillation and weakness. But he relied on the advice of his state council, itself divided, and on the dubious loyalty of tributary communities. When Cortés—with incredible boldness—took Montezuma hostage, the emperor's influence over his people crumbled.

The major explanation for the collapse of the Aztec Empire to six hundred Spaniards lies in the Aztecs' notion of warfare and their level of technology. Forced to leave Tenochtitlán to settle a conflict elsewhere, Cortés placed his lieutenant, Alvarado, in charge. Alvarado's harsh rule drove the Aztecs to revolt, and they almost succeeded in destroying the Spanish garrison. When Cortés re-

turned just in time, the Aztecs allowed his reinforcements to join Alvarado's besieged force. No threatened European or Asian state would have conceived of doing such a thing: dividing an enemy's army and destroying the separate parts was basic to their military tactics. But for the Aztecs warfare was a ceremonial act in which "divide and conquer" had no place.

Having allowed the Spanish forces to reunite, the entire population of Tenochtitlán attacked the invaders. The Aztecs killed many Spaniards. In retaliation, the Spaniards executed Montezuma. The Spaniards escaped from the city and inflicted a crushing defeat on the Aztec army at Otumba near Lake Texcoco on July 7, 1520. The Spaniards won because "the simple Indian methods of mass warfare were of little avail against the manoeuvring of a well-drilled force."[15] Aztec weapons proved no match for the terrifyingly noisy and lethal Spanish cannon, muskets, crossbows, and steel swords. European technology decided the battle. Cortés began the systematic conquest of Mexico.

From 1493 to 1527 the Inca Huayna Capac ruled as a benevolent despot (the word *Inca* refers both to the ruler of the Amerindians who lived in the valleys of the Andes Mountains in present-day Peru and to the people themselves). His power was limited only by custom. His millions of subjects considered him a god, firm but just to his people, merciless to his enemies. Only a few of the Inca's closest relatives dared look at his divine face. Nobles approached him on their knees, and the masses kissed the dirt as he rode by in his litter. The borders of his vast empire were well fortified and threatened by no foreign invaders. Grain was plentiful, and apart from an outbreak of smallpox in a distant province—introduced by the Spaniards—no natural disaster upset the general peace. An army of fifty thousand loyal troops stood at the Inca's disposal. Why did this powerful empire fall so easily to Francisco Pizarro and his band of 175 men armed with one small, ineffective cannon?

The Incas were totally isolated. They had no contact with other Amerindian cultures and knew nothing at all of Aztec civilization or its collapse to the Spaniards in 1521. Since about the year 1500, Inca scouts had reported "floating houses" on the seas, manned by white men with beards. Tradesmen told of strange large animals with feet of silver (as horseshoes appeared in the brilliant sunshine). Having observed a border skirmish between Indians and white men, intelligence sources advised

Huayna Capac that the Europeans' swords were as harmless as women's weaving battens. A coastal chieftain had poured chicha, the native beer, down the barrel of a gun to appease the god of thunder. These incidents suggest that Inca culture provided no basis for understanding the Spaniards and the significance of their arrival. Moreover, even if the strange pale men planned war, there were very few of them, and the Incas believed that they could not be reinforced from the sea.[16]

At first the Incas did not think that the strangers intended trouble. They believed the old Inca legend that the creator-god Virocha—who had brought civilization to them, become displeased, and sailed away promising to return someday—had indeed returned. Belief in a legend prevented the Incas, like the Aztecs, from taking prompt action.

Religious ideology contributed to grave domestic crisis within the empire. When the ruler died, his corpse was preserved as a mummy. The mummy was both a holy object and a dynamic force in Inca society. It was housed in a sacred chamber and dressed in fine clothing. It was carried in procession to state ceremonies and was asked for advice in times of trouble. This cult of the royal mummies left a new Inca (ruler) with the title and insignia of his office but little else. Because each dead Inca retained possession of the estates and properties he had held in life, each new Inca lacked land. Thus, to strengthen his administration, secure the means to live in the royal style, and reward his supporters, a new Inca had to engage in warfare to acquire land.

In 1525, Huascar succeeded his father Huayna Capac as Inca and was crowned at Cuzco, the Incas' capital city, with the fringed headband symbolizing his imperial office. By this time, the dead rulers controlled most of Peru's land and resources. The nobility managed the estates of the dead Inca rulers. Needing land and other possessions, Huascar proposed burying the mummies of all of the dead Incas and using the profits from their estates for the living.

According to Inca law, the successor of a dead Inca had to be a son by the ruler's principal wife, who had to be the ruler's full sister. Huascar was the result of such an incestuous union. His half-brother Atauhualpa was not. Atauhualpa tried to persuade Huascar to split the kingdom with him, claiming that their father's dying wish was for both sons to rule. Huascar rejected this claim. The great nobles responsible for the cult of the royal mum-

mies, however, were alarmed and outraged by Huascar's proposal to bury the mummies. Not only would Huascar be insulting the dead mummies and thus provoke their anger and retaliation, but the nobility would be deprived of the wealth and power they enjoyed as custodians of the cult. Willing to ignore the fact that Atauhualpa had not been born of an incestuous union, the nobles supported Atauhualpa's claim to rule. Civil war ensued, and Atauhualpa emerged victorious.[17] The five-year struggle may have exhausted him and damaged his judgment.

Francisco Pizarro (ca 1475–1541) landed on the northern coast of Peru on May 13, 1532, the very day Atauhualpa won the decisive battle against his brother. The Spaniard soon learned about the war and its outcome. As Pizarro advanced across the steep Andes toward Cuzco, Atauhualpa was proceeding to the capital for his coronation. Atauhualpa stopped at the provincial town of Cajamarca. He, like Montezuma in Mexico, was kept fully informed of the Spaniards' movements. His plan was to lure the Spaniards into a trap, seize their horses and ablest men for his army, and execute the rest. What had the Inca, surrounded by his thousands of troops, to fear? Atauhualpa thus accepted Pizarro's invitation to meet in the central plaza of Cajamarca with his bodyguards "unarmed so as not to give offense." He rode right into the Spaniard's trap. Pizarro knew that if he could capture that Inca, from whom all power devolved, he would have the "Kingdom of Gold" for which he had come to the New World.

The Inca's litter arrived in the ominously quiet town square. One cannon blast terrified the Indians. The Spaniards rushed out of hiding and slaughtered them. Atauhualpa's fringed headband was instantly torn from his head. He offered to purchase his freedom with a roomful of gold. Pizarro agreed to this ransom, and an appropriate document was drawn up and signed. But after the gold had been gathered from all parts of the empire to fill the room—its dimensions were 17 feet by 22 feet by 9 feet—the Spaniards trumped up charges against Atauhualpa and strangled him. The Inca Empire lay at Pizarro's feet.

The South American Holocaust

In the sixteenth century, about 200,000 Spaniards emigrated to the New World. Soldiers demobilized from the Spanish and Italian campaigns, adventurers and drifters unable to find work in Spain, they did not intend to work in the New World. After assisting in the conquest of the Aztecs and the subjugation of the Incas, these drifters wanted to settle down and become a ruling class. In temperate grazing areas they carved out vast estates and imported Spanish sheep, cattle, and horses for the kinds of ranching with which they were familiar. In the coastal tropics, unsuited for grazing, the Spanish erected huge sugar plantations. Columbus had introduced sugar into the West Indies; Cortés had introduced it into Mexico. Sugar was a great luxury in Europe, and demand for it was high. Around 1550 the discovery of silver at Zacatecas and Guanajuato in Mexico and Potosí in present-day Bolivia stimulated silver rushes. How were the cattle ranches, sugar plantations, and silver mines to be worked? Obviously, by the Indians.

The Spanish quickly established the *encomienda* system, whereby the Crown granted the conquerors the right to employ groups of Indians in a town or area as agricultural or mining laborers or as tribute-payers. Theoretically, the Spanish were forbidden to enslave the Indian natives; in actuality, the encomiendas were a legalized form of slavery. The European demand for sugar, tobacco, and silver prompted the colonists to exploit the Indians mercilessly. Unaccustomed to forced labor, especially in the blistering heat of tropical cane fields or the dark, dank, and dangerous mines, Indians died like flies. Recently scholars have tried to reckon the death rate of the Amerindians in the sixteenth century. Some historians maintain that the Indian population of Peru fell from 1.3 million in 1570 to 600,000 in 1620; central Mexico had 25.3 million Indians in 1519 and 1 million in 1605.[18] Some demographers dispute these figures, but all agree that the decline of the native Indian population in all of Spanish-occupied America amounted to a catastrophe greater in scale than any that has occurred even in the twentieth century.

What were the causes of this devastating slump in population? Students of the history of medicine have suggested the best explanation: disease. The

✤ **Indians Panning for Gold**   The Flemish engraver Theodore de Bry (1528–1598) produced many scenes of American life based on geographers' accounts; he was not an eyewitness of what he illustrated. Here native Americans working in a stream on Hispaniola dredge up and sift alluvial sand for gold dust and nuggets. The island had very little of either. *(Source: By permission of the Houghton Library, Harvard University)*

major cause of widespread epidemics is migration, and those peoples isolated longest from other societies suffer most. Contact with disease builds up bodily resistance. At the beginning of the sixteenth century, Amerindians probably had the unfortunate distinction of longer isolation from the rest of humankind than any other people on earth. Crowded concentrations of laborers in the mining camps bred infection, which the miners carried to their home villages. With little or no resistance to diseases brought from the Old World, the inhabitants of the highlands of Mexico and Peru, especially, fell victim to smallpox. According to one expert, smallpox caused "in all likelihood the most severe single loss of aboriginal population that ever occurred."[19]

Although disease was the prime cause of the Indian holocaust, the Spaniards themselves contributed heavily to the Indians' death rate.[20] According to the Franciscan missionary Bartolomé de Las Casas (1474–1566), the Spanish maliciously murdered thousands:

This infinite multitude of people [the Indians] was . . . without fraud, without subtilty or malice . . . toward the Spaniards whom they serve, patient, meek and peaceful. . . .

To these quiet Lambs . . . came the Spaniards like most c(r)uel Tygres, Wolves and Lions, enrag'd with a sharp and tedious hunger; for these forty years past, minding nothing else but the slaughter of these unfortunate wretches, whom with divers kinds of torments neither seen nor heard of before, they have so cruelly and inhumanely butchered, that of three millions of people which Hispaniola it self did contain, there are left remaining alive scarce three hundred persons.[21]

Las Casas's remarks concentrate on the tropical lowlands, but the death rate in the highlands was also staggering.

The Christian missionaries who accompanied the conquistadors and settlers—Franciscans, Dominicans, and Jesuits—played an important role in converting the Indians to Christianity, teaching them European methods of agriculture, and inculcating loyalty to the Spanish crown. In terms of numbers of people baptized, missionaries enjoyed phenomenal success, though the depth of the Indians' understanding of Christianity remains debatable. Missionaries, especially Las Casas, asserted that the Indians had human rights, and through Las Casas's persistent pressure the emperor Charles

V in 1531 abolished the worst abuses of the encomienda system.

Some scholars offer a psychological explanation for the colossal death rate of the Indians, suggesting that they simply lost the will to survive because their gods appeared to have abandoned them to a world over which they had no control. Hopelessness, combined with abusive treatment and overwork, pushed many men to suicide, many women to abortion or infanticide.

Whatever its precise causes, the astronomically high death rate created a severe labor shortage in Spanish America. As early as 1511, King Ferdinand of Spain observed that the Indians seemed to be "very frail" and that "one black could do the work of four Indians."[22] Thus was born an absurd myth and the massive importation of black slaves from Africa (see pages 665–674).

Colonial Administration

Having seized the great Indian ceremonial centers in Mexico and Peru, the Spanish conquistadors proceeded to subdue the main areas of native American civilization in the New World. Columbus, Cortés, and Pizarro claimed the lands they had "discovered" for the crown of Spain. How were these lands to be governed?

According to the Spanish theory of absolutism, the Crown was entitled to exercise full authority over all imperial lands. In the sixteenth century the Crown divided Spain's New World territories into four *viceroyalties,* or administrative divisions. New Spain, with its capital at Mexico City, consisted of Mexico, Central America, and present-day California, Arizona, New Mexico, and Texas. Peru, with its viceregal seat at Lima, originally consisted of all the lands in continental South America but later was reduced to the territory of modern Peru, Chile, Bolivia, and Ecuador. New Granada, with Bogotá as its administrative center, included present-day Venezuela, Colombia, Panama, and, after 1739, Ecuador. La Plata, with Buenos Aires as its capital, consisted of Argentina, Uruguay, and Paraguay. Within each territory a *viceroy,* or imperial governor, had broad military and civil authority as the Spanish sovereign's direct representative. The viceroy presided over the *audiencia,* twelve to fifteen judges who served as advisory council and as the highest judicial body.

From the early sixteenth century to the beginning of the nineteenth, the Spanish monarchy acted on the mercantilist principle that the colonies existed for the financial benefit of the mother country. The mining of gold and silver was always the most important industry in the colonies. The Crown claimed the *quinto,* one-fifth of all precious metals mined in the Americas. Gold and silver yielded the Spanish monarchy 25 percent of its total income. In return, Spain shipped manufactured goods to the New World and discouraged the development of native industries.

The Portuguese governed their colony of Brazil in a similar manner. After the union of the crowns of Portugal and Spain in 1580, Spanish administrative forms were introduced. Local officials called *corregidores* held judicial and military powers. Mercantilist policies placed severe restrictions on Brazilian industries that might compete with those of Portugal. In the seventeenth century the use of black slave labor made possible the cultivation of coffee, cotton, and sugar. In the eighteenth century Brazil led the world in the production of sugar. The unique feature of colonial Brazil's culture and society was its thoroughgoing mixture of Indians, whites, and blacks.

The Economic Effects of Spain's Discoveries on Europe

The sixteenth century has often been called Spain's golden century. The influence of Spanish armies, Spanish Catholicism, and Spanish wealth was felt all over Europe. This greatness rested largely on the influx of precious metals from the Americas.

The mines at Zacatecas, Guanajuato, and Potosí in Peru poured out huge quantities of precious metals. To protect this treasure from French and English pirates, armed convoys transported it each year to Spain. Between 1503 and 1650, 16 million kilograms of silver and 185,000 kilograms of gold entered Seville's port. Spanish predominance, however, proved temporary.

In the sixteenth century, Spain experienced a steady population increase, creating a sharp rise in the demand for food and goods. Spanish colonies in the Americas also represented a demand for products. Since Spain had expelled some of the best farmers and businessmen—the Muslims and Jews—in the fifteenth century, the Spanish economy was suffering and could not meet the new demands. Prices rose. Because the cost of manufacturing cloth and other goods increased, Spanish products could not compete in the international market with cheaper products made elsewhere. The textile industry was badly hurt. Prices spiraled upward faster than the government could levy taxes to dampen the economy. (Higher taxes would have cut the public's buying power; with fewer goods sold, prices would have come down.)

Did the flood of silver bullion from America cause the inflation? Prices rose most steeply before 1565, but bullion imports reached their peak between 1580 and 1620. Thus there is no direct correlation between silver imports and the inflation rate. Did the substantial population growth accelerate the inflation rate? It may have done so. After 1600, when the population pressure declined, prices gradually stabilized. One fact is certain: the price revolution severely strained government budgets. Several times between 1557 and 1647, Spain's king Philip II and his successors repudiated the state debt, thereby undermining confidence in the government and leading the economy into shambles.

As Philip II paid his armies and foreign debts with silver bullion, Spanish inflation was transmitted to the rest of Europe. Between 1560 and 1600, much of Europe experienced large price increases. Prices doubled and in some cases quadrupled. Spain suffered most severely, but all European countries were affected. People who lived on fixed incomes, such as the continental nobles, were badly hurt because their money bought less. Those who owed fixed sums of money, such as the middle class, prospered: in a time of rising prices, debts had less value each year. Food costs rose most sharply, and the poor fared worst of all.

Seaborne Trading Empires

By 1550, European overseas reconnaissance had led to the first global seaborne trade. For centuries the Muslims had controlled the rich spice trade of the Indian Ocean; Muslim expeditions had been across Asian and African land routes. The Europeans' discovery of the Americas and their exploration of the Pacific for the first time linked the entire world by intercontinental seaborne trade. That trade brought into being three successive commercial empires: the Portuguese, the Spanish, and the Dutch.

In the sixteenth century, naval power and shipborne artillery gave Portugal hegemony over the sea route to India. To Lisbon the Portuguese fleet brought spices, which the Portuguese paid for with

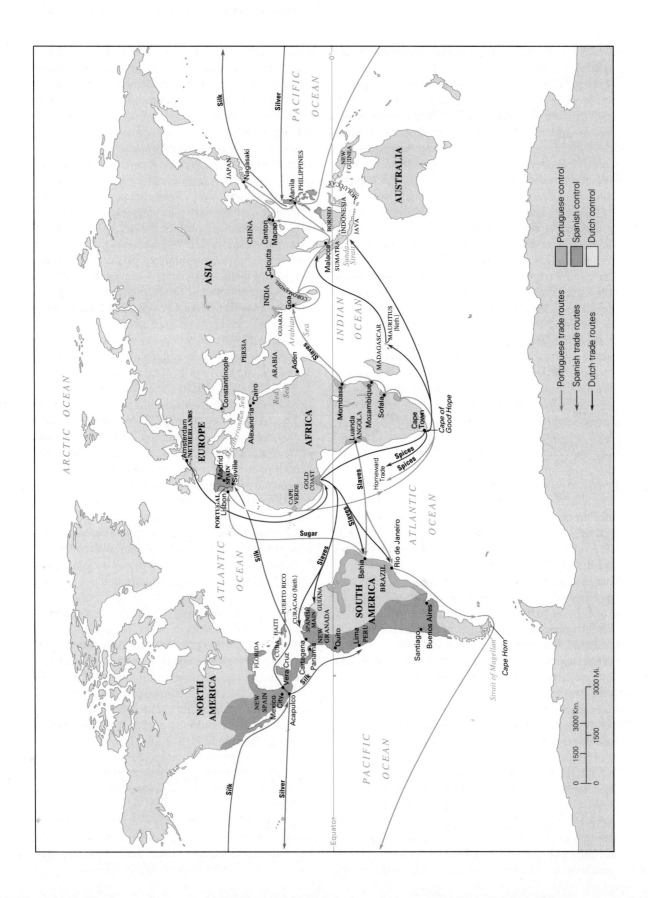

ARCTIC OCEAN

NORTH AMERICA

NEW SPAIN

Mexico City

Acapulco

Vera Cruz

FLORIDA

CUBA

HAITI

PUERTO RICO

CURACAO (Neth.)

Cartagena

Panama

SPANISH MAIN

NEW GRANADA

Quito

Lima

PERU

SOUTH AMERICA

Santiago

Buenos Aires

Rio de Janeiro

BRAZIL

Bahia

GUIANA

Silver

Silk

Silk

Silver

PACIFIC OCEAN

ATLANTIC OCEAN

Strait of Magellan

Cape Horn

Equator

Silk

Sugar

Slaves

Slaves

Slaves

Slaves

Spices

Spices

Homeward Trade

CAPE VERDE

GOLD COAST

PORTUGAL

Lisbon

SPAIN

Madrid

Seville

Amsterdam

NETHERLANDS

EUROPE

Mediterranean Sea

Constantinople

Alexandria

Cairo

Red Sea

ARABIA

Aden

PERSIA

AFRICA

Luanda

ANGOLA

Mombasa

Mozambique

Sofala

MADAGASCAR

MAURITIUS (Neth.)

Cape Town

Cape of Good Hope

INDIAN OCEAN

ASIA

Slaves

Arabian Sea

GUJARAT

INDIA

Goa

COROMANDEL

Calcutta

CHINA

Canton

Macao

JAPAN

Nagasaki

Manila

PHILIPPINES

Malacca

SUMATRA

Sunda Strait

INDONESIA

JAVA

BORNEO

MOLUCCAS

NEW GUINEA

AUSTRALIA

PACIFIC OCEAN

Silk

Silver

ATLANTIC OCEAN

Portuguese control

Spanish control

Dutch control

Portuguese trade routes

Spanish trade routes

Dutch trade routes

0   1500   3000 Km.

0   1500   3000 Mi.

textiles produced at Gujarat and Coromandel in India and with gold and ivory from East Africa (Map 16.2). From their fortified bases at Goa on the Arabian Sea and at Malacca on the Malay Peninsula, ships of Malabar teak carried goods to the Portuguese settlement at Macao in the South China Sea. From Macao, loaded with Chinese silks and porcelains, Portuguese ships sailed to the Japanese port of Nagasaki and to the Philippine port of Manila, where Chinese goods were exchanged for Spanish (that is, Latin American) silver. Throughout Asia, the Portuguese traded in slaves—black Africans, Chinese, and Japanese. The Portuguese imported to India horses from Mesopotamia and copper from Arabia; from India they exported hawks and peacocks for the Chinese and Japanese markets.

Across the Atlantic, Portuguese Brazil provided most of the sugar consumed in Europe in the sixteenth and early seventeenth centuries. African slave labor produced the sugar on the plantations of Brazil, and Portuguese merchants, some of them Jewish, controlled both the slave trade between West Africa and Brazil (see pages 545–546) and the commerce in sugar between Brazil and Portugal. The Portuguese were the first worldwide traders, and Portuguese was the language of the Asian maritime trade.

Spanish possessions in the New World constituted basically a land empire and, as already described, in the sixteenth century the Spaniards devised a method of governing that empire. But across the Pacific the Spaniards also built a seaborne empire, centered at Manila in the Philippines, which had been "discovered" by Ferdinand Magellan in 1521. Between 1564 and 1571, the Spanish navigator Miguel Lopez de Legazpi sailed from Mexico and through a swift and almost bloodless conquest took over the Philippine Islands. Legazpi founded Manila, which served as the trans-Pacific bridge between Spanish America and the extreme Eastern trade.

Chinese silk, sold by the Portuguese in Manila for American silver, was transported to Acapulco in Mexico, from which it was carried overland to Vera Cruz for re-export to Spain. Because hostile Pacific winds prohibited direct passage from the Philippines to Peru, large shipments of silk also went south from Acapulco to Peru (see Map 16.2). Spanish merchants could never satisfy the European demand for silk, so huge amounts of bullion went from Acapulco to Manila. For example, in 1597, 12 million pesos of silver, almost the total value of the transatlantic trade, crossed the Pacific. After about 1640, the Spanish silk trade declined because it could not compete with Dutch imports.

In the latter half of the seventeenth century, the worldwide Dutch seaborne trade predominated. The Dutch Empire was built on spices. In 1599 a Dutch fleet returned to Amsterdam carrying 600,000 pounds of pepper and 250,000 pounds of cloves and nutmeg. Those who had invested in the expedition received a 100 percent profit. The voyage led to the establishment in 1602 of the Dutch East India Company, founded with the stated intention of capturing the spice trade from the Portuguese.

The Dutch fleet, sailing from the Cape of Good Hope and avoiding the Portuguese forts in India, steered directly for the Sunda Strait in Indonesia (see Map 16.2). The Dutch wanted direct access to and control of the Indonesian sources of spices. In return for assisting Indonesian princes in local squabbles and disputes with the Portuguese, the Dutch won broad commercial concessions. Through agreements, seizures, and outright war, they gained control of the western access to the Indonesian archipelago. Gradually, they acquired political domination over the archipelago itself. Exchanging European manufactured goods—armor, firearms, linens, and toys—the Dutch soon had a monopoly on the very lucrative spice trade.[23]

The seaborne empires profited from the geographical reconnaissance and technological developments of the sixteenth century. The empires of Portugal, Spain, and Holland had strong commercial ambitions. They also paved the way for the eighteenth-century mercantilist empires of France and Great Britain.

MAP 16.2 Seaborne Trading Empires in the Sixteenth and Seventeenth Centuries In the sixteenth century, for the first time, the entire globe was linked by seaborne trade. In the seventeenth century American silver paid for Asian silks and spices, and African slaves in Latin America produced sugar for the tables of Europe.

The Chinese and Japanese Discovery of the West

The desire to Christianize pagan peoples was a major motive in Europeans' overseas expansion. The Indians of Central and South America, the

Muslims and polytheistic peoples of the Pacific, and the Confucian, Buddhist, and Shinto peoples of China and Japan became objects of Christianizing efforts. In this missionary activity the new Jesuit Order was dominant and energetic.

In 1582 the Jesuit Matteo Ricci (1552–1610) settled at Macao on the mouth of the Canton River. Like the Christian monks who had converted the Germanic tribes of early medieval Europe, Ricci sought first to convert the emperor and elite groups and then, through gradual assimilation, to win the throngs of Chinese. He tried to present Christianity to the Chinese in Chinese terms. He understood the Chinese respect for learning and worked to win converts among the scholarly class. When Ricci was admitted to the Imperial City at Beijing (Peking), he addressed the emperor Wan-li:

Li Ma-tou [Ricci's name transliterated into Chinese], your Majesty's servant, comes from the Far West, addresses himself to Your Majesty with respect, in order to offer gifts from his country. Despite the distance, fame told me of the remarkable teaching and fine institutions with which the imperial court has endowed all its peoples. I desired to share these advantages and live out my life as one of Your Majesty's subjects, hoping in return to be of some small use.[24]

Ricci presented the emperor with two clocks, one of them decorated with dragons and eagles in the Chinese style. The emperor's growing fascination with clocks gave Ricci the opportunity to display other examples of Western technology. He instructed court scholars about astronomical equipment and the manufacture of cannon and drew for them a map of the world—with China at its center. These inventions greatly impressed the Chinese intelligentsia. Over a century later a Jesuit wrote, "The Imperial Palace is stuffed with clocks, . . . watches, carillons, repeaters, organs, spheres, and astronomical clocks of all kinds—there are more than four thousand pieces from the best masters of Paris and London."[25] The Chinese first learned about Europe from the Jesuits.

But the Christians and the Chinese did not understand one another. Because the Jesuits served the imperial court as mathematicians, astronomers, and cartographers, the Chinese emperors allowed them to remain in Beijing. The Jesuits, however, were primarily interested in converting the Chinese to Christianity. The missionaries thought that

by showing the pre-eminence of Western science, they were demonstrating the superiority of Western religion. This was a relationship that the Chinese did not acknowledge. They could not accept a religion that required total commitment and taught the existence of an absolute. Only a small number of the highly educated, convinced of a link between ancient Chinese tradition and Christianity, became Christians. Most Chinese were hostile to the Western faith. They accused Christians of corrupting Chinese morals because they forbade people to honor their ancestors—and corruption of morals translated into disturbing the public order. They also accused Christians of destroying Chinese sanctuaries, of revering a man (Christ) who had been executed as a public criminal, and of spying on behalf of the Japanese.

The "Rites Controversy," a dispute over ritual between the Jesuits and other Roman Catholic religious orders, sparked a crisis. The Jesuits supported the celebration of the Mass in Chinese and the performance of other ceremonies in terms understandable to the Chinese. The Franciscans and other missionaries felt that the Jesuits had sold out the essentials of the Christian faith in order to win converts.

One burning issue was whether Chinese reverence for ancestors was homage to the good that the dead had done during their lives or an act of worship. The Franciscans secured the support of Roman authorities who considered themselves authorities on Chinese culture and decided against the Jesuits. In 1704 and again in 1742 Rome decreed that Roman ceremonial practice in Latin (not in Chinese) was to be the law for Chinese missions. (This decision continued to govern Roman Catholic missionary activity until the Second Vatican Council in 1962.) Papal letters also forbade Chinese Christians from participating in the rites of ancestor worship. The emperor in turn banned Christianity in China, and the missionaries were forced to flee.

The Christian West and the Chinese world learned a great deal from each other. The Jesuits probably were "responsible for the rebirth of Chinese mathematics in the seventeenth and eighteenth centuries," and Western contributions stimulated the Chinese development of other sciences.[26] From the Chinese, Europeans got the idea of building bridges suspended by chains. The first Western experiments in electrostatics and magnetism in the seventeenth century derived from

Chinese models. Travel accounts about Chinese society and customs had a profound impact on Europeans, making them more sensitive to the beautiful diversity of peoples and manners, as the essays of Montaigne (see pages 546–547) and other Western thinkers reveal.

Initial Japanese contacts with Europeans paralleled those of the Chinese. In 1542, Portuguese merchants arrived in Japan and quickly won large profits carrying goods between China and Japan. Dutch and English ships followed, also enjoying the rewards of the East Asian trade. The Portuguese merchants vigorously supported Christian missionary activity, and in 1547 the Jesuit missionary Saint Francis Xavier landed at Kagoshima, preached widely, and in two years won many converts. From the beginning, however, the Japanese government feared that native converts might have conflicting political loyalties. Divided allegiance could encourage European invasion of the islands—the Japanese authorities had the example of the Philippines, where Spanish conquest followed missionary activity.

Convinced that European merchants and missionaries had contributed to the general civil disorder, which the regime was trying to eradicate, the Japanese government decided to expel the Spanish and Portuguese and to close Japan to all foreign influence. A decree of 1635 was directed at the commissioners of the port of Nagasaki, a center of Japanese Christianity:

If there is any place where the teachings of the padres (Catholic priests) is practiced, the two of you must order a thorough investigation. . . . If there are any Southern Barbarians (Westerners) who propagate the teachings of the padres, or otherwise commit crimes, they may be incarcerated in the prison.[27]

In 1639, an imperial memorandum decreed: "hereafter entry by the Portuguese galeota [galleon or large oceangoing warship] is forbidden. If they insist on coming [to Japan], the ships must be destroyed and anyone aboard those ships must be beheaded.[28]

When tens of thousands of Japanese Christians made a stand on the peninsula of Shimabara, the Dutch lent the Japanese government cannon. The Protestant Dutch hated Catholicism, and as businessmen they hated the Portuguese, their great commercial rivals. Convinced that the Dutch had come only for trade and did not want to proselytize, the imperial government allowed the Dutch to remain. But Japanese authorities ordered them to remove their factory-station from Hirado on the western tip of Kyushu to the tiny island of Deshima, which covered just 2,100 square feet. The government limited Dutch trade to one ship a year, watched the Dutch very closely, and required Dutch officials to pay an annual visit to the capital to renew their loyalty. The Japanese also compelled the Dutch merchants to perform servile acts that other Europeans considered humiliating.

Long after Christianity ceased to be a potential threat to the Japanese government, the fear of Christianity sustained a policy of banning Western books on science or religion. Until well into the eighteenth century, Japanese intellectuals were effectively cut off from Western developments. The Japanese opinion of Westerners was not high. What little the Japanese knew derived from the few Dutch businessmen at Deshima. Very few Japanese people ever saw Europeans. If they did, they considered them "a special variety of goblin that bore only a superficial resemblance to a normal human being." The widespread rumor was that when Dutchmen urinated they raised one leg like dogs.[29]

✦ POLITICS, RELIGION, AND WAR

In 1559 France and Spain signed the Treaty of Cateau-Cambrésis, which ended the long conflict known as the Habsburg-Valois Wars. This event marks a watershed in early modern European history. Spain (the Habsburg side) was the victor. France, exhausted by the struggle, had to acknowledge Spanish dominance in Italy, where much of the war had been fought. Spanish governors ruled in Sicily, Naples, and Milan, and Spanish influence was strong in the Papal States and Tuscany. The Treaty of Cateau-Cambrésis ended an era of strictly dynastic wars and initiated a period of conflicts in which politics and religion played the dominant roles.

The wars of the late sixteenth century differed considerably from earlier wars. Sixteenth- and seventeenth-century armies were bigger than medieval ones; some forces numbered as many as fifty thousand men. Because large armies were expensive, governments had to reorganize their administrations to finance them. The use of gunpowder altered both the nature of warfare and popular attitudes toward it. Guns and cannon killed and wounded from a distance, indiscriminately. Writers scorned gunpowder as a coward's weapon that allowed a common soldier to kill a gentleman. Gunpowder weakened the notion, common during the Hundred Years' War (1337–1453), that warfare was an ennobling experience. Governments utilized propaganda, pulpits, and the printing press to arouse public opinion to support war.[30]

Late sixteenth-century conflicts fundamentally tested the medieval ideal of a unified Christian society governed by one political ruler—the emperor—to whom all rulers were theoretically subordinate, and one church, to which all people belonged. The Protestant Reformation had killed this ideal, but few people recognized it as dead. Catholics continued to believe that Calvinists and Lutherans could be reconverted; Protestants persisted in thinking that the Roman church should be destroyed. Most people believed that a state could survive only if its members shared the same faith. The settlement finally achieved in 1648, known as the Peace of Westphalia, signaled the end of the medieval ideal.

The Origins of Difficulties in France (1515–1559)

In the first half of the sixteenth century, France continued the recovery begun during the reign of Louis XI (r. 1461–1483). The population losses caused by the plague and the disorders accompanying the Hundred Years' War had created such a labor shortage that serfdom virtually disappeared. Cash rents replaced feudal rents and servile obligations. This development clearly benefited the peasantry. Meanwhile, the declining buying power of money hurt the nobility. Domestic and foreign trade picked up; mercantile centers expanded.

The charming and cultivated Francis I (r. 1515–1547) and his athletic, emotional son Henry II (r. 1547–1559) governed through a small, efficient council. In 1539 Francis issued an ordinance that placed the whole of France under the jurisdiction of the royal law courts and made French the language of those courts. This act had a powerful centralizing impact. The *taille,* a tax on land, provided what strength the monarchy had and supported a strong standing army. Unfortunately, the tax base was too narrow to support France's extravagant promotion of the arts and ambitious foreign policy.

Deliberately imitating the Italian Renaissance princes, the Valois monarchs lavished money on a vast building program and on Italian artists. Francis I commissioned the Paris architect Pierre Lescot to rebuild the palace of the Louvre and Michelangelo's star pupil, Il Rosso, to decorate the wing of the Fontainebleau chateau. After acquiring Leonardo da Vinci's painting *Mona Lisa,* Francis brought Leonardo himself to France. Whatever praise Francis I and Henry II deserve for importing Italian Renaissance art and architecture to France, they spent far more than they could afford.

The Habsburg-Valois Wars, which had begun in 1522, also cost more than the government could afford. In addition to the time-honored practices of increasing taxes and heavy borrowing, Francis I tried two new devices to raise revenue: the sale of public offices and a treaty with the papacy. The former proved to be only a temporary source of money. The offices sold tended to become hereditary within a family, and once a man bought an office he and his heirs were tax-exempt. The sale of public offices thus created a tax-exempt class known as the "nobility of the robe."

The treaty with the papacy was the Concordat of Bologna (1516), in which Francis agreed to recognize the supremacy of the papacy over a universal council, thereby accepting a monarchial, rather than a conciliar view of church government. In return, the French crown gained the right to appoint all French bishops and abbots. This understanding gave the monarchy a rich supplement of money and offices and power over ecclesiastical organization that lasted until the Revolution of 1789. The Concordat of Bologna helps to explain why France did not later become Protestant: in effect, it established Catholicism as the state religion. The Concordat, however, perpetuated disorders within the French church. The government used ecclesiastical offices to pay and reward civil servants, who were likely to be worldly priests who possessed few special spiritual qualifications and were not inclined to work to elevate the intellectual and moral standards of the parish clergy. Thus the teachings of Luther and Calvin, spread far and wide because of the invention of printing from movable type some sixty years before, found a receptive audience.

After the publication of Calvin's *Institutes of the Christian Religion* in 1536, sizable numbers of French people were attracted to the "reformed religion," as Calvinism was called. Because Calvin wrote in French rather than Latin, his ideas gained wide circulation. At first, Calvinism drew converts from among reform-minded members of the

✤ **Rossi and Primaticcio: The Gallery of Francis I**   Flat paintings alternating with rich sculpture provide a rhythm that directs the eye down the long gallery at Fontainebleau, constructed between 1530 and 1540. Francis I sought to re-create in France the elegant Renaissance lifestyle found in Italy. *(Source: Art Resource, NY)*

Catholic clergy, the industrious middle classes, and artisan groups. Most Calvinists lived in Paris, Lyons, Meaux, Grenoble, and other major cities.

In spite of condemnation by the universities, government bans, and massive burnings at the stake, the numbers of Protestants in France grew steadily. When Henry II died in 1559, perhaps one-tenth of the population had become Calvinist.

Religious Riots and Civil War in France (1559–1589)

For thirty years, from 1559 to 1589, violence and civil war divided and shattered France. The feebleness of the monarchy was the seed from which the weeds of civil violence germinated. The three weak sons of Henry II could not provide the necessary leadership, and the French nobility took advantage of this monarchial weakness. In the second half of the sixteenth century, between two-fifths and one-half of the nobility at one time or another became Calvinist, frequently adopting the "reformed religion" as a religious cloak for their independence from the monarchy. Armed clashes between Catholic royalist lords and Calvinist antimonarchial lords occurred in many parts of France.

Among the upper classes, the fundamental object of the struggle was power. At lower social levels, however, religious concerns were paramount.

Working-class crowds composed of skilled craftsmen and the poor wreaked terrible violence on people and property. Both Calvinists and Catholics believed that the others' books, services, and ministers polluted the community. Preachers incited violence, and ceremonies like baptisms, marriages, and funerals triggered it. Protestant pastors encouraged their followers to destroy statues and liturgical objects in Catholic churches. Catholic priests urged their flocks to shed the blood of the Calvinist heretics.

In the fourteenth and fifteenth centuries, crowd action—attacks on great nobles and rich prelates—had expressed economic grievances. In contrast, religious rioters of the sixteenth century believed that they could assume the power of public magistrates and rid the community of corruption. Municipal officials criticized the crowds' actions, but the participation of pastors and priests in these riots lent them some legitimacy.[31]

A savage Catholic attack on Calvinists in Paris on August 24, 1572 (Saint Bartholomew's Day), followed the usual pattern. The occasion was a religious ceremony—the marriage of the king's sister Margaret of Valois to the Protestant Henry of Navarre—that was intended to help reconcile Catholics and Huguenots, as French Calvinists were called. The night before the wedding, the leader of the Catholic aristocracy, Henry of Guise, had Gaspard de Coligny, leader of the Huguenot party, attacked. Rioting and slaughter followed. The Huguenot gentry in Paris was massacred, and religious violence spread to the provinces. Between August 25 and October 3, perhaps twelve thousand Huguenots perished at Meaux, Lyons, Orléans, and Paris.

The Saint Bartholomew's Day massacre led to the War of the Three Henrys, a civil conflict among factions led by the Protestant Henry of Navarre, by King Henry III (who succeeded the tubercular Charles IX), and by the Catholic Henry of Guise. The Guises wanted not only to destroy Calvinism but to replace Henry III with a member of the Guise family. France suffered fifteen more years of religious rioting and domestic anarchy. Agriculture in many areas was destroyed; commercial life declined severely; starvation and death haunted the land.

What ultimately saved France was a small group of Catholic moderates called *politiques.* They believed that no religious creed was worth the incessant disorder and destruction and that only the restoration of a strong monarchy could reverse the trend toward collapse. The death of Queen Catherine de' Medici, followed by the assassinations of Henry of Guise and King Henry III, paved the way for the accession of the politique and Protestant Henry of Navarre, who ascended the throne as Henry IV (r. 1589–1610).

This glamorous prince, "who knew how to fight, to make love, and to drink," as a contemporary remarked, knew that the majority of the French were Roman Catholics. Declaring "Paris is worth a Mass," Henry knelt before the archbishop of Bourges and was received into the Roman Catholic church. Henry's willingness to sacrifice religious principles in the interest of a strong monarchy saved France. The Edict of Nantes, which Henry published in 1598, granted to Huguenots liberty of conscience and liberty of public worship in two hundred fortified towns, such as La Rochelle. The reign of Henry IV and the Edict of Nantes prepared the way for French absolutism in the seventeenth century (see page 558) by helping to restore internal peace in France.

The Revolt of the Netherlands and the Spanish Armada

In the last quarter of the sixteenth century, the political stability of England, the international prestige of Spain, and the moral influence of the Roman papacy all became mixed up with a religious crisis in the Low Countries. By this time, the Netherlands was the pivot around which European money, diplomacy, and war revolved. What began as a movement for the reformation of the Catholic church developed into a struggle for Dutch independence from Spanish rule.

The Habsburg emperor Charles V (r. 1519–1556) had inherited the seventeen provinces that compose present-day Belgium and Holland. The French-speaking southern towns produced fine linens and woolens; the wealth of the Dutch-speaking northern cities rested on fishing, shipping, and international banking. In the cities of both regions of the Low Countries, trade and commerce had produced a vibrant cosmopolitan atmosphere.

Each of the seventeen provinces of the Netherlands was self-governing and enjoyed the right to make its own laws and collect its own taxes. Only economic connections and the recognition of a common ruler in the person of the emperor Charles V united the provinces. Delegates from each province met together in the Estates General, but important decisions had to be referred back to each provincial Estate for approval. In the middle of the sixteenth century, the provinces of the Netherlands had a limited sense of federation.

In the Low Countries, as elsewhere, corruption in the Roman church and the critical spirit of the Renaissance provoked pressure for reform. Lutheran tracts and Dutch translations of the Bible flooded the seventeen provinces in the 1520s and 1530s, and Protestant ideas circulated freely in the cosmopolitan atmosphere of the commercial centers. But Charles's Flemish loyalty checked the spread of Lutheranism. Charles had been born in Ghent and raised in the Netherlands; he was Flemish in language and culture. He identified with the Flemish and they with him.

In 1556, however, Charles V abdicated and divided his territories. His younger brother Ferdinand received Austria and the Holy Roman Empire and ruled as Ferdinand I (r. 1558–1564). His son Philip inherited Spain, the Low Countries, Milan and the kingdom of Sicily, and the Spanish possessions in America and ruled as Philip II (r. 1556–1598).

Lutheranism posed no serious threat to Spanish rule in the Low Countries; it was the spread of Calvinism that upset the applecart. By the 1560s,

To Purify the Church   The destruction of pictures and statues representing biblical events, Christian doctrine, or sacred figures was a central feature of the Protestant Reformation. Here Dutch Protestant soldiers destroy what they consider idols in the belief that they are purifying the church. *(Source: Fotomas Index)*

there was a strong, militant minority of Calvinists to whom Calvinism appealed because of its intellectual seriousness, moral gravity, and approval of any form of labor well done. Many working-class people converted because Calvinist employers would hire only fellow Calvinists. Well organized and with the backing of rich merchants, Calvinists quickly gained a wide following, and the Calvinist reformed religion tended in the 1570s to encourage opposition to "illegal" civil authorities.

In August of 1566, a year of very high grain prices, fanatical Calvinists, primarily of the poorest classes, embarked on a rampage of frightful destruction. As in France, Calvinist destruction in the Low Countries was incited by popular preaching, and attacks were aimed at religious images as symbols of false doctrines, not at people. The cathedral of Notre Dame at Antwerp was the first target. Begun in 1124 and finished only in 1518, this church stood as a monument to the commercial prosperity of Flanders, the piety of the business classes, and the artistic genius of centuries. On six succes-

sive summer evenings, crowds swept through the nave, attacking the greatest concentration of artworks in northern Europe: altars, paintings, books, tombs, ecclesiastical vestments, missals, manuscripts, ornaments, stained-glass windows, and sculptures. Before the havoc was over, thirty more churches had been sacked and irreplaceable libraries burned. From Antwerp the destruction spread to Brussels and Ghent and north to the provinces of Holland and Zeeland.

From Madrid, Philip II sent twenty thousand Spanish troops led by the duke of Alva to pacify the Low Countries. Alva interpreted "pacification" to mean the ruthless extermination of religious and political dissidents. His repressive measures and heavy taxation triggered widespread revolt.

For ten years, between 1568 and 1578, civil war raged in the Netherlands between Catholics and Protestants and between the seventeen provinces and Spain. Spanish generals could not halt the fighting. In 1576 the seventeen provinces united under the leadership of Prince William of Orange, called "the Silent" because of his remarkable discretion. In 1578 Philip II sent his nephew Alexander Farnese, duke of Parma, with an army of German mercenaries to crush the revolt once and for all. Avoiding pitched battles, Farnese fought by patient sieges. One by one the cities of the south fell and finally Antwerp, the financial capital of northern Europe.

Antwerp marked the farthest extent of Spanish jurisdiction and ultimately the religious division of the Netherlands. The ten southern provinces, the Spanish Netherlands (the future Belgium), remained Catholic and under the control of the Spanish Habsburgs. The seven northern provinces were Protestant and, led by Holland, formed the Union of Utrecht and in 1581 declared their independence from Spain. Thus was born the United Provinces of the Netherlands (Map 16.3).

Geography and sociopolitical structure differentiated the two countries. The northern provinces were ribboned with sluices and canals and therefore were highly defensible. Several times the Dutch had broken the dikes and flooded the countryside to halt the advancing Farnese. In the southern provinces the Ardennes Mountains interrupt the otherwise flat terrain. In the north the commercial aristocracy possessed the predominant power; in the south the landed nobility had the greater influence. The north was Protestant; the south remained Catholic.

Philip II and Alexander Farnese did not accept the division of the Low Countries, and the strug-

The Battle of Lepanto On October 7, 1571, the fleet of the Holy League (Spain, Venice, the papacy), under Don Juan of Austria, met the Ottoman Turkish navy at a bay in the mouth of the Gulf of Patros off Lepanto in western Greece. Since most of the Ottoman sailors had been sent home for the winter, the Turkish fleet was not ready for battle. Superior European numbers and command prevailed, and the Ottomans were routed. The battle broke the spell of complete Turkish supremacy in the Mediterranean, Europe celebrated a great victory, and the Christian galleys gained a huge crop of prisoners to man the oars. But the Turks quickly rebuilt their navy and regained effective control of the Mediterranean. *(Source: National Maritime Museum, London)*

gle continued after 1581. The Protestant United Provinces repeatedly asked the Protestant Queen Elizabeth of England for assistance. But she was reluctant to antagonize Philip II by supporting the Dutch against the Spanish. The Spanish king had the steady flow of silver from the Americas at his disposal, and Elizabeth, lacking such treasure, wanted to avoid war. She realized, however, that if she did not help the Protestant Netherlands and they were crushed by Farnese, the Spanish were likely to invade England.

Three developments forced Elizabeth's hand. First, the wars in the Low Countries—the chief market for English woolens—badly hurt the English economy. When wool was not exported, the Crown lost valuable customs revenues. Second, the murder of William the Silent in July 1584 eliminated not only a great Protestant leader but the chief military check on the Farnese advance. Third, the collapse of Antwerp appeared to signal a Catholic sweep through the Netherlands. The next step, the English feared, would be a Spanish invasion of their island. For these reasons, Elizabeth pumped £250,000 and two thousand troops into the Protestant cause in the Low Countries between 1585 and 1587. Increasingly fearful of plots orchestrated by the Catholic Mary, Queen of Scots, Elizabeth's cousin and probable heir, Elizabeth finally signed her death warrant. Mary was beheaded on February 18, 1587. Sometime between March 24 and 30, the news of Mary's death reached Philip II.

Philip of Spain considered himself the international defender of Catholicism and heir to the medieval imperial power. When Pope Sixtus V (r. 1585–1590) heard of the death of the Queen of Scots, he promised to pay Philip a million gold ducats the moment Spanish troops landed in England. Alexander Farnese had repeatedly warned that, to subdue the Dutch, he would have to conquer England and cut off the source of Dutch support.

In these circumstances Philip prepared a vast fleet to sail from Lisbon to Flanders, fight off Elizabeth's navy *if* it attacked, rendezvous with Farnese, and escort his barges across the English Channel. The expedition's purpose was to transport the Flemish army for a cross-Channel assault. Philip expected to receive the support of English Catholics and anticipated a great victory for Spain.

On May 9, 1588, *la felicissima armada*—"the most fortunate fleet" of 130 vessels as it was called in official documents—sailed from Lisbon harbor.

MAP 16.3 The Netherlands, 1578–1609
Though small in geographical size, the Netherlands held a strategic position in the religious struggles of the sixteenth century.

An English fleet of about 150 ships—smaller, faster, and more maneuverable than the Spanish ships, and many having greater firepower—met the Spanish fleet in the Channel. A combination of storms and squalls, spoiled food and rank water aboard the Spanish ships, inadequate Spanish ammunition, and, to a lesser extent, English fire ships that caused the Spanish to scatter gave England the victory. Many Spanish ships sank on the journey home around Ireland; perhaps 65 managed to reach home ports.

The battle in the Channel had mixed consequences. Spain soon rebuilt its navy, and after 1588 the quality of the Spanish fleet improved. More silver reached Spain from the New World between 1588 and 1603 than in any other fifteen-year period. The war between England and Spain dragged on for years.

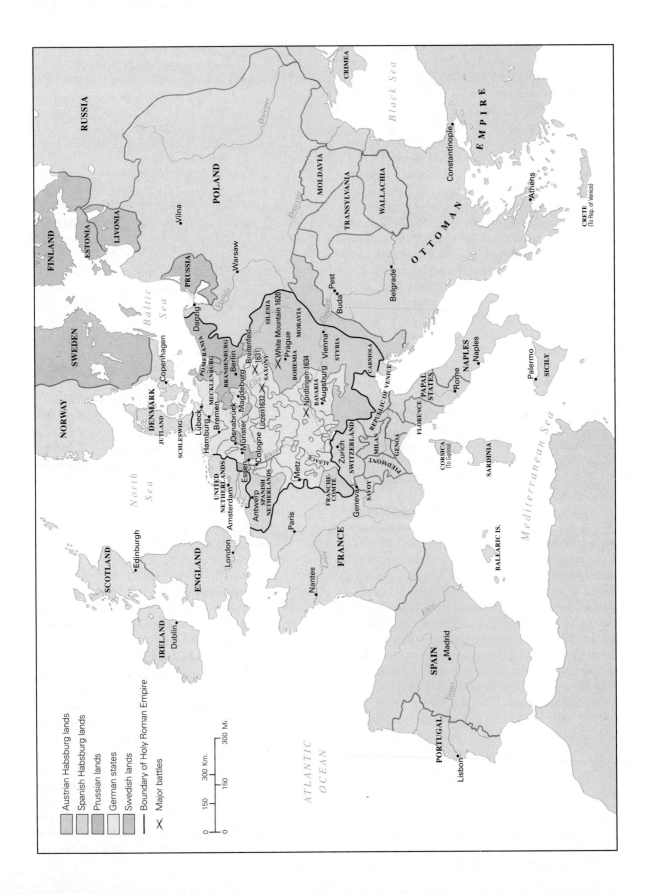

RUSSIA

FINLAND

SWEDEN

NORWAY

ESTONIA

LIVONIA

•Vilna

POLAND

•Warsaw

PRUSSIA

Baltic Sea

Danzig

DENMARK

JUTLAND

SCHLESWIG

Copenhagen

POMERANIA

MECKLENBURG

BRANDENBURG

Berlin

SILESIA

White Mountain 1620

Breitenfeld

1631

SAXONY

Prague

BOHEMIA

MORAVIA

Magdeburg

Lützen 1632

Elbe

CRIMEA

Black Sea

OTTOMAN EMPIRE

Constantinople

Athens

CRETE
(To Rep. of Venice)

MOLDAVIA

TRANSYLVANIA

WALLACHIA

Belgrade

Buda

Pest

Danube

Vienna

STYRIA

CARNIOLA

Nördlingen 1634

BAVARIA

Augsburg

NORTH Sea

Lübeck

Hamburg

Bremen

Osnabrück

Münster

Cologne

Essen

Rhine

UNITED
NETHERLANDS

Amsterdam

Antwerp

SPANISH
NETHERLANDS

Paris

FRANCE

Loire

Nantes

Metz

FRANCHE-
COMTÉ

ALSACE

Geneva

SAVOY

Zurich

SWITZERLAND

PIEDMONT

MILAN

GENOA

REPUBLIC OF VENICE

FLORENCE

PAPAL
STATES

Rome

NAPLES

Naples

CORSICA
(To Genoa)

SARDINIA

SICILY

Palermo

Mediterranean Sea

BALEARIC IS.

SPAIN

Madrid

Tagus

Ebro

PORTUGAL

Lisbon

SCOTLAND

Edinburgh

ENGLAND

London

IRELAND

Dublin

ATLANTIC OCEAN

Austrian Habsburg lands
Spanish Habsburg lands
Prussian lands
German states
Swedish lands
Boundary of Holy Roman Empire
X Major battles

0   150   300 Km.
0   150   300 Mi.

The defeat of the Spanish Armada was decisive, however, in the sense that it prevented Philip II from reimposing unity on western Europe by force. He did not conquer England, and Elizabeth continued her financial and military support of the Dutch. In the Netherlands neither side gained significant territory. The borders of 1581 tended to become permanent. In 1609 Philip III of Spain (r. 1598–1621) agreed to a truce, in effect recognizing the independence of the United Provinces. In seventeenth-century Spain the memory of the defeat of the Armada contributed to a spirit of defeatism. In England the victory gave rise to a David and Goliath legend that enhanced English national sentiment.

The Thirty Years' War (1618–1648)

Meanwhile, the political-religious situation in central Europe deteriorated. An uneasy truce had prevailed in the Holy Roman Empire since the Peace of Augsburg of 1555. The Augsburg settlement, recognizing the independent power of the German princes, had undermined the authority of the central government. According to the Augsburg settlement, the faith of the prince determined the religion of his subjects. There was no freedom of religion. If a prince was Lutheran, his subjects would be Lutheran. If a prince was Catholic, his subjects would be too. Dissidents had to convert or move to an area where their religion was recognized. Later in the century, Catholics grew alarmed because Lutherans, in violation of the Peace of Augsburg, were steadily acquiring German bishoprics. And Protestants were not pleased by militant Jesuits' success in reconverting several Lutheran princes to Catholicism. The spread of Calvinism further confused the issue. Lutherans feared that Catholic and Calvinist gains would totally undermine the Augsburg principles. In an increasingly tense situation, Lutheran princes formed the Protestant Union (1608). Catholics retaliated with the Catholic League (1609). The Holy Roman Empire was divided into two armed camps.

❋ **MAP 16.4 Europe in 1648**   Which country emerged from the Thirty Years' War as the strongest European power? What dynastic house was that country's major rival in the early modern period?

Dynastic interests were also at stake. The Spanish Habsburgs strongly supported the goals of the Austrian Habsburgs: the unity of the empire under Habsburg rule and the preservation of Catholicism within the empire.

Violence erupted first in Bohemia (Map 16.4). The Bohemians were Czech and German in nationality, and Lutheran, Calvinist, Catholic, and Hussite in religion; all these faiths enjoyed a fair degree of religious freedom in Bohemia. In 1617 Ferdinand of Styria, the new Catholic king of Bohemia, closed some Protestant churches. In retaliation, on May 23, 1618, Protestants hurled two of Ferdinand's officials from a castle window in Prague. They fell 70 feet but survived: Catholics claimed that angels had caught them; Protestants said the officials fell on a heap of soft horse manure. Called the "defenestration of Prague," this event marked the beginning of the Thirty Years' War (1618–1648).

Historians traditionally divide the war into four phases. The first, or Bohemian, phase (1618–1625) was characterized by civil war in Bohemia, as Bohemians fought for religious liberty and independence from Austrian Habsburg rule. In 1620 Ferdinand, newly elected Holy Roman Emperor Ferdinand II (r. 1619–1637), totally defeated Protestant forces at the Battle of the White Mountain and followed up his victories by wiping out Protestantism in Bohemia.

The second, or Danish, phase of the war (1625–1629)—so called because of the participation of King Christian IV of Denmark (r. 1588–1648), the ineffective leader of the Protestant cause—witnessed additional Catholic victories. The year 1629 marked the peak of Habsburg power. The Jesuits persuaded Ferdinand to issue the Edict of Restitution. It specified that all Catholic properties lost to Protestantism since 1552 were to be restored and only Catholics and Lutherans (*not* Calvinists, Hussites, or other sects) were to be allowed to practice their faiths. Ferdinand appeared to be embarked on a policy to unify the empire. Protestants throughout Europe feared collapse of the balance of power in north-central Europe.

The third, or Swedish, phase of the war (1630–1635) began when Swedish king Gustavus Adolphus (1594–1632) intervened to support the Protestant cause within the empire. In 1631, with French support, Gustavus Adolphus won a brilliant victory at Breitenfeld (see Map 16.4). Again in

1632 he was victorious at Lützen, though he was fatally wounded in the battle. The participation of the Swedes in the Thirty Years' War proved decisive for the future of Protestantism and later German history. The Swedish victories ended the Habsburg ambition of uniting all the German states under imperial authority.

The death of Gustavus Adolphus, followed by the defeat of the Swedes at the Battle of Nördlingen in 1634, prompted the French to enter the war on the side of the Protestants. Thus began the French, or international, phase of the Thirty Years' War (1635–1648). For almost a century, French foreign policy had been based on opposition to the Habsburgs, because a weak Holy Roman Empire enhanced France's international stature. Now, in 1635, France declared war on Spain and again sent financial and military assistance to the Swedes and the German Protestant princes. The war dragged on; neither side had the resources to win a quick, decisive victory. French, Dutch, and Swedes, supported by Scots, Finns, and German mercenaries, burned, looted, and destroyed German agriculture and commerce.

Finally, in October 1648, peace was achieved. The treaties signed at Münster and Osnabrück— the Peace of Westphalia—mark a turning point in European political, religious, and social history. The treaties recognized the sovereign, independent authority of the German princes. Each ruler could govern his particular territory and make war and peace as well. With power in the hands of more than three hundred princes, with no central government, courts, or means of controlling unruly rulers, the Holy Roman Empire as a real state was effectively destroyed.

The independence of the United Provinces of the Netherlands was acknowledged. The political divisions within the empire, and the acquisition of the province of Alsace increased France's size and prestige, and the treaties allowed France to intervene at will in German affairs. Sweden achieved a powerful presence in northeastern Germany (see Map 16.4). The treaties also denied the papacy the right to participate in German religious affairs— a restriction symbolizing the reduced role of the church in European politics.

The Westphalian treaties stipulated that the Augsburg religious agreement of 1555 should stand permanently. The sole modification made Calvinism, along with Catholicism and Lutheranism, a legally permissible creed. In practice, the north German states remained Protestant, the south German states Catholic.

The Thirty Years' War settled little but was a disaster for the German economy and society—probably the most destructive event in German history before the twentieth century. Population losses were frightful. Perhaps one-third of the urban residents and two-fifths of the inhabitants of rural areas died. Entire areas of Germany were depopulated, partly by military actions, partly by disease— typhus, dysentery, bubonic plague, and syphilis (brought to Europe from the Americas) accompanied the movements of armies—and partly by the thousands of refugees who fled to safer areas.

In Germany the European-wide economic crisis caused primarily by the influx of silver from South America was badly aggravated by the war. Scholars still cannot estimate the value of losses in agricultural land and livestock, in trade and commerce. Those losses, compounded by the flood of Spanish silver, brought on severe price increases. Inflation was worse in Germany than anywhere else in Europe.

The population decline caused a rise in the value of labor. Owners of great estates had to pay more for agricultural workers. Farmers who needed only small amounts of capital to restore their lands started over again. Many small farmers, however, lacked the revenue to rework their holdings and became day laborers. Nobles and landlords were able to buy up many small holdings and amass great estates. In some parts of Germany, especially east of the Elbe River in areas like Mecklenburg and Pomerania, peasants' loss of land led to a new serfdom.[32] The Thirty Years' War contributed to the legal and economic decline of the largest segment of German society.

❖ CHANGING ATTITUDES

What were the cultural consequences of the religious wars and of the worldwide discoveries? What impact did the discoveries and wars have on Europeans' attitudes? The clash of traditional religious and geographical beliefs with the new knowledge provided by explorers—combined with decades of devastation and disorder within Europe—bred confusion, uncertainty, and insecurity. Geographical evidence based on verifiable scientific proofs contradicted the evidence of the Scriptures and of the classical authors.

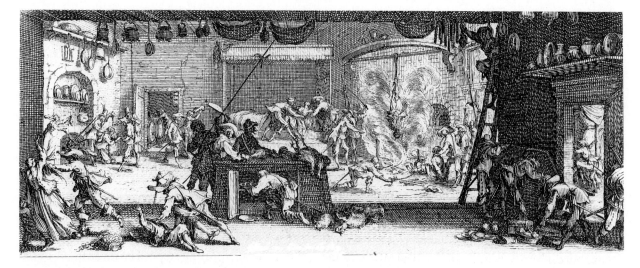

❋ **The Horrors of War**   Following Richelieu's invasion of Lorraine in 1633, the French engraver Jacques Callot (1592/3–1635) produced a series of etchings collectively titled *The Great Miseries of War,* depicting the theft, rape, and brutality for which soldiers of the Thirty Years' War gained an enduring reputation. *(Source: Courtesy of the Trustees of the British Museum)*

The age of religious wars revealed extreme and violent contrasts. It was a deeply religious period in which men fought passionately for their beliefs; 70 percent of the books printed dealt with religious subjects. Yet the times saw the beginnings of religious skepticism. Europeans explored new continents, partly with the missionary aim of Christianizing the peoples they encountered. Yet the Spanish, Portuguese, Dutch, and English proceeded to dominate and enslave the Indians and blacks they encountered. While Europeans indulged in gross sensuality, the social status of women declined. The exploration of new continents reflects deep curiosity and broad intelligence. Yet Europeans believed in witches and burned thousands at the stake. Sexism, racism, and skepticism had all originated in ancient times. But late in the sixteenth century they began to take on their familiar modern forms.

The Status of Women

Did new ideas about women appear in this period? Theological and popular literature on marriage published in Reformation Europe helps to answer this question. Manuals emphasized the qualities expected of each partner. A husband was obliged to provide for the material welfare of his wife and children, to protect his family while remaining steady and self-controlled. He was to rule his household firmly but justly; he was not to behave like a tyrant—a guideline that counselors repeated frequently. A wife was to be mature, a good household manager, and subservient and faithful to her spouse. The husband also owed fidelity. Both Protestant and Catholic moralists rejected the double standard of sexual morality, considering it a threat to family unity. Counselors believed that marriage should be based on mutual respect and trust. Although they discouraged impersonal unions arranged by parents, they did not think romantic attachments—based on physical attraction and love—a sound basis for an enduring relationship.

A woman might assist in her own or her husband's business and do charitable work. But moralists held that involvement in social or public activities was inappropriate because it distracted the wife from her primary responsibility: her household. If a woman suffered under her husband's yoke, writers explained, her submission, like the pain of childbearing, was a punishment inherited from Eve, penance for man's fall. Moreover, they said, a woman's lot was no worse than a man's: he had to earn the family's bread by the sweat of his brow.[33]

Catholics viewed marriage as a sacramental union; validly entered into, it could not be dissolved. Protestants stressed the contractual nature of marriage: each partner promised the other support, companionship, and the sharing of mutual property. Protestants recognized the right of both parties to divorce and remarry for various reasons, including adultery and irreparable breakdown.[34]

Society in the early modern period was patriarchal. Women neither lost their identity nor lacked meaningful work, but the all-pervasive assumption was that men ruled. Leading students of the Lutherans, Catholics, French Calvinists, and English Puritans tend to agree that there was no improvement in women's long-standing subordinate status.

Artists' drawings of plump, voluptuous women and massive, muscular men reveal the contemporary standards of physical beauty. It was a sensual age that gloried in the delights of the flesh. Some people, such as the humanist poet Pietro Aretino (1492–1556), found sexual satisfaction with people of either sex. Reformers and public officials simultaneously condemned and condoned sexual "sins."

Prostitution was common because desperate poverty forced women and young men into it. Since the later Middle Ages, licensed houses of prostitution had been common in urban centers. When in 1566 Pope Pius IV (r. 1559–1565) expelled all the prostitutes from Rome, so many people left and the city suffered such a loss of revenue that in less than a month the pope was forced to rescind the order. Scholars debated Saint Augustine's notion that prostitutes serve a useful social function by preventing worse sins. Civil authorities in both Catholic and Protestant countries licensed houses of public prostitution. These establishments were intended for the convenience of single men, and some Protestant cities, such as Geneva and Zurich, installed officials in the brothels with the express purpose of preventing married men from patronizing them.

Single women of the middle and working classes in the sixteenth and seventeenth centuries worked in many occupations and professions—as butchers, shopkeepers, nurses, goldsmiths, and midwives and in the weaving and printing industries. Most women who were married assisted in their husbands' businesses. What became of the thousands of women who left convents and nunneries during the Reformation? This question pertains primarily to women of the upper classes, who formed the dominant social group in the religious houses of late medieval Europe. Luther and the Protestant reformers believed that celibacy had no scriptural

basis and that young girls were forced by their parents into convents and, once there, were bullied by men into staying. Therefore, reformers favored the suppression of women's religious houses and encouraged former nuns to marry. Marriage, the reformers maintained, not only gave women emotional and sexual satisfaction but freed them from clerical domination, cultural deprivation, and sexual repression.[35] It appears that these women passed from clerical domination to subservience to husbands.

Some nuns in the Middle Ages probably did lack a genuine religious vocation, and some religious houses did witness financial mismanagement and moral laxness. Nevertheless, convents had provided women of the upper classes with an outlet for their literary, artistic, medical, or administrative talents if they could not or would not marry. When the convents were closed, marriage became virtually the only occupation available to upper-class Protestant women.

The great European witch scare reveals more about contemporary attitudes toward women.

The Great European Witch-Hunt

The period of the religious wars witnessed a startling increase in the phenomenon of witch-hunting, whose prior history was long but sporadic. "A witch," according to Chief Justice Edward Coke of England (1552–1634), "was a person who hath conference with the Devil to consult with him or to do some act." This definition by the highest legal authority in England demonstrates that educated people, as well as the ignorant, believed in witches. Witches were thought to be individuals who could mysteriously injure other people or animals—by causing a person to become blind or impotent, for instance, or by preventing a cow from giving milk.

Belief in witches dates back to the dawn of time. For centuries, tales had circulated about old women who made nocturnal travels on greased broomsticks to *sabbats*, or assemblies of witches, where they participated in sexual orgies and feasted on the flesh of infants. In the popular imagination witches had definite characteristics. The vast majority were married women or widows between fifty and seventy years old, crippled or bent with age, with pockmarked skin. They often practiced midwifery or folk medicine, and most had sharp tongues and were quick to scold.

Religious reformers' extreme notions of the Devil's powers and the insecurity created by the religious wars contributed to the growth of belief in witches. The idea developed that witches made pacts with the Devil in return for the power to work mischief on their enemies. Since pacts with the Devil meant the renunciation of God, witchcraft was considered heresy, and persecution for it had actually begun in the later fourteenth century when it was so declared. Persecution reached its most virulent stage in the late sixteenth and seventeenth centuries.

Fear of witches took a terrible toll of innocent lives in several parts of Europe. In southwestern Germany, 3,229 witches were executed between 1561 and 1670, most by burning. The communities of the Swiss Confederation in central Europe tried 8,888 persons between 1470 and 1700 and executed 5,417 of them as witches. In all the centuries before 1500, witches in England had been suspected of causing perhaps "three deaths, a broken leg, several destructive storms and some bewitched genitals." Yet between 1559 and 1736, almost 1,000 witches were executed in England.[36]

Historians and anthropologists have offered a variety of explanations for the great European witch-hunt. Some scholars maintain that charges of witchcraft were a means of accounting for inexplicable misfortunes. The English in the fifteenth century had blamed their military failures in France on Joan of Arc's witchcraft. In the seventeenth century the English Royal College of Physicians attributed undiagnosable illnesses to witchcraft. Some scholars think that in small communities, which typically insisted on strict social conformity, charges of witchcraft were a means of attacking and eliminating the nonconformist; witches, in other words, served the collective need for scapegoats. The evidence of witches' trials, some writers suggest, shows that women were not accused because they harmed or threatened their neighbors; rather, people believed such women worshiped the Devil, engaged in wild sexual activities with him, and ate infants. Other scholars argue the exact opposite: that people were tried and executed as witches because their neighbors feared their evil powers. According to still another theory, the unbridled sexuality attributed to witches was a figment of their accusers' imagination—a psychological projection by their accusers resulting from Christianity's repression of sexuality.

❈ **Witches Worshiping the Devil** In medieval Christian art, a goat symbolizes the damned at the Last Judgment, following Christ's statement that the Son of Man would separate believers from nonbelievers as a shepherd separates the sheep from the goats (Matthew 25:31–32). In this manuscript illustration, a witch arrives at a sabbat and prepares to venerate the Devil in the shape of a goat by kissing its anus. *(Source: The Bodleian Library, Oxford)*

Despite an abundance of hypotheses, scholars cannot fully understand the phenomenon. Specific reasons for the persecution of women as witches probably varied from place to place. Nevertheless, given the broad strand of misogyny (hostility to women) in Western religion, the ancient belief in the susceptibility of women (the so-called weaker vessels) to the Devil's allurements, and the pervasive seventeenth-century belief about women's multiple and demanding orgasms and thus their sexual insatiability, it is not difficult to understand why women were accused of all sorts of mischief and witchcraft. Charges of witchcraft provided a legal basis for the execution of tens of thousands of women. The most important capital crime for women in early modern times, witchcraft has considerable significance for the history and status of women.[37]

African Slave and Indian Woman   A black slave approaches an Indian prostitute. Unable to explain what he wants, he points with his finger; she eagerly grasps for the coin. The Spanish caption above moralizes on the black man using stolen money—yet the Spaniards ruthlessly expropriated all South American mineral wealth. *(Source: New York Public Library)*

European Slavery and the Origins of American Racism

Except for the Aborigines of Australia, almost all peoples in the world have engaged in the enslavement of other human beings at some time in their histories. Since ancient times, victors in battle have enslaved conquered peoples. In the later Middle Ages slavery was deeply entrenched in southern Italy, Sicily, Crete, and Mediterranean Spain. The bubonic plague, famines, and other epidemics created a severe shortage of agricultural and domestic workers throughout Europe, encouraging Italian merchants to buy slaves from the Balkans, Thrace,

southern Russia, and central Anatolia for sale in the West. In 1364 the Florentine government allowed the unlimited importation of slaves as long as they were not Catholics. Between 1414 and 1423, at least ten thousand slaves were sold in Venice alone. The slave trade was a lucrative business enterprise in Italy during the Renaissance. Where profits were high, papal threats of excommunication completely failed to stop it. Genoese slave traders set up colonial stations in the Crimea and along the Black Sea, and according to an international authority on slavery, these outposts were "virtual laboratories" for the development of slave plantation agriculture in the New World.[38] This form of slavery had nothing to do with race; almost all of these slaves were white. How, then, did black African slavery enter the European picture and take root in the New World?

The capture of Constantinople by the Ottoman Turks in 1453 halted the flow of white slaves from the Black Sea region and the Balkans. Mediterranean Europe, cut off from its traditional source of slaves, had no alternative source for slave labor but sub-Saharan Africa. The centuries-old trans-Saharan trade in slaves was greatly stimulated by the existence of a ready market for slaves in the vineyards and sugar plantations of Sicily and Majorca. By the later fifteenth century, before the discovery of America, the Mediterranean had developed an "American" form of slavery.

Meanwhile, the Genoese and other Italians had colonized the Canary Islands in the western Atlantic. And sailors working for Portugal's Prince Henry the Navigator (see page 517) discovered the Madeira Islands and made settlements there. In this stage of European expansion, "the history of slavery became inextricably tied up with the history of sugar."[39] Population increases and monetary expansion in the fifteenth century led to an increasing demand for sugar even though it was an expensive luxury that only the affluent could afford. Between 1490 and 1530, between 300 and 2,000 black slaves arrived annually at the port of Lisbon (Map 16.5). From Lisbon, where African slaves performed most of the manual labor and constituted 10 percent of the city's population, slaves were transported to the sugar plantations of Madeira, the Azores, the Cape Verde Islands, and then Brazil. Sugar and those small Atlantic islands gave slavery in the Americas its distinctive shape. Columbus himself spent a decade in Madeira and took sugar plants on his voyages to "the Indies."

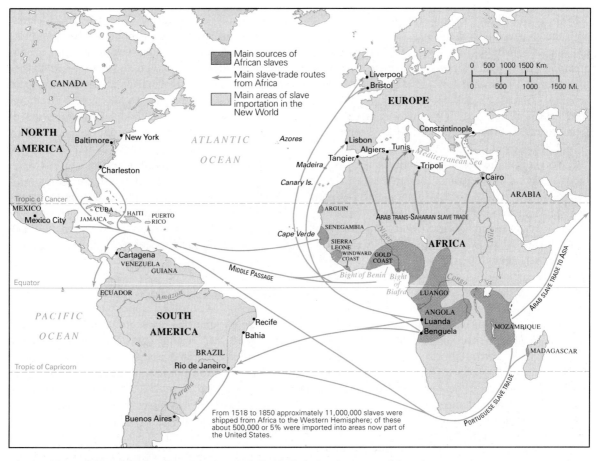

Main sources of African slaves

Main slave-trade routes from Africa

Main areas of slave importation in the New World

From 1518 to 1850 approximately 11,000,000 slaves were shipped from Africa to the Western Hemisphere; of these about 500,000 or 5% were imported into areas now part of the United States.

✳ **MAP 16.5 The African Slave Trade** Decades before the discovery of America, Greek, Russian, Bulgarian, Armenian, and then black slaves worked the plantation economies of southern Italy, Sicily, Portugal, and Mediterranean Spain—thereby serving as models for the American form of slavery.

As European economic exploitation of the Americas proceeded, the major problem settlers faced was a shortage of labor. As early as 1495, the Spanish solved the problem by enslaving the native Indians. In the next two centuries, the Portuguese, Dutch, and English followed suit.

Unaccustomed to any form of forced labor, certainly not to panning gold for more than twelve hours a day in the broiling sun, the Indians died "like fish in a bucket," as one Spanish settler reported.[40] In 1515 the Spanish missionary Bartolomé de Las Casas (see page 526), who had seen the evils of Indian slavery, urged the future emperor Charles V to end Indian slavery in his American dominions. Las Casas recommended the importation of blacks from Africa, both because church law did not strictly forbid black slavery and

because he thought blacks could better survive under South American conditions. Charles agreed, and in 1518 the African slave trade began. (When the blacks arrived, Las Casas immediately regretted his suggestion.) Columbus's introduction of sugar plants, moreover, stimulated the need for black slaves, and the experience and model of plantation slavery in Portugal and on the Atlantic islands encouraged the establishment of a similar agricultural pattern in the New World.

Several European nations participated in the African slave trade. Portugal brought the first slaves to Brazil; by 1600, 4,000 were being imported annually. After its founding in 1621, the Dutch West India Company, with the full support of the government of the United Provinces, transported thousands of Africans to Brazil and the

Caribbean. Only in the late seventeenth century, with the chartering of the Royal African Company, did the English get involved. Thereafter, large numbers of African blacks poured into the West Indies and North America. In 1790 there were 757,181 blacks in a total U.S. population of 3,929,625. When the first census was taken in Brazil in 1798, blacks numbered about 2 million in a total population of 3.25 million.

European settlers brought to the Americas the racial attitudes they had absorbed in Europe. Their beliefs and attitudes toward blacks derived from two basic sources: Christian theological speculation about the nature of God (light) and the Devil (black), and Muslim ideas. In the sixteenth and seventeenth centuries, the English, for example, were extremely curious about Africans' lives and customs, and slavers' accounts were extraordinarily popular. Travel literature depicted Africans as savages because of their eating habits, morals, clothing, and social customs; as barbarians because of their language and methods of war; and as heathens because they were not Christian. English people saw similarities between apes and Africans; thus the terms *bestial* and *beastly* were frequently applied to Africans. Africans were believed to possess a potent sexuality. One seventeenth-century observer considered Africans "very lustful and impudent, . . . their members' extraordinary greatness is a token of their lust." African women were considered sexually aggressive with a "temper hot and lascivious."[41]

"At the time when Columbus sailed to the New World, Islam was the largest world religion, and the only world religion that showed itself capable of expanding rapidly in areas as far apart and as different from each other as Senegal [in northwest Africa], Bosnia [in the Balkans], Java, and the Philippines."[42] Medieval Arabic literature emphasized blacks' physical repulsiveness, mental inferiority, and primitivism. In contrast to civilized peoples from the Mediterranean to China, some Muslim writers claimed, sub-Saharan blacks were the only peoples who had produced no sciences or stable states. The fourteenth-century Arab historian Ibn Khaldun (1332–1406) wrote that "the only people who accept slavery are the Negroes, owing to their low degree of humanity and their proximity to the animal stage." Though black kings, Khaldun alleged, sold their subjects without even a pretext of crime or war, the victims bore no resentment because they gave no thought to the

future and had "by nature few cares and worries; dancing and rhythm are for them inborn."[43] It is easy to see how such absurd images developed into the classic stereotypes used to justify black slavery in South and North America in the seventeenth, eighteenth, and nineteenth centuries. Medieval Christians and Muslims had similar notions of blacks as inferior and primitive people ideally suited to enslavement. Perhaps centuries of commercial contacts between Muslim and Mediterranean peoples had familiarized the latter with Muslim racial attitudes. The racial beliefs that the Portuguese, Spanish, Dutch, and English brought to the New World, however, derive primarily from Christian theological speculation.

LITERATURE AND ART

The age of religious wars and overseas expansion also witnessed extraordinary intellectual and artistic ferment. This effervescence can be seen in prose, poetry, and drama, in art, and in music. In many ways, the literature, visual arts, music, and drama of the period mirrored the social and cultural conditions that gave rise to them.

The Essay: Michel de Montaigne

Decades of religious fanaticism brought famine, civil anarchy, and death and led both Catholics and Protestants to doubt that any one faith contained absolute truth. The late sixteenth and seventeenth centuries witnessed the beginning of modern *skepticism,* a school of thought founded on doubt that total certainty or definitive knowledge is ever attainable. The skeptic is cautious and critical and suspends judgment. Perhaps the finest representative of early modern skepticism is the Frenchman Michel de Montaigne (1533–1592).

Montaigne came from a bourgeois family that had made a fortune selling salted herring and wine and in 1477 had purchased the title and property of Montaigne in Gascony; his mother descended from a Jewish family that had been forced to flee Spain. Montaigne received a classical education before studying law and securing a judicial appointment in 1554. At the age of thirty-eight, Montaigne resigned his judicial post, retired to his estate, and devoted the rest of his life to study, contemplation, and the effort to understand himself. His wealth provided him the leisure time to do so. Like the Greeks, he believed that the object of life was to "know thyself," for self-knowledge teaches men and women how to live in accordance with nature and God.

Montaigne developed a new literary genre, the essay—from the French word *essayer,* meaning "to test or try"—to express his thoughts and ideas. His *Essays* provide insight into the mind of a remarkably humane, tolerant, and civilized man. Montaigne was a humanist; he loved the Greek and Roman writers and was always eager to learn from them. From the ancient authors, especially the Roman Stoic Seneca, he acquired a sense of calm, inner peace, and patience and broad-mindedness.

Montaigne grew up during the French civil wars—a period when religious ideology had set family against family, even brother against brother. He wrote:

In this controversy . . . France is at present agitated by civil wars. . . . [Even] among the good men . . . we see many whom passion drives outside the bounds of reason, and makes them sometimes adopt unjust, violent, and even reckless courses.[44]

Though he remained a Catholic, Montaigne possessed a detachment and a willingness to look at all sides of a question:

I listen with attention to the judgment of all men; but so far as I can remember, I have followed none but my own. Though I set little value upon my own opinion, I set no more on the opinions of others.

In the book-lined tower where he passed his days, Montaigne became a deeply learned man. Yet he was not ignorant of the world of affairs, and he criticized scholars and bookworms who ignored the life around them. His essay "On Cannibals" reflects the impact of overseas discoveries on Europeans' consciousness. His tolerant mind rejected the notion that one culture is superior to another:

I long had a man in my house that lived ten or twelve years in the New World, discovered in these latter days, and in that part of it where Villegaignon landed [Brazil]. . . .

I find that there is nothing barbarous and savage in [that] nation, by anything that I can gather, excepting, that every one gives the title of barbarism to everything that is not in use in his own country. As, indeed, we have no other level of truth and reason, than the example and idea of the opinions and customs of the place wherein we live.[45]

In his belief in the nobility of human beings in the state of nature, uncorrupted by organized society, and in his cosmopolitan attitude toward different civilizations, Montaigne anticipated many eighteenth-century thinkers.

The thought of Michel de Montaigne marks a sharp break with the past. Faith and religious certainty had characterized the intellectual attitudes of Western society for a millennium. Montaigne's rejection of any kind of dogmatism, his secularism, and his skepticism thus represent a basic change. In his own time and throughout the seventeenth century, few would have agreed with him. Montaigne inaugurated an era of doubt. "Wonder," he said, "is the foundation of all philosophy, research is the means of all learning, and ignorance is the end."[46]

Elizabethan and Jacobean Literature

In addition to the development of the essay as a literary genre, the period fostered remarkable creativity in other branches of literature. England, especially in the latter part of Elizabeth's reign and in the first years of her successor James I (r. 1603–1625), witnessed unparalleled brilliance. The terms *Elizabethan* and *Jacobean* (the latter refers to the reign of James) are used to designate the English music, poetry, prose, and drama of this period. The poetry of Sir Philip Sidney (1554–1586), such as *Astrophel and Stella,* strongly influenced later poetic writing. *The Faerie Queene* of Edmund Spenser (1552–1599) endures as one of the greatest moral epics in any language. Above all, the immortal dramas of Shakespeare and the stately prose of the Authorized or King James Version of the Bible mark the Elizabethan and Jacobean periods as the golden age of English literature.

William Shakespeare (1564–1616), the son of a successful glove manufacturer who rose to the highest municipal office in the Warwickshire town of Stratford-on-Avon, chose a career on the London stage. By 1592 he had gained recognition as an actor and playwright. Between 1599 and 1603, Shakespeare performed in the Lord Chamberlain's Company and became co-owner of the Globe Theatre, which after 1603 presented his plays.

Shakespeare's genius lies in the originality of his characterizations, the diversity of his plots, his understanding of human psychology, and his unexcelled gift for language. Shakespeare was a Renaissance man in his deep appreciation for classical culture, individualism, and humanism. Such plays as *Julius Caesar, Pericles,* and *Antony and Cleopatra* deal with classical subjects and figures. Several of his comedies have Italian Renaissance settings. The nine history plays, including *Richard II, Richard III,* and *Henry IV,* enjoyed the greatest popularity among Shakespeare's contemporaries. Written during the decade after the defeat of the Spanish Armada, the history plays express English national consciousness. Lines such as these from *Richard II* reflect this sense of national greatness with unparalleled eloquence:

This royal Throne of Kings, this sceptre'd Isle,
This earth of Majesty, this seat of Mars,
This other Eden, demi-paradise,
This fortress built by Nature for herself,
Against infection and the hand of war:
This happy breed of men, this little world,
This precious stone, set in the silver sea,
Which serves it in the office of a wall,
Or as a moat defensive to a house,
Against the envy of less happier Lands,
This blessed plot, this earth, this Realm, this
*   England.*

Shakespeare's later plays, above all the tragedies *Hamlet, Othello,* and *Macbeth,* explore an enormous range of human problems and are open to an almost infinite variety of interpretations. *Othello,* which the nineteenth-century historian Thomas Macaulay called "perhaps the greatest work in the world," portrays an honorable man destroyed by a flaw in his own character and the satanic evil of his supposed friend Iago. The central figure in *Hamlet,* a play suffused with individuality, wrestles with moral problems connected with revenge and with man's relationship to life and death. The soliloquy in which Hamlet debates suicide is perhaps the most widely quoted passage in English literature:

To be, or not to be: that is the question:
Whether 'tis nobler in the mind to suffer
The slings and arrows of outrageous fortune,
Or to take arms against a sea of troubles,
And by opposing end them?

Hamlet's sad cry, "There is nothing either good or bad but thinking makes it so," expresses the anguish and uncertainty of modern man. *Hamlet* has always enjoyed great popularity, because in his many-faceted personality people have seen an aspect of themselves.

In 1929, in lectures at Oxford University, the novelist Virginia Woolf created an imaginary situation. What would have happened, she wondered, if Shakespeare had had a gifted sister who wanted to be an actress and to write poetry or plays? Unlike her brother, she would not have been sent to grammar school. If on her own she learned to read and write and occasionally picked up a book, her parents soon would have interrupted and told her to mend the stockings or mind the stew. Before she was out of her teens, her parents, loving though they were, would have selected a husband for her. If the force of her gift for learning and the stage was strong enough, she would have the choice of obeying her parents or leaving their home. If she succeeded in getting to London, she would discover that the theater did not hire women. Dependent on the kindness of strangers even for food, she probably would have found herself pregnant. And then "who shall measure the heat and violence of the poet's heart when caught and tangled in a woman's body?—she kills herself." Woolf concludes her story:

This may be true or it may be false—who can say?—
but what is true in it, so it seemed to me, reviewing the
story of Shakespeare's sister as I have made it, is that
any woman born with a great gift in the sixteenth cen-
tury would certainly have gone crazed, shot herself,
or ended her days in some lonely cottage outside the
village, half witch, half wizard, feared and mocked
at.[47]

Unlike her contemporary Montaigne, Shakespeare's sister would not have had "a room of her own"— that is, the financial means to study and to write, even apart from the social and cultural barriers against a woman doing so.

The other great masterpiece of the Jacobean period was the Authorized or King James Version of the Bible (1611). Based on the best scriptural research of the time and divided into chapters and verses, the Authorized Version is actually a revision of earlier versions of the Bible rather than an original work. Yet it provides a superb expression of the mature English vernacular in the early seventeenth century. Thus Psalm 37:

Fret not thy selfe because of evill doers, neither bee
*   thou envious against the workers of iniquitie.*
For they shall soone be cut downe like the grasse;
*   and wither as the greene herbe.*

*Trust in the Lord, and do good, so shalt thou dwell in
the land, and verely thou shalt be fed.*
*Delight thy selfe also in the Lord; and he shall give
thee the desires of thine heart.*
*Commit thy way unto the Lord: trust also in him, and
he shall bring it to passe.*
*And he shall bring forth thy righteousness as the
light, and thy judgement as the noone day.*

The Authorized Version, so called because it was
produced under royal sponsorship—it had no official ecclesiastical endorsement—represented the
Anglican and Puritan desire to encourage lay people to read the Scriptures. It quickly achieved great
popularity and displaced all earlier versions. British
settlers carried this Bible to the North American
colonies, where it became known as the "King
James Bible." For centuries this version of the
Bible has had a profound influence on the language and lives of English-speaking peoples.

Baroque Art and Music

Throughout European history, the cultural tastes
of one age have often seemed quite unsatisfactory
to the next. So it was with the baroque. The term
baroque may have come from a Portuguese word

for an "odd-shaped, imperfect pearl." Late-eighteenth-century art critics used it as an expression of
scorn for what they considered an overblown, unbalanced style. The hostility of these critics has
long since passed, and modern specialists agree
that the triumphs of the baroque mark one of the
high points in the history of Western culture.

The early development of the baroque is complex. Most scholars stress the influence of Rome
and the revitalized Catholic church of the later sixteenth century. The papacy and the Jesuits encouraged the growth of an intensely emotional, exuberant art. These patrons wanted artists to go beyond
the Renaissance focus on pleasing a small, wealthy
cultural elite. They wanted artists to appeal to the
senses and thereby touch the souls and kindle the
faith of ordinary churchgoers while proclaiming
the power and confidence of the reformed Catholic church. In addition to this underlying religious emotionalism, the baroque drew its sense of
drama, motion, and ceaseless striving from the
Catholic Reformation. The interior of the famous
Jesuit Church of Jesus in Rome—the Gesù—combined all these characteristics in its lavish, shimmer-
ing, wildly active decorations and frescoes.

Taking definite shape in Italy after 1600, the
baroque style in the visual arts developed with

Veronese: Feast in the House of Levi   Using the story in Mark 2:15, which says
that many tax collectors and sinners joined Jesus at dinner, the Venetian painter celebrated patrician wealth and luxury in Venice's golden age. The black servants,
dwarfs, and colonnades all contribute to the sumptuous setting. *(Source: Gallerie
dell'Accademia/Archivio Cameraphoto Venezia/Art Resource, NY)*

✤ **Velázquez: Juan de Pareja** This portrait (1650) of the Spanish painter Velázquez's one-time assistant, a black man of obvious intellectual and sensual power and himself a renowned religious painter, suggests the integration of some blacks in seventeenth-century society. The elegant lace collar attests to his middle-class status. *(Source: The Metropolitan Museum of Art)*

exceptional vigor in Catholic countries—in Spain and Latin America, Austria, southern Germany, and Poland. Yet baroque art was more than just "Catholic art" in the seventeenth century and the first half of the eighteenth. True, neither Protestant England nor the Netherlands ever came fully under the spell of the baroque, but neither did Catholic France. And Protestants accounted for some of the finest examples of baroque style, especially in music. The baroque style spread partly because its tension and bombast spoke to an agitated age, which was experiencing great violence and controversy in politics and religion.

In painting, the baroque reached maturity early in the work of Peter Paul Rubens (1577–1640), the most outstanding and representative of baroque painters. Studying in his native Flanders and in Italy, where he was influenced by such masters as Michelangelo, Rubens developed his own rich,

sensuous, colorful style, characterized by animated figures, melodramatic contrasts, and monumental size. Rubens excelled in glorifying monarchs such as Queen Mother Marie de' Medici of France. He was a devout Catholic—nearly half of his pictures treat Christian subjects—yet among his trademarks are the fleshy, sensual nudes who populate his canvases as Roman goddesses, water nymphs, and remarkably voluptuous saints and angels.

In music, the baroque style reached its culmination almost a century later in the dynamic, soaring lines of the endlessly inventive Johann Sebastian Bach (1685–1750), one of the greatest composers of the Western world. Organist and choirmaster of several Lutheran churches across Germany, Bach was equally at home writing secular concertos and sublime religious cantatas. Bach's organ music, the greatest ever written, combines the baroque spirit of invention, tension, and emotion in an unforgettable striving toward the infinite. Unlike Rubens, Bach was not fully appreciated in his lifetime, but since the early nineteenth century his reputation has grown steadily.

SUMMARY

In the sixteenth and seventeenth centuries, Europeans for the first time gained access to large parts of the globe. European peoples had the intellectual curiosity, driving ambition, and scientific technology to attempt feats that were as difficult and expensive then as going to the moon is today. Exploration and exploitation contributed to a more sophisticated standard of living in the form of spices and Asian luxury goods and to a terrible international inflation resulting from the influx of South American silver and gold. Governments, the upper classes, and especially the peasantry were badly hurt by the inflation. Meanwhile, the middle class of bankers, shippers, financiers, and manufacturers prospered for much of the seventeenth century.

Europeans' technological development contributed to their conquest of Aztec Mexico and Inca Peru. Along with technology, Europeans brought disease to the New World and thereby caused a holocaust among the Indians. Overseas reconnaissance led to the first global seaborne commercial empires of the Portuguese, the Spanish, and the Dutch.

European expansion and colonization took place against a background of religious conflict and rising national consciousness. The sixteenth and seventeenth centuries were by no means a secular period. Although the medieval religious framework had broken down, people still thought largely in religious terms. Europeans used religious doctrine to explain what they did politically and economically. Religious ideology served as a justification for a variety of conflicts: the French nobles' opposition to the Crown, the Dutch struggle for political and economic independence from Spain. In Germany, religious pluralism and foreign ambitions added to political difficulties. After 1648 the divisions between Protestants and Catholics tended to become permanent. Sexism, racism, and religious skepticism were harbingers of developments to come.

NOTES

1. Quoted in C. M. Cipolla, *Guns, Sails, and Empires: Technological Innovation and the Early Phases of European Expansion, 1400–1700* (New York: Minerva Press, 1965), pp. 115–116.
2. J. H. Parry, *The Age of Reconnaissance* (New York: Mentor Books, 1963), Chs. 3 and 5.
3. See C. R. Phillips, *Ciudad Real, 1500–1750: Growth, Crisis, and Readjustment in the Spanish Economy* (Cambridge, Mass.: Harvard University Press, 1979), pp. 103–104, 115.
4. Quoted in Cipolla, *Guns, Sails, and Empires,* p. 132.
5. Quoted in F. H. Littell, *The Macmillan Atlas History of Christianity* (New York: Macmillan, 1976), p. 75.
6. Quoted in Cipolla, *Guns, Sails, and Empires,* p. 133.
7. Quoted in S. E. Morison, *Admiral of the Ocean Sea: A Life of Christopher Columbus* (Boston: Little, Brown, 1942), p. 339.
8. T. K. Rabb, "Columbus: Villain or Hero," *Princeton Alumni Weekly,* October 14, 1992, pp. 12–17.
9. J. M. Cohen, ed. and trans., *The Four Voyages of Christopher Columbus* (New York: Penguin Books, 1969), p. 37.
10. Quoted in R. L. Kagan, "The Spain of Ferdinand and Isabella," in *Circa 1492: Art in the Age of Exploration,* ed. J. A. Levenson (Washington, D.C.: National Gallery of Art, 1991), p. 60.
11. Quoted in F. Maddison, "Tradition and Innovation: Columbus' First Voyage and Portuguese Navigation in the Fifteenth Century," ibid., p. 69.
12. W. D. Phillips and C. R. Phillips, *The Worlds of Christopher Columbus* (Cambridge: Cambridge University Press, 1992), p. 273.
13. See ibid.
14. See G. W. Conrad and A. A. Demarest, *Religion and Empire: The Dynamics of Aztec and Inca Expansionism* (New York: Cambridge University Press, 1993), pp. 67–69.
15. G. C. Vaillant, *Aztecs of Mexico* (New York: Penguin Books, 1979), p. 241. Chapter 15, on which this section leans, is fascinating.
16. V. W. Von Hagen, *Realm of the Incas* (New York: New American Library, 1961), pp. 204–207.
17. Conrad and Demarest, *Religion and Empire,* pp. 135–139.
18. N. Sanchez-Albornoz, *The Population of Latin America: A History,* trans. W. A. R. Richardson (Berkeley: University of California Press, 1974), p. 41.
19. Quoted in A. W. Crosby, *The Columbian Exchange: Biological and Cultural Consequences of 1492* (Westport, Conn.: Greenwood, 1972), p. 39.
20. Ibid., pp. 35–59.
21. Quoted in C. Gibson, ed., *The Black Legend: Anti-Spanish Attitudes in the Old World and the New* (New York: Knopf, 1971), pp. 74–75.
22. Quoted in L. B. Rout, Jr., *The African Experience in Spanish America* (New York: Cambridge University Press, 1976), p. 23.
23. See Parry, *The Age of Reconnaissance,* Chs. 12, 14, and 15.
24. Quoted in S. Neill, *A History of Christian Missions* (New York: Penguin Books, 1977), p. 163.
25. Quoted in C. M. Cipolla, *Clocks and Culture: 1300–1700* (New York: Norton, 1978), p. 86.
26. J. Gernet, *A History of Chinese Civilization* (New York: Cambridge University Press, 1982), p. 458.
27. Quoted in A. J. Andrea and J. H. Overfield, *The Human Record,* vol. 1 (Boston: Houghton Mifflin, 1990), pp. 406–407.
28. Ibid., p. 408.
29. See D. Keene, *The Japanese Discovery of Europe,* rev. ed. (Stanford, Calif.: Stanford University Press, 1969), pp. 1–17. The quotation is on page 16.
30. See J. Hale, "War and Public Opinion in the Fifteenth and Sixteenth Centuries," *Past and Present* 22 (July 1962): 29.
31. See N. Z. Davis, "The Rites of Violence: Religious Riot in Sixteenth Century France," *Past and Present* 59 (May 1973): 51–91.
32. H. Kamen, "The Economic and Social Consequences of the Thirty Years' War," *Past and Present* 39 (April 1968): 44–61.
33. This passage is based heavily on S. E. Ozment, *When Fathers Ruled: Family Life in Reformation*

Europe (Cambridge, Mass.: Harvard University Press, 1983), pp. 50–99.

34. Ibid., pp. 85–92.

35. Ibid., pp. 9–14.

36. N. Cohn, *Europe's Inner Demons: An Enquiry Inspired by the Great Witch-Hunt* (New York: Basic Books, 1975), pp. 253–254; K. Thomas, *Religion and the Decline of Magic* (New York: Charles Scribner's Sons, 1971), pp. 450–455.

37. See E. W. Monter, "The Pedestal and the Stake: Courtly Love and Witchcraft," in *Becoming Visible: Women in European History,* ed. R. Bridenthal and C. Koonz (Boston: Houghton Mifflin, 1977), pp. 132–135; and A. Fraser, *The Weaker Vessel* (New York: Random House, 1985), pp. 100–103.

38. C. Verlinden, *The Beginnings of Modern Colonization,* trans. Y. Freccero (Ithaca, N.Y.: Cornell University Press, 1970), pp. 5–6, 80–97.

39. This section leans heavily on D. B. Davis, *Slavery and Human Progress* (New York: Oxford University Press, 1984), pp. 54–62.

40. Quoted in D. P. Mannix with M. Cowley, *Black Cargoes: A History of the Atlantic Slave Trade* (New York: Viking Press, 1968), p. 5.

41. Ibid., p. 19.

42. See P. Brown, "Understanding Islam," *New York Review of Books,* February 22, 1979, pp. 30–33.

43. Davis, *Slavery and Human Progress,* pp. 43–44.

44. D. M. Frame, trans., *The Complete Works of Montaigne* (Stanford, Calif.: Stanford University Press, 1958), pp. 175–176.

45. C. Cotton, trans., *The Essays of Michel de Montaigne* (New York: A. L. Burt, 1893), pp. 207, 210.

46. Ibid., p. 523.

47. V. Woolf, *A Room of One's Own* (New York: Harcourt, Brace & World, 1957), p. 51.

Suggested Reading

Perhaps the best starting point for the study of European society in the age of exploration is Parry's *Age of Reconnaissance,* cited in the Notes, which treats the causes and consequences of the voyages of discovery. Parry's splendidly illustrated *The Discovery of South America* (1979) examines Europeans' reactions to the maritime discoveries and treats the entire concept of new discoveries. For the earliest British reaction to the Japanese, see *A World Elsewhere: Europe's Encounter with Japan in the Sixteenth and Seventeenth Centuries* (1990). The urbane studies of C. M. Cipolla present fascinating material on technological

and sociological developments written in a lucid style. In addition to the titles cited in the Notes, see *Cristofano and the Plague: A Study in the History of Public Health in the Age of Galileo* (1973) and *Public Health and the Medical Profession in the Renaissance* (1976). Morison's *Admiral of the Ocean Sea,* also listed in the Notes, is the standard biography of Columbus. The advanced student should consult F. Braudel, *Civilization and Capitalism, 15th–18th Century,* trans. S. Reynolds, vol. 1, *The Structures of Everyday Life* (1981); vol. 2, *The Wheels of Commerce* (1982); and vol. 3, *The Perspective of the World* (1984). These three fat volumes combine vast erudition, a global perspective, and remarkable illustrations. For the political ideas that formed the background of the first Spanish overseas empire, see A. Pagden, *Spanish Imperialism and the Political Imagination* (1990).

For the religious wars, in addition to the references cited in the Notes to this chapter, see J. H. M. Salmon, *Society in Crisis: France in the Sixteenth Century* (1975), which traces the fate of French institutions during the civil wars. A. N. Galpern, *The Religions of the People in Sixteenth-Century Champagne* (1976), is a useful case study in religious anthropology, and W. A. Christian, Jr., *Local Religion in Sixteenth Century Spain* (1981), traces the attitudes and practices of ordinary people.

A cleverly illustrated introduction to the Low Countries is K. H. D. Kaley, *The Dutch in the Seventeenth Century* (1972). The study by J. L. Motley, *The Rise of the Dutch Republic,* vol. 1 (1898), still provides a good comprehensive treatment and is fascinating reading. For Spanish military operations in the Low Countries, see G. Parker, *The Army of Flanders and the Spanish Road, 1567–1659: The Logistics of Spanish Victory and Defeat in the Low Countries' Wars* (1972). The same author's *Spain and the Netherlands, 1559–1659: Ten Studies* (1979), contains useful essays, of which students may especially want to consult "Why Did the Dutch Revolt Last So Long?" For the later phases of the Dutch-Spanish conflict, see J. I. Israel, *The Dutch Republic and the Hispanic World, 1606–1661* (1982), which treats the struggle in global perspective.

Of the many biographies of Elizabeth of England, W. T. MacCaffrey, *Queen Elizabeth and the Making of Policy, 1572–1588* (1981), examines the problems posed by the Reformation and how Elizabeth solved them. J. E. Neale, *Queen Elizabeth I* (1957), remains valuable, and L. B. Smith, *The Elizabethan Epic* (1966), is a splendid evocation of the age of Shakespeare with Elizabeth at the center. The best recent biography is C. Erickson, *The First Elizabeth* (1983), a fine, psychologically resonant portrait.

Nineteenth- and early-twentieth-century historians described the defeat of the Spanish Armada as a great victory for Protestantism, democracy, and capitalism, which those scholars tended to link together. Recent historians have focused on its contemporary significance. For a sympathetic but judicious portrait of the man who launched the Armada, see G. Parker, *Philip II* (1978). The best recent study of the leader of the Armada is P. Pierson, *Commander of the Armada: The Seventh Duke of Medina Sidonia* (1989). D. Howarth, *The Voyage of the Armada* (1982), discusses the expedition largely in terms of the individuals involved, and G. Mattingly, *The Armada* (1959), gives the diplomatic and political background; both Howarth and Mattingly tell very exciting tales. M. Lewis, *The Spanish Armada* (1972), also tells a good story, but strictly from the English perspective. Significant aspects of Portuguese culture are treated in A. Hower and R. Preto-Rodas, eds., *Empire in Transition: The Portuguese World in the Time of Camões* (1985).

C. V. Wedgwood, *The Thirty Years' War* (1961), must be qualified in light of recent research on the social and economic effects of the war, but it is still a good (though detailed) starting point on a difficult period. Various opinions on the causes and results of the war are given in T. K. Rabb's anthology, *The Thirty Years' War* (1981). In addition to the articles by Hale and Kamen cited in the Notes, the following articles, both of which appear in the scholarly journal *Past and Present,* provide some of the latest important findings: J. V. Polisensky, "The Thirty Years' War and the Crises and Revolutions of Sixteenth Century Europe," 39 (1968), and M. Roberts, "Queen Christina and the General Crisis of the Seventeenth Century," 22 (1962).

As background to the intellectual changes instigated by the Reformation, D. C. Wilcox, *In Search of God and Self: Renaissance and Reformation Thought* (1975), contains a perceptive analysis, and T. Ashton, ed., *Crisis in Europe, 1560–1660* (1967), is fundamental. For women, marriage, and the family, see L. Stone, *The Family, Sex, and Marriage in England, 1500–1800* (1977), an important but controversial work; D. Underdown, "The Taming of the Scold," and S. Amussen, "Gender, Family, and the Social Or-

der," in *Order and Disorder in Early Modern England,* ed. A. Fletcher and J. Stevenson (1985); A. Macfarlane, *Marriage and Love in England: Modes of Reproduction, 1300–1848* (1986); C. R. Boxer, *Women in Iberian Expansion Overseas, 1415–1815* (1975), an invaluable study of women's role in overseas immigration; and S. M. Wyntjes, "Women in the Reformation Era," a quick survey of conditions in different countries, in Bridenthal and Koonz's *Becoming Visible.* Ozment's *When Fathers Ruled,* cited in the Notes, is a seminal study concentrating on Germany and Switzerland.

On witches and witchcraft see, in addition to the titles by Cohn and Thomas in the Notes, J. B. Russell, *Witchcraft in the Middle Ages* (1976) and *Lucifer: The Devil in the Middle Ages* (1984); M. Summers, *The History of Witchcraft and Demonology* (1973); and H. R. Trevor-Roper, *The European Witch-Craze of the Sixteenth and Seventeenth Centuries* (1967), an important collection of essays.

As background to slavery and racism in North and South America, students should see J. L. Watson, ed., *Asian and African Systems of Slavery* (1980), a valuable collection of essays. Davis's *Slavery and Human Progress,* cited in the Notes, shows how slavery was viewed as a progressive force in the expansion of the Western world. For North American conditions, interested students should consult W. D. Jordan, *The White Man's Burden: Historical Origins of Racism in the United States* (1974), and the title by Mannix listed in the Notes, a hideously fascinating account. For Caribbean and South American developments, see F. P. Bowser, *The African Slave in Colonial Peru* (1974); J. S. Handler and F. W. Lange, *Plantation Slavery in Barbados: An Archeological and Historical Investigation* (1978); and R. E. Conrad, *Children of God's Fire: A Documentary History of Black Slavery in Brazil* (1983).

The leading authority on Montaigne is D. M. Frame. In addition to his translation of Montaigne's works cited in the Notes, see his *Montaigne's Discovery of Man* (1955).

Columbus Describes His First Voyage

On his return voyage to Spain in January 1493, Christopher Columbus composed a letter intended for wide circulation and had copies of it sent ahead to Isabella and Ferdinand and others when the ship docked at Lisbon. Because the letter sums up Columbus's understanding of his achievements, it is considered the most important document of his first voyage. Remember that his knowledge of Asia rested heavily on Marco Polo's Travels, *published around 1298.*

Since I know that you will be pleased at the great success with which the Lord has crowned my voyage, I write to inform you how in thirty-three days I crossed from the Canary Islands to the Indies, with the fleet which our most illustrious sovereigns gave me. I found very many islands with large populations and took possession of them all for their Highnesses; this I did by proclamation and unfurled the royal standard. No opposition was offered.

I named the first island that I found 'San Salvador,' in honour of our Lord and Saviour who has granted me this miracle. . . . When I reached Cuba, I followed its north coast westwards, and found it so extensive that I thought this must be the mainland, the province of Cathay.[1] . . . From there I saw another island eighteen leagues eastwards which I then named 'Hispaniola.'[2] . . .

Hispaniola is a wonder. The mountains and hills, the plains and meadow lands are both fertile and beautiful. They are most suitable for planting crops and for raising cattle of all kinds, and there are good sites for building towns and villages. The harbours are incredibly fine and there are many great rivers with broad channels and the majority contain gold.[3] The trees, fruits and plants are very different from those of Cuba. In Hispaniola there are many spices and large mines of gold and other metals. . . .[4]

The inhabitants of this island, and all the rest that I discovered or heard of, go naked, as their mothers bore them, men and women alike. A few of the women, however, cover a single place with a leaf of a plant or piece of cotton which they weave for the purpose. They have no iron or steel or arms and are not capable of using them, not because they are not strong and well built but because they are amazingly timid. All the weapons they have are canes cut at seeding time, at the end of which they fix a sharpened stick, but they have not the courage to make use of these, for very often when I have sent two or three men to a village to have conversation with them a great number of them have come out. But as soon as they saw my men all fled immediately, a father not even waiting for his son. And this is not because we have harmed any of them; on the contrary, wherever I have gone and been able to have conversation with them, I have given them some of the various things I had, a cloth and other articles, and received nothing in exchange. But they have still remained incurably timid. True, when they have been reassured and lost their fear, they are so ingenuous and so liberal with all their possessions that no one who has not seen them would believe it. If one asks for anything they have they never say no. On the contrary, they offer a share to anyone with demonstrations of heartfelt affection, and they are immediately content with any small thing, valuable or valueless, that is given them. I forbade the men to give them bits of broken crockery, fragments of glass or tags of laces, though if they could get them they fancied them the finest jewels in the world.

I hoped to win them to the love and service of their Highnesses and of the whole Spanish nation and to persuade them to collect and give us of the things which they possessed in abundance and which we needed. They have no religion and are not idolaters; but all believe that power and goodness dwell in the sky and they are firmly convinced that I have come from the sky with these ships and people. In this belief they gave me a good reception everywhere, once they had overcome their fear; and this is not because they are stupid—far from it, they are men of great intelligence, for they navigate all those seas, and give a marvellously good account of everything—but because they have never before seen men clothed or ships like these. . . .

In all these islands the men are seemingly content with one woman, but their chief or king is allowed more than twenty. The women appear to work more than the men and I have not been able to find out if they have private property. As far as I could see whatever a man had was shared among all the rest and this particularly applies to food. . . . In another island, which I am told is larger than Hispaniola, the people have no hair. Here there is a vast quantity of gold, and from here and the other islands I bring Indians as evidence.

In conclusion, to speak only of the results of this very hasty voyage, their Highnesses can see that I will give them as much gold as they require, if they will render me some very slight assistance; also I will give them all the spices and cotton they want . . . I will also bring them as much aloes as they ask and as many slaves, who will be taken from the idolaters. I believe also that I have found rhubarb and cinnamon and there will be countless other things in addition . . .

So all Christendom will be delighted that our Redeemer has given victory to our most illustrious King and Queen and their renowned kingdoms, in this great matter. They should hold great celebrations and render solemn thanks to the Holy Trinity with many solemn prayers, for the great triumph which they will have, by the conversion of so many peoples to our holy faith and for the temporal benefits which will follow, for not only Spain, but all Christendom will receive encouragement and profit.

This is a brief account of the facts.
Written in the caravel off the Canary Islands.[5]

15 February 1493

At your orders
THE ADMIRAL

Questions for Analysis

1. How did Columbus explain the success of his voyage?

German woodcut depicting Columbus's landing at San Salvador. *(Source: John Carter Brown Library)*

2. What was Columbus's view of the native Americans he met?

3. Evaluate Columbus's statements that the Caribbean islands possessed gold, cotton, and spices.

4. Why did Columbus cling to the idea that he had reached Asia?

Source: J. M. Cohen, ed. and trans., *The Four Voyages of Christopher Columbus*. Copyright © 1969 Penguin Books Ltd.

1. Cathay is the old name for China. In the logbook and later in this letter Columbus accepts the native story that Cuba is an island which they can circumnavigate in something more than twenty-one days, yet he insists here and later, during the second voyage, that it is in fact part of the Asiatic mainland. 2. Hispaniola is the second largest island of the West Indies; Haiti occupies the western third of the island, the Dominican Republic the rest. 3. This did not prove to be true. 4. These statements are also inaccurate. 5. Actually Columbus was off Santa Maria in the Azores.

CHAPTER

17

Absolutism and Constitutionalism in Europe, ca 1589–1725

❖

The Queen's Staircase is among the grandest of the surviving parts of Louis XIV's palace at Versailles. *(Source: © Photo R.M.N.)*

The seventeenth century in Europe was an age of intense conflict and crisis. The crisis had many causes, but the era's almost continuous savage warfare was probably the most important factor. War drove governments to build enormous armies and levy ever higher taxes on an already hard-pressed, predominately peasant population. Deteriorating economic conditions also played a major role. Europe as a whole experienced an unusually cold and wet climate over many years—a "little ice age" that brought small harvests, periodic food shortages, and even starvation. Not least, the combination of war, increased taxation, and economic suffering triggered social unrest and widespread peasant revolts, which were both a cause and an effect of profound dislocation.

The many-sided crisis of the seventeenth century posed a grave challenge to European governments: how were they to maintain order? The most common response of monarchial governments was to seek more power to deal with the problems and the threats that they perceived. Indeed, European rulers in this period generally sought to attain *absolute,* or complete, power and build absolutist states. Thus monarchs regulated religious sects, and they abolished the liberties long held by certain areas, groups, or provinces. Absolutist rulers also created new state bureaucracies to enhance their power and to direct the economic life of the country in the interest of the monarch. Above all, monarchs fought to free themselves from the restrictions of custom, competing institutions, and powerful social groups. In doing so, they sought freedom from the nobility and from traditional representative bodies—most commonly known as Estates or Parliament—that were usually dominated by the nobility.

The monarchial demand for freedom of action upset the status quo and led to bitter political battles. Nobles and townspeople sought to maintain their traditional rights, claiming that monarchs could not rule at will but rather had to respect representative bodies and follow established constitutional practices. Thus opponents of absolutism argued for *constitutionalism*—the limitation of the state by law. In seventeenth-century Europe, however, advocates of constitutionalism generally lost out and would-be absolutists triumphed in most countries.

There were important national variations in the development of absolutism. The most spectacular example occurred in western Europe, where Louis XIV built on the heritage of a well-developed monarchy and a strong royal bureaucracy. Moreover, when Louis XIV came to the throne, the powers of the nobility were already somewhat limited, the French middle class was relatively strong, and the peasants were generally free from serfdom. In eastern Europe and Russia, absolutism emerged out of a very different social reality: a powerful nobility, a weak middle class, and an oppressed peasantry composed of serfs. Eastern monarchs generally had to compromise with their nobilities as they fashioned absolutist states. Finally, in Holland and England, royal absolutism did not triumph. In England especially, the opponents of unrestrained monarchial authority succeeded in firmly establishing a constitutional state, which guaranteed that henceforth Parliament and the monarch would share power.

Thus in the period between roughly 1589 and 1725, two basic patterns of government emerged in Europe: absolute monarchy and the constitutional state. Almost all subsequent governments in the West have been modeled on one of these patterns, which have also influenced greatly the rest of the world in the last three centuries.

- How and why did Louis XIV of France lead the way in forging the absolute state?

- How did Austrian, Prussian, and Russian rulers in eastern Europe build absolute monarchies—monarchies that proved even more durable than that of Louis XIV?

- How did the absolute monarchs' interaction with artists, architects, and writers contribute to the splendid cultural achievements of both western and eastern Europe in this period?

- How and why did the constitutional state triumph in Holland and England?

This chapter explores these questions.

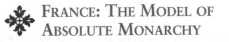

FRANCE: THE MODEL OF ABSOLUTE MONARCHY

France had a long history of unifying and centralizing monarchy, although the actual power and effectiveness of the French kings had varied enormously over time. Passing through a time of troubles and civil war after the death of Henry II in

1559, both France and the monarchy recovered under Henry IV and Cardinal Richelieu in the early seventeenth century. They laid the foundations for fully developed French absolutism under the "Great Monarch," Louis XIV. Providing inspiration for rulers all across Europe, Louis XIV and the mighty machine he fashioned deserve special attention

The Foundations of French Absolutism

Henry IV, the ingenious Huguenot-turned-Catholic, ended the French religious wars with the Edict of Nantes in 1598 (see page 534). The first of the Bourbon dynasty, Henry IV and his great minister Maximilian de Béthune, duke of Sully (1560–1641), then laid the foundations of later French absolutism.

Henry denied influence on the royal council to the nobility, which had harassed the countryside for half a century. Maintaining that "if we are without compassion for the people, they must succumb and we all perish with them," Henry also lowered taxes paid by the overburdened peasantry. Sully reduced the crushing royal debt accumulated during the era of religious conflict, encouraged French trade, and started a countrywide highway system. Within twelve years, Henry IV and his minister had restored public order in France and laid the foundation for economic prosperity. Unfortunately, the murder of Henry IV in 1610 by a crazed fanatic led to a severe crisis.

After the death of Henry IV, the queen-regent Marie de' Medici led the government for the child-king Louis XIII (r. 1610–1643), but feudal nobles and princes of the blood dominated the political scene. In 1624 Marie de' Medici secured the appointment of Armand Jean du Plessis—Cardinal Richelieu (1585–1642)—to the council of ministers. It was a remarkable appointment. The next year Richelieu became president of the council, and after 1628 he was first minister of the French crown. Richelieu used his strong influence over King Louis XIII to exalt the French monarchy as the embodiment of the French state.

Richelieu's policy was the total subordination of all groups and institutions to the French monarchy. The French nobility, with its selfish and independent interests, had long constituted the foremost threat to the centralizing goals of the Crown and to a strong national state. Now Richelieu crushed aristocratic conspiracies with quick execu-

tions, and he never called a session of the Estates General—the ancient representative body of the medieval orders that was primarily a representative of the nobility.

The genius of Cardinal Richelieu was reflected in the administrative system he established. He extended the use of the royal commissioners called *intendants,* each of whom held authority in one of France's thirty-two *généralités* (districts). The intendants were authorized "to decide, order and execute all that they see good to do." Usually members of the upper middle class or minor nobility, the intendants were appointed directly by the monarch, to whom they were solely responsible. They recruited men for the army, supervised the collection of taxes, presided over the administration of local law, checked up on the local nobility, and regulated economic activities—commerce, trade, the guilds, marketplaces—in their districts. As the intendants' power grew during Richelieu's administration, so did the power of the centralized state.

The cardinal perceived that Protestantism often served as a cloak for the political intrigues of ambitious lords. When the Huguenots revolted in 1625, Richelieu personally supervised the siege of their walled city, La Rochelle, and forced it to surrender. Thereafter, fortified cities were abolished. Huguenots were allowed to practice their faith, but they no longer possessed armed strongholds or the means to be an independent party in the state.

French foreign policy under Richelieu was aimed at the destruction of the fence of Habsburg territories that surrounded France. Consequently, in the Thirty Years' War Richelieu supported the Habsburgs' enemies, like the Lutheran king Gustavus Adolphus (see page 539). French influence became an important factor in the political future of the German Empire.

These new policies, especially war, cost money. Richelieu fully realized the need for greater revenues through increased taxation. But seventeenth-century France remained "a collection of local economies and local societies dominated by local elites." The government's power to tax was limited by the rights of assemblies in some provinces (such as Brittany) to vote their own taxes, the hereditary exemption from taxation of many wealthy members of the nobility and the middle class, and the royal pension system. Therefore, Richelieu—and later Louis XIV—temporarily solved their financial problems by securing the cooperation of local elites. Even in France royal absolutism was restrained by its need to compromise with the financial interests of well-entrenched groups.[1]

In building the French state, Richelieu believed that he had to take drastic measures against persons and groups within France and conduct a tough anti-Habsburg foreign policy. He knew that his actions sometimes seemed to contradict traditional Christian teaching. As a priest and bishop, how did he justify his policies? He developed his own *raison d'état* (reason of state): "What is done for the state is done for God, who is the basis and foundation of it." This being so, Richelieu maintained that, "Where the interests of the state are concerned, God absolves actions which, if privately committed, would be a crime."[2]

Richelieu persuaded Louis XIII to appoint his protégé Jules Mazarin (1602–1661) as his successor. Governing for the child-king Louis XIV, Mazarin became the dominant power in the government. He continued the centralizing policies of Richelieu, but in 1648 his unpopular attempts to increase royal revenues and expand the state bureaucracy resulted in a widespread rebellion known as the Fronde. Bitter civil war ensued between the monarchy and the opposition, led by the nobility and middle class. Riots and turmoil wracked Paris and the nation. Violence continued intermittently for the next twelve years.

Conflicts during the Fronde had a traumatic effect on the young Louis XIV. The king and his mother were frequently threatened and sometimes treated as prisoners by aristocratic factions. This period formed the cornerstone of Louis's political education and of his conviction that the sole alternative to anarchy was to concentrate as much power as possible in his own hands. Yet Louis XIV also realized that he would have to compromise with the bureaucrats and social elites who controlled local institutions and constituted the state bureaucracy. And he did so.

The Monarchy of Louis XIV

In the reign of Louis XIV (r. 1643–1715), the longest in European history, the French monarchy reached the peak of its absolutist development. In the magnificence of his court, in his absolute power, in the brilliance of the culture over which he presided and which permeated all of Europe, and in his remarkably long life, the "Sun King"

Philippe de Champaigne: Cardinal Richelieu
This portrait, with its penetrating eyes, expression of haughty and imperturbable cynicism, and dramatic sweep of red robes, suggests the authority, grandeur, and power that Richelieu wished to convey as first minister of France. *(Source: Reproduced by courtesy of the Trustees, The National Gallery, London)*

dominated his age. It was said that when Louis sneezed, all Europe caught cold.

Born in 1638, king at the age of five, Louis entered into personal, or independent, rule in 1661. Always a devout Catholic, Louis believed that God had established kings as his rulers on earth. The royal coronation consecrated Louis to God's service, and he was certain that although kings were a race apart, they had to obey God's laws and rule for the good of the people.

Louis's education was more practical than formal. He learned statecraft by direct experience.

❖ **Louis XIV** A skilled horseman and an enthusiastic hunter, Louis XIV rode with his armies on their many campaigns. This painting of Louis as a Roman general by Mignard Pierre (1612–1695) captures the king's enormous physical energy and proud self-confidence. *(Source: Galleria Sabauda, Turin/Scala/Art Resource, NY)*

The misery he suffered during the Fronde gave him an eternal distrust of the nobility and a profound sense of his own isolation. Accordingly, silence, caution, and secrecy became political tools for the achievement of his goals. His characteristic answer to requests of all kinds became the enigmatic "Je verrai" ("I shall see").

Louis XIV installed his royal court at Versailles, an old hunting lodge ten miles from Paris. His architects, Le Nôtre and Le Vau, turned what the duke of Saint-Simon called "the most dismal and thankless of sights" into a veritable paradise. Louis XIV required all the great nobility of France—at the peril of social, political, and sometimes economic disaster—to live at Versailles for at least part of the year. Versailles became a model of rational order, the center of France, and the perfect symbol of the king's power. In the gigantic Hall of Mirrors

hundreds of candles illuminated the domed ceiling, where allegorical paintings celebrated the king's victories. Louis skillfully used the art and architecture of Versailles to overawe his subjects and visitors and reinforce his power. Many monarchs subsequently imitated Louis XIV's example, and French became the language of diplomatic exchange and of royal courts all across Europe.

Historians have often said that Louis XIV was able to control completely the nobility, which historically had opposed the centralizing goals of the French monarchy. The duke of Saint-Simon, a high-ranking noble and fierce critic of the king, wrote in his memoirs, that Louis XIV

reduced everyone to subjection, and brought to his court those very persons he cared least about. Whoever was old enough to serve did not dare demur. It was still another device to ruin the nobles by accustoming them to equality and forcing them to mingle with everyone indiscriminately. . . .

Upon rising, at bedtime, during meals, in his apartments, in the gardens of Versailles, everywhere the courtiers had a right to follow, he would glance right and left to see who was there; he saw and noted everyone; he missed no one, even those who were hoping they would not be seen. . . .

Louis XIV took great pains to inform himself on what was happening everywhere, in public places, private homes, and even on the international scene. . . . Spies and informers of all kinds were numberless.[3]

As Saint-Simon suggests, the king did use court ceremonial to curb the great nobility. By excluding the highest nobles from his councils, he also weakened their ancient right to advise the king and to participate in government. They became mere instruments of policy, their time and attention occupied with operas, balls, gossip, and trivia.

Recent research, however, has demonstrated that Louis XIV actually secured the active collaboration of the nobility. Thus Louis XIV separated power from status and grandeur at Versailles: he secured the nobles' cooperation, and the nobility enjoyed their status and the grandeur in which they lived. The nobility agreed to participate in projects that both exalted the monarchy and reinforced their own ancient aristocratic prestige. Thus French government in the seventeenth century rested on a social and political structure in which the nobility continued to exercise great influence.[4]

In day-to-day government Louis utilized several councils of state, which he personally attended, and the intendants, who acted for the councils throughout France. A stream of questions and instructions flowed between local districts and Versailles, and under Louis XIV a uniform and centralized administration was imposed on the country. The councilors of state came from the upper middle class or from the recently ennobled, who were popularly known as "nobility of the robe" (because of the long judicial robes many of them wore). These ambitious professional bureaucrats served the state in the person of the king.

Throughout Louis's long reign and despite increasing financial problems, he never called a meeting of the Estates General. Thus his critics had no means of united action. French government remained highly structured, bureaucratic, centered at Versailles, and responsible to Louis XIV.

Economic Management and Religious Policy

Louis XIV's bureaucracy, court, and army cost a great amount of money, and the French method of collecting taxes consistently failed to produce the necessary revenue. An old agreement between the Crown and the nobility permitted the king to tax the common people if he did not tax the nobles. Because many among the rich and prosperous classes were exempt, the tax burden fell heavily on those least able to pay: the poor peasants.

The king named Jean-Baptiste Colbert (1619–1683), the son of a wealthy merchant-financier, as controller-general of finances. Colbert came to manage the entire royal administration and proved himself a financial genius. His central principle was that the French economy should serve the state, and he rigorously applied to France the system called mercantilism.

Hall of Mirrors, Versailles   The grandeur and elegance of the Sun King's reign are reflected in the Hall of Mirrors at the Versailles palace. The king's victories were celebrated in paintings on the domed ceiling. Hundreds of candles lit up the dome. *(Source: Giraudon/Art Resource, NY)*

Mercantilism is a collection of government policies for the regulation of economic activities, especially commercial activities, by and for the state. In the seventeenth and eighteenth centuries, a nation's international power was thought to be based on its wealth—specifically on the gold so necessary for fighting wars. To accumulate gold, economic theory suggested, a country should always sell more goods abroad than it bought. Colbert insisted that France should be self-sufficient, able to produce within its borders everything needed by the subjects of the French king. If France were self-sufficient, the outflow of gold would be halted, debtor states would pay in bullion, and, with the wealth of the nation increased, France's power and prestige would be enhanced.

Colbert attempted to accomplish self-sufficiency through state support for both old industries and newly created ones. New factories in Paris manufactured mirrors to replace Venetian imports, for example. To ensure a high-quality finished product, Colbert set up a system of state inspection and regulation. He compelled all craftsmen to organize into guilds, and he encouraged skilled foreign craftsmen and manufacturers to immigrate to France. To improve communications, he built roads and canals. To protect French products, he placed high tariffs on foreign goods. His most important accomplishment was the creation of a powerful merchant marine to transport French goods. Colbert tried to organize and regulate the entire French economy for the glory of the French state as embodied in the king.

Colbert's achievement in the development of manufacturing was prodigious. The commercial classes prospered, and between 1660 and 1700 their position steadily improved. The national economy, however, rested on agriculture. Although French peasants were not serfs, as were the peasants of eastern Europe, they were mercilessly taxed. After 1685 other hardships afflicted them: savage warfare, poor harvests, continuing deflation of the currency, and fluctuation in the price of grain. Many peasants emigrated. A totally inadequate tax base and heavy expenditure for war in the later years of Louis's reign made Colbert's goals unattainable.

Economic policy was complicated in 1685 by Louis XIV's revocation of the Edict of Nantes. The new law ordered the destruction of churches, the closing of schools, the Catholic baptism of Huguenots, and the exile of Huguenot pastors who refused to renounce their faith. Why did Louis, by revoking the edict, persecute some of his most loyal and industrially skilled subjects?

Recent scholarship has convincingly shown that Louis XIV was basically tolerant. He insisted on religious unity not for religious but for political reasons. His goal was "one king, one law, one faith." He hated division within the realm and insisted that religious unity was essential to his royal dignity and to the security of the state. Thus after permitting religious liberty in the early years of his reign, Louis finally decided to crack down on Protestants.

Although France's large Catholic majority applauded Louis XIV, writers in the eighteenth century and later damned him for intolerance and for the adverse impact that revocation had on the economy and foreign affairs. They claimed that tens of thousands of Huguenot craftsmen, soldiers, and business people emigrated, depriving France of their skills and tax revenues and carrying their bitterness to Holland, England, and Prussia. Although the claims of economic damage were exaggerated, the revocation of the Edict of Nantes certainly aggravated Protestant hatred for Louis and for his armies.

French Classicism

Scholars characterize French art and literature during the age of Louis XIV as "French classicism." French artists and writers of the late seventeenth century deliberately imitated the subject matter and style of classical antiquity; their work resembled that of Renaissance Italy. French art possessed the classical qualities of discipline, balance, and restraint. Classicism was the official style of Louis's court.

After Louis's accession to power, the principles of absolutism molded the ideals of French classicism. Individualism was not allowed, and artists glorified the state as personified by the king. Precise rules governed all aspects of culture. Formal and restrained perfection was the goal.

Contemporaries said that Louis XIV never ceased playing the role of grand monarch on the stage of his court, and he used music and theater as a backdrop for court ceremonial. Among composers Louis favored Jean-Baptiste Lully (1632–1687), whose orchestral works and court ballets combine lively animation with the restrained austerity typical of French classicism. His operatic productions were a powerful influence throughout Europe. Louis also supported François Couperin (1668–1733), whose harpsichord and organ works possess the grandeur the king loved, and Marc-Antoine Charpentier (1634–1704), whose solemn religious music entertained him at meals.

Louis XIV loved the stage, and in the plays of Molière and Racine his court witnessed the finest achievements of the French theater. Playwright, stage manager, director, and actor, Molière produced comedies that exposed the hypocrisies and follies of society through brilliant caricature. *Tartuffe* satirized the religious hypocrite; *Les Femmes Savantes (The Learned Women)* mocked the fashionable pseudointellectuals of the day. Molière made the bourgeoisie the butt of his ridicule; he stopped short of criticizing the nobility, thus reflecting the policy of his royal patron.

While Molière dissected social mores, his contemporary Jean Racine (1639–1699) analyzed the power of love. Racine based his tragic dramas on Greek and Roman legends, and his persistent theme is the conflict of good and evil. Several of his plays—*Andromaque, Bérénice, Iphigénie,* and *Phèdre*—bear the names of women and deal with the power of passion in women. For simplicity of language, symmetrical structure, and calm restraint, the plays of Racine represent the finest examples of French classicism.

The Wars of Louis XIV

Visualizing himself as a great military hero, Louis XIV used almost endless war to exalt himself above the other rulers of Europe. Military glory was his aim. In 1666 Louis appointed François le Tellier (later marquis of Louvois) secretary of war. Louvois created a professional army, which was modern in the sense that the French state, rather than private nobles, employed the soldiers.

A commissariat was established to feed the troops, taking the place of the usual practice of living off the countryside. Uniforms and weapons were standardized. A rational system of recruitment, training, discipline, and promotion was imposed. With this new military machine, one national state, France, was able to dominate the politics of Europe for the first time.

Louis continued on a broader scale the expansionist policy begun by Cardinal Richelieu. In 1667, using a dynastic excuse, he invaded Flanders, part of the Spanish Netherlands, and

Jean-Baptiste Poquelin, also known as Molière This is an elegant, sensuous, and romantic portrait of the playwright whose works set the moral tone of Louis's court. Louis basked in Molière's admiration, approved his social criticism, and amply rewarded him. *(Source: Musée de Versailles/Photographie Bulloz)*

Franche-Comté. He thus acquired twelve towns, including the important commercial centers of Lille and Tournai (Map 17.1). Five years later, Louis personally led an army of over a hundred thousand men into Holland. The Dutch ultimately saved themselves only by opening the dikes and flooding the countryside. This war, which lasted six years and eventually involved the Holy Roman Empire and Spain, was concluded by the Treaty of Nijmegen (1678). Louis gained additional Flemish towns and all of Franche-Comté.

Encouraged by his successes, by the weakness of the German Empire, and by divisions among the other European powers, Louis continued his aggression. In 1681 he seized the city of Strasbourg and three years later sent his armies into the province of Lorraine. At that moment the king seemed invincible. In fact, Louis had reached the limit of his expansion at Nijmegen. The wars of the

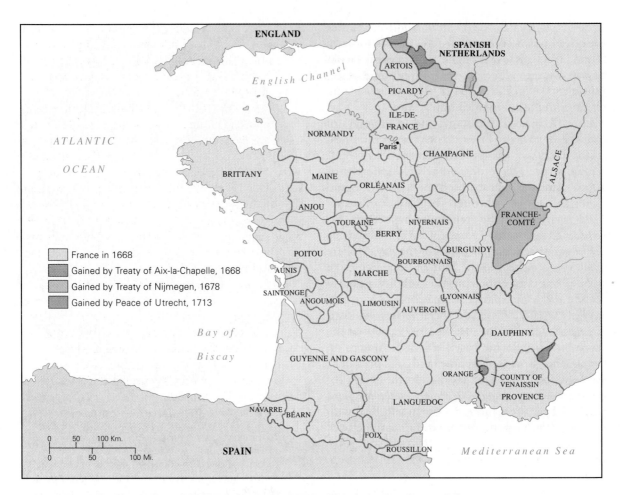

MAP 17.1 Acquisitions of Louis XIV, 1668–1713 The desire for glory and the weakness of his German neighbors encouraged Louis's expansionist policy. But he paid a high price for his acquisitions.

1680s and 1690s brought him no additional territories. In 1689 the Dutch prince William of Orange, a bitter foe, became king of England. William joined the League of Augsburg—which included the Habsburg emperor, the kings of Spain and Sweden, and the electors of Bavaria, Saxony, and the Palatinate—adding British resources and men to the alliance. Neither the French nor the league won any decisive victories. France lacked the means to win; it was financially exhausted.

At the same time a series of bad harvests between 1688 and 1694 brought catastrophe. Cold, wet summers reduced the harvests by an estimated one-third to two-thirds, and in many provinces the death rate rose to several times the normal figure. Rising grain prices, new taxes, a slump in manufac-

turing, and the constant nuisance of pillaging troops—all these meant great suffering for the French people. France wanted peace at any price. Louis XIV granted a respite for five years while he prepared for the conflict later known as the War of the Spanish Succession.

This struggle (1701–1713) involved the dynastic question of the succession to the Spanish throne. When Charles I (r. 1665–1700) died in 1700, his will left the Spanish crown and the worldwide Spanish Empire to Philip of Anjou, Louis XIV's grandson. By accepting this will, Louis obviously would gain power in Spain; he would also be reneging on an earlier treaty to divide the vast Spanish possessions between himself and the Holy Roman emperor. He accepted the will, thereby provoking a great war.

The Dutch and the English would not accept French acquisition of the Spanish Netherlands and of the rich trade with the Spanish colonies, which would make France too strong in Europe and in North America. Thus in 1701 they joined with the Austrians and Prussians in the Grand Alliance. In the ensuing series of conflicts, Louis suffered major defeats and finally sued for peace.

The war was concluded at Utrecht in 1713, where the principle of partition was applied. Louis's grandson Philip remained the first Bourbon king of Spain on the understanding that the French and Spanish crowns would never be united. France surrendered Newfoundland, Nova Scotia, and the Hudson Bay territory to England, which also acquired Gibraltar, Minorca, and control of the African slave trade from Spain. The Dutch gained little because Austria received the former Spanish Netherlands (Map 17.2).

The Peace of Utrecht represented the balance-of-power principle in operation, setting limits on the extent to which any one power, in this case France, could expand. The treaty completed the decline of Spain as a great power. It vastly expanded the British Empire. The Peace of Utrecht also marked the end of French expansionist policy. In Louis's thirty-five-year quest for military glory, his main territorial acquisition after 1678 was Strasbourg. Even revisionist historians sympathetic to Louis acknowledge "that the widespread misery in France during the period was in part due to royal policies, especially the incessant wars."[5] The news of Louis's death in 1715 brought rejoicing throughout France.

THE DECLINE OF ABSOLUTIST SPAIN IN THE SEVENTEENTH CENTURY

Spanish absolutism and greatness had preceded that of the French. In the sixteenth century, Spain (or, more precisely, the kingdom of Castile) had developed the standard features of absolute monarchy: a permanent professional bureaucracy, a standing army, and national taxes that fell most heavily on the poor. Spain developed its mighty international absolutism on the basis of silver bullion from Peru. But by the 1590s the seeds of disaster were sprouting, and in the seventeenth century Spain experienced a steady decline. The lack of a strong middle class (largely the result of the expulsion of the Jews and Moors), agricultural crisis and population decline, failure to invest in productive enterprises, intellectual isolation and psychological malaise—by 1715 all combined to reduce Spain to a second-rate power.

The fabulous flow of silver from Mexico and Peru had led Philip II to assume the role of defender of Roman Catholicism in Europe (see pages 534–539). But when the "Invincible Armada" went down in 1588, a century of Spanish pride and power went with it. After 1590 a spirit of defeatism and disillusionment crippled most reform efforts.

Philip II's Catholic crusade had been financed by the revenues of the Spanish-Atlantic economy. In the early seventeenth century, the Dutch and English began to trade with the Spanish colonies, and Mexico and Peru developed local industries. Between 1610 and 1650, Spanish trade with the colonies fell 60 percent, and the American silver lodes started to run dry. Yet in Madrid royal expenditures remained high. The result was chronic deficits and frequent cancellations of Spain's national debt. These brutal cancellations—a form of bankruptcy—shook public confidence in the state.

Spain, in contrast to the other countries of western Europe, developed only a tiny middle class. Public opinion, taking its cue from the aristocracy, condemned moneymaking as vulgar and undignified. Those with influence or connections sought titles of nobility and social prestige, or they became priests, monks, and nuns. The flood of gold and silver had produced severe inflation, and many businessmen found so many obstacles in the way of profitable enterprise that they simply gave up.

Spanish aristocrats, attempting to maintain an extravagant lifestyle that they could no longer afford, increased the rents on their estates. High rents and heavy taxes in turn drove the peasants from the land. Agricultural production suffered, and the peasants departed for the large cities, where they swelled the ranks of beggars.

Their most Catholic majesties, the kings of Spain, had no solutions to these dire problems. Philip IV (r. 1622–1665) left the management of his several kingdoms to Count Olivares. An able administrator, the count devised new sources of revenue, but he clung to the grandiose belief that the solution to Spain's difficulties rested in a return to the imperial tradition. Unfortunately, the imperial tradition demanded the revival of war with the Dutch in 1622 and a long war with France over Mantua (1628–1659). These conflicts, on top of

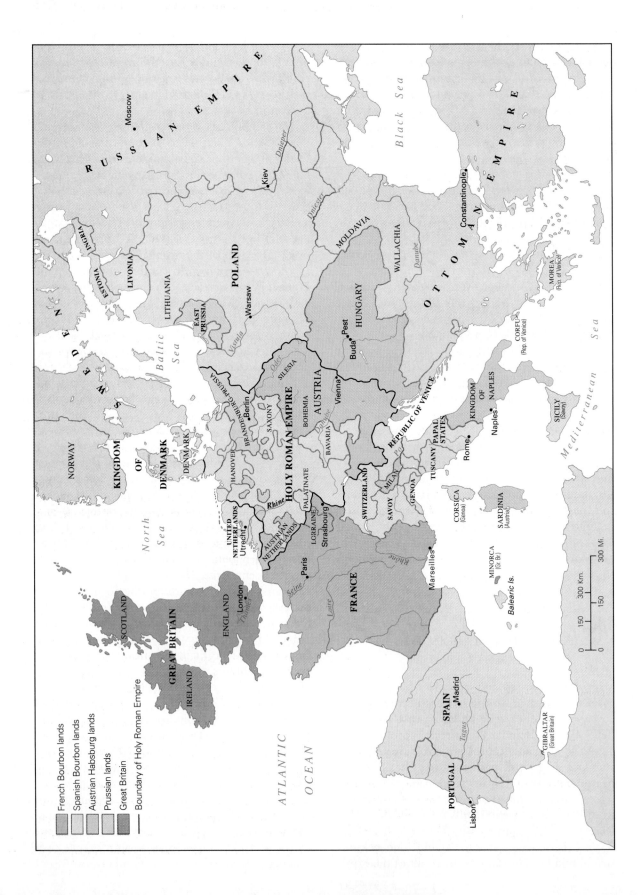

RUSSIAN EMPIRE

Moscow

Dnieper

Kiev

Black Sea

OTTOMAN EMPIRE

Constantinople

MOREA
(Rep. of Venice)

CORFU
(Rep. of Venice)

Dniester

MOLDAVIA

WALLACHIA

Danube

POLAND

Warsaw

EAST PRUSSIA

LITHUANIA

LIVONIA

ESTONIA

INGRIA

Baltic Sea

Vistula

Oder

BRANDENBURG-PRUSSIA

Berlin

SILESIA

SAXONY

BOHEMIA

HUNGARY

Pest
Buda

AUSTRIA

Vienna

HOLY ROMAN EMPIRE

BAVARIA

Danube

HANOVER

KINGDOM OF DENMARK

DENMARK

NORWAY

S W E D E N

North Sea

Rhine

PALATINATE

UNITED NETHERLANDS
Utrecht

AUSTRIAN NETHERLANDS

LORRAINE
Strasbourg

SWITZERLAND

SAVOY

MILAN

GENOA

REPUBLIC OF VENICE

Po

TUSCANY

PAPAL STATES

Rome

KINGDOM OF NAPLES

Naples

SICILY
(Savoy)

CORSICA
(Genoa)

SARDINIA
(Austria)

Mediterranean Sea

MINORCA
(Gr. Br.)

Balearic Is.

FRANCE

Paris

Seine

Loire

Rhône

Marseilles

GREAT BRITAIN

SCOTLAND

ENGLAND

London

Thames

IRELAND

ATLANTIC OCEAN

SPAIN

Madrid

PORTUGAL

Lisbon

Tagus

GIBRALTAR
(Great Britain)

French Bourbon lands
Spanish Bourbon lands
Austrian Habsburg lands
Prussian lands
Great Britain
—— Boundary of Holy Roman Empire

0   150   300 Km.
0   150   300 Mi.

an empty treasury, brought disaster. The Treaty of the Pyrenees of 1659, which ended the French-Spanish wars, compelled Spain to surrender extensive territories to France. After this treaty, Spain's decline as a great power became irreversible.

Seventeenth-century Spain was the victim of its past. It could not forget the grandeur of the sixteenth century and look to the future. The most cherished Spanish ideals were military glory and strong Roman Catholic faith. In the seventeenth century, Spain lacked the finances and the manpower to fight long, expensive wars. Spain also ignored the new mercantile ideas and scientific methods because they came from heretical nations, Holland and England.

In the brilliant novel *Don Quixote,* the Spanish writer Miguel de Cervantes (1547–1616) produced one of the masterpieces of world literature. *Don Quixote* delineates the whole fabric of sixteenth-century Spanish society. The main character, Don Quixote, lives in a dream world, traveling about the countryside seeking military glory. A leading scholar wrote, "The Spaniard convinced himself that reality was what he felt, believed, imagined. He filled the world with heroic reverberations. Don Quixote was born and grew."[6]

❁ ABSOLUTISM IN EASTERN EUROPE: AUSTRIA, PRUSSIA, AND RUSSIA

The rulers of eastern Europe also labored to build strong absolutist states in the seventeenth century. But they built on social and economic foundations different from those in western Europe. These foundations were laid between 1400 and 1650,

MAP 17.2 Europe in 1715 The Peace of Utrecht ended the War of the Spanish Succession and redrew the map of Europe. A French Bourbon king succeeded to the Spanish throne on the understanding that the French would not attempt to unite the French and Spanish crowns. France surrendered to Austria the Spanish Netherlands (later Belgium), then in French hands; and France recognized the Hohenzollern rulers of Prussia. Spain ceded Gibraltar to Great Britain, for which it has been a strategic naval station ever since. Spain also granted to Britain the *asiento,* the contract for supplying African slaves to America.

when the princes and the landed nobility of eastern Europe rolled back the gains made by the peasantry during the High Middle Ages and reimposed serfdom on the rural masses. The nobility also enhanced its power as the primary social force by reducing the importance of the towns and the middle classes.

Despite the strength of the nobility, strong kings did begin to emerge in many eastern European lands in the course of the seventeenth century. There were endless wars, and in this atmosphere of continuous military emergency monarchs found ways to reduce the political power of the landlord nobility. Cautiously leaving the nobles the unchallenged masters of their peasants, eastern monarchs gradually monopolized political power in three key areas. They imposed and collected permanent taxes without consent. They maintained permanent standing armies, which policed their subjects in addition to fighting abroad. And they conducted relations with other states as they pleased.

There were important variations on the absolutist theme in eastern Europe. The royal absolutism created in Prussia was stronger and more effective than that established in Austria. This advantage gave Prussia a thin edge over Austria in the struggle for power in east-central Europe in the eighteenth century, and it prepared the way for Prussia's unification of the German people in the nineteenth century. As for Russia, it developed its own form of autocratic government at an early date, and its political absolutism was quite different from that of France or even Prussia.

Lords and Peasants

Lords and peasants were the basic social groups in eastern Europe, a vast region including Bohemia, Silesia, Hungary, eastern Germany, Poland, Lithuania, and Russia. Peasants in eastern Europe had done relatively well in the period from roughly 1050 to 1300, a time of gradual economic expansion and population growth. Eager to attract German settlers to their sparsely populated lands, the rulers and nobles of eastern Europe had offered potential newcomers economic and legal incentives. Large numbers of incoming settlers had obtained land on excellent terms and gained much personal freedom. These benefits were gradually extended to the local Slavic populations, even

THE RISE OF WESTERN ABSOLUTISM AND CONSTITUTIONALISM

1581	Formation of the Republic of the United Provinces of the Netherlands
1588	Defeat of the Spanish Armada
1589–1610	Reign of Henry IV of France; economic reforms help to restore public order, lay foundation for absolutist rule
1598	Edict of Nantes: Henry IV ends the French wars of religion
1610–1650	Spanish trade with the New World falls by 60 percent
1618–1648	Thirty Years' War
1624–1642	Richelieu dominates French government
1625	Huguenot revolt in France; siege of La Rochelle
1629–1640	Charles I attempts to rule England without Parliament
1640–1660	Long Parliament in England
1642–1649	English civil war
1643–1715	Reign of Louis XIV
1648–1660	The Fronde: French nobility opposes centralizing efforts of monarchy
1648	Peace of Westphalia confirms Dutch independence from Spain
1649	Execution of Charles I; beginning of the Interregnum in England
1653–1658	Cromwell rules England as military dictator
1659	Treaty of the Pyrenees forces Spain to cede extensive territories to France
1660	Restoration of the English monarchy: Charles II returns from exile
1661	Louis XIV enters into independent rule
ca 1663–1683	Colbert directs Louis XIV's mercantilist economic policy
1667	France invades Holland
1673	Test Act excludes Roman Catholics from public office in England
1685	Louis XIV revokes the Edict of Nantes
1685–1688	James II rules England, attempts to restore Roman Catholicism as state religion
1688	The Glorious Revolution establishes a constitutional monarchy in England under Mary and William III
1689	Enactment of the Bill of Rights in England
1701–1713	War of the Spanish Succession
1713	Peace of Utrecht ends French territorial acquisitions, expands the British Empire, completes decline of Spain as a great power

THE RISE OF ABSOLUTISM IN EASTERN EUROPE

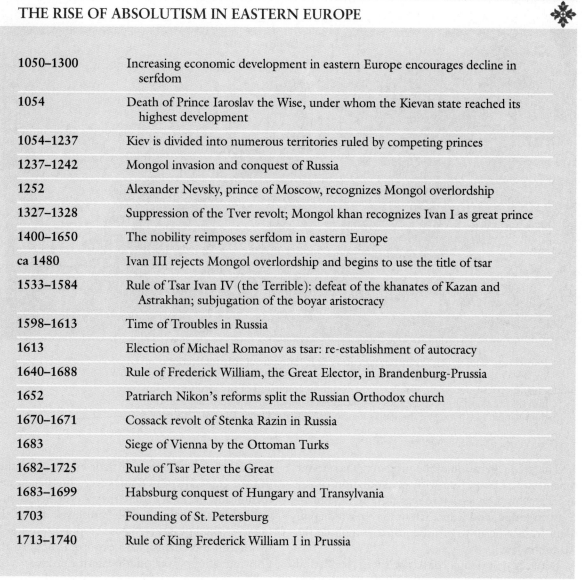

1050–1300	Increasing economic development in eastern Europe encourages decline in serfdom
1054	Death of Prince Iaroslav the Wise, under whom the Kievan state reached its highest development
1054–1237	Kiev is divided into numerous territories ruled by competing princes
1237–1242	Mongol invasion and conquest of Russia
1252	Alexander Nevsky, prince of Moscow, recognizes Mongol overlordship
1327–1328	Suppression of the Tver revolt; Mongol khan recognizes Ivan I as great prince
1400–1650	The nobility reimposes serfdom in eastern Europe
ca 1480	Ivan III rejects Mongol overlordship and begins to use the title of tsar
1533–1584	Rule of Tsar Ivan IV (the Terrible): defeat of the khanates of Kazan and Astrakhan; subjugation of the boyar aristocracy
1598–1613	Time of Troubles in Russia
1613	Election of Michael Romanov as tsar: re-establishment of autocracy
1640–1688	Rule of Frederick William, the Great Elector, in Brandenburg-Prussia
1652	Patriarch Nikon's reforms split the Russian Orthodox church
1670–1671	Cossack revolt of Stenka Razin in Russia
1683	Siege of Vienna by the Ottoman Turks
1682–1725	Rule of Tsar Peter the Great
1683–1699	Habsburg conquest of Hungary and Transylvania
1703	Founding of St. Petersburg
1713–1740	Rule of King Frederick William I in Prussia

those of central Russia. Thus by 1300 serfdom had all but disappeared in eastern Europe. Peasants were able to bargain freely with their landlords and move about as they pleased.

After about 1300, however, as Europe's population and economy declined grievously, mainly because of the Black Death, noble landlords sought to solve their tough economic problems by more heavily exploiting the peasantry. In western Europe this attempt generally failed, but in the vast region east of the Elbe River in Germany the landlords were successful in degrading peasants. By 1500 eastern peasants were on their way to becoming serfs again.

Eastern lords triumphed because they made their kings and princes issue laws that restricted the right of their peasants to move to take advantage of better opportunities elsewhere. In Prussian territories by 1500, the law required that runaway peasants be hunted down and returned to their lords, and a runaway servant was to be nailed to a post by one ear and given a knife to cut himself loose. Moreover, lords steadily took more and more of their peasants' land and arbitrarily imposed heavier and heavier labor obligations. By the early 1500s, lords in many territories could command their peasants to work for them without pay for as many as six days a week.

Punishing Serfs This seventeenth-century illustration from Adam Olearius's *Travels in Moscovy* suggests what eastern serfdom really meant. The scene is eastern Poland. There, according to Olearius, a common command of the lord was, "Beat him till the skin falls from the flesh." Selections from Olearius's book are found in this chapter's Listening to the Past. *(Source: University of Illinois Library, Champaign)*

The gradual erosion of the peasantry's economic position was bound up with manipulation of the legal system. The local lord was also the local prosecutor, judge, and jailer. There were no independent royal officials to provide justice or uphold the common law.

Between 1500 and 1650, the social, legal, and economic conditions of peasants in eastern Europe continued to decline. In Poland, for example, nobles gained complete control over their peasants in 1574. In Russia the right of peasants to move from a given estate was abolished in 1603. In 1649 a new law code completed the legal re-establishment of permanent hereditary serfdom. The common fate of peasants in eastern Europe by the middle of the seventeenth century was serfdom.

The consolidation of serfdom between 1500 and 1650 was accompanied by the growth of estate agriculture, particularly in Poland and eastern Germany. In the sixteenth century, European economic expansion and population growth resumed after the great declines of the late Middle Ages. Eastern lords had powerful economic incentives to increase the production of their estates, and they did so. Generally, the estates were inefficient and technically backward, but they nevertheless succeeded in squeezing sizable surpluses out of the impoverished peasants. These surpluses were sold to foreign merchants, who exported them to the growing cities of wealthier western Europe.

The re-emergence of serfdom in eastern Europe in the early modern period was a momentous human development. Above all, it reflected the fact that eastern lords enjoyed much greater political power than their western counterparts. In the late Middle Ages, when much of eastern Europe was experiencing innumerable wars and general political chaos, the noble landlord class had greatly increased its political power at the expense of the ruling monarchs. Moreover, the western concept and reality of sovereignty, as embodied in a king who protected the interests of all his people, was not well developed in eastern Europe before 1650.

Finally, with the approval of weak kings, the landlords systematically undermined the medieval privileges of the towns and the power of the urban classes. For example, instead of selling their products to local merchants in the towns, as required in the Middle Ages, the landlords often sold directly to foreign capitalists. Eastern towns also lost their medieval right of refuge and were compelled to return runaways to their lords. The population of the towns and the urban middle classes declined greatly. This development both reflected and promoted the supremacy of noble landlords in most of eastern Europe in the sixteenth century.

Austria and the Ottoman Turks

The Habsburgs of Austria emerged from the Thirty Years' War (see pages 539–540) impoverished and exhausted. The effort to root out Protestantism in the German lands had failed utterly, and the authority of the Holy Roman Empire and its Habsburg emperors had declined almost to the vanishing point. Yet defeat in central Europe also opened new vistas. The Habsburg monarchs were forced to turn inward and eastward in an attempt to fuse their diverse holdings into a strong, unified state.

An important step in this direction had actually been taken in Bohemia during the Thirty Years' War. Protestantism had been strong among the Czechs, a Slavic people concentrated in Bohemia. In 1618 the Czech nobles who controlled the Bohemian Estates—the representative body of the different legal orders—had risen up against their Habsburg king. This revolt was crushed, and then the Czech nobility was totally restructured to ensure its loyalty to the monarchy. With the help of this new nobility, the Habsburgs established strong direct rule over reconquered Bohemia. The condition of the enserfed peasantry worsened. Protestantism was also stamped out, and religious unity began to emerge. The reorganization of Bohemia was a giant step toward royal absolutism.

After the Thirty Years' War, Ferdinand III (r. 1637–1657) centralized the government in the hereditary German-speaking provinces, most notably Austria, Styria, and the Tyrol. The king created a permanent standing army ready to put down any internal opposition. The Habsburg monarchy was then ready to turn toward the vast plains of Hungary, in opposition to the Ottoman Turks.

The Ottomans had come out of Anatolia, in present-day Turkey, to create one of history's greatest military empires. Their armies had almost captured Vienna in 1529, and for more than 150 years thereafter the Ottomans ruled all of the Balkan territories, almost all of Hungary, and part of southern Russia. In the late seventeenth century, under vigorous reforming leadership, the Ottoman Empire succeeded in marshaling its forces for one last mighty blow at Christian Europe. A huge Turkish army surrounded Vienna and laid siege to it in 1683. After holding out against great odds for two months, the city was relieved at the last minute, and the Ottomans were forced to retreat. As their Russian and Venetian allies attacked on other fronts, the Habsburgs conquered all of Hungary and Transylvania (part of present-day Romania) by 1699 (Map 17.3).

The Turkish wars and this great expansion strengthened the Habsburg army and promoted some sense of unity in the Habsburg lands. But Habsburg efforts to create a fully developed, highly centralized, absolutist state were only partly successful. The Habsburg state remained a composite of three separate and distinct territories: the old "hereditary provinces" of Austria, the kingdom of Bohemia, and the kingdom of Hungary. Each part had its own laws and political life, for the three noble-dominated Estates continued to exist, though with reduced powers. Above all, the Hungarian nobility effectively thwarted the full development of Habsburg absolutism. Time and again throughout the seventeenth century, Hungarian nobles rose in revolt against the attempts of Vienna to impose absolute rule. They never triumphed decisively, but neither were they ever crushed.

Hungarians resisted because many of them were Protestants, especially in the area long ruled by the more tolerant Turks, and they hated the heavy-handed attempts of the conquering Habsburgs to re-Catholicize everyone. Moreover, the lords of Hungary and even part of the Hungarian peasantry had become attached to a national ideal long before most of the other European peoples. They were determined to maintain as much independence and local control as possible. Thus when the Habsburgs were bogged down in the War of the Spanish Succession (see page 564), the Hungarians rose in one last patriotic rebellion under Prince Francis Rákóczy in 1703. Rákóczy and his forces were eventually defeated, but this time the Habsburgs had to accept many of the traditional privileges of the Hungarian aristocracy in return for Hungarian acceptance of hereditary Habsburg rule. Thus Hungary, unlike Austria or Bohemia,

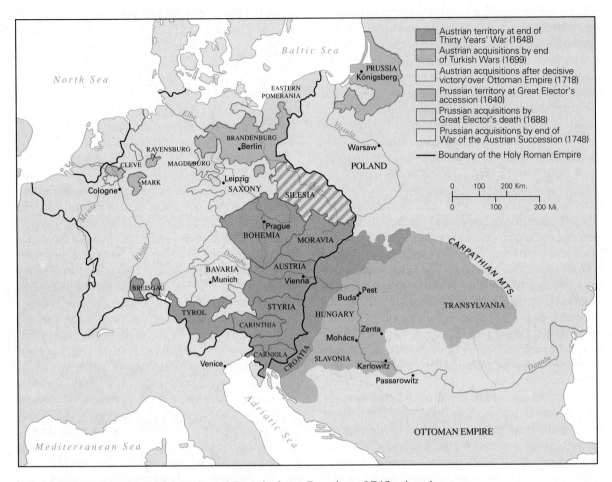

❋ **MAP 17.3 Growth of Austria and Brandenburg-Prussia to 1748**   Austria expanded to the southwest into Hungary and Transylvania at the expense of the Ottoman Empire. It was unable to hold the rich German province of Silesia, however, which was conquered by Brandenburg-Prussia.

never came close to being fully integrated into a centralized, absolute Habsburg state.

The Emergence of Prussia

As the status of east German peasants declined steadily after 1400, local princes lost political power, and a revitalized landed nobility became the undisputed ruling class. The Hohenzollern family, which ruled through different branches as the electors of Brandenburg and the dukes of Prussia, were little more than the largest landowners in a landlord society. Nothing suggested that the Hohenzollerns and their territories would ever play an important role in European or even German affairs.

Brandenburg was a helpless spectator in the Thirty Years' War, its territory alternately ravaged by Swedish and Habsburg armies. Yet the country's devastation prepared the way for Hohenzollern absolutism, because foreign armies dramatically weakened the political power of the Estates—the representative assemblies of the realm. The weakening of the Estates helped the very talented young elector Frederick William (r. 1640–1688), later known as the "Great Elector," to ride roughshod over traditional constitutional liberties and to take a giant step toward royal absolutism.

When Frederick William came to power in 1640, the twenty-year-old ruler was determined to unify his three quite separate provinces and to add to them by diplomacy and war. These provinces were Brandenburg itself, the area around Berlin; Prussia, inherited in 1618 when the junior branch of the Hohenzollern family died out; and scattered holdings along the Rhine in western Germany (see Map 17.3). Each province was inhabited by Germans; but each had its own Estates, dominated by the nobility and the landowning classes.

The struggle between the Great Elector and the provincial Estates was long, complicated, and intense. After the Thirty Years' War, the representatives of the nobility zealously reasserted the right of the Estates to vote taxes, a right the Swedish armies of occupation had simply ignored. Yet first in Brandenburg and then in Prussia, the Great Elector eventually had his way. To pay for the permanent standing army that he first established in 1660, Frederick William forced the Estates to accept the introduction of permanent taxation without consent. The soldiers doubled as tax collectors and policemen, becoming the core of the expanding state bureaucracy. The power of the Estates declined rapidly thereafter, and the Great Elector turned the screws of taxation. State revenue tripled and the size of the army leaped about tenfold during his reign.

In accounting for the Great Elector's fateful triumph, two factors appear central. First, as in the formation of every absolutist state, war was a decisive factor. The ongoing struggle between Sweden and Poland for control of the Baltic after 1648 and the wars of Louis XIV in western Europe created an atmosphere of permanent crisis. It was no accident that, except in commercially minded Holland, constitutionalism won out only in England, the only major country to escape devastating foreign invasions in the seventeenth century.

Second, the nobility had long dominated the government through the Estates but only for its own narrow self-interest. When, therefore, the Great Elector reconfirmed the nobility's freedom from taxation and its unlimited control over the peasants in 1653 and after, the nobility accepted a self-serving compromise. While Frederick William reduced the nobility's political power, the bulk of the Great Elector's new taxes fell on towns, and royal authority stopped at the landlords' gates.

By the time of his death in 1688, the Great Elector had created a single state out of scattered principalities. But his new creation was still small and fragile. It was Frederick William I, "the Soldiers' King" (r. 1713–1740), who truly established

A Prussian Giant Grenadier   Frederick William I wanted tall, handsome soldiers. He dressed them in tight, bright uniforms to distinguish them from the peasant population from which most soldiers came. He also ordered several portraits of his favorites from his court painter, J. C. Merk. Grenadiers wore the distinctive mitre cap instead of an ordinary hat so that they could hurl their heavy hand grenades unimpeded by a broad brim. *(Source: Copyright reserved to Her Majesty Queen Elizabeth II)*

Prussian absolutism and gave it its unique character. A dangerous psychoneurotic as well as a talented reformer, Frederick William I created the best army in Europe, for its size, and he infused military values into a whole society.

Frederick William's attachment to the army and military life was intensely emotional. He had, for example, a bizarre, almost pathological love for tall soldiers, whom he credited with superior strength and endurance. Like some fanatical modern-day basketball coach in search of a championship team, he sent his agents throughout both Prussia and all of Europe, tricking, buying, and kidnapping top recruits. Neighboring princes sent him their giants as gifts to win his gratitude. Prussian mothers told their sons: "Stop growing or the recruiting agents will get you."[7] Frederick William's love of the army was also based on a hardheaded conception of the struggle for power and a dog-eat-dog view of international politics. Throughout his long reign he never wavered in his conviction that the welfare of king and state depended above all else on the army.

As in France, the cult of military power provided the rationale for a great expansion of royal absolutism. As the ruthless king himself put it: "I must be served with life and limb, with house and wealth, with honour and conscience, everything must be committed except eternal salvation—that belongs to God, but all else is mine."[8] To make good these extraordinary demands, Frederick William created a strong and exceptionally honest bureaucracy, which administered the country and tried to develop it economically. The last traces of the parliamentary Estates and local self-government vanished.

The king's grab for power brought him into considerable conflict with the noble landowners, the Junkers. In the end the Prussian nobility responded to a combination of threats and opportunities and became the officer caste. By 1739 all but 5 of 245 officers with the rank of major or above were aristocrats. A new compromise had been worked out: the nobility imperiously commanded the peasantry in the army as well as on its estates.

Coarse and crude, penny-pinching and hard working, Frederick William achieved results. Above all, he built a first-rate army out of third-rate resources. Twelfth in Europe in population, Prussia had the fourth largest army by 1740, behind France, Russia, and Austria. Soldier for soldier, the Prussian army became the best in Europe, astonishing foreign observers with its precision, skill, and discipline. Curiously, the king loved his "blue boys" so much that he hated to "spend" them. This most militaristic of kings was, paradoxically, almost always at peace.

Nevertheless, the Prussian people paid a heavy and lasting price for the obsessions of the royal drillmaster. Civil society became rigid and highly disciplined. Prussia became the "Sparta of the North"; unquestioning obedience was the highest virtue. As a Prussian minister later summed up, "To keep quiet is the first civic duty."[9] Thus the absolutism of Frederick William I combined with harsh peasant bondage and Junker tyranny to lay the foundations for probably the most militaristic country of modern times.

The Rise of Moscow

In the ninth century, the Vikings, those fearless warriors from Scandinavia, appeared in the lands of the eastern Slavs. Called "Varangians" in the old Russian chronicles, the Vikings were interested primarily in international trade. In order to increase and protect their international commerce, they declared themselves the rulers of the eastern Slavs. The Varangian ruler Oleg (r. 878–912) established his residence at Kiev. He and his successors ruled over a loosely united confederation of Slavic territories—the Kievan state—which reached its height under Prince Iaroslav the Wise (r. 1019–1054).

After Iaroslav's death in 1054, Kiev disintegrated into more and more competing units, each ruled by a prince. A given prince owned a certain number of farms or landed estates and had them worked directly by his people, mainly slaves, called *kholops* in Russian. Outside of these estates, the prince exercised limited authority in his principality. Excluding the clergy, two kinds of people lived there: the noble boyars and the commoner peasants.

Like the Germans and the Italians, the eastern Slavs might have emerged from the Middle Ages weak and politically divided had it not been for the Mongol conquest of the Kievan state. Wild nomadic tribes from present-day Mongolia, the Mongols were temporarily unified in the thirteenth century by Jenghiz Khan (1162–1227), one of history's greatest conquerors. In five years his armies subdued all of China. His successors then wheeled westward, smashing everything in their path and reaching the plains of Hungary victorious before they pulled back in 1242. The Mongol army—the

Golden Horde—was savage in the extreme, often slaughtering entire populations of cities before burning them to the ground.

Having devastated and conquered, the Mongols ruled the eastern Slavs for more than two hundred years. They forced all the bickering Slavic princes to submit to their rule and to give them tribute and slaves. If the conquered peoples rebelled, the Mongols were quick to punish with death and destruction. Thus the Mongols unified the eastern Slavs, for the Mongol khan was acknowledged by all as the supreme ruler.

Beginning with Alexander Nevsky in 1252, the previously insignificant princes of Moscow became particularly adept at serving the Mongols. They loyally put down popular uprisings and collected the khan's harsh taxes. By way of reward, the princes of Moscow emerged as hereditary great princes. Eventually the Muscovite princes were able to destroy their princely rivals and even to replace the khan as supreme ruler.

One of the more important Muscovite princes was Ivan I (r. 1328–1341), popularly known as "Ivan the Moneybag." Extremely stingy, Ivan I built up a large personal fortune and increased his influence by loaning money to less frugal princes to pay their Mongol taxes. Ivan's most serious rival was the prince of Tver, who joined his people in 1327 in a revolt against Mongol oppression. Appointed commander of a large Russian-Mongol army, Ivan laid waste to Tver and its lands. For this proof of devotion, the Mongols made Ivan the general tax collector for all the Slavic lands they had subjugated and named him great prince. Ivan also convinced the metropolitan of Kiev, the leading churchman of all eastern Slavs, to settle in Moscow. Ivan I thus gained greater prestige.

In the next hundred-odd years, the great princes of Moscow significantly increased their holdings. Then, in the reign of Ivan III (r. 1462–1505), the process of gathering in the territories around Moscow was largely completed. Of the principalities that Ivan III purchased and conquered, Novgorod with its lands extending almost to the Baltic Sea was most crucial (Map 17.4). Thus the princes of Moscow defeated all rivals to win complete princely authority.

Not only was the prince of Moscow the *unique* ruler, he was the *absolute* ruler, the autocrat, the *tsar*—the Slavic contraction for "caesar," with all its connotations. This imperious conception of absolute power was powerfully reinforced by two de-velopments. First, about 1480 Ivan III stopped acknowledging the khan as his supreme ruler. There is good evidence to suggest that Ivan and his successors saw themselves as khans. Certainly they assimilated the Mongol concept of kingship as the exercise of unrestrained and unpredictable power.

Second, after the fall of Constantinople to the Turks in 1453, the tsars saw themselves as the heirs of both the caesars and Orthodox Christianity, the one true faith. All the other kings of Europe were heretics: only the tsars were rightful and holy rulers. This idea was promoted by Orthodox churchmen, who spoke of "holy Russia" as the "Third Rome." Ivan's marriage to the daughter of the last Byzantine emperor further enhanced the aura of an imperial inheritance for Moscow. Worthy successor to the mighty khan and the true Christian emperor, the Muscovite tsar was a king claiming unrestricted power as his God-given right. The Mongol inheritance weighed heavily on Russia.

As peasants had begun losing their freedom of movement in the fifteenth century, so had the noble boyars begun losing power and influence. For example, when Ivan III conquered the principality of Novgorod in the 1480s, he confiscated fully 80 percent of the land, executing the previous owners or resettling them nearer Moscow. He then kept more than half of the confiscated land for himself and distributed the remainder to members of a newly emerging service nobility, who held the tsar's land on the explicit condition that they serve in the tsar's army. Moreover, Ivan III began to require boyars outside Novgorod to serve him if they wished to retain their lands.

The rise of the new service nobility accelerated under Ivan IV (r. 1533–1584), the famous "Ivan the Terrible." Having ascended the throne at age three, Ivan suffered insults and neglect at the hands of the haughty boyars after his mother died. But at age sixteen he suddenly pushed aside his hated boyar advisers and crowned himself. Selecting the beautiful and kind Anastasia of the popular Romanov family for his wife and queen, the young tsar soon declared war on the remnants of Mongol power. He defeated the faltering khanates of Kazan and Astrakhan between 1552 and 1556, adding vast new territories to Russia. In the course of these wars, Ivan virtually abolished the old distinction between hereditary boyar private property and land granted temporarily for service. All nobles, old and new, had to serve the tsar in order to hold any land.

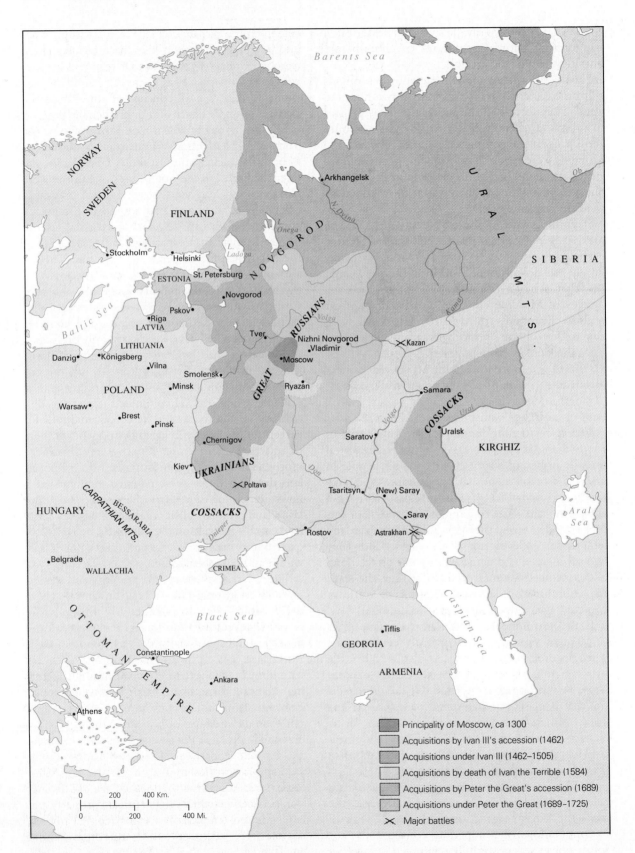

NORWAY

SWEDEN

FINLAND

Barents Sea

•Arkhangelsk

URAL

N. Dvina

Ob

SIBERIA

L. Onega

NOVGOROD

•Stockholm

•Helsinki

ESTONIA

St. Petersburg•

L. Ladoga

•Novgorod

Baltic Sea

•Riga

LATVIA

•Pskov

•Tver

RUSSIANS

Volga

Kama

LITHUANIA

Danzig• •Königsberg

•Vilna

•Smolensk

•Minsk

GREAT

Nizhni Novgorod•
•Vladimir

•Moscow

✕ Kazan

Ural

Samara•

POLAND

Warsaw•

•Brest

•Pinsk

•Ryazan

COSSACKS

•Uralsk

KIRGHIZ

Saratov•

Volga

•Chernigov

Kiev•

UKRAINIANS

✕ Poltava

Don

HUNGARY

CARPATHIAN MTS.

BESSARABIA

COSSACKS

Dnieper

Tsaritsyn•

(New) Saray

•Rostov

Astrakhan•✕

•Saray

*Aral
Sea*

•Belgrade

WALLACHIA

CRIMEA

Black Sea

•Tiflis

GEORGIA

Caspian Sea

OTTOMAN EMPIRE

Constantinople•

•Ankara

ARMENIA

•Athens

| | Principality of Moscow, ca 1300 |
| Acquisitions by Ivan III's accession (1462) |
| Acquisitions under Ivan III (1462–1505) |
| Acquisitions by death of Ivan the Terrible (1584) |
| Acquisitions by Peter the Great's accession (1689) |
| Acquisitions under Peter the Great (1689–1725) |
| ✕ Major battles |

0   200   400 Km.

0   200   400 Mi.

Ivan the Terrible Ivan IV, the first to take the title Tsar of Russia, executed many Muscovite boyars and their peasants and servants. His control of all land, trade, and industry restricted Russian social and economic development. *(Source: National Museum, Copenhagen, Denmark)*

The transformation of the entire nobility into a service nobility was completed in the second part of Ivan the Terrible's reign. In 1557 Ivan turned westward, and for the next twenty-five years Muscovy waged an exhausting, unsuccessful war primarily with the large Polish-Lithuanian state, which controlled not only Poland but much of the Ukraine in the sixteenth century. Quarreling with the boyars over the war and blaming them for the sudden death of his beloved Anastasia in 1560, the increasingly cruel and demented Ivan turned to strike down all who stood in his way.

Above all, he reduced the ancient Muscovite boyar families with a reign of terror. Leading boyars, their relatives, and even their peasants were executed en masse by a special corps of unquestioning servants. Dressed in black and riding black horses, they were forerunners of the modern dictator's secret police. Large estates were confiscated, broken up, and reapportioned to the lower service nobility, which was totally dependent on the autocrat.

Ivan also took giant strides toward making all commoners servants of the tsar. As the service nobles demanded more from their peasants, more and more peasants fled toward the wild, recently conquered territories to the east and south. There they formed free groups and outlaw armies known as Cossacks. The Cossacks maintained a precarious independence beyond the reach of the oppressive landholders and the tsar's hated officials. The solution to this problem was to complete the tying of the peasants to the land, making them serfs perpetually bound to serve the noble landholders, who were bound in turn to serve the tsar.

In the time of Ivan the Terrible, urban traders and artisans were also bound to their towns and

MAP 17.4 Expansion of Russia to 1725 After the disintegration of the Kievan state and the Mongol conquest, the princes of Moscow and their descendants gradually extended their rule over an enormous territory.

jobs so that the tsar could tax them more heavily. The urban classes had no security in their work or property and remained weak and divided. Even the wealthiest merchants were basically dependent agents of the tsar.

As has so often occurred in Russia, the death of an iron-fisted tyrant—in this case, Ivan the Terrible in 1584—ushered in an era of confusion and violent struggles for power. Events were particularly chaotic after Ivan's son Theodore died in 1598 without an heir. The years 1598 to 1613 are aptly called the Time of Troubles.

Close relatives of the deceased tsar intrigued against and murdered each other, alternately fighting and welcoming the invading Swedes and Poles, who even occupied Moscow. Most serious for the cause of autocracy, there was a great social upheaval as Cossacks marched northward, rallying peasants and slaughtering nobles and officials. This social explosion from below, which combined with a belated surge of patriotic opposition to the Polish invaders, brought the nobles to their senses. In 1613 they elected Ivan's sixteen-year-old grandnephew, Michael Romanov, the new hereditary tsar and rallied around him in the face of common internal and external threats.

Michael's reign saw the gradual re-establishment of tsarist autocracy (see Listening to the Past). The recently rebellious peasants were ground down further, while Ivan's heavy military obligations on the nobility were relaxed considerably, a trend that continued after his death. The result was a second round of mass upheaval and protest.

In the mid-seventeenth century, the unity of the Russian Orthodox church was torn apart by the religious reforms of the patriarch Nikon, a dogmatic purist who wished to bring "corrupted" Russian practices of worship into line with the Greek Orthodox model. The self-serving church hierarchy quickly went along, but the intensely religious common people resisted. Great numbers left the church and formed illegal communities of "Old Believers," who were hunted down and persecuted. After the great split, the Russian masses were alienated from the established church, which became totally dependent on the state for its authority.

Again the Cossacks revolted against the state, which was doggedly trying to catch up with them on the frontiers and reduce them to serfdom. Under the leadership of Stenka Razin they moved up the Volga River in 1670 and 1671, attracting a great undisciplined army of peasants, murdering landlords, and high church officials, and proclaiming freedom from oppression. In response to this rebellion, finally defeated by the government, the thoroughly scared upper classes tightened the screws of serfdom even further.

The Reforms of Peter the Great

It is now possible to understand the reforms of Peter the Great (r. 1682–1725) and his kind of monarchial absolutism. Contrary to some historians' assertions, Peter was interested primarily in military power and not in some grandiose westernization plan. A giant for his time, at six feet seven inches, and possessing enormous energy and determination, Peter was determined to increase Russia's power and to continue the territorial expansion that had gained a large part of the Ukraine in 1667 and had completed the conquest of Siberia in the seventeenth century. Little wonder that the forty-three years of Peter's rule knew only one year of peace.

When Peter took full control in 1689, the heart of his part-time army still consisted of cavalry made up of boyars and service nobility. The Russian army was lagging behind the professional standing armies being formed in Europe in the seventeenth century. The core of such armies was a highly disciplined infantry—an infantry that fired and refired rifles as it fearlessly advanced, before charging with fixed bayonets. Such a large, permanent army was enormously expensive. Given the desire to conquer more territory, Peter's military problem was serious.

Peter's solution was, in essence, to tighten up Muscovy's old service system and really make it work. He put the nobility back in harness with a vengeance. Every nobleman, great or small, was once again required to serve in the army or in the civil administration—for life. Since a more modern army and government required skilled technicians and experts, Peter created schools and even universities. One of his most hated reforms required five years of compulsory education away from home for every young nobleman. Peter established a merit-based military-civilian bureaucracy in which some people of non-noble origin rose to high positions. He also searched out talented foreigners—twice in his reign he went abroad to study and observe—and placed them in his service. These measures combined to make the army and government more powerful and efficient.

Peter also greatly increased the service requirements of the commoners. He established a regular standing army of more than 200,000 soldiers. In addition, special forces of Cossacks and foreigners numbered more than 100,000. The departure of a drafted peasant boy was regarded by his family and village as almost like a funeral, as indeed it was, since the recruit was drafted for life. The peasantry also served with its taxes, which increased three-fold during Peter's reign. Serfs were arbitrarily assigned to work in the growing number of factories and mines.

The constant warfare of Peter's reign consumed from 80 to 85 percent of all revenues but brought only modest territorial expansion. Yet after initial losses in the Great Northern War with Sweden, which lasted from 1700 to 1721, Peter's new war machine crushed Sweden's smaller army in the Ukraine at Poltava in 1709, one of the most significant battles in Russian history. Sweden never really regained the offensive. Annexing Estonia and much of present-day Latvia (see Map 17.4), Russia became the dominant power on the Baltic Sea and very much a European Great Power. If victory or defeat is the ultimate historical criterion, Peter's reforms were a success.

There were other important consequences of Peter's reign. Because of his feverish desire to use modern technology to strengthen the army, many Westerners and Western ideas flowed into Russia for the first time. A new class of educated Russians began to emerge. At the same time, vast numbers of Russians, especially among the poor and weak, hated Peter's massive changes. The split between the enserfed peasantry and the educated nobility thus widened, even though all were caught up in the endless demands of the sovereign.

A new idea of state interest, distinct from the tsar's personal interests, began to take hold. Peter claimed to act for the common good, and he attached explanations to his decrees in an attempt to gain the support of the populace. Yet, as before, the tsar alone decided what the common good was.

In sum, Peter built on the service obligations of old Muscovy. His monarchial absolutism was truly the culmination of the long development of a unique Russian civilization. Yet the creation of a more modern army and state introduced much that was new and Western to that civilization. This development paved the way for Russia to move much closer to the European mainstream in its thought and institutions during the Enlightenment under Catherine the Great.

Absolutism and the Baroque

The rise of royal absolutism in eastern Europe had major cultural consequences. Inspired in part by Louis XIV of France, the great and not-so-great rulers called on the artistic talent of the age to glorify their power and magnificence. This exaltation of despotic rule was particularly striking in architecture and city planning.

As soaring Gothic cathedrals expressed the idealized spirit of the High Middle Ages, so dramatic baroque palaces symbolized the age of absolutist power. By 1700 palace building had become an obsession for the rulers of central and eastern Europe. Their baroque palaces were clearly intended to overawe the people with the monarch's strength. One such palace was Schönbrunn, an enormous Viennese Versailles begun in 1695 by Emperor Leopold I to celebrate Austrian military victories and Habsburg might.

Petty princes also contributed mightily to the mania of palace building. The not-very-important elector-archbishop of Mainz, the ruling prince of that city, confessed apologetically that "building is a craze which costs much, but every fool likes his own hat."[10] The archbishop of Mainz's own "hat" was an architectural gem, like that of another churchly ruler, the prince-bishop of Würzburg. In central and eastern Europe, the favorite noble servants of royalty became extremely rich and powerful, and they, too, built grandiose palaces in the capital cities. These palaces were in part an extension of the monarch, for they surpassed the buildings of less favored nobles.

Palaces like Schönbrunn and Würzburg were magnificent examples of the baroque style. They expressed the baroque delight in bold, sweeping statements intended to provide a dramatic emotional experience. To create this experience, baroque masters dissolved the traditional artistic frontiers: the architect permitted the painter and the artisan to cover the undulating surfaces with wildly colorful paintings, graceful sculptures, and fanciful carvings. Space was used in a highly original way, to blend everything together in a total environment.

Not content with fashioning ostentatious palaces, absolute monarchs and baroque architects remodeled existing capital cities or built new ones to

❋ **Würzburg, the Prince-Bishop's Palace** The baroque style brought architects, painters, and sculptors together in harmonious, even playful partnership. This magnificent monumental staircase, designed by Johann Balthasar Neumann in 1735, merges into the vibrant ceiling frescoes by Giovanni Battista Tiepolo. A man is stepping out of the picture, and a painted dog resembles a marble statue. *(Source: Erich Lessing/Art Resource, NY)*

reflect royal magnificence and the centralization of political power. Karlsruhe, founded in 1715 as the capital city of a small German principality, is one extreme example. There, broad, straight avenues radiated out from the palace, so that all roads—like all power—were focused on the ruler. More typically, the monarch's architects added new urban areas alongside the old city, and these areas became the real heart of the expanding capital.

The distinctive features of the new additions were their broad avenues, their imposing government buildings, and their rigorous mathematical layout. Along major thoroughfares the nobles built elaborate townhouses; stables and servants' quarters were built on the alleys behind. Under arcades along the avenues appeared smart and expensive

shops, the first department stores, with plate-glass windows and fancy displays. The additions brought reckless speed to the European city. Whereas everyone had walked through the narrow, twisting streets of the medieval town, the high and mighty raced down the broad boulevards in elegant carriages. A social gap opened between the wealthy riders and the gaping, dodging pedestrians.

No city illustrates better than St. Petersburg the close ties among politics, architecture, and urban development in this period. In 1702 Peter the Great's armies seized a desolate Swedish fortress on one of the water-logged islands at the mouth of the Neva River on the Baltic Sea. Within a year the tsar had decided to build a new city there and to make it, rather than ancient Moscow, his capital. The land was swampy and inhospitable. But for Peter it was a future metropolis gloriously bearing his name. After the decisive Russian victory at Poltava in 1709, he moved into high gear. In one imperious decree after another, he ordered his people to build a new city, his "window on Europe."

Peter believed that it would be easier to reform the country militarily and administratively from such a city than from Moscow, and his political goals were reflected in his architectural ideas. First Peter wanted a comfortable, "modern" city. Modernity meant broad, straight, stone-paved avenues, houses built in a uniform line, large parks, canals for drainage, stone bridges, and street lighting. Second, all building had to conform strictly to detailed architectural regulations set down by the government. Finally, each social group—the nobility, the merchants, the artisans, and so on—was to live in a certain section of town. In short, the city and its population were to conform to a carefully defined urban plan of the baroque type.

Peter used the methods of Russian autocracy to build his modern capital. The creation of St. Petersburg was just one of the heavy obligations he dictatorially imposed on all social groups in Russia. The peasants bore the heaviest burdens. Just as the government drafted peasants for the army, it also drafted from 25,000 to 40,000 men each summer to labor in St. Petersburg for three months, without pay. Peasants hated forced labor in the capital, and each year from one-fourth to one-third of those sent risked brutal punishment and ran away. Many peasant construction workers died each summer from hunger, sickness, and accidents. Beautiful St. Petersburg was built on the shoveling, carting, and paving of a mass of conscripted serfs.

Peter also drafted more privileged groups to his city, but on a permanent basis. Nobles were sum-

St. Petersburg, ca 1760   Rastrelli's remodeled Winter Palace, which housed the royal family until the Russian Revolution of 1917, stands on the left along the Neva River. The Navy Office with its golden spire and other government office buildings are nearby and across the river. Russia became a naval power and St. Petersburg a great port. *(Source: Michael Holford)*

marily ordered to build costly stone houses and palaces in St. Petersburg and to live in them most of the year. Merchants and artisans were also commanded to settle and build in St. Petersburg. These nobles and merchants were then required to pay for the city's avenues, parks, canals, embankments, pilings, and bridges. The building of St. Petersburg was, in truth, an enormous direct tax levied on the wealthy, who in turn forced the peasantry to do most of the work. No wonder so many Russians hated Peter's new city.

Yet the tsar had his way. By the time of his death in 1725, there were at least six thousand houses and numerous impressive government buildings in St. Petersburg. Under the remarkable women who ruled Russia throughout most of the eighteenth century, St. Petersburg blossomed as a majestic and well-organized city, at least in its wealthy showpiece sections. Chief architect Bartolomeo Rastrelli combined Italian and Russian traditions into a unique, wildly colorful St. Petersburg style in many noble palaces and government buildings. All the while St. Petersburg grew rapidly, and its almost 300,000 inhabitants in 1782 made it one of the world's largest cities. A magnificent and harmonious royal city, St. Petersburg proclaimed the power of Russia's rulers and the creative potential of the absolutist state.

❖ ENGLAND: THE TRIUMPH OF CONSTITUTIONAL MONARCHY

In 1588 Queen Elizabeth I of England exercised great personal power, but by 1689 the power of the English monarchy was severely limited. Change in England was anything but orderly. Seventeenth-century England displayed little political stability. It executed one king, experienced a bloody civil war, experimented with military dictatorship, then restored the son of the murdered king, and finally, after a bloodless revolution, established constitutional monarchy. Political stability came only in the 1690s. Yet out of this tumultuous century England built the foundations for a strong and enduring constitutional monarchy.

In the middle years of the seventeenth century, the problem of sovereignty was vigorously debated. In *Leviathan,* the English philosopher and political theorist Thomas Hobbes (1588–1679) maintained that sovereignty is ultimately derived from the people, who transfer it to the monarchy by implicit contract. The power of the ruler is absolute, Hobbes said, but kings do not hold their power by divine right. This abstract theory pleased no one in the seventeenth century, but it did stimulate fruitful thinking about England's great seventeenth-century problem—the problem of order and political power.

The Decline of Absolutism in England (1603–1660)

Elizabeth I's extraordinary success was the result of her political shrewdness and flexibility, her careful management of finances, her wise selection of ministers, her clever manipulation of Parliament, and her sense of royal dignity and devotion to hard work. After her Scottish cousin James Stuart succeeded her as James I (r. 1603–1625), Elizabeth's strengths seemed even greater.

King James was learned and, with thirty-five years' experience as king of Scotland, politically shrewd. But he was not as interested in displaying the majesty and mystique of monarchy as Elizabeth had been, and he lacked the common touch. Moreover, James was a dogmatic proponent of the theory of divine right of kings. "There are no privileges and immunities," said James, "which can stand against a divinely appointed King." This typically absolutist notion implied total royal jurisdiction over the liberties, persons, and properties of English men and women. Such a view ran directly counter to many long-standing English ideas, including the belief that a person's property could not be taken away without due process of law. And in the House of Commons the English had a strong representative body to question these absolutist pretensions.

The House of Commons guarded the state's pocketbook, and James and later Stuart kings badly needed to open that pocketbook. James I looked on all revenues as a windfall to be squandered on a lavish court and favorite courtiers. The extravagance displayed in James's court, as well as the public flaunting of his male lovers, weakened respect for the monarchy. These actions also stimulated the knights and burgesses who sat in the House of Commons at Westminster to press for a thorough discussion of royal expenditures, religious reform, and foreign affairs. In short, the Commons aspired to sovereignty—the ultimate political power in the realm.

During the reigns of James I and his son Charles I (r. 1625–1649) the English House of Commons was very different from the assembly that Henry VIII had manipulated into passing his Reformation legislation. The class that dominated the Commons during the Stuarts' reign wanted political power corresponding to its economic strength. A social revolution had brought about this change. The dissolution of the monasteries and the sale of monastic land had enriched many people. Agricultural techniques like the draining of wasteland had improved the land and increased its yield. In the seventeenth century old manorial common land was enclosed and profitably turned into sheep runs. Many invested in commercial ventures at home, such as the expanding cloth industry, and in foreign trade. Many also made prudent marriages. These developments increased social mobility. The typical pattern was for the commercially successful to set themselves up as country gentry. This elite group possessed a far greater proportion of the land and of the nation's wealth in 1640 than in 1540. Increased wealth resulted in a better-educated and more articulate House of Commons.

In England, unlike France, no social stigma was attached to paying taxes. Members of the House of Commons were willing to tax themselves provided they had some say in state spending and state policies. The Stuart kings, however, considered such ambitions intolerable presumption and a threat to their divine-right prerogative. Consequently, at every Parliament between 1603 and 1640, bitter squabbles erupted between Crown and Commons. Like the Great Elector in Prussia, Charles I tried to govern without Parliament (1629–1640) and to finance his government by arbitrary levies. And as in Prussia these absolutist measures brought intense political conflict.

Religion was another source of conflict. In the early seventeenth century, increasing numbers of English people felt dissatisfied with the Church of England established by Henry VIII and reformed by Elizabeth. Many Puritans (see page 535) remained committed to "purifying" the Anglican church of Roman Catholic elements—elaborate vestments and ceremonies, the position of the altar in the church, even the giving and wearing of wedding rings.

Many Puritans were also attracted by the socioeconomic implications of John Calvin's theology. Calvinism emphasized hard work, sobriety, thrift, competition, and postponement of pleasure, and it tended to link sin and poverty with weakness and moral corruption. These attitudes, which have frequently been called the "Protestant ethic," "middle-class ethic," or "capitalist ethic," fit in precisely with the economic approaches and practices of many (successful) business people and farmers. These "Protestant virtues" represented the prevailing values of members of the House of Commons.

James I and Charles I both gave the impression of being highly sympathetic to Roman Catholicism. Charles supported the policies of Archbishop of Canterbury William Laud (1573–1645), who tried to impose elaborate ritual and rich ceremonial on all churches. People believed that the country was being led back to Roman Catholicism. In 1637 Laud attempted to impose two new elements on the church organization in Scotland: a new prayer book, modeled on the Anglican Book of Common Prayer, and bishoprics, which the Presbyterian Scots firmly rejected. The Scots revolted. To finance an army to put down the Scots, King Charles was compelled to summon Parliament in November 1640. It was a fatal decision.

For eleven years Charles I had ruled without Parliament, financing his government through extraordinary stopgap levies considered illegal by most English people. Most members of Parliament believed that such taxation without consent amounted to absolutist despotism. Thus they were not willing to trust the king with an army. Accordingly, the Parliament summoned in November 1640 (commonly called the Long Parliament because it sat from 1640 to 1660) enacted legislation that limited the power of the monarch and made arbitrary government impossible.

In 1641 the Commons passed the Triennial Act, which compelled the king to summon Parliament every three years. The Commons impeached Archbishop Laud and abolished the House of Lords and the ecclesiastical Court of High Commission. King Charles reluctantly accepted these measures. But understanding and peace were not achieved, and an uprising in Ireland precipitated civil war.

Ever since Henry II had conquered Ireland in 1171, English governors had mercilessly ruled the land, and English landlords had ruthlessly exploited the Irish people. The English Reformation had made a bad situation worse: because the Irish remained Catholic, religious differences united with economic and political oppression. Without an army, Charles I could neither come to terms with the Scots nor put down the Irish rebellion, and the Long Parliament remained unwilling to place an army under a king it did not trust. Charles thus recruited an army drawn from the nobility and the nobility's cavalry staff, the rural gentry, and mercenaries. The parliamentary army that rose in opposition was composed of the militia of the city of London, country squires with business connections, and men with a firm belief that serving was their spiritual duty.

The English civil war (1642–1649) tested whether ultimate political power in England was to reside in the king or in Parliament. The civil war did not resolve that problem, although it ended in 1649 with the execution of King Charles on the charge of high treason and thus dealt a severe blow to the theory of divine-right, absolute monarchy in England. Kingship was abolished in England, and a *commonwealth,* or republican form of government, was proclaimed.

In fact, the army that had defeated the royal forces controlled the government, and Oliver Cromwell controlled the army. Indeed, the period from 1649 to 1660, known as the Interregnum because it separated two monarchial periods, was a transitional time of military dictatorship, and for most of that time Cromwell was head of state.

Oliver Cromwell (1599–1658) came from the country gentry, the class that dominated the House of Commons in the early seventeenth century. He was a member of the Long Parliament. Cromwell rose in the parliamentary army and achieved nationwide fame by infusing the army with his Puritan convictions and molding it into the highly effective military machine, called the New Model Army, that defeated the royalist forces. The army prepared a constitution, the Instrument of Government (1653), that invested executive power in a lord protector (Cromwell) and a council of state. The instrument provided for triennial parliaments and gave Parliament the sole power to raise taxes. But after repeated disputes, Cromwell tore up the document and proclaimed quasi-martial law.

On the issue of religion, Cromwell favored broad toleration, and the Instrument of Government gave all Christians, except Roman Catholics, the right to practice their faith. Cromwell welcomed the immigration of Jews, because of their skills, and they began to return to England after four centuries of absence. As for Irish Catholicism, Cromwell identified it with sedition. In 1649 he crushed rebellion in Ireland with merciless savagery, leaving a legacy of Irish hatred for England. He also rigorously censored the press, forbade sports, and kept the theaters closed in England.

Cromwell pursued mercantilist economic policies similar to those that Colbert established in France. He enforced a navigation act requiring that English goods be transported on English ships. The navigation act was a great boost to the development of an English merchant marine and brought about a short but successful war with the commercially threatened Dutch.

Periodical Sheet on the English Civil War Single sheets or broadsides spread the positions of the opposing sides to the nonliterate public. *Mercurius Rusticus,* intended for country people, conveyed the royalist argument. *(Source: The British Library)*

Military government collapsed when Cromwell died in 1658. Fed up with military rule, the English longed for a return to civilian government, restoration of the common law, and social and religious stability. Moreover, the strain of creating a community of puritanical saints proved too psychologically exhausting. Government by military dictatorship was an experiment in absolutism that the English never forgot or repeated. By 1660 they were ready to try a restoration of monarchy.

The Restoration of the English Monarchy

The Restoration of 1660 re-established the monarchy in the person of Charles II (r. 1660–1685), eldest son of Charles I. At the same time both houses of Parliament were also restored, together with the established Anglican church. The Restoration failed to resolve two serious problems. What was to be the attitude of the state toward Puritans, Catholics, and dissenters from the established church? And what was to be the constitutional relationship between the king and Parliament?

Charles II, a relaxed, easygoing, and sensual man, was basically not much interested in religious issues. But the new members of Parliament were, and they proceeded to enact a body of laws that sought to compel religious uniformity. Those who refused to receive the sacrament of the Church of England could not vote, hold public office, preach, teach, attend the universities, or even assemble for meetings, according to the Test Act of 1673.

In politics, Charles II was at first determined to get along with Parliament and share power with it. His method for doing so had profound importance for later constitutional development. The king appointed a council of five men who served both as his major advisers and as members of Parliament, thus acting as liaison agents between the executive and the legislature. It gradually came to be accepted that the council of five was answerable in Parliament for the decisions of the king.

Harmony between the Crown and Parliament rested on the understanding that Charles would summon Parliament frequently and Parliament would vote him sufficient revenues. However, although Parliament believed that Charles should have large powers, it did not grant him an adequate income. Accordingly, in 1670 Charles entered into a secret agreement with Louis XIV. The French king would give Charles £200,000 annually. In return Charles would relax the laws against Catholics, gradually re-Catholicize England, support French policy against the Dutch, and convert to Catholicism himself.

When the details of this secret treaty leaked out, a wave of anti-Catholic fear swept England. Charles had produced only bastards, and therefore it appeared that his brother and heir, James, duke of York, who had publicly acknowledged his Catholicism, would inaugurate a Catholic dynasty. The combination of hatred for the French absolutism embodied in Louis XIV and hostility to Roman Catholicism led the Commons to pass an exclusion bill denying the succession to a Roman Catholic. But Charles quickly dissolved Parliament, and the bill never became law.

James II (r. 1685–1688) succeeded his brother. Almost at once the worst English anti-Catholic fears, already aroused by Louis XIV's recent revocation of the Edict of Nantes, were realized. In direct violation of the Test Act, James appointed Roman Catholics to positions in the army, the universities, and local government. The king was suspending the law at will and appeared to be reviving the absolutism of his father (Charles I) and grandfather (James I). He went further. Attempting to broaden his base of support with Protestant dissenters and nonconformists, James issued a declaration of indulgence granting religious freedom to all.

Two events gave the signals for revolution. First, seven bishops of the Church of England petitioned the king that they not be forced to read the declaration of indulgence because of their belief that it was an illegal act. They were imprisoned in the Tower of London but subsequently acquitted amid great public enthusiasm. Second, in June 1688 James's second wife produced a male heir. A Catholic dynasty seemed assured. The fear of a Roman Catholic monarchy, supported by France and ruling outside the law, prompted a group of eminent persons to offer the English throne to James's Protestant daughter, Mary, and her Dutch husband, Prince William of Orange. In December 1688 James II, his queen, and their infant son fled to France and became pensioners of Louis XIV. Early in 1689, William and Mary were crowned king and queen of England.

The English call the events of 1688 to 1689 the "Glorious Revolution." The revolution was indeed glorious in the sense that it replaced one king with another with a minimum of bloodshed. It also represented the destruction, once and for all, of the idea of divine-right absolutism in England. William and Mary accepted the English throne from Parliament and in so doing explicitly recognized the supremacy of Parliament.

The men who brought about the revolution quickly framed their intentions in the Bill of Rights, the cornerstone of the modern British constitution. The basic principles of the Bill of Rights were formulated in direct response to Stuart absolutism. Law was to be made in Parliament; once made, it could not be suspended by the Crown. Parliament had to be called at least every three years. Both elections to and debate in Parliament were to be free, in the sense that the Crown was not to interfere in them. Judges would hold their offices "during good behavior," a provision that assured judicial independence.

In striking contrast to the states of continental Europe, there was to be no standing army that could be used against the English population in peacetime. Moreover, the Bill of Rights granted Protestants the right to possess firearms. Additional legislation granted freedom of worship to Protestant dissenters and nonconformists and required that the English monarch always be Protestant.

The Glorious Revolution found its best defense in John Locke's *Second Treatise of Civil Government* (1690). The political philosopher Locke (1632–1704) maintained that people set up civil governments in order to protect life, liberty, and property. A government that oversteps its proper function —protecting the natural rights of life, liberty, and property—becomes a tyranny. (By "natural" rights, Locke meant rights basic to all men because all have the ability to reason.) Under a tyrannical government, the people have the natural right to rebellion. Recognizing the close relationship between economic and political freedom, Locke linked economic liberty and private property with political freedom.

Locke served as the great spokesman for the liberal English revolution of 1688 to 1689 and for representative government. His idea, inherited from ancient Greece and Rome, that there are natural or universal rights equally valid for all peoples and societies, played a powerful role in eighteenth-century Enlightenment thought. His ideas on liberty and tyranny were especially popular in colonial America.

The events of 1688 to 1689 did not constitute a *democratic* revolution. The revolution formalized Parliament's great power, and Parliament represented the upper classes. The great majority of English people had little say in their government. The English revolution established a constitutional monarchy; it also inaugurated an age of aristocratic government.

In the course of the eighteenth century, the cabinet system of government evolved out of Charles II's old council-of-five system. The term *cabinet* derives from the small private room in which English rulers consulted their chief ministers. In a cabinet system, the leading ministers formulate common policy and conduct the business of the country. During the administration of one royal minister, Sir Robert Walpole, who led the cabinet from 1721 to 1742, the idea developed that the cabinet was responsible to the House of Commons. Walpole enjoyed the favor of the monarchy and of the House of Commons and came to be called the king's first, or "prime," minister. In the English cabinet system, both legislative and executive power are held by the leading ministers, who form the government.

THE DUTCH REPUBLIC IN THE SEVENTEENTH CENTURY

In the late sixteenth century, the seven northern provinces of the Netherlands, of which Holland and Zeeland were the most prosperous, had thrown off Spanish domination (see pages 534–539). The seventeenth century then witnessed an unparalleled flowering of Dutch scientific, artistic, and literary achievement. In this period, often called the golden age of the Netherlands, Dutch ideas and attitudes played a profound role in shaping a new and modern world-view.

The Republic of the United Provinces of the Netherlands represents a variation in the development of the modern constitutional state. Within each province an oligarchy of wealthy merchants called regents handled domestic affairs in the local Estates. The provincial Estates held virtually all the power. A federal assembly, or States General, handled matters of foreign affairs, such as war, but all issues had to be referred back to the local Estates for approval. The regents in each province jealously guarded local independence and resisted efforts at centralization. Nevertheless, Holland, which had the largest navy and the most wealth, dominated the republic and the States General.

The government of the United Provinces conforms to none of the standard categories of seventeenth-century political organization. The Dutch were not monarchial but fiercely republican. The government was controlled by wealthy merchants and financiers. Though rich, their values were not aristocratic but strongly middle class. The political success of the Dutch rested on the phenomenal commercial prosperity of the Netherlands. The moral and ethical bases of that commercial wealth were thrift, hard work, and simplicity in living.

John Calvin had written, "From where do the merchant's profits come except from his own diligence and industry." This attitude undoubtedly encouraged a sturdy people who had waged a centuries-old struggle against the sea. Louis XIV's hatred of the Dutch was proverbial. They represented all that he despised—middle-class values, religious toleration, and independent political institutions.

Alone of all European peoples in the seventeenth century, the Dutch practiced religious toleration. Peoples of all faiths were welcome within their borders. Jews enjoyed a level of acceptance and absorption in Dutch business and general culture unique in early modern Europe. It is a testimony to the urbanity of Dutch society that in a century when patriotism was closely identified with religious uniformity, the Calvinist province of Holland allowed its highest official, Jan van Oldenbarneveldt, to continue to practice his Roman Catholic faith. As long as business people conducted their religion in private, the government did not interfere with them.

Toleration paid off. It attracted a great amount of foreign capital and business expertise. The Bank of Amsterdam became Europe's best source of cheap credit and commercial intelligence and the main clearing-house for bills of exchange. People of all races and creeds traded in Amsterdam, at whose docks on the Amstel River five thousand ships were berthed. Joost van den Vondel, the poet of Dutch imperialism, exulted:

Rembrandt: The Jewish Bride Holland's greatest painter, Rembrandt (1606–1669) combined an expressive mastery of technique, emotional depth, psychological penetration, and enormous range—religious scenes, still lifes, portraits. The so-called Jewish Bride (ca 1665), perhaps a wedding portrait of two wealthy people, reveals the artist's unsurpassed handling of light, so characteristic of his later work. *(Source: Rijksmuseum-Stichting)*

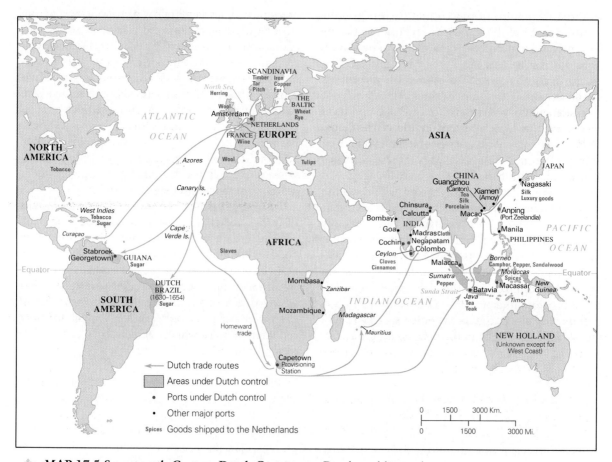

MAP 17.5 Seventeenth-Century Dutch Commerce Dutch wealth rested on commerce, and commerce depended on the huge Dutch merchant marine, manned by perhaps forty-eight thousand sailors. The fleet carried goods from all parts of the globe to the port of Amsterdam.

God, God, the Lord of Amstel cried, hold every
*   conscience free;*
And Liberty ride, on Holland's tide, with billowing
*   sails to sea,*
And run our Amstel out and in; let freedom gird the
*   bold,*
And merchant in his counting house stand elbow deep
*   in gold.*[11]

The fishing industry was a cornerstone of the Dutch economy. For half of the year, from June to December, fishing fleets combed the dangerous English coast and the North Sea, raking in tiny herring. Profits from herring stimulated shipbuilding, and even before 1600 the Dutch were offering the lowest shipping rates in Europe. In 1650 the Dutch merchant marine was the largest in Europe, comprising roughly half of the European total. All the wood for these ships had to be imported: the Dutch bought whole forests from Norway. They controlled the Baltic grain trade, buying entire wheat and rye crops in Poland, east Prussia, and Swedish Pomerania. Foreign merchants coming to Amsterdam could buy anything from precision lenses for the newly invented microscope to muskets for an army of five thousand.

In 1602 a group of the regents of Holland formed the Dutch East India Company, a joint stock company. Each investor received a percentage of the profits proportional to the amount of money he had put in. Within a half-century, the Dutch East India Company had cut heavily into Portuguese trading in East Asia. The Dutch seized the Cape of Good Hope, Ceylon, and Malacca and established trading posts in each place. In the 1630s the Dutch East India Company was paying its investors about a 35 percent annual return on their investments. The Dutch West India Company, founded in 1621, traded extensively with Latin America and Africa (Map 17.5).

Trade and commerce brought the Dutch prodigious wealth. In the seventeenth century, the Dutch enjoyed the highest standard of living in Europe, perhaps in the world. Amsterdam and Rotterdam built massive granaries where the surplus of one year could be stored against possible shortages the next. Thus food prices fluctuated very little, except during the 1650s when several bad harvests reduced supplies. By the standards of Cologne, Paris, or London, salaries were high for all workers, except women. All classes of society, including unskilled laborers, ate well. The low price of bread meant that, compared with other places in Europe, a higher percentage of a worker's income could be spent on fish, cheese, butter, vegetables, even meat. A scholar recently described the Netherlands as "an island of plenty in a sea of want."[12]

Dutch economic leadership was eventually sapped by wars, beginning with those with France and England in the 1670s. The long War of the Spanish Succession, in which the Dutch supported England against France, was a costly drain on Dutch manpower and financial resources. The peace signed in 1713 to end that war marked the beginning of Dutch economic decline.

SUMMARY

War, religious strife, economic depression, and peasant revolts were all aspects of a deep crisis in seventeenth-century Europe. Rulers responded by aggressively seeking to expand their power, which they claimed was essential to meet emergencies and quell disorders. Claiming also that they ruled by divine right, monarchs sought the freedom to wage war, levy taxes, and generally make law as they saw fit. Although they were limited by technology and inadequate financial resources, monarchial governments on the European continent succeeded to a large extent, overpowering organized opposition and curbing the power of the nobility and the traditional representative institutions.

The France of Louis XIV led the way to royal absolutism. France developed a centralized bureaucracy, a professional army, a state-directed economy, all of which Louis personally supervised. The king saw himself as the representative of God on earth and accountable to no one here below. His majestic bearing and sumptuous court dazzled contemporaries. Yet behind the grand façade of unchallenged personal rule and obedient bureaucrats working his will there stood major limitations on Louis XIV's power. Most notable were the financial independence of some provinces and the nobility's traditional freedom from taxation, which Louis himself was compelled to reaffirm.

Within a framework of resurgent serfdom and entrenched nobility, Austrian and Prussian monarchs also fashioned absolutist states in the seventeenth and early eighteenth centuries. These monarchs won absolutist control over standing armies, permanent taxes, and legislative bodies. But they did not question the underlying social and economic relationships. Indeed, they enhanced the privileges of the nobility, which furnished the leading servitors for enlarged armies and growing government bureaucracies.

In Russia, social and economic trends were similar to those in Austria and Prussia. Unlike those two states, however, Russia had a long history of powerful princes. Tsar Peter the Great succeeded in tightening up Russia's traditional absolutism and modernizing it by reforming the army, the bureaucracy, and the defense industry. In Russia and throughout eastern Europe, war and the needs of the state in time of war weighed heavily in the triumph of absolutism.

Triumphant absolutism interacted spectacularly with the arts. It molded the ideals of French classicism, which glorified the state as personified by Louis XIV. Baroque art, which had grown out of the Catholic Reformation's desire to move the faithful and exalt the faith, admirably suited the secular aspirations of eastern European rulers. Thus baroque art attained magnificent heights in eastern Europe, symbolizing the ideal and harmonizing with the reality of imperious royal absolutism.

Holland and England defied the general trend toward absolute monarchy. While Holland prospered under a unique republican confederation that placed most power in the hands of the different provinces, England—fortunately shielded from continental armies and military emergencies by its navy and the English Channel—evolved into the first modern constitutional state. The bitter conflicts between Parliament and the first two Stuart rulers, James I and Charles I, tested where supreme power would rest in the state. The resulting civil war deposed the king, but it did not settle the question. A revival of absolutist tendencies under James II brought on the Glorious Revolution of 1688, and the people who made that revolution settled three basic issues. Power was divided between king and Parliament, with Parliament enjoying the greater share. Government was to be based on the rule of law. And the liberties of English people were to be made explicit in written form, in the Bill of Rights. This constitutional settlement marked an important milestone in world history, although the framers left to later generations the task of making constitutional government work.

NOTES

1. J. B. Collins, *Fiscal Limits of Absolutism: Direct Taxation in Early Seventeenth Century France* (Berkeley: University of California Press, 1988), pp. 1, 3–4, 215–222.
2. Quoted in J. H. Elliot, *Richelieu and Olivares* (Cambridge: Cambridge University Press, 1984), p. 135; and in W. F. Church, *Richelieu and Reason of State* (Princeton, N.J.: Princeton University Press, 1972), p. 507.
3. S. de Gramont, ed., *The Age of Magnificence: Memoirs of the Court of Louis XIV by the Duc de Saint Simon* (New York: Capricorn Books, 1964), pp. 141–145.
4. See W. Beik, *Absolutism and Society in Seventeenth Century France: State Power and Provincial Aristocracy in Languedoc* (Cambridge: Cambridge University Press, 1985), pp. 279–302.
5. W. F. Church, *Louis XIV in Historical Thought: From Voltaire to the Annales School* (New York: Norton, 1976), p. 92.
6. B. Bennassar, *The Spanish Character: Attitudes and Mentalities from the Sixteenth to the Nineteenth Century,* trans. B. Keen (Berkeley: University of California Press, 1979), p. 125.
7. Quoted in R. Ergang, *The Potsdam Fuhrer: Frederick William I, Father of Prussian Militarism* (New York: Octagon Books, 1972), pp. 85, 87.
8. Quoted in R. A. Dorwart, *The Administrative Reforms of Frederick William I of Prussia* (Cambridge, Mass.: Harvard University Press, 1953), p. 226.
9. Quoted in H. Rosenberg, *Bureaucracy, Aristocracy, and Autocracy: The Prussian Experience, 1660–1815* (Boston: Beacon Press, 1966), p. 38.
10. Quoted in J. Summerson, in *The Eighteenth Century: Europe in the Age of Enlightenment,* ed. A. Cobban (New York: McGraw-Hill, 1969), p. 80.
11. Quoted in D. Maland, *Europe in the Seventeenth Century* (New York: Macmillan, 1967), pp. 198–199.
12. S. Schama, *The Embarrassment of Riches: An Interpretation of Dutch Culture in the Golden Age* (New York: Knopf, 1987), pp. 165–170.

SUGGESTED READING

Students who wish to explore the problems presented in this chapter will find a rich and exciting literature. G. Parker, *Europe in Crisis, 1598–1618* (1980), provides a sound introduction to the social, economic, and religious tensions of the period, as does R. S. Dunn, *The Age of Religious Wars, 1559–1715,* 2d ed. (1979). T. Aston, ed., *Crisis in Europe, 1560–1660* (1967), contains essays by leading historians. P. Anderson, *Lineages of the Absolutist State* (1974), is a stimulating Marxist interpretation of absolutism in western and eastern Europe.

Louis XIV and his age have attracted the attention of many scholars. J. Wolf, *Louis XIV* (1968), remains the best available biography. Two works of W. H. Lewis, *The Splendid Century* (1957) and *The Sunset of the Splendid Century* (1963), make delightful light reading. The advanced student will want to consult the excellent historiographical analysis by W. F. Church mentioned in the Notes, *Louis XIV in Historical Thought*. Perhaps the best works of the Annales school on the period are P. Goubert, *Louis XIV and Twenty Million Frenchmen* (1972), and Goubert's heavily detailed *The Ancien Régime: French Society, 1600–1750,* 2 vols. (1969–1973), which contains invaluable material on the lives and work of ordinary people. R. Bonney, *The King's Debts: Finance and Politics in France, 1589–1661* (1981), and A. Trout, *Jean-Baptiste Colbert* (1978), consider economy and financial conditions. R. Hatton, *Europe in the Age of Louis XIV* (1979), is a splendidly illustrated survey of many aspects of seventeenth-century European culture.

For Spain, M. Defourneaux, *Daily Life in Spain in the Golden Age* (1976), is extremely useful. See also C. R. Phillips, *Ciudad Real, 1500–1750: Growth, Crisis, and Readjustment in the Spanish Economy* (1979), a significant case study. V. L. Tapie, *The Age of Grandeur: Baroque Art and Architecture* (1960), emphasizes the relationship between art and politics with excellent illustrations. Art and architecture are also treated admirably in E. Hempel, *Baroque Art and Architecture in Central Europe* (1965), and G. Hamilton, *The Art and Architecture of Russia* (1954).

The best study on early Prussian history is still F. L. Carsten, *The Origin of Prussia* (1954). Rosenberg, *Bureaucracy, Aristocracy, and Autocracy,* cited in the Notes, is a masterful analysis of the social context of Prussian absolutism. Ergang, *The Potsdam Fuhrer,* also cited in the Notes, is an exciting and critical biography of ramrod Frederick William I. G. Craig, *The Politics of the Prussian Army, 1640–1945* (1964), expertly traces the great influence of the military on the Prussian state over three hundred years. R. J. Evans, *The Making of the Habsburg Empire, 1550–1770* (1979), analyzes the development of absolutism in Austria, as does A. Wandruszka, *The House of Habsburg* (1964). D. McKay and H. Scott, *The Rise of the Great Powers, 1648–1815* (1983), is a good general account. R. Vierhaus, *Germany in the Age of Absolutism* (1988), offers a thorough survey of the different German states.

On eastern European peasants and serfdom, D. Chirot, ed., *The Origins of Backwardness in Eastern Europe: Economics and Politics from the Middle Ages Until the Twentieth Century* (1989), is a wide-ranging introduction. E. Levin, *Sex and Society in the World of the Orthodox Slavs, 900–1700* (1989), carries family history to eastern Europe. J. Blum, *Lord and Peasant in Russia from the Ninth to the Nineteenth Century* (1961), provides a good look at conditions in rural Russia, and P. Avrich, *Russian Rebels, 1600–1800* (1972), treats some of the violent peasant upheavals that those conditions produced. R. Hellie, *Enserfment and Military Change in Muscovy* (1971), is outstanding. In addition to the fine survey by N. V. Riasanovsky, *A History of Russia* (1963), J. Billington, *The Icon and the Axe* (1970), is a stimulating history of early Russian intellectual and cultural developments. B. H. Sumner, *Peter the Great and the Emergence of Russia* (1962), is a good brief introduction, which may be compared with N. V. Riasanovsky, *The Image of Peter the Great in Russian History and Thought* (1985).

English political and social issues of the seventeenth century are considered by M. Ashley, *The House of Stuart: Its Rise and Fall* (1980); C. Hill, *A Century of Revolution* (1961); and K. Wrightson, *English Society, 1580–1680* (1982). Comprehensive treatments of Parliament include C. Russell's *Crisis of Parliaments, 1509–1660* (1971), and *Parliaments and English Politics, 1621–1629* (1979). L. Stone, *The Causes of the English Revolution* (1972), and B. Manning, *The English People and the English Revolution* (1976), are recommended. D. Underdown, *Revel, Riot, and Rebellion* (1985), discusses the extent of popular involvement. For English intellectual currents, see J. O. Appleby, *Economic Thought and Ideology in Seventeenth Century England* (1978). Other recommended works include P. Collinson, *The Religion of Protestants* (1982); R. Thompson, *Women in Stuart England and America* (1974); and A. Fraser, *The Weaker Vessel* (1985). For Cromwell and the Interregnum, A. Fraser, *Cromwell, the Lord Protector* (1973), is valuable. C. Hill, *The World Turned Upside Down* (1972), discusses radical thought during the period. For the Restoration and the Glorious Revolution, see R. Hutton, *Charles II: King of England, Scotland and Ireland* (1989); J. Childs, *The Army, James II, and the Glorious Revolution* (1980); and L. G. Schwoerer, *The Declaration of Rights, 1689* (1981), a fine assessment of that fundamental document. The ideas of John Locke are analyzed by J. P. Kenyon, *Revolution Principles: The Politics of Party, 1689–1720* (1977).

On Holland, K. H. D. Haley, *The Dutch Republic in the Seventeenth Century* (1972), is a splendidly illustrated appreciation of Dutch commercial and artistic achievements, and Schama, *The Embarrassment of Riches,* cited in the Notes, is a lively recent synthesis. R. Boxer, *The Dutch Seaborne Empire* (1980), is useful for Dutch overseas expansion. V. Barbour, *Capitalism in Amsterdam in the Seventeenth Century* (1950), and D. Regin, *Traders, Artists, Burghers: A Cultural History of Amsterdam in the Seventeenth Century* (1977), focus on the leading Dutch city. The leading statesmen of the period may be studied in these biographies: H. H. Rowen, *John de Witt, Grand Pensionary of Holland, 1625–1672* (1978); S. B. Baxter, *William the III and the Defense of European Liberty, 1650–1702* (1966); and J. den Tex, *Oldenbarnevelt,* 2 vols. (1973).

A Foreign Traveler in Russia

Russia in the seventeenth century remained a remote and mysterious land for western and even central Europeans, who had few direct contacts with the tsar's dominion. Knowledge of Russia came mainly from occasional travelers who had visited Muscovy and sometimes wrote accounts of what they had seen.

The most famous of these accounts was by the German Adam Olearius (ca 1599–1671), who was send to Moscow by the duke of Holstein on three diplomatic missions in the 1630s. These missions ultimately proved unsuccessful, but they provided Olearius with a rich store of information for his Travels in Moscovy, *from which the following excerpts are taken. Published in German in 1647 and soon translated into several languages (but not Russian), Olearius's unflattering but well-informed study played a major role in shaping European ideas about Russia.*

The government of the Russians is what political theorists call a "dominating and despotic monarchy," where the sovereign, that is, the tsar or the grand prince who has obtained the crown by right of succession, rules the entire land alone, and all the people are his subjects, and where the nobles and princes no less than the common folk—townspeople and peasants—are his serfs and slaves, whom he rules and treats as a master treats his servants. . . .

If the Russians be considered in respect to their character, customs, and way of life, they are justly to be counted among the barbarians. . . . The vice of drunkenness is so common in this nation, among people of every station, clergy and laity, high and low, men and women, old and young, that when they are seen now and then lying about in the streets, wallowing in the mud, no attention is paid to it, as something habitual. If a cart driver comes upon such a drunken pig whom he happens to know, he shoves him onto his cart and drives him home, where he is paid his fare. No one ever refuses an opportunity to drink and to get drunk, at any time and in any place, and usually it is done with vodka. . . .

The Russians being naturally tough and born, as it were, for slavery, they must be kept under a harsh and strict yoke and must be driven to do their work with clubs and whips, which they suffer without impatience, because such is their station, and they are accustomed to it. Young and half-grown fellows sometimes come together on certain days and train themselves in fisticuffs, to accustom themselves to receiving blows, and, since habit is second nature, this makes blows given as punishment easier to bear. Each and all, they are slaves and serfs. . . .

Because of slavery and their rough and hard life, the Russians accept war readily and are well suited to it. On certain occasions, if need be, they reveal themselves as courageous and daring soldiers. . . .

Although the Russians, especially the common populace, living as slaves under a harsh yoke, can bear and endure a great deal out of love for their masters, yet if the pressure is beyond measure, then it can be said of them: "Patience, often wounded, finally turned into fury." A dangerous indignation results, turned not so much against their sovereign as against the lower authorities, especially if the people have been much oppressed by them and by their supporters and have not been protected by the higher authorities. And once they are aroused and enraged, it is not easy to appease them. Then, disregarding all dangers that may ensue, they resort to every kind of violence and behave like madmen. . . . They own little; most of them have no feather beds; they lie on cushions, straw, mats, or their clothes; they sleep on benches and, in winter, like the non-Germans [i.e., natives] in Livonia, upon the oven, which serves them for cooking and is flat on the top; here husband, wife, children, servants, and maids huddle together. In some houses in the countryside we saw chickens and pigs under the benches and the ovens. . . .

Russians are not used to delicate food and dainties; their daily food consists of porridge, turnips, cabbage, and cucumbers, fresh and pickled, and in Moscow mostly of big salt fish which stink badly, because of the thrifty use of salt, yet are eaten with relish. . . .

The Russians can endure extreme heat. In the bathhouse they stretch out on benches and let themselves be beaten and rubbed with bunches of birch twigs and wisps of bast (which I could not stand); and when they are hot and red all over and so exhausted that they can bear it no longer in the bathhouse, men and women rush outdoors naked and pour cold water over their bodies; in winter they even wallow in the snow and rub their skin with it as if it were soap; then they go back into the hot bathhouse. And since bathhouses are usually near rivers and brooks, they can throw themselves straight from the hot into the cold bath. . . .

Generally noble families, even the small nobility, rear their daughters in secluded chambers, keeping them hidden from outsiders; and a bridegroom is not allowed to have a look at his bride until he receives her in the bridal chamber. Therefore some happen to be deceived, being given a misshapen and sickly one instead of a fair one, and sometimes a kinswoman or even a maidservant instead of a daughter; of which there have been examples even among the highborn. No wonder therefore that often they live together like cats and dogs and that wife-beating is so common among Russians. . . .

In the Kremlin and in the city there are a great many churches, chapels, and monasteries, both within and without the city walls, over two thousand in all. This is so because every nobleman who has some fortune has a chapel built for himself, and most of them are of stone. The stone churches are round and vaulted inside. . . . They allow neither organs nor any other musical instruments in their churches, saying: Instruments that have neither souls nor life cannot praise God. . . .

In their churches there hang many bells, sometimes five or six, the largest not over two hundredweights. They ring these bells to

V. Vasnetsou (1848–1926), Red Square in the late seventeenth century. (*Source: Sovfoto/Eastfoto*)

summon people to church, and also when the priest during mass raises the chalice. In Moscow, because of the multitude of churches and chapels, there are several thousand bells, which during the divine service create such a clang and din that one unaccustomed to it listens in amazement.

Questions for Analysis

1. In what ways were all social groups in Russia similar, according to Olearius?

2. How did Olearius characterize the Russians in general? What supporting evidence did he offer for his judgment?

3. Did Olearius find any positive or admirable traits in the Russian people? What were they?

4. On the basis of these representative passages, why do you think Olearius's book was so popular and influential in central and western Europe?

Source: G. Vernadsky and R. T. Fisher Jr., eds., *A Source Book for Russian History*. Copyright © 1972 by Yale University Press. Reprinted by permission.

18

Toward a New World-View in the West

Painting by Jean-Honoré Fragonard (1732–1806) of Denis Diderot, one of the editors of the *Encyclopedia,* the greatest intellectual achievement of the Enlightenment. *(Source: Louvre © Photo R.M.N.)*

Most people are not philosophers, but they nevertheless have a basic outlook on life, a more or less coherent world-view. At the risk of oversimplification, one may say that the world-view of medieval and early modern Europe was primarily religious and theological. Not only did Christian or Jewish teachings form the core of people's spiritual and philosophical beliefs, but religious teachings also permeated all the rest of human thought and activity. Political theory relied on the divine right of kings, for example, and activities ranging from marriage and divorce to eating habits and hours of business were regulated by churches and religious doctrines.

In the course of the eighteenth century, this religious and theological world-view underwent a fundamental transformation among the European upper and comfortable classes. Economically secure and increasingly well educated, these privileged groups of preindustrial Europe often came to see the world primarily in secular and scientific terms. And while few individuals abandoned religious beliefs altogether, the role of churches and religious thinking in earthly affairs and in the pursuit of knowledge was substantially reduced. Among many in the aristocracy and solid middle classes, a new critical, scientific, and very modern world-view took shape.

- Why did this momentous change occur?
- How did this new world-view affect the way people thought about society and human relations?
- What impact did this new way of thinking have on political developments and monarchial absolutism?

This chapter will focus on these questions.

 THE SCIENTIFIC REVOLUTION

The foremost cause of the change in world-view was the scientific revolution. Modern science—precise knowledge of the physical world based on the union of experimental observations with sophisticated mathematics—crystallized in the seventeenth century. Whereas science had been secondary and subordinate in medieval intellectual life, it became independent and even primary for many educated people in the eighteenth century.

The emergence of modern science was a development of tremendous long-term significance. A noted historian has even said that the scientific revolution of the late sixteenth and seventeenth centuries "outshines everything since the rise of Christianity" and was "the real origin both of the modern world and the modern mentality."[1] This statement is an exaggeration, but not much of one. Of all the great civilizations, only that of the West developed modern science. With the scientific revolution Western society began to acquire its most distinctive traits. Let us examine the milestones on the fateful march toward modern science first and then search for the nonscientific influences along the route.

Scientific Thought in 1500

Since developments in astronomy and physics were at the heart of the scientific revolution, one must begin with the traditional European conception of the universe and movement within it. In the early 1500s, traditional European ideas about the universe were still based primarily on the ideas of Aristotle, the great Greek philosopher of the fourth century B.C. These ideas had been recovered gradually during the Middle Ages and then brought into harmony with Christian doctrines by medieval theologians. According to this revised Aristotelian view, a motionless earth was fixed at the center of the universe. Around it moved ten separate transparent crystal spheres. In the first eight spheres were embedded, in turn, the moon, the sun, the five known planets, and the fixed stars. Then followed two spheres that theologians added during the Middle Ages to account for slight changes in the positions of the stars over the centuries. Beyond the tenth sphere was heaven, with the throne of God and the souls of the saved. Angels kept the spheres moving in perfect circles.

Aristotle's views, suitably revised by medieval philosophers, also dominated thinking about physics and motion on earth—the sublunar world. The sublunar world was made up of four imperfect, changeable elements. The "light" elements (air and fire) naturally moved upward; the "heavy" elements (water and earth) naturally moved downward. These natural directions of motion did not always prevail, however, for elements were often mixed together and could be affected by an outside force such as a human being. Aristotle and his

Ptolemy's System This 1543 drawing shows how the changing configurations of the planets moving around the earth form the twelve different constellations, or "signs," of the zodiac. The learned astronomer on the right is using his knowledge to predict the future for the king on the left. *(Source: Mary Evans Picture Library/Photo Researchers)*

followers also believed that a uniform force moved an object at a constant speed and that the object would stop as soon as that force was removed.

Aristotle's science as interpreted by Christian theologians fit neatly with Christian doctrines. It established a home for God and a place for Christian souls. It put human beings at the center of the universe and made them the critical link in a "great chain of being" that stretched from the throne of God to the most lowly insect on earth. Thus science was primarily a branch of theology, and it reinforced religious thought.

The Copernican Hypothesis

The desire to explain and thereby glorify God's handiwork led to the first great departure from the medieval system. This departure was the work of the Polish clergyman and astronomer Nicolaus Copernicus (1473–1543). As a young man, Copernicus studied church law and astronomy in various European universities. He saw how professional astronomers still depended for their most accurate calculations on the work of Ptolemy, the last great ancient astronomer, who had lived in Alexandria in the second century A.D. Ptolemy's achievement had been to work out complicated rules to help stargazers and astrologers to track the planets with greater precision. Many people then (and now) believed that the changing relationships between planets and stars influenced and even determined the future.

The young Copernicus was uninterested in astrology and felt that Ptolemy's cumbersome and occasionally inaccurate rules detracted from the majesty of a perfect Creator. He preferred an old Greek idea being discussed in Renaissance Italy—the idea that the sun, rather than the earth, was at the center of the universe. Working on his hypothesis from 1506 to 1530, Copernicus indeed theorized that the stars and planets, including the earth, revolve around a fixed sun. Yet Copernicus was a cautious man. Fearing the ridicule of other astronomers, he did not publish his *On the Revolutions of the Heavenly Spheres* until 1543, the year of his death.

Copernicus's theory had enormous scientific and religious implications, many of which the conservative Copernicus did not anticipate. Perhaps most significant from a religious standpoint was that by characterizing the earth as just another planet in an immense universe, Copernicus destroyed the basic idea of Aristotelian physics—the idea that the earthly world was quite different from the heavenly one. Where was the realm of perfection? Where were heaven and the throne of God?

The Copernican theory quickly brought sharp attacks from religious leaders, especially Protestants. Hearing of Copernicus's work even before it was published, Martin Luther spoke of him as the "new astrologer who wants to prove that the earth moves and goes round. . . . The fool wants to turn the whole art of astronomy upside down." Luther noted that "as the Holy Scripture tells us, so did Joshua bid the sun stand still and not the earth."[2]

John Calvin also condemned Copernicus. Catholic reaction was milder at first, but in 1616 the church officially declared the Copernican theory false.

Other events were almost as influential in creating doubts about traditional astronomical ideas. In 1572 a new star appeared and shone very brightly for almost two years. The new star, which was actually a distant exploding star, made an enormous impression on people. It seemed to contradict the idea that the heavenly spheres were unchanging and therefore perfect. In 1577 a new comet suddenly moved through the sky, cutting a straight path across the supposedly impenetrable crystal spheres. It was time, as a typical scientific writer put it, for "the radical renovation of astronomy."[3]

From Brahe to Galileo

One astronomer who agreed was Tycho Brahe (1546–1601) of Denmark. He established himself as Europe's leading astronomer with his detailed observations of the new star of 1572. For twenty years thereafter he meticulously observed the stars and planets with the naked eye. An imposing man who had lost a piece of his nose in a duel and replaced it with a special bridge of gold and silver alloy, Brahe was a noble who exploited his peasants arrogantly and approached the heavens humbly. His great contribution was his mass of data. His limited understanding of mathematics, however, prevented him from making much sense out of his data. That was left to his brilliant young assistant, the German Johannes Kepler (1571–1630).

Working and reworking Brahe's mountain of observations in a staggering sustained effort, Kepler formulated three famous laws of planetary motion. First, building on Copernican theory, he demonstrated in 1609 that the orbits of the planets around the sun are elliptical rather than circular. Second, he demonstrated that the planets do not move at a uniform speed in their orbits. Third, in 1619 he showed that the time a planet takes to make its complete orbit is precisely related to its distance from the sun. Kepler's contribution was monumental. Whereas Copernicus had speculated, Kepler proved mathematically the precise relations of a sun-centered (solar) system. His work demolished the old system of Aristotle and Ptolemy, and in his third law he came close to formulating the idea of universal gravitation.

While Kepler was unraveling planetary motion, a young Florentine named Galileo Galilei (1564–

1642) was challenging all the old ideas about motion. Like so many early scientists, Galileo was a poor nobleman first marked for a religious career. However, he soon became fascinated by mathematics. A brilliant student, Galileo became a professor of mathematics in 1589 at age twenty-five. He proceeded to examine motion and mechanics in a new way. Indeed, his great achievement was the elaboration and consolidation of the modern experimental method: rather than speculate about what might or should happen, Galileo conducted controlled experiments to find out what actually *did* happen.

In his famous acceleration experiment, by rolling brass balls down an inclined plane, he showed that a uniform force—in this case, gravity—produces a uniform acceleration. With this and other experiments, Galileo went on to formulate the law of inertia: rather than rest being the natural state of objects, an object continues in motion forever unless stopped by some external force. Aristotelian physics was in a shambles.

On hearing details about the invention of the telescope in Holland, Galileo made one for himself and trained it on the heavens. He quickly discovered the first four moons of Jupiter, providing new evidence for the Copernican theory, in which Galileo already believed. Galileo then pointed his telescope at the moon. He wrote in 1610 in *Siderus Nuncius*:

I feel sure that the moon is not perfectly smooth, free from inequalities, and exactly spherical, as a large school of philosophers considers with regard to the moon and the other heavenly bodies. On the contrary, it is full of inequalities, uneven, full of hollows and protuberances, just like the surface of the earth itself, which is varied. . . . The next object which I have observed is the essence or substance of the Milky Way. By the aid of a telescope anyone may behold this in a manner which so distinctly appeals to the senses that all the disputes which have tormented philosophers through so many ages are exploded by the irrefutable evidence of our eyes, and we are freed from wordy disputes upon the subject. For the galaxy is nothing else but a mass of innumerable stars planted together in clusters.[4]

Reading these famous lines, one feels a crucial corner in Western civilization being turned. The traditional religious and theological world-view, which rested on identifying and accepting the proper established authority, was beginning to give way in certain fields to a critical, scientific method. This new method of learning and investigating was the greatest accomplishment of the entire scientific revolution, for it proved capable of great extension. A historian investigating documents of the past, for example, is not so different from a Galileo studying stars and rolling balls.

Galileo's work eventually aroused the ire of some theologians. After the publication in Italian of his widely read *Dialogue on the Two Chief Systems of the World* in 1632, which openly lampooned the traditional views of Aristotle and Ptolemy and defended those of Copernicus, Galileo was tried for heresy by the papal Inquisition. Imprisoned and threatened with torture, the aging Galileo recanted, "renouncing and cursing" his Copernican errors. Of minor importance in the development of science, Galileo's trial later became for some writers the perfect symbol of the inherent conflict between religious belief and scientific knowledge.

Newton's Synthesis

The accomplishments of Kepler, Galileo, and other scientists had taken effect by about 1640. The old astronomy and physics were in ruins, and several fundamental breakthroughs had been made. The fusion of the new findings in a new synthesis, a single explanatory system that would comprehend motion both on earth and in the skies, was the work of Isaac Newton (1642–1727).

Newton was born into lower English gentry and attended Cambridge University. Fascinated by alchemy, he sought the elixir of life and a way to change base metals into gold and silver. Not without reason did the twentieth-century economist John Maynard Keynes call him the "last of the magicians." Newton was also intensely religious. He

Galileo's Paintings of the Moon   When Galileo published the results of his telescopic observations of the moon, he added these paintings to illustrate the marvels he had seen with his telescopes. *(Source: Biblioteca Nazionale Centrale, Florence/Scala/Art Resource, NY)*

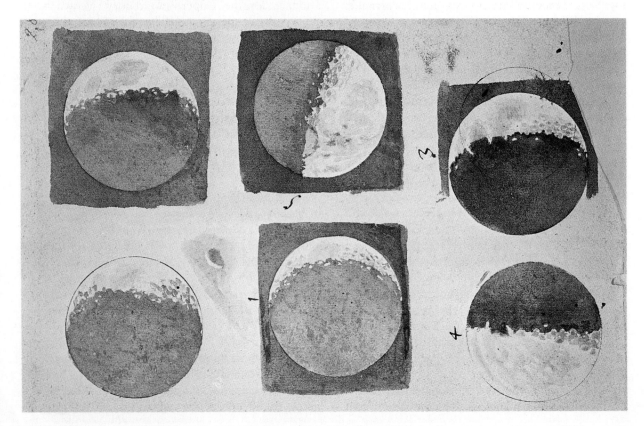

had a highly suspicious nature, lacked interest in women and sex, and in 1693 suffered a nervous breakdown from which he later recovered. He was far from being the perfect rationalist so endlessly eulogized by writers in the eighteenth and nineteenth centuries.

Of his intellectual genius and incredible powers of concentration there can be no doubt, however. Arriving at some of his most basic ideas about physics in 1666 at age twenty-four, but unable to prove these theories mathematically, he attained a professorship and studied optics for many years. In 1684 Newton returned to physics for eighteen extraordinarily intensive months. Seldom leaving his room, he neglected even the meals sent up, his mind fastened like a vise on the laws of the universe. He opened the third book of his immortal *Principia,* published in Latin in 1687, with these lines: "In the preceding books I have laid down the principles . . . [that] are the laws of certain motions, and powers or forces. . . . It remains that from the same principles I now demonstrate the frame of the System of the World."

Newton made good his grandiose claim. He integrated the astronomy of Copernicus, as corrected by Kepler's laws, with the physics of Galileo and his predecessors. Newton did this by means of a set of mathematical laws that explain motion and mechanics. These laws of dynamics are complex, and it took scientists and engineers two hundred years to work out all their implications. Nevertheless, the key feature of the Newtonian synthesis was the law of universal gravitation. According to this law, every body in the universe attracts every other body in the universe in a precise mathematical relationship, based on mass and distance. The whole universe—from Kepler's elliptical orbits to Galileo's rolling balls—was unified in one majestic system.

Causes of the Scientific Revolution

With a charming combination of modesty and self-congratulation, Newton once wrote, "If I have seen further [than others], it is by standing on the shoulders of Giants."[5] Surely the path from Copernicus to Newton confirms the "internal" view of the scientific revolution as the product of towering individual genius. Yet there were certainly broader causes as well.

First, the long-term contribution of medieval intellectual life and medieval universities to the scien-

Isaac Newton   This portrait suggests the depth and complexity of the great genius. Is the powerful mind behind those piercing eyes thinking of science or of religion, or perhaps of both? *(Source: Scala/Art Resource, NY)*

tific revolution was much more considerable than historians unsympathetic to the Middle Ages once believed. By the thirteenth century, permanent universities with professors and large student bodies had been established in western Europe to train the lawyers, doctors, and church leaders that society required. By 1300 philosophy had taken its place alongside law, medicine, and theology. Medieval philosophers developed a limited but real independence from theologians and a sense of free inquiry. They nobly pursued a body of knowledge and tried to arrange it meaningfully by means of abstract theories.

Within this framework, science was able to emerge as a minor but distinct branch of philosophy. In the fourteenth and fifteenth centuries, first in Italy and then elsewhere in Europe, leading universities established new professorships of mathematics, astronomy, and physics (natural philosophy) within their faculties of philosophy. Although the prestige of the new fields was low among both professors and students, rational, critical thinking was applied to scientific problems by a permanent community of scholars. And an outlet existed for the talents of a Galileo or a Newton: all the great pathfinders either studied or taught at universities.

Second, the Renaissance also stimulated scientific progress. The recovery of the finest works of Greek mathematics—a byproduct of Renaissance humanism's ceaseless search for the knowledge of antiquity—greatly improved European mathematics well into the early seventeenth century. Finally, in the Renaissance pattern of patronage, especially in Italy, various rulers and wealthy business people supported scientific investigations, as the Medicis of Florence, for instance, did those of Galileo.

The navigational problems of long sea voyages in the age of overseas expansion were a third factor in the scientific revolution. As early as 1484, the king of Portugal appointed a commission of mathematicians to perfect tables to help seamen find their latitude. This resulted in the first European navigation manual.

The problem of fixing longitude was much more difficult. In England the government and the great capitalistic trading companies turned to science and scientific education in an attempt to solve this pressing practical problem. At Gresham College in London, the main center of scientific activity in England in the first half of the seventeenth century, the professor of astronomy was directed to teach courses on the science of navigation. Scientists at Gresham College enjoyed close ties with top officials of the Royal Navy and with leading merchants and shipbuilders. The close tie between practical men and scientists also led to the establishment in 1662 of the Royal Society of London, which published scientific papers and sponsored scientific meetings.

Navigational problems were also critical in the development of many new scientific instruments, such as the telescope, barometer, thermometer, pendulum clock, microscope, and air pump. Better instruments, which permitted more accurate observations, were part of a fourth factor in the scientific revolution, the development of better ways of obtaining knowledge about the world. Two important thinkers, Francis Bacon (1561–1626) and René Descartes (1596–1650), represented key aspects of this improvement in scientific methodology.

The English politician and writer Francis Bacon was the greatest early propagandist for the new experimental method, as Galileo was its greatest early practitioner. Rejecting the Aristotelian and medieval method of using speculative reasoning to build general theories, Bacon argued that new knowledge had to be pursued through empirical, experimental research. A researcher who wants to learn more about leaves or rocks should not speculate about the subject but rather collect a multitude of specimens and then compare and analyze them. Thus freed from sterile medieval speculation, the facts will speak for themselves, and important general principles will then emerge. Knowledge will increase. Bacon's contribution was to formalize the empirical method, which had already been used by Brahe and Galileo, into the general theory of inductive reasoning known as *empiricism.*

Bacon claimed that the empirical method would result not only in more knowledge but also in highly practical, useful knowledge. According to Bacon, scientific discoveries would bring about much greater control over the physical environment and make people rich and nations powerful. Thus Bacon helped provide a radically new and effective justification for private and public support of scientific inquiry.

The French philosopher René Descartes was a true genius who made his first great discovery in mathematics. As a twenty-three-year-old soldier serving in the Thirty Years' War, he experienced on a single night in 1619 a life-changing intellectual vision. Descartes saw that there was a perfect correspondence between geometry and algebra and that geometrical, spatial figures could be expressed as algebraic equations and vice versa. A major step forward in the history of mathematics, Descartes' discovery of analytic geometry provided scientists with an important new tool. But his greatest achievement was to develop his initial vision into a whole philosophy of knowledge and science.

Like Bacon, Descartes scorned traditional science and had great faith in the powers of the human mind. Yet Descartes was much more systematic and mathematical than Bacon. He decided it was necessary to doubt everything that could reasonably be doubted and then, as in geometry, to use deductive reasoning from self-evident principles to ascertain scientific laws. Descartes' reasoning ultimately reduced all substances to "matter" and "mind"—that is, to the physical and the spiri-

Descartes in Sweden   Queen Christina of Sweden (r. 1632–1654) encouraged art and science and invited many foreign artists and scholars to visit her court. She speaks here with French mathematician and philosopher René Descartes in 1649. The strong-minded daughter of Protestant hero Gustavus Adolphus, Christina rejected marriage, abdicated in 1654, converted to Catholicism, and died in Rome. *(Source: Versailles/Photographie Bulloz)*

tual. His view of the world as consisting of two fundamental entities is known as *Cartesian dualism*. Descartes was a profoundly original and extremely influential thinker.

Bacon's inductive experimentalism and Descartes' deductive, mathematical rationalism are combined in the modern scientific method, which began to crystallize in the late seventeenth century. Neither man's extreme approach was sufficient by itself. Thus the modern scientific method has joined precise observations and experimentalism with the search for general laws that may be expressed in rigorously logical, mathematical language.

Finally, there is the question of the role of religion in the development of science. Just as some historians have argued that Protestantism led to the rise of capitalism, others have concluded that Protestantism, by supposedly making scientific inquiry a question of individual conscience and not of religious doctrine, was a fundamental factor in the rise of modern science. However, all religious authorities in the West—Catholic, Protestant, and Jewish—opposed the Copernican system to a greater or lesser extent until about 1630, by which time the scientific revolution was definitely in progress. The Catholic church was initially less hostile than Protestant and Jewish religious leaders. This early Catholic toleration and the scientific interests of Renaissance Italy helped account for the crucial role that Italian scientists played in scientific progress right up to the trial of Galileo in 1633. Thereafter, the Counter-Reformation church became more hostile to science, a change that helped account for the decline of science in Italy (but not in Catholic France) after 1640. At the same time, some Protestant countries became quite proscience, especially if the country lacked a strong religious authority capable of imposing religious orthodoxy on scientific questions, as did Protestant England after 1630. English religious conflicts became so intense that the authorities could not impose religious unity on anything, including science. Neutral and useful, science became an accepted part of life and developed rapidly in England after about 1640.

Some Consequences of the Scientific Revolution

The rise of modern science had many consequences, some of which are still unfolding. First, it went hand in hand with the rise of a new and expanding social group—the international scientific community. Members of this community were linked together by common interests and shared values as well as by journals and the learned scientific societies founded in many countries in the later seventeenth and the eighteenth centuries. Expansion of knowledge was the primary goal of this community, and scientists' material and psychological rewards depended on their success in this endeavor. Thus science became quite competitive, and even more scientific advance was inevitable.

Second, the revolutionary modern scientific method, in addition to being both theoretical and experimental, was highly critical, and it differed profoundly from the old way of getting knowledge about nature. It refused to base its conclusions on tradition and established sources, on ancient authorities and sacred texts.

The scientific revolution had few consequences for economic life and the living standards of the masses until the late eighteenth century at the very earliest. True, improvements in the techniques of navigation facilitated overseas trade and helped enrich leading merchants. But science had relatively few practical economic applications, and the hopes of the early Baconians were frustrated. The close link between theoretical, or pure, science and applied technology, which we take for granted today, simply did not exist before the nineteenth century. Thus the scientific revolution of the seventeenth century was first and foremost an intellectual revolution. For more than a hundred years its greatest impact was on how people thought and believed.

✷ THE ENLIGHTENMENT

The scientific revolution was the single most important factor in the creation of the new world-view of the eighteenth-century Enlightenment. This world-view, which has played a large role in shaping the modern mind, grew out of a rich mix of ideas. These ideas were diverse and often conflicting, for the talented (and not-so-talented) writers who espoused them competed vigorously for the attention of a growing public of well-educated but fickle readers, who remained a small minority of the population. Despite this diversity, three central concepts stand at the core of Enlightenment thinking.

The most important and original idea of the Enlightenment was that the methods of natural science could and should be used to examine and understand all aspects of life. This was what intellectuals meant by *reason,* a favorite word of Enlightenment thinkers. Nothing was to be accepted on faith. Everything was to be submitted to the rational, critical, scientific way of thinking. This approach often brought the Enlightenment into a head-on conflict with established churches, which rested their beliefs on the special authority of the Bible and Christian theology. A second important Enlightenment concept was that the scientific method was capable of discovering the laws of human society as well as those of nature. Thus was social science born. Its birth led to the third key idea, that of progress. Armed with the proper method of discovering the laws of human existence, Enlightenment thinkers believed it was at least possible for human beings to create better societies and better people. Their belief was strengthened by some modest improvements in economic and social life during the eighteenth century.

The Enlightenment was therefore profoundly secular. It revived and expanded the Renaissance concentration on worldly explanations. In the course of the eighteenth century, the Enlightenment had a profound impact on the thought and culture of the urban middle classes and the aristocracy. It did not, however, have much appeal for the urban poor and the peasants, who were preoccupied with the struggle for survival and who often resented the Enlightenment attack on traditional popular beliefs (see Chapter 19).

The Emergence of the Enlightenment

Loosely united by certain key ideas, the European Enlightenment was a broad intellectual and cultural movement that gained strength gradually and did not reach its maturity until about 1750. Yet it was the generation that came of age between the publication of Newton's *Principia* in 1687 and the death of Louis XIV in 1715 that tied the crucial knot between the scientific revolution and a new outlook on life. Talented writers of that generation popularized hard-to-understand scientific achievements for the educated elite.

The most famous and influential popularizer was a versatile French man of letters, Bernard de Fontenelle (1657–1757). He set out to make science witty and entertaining for a broad nonscientific audience—as easy to read as a novel. This was a tall order, but Fontenelle largely succeeded. His most famous work, *Conversations on the Plurality of Worlds* (1686), begins with two elegant figures walking in the gathering shadows of a large park. One is a woman, a sophisticated aristocrat, and the other is her friend, perhaps even her lover. They gaze at the stars, and their talk turns to a passionate discussion of . . . astronomy! He confides that "each star may well be a different world," then gently stresses how error is giving way to truth. At one point he explains:

There came on the scene . . . one Copernicus, who made short work of all those various circles, all those solid skies, which the ancients had pictured to themselves. . . . Fired with the noble zeal of a true astronomer, he took the earth and spun it very far away from the center of the universe, where it had been installed, and in that center he put the sun, which had a far better title to the honor.[6]

Rather than despair at this dismissal of traditional understanding, Fontenelle's lady rejoices in the knowledge that the human mind is capable of making great progress.

Fontenelle and other writers of his generation were instrumental in bringing science into conflict with religion. Many seventeenth-century scientists, both Catholic and Protestant, believed that their work exalted God. They did not draw antireligious implications from their scientific findings. Fontenelle, in contrast, was skeptical about absolute truth and cynical about the claims of organized religion. In *Eulogies of Scientists,* Fontenelle exploited with endless variations the basic theme of rational, progressive scientists versus prejudiced, reactionary priests.

The progressive and antireligious implications that writers such as Fontenelle drew from the scientific revolution reflected a crisis in European thought at the end of the seventeenth century. This crisis had its roots in several intellectual uncertainties and dissatisfactions, of which the demolition of Aristotelian-medieval science was only one.

A second uncertainty involved the whole question of religious truth. The destructive wars of religion had been fought, in part, because religious freedom was an intolerable idea in Europe in the early seventeenth century. Both Catholics and Protestants had believed that religious truth was absolute and therefore worth fighting and dying for. Most Catholics and Protestants also believed that a strong state required unity in religious faith. Yet the disastrous results of the many attempts to impose such religious unity led some people to ask if it was really necessary. Others skeptically asked if religious truth could ever be known with absolute certainty and concluded that it could not.

The most famous of these skeptics was Pierre Bayle (1647–1706), a French Huguenot who despised Louis XIV and found refuge in the Netherlands. Critically examining the religious beliefs and

Popularizing Science The frontispiece illustration of Fontenelle's *Conversations on the Plurality of Worlds* invites the reader to share the pleasures of astronomy with an elegant lady and an entertaining teacher. The drawing shows the planets revolving around the sun. *(Source: University of Illinois Library, Champaign)*

persecutions of the past, Bayle demonstrated that human beliefs had been extremely varied and very often mistaken. He concluded that nothing can ever be known beyond all doubt and that in religion, as in philosophy, humanity's best hope was open-minded toleration. Bayle's skeptical views were very influential. Many eighteenth-century writers mined his inexhaustible vein of critical skepticism for ammunition in their attacks on superstition and theology.

The rapidly growing travel literature on non-European lands and cultures was a third cause of uncertainty. In the wake of the great discoveries, Europeans were learning that the peoples of China, India, Africa, and the Americas all had their own very different beliefs and customs. Europeans shaved their faces and let their hair grow. Turks shaved their heads and let their beards grow. In Europe a man bowed before a woman to show respect. In Siam a man turned his back on a woman when he met her because it was disrespectful to look directly at her. Countless similar examples discussed in the travel accounts helped change the perspective of educated Europeans. They began to look at truth and morality in relative, rather than absolute, terms. If anything was possible, who could say what was right or wrong?

A fourth cause and manifestation of European intellectual turmoil was John Locke's epoch-making *Essay Concerning Human Understanding.* Published in 1690—the same year Locke published his *Second Treatise of Civil Government* (see page 586) —Locke's essay brilliantly set forth a new theory about how human beings learn and form their ideas. In doing so, he rejected the prevailing view of Descartes, who had held that all people are born with certain basic ideas and ways of thinking. Locke insisted that all ideas are derived from experience. The human mind at birth is like a blank tablet (*tabula rasa*) on which the environment writes the individual's understanding and beliefs. Human development is therefore determined by education and social institutions, for good or for evil. Locke's *Essay* was, along with Newton's *Principia,* one of the dominant intellectual inspirations of the Enlightenment.

The Philosophes and the Public

By the time Louis XIV died in 1715, many of the ideas that would soon coalesce into the new world-view had been assembled. Yet Christian Europe was still strongly attached to its traditional beliefs, as witnessed by the powerful revival of religious orthodoxy in the first half of the eighteenth century (see Chapter 19). By the outbreak of the American Revolution in 1775, however, a large portion of western Europe's educated elite had embraced many of the new ideas. This acceptance was the work of one of history's most influential groups of intellectuals, the philosophes. It was the philosophes who proudly and effectively proclaimed that they, at long last, were bringing the light of knowledge to their ignorant fellow creatures in a great age of enlightenment.

Philosophe is the French word for "philosopher," and it was in France that the Enlightenment reached its highest development. The French philosophes were indeed philosophers, asking fundamental philosophical questions about the meaning of life, God, human nature, good and evil, and cause and effect. But in the tradition of Bayle and Fontenelle, they were not content with abstract arguments or ivory-tower speculations. They were determined to reach and influence all the economic and social elites, whom they perceived as the educated or enlightened public, or simply the "public."

As a wealth of recent scholarship has shown, this public was quite different from the great majority of the population, which was known as the common people, or simply the "people." French philosophe Jean le Rond d'Alembert (1717–1783) characteristically made a sharp distinction between "the truly enlightened public" and "the blind and noisy multitude."[7] The philosophes believed that the great majority of the common people was doomed to superstition and confusion because it lacked the money and leisure to look beyond its bitter struggle with grinding poverty (see Chapter 19).

The great philosophes and their imitators were not free to write as they wished, for it was illegal in France to criticize openly either church or state. Their most radical works had to circulate in manuscript form. Knowing that direct attacks would probably be banned or burned, the philosophes wrote novels and plays, histories and philosophies, dictionaries and encyclopedias, all filled with satire and double meanings to spread their message to the public.

One of the greatest philosophes, the baron de Montesquieu (1689–1755), brilliantly pioneered this approach in *The Persian Letters,* an extremely influential social satire published in 1721. Montesquieu's work consisted of amusing letters supposedly written by Persian travelers, who see European customs in unique ways and thereby cleverly criticize existing practices and beliefs. Having gained fame by using wit as a weapon against cruelty and superstition, Montesquieu settled down on his family estate to study history and politics. He was also inspired by the example of the physical sciences, and he set out to apply the critical method to the problem of government in *The Spirit of Laws* (1748). The result was a complex comparative study of republics, monarchies, and despotisms.

Dismayed by the triumph of royal absolutism under Louis XIV, Montesquieu focused on the conditions that would promote liberty and prevent tyranny. He argued that despotism could be avoided if political power was divided and shared by a variety of classes and legal orders holding unequal rights and privileges. A strong, independent upper class was especially important, according to Montesquieu, because in order to prevent the abuse of power, "it is necessary that by the arrangement of things, power checks power." Admiring greatly the English balance of power among the king, the houses of Parliament, and the independent courts, Montesquieu believed that in France the thirteen high courts—the *parlements*—were front-line defenders of liberty against royal despotism. Apprehensive about the uneducated poor, Montesquieu was clearly no democrat, but his theory of separation of powers had a great impact on France's wealthy, well-educated elite. The constitutions of the young United States in 1789 and of France in 1791 were based in large part on this theory.

The most famous and in many ways most representative philosophe was François Marie Arouet, who was known by the pen name Voltaire (1694–1778). In his long career, this son of a comfortable middle-class family wrote more than seventy witty volumes, hobnobbed with kings and queens, and died a millionaire because of shrewd business speculations. His early career, however, was turbulent. In 1717 Voltaire was imprisoned for eleven months in the Bastille in Paris for insulting the regent of France. In 1726 a barb from his sharp tongue led a great French nobleman to have him beaten and arrested. This experience made a deep impression on Voltaire. All his life he struggled against legal injustice and unequal treatment be-

Madame du Châtelet   Fascinated by the new world system of Isaac Newton, this aristocratic woman helped to spread Newton's ideas in France by translating his *Principia* into French and by influencing Voltaire, her companion for fifteen years until her death. (*Source: Private Collection/Photographie Bulloz*)

fore the law. Released from prison after promising to leave the country, Voltaire lived in England for three years and came to share Montesquieu's enthusiasm for English institutions.

Returning to France and soon threatened again with prison in Paris, Voltaire had the great fortune of meeting Gabrielle-Emilie Le Tonnelier de Breteuil, marquise du Châtelet (1706–1749), an intellectually gifted woman from the high aristocracy with a passion for science. Inviting Voltaire to live in her country house at Cirey in Lorraine and becoming his long-time companion (under the eyes of her tolerant husband), Madame du Châtelet studied physics and mathematics and published scientific articles and translations.

Perhaps the finest representative of a small number of elite French women and their scientific accomplishments during the Enlightenment, Madame du Châtelet suffered nonetheless because of her gender. Excluded on principle from the Royal

Academy of Sciences and from stimulating interchange with other scientists because she was a woman, she depended on private tutors for instruction and became uncertain of her ability to make important scientific discoveries. Madame du Châtelet therefore concentrated on spreading the ideas of others, and her translation with an accompanying commentary of Newton's *Principia* into French for the first (and only) time was her greatest work. But she had no doubt that women's limited scientific contributions in the past were due to limited and unequal education. Imagining a scientific experiment that she would make if she were a ruler, Madame du Châtelet wrote, "I would reform an abuse which cuts off, so to speak, half the human race. I would make women participate in all the rights of humankind, and above all in those of the intellect."[8]

While living at Cirey, Voltaire wrote various works praising England and popularizing English scientific progress. Newton, he wrote, was history's greatest man, for he had used his genius for the benefit of humanity. In the true style of the Enlightenment, Voltaire mixed the glorification of science and reason with an appeal for better individuals and institutions. Yet like almost all of the philosophes, Voltaire was a reformer, not a revolutionary, in social and political matters. He was eventually appointed royal historian in 1743, and his *Age of Louis XIV* portrayed Louis as the dignified leader of his age. Voltaire also began a long correspondence with Frederick the Great and, after the death of his beloved Emilie, accepted Frederick's invitation to come brighten up the Prussian court in Berlin. The two men later quarreled, but Voltaire always admired Frederick as a free thinker and an enlightened monarch.

Unlike Montesquieu, Voltaire pessimistically concluded that the best one could hope for in the way of government was a good monarch since human beings "are very rarely worthy to govern themselves." Nor did he believe in social and economic equality in human affairs. The idea of making servants equal to their masters was "absurd and impossible." The only realizable equality, Voltaire thought, was that "by which the citizen only depends on the laws which protect the freedom of the feeble against the ambitions of the strong."[9]

Voltaire's philosophical and religious positions were much more radical. In the tradition of Bayle, Voltaire's voluminous writings challenged, often indirectly, the Catholic church and Christian theology at almost every point. Though he was considered by many devout Christians to be a shallow blasphemer, Voltaire's religious views were influential and quite typical of the mature Enlightenment. Voltaire clearly believed in a God, but his was a distant, deistic God, a great Clockmaker who built an orderly universe and then stepped aside and let it run. Above all, Voltaire and most of the philosophes hated all forms of religious intolerance, which, they believed, often led to fanaticism and savage, inhuman action. Simple piety and human kindness—as embodied in Christ's great commandments to "love God and your neighbor as yourself"—were religion enough, even Christianity enough, as may be seen in Voltaire's famous essay on religion (see Listening to the Past).

The philosophes' greatest and most representative intellectual achievement was, quite fittingly, a group effort—the seventeen-volume *Encyclopedia: The Rational Dictionary of the Sciences, the Arts, and the Crafts,* edited by Denis Diderot (1713–1784) and Jean le Rond d'Alembert. Diderot and d'Alembert set out to teach people how to think critically and objectively about all matters. As Diderot said, he wanted the *Encyclopedia* to "change the general way of thinking."[10]

The editors of the *Encyclopedia* had to conquer innumerable obstacles. After the appearance in 1751 of the first volume, which dealt with such controversial subjects as atheism, the soul, and blind people, the timid publisher watered down some of the articles in the last ten volumes without the editors' consent. Yet Diderot's unwavering belief in the importance of his mission held the encyclopedists together for fifteen years, and the enormous work was completed in 1765. Hundreds of thousands of articles by leading scientists, famous writers, skilled workers, and progressive priests treated every aspect of life and knowledge.

Not every article was daring or original, but the overall effect was little short of revolutionary. Science and the industrial arts were exalted, religion and immortality questioned. Intolerance, legal injustice, and out-of-date social institutions were openly criticized. The encyclopedists were convinced that greater knowledge would result in greater human happiness, for knowledge was useful and made possible economic, social, and political progress. The *Encyclopedia,* widely read and extremely influential throughout western Europe, summed up the new world-view of the Enlightenment.

figure 1ère

✤ **Canal with Locks**   Articles on science and the industrial arts in the *Encyclopedia* carried lavish explanatory illustrations. This engraving from the section on water and its uses shows advances in canal building and reflects the encyclopedists' faith in technical progress. *(Source: University of Illinois Library, Champaign)*

The Later Enlightenment

After about 1770, the harmonious unity of the philosophes and their thought began to break down. As the new world-view became increasingly accepted by the educated public, some thinkers sought originality by exaggerating certain Enlightenment ideas to the exclusion of others. These latter-day philosophes often built rigid, dogmatic systems.

In his *System of Nature* (1770) and other works, the wealthy German-born but French-educated Baron Paul d'Holbach (1723–1789) argued that human beings were machines completely determined by outside forces. Free will, God, and immortality of the soul, he claimed, were foolish myths. D'Holbach's aggressive atheism and determinism dealt the unity of the Enlightenment movement a severe blow. Deists such as Voltaire, who believed in God but not in established

churches, were repelled by the inflexible atheism they found in the *System of Nature*. They saw in it the same dogmatic intolerance they had been fighting all their lives.

Nevertheless, D'Holbach was a generous patron and witty host of writers and intellectuals. At his twice-weekly dinner parties, an inner circle of regulars exchanged ideas with aspiring philosophes and distinguished visitors. One whose carefully argued skepticism had a powerful long-term influence was the Scottish philosopher David Hume (1711–1776).

Building on Locke's teachings on learning, Hume argued that the human mind is really nothing but a bundle of impressions. These impressions originate only in sense experiences and our habits of joining these experiences together. Reason, therefore, cannot tell us anything about questions that cannot be verified by sense experience (in the form of controlled experiments or mathematics), such as the origin of the universe or the existence of God. Paradoxically, Hume's rationalistic inquiry ended up undermining the Enlightenment's faith in the power of reason.

Another French aristocrat, Marie-Jean Caritat, the marquis de Condorcet (1743–1794), transformed the Enlightenment belief in gradual, hard-won progress into fanciful utopianism. In his *Progress of the Human Mind,* written in 1793 during the French Revolution, Condorcet hypothesized and tracked nine stages of human progress that had already occurred, and he predicted that the tenth would bring perfection. Ironically, Condorcet wrote this work while fleeing for his life. Caught and condemned by revolutionary extremists, he preferred death by his own hand to the blade of the guillotine.

Other thinkers and writers after about 1770 began to attack the Enlightenment's faith in reason, progress, and moderation. The most famous of these was the Swiss Jean-Jacques Rousseau (1712–1778), a brilliant and difficult thinker, an appealing but neurotic individual. Born into a poor family of watchmakers in Geneva, Rousseau went to Paris and was greatly influenced by Diderot and Voltaire. Always extraordinarily sensitive and suspicious, Rousseau came to believe that his philosophe friends and the women of the Parisian salons were plotting against him. In the mid-1750s, he broke with them personally and intellectually, living thereafter as a lonely outsider with his uneducated common-law wife and going in his own highly original direction.

Like other Enlightenment thinkers, Rousseau was passionately committed to individual freedom. Unlike them, however, he attacked rationalism and civilization as destroying, rather than liberating, the individual. Warm, spontaneous feeling had to complement and correct cold intellect, he believed. Moreover, the basic goodness of the individual and the unspoiled child had to be protected from the cruel refinements of civilization. These ideas greatly influenced the early romantic movement (see Chapter 25), which rebelled against the culture of the Enlightenment in the late eighteenth century. They also had a powerful impact on the development of child psychology and modern education (see Chapter 19, Listening to the Past).

Rousseau's contribution to political theory in *The Social Contract* (1762) was equally significant. His contribution was based on two fundamental concepts: the general will and popular sovereignty.

According to Rousseau, the general will is sacred and absolute, reflecting the common interests of all the people, who have displaced the monarch as the holder of sovereign power. The general will is not necessarily the will of the majority, however. At times, the general will may be the authentic, long-term needs of the people as correctly interpreted by a farseeing minority. Little noticed before the French Revolution, Rousseau's concept of the general will appealed greatly to democrats and nationalists after 1789. The concept has also been used since 1789 by many dictators claiming that they, rather than some momentary majority of the voters, represent the general will and thus the true interests of democracy and the sovereign masses.

Urban Culture and Public Opinion

The writings and press campaigns of the philosophes were part of a profound cultural transformation. The object of impressive ongoing research and scholarly debate in recent years, this transformation had several interrelated aspects.

Of great importance, the European market for books grew dramatically in the eighteenth century. In Germany the number of new titles appearing annually grew substantially and at an accelerating rate, from roughly six hundred new titles in 1700 to about eleven hundred in 1764 and about twenty-six hundred in 1780. Well-studied France, which was indicative of general European trends, witnessed an explosive growth in book consumption. The solid and upper middle classes, the clergy, and the aristocracy accounted for most of the change. The number of books in the hands of these privileged groups increased eight- to tenfold between the 1690s and the 1780s. Moreover, the number of religious and devotional books published legally in Paris declined precipitously. History and law held constant, while the proportion of legally published books treating the arts and sciences surged.

In addition, France's unpredictable but pervasive censorship caused many books to be printed abroad and then smuggled back into the country for "under-the-cloak" sale. Experts believe that perhaps the majority of French books produced between 1750 and 1789 came from publishing companies located outside France. These publishers also smuggled forbidden books in French and other languages into the absolutist states of central, southern, and eastern Europe. The recently discovered catalogues of some of these foreign publishers reveal a massive presence of the famous French philosophes, reaffirming the philosophes' central role in the spread of critical secular attitudes.

The illegal book trade in France also featured an astonishing growth of scandalmongering denunciations of high political figures and frankly pornographic works. These literary forms frequently came together in scathing pornographic accounts of the moral and sexual depravity of the French court, allegedly mired in luxury, perversion, and adultery. A favorite theme was the way that some beautiful but immoral aristocratic women used their sexual charms to gain power over weak rulers and high officials, thereby corrupting the process of government. Spurred by repeated royal directives, the French police did its best to stamp out this underground literature, but new slanders kept cropping up, like the wild tabloid fantasies at checkout counters in today's supermarkets.

Reading more books on many more subjects, the educated public in France and throughout Europe increasingly approached reading in a new way. The result was what some German scholars have called a "reading revolution." The old style of reading in Europe had been centered on sacred texts read slowly aloud with the audience reverently savoring each word. Now reading involved many texts, which were constantly changing and commanded no special respect. Reading became individual, silent, and rapid. The well-educated classes were reading insatiably, skeptically, and carelessly. Subtle but profound, the reading revolution was closely linked to the rise of a critical world-view.

As the reading public developed, it joined forces with the philosophes to call for the autonomy of the printed word. Outside Prussia, the Netherlands, and Great Britain, however, censorship was the rule. And the philosophes and the public resorted to discussion and social interchange in order to circumvent censorship and create an autonomous cultural sphere. Indeed, sparkling conversation in private homes spread Enlightenment ideas to Europe's upper middle class and aristocracy. Paris set the example, and other French and European cities followed. In Paris a number of talented and often rich women presided over regular social gatherings in their elegant drawing rooms, or *salons*. There they encouraged the exchange of witty, uncensored observations on literature, science, and philosophy.

Elite women also exercised an unprecedented feminine influence on artistic taste. Soft pastels, ornate interiors, sentimental portraits, and starry-eyed lovers protected by hovering Cupids were all hallmarks of the style they favored. This style, known as the rococo, was popular throughout Europe in the eighteenth century. Some philosophes championed greater rights and expanded education for women, claiming that the position and treatment of women were the best indicators of a society's level of civilization and decency.[11] To be sure, to these male philosophes greater rights for women did not mean equal rights, and the philosophes were not particularly disturbed by the fact that elite women remained legally subordinate to men in economic and political affairs. Elite women lacked many rights, but so did most men.

One of the most famous salons was that of Madame Geoffrin, the unofficial godmother of the *Encyclopedia*. Madame Geoffrin was married by arrangement at fifteen to a rich and boring businessman of forty-eight. After dutifully raising her children, and in spite of her husband's loud protests, she developed a twice-weekly salon that counted Fontenelle and Montesquieu among its regular guests. Inheriting a large fortune after her husband's death, Madame Geoffrin gave the encyclopedists generous financial aid and helped save their enterprise from collapse. Corresponding with the king of Sweden and Catherine the Great of Russia, Madame Geoffrin remained her own woman, a practicing Christian who would not tolerate attacks on the church in her house.

The talented Julie de Lespinasse epitomized the skills of the Enlightenment hostess. Her highly informal salon attracted the keenest minds in France and Europe. As one philosophe wrote:

She could unite the different types, even the most antagonistic, sustaining the conversation by a well-aimed phrase, animating and guiding it at will. . . . Politics, religion, philosophy, news: nothing was excluded. Her circle met daily from five to nine. There one found men of all ranks in the State, the Church, and the Court, soldiers and foreigners, and the leading writers of the day.[12]

As that passage suggests, the salons created an independent cultural realm freed from religious dogma and political censorship. There educated members of the intellectual, economic, and social elites could debate issues and form their own ideas.

Enlightenment Culture The culture of the Enlightenment was elegant, intellectual, and international. This painting shows the seven-year-old Austrian child prodigy, Wolfgang Amadeus Mozart (1756–1791), playing his own composition at an "English tea" given by the Princess de Conti near Paris. Mozart's phenomenal creative powers lasted a lifetime, and he produced a vast range of symphonies, operas, and chamber music. *(Source: Versailles/Photographie Bulloz)*

In this gracious atmosphere, the *public* of philosophes, the French nobility, and the prosperous middle classes intermingled and increasingly influenced one another. Critical thinking about almost any question became fashionable and flourished with hopes for human progress through greater knowledge and enlightened public opinion.

THE ENLIGHTENMENT AND ABSOLUTISM

How did the Enlightenment influence political developments? To this important question there is no easy answer. On the one hand, the French philosophes and kindred spirits in most European countries were primarily interested in converting people to critical, scientific thinking and were not particularly concerned with politics. On the other hand, such thinking naturally led to political criticism and interest in political reform as both possible and desirable.

Some Enlightenment thinkers, led by the nobleman Montesquieu, argued for curbs on monarchial power in order to promote liberty. Until the American Revolution, however, most Enlightenment thinkers outside England and the Netherlands believed that political change could best come from above—from the ruler—rather than from below, especially in central and eastern Europe. Royal absolutism was a fact of life, and the kings and queens of Europe's leading states clearly had no intention of giving up their great powers. Therefore, the philosophes and their sympathizers realistically concluded that a benevolent absolutism offered the best opportunities for improving society. Critical thinking was turning the art of good government into an exact science. It was necessary only to educate and "enlighten" the monarch, who could then make good laws and promote human happiness. Enlightenment thinkers also turned toward rulers because rulers seemed to be listening, treating them with respect, and seeking their advice. Finally, the philosophes distrusted "the people," who they believed were deluded by superstitions and driven by violent passions, little children in need of firm parental guidance.

Encouraged and instructed by the philosophes, many absolutist rulers of the later eighteenth century tried to govern in an "enlightened" manner. Yet the actual programs and accomplishments of these rulers varied greatly. Let us therefore examine the evolution of monarchial absolutism at close range before trying to form any overall judgment about the Enlightenment's effect on it.

Absolutism in Central and Eastern Europe

Enlightenment teachings inspired European rulers in small as well as large states in the second half of the eighteenth century. Yet by far the most influential of the new-style monarchs were in Prussia, Russia, and Austria, and they deserve primary attention.

Frederick the Great of Prussia   Frederick II (r. 1740–1786), commonly known as Frederick the Great, built masterfully on the work of his father, Frederick William I (see pages 573–574). This was somewhat surprising, for like many children with tyrannical parents he rebelled against his family's wishes in his early years. Rejecting the crude life of the barracks, Frederick embraced culture and literature, even writing poetry and fine prose in French, a language his father detested. After trying unsuccessfully to run away in 1730 at age eighteen, he was virtually imprisoned and even compelled to watch his companion in flight beheaded at his father's command. Yet like many other rebellious youths, Frederick eventually reached a reconciliation with his father, and by the time he came to the throne ten years later, Frederick was determined to use the splendid army that his father had left him.

Therefore, when the ruler of Austria, Charles VI, also died in 1740 and his young and charismatic daughter, Maria Theresa, inherited the Habsburg dominions, Frederick suddenly and without warning invaded her rich, mainly German province of Silesia. This action defied solemn Prussian promises to respect the Pragmatic Sanction, which guaranteed Maria Theresa's succession. Maria Theresa's ethnically diverse army was no match for Prussian precision. In 1742 as other greedy powers were falling on her lands in the general European War of the Austrian Succession (1740–1748), she was forced to cede almost all of Silesia to Prussia (see Map 17.3). In one stroke Prussia doubled its population to 6 million people. Now Prussia unquestionably towered above all the other German states and stood as a European Great Power.

Though successful in 1742, Frederick had to spend much of his reign fighting against great odds to save Prussia from total destruction. Maria Theresa was determined to regain Silesia, and when the ongoing competition between Britain and France for colonial empire brought renewed conflict in 1756, Austria fashioned an aggressive alliance with France and Russia. During the Seven Years' War (1756–1763), the aim of the alliance was to conquer Prussia and divide up its territory. Frederick led his army brilliantly, striking repeatedly at vastly superior forces invading from all sides. At times he believed all was lost, but he fought on with stoic courage. In the end, he was miraculously saved: Peter III came to the Russian throne in 1762 and called off the attack against Frederick, whom he greatly admired.

In the early years of his reign, Frederick II had kept his enthusiasm for Enlightenment culture strictly separated from a brutal concept of international politics. He wrote:

Of all States, from the smallest to the biggest, one can safely say that the fundamental rule of government is the principle of extending their territories. . . . The passions of rulers have no other curb but the limits of their power. Those are the fixed laws of European politics to which every politician submits.[13]

But the terrible struggle of the Seven Years' War tempered Frederick and brought him to consider how more humane policies for his subjects might also strengthen the state.

Thus Frederick went beyond a superficial commitment to Enlightenment culture for himself and his circle. He tolerantly allowed his subjects to believe as they wished in religious and philosophical matters. He promoted the advancement of knowledge, improving his country's schools and permitting scholars to publish their findings. Moreover, Frederick tried to improve the lives of his subjects more directly. As he wrote his friend Voltaire, "I must enlighten my people, cultivate their manners and morals, and make them as happy as human beings can be, or as happy as the means at my disposal permit." Prussia's laws were simplified, torture of prisoners was abolished, and judges decided cases quickly and impartially. Prussian officials became famous for their hard work and honesty. Frederick himself set a good example. He worked hard and lived modestly, claiming that he was "only the first servant of the state." Thus Frederick justified monarchy in terms of practical results and said nothing of the divine right of kings.

Frederick's dedication to high-minded government went only so far, however. He never tried to change Prussia's existing social structure. True, he condemned serfdom in the abstract, but he accepted it in practice and did not even free the serfs on his own estates. He accepted and extended the privileges of the nobility, which he saw as his primary ally in the defense and extension of his realm. It became practically impossible for a middle-class person to gain a top position in the government. The Junker nobility remained the backbone of the army and the entire Prussian state.

Catherine the Great of Russia   Catherine the Great of Russia (r. 1762–1796) was one of the most remarkable rulers who ever lived, and the French philosophes adored her. Catherine was a German princess from Anhalt-Zerbst, a totally insignificant principality sandwiched between Prussia and Saxony. Her father commanded a regiment of the Prussian army, but her mother was related to the Romanovs of Russia, and that relationship proved to be Catherine's chance.

Peter the Great had abolished the hereditary succession of tsars so that he could name his successor and thus preserve his policies. This move opened a period of palace intrigue and a rapid turnover of rulers until Peter's youngest daughter, Elizabeth, came to the Russian throne in 1741. A shrewd but crude woman—one of her official lovers was an illiterate shepherd boy—Elizabeth named her nephew Peter heir to the throne and chose Catherine to be his wife in 1744. It was a mismatch from the beginning. The fifteen-year-old Catherine was intelligent and attractive; her husband was stupid and ugly, his face badly scarred by smallpox. Ignored by her childish husband, Catherine carefully studied Russian, endlessly read writers such as Bayle and Voltaire, and made friends at court. Soon she knew what she wanted. "I did not care about Peter," she wrote in her *Memoirs,* "but I did care about the crown."[14]

As the old empress Elizabeth approached death, Catherine plotted against her unpopular husband. She selected as her new lover a tall, dashing young officer named Gregory Orlov, who with his four officer brothers commanded considerable support among the soldiers stationed in St. Petersburg. When Peter came to the throne in 1762, his decision to withdraw Russian troops from the coalition against Prussia alienated the army. Nor did Peter III's attempt to gain support from the Russian nobility by freeing it from compulsory state service succeed. At the end of six months, Catherine and

Catherine as Equestrian   Catherine took advantage of her intelligence and good looks to overthrow her husband Peter III and become empress of Russia. Strongly influenced by the Enlightenment, she cultivated the French philosophes and instituted moderate reforms only to reverse them in the aftermath of Pugachev's rebellion. Catherine's portrait hangs above her throne. *(Source: Novosti)*

her military conspirators deposed Peter III in a palace revolution. Then the Orlov brothers murdered him. The German princess became empress of Russia.

Catherine had drunk deeply at the Enlightenment well. Never questioning the common assumption that absolute monarchy was the best form of government, she set out to rule in an enlightened manner. She had three main goals. First, she worked hard to bring the sophisticated culture of western Europe to backward Russia. To do so, she imported Western architects, sculptors, musicians, and intellectuals. She bought masterpieces of Western art in wholesale lots and patronized the philosophes. An enthusiastic letter writer, she corresponded extensively with Voltaire and praised him as the "champion of the human race." When the French government banned the *Encyclopedia,* she offered to publish it in St. Petersburg. She sent money to Diderot when he needed it. With these and countless similar actions, Catherine won good press in the West for herself and for her country. Moreover, this intellectual ruler, who wrote plays and loved good talk, set the tone for the entire Russian nobility. Peter the Great westernized Russian armies, but it was Catherine who westernized the thinking of the Russian nobility.

Catherine's second goal was domestic reform, and she began her reign with sincere and ambitious projects. Better laws were a major concern. She appointed a special legislative commission to prepare a new law code. No new unified code was ever produced, but Catherine did restrict the practice of torture and allowed limited religious toleration. She also tried to improve education and strengthen local government. The philosophes applauded these measures and hoped more would follow.

Such was not the case. In 1773 a common Cossack soldier named Emelian Pugachev sparked a gigantic uprising of serfs, very much as Stenka Razin had done a century earlier (see page 578). Proclaiming himself the true tsar, Pugachev issued "decrees" abolishing serfdom, taxes, and army service. Thousands joined his cause, slaughtering landlords and officials over a vast area of southwestern Russia. Pugachev's untrained hordes eventually proved no match for Catherine's noble-led regular army. Betrayed by his own company, Pugachev was captured and savagely executed.

Pugachev's rebellion was a decisive turning point in Catherine's domestic policy. On coming to the throne, she had condemned serfdom in theory, but Pugachev's rebellion put an end to any illusions she might have had about attempting reform. The peasants were clearly dangerous, and her empire rested on the support of the nobility. After 1775 Catherine gave the nobles absolute control of their serfs. She extended serfdom into new areas, such as Ukraine. In 1785 she formalized the nobility's privileged position, freeing nobles forever from taxes and state service. She also confiscated the lands of the Russian Orthodox church and gave them to favorite officials. Under Catherine the Russian nobility attained its most exalted position, and serfdom entered its most oppressive phase.

Catherine's third goal was territorial expansion, and in this she was extremely successful. Her armies subjugated the last descendants of the Mongols, the Crimean Tartars, and began the conquest of the Caucasus. Her greatest coup by far was the partitioning of Poland, whose fate in the late eighteenth century demonstrated the dangers of failing to build a strong absolutist state. All important decisions continued to require the unanimous agreement of all nobles elected to the Polish Diet, which meant that nothing could ever be done to strengthen the state. When Frederick of Prussia proposed that Prussia, Austria, and Russia each take a gigantic slice of Polish territory, Catherine jumped at the chance. The first partition of Poland took place in 1772. Two more partitions, in 1793 and 1795, gave all three powers more Polish territory, and the ancient republic of Poland simply vanished from the map.

Expansion helped Catherine keep the nobility happy, for it provided her with vast new lands to give to her faithful servants and her many lovers. On all the official royal favorites she lavished large estates with many serfs, as if to make sure there were no hard feelings when her interest cooled. Until the end this remarkable woman—who always believed that, in spite of her domestic setbacks, she was slowly civilizing Russia—kept her zest for life. Fascinated by a new twenty-two-year-old flame when she was a roly-poly grandmother in her sixties, she happily reported her good fortune to a favorite former lover: "I have come back to life like a frozen fly; I am gay and well."[15]

The Austrian Habsburgs In Austria, two talented rulers did manage to introduce major reforms, although traditional power politics was more important than Enlightenment teachings. One was Joseph II (r. 1780–1790), a fascinating individual. For an earlier generation of historians he was the "revolutionary emperor," a tragic hero whose lofty reforms were undone by the landowning nobility he challenged. More recent scholarship has revised this romantic interpretation and stressed how Joseph II continued the state-building work of his mother, the empress Maria Theresa (r. 1740–1780), a remarkable but old-fashioned absolutist.

Emerging from the long War of the Austrian Succession in 1748 with only the serious loss of Silesia, Maria Theresa and her closest ministers were determined to introduce reforms that would make the state stronger and more efficient. Three aspects of these reforms were most important. First, Maria Theresa introduced measures aimed at limiting the papacy's political influence in her realm. Second, a whole series of administrative reforms strengthened the central bureaucracy,

Maria Theresa   The empress of Austria and her husband pose with eleven of their sixteen children at Schönbrunn palace in this family portrait by court painter Martin Meytens (1695–1770). Joseph, the heir to the throne, stands at the center of the star pattern. Wealthy women often had very large families, in part because they seldom nursed their babies as poor women usually did. *(Source: Kunsthistorisches Museum, Vienna)*

smoothed out some provincial differences, and revamped the tax system, taxing even the lands of nobles without special exemptions. Third, the government sought to improve the lot of the agricultural population, cautiously reducing the power of lords over their hereditary serfs and their partially free peasant tenants.

Coregent with his mother from 1765 onward and a strong supporter of change, Joseph II moved forward rapidly when he came to the throne in 1780. He controlled the established Catholic church even more closely in an attempt to ensure that it produced better citizens. He granted religious toleration and civic rights to Protestants and Jews—a radical innovation that impressed his contemporaries. In even more spectacular peasant reforms, Joseph abolished serfdom in 1781, and in 1789 he decreed that all peasant labor obligations be converted into cash payments. This ill-conceived measure was violently rejected not only by the nobility but also by the peasants it was intended to help, for their primitive barter economy was woefully lacking in money. When a disillusioned Joseph died prematurely at forty-nine, the entire Habsburg Empire was in turmoil. His brother Leopold II (r. 1790–1792) was forced to cancel Joseph's radical edicts in order to re-establish order. Peasants once again were required to do forced labor for their lords.

Absolutism in France

The Enlightenment's influence on political developments in France was complex. The monarchy maintained its absolutist claims, and some philosophes, such as Voltaire, believed that the king was still the best source of needed reform. At the same time, discontented nobles and learned judges drew on thinkers such as Montesquieu for liberal arguments. They sought with some success to limit the king's power, as France diverged from the absolutist states just considered.

When Louis XIV finally died in 1715, to be succeeded by his five-year-old great-grandson, Louis XV (r. 1715–1774), the Sun King's elaborate system of absolutist rule was challenged in a general reaction. Favored by the duke of Orléans (1674–1723), a licentious rake and nephew of Louis XIV who governed as regent until 1723, the nobility made a strong comeback.

Most important, in 1715 the duke restored to the high court of Paris—the Parlement—the an-

cient right to evaluate royal decrees publicly before they were given the force of law. The restoration of this right, which had been suspended under Louis XIV, was a fateful step. The judges of the Parlement of Paris had originally come from the middle class, and their high position reflected the way that Louis XIV (and earlier French monarchs) had chosen to use that class to build the royal bureaucracy so necessary for an absolutist state. By the eighteenth century, however, these middle-class judges had risen to become hereditary nobles. Moreover, although Louis XIV had curbed the political power of the nobility, he had never challenged its enormous social prestige. Thus high position in the government continued to bestow the noble status that middle-class officials wanted. The judges of Paris, like many high-ranking officials, actually owned their government jobs and freely passed them on as private property from father to son. By allowing this well-entrenched and increasingly aristocratic group to evaluate the king's decrees, the duke of Orléans sanctioned a counterweight to absolute power.

These implications became clear when the heavy expenses of the War of the Austrian Succession plunged France into financial crisis. In 1748 Louis XV appointed a finance minister who decreed a 5 percent income tax on every individual regardless of social status. Exemption from most taxation had long been a hallowed privilege of the nobility, and other important groups—the clergy, the large towns, and some wealthy bourgeoisie—had also gained special tax advantages over time. The result was a vigorous protest from many sides, led by the Parlement of Paris. The monarchy retreated; the new tax was dropped.

After the disastrously expensive Seven Years' War, the conflict re-emerged. The government tried to maintain emergency taxes after the war ended. The Parlement of Paris protested and even challenged the basis of royal authority, claiming that the king's power had to be limited to protect liberty. Once again the government caved in and withdrew the wartime taxes in 1764. Emboldened by this striking victory, the judicial opposition asserted that the king could not levy taxes without the consent of the Parlement of Paris acting as the representative of the entire nation.

Indolent and sensual by nature, more interested in his many mistresses than in affairs of state, Louis XV finally roused himself for a determined defense of his absolutist inheritance. "The magistrates," he angrily told the Parlement of Paris in a famous face-to-face confrontation, "are my officers. . . . In my person only does the sovereign power rest."[16] In 1768 Louis appointed a tough career official named René de Maupeou as chancellor and ordered him to crush the judicial opposition.

Maupeou abolished the Parlement of Paris and exiled its members to isolated backwaters in the provinces. He created a new and docile Parlement of royal officials, and he began once again to tax the privileged groups. Most philosophes and educated public opinion as a whole sided with the old Parlement, however, and there was widespread criticism of "royal despotism." The illegal stream of scandalmongering, pornographic attacks on the king and his court became a torrent, and some scholars now believe these lurid denunciations ate away at the foundations of royal authority. Yet the monarchy's power was still great enough for Maupeou simply to ride over the opposition, and Louis XV would probably have prevailed—if he had lived to a very ripe old age.

But Louis XV died in 1774. The new king, Louis XVI (r. 1774–1792), was a shy twenty-year-old with good intentions. Taking the throne, he is reported to have said, "What I should like most is to be loved."[17] The eager-to-please monarch decided to yield in the face of such strong criticism from so much of France's educated elite. He dismissed Maupeou and repudiated the strong-willed minister's work. The old Parlement of Paris was reinstated as enlightened public opinion cheered and anticipated moves toward more representative government. But such moves were not forthcoming. Instead, a weakened but unreformed monarchy faced a judicial opposition that claimed to speak for the entire French nation. Increasingly locked in stalemate, the country was drifting toward renewed financial crisis and political upheaval.

The Overall Influence of the Enlightenment

Having examined the evolution of monarchial absolutism in four leading states, we can begin to look for meaningful generalizations and evaluate the overall influence of Enlightenment thought on politics.

France clearly diverged from its eastern neighbors in its political development in the eighteenth century. The capacity of the French monarch to govern in a truly absolutist manner declined substantially. The political resurgence of the French nobility after 1715 and the growth of judicial opposition drew crucial support from educated public opinion, which increasingly made the liberal critique of unregulated royal authority its own.

The situation in eastern and east-central Europe was different. The liberal critique of absolute monarchy remained an intellectual curiosity, and proponents of reform from above held sway. Moreover, despite differences, the leading eastern European monarchs of the later eighteenth century all claimed that they were acting on the principles of the Enlightenment. The philosophes generally agreed with this assessment and cheered them on. Beginning in the mid-nineteenth century, historians developed the idea of a common "enlightened despotism" or "enlightened absolutism," and they canonized Frederick, Catherine, and Joseph as its most outstanding examples. More recent research has raised doubts about this old interpretation and has led to a fundamental reevaluation.

There is general agreement that these absolutists, especially Catherine and Frederick, did encourage and spread the cultural values of the Enlightenment. They were proud of their intellectual accomplishments and good taste, and they supported knowledge, education, and the arts. Historians also agree that the absolutists believed in change from above and tried to enact needed reforms. Yet the results of these efforts brought only very modest improvements, and the life of the peasantry remained very hard in the eighteenth century. Thus some historians have concluded that these monarchs were not really sincere in their reform efforts. Others disagree, arguing that powerful nobilities blocked the absolutists' genuine commitment to reform. (The old interpretation of Joseph II as the tragic revolutionary emperor forms part of this argument.)

The emerging answer to this controversy is that the later eastern absolutists were indeed committed to reform but that humanitarian objectives were of quite secondary importance. Above all, the absolutists wanted reforms that would strengthen the state and allow them to compete militarily with their neighbors. Modern scholarship has therefore stressed how Catherine, Frederick, and Joseph were in many ways simply continuing the state building of their predecessors, reorganizing armies and expanding bureaucracies to raise more taxes and troops. The reason for this continuation was simple. The international political struggle was

THE ENLIGHTENMENT

1686	Fontenelle, *Conversations on the Plurality of Worlds*
1687	Newton, *Principia*
1690	Locke, "Essay Concerning Human Understanding" and "Second Treatise on Civil Government"
1715–1774	Rule of Louis XV in France
1721	Montesquieu, *The Persian Letters*
1740–1748	War of the Austrian Succession
1740–1780	Rule of Maria Theresa in Austria
1740–1786	Rule of Frederick II (the Great) in Prussia
1742	Austria cedes Silesia to Prussia
1743	Voltaire, *Age of Louis XIV*
1748	Montesquieu, *The Spirit of the Laws* Hume, *An Enquiry Concerning Human Understanding*
1751–1765	Publication of the *Encyclopedia,* edited by Diderot and d'Alembert
1756–1763	Seven Years' War
1762	Rousseau, *Social Contract*
1762–1796	Rule of Catherine II (the Great) in Russia
1770	D'Holbach, *The System of Nature*
1771	Maupeou, Louis XV's chancellor, abolishes Parlement of Paris
1772	First partition of Poland among Russia, Prussia, and Austria
1774	Ascension of Louis XVI in France; restoration of Parlement of Paris
1780–1790	Rule of Joseph II in Austria
1781	Abolition of serfdom in Austria
1785	Catherine the Great frees the nobles from taxes and state service
1790–1792	Rule of Leopold II in Austria; serfdom is re-established
1793, 1795	Second and third partitions of Poland, which completes its absorption

brutal, and the stakes were high. First Austria under Maria Theresa and then Prussia under Frederick the Great had to engage in bitter fighting to escape dismemberment. Decentralized Poland was coldly divided and eventually liquidated.

Yet in this drive for more state power, the later absolutists were also innovators, and the idea of an era of enlightened absolutism retains a certain validity. Sharing the Enlightenment faith in critical thinking and believing that knowledge meant power, these absolutists really were more enlightened than their predecessors because they put state-building reforms in a new, broader perspective. Above all, the later absolutists considered how more humane laws and practices could help their populations become more productive and satisfied and thus able to contribute more substantially to the welfare of the state. It was from this perspective that they introduced many of their most progressive reforms, tolerating religious minorities, simplifying legal codes, and promoting practical education. Nevertheless, reforms had to be grafted on to existing political and social structures. Thus each enlightened absolutist sought greater state power, but each believed a different policy would attain it.

The eastern European absolutists of the later eighteenth century combined old-fashioned state building with the culture and critical thinking of the Enlightenment. In doing so, they succeeded in expanding the role of the state in the life of society. Unlike the successors of Louis XIV, they perfected bureaucratic machines that were to prove surprisingly adaptive and capable of enduring into the twentieth century.

SUMMARY

This chapter has focused on the complex development of a new world-view in Western civilization. This new view was essentially critical and secular, drawing its inspiration from the scientific revolution and crystallizing in the Enlightenment.

Decisive breakthroughs in astronomy and physics in the seventeenth century, which demolished the imposing medieval synthesis of Aristotelian philosophy and Christian theology, had only limited practical consequences despite the expectations of scientific enthusiasts. Yet the impact of new scientific knowledge on intellectual life became great. Interpreting scientific findings and Newtonian laws in an antitraditional, antireligious manner, the French philosophes of the Enlightenment extolled the superiority of rational, critical thinking. This new method, they believed, promised not just increased knowledge but even the discovery of the fundamental laws of human society. Although they reached different conclusions when they turned to social and political realities, they did stimulate absolute monarchs to apply reason to statecraft and the search for useful reforms. Above all, the philosophes succeeded in shaping an emerging public opinion and spreading their radically new world-view. These were momentous accomplishments.

NOTES

1. H. Butterfield, *The Origins of Modern Science* (New York: Macmillan, 1951), p. viii.
2. Quoted in A. G. R. Smith, *Science and Society in the Sixteenth and Seventeenth Centuries* (New York: Harcourt Brace Jovanovich, 1972), p. 97.
3. Quoted in Butterfield, *The Origins of Modern Science,* p. 47.
4. Quoted in Smith, *Science and Society in the Sixteenth and Seventeenth Centuries,* p. 120.
5. A. R. Hall, *From Galileo to Newton, 1630–1720* (New York: Harper & Row, 1963), p. 290.
6. Quoted in P. Hazard, *The European Mind, 1680–1715* (Cleveland: Meridian Books, 1963), pp. 304–305.
7. Quoted in R. Chartier, *The Cultural Origins of the French Revolution* (Durham, N.C.: Duke University Press, 1991), p. 27.
8. Quoted in L. Schiebinger, *The Mind Has No Sex?: Women in the Origins of Modern Science* (Cambridge, Mass.: Harvard University Press, 1989), p. 64.
9. Quoted in G. L. Mosse et al., eds., *Europe in Review* (Chicago: Rand McNally, 1964), p. 156.
10. Quoted in P. Gay, "The Unity of the Enlightenment," *History* 3 (1960): 25.
11. See E. Fox-Genovese, "Women in the Enlightenment," in *Becoming Visible: Women in European History,* 2d ed., ed. R. Bridenthal, C. Koonz, and S. Stuard (Boston: Houghton Mifflin, 1987), esp. pp. 252–259 and 263–265.
12. Quoted in G. P. Gooch, *Catherine the Great and Other Studies* (Hamden, Conn.: Archon Books, 1966), p. 149.
13. Quoted in L. Krieger, *Kings and Philosophers, 1689–1789* (New York: Norton, 1970), p. 257.
14. Quoted in Gooch, *Catherine the Great and Other Studies,* p. 15.
15. Ibid., p. 53.
16. Quoted in R. R. Palmer, *The Age of Democratic Revolution,* vol. 1 (Princeton, N.J.: Princeton University Press, 1959), pp. 95–96.
17. Quoted in G. Wright, *France in Modern Times,* 4th ed. (New York: Norton, 1987), p. 34.

SUGGESTED READING

The first three authors cited in the Notes—H. Butterfield, A. G. R. Smith, and A. R. Hall—have written excellent general interpretations of the scientific revolution. These may be compared with an outstanding recent work by M. Jacob, *The Cultural Meaning of the*

Scientific Revolution (1988), which has a useful bibliography. L. Schiebinger, *The Mind Has No Sex?: Women in the Origins of Modern Science* (1989), provides a brilliant analysis of how the new science gradually excluded women interested in science, a question completely neglected in older studies. A. Debus, *Man and Nature in the Renaissance* (1978), is good on the Copernican revolution, whereas M. Boas, *The Scientific Renaissance, 1450–1630* (1966), is especially insightful about the influence of magic on science. S. Drake, *Galileo* (1980), is a good short biography. T. Kuhn, *The Structure of Scientific Revolutions* (1962), is a challenging, much-discussed attempt to understand major breakthroughs in scientific thought over time. E. Andrade, *Sir Isaac Newton* (1958), is a good brief biography, which may be compared with F. Manuel, *The Religion of Isaac Newton* (1974).

The work of P. Hazard listed in the Notes is a classic study of the formative years of Enlightenment thought, and his *European Thought in the Eighteenth Century* (1954) is also recommended. P. Gay has written several major studies on the Enlightenment: *Voltaire's Politics* (1959) and *The Party of Humanity* (1971) are two of the best. J. Sklar, *Montesquieu* (1987), is an engaging biography. I. Wade, *The Structure and Form of the French Enlightenment* (1977), is a major synthesis. F. Baumer, *Religion and the Rise of Skepticism* (1969); H. Payne, *The Philosophes and the People* (1976); and H. Chisick, *The Limits of Reform in the Enlightenment: Attitudes Toward the Education of the Lower Classes in Eighteenth-Century France* (1981), are interesting studies of important aspects of Enlightenment thought. The changing attitudes of the educated public are imaginatively analyzed by R. Chartier in *The Cultural Origins of the French Revolution,* cited in the Notes, and in *French Historical Studies* (Fall 1992). R. Danton, *The Literary Underground of the Old Regime* (1982), provides a fascinating glimpse of low-life publishing. On women, see the stimulating study by E. Fox-Genovese cited in the Notes as well as S. Spencer, ed., *French Women and the Age of Enlightenment* (1984), and K. Rogers, *Feminism in Eighteenth-Century England* (1982). J. Landes, *Women and the Public Sphere in the Age of the French Revolution* (1988), is a fascinating and controversial study of women and politics. Above all, one should read some of the philosophes and let them speak for themselves. Two good anthologies are C. Brinton, ed., *The Portable Age of Reason* (1956), and F. Manuel, ed., *The Enlightenment* (1951). Voltaire's most famous and very amusing novel *Candide* is

highly recommended, as is S. Gendzier, ed., *Denis Diderot: The Encyclopedia: Selections* (1967). A. Wilson's biography, *Diderot* (1972), is long but rewarding.

In addition to the works mentioned in the Suggested Reading for Chapter 17, the monarchies of Europe are carefully analyzed in H. Scott, *Enlightened Absolutism* (1990); in C. Tilly, ed., *The Formation of National States in Western Europe* (1975); and in J. Gagliardo, *Enlightened Despotism* (1967), all of which have useful bibliographies. M. Anderson, *Historians and Eighteenth-Century Europe* (1979), is a valuable introduction to modern scholarship, and C. Behrens, *Society, Government, and the Enlightenment: The Experience of Eighteenth-Century France and Prussia* (1985), is a stimulating comparative study. A recommended study on the struggle for power and reform in France is F. Ford, *Robe and Sword* (1953), which discusses the resurgence of the French nobility after the death of Louis XIV. J. Lynch, *Bourbon Spain, 1700–1808* (1989), and R. Herr, *The Eighteenth-Century Revolution in Spain* (1958), skillfully analyze the impact of Enlightenment thought in Spain. Important works on Austria include C. Macartney, *Maria Theresa and the House of Austria* (1970); P. Bernard, *Joseph II* (1968); and T. Blanning, *Joseph II and Enlightened Absolutism* (1970). There are several fine works on Russia. J. Alexander, *Catherine the Great: Life and Legend* (1989), is the best biography of the famous ruler, which may be compared with the empress's own story, *The Memoirs of Catherine the Great,* edited by D. Maroger (1961). I. de Madariaga, *Russia in the Age of Catherine the Great* (1981); and P. Dukes, *The Making of Russian Absolutism, 1613–1801* (1982), are strongly recommended. The ambitious reader should also look at A. N. Radishchev, *A Journey from St. Petersburg to Moscow* (English trans., 1958), a famous 1790 attack on Russian serfdom and an appeal to Catherine the Great to free the serfs, for which Radishchev was exiled to Siberia.

The culture of the time may be approached through A. Cobban, ed., *The Eighteenth Century* (1969), a richly illustrated work with excellent essays, and C. B. Behrens, *The Ancien Régime* (1967). T. Crow, *Painters and Public Life in Eighteenth-Century Paris* (1985), examines artists and cultural politics. C. Rosen, *The Classical Style: Haydn, Mozart, Beethoven* (1972), brilliantly synthesizes music and society, as did Mozart himself in his great opera *The Marriage of Figaro,* where the count is the buffoon and his servant the hero.

Voltaire on Religion

Voltaire was the most renowned and probably the most influential of the French philosophes. His biting, satirical novel Candide *(1759) is still widely assigned in college courses, and his witty yet serious* Philosophical Dictionary *remains a source of pleasure and stimulation. The* Dictionary *consists of a series of essays on topics ranging from Adam to Zoroaster, from certainty to circumcision. The following passage is taken from the essay on religion.*

Voltaire began writing the Philosophical Dictionary *in 1752, at the age of fifty-eight, after arriving at the Prussian court in Berlin. Frederick the Great applauded Voltaire's efforts, but Voltaire put the project aside after leaving Berlin. The first of several revised editions was published anonymously in 1764. It was an immediate, controversial success. Snapped up by an "enlightened" public, it was denounced by religious leaders as a threat to the Christian community and was burned in Geneva and Paris.*

I meditated last night; I was absorbed in the contemplation of nature; I admired the immensity, the course, the harmony of those infinite globes which the vulgar do not know how to admire.

I admired still more the intelligence which directs these vast forces. I said to myself: "One must be blind not to be dazzled by this spectacle; one must be stupid not to recognize its author; one must be mad not to worship the Supreme Being. What tribute of worship should I render Him? Should not this tribute be the same in the whole of space, since it is the same Supreme Power which reigns equally in all space?

Should not a thinking being who dwells on a star in the Milky Way offer Him the same homage as a thinking being on this little globe of ours? Light is the same for the star Sirius as for us; moral philosophy must also be the same. If a feeling, thinking animal on Sirius is born of a tender father and mother who have been occupied with his happiness, he owes them as much love and care as we owe to our parents. If someone in the Milky Way sees a needy cripple, and if he can aid him and does not do so, then he is guilty toward all the globes.

Everywhere the heart has the same duties: on the steps of the throne of God, if He has a throne; and in the depths of the abyss, if there is an abyss."

I was deep in these ideas when one of those genii who fill the spaces between the worlds came down to me. I recognized the same aerial creature who had appeared to me on another occasion to teach me that the judgments of God are different from our own, and how a good action is preferable to a controversy.

The genii transported me into a desert all covered with piles of bones. . . . He began with the first pile. "These," he said, "are the twenty-three thousand Jews who danced before a calf, together with the twenty-four thousand who were killed while fornicating with Midianitish women. The number of those massacred for such errors and offences amounts to nearly three hundred thousand.

"In the other piles are the bones of the Christians slaughtered by each other because of metaphysical disputes. They are divided into several heaps of four centuries each. One heap would have mounted right to the sky; they had to be divided."

"What!" I cried, "brothers have treated their brothers like this, and I have the misfortune to be of this brotherhood!"

"Here," said the spirit, "are the twelve million native Americans killed in their own land because they had not been baptized."

"My God! . . . Why assemble here all these abominable monuments to barbarism and fanaticism?"

"To instruct you. . . . Follow me now." [The genii takes Voltaire to the "heroes of humanity, who tried to banish violence and plunder from the world," and tells Voltaire to question them.]

[At last] I saw a man with a gentle, simple face, who seemed to me to be about thirty-five years old. From afar he looked with compassion upon those piles of whitened bones, through which I had been led to reach the sage's dwelling place. I was astonished to find his feet swollen and bleeding, his hands likewise, his side pierced, and his ribs laid bare by the cut of the lash. "Good God!" I said to him, "is it possible for a just man, a sage, to be in this state? I have just seen one who was treated in a very hateful way, but there is no comparison between his torture and yours. Wicked priests and wicked judges poisoned him; is it by priests and judges that you were so cruelly assassinated?"

With great courtesy he answered, "Yes."

"And who were these monsters?"

"They were hypocrites."

"Ah! that says everything; I understand by that one word that they would have condemned you to the cruelest punishment. Had you then proved to them, as Socrates did, that the Moon was not a goddess, and that Mercury was not a god?"

"No, it was not a question of planets. My countrymen did not even know what a planet was; they were all arrant ignoramuses. Their superstitions were quite different from those of the Greeks."

"Then you wanted to teach them a new religion?"

"Not at all; I told them simply: 'Love God with all your heart and your neighbor as yourself, for that is the whole of mankind's duty.' Judge yourself if this precept is not as old as the universe; judge yourself if I brought them a new religion." . . .

"But did you say nothing, do nothing that could serve them as a pretext?"

"To the wicked everything serves as pretext."

"Did you not say once that you were come not to bring peace, but a sword?"

"It was a scribe's error; I told them that I brought peace and not a sword. I never wrote anything; what I said can have been changed without evil intention."

"You did not then contribute in any way by your teaching, either badly reported or badly

✤ Voltaire dining at Sans Souci palace.
(Source: Bildarchiv Preussischer Kulturbesitz)

interpreted, to those frightful piles of bones which I saw on my way to consult with you?"

"I have only looked with horror upon those who have made themselves guilty of all these murders."

. . . [Finally] I asked him to tell me in what true religion consisted.

"Have I not already told you? Love God and your neighbor as yourself."

"Is it necessary for me to take sides either for the Greek Orthodox Church or the Roman Catholic?"

"When I was in the world I never made any difference between the Jew and the Samaritan."

"Well, if that is so, I take you for my only master." Then he made a sign with his head that filled me with peace. The vision disappeared, and I was left with a clear conscience.

Questions for Analysis

1. Why did Voltaire believe in a Supreme Being? How does this passage reflect the influence of Isaac Newton's scientific system?

2. Was Voltaire trying to entertain or teach or do both? Was he effective? Explain.

3. If Voltaire was trying to convey serious ideas about religion and morality, what were those ideas? What was he attacking?

4. If a person today thought and wrote like Voltaire, would that person be called a defender or a destroyer of Christianity? Why?

Source: F. M. Arouet de Voltaire, *Oeuvres completes* (Paris: Firmin-Didot, 1875), vol. 8, pp. 188–190; translated into English by John McKay.

CHAPTER

19

The Changing Life of the People in Europe

The Spanish artist Francisco de Goya y Lucientes painted *The Stilts (Los Zacos)* in 1791–1792. *(Source: Museo del Prado, Madrid)*

The world of European absolutism and aristocracy, a combination of raw power and elegant refinement, was a world apart from that of common people. Weakness and uncertainty, poverty and pain—these enduring realities weighed heavily on the vast majority. Yet the common people in Western societies were by no means helpless victims of fate, ignorance, and inequality. With courage and intelligence, with hard work and family loyalties, ordinary men and women struggled and survived. There is a dignity in these efforts that is deeply moving.

This, then, is the story of those ordinary lives at a time when the idea of far-reaching scientific and material progress was only the sweet dream of a privileged elite in fashionable salons.

- How did the common people of Europe wring a living out of the land, and how was cottage industry growing to complement these efforts?

- What changes occurred in marriage and the family in the course of the eighteenth century?

- What was life like for children, and how did attitudes toward children evolve?

- What did people eat, and how did changes in diet and medical care affect their lives?

- What were the patterns of popular religion and culture? How did these patterns come into contact—and conflict—with the critical worldview of the educated public and thereby widen the cultural divide between rich and poor in the era of the Enlightenment?

Such questions help us better understand how the peasant masses and urban poor really lived in western Europe before the age of revolution opened at the end of the eighteenth century. These questions will be the focus of this chapter.

AGRICULTURE AND POPULATION

At the end of the seventeenth century, at least 80 percent of the people of all western European countries, with the possible exception of Holland, drew their livelihood from agriculture. In eastern Europe the percentage was considerably higher. Men and women lavished their attention on the land, and the land repaid their efforts, yielding the food and most of the raw materials for industry that made life possible. But the land was stingy and capricious. Yields were low even in good years, finding enough to eat was an endless challenge, and disease or starvation was the price of failure. As a result, most peasant communities had learned to keep family size under control. If total population grew even modestly, as it did in the eighteenth century, people had to find new sources of food and income.

Working the Land

The greatest accomplishment of medieval agriculture was the open-field system of village agriculture developed by European peasants. That system divided the land to be cultivated by the peasants into a few large fields that in turn were cut up into long narrow strips. The fields and strips were not enclosed. An individual peasant family—if it was fortunate—held a number of strips scattered throughout the large fields. The land of those who owned but did not till—primarily the nobility, the clergy, and wealthy townsmen—was also in scattered strips. The peasants farmed each large field as a community, plowing, sowing, and harvesting in accordance with tradition and the village leaders.

The ever-present problem was exhaustion of the soil. If a community planted wheat year after year in the same field, the nitrogen in the soil was soon depleted, and crop failure and starvation were certain. Since the supply of manure for fertilizer was limited, the only way for land to recover its life-giving fertility was for a field to lie fallow for a period of time. In the early Middle Ages, a year of fallow was alternated with a year of cropping, so that in any given year half of the land stood idle. Eventually, three-year rotations were introduced. This system permitted a year of wheat or rye followed by a year of oats or beans or peas and then a year of fallow. The results of this change were modest, however. In a rich agricultural region like the Po Valley in northern Italy, every bushel of wheat sown yielded on average only five or six bushels of grain at harvest during the seventeenth century. Such yields were no more than those attained in fertile, well-watered areas in the thirteenth century or in ancient Greece. By modern standards, output in 1700 was distressingly low. (Today an American or French farmer with similar land can expect roughly fifty bushels of wheat for each bushel of wheat sown.) Only awareness of the tragic consequences of continuous cropping forced undernourished populations to let a third of their land lie idle at any given time.

Traditional rights reinforced the traditional pattern of farming. In addition to rotating the field crops in a uniform way, villages held open meadows in common to provide animals with hay and natural pasture. After the harvest, the people of the village also pastured their animals on the wheat or rye stubble. In many places such pasturing followed a brief period, also established by tradition, for the gleaning of grain. Poor women would go through the fields picking up the few single grains that had fallen to the ground in the course of the harvest. This backbreaking labor provided the slender margin of survival for some people in the winter months.

In the age of absolutism and nobility, state and landlord levied heavy taxes and high rents as a matter of course. In so doing, they stripped the peasants of much of their meager earnings. Generally speaking, the peasants of eastern Europe were worst off. As discussed in Chapter 18, they were serfs, bound to their lords in hereditary service. Five or six days of unpaid work per week on the lord's land was not uncommon. Well into the nine-

Millet: The Gleaners   Poor French peasant women search for grains and stalks that the harvesters (in the background) have missed. The open-field system seen here could still be found in parts of Europe in 1857, when this picture was painted. Jean-François Millet is known for his great paintings expressing social themes. *(Source: Louvre © Photo R. M. N.)*

teenth century, individual Russian serfs and serf families were regularly sold with and without land. Serfdom was often very close to slavery.

Social conditions were considerably better in western Europe. Peasants were generally free from serfdom. In France and western Germany, they owned land and could pass it on to their children. Yet life was hard and poverty was the great reality for most people. In the Beauvais region of France at the beginning of the eighteenth century, only a tenth of the peasants could live satisfactorily off the fruits of their landholdings. Owning less than half of the land, the peasants had to pay heavy royal taxes, the church's tithe, and dues to the lord, as well as set aside seed for the next season. Left with only half of their crop for their own use, they had to toil for others and seek work far afield in a constant scramble for a meager living.

Technological progress offered a possible way for European peasants to improve their difficult position by producing more. The uncultivated fields were the heart of the matter. If peasants could replace the fallow with crops, they could increase the land under cultivation by 50 percent. The secret was to eliminate the fallow by alternating grain with certain nitrogen-storing crops, such as turnips and potatoes, clovers and grasses, which rejuvenate the soil while still giving produce.

Technological progress, however, did not come easily. To wait for the entire village to agree to a new crop rotation might mean waiting forever. Thus an innovating agriculturalist sought to enclose and consolidate his scattered holdings into a compact, fenced-in field, and he also sought to enclose his share of the natural pasture—known as the common. But because the common rights, like gleaning, were precious to many rural people, only powerful social and political pressures could overcome the traditionalism of rural communities. The old system of open fields held on tenaciously. Indeed, until the end of the eighteenth century, the promise of the new system was extensively realized only in the Low Countries and in England. Across the rest of Europe, technological progress was limited largely to the introduction of a single new but extremely important crop—the potato (see page 614).

The Balance of Numbers

Until 1700 the total population of Europe grew slowly much of the time and by no means con-

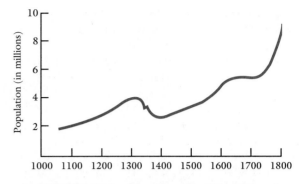

FIGURE 19.1   The Growth of Population in England, 1000–1800   England is a good example of both the uneven increase of European population before 1700 and the third great surge of growth, which began in the eighteenth century. (*Source: Data from E. A. Wrigley,* Population and History, *McGraw-Hill, New York, 1969*)

stantly (Figure 19.1). In seventeenth-century Europe, births and deaths were in a crude but effective balance. The birthrate—annual births as a proportion of the population—was fairly high but far lower than it would have been if all women had been having as many children as biologically possible. The death rate in normal years was also high, though somewhat lower than the birthrate. As a result, the population grew modestly in normal years at a rate of perhaps 0.5 to 1 percent. Yet even fairly modest population growth of 1 percent per year produces a large increase over a long period—a fourfold increase in 150 years, for example. Such gigantic increases did not occur in agrarian Europe because in certain tragic periods, many more people died than were born; total population fell sharply, even catastrophically.

The grim reapers of demographic crisis were famine, epidemic disease, and war. Famine, the inevitable result of poor farming methods and periodic crop failures, was particularly murderous because it was accompanied by disease. With a brutal one-two punch, famine stunned and weakened a population, and disease finished it off. Disease, including epidemics of bubonic plague, dysentery, and smallpox, could also ravage independently, even in years of adequate harvests.

War was another scourge. The indirect effects were more harmful than the organized killing. War spread disease. Soldiers and camp followers passed venereal disease throughout the countryside to scar and kill. Armies requisitioned scarce food

Albrecht Dürer: The Four Horsemen of the Apocalypse   Dürer combines emotional power and unsurpassed technical skill in this famous 1498 woodcut. Dürer's terrifying vision of Death and his henchmen periodically became reality in Europe well into the eighteenth century. *(Source: Courtesy of Museum of Fine Arts, Boston)*

supplies for their own use and disrupted the agricultural cycle. The Thirty Years' War (see pages 539–540) witnessed all possible combinations of distress. In the German states, the number of inhabitants declined by more than *two-thirds* in some large areas and by at least one-third almost everywhere else. The great sixteenth-century artist Albrecht Dürer captured the horror of demographic crisis in his chilling woodcut *The Four Horsemen of the Apocalypse.* Death, accompanied by his trusty companions War, Famine, and Conflict, takes his merciless ride of destruction. The narrow victory of life over death that prevails in normal times is being undone.

In the eighteenth century, the population of Europe began to grow markedly. This increase in numbers occurred in all areas of Europe: western and eastern, northern and southern, dynamic and stagnant. Growth was especially dramatic after about 1750, as Figure 19.2 shows. Why was this so? In some areas some women did have more babies than before because new opportunities for employment in rural industry allowed them to marry at an earlier age, as we shall see (pages 633–634). But the basic cause for Europe as a whole was a decline in mortality—fewer deaths.

The bubonic plague mysteriously disappeared. After the Black Death in the fourteenth century, plagues had remained a part of the European experience, striking again and again with savage force, particularly in towns. As late as 1720 an epidemic swept southern France, killing one-third, one-half, even three-fourths of those in the larger towns. Once again an awful fear swept across Europe. But the epidemic passed, and that was the last time plague fell on western and central Europe. The final disappearance of plague was due in part to stricter measures of quarantine in plague-prone Mediterranean ports and along the Austrian border with Turkey. Chance and plain good luck were more important, however.

After 1600, for reasons unknown, a new rat of Asiatic origin—the brown, or wander, rat—began to drive out and eventually eliminate the black rat whose flea is the principal carrier of the plague bacillus. Although the brown rat also carries the plague bacillus, another kind of flea is its main parasite. That flea carries the plague poorly and, for good measure, has little taste for human blood.

Advances in medical knowledge did not contribute much to reducing the death rate in the eighteenth century (see pages 642–645). However, improvements in the water supply and sewerage promoted somewhat better public health and helped reduce such diseases as typhoid and typhus in some urban areas of western Europe. These improvements and the drainage of many swamps and marshes reduced the large population of flies and mosquitoes that helped spread serious epidemics and common diseases, especially those striking children and young adults.

Human beings also became more successful in their efforts to safeguard the supply of food and protect against famine. The eighteenth century was a time of considerable canal and road building in western Europe. These advances in transportation, which were among the more positive aspects of strong absolutist states, lessened the impact of local crop failure and famine. Emergency supplies could be brought in. The age-old spectacle of localized starvation became less frequent. Wars became more gentlemanly and less destructive than in the seventeenth century and spread fewer epidemics. New foods, particularly the potato from South America, were introduced. In short, population grew in the eighteenth century primarily because years of abnormal death rates were less catastrophic. Famines, epidemics, and wars continued to occur, but their severity moderated.

The growth of population in the eighteenth century cannot be interpreted as a sign of human progress, however. Serious population pressures on resources were in existence by 1600 and continued throughout the seventeenth and eighteenth cen-

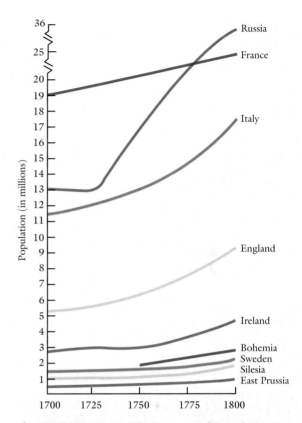

FIGURE 19.2   The Increase of Population in Europe in the Eighteenth Century   France's large population continued to support French political and intellectual leadership. Russia emerged as Europe's most populous state because natural increase was complemented by growth from territorial expansion.

turies. Only so much land was available, and tradition slowed the adoption of better farming methods. Thus agriculture could not provide enough work for the rapidly growing labor force, and poor people in the countryside had to look for new ways to make a living.

The Growth of Cottage Industry

The growth of population increased the number of rural workers with little or no land and this in turn contributed to the development of industry in rural areas. To be sure, peasant communities had always made some clothing, processed some food, and constructed some housing for their own use. But in the Middle Ages, peasants did not produce manufactured goods on a large scale for sale in a market. Instead, industry was dominated and organized by urban craft guilds and urban merchants, who jealously regulated handicraft production and sought to maintain it as an urban monopoly. By the eighteenth century, however, the pressures of rural poverty and the need for employment in the countryside had proved too great, and a new system was expanding lustily.

The new system had many names. It has often been called "cottage industry" or "domestic industry," to distinguish it from the factory industry that came later. In recent years, some scholars have preferred to speak of "protoindustrialization," by which they usually mean a stage of rural industrial development with wage workers and hand tools that necessarily preceded the emergence of large-scale factory industry. This focus has sparked renewed interest in Europe's early industrial development and shown again that the mechanized factories grew out of a vibrant industrial tradition. However, the evolving concept of protoindustrialization has different versions; thus the phrase "putting-out system," widely used by contemporaries to describe the key features of eighteenth-century rural industry, still seems an appropriate term for the new form of industrial production.

The two main participants in the *putting-out system* were the merchant-capitalist and the rural worker. The merchant loaned or "put out" raw materials—raw wool, for example—to several cottage workers. Those workers processed the raw material in their own homes, spinning and weaving the wool into cloth in this case, and returned the finished product to the merchant. The merchant

The Weaver's Repose   This painting by Decker Cornelis Gerritz (1594–1637) captures the pleasure of release from long hours of toil in cottage industry. The loom realistically dominates the cramped living space and the family's modest possessions. *(Source: Musées Royaux des Beaux-Arts, Brussels. Copyright A.C.I.)*

then paid the workers by the piece and sold the finished products. There were endless variations on this basic relationship. Sometimes rural workers would buy their own materials and work as independent producers before they delivered finished goods to the merchant. Sometimes several workers toiled together in a workshop to perform a complicated process. The relative importance of earnings from the land and from industry varied greatly for handicraft workers. In all cases, however, the putting-out system was a kind of capitalism. Merchants sold finished goods in distant markets, seeking to make profits and increase their capital in their businesses.

The putting-out system grew because it offered competitive advantages. Underemployed rural labor was abundant, and poor peasants and landless laborers would work for low wages. Since production in the countryside did not need to meet rigid guild standards, which maintained quality but discouraged the development of new methods, workers and merchants could change procedures and experiment as they saw fit. Textiles and all manner of everyday articles such as knives, forks, housewares, buttons and gloves, and clocks and musical instruments could be produced quite satisfactorily in the countryside.

Rural manufacturing did not spread across Europe at an even rate. It appeared first in England and developed most successfully there, particularly for the spinning and weaving of woolen cloth. Continental countries developed rural industry more slowly. In France at the time of Louis XIV, Colbert had revived the urban guilds and used them as a means to control the cities and collect taxes (see page 562). But the pressure of rural poverty proved too great. In 1762 the special privileges of urban manufacturing were severely restricted in France, and the already-developing rural industries were given free rein from then on. Thus in France, as in Germany and other areas, the later part of the eighteenth century witnessed a remarkable expansion of rural industry in certain densely populated regions (Map 19.1). The pattern established in England was spreading to the European continent.

Cottage industry, like peasant agriculture from which it evolved, was based on family enterprise. All the members of the family helped in the work, especially in textiles, the most important cottage industry. Children and aged relatives carded and combed the cotton or wool, women and older daughters spun the thread, and the man of the house wove the cloth. The availability of work for everyone, even the youngest, encouraged cottage workers to marry early and have large families. After the dirt was beaten out of the raw material, for example, it had to be thoroughly cleaned with strong soap in a tub, where tiny feet took the place of the agitator in a washing machine. A famous English textile inventor recalled that "soon after I was able to walk I was employed in the cotton manufacture. . . . My mother tucked up my petticoats about my waist, and put me into the tub to tread upon the cotton at the bottom."[1] Each family member had a task, and family life overlapped with the work experience.

❖ MARRIAGE AND THE FAMILY

The family is the basic unit of social organization. It is within the structure of the family that human beings love, mate, and reproduce themselves. It is primarily the family that teaches each child, imparting values and customs that condition an individual's behavior for a lifetime. The family is also an institution woven into the web of history.

Extended and Nuclear Families

In many traditional Asian and African societies, the typical family has often been an extended family. A newly married couple, instead of establishing a home, goes to live with either the bride's or the groom's family. The wife and husband raise their children while living under the same roof with their own brothers and sisters, who may also be married. The extended family is a big, three- or four-generation clan, headed by a patriarch or perhaps a matriarch and encompassing everyone from the youngest infant to the oldest grandparent.

Extended families, it is often said, provide security for adults and children in traditional agrarian peasant economies. Everyone has a place within the extended family, from cradle to grave. Sociologists frequently assume that the extended family gives way to the nuclear family with the advent of industrialization and urbanization. In a society characterized by nuclear families, couples establish their own households when they marry, and they raise their children apart from their parents. A similar process has indeed been occurring in much of

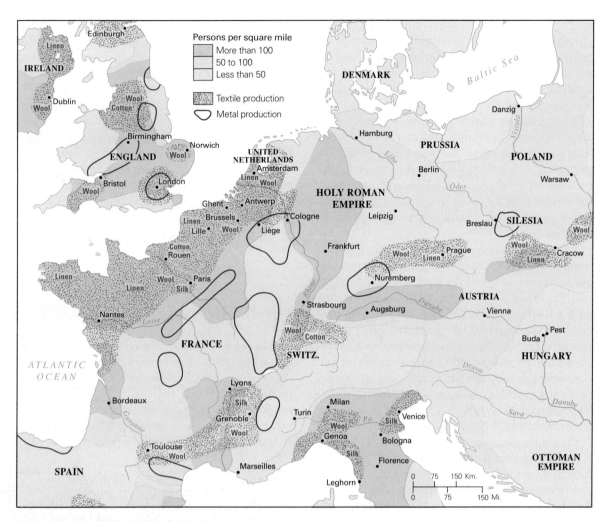

MAP 19.1 Industry and Population in Eighteenth-Century Europe The growth of cottage manufacturing in rural areas helped country people to increase their income and contributed to increases in the population. This putting-out system began in England. Most of the work was in the textile industry. Cottage industry was also strong in the Low Countries—modern-day Belgium and Holland.

Asia and Africa today. And since Europe was once agrarian and preindustrial, it has often been believed that the extended family must also have prevailed in Europe before being destroyed by the Industrial Revolution.

In recent years, innovative historians, analyzing previously neglected parish registers of births, deaths, and marriages, have greatly increased knowledge about the details of family life for the great majority of people before the nineteenth century. It seems clear that the extended, three-generation family was a rarity in western and central Europe by 1700. Indeed, the extended family may

never have been common in Europe, although it is hard to know about the early Middle Ages because relatively few records survive. When young European couples married, they normally established their own households and lived apart from their parents. When a three-generation household came into existence, it usually resulted from a parent moving in with a married child rather than a newly married couple moving in with either set of parents.

Most people did not marry young in the seventeenth and early eighteenth centuries. The average person, who was neither rich nor aristocratic, married surprisingly late, many years after reaching adulthood and many more after beginning to work. In one well-studied, apparently typical English village, both men and women married for the first time at an average age of twenty-seven or older in the seventeenth and eighteenth centuries. A similar pattern existed in early-eighteenth-century France. Moreover, a substantial portion of men and women never married at all.

The custom of late marriage in combination with a nuclear-family household was a distinctive characteristic of European society. It seems likely that the aggressiveness and creativity that have characterized European society have been due in part to a pattern of marriage and family that fosters and requires self-reliance and independence. In preindustrial western Europe in the sixteenth through eighteenth centuries, marriage normally joined a mature man and a mature woman—two adults who had already experienced a great deal of life and could transmit self-reliance and real skills to the next generation.

Why was marriage delayed? The main reason was that couples normally could not marry until they could support themselves economically. The land was still the main source of income. The peasant son often needed to wait until his father's death to inherit the family farm and marry his sweetheart. Similarly, the peasant daughter and her family needed to accumulate a small dowry to help her fiancé buy land or build a house.

There were also laws and community controls to temper impetuous love and physical attraction. In some areas, couples needed the legal permission or tacit approval of the local lord or landowner in order to marry, and poor couples had particular difficulty securing the approval of local officials. These officials believed that freedom to marry for the lower classes would mean more landless paupers, more abandoned children, and more money for welfare. Village elders often agreed. Thus prudence, law, and custom combined to postpone the march to the altar. This pattern helped society maintain some kind of balance between the number of people and the available economic resources.

Work Away from Home

Many young people worked within their families until they could start their own households. Boys plowed and wove; girls spun and tended the cows.

Many others left home temporarily to work elsewhere. In the towns, a lad might be apprenticed to a craftsman for seven or fourteen years to learn a trade. During that time, he would not be permitted to marry. In most trades he earned little and worked hard, but if he was lucky, he might eventually be admitted to a guild and establish his economic independence. More often, a young man would drift from one tough job to another: hired hand for a small farmer, wage laborer on a new road, carrier of water in a nearby town. He was always subject to economic fluctuations, and unemployment was a constant threat.

Girls also temporarily left their families to work, at an early age and in large numbers. The range of opportunities open to them was more limited, however. Service in another family's household was

Chardin: The Kitchen Maid   Lost in thought as she pauses in her work, perhaps this young servant is thinking about her village and loved ones there. Jean-Baptiste Chardin was one of eighteenth-century France's greatest painters. His scenes from everyday life provide valuable evidence for the historian. *(Source: National Gallery of Art, Washington, D.C. Samuel H. Kress Collection)*

by far the most common job, and even middle-class families often sent their daughters into service. Thus a few years away from home as a servant were often a normal part of growing up.

The legions of young servant girls worked hard but had little real independence. Sometimes the employer paid the girl's wages directly to her parents. Constantly under the eye of her mistress, the servant girl found her tasks were many—cleaning, shopping, cooking, caring for the baby. Often the work was endless, for there were no laws to limit exploitation. Rarely were girls so brutalized that they snapped under the strain of such treatment like Varka—the Russian servant girl in Anton Chekhov's chilling story "Sleepy"—who, driven beyond exhaustion, finally quieted her mistress's screaming child by strangling it in its cradle. But court records are full of complaints by servant girls of physical mistreatment by their mistresses. There were many others like the fifteen-year-old English girl in the early eighteenth century who told the judge that her mistress had not only called her "very opprobrious names, as Bitch, Whore and the like," but also "beat her without provocation and beyond measure."[2]

There was also the pressure of seducers and sexual attack. In theory, domestic service offered protection and security within a new family for a young girl leaving home. But in practice, she was often the easy prey of a lecherous master or his sons or his friends. Indeed, "the evidence suggests that in all European countries, from Britain to Russia, the upper classes felt perfectly free to exploit sexually girls who were at their mercy."[3] If the girl became pregnant, she was quickly fired and thrown out in disgrace to make her own way. Prostitution and petty thievery were often the harsh consequences of unwanted pregnancy. "What are we?" exclaimed a bitter Parisian prostitute. "Most of us are unfortunate women, without origins, without education, servants and maids for the most part."[4]

Premarital Sex and Community Controls

Did the plight of some former servant girls mean that late marriage in preindustrial Europe went hand in hand with premarital sex and many illegitimate children? For most of western and central Europe until at least 1750, the answer seems to have been no. English parish registers seldom listed more than one bastard out of every twenty children baptized. Some French parishes in the seventeenth century had extraordinarily low rates of illegitimacy: less than 1 percent of all babies were born out of wedlock. Illegitimate babies were apparently a rarity, at least as far as the official church records are concerned.

At the same time, premarital sex was clearly commonplace. In one well-studied English village, 33 percent of all first children were conceived before the couple was married, and many were born within three months of the marriage ceremony. In the mid-eighteenth century, 20 percent of the French women in the village of Auffay, in Normandy, were pregnant when they got married, although only 2 percent of all babies in the village were born to unwed mothers.

The combination of very low rates of illegitimate birth and large numbers of pregnant brides reflected the powerful social controls of the traditional village. The prospect of an unwed (and therefore poor) mother with an illegitimate child was inevitably viewed as a grave threat to the economic, social, and moral stability of the closely knit community. Irate parents and anxious village elders, indignant priests and authoritative landlords, all combined to pressure any young people who wavered about marriage in the face of unexpected pregnancy. In the countryside, premarital sex was not entered into lightly, and it was generally limited to those contemplating marriage.

The concerns of the village and the family weighed heavily on most aspects of a couple's life, both before and after marriage. One leading authority describes the traditional French peasant household in these terms:

The individuality of the couple, or rather, its tendency towards individuality, was crushed by the family institutions, and also by the social pressures exercised by the village community as a whole, and by the neighborhood in particular. Anything that might endanger the [couple's] household might also prejudice the village community, and the community reacted, occasionally violently, to punish those who contravened the rules. The intrusion of the community into every aspect of family life was very noticeable.[5]

Thus whereas uninvolved individuals today are inclined to ignore the domestic disputes and marital scandals of others, the people in peasant communities gave such affairs the loudest and most unfavorable publicity, either at the time of the event or during the Carnival season (see page 000). Re-

✳ **David Allan: The Penny Wedding (1775)**   The spirited merry-making of a peasant wedding was a popular theme of European artists. In rural Scotland "penny weddings" were common. Guests paid a fee for the food and fun; the money left over went to the newlyweds to help them get started. The dancing, feasting, and drinking that took place at these community parties led the stern elders of the Presbyterian church to oppose them and hastened their decline. *(Source: National Gallery of Scotland)*

lying on degrading public rituals, the young men of the village would typically gang up on the person they wanted to punish and force him or her to sit astride a donkey facing backward and holding up the donkey's tail. They would parade the overly brutal spouse-beating husband (or wife), or the couple whose adultery had been discovered, all around the village, loudly proclaiming the offender's misdeeds with scorn and ridicule. The donkey ride and similar colorful humiliations ranging from rotten vegetables splattered on the doorstep to obscene and insulting midnight serenades were common punishments throughout much of Europe. They epitomized the community's far-reaching effort to police personal behavior and maintain community standards.

Community controls did not extend to family planning, however. Once a man and woman married they generally had several children. Birth con-

trol within marriage was not unknown in western and central Europe before the nineteenth century, but it was primitive and quite undependable. The most common method was *coitus interruptus*— withdrawal by the male before ejaculation. Mechanical and other means of contraception were also used in the eighteenth century, but mainly by certain sectors of the urban population. The "fast set" of London used the "sheath" regularly, though primarily to protect against venereal disease, not pregnancy. Prostitutes used various contraceptive techniques to prevent pregnancy, and such information was available in large towns if a person really sought it.

New Patterns of Marriage and Illegitimacy

In the second half of the eighteenth century, the pattern of late marriage and few births out of wedlock began to change and break down. The number of illegitimate births soared between about 1750 and 1850 as much of Europe experienced an "illegitimacy explosion." In Frankfurt, Germany, for example, illegitimate births rose steadily from about 2 percent of all births in the early 1700s to a peak of about 25 percent around 1850. In Bordeaux, France, 36 percent of all babies were being born out of wedlock by 1840. Small towns and villages experienced less startling climbs, but increases from a range of 1 to 3 percent initially to 10 to 20 percent between 1750 and 1850 were commonplace. Fewer young women were abstaining from premarital intercourse, and, more important, fewer young men were marrying the women they got pregnant. Thus a profound sexual and cultural transformation took place.

Historians are still debating the meaning of this transformation, but two interrelated ideas dominate most interpretations. First, the growth of cottage industry created new opportunities for earning a living, opportunities not tied to the land. Young people attained greater independence and did not have to wait to inherit a farm in order to get married and have children. A scrap of ground for a garden and a cottage for the loom and spinning wheel could be quite enough for a modest living. These circumstances worked against the businesslike, calculating peasant marriage that was often dictated by the needs of the couple's families. After 1750, courtship became more extensive and freer as cottage industry grew. It was easier to yield to the attraction of the opposite sex and fall in love. Sexual activity might follow, and in most cases marriage for love rather than economic considerations also did, as cottage workers blazed a path that factory workers would follow in the nineteenth century.

Second, the needs of a growing population sent many young villagers to towns and cities in search of temporary or permanent employment. Mobility in turn encouraged new sexual and marital relationships, which were less subject to village tradition and resulted in more illegitimate births. Yet most young women in urban areas found work only as servants or textile workers. Poorly paid, insecure, and with little possibility of living truly independent, "liberated" lives, they looked mainly to marriage and family life as an escape from hard work and as the foundation of a satisfying life.

Promises of marriage from a man of the working girl's own class led naturally enough to sex, which was widely viewed as part of serious courtship. In one medium-size French city from 1787 to 1788, the great majority of unwed mothers stated that sexual intimacy had followed promises of marriage. Their sisters in rural Normandy reported again and again that they had been "seduced in anticipation of marriage."[6] Many soldiers, day laborers, and male servants were no doubt sincere in their proposals. But their lives were also insecure, and many hesitated to take on the heavy economic burdens of wife and child.

Thus it became increasingly difficult for a woman to convert pregnancy into marriage, and in a growing number of cases the intended marriage did not take place. The romantic yet practical dreams and aspirations of many young working men and women in towns and villages were frustrated by low wages, inequality, and changing economic and social conditions. Old patterns of marriage and family were breaking down among the common people. Only in the late nineteenth century would more stable patterns reappear.

CHILDREN AND EDUCATION

In the traditional framework of agrarian Europe, women married late but then began bearing children rapidly. If a woman married before she was thirty, and if both she and her husband lived to forty-five, the chances were roughly one in two that she would give birth to six or more children. The newborn child entered a dangerous world. Infant mortality was high. One in five was sure to die, and one in three was quite likely to die in the poorest areas. Newborn children were very likely to catch mysterious infectious diseases of the chest and stomach, and many babies died of dehydration brought about by a bad bout of ordinary diarrhea. Even in rich families little could be done for an ailing child. Childhood itself was dangerous because of adult indifference, neglect, and even abuse.

Schools and formal education played only a modest role in the lives of ordinary children, and many boys and many more girls never learned to read. Nevertheless, basic literacy was growing among the popular classes, whose reading habits have been intensively studied in recent years. Attempting to peer into the collective attitudes of the common people and compare them with those of the book-hungry cultivated public, historians have produced some fascinating insights.

Child Care and Nursing

Women of the lower classes generally breast-fed their infants and for a much longer period than is customary today. Breast-feeding decreases the likelihood of pregnancy for the average woman by delaying the resumption of ovulation. By nursing their babies, women limited their fertility and spaced their children—from two to three years apart. If a newborn baby died, nursing stopped and a new life could be created. Nursing also saved lives: an infant who was breast-fed and received precious immunity-producing substances with its mother's milk was more likely to survive than an infant who was given any other food. In many areas of Russia, where the common practice was to give a new child a sweetened (and germ-laden) rag to suck on for its subsistence, half of the babies did not survive the first year.

In contrast to the laboring poor, the women of the aristocracy and upper middle class seldom nursed their own children. The upper-class woman felt that breast-feeding was crude, common, and undignified. Instead, she hired a wet nurse to suckle her child. The urban mother of more modest means—the wife of a shopkeeper or an artisan—also commonly used a wet nurse in order to facilitate full-time work in the shop.

Wet-nursing was a very widespread and flourishing business in the eighteenth century, a dismal business within the framework of the putting-out system. The traffic was in babies rather than in wool and cloth, and two or three years often passed before the wet-nurse worker finished her task. In the process the poor wet-nurse worker was often exploited and abused. For example, she had little contact with the family that hired her and could be dismissed on a whim by the mother or the family doctor.

Many observers stressed the flaws of wet nurses. It was a common belief that with her milk a nurse passed her bad traits to a baby. When a child turned out poorly, it was assumed that "the nurse had changed it." Many observers charged that nurses were often negligent and greedy. They claimed that there were large numbers of "killing nurses" with whom no child ever survived. Such a nurse let a child die quickly so that she could take another child and another fee.

Foundlings and Infanticide

In the ancient world it was not uncommon to allow or force newborn babies, particularly girl babies, to die when there were too many mouths to feed. To its great and eternal credit, the early medieval church, strongly influenced by Jewish law, denounced infanticide as a pagan practice and insisted that every human life was sacred. The willful destruction of newborn children became a crime

Abandoned Children At this Italian foundlings' home a frightened mother could discreetly deposit her baby on a revolving table, turn the table to move the baby into the home, and hurry away without being seen. *(Source: The Bettmann Archive)*

punishable by death. And yet, as the previous reference to killing nurses suggests, direct and indirect methods of eliminating unwanted babies did not disappear. There were, for example, many cases of "overlaying"—parents rolling over and suffocating the child placed between them in their bed. Such parents claimed they had been drunk and had acted unintentionally. In Austria in 1784, suspicious authorities made it illegal for parents to take children under five into bed with them. Severe poverty, on the one hand, and increasing illegitimacy, on the other, conspired to force the very poor to thin their own ranks.

The young girl—very likely a servant—who could not provide for her child had few choices. If she would not have an abortion or employ the services of a killing nurse, she could bundle up her baby and leave it on the doorstep of a church. In the late seventeenth century, Saint Vincent de Paul was so distressed by the number of babies brought to the steps of Notre Dame in Paris that he established a home for foundlings. Others followed his example. In England the government acted on a petition calling for a foundling hospital "to prevent the frequent murders of poor, miserable infants at birth" and "to suppress the inhuman custom of exposing newborn children to perish in the streets."

In much of Europe in the eighteenth century, foundling homes emerged as a favorite charity of the rich and powerful. Great sums were spent on them. The foundling home in St. Petersburg, perhaps the most elaborate and lavish of its kind, occupied the former palaces of two members of the high nobility. In the early nineteenth century it had twenty-five thousand children in its care and was receiving five thousand new babies a year. At their best, foundling homes in the eighteenth century were a good example of Christian charity and social concern in an age of great poverty and inequality.

Yet the foundling home was no panacea. By the 1770s one-third of all babies born in Paris were immediately abandoned to the foundling home by their mothers. Fully one-third of all those foundlings were abandoned by married couples, a powerful commentary on the standard of living among the working poor, for whom an additional mouth to feed often meant tragedy.

Furthermore, great numbers of babies entered the foundling homes, but few left. Even in the best of these homes, 50 percent of the babies normally died within a year. In the worst, fully 90 percent did not survive. They succumbed to long journeys over rough roads, the intentional and unintentional neglect of their wet nurses, and the customary childhood illnesses. So great was the carnage that some contemporaries called the foundling hospitals "legalized infanticide."

Attitudes Toward Children

What were the typical circumstances of children's lives? Did the treatment of foundlings reflect the attitudes of typical parents? Although some scholars argue otherwise, it seems that the young child was often of little concern to its parents and to society in the eighteenth century. This indifference toward children was found in all classes; rich children were by no means exempt. The practice of using wet nurses, who were casually selected and often negligent, is one example of how even the rich and the prosperous put the child out of sight and out of mind. One French moralist, writing in 1756 about how to improve humanity, observed that "one blushes to think of loving one's children." It has been said that the English gentleman of the period "had more interest in the diseases of his horses than of his children."[7]

Feelings toward children were greatly influenced by the terrible frequency of death among children of all classes. Doctors and clergymen urged parents not to become too emotionally involved with their children, who were so unlikely to survive. Mothers especially did not always heed such warnings, but the risk of emotional devastation was very real for them. The great eighteenth-century English historian Edward Gibbon (1737–1794) wrote that "the death of a new born child before that of its parents may seem unnatural but it is a strictly probable event, since of any given number the greater part are extinguished before the ninth year, before they possess the faculties of the mind and the body." Gibbon's father named all his boys Edward after himself, hoping that at least one of them would survive to carry his name. His prudence was not misplaced. Edward the future historian and eldest survived. Five brothers and sisters who followed him all died in infancy.

The medical establishment was seldom interested in the care of children. One contemporary observer quoted a famous doctor as saying that "he never wished to be called to a young child because he was really at a loss to know what to offer for it." There were "physicians of note who make no scruple to assert that there is nothing to be done for children when they are ill." The best hope for children was often treatment by women healers and midwives, who helped many women deliver their babies and provided advice on child care. Nevertheless, children were still caught in a vicious circle: they were neglected because they were very likely to die, and they were likely to die because they were neglected.

Emotional detachment from children often shaded off into abuse. When parents and other adults did turn toward children, it was normally to discipline and control them. The novelist Daniel Defoe (1660?–1731), who was always delighted when he saw very young children working hard in cottage industry, coined the axiom "Spare the rod and spoil the child." He meant it. So did Susannah Wesley (1669–1742), mother of John Wesley, the founder of Methodism. According to her, the first task of a parent toward her children was "to conquer the will, and bring them to an obedient temper." She reported that her babies were "taught to fear the rod, and to cry softly."[8]

It was hardly surprising that when English parish officials dumped their paupers into the first factories late in the eighteenth century, the children were beaten and brutalized. That was part of the child-rearing pattern—considerable indifference, on the one hand, and strict physical discipline, on the other—that prevailed throughout most of the eighteenth century.

From the middle of the century, this pattern came under increasing attack and began to change. Critics, led by Jean-Jacques Rousseau in his famous treatise *Emile* (see Listening to the Past), called for greater love, tenderness, and understanding toward children. In addition to supporting foundling homes to discourage infanticide and urging wealthy women to nurse their own babies, these new voices ridiculed the practice of swaddling: wrapping youngsters in tight-fitting clothes and blankets was generally believed to form babies properly by "straightening them out." By the end of the eighteenth century, small children were often being dressed in simpler, more comfortable clothing, allowing much greater freedom of movement. More parents expressed a delight in the love and intimacy of the child and found real pleasure in raising their offspring. These changes were part of the general growth of humanitarianism and cautious optimism about human potential that characterized the eighteenth-century Enlightenment.

Schools and Popular Literature

The role of schools and formal education outside the home was also growing more important. The aristocracy and the rich had led the way in the sixteenth century with special colleges, often run by Jesuits. But schools charged specifically with elementary education of the children of the common people usually did not appear until the seventeenth century. Unlike medieval schools, which mingled all age groups, these elementary schools specialized in boys and girls from seven to twelve, who were instructed in basic literacy and religion. The growth of popular education quickened in the eighteenth century, but there was no revolutionary acceleration, and many common people received no formal education.

Prussia led the way in the development of universal education, inspired by the old Protestant idea that every believer should be able to read and study the Bible in the quest for personal salvation and by the new idea of a population capable of effectively serving the state. As early as 1717, Prussia made attendance at elementary schools compulsory, and more Protestant German states, such as Saxony and Württemberg, followed in the eighteenth century. Religious motives were also extremely important elsewhere. From the middle of the seventeenth century, Presbyterian Scotland was convinced that the path to salvation lay in careful study of the Scriptures, and it established an effective network of parish schools for rich and poor alike. The Church of England and the dissenting congregations established "charity schools" to instruct the children of the poor, and in 1682 France began setting up Christian schools to teach the catechism and prayers as well as reading and writing. In 1774 Habsburg empress Maria Theresa established a general system of elementary education that called for compulsory education and a school in every community. Thus some elementary education was becoming a reality for European peoples, and schools were of growing significance in the life of the child.

The result of these efforts was a remarkable growth in basic literacy between 1600 and 1800, especially after 1700. Whereas in 1600 only one male in six was barely literate in France and Scotland, and one in four in England, by 1800 almost nine out of ten Scottish males, two out of three males in France, and more than half of English males were literate. In all three countries the bulk of the jump occurred in the eighteenth century. Women were also increasingly literate, although they lagged behind men in most countries.

The growth in literacy promoted a growth in reading, and historians have carefully examined what the common people read in an attempt to discern what they were thinking. One thing seems certain: the major philosophical works of the Enlightenment had little impact on peasants and workers, who could neither afford nor understand those favorites of the book-hungry educated public.

Although the Bible remained the overwhelming favorite, especially in Protestant countries, the staple of popular literature was short pamphlets known as chapbooks. Printed on the cheapest paper available, many chapbooks dealt with religious subjects. They featured Bible stories, prayers, devotions, and the lives of saints and other exemplary Christians. Promising happiness after death, devotional literature was also intensely practical. It gave the believer moral teachings and a confidence in God that helped in daily living.

Entertaining, often humorous stories formed a second element of popular literature. Fairy tales, medieval romances, fictionalized history, and fantastic adventures—these were some of the delights that filled the peddler's pack as he approached a village. Both heroes and villains possessed superhuman powers in this make-believe world, a world of

A Peasant Family Reading the Bible   Praised by the philosophe Diderot for its moralistic message, this engraving of a painting by Jean-Baptiste Greuze (1725–1805) captures the power of sacred texts and the spoken word. The peasant patriarch reads aloud from the massive family Bible, and the close-knit circle of absorbed listeners concentrates on every word. Only the baby is distracted by the dog. *(Source: Bibliothèque Nationale/Giraudon/Art Resource, NY)*

danger and magic, of fairy godmothers and evil trolls. But the good fairies always triumphed over the evil ones in the story's marvelous resolution. The significance of these entertaining stories for the peasant reader is not clear, however. Many scholars see them reflecting a desire for pure escapism and a temporary flight from harsh everyday reality. Others see these tales reflecting ancient folk wisdom and counseling prudence in a world full of danger and evil, where wolves dress up like grandmothers and eat Little Red Riding Hoods.

Some popular literature was highly practical, dealing with rural crafts, household repairs, useful plants, and similar matters. Much of such lore was stored in almanacs. With calendars listing secular, religious, and astrological events mixed in with agricultural schedules, bizarre bits of information, and jokes, the almanac was universal, noncontroversial, and highly appreciated, even by many in the comfortable classes. "Anyone who could would read an almanac."[9]

In general, however, the reading of the common people had few similarities with that of educated elites. Popular literature was simple and it was practical, both as devotional self-help and as how-to instruction. It was also highly escapist. Yet the common people were apparently content with works that reinforced traditional values and did not foster social or religious criticism. These results fit well with the modest educational objectives of rulers and educated elites. They believed that carefully limited instruction stressing religion and morals was useful to the masses and that too much study would disorient them and foster discontent.

✳ FOOD AND MEDICAL PRACTICE

The European population increased rapidly in the eighteenth century. Plague and starvation gradually disappeared, and Europeans lived longer lives. What were the characteristics of diets and nutrition in this era of improving health and longevity? Although it played only a small part, what was medical practice like in the eighteenth century? What does a comparison of rich and poor reveal?

Diets and Nutrition

At the beginning of the eighteenth century, ordinary men and women depended on grain as fully as they had in the past. Bread was quite literally the staff of life. Peasants in the Beauvais region of France ate two pounds of bread a day, washing it down with water, green wine, beer, or a little skimmed milk. Their dark bread was made from a mixture of roughly ground wheat and rye—the standard flour of the common people. The poor also ate grains in soup and gruel. In rocky northern Scotland, for example, people depended on oatmeal, which they often ate half-cooked so that it would swell in their stomachs and make them feel full.

Not surprisingly, an adequate supply of grain and an affordable price for bread loomed in the popular imagination. Peasants, landless laborers, and urban workers all believed in the old medieval idea of the "just price"—that is, a price that was "fair" to both consumers and producers. But in the later eighteenth century, this traditional, moral view of prices and the economy clashed repeatedly with the emerging free-market philosophy of unregulated supply and demand, which government officials, large landowners, and early economists increasingly favored. In years of poor harvests and soaring prices, this clash often resulted in food riots and popular disturbances. Peasants and workers would try to stop wagons loaded with grain from leaving their region, or they would seize grain held by speculators and big merchants accused of hoarding and rigging the market. (Usually the tumultuous crowd paid what it considered to be a fair price for what it took.) Governments were keenly aware of the problem of adequate grain supplies, and they would sometimes try to control prices to prevent unrest in crisis years.

Although breadstuffs were all-important for the rural and urban poor, they also ate a fair quantity of vegetables. Indeed, vegetables were considered "poor people's food." Peas and beans were probably the most common and were eaten fresh in late spring and summer. Dried, they became the basic ingredients in the soups and stews of the long winter months. In most regions, other vegetables appeared in season on the tables of the poor—primarily cabbages, carrots, and wild greens. Fruit was uncommon and limited to the summer months.

The common people of Europe loved meat and eggs, but they seldom ate their fill. Indeed, as the population surged in the sixteenth century, meat became more expensive, and the poor ate less meat in 1700 than in 1500. Moreover, in most European countries harsh game laws deprived the poor of the right to hunt and eat edible game such as rabbits, deer, and partridges. Only nobles and large landowners could legally kill game. Few laws were more bitterly resented—or more frequently broken—by ordinary people than those governing hunting.

Milk was rarely drunk. Perhaps because some individuals do suffer seriously from dairy allergies, it was widely believed that milk caused sore eyes, headaches, and a variety of ills, except among the very young and very old. Milk was used primarily to make cheese and butter, which the poor liked but could afford only occasionally. Medical and popular opinion considered whey, the watery liquid left after milk was churned, "an excellent temperate drink."

The diet of the rich—aristocrats, officials, and the comfortable bourgeoisie—was traditionally quite different from that of the poor. The men and women of the upper classes were rapacious carnivores. A truly elegant dinner among the great and powerful consisted of one rich meat after another: a chicken pie, a leg of lamb, a grilled steak, for example, perhaps followed by three fish courses, all complemented with sweets, cheeses, and nuts of all kinds. Fruits and vegetables were not often found on the tables of the rich.

There was also an enormous amount of overdrinking among the rich. The English squire who loved to hunt with his hounds loved to drink with a similar passion. With his dinner he drank red wine from France or white wine from the Rhineland, and with his dessert he took sweet but strong port or Madeira from Portugal. Sometimes he ended the evening under the table in a drunken stupor.

The diet of small traders, master craftsmen, minor bureaucrats—the people of the towns and cities—was generally less monotonous than that of the peasantry. The markets, stocked by market gardens on the outskirts, provided a substantial variety of meats, vegetables, and fruits, although bread and beans still formed the bulk of such families' diet.

There were also regional dietary differences in 1700. Generally speaking, northern, Atlantic Europe ate better than southern, Mediterranean Europe. The poor of England probably ate best of all. The Dutch were also considerably better fed than the average European, in large part because of their advanced agriculture and diversified gardens.

The Impact of Diet on Health

How were the poor and the rich served by their quite different diets? At first glance, the diet of the laboring poor, relying as it did on grains and vegetables, might seem low in protein. However, the whole-grain wheat or rye flour used in eighteenth-century bread retained most of the bran—the ground-up husk—and the all-important wheat germ, which contains higher proportions of some minerals, vitamins, and good-quality proteins than does the rest of the grain. In addition, the field peas and beans eaten by poor people since the early Middle Ages contained protein that complemented the proteins in whole-grain bread. The proteins in whey, cheese, and eggs, which the poor ate at least occasionally, also supplemented the bread and vegetables.

The basic bread-and-vegetables diet of the poor *in normal times* was adequate. But a key dietary problem in some seasons, particularly in the late winter and early spring, was probably getting enough green vegetables (or milk) to ensure adequate supplies of vitamins A and C. A severe deficiency of vitamin C produces scurvy, a disease that leads to rotting gums, swelling of the limbs, and great weakness. Before the season's first vegetables, many people had used up their bodily reserves of vitamin C and were suffering from mild cases of scurvy. (Scurvy was an acute problem for sailors on long voyages and by the end of the sixteenth century was being controlled on ships by a daily ration of lime juice for crew members.)

The practice of gorging on meat, sweets, and spirits caused the rich their own nutritional problems. Because of their great disdain for fresh vegetables, they, too, were very often deficient in vitamins A and C. Gout was a common affliction of the overfed and underexercised rich. No wonder they were often caricatured as dragging their flabby limbs and bulging bellies to the table to stuff their swollen cheeks and poison their livers. People of moderate means, who could afford some meat and dairy products with fair regularity but who had not abandoned the bread and vegetables of the poor, were probably best off from a nutritional standpoint.

Patterns of food consumption changed rather markedly as the century progressed. More varied diets associated with new methods of farming were confined largely to the Low Countries and Eng-

✳ **Royal Interest in the Potato**   Frederick the Great of Prussia, shown here supervising cultivation of the potato, used his influence and position to promote the new food on his estates and throughout Prussia. Peasants could grow potatoes with the simplest hand tools. But doing so was backbreaking labor, as this painting by R. Warthmüller suggests. *(Source: Private Collection, Hamburg/Archiv für Kunst und Geschichte, Berlin)*

land, but a new food—the potato—came to the aid of the poor everywhere. Introduced into Europe from the Americas—along with corn, squash, tomatoes, and many other useful plants—the humble potato is an excellent food. Containing a good supply of carbohydrates, calories, and vitamins A and C (especially if it is not overcooked and the skin is eaten), the potato offset the lack of vitamins from green vegetables in the poor person's winter and early spring diet, and it provided a much higher caloric yield than grain for a given piece of land.

For some desperately poor peasants who needed to get every possible calorie from a tiny plot of land, the potato replaced grain as the primary food in the eighteenth century. This happened first in Ireland, where English (Protestant) repression and exploitation forced large numbers of poor (and Catholic) peasants to live off tiny scraps of rented ground. Elsewhere in Europe, potatoes took hold

more slowly because many people did not like them. Thus potatoes were first fed to pigs and livestock, and there was even debate about whether they were fit for humans. In Germany the severe famines caused by the Seven Years' War settled the matter: potatoes were edible and not just "famine food." By the end of the century, the potato had become an important dietary supplement in much of Europe.

There was also a general growth of market gardening, and a greater variety of vegetables appeared in towns and cities. In the course of the eighteenth century, the large towns and cities of maritime Europe began to receive semitropical fruits, such as oranges and lemons, from Portugal and the West Indies, although they were not cheap.

Not all changes in the eighteenth century were for the better, however. Bread began to change, most noticeably for the English and for the comfortable groups on the European continent. Rising incomes and new tastes led to a shift from whole-grain black or brown bread to "bread as white as snow" and started a decline in bread's nutritional value. The high-roughage bran and some of the dark but high-vitamin germ were increasingly sifted out by millers. This foretold further "improvements" in the nineteenth century, which would leave bread perfectly white and greatly reduced in nutritional value.

Another sign of nutritional decline was the growing consumption of sugar. Initially a luxury, sugar dropped rapidly in price as slave-based production increased in the Americas, and the sweetener was much more widely used in the eighteenth century. This development probably led to an increase in cavities and to other ailments as well, although the greater or lesser poverty of the laboring poor still protected most of them from the sugar-tooth virus of the rich and well-to-do.

Medical Practitioners

Although sickness, pain, and disease—intractable challenges built into the human condition—permeated the European experience in the eighteenth century, medical science played a very small part in improving the health of most people. Yet the Enlightenment's growing focus on discovering the laws of nature and on human problems did give rise to a great deal of research and experimentation. The century also saw a remarkable rise in the number of medical practitioners, and a high value was placed on their services. Therefore, when the great breakthroughs in knowledge came in the middle and late nineteenth century, they could be rapidly evaluated and diffused.

Care of the sick in the eighteenth century was the domain of several competing groups: faith healers, apothecaries (or pharmacists), surgeons, and physicians. Since the great majority of common ailments have a tendency to cure themselves, each group could point to successes and win adherents. When a doctor's treatment made the patient worse, as it often did, the original medical problem could always be blamed.

Faith healers, who had been among the most important kinds of physicians in medieval Europe, remained active. They and their patients believed that demons and evil spirits caused disease by lodging in people and that the proper treatment was to exorcise, or drive out, the offending devil. This demonic view of disease was strongest in the countryside, where popular belief placed great faith in the healing power of religious relics, prayer, and the laying on of hands. Faith healing was particularly effective in the treatment of mental disorders such as hysteria and depression, where the link between attitude and illness is most direct.

Apothecaries sold a vast number of herbs, drugs, and patent medicines for every conceivable "temperament and distemper." Early pharmacists were seldom regulated, and they frequently diagnosed freely. Their prescriptions were incredibly complex—a hundred or more drugs might be included in a single prescription—and often very expensive. Some of the drugs and herbs undoubtedly worked. For example, strong laxatives were given to the rich for their constipated bowels. Indeed, the medical profession continued to believe that regular "purging" of the bowels was essential for good health and the treatment of illness. Much purging was harmful, however, and only bloodletting for the treatment of disease was more effective in speeding patients to their graves.

Surgeons, in contrast, made considerable medical and social progress. Long considered as ordinary artisans comparable to butchers and barbers, surgeons began studying anatomy seriously and improved their art. With endless opportunities to practice, army surgeons on gory battlefields led the way. They learned that a soldier with an extensive wound, such as a shattered leg or arm, could perhaps be saved if the surgeon could obtain above the wound a flat surface that could be cauterized with fire. Thus if a soldier (or a civilian) had a broken limb and the bone stuck out, the surgeon amputated so that the remaining stump could be cauterized and the likelihood of death reduced.

The eighteenth-century surgeon (and patient) labored in the face of incredible difficulties. Almost all operations were performed without any painkiller, for the anesthesias of the day were hard to control and were believed too dangerous for general use. The terrible screams of people whose limbs were being sawed off echoed across battlefields and through hospitals. Many patients died from the agony and shock of such operations. Surgery was also performed in the midst of filth and dirt, for there simply was no knowledge of bacteriology and the nature of infection. The simplest wound treated by a surgeon could fester and lead to death.

Physicians, the fourth major group, were apprenticed in their teens to a practicing physician for several years of on-the-job training. This training was then rounded out with hospital work or some university courses. Because such prolonged training was expensive, physicians continued to come mainly from prosperous families, and they usually concentrated on urban patients from similar social backgrounds. They had little contact with urban workers and even less with peasants.

To their credit, physicians in the eighteenth century were increasingly willing to experiment with new methods, but time-honored practices lay heavily on them. Physicians, like apothecaries, laid great stress on purging. And bloodletting was still considered a medical cure-all. It was the way "bad blood," the cause of illness, was removed and the balance of humors necessary for good health was restored. According to a physician practicing medicine in Philadelphia in 1799, bleeding was proper at the onset of all inflammatory fevers, in all inflammations, and for "asthma, sciatic pains, coughs, head-aches, rheumatisms, the apoplexy, epilepsy, and bloody fluxes."[10] It was also necessary after all falls, blows, and bruises.

While ordinary physicians were bleeding, apothecaries purging, surgeons sawing, and faith healers praying, the leading medical thinkers were attempting to pull together and assimilate all the information and misinformation they had been accumulating. The attempt was ambitious: to systematize medicine around simple, basic principles, as Newton had done in physics. But the schools of thought resulting from such speculation and theorizing did little to improve medical care.

Hospitals and Medical Experiments

Hospitals were terrible places throughout most of the eighteenth century. There was no isolation of patients. Operations were performed in a patient's bed. Nurses were old, ignorant, greedy, and often drunk women. Fresh air was considered harmful, and infections of every kind were rampant. Diderot's article in the *Encyclopedia* on the Hôtel-Dieu in Paris, the "richest and most terrifying of all French hospitals," vividly describes normal conditions of the 1770s:

Imagine a long series of communicating wards filled with sufferers of every kind of disease who are some-times packed three, four, five or even six into a bed, the living alongside the dead and dying, the air polluted by this mass of unhealthy bodies, passing pestilential germs of their afflictions from one to the other, and the spectacle of suffering and agony on every hand. That is the Hôtel-Dieu.[11]

No wonder the poor of Paris hated hospitals and often saw confinement there as a plot to kill paupers.

In the last years of the century, the humanitarian concern already reflected in Diderot's description of the Hôtel-Dieu led to a movement for hospital reform throughout western Europe. Efforts were made to improve ventilation and eliminate filth in the belief that bad air caused disease. The theory was wrong, but the results were beneficial, for the spread of infection was somewhat reduced.

Mental hospitals, too, were incredibly savage institutions. The customary treatment for mental illness was bleeding and cold water, administered more to maintain discipline than to effect a cure. Violent persons were chained to the wall and forgotten. A breakthrough of sorts occurred in the 1790s when William Tuke founded the first humane sanatorium in England. In Paris an innovative warden, Philippe Pinel, took the chains off the mentally disturbed in 1793 and tried to treat them as patients rather than as prisoners.

In the eighteenth century, all sorts of wildly erroneous ideas about mental illness circulated. One was that moonlight caused madness, a belief reflected in the word *lunatic*—someone harmed by lunar light. Another mid-eighteenth-century theory, which lasted until at least 1914, was that masturbation caused madness, not to mention acne, epilepsy, and premature ejaculation. Thus parents, religious institutions, and schools waged relentless war on masturbation by males, although they were curiously uninterested in female masturbation.

In the second half of the eighteenth century, medicine in general turned in a more practical and experimental direction. Some of the experimentation was creative quackery involving the recently discovered phenomenon of electricity. One magnificent quack in London promoted sleep on a cure-all Celestial Bed, which was lavishly decorated with magnets and electrical devices. A single night on the bed cost a small fortune. The rich could buy expensive treatments, but the prevalence of quacks and the general lack of knowledge meant they often got little for their money. Because so

Hospital Life　Patients crowded into hospitals like this one in Hamburg in 1746 had little chance of recovery. A priest by the window administers last rites, while in the center a surgeon coolly saws off the leg of a man who has received no anesthesia. *(Source: Germanisches Nationalmuseum, Nuremberg)*

many treatments were harmful, the common people were probably much less deprived by their reliance on faith healers and folk medicine than one might think.

Experimentation and the intensified search for solutions to human problems led to some real advances in medicine after 1750, however. The eighteenth century's greatest medical triumph was the conquest of smallpox. With the progressive decline of bubonic plague, smallpox became the most terrible of the infectious diseases. In the words of historian Thomas Macaulay, "Smallpox was always present, filling the churchyard with corpses, tormenting with constant fears all whom it had not stricken." It is estimated that 60 million Europeans died of smallpox in the eighteenth century. Fully 80 percent of the population was stricken at some point in life, and 25 percent of the total population was left permanently scarred. If ever a human problem cried out for solution, it was smallpox.

Inoculation against smallpox was already practiced in China and the Muslim lands of western Asia. Something approaching mass inoculation took place in England in the 1760s and the practice spread to the continent of Europe. By the later years of the century, smallpox inoculation was playing some part in the decline of the death rate and the general increase in European population. However, the method of inoculation—using active smallpox to stimulate immunity—could cause a mild, and potentially infectious, case of the disease.

The final breakthrough against smallpox came at the end of the century. Edward Jenner (1749–1823), a talented country doctor, noted that in the English countryside there was a long-standing belief that dairy maids who had contracted cowpox did not get smallpox. Cowpox produces sores on the cow's udder and on the hands of the milker. The sores resemble those of smallpox, but the disease is mild and not contagious. In 1796, using matter taken from a milkmaid with cowpox, Jenner performed his first vaccination on a young boy. In the next two years, he performed twenty-three successful vaccinations and in 1798 published his findings. After Austrian medical authorities replicated Jenner's results, the new method of treatment spread rapidly. Smallpox soon declined to the point of disappearance in Europe and then throughout the world. For his great discovery, Jenner eventually received prizes totaling £30,000 from the British government, a fitting recompense for a man who gave an enormous gift to humanity and helped lay the foundation for the science of immunology in the nineteenth century.

RELIGION AND POPULAR CULTURE

Though the critical spirit of the Enlightenment spread among the educated elite in the eighteenth century, the majority of ordinary men and women remained firmly committed to the Christian religion, especially in rural areas. Religion offered answers to life's mysteries and gave comfort and courage in the face of sorrow and fear. Religion also remained strong because it was usually embedded in local traditions, everyday social experience, and popular culture.

Yet the popular religion of village Europe was everywhere enmeshed in a larger world of church hierarchies and state power. These powerful outside forces sought to regulate religious life at the local level. Their efforts created tensions that helped set the scene for a vigorous religious revival in Germany and England. Similar tensions arose in Catholic countries, where powerful elites criticized and attacked popular religious practices that their increasingly rationalistic minds deemed foolish and superstitious.

The Institutional Church

As in the Middle Ages, the local parish church remained the basic religious unit all across Europe. Still largely coinciding with the agricultural village, the parish fulfilled many needs. Whether Catholic or Protestant, the parish church was the focal point of religious devotion and much more. Villagers came together at services and gossiped and swapped stories afterward, and neighbors joined in church for baptisms, marriages, funerals, and other special events. Thus the parish church was woven into the very fabric of community life.

Moreover, the local church had important administrative tasks. It is because priests and parsons kept such complete parish registers that historians have learned so much about population and family life. Parishes also normally distributed charity to the destitute, looked after orphans, and provided whatever primary education was available for the common people.

The many tasks of the local church were usually the responsibility of a resident priest or pastor, a full-time professional working with assistants and lay volunteers. All clerics—whether Roman Catholic, Protestant, or Orthodox—also shared the fate of middlemen in a complicated institutional system. Charged most often with ministering to poor peasants, the priest or parson was the last link in a powerful church-state hierarchy that was everywhere determined to control religion down to the grassroots. However, the regulatory framework of belief, which went back at least to the fourth century when Christianity became the official religion of the Roman Empire, had undergone important changes since 1500.

The Protestant Reformation had burst forth as a culmination of medieval religiosity and a desire to purify Christian belief. Martin Luther, the greatest of the reformers, preached that all men and women were saved from their sins and God's damnation only by personal faith in Jesus Christ. The individual could reach God directly, without need of priestly intermediaries. This was the revolutionary meaning of Luther's "priesthood of all believers," which broke forever the monopoly of the priestly class over medieval Europe's most priceless treasure—eternal salvation.

As the Reformation gathered force, with peasant upheaval and doctrinal competition, German princes and monarchs in northern Europe put themselves at the head of official churches in their territories. Protestant authorities, with generous assistance from state-certified theologians, then proceeded to regulate their "territorial churches" strictly, selecting personnel and imposing detailed rules. They joined with Catholics to crush the Anabaptists, who, with their belief in freedom of conscience and separation of church and state, had become the real revolutionaries. Thus the Reformation, initially so radical in its rejection of Rome and its stress on individual religious experience, eventually resulted in a bureaucratization of the church and local religious life in Protestant Europe.

The Reformation era also increased the practical power of Catholic rulers over "their" churches, but

A Religious Festival in Urban France This vibrant painting suggests how religious life interacted with powerful institutions in Catholic Europe. Moving past crowds and through the city, this procession is celebrating the Blessed Sacrament on the Feast of Corpus Christi (the Body of Christ). Church dignitaries are grouped in the center; the colorful nobility is on the left; and the middle orders, with their sober black suits, are on the right. Both participation and hierarchical inequality are the rule. *(Source: Bibliothèque des Arts Décoratifs/Jean-Loup Charmet)*

it was only in the eighteenth century that some Catholic monarchs began to impose striking reforms. These reforms, which had their counterparts in Orthodox Russia, had a very "Protestant" aspect. They increased state control over the Catholic church, making it less subject to papal influence. For instance, Spain, a deeply Catholic country with devout rulers, took firm control of ecclesiastical appointments. Papal proclamations could not even be read in Spanish churches without prior approval from the government. Spain also asserted state control over the Spanish Inquisition, which had been ruthlessly pursuing heresy as an independent agency under Rome's direction for two hundred years. In sum, Spain went far toward creating a "national" Catholic church, as France had done earlier.

Some Catholic rulers also turned their reforming efforts on certain religious orders and monasteries and convents. Following the earlier example of Portugal, the French king ordered the politically influential Jesuits out of France in 1763 and confiscated their property. Believing that the large monastic clergy should make a more practical contribution to social and religious life, Maria Theresa of Austria (see page 000) sharply restricted entry into "unproductive" orders, and her son Joseph II abolished contemplative orders, henceforth permitting only orders that were engaged in teaching, nursing, or other practical work. The state also expropriated the dissolved monasteries and used their great wealth for charitable purposes and higher salaries for ordinary priests.

Protestant Revival

In their attempt to recapture the vital core of the Christian religion, the Protestant reformers had rigorously suppressed all the medieval practices that they considered nonessential or erroneous because they were not founded on Scripture. Relics and crucifixes had been permanently removed from crypt and altar. Stained-glass windows had been smashed, walls and murals covered with whitewash, and processions and pilgrimages eliminated. Such revolutionary changes had often troubled ordinary churchgoers, but by the late seventeenth century the vast reforms of the Reformation had been completed and thoroughly routinized in most Protestant churches.

Indeed, official Protestant churches had generally settled into a smug complacency. In the Reformation heartland, one concerned German minister wrote that the Lutheran church "had become paralyzed in forms of dead doctrinal conformity" and badly needed a return to its original inspiration.[12] This voice was one of many that would prepare and then guide a powerful Protestant revival, which was largely successful because it answered the intense but increasingly unsatisfied needs of common people.

The Protestant revival began in Germany. It was known as Pietism, and three aspects account for its powerful appeal. First, Pietism called for a warm, emotional religion that everyone could experience. Enthusiasm—in prayer, in worship, in preaching, in life itself—was the key concept. "Just as a drunkard becomes full of wine, so must the congregation become filled with spirit," declared one exuberant writer. Another said simply, "The heart must burn."[13]

Second, Pietism reasserted the earlier radical stress on the priesthood of all believers, thereby reducing the wide gulf between the official clergy and the Lutheran laity. Bible reading and study were enthusiastically extended to all classes, and this provided a powerful spur for popular education as well as individual religious development. Third, Pietists believed in the practical power of Christian rebirth in everyday affairs. Reborn Christians were expected to lead good, moral lives and come from all social classes.

Pietism had a major impact on John Wesley (1703–1791), who served as the catalyst for popular religious revival in England. Wesley, who came from a long line of ministers, mapped a fanatically earnest "scheme of religion." As a teaching fellow at Oxford University, he organized a Holy Club for similarly minded students. They were soon known contemptuously as "Methodists" because they were so methodical in their devotion. Yet like the young Luther, Wesley remained intensely troubled about his own salvation, even after his ordination as an Anglican priest in 1728.

Wesley's anxieties related to grave problems of the faith in England. The government shamelessly used the Church of England to provide favorites with high-paying jobs and sinecures. The building of churches practically stopped even though the population was growing and in many parishes there was a grave shortage of pews. Services and sermons had settled into an uninspiring routine, while the skepticism of the Enlightenment was making inroads among the educated classes and deism was becoming popular. Some bishops and church leaders acted as if they believed that doctrines such as the Virgin Birth or the Ascension were little more than elegant superstitions.

Spiritual counseling from a sympathetic Pietist minister from Germany prepared Wesley for a mystical, emotional "conversion" in 1738. He described this critical turning point in his *Journal*:

In the evening I went to a [Christian] society in Aldersgate Street where one was reading Luther's preface to the Epistle to the Romans. About a quarter before nine, while he was describing the change which God works in the heart through faith in Christ, I felt my heart strangely warmed. I felt I did trust in Christ, Christ alone for salvation; and an assurance was given me that he had taken away my sins, even mine, and saved me from the law of sin and death.[14]

Wesley's emotional experience resolved his intellectual doubts. Moreover, he was convinced that any person, no matter how poor or uneducated, might have a similarly heartfelt conversion and gain the same blessed assurance.

Wesley took the good news to the people, traveling some 225,000 miles by horseback and preaching more than forty thousand sermons in fifty years. Since existing churches were often overcrowded and the church-state establishment was hostile, Wesley preached in open fields. People came in large numbers. Of critical importance was Wesley's rejection of Calvinist predestination—the doctrine of salvation granted only to a select few. Expanding on earlier Dutch theologians' views, he preached that *all* men and women who earnestly sought salvation might be saved. It was a message of hope and joy, of free will and universal salvation. Wesley's ministry won converts and eventually resulted in a new denomination.

And as Wesley had been inspired by Pietist revival in Germany, so evangelicals in the Church of

✳ **A Midsummer Afternoon with a Methodist Preacher**   This detail from a painting by Philippe de Loutherbourg portrays in a humorous manner how John Wesley and his followers took their optimistic Christianity to the people of England. Methodist ministers championed open-air preaching and week-long revivals. *(Source: Royal Ontario Museum)*

England and the old dissenting groups followed his example, giving impetus to an even broader awakening among the lower classes. In Protestant countries religion remained a vital force in the lives of the people.

Catholic Piety

Religion also flourished in Catholic Europe around 1700, but there were important differences with Protestant practice. First of all, the visual contrast was striking. Baroque artists had lavished rich and emotionally exhilarating figures and images on Catholic churches; Protestants excluded such works from their places of worship. Catholics in Europe remained intensely religious. More than 95 percent of the Catholic population probably attended church for Easter Communion, the climax of the Catholic church year.

The tremendous popular strength of religion in Catholic countries reflected religion's integral role in community life and popular culture. Thus although Catholics reluctantly confessed their sins to priests, they enthusiastically joined together in religious festivals to celebrate the passage of the liturgical year. In addition to the great processional days—such as Palm Sunday, the joyful re-enactment of Jesus' triumphal entry into Jerusalem, or Rogations, with its chanted supplications and penances three days before the bodily ascent of Jesus into heaven on Ascension Day—each parish had its own saints' days, processions, and pilgrimages. Led by its priest, a congregation might march around the village or across the countryside to a local shrine or chapel, perhaps closing the event with an enormous picnic. Before each procession or feast day, the priest explained its religious significance to kindle group piety. But processions were also part of folklore and tradition, an escape from work, and a form of recreation. A holiday atmosphere sometimes reigned on longer processions. People drank and danced, and couples disappeared into the woods.

Indeed, devout Catholics had many religious beliefs that were marginal to the Christian faith, often of obscure or even pagan origin. On the feast of Saint Anthony, for example, priests were expected to bless salt and bread for farm animals to protect them from disease. One saint's relics could help cure a child of fear, and there were healing springs for many ailments. Ordinary people combined a strong Christian faith with a wealth of time-honored superstitions.

Inspired initially by the fervor of the Catholic Counter-Reformation and then to some extent by the critical rationalism of the Enlightenment, parish priests and Catholic hierarchies sought increasingly to "purify" popular religious practice and to detach that purified religion from everyday life in the eighteenth century. Thus one parish priest in France lashed out at his parishioners, claiming that they were "more superstitious than devout . . . and sometimes appear as baptized idolators."[15] French priests particularly denounced the "various remnants of paganism" found in popular bonfire ceremonies during Lent in which young men, "yelling and screaming like madmen," tried to jump over the bonfires in order to help the crops grow and protect themselves from illness. One priest saw rational Christians regressing into pagan animals—"the triumph of Hell and the shame of Christianity."[16]

In contrast with Protestant reformers, who had already used the power of the territorial state to crush such practices, many Catholic priests and bishops preferred a compromise between theological purity and the people's piety, perhaps realizing that the line between divine truth and mere superstition is not easily drawn. Thus the severity of the formal attack on popular Catholicism varied widely by country and region. Where authorities pursued purification vigorously, as in Austria under Joseph II, pious peasants saw only an incomprehensible attack on the true faith and drew back in anger. Their reaction dramatized the growing tension between the educated elites and the common people.

Leisure and Recreation

The combination of religious celebration and popular recreation seen in festivals and processions was most strikingly displayed at Carnival, a time of reveling and excess in Catholic and Mediterranean Europe. Carnival preceded Lent—the forty days of fasting and penitence before Easter—and for a few days in January or February a wild release of drinking, masquerading, and dancing reigned. A combination of plays, processions, and rowdy spectacles turned the established order upside-down. Peasants became nobles, fools turned into philosophers, and the rich were humbled. These once-a-year rituals gave people a much-appreciated chance to release their pent-up frustrations and aggressions before life returned to the usual pattern of leisure and recreation.

That pattern featured socializing in groups, for despite the spread of literacy the culture of the common people was largely oral rather than written. In the cold dark winter months families gathered around the fireplace to talk, sing, tell stories, do craftwork, and keep warm. In some parts of Europe, women gathered together in groups in someone's cottage to chat, sew, spin, and laugh. Sometimes a few young men would be invited so that the daughters (and mothers) could size up potential suitors in a supervised atmosphere. A favorite recreation of men was drinking and talking with buddies in public places. It was a sorry village that had no tavern. In addition to old favorites such as beer and wine, the common people turned with gusto toward cheap and potent hard liquor, which in the eighteenth century fell in price because of the greatly improved techniques for distilling grain.

Towns and cities offered a wide range of amusements. Participants had to pay for many of these because the eighteenth century saw a sharp increase in the commercialization of leisure-time activities—a trend that continues to this day. Urban fairs featured prepared foods, acrobats, freak shows, open-air performances, optical illusions, and the like. Such entertainments attracted a variety of social classes. So did the growing number of commercial, profit-oriented spectator sports. These ranged from traveling circuses and horse races to boxing matches and bullfights. Sports heroes such as hefty heavyweight champions and haughty matadors made their appearance on the historical scene.

"Blood sports," such as bullbaiting and cockfighting, remained popular with the masses. In bullbaiting, a bull, usually chained to a stake in the courtyard of an inn, was attacked by ferocious dogs for the amusement of the innkeeper's guests. Eventually the maimed and tortured animal was slaughtered by a butcher and sold as meat. In a cockfight, two roosters, carefully trained by their owners and armed with razor-sharp steel spurs, slashed and clawed each other in a small ring until the victor won—and the loser died. An added attraction of cockfighting was that the screaming spectators could bet on the lightning-fast combat and its uncertain outcome.

In trying to place the vibrant popular culture of the common people in broad perspective, historians have stressed the growing criticism levied against it by the educated elites in the second half of the eighteenth century. These elites, which had previously shared the popular enthusiasm for religious festivals, Carnival, drinking in taverns, blood sports, and the like, now tended to see only superstition, sin, disorder, and vulgarity.[17] The resulting attack on popular culture, which had its more distant origins in the Protestant clergy's efforts to eliminate frivolity and superstition, was intensified as educated elites embraced the critical world-view of the Enlightenment. This shift in cultural attitudes was yet another aspect of the widening separation between the common people and the educated public. The mutual hostility that this separation engendered played an important role in the emergence of sharp class conflict in the era of the French and the Industrial Revolutions.

Cockfighting in England This engraving by William Hogarth (1697–1764) satirizes the popular taste for blood sports, which Hogarth despised and lampooned in his famous *Four Stages of Cruelty*. The central figure in the wildly excited gathering is a blind nobleman, who actually existed and seldom missed a fight. Notice the steel spurs on the birds' legs. *(Source: Courtesy of Trustees of the British Museum)*

SUMMARY

In recent years, imaginative research has greatly increased the specialist's understanding of ordinary life and social patterns in the past. The human experience as recounted by historians has become richer and more meaningful, and many mistaken ideas have fallen by the wayside. This has been particularly true of eighteenth-century, predominately agrarian Europe, which combined a fascinating mixture of continuity and change.

The life of the people remained primarily rural and oriented toward the local community. Tradition, routine, and well-established codes of behavior framed much of the everyday experience of the typical villager. Thus just as the three-field agricultural cycle and its pattern of communal rights had determined traditional patterns of grain production, so did community values in the countryside strongly encourage a late age for marriage, a low rate of illegitimate births, and a strict attitude toward children. Patterns of recreation and leisure, from churchgoing and religious festivals to sewing and drinking in groups, also reflected and reinforced community ties and values. Many long-standing ideas and beliefs, ranging from obscure religious customs to support for fair prices, remained strong forces and sustained continuity in popular life.

Yet powerful forces also worked for change. Many of these came from outside and above, from the aggressive capitalists, educated elites, and government officials discussed in the last two chapters. Closely knit villages began to lose control over families and marital practices, as could be seen in the earlier, more romantic marriages of cottage workers and in the beginning of the explosion in illegitimate births. Although the new, less rigorous attitudes toward children that were emerging in elite culture did not reach the common people, the elite belief in the usefulness of some education did result in growing popular literacy. The grain-based diet became more varied with the grudging acceptance of the potato, and the benefits of the spectacular conquest of smallpox began to reach the common people in the late eighteenth century. Finally, the common people found that their beliefs and customs were being increasingly attacked by educated elites, which thought they knew best. The popular reaction to these attacks generally remained muted in the eighteenth century, but the common people and their advocates would offer vigorous responses and counterattacks in the revolutionary era (see Chapter 23).

NOTES

1. Quoted in S. Chapman, *The Lancashire Cotton Industry* (Manchester, Eng.: Manchester University Press, 1903), p. 13.
2. Quoted in J. M. Beattie, "The Criminality of Women in Eighteenth-Century England," *Journal of Social History* 8 (Summer 1975): 86.
3. W. L. Langer, "Infanticide: A Historical Survey," *History of Childhood Quarterly* 1 (Winter 1974): 357.
4. Quoted in R. Cobb, *The Police and the People: French Popular Protest, 1789–1820* (Oxford: Clarendon Press, 1970), p. 238.
5. M. Segalen, *Love and Power in the Peasant Family: Rural France in the Nineteenth Century* (New York: Basil Blackwell, 1983), p. 41. The passage cited here has been edited into the past tense.
6. G. Gullickson, *Spinners and Weavers of Auffay: Rural Industry and the Sexual Division of Labor in a French Village, 1750–1850* (Cambridge: Cambridge University Press, 1986), p. 186. See also L. A. Tilly, J. W. Scott, and M. Cohen, "Women's Work and European Fertility Patterns," *Journal of Interdisciplinary History* 6 (Winter 1976): 447–476.
7. Quoted in B. W. Lorence, "Parents and Children in Eighteenth-Century Europe," *History of Childhood Quarterly* 2 (Summer 1974): 1–2.
8. Quoted ibid., pp. 13, 16.
9. E. Kennedy, *A Cultural History of the French Revolution* (New Haven, Conn.: Yale University Press, 1989), p. 47.
10. Quoted in L. S. King, *The Medical World of the Eighteenth Century* (Chicago: University of Chicago Press, 1958), p. 320.
11. Quoted in R. Sand, *The Advance to Social Medicine* (London: Staples Press, 1952), pp. 86–87.
12. Quoted in K. Pinson, *Pietism as a Factor in the Rise of German Nationalism* (New York: Columbia University Press, 1934), p. 13.
13. Quoted ibid., pp. 43–44.
14. Quoted in S. Andrews, *Methodism and Society* (London: Longmans, Green, 1970), p. 327.
15. Quoted in I. Woloch, *Eighteenth-Century Europe: Tradition and Progress, 1715–1789* (New York: Norton, 1982), p. 292.
16. Quoted in T. Tackett, *Priest and Parish in Eighteenth-Century France* (Princeton, N.J.: Princeton University Press, 1977), p. 214.

17. Woloch, *Eighteenth-Century Europe,* pp. 220–221; see also pp. 214–220.

SUGGESTED READING

Though long ignored in many general histories of the world, social topics of the kind considered in this chapter have come into their own in recent years. The reader is strongly advised to take time to look through recent volumes of journals such as *Journal of Social History, Past and Present, History of Childhood Quarterly,* and *Journal of Interdisciplinary History.* In addition, the number of book-length studies has expanded rapidly and continues to do so.

Two fine books on the growth of population are C. Cipolla's short and lively *The Economic History of World Population* (1962) and T. McKeown's scholarly *The Modern Rise of Population* (1977). W. McNeill, *Plagues and Peoples* (1976), is also noteworthy. B. H. Slicher van Bath, *The Agrarian History of Western Europe, A.D. 500–1850* (1963), is a wide-ranging general introduction to the gradual transformation of European agriculture. J. Blum, *The End of the Old Order in Rural Europe* (1978), is an impressive comparative study. Two recommended and complementary studies on landowning nobilities are R. Forster, *The Nobility of Toulouse in the Eighteenth Century* (1960), and G. E. Mingay, *English Landed Society in the Eighteenth Century* (1963). E. L. R. Ladurie, *The Peasants of Languedoc* (1976), a brilliant and challenging study of rural life in southern France for several centuries, complements J. Goody et al., eds., *Family and Inheritance: Rural Society in Western Europe, 1200–1800* (1976). Life in small-town preindustrial France comes alive in P. Higonnet, *Pont-de-Montvert: Social Structure and Politics in a French Village, 1700–1914* (1971), and O. Hufton deals vividly and sympathetically with rural migration, work, women, and much more in *The Poor in Eighteenth-Century France* (1974). F. Braudel, *Civilization and Capitalism, 15th–18th Century* (1981–1984), is a monumental and highly recommended three-volume synthesis of social and economic development. Another exciting work is J. Nef, *War and Human Progress* (1968), which examines the impact of war on economic and industrial development in European history between about 1500 and 1800 and may be compared with M. Gutmann, *War and Rural Life in the Early Modern Low Countries* (1980).

Among general introductions to the history of the family, women, and children, J. Casey, *The History of the Family* (1989), is recommended. P. Laslett, *The World We Have Lost* (1965), is an exciting, pioneering investigation of England before the Industrial Revolution, though further research has weakened some of his conclusions. L. Stone, *The Family, Sex and Marriage in England, 1500–1800* (1977), is a provocative general interpretation, and L. Tilly and J. Scott, *Women, Work and Family* (1978), is excellent. Two valuable works on women, both with good bibliographies, are M. Boxer and J. Quataert, eds., *Connecting Spheres: Women in the Western World, 1500 to the Present* (1987), and R. Bridenthal, C. Koonz, and S. Stuard, eds., *Becoming Visible: Women in European History,* 2d ed. (1987). P. Ariès, *Centuries of Childhood: A Social History of Family Life* (1962), is another stimulating study. E. Shorter, *The Making of the Modern Family* (1975), is a lively, controversial interpretation, which should be compared with the excellent study by M. Segalen, *Love and Power in the Peasant Family: Rural France in the Nineteenth Century* (1983). T. Rabb and R. I. Rothberg, eds., *The Family in History* (1973), is a good collection of articles dealing with both Europe and the United States. A. MacFarlane, *The Family Life of Ralph Josselin* (1970), is a brilliant re-creation of the intimate family circle of a seventeenth-century English clergyman who kept a detailed diary; MacFarlane's *Origins of English Individualism: The Family, Property and Social Transition* (1978) is a major work. I. Pinchbeck and M. Hewitt, *Children in English Society* (1973), is a good introduction. B. Lorence-Kot, *Child-Rearing and Reform: A Study of Nobility in Eighteenth-Century Poland* (1985), stresses the harshness of parental discipline.

Various aspects of sexual relationships are treated imaginatively by M. Foucault, *The History of Sexuality* (1981), and R. Wheaton and T. Hareven, eds., *Family and Sexuality in French History* (1980). L. Moch, *Moving Europeans: Migration in Western Europe Since 1650* (1992), offers a rich, human, and highly recommended account of the movements of millions of ordinary people. J. Burnett, *A History of the Cost of Living* (1969), has a great deal of interesting information about what people spent their money on in the past, and complements J. C. Drummond and A. Wilbraham, *The Englishman's Food: A History of Five Centuries of English Diet,* 2d ed. (1958). J. Knyveton, *Diary of a Surgeon in the Year 1751–1752* (1937), gives a contemporary's unforgettable picture of both eighteenth-century medicine and social customs, as do D. Porter and R. Porter, *Patient's Progress: Doctors and Doctoring in Eighteenth-Century England* (1989), and M. Romsey, *Professional and Popular Medicine in France, 1770–1830: The Social World of Medical Practice* (1988). Good introductions to the evolution of medical practices are B. Ingles, *History of Medicine* (1965); O. Bettmann, *A Pictorial History of Medicine* (1956); and L. King, *The Medical World of the Eight-*

eenth Century (1958). W. Boyd, *History of Western Education* (1966), is a standard survey; R. Houston, *Literacy in Early Modern Europe: Culture and Education, 1500–1800* (1988), is brief and engaging.

The study of popular culture is expanding. Among older studies, M. George, *London Life in the Eighteenth Century* (1965), is a delight, and D. Roche, *The People of Paris: An Essay in Popular Culture in the 18th Century* (1987), presents an unforgettable portrait of the Paris poor. I. Woloch, *Eighteenth-Century Europe: Tradition and Progress, 1715–1789* (1982), includes a survey of popular culture and a good bibliography; E. Kennedy, *A Cultural History of the French Revolution* (1989), beautifully captures rural and urban attitudes in France before and during the French Revolution. R. Malcolmson, *Popular Recreation in English Society, 1700–1850* (1973), provides a colorful account of boxers, bettors, bullbaiting, and more. L. Hunt, *The New Cultural History* (1989), provides an engaging discussion of conceptual issues. G. Rude, *The Crowd in History, 1730–1848* (1964), is an influential effort to see politics and popular protest from below. An important series edited by R. Forster and O. Ranuum considers neglected social questions such as diet, abandoned children, and deviants, as does P. Burke's excellent study, *Popular Culture in Early Modern Europe* (1978). J. Gillis, *For Better, for Worse: Marriage in Britain Since 1500* (1985), and R. Philips, *Untying the Knot: A Short History of Divorce* (1991), are good introductions to institutional changes.

Good works on religious life include Tackett, cited in the Notes; J. Delumeau, *Catholicism Between Luther and Voltaire: A New View of the Counter-Reformation* (1977); B. Semmel, *The Methodist Revolution* (1973); and J. Bettey, *Church and Community: The Parish Church in English Life* (1979).

LISTENING TO THE
PAST

A New Way to Educate Children

Emile, by Jean-Jacques Rousseau, is one of history's most original books. Sometimes called a declaration of rights for children, Emile *challenged existing patterns of child rearing and pleaded for humane treatment of children.*

Rousseau's work also had a powerful impact on theories of education. As the following passage suggests, Emile *argued that education must shield the unspoiled child from the corrupting influences of civilization and allow the child to develop naturally and spontaneously. It is eloquent testimony to Rousseau's troubled life that he neglected his own children and placed all five of them in orphanages.*

Rousseau believed that the sexes were by nature intended for different occupations. Thus Emile might eventually tackle difficult academic subjects, but Sophie, his future wife in the book, needed to learn only how to manage the home and be a good mother and an obedient wife. The idea that girls and boys should be educated to operate in "separate spheres" was to gain wide acceptance in the nineteenth century.

A man must know many things which seem useless to a child, but need the child learn, or can he indeed learn, all that the man must know? Try to teach the child what is of use to a child and you will find that it takes all his time. Why urge him to the studies of an age he may never reach, to the neglect of those studies which meet his present needs? "But," you ask, "will it not be too late to learn what he ought to know when the time comes to use it?" I cannot tell; but this I do know, it is impossible to teach it sooner, for our real teachers are experience and emotion, and man will never learn what befits a man except under its own conditions. A child knows he must become a man; all the ideas he may have as to man's place in life are so many opportunities for his instruction, but he should remain in complete ignorance of those ideas which are beyond his grasp. My whole book is one continued argument in support of this fundamental principle of education.

As soon as we have contrived to give our pupil [Emile] an idea of the word "useful," we have got an additional means of controlling him, for this word makes a great impression on him, provided that its meaning for him is a meaning relative to his own age, and provided he clearly sees its relation to his own well-being. . . . "What is the use of that?" In the future this is the sacred formula, the formula by which he and I test every action of our lives. . . .

I do not like verbal explanations. Young people pay little heed to them, nor do they remember them. Things! Things! I cannot repeat it too often. We lay too much stress upon words; we teachers babble, and our students follow our example.

Suppose we are studying the course of the sun and the way to find our bearings, when all at once Emile interrupts me with the question, "What is the use of that?" What a fine lecture I might give [going on and on]! . . . When I have finished I shall have shown myself a regular pedant, I shall have made a great display of learning, and not one single idea has he understood. . . .

But Emile is educated in a simpler fashion. We take so much pains to teach him a difficult idea that he will have heard nothing of all this. At the first word he does not understand, he will run away, he will prance about room, and leave me to speechify by myself. Let us seek a more commonplace explanation; my scientific learning is of no use to him.

We were observing the position of the forest to the north of Montmorency when he interrupted me with the usual question, "What is the use of that?" "You are right," I said. "Let us take time to think it over, and if we find it is no use we will drop it, for we only want useful games." We find something else to do and geography is put aside for the day.

Next morning I suggest a walk; there is nothing he would like better; children are always ready to run about, and he is a good walker. We climb up to the forest, we wander through its clearings and lose ourselves. . . . At last we [are exhausted and] sit down to rest and to consider our position. I assume that Emile has been educated like an ordinary child. He does not think, he begins to cry; he has no idea we are close to Montmorency, which is hidden from our view by a mere thicket. . . .

Jean-Jacques. "My dear Emile, what shall we do to get out?"

Emile. "I am sure I do not know. I am tired, I am hungry, I am thirsty, I cannot go any further."

Jean-Jacques. "Do you suppose I am any better off? I would cry too if I could make my lunch off tears. Crying is no use, we must look about us. What time is it?"

Emile. "It is noon and I am so hungry!"

Jean-Jacques. "I am so hungry too. . . . Unluckily my dinner won't come to find me. It is twelve o'clock. This time yesterday we were observing the position of the forest from Montmorency. If only we could see the position of Montmorency from the forest—"

Emile. "But yesterday we could see the forest, and here we cannot see the town."

Jean-Jacques. "That is just it. If we could only find it without seeing it. . . . Did not we say the forest was—"

Emile. "North of Montmorency."

Jean-Jacques. "Then Montmorency must lie—"

Emile. "South of the forest."

Jean-Jacques. "We know how to find the north at midday."

Emile. "Yes, by the direction of the shadows."

Jean-Jacques. "But the south?"

Emile. "What shall we do?"

Jean-Jacques. "The south is opposite the north."

Emile. "That is true; we need only find the opposite of the shadows. That is the south! That is the south! Montmorency must be over there! Let us look for it there!"

Jean-Jacques. "Perhaps you are right; let us follow this path through the wood."

This illustration depicts children learning about the five senses. *(Source: Caroline Buckler)*

Emile. (Clapping his hands.) "Oh, I can see Montmorency! there it is, quite plain, just in front of us! Come to lunch, come to dinner, make haste! Astronomy is some use after all."

Be sure that he thinks this if he does not say it; no matter which, provided I do not say it myself. He will certainly never forget this day's lesson as long as he lives, while if I had only led him to think of all this at home, my lecture would have been forgotten the next day. Teach by doing whenever you can, and only fall back upon words when doing is out of the question.

Questions for Analysis

1. What criticism did Rousseau direct at the social and educational practices of his time?

2. How did Rousseau propose to educate his pupil?

3. Do you think Rousseau's plan appealed to peasants and urban workers in the eighteenth century? Why or why not?

4. In what ways did Rousseau's plan of education and his assumptions about human nature reflect some major ideas of the Enlightenment?

Source: Slightly adapted from J.-J. Rousseau, *Emile, or Education,* trans. B. Foxley (New York: E. P. Dutton, 1911), pp. 141–144.

20

Africa, 1400–1800

This bronze figure of a hornblower was created by a royal artisan for the court of Benin (A.D. 1500–1700). *(Source: Courtesy of the Trustees of the British Museum)*

African states and societies of the fifteenth through eighteenth centuries comprised a wide variety of languages, cultures, and kinds of economic and political development. Modern European intrusion into Africa beginning in the fifteenth century led to the transatlantic slave trade, one of the great forced migrations in world history. Africa made a substantial, though involuntary, contribution to the building of the West's industrial civilization. In the seventeenth century, an increasing desire for sugar in Europe resulted in an increasing demand for slave labor in South America and the West Indies. In the eighteenth century, Western technological changes created a demand for cotton and other crops that required extensive human labor. As a result, the West's "need" for slaves from Africa increased dramatically.

Africa's relationship with Asia, the Islamic world, and the West stretches back a very long time, but only recently have anthropologists, economists, and historians begun to ask critical questions about African societies in early modern times.

- What kinds of economic and social structures did African societies have?
- What impact did Islam have on African societies?
- What kinds of literary sources survive?
- What role did slavery play in African societies before European intrusion?
- What were the geographical and societal origins of the slaves involuntarily shipped to America and to Asia?

This chapter explores these questions.

SENEGAMBIA AND BENIN

In Africa in the mid-fifteenth century, there were societies held together by family or kinship ties, and there were kingdoms and states ruled by princes who governed defined areas through bureaucratic hierarchies. Along the 2,000-mile west coast between Senegambia and the northeastern shore of the Gulf of Guinea, a number of kingdoms flourished. Because much of that coastal region is covered by tropical rain forest, in contrast to the western Sudan, it is called the West African Forest Region (Map 20.1). The Senegambian states in the north possessed a homogeneous culture and a common history. For centuries Senegambia—named for the Senegal and Gambia Rivers—had served as an important entrepôt for desert caravan contact with the Islamic civilizations of North Africa and the Middle East. Through the transatlantic slave trade, Senegambia contributed heavily to New World population in the early seventeenth century. That trade brought Senegambia into contact with the Americas and Europe. Thus Senegambia felt the impact of Islamic culture to the north and of European influences from the maritime West.

In the thirteenth century, the kingdoms of Ghana and Mali had incorporated parts of Senegambia. Mali's influence disintegrated after 1450, and successor kingdoms that were independent but connected to one another through family ties emerged. Stronger states rose and temporarily exercised power over weaker ones.

Scholars are still exploring the social and political structures of the various Senegambian states. The peoples of Senegambia spoke Wolof, Serer, and Pulaar, which are all members of the West African language group. Both the Wolof-speakers and the Serer-speakers had clearly defined social classes: royalty, nobility, warriors, peasants, low-caste artisans such as blacksmiths and leatherworkers, and slaves. Slaves were individuals who were pawned for debt, house servants who could not be sold, and people who were acquired through war or purchase. Senegambian slavery varied from society to society but generally was not a benign institution. In some places the treatment of slaves was as harsh as treatment in the Western world later would be. However, many Senegambian slaves were not considered property to be bought and sold, and some served as royal advisers and enjoyed great power and prestige.[1]

The king of the Wolof was elected by the nobility. After his election the king immediately acquired authority and a special religious charisma. He commanded contingents of soldier-slaves and appointed village chiefs. The king gained his revenue from the chiefs, from merchants, and from taxes levied on defeated peoples.[2] The Wolof had a well-defined government hierarchy.

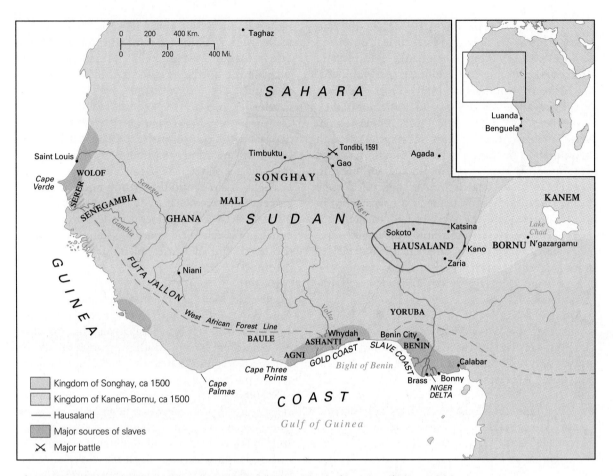

MAP 20.1 West African Kingdoms and the Slave Trade from ca 1500 to 1800
Consider the role that rivers and other geographical factors played in the develop-
ment of the West African slave trade. Why were Luanda and Benguela the logical
Portuguese source for slaves?

Among the stateless societies of Senegambia,
where kinship and lineage groups tended to fragment communities, age-grade systems evolved.
Age-grades were groups of men and women whom
the society initiated into adulthood at the same
time. Age-grades cut across family ties, created
community-wide loyalties, and provided a means
of local law enforcement, because the group was
responsible for the behavior of all its members.

The typical Senegambian community was a small
self-supporting agricultural village of closely related families. Custom assigned a high value to cultivation of the land—the shared objective of the
group. Fields were cut from the surrounding forest, and the average farm of six or eight acres sup-

ported a moderate-size family. Often the family
worked the land for a common harvest; sometimes
individuals had their own private fields. Millet and
sorghum were the staple grains in northern Senegambia; farther south, forest dwellers cultivated
yams as a staple. Senegambians supplemented their
diet with plantains, beans, and bananas, fish, oys-
ters, and small game such as rabbits and monkeys.
Along the Guinea coast rice was the basic cereal,
and okra, onions, melons, and pepper spiced the
regular diet. Frequent fairs in neighboring villages
served as markets for the exchange of produce and
opportunities for receiving outside news and social
diversion. As one scholar has put it, "Life was simple, government largely limited to the settlement

The Oba of Benin   The walls of the Oba's palace were decorated with bronze plaques that may date to the period from the sixteenth to the eighteenth century. This plaque vividly conveys the Oba's power, majesty, and authority. The necklace (or choker) is his symbol of royalty. Attendants hold up his hands, and warriors raise shields over his head as sunshades. *(Source: The Metropolitan Museum of Art, The Michael C. Rocke-feller Memorial Collection, Gift of Nelson A. Rockefeller, 1965)*

of disputes by family heads or elders . . . social life centered on the ceremony accompanying birth, death, and family alliance."[3]

The fifteenth and sixteenth centuries saw the emergence of the great forest kingdom of Benin (see Map 20.1) in what is now southern Nigeria. Although scholars still know little about Benin's origins, its history seems to have been character-ized by power struggles between the king and the nobility that neither side ever completely won. An elaborate court ceremonial exalted the position of the *oba,* or king, and brought stability to the state. In the later fifteenth century, the oba Ewuare played off his palace chiefs against the village chiefs and thereby maintained a balance of power. A great warrior, Ewuare strengthened his army and pushed Benin's borders as far as the Niger River on the east, westward into Yoruba country, and south to the Gulf of Guinea. During the late sixteenth and seventeenth centuries the office of the oba evolved from a warrior kingship to a position of spiritual leadership.

At its height in the late sixteenth century, Benin controlled a vast territory, and European visitors described a sophisticated society. According to a modern historian, the capital, Benin City, "was a stronghold twenty-five miles in circumference, protected by walls and natural defenses, containing an elaborate royal palace and neatly laid-out houses with verandas and balustrades, and divided by broad avenues and smaller intersecting streets."[4] Visitors also noted that Benin City was kept scrupulously clean and had no beggars and that public security was so effective that theft was unknown. The period also witnessed remarkable artistic creativity in ironwork, in carved ivory, and especially in bronze portrait busts. Over nine hundred brass plaques survive, providing important information about Benin court life, military triumphs, and cosmological ideas.

In 1485 the Portuguese and other Europeans in pursuit of trade began to appear in Benin. A small exchange in pepper and slaves developed but never acquired importance in the Benin economy. Nor did the Portuguese have much success in converting the staunchly animistic people to Christianity. Europe's impact on Benin was minimal. In the early eighteenth century, as tributary states and stronger neighbors nibbled at Benin's frontiers, the kingdom underwent a crisis. Benin, however, survived as an independent entity until the British conquered and burned Benin City in 1898.

❖ THE SUDAN: SONGHAY, KANEM-BORNU, AND HAUSALAND

The kingdom of Songhay, a successor state of Ghana and Mali, dominated the whole Niger region of the western and central Sudan (see Map 20.1). Muhammad Toure (1492–1528) completed the expansionist and administrative consolidation begun by his predecessors. Muhammad Toure's power rested on his successful military expeditions. From his capital at Gao he extended his lordship as far north as the salt-mining center at Taghaz in the mid-Sahara and as far east as Agada and Kano. A convert to Islam, Muhammad made a pilgrimage to Mecca. Impressed by what he saw there, he tried to bring about greater centralization in his own territories. In addition to building a strong army and improving taxation procedures, he re-

placed local Songhay officials with more efficient Arab ones in an effort to substitute royal institutions for ancient kinship ties.

What kind of economy existed in the Songhay Empire? What social structures? What role did women play in Songhay society? What is known of Songhay education and culture? The paucity of written records and of surviving artifacts prevent scholars from satisfactorily exploring these questions. Some information is provided by Leo Africanus (ca. 1465–1550), a Moroccan captured by pirates and given as a slave to Pope Leo X. Leo Africanus became a Christian, taught Arabic in Rome, and in 1526 published an account of his many travels, including a stay in the Songhay kingdom.

As a scholar Leo was naturally impressed by Timbuktu, the second city of the empire, which he visited in 1513. "Here [is] a great store of doctors, judges, priests, and other learned men, that are bountifully maintained at the King's court," Leo reported.[5] Many of these Islamic scholars had studied in Cairo and other centers of Muslim learning. They gave Timbuktu a reputation for intellectual sophistication, religious piety, and moral justice.

Songhay under Muhammad Toure seems to have enjoyed economic prosperity. Leo Africanus noted the abundant food supply, which was produced in the southern savanna and carried to Timbuktu by a large fleet of canoes controlled by the king. The Sudanese had large amounts of money to spend, and expensive North African and European luxuries were much in demand: clothes, copperware, glass and stone beads, perfumes, and horses. The existence of many shops and markets implies the development of an urban culture. At Timbuktu, merchants, scholars and judges, and artisans constituted a distinctive bourgeoisie. The presence of many foreign merchants, including Jews and Italians, gave the city a cosmopolitan atmosphere. Jews largely controlled the working of gold.

Slaves played a very important part in the economy of Songhay. On the royal farms scattered throughout the kingdom, slaves produced rice—the staple crop—for the royal granaries. Although slaves could possess their own slaves, land, and cattle, they could not bequeath any of this property; the king inherited all of it. Muhammad Toure greatly increased the number of royal slaves through raids on the pagans (non-Muslims). He

✳ **Queen Mother and Attendants**   As in Ottoman, Chinese, and European societies, so the mothers of rulers in Africa sometimes exercised considerable political power because of their influence on their sons. African kings granted the title "Queen Mother" as a badge of honor. The long beaded cap, called "chicken's beak," symbolizes her rank as do her elaborate neck jewelry and attendants. *(Source: Metropolitan Museum of Art. Gift of Mr. and Mrs. Klaus G. Perls, 1991)*

gave slaves to favorite Muslim scholars, who thus gained a steady source of income. Or the slaves were sold at the large market at Gao. Traders from North Africa bought them for sale in Cairo, Constantinople, Lisbon, Naples, Genoa, and Venice.

The kingdom of Songhay had considerable economic and cultural strengths, but it also had serious internal problems. Islamic institutions never took root in the countryside, and Muslim officials alienated the king from his people. Muhammad Toure's reforms were a failure. He governed a diverse group of peoples—Tuareg, Malinke, Fulani, as well as Songhai—who were often hostile to one another, and no cohesive element united them. Finally, the Songhai never developed an effective method of transferring power. Revolts, conspira-

cies, and palace intrigues followed the deaths of every king, and only three of the nine rulers in the dynasty begun by Muhammad Toure died natural deaths. Muhammad himself was murdered by one of his sons. His death began a period of political instability that led to the slow disintegration of the kingdom.[6]

In 1582 the sultanate of Morocco began to press southward in search of a greater share of the trans-Saharan trade. The people of Songhay, lacking effective leadership and believing the desert to be a sure protection against invasion, took no defensive precautions. In 1591 a Moroccan army of three thousand soldiers—many of whom were slaves of European origin equipped with European muskets—crossed the Sahara and inflicted a

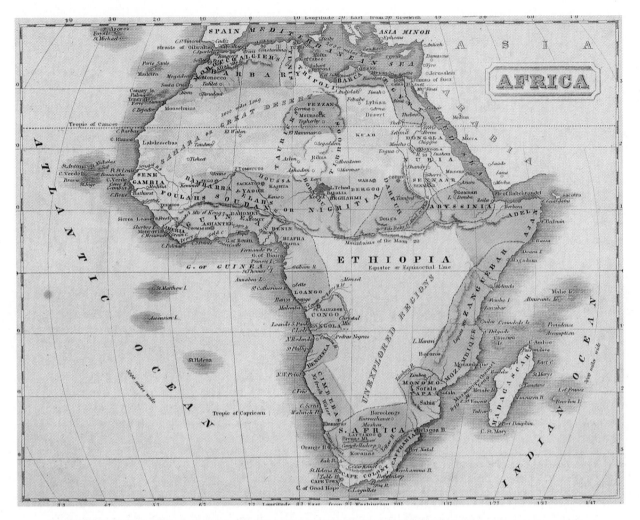

"Africa, 1829" For most of the nineteenth century, what Americans learned of African geography derived from "maps" such as this one, a perfect example of abysmal Western ignorance—or carelessness, since even seventeenth–century Portuguese and British traders knew that Luanda and Benguela are in Angola. Because of its errors, this "map" is now a collector's item. By comparing it to Maps 20.1 and 20.2, you should be able to discover at least ten serious mistakes. *(Source: A private collection)*

crushing defeat on the Songhai at Tondibi. This battle spelled the end of the Songhay Empire. Although a moderate-size kingdom lingered on in the south for a century or so and weak political units arose, not until the eighteenth century did kingdoms able to exercise wide authority emerge again.

To the east of Songhay lay the kingdoms of Kanem-Bornu and Hausaland (see Map 20.1). Under the dynamic military leader Idris Alooma (1571–1603), Kanem-Bornu subdued weaker peoples and gained jurisdiction over an extensive area. Well drilled and equipped with firearms, camel-mounted cavalry and a standing army decimated warriors fighting with spears and arrows. Idris Alooma perpetuated the feudal pattern of government in which lands were granted to able fighters in return for loyalty and the promise of future military assistance. Meanwhile, agriculture occupied most people, peasants and slaves alike. Kanem-Bornu shared in the trans-Saharan trade, shipping eunuchs and young girls to North Africa in return for horses and firearms. A devout Muslim, Idris Alooma elicited high praise from Ibn Fartura, who wrote a history of his reign called *The Kanem Wars:*

So he made the pilgrimage and visited Medina with delight. . . . Among the benefits which God . . . conferred upon the Sultan Idris Alooma was the acquisition of Turkish musketeers and numerous household slaves who became skilled in firing muskets. . . .

Among the most surprising of his acts was the stand he took against obscenity and adultery, so that no such thing took place openly in his time. Formerly the people had been indifferent to such offences. . . . In fact he was a power among his people and from him came their strength.

The Sultan was intent on the clear path laid down by the Qur'an . . . in all his affairs and actions.[7]

Idris Alooma built mosques at his capital city of N'gazargamu and substituted Muslim courts and Islamic law for African tribunals and ancient customary law. His eighteenth-century successors lacked his vitality and military skills, however, and the empire declined.

Between Songhay and Kanem-Bornu were the lands of the Hausa. An agricultural people living in small villages, the Hausa grew millet, sorghum, barley, rice, cotton, and citrus fruit and raised livestock. Some Hausa merchants carried on a heavy trade in slaves and kola nuts with North African communities across the Sahara. Obscure trading posts evolved into important Hausa city-states like Kano and Katsina, through which Islamic influences entered the region. Kano and Katsina became Muslim intellectual centers and in the fifteenth century attracted scholars from Timbuktu. The Muslim chronicler of the reign of King Muhammad Rimfa of Kano (r. 1463–1499) records that Muhammad introduced the Muslim practices of *purdah,* or seclusion of women, of the *idal-fitr,* or festival after the fast of Ramadan, and of assigning eunuchs to the high offices of state.[8] As in Songhay and Kanem-Bornu, however, Islam made no strong imprint on the mass of the Hausa people until the nineteenth century.

ETHIOPIA

At the beginning of the sixteenth century, the powerful East African Christian kingdom of Ethiopia extended from Massawa in the north to several tributary states in the south (Map 20.2). The ruling Solomonid Dynasty, however, faced serious troubles. Adal, a Muslim state along the southern base of the Red Sea, began incursions into Ethiopia, and in 1529 the Adal general Ahmad ibn-Ghazi inflicted a disastrous defeat on the Ethiopian emperor Lebna Dengel (r. 1508–1540). Ahmad followed up his victory with systematic devastation of the land, destruction of many Ethiopian artistic and literary works, and the forced conversion of thousands to Islam. Lebna Dengel fled to the mountains and appealed to Portugal for assistance. The Portuguese, eager for a share in the wealth of the East African coast and interested in the conversion of Ethiopia to Roman Catholicism, responded with a force of musketeers. In 1541 they decisively defeated the Muslims near Lake Tana.

No sooner had the Muslim threat ended than Ethiopia encountered three more dangers. The Galla, Cushitic-speaking peoples, moved northward in great numbers, occupying portions of Harar, Shoa, and Amhara. The Ethiopians could not defeat them militarily, and the Galla were not interested in assimilation. For the next two centuries the two peoples lived together in an uneasy truce. Simultaneous with the Galla migrations was the Ottoman Turks' seizure of Massawa and other coastal cities. Then the Jesuits arrived, eager to capitalize on earlier Portuguese support, and attempted to force Roman Catholicism on a proud people whose Coptic form of Christianity long antedated the European version. The overzealous Jesuit missionary Alphonse Mendez tried to revamp the Ethiopian liturgy, rebaptize the people, and replace ancient Ethiopian customs and practices with Roman ones. Since Ethiopian national sentiment was closely tied to Coptic Christianity, violent rebellion and anarchy ensued.

In 1633 the Jesuit missionaries were expelled. For the next two centuries hostility to foreigners, weak political leadership, and regionalism characterized Ethiopia. Civil conflicts between the Galla and the Ethiopians erupted continually. The Coptic church, though lacking strong authority, survived as the cornerstone of Ethiopian national identity.

THE SWAHILI CITY-STATES

The word *Swahili,* meaning "People of the Coast," refers to the people living along the East African coast and on the nearby islands. Their history, unlike that of most African peoples, exists in writing. By the eleventh century, the Swahili had accepted

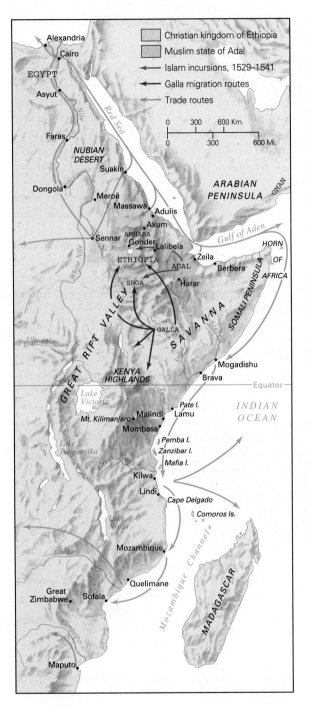

MAP 20.2 East Africa in the Sixteenth Century In early modern times, the Christian kingdom of Ethiopia, first isolated and then subjected to Muslim and European pressures, played an insignificant role in world affairs. But the East African city-states, which stretched from Sofola in the south to Mogadishu in the north, had powerfully important commercial relations with Mughal India, China, the Ottoman world, and southern Europe.

Islam, and "its acceptance was the factor that marked the acquisition of 'Swahili' identity: Islam gave the society coherent cultural form."[9] The Swahili language is studied today by North Americans who want to identify themselves as having African ancestry, but slaves shipped from East Africa came from inland, not from Swahili-speaking coastal peoples; virtually no Swahili people went to North America. As a people living on the shores of the Indian Ocean, the Swahili felt the influences of Indians, Indonesians, Persians, and especially Arabs.

Swahili civilization was overwhelmingly maritime. A fertile, well-watered, and intensely cultivated stretch of land no more than ten miles wide extends down the coast: it yielded rice, grains, citrus fruit, and cloves. The sea provided fish. But the considerable prosperity of the region rested on trade and commerce. The Swahili acted as middlemen in an Indian Ocean–East African protocapitalism, exchanging ivory, rhinoceros horn, tortoise shells, inlaid ebony chairs, copra (dried coconut meat that yields coconut oil), and inland slaves for Arabian and Persian perfumes and toilet articles, ink and paper, and for Indian textiles, beads, and iron tools. In the fifteenth century, the city-states of Mogadishu, Pate, Lamu, Mombasa, and especially Kilwa enjoyed a worldwide reputation for commercial prosperity.[10] These cities were cosmopolitan, and their standard of living was very high.

The arrival of the Portuguese explorer Vasco da Gama (see Map 16.1, page 517) in 1498 spelled the end of the Swahili cities' independence. Da Gama, lured by the spice trade, wanted to build a Portuguese maritime empire in the Indian Ocean, and between 1502 and 1507 the southern ports of Kilwa, Zanzibar, and Sofala fell before Portuguese guns and became Portuguese tributary states. The better-fortified northern cities, such as Mogadishu, survived as important entrepôts for goods to India.

The Portuguese victory in the south proved hollow, however. Rather than accept Portuguese commercial restrictions, the residents deserted the towns, and the town economies crumbled. Large numbers of Kilwa's people, for example, immigrated to northern cities. The flow of gold from inland mines to Sofala slowed to a trickle. Swahili passive resistance successfully prevented the Portuguese from gaining control of the local coastal trade.

After the intermittent bombardment of several cities, Portugal finally won an administrative

 **Saint George in Ethiopian Art** This image of a black Saint George slaying a dragon from a seventeenth-century Ethiopian manuscript attests to the powerful and pervasive Christian influence in Ethiopian culture. (*Source: The British Library*)

stronghold near Mombasa in 1589. Called Fort Jesus, it remained a Portuguese base for over a century. In the late seventeenth century, pressures from the northern European maritime powers—the Dutch, French, and English—aided greatly by the Arabs of Oman, combined with local African rebellions to bring about the collapse of Portuguese influence in Africa. A Portuguese presence remained only at Mozambique in the far south.

The Portuguese made no religious or cultural impact on the Swahili cities. Their sole effect was the cities' economic decline.

THE SLAVE TRADE

Slavery had a long history within Africa, and the transatlantic slave trade that began in the late fifteenth century is properly understood against that background. "Slavery was . . . fundamental to the social, political, and economic order of parts of the northern savanna, Ethiopia and the East African coast. . . . Enslavement was an organized activity, sanctioned by law and custom. Slaves were a principal commodity in trade, including the export

Dutch Colony, Cape of Good Hope Founded in 1657, by the mid-eighteenth century the Cape Colony had fifteen thousand inhabitants and may have been the largest European settlement on the African continent. Crews took on fresh provisions there, repaired their ships, and awaited favorable winds for crossing the Indian Ocean. *(Source: William Fehr Collection)*

sector, and slaves were important in the domestic sphere" as concubines, servants, soldiers, and ordinary laborers.[11]

Islam had heavily influenced African slavery. African rulers justified enslavement with the Muslim argument that prisoners of war could be sold; and, since captured peoples were considered chattel, they could be used in the same positions that prevailed in the Muslim world. Between 650 and 1600, black as well as white Muslims transported perhaps as many as 4.82 million black slaves across the trans-Saharan trade route.[12] When the transatlantic slave trade began, it represented little that was new.

The African slave trade, extending from the sixteenth to the nineteenth century and involving the forced migration of millions of human beings, represents one of the most inhumane, unjust, and tragic blots on the histories of human societies. The African diaspora immediately provokes a host of questions. What regions of Africa were the sources of slaves? What goods and business procedures were involved in the exchange of slaves? What were the economic, social, political, and demographic effects of the slave trades on African societies? In a period when the enslavement of peoples was dying out in Asian and European societies, when serfdom was declining in western Europe, why were *African* peoples enslaved, when land was so widely available and much of the African continent had a labor *shortage?*

The answer to the last question seems to lie in a technical problem related to African agriculture. Partly because of the tsetse fly, which causes sleeping sickness and other diseases, partly because of easily leached lateritic soils (containing high concentrations of oxides), farmers had great difficulty using draft animals. Tropical soils responded poorly to plowing, and most work had to be done with the hoe. Productivity, therefore, was low. Economists maintain that in most societies the value of a worker's productivity determines the value of his or her labor. In precolonial Africa, the individual's agricultural productivity was low, so his or her economic value to society was less than the economic value of a European peasant in Europe. *Slaves* in the Americas were more productive than free producers in Africa. And European slave dealers were very willing to pay a price higher than the value of an African's productivity in Africa.

The incidence of disease in the Americas also helps to explain the enslavement of Africans. Smallpox took a terrible toil on native Americans (see page 525), and between 30 percent and 50 percent of Europeans exposed to malaria succumbed to that sickness. Africans had developed some immunity to both diseases, and in the New World they experienced the lowest mortality rate of any people. Europeans wanted workers for mines and sugar cane plantations. A coerced (or slave) labor force proved easier to exploit than a wage labor force.[13] As the demand for sugar increased, as the technology for sugar production improved and shipping rates declined, the pressure for slave labor accelerated.

The search for a sea route to India led the Portuguese in the fifteenth century to explore the West African coast. Having "discovered" Brazil in 1500, the Portuguese founded a sugar colony at Bahia in 1551. Between 1551 and 1575, before the traffic to North America had gotten under way, the Portuguese delivered more African slaves to Brazil than would ever reach British North America (Table 20.1). Portugal essentially monopolized the slave trade until 1600 and continued to play a large role in the seventeenth century, though increasingly threatened by the Dutch, French, and English. From 1690 until the House of Commons abolished the slave trade in 1807, England was the leading carrier of African slaves.

Population density and supply conditions along the West African coast and the sailing time to New World markets determined the sources of slaves. As

TABLE 20.1 ESTIMATED SLAVE IMPORTS BY DESTINATION, 1451–1870

Destination	Estimated Total Slave Imports
British North America	399,000
Spanish America	1,552,100
British Caribbean	1,665,000
French Caribbean	1,600,200
Dutch Caribbean	500,000
Danish Caribbean	28,000
Brazil	3,646,800
Old World	175,000
	9,566,100

Source: P. D. Curtin, The Atlantic Slave Trade: A Census *(Madison, Wis.: University of Wisconsin Press, 1969), p. 268. Used with permission.*

the demand for slaves rose, slavers moved down the West African coast from Senegambia to the more densely populated hinterlands of the Bight of Benin and the Bight of Biafra (see Map 16.5, page 545). In the sixteenth and early seventeenth centuries, the Senegambian coast and the area near the mouth of the Congo River yielded the greatest numbers. By the late seventeenth century the British found the Ivory Coast region the most profitable territory. A century later the Bight of Benin and the Gold Coast had become the largest suppliers. The abundant supply of slaves in Angola, the region south of the Congo River, however, and the quick passage from Angola to Brazil and the Caribbean established that region as the major coast for Portuguese slavers.

Transatlantic wind patterns partly determined the routes of exchange. Shippers naturally preferred the swiftest crossing—that is, from the African port nearest the latitude of the intended

American destination. Thus Portuguese shippers carried their cargoes from Angola to Brazil, and British merchants sailed from the Bight of Benin to the Caribbean. The great majority of slaves were intended for the sugar and coffee plantations extending from the Caribbean islands to Brazil.[14]

Angola produced 26 percent of all African slaves and 70 percent of all Portuguese slaves. Trading networks extending deep into the interior culminated at two major ports on the Angolan coast, Luanda and Benguela (see inset to Map 20.1). Between the 1730s and 1770s Luanda shipped between 8,000 and 10,000 slaves each year; at the end of the eighteenth century Benguela's numbers equaled those of Luanda. In 1820, the peak year, 18,957 blacks left Luanda. The Portuguese acquired a few slaves through warfare but secured the vast majority through trade with African dealers. Whites did not participate in the inland markets.

Almost all Portuguese shipments went to satisfy the virtually insatiable Brazilian demand for slaves.[15] The transatlantic slave trade lasted for almost four centuries and involved the brutalization and exploitation of millions of human beings. Here is an excerpt from the report in 1793 of a Portuguese doctor with experience on the Middle Passage between Angola and Brazil:

When the slaves coming from many different parts of the interior reach the maritime ports of Africa, they are there once more traded for goods and merchandise. . . .

Here takes place the second round of hardships that these unlucky people are forced to suffer. . . . They are terribly handled and most scantily provided for . . . their human nature entirely overlooked. The dwelling place of the slave is simply the dirt floor of the compound, and he remains there exposed to harsh conditions and bad weather, and at night there are only a lean-to and some sheds . . . which they are herded into like cattle.

Their food continues scarce as before . . . limited at times to badly cooked beans, at other times to corn. . . . They also add to the diet a small amount of salted fish. . . .

They suffer in other ways. When they are first traded, they are made to bear the brand mark of the backlander who enslaved them, so that they can be recognized in case they run away. And when they reach a port . . . , they are branded on the right breast with the coat of arms of the king and nation, of whom they have become vassals. . . . This mark is made with a hot silver instrument in the act of paying the king's duties, and this brand mark is called a carimbo.

They are made to bear one more brand mark. This one is ordered by their private master, under whose name they are transported to Brazil. . . .

In this miserable and deprived condition the terrified slaves remain for weeks and months, and the great number of them who die is unspeakable. With some ten or twelve thousand arriving at Luanda each year, it often happens that only six or seven thousand are finally transported to Brazil. . . .

Shackled in the holds of ships, the black slaves . . . are far more deprived than when on land. First of all, with two or three hundred slaves placed under the deck, there is hardly room enough to draw a breath. . . . The captains, aware of their own (financial) interests, recognize the seriousness of the problem, and they try to remedy it to some extent. . . . Each day they order a certain number of slaves brought on deck in chains to get some fresh air, not allowing more because of their fear of rebellion. . . .

Second, the slaves are afflicted with a very short ration of water, of poor quality and lukewarm because of the climate—hardly enough to water their mouths. The suffering that this causes is extraordinary, and their dryness and thirst cause epidemics which, beginning with one person, soon spread to many others. Thus, after only a few days at sea, they start to throw the slaves into the ocean.

Third, they are kept in a state of constant hunger. Their small ration of food, brought over from Brazil on the outward voyage, is spoiled and damaged. . . . They add to each ration a small portion of noxious fish from the Atlantic Ocean, which decays during the voyage.[16]

Unlike Great Britain, France, and the Netherlands, Portugal did not have a strong mercantile class involved in slaving in the eighteenth century. Instead, the Portuguese colony of Brazil provided the ships, capital, and goods for the slave trade. Credit played a major role in the trade: Brazilian-controlled firms in Luanda extended credit to African operators, who had to make payments in slaves six or eight months later. Portuguese ironware and wine, Brazilian tobacco and brandies, European and Asian textiles, firearms, and beads were the main goods exchanged for slaves. All commodities entered Angola from Brazil. The Luandan (or Benguelan) merchants pegged the value of the goods to the value of prime young slaves but then undervalued the worth of the slaves and over-priced the goods. As a result, the African operators frequently ended up in debt to the merchants.

Although the demand was great, Portuguese merchants in Angola and Brazil sought to maintain only a steady trickle of slaves from the African interior to Luanda and across the ocean to Bahia and Rio de Janeiro: a flood of slaves would have depressed the American market. Rio, the port capital through which most slaves passed, commanded the Brazilian trade. Planters and mine operators from the provinces traveled to Rio to buy slaves. Between 1795 and 1808, approximately 10,000 An-

golans per year stood in the Rio slave market. In 1810 the figure rose to 18,000; in 1828 it reached 32,000.[17]

The English ports of London, Bristol, and particularly Liverpool dominated the British slave trade. In the eighteenth century Liverpool was the world's greatest slave-trading port. In all three cities, small and cohesive merchant classes exercised great public influence. The cities also had huge stores of industrial products for export, growing shipping industries, and large amounts of ready cash for investment abroad. Merchants generally formed partnerships to raise capital and to share the risks; each voyage was a separate enterprise or venture.

City of Luanda, Angola   Founded by the Portuguese in 1575, Luanda was a center of the huge slave trade to Brazil. In this eighteenth-century print, offices and warehouses line the streets, and (right foreground) slaves are dragged to the ships for transportation to America. (*Source: New York Public Library, Astor, Lenox, and Tilden Foundations*)

Ashanti Staff Top In the early eighteenth century, the Ashanti of central Ghana expanded northward, subdued various peoples, and established a powerful successor state to the medieval African kingdoms of Ghana and Mali. The gold trade was the linchpin of its economic and political power. A splendid example of the Ashanti's superb skill in goldworking, this staff top reflects the region's proverbial wealth. *(Source: Lee Boltin Picture Library)*

Slaving ships from Bristol searched the Gold Coast, the Bight of Benin, Bonny, and Calabar. The ships of Liverpool drew slaves from Gambia, the Windward Coast, and the Gold Coast. To Africa, British ships carried textiles, gunpowder and flint, beer and spirits, British and Irish linens, and woolen cloth. A collection of goods was

grouped together into what was called the "sorting." An English sorting might include bolts of cloth, firearms, alcohol, tobacco, and hardware; this batch of goods would be traded for an individual slave or a quantity of gold, ivory, or dyewood. When Europeans added a markup for profit, Africans followed suit. Currency was not exchanged; it served as a standard of value and a means of keeping accounts.[18]

European traders had two systems for exchange. First, especially on the Gold Coast, they established factory-forts. These fortified trading posts were expensive to maintain but proved useful for fending off rival Europeans. In the second, or shore, method of trading, European ships sent boats ashore or invited African dealers to bring traders and slaves out to the ships. The English captain John Adams, who made ten voyages to Africa between 1786 and 1800, described the shore method of trading at Bonny:

This place is the wholesale market for slaves, as not fewer than 20,000 are annually sold here; 16,000 of whom are natives of one nation called Ibo. . . . Fairs where the slaves of the Ibo nation are obtained are held every five or six weeks at several villages, which are situated on the banks of the rivers and creeks in the interior, and to which the African traders of Bonny resort to purchase them.

. . . The traders augment the quantity of their merchandise, by obtaining from their friends, the captains of the slave ships, a considerable quantity of goods on credit. . . . Evening is the period chosen for the time of departure, when they proceed in a body, accompanied by the noise of drums, horns, and gongs. At the expiration of the sixth day, they generally return bringing with them 1,500 or 2,000 slaves, who are sold to Europeans the evening after their arrival, and taken on board the ships. . . .

It is expected that every vessel, on her arrival at Bonny, will fire a salute the instant the anchor is let go, as a compliment to the black monarch who soon afterwards makes his appearance in a large canoe, at which time, all those natives who happen to be alongside the vessel are compelled to proceed in their canoes to a respectful distance, and make way for his Majesty's barge. After a few compliments to the captain, he usually enquires after brother George, meaning the King of England, George III, and hopes he and his family are well. He is not pleased unless he is re-

galed with the best the ship affords. . . . His power is absolute; and the surrounding country, to a considerable distance, is subject to his dominion.[19]

The shore method of buying slaves allowed the ship to move easily from market to market. The final prices of the slaves depended on their ethnic origin, their availability when the shipper arrived, and their physical health when offered for sale in the West Indies or the North or South American colonies.

Meanwhile, according to one scholar, the northbound trade in slaves across the Sahara "continued without serious disruption until the late nineteenth century, and in a clandestine way and on a much reduced scale it survived well into the twentieth century."[20] The present scholarly consensus is that the trans-Saharan slave trade in the seventeenth and eighteenth centuries was never as important as the transatlantic trade.

The Savanna and the Horn regions of East Africa experienced a great expansion of the slave trade in the late eighteenth century, and in the first half of the nineteenth century, slave exports from these areas and from the eastern coast amounted to perhaps 30,000 a year. Why this demand? Merchants and planters wanted slaves to work the sugar plantations on the Mascarene Islands, located east of Madagascar, the clove plantations on Zanzibar and Pemba, the food plantations along the Kenya coast. The eastern coast also exported slaves for the Americas, when Brazilian businessmen significantly increased their purchases. Thus, in the late eighteenth and early nineteenth centuries, precisely when the slave trade to North America and the Caribbean declined, the Eastern and Asian markets expanded. Only with colonial conquest by Great Britain, Germany, and Italy after 1870 did suppression begin. Slavery, however, persists. Recent reports (1994) by the United Nations International Labor Organization, the British Anti-Slavery Society, and the U.S. Department of State reveal slavery on an extensive scale in Mauritania (northwestern Africa) and in the Sudan (eastern Africa).[21] The past isn't dead; it's not even past.

Supplying slaves for the foreign market was in the hands of a small wealthy merchant class or was a state monopoly. Gathering a band of raiders and the capital for equipment, guides, tolls, and supplies involved considerable expense. By contemporary standards, slave raiding was a costly operation. Only black entrepreneurs with sizable capital and labor could afford to finance and direct raiding drives. They exported slaves because the profits on exports were greater than the profits to be made from using labor in the domestic economy:

The export price of slaves never rose to the point where it became cheaper for Europeans to turn to alternative sources of supply, and it never fell to the point where it caused more than a temporary check to the trade. . . . The remarkable expansion of the slave trade in the eighteenth century provides a horrific illustration of the rapid response of producers in an underdeveloped economy to price incentives.[22]

Other factors that might result in slavery were kidnapping; judicial enslavement by the state for serious crimes, such as murder or threats to royal authority; state demand for slaves as tribute from subject peoples; destitution following a natural disaster, such as famine or plague, which might force parents to sell "surplus" children; and, as in Russia or China, severe debt, which might lead a person to surrender his or her freedom in return for settlement of the debt. Europeans initiated the Atlantic slave trade, but its continuation was made possible through an alliance between European shippers and African suppliers.

African peoples, captured and forcibly brought to the Americas, played an integral part in the formation of the Atlantic world. They had an enormous impact on the economics of the Portuguese and Spanish colonies of South America and in the Dutch, French, and British colonies of the Caribbean and North America. For example, in the sugar plantations of Mexico and the Caribbean, on the cotton, rice, and tobacco plantations of North America, in the silver and gold mines of Peru and Mexico, slaves of African descent not only worked in the mines and fields, they filled skilled, supervisory, and administrative positions, as well as performing domestic service. African slaves also transmitted their cultures to the Americas. Through language, religion, music, and art they contributed to the cultures of their particular regions and to the development of an Afro-Atlantic civilization.[23]

What economic impact did European trade have on African societies? Africans possessed technology well suited to their environment. Over the centuries they had cultivated a wide variety of plant foods, developed plant and animal husbandry techniques, and mined, smelted, and otherwise worked a great variety of metals. Apart from firearms, American tobacco and rum, and the cheap brandy brought by the Portuguese, European goods presented no novelty to Africans. What made foreign products desirable to Africans was their price. Traders of hand-woven Indian cotton textiles, Venetian imitations of African beads, and iron bars from European smelters could undersell African manufacturers. Africans exchanged slaves, ivory, gold, pepper, and animal skins for those goods. Their earnings usually did not remain in Africa. African states eager to expand or to control commerce bought European firearms, although the difficulty of maintaining guns often gave gun owners only marginal superiority over skilled bowmen.[24] The kingdom of Dahomey, however, built its power on the effective use of firearms.

The African merchants who controlled the production of exports gained from foreign trade. The king of Dahomey, for example, had a gross income in 1750 of £250,000 from the overseas export of slaves. A portion of his profit was spent on goods that improved the living standards of his people.

Three Traders   This sixteenth-century brass plaque shows three traders, probably appointed to deal with Europeans. The one in the center carries his staff of office; the two on the sides hold manillas, an early form of currency. Just as the crocodile holding a fish represents power over the seas, so the traders symbolize royal authority over commerce with outsiders. *(Source: Courtesy of the Trustees of the British Museum)*

Slave-trading entrepôts, which provided opportunities for traders and for farmers who supplied foodstuffs to towns, caravans, and slave ships, prospered. But such economic returns did not spread very far.[25] International trade did not lead to the economic development of Africa. Neither technological growth nor the gradual spread of economic benefits occurred in Africa in early modern times.

The arrival of Europeans did cause basic social changes in some West African societies. In Senegambia, chattel slavery seems to have been unknown before the growth of the transatlantic trade (see page 657). By the late eighteenth century, however, chiefs were using the slave labor of craftsmen, sailors, and farm workers. If the price was right, they were sold off. Those who committed crimes had traditionally paid fines, but because of the urgent demand for slaves, many misdemeanors became punishable by sale to slave dealers. Europeans introduced corn, pineapple, cassava, and sweet potatoes to West Africa, which had important consequences for population growth.

The intermarriage of French traders and Wolof women in Senegambia created a *métis,* or mulatto class. In the emerging urban centers at Saint-Louis, this small class adopted the French language, the Roman Catholic faith, and a French manner of life. The métis exercised considerable political and economic power. When granted French citizenship in the late eighteenth century, its members sent Senegalese grievances to the Estates General of 1789.[26] However, European cultural influences did not penetrate West African society beyond the seacoast.

The political consequences of the slave trade varied from place to place. The trade enhanced the power and wealth of some kings and warlords in the short run but promoted conditions of instability and collapse over the long run. In the kingdom of the Congo the perpetual Portuguese search for slaves undermined the monarchy, destroyed political unity, and led to constant disorder and warfare; power passed to the village chiefs. Likewise in Angola, which became a Portuguese proprietary colony, the slave trade decimated and scattered the population and destroyed the local economy. By contrast, the military kingdom of Dahomey, which entered into the slave trade in the eighteenth century and made it a royal monopoly, prospered enormously from trading in slaves. The economic

TABLE 20.2 THE TRANS-ATLANTIC SLAVE TRADE, 1450–1900

Period	Volume	Percent
1450–1600	367,000	3.1
1601–1700	1,868,000	16.0
1701–1800	6,133,000	52.4
1801–1900	3,330,000	28.5
Total	11,698,000	100.0

Source: P. E. Lovejoy, Transformations in Slavery: A History of Slavery in Africa *(Cambridge: Cambridge University Press, 1983), p. 19. Used with permission.*

strength of the state rested on the slave trade. The royal army raided deep into the interior, and in the late eighteenth century Dahomey became one of the major West African sources of slaves. When slaving expeditions failed to yield sizable catches, and when European demands declined, the resulting depression in the Dahomeyan economy caused serious political unrest. Iboland inland from the Niger Delta, from whose great port cities of Bonny and Brass the British drained tens of thousands of slaves, experienced minimal political effects and suffered no permanent population loss. A high birthrate kept pace with the incursions of the slave trade, and Ibo societies remained demographically and economically strong.

What demographic impact did the slave trade have on Africa? In all, between approximately 1500 and 1900, about 12 million Africans were exported to the Americas, 6 million were exported to Asia, and 8 million were retained within Africa. Tables 20.1 and 20.2 report the somewhat divergent findings of two careful scholars on the number of slaves shipped to the New World. Export figures do not include the approximately 10 to 15 percent who died during procurement or in transit.

Western or American markets wanted young male slaves. The Asian and African markets preferred young females. Women were sought for their reproductive value, as sex objects, and because their economic productivity was not threatened by the possibility of physical rebellion, as might be the case with young men. Consequently, two-thirds of those exported to the Americas were male, one-third female. The population on the western coast of Africa became predominantly female; in the east African Savanna and the Horn regions the population was predominantly male. The slave trade therefore had significant consequences for the institutions of marriage, slavery itself, and the sexual division of labor—topics scholars have yet to explore. Although overall population growth may have shown modest growth from roughly 1650 to 1900, that growth was offset by declines in the Horn and on the eastern and western coasts. While Europe and Asia experienced considerable demographic and economic expansion in the eighteenth century, Africa suffered decline.[27]

SUMMARY

The period between 1400 and 1800 saw the rise of several different African societies. French culture influenced the coastal fringes of Senegambia; the English maintained factories along the Gold Coast; and the Portuguese held Angola as a colony and maintained an insecure grip on Mozambique in East Africa. Yet despite the export of as many as 12 million slaves from Africa to meet the labor needs of South and North America, European influence hardly penetrated the African interior. The overall impact of the slave trade on Africa was devastating for some regions and societies but marginal for others. It appeared around 1810 that Africa's development would be entirely autonomous.

NOTES

1. P. D. Curtin, *Economic Change in Precolonial Africa: Senegambia in the Era of the Slave Trade* (Madison: University of Wisconsin Press, 1975), pp. 34–35; and J. A. Rawley, *The Transatlantic Slave Trade: A History* (New York: Norton, 1981), p. 12.

2. R. W. July, *A History of the African People,* 3d ed. (New York: Scribner's, 1980), pp. 128–129.

3. R. W. July, *Precolonial Africa: An Economic and Social History* (New York: Scribner's, 1975), p. 99.

4. July, *A History of the African People,* p. 141.

5. Quoted in R. Hallett, *Africa to 1875* (Ann Arbor: University of Michigan Press, 1970), p. 151.

6. See *The Cambridge History of Africa,* vol. 3, *ca 1050 to 1600,* ed. R. Oliver (Cambridge: Cambridge University Press, 1977), pp. 427–435.

7. A. ibn-Fartura, "The Kanem Wars," in *Nigerian Perspectives,* ed. T. Hodgkin (London: Oxford University Press, 1966), pp. 111–115.

8. "The Kano Chronicle," quoted in Hodgkin, *Nigerian Perspectives,* pp. 89–90.

9. J. Middleton, *The World of Swahili: An African Mercantile Civilization* (New Haven, Conn.: Yale University Press, 1992), p. 27.

10. Ibid., pp. 35–38.

11. P. E. Lovejoy, *Transformations in Slavery: A History of Slavery in Africa* (Cambridge: Cambridge University Press, 1983), p. 19. This section leans heavily on Lovejoy's work.

12. See Table 2.1, "Trans-Saharan Slave Trade, 650–1600," ibid., p. 25.

13. P. Manning, *Slavery and African Life: Occidental, Oriental, and African Slave Trades* (New York: Cambridge University Press, 1990), pp. 31–37.

14. Rawley, *The Transatlantic Slave Trade,* p. 45.

15. Ibid., pp. 41–47.

16. R. E. Conrad, *Children of God's Fire: A Documentary History of Black Slavery in Brazil* (Princeton, N.J.: Princeton University Press, 1983), pp. 20–23.

17. Rawley, *The Transatlantic Slave Trade,* pp. 45–47.

18. July, *A History of the African People,* p. 208.

19. J. Adams, "Remarks on the Country Extending from Cape Palmas to the River Congo," in Hodgkin, *Nigerian Perspectives,* pp. 178–180.

20. A. G. Hopkins, *An Economic History of West Africa* (New York: Columbia University Press, 1973), p. 83.

21. See Lori Grinker, "Disaster in the Sudan," *New York Times,* February 12, 1993, p. A33; Stanley Miller, "U.N. Agency Assails Mauritania on Slavery," *Los Angeles Times,* March 9, 1993, p. 3; Augustine Lado and Betty Hinds, "Where Slavery Isn't History," *Washington Post,* October 17, 1993, section 3, p. 13; and Charles Jacobs and Mohamed Athie, "Bought and Sold," *New York Times,* July 13, 1994, p. A19.

22. Hopkins, *An Economic History of West Africa,* p. 105.
23. J. Thornton, *Africa and Africans in the Making of the Atlantic World* (New York: Cambridge University Press, 1992), pp. 138–142.
24. July, *Precolonial Africa,* pp. 269–270.
25. Hopkins, *An Economic History of West Africa,* p. 119.
26. July, *A History of the African People,* pp. 201–202.
27. Manning, *Slavery and African Life,* pp. 22–23 and Ch. 3, pp. 38–59.

SUGGESTED READING

Students wishing to explore more fully some of the issues raised in this chapter might begin with *African History: Text and Readings:* vol. 1, *Western African History;* vol. 2, *Eastern African History;* and vol. 3, *Central and Southern African History* (1990), all edited by R. O. Collins. This work gives a useful introduction to the geography and history of the continent and brings together a solid collection of primary documents and scholarly commentaries. *African Civilization Revisited,* ed. B. Davidson (1991), also contains interesting source readings on many facets of African history and cultures from antiquity to the present. K. Shillington, *History of Africa* (1989) provides a soundly researched, highly readable, and well-illustrated survey, while R. Oliver, *The African Experience* (1991) traces African history through particular historical problems. Although many of the articles in *The Cambridge History of Africa,* vol. 4, *From 1600–1790,* ed. R. Gray (1975), are now dated, the following articles are still useful: "The Central Sahara and Sudan," "North-West Africa," and "Southern Africa and Madagascar." V. B. Thompson, *Africa and Unity* (1969), offers an African and African-American response to the traditional Eurocentric interpretation of African history and culture.

J. Thornton, *Africa and Africans in the Making of the Atlantic World, 1400–1680* (1992), places African developments in an Atlantic context. Likewise, both *Atlantic American Societies: From Columbus Through Abolition, 1492–1888,* ed. A. L. Karras and J. R. McNeill (1992), and *Slavery and the Rise of the Atlantic System,* ed. B. Solow (1991), contain important and valuable articles on many of the economic and cultural factors that linked Africa and the Western Hemisphere. For Ethiopia, see H. G. Marcus, *A History of Ethiopia* (1994), a concise but highly readable study. The standard study of the Savanna is probably J. Vansina, *Kingdoms of the Savanna* (1966). For East Africa and the Horn region, see J. Middleton, *The World of Swahili: An African Mercantile Civilization* (1992), which provides an expert synthesis of recent scholarly literature by a social anthropologist; the older study of C. S. Nicholls, *The Swahili Coast* (1971), is still useful. J. Knappert, *Four Centuries of Swahili Verse: A Literary History and Anthology* (1979), is a most interesting celebration of literary manifestations of Swahili culture.

The literature of slavery continues to grow. In addition to the titles by P. Manning and J. Middleton cited in the Notes, see P. Manning, *Slavery, Colonialism and Economic Growth in Dahomey, 1640–1960* (1982), an in-depth study of the kingdom of Dahomey, which, after Angola, was the largest exporter of slaves to the Americas. J. F. Searing, *West African Slavery and Atlantic Commerce, 1700–1860* (1993), explores the effects of the Atlantic slave trade on the societies of the Senegal River Valley. The theme of R. L. Stein's *The French Slave Trade in the Eighteenth Century: An Old Regime Business* (1979) is indicated by its title.

Although the emphasis in *Global Dimensions of African Diaspora,* ed. J. E. Harris (1982), is heavily on the U.S. and the Caribbean, with very little on South America, East or South Asia, some of the articles are very important: see, especially, those by J. E. Harris, L. W. Levine, and S. C. Drake.

The Abolition of the Slave Trade

Several Western nations outlawed the slave trade in the early nineteenth century. Great Britain took the lead. Laws, however, cannot be enforced if strong sentiment opposes them. And in the nineteenth century the economies of several African kingdoms rested on the slave trade, which thrived because of demands in the Americas for workers on cotton, coffee, and sugar cane plantations and in East Africa for laborers in the spice fields. Just as today the United States subsidizes the development of agricultural products in Colombia and Turkey in order to encourage farmers to stop growing opium and coca (the sources of heroin and cocaine for American users), so in the nineteenth century the British in Africa promoted farming and the production of nonhuman commodities as alternatives to the slave trade.

In 1839, the British government sent Robert Craigie, a naval officer, to discuss the end of the slave trade with King Pepple of Bonny, an area in the Niger Delta now part of Nigeria. Bonny had continued to export thousands of slaves after Britain abolished the trade in 1807. This document reports the negotiations between King Pepple and Captain Craigie.

King Pepple, of Bonny, accompanied by Anna Pepple,[1] by his Juju man or high priest, and Hee Chee, Anna Pepple's secretary, for the first time went on board a man-of-war, for the purpose of paying a visit to Captain Craigie, where he was received with the usual salutes.

When the King and suite had finished breakfast, Captain Craigie presented to His Majesty a box containing presents from the English Government, which the King desired might be opened. As the bales of scarlet and green broad cloth were being lifted out of the case, the King and Anna Pepple especially were struck with the magnificence of the gifts, and Captain Craigie made a request of His Majesty

to allow Anna Pepple to have one piece of cloth and a shawl, which the King at once complied with.

Captain Craigie then proceeded to read to King Pepple and suite the despatch of Lord Palmerston[2] dated 14th April, 1838, relative to Slave abolition, and strongly impressed upon His Majesty that part which states that treaties had already been made between England and other African Princes for the purpose of putting an end to the Slave Trade, and that in those cases the Articles of Treaty had been faithfully maintained.

Captain Craigie assured the King that England . . . . would send out ships in abundance for their palm-oil and other products; and if the Bonny men directed their attention properly to these, he was certain they could easily get rich without exporting slaves. . . .

The King, Anna Pepple, and the Juju man for some time remained silent; their countenances, however, were indicative of their consternation; the idea of making such a proposal seemed to them to be incomprehensible. At length Anna Pepple said—

"If we cease to sell slaves to foreign ships, our principal source of wealth will be gone; the English were our first customers, and the trade has since been our chief means of support."

Captain Craigie: "How much would you lose if you gave up selling slaves for exportation?"

Anna Pepple: "Too much—very much—we gain more by one slave-ship than by five palm-oil ships."

Hee Chee, Anna Pepple's Secretary: "We depend entirely on selling slaves and palm oil for our subsistence; suppose then the Slave Trade done away with, the consumption of palm-oil in England to stop, the crop to fail, or that the English ships did not come to the Bonny, what are we to do? We must starve, as it is contrary to our religion to cultivate the ground."

Captain Craigie: "There need be no apprehension of the demand for palm-oil in England ceasing, or of English ships not coming out to the Bonny to take from you your products in exchange for British merchandise; but if you can show clearly that your losses will be so great by giving up slave exportation, I think it possible that the Queen of England may in some measure remunerate you for such loss. . . . I only wish to know if you are disposed to treat[4] for the abolition of the Slave Trade."

Juju Man: "Suppose a Spanish ship's coming to Bonny with goods to exchange for slaves; are we to send her away? This morning, if the Spanish ship had things which we stood in need of, it would be equally foolish not to take them."

Captain Craigie: "How would the abolition of the slave exportation so materially affect you?"

King Pepple: "It would affect myself and chiefs thus—

"First, by stopping the revenues arising from slaves being exported.

"Secondly, our own profit on slaves, and that arising from piloting slave-ships up and out of Bonny would be lost."

Captain Craigie: ". . . If your requests are within reasonable limits, to make you an annual 'dash,' or remuneration, for a term of years (perhaps five years), how much would you consider to be sufficient?"

After some consultation among themselves, Hee Chee, Anna Pepple's Secretary, said "The King will take 4,000 dollars yearly."

Captain Craigie: . . . I am certain 4,000 would be considered too much; indeed I would not venture to propose more than 2,000 dollars. If you will say that this sum (for the time above specified) will be sufficient, I shall lay the matter before the English Government."

The King, Anna Pepple, the Juju man, and Hee Chee, had a discussion for some time.

Anti-slavery medallion. *(Source: Josiah Wedgwood and Sons, Limited)*

They for a long while insisted on not naming less than 3,000 dollars, till they at last came down to 2,000. . . .

King Pepple and suite then returned to the shore under the same salute as that with which they were received.

Just as today Colombian and Turkish farmers accept American aid for not producing opium and coca but continue to produce them; so (according to a report to the British Parliament in 1849) did King Pepple accept British aid for not selling slaves but continued to sell them to the Spanish and Portuguese.

Questions for Analysis

1. What arguments does Captain Craigie give for the abolition of the slave trade?

2. What is the reaction of King Pepple to Craigie's remarks?

3. Compare efforts to end slave trade in the nineteenth century with recent government efforts to end the drug trade.

Source: A. J. Andrea and J. H. Overfield, eds., *The Human Record: Sources of Global History*, vol. 2 (Boston: Houghton Mifflin, 1990), pp. 316–318.

Notes: 1. A male relative of the king who held some sort of position in directing the family's slaving operations. 2. Palmerston (1789–1865) was British foreign secretary at the time. 3. Negotiate.

21

The Middle East and India, ca 1450–1800

Wedding Celebrations of Prince Dara Shikoh, 1633, from the Padshah-nama, Mughal, ca. 1645. The marriage of Shah Jahan's favorite son and intended heir. *(Source: The Royal Collection © Her Majesty Queen Elizabeth II)*

Around 1450, the spiritual descendants of the Prophet Muhammad controlled three vast and powerful empires: the Ottoman Empire centered in Anatolia, the Safavid Empire of Persia, and the Mughal Empire of India. From West Africa to central Asia, from the Balkans to Southeast Asia, Muslim armies pursued policies of territorial expansion. Between 1450 and 1800, these powerful Muslim kingdoms reached the zenith of their territorial extension and of their intellectual and artistic vitality. With the conquest of Constantinople in 1453 the Ottoman Turks gained an impregnable capital and the respect of all Islam. The Ottomans soon overran much of Anatolia, North Africa, and the Balkans. Lasting almost five hundred years (1453–1918), the Ottoman Empire was one of the largest and most enduring political entities in world history. In Persia the Safavid Dynasty created a theocracy and presided over a brilliant culture. A theological dispute between the Ottomans and the Safavids brought bitter division in the Islamic world and weakened both powers. Meanwhile, the Mughal leader Babur and his successors conquered the Indian subcontinent, and Mughal rule inaugurated a period of radical administrative reorganization in India and the flowering of intellectual and architectural creativity.

In 1450 all the great highways of international trade were in Muslim hands, and the wealth of the Muslim states derived largely from commerce. By 1750 the Muslims had lost that control, and the Muslim states were declining economically, politically, and culturally.

- Who were the Ottomans and the Safavids?
- What political and religious factors gave rise to the Ottoman and Safavid Empires, and how were the two empires governed?
- What intellectual developments characterized the Ottoman and Safavid cultures?
- What external and domestic difficulties caused the decline of the Ottoman Empire and Safavid Persia?
- How did Muslim government reform and artistic inspiration affect the dominant Hindu population in India?
- What political and social conditions in India enabled the British to expand their empire?

These are the questions explored in this chapter.

✤ THE SPLENDOR OF THE OTTOMAN STATE

The Ottomans took their name from Osman (1299–1326), the ruler of a Turkish-speaking people in western Anatolia who began expansionist moves in the fourteenth century. The Ottomans gradually absorbed other peoples on the Anatolian peninsula, and the Ottoman state emerged as one of many small Turkish states during the breakup of the empire of the Seljuk Turks. The first Ottoman state thus occupied the border between Islam and Byzantine Christendom. The Ottoman ruler called himself "border chief," or leader of the *gazis,* frontier fighters in the *jihad,* or holy war. The earliest Ottoman historical source, a fourteenth-century saga, describes the gazis as the "instrument of God's religion . . . God's scourge who cleanses the earth from the filth of polytheism . . . God's pure sword."[1]

The principle of jihad was the cornerstone of Ottoman political theory and then of the Ottoman state. Europe was the frontier of the Muslim crusading mission. In 1389 in what is today the former Yugoslavia the Ottomans defeated a combined force of Serbs and Bosnians. In 1396, on the Danube River in modern Bulgaria, they crushed King Sigismund of Hungary, who was supported by French, German, and English knights. The reign of Sultan Mehmet II (r. 1451–1481) saw the end of all Turkish dynasties in Anatolia and the Ottoman conquest of Constantinople, capital of the Byzantine Empire, which had lasted a thousand years.

The six-week siege of Constantinople in 1453 remains one of the dramatic events in world history because Constantinople symbolized the continuation of imperial Rome. The Byzantine emperor Constantine IX Palaeologus (r. 1449–1453), with only about 10,000 men, relied on the magnificent system of circular walls and stone fortifications that had protected the city for a thousand years. Mehmet II had over 100,000 men and a large fleet, but iron chains spanning the harbor kept him out of the Golden Horn, the inlet of the Bosporus Strait that connects the Black and Marmona Seas and forms the harbor of Istanbul.

Western technology eventually decided the battle. A Transylvanian cannon founder who deserted the Byzantines for Ottoman service cast huge bronze cannons on the spot (bringing raw materials to the scene of military action was easier than moving guns long distances).[2] When a cannon shot shattered a city gate, the Turks forced an entry. For three days the city suffered looting and rape. The Muslim historian Oruc described the conquest of Constantinople:

Sultan Mehmet, the son of Sultan Murad, inspired by zeal, said "in the cause of God" and commanded plunder. The gazis, entering by force on every side, found a way in through the breaches in the fortress made by the guns and put the infidels in the fortress to the sword. . . . Mounting on the tower they destroyed the infidels who were inside and entered the city. They looted and plundered. They seized their money and possessions and made their sons and daughters slaves. The Muslims took so much booty that the wealth gathered in Istanbul (Constantinople) since it was built 2400 years before became the portion of the gazis. They plundered for three days, and after three days plunder was forbidden.[3]

The conquest of Constantinople inaugurated the imperial phase of the Ottoman military state. The Ottoman emperors considered themselves successors of the Byzantine emperor, as their title *Sultan-i-Rum* ("Sultan of Rome") attests. They renamed the city Istanbul, "city of Islam," though the name was not officially changed until 1930. Mehmet began the transformation of the city into an Ottoman imperial capital. He ordered Constantinople cleaned up and the walls repaired. He appointed Turkish officials to adapt the city administration to Turkish ways, and he nominated a Greek patriarch over the Greek Orthodox church, giving its members virtual freedom of religion as long as they paid the *jitza,* a tax on non-Muslims. Mehmet's installation of the supreme authority over all Orthodox Christians meant that the patriarch acknowledged Turkish rule; Greek resistance to that rule was rendered virtually impossible.

Because the conquest had severely depopulated the city and many survivors had been sold into slavery, inhabitants of territories later conquered by the Ottomans were transplanted to Constantinople. Jews cruelly oppressed in western Europe found Turkey "a paradise." In 1454, one Jewish resident, Isaac Sarfati, sent a circular letter to his coreligionists in the Rhineland, Swabia, Moravia, and Hungary praising the happy conditions of the Jews under the crescent in contrast to the "great torture chamber" under the cross and urging them to come to Turkey.[4] A massive migration to Ottoman lands followed. When Ferdinand and Isabella of Spain expelled the Jews in 1492 (see page 485), many emigrated to Turkey.

The Ottomans also continued to expand. In 1453, they controlled only the northwest quadrant of Anatolia. Mehmet II completed the conquest of Anatolia. From Constantinople, their new capital, the Ottomans pushed down the Aegean and up the Adriatic. They so severely threatened Italy and southeastern Europe that the aged Pope Pius II himself shouldered the cross of the Crusader in 1464. In 1480 an Ottoman fleet took the Italian port of Otranto, and serious plans were laid for the conquest of all Italy. Only a disputed succession following the death of Mehmet II in 1481 caused the postponement of that conquest and, later, the cancellation of those plans. The Ottoman Turks inspired such fear that even in distant Iceland the Lutheran Book of Common Prayer begged God for protection not only from "the cunning of the Pope" but also from "the terror of the Turk."

Selim the Grim (r. 1512–1520) gained the Ottoman throne by forcing his father's abdication and murdering his brother. A bloodthirsty and inflexible despot, Selim was a superb military commander. Under his leadership, the Ottomans added Syria and Palestine (1516) and Egypt (1517) to their empire and extended their rule across North Africa to Cyrenaica, Tripolitania, Tunisia, and Algeria. Selim's reign marks the beginning of four centuries when most Arabs were under Ottoman rule.

Suleiman (r. 1520–1566), who brought to the throne great experience as a provincial administrator and enormous energy as a soldier, extended Ottoman jurisdiction to its widest geographical extent (Map 21.1). With Greece and the Balkans already under Ottoman domination, Suleiman's army crushed the Hungarians at Mohács in 1526, killing the king and thousands of his nobles. Suleiman seems to have taken this victory entirely as his due. Not long after the battle he recorded laconically in his diary, "The emperor, seated on a

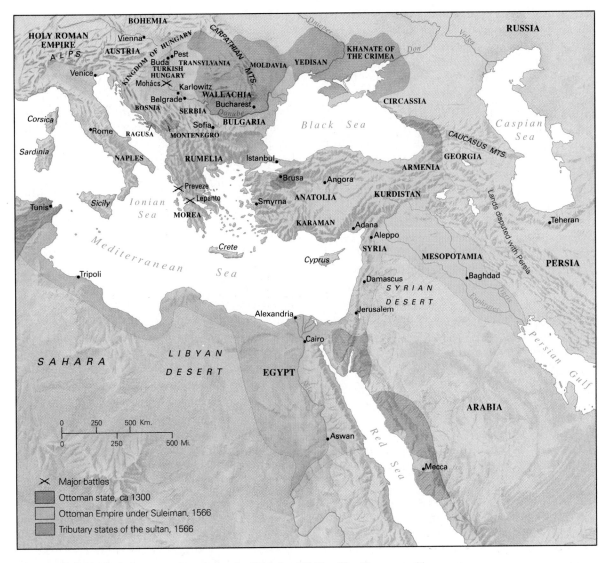

❋ **MAP 21.1 The Ottoman Empire at Its Height, 1566**   The Ottomans, like their great rivals the Habsburgs, rose to rule a vast dynastic empire encompassing many different peoples and ethnic groups. The army and the bureaucracy served to unite the disparate territories into a single state.

golden throne, receives the homage of the vizirs and beys: massacre of 2,000 prisoners: the rains fall in torrents." Three years later the Turks besieged the Habsburg capital at Vienna. Only an accident—the army's insistence on returning home before winter—prevented Muslim control of all central Europe.

In virtually every area, the Ottomans' success was due to the weakness and political disunity of their enemies and to the superiority of Turkish military organization and artillery. Gunpowder, invented by the Chinese and adapted to artillery use by Europeans, played an influential role in the expansion of the Ottoman state.

Though victorious on land, the Ottomans did not enjoy complete dominion on the sea. The middle decades of the sixteenth century witnessed a titanic struggle between the Ottoman and

Habsburg empires for control of the Mediterranean. In September 1538 an Ottoman naval victory at Preveze, the chief Turkish port in Albania, assured Turkish control of the Ionian and Aegean Seas. Meanwhile, attacks from the island of Cyprus by Christian pirates on Ottoman shipping in the eastern Mediterranean provoked the sultan to conquer Cyprus in 1570. He introduced Ottoman administration and settled thousands of Turks from Anatolia there. (Thus began the large Turkish presence on Cyprus that continues to the present day.) In response, Pope Pius V organized the Holy League against the Turks. On October 7, 1571, an armada of over 200 Spanish, Venetian, and papal galleys smashed the Turks at Lepanto at the mouth of the Gulf of Patras in Greece (see Map 21.1). About 15,000 Turks were killed or captured, 10,000 Christian galley slaves were liberated, and the victors lost about 7,000 men. European churches rang with victory celebrations for the first major Ottoman defeat by Christian forces. Lepanto, however, marked no decisive change in Turkish hegemony: the Turks remained supreme on land and quickly rebuilt their entire fleet.

Military organization dominated the Ottoman social and administrative systems, which reached classic form under Suleiman I. The seventeenth-century Ottoman historian Mustafa Naima divided Muslim society into producers of wealth, Muslim and non-Muslim, and the military. In Naima's view there could be no state without the military; wealth was needed to support the military; the state's subjects raised the wealth; subjects could prosper only through justice; and without the state there could be no justice.[5]

The ruling class consisted exclusively of Muslims, theoretically totally loyal to the sultan and fully immersed in the complex Islamic culture. Under Suleiman I, the Ottoman ruling class consisted in part of descendants of Turkish families that had formerly ruled parts of Anatolia. In return for bureaucratic service to the sultan, they held *trimars* (landed estates) on *sipahinek* (property) for the duration of their lifetimes. The ruling class had the usufruct but not the ownership of the land. Since all property belonged to the sultan and reverted to him on the holder's death, Turkish nobles—unlike their European counterparts—could not put down

Procession of Suleiman   In 1533 the Dutch painter and print maker Pieter Coecke van Aelst visited Constantinople, where he sketched the design for this elegant scene. The triumphant procession of the sultan, with his officials and courtiers, through monuments brought from all over the Mediterranean world (notice the column with Egyptian hieroglyphics) captures the power of the Grand Turk. *(Source: The Metropolitan Museum of Art, Harris Brisbane Dick Fund, 1928)*

roots. Because there was no security of landholding and no hereditary nobility, the Ottoman Empire did not develop a feudal structure before 1600.

Slaves who had been purchased from Spain, North Africa, and Venice, captured in battle, and acquired through the system known as *devshirme*—by which the sultan's agents swept the provinces for Christian youths—were recruited for the imperial civil service and the army. Southern Europeans did not shrink from selling people into slavery, and, as the Ottoman jihad advanced in the fifteenth and sixteenth centuries, Albanian, Bosnian, Wallachian, and Hungarian slave boys filled Ottoman imperial needs. Moreover, because devshirme recruitment often meant social advancement, some Christian and Muslim parents bribed government officials to accept their children. All were converted to Islam. (Islamic law forbade the enslavement of Muslims but not of converts.) The brightest 10 percent entered the palace school. There they learned to read and write Arabic, Ottoman Turkish, and Persian, received special religious instruction, and were trained for the civil service. Other boys were sent to Turkish farms, where they acquired physical toughness in preparation for military service. Known as *janissaries* (Turkish for "recruits"), they formed the elite army corps. Thoroughly indoctrinated and absolutely loyal to the sultan, the janissary slave corps eliminated the influence of old Turkish families and played the central role in Ottoman military affairs in the sixteenth century.

All authority theoretically emanated from the sultan and flowed from him to his state servants: police officers, provincial governors, heads of the treasury, generals. The sultan frequently designated these men *pashas,* a title of distinction.

The reign of Suleiman I witnessed an extraordinary artistic flowering and represents the peak of Ottoman influence and culture. In Turkish history Suleiman is known as *Kanuni* ("Lawgiver") because of his profound influence on the civil law. He ordered Lütfi Paşa (d. 1562), a poet of slave origin and juridical scholar, to draw up a new general code of laws. Published in Suleiman's name, this sultanic legal code prescribed penalties for routine criminal acts such as robbery, adultery, and murder. It also sought to reform bureaucratic and financial corruption in areas such as harem interven-

tion in administrative affairs, foreign merchants' payment of bribes to avoid customs duties, imprisonment without trial, and promotion in the provincial administration because of favoritism rather than ability. The legal code also introduced the idea of balanced financial budgets. Suleiman's legal acts influenced many legal codes, including that of the United States. Today, Suleiman's image, along with the images of Solon, Moses, and Thomas Jefferson, and other great lawgivers, appears in the chamber of the U.S. House of Representatives.

Europeans called Suleiman "the Magnificent" because of the grandeur of his court. With annual state revenues of about $80 million (at a time when Elizabeth I of England could expect $150,000 and Francis I of France perhaps $1 million), with thousands of servants to cater to his whims, and with a lifestyle no European monarch could begin to rival, Suleiman was indeed magnificent. He used his fabulous wealth and power to adorn Constantinople with palaces and mosques. Some of his undertakings, such as his reconstruction of the water systems of the great pilgrimage sites at Mecca and Jerusalem, benefited his subjects.

The Ottomans under Suleiman demonstrated splendid creativity in carpet weaving, textiles, ceramics, and, above all, architecture. In the buildings of Pasha Sinan (1491–1588), a Christian slave who rose to become imperial architect, the Ottoman spirit is powerfully expressed. A contemporary of Michelangelo, Sinan designed 312 public buildings—mosques, schools, hospitals, public baths, palaces, and burial chapels. His masterpieces, the Shehzade and Suleimaniye mosques at Constantinople, represented solutions to spatial problems unique to domed buildings and expressed the discipline, power, and devotion to Islam that characterized the Ottoman Empire under Suleiman the Magnificent. With pardonable exaggeration, Suleiman began a letter to the king of France, with whom he was allied against the Habsburgs after 1536, by saying, "I who am the sultan of sultans, the sovereign of sovereigns, the dispenser of crowns to the monarchs on the face of the earth . . . to thee who are Francis, King of the land of France."[6]

The age of Suleiman witnessed a tremendous cultural explosion that may have rivaled the artistic and literary achievements of the European Renaissance. In addition to architecture, Ottoman scholars and artists showed great distinction in poetry, painting, history, mathematics, geographical literature, astronomy, medicine, and the religious sciences.

Poetry, rather than prose, was the main vehicle of Ottoman literary expression. *Diwan* poetry, so called because it consisted of collections of poems, though written by intellectuals in Turkish, followed classical Islamic (Arabic) forms and rules and addressed the ruling class. Şeyhi of Kütahya (d. 1429) compiled a large Diwan collection and in his *Book of the Donkey* used animals to personify and satirize his political enemies. Modern scholars consider Bursah Ahmet Pasa, an imperial judge and confidential adviser to the sultan Mehmet II, to be the greatest Ottoman poet of the fifteenth century. Bursah Ahmet Pasa's beautiful odes and diversified style won him widespread popularity.

Folk literature, produced by traveling troubadours, described the traditions and wisdom of the people in humorous short stories and anecdotes. The folk collection of Dede Korkut, set down in Turkish prose, includes tribal epics describing the conflicts with the Georgians, Circassians, and Byzantines and serves as a major source for the history of the fourteenth century.

Just as Western historical writing in the early modern period often served to justify the rights of ruling dynasties, so Ottoman historical scholarship under Mehmet II and Suleiman promoted the claims of the family of Osman. Perhaps the greatest historian of the early sixteenth century was Ahmet Semseddin Iba-i Kemal, or Kemalpasazêde (d. 1526), the Muslim judge and administrator whose *History of the House of Osman* gives original source material for the reigns through which he himself lived. Building on the knowledge of earlier Islamic writers and stimulated by Ottoman naval power, the geographer and cartographer Piri Reis produced a map that showed all the known world (1513); another of his maps detailed Columbus's third voyage to the New World. Piri Reis's *Book of the Sea* (1521) contained 129 chapters, each with a map incorporating all Islamic (and Western) knowledge of the seas and navigation and describing harbors, tides, dangerous rocks and shores, and storm areas. Takiyuddin Mehmet (1521–1585), who served as the sultan's chief astronomer, built an observatory at Constantinople. His *Instruments of the Observatory* catalogued astronomical instruments and described an astronomical clock that fixed the location of heavenly bodies with greater precision than ever before.

What medical treatment or health care was available to the sick in the Ottoman world? Muslim medical education was practical, not theoretical: students received their training not in the *madrasas,* or mosque schools, but by apprenticeship to experienced physicians or in the *bimaristans,* the hospitals. Under a senior's supervision, medical students studied the course of various diseases, learned the techniques of surgery, and especially mastered pharmacology—the preparation of drugs from plants. The Muslim knowledge of pharmacology derived from centuries-old traditions, and modern students of the history of medicine believe that pharmacology as an institution is an Islamic invention.

By the fifteenth century, Muslims knew the value of quarantine. Yet when devastating epidemics, such as the bubonic plague, struck the empire during Mehmet II's reign, he and the court fled to the mountains of the Balkans, and the imperial government did little to fight the plague. Under Suleiman, however, the imperial palace itself became a center of medical science, and the large number of hospitals established in Constantinople and throughout the empire testifies to his support for medical research and his concern for the sick. Abi Ahmet Celebi (1436–1523), the chief physician of the empire, produced a study on kidney and bladder stones and supported the research of the Jewish doctor Musa Colinus ul-Israil on the application of drugs. Celebi founded the first Ottoman medical school, which served as a training institution for physicians of the empire.[7] The sultans and the imperial court usually relied on Jewish physicians.

To fight smallpox, the Chinese had successfully practiced inoculation in the sixteenth century, and the procedure spread to Turkey in the seventeenth. Lady Mary Wortley Montague, wife of the British ambassador to Constantinople, had her son inoculated in 1717. Here is her description of the method:

The smallpox, so fatal and so general amongst us (in England), is here entirely harmless by the invention of engrafting. . . . Every autumn . . . people send one another to know if any of their family has a mind to have the smallpox (get inoculated). . . . An old woman comes with a nutshell full of the matter of the best sort of smallpox and asks what veins you please (want) to have opened. She immediately rips open what you offer to her with a large needle (which gives you no more pain than a common scratch) and puts into the vein as much venom as can lie upon the head of the needle, and after binds up the little wound. . . . The children or young patients play together all the rest of the day and are in perfect health till the eighth. Then the fever begins to seize 'em and they keep their beds two days, very seldom three. They have very rarely twenty or thirty (pockmarks) in their faces, which never mark (leave a permanent scar), and in eight days' time they are as well as before their illness. . . . Every year thousands undergo this operation, and the French ambassador says pleasantly that they take the smallpox here by way of diversion as they take the waters in other countries (at spas). . . . There is no example of anyone that has died in it.[8]

This was eighty years before the English physician Edward Jenner (see page 644) tried the procedure using cowpox in England.

Lady Mary Wortley Montague marveled at the splendor of Ottoman culture. Remarkably intelligent and fluent in several languages, a pioneer feminist, Lady Mary also had a mind exceptionally open to different cultures. As an aristocrat, the wife of an official foreign representative, and a woman, she had access to people and places (such as the imperial seraglio or harem) off-limits to ordinary tourists. Her many letters to relatives and friends in England provide a wealth of information about upper-class Ottoman society.

On January 19, 1718, Lady Mary gave birth to a daughter and described the experience in a letter to an English friend:

I was brought to bed of a daughter. . . . I must own that it was not half so mortifying here as in England, there being as much difference as there is between a little cold in the head, which sometimes happens here, and the consumptive coughs so common in London.[9]

The naturalness of childbirth in Turkey, Lady Mary suggests, may have been because Turkish women

Lady Mary Wortley Montague   Famous in her own time for her letters from Constantinople and, after her return to England, for her efforts to educate the English public about inoculation against smallpox, Lady Mary is praised by twentieth-century scholars as a brilliant and urbane woman struggling for emancipation. *(Source: Boston Athenaeum)*

had much more experience of it than English-women:

in this country 'tis more despicable to be married and not fruitful than 'tis with us to be fruitful before marriage. They have a notion that whenever a woman leaves off bearing children, 'tis because she is too old for that business, whatever her face says to the contrary, and this opinion makes the ladies here so ready to make proofs of their youth. . . . Without any exaggeration, all the women of my acquaintance that have been married ten years have twelve or thirteen children, and the old ones boast of having had five and twenty or thirty apiece and are respected according to the number they have produced.[10]

Turkish women's sense of self-worth seems to have been closely tied to their production of children, as was common in many cultures at the time. As for Turkish morality, "'Tis just as 'tis with you; and the Turkish ladies don't commit one sin the less for not being Christians." In other words, Turkish women are neither better nor worse than European ones. Moreover,

'Tis very easy to see that they have more liberty than we have, . . . and their shapes are wholly concealed by a thing they call a ferigee, which no woman of any sort (class) appears without. . . . You may guess how effectively this disguises them, that there is no distinguishing the great lady from her slave, and 'tis impossible for the most jealous husband to know his wife when he meets her, and no man dare either touch or follow a woman in the street.

This perpetual masquerade gives them entire liberty of following their inclinations without danger of discovery. The most usual method of intrigue is to send an appointment to the lover to meet the lady at a Jew's shop, which are as notoriously convenient as our Indian houses. . . .

You may easily imagine the number of faithful wives very small in a country where they have nothing to fear from their lovers' indiscretion. . . . Neither have they much to apprehend from the resentment of their husbands, those ladies that are rich having all their money in their own hands, which they take with 'em upon a divorce with an addition which he is obliged to give 'em. Upon the whole, I look upon the Turkish woman as the only free people in the empire.[11]

In short, in spite of the legal restrictions of the harem, upper-class ladies found ways to go out and even to have affairs.

In the seventeenth and eighteenth centuries, grave political, social, and economic difficulties afflicted the Ottoman Empire. Ottoman government depended heavily on the sultan, and the matter of the dynastic succession posed a major political problem. In earlier centuries heirs to the throne had gained administrative experience as governors of provinces and military experience on the battlefield as part of their education. After Suleiman's reign, however, this tradition was abandoned. To prevent threats of usurpation, heirs were brought up in the harem and were denied a role in government. By the time a prince succeeded his father, years of dissipation were likely to have rendered the prince alcoholic, insane, or exhausted from excessive sexual activity. Selim II (r. 1566–1574), whom the Turks called "Selim the Drunkard," left the conduct of public affairs to his vizier while he pursued the pleasures of the harem. Turkish sources attribute his death to a fall in his bath caused by dizziness when he tried to stop drinking. The Ottomans, moreover, abandoned the system whereby the eldest son inherited and instead gave the throne to the member of the dynasty with the greatest political influence at the time of the sultan's death. As the sultan's brothers and sons formed factions, harem coalitions conspired for the throne.

A series of incompetent rulers enabled the janissaries to destroy the influence of the old Turkish families. Members of the elite army corps secured permanent military and administrative offices for their sons through bribery, making their positions hereditary. The janissaries thus became the powerful feudal class in Ottoman Turkey.

Under the very competent vizier Muhammad Kuprili (ca 1570–1661) Ottoman fortunes revived. Kuprili abolished the corruption pervasive throughout the imperial administration, maintained domestic peace, and pursued a vigorous foreign policy. When Kuprili died, his brother-in-law Kara Mustafa directed the empire's military operations. His objective was an attack on the Habsburg capital, Vienna. When battle came on September 12, 1683, the combination of a strong allied Christian force (see page 571) and Habsburg heavy artillery, which the Turks lacked, gave the Europeans the victory. The Ottomans rallied again, but defeat at Vienna and domestic disorders led to the decline of Ottoman power in the Balkans. In the words of one historian, "The Ottoman state was predicated upon, committed to, and organized for conquest. . . . An end to significant and sustained conquest rocked the entire state structure and sent aftershocks through all its institutions."[12]

The peace treaty signed at Karlowitz (1699) marks a watershed in Ottoman history. By its terms the empire lost (to Austria) the major European provinces of Hungary and Transylvania along with the vast tax revenues they had provided. Karlowitz

Visit to the Lunatic Asylum   Beginning in the ninth century, Islamic hospitals had special wards for the insane. Therapy consisted of baths, massages, bleeding (for the violently agitated), and drugs given as sedatives, stimulants, or antidepressants. Fear that the violent would harm themselves or others led to shackling. In this scene from an album produced for Sultan Ahmed I (r. 1603–1617) three violent patients are chained; the nearly naked appearance of two of them (which would have shocked Muslim sensibilities) is a sure sign of their insanity. The Jewish doctor (right) is threatened with a knife; his assistant is caught in the stocks from which the third lunatic tries to escape. Two visitors observing the mayhem through the window put their forefingers to their mouths, a common gesture in Muslim society indicating astonishment and a defense against evil. *(Source: Topkapi Saray Museum, Istanbul)*

also shattered Ottoman morale. Eighteenth-century wars against European powers—Venice (1714–1718), Austria and Russia (1736–1739), and Russia (1768–1774 and 1787–1792)—proved indecisive but contributed to general Ottoman internal disintegration.

Rising population caused serious social problems. A long period of peace in the later sixteenth century and again in the mid-eighteenth century—while the War of the Austrian Succession (1740–1748) and the Seven Years' War (1756–1763) were preoccupying the European powers (see page 611)—and a decline in the frequency of visits of

the plague led to a doubling of the population. The land could not sustain so many people, nor could the towns provide jobs for the thousands of agricultural workers who fled to them. The return of demobilized soldiers from the West aggravated the situation. Inflation, famine, and widespread revolts resulted.

Inability to respond to European and worldwide economic changes contributed to Ottoman weakness and decline. The empire did not modernize and thus could not compete effectively with European capitalistic powers. European trade with the Americas, Asia, and Africa by means of the Atlantic

✧ **Polo** Two teams of four on horseback ride back and forth on a grass field 200 by 400 yards trying to hit a 4½-ounce wooden ball with a four-foot mallet through the opponents' goal. Because a typical match involves many high-speed collisions among the horses, each player has to maintain a string of expensive ponies in order to change mounts several times during the game. Students of the history of sports believe the game originated in Persia, as shown in this eighteenth-century miniature, whence it spread to India, China, and Japan. Brought from India to England where it became very popular among the aristocracy in the nineteenth century, polo is a fine example of cross-cultural influences. *(Source: Private Collection)*

Ocean meant that the ancient Middle Eastern trade routes—with their heavy customs duties—were bypassed. The Ottoman state lost vast revenues. Meanwhile, Ottoman guilds set the prices of commodities such as wheat, wool, copper, and precious metals, and European willingness to pay high prices pulled those commodities out of the Ottoman Empire. The result was scarcity, which led to a decline in Turkish industrial production. Likewise in the craft industries, Europeans bought Ottoman raw materials, used them to manufacture textiles and metallurgical goods, and sold them in Turkish lands, thereby destroying Ottoman craft industries in the early nineteenth century. Prices rose; inflation increased; and the government devalued the currency, causing new financial crises.

More than any other single factor, a series of agreements known as capitulations, which the Ottoman government signed with European powers, contributed to the Ottoman decline. A trade compact signed in 1536 and renewed in 1569 virtually exempted French merchants from Ottoman law and allowed them to travel and buy and sell throughout the sultan's dominions and to pay low customs duties on French imports and exports. In 1590, in spite of strong French opposition, a group of English merchants gained the right to trade in Ottoman territory in return for supplying the sultan with iron, steel, brass, and tin for his war with Persia. In 1615, as part of a twenty-year peace treaty, the capitulation rights already given to French and English businessmen were extended to the Habsburgs. These capitulations progressively gave European merchants an economic stranglehold on Ottoman trade and commerce. In the nineteenth century, the Ottoman empire was beset by the loss of territory, the pressures of European capitalistic imperialism, and unresolved internal problems; Tsar Nicholas I of Russia (1825–1855) called it "the sick man of Europe."[13]

THE PERSIAN THEOCRATIC STATE

Describing the Mongol destruction of Persia in the thirteenth century, the Persian historian Juvaini wrote, "With one stroke, a world which billowed with fertility was laid desolate, and the regions thereof became a desert, and the greater part of the living dead, and their skin and bones crumbling dust."[14] Pursuing a scorched-earth policy toward the land and a psychological reign of terror over the people, the Mongols, so modern demographers estimate, reduced the population of Persia, Khurasan, Iraq, and Azerbaijan (Map 21.2) from 2,500,000 to 250,000. Mongol devastation represents the last great sweep of Turkish steppe nomads from central Asia into the European and Islamic heartlands. Turkish tribes in central Asia far outnumbered the ethnic Mongols. The Turks joined Jenghiz Khan partly because he had defeated them, partly because westward expansion with the Mongols offered adventure and rich pasturelands for their herds of sheep and horses.[15]

The rehabilitation of Persia began under Ghazan (r. 1295–1304), the *Ilkhan,* as the Mongol rulers of Persia were called. A descendant of Jenghiz Khan, Ghazan reduced peasants' taxes and thereby encouraged their will to produce. He also worked to improve the fiscal and administrative systems. His declaration of Islam as the state religion had profound political and cultural consequences: native (and Muslim) Persians willingly served the state government; they alone had the literacy needed to run a bureaucracy. Turkish-Mongol soldiers adapted to Persian ways. The court patronized Persian art. Across the central Asian heartlands hundreds of Chinese doctors, engineers, artists, and potterymakers came seeking opportunity in the Persian-Mongol-Turkish capital at Tabriz. Chinese artistic influences left a permanent mark on Persian miniature painting, calligraphy, and pottery design.

But Mongol rule of Persia did not last long. While Mehmet II was extending Ottoman jurisdiction through eastern Anatolia, the Safavid movement advanced in Persia. The Safavid Dynasty, which takes its name from Safi al-Din (1252–1334), a supposed descendant of Ali (the fourth caliph), began as leaders of a contemplative Sufi sect; gradually the dynasty evolved into a militant and heretical Shi'ite regime. The attraction of the masses to Shi'ism perhaps reflects the role of religion as a vehicle for the expression of political feeling—in this case opposition to Mongol domination. In the early sixteenth century, Persia emerged as a powerful Muslim state under the Safavids. (Since 1935 Persia has been known as Iran.)

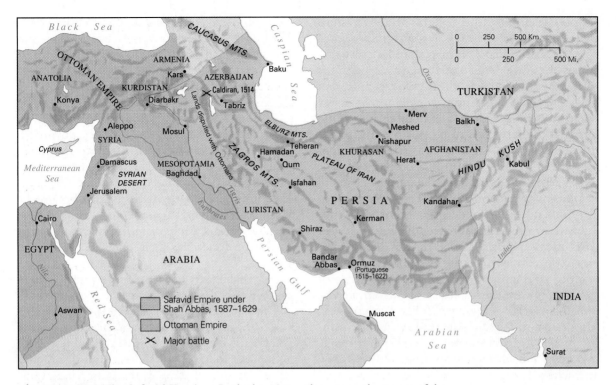

✳ **MAP 21.2 The Safavid Empire** In the late sixteenth century, the power of the Safavid kingdom of Persia rested on its strong military force, its Shi'ite Muslim faith, and its extraordinarily rich trade in rugs and pottery. Many of the cities on the map, such as Tabriz, Qum, and Shiraz, were great rug-weaving centers.

Between 1502 and 1510, Ismail (r. 1502–1524) defeated petty Turkish leaders, united Persia under his sovereignty, and proclaimed himself *shah,* or king.

The strength of the Safavid state rested on three crucial features. First, it had the loyalty and military support of Qizilbash nomadic tribesmen. (*Qizilbash,* a Turkish word meaning "redheads," was applied to these people because of the red hats they wore.) The shah secured the loyalty of the Qizilbash by granting them vast grazing lands, especially on the troublesome Ottoman frontier. In return, the Qizilbash supplied him troops. Second, the Safavid state utilized the skills of urban bureaucrats and made them an essential part of the civil machinery of government.

The third source of Safavid strength was the Shi'ite faith. The Shi'ites claimed descent from Ali, Muhammad's cousin and son-in-law, and believed that leadership among Muslims rightfully belonged to the Prophet's descendants. Ismail claimed descent from a line of twelve infallible *imams* (leaders) beginning with Ali and was officially regarded as their representative on earth. When Ismail conquered Tabriz in 1501, he declared Shi'ism the official and compulsory religion of his new empire under penalty of death. Today, in the late twentieth century, Iran remains the only Muslim state in which Shi'ism is the official religion.

Shi'ism gradually shaped the cultural and political identity of Persia (and later Iran). Recent scholarship asserts that Ismail was not "motivated by cynical notions of political manipulation."[16] Shah Ismail imported Shi'ite *ulema* (scholars outstanding in learning and piety) from other Arab lands to instruct and guide his people. With its puritanical emphasis on the holy law and on self-flagellation in penance for any disloyalty to Ali, the Safavid state represented theocracy triumphant throughout the first half century of its existence.

Safavid power reached its height under Shah Abbas (r. 1587–1629), whose military achievements, support for trade and commerce, and endowment of the arts earned him the epithet "the Great." The Persian army had hitherto consisted of tribal units under tribal leadership. Shah Abbas built a national army on the Ottoman model, composed of Armenian and Georgian recruits paid by and loyal to himself. Shah Abbas campaigned against the Turks and captured Baghdad, Mosul, and Diarbakr in Mesopotamia (see Map 21.2).

Military victories account for only part of Shah Abbas's claim to greatness. Determined to improve his country's export trade, he built the small cottage business of carpet weaving into a national industry. In the capital city of Isfahan alone, factories employed over twenty-five thousand weavers who produced woolen carpets, brocades, and silks of brilliant color, design, and quality. Armenians controlled the carpet industry; the Safavids had brought them to Isfahan to protect them from Turkish persecution. Three hundred Chinese potters were imported to make glazed building tiles, which adorned the great Safavid buildings. They captured much of the European tile market.

The jewel of the empire was Isfahan, whose prosperity and beauty rested on trade and industry. A seventeenth-century English visitor described Isfahan's bazaar as "the surprisingest piece of Greatness in Honour of commerce the world can boast of." Besides splendid rugs, stalls displayed pottery and fine china, metalwork of exceptionally high quality, silks and velvets of stunning weave and design. A city of perhaps 750,000 people, Isfahan contained 162 mosques, 48 schools where future members of the ulema learned the sacred Muslim sciences, 273 public baths, and the vast imperial palace. Private houses had their own garden courts; and public gardens, pools, and parks adorned the wide streets. Tales of the beauty of Isfahan circulated worldwide, attracting thousands of tourists annually in the seventeenth and eighteenth centuries.

Shah Abbas was succeeded by inept rulers whose heavy indulgence in wine and the pleasures of the harem weakened the monarchy and fed the slow disintegration of the state. Internal weakness encouraged increased foreign aggression. In the eighteenth century the Turks, Afghans, and Russians invaded and divided Persia among themselves, and political anarchy and social chaos characterized Persian life.

INDIA, FROM MUGHAL DOMINATION TO BRITISH DOMINION (CA 1498–1805)

While powerful Muslim empires developed in Ottoman Turkey and Safavid Persia in the early sixteenth century, the Asian subcontinent of India experienced the intrusion of two vigorous foreign cultures. In 1510 the Portuguese occupied the island of Goa and shortly afterward under Alfonso de Albuquerque (see pages 517–518) extended Portuguese influence on the Indian mainland. The Portuguese soon controlled the trade of the Indian Ocean. On the mainland they used persuasion and force to convert the Indian peoples to Christianity. Fifteen years after the arrival of the Portuguese, an army from Afghanistan and central Asia invaded northern India.

In 1504 Babur (r. 1483–1530), ruler of the small Mughal territory in central Asia, captured Kabul and established a kingdom in Afghanistan. From Kabul he moved southward into India. In 1526 with a force of only twelve thousand men, Babur defeated the decrepit sultan of Delhi at Panipat. Babur's capture of the cities of Agra and Delhi, the key fortresses of the north, paved the way for further conquests in northern India. Thus began Mughal rule, which lasted until the eighteenth century, when domestic disorder and incompetent government opened the door to lengthy European intervention. (*Mughal* refers to the Muslim empire of India. Although the name *Mughal* is a variant of *Mongol,* the founders of the Mughal Empire were mainly Turks and Afghans, not Mongol descendants of Jenghiz Khan.)

The Rule of the Mughals

By the start of the sixteenth century, India had been the object of foreign conquest for almost a millennium. Muslims first invaded India in the seventh century. The Turkish chieftain Mahmud conquered the Punjab in the tenth century, and in the thirteenth century the Turkish Muslim Qutb-ud-din established the sultanate of Delhi, which gained control over most of the subcontinent. In 1398, central Asian armies under Timur the Lame (Tamerlane) swept down through the northwest, looted Delhi, and seized tens of thousands of

Masji-Shah Mosque   Just as the Gothic cathedrals manifested the civic pride of medieval European towns, so this mosque with its magnificent tile work and delicate stone tracery celebrated the commercial dynamism of Isfahan and the political power of the Safavid Dynasty of Persia. (*Source: Erwin Böhm, Mainz*)

slaves as booty. Timur, Babur's grandfather, left Delhi completely destroyed with "not a bird moving" and all India politically fragmented. Although the vast majority of the people remained Hindu, Islam had a strong impact on the culture of India, especially in art and architecture.

Babur's son Humayun reigned from 1530 to 1540 and from 1555 to 1556. When the Afghans of northern India rebelled, he lost most of the territories that his father had acquired. Humayun went into temporary exile in Persia, where he developed a deep appreciation for Persian art and literature. This interest led to a remarkable flowering of Mughal art under his son Akbar.

The reign of Akbar (r. 1556–1605) may well have been the greatest in the history of India. Under his dynamic leadership the Mughal state took

definite form. A boy of thirteen when he became *badshah,* or imperial ruler, Akbar was ably assisted during his early years by his father's friend Bairam Khan, a superb military leader. In 1555 Bairam Khan had defeated Hindu forces at Panipat and shortly afterward recaptured Delhi and Agra. Before falling from power in 1560, Bairam Khan took the great fortress of Gwalior, annexed the rich city of Janupur, and prepared for war against Malwa. Akbar continued this expansionist policy throughout this time, gradually adding the territories of Malwa, Gondwana, and Gujarat. Because the Afghan tribesmen put up tremendous resistance, it took Akbar several years to acquire Bengal. The Mughal Empire under Akbar eventually included most of the subcontinent north of the Godavari River (see Map 21.3).

To govern this vast region, Akbar developed an efficient bureaucracy staffed by able and well-trained officials, both Muslim and non-Muslim. As in the early modern nations of Europe, solvency in the Mughal state depended on the establishment of a careful system for recording income and expenditures. Under Akbar's finance minister Raja Todar Mal, a Hindu, a *diwan* (bureau of finance) and royal mint came into existence. Raja Todar Mal devised methods for the assessment and collection of taxes, and those methods were applied throughout the empire. To administer the provinces, Akbar appointed about 800 *mansabdars,* imperial officials who performed a wide variety of financial, military, and judicial functions at the local level. The central government, however, rarely interfered in the life of village communities. Akbar's policies laid the basis for all later Mughal administration in India.

A mark of Akbar's cosmopolitanism was his appointment of the Spanish Jesuit Antonio Monserrate (1536–1600) as tutor to his second son, Prince Murad (see Listening to the Past). The cornerstone of Akbar's policies was religious toleration: he sought the peaceful mutual assimilation of Hindus and Muslims, especially in his government. Although this was not a radical innovation—a few Hindus had long been employed in the imperial army and in the administration—very deep prejudices divided the two peoples. When the refusal of many Hindus to serve under a Muslim ruler or to learn Persian (the court language) thwarted Akbar's goal, he took decisive steps to heal the breach, because, according to his principle of *sulahkul* (universal tolerance), the badshah was responsible for all the people, regardless of their religion.

In 1564 the Muslim ruler ended the pilgrim tax and thus won the gratitude of the many Hindus who traveled to various pilgrimage sites. And by abolishing the *jizya,* a tax imposed on non-Muslim adult males, he immediately earned the support of the Hindu warrior class and the goodwill of the general Hindu population. Twice Akbar married Hindu princesses, one of whom became the mother of his heir Jahangir. Hindus eventually accounted for 30 percent of the imperial bureaucracy.

Scholars have heatedly debated Akbar's own religious beliefs. He considered himself an orthodox Muslim and demonstrated great devotion at the shrine of an Islamic mystic at Ajmer. Yet he supported an eclectic assortment of theological ideas, a policy that caused serious domestic difficulties. Orthodox Muslims became alarmed. After 1579 Akbar invited Jains, Zoroastrians, Hindus, and Jesuits to join the Muslim ulema in debate. From these discussions Akbar created the *Din-i-Ilahi* (literally, "divine discipleship"), which some advisers called a syncretic religion (a religion that reconciles different beliefs).

The Din-i-Ilahi borrowed the concept of great respect for animal life from the Jains and reverence for the sun from the Zoroastrians, but it was primarily based on the rationalistic elements in the Islamic tradition and stressed the emperor as a Perfect Man. Some scholars interpret it as a reflection of Akbar's "cult of personality," intended to serve as a common bond for the court nobility. In any case, the Din-i-Ilahi antagonized all sects and provoked serious Muslim rebellions.

Akbar often sought the spiritual advice of the Sufi mystic Shaykh Salim Chishti. The birth of a long-awaited son, Jahangir, which Akbar interpreted as fulfillment of the shaykh's prophecy, inspired Akbar to build a new city, Fatehpur-Sikri, to symbolize the regime's Islamic foundations. He personally supervised the construction of the new city. It combined the Muslim tradition of domes, arches, and spacious courts with the Hindu tradition of flat stone beams, ornate decoration, and solidity. According to Abu-l-Fazl, the historian of Akbar's reign, "His majesty plans splendid edifices, and dresses the work of his mind and heart in the garment of stone and clay."[17] Completed in 1578, the city included an imperial palace, a mosque, lavish gardens, and a hall of worship, as well as thousands of houses for ordinary people. Akbar placed Shaykh Salim Chishti's tomb inside the great mosque in order to draw on its presumed sanctity. Just as medieval European rulers such as Charlemagne and Phillip the Fair sought to strengthen their political power through association with Christian saints, so Akbar tried to identify Mughal authority with a Muslim saint. Along with the ancient cities of Delhi and Agra, Fatehpur-Sikri served as an imperial capital and the center of Akbar's lavish court.

Akbar was gifted with a creative intellect and imagination. He replaced Barlas Turkish with Persian as the offical language of the Mughal Empire; Persian remained the official language until the

British replaced it with English in 1835. He enthusiastically supported artists who produced magnificent paintings and books in the Indo-Persian style. In Mughal India, as throughout the Muslim world, books were regarded as precious objects. Time, talent, and expensive materials went into their production, and they were highly coveted because they reflected wealth, learning, and power.

Akbar reportedly possessed twenty-four thousand books when he died. Abu-l-Fazl, the historian, described the library and Akbar's love of books:

His Majesty's library is divided into several parts. . . . Prose works, poetical works, Hindi, Persian, Greek, Kashmirian, Arabic, are all separately placed. In this order they are also inspected. Experienced people

City of Fatehpur-Sikri   In 1569 Akbar founded the city of Fatehpur-Sikri to honor the Muslim holy man Shaikh Salim Chishti, who had foretold the birth of Akbar's son and heir, Jahangir. The red sandstone city, probably the finest example of Mughal architecture still intact, was Akbar's capital for fifteen years. *(Source: Nrupen Madhvani/Dinodia Picture Agency, Bombay)*

bring them daily and read them before His Majesty, who hears every book from beginning to end . . . and rewards the readers with presents of cash either in gold or silver, according to the number of leaves read out by them. Among books of renown there are few that are not read in His Majesty's assembly hall; and there are no historical facts of past ages, or curiosities of science, or interesting points of philosophy, with which His Majesty, a leader of impartial sages, is unacquainted.[18]

Akbar's son Jahangir (r. 1605–1628) lacked his father's military abilities and administrative genius but did succeed in consolidating Mughal rule in Bengal. His patronage of the arts and lavish court have led scholars to characterize his reign as an "age of splendor."

Jahangir's son Shah Jahan (r. 1628–1658) launched fresh territorial expansion. Faced with dangerous revolts by the Muslims in Ahmadnagar and the resistance of the newly arrived Portuguese in Bengal, Shah Jahan not only crushed them but strengthened his northwestern frontier. He reasserted Mughal authority in the Deccan and Golkunda.

The new capital that Shah Jahan founded at Delhi superseded Agra, Akbar's main capital. Situated on the rich land linking the Indus and Ganges Valleys, Delhi eventually became one of the great cities of the Muslim world. The city boasted one of the finest mosques in Islam, the Juma Masjid, and magnificent boulevards. The Red Fort, named for its red sandstone walls, housed the imperial palace, the headquarters of the imperial administration, the imperial treasury, an arsenal, and a garrison. Subsequent Mughal rulers held their *durbar,* or court, at Delhi.

Shah Jahan ordered the construction of the Peacock Throne. This famous piece, actually a cot resting on golden legs, was encrusted with emeralds, diamonds, pearls, and rubies. It took seven years to fashion and cost the equivalent of $5 million. It served as the imperial throne of India until 1739, when the Persian warrior Nadir Shah seized it as plunder and carried it to Persia.

Shah Jahan's most enduring monument is the Taj Mahal, the supreme example of a garden tomb. The English word *paradise* derives from the old Persian *pairidaeza,* a walled garden. The Mughals sought to bring their vision of paradise alive in the walled garden tombs in which they buried their

Jesuits at the Court of Akbar   Akbar considered the creation of a new faith, synthesizing his Muslim beliefs, Hindu, Parsee, and Christian creeds, but the scheme encountered fierce opposition. The Jesuits' black robes fascinated Mughal artists, and the splendor of the imperial court astounded the Jesuits. *(Source: Reproduced by kind permission of the Trustees of the Chester Beatty Library, Dublin)*

dead. Twenty thousand workers toiled eighteen years to build this memorial in Agra to Shah Jahan's favorite wife, Mumtaz Mahal, who died giving birth to their fifteenth child. One of the most beautiful structures in the world, the Taj Mahal is

❊ **Taj Mahal at Agra** This tomb is the finest example of Muslim architecture in India. Its white marble exterior is inlaid with semiprecious stones in Arabic inscriptions and floral designs. The oblong pool reflects the building, which asserts the power of the Mughal Dynasty. *(Source: Ira Kirschenbaum/Stock, Boston)*

both an expression of love and a superb architectural blending of Islamic and Indian culture. It also asserted the power of the Mughal Dynasty.

The Mughal state never developed a formal procedure for the imperial succession, and a crisis occurred toward the end of Shah Jahan's reign. Competition among his sons ended with the victory of Aurangzeb, who executed his elder brother and locked his father away until death in 1666. A puritanically devout and strictly orthodox Muslim, a skillful general and a clever diplomat, Aurangzeb (r. 1658–1707) ruled more of India than did any previous badshah. His reign witnessed the culmination of Mughal power and the beginning of its decline (Map 21.3).

A combination of religious zeal and financial necessity seems to have prompted Aurangzeb to introduce a number of reforms. He appointed censors of public morals in important cities to enforce Islamic laws against gambling, prostitution, drinking, and the use of narcotics. He forbade *suttee*—the self-immolation of widows on their husbands' funeral pyres—and the castration of boys to be sold as eunuchs. He also abolished all taxes not authorized by Islamic law. This measure led to a serious loss of state revenues. To replace them, Aurangzeb in 1679 reimposed the jizya, the tax on non-Muslims. It fell most on the Hindu majority.

Regulating Indian society according to Islamic law meant modifying the religious toleration and cultural cosmopolitanism instituted by Akbar. Aurangzeb ordered the destruction of some Hindu temples. He required Hindus to pay higher customs duties than Muslims. Out of fidelity to Islamic law, he even criticized his mother's tomb, the Taj Mahal: "The lawfulness of a solid construction

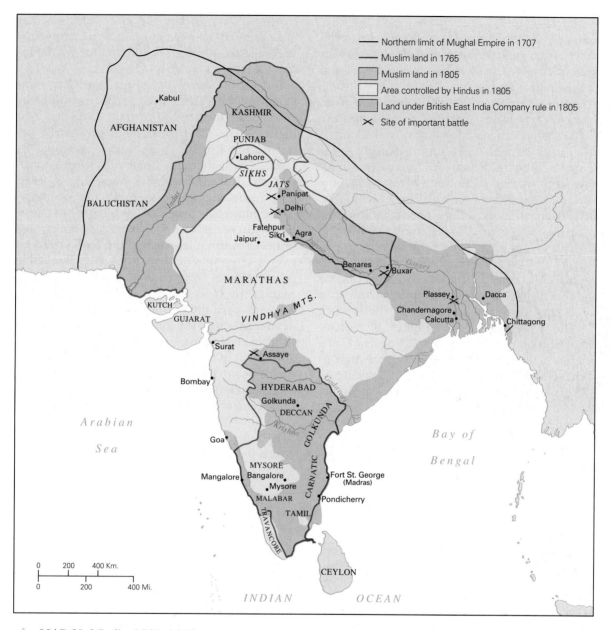

Northern limit of Mughal Empire in 1707
Muslim land in 1765
Muslim land in 1805
Area controlled by Hindus in 1805
Land under British East India Company rule in 1805
✕ Site of important battle

Kabul

AFGHANISTAN

KASHMIR

PUNJAB
•Lahore
SIKHS
JATS
✕•Panipat
✕•Delhi
BALUCHISTAN
Fatehpur
Jaipur• Sikri •Agra
•

MARATHAS
Benares
✕Buxar
Ganges
Plassey✕ •Dacca
Chandernagore•
Calcutta• •Chittagong

KUTCH
GUJARAT
VINDHYA MTS.

Surat•
✕ Assaye
Bombay•

Arabian

Sea

HYDERABAD
Golkunda
• DECCAN
Krishna
GOLKUNDA

Bay of
Bengal

Goa•

MYSORE
Mangalore• Bangalore•
•Mysore
MALABAR
TAMIL
TRAVANCORE

CARNATIC

Fort St. George
(Madras)•
•Pondicherry

0   200   400 Km.
0   200   400 Mi.

CEYLON

INDIAN   OCEAN

❁ **MAP 21.3 India, 1707–1805**   In the eighteenth century Mughal power gradually
yielded to the Hindu Marathas and to the British East India Company.

over a grave is doubtful, and there can be no doubt
about the extravagance involved."[19] Aurangzeb
employed more Hindus in the imperial administration than any previous Mughal ruler. But his religious policy proved highly unpopular with the majority of his subjects and created problems that
weaker successors could not handle.

Aurangzeb's military ventures also had mixed
results. A tireless general, he pushed the conquest
of the south and annexed the Golkunda and Bi-
japur sultanates. The stiffest opposition came from
the Marathas, a militant Hindu group centered in
the western Deccan. From 1681 until his death in
1707 at the age of ninety, Aurangzeb led repeated

sorties through the Deccan. He took many forts and won several battles, but total destruction of the Maratha guerrilla bands eluded him. After his death they played an important role in the collapse of the Mughal Empire.

Aurangzeb's eighteenth-century successors faced formidable problems. Repeated disputes over the succession undermined the stability of the monarchy. Court intrigues replaced the battlefield as the testing ground for the nobility. Mughal provincial governors began to rule independently, giving only minimal allegiance to the badshah at Delhi. The Marathas, who revolted and pressed steadily northward, constituted the gravest threat to Mughal authority. No ruler could defeat them.

In 1739 the Persian adventurer Nadir Shah invaded India, defeated the Mughal army, looted Delhi, and after a savage massacre carried off a huge amount of treasure, including the Peacock Throne. When Nadir Shah withdrew to Afghanistan, he took with him the Mughal government's prestige. Constant skirmishes between the Afghans and the Marathas for control of the Punjab and northern India ended in 1761 at Panipat, where the Marathas were crushingly defeated by the Afghans. At this point, India no longer had any power capable of imposing order on the subcontinent or checking the penetration of the rapacious Europeans.

European Rivalry for the Indian Trade

Shortly before Babur's invasion of India, the Portuguese under the navigator Pedro Alvares Cabral had opened the subcontinent to Portuguese trade. In 1510 they established the port of Goa on the Arabian Sea as their headquarters and through a policy of piracy and terrorism swept the Muslims off the Indian and Arabian Oceans (see Map 21.3). The Portuguese historian Barroes attempted to justify Portugal's seizure of commercial traffic that the Muslims had long dominated:

It is true that there does exist a common right to all to navigate the seas and in Europe we recognize the rights which others hold against us; but the right does not extend beyond Europe and therefore the Portuguese as Lords of the Sea are justified in confiscating the goods of all those who navigate the seas without their permission.[20]

In short, Western principles of international law did not apply in Asia. For almost a century the Portuguese controlled the spice trade over the Indian Ocean.

In 1602 the Dutch formed the Dutch East India Company with the stated goal of wresting the enormously lucrative spice trade from the Portuguese. The scent of fabulous profits also attracted the English. With a charter signed by Queen Elizabeth, eighty London merchants organized the British East India Company. In 1619 Emperor Jahangir granted a British mission important commercial concessions at Surat on the western coast of India. Gifts, medical services, and bribes to Indian rulers enabled the British to set up twenty-seven other coastal forts. Fort St. George on the eastern coast became the modern city of Madras. In 1668 the city of Bombay—given to England when the Portuguese princess Catherine of Braganza married King Charles II—was leased to the company, marking the virtually total British absorption of Portuguese power in India. In 1690 the company founded a fort that became the city of Calcutta. Thus the three places that later became centers of British economic and political imperialism—Madras, Bombay, and Calcutta—existed before 1700. The Dutch concentrated their efforts in Indonesia.

Factory-Fort Societies

The British called their trading post at Surat a "factory," and the word was later used for all European settlements in India. The term did not signify manufacturing; it designated the walled compound containing the residences, gardens, and offices of British East India Company officials and the warehouses where goods were stored before being shipped to Europe. The company president exercised political authority over all residents.

Factory-forts existed to make profits from the Asian-European trade, and they evolved into flourishing centers of economic profit. The British East India Company sold silver, copper, zinc, lead, and fabrics to the Indians and bought cotton goods, silks, pepper and other spices, sugar, and opium from them. By the late seventeenth century the company was earning substantial profits. Profitability increased after 1700 when it began to trade with China. Some Indian merchants in Calcutta and Bombay made gigantic fortunes from trade within Asia.

Because the directors of the British East India Company in London discouraged all unnecessary expenses and financial risks, they opposed any interference in local Indian politics and even missionary activities. Conditions in India, however, brought about a fundamental change in the nature of the company's factories. The violent disorders and political instability that wracked India during Aurangzeb's reign and in the early eighteenth century caused the factories to evolve into defensive installations manned by small garrisons of native troops. When warlords appeared or an uprising occurred, people from the surrounding countryside flocked into the fort, and the company factory-forts gradually came to exercise political authority over the territories around them.

Indian and Chinese wares enjoyed great popularity in England and on the European continent in the late seventeenth and early eighteenth centuries. The middle classes wanted Indian textiles,

English Factory at Surat   The factory began as a storage place for goods before they were bought and transported abroad; it gradually expanded to include merchants' residences and some sort of fortification. By 1650, the English had twenty-three factories in India. Surat, in the Gujarat region on the Gulf of Cambay, was the busiest factory and port until it was sacked by the Marathas in 1664. *(Source: The Mansell Collection)*

which were colorful, durable, cheap, and washable. The upper classes desired Chinese wallpaper and porcelains, Indian silks and brocades. In the European economies, however, Asian goods created serious problems. As early as 1695 English manufacturers called for an embargo on Indian cloth, and silk weavers picketed the House of Commons.

Trade with Asia was one-way: Asians had little interest in European manufactured articles. Finding the Siamese completely uninterested in traditional Dutch goods, the Dutch East India Company tried to interest them in collections of pornography. Europeans had to pay for everything they bought from Asia with precious metals. Thus there was insistent pressure in England, France, and the Netherlands against the importation of Asian goods. As one authority explains it: "The root of the argument from which grew a tree of many branches was the old fear of the drain of gold."[21]

The Rise of the British East India Company

The French were the last to arrive in India. Louis XIV's financial wizard Colbert (see pages 561–562) planned the French East India Company for trade in the Eastern Hemisphere, and in the 1670s the company established factories at Chandernagore in Bengal, Pondicherry, and elsewhere. Joseph Dupleix (1697–1764), who was appointed governor general at Pondicherry in 1742, made allies of Indian princes and built an army of native troops, called *sepoys,* who were trained as infantrymen. The British likewise built an army with Indian surrogates trained in Western military drill and tactics. War broke out at midcentury.

From 1740 to 1763 Britain and France were almost continually engaged in a tremendous global struggle. India, like North America in the Seven Years' War, became a battlefield and a prize. The French won land battles, but English seapower decided the first phase of the war. Then a series of brilliant victories destroyed French power in southern India. By preventing French reinforcements from arriving, British seapower again proved to be the determining factor, and British jurisdiction soon extended over the important northern province of Bengal. The Treaty of Paris of 1763 recognized British control of much of India, and

scholars acknowledge the treaty as the beginning of the British Empire in India.

How was the vast subcontinent to be governed? Parliament believed that the British East India Company had too much power and considered the company responsible for the political disorders in India, which were bad for business. Parliament attempted to solve Indian problems with special legislation. The Regulating Act of 1773 created the office of governor general, with an advisory council, to exercise political authority over the territory controlled by the company. The India Act of 1784 required that the governor general be chosen from outside the company, and it made company directors subject to parliamentary supervision.

Implementation of these reforms fell to Warren Hastings, the governor of Bengal and first governor general (r. 1774–1785) with jurisdiction over Bombay and Madras. Hastings tried to build an effective administrative system and to turn the British East India Company into a government. He laid the foundations for the first Indian civil service, abolished tolls to facilitate internal trade, placed the salt and opium trades under government control, and planned a codification of Muslim and Hindu laws. He sought allies among Indian princes. The biggest problem facing Hastings's administration was a coalition of the rulers of Mysore and the Marathas aimed at the expulsion of the British. Hastings's skillful diplomacy offset this alliance temporarily.

Hastings's successor Lord Charles Cornwallis served as governor general of India from 1786 to 1794. Cornwallis continued the work of building a civil service and the war against Mysore. His introduction of the British style of property relations in effect converted a motley collection of former Mughal officers, tax collectors, and others into English-style landlords. The result was a new system of landholding, in which the rents of tenant farmers supported the landlords.

The third governor general, the marquess Richard Wellesley (r. 1797–1805), defeated Mysore in 1799 and four years later crushed the Marathas at the Battle of Assaye (see Map 21.3). Building on the work of his predecessors, he vastly extended British influence in India. Like most nineteenth-century British governors of India, Wellesley believed that British rule strongly benefited the Indians. With supreme condescension he wrote that

Textile from Kalamkari   Containing a rich variety of Persian, Hindu, Muslim, and Christian motifs, this superb example of seventeenth-century painted cotton suggests the beauty and complexity of Indian textile manufacture as well as the diversity of influences in Indian culture itself. *(Source: The Metropolitan Museum of Art)*

British power should be established over the Indian princes in order

to deprive them of the means of prosecuting any measure or of forming any confederacy hazardous to the security of the British empire, and to enable us to preserve the tranquility of India by exercising a general control over the restless spirit of ambition and violence which is characteristic of every Asiatic government.[22]

By the beginning of the nineteenth century, the authority and power of the British East India Company had yielded to the government in London. Subsequent British rule of India rested on three foundations: the support of puppet Indian princes, who exercised the trappings but not the reality of power; a large army of sepoys of dubious loyalty; and an increasingly effective civil service, staffed largely by Englishmen with Hindus and Muslims in minor positions.

SUMMARY

In the eighteenth century, the Ottoman Turks lived almost entirely within a closed Islamic environment. Very few knew European languages or had firsthand knowledge of Europe. Diplomatic relations with any European power did not exist before 1793. When the Ottomans thought of Europe at all, they believed it inferior to Islamic civilization, despite the plea in 1653 of Katib Chelebi, a renowned Ottoman historian, for greater Muslim knowledge of geography: "Sufficient and compelling proof of the necessity for learning this science is the fact that the unbelievers, by their application to and esteem for those branches of learning, have discovered the New World and have overrun the ports of India and the East Indies."[23] Everyone looked backward to the period of Suleiman the Magnificent, when the empire was at its height. There was little thought of innovation or experimentation. Some scholars believe that Islam's hostility to innovation is traceable to a saying of Muhammad: "The worst things are those that are novelties, every novelty is an innovation, every innovation is an error, and every error leads to Hell-fire." After war with Russia (1736–1739), in which the Turks were largely successful, the Ottomans entered a long period of peace on their western frontier. Not until the reign of Sultan Selim III (r. 1761–1808), during which the imperial administration and the army were restructured, European languages studied, and relations established with European powers, did the Ottoman Empire begin to become a modern state.

In the seventeenth century, the Shi'ite state of Persia enjoyed military success, economic boom, and cultural pre-eminence. The wealth and magnificence of the shah was a legend in sophisticated China and in primitive North America. In the eighteenth century, however, political weakness attracted Russian and Ottoman invasion and led to Persia's dismemberment.

The contemporary Indian writer V. S. Naipaul has called India "a wounded civilization." For centuries the economic prize of European commercial interests, in the 1700s the Indian subcontinent began to experience British political domination. Bitter hostility between Hindus and Muslims persisted as a dominant theme of Indian life.

NOTES

1. Quoted in B. Lewis, *The Muslim Discovery of Europe* (New York: Norton, 1982), p. 29.
2. W. H. McNeill, *The Pursuit of Power: Technology, Armed Force, and Society Since A.D. 1000* (Chicago: University of Chicago Press, 1982), p. 87.
3. Quoted in Lewis, *The Muslim Discovery of Europe,* p. 30.
4. F. Babinger, *Mehmed the Conqueror and His Times,* trans. R. Manheim. (Princeton, N.J.: Princeton University Press, 1978), p. 107.
5. F. Robinson, *Atlas of the Islamic World Since 1500* (New York: Facts on File, 1982), p. 72.
6. Quoted in P. K. Hitti, *The Near East in History* (Princeton, N.J.: Van Nostrand, 1961), p. 336.
7. See S. J. Shaw, *History of the Ottoman Empire and Modern Turkey,* vol. 1, *Empire of the Gazis: The Rise and Decline of the Ottoman Empire, 1208–1808* (Cambridge: Cambridge University Press, 1988), pp. 139–151.
8. *The Selected Letters of Lady Mary Wortley Montagu,* ed. R. Halsband. (London: Longman Group, 1970), pp. 98–99.
9. Ibid., p.106.
10. Ibid., p. 105.
11. Ibid., p. 96–97.
12. N. Itzkowitz, *Ottoman Empire and Islamic Tradition* (Chicago: University of Chicago Press, 1980), p. 95.
13. See Shaw, *Empire of the Gazis,* pp. 171–175, 225, 246–247; V. H. Parry, H. Inalcik, A. N. Kurat, and J. S. Bromley, *A History of the Ottoman Empire to 1715* (New York: Cambridge University Press, 1976), pp. 126, 139–140.
14. Quoted in R. E. Dunn, *The Adventures of Ibn Battuta: A Muslim Traveler of the 14th Century* (Berkeley: University of California Press, 1986), p. 81.
15. Ibid., pp. 83–87.
16. D. Morgan, *Medieval Persia, 1040–1797* (New York: Longman, 1988), pp. 112–113.
17. Quoted in V. A. Smith, *The Oxford History of India* (Oxford: Oxford University Press, 1967), p. 398.
18. Quoted in M. C. Beach, *The Imperial Image: Paintings for the Mughal Court* (Washington, D.C.: Freer Gallery of Art, Smithsonian Institution, 1981), pp. 9–10.
19. Quoted in S. K. Ikram, *Muslim Civilization in India* (New York: Columbia University Press, 1964), p. 202.
20. Quoted in K. M. Panikkar, *Asia and Western*

Domination (London: George Allen & Unwin, 1965), p. 35.

21. Quoted ibid., p. 53.
22. Quoted in W. Bingham, H. Conroy, and F. W. Iklé, *A History of Asia,* vol. 2 (Boston: Allyn and Bacon, 1967), p. 74.
23. Quoted ibid., p. 106.

SUGGESTED READING

The curious student interested in the Ottoman world might begin with A. Wheatcroft, *The Ottomans* (1993), an excitingly written and beautifully illustrated popular account of many facets of Ottoman culture that separates Western myths from Turkish reality; this book also has a helpful bibliography. In addition to the titles by Babinger, Itkowitz, and Shaw cited in the Notes, H. Inalcik, *The Ottoman Empire: the Classical Age, 1300–1600* (1973) and chapters 13, 14, and 15 of A. Hourani, *A History of the Arab Peoples* (1991) should also prove helpful. For Suleiman the Magnificent, E. Atil, *The Age of Sultan Suleyman the Magnificent* (1987) is a splendidly illustrated celebration of the man and his times, while A. Bridge, *Suleiman the Magnificent. Scourge of Heaven* (1972) presents a highly readable, if romantic, view; *Circa 1492. Art in the Age of Exploration,* ed. J. A. Levenson (1991) has several stimulating chapters on the Ottomans and Constantinople. For the later empire, see L. Cassels, *The Struggle for the Ottoman Empire, 1710–1740* (1966) and S. J. Shaw, *Between Old and New: The Ottoman Empire under Sultan Selim III, 1789–1807* (1971).

The literature on women is growing, though still largely restricted to the upper classes. See F. Davis, *The Ottoman Lady: A Social History from 1718 to 1918* (1986); A. L. Croutier, *Harem: The World Behind the Veil* (1989); L. P. Pierce, *The Imperial Harem: Woman and Sovereignty in the Ottoman World* (1993), a fine achievement which treats not only the political roles of Turkish women, but marriage, concubines, and childbirth; and *The Selected Letters of Lady Mary Wortley Montagu,* ed. R. Halsband (1970), which gives the invaluable impressions of a sophisticated English-woman.

For slavery in the Ottoman world, see the appropriate pages of B. Lewis, *Race and Slavery in the Middle East* (1990), and E. R. Toledano, *The Ottoman Slave Trade and Its Suppression: 1840–1890* (1982), which although dealing with a period later than this chapter, offers useful references to earlier centuries.

Perhaps the best general introduction to the history and civilization of India is S. Wolpert's elegant appreciation *India* (1990), but see also P. Spears, *A History of India,* vol. II (1986). The titles by V. A. Smith and S. K. Ikram, cited in the Notes, provide broad general treatments, as do P. M. Holt *et al.,* eds., *The Cambridge History of India* 2 vols. (1970), M. Mujeeb, *The Indian Muslims* (1967), and I. Habib, *The Agrarian System of Mughal India, 1556–1707* (1963) whose theme and scope are indicated by the title. Many of the essays in J. F. Richards, *Power, Administration and Finance in Mughal India* (1993) are useful and authoritative. For the decline of imperial authority in eighteenth century India, see the important study of M. Alam, *The Crisis of Empire in Mughal North India: Awadh and the Punjab, 1707–48* (1986). Students wishing to study Indian culture through its architecture, should consult two splendid and recent achievements: C. Tadgell, *The History of Architecture in India: from the Dawn of Civilization to the End of the Raj* (1995) and G. Mitchell, *The Royal Palaces of India* (1995). E. B. Findly, *Nur Jahan. Empress of Mughal India* (1993) provides a vivid picture of one powerful and influential woman. E. Maclagan, *The Jesuits and the Great Mogul* (1932) discusses the Jesuits at the courts of Akbar, Jahangir, and Shah Jahan. B. Gascoigne, *The Great Moghuls* (1971) and G. Hambly, *The Cities of Mughal India: Delhi, Agra, and Fatehpur Sikri* (1968) are well illustrated and highly readable. For the impact of Portuguese, Dutch, and English mercantile activities in India, see M. N. Pearson, *Merchants and Rulers in Gujarat: The Response to the Portuguese in the Sixteenth Century* (1976).

Culture Shock

A keen student of comparative religion, the Mughal emperor Akbar invited Jain teachers, Sikh gurus, and Catholic Jesuits to his court. The Jesuits had recently established a mission and college in Goa. One of the Jesuits, Antonio Monserrate, who eventually served as an adviser to the emperor and accompanied him on several military expeditions, had been ordered by the Superior of the Society of Jesus in India to keep a careful record of his experiences at the Mughal court. Monserrate's Commentary *has proved invaluable to scholars for its picture of Akbar's personality and policies and Westerners' reaction to Indian culture in the late sixteenth century.*

The wives of the Brachmans—a famous class of nobly-born Hindus—are accustomed, in accordance with an ancient tradition of their religion, to burn themselves on the same pyres as their dead husbands. The King ordered the priests to be summoned to see an instance of this. They went in ignorance of what was to take place; but when they found out, they plainly indicated by their saddened faces how cruel and savage they felt that crime to be. Finally Rudolf[1] publicly reprimanded the King for showing openly by his presence there that he approved of such a revolting crime, and for supporting it by his weighty judgment and explicit approbation, (for he was heard to say that such fortitude could only come from God). Such was Zelaldinus'[2] kindness and favour towards the priests that he showed no resentment; and a certain chief, a great favourite of his, a Brachman by birth, who held the office of Superintendent of sacred observances, could no longer persuade him to attend such spectacles. The wretched women are rendered quite insensible by means of certain drugs, in order that they may feel no pain. For this purpose opium is used, or a soporific herb named bang, or—more usually—the herb 'duturo,' which is known to the Indians, although entirely unfamiliar alike to modern Europeans and to the ancients. Sometimes they are half-drugged: and, before they lose their resolution, are hurried to the pyre with warnings, prayers and promises of eternal fame. On arriving there they cast themselves into the flames. If they hesitate, the wretched creatures are driven on to the pyre: and if they try to leap off again, are held down with poles and hooks. The nobles who were present were highly incensed at the Fathers' interference. They did not dare to gainsay the King; but they grumbled loudly amongst themselves, saying, 'Away with you, black-clothed Franks.' The whole city was filled with praise and admiration when news was brought that the Franks had dared to rebuke the King regarding this affair.

On one occasion, the Fathers met a crowd of worthless profligates,[3] some of those who dress and adorn themselves like women. The priests were rightly disgusted at this, and took the first opportunity of privately complaining to the King (since he was so favourable to them) about this disgraceful matter. They declared with the greatest emphasis that they were astonished at his permitting such a class of men to live in his kingdom, let alone in his city, and almost under his eyes. They must be banished, as though they were a deadly plague, to his most distant territories; even better, let them be burnt up by devouring flames. They never would have believed that such men could be found in the court itself and in the royal city, where lived a king of such piety, integrity and prudence. Therefore let him give orders that these libertines should never again be seen in Fattepurum, seeing that his remarkable prophet[4] had guaranteed that good men should never suffer for their good actions. The King laughed at this piece of sarcasm and retired, saying that he would attend to the matter.

Questions for Analysis

1. What does the document reveal about the Jesuits' relations with Akbar?

2. Consider the Jesuits' reactions to the Hindu practice of suttee.[5] Should they have interfered?

3. Contrast the Jesuits' reaction to suttee and to the transvestite prostitutes.

Source: *The Commentary of Father Monseratte, S.J., on His Journey to the Court of Akbar* (London: Oxford University Press, 1922), pp. 61–63.

1. One of the Jesuits.
2. The Jesuits' name for Akbar.
3. Male prostitutes, common in almost all societies.
4. A reference to the Prophet Muhammad. The Jesuits' logic and charity is somewhat faulty here.
5. *Suttee* means "true one" in Sanskrit. The term was used to describe a Hindu widow's self-immolation on the funeral pyre of her dead husband, without whom her life had supposedly lost all meaning. The British abolished suttee in 1829, but even today women whose dowries are not paid are sometimes burned to death.

Antonio at the court of Akbar. *(Source: Reproduced by kind permission of the Trustees of the Chester Beatty Library, Dublin)*

22 China and Japan, ca 1400–1800

❖ Toyotomi Hideyoshi (1530–1598) is represented as a knightly archer in this statue in a niche of the Yomei-mon, a gate leading to the Toshogu Shrine at Nikko. *(Source: Photographer, Martin Hürlimann. Courtesy of Reich Verlag, Switzerland.)*

The period from about 1400 to 1800 witnessed growth and dynamic change in East Asia. In China the native Ming Dynasty (1368–1644) had replaced the Yuan (1271–1368) and in 1644 was replaced by the foreign Manchu Dynasty. The early Ming period was a time of remarkable economic reconstruction and of the establishment of new and original social institutions. Over time, however, the bureaucracy prevented the changes necessary to meet new demands on the empire. The Manchus inaugurated a long period of peace, relative prosperity, and population expansion. In the Manchu period the Chinese Empire reached its greatest territorial extent, and literary and artistic creativity reached their apogee.

In the Japanese islands, united by Nobunaga and later the Tokugawa Shogunate (1600–1867), the feudal military aristocracy continued to evolve. Although Japan developed largely in isolation from outside influences, its sociopolitical system bore striking similarities to medieval European feudalism. The period of the Tokugawa Shogunate, like that of the Ming Dynasty in China, was marked by remarkable agricultural productivity and industrial growth.

- What features characterized the governments of the Ming and Manchu Dynasties in China and the Tokugawa Shogunate in Japan?

- How did agricultural and commercial developments affect Chinese and Japanese societies?

- How did Chinese thinkers interpret and explain the shift from the Ming to the Manchus?

This chapter explores these questions.

CHINA, FROM THE MING TO THE MID-MANCHU DYNASTY (CA 1368–1795)

Mongol repression under the Yuan Dynasty, rapid inflation of the currency, disputes over succession among the khans, and the growth of peasant secret societies led to the decay of Mongol government in China. By 1368, Hong Wu, the leader of a secret society called the Red Turbans, had pushed the Mongols out of China. Hong Wu (r. 1368–1398), founder of the Ming Dynasty, and Liu Bang (r. 206–195 B.C.), founder of the Han Dynasty, were the only peasants to found major dynasties in China. The Ming Dynasty (1368–1644) was the only dynasty that originated south of the Yangtze River (see Map 22.1).

Under the Ming, China experienced dynamic change. Agricultural development and commercial reconstruction followed a long period of chaos and disorder. Hong Wu introduced far-reaching social and political institutions. By the middle of the fifteenth century, however, his administrative framework had begun to decay. Externally, defeats in Mongolia in the later fifteenth century led to a long period of Chinese withdrawal. Nevertheless, the Ming period stands out because of its social and cultural achievements.

The Ming Agricultural and Commercial Revolutions

Mongol exploitation and the civil disorders that accompanied the breakdown of Yuan rule left China in economic chaos in the mid-fourteenth century. Vast stretches of farmland were laid waste, some entirely abandoned. Damaged dikes and canals proved unusable, causing trade to decline.

Between 1370 and 1398, a profound economic reconstruction occurred. The agricultural revolution that China underwent in the Ming period was part of a gigantic effort at recovery after the disaster of Mongol rule. At the heart of this revolution was radical improvement in methods of rice production.

More than bread in Europe, rice supplied almost the total nourishment of the population in central and south China. (In north China, wheat, made into steamed or baked bread or into noodles, served as the staple of the diet.) Terracing and irrigation of mountain slopes, introduced in the eleventh century, had increased rice harvests. The introduction of drought-resistant Indochinese, or Champa, rice proved an even greater boon. Although Champa rice was of lower nutritional quality than the native rice, it considerably increased the total output of food. Ming farmers experimented with Champa rice that required only sixty days from planting to harvesting instead of the usual hundred days. Peasants soon reaped two harvests a year, an enormous increase in production.

Other innovations also brought good results. Ming-era peasants introduced irrigation pumps worked by pedals. Farmers began to stock the rice paddies with fish, which continuously fertilized the

Chinese Peasants at Work The Western artist who sketched this picture in the seventeenth century seems to be telling us that human power in agriculture was as common in China as animal power. Notice that a woman also pulls the plow; she might have been pregnant. Coco palms (left) are not usually found as far north as China. The pigtailed men date the picture from the Manchu period. *(Source: Caroline Buckler)*

rice fields, destroyed malaria-bearing mosquitoes, and enriched the diet. Fish farming in the paddies eventually enabled large, previously uninhabitable parts of southern China to be brought under cultivation. Farmers discovered the possibilities of commercial cropping in cotton, sugar cane, and indigo. And new methods of crop rotation allowed for continuous cultivation and for more than one harvest per year from a single field.

The Ming rulers promoted the repopulation and colonization of devastated regions through massive transfers of people. Immigrants received large plots of land and exemption from taxation for many years. Table 22.1, based on fourteenth-century records of newly reclaimed land, helps tell the story.[1]

Reforestation was a dramatic aspect of the agricultural revolution. In 1391 the Ming government ordered 50 million trees planted in the Nanjing (Nanking) area. Lumber from the trees was intended for the construction of a maritime fleet. In 1392 each family holding colonized land in Anhwei province had to plant 200 each of mulberry, jujube, and persimmon trees. In 1396 peasants in the present-day provinces of Hunan and Hupeh in

the east planted 84 million fruit trees. Historians have estimated that 1 billion trees were planted during Hong Wu's reign.[2]

What were the social consequences of agricultural development? Increased food production led to steady population growth. Demographers date the start of the Chinese population boom at about 1550, as a direct result of improved methods of rice production. Increases in total yields differed fundamentally, however, from comparable agricultural growth in Europe: Chinese grain harvests were improved through intensification of peasant labor. This meant lower income per capita.

Population increase seems to have led to the multiplication of towns and small cities. Urbanization in the Ming era (and, later, in the Manchu period) meant the proliferation of market centers and small towns rather than the growth of "large" cities like those in Europe in the High Middle Ages and China in the Song (Sung) period (960–1279). Most people lived in tiny hamlets or villages that had no markets. What distinguished a village from a town was the existence of a market in a town.

Towns held markets twice a week; in southern China, where a week was ten days long, markets were held three times a week. Town markets consisted of little open-air shops that sold essential goods—pins, matches, oil for lamps, candles, paper, incense, tobacco—to country people from surrounding hamlets. The market usually included a tearoom or tavern where tea and rice wine were sold, entertainers performed, and moneylenders and pawnshops sometimes did business.

Tradesmen, who carried their wares on their backs, and craftsmen—carpenters, barbers, joiners, locksmiths—moved constantly from market to market. Itinerant salesmen depended on the city market for their wares. In large towns and cities foodstuffs from the countryside and rare and precious goods from distant places were offered for sale. Cities gradually became islands of sophistication in the highly localized Chinese economy. Nanjing, for example, spread out enormously because the presence of the imperial court and bureaucracy generated a great demand for goods. The concentration of people in turn created demand for goods and services. Industrial development was stimulated. Small businesses manufactured textiles, paper, and luxury goods such as silks and porcelains. Nanjing and Shanghai became centers for the production of cotton and silks; Xiangtan specialized in the grain and salt trade and in silver. Small towns remained embedded in peasant culture, but large towns and cities pursued contacts with the wider world.

The Government of Hong Wu

Hong Wu's government reforms rested on a few strong centralizing principles. Hong Wu established China's capital at Nanjing (literally, "southern capital"), his old base on the Yangtze River. He stripped many nobles of their estates and divided the estates among the peasantry. Although Hong Wu had been a monk, he confiscated many of the temples' tax-exempt lands, thereby increasing the proceeds of the state treasury. In the Song period, commercial taxes had fed the treasury. In the Ming and, later, the Manchu periods, imperial revenues came mainly from agriculture: farmers produced the state's resources.

Hong Wu ordered a general survey of all China's land and several censuses of the population. The data gathered were recorded in official

TABLE 22.1 LAND RECLAMATION IN EARLY MING CHINA ✷

Year	Reclaimed Land (in hectares; 1 hectare = 2.5 acres)
1371	576,000
1373	1,912,000
1374	4,974,000
1379	1,486,000

Source: J. Gernet, A History of Chinese Civilization, trans. J. R. Foster (Cambridge: Cambridge University Press, 1982), p. 391. Used with permission.

registers, which provided valuable information about the taxes that landlords, temples, and peasants owed. According to the registers, the capital was owed 8 million *shih,* or 160,000 tons, of rice per year. Such thorough fiscal information contributed to the efficient operation of the state.

To secure soldiers for the army and personnel for his administration and to generate revenue, Hong Wu adopted the Yuan practice of requiring service to the state. He made all occupations hereditary, classifying the entire Chinese population into three hereditary categories: peasants, artisans, and soldiers. The state ministry that had jurisdiction over a particular category designated an individual's obligations to the state.

The ministry of finance oversaw the peasants, who provided the bulk of the taxes and performed public labor services. The ministry of public works supervised artisans and all people who had special skills and crafts. The ministry of the army controlled the standing army of 2 million men. Each social category prevailed in a particular geographical region. Peasants lived in the countryside. Craftsmen lived mainly in the neighborhoods of the cities for which they produced goods. Army families lived along the coasts and lengthy frontiers that they defended. When a soldier died or proved unable to fight, his family had to provide a replacement.

The Ming emperor wielded absolute and despotic power. Access to his personal favor was the only means of acquiring privilege or some limited derivative power. The complex ceremonial and court ritual surrounding any public appearance by the emperor, the vast imperial palace staffed only by servile women and eunuchs, and the precise procedures of the imperial bureaucracy, which blamed any difficulties on the emperor's advisers— all lent the throne a rarefied aura and exalted the emperor's authority. In addition, Hong Wu demanded that the military nobles (his old rebel comrades-in-arms) live at his court in Nanjing, where he could keep an eye on them. He raised many generals to the nobility, a position that bestowed honor and financial benefits but no political power whatsoever.

Late in his reign Hong Wu executed many nobles and divided China into principalities, putting one of his sons in charge of each. Suspicious even of his sons' loyalty, he carefully limited their power. Positions in the imperial administration were filled in part by means of civil service examinations, which proved to be Hong Wu's most enduring reform. The examination system, which lasted until the twentieth century, later became the exclusive channel for official recruitment. Examinations were given every three years at the district, provincial, and state (imperial) levels; candidates had to pass the lower levels before trying for the imperial level where the success rate in late imperial China was between one and two percent. In the Ming period the examinations required a minute knowledge of the ancient Chinese classics and a formal and precise literary style: they discouraged all originality. In the bureaucrats who passed them, the examinations promoted conservatism and opposition to innovation. To prevent nepotism and corruption, civil service positions were filled according to the "Rule of Avoidance": a candidate could

An Acrobat Entertains   The hard, dull routine of country or town people could be temporarily lightened by a traveling juggler, gymnast, or comedian who performed skits and then passed the hat for payment. Here an acrobat demonstrates his skill with the lance as spectators watch: at the top, a handicapped person, two beggars, and a boy who calls them; at the left, a group of porters with poles for carrying merchandise on their shoulders; on the right, a group of the well-to-do. (*Source: Art Institute of Chicago/Photo: Wan-go Weng*)

not be appointed to a position in his native province, nor could two members of the same family serve in the same province.

After 1426 the eunuch-dominated secret police controlled the palace guards and the imperial workshops, infiltrated the civil service, and headed all foreign missions. Through blackmail, espionage, and corruption, the secret police exercised enormous domestic power. How did eunuchs acquire such power? Without heirs, they had no immediate family concerns. Drawn from the lowest classes of society, viewed with distaste by respectable people, eunuchs had no hope of gaining status except by satisfying every whim of the emperor. They were indifferent to public opinion. Because of their total submission to the emperor, the emperors believed them absolutely trustworthy. Several eunuchs—Wang Chih in the 1470s, Liu Zhi in the 1500s, and Wei Zhong-xian in the 1620s—gained dictatorial power when their emperors lost interest in affairs of state.

Foreign affairs occupied much of Hong Wu's attention. He sought to control all Chinese contacts with the outside world, and he repeatedly invaded Mongolia. But the strengthening and extension of the Great Wall stands as Hong Wu's and his Ming successors' most visible achievement. According to one record, the defense system of the Great Wall throughout the Ming period formed a protective girdle "10,000 *li* (a *li* is about one-third of a mile) in an unbroken chain from the Yalu River in the east to Jiayuguan in the west."[3] The forts, beacon towers, and garrisons that pierced the wall at militarily strategic spots kept in close contact with the central government. Because of the steady pressure of Mongol attacks in the fifteenth century, Hong Wu's successors continued the work of reinforcing the Great Wall.

Hong Wu forbade free commercial contacts along the coasts between Chinese and foreign merchants. He insisted that foreign states eager to trade with China acknowledge his suzerainty by offering tribute. The early Ming emperors displayed greater military and diplomatic efficiency than had Chinese rulers for centuries. By the mid-fifteenth century, however, Mongol raids by land and Japanese piracy at sea, often with the hidden cooperation of the local Chinese, were commonplace. Along the coasts Koreans, Vietnamese, Malays, Sumatrans, and Japanese entered China disguised as merchants. If they were dissatisfied with the official rates of exchange, they robbed and destroyed. Neither fortresses and the transfer of coastal settlements inland nor precautionary attacks on pirate merchant raiders could suppress the problem. The imperial court came to regard foreigners arriving by ship, including Europeans when they arrived in the sixteenth century, as "barbarians."

Maritime Expansion

Another dramatic development of the Ming period was the series of naval expeditions sent out between 1405 and 1433 under Hong Wu's son Yong Lu and Yong Lu's successor. China had a strong maritime history stretching back to the eleventh century, and these early fifteenth-century voyages were a continuation of that tradition. The Ming expeditions established China as the greatest maritime power in the world—considerably ahead of Portugal, whose major seafaring reconnaissances began a half-century later.

In contrast to Hong Wu, Yong Lu broadened diplomatic and commercial contacts within the tribute system. Yong Lu had two basic motives for launching overseas voyages. First, he sent them in search of Jian Wen, a serious contender for the throne whom he had defeated but who, rumor claimed, had escaped to Southeast Asia. Second, he launched the expeditions to explore, to expand trade, and to provide the imperial court with luxury objects. Led by the Muslim eunuch admiral Zheng He and navigating by compass, seven fleets sailed to East and South Asia. The first expedition (which carried 27,800 men) involved 62 major ships, the largest of which was 440 feet in length and 180 feet in the beam and had 9 masts. The expeditions crossed the Indian Ocean to Ceylon, the Persian Gulf, and the east coast of Africa.

These voyages had important consequences. They extended the prestige of the Ming Dynasty throughout Asia. Trade, in the form of tribute from as far as the west coast of southern India, greatly increased. Diplomatic contacts with the distant Middle East led to the arrival in Nanjing of embassies from Egypt. The maritime expeditions also led to the publication of geographical works such as the *Treatise on the Barbarian Kingdoms on the Western Oceans* (1434) and *The Marvels Discovered by the Boat Bound for the Galaxy* (1436). The information acquired from the voyages served as the basis of Chinese knowledge of the maritime world until the nineteenth century. Finally, these expeditions resulted in Chinese emigration to the countries of Southeast Asia and the ports of southern India. The voyages were terminated because Confucian court intellectuals persuaded the emperor that his quest for strange and exotic things signaled the collapse of the dynasty.[4] After 1435, China returned to a policy of isolation.

Decline of the Ming Dynasty

A bitter struggle for the throne ensued when Hong Wu died. The bloody wars that brought his son Yong Lu to the throne devastated the territory between the Yellow and the Yangtze Rivers. Yong Lu (1403–1424) promoted a policy of resettlement there. He continued his father's policies of requiring civil service examinations, controlling the nobility, and trying to restrain pirates. He also transferred the capital back to Beijing (Peking). A former governor *(wang)* of the north, Yong Lu felt he had greater support there than in the south. Beijing was also closer to the northern frontier and thus was a better place for strategic defense against China's ancient enemies, the Mongols. The move pleased the military faction but hurt the new gentry and mercantile groups, whose economic interests centered around Nanjing.

The extravagance of the imperial court caused economic difficulties. Hong Wu had exercised fiscal restraint, but Yong Lu and his successors tried to outdo the splendor and magnificence of the Mongols. The emperor and his court lived in the Forbidden City, a quarter-mile compound filled with palatial buildings, ceremonial halls, marble terraces, and lengthy galleries; their grandeur surpassed that of Louis XIV's Versailles. Surrounding the Forbidden City and occupying some three square smiles was the Imperial City, where, in the words of a modern historian,

there were also supply depots and material-processing plants. Among them was the court of Imperial Entertainments, which had the capacity to serve banquets for up to 15,000 men on short notice. Next to the bakery, distillery, and confectionery were the emperor's stable, armory, printing-office, and book depository.[5]

A century and a half later, in the reign of the emperor Wan-li, everything required for the maintenance of the Imperial City was manufactured or deposited there. Approximately twenty thousand eunuchs worked there, and some three thousand female domestics performed household tasks. The emperor's immediate court—councilors, bodyguards, relatives, official wives, and concubines—numbered several thousand people. Supporting so many people on a lavish scale placed a great burden on the treasury. Financial difficulties thus played a major role in the decline of the Ming.

Yong Lu's successors lacked his drive and ability. The Mongols continued to press on the northern borders, and the Chinese had to yield some territory. In 1450, during an ill-conceived expedition against the Mongols, the inexperienced young emperor Ying-Zoung (r. 1436–1450 and 1457–1464) was captured and remained a prisoner of the Mongols for seven years. In the south, a Chinese army of 200,000 had pressed into northern Vietnam in 1406. This imperialistic move led to temporary Chinese domination of the Red River basin and of much of central Vietnam. A Vietnamese liberation movement retaliated and by 1427 had driven the occupiers out. In the sixteenth century the Japanese accelerated their coastal raids and even sacked the cities of Ningbo (Ningpo) and Yangzhou (Yangchow). Difficulties in collecting taxes hindered the government's ability to strengthen the army. It was commonplace in the eleven hundred counties of Ming China for people to delay or refuse to pay taxes, aware that no magistrate could prosecute thousands of delinquents. Their taxes were eventually written off.

In spite of these pressures, the empire did not fall apart. In fact, southern China enjoyed considerable prosperity in the late sixteenth and early seventeenth centuries. Japanese, Portuguese, and Dutch merchants paid in silver for the Chinese silks and ceramics they bought. However, because of the steady flow of silver into China from the trade with Japan and, later, from the mines of Mexico and Peru by way of Spain, the value of Chinese paper currency, which had been in circulation since the eleventh century, drastically declined. Unable to control either the state economy or local commercial activity, the imperial government had to acquiesce in foreign trade. The emperor also had to recognize the triumph of silver as a medium of exchange.

By the late sixteenth century China was participating in the emerging global economy. Portuguese ships carried Chinese silks and ceramics to Nagasaki and returned with Japanese silver. The huge Ming merchant marine fleet, built from the trees planted by Hong Wu and technically more

Silkworm Culture   Women traditionally handled silkworm culture, though men helped pick the mulberry leaves that fed the worms. At the left, silkworms are cultivated, graded, and harvested. At the right, the cocoons are boiled in a cauldron before the threads can be drawn, and a boy fans the fire under the pot. *(Source: Library of Congress/Laurie Platt Winfrey, Inc.)*

proficient for long sea voyages than were the Spanish and Portuguese fleets, transported textiles, porcelains, silk, and paper to Manila in the Philippines and brought back sweet potatoes, tobacco, firearms, and silver. From Manila the Spanish fleet carried Chinese goods to the markets of Barcelona, Antwerp, and Venice. The Dutch transported tea by the boatload from Fujian (Fukien) and Zhejiang (Chekiang) for the castles and drawing rooms of Europe.[6] Europeans paid for most of their imports with silver. Scholars argue that between one-third and one-half of all the silver mined in the Americas between 1527 and 1821 wound up in China. Spanish galleons carried it from Acapulco to Manila and from there to Chinese ports[7].

In the middle of the sixteenth century, China showed many signs of developing into an urban mercantile society. Merchants and businessmen had large amounts of capital, and they invested it not in land, as in the past, but in commercial and craft industries. Silk making, cotton weaving, porcelain manufacture, printing, and steel production

assumed a definite industrial character. So many peasants seeking employment migrated to the towns that agriculture declined. Some businesses employed several hundred workers, many of them women. According to a French scholar, "Peasant women took jobs at Sung-chiang, southwest of Shanghai in the cotton mills. According to contemporary descriptions, in the big workshops the employees were already the anonymous labor force that we regard as characteristic of the industrial age."[8]

Technical treatises reveal considerable progress in manufacturing procedures. Silk looms had three or four shuttle winders. Printers could produce a sheet of paper with three or four different colors, similar to the page of a modern magazine. Chinese ceramics displayed astonishing technology—which helps explain the huge demand for them. Likewise, agricultural treatises described new machines for working the soil, sowing seed, and irrigation. Population, which stood at roughly 70 million at the start of the Ming period, increased to about 130 million by 1600.

With population, technology, and capital, why did China fail to develop something comparable to what Westerners later called an industrial or commercial revolution? The traditional Chinese value system did not esteem commerce, industry, or social change.

China never experienced a scientific revolution or an Enlightenment, as the European West did in the seventeenth and eighteenth centuries (Ch. 18). Lacking a spirit that criticized existing ideas and institutions, China remained culture bound and conservative. The Chinese practice of partible inheritance in which sons divided parents' estates thwarted, or at least slowed, the accumulation of capital. (The English system of primogeniture by which only the eldest son inherited promoted the accumulation of capital.) Likewise, the extensive pursuit of the Confucian civil service examinations as the path to socio-economic advancement diverted capital from industrial, technical, and even agricultural innovation. The fundamental axiom that China, the Central Kingdom of the universe, was superior to other states and contained within its borders all that was needed for a happy existence likewise discouraged change.

Hostility to the artisan and merchant classes had very deep roots in traditional China. The sixth century B.C. scholar Han Fei had listed merchants and craftsmen among "The Five Vermin of the State," writing:

An enlightened ruler will administer his state in such a way as to decrease the number of merchants, artisans and other men who make their living by wandering from place to place, and will see to it that such men are looked down upon. In this way he lessens the number of people who abandon primary pursuits (agriculture) to take up secondary occupations. . . . When wealth and money, no matter how dishonestly gotten, can buy what is in the market, you may be sure that the number of merchants will not remain small. . . . These are the customs of a disordered state.[9]

Revering such classical Confucian texts, officials in the seventeenth and eighteenth centuries looked on merchants with distrust and distaste.

Wealth was based on agriculture, and from agriculture the state derived its taxes and the ruling class its income. Could trade and manufacturing also be taxed? No, they could not. According to Confucian philosophy, any promotion of trade would encourage people to aspire to a different lifestyle and to a higher social status, and such aspirations would bring change and social disorder. Moreover, Chinese thinkers held that merchants produced nothing: they bought something from its grower or maker and sold it at a higher price than they had paid; thus they were parasites living off the labor of others. In addition, the proliferation of luxury goods, which people did not really need, would lead to extravagance and excessive consumption and in turn to moral decay.

Believing that virtue lies in frugality, vice in extravagance, the Ming emperors issued sumptuary laws restricting or prohibiting certain styles of clothing, tableware, means of conveyance, and articles of household decoration. The effect of these laws, however, was *increased* social stratification: the richer became richer, the poor poorer. Nevertheless, the Confucian ideal remained intact: a "successful merchant" was, by definition, one who had stopped trading and had invested his wealth in agriculture.[10] By contrast, in England, and later in western and central Europe, the upper middle classes gained increasing influence in representative assemblies and passed laws that facilitated commerce, business, and industry.

In 1600 the Ming Dynasty faced grave political and economic problems. The Manchus, a Tungusic people from Manchuria, threatened from the north. Wars against the Japanese and Koreans had depleted the imperial treasury. As rich landowners bought up the lands assigned to farm families, the social structures set up by Hong Wu broke down. The military, considered a disreputable profession, attracted the dregs of society, so the government had to hire mercenaries. According to the Italian Jesuit missionary Matteo Ricci (1552–1610), "All those under arms lead a despicable life, for they have not embraced this profession out of love of their country or devotion to their king or love of honour and glory, but as men in the service of a provider of employment."[11] Maintenance of the army placed a heavy burden on the state.

Meanwhile, the imperial court continued to squander vast sums on an ostentatious lifestyle. Under the emperor Wan-li, forty-five princes of the first rank received annual incomes of 10,000 shih (the money equivalent of 10,000 tons of grain), and 21,000 lesser nobles also received large allowances. The emperors increased domestic sales taxes, established customs posts for export-import duties, and laid ever-more-crushing taxes on the peasants. New taxes provoked violent riots in the large commercial centers of Suzhou (Soochow), Hangzhou (Hangchow), and Beijing.

Finally, the emperors became the victims of the bureaucracy and of Confucian ideology. A Ming emperor was taught that his primary duties were to venerate the heavens, the abode of his ancestors who watched over him; and to follow the precedents set by his ancestors. As long as the emperor performed certain time-honored rituals, he retained the Mandate of Heaven, the traditional legitimization of Chinese rulers. Imperial ritual connected the ordinary person to the state by inspiring awe, respect and loyalty. Thus successive emperors spent a large part of each day in the performance of imperial ceremonies which they began to resent.

The dynastic shift from the Ming to the Qing (Ch-ing) Dynasty established by the Manchus seemed to fulfill the Han Confucian doctrine that history operates in a cyclical fashion. The Ming emperor apparently had forfeited the Mandate of Heaven. According to Han Confucian scholars, a wise ruler satisfies Heaven's mandate by observing the proper Confucian rites of social intercourse. If the emperor is respectful to his parents, attentive to his ministers, and concerned for his subjects, then the empire and the civilized world will flourish. The emperor was supposed to be a model. If he was virtuous, his officials were likely to be so too. If he looked to his own self-interest, his civil servants would probably do likewise, to the cost of the general welfare: corruption would spread, taxes would be oppressive, and peasants would revolt.

The reign of Wan-li (r. 1573–1619), who ruled longer than any other member of the Ming Dynasty, illustrates what happened when the emperor was at odds with the system. An intelligent man with some good ideas, Wan-li felt that the bureaucrats opposed everything he wanted to do. When he tried to increase the size of the army and to improve its effectiveness through drills and maneuvers, civil service officials sent him lengthy petitions calling for an end to such exercises. When he wanted to take personal command of the army at a time of foreign invasion, bureaucrats told him that precedent forbade his leaving the Imperial City. Wan-li gradually reached the conclusion that the monarchy had become no more than a set of stylized performances.

Stymied in whatever he wanted to do, he simply refused to make state decisions. He devoted his time to his horses and, though still a young man, to the construction of his tomb. Imperial decisions were postponed. Factional strife among the court eunuchs and bureaucrats increased. The wheels of government ground to a halt.[12] Between 1619 and 1627, greedy court eunuchs helped precipitate a crisis. The eunuch Wei Zhong-xian (1568–1627) exercised a two-year reign of terror and sent hundreds of honest civil servants to their deaths as conspirators. The bureaucracy, which the eunuchs controlled, was so torn by factions that it could not function.

Meanwhile, the Manchus pressed against China's northeastern border. Under their leader Nurhachi (1559–1626), they built a powerful military and administrative organization and gained the allegiance of the Mongols and other tribes. As the Ming government in Beijing floundered, public anger at bureaucratic corruption mounted. The gentry and business classes, centered in the south around Nanjing, had been alienated by the Ming court's fiscal mismanagement and demands for more taxes. Ming troops, their pay in arrears, turned outlaw. Droughts led to crop failures, which in turn caused widespread famines. Starving peasants turned to banditry, and entire provinces revolted. The general decay paved the way for Manchu conquest.

In the popular understanding of the Mandate of Heaven, the natural and political orders were closely linked. Events such as droughts, famines, earthquakes, floods, and volcanic eruptions were considered signs of Heaven's displeasure and signaled that conditions were ripe for the appearance of a new dynasty. Predictably, when it seemed that the Mandate of Heaven had been withdrawn from the Ming emperor and was about to redescend on someone worthy, ambitious generals, bandit warlords, and popular movements appeared. According to a modern historian, "The prospect of a new mandate feverishly excited rebellions, which seemed in turn to prove that the previous dynastic cycle had reached its term."[13] Such events had accompanied the collapse of the Yuan and the rise of the Ming. Similar developments greeted the fall of the Ming and the emergence of the Manchus.

Manchu Rule

Capitalizing on the internal weaknesses of the Ming, in 1644 the Manchus declared a new dynasty, the Qing. They went on to capture Beijing and slowly gained control of all China. Although various Ming princes and local bandit groups had

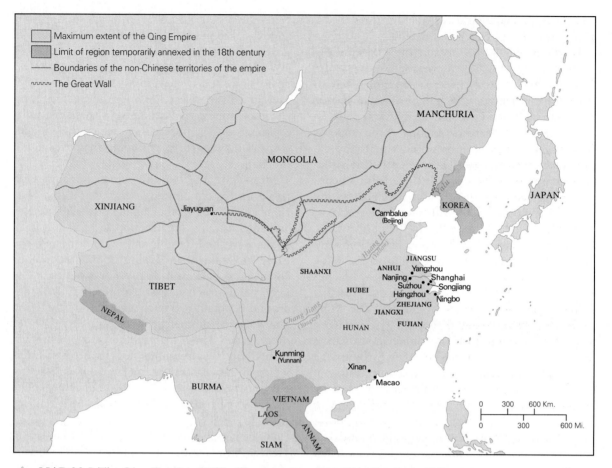

MAP 22.1 The Qing Empire, 1759   The sheer size of the Qing Empire in China almost inevitably led to its profound cultural influence on the rest of Asia. What geographical and political factors limited the extent of the empire?

risen against the Manchus, the army lacked good equipment and staying power and gradually collapsed. The entry of the Manchus' imperial armies into Yunnan in 1681 marked their complete military triumph.

By purging the civil service of the old court eunuchs and troublesome factions, and by offering Chinese intellectuals positions in the bureaucracy, the Manchus gained the support of the influential academic and intellectual classes. Chinese scholars flocked to Beijing. The Manchu government, staffed by able and honest Chinese, became much more efficient than the Ming.

The Qing Dynasty—the name adopted by the Manchus means "pure" or "unsullied"—ruled until 1912. In its heyday in the eighteenth century, the Qing Empire covered much of Asia—China proper, Manchuria, Mongolia, Tibet, and Xinjiang

(Sinkiang)—and enjoyed tribute from Burma, Nepal, Laos, Siam, Annam, and Korea (Map 22.1). China had the largest population on earth and achieved an unprecedented degree of prosperity.

How did a million Manchus govern 350 million Chinese? The Qing Dynasty retained the basic structures of Ming and Confucian government. The emperor, possessor of the Mandate of Heaven, governed as a supreme and autocratic ruler. The bureaucracies continued as they had in Ming and earlier times: the imperial household bureaucracy managed the emperor's palaces and households; the central bureaucracy administered his vast empire. Most positions in the empire were assigned on the basis of candidates' performances in the civil service examinations in the Confucian classics. The highest positions in Beijing and in the provinces of China were open to Chinese as well as to Manchus. These measures pacified the Chinese economic and intellectual elites. The Manchus, however, maintained a privileged status in society. They wore distinctive clothes, did not practice footbinding, retained their own language and alphabet, and maintained ethnic separatism by forbidding intermarriage with the Chinese. The Manchus required Chinese males to wear their hair in a pigtail as a sign of subservience.

Along with the agricultural improvements begun in the Ming period, internal peace, relative prosperity, and engineering methods that prevented flooding of the countryside contributed to a population explosion in the eighteenth century, as the statistics in Table 22.2 illustrate. But in the late eighteenth century growth without increased agricultural output led to rebellions and uprisings that eventually weakened the Qing Dynasty.

The reign of the emperor Kang-xi (r. 1662–1722) launched a period of great achievement. A contemporary of the Indian ruler Aurangzeb, the French king Louis XIV, and the Russian tsar Peter the Great, Kang-xi demonstrated exceptional intelligence, energy, and concern for the welfare of his people. He also enjoyed much greater freedom of action than had the Ming emperor Wan-li a century earlier. Whereas Wan-li had been a captive of precedent, incapable of making changes, Kang-xi cut both court expenses and taxes and traveled extensively throughout his domain. On these trips he investigated the conduct of local bureaucrats in an effort to prevent them from oppressing the people. Kang-xi squarely faced and thoroughly crushed a massive rebellion in southern China in 1678. He personally led an army into Mongolia and smashed the forces of the Mongol leader Galdan. This victory permanently eliminated the danger of a reinvigorated Mongolian empire on China's borders.

Kang-xi also cultivated the arts of peace. He invited scholars to his court and subsidized the compilation of a huge encyclopedia and two monumental dictionaries. *The Complete Library of the Four Treasuries,* a collection of all of Chinese literature, required the work of 15,000 calligraphers and 361 editors. It preserved the Chinese literary tradition. Kang-xi's contributions to literature hold a distinguished place in the long history of Chinese culture. Europeans and Americans, however, appreciate this period primarily for its excellent porcelain. An imperial factory at Jiangxi (Kiangsi), directly controlled by Kang-xi's court, produced porcelain masterpieces. Monochrome vases, bowls,

TABLE 22.2 POPULATION OF CHINA, 1578–1989

Year	Government	Population (in millions)	
		Families	Individuals
1578	Ming Dynasty	10.6	60.7
1662	Qing Dynasty	19.2	100.0
1710		23.3	116.0
1729		25.5	127.0
1741			143.4
1754			184.5
1778			243.0
1796			275.7
1814			374.6
1850			414.5
1953	People's Republic		601.9
1974			800.0
1989			1,064.0

and dishes in oxblood, pale green, and dark blue, and polychromes in blue and white, enjoyed great popularity in Paris, London, and New York in the eighteenth century and ever since.

The long reign of the emperor Qian-long (r. 1736–1795) marked the zenith of the Qing Dynasty. The cultivation of new crops from the Americas—white potatoes, corn, peanuts—on marginal lands helped to support the steadily expanding population. Chinese rule was extended into central Asia. The imperial court continued to support arts and letters. In the last two decades of his reign, however, Qian-long showered titles, gifts, and offices on a handsome young Manchu named He-shen. Contemporaries considered He-shen uncultured, greedy, and ambitious. The corruption of the imperial civil service under He-shen, combined with heavy taxation, sparked revolts that continued to the end of the dynasty in 1912.

The Qianlong Emperor at an Archery Contest Executed by the Italian Jesuit Giuseppe Castiglione, whose portraits and panoramas combine Chinese composition with Western perspective and coloration, this painting—with the elegant garden, stately uniforms of the attendants, and dignified image of the emperor—suggests the formal ritual of the imperial court. Castiglione was a special favorite of the Qianlong emperor, who also supported Jesuit architects and designers. *(Source: A private collection/Photo: Wan-go Weng)*

External Pressures

By the middle years of the eighteenth century, Qianlong also faced increasing foreign pressures. In the north and northwest, the region from which invaders had historically entered China, Mongols, Russians, and ethnic minority peoples pressed the borders. Christian missionaries, notably the Jesuits, wanted greater scope for their proselytizing activities. Nearby Asian countries that had many cultural affinities with China—Korea, Burma, Siam, Vietnam—desired greater trade with China. So, too, did European merchants: the European demand for Chinese silk, porcelain, and tea was enormous. The British East India Company, for example, had by 1740 become an international corporation with global activities, backed by eager investors in Great Britain. What was the response of the imperial government to these increasing foreign pressures?

The Qing government had no ministry of foreign affairs. Chinese relations with all foreign countries reflected the Chinese belief that China was the "central kingdom" and that all other countries were "peripheral" and removed from the cultural center of the universe. The Office of Border Affairs conducted relations with peoples in the northwest crescent (Mongols and Russians). It took police action when necessary and used the marriages of imperial daughters as the means of making alliance and maintaining peace in the north. Acting on the theory that religious evangelization by foreigners reflected on the prestige of the emperor, the imperial household itself supervised the activities of Jesuit missionaries. The Ministry of Rituals managed commercial relations with the nations of East Asia. Business delegations from Korea, Burma, Siam were termed "tribute missions." As long as they used a language of subservience to the emperor and his ministers and made the ritual prostrations, they were allowed limited amounts of trade with China in precisely defined times and places—in the port of Canton from October to March.[14] As mentioned above, the Chinese value system did not respect business and commerce and distrusted traders.

Sniffing fat profits to be made from expanded trade, the aggressive merchants of London and Liverpool could not comprehend the Chinese attitude. Accordingly, the British East India Company, with the support of King George III's government, resolved on a personal appeal to Qian-long through a delegation headed by an experienced diplomat, Lord George Macartney. Three ships sailed from Portsmouth in September 1792 carrying rich gifts for the emperor: a huge imperial state coach fashioned after George III's own vehicle; a variety of heavily jeweled pocket, wrist, and neck watches; and a planetarium, a working model of the entire solar system. The dazzling array of gifts was intended to show that England was the most scientifically advanced and economically powerful nation on earth. Delivered in a diamond-encrusted gift box, George III's respectful letter to the emperor stated in part:

His Most Sacred Majesty George III ... to the Supreme Emperor of China Qianlong, worthy to live tens of thousands and tens of thousands thousand years, sendeth

Greeting ...

We have been still more anxious to inquire into the arts and manners of countries where civilization has been perfected by the wise ordinances and virtuous examples of their Sovereigns thro a long series of ages; and, above all, Our ardent wish had been to become acquainted with those celebrated institutions of Your Majesty's populous and extensive Empire which have carried its prosperity to such a height as to be the admiration of all surrounding nations. ...

We have the happiness of being at peace with all the World ... Many of our subjects have also frequented for a long time past a remote part of your Majesty's dominions for the purpose of Trade. No doubt the interchange of commodities between Nations distantly situated tends to their mutual convenience, industry, and wealth.[15]

The letter went on to ask for the establishment of permanent Chinese-British diplomatic relations; broader trade, including the opening of new ports for international commerce; and a fair system of tariffs or customs duties.

The mission that reached Canton in June 1793 (the long journey is an indication of the time involved in eighteenth-century travel) almost floundered over the issue of ritual and procedure. Court officials agreed that Macartney might see the emperor at his summer palace, if the British emissaries acknowledged that they came as a "tributary nation" and performed the *kowtow*—kneeling and striking their heads on the ground nine times in front of the emperor. Macartney protested that he was not required to show such obeisance even to George III. A compromise was finally reached when Macartney agreed to bow on one knee as he would bow to his English sovereign. Qian-long however, was not pleased. The ruler of China considered himself supreme and all other kings his subordinates. Though thoroughly courteous to his guests, he denied all their requests (see Listening to the Past).

The Macartney mission represented the clash of two different cultures. On the one side was China, "an immobile empire," convinced of its superiority, opposed to all innovation, and convinced that the ancient Confucian texts contained the answers to all problems. On the other side was Great Britain, equally convinced of its superiority "because it was modern: founded on science, the free exchange of ideas, and the mastery of commercial exchange."[16] Understanding and communication proved impossible.

The Life of the People

The family is the fundamental unit of every society. In Ming and Qing China, however, the family exercised greater social influence than it did anywhere else—and far more than in Western societies. The family directed the moral education of the child, the economic advancement and marriage of the young, and religious life through ceremonial rites honoring family ancestors. The Chinese family discharged many of the roles that the Christian church performed in Europe in the Middle Ages and that the state carries out today. It assumed total responsibility for the sick, the indigent, and the aged. The family expected and almost invariably received the full devotion and loyalty of its members. A person without a family had no material or psychological support.

Poor families tended to be nuclear: couples established their own households and raised their own children. The educated, the middle class, and the wealthy frequently resided in extended families: several generations of patrilineal relatives and their wives lived together in one large house or compound, individual families occupying different sections. In both kinds of families, the paternal head of the family held autocratic power over all members of the household. Apart from crimes against the emperor and his family, the worst crimes were those committed by children against their parents. Fathers who harmed their sons received lighter punishment than sons who harmed (or even insulted) their fathers. In one instance the Ministry of Punishments reviewed a local governor's sentence that a father be beaten for burying his son alive. The son had used foul language to his father. The ministry concluded that "although the killing (by the father) was done intentionally, it was the killing of a son who had committed a capital crime by reviling his father. The father was acquitted."[17] When a father died, his authority over the household passed to his eldest son.

The father led the family in the ancient Confucian rites honoring the family ancestors. If these ceremonies were not continued by the next generation, the family suffered social disgrace and, it was believed, the dead endured great misery. Thus marriage and childbearing were extremely important.

Almost everyone married. Reverence for one's parents, maintenance of the family, and perpetuation of the line required that sons marry shortly after reaching puberty. The father and family elders discussed the possibilities and employed a local go-between to negotiate with the prospective bride's family. The go-between drew up a marriage contract specifying the property, furniture, clothing, and gifts that the two young people would bring to the union. As elsewhere, parents wanted to make the most economically and socially advantageous union for their children. The couple had no part in these arrangements. Often they had never met each other until the groom lifted the bride's veil on their wedding day. But they had been brought up to accept this custom.

A Chinese bride became part of her husband's family, subject to him and to her in-laws. Her first duty was to bear sons. If she did not, she might adopt a son. Failure to provide heirs gave her husband grounds for divorce, which brought great disgrace on her family. A woman, however, could not divorce her husband for any reason. Divorce was extremely rare in Chinese society, but a wealthy man with a "nonproductive" wife might bring concubines to live in the house along with his wife.

Men held a much higher position in society than did women. The desperately poor often killed girl babies or sold their daughters as servants or concubines. Young brides came under the direct control of their mothers-in-law, whose severity and cruelty are a common theme in Chinese literature. Once a strong-willed woman had sons, she gained increasing respect as the years went by. The Chinese deeply respected age. Some women of the wealthy classes, with servants to do the household chores, spent their days in semiseclusion nibbling dainties, smoking opium, and gambling. Women who brought large dowries to their marriages could dispose of part of those dowries as they wished. Some invested in profitable business activities. Poor women worked in the fields beside their husbands, in addition to bearing children and managing the household.

The educational system during the Ming and Qing periods had both virtues and weaknesses. Most villages and all towns and cities operated schools that prepared boys for the all-important civil service examinations. Boys learned to write with a brush the approximately three thousand commonly used characters of literary Chinese; and they learned the standard texts of Confucian philosophy, ethics, and history. The curriculum was very limited, and the instructional method stressed memorization and discouraged imagination. The civil service aspirant received no practical training in the work of government. But the system yielded a high percentage of literate men (relative to Europe at the same time) and gave Chinese society cohesion and stability. All educated Chinese shared the same basic ethical and literary culture, much as medieval Europeans were formed by Latin Christian culture.

In China, as in medieval Europe, educational opportunities for girls were severely limited. Rich men occasionally hired tutors for their daughters, and a few women achieved exceptional knowledge. Most women of all classes received training that prepared them for roles as wives and mothers: courteous behavior, submission to their husbands, and the administration of a household.

What of health and medical care in imperial China? Although Egyptian and Babylonian medicine predate Chinese medicine by perhaps a millennium, the Chinese medical tradition is the oldest continuing usage in the world. Chinese medical theory deriving from the Han period (from the third century B.C. to the third century A.D.) attributes all ailments to a lack of harmony in the body; cure, then, rests on restoring harmony. Diagnosis of disease depended on visual observation, studying the case history, auditory symptoms, and taking the pulse. Physicians held that three spots along the wrist gave the pulse readings of different organs, and the experienced physician could diagnose the malfunction of any internal organ by checking the pulse. Two basic forms of therapy (treatment) existed. Medicinal therapy was based on the curative effects of herbs. This treatment entailed taking pills or powders in a boiled broth. The other therapy was acupuncture, the insertion of needles into specific parts of the body.

The theory behind acupuncture was that twelve channels run over the body close to the skin, each channel is related to a specific organ, and the needle stimulates a sluggish or pacifies an overactive organ. The acupuncturist used fine needles and avoided vital organs. Certainly acupuncture was no more dangerous than the widespread European practice of bleeding.

Reliance on acupuncture and the Confucian principle that the body is the sacred gift of parents to child made dissection a terrible violation of filial piety and thus strongly discouraged serious surgery. Another factor militating against surgery was the Chinese culture's disdain for manual work of any kind. A "wise" doctor mastered a body of classical texts, prescribed medicine for treatment, and "did not lower himself to perform manual, surgical operations."[18] Nor should a doctor accept fees for service.

Confucian policy did not allow any experts with specialized knowledge to rise socially as a group: social mobility, it was thought, led to social tensions and demands for restructuring.[19] Thus, while physicians in the Islamic and European worlds enjoyed respect and sometimes modest wealth, the

Ch'en Shu: The White Cockatoo   Like Italy and France in the early modern period, China and Japan can boast of distinguished women artists. This painting in ink and color on a hanging scroll depicts a highly prized species of parrot. The work by Ch'en Shu, a Chinese artist famous in her time, is very much in the Chinese artistic tradition. (*Source: The Metropolitan Museum of Art, 13.220.31*)

position of Chinese doctors was deemed insignificant, and they were considered mere artisans. Rather than consulting medical experts, each person had to acquire sufficient knowledge, including pharmacological knowledge, to help members of his or her family in time of illness.

Several emperors decreed that medical colleges should be established and that annual examinations should test physicians' skills so that the needs of the people, as well as the needs of the imperial court, would be served. But these orders were never implemented. As a result, although the idea of state-supported hospitals was an ancient one in China, the first institutions to provide medical care for the sick of a community were established by

Chinese Scholars The civil service examinations, the chief means of access to government positions and social status, inculcated total submission to the autocratic state. The largest number of candidates took the examinations in general knowledge and literary ability. Here candidates stand at writing desks, composing essays. *(Source: Bibliothèque Nationale, Paris)*

Christian medical missionaries in the nineteenth century.

In sharp contrast to Europe, China had few social barriers. The emperors fought the development of a hereditary aristocracy which could have undermined their absolute monarchy, and they granted very few titles of nobility in perpetuity. Though China had no legally defined aristocracy, she did have an "upper class" based on a *combination* of wealth, education, lineage, and bureaucratic position. Agricultural land remained the most highly prized form of wealth, but silver ingots, jade, libraries of classical works, porcelain, and urban real estate also indicated status. Wealth alone, however, did not bring status. Offices in the state bureaucracy provided opportunities and motivation for upward mobility. Family members encouraged intelligent sons to prepare for the civil service examinations, and the work and sacrifice of parents bore fruit in their sons' success. Positions in the bureaucracy brought salaries and gifts which a family invariably invested in land. The competitive examinations with few exceptions were open to all classes, and that accessibility prevented the formation of a ruling caste. China did not develop a politically articulate bourgeoisie. Because everyone accepted the Confucian principle that the learned and civilized should rule the state, scholars ranked highest in the social order. They, along with Heaven, Earth, the emperor, parents deserved special veneration. With the possible exception of the Jewish people, no people has respected learning as much as the Chinese. Merchants tried to marry into the scholar class in order to rise in the world. At the bottom of society were actors, prostitutes, and beggars.

The Chinese found recreation and relaxation in many ways. All classes gambled at cards and simple numbers games. The teahouse served as the local meeting place for exchanging news and gossip and listening to the tales of professional storytellers, who enjoyed great popularity. The affluent indulged in an alcoholic drink made from fermented and distilled rice, and both men and women liked pipes and tobacco. Everyone who could afford to do so went to the theater. The actors, like their ancient Greek counterparts, wore happy and sad masks, and their gestures were formal and stylized. The plays typically dramatized episodes from Chinese history and literature. The Chinese associated athletics, riding, and horse racing with soldiers, at best a necessary evil, and regarded the active life as

Chinese Cookery Everywhere in the world, until very recently, meat was scarce and thus a luxury. In China, the shortage of meat encouraged great sophistication in the preparation of foods, especially vegetables. Although European travelers interpreted the frequent servings of vegetables and fish as a sign of poverty, the Chinese, if we can trust modern nutritionists, probably had a healthier diet than the Europeans. Notice the variety of dishes. Women obviously ate separately from men. *(Source: Roger-Viollet)*

the direct antithesis of the scholarly contemplation they most valued.

JAPAN (CA 1400–1800)

The Ashikaga Shogunate lasted from the middle of the fourteenth to the late sixteenth century. During this period, Japanese society experienced almost continual violence and civil war. Weak central governments could not maintain order. Throughout the islands, local strongmen took charge. Around 1450, 250 *daimyos,* or lords, held power; by 1600, only 12 survivors could claim descent from daimyo families of the earlier date. Successful military leaders carved out large territories and governed them as independent rulers. Political and social conditions in fifteenth- and sixteenth-century Japan strongly resembled conditions in western Europe in the tenth and eleventh centuries. Political power was in the hands of a small group of military leaders. Historians often use the same term—*feudalism*—to describe the Japanese and European experience. As in medieval Europe, feudalism paved the way for the rise of a strong centralized state in seventeenth-century Japan.

Feudalism in Japan

Feudalism played a powerful role in Japanese culture until the nineteenth century. The similarities between feudalism in Japan and in medieval Europe have fascinated scholars, as have the very significant differences. In Europe, feudalism emerged out of the fusion of Germanic and Roman social institutions and flowered under the impact of Muslim and Viking invasions. In Japan, feudalism evolved from a combination of the native warrior tradition and Chinese Confucian ethics. Japanese society had adopted the Confucian emphasis on filial respect for the head of the family, for the local civil authorities, and for the supreme authority at the head of the state.

The two constituent elements of Japanese feudalism appeared between the eighth and the twelfth centuries: (1) the *shoen* (private land outside imperial control) with its *shiki* (rights) and (2) the *samurai* (the military warrior clique). Some scholars have equated the shoen with the European manor, but the comparison needs careful qualification. A manor usually corresponded to one composite village; a particular family's shoen was widely scattered. Those who held shoen possessed the shiki there—that is, the right to the income or rice produced by the land. But, just as several persons might hold rights—military, judicial, grazing—on a medieval European manor and all these rights yielded income, so several persons frequently held shiki rights on a Japanese estate.

By the sixteenth century, only a small proportion of samurai had attained the rank of daimyo and possessed a shoen. Most warriors were salaried

✱ **Women Husking Rice** Rice was basic to Japanese culture. Farmers paid their taxes to the daimyo's agent in rice, and the daimyo paid the salaries of the samurai in rice. It was the staple of the diet eaten by all classes. Here women husk the rice, separate the grains from the chaff using a primitive machine, and clean and pack the rice in bales made of rice stalks. *(Source: Laurie Platt Winfrey, Inc.)*

fighters with no connection to land. From their daimyos, they received stipends in rice, not in land; and in this respect they resembled European knights, who were supported by cash or money fiefs.

The Japanese samurai warrior resembled the knight of twelfth-century France in other ways as well. Both were armed with expensive weapons, and both fought on horseback. Just as the knight was supposed to live according to the chivalric code, so Japanese samurai were expected to live according to *Bushido,* or "Way of the Warrior," a code that stressed military honor, courage, stoic acceptance of hardship, and, above all, loyalty. Disloyalty brought social disgrace, which the samurai could avoid only through *seppuku,* ritual suicide by slashing his belly. Both samurai and knights were highly conscious of themselves as aristocrats. But knights fought as groups, and samurai fought as individuals.

By the middle of the sixteenth century Japanese feudalism had taken on other distinctive features. As the number of shoen decreased and the powerful daimyos consolidated their territories, the practice of *primogeniture* became common, keeping an estate intact under the eldest or ablest son. Around 1540 the introduction of the musket from Europe made infantrymen effective against mounted samurai, and the use of Western cannon required more elaborately fortified castles. Thus, in addition to armed cavalrymen, daimyos began to employ large numbers of foot soldiers equipped with spears, and they constructed new castles. These military and social developments occurred during a century of turbulence and chronic disorder, out of which emerged a leader who ended the chaos and began the process of unification, laying the foundation of the modern Japanese national state.

Nobunaga and National Unification

Oda Nobunaga (1534–1582), a samurai of the lesser daimyo class, won control of his native province of Owari in 1559. He began immediately to extend his power, defeating a powerful daimyo in 1560 and eight years later seizing Kyoto, the capital city, where the emperor and his court resided. As a result, Nobunaga became the virtual ruler of central Japan.

Scholars have called the years from 1568 to 1600 the period of "national unification." During this time Japan underwent aggressive and dynamic change. Adopting the motto "Rule the empire by force," Nobunaga set out to subdue all real and potential rivals and to replace them with his vassals. With the support of Toyotomi Hideyoshi (1537–1598), a brilliant general, he subdued first western and then eastern and northern Japan.

The great Buddhist temple-fortresses proved to be Nobunaga's biggest problem. Some of these monasteries possessed vast wealth and armed retainers. During the civil wars the Buddhists had supported various daimyos in their private wars, but Nobunaga would tolerate no such interference. The strategically located monastery on Mount Hiei near Kyoto had long provided sanctuary for political factions. Previous daimyos had refused to attack it because it was sacred. Nobunaga, however, used fire to reduce it, and his men slaughtered thousands of its occupants.

Although Nobunaga won control of most of Japan by the sword, he backed up his conquests with government machinery and a policy of conciliation. He gave lands and subordinate positions in the army to his defeated enemies. Trusted daimyos received complete civil jurisdiction over entire provinces. At strategic points, such as Nijo near Kyoto and Azuchi on the shore of Lake Biwa, Nobunaga built castles to serve as key administrative and defensive centers for the surrounding territories. He opened the little fishing village of Nagasaki to foreign commerce; it soon grew into the nation's largest port. He standardized the currency, eliminated customs barriers, and encouraged the development of trade and industry. In 1582, when Nobunaga was murdered by one of his vassals, his general and staunchest adherent, Hideyoshi, carried on his work.

A peasant's son who had risen to power by his military bootstraps, Hideyoshi advanced the unification and centralization of Japan in two important ways. First, in 1582 he attacked the great fortress at Takamatsu. When direct assault failed, his troops flooded the castle and forced its surrender. When Takamatsu fell, so did the large province of Mori. A successful siege of the town of Kagoshima then brought the southern island of Kyushu under his domination. Hideyoshi soothed the vanquished daimyos as Nobunaga had done—with lands and military positions—but he also required them to swear allegiance and to obey him "down to the smallest particular."[20]

Having reduced his most dangerous adversaries, Hideyoshi ordered a survey of the entire country. The military power of the unified Japanese state depended on a strong agricultural base, and Hideyoshi wanted to exploit the peasantry fully. His agents collected detailed information about the daimyos' lands and about towns, villages, agricultural produce, and industrial output all over Japan. This material enabled Hideyoshi to assess military quotas and taxable property. His surveys tied the peasant population to the land and tightened the collection of the land tax. When Hideyoshi died in 1598, he left a strong centralized state. Brute force had created a unified Japan.

On his deathbed the old soldier had set up a council of regents to govern during the minority of his infant son. The strongest regent was Hideyoshi's long-time supporter Tokugawa Ieyasu (1543–1616), who ruled vast territories around Edo (modern-day Tokyo). Ieyasu quickly eliminated the young ruler and in 1600 at Sekigahara smashed a coalition of daimyo defenders of the heir. This battle was the beginning of the Tokugawa regime.

The Tokugawa Regime

Japanese children are taught that "Ieyasu ate the pie that Nobunaga made and Hideyoshi baked." As the aphorism suggests, Ieyasu took over and completed the work begun by his able predecessors. He took decisive steps to solidify his dynasty and control the feudal nobility and to maintain peace and prosperity in Japan. The Tokugawa regime that Ieyasu fashioned worked remarkably well, lasting until 1867.

Ieyasu obtained from the emperor the title of *shogun,* or general-in-chief. Constitutionally, the emperor exercised sovereign authority. In practice, authority and power—both the legal right and the physical means—were held by the Tokugawa shogun. Ieyasu declared the emperor and his court at Kyoto "very precious and decorative, like gold and silver," and surrounded the imperial court with all the ceremonial trappings but none of the realities of power.

In a scheme resembling the later residency requirements imposed by Louis XIV (see page 560)

Tokugawa Ieyasu   A short, stocky man who had spent most of his life on horseback, Ieyasu was sixty-two when he secured appointment as shogun. Having unified Japan and established a peace that lasted 250 years, he ranks with George Washington and Peter the Great of Russia as one of the great nation builders in world history. In this iconic style of Shinto painting, the elderly Ieyasu is depicted as a deity. *(Source: The Tokugawa Foundation)*

and Peter the Great (see page 581), Ieyasu forced the feudal lords to establish "alternate residence" at his capital city of Edo, to spend part of each year there, and to leave their wives and sons there—essentially as hostages. This requirement had obvious advantages: the shogun could keep close tabs on the daimyos, control them through their children, and weaken them financially with the burden of maintaining two residences. Ieyasu justified this course of action by invoking the *Bushido* code, with its emphasis on loyalty. He forbade members of the nobility to marry without his consent, thus preventing the formation of dangerous alliances.

The early Tokugawa shoguns also restricted the construction of castles—symbols, in Japan as in medieval Europe, of feudal independence. Later, the practice of alternate residence led to considerable castle building, castles that represented demands for goods and services and which turned Edo and other cities into huge commercial centers. Members of the aristocratic class exercised full administrative powers within their domains. In effect, the country was governed by martial law in peacetime. Only warriors could hold official positions in the state bureaucracy. A network of spies kept close watch on those lords whose loyalty the shogun suspected.

As in medieval Europe and early modern China, the agricultural class held a respected position because its members provided Japanese society with sustenance. Even so, farmers had to mind their betters, and they bore a disproportionate share of the tax load. According to the survey made by Hideyoshi, taxes were imposed on villages, not on individuals; the tax varied between 30 and 40 percent of the rice crop. Also as in Europe and China, the commercial classes in Japan occupied the lowest rungs on the social ladder because they profited from the toil of others.

The peace that the Tokugawa Shogunate imposed brought a steady rise in population and prosperity. As demand for goods grew, so did the numbers of merchants. To maintain stability, the early Tokugawa shoguns froze the four ancient social categories: imperial court nobility, samurai, peasants, and merchants. Laws rigidly prescribed what each class could and could not do. Nobles, for example, were "strictly forbidden, whether by day or by night, to go sauntering through the streets or lanes in places where they have no business to be." Daimyos were prohibited from moving troops outside their frontiers, making alliances, and coining money. Designated dress and stiff rules of etiquette distinguished one class from another.[21] As intended, this stratification protected the Tokugawa shoguns from daimyo attack and inaugurated a long era of peace.

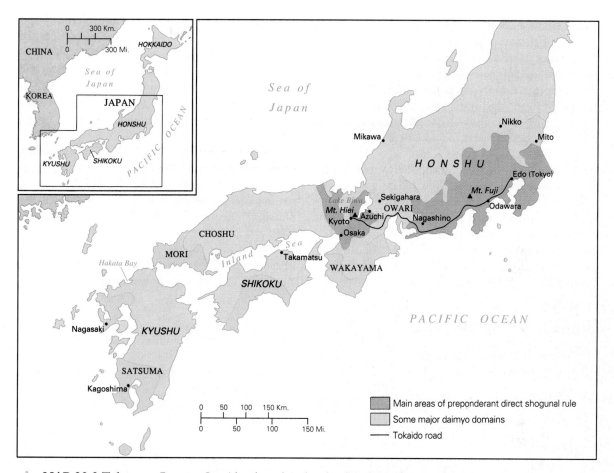

MAP 22.2 Tokugawa Japan   Consider the cultural and political significance of the fact that Japan is an island. How did the concentration of shogunate lands affect the shogunate's government of Japan?

In the interests of stability and peace, Ieyasu's descendants also imposed measures called *sakoku*. This "closed country policy" sealed Japan's borders around 1636. Japanese were forbidden to leave the country. Foreigners were excluded.

In 1549 the Jesuit missionary Francis Xavier had landed at Kagoshima. He soon made many converts among the poor and even some among the daimyos. By 1600 there were 300,000 baptized Christians in Japan. Most of them lived on Kyushu, the southernmost island (Map 22.2), where the shogun's power was weakest and the loyalty of the daimyos most doubtful. In 1615 bands of Christian samurai supported Ieyasu's enemies at the fierce Battle of Osaka. In 1637, 30,000 peasants in the heavily Catholic area of northern Kyushu revolted. The shoguns thus came to associate Christianity with domestic disorder and feu-

dal rebellion. Accordingly, what had been mild persecution of Christians became ruthless repression after 1639. Foreign priests were expelled or tortured, and thousands of Japanese Christians suffered crucifixion. The "closed country policy" remained in force for almost two centuries. The shogunate kept Japan isolated—but not totally.

Through the Dutch factory on the tiny island of Deshima in Nagasaki harbor (see page 531), a stream of Western ideas and inventions trickled into Japan in the eighteenth century. Western writings, architectural illustrations, calendars, watches, medicine, and paintings deeply impressed the Japanese. Western portraits and other paintings introduced the Japanese to perspective and shading. When the Swedish scientist C. P. Thunberg, physician to the Dutch at Deshima, visited Nagasaki and Edo, the Japanese looked on him as a scientific oracle and plied him with questions. Japanese scholars believed that Western inventions were more efficient than their Japanese equivalents and that these inventions contributed to the prosperity of European nations. Japanese curiosity about things Western gave rise to an intellectual movement known as *rangaku,* foreign studies, which urged that these Western ideas and inventions be adopted by the Japanese.

Japanese understanding of the West was severely limited and often fanciful, as was Western knowledge of Asian civilizations. Like eighteenth-century Europeans who praised Chinese and Persian customs to call attention to shortcomings at home, Japanese scholars idealized Western conditions. Both peoples wanted to create within their countries the desire for reform and progress.[22]

The Life of the People

Two hundred years of peace is no mean achievement in the history of world societies. There is nothing comparable to it in all of medieval and modern times. Moreover, profound social and economic development occurred in spite of Japan's isolation.

The Tokugawa Shogunate subdued the nobility by emasculating it politically. Stripped of power and required to spend part of each year at Edo, the daimyos and samurai passed their lives pursuing pleasure. They spent frantically on fine silks, paintings, concubines, boys, the theater, and the redecoration of their castles. Around 1700 one scholar observed that the entire military class was living "as in an inn, that is, consuming now and pay-

Women Weaving   Often working at home, women made an enormous contribution to the Japanese silk industry: their small, delicate hands (in contrast to the larger and possibly callused hands of men) seemed suited to working with fine silk threads. In an age when public-assisted child care was not dreamed of, working mothers relied on the help of female relatives, or, as here, infants were tied to mothers' backs, an added burden for mothers and probably not ideal for the child. Notice the spinning wheel in the corner and various spindles on the floor. *(Source: By kind permission of the East-West Gallery, New Hope, PA)*

A Male Prostitute   He writes a poem as a female prostitute massages their patron's back. Notice the elaborate hairstyles, the rich material of the kimonos, and the boxes of writing instruments. *(Source: The Fine Arts Museums of San Francisco. Achenbach Foundation for Graphic Arts purchase, 1969. 32.20)*

ing later."[23] Eighteenth-century Japanese novels, plays, and histories portray the samurai engrossed in tavern brawls and sexual orgies. These frivolities, plus more sophisticated pleasures and the heavy costs of maintaining an alternate residence at Edo, gradually ruined the warrior class.

In traditional Japanese society, women were subordinate to men, and the civil disorders of the sixteenth century strengthened male domination. Parents in the samurai class arranged their daughters' marriages to advance family interests. Once a woman married, her life centered on her children and domestic chores. The management of a large household with several children and many servants imposed heavy responsibilities on women. An upper-class wife rarely left home unchaperoned. "Middle class" women, however, began to emerge from the home. The development of an urban commercial culture in the cities (see page 732) in the Tokugawa period led to the employment of women in silk and textile manufacture, in publishing, in restaurants and various shops, and especially in entertainment.

All major cities contained places of amusement for men—teahouses, theaters, restaurants, houses of prostitution. Desperately poor parents sometimes sold their daughters to entertainment houses, and the most attractive or talented girls, trained in singing, dancing, and conversational arts, became courtesans called *geishas*, or "accomplished persons," in modern times. The Tokugawa period saw the beginnings for men of the separation of family and business life on the one hand, and leisure and amusement on the other. That separation is still evident in Japanese society.[24]

The samurai spent heavily on kabuki theater. An art form created by townspeople, kabuki consisted of crude, bawdy skits dealing with love and romance or aspects of prostitution, an occupation in which many actors and actresses had professional experience. Performances featured elaborate costumes, song, dance, and poetry. Because actresses were thought to be corrupting the public morals, the Tokugawa government banned them from the stage in 1629. From that time on, men played all the parts. Male actors in female dress and makeup performed as seductively as possible to entice the burly samurai who thronged the theaters. Homosexuality, long accepted in Japan, was widely practiced among the samurai, who pursued the actors and spent profligately on them. According to one seventeenth-century writer:

"Youth's kabuki" began with beautiful youths being made to sing and dance, whereupon droll fools . . . had their hearts captivated and their souls stolen. . . . There were many of these men who soon had run through their fortunes.[25]

Some moralists and bureaucrats complained from time to time, but the Tokugawa government decided to accept kabuki and prostitution as necessary evils. The practices provided employment, gratified the tastes of samurai and townspeople, and diverted former warriors from potential criminal and political mischief.[26] The samurai paid for their costly pleasures in the way their European counterparts did—by fleecing the peasants and borrowing from the merchants.

According to Japanese tradition, farmers deserved respect. In practice, peasants were sometimes severely oppressed and led miserable lives. It was government policy to tax them to the level of bare subsistence, and official legislation repeatedly redefined their duties. In 1649 every village in Japan received these regulations:

Peasants are people without sense or forethought. Therefore they must not give rice to their wives and children at harvest time, but must save food for the future. They should eat millet, vegetables, and other coarse food instead of rice. Even the fallen leaves of plants should be saved as food against famine. . . . During the seasons of planting and harvesting, however, when the labor is arduous, the food taken may be a little better. . . .

They must not buy tea or sake [a fermented liquor made from rice] to drink nor must their wives.

The husband must work in the fields, the wife must work at the loom. Both must do night work. However good-looking a wife may be, if she neglects her household duties by drinking tea or sightseeing or rambling on the hillsides, she must be divorced.

Peasants must wear only cotton or hemp—no silk. They may not smoke tobacco. It is harmful to health, it takes up time, and costs money. It also creates a risk of fire.[27]

The conspicuous consumption of the upper classes led them during the seventeenth and eighteenth centuries to increase taxes from 30 or 40 percent of the rice crop to 50 percent. Merchants who bought farm produce fixed the price of rice so low that it seemed to farmers that the more they produced, the less they earned. They found release only by flight or revolt.

After 1704, peasant rebellions were chronic. Oppressive taxation provoked 84,000 farmers in the province of Iwaki to revolt in 1739. After widespread burning and destruction, their demands were met. In other instances the shoguns ordered savage repression.

Natural disasters also added to the peasants' misery. In the 1770s fires, floods, and volcanic eruptions hit all parts of Japan. Drought and torrential rain led to terrible famines between 1783 and 1788 and again between 1832 and 1836. Taxation, disaster, and oppression often combined to make the lot of peasants one of unrelieved wretchedness.

This picture of the Japanese peasantry tells only part of the story, however. Scholarship has demonstrated that in the Tokugawa period peasant society was "a pyramid of wealth and power . . . that rose from the tenant farmer at the bottom through small landholders to wealthy peasants at the top."[28] Agricultural productivity increased substantially, and assessed taxes were fixed, though they remained high. Peasants who improved their lands and increased their yields continued to pay the same assessed tax and could pocket the surplus as profit. Their social situation accordingly improved. By the early nineteenth century there existed a large class of relatively wealthy, educated, and ambitious peasant families who resembled the middle ranks of the warrior class.

Likewise, local economic conditions and family social status shaped the lives of Japanese women. The existence of a rich peasant's wife, daughter, or sister differed considerably from that of poor peasant women. The well-to-do seem to have made few distinctions in the early upbringing of male and female children. Regional prosperity determined the amounts of money spent on the education of both sexes in their early years. In the early nineteenth century the regions around flourishing Edo and Kyoto spent far more than the poor Toh-ku region; and parents in thriving areas devoted considerable sums on their daughters' education. Girls from middle-level peasant families may have had from two to five years of formal schooling. But they were thought incapable of learning the difficult

Kitagawa Utamaro: Ladies at a Tea Shop   Famous for his book of insects reflecting remarkable powers of observation, Utamaro (1753–1806) is best known for his portrayal of women in which he accented their sensuous beauty. First of the great masters of the *ukiyo-e* school, "pictures of the floating world," the dominant movement in Japanese art of the Tokugawa period, Utamaro produced wood-block prints such as this with subjects drawn from everyday life. Notice the dress of the ladies and the various activities of the servants. *(Source: Private Collection)*

Chinese characters, so their education focused on moral instruction intended to instill the virtue of obedience. Daughters of wealthy peasant families learned penmanship, the Chinese classics, poetry, and the proper forms of correspondence, and they rounded off their education with travel.[29]

Scholars of the Japanese family, like students of the late medieval and early modern European family (see pages 632–634), have explored the extent of premarital sex, the age at which people married, the frequency with which they married someone from another village, and the level of divorce. For Tokugawa Japan, considerable regional variations make broad generalizations dangerous; research continues. It is clear, however, that marriage linked families of equal status and class; Japanese marriages, therefore, strengthened economic and social divisions. This practice gave Japanese women an advantage over their Chinese counterparts: the Japanese bride had to learn the special ways of her new household, but she was unlikely to be intimidated by her new family. Chinese women married "up" into families of a higher status and thus tended to be overawed by the wealth and status of their in-laws.

On the Japanese bride fell the responsibility of bringing harmony to the household. Harmony "meant that she had to refrain from quarreling with the members of her new household, do the work expected of her position, and conform to family custom."[30] Both samurai and peasant teaching stressed that "the married couple was the foundation of morality" and that the basis for harmony in the couple rested on good connubial relations. Once the author of *Observations of Agricultural Practices,* a study of rural life, stayed overnight at a farmhouse. Newlyweds in the family went to bed early and, separated from the others by only a screen, began noisy lovemaking. "Outrageous," exclaimed the guest, whereupon the old woman of the family got angry. "Harmony between husband and wife is the basis for prosperity for the descendants. . . . I permit this coupling day and night. People who laugh at their passion are themselves outrageous. Get out!"[31] Domestic harmony and social necessity were closely linked.

A peasant wife shared with her husband responsibility for the family's economic well-being. If of poor or middling status, she worked alongside her husband in the fields, doing the routine work while he did the heavy work. If they were tenant farmers and worked for salaries, the wife invariably earned half or a third less than her husband. Wives of prosperous farmers never worked in the fields, but they spun silk, wove cloth, helped in any family business, and supervised the maids. Whatever their economic status, Japanese women, like women everywhere in the world, tended the children; they were her special responsibility. The production of children, especially sons, strengthened a wife's prestige, but among well-to-do Japanese farm women, the bride's skill in prudent household management was the most desired talent.

How was divorce initiated, and how frequent was it? Customs among the noble class differed considerably from peasant practices. Widows and divorcees of the samurai aristocracy—where female chastity was the core of fidelity—were not expected to remarry. The husband alone could initiate divorce by ordering his wife to leave or by sending her possessions to her natal home. The wife could not prevent divorce or ensure access to her children.

Among the peasant classes, divorce seems to have been fairly common—at least 15 percent in the villages near Osaka in the eighteenth century. Women as well as men could begin the procedure. Wives' reasons were husbands' drunkenness, physical abuse, or failure to support the family. Many women secured divorce from temples whose function was to dissolve marriages: if a married woman entered the temple and performed its rites for three years, her marriage bond was dissolved. Sometimes Buddhist temple priests served as divorce brokers: they went to the village headman and had him force the husband to agree to a divorce. News of the coming of temple officials was usually enough to produce a letter of separation. A poor woman wanting a divorce simply left her husband's home. Opportunities for remarriage were severely limited. Divorce in samurai society carried social stigma; it did not among the peasantry.[32]

The Tokugawa period witnessed a major transformation of agriculture, a great leap in productivity and specialization. The rural population increased, but the agricultural population did not; surplus labor was drawn to other employment and to the cities. In fact, Japan suffered an acute shortage of farm labor from 1720 to 1868. In some villages, industry became almost as important as agriculture. At Hirano near Osaka, for example, 61.7 percent of all arable land was sown in cotton. The peasants had a thriving industry: they ginned the cotton locally before transporting it to wholesalers in Osaka. In many rural places, as many peasants worked in the manufacture of silk, cotton, or vegetable oil as in the production of rice.[33] In theory, the urban commercial classes, scorned for benefiting from the misery of the peasants and the appetites of the samurai, occupied the bottom rung of the social ladder. Merchants had no political power, but they accumulated wealth, sometimes great wealth. They also demonstrated the possibility of social mobility and thus the inherent weakness of the regime's system of strict social stratification.

The commercial class grew in response to the phenomenal development of urban life. In the seventeenth century, the surplus rural population, together with underemployed samurai and the ambitious and adventurous, thronged to the cities. All wanted a better way of life than could be found in the dull farming villages. Japan's cities grew tremendously: Kyoto, home to the emperor and his pleasure-loving court; Edo (modern Tokyo), the political capital, with its multitudes of government bureaucrats, daimyos in alternate residence, intellectuals, and police; and Osaka, by this time the greatest commercial city in Japan, with its huge grain exchange and commercial banks. In the eighteenth century, Edo's population of almost a million represented the largest demand for goods and services in the world.

The Tokugawa shoguns turned the samurai into urban consumers by denying them military opportunities. Merchants stood ready to serve them. Towns offered all kinds of luxury goods and catered to every extravagant and exotic taste. By marketing the daimyos' grain, town merchants gave the aristocrats the cash they needed to support their rich establishments. Merchants formed guilds and banks and lent money to the samurai. Those who defaulted on their debts found themselves cut off from further credit.[34]

As the ruling samurai with their fixed stipends became increasingly poorer, the despised merchants grew steadily wealthier. By contemporary standards anywhere in the world, the Japanese "middle" class lived very well. In 1705 the shogunate confiscated the property of a merchant in Osaka "for conduct unbecoming a member of the commercial class." In fact, the confiscation was at the urging of influential daimyos and samurai who owed the merchant gigantic debts. The government seized 50 pairs of gold screens, 360 carpets, several mansions, 48 granaries and warehouses scattered around the country, and hundreds of thousands of gold pieces. This merchant possessed fabulous wealth, but other merchants too enjoyed a rich lifestyle.[35]

SUMMARY

In the eighteenth and early nineteenth centuries China experienced a rapid increase in both prosperity and population. On the basis of highly developed agriculture, the Qing Empire supported a population of 200 million in 1762 and 374 million in 1812, compared with only 193 million in all of Europe in 1800. Qing China was geographically larger than the People's Republic of China today, encompassing some of the present-day Russian federation.

China's political and economic systems began to deteriorate in the late eighteenth and early nineteenth centuries. The country suffered from excessive centralization: all local questions had to be referred to Beijing. The extravagant court was an intolerable drain on the state treasury. Graft and corruption pervaded the imperial bureaucracy, provincial administration, and army. Population explosion led to a severe land shortage, causing tension and revolts in the countryside.

In 1800 Tokugawa Japan was reaping the rewards of two centuries of peace and social order. Steady economic growth and improved agricultural technology had swelled the population. The samurai had been transformed into peaceful city dwellers and civil bureaucrats. The wealth of the business classes grew, and the samurai, dependent on fixed agricultural rents or stipends in rice in a time of rising standards of living, fell into debt. The Tokugawa regime formed submissive citizens whose discipline is apparent even today.

Although the shogunate maintained a policy of national isolation and no foreign power influenced Japan's political or social life, Japan was not really cut off from outside cultural contacts. Through the port of Nagasaki, Western scientific ideas and some Western technology entered Japan in response to the persistent interest of Japanese scholars. The Japanese readily absorbed foreign technological ideas.

NOTES

1. J. Gernet, *A History of Chinese Civilization,* trans. J. R. Foster (New York: Cambridge University Press, 1982), p. 391.
2. Ibid.
3. L. Zewen et al., *The Great Wall* (New York: McGraw-Hill, 1981), p. 140.
4. See E. L. Dreyer, *Early Ming China: A Political History, 1355–1435* (Stanford, Calif.: Stanford University Press, 1982), pp. 194–205.
5. R. Huang, *1587: A Year of No Significance: The Ming Dynasty in Decline* (New Haven, Conn.: Yale University Press, 1981), p. 13.
6. J. E. Wills, Jr., "Maritime China from Wang Chih to Shih Long," in *From Ming to Ch'ing: Conquest, Region, and Continuity in Seventeenth-Century China,* ed. J. D. Spence and J. E. Wills, Jr. (New Haven, Conn.: Yale University Press, 1979), pp. 203–216.
7. F. Braudel, *The Wheels of Commerce: Civilization and Capitalism, 15th–18th Century,* vol. 2, trans. S. Reynolds (New York: Harper & Row, 1982), pp. 198–199.
8. Gernet, *A History of Chinese Civilization,* pp. 425–426.
9. Quoted in C. Clunas, *Superfluous Things: Material Culture and Social Status in Early Modern China* (Urbana: University of Illinois Press, 1991), pp. 141–142.
10. Ibid., pp. 147–165.
11. Quoted in Gernet, *A History of Chinese Civilization,* p. 431.
12. See Huang, *1587,* pp. 120–129.
13. F. Wakeman, Jr., *The Fall of Imperial China* (New York: Free Press, 1975), pp. 58–64.
14. J. D. Spence, *The Search for Modern China* (New York: Norton, 1991), pp. 117–122.
15. Quoted in A. Peyrefitte, *The Immobile Empire,* trans. J. Rothschild (New York: Knopf, 1992), pp. 195–196.
16. Ibid., p. 539.
17. Quoted in Spence, *The Search for Modern China,* p. 125.
18. See R. C. Croizier, *Traditional Medicine in Modern China* (Cambridge, Mass.: Harvard University Press, 1968), pp. 19–27.
19. P. U. Unschuld, *Medicine in China: A History of Pharmaceutics* (Berkeley: University of California Press, 1986), p. 4.
20. See G. B. Sansom, *A History of Japan, 1344–1615,* vol. 2 (Stanford, Calif.: Stanford University Press, 1961), Chs. 20–21.
21. Ibid., Ch. 25.
22. See D. Keene, *The Japanese Discovery of Europe, 1720–1830* (Stanford, Calif.: Stanford University Press, 1969), pp. 24–25, Ch. 4, and passim.
23. Quoted in D. H. Shively, "Bakufu Versus Kabuki," in *Studies in the Institutional History of Early Modern Japan,* ed. J. W. Hall (Princeton, N.J.: Princeton University Press, 1970), p. 236.
24. E. O. Reischauer and A. M. Craig, *Japan: Tradition and Transformation,* rev. ed. (Boston: Houghton Mifflin, 1989), pp. 104–105.
25. Quoted in Shively, "Bakufu Versus Kabuki," pp. 241–242.

LISTENING TO THE
PAST

The Macartney Mission to China

Lord George Macartney's embassy to China (1792–1794) sought to establish permanent diplomatic relations between China and Great Britain and to expand trade between the two countries. The mission failed when the emperor rejected the British proposals for the reasons that he states in the letter that follows. Although Macartney later wrote, "Nothing could be more fallacious than to judge of China by any European standard," the British refused to recognize the right of Chinese civilization to be different. The Macartney mission thus serves as a parading of the cultural clashes between the West and Asia that marked the next two centuries.

You, O King, from afar have yearned after the blessings of our civilization, and in your eagerness to come into touch with our converting influence have sent an Embassy across the sea bearing a memorial.[1] I have already taken note of your respectful spirit of submission, have treated your mission with extreme favor and loaded it with gifts . . . .

Yesterday your Ambassador petitioned my Ministers to memorialize me regarding your trade with China, but his proposal is not consistent with our dynastic usage and cannot be entertained. Hitherto, all European nations, including your own country's barbarian merchants, have carried on their trade with our Celestial Empire at Canton. Such has been the procedure for many years, although our Celestial Empire possesses all things in prolific abundance and lacks no product within its own borders. There was therefore no need to import the manufactures of outside barbarians in exchange for our own produce. But as the tea, silk and porcelain which the Celestial Empire produces, are absolute necessities to European nations and to yourselves, we have permitted, as a signal mark of favor, that foreign *hongs*[2] should be established at Canton, so that your wants might be supplied and your

country thus participate in our beneficence. But your Ambassador has now put forward new requests which completely fail to recognize the Throne's principle to "treat strangers from afar with indulgence," and to exercise a pacifying control over barbarian tribes, the world over. Moreover, our dynasty, swaying the myriad races of the globe, extends the same benevolence towards all. Your England is not the only nation trading at Canton. If other nations, following your bad example, wrongfully importune my ear with further impossible requests, how will it be possible for me to treat them with easy indulgence? Nevertheless, I do not forget the lonely remoteness of your island, cut off from the world by intervening wastes of sea, nor do I overlook your excusable ignorance of the usages of our Celestial Empire. I have consequently commanded my Ministers to enlighten your Ambassador on the subject, and have ordered the departure of the mission. . . .

Your request for a small island near Chusan,[3] where your merchants may reside and goods be warehoused, arises from your desire to develop trade. As there are neither foreign *hongs* nor interpreters in or near Chusan, where none of your ships have ever called, such an island would be utterly useless for your purposes. Every inch of the territory of our Empire is marked on the map and the strictest vigilance is exercised over it all: even tiny islets and far-lying sand-banks are clearly defined as part of the provinces to which they belong. Consider, moreover, that England is not the only barbarian land which wishes to establish . . . trade with our Empire. . . .

The next request, for a small site in the vicinity of Canton city, where your barbarian merchants may lodge or, alternatively, that there be no longer any restrictions over their movements at Aomen,[4] has arisen from the following causes. Hitherto, the barbarian merchants of Europe have had a definite locality assigned to them at Aomen for residence and trade, and have been forbidden to encroach an inch beyond the limits assigned to that locality.... If these restrictions were withdrawn, friction would inevitably occur between the Chinese and your barbarian subjects, and the results would militate against the benevolent regard that I feel towards you. From every point of view, therefore, it is best that the regulations now in force should continue unchanged....

Regarding your nation's worship of the Lord of Heaven, it is the same religion as that of other European nations. Ever since the beginning of history, sage Emperors and wise rulers have bestowed on China a moral system and inculcated a code, which from time immemorial has been religiously observed by the myriads of my subjects.[5] There has been no hankering after heterodox doctrines. Even the European (missionary) officials in my capital are forbidden to hold intercourse with Chinese subjects; they are restricted within the limits of their appointed residences, and may not go about propagating their religion. The distinction between Chinese and barbarian is most strict, and your Ambassador's request that barbarians shall be given full liberty to disseminate their religion is utterly unreasonable.

It may be, O King, that the above proposals have been wantonly made by your Ambassador on his own responsibility, or peradventure you yourself are ignorant of our dynastic regulations and had no intention of transgressing them when you expressed these wild ideas and hopes.... If, after the receipt of this explicit decree, you lightly give ear to the representations of your subordinates and allow your barbarian merchants to proceed to Chêkiang and Tientsin,[6] with the object of landing and trading there, the ordinances of my Celestial Empire are strict in the extreme, and the local officials, both civil and military, are bound reverently to obey the law of the land. Should your vessels touch the shore, your merchants will assuredly never be permitted to land or to reside there, but will be subject to instant expulsion. In that event your barbarian merchants will have had a long journey for nothing. Do not say that you were not warned in due time! Tremblingly obey and show no negligence! A special mandate!

Lord Macartney tries to impress the emperor Ch'ien-lung with an array of expensive presents. (*Source: National Maritime Museum, London*)

Questions for Analysis

1. Consider the basic premises of eighteenth-century European Enlightenment culture and the premises of Chinese culture.

2. What reasons does the emperor give for denying the British requests? What is the basis for the emperor's position?

3. How does the emperor view China's economic and cultural position in the world?

Source: A. J. Andrea and J. H. Overfield, eds., *The Human Record: Sources of Global History*, vol. 2 (Boston: Houghton Mifflin, 1990), pp. 262–264. Reprinted from E. Backhouse and J. O. P. Brand, *Annals and Memoirs of the Court of Peking* (Boston: Houghton Mifflin, 1914), pp. 325–331.

Notes: **1.** Memorandum. **2.** Groups of merchants. **3.** A group of islands in the East China Sea at the entrance to Hangchow Bay. **4.** A city some 45 miles to the south of Canton, at the lower end of the Pearl (Zhu) River delta. **5.** The reference is to Confucianism. **6.** Two Chinese port cities.

LISTENING TO THE
PAST

The Macartney Mission to China

Lord George Macartney's embassy to China (1792–1794) sought to establish permanent diplomatic relations between China and Great Britain and to expand trade between the two countries. The mission failed when the emperor rejected the British proposals for the reasons that he states in the letter that follows. Although Macartney later wrote, "Nothing could be more fallacious than to judge of China by any European standard," the British refused to recognize the right of Chinese civilization to be different. The Macartney mission thus serves as a parading of the cultural clashes between the West and Asia that marked the next two centuries.

You, O King, from afar have yearned after the blessings of our civilization, and in your eagerness to come into touch with our converting influence have sent an Embassy across the sea bearing a memorial.[1] I have already taken note of your respectful spirit of submission, have treated your mission with extreme favor and loaded it with gifts . . . .

Yesterday your Ambassador petitioned my Ministers to memorialize me regarding your trade with China, but his proposal is not consistent with our dynastic usage and cannot be entertained. Hitherto, all European nations, including your own country's barbarian merchants, have carried on their trade with our Celestial Empire at Canton. Such has been the procedure for many years, although our Celestial Empire possesses all things in prolific abundance and lacks no product within its own borders. There was therefore no need to import the manufactures of outside barbarians in exchange for our own produce. But as the tea, silk and porcelain which the Celestial Empire produces, are absolute necessities to European nations and to yourselves, we have permitted, as a signal mark of favor, that foreign *hongs*[2] should be established at Canton, so that your wants might be supplied and your

country thus participate in our beneficence. But your Ambassador has now put forward new requests which completely fail to recognize the Throne's principle to "treat strangers from afar with indulgence," and to exercise a pacifying control over barbarian tribes, the world over. Moreover, our dynasty, swaying the myriad races of the globe, extends the same benevolence towards all. Your England is not the only nation trading at Canton. If other nations, following your bad example, wrongfully importune my ear with further impossible requests, how will it be possible for me to treat them with easy indulgence? Nevertheless, I do not forget the lonely remoteness of your island, cut off from the world by intervening wastes of sea, nor do I overlook your excusable ignorance of the usages of our Celestial Empire. I have consequently commanded my Ministers to enlighten your Ambassador on the subject, and have ordered the departure of the mission. . . .

Your request for a small island near Chusan,[3] where your merchants may reside and goods be warehoused, arises from your desire to develop trade. As there are neither foreign *hongs* nor interpreters in or near Chusan, where none of your ships have ever called, such an island would be utterly useless for your purposes. Every inch of the territory of our Empire is marked on the map and the strictest vigilance is exercised over it all: even tiny islets and far-lying sand-banks are clearly defined as part of the provinces to which they belong. Consider, moreover, that England is not the only barbarian land which wishes to establish . . . trade with our Empire. . . .

The next request, for a small site in the vicinity of Canton city, where your barbarian merchants may lodge or, alternatively, that there be no longer any restrictions over their movements at Aomen,[4] has arisen from the following causes. Hitherto, the barbarian

The Revolution in Western Politics, 1775–1815

The mayor of Rouen protects access to the townhall from the onslaught of a crowd rioting over the lack of bread, August 29, 1792. *(Source: Musée des Beaux Arts, Rouen/Laurie Platt Winfrey, Inc.)*

The last years of the eighteenth century were a time of great upheaval in the West. A series of revolutions and revolutionary wars challenged the old order of monarchs and aristocrats. The ideas of freedom and equality, ideas that have not stopped shaping the world since that era, flourished and spread. The revolutionary era began in North America in 1775. Then in 1789 France, the most influential country in Europe, became the leading revolutionary nation. It established first a constitutional monarchy, then a radical republic, and finally a new empire under Napoleon. The armies of France also joined forces with patriots and radicals abroad in an effort to establish throughout much of Europe new governments based on new principles. The world of modern domestic and international politics was born.

- What caused this era of revolution?
- What were the ideas and objectives of the men and women who rose up violently to undo the established system?
- What were the gains and losses for privileged groups and for ordinary people in a generation of war and upheaval?

These are the questions underlying this chapter's examination of the revolutionary era.

❖ LIBERTY AND EQUALITY

Two ideas fueled the revolutionary period in both America and Europe: liberty and equality. What did eighteenth-century politicians and other people mean by liberty and equality, and why were those ideas so radical and revolutionary in their day?

The call for liberty was first of all a call for individual human rights. Even the most enlightened monarchs customarily claimed that it was their duty to regulate what people wrote and believed. Liberals of the revolutionary era protested such controls from on high. They demanded freedom to worship according to the dictates of their consciences, an end to censorship, and freedom from arbitrary laws and from judges who simply obeyed orders from the government. The Declaration of the Rights of Man, issued at the beginning of the French Revolution, proclaimed, "Liberty consists in being able to do anything that does not harm another person." In theory, therefore, a citizen's

rights had "no limits except those which assure to the other members of society the enjoyment of these same rights." In the context of the monarchial and absolutist forms of government then dominating Europe, this was a truly radical idea.

The call for liberty was also a call for a new kind of government. Revolutionary liberals believed that the people were sovereign—that is, that the people alone had the authority to make laws limiting an individual's freedom of action. In practice, this system of government meant choosing legislators who represented the people and were accountable to them.

Equality was a more ambiguous idea. Eighteenth-century liberals argued that, in theory, all citizens should have identical rights and civil liberties and that the nobility had no right to special privileges based on the accident of birth. However, liberals accepted some well-established distinctions.

First, most eighteenth-century liberals were *men* of their times, and they generally shared with other men the belief that equality between men and women was neither practical nor desirable. Women played an important political role in the French Revolution at several points, but the men of the French Revolution limited formal political rights—the right to vote, to run for office, to participate in government—to men.

Second, liberals never believed that everyone should be equal economically. Quite the contrary. As Thomas Jefferson wrote in an early draft of the American Declaration of Independence (before he changed "property" to the more noble-sounding "happiness"), everyone was equal in "the pursuit of property." Jefferson and other liberals certainly did not expect equal success in that pursuit. Great differences in wealth and income between rich and poor were perfectly acceptable to liberals. The essential point was that everyone should legally have an equal chance.

In eighteenth-century Europe, however, such equality of opportunity was a truly revolutionary idea. Society was still legally divided into groups with special privileges, such as the nobility and the clergy, and groups with special burdens, such as the peasantry. And in most countries, various middle-class groups—professionals, business people, townspeople, and craftsmen—enjoyed privileges that allowed them to monopolize all sorts of economic activity. Liberals criticized not economic inequality itself but this kind of economic inequality based on artificial legal distinctions.

The ideas of liberty and equality—the central ideas of classical liberalism—had deep roots in Western history. The classical and Judeo-Christian traditions had affirmed for hundreds of years the sanctity and value of the individual human being, as well as personal responsibility on the part of both common folk and exalted rulers. The hounded and persecuted Protestant radicals of the later sixteenth century had died for the revolutionary idea that individuals were entitled to their own religious beliefs.

Although the liberal creed was rooted in the Western tradition, classical liberalism first crystallized at the end of the seventeenth century and during the Enlightenment of the eighteenth century. Liberal ideas reflected the Enlightenment's stress on human dignity and human happiness on earth and its faith in science, rationality, and progress. Almost all the writers of the Enlightenment were passionately committed to greater personal liberty and equal treatment before the law.

Certain English and French thinkers were mainly responsible for joining the Enlightenment's concern for personal freedom and legal equality to a theoretical justification of liberal self-government. The two most important were John Locke and the baron de Montesquieu. Locke maintained that England's long political tradition rested on "the rights of Englishmen" and on representative government through Parliament. He admired especially the great Whig nobles who had deposed James II and made the bloodless revolution of 1688–1689, and he argued that if a government oversteps its proper function of protecting the natural rights of life, liberty, and private property, it becomes a tyranny. Montesquieu was also inspired by English constitutional history. He, too, believed that powerful "intermediary groups"—such as the judicial nobility of which he was a proud member—offered the best defense of liberty against despotism.

The Marquis de Lafayette   The most famous great noble to embrace the liberal revolution is shown here directing a battle in the American Revolution. He later returned to France to champion liberty and equality there. The elegant black man is Lafayette's servant, a free man in an age of widespread slavery. *(Source: Jean-Loup Charmet)*

The belief that representative institutions could defend their liberty and interests appealed powerfully to well-educated, prosperous groups, which historians have traditionally labeled as the bourgeoisie. Yet liberal ideas about individual rights and political freedom also appealed to much of the hereditary nobility, at least in western Europe and as formulated by Montesquieu. Representative government did not mean democracy, which liberal thinkers tended to equate with mob rule. Rather, they envisioned voting for representatives as being restricted to those who owned property— those with "a stake in society." England had shown the way. After 1688 it had combined a parliamentary system and considerable individual liberty with a restricted franchise and unquestionable aristocratic pre-eminence. In the course of the eighteenth century, many leading French nobles, led by a judicial nobility inspired by the doctrines of Montesquieu, were increasingly eager to follow the English example. Thus eighteenth-century liberalism found broad support among the prosperous, well-educated elites in western Europe.

What liberalism lacked from the beginning was strong popular support. At least two reasons account for the people's wary attitude. First, for common people, the great questions were not theoretical and political but immediate and economic; getting enough to eat was a crucial challenge. Second, some of the traditional practices and institutions that liberals wanted to abolish were dear to peasants and urban workers. Comfortable elites had already come into conflict with the people in the eighteenth century over the enclosure of common lands and the regulation of food prices. This conflict would sharpen in the revolutionary era as differences in outlook and well-being led to many misunderstandings and disappointments for both groups.

✤ THE AMERICAN REVOLUTION (1775–1789)

The era of liberal political revolution began in the New World. The thirteen mainland colonies of British North America revolted against their home country and then succeeded in establishing a new unified government.

The American revolutionaries believed that they were demanding only the traditional rights of English men and women. But those traditional rights were liberal rights, and in the American context they had very strong democratic and popular overtones that made them quite radical. In founding a government firmly based on liberal principles, the Americans set an example that had a forceful impact on Europe and sped up political development there.

The Origins of the Revolution

The American Revolution had its immediate origins in a squabble over increased taxes. The British government had fought and decisively won the Seven Years' War on the strength of its professional army and navy. The American colonists had furnished little real aid. The high cost of the war to the British, however, had led to a doubling of the British national debt. Anticipating further expense defending its recently conquered western lands from native American uprisings, the British government in London set about reorganizing the empire with a series of bold, largely unprecedented measures. Breaking with tradition, the British decided to maintain a large army in North America after peace was restored in 1763. Moreover, they sought to exercise strict control over their newly conquered western lands and to tax the colonies directly. In 1765 the government pushed through Parliament the Stamp Act, which levied taxes on a long list of commercial and legal documents, diplomas, pamphlets, newspapers, almanacs, dice, and playing cards. A stamp glued to each article indicated the tax had been paid.

This effort to increase taxes as part of a tightening-up of the empire seemed perfectly reasonable to the British. Americans were being asked to pay only a share of their own defense costs. Moreover, Americans had been paying only very low local taxes. The Stamp Act would have doubled taxes to about 2 shillings per person per year. No other people in the European or colonial world (except the Poles) paid so little. In contrast, the British paid the highest taxes in the Western world—26 shillings per person. The colonists protested the Stamp Act vigorously and violently, however, and after rioting and boycotts against British goods, Parliament reluctantly repealed the new tax.

As the fury over the Stamp Act revealed, much more was involved than taxes. The key questions were political. To what extent could the home government reassert its power while limiting the authority of colonial legislatures and their elected representatives? Who had the right to make laws for Americans? While a troubled majority of Americans searched hard for a compromise, some radicals began to proclaim that "taxation without representation is tyranny." The British government replied that Americans were represented in Parliament, albeit indirectly (like most English people themselves), and that the absolute supremacy of Parliament throughout the empire could not be questioned. Many Americans felt otherwise. As John Adams of Massachusetts put it, "A Parliament of Great Britain can have no more rights to tax the colonies than a Parliament of Paris." At risk were Americans' existing liberties and time-honored institutions.

Americans had long exercised a great deal of independence and gone their own way. The colonial assemblies made the important laws, which were seldom overturned by the home government. The right to vote was much more widespread than in England. In many parts of colonial Massachusetts, for example, as many as 95 percent of the adult males could vote. Moreover, greater political

Toward Revolution in Boston The Boston Tea Party was one of many angry confrontations between British officials and Boston patriots. On January 27, 1774, a crowd seized and then tarred and feathered a British customs collector. This French engraving from 1784 commemorates the defiant and provocative action. *(Source: The Granger Collection, New York)*

equality was matched by greater social and economic equality. Neither a hereditary nobility nor a hereditary serf population existed, although the slavery of the Americas consigned blacks to a legally oppressed caste. Independent farmers were the largest group in the country and set much of its tone. In short, the colonial experience had slowly formed a people who felt themselves separate and distinct from the home country. The controversies over taxation intensified those feelings of distinctiveness and separation and brought them to the fore.

In 1773 the dispute over taxes and representation flared up again. The British government had permitted the financially hard-pressed East India Company to ship its tea from China directly to its agents in the colonies, rather than through London middlemen who sold to independent colonial merchants. Thus the company secured a monopoly on the tea trade and colonial merchants were suddenly excluded from a highly profitable business. The colonists were quick to protest.

In Boston men disguised as Indians had a rowdy "tea party" and threw the company's tea into the harbor. This action led to extreme measures. Parliament passed the so-called Coercive Acts, which closed the port of Boston, curtailed local elections and town meetings, and greatly expanded the royal governor's power. County conventions in Massachusetts protested vehemently and urged that the acts be "rejected as the attempts of a wicked administration to enslave America." Other colonial assemblies joined in the denunciations. In September 1774, the First Continental Congress met in Philadelphia, where the more radical members argued successfully against concessions to the Crown. Compromise was also rejected by the British Parliament, and in April 1775 fighting began in Massachusetts, at Lexington and Concord.

Independence

The fighting spread, and the colonists moved slowly but inevitably toward open rebellion and a declaration of independence. The uncompromising attitude of the British government and its use of German mercenaries went a long way toward dissolving long-standing loyalties to the home country and rivalries among the separate colonies. *Common Sense* (1775), a brilliant attack by the recently arrived English radical Thomas Paine (1737–1809), also mobilized public opinion in favor of independence. A runaway bestseller, Paine's tract ridiculed the idea of a small island ruling a great continent. In his call for freedom and republican government, Paine expressed Americans' growing sense of separateness and moral superiority.

On July 4, 1776, the Second Continental Congress adopted the Declaration of Independence, which boldly listed the tyrannical acts committed by King George III (r. 1760–1820) and confidently proclaimed the natural rights of mankind and the sovereignty of the American states. Sometimes called the world's greatest political editorial, the Declaration of Independence in effect universalized the traditional rights of English people and made them the rights of all mankind. It stated "that all men are created equal; that they are endowed by their Creator with certain unalienable rights; that among these are life, liberty, and the pursuit of happiness." No other American political document has ever caused such excitement, either at home or abroad.

Many American families remained loyal to Britain; many others divided bitterly. After the Declaration of Independence, the conflict often took the form of a civil war pitting patriots against those who remained loyal to the King. The loyalists tended to be wealthy and politically moderate. Many patriots, too, were wealthy—individuals such as John Hancock and George Washington—but willingly allied themselves with farmers and artisans in a broad coalition. This coalition harassed the loyalists and confiscated their property to help pay for the American war effort. The broad social base of the revolutionaries tended to make the liberal revolution democratic. State governments extended the right to vote to many more men in the course of the war and re-established themselves as republics.

On the international scene, the French sympathized with the rebels from the beginning. They wanted revenge for the humiliating defeats of the Seven Years' War. Officially neutral until 1778, they supplied the great bulk of guns and gunpowder used by the American revolutionaries, very much as foreign great powers have supplied weapons for "wars of national liberation" in our time. By 1777 French volunteers were arriving in Virginia, and a dashing young nobleman, the marquis de Lafayette (1757–1834), quickly became one of Washington's most trusted generals. In 1778 the French government offered a formal alliance to the American ambassador in Paris, Benjamin Franklin, and in 1779 and 1780 the Spanish and Dutch declared war on Britain. Catherine the

The Signing of the Declaration, July 4, 1776   John Trumbull's famous painting shows the dignity and determination of America's revolutionary leaders. An extraordinarily talented group, they succeeded in rallying popular support without losing power to more radical forces in the process. *(Source: Yale University Art Gallery)*

Great of Russia helped organize the League of Armed Neutrality in order to protect neutral shipping rights, which Britain refused to recognize.

Thus by 1780 Great Britain was engaged in an imperial war against most of Europe as well as the thirteen colonies. In these circumstances, and in the face of severe reverses in India, the West Indies, and at Yorktown in Virginia, a new British government decided to cut its losses. American negotiators in Paris were receptive. They feared that France wanted a treaty that would bottle up the new United States east of the Allegheny Mountains and give British holdings west of the Alleghenies to France's ally, Spain. Thus the American negotiators separated themselves from their French allies and accepted the extraordinarily favorable terms Britain offered.

By the Treaty of Paris of 1783, Britain recognized the independence of the thirteen colonies and ceded all its territory between the Allegheny Mountains and the Mississippi River to the Americans. Out of the bitter rivalries of the Old World, the Americans snatched dominion over almost half a continent.

Framing the Constitution

The liberal program of the American Revolution was consolidated by the federal Constitution, the Bill of Rights, and the creation of a national republic. Assembling in Philadelphia in the summer of 1787, the delegates to the Constitutional Convention were determined to end the period of economic depression, social uncertainty, and very weak central government that had followed independence. The delegates decided, therefore, to grant the federal, or central, government important powers: regulation of domestic and foreign trade, the right to levy taxes, and the means to enforce its laws.

Strong rule would be placed squarely in the context of representative self-government. Senators and congressmen would be the lawmaking delegates of the voters, and the president of the republic would be an elected official. The central government would operate in Montesquieu's framework of checks and balances. The executive, legislative, and judicial branches would systematically balance one another. The power of the federal government would in turn be checked by the powers of the individual states.

When the results of the secret deliberations of the Constitutional Convention were presented to the states for ratification, a great public debate began. The opponents of the proposed constitution—the Anti-Federalists—charged that the new document took too much power from the individual states and made the federal government too strong. Moreover, many Anti-Federalists feared for the personal liberties and individual freedoms for which they had just fought. In order to overcome these objections, the Federalists solemnly promised to spell out these basic freedoms as soon as the new constitution was adopted. The result was the first ten amendments to the Constitution, which the first Congress passed shortly after it met in New York in March 1789. These amendments formed an effective bill of rights to safeguard the individual. Most of them—trial by jury, due process of law, right to assemble, freedom from unreasonable search—had their origins in English law and the English Bill of Rights of 1689. Others—the freedoms of speech, the press, and religion—reflected natural-law theory and the American experience.

The American Constitution and the Bill of Rights exemplified the great strengths and the limits of what came to be called classical liberalism. Liberty meant individual freedoms and political safeguards. Liberty also meant representative government but did not necessarily mean democracy, with its principle of one person, one vote. Equality—slaves excepted—meant equality before the law, not equality of political participation or economic well-being. Indeed, economic inequality was resolutely defended by the elite that framed the Constitution. The right to own property was guaranteed by the Fifth Amendment, and if the government took private property, the owner was to receive "just compensation." The radicalism of liberal revolution in America was primarily legal and political, *not* economic or social.

THE FRENCH REVOLUTION (1789–1791)

In Europe, hundreds of books, pamphlets, and articles analyzed and romanticized the American upheaval. Thoughtful Europeans noted, first of all, its enormous long-term implications for international politics. A secret report by the Venetian ambassador to Paris in 1783 stated what many felt: if the new nation survived in unity, it might "become the most formidable power in the world."[1] More generally, American independence fired the imaginations of those aristocrats who were uneasy with their hereditary privileges and those commoners who yearned for equality. Many Europeans believed that the world was advancing and that America was leading the way. As one French writer put it in 1789, "This vast continent which the seas surround will soon change Europe and the universe." The Americans had shown how rational beings could assemble together to exercise sovereignty and write a permanent constitution—a new social contract. All this gave greater reality to the concepts of individual liberty and representative government and reinforced one of the primary ideas of the Enlightenment: that a better world was possible.

No country felt the consequences of the American Revolution more directly than France. Hundreds of French officers served in America and were inspired by the experience. The most famous of these, the young and impressionable marquis de Lafayette, left home as a great aristocrat determined to fight only France's traditional foe, England. He returned with a love of liberty and firm republican convictions. French intellectuals and publicists engaged in passionate analysis of the federal and state constitutions. The American Revolution undeniably hastened upheaval in France.

Yet the French Revolution did not mirror the American example. It was more radical and more complex, more influential and more controversial, more loved and more hated. For Europeans and most of the rest of the world, it was the great revolution of the eighteenth century, *the* revolution that opened the modern era in politics.

The Breakdown of the Old Order

Like the American Revolution, the French Revolution had its immediate origins in the financial difficulties of the government. With both the high court of Paris—the Parlement—and public opinion successfully resisting increased taxes, the government was forced to finance all of its enormous expenditures during the American war with borrowed money. As a result, the national debt and the annual budget deficit soared. By the 1780s, fully 50 percent of France's annual budget went for interest on the ever-increasing debt. Another 25 percent went to maintain the military, while 6 percent was absorbed by the costly and extravagant king and his court at Versailles. Less than 20 percent of the entire national budget was available for the productive functions of the state, such as transportation and general administration. This was an impossible financial situation.

One way out would have been for the government to declare partial bankruptcy, forcing its creditors to accept greatly reduced payments on the debt. Both the Spanish and the French monarchies had done this in earlier times. By the 1780s, however, the French debt was being held by an army of aristocratic and bourgeois creditors, and the French monarchy, though absolute in theory, had become far too weak for such a drastic and unpopular action.

Nor could the king and his ministers, unlike modern governments, print money and create inflation to cover their deficits. Unlike England and Holland, which had far larger national debts relative to their populations, France had no central bank, no paper currency, and no means of creating credit. French money was good gold coin. Therefore, when a depressed economy and a lack of public confidence made it increasingly difficult for the government to obtain new gold loans in 1786, it had no alternative but to try increasing taxes. But since France's tax system was unfair and out-of-date, increased revenues were possible only through fundamental reforms. Such reforms, which would affect all groups in France's complex and fragmented society, opened a Pandora's box of social and political demands.

Legal Orders and Social Realities

As in the Middle Ages, France's 25 million inhabitants were still legally divided into three orders, or *estates*—the Roman Catholic clergy, the nobility, and everyone else. As the nation's first estate, the clergy numbered about 100,000 and had important privileges. It owned about 10 percent of the land and paid only a "voluntary gift," rather than regular taxes, to the government every five years. Moreover, the church levied a tax (the tithe) on landowners, which averaged somewhat less than 10 percent. Much of the church's income was actually drained away from local parishes by political appointees and worldly aristocrats at the top of the church hierarchy—to the intense dissatisfaction of the poor parish priests.

The second legally defined estate consisted of some 400,000 noblemen and noblewomen. The nobles owned outright about 25 percent of the land in France, and they, too, were taxed very lightly. Moreover, nobles continued to enjoy certain manorial rights, or privileges of lordship, that dated back to medieval times and allowed them to tax the peasantry for their own profit. They did this by means of exclusive rights to hunt and fish, village monopolies on baking bread and pressing grapes for wine, fees for justice, and a host of other "useful privileges." In addition, nobles had "honorific privileges," such as the right to precedence on public occasions and the right to wear a sword. These rights conspicuously proclaimed the nobility's legal superiority and exalted social position.

Everyone else was a commoner, legally a member of the third estate. A few commoners—prosperous merchants or lawyers and officials—were well educated and rich, and might even buy up manorial rights as profitable investments. Many more commoners were urban artisans and unskilled day laborers. The vast majority of the third estate consisted of the peasants and agricultural workers in the countryside. Thus the third estate was a conglomeration of vastly different social groups united only by their shared legal status as distinct from the nobility and clergy.

In discussing the long-term origins of the French Revolution, historians have long focused on growing tensions between the nobility and the comfortable members of the third estate, usually known as the *bourgeoisie,* or middle class. A dominant historical interpretation, which has held sway for at least two generations, maintains that the bourgeoisie was basically united by economic position and class interest. Aided by a general economic expansion, the middle class grew rapidly in the eighteenth century, tripling to about 2.3 million persons, or about 8 percent of France's population. Increasing in size, wealth, culture, and self-confidence, this rising bourgeoisie became progressively exasperated by archaic "feudal" laws and customs that restrained the economy and their needs and aspirations. As a result, the French bourgeoisie eventually rose up to lead the entire third estate in a great social revolution, a revolution that destroyed feudal privileges and established a capitalist order based on individualism and a market economy.

In recent years, a flood of new research has challenged these accepted views, and once again the French Revolution is a subject of heated scholarly debate. Above all, revisionist historians have questioned the existence of a growing social conflict between a progressive capitalistic bourgeoisie and a reactionary feudal nobility in eighteenth-century France. Instead, these historians see both bourgeoisie and nobility as highly fragmented, riddled with internal rivalries. Rather than standing as unified blocs against each other, nobility and bourgeoisie formed two parallel social ladders increasingly linked together at the top by wealth, marriage, and Enlightenment culture.

Revisionist historians stress three developments in particular. First, the nobility remained a fluid and relatively open order. Throughout the eighteenth century, substantial numbers of successful commoners continued to seek and obtain noble status through government service and purchase of expensive positions conferring nobility. Thus the nobility continued to attract the wealthiest members of the middle class and to permit social mobility. Second, key sections of the nobility and the prosperous bourgeoisie formed together the core of the book-hungry Enlightenment public. Both groups saw themselves as forming part of the educated elite and standing well above the common people—the peasants and the urban poor. Both groups were also equally liberal until revolution actually began, and they generally supported the judicial opposition to the government. Third, the nobility and the bourgeoisie were not really at odds in the economic sphere. Both looked to investment in land and to government service as their preferred activities, and the goal of the merchant capitalist was to gain enough wealth to live nobly as a large landowner. At the same time, wealthy nobles often acted as aggressive capitalists, investing especially in mining, metallurgy, and foreign trade.

The revisionists have clearly shaken the belief that the bourgeoisie and the nobility were inevitably locked in growing conflict before the French Revolution. But in stressing the similarities between the two groups, especially at the top, revisionists have also reinforced the view, long maintained by historians, that the Old Regime had ceased to correspond with social reality by the 1780s. Legally, society was still based on rigid orders inherited from the Middle Ages. But France had moved far toward being a society based on wealth and education, where an emerging elite that included both aristocratic and bourgeois notables was frustrated by a bureaucratic monarchy that continued to claim the right to absolute power.

The Formation of the National Assembly

The Revolution was under way by 1787, though no one could have realized what was to follow. Spurred by a depressed economy and falling tax receipts, Louis XVI's minister of finance convinced the king to call an assembly of notables to gain support for a general tax on all landed property. The assembled notables, who were mainly important noblemen and high-ranking clergy, ultimately responded that such sweeping tax changes required the approval of the Estates General, the representative body of all three estates, which had not met since 1614.

Facing imminent bankruptcy, the king tried to reassert his authority. He dismissed the notables and established new taxes by decree. In stirring language, the Parlement of Paris promptly declared the royal initiative null and void. When the king tried to exile the judges, a tremendous wave of protest swept the country. Frightened investors also refused to advance more loans to the state. Finally in July 1788, a beaten Louis XVI bowed to public opinion and called for a spring session of the Estates General. Absolute monarchy was collapsing.

What would replace it? Throughout the unprecedented election campaign of 1788 and 1789, that question excited France. All across the country, clergy, nobles, and commoners met together in their respective orders to draft petitions for change and to elect their respective delegates to the Estates General. The local assemblies of the clergy chose two-thirds of the delegates from among the poorer parish priests, who were commoners by birth. Among the nobles, already badly split by wealth and education, a conservative majority was drawn from the poorer and more numerous provincial nobility. But fully one-third of the nobility's representatives were liberals committed to major changes.

As for the third estate, there was great popular participation in the elections. Almost all male commoners twenty-five years or older had the right to vote. Still, most of the representatives finally selected were well-educated, prosperous lawyers and government officials. There were no delegates elected from the great mass of laboring poor, an exclusion that would encourage the peasants and also the urban artisans to intervene directly and dramatically at numerous points in the Revolution, as we shall see.

The petitions for change coming from the three estates showed a surprising degree of consensus on most issues. There was general agreement that royal absolutism should give way to constitutional monarchy, in which laws and taxes would require the consent of the Estates General meeting regularly. All agreed that in the future individual liberties would have to be guaranteed by law and that the economic position of the parish clergy would have to be improved. It was generally acknowledged that economic development required reforms, such as the abolition of internal trade barriers. The striking similarities in the grievance petitions of the clergy, nobility, and third estate reflected the broad commitment of France's educated elite to liberalism.

Yet an increasingly bitter quarrel undermined this consensus during the intense electoral campaign. *How* would the Estates General vote, and precisely *who* would lead in the political reorganization that was generally desired? The Estates General of 1614 had sat as three separate houses. Any action had required the agreement of at least two branches, a requirement that had virtually guaranteed control by the nobility and the clergy. The aristocratic Parlement of Paris ruled that the Estates General should once again sit separately. Certain middle-class intellectuals and some liberal nobles demanded instead a single assembly dominated by representatives of the third estate. Amid increased political competition and a growing hostility toward aristocratic aspirations, the government agreed that the third estate should have as many delegates as the clergy and the nobility combined. When it then rendered this act meaningless by upholding voting by separate order, middle-class leaders saw fresh evidence of an aristocratic conspiracy.

The Estates General opened in May 1789 at Versailles with twelve hundred delegates. The estates were almost immediately deadlocked. Delegates of the third estate refused to transact any business until the king ordered the clergy and nobility to sit with them in a single body. Finally, after a six-week war of nerves, the third estate on June 17 voted to call itself the National Assembly. On June 20, the delegates of the third estate, excluded from their hall because of "repairs," moved to a large indoor tennis court. There they swore

The Oath of the Tennis Court This painting, based on an unfinished work by Jacques-Louis David (1748–1825), enthusiastically celebrates the revolutionary rupture of June 20, 1789. Locked out of their assembly hall at Versailles and joined by some sympathetic priests, the delegates of the third estate have moved to an indoor tennis court and are swearing never to disband until they have written a new constitution and put France on a firm foundation. (*Source: Musée Carnavalet/Photographie Bulloz*)

the Oath of the Tennis Court, pledging not to disband until they had written a new constitution.

The indecisive king's actions were then somewhat contradictory. On June 23 he made a conciliatory speech urging reforms to a joint session and then ordered the three estates to meet together. Then, apparently following the advice of relatives and court nobles that he dissolve the Estates General by force, the king called an army of eighteen thousand troops toward Versailles. On July 11 he dismissed his finance minister and his other more liberal ministers. Having resigned himself to bankruptcy, Louis XVI belatedly sought to reassert his historic "divine right" to rule. The middle-class delegates and their allies from the liberal nobility had done their best, but they were resigned to being disbanded at bayonet point. One third-estate delegate reassured a worried colleague, "You won't hang—you'll only have to go back home."[2]

The Revolt of the Poor and the Oppressed

While the educated delegates of the third estate pressed for symbolic equality with the nobility and clergy in a single legislative body at Versailles, economic hardship gripped the common people of France in a tightening vise. Grain was the basis of the diet of ordinary people in the eighteenth century, and in 1788 the harvest had been extremely poor. The price of bread, which had been rising gradually since 1785, began to soar. By July 1789 it had climbed as high as 8 sous per pound in the provinces. In Paris, where bread was regularly subsidized by the government in an attempt to prevent popular unrest, the price rose to 4 sous, a price at which a laborer with a wife and three children had to spend most of his wages to buy the family's bread.

Harvest failure and high bread prices unleashed a classic economic depression of the preindustrial age. With food so expensive and with so much uncertainty, the demand for manufactured goods collapsed, resulting in thousands of artisans and small traders being thrown out of work. By the end of 1789, almost half of the French people were in need of relief. In Paris the situation was so desperate in July 1789 that perhaps 150,000 of the city's 600,000 people were without work.

Against this background of dire poverty and excitement generated by the political crisis, the people of Paris entered decisively onto the revolutionary stage. They believed in a general, though ill-defined, way that the economic distress had human causes. They believed that they should have steady work and enough bread at fair prices to survive. Specifically, they feared that the dismissal of the king's moderate finance minister would put them at the mercy of aristocratic landowners and grain speculators. Stories like that quoting the wealthy financier Joseph François Foulon as saying that the poor "should eat grass, like my horses" and rumors that the king's troops would sack the city began to fill the air. Angry crowds formed, and passionate voices urged action. On July 13 the people began to seize arms for the defense of the city, and on July 14 several hundred of the most determined people marched to the Bastille to search for gunpowder.

Storming the Bastille This representation by an untrained contemporary artist shows civilians and members of the Paris militia—the "conquerors of the Bastille"—on the attack. Their successful action had enormous practical and symbolic significance, and July 14 has long been France's most important national holiday. *(Source: Musée Carnavalet/Photo Hubert Josse)*

The governor of the medieval fortress-prison refused to hand over the powder, panicked, and ordered his men to fire, killing ninety-eight people attempting to enter. Cannons were brought to batter the main gate, and fighting continued until the prison surrendered. The governor of the prison was later hacked to death, and his head was stuck on a pike and paraded through the streets. The next day a committee of citizens appointed the marquis de Lafayette commander of the city's armed forces. Paris was lost to the king, who was forced to recall the finance minister and disperse his troops. The popular uprising had saved the National Assembly.

As the delegates resumed their long-winded and inconclusive debates at Versailles, the people in the countryside sent them a radical and unmistakable message. All across France, peasants began to rise in spontaneous, violent, and effective insurrection against their lords. Neither middle-class landowners nor the larger, more prosperous farmers were spared. In some areas, peasants reinstated traditional village practices, undoing recent enclosures and reoccupying old common lands. Peasants seized forests, and taxes went unpaid. Fear of vagabonds and outlaws—called the Great Fear by contemporaries—seized the countryside and fanned the flames of rebellion.

Faced with chaos yet afraid to call on the king to restore order, some liberal nobles and middle-class delegates at Versailles responded to peasant demands with a surprise maneuver on the night of August 4, 1789. The duke of Aiguillon, one of France's greatest noble landowners, declared that

in several provinces the whole people forms a kind of league for the destruction of the manor houses, the ravaging of the lands, and especially for the seizure of the archives where the title deeds to feudal properties are kept. It seeks to throw off at last a yoke that has for many centuries weighted it down.[3]

He urged equality in taxation and the elimination of feudal dues. In the end, all the old exactions imposed on the peasants—serfdom where it still existed, village monopolies, the right to make peasants work on the roads, and a host of other dues—were abolished. Though a clarifying law passed a week later was less generous, the peasants ignored the "fine print." They never paid feudal dues again. Thus the French peasantry, which already owned about 30 percent of all the land, achieved a great and unprecedented victory in the early days of revolutionary upheaval. Henceforth, the French peasants would seek mainly to protect and consolidate their triumph. As the Great Fear subsided in the countryside, they became a force for order and stability.

A Limited Monarchy

The National Assembly moved forward. On August 27, 1789, it issued the Declaration of the Rights of Man, which stated, "Men are born and remain free and equal in rights." The declaration also maintained that mankind's natural rights are "liberty, property, security, and resistance to oppression" and that "every man is presumed innocent until he is proven guilty." As for law, "it is an expression of the general will; all citizens have the right to concur personally or through their representatives in its formation. . . . Free expression of thoughts and opinions is one of the most precious rights of mankind: every citizen may therefore speak, write, and publish freely." In short, this clarion call of the liberal revolutionary ideal guaranteed equality before the law, representative government for a sovereign people, and individual freedom. This revolutionary credo, only two pages long, was propagandized throughout France and the rest of Europe and around the world.

Moving beyond general principles to draft a constitution proved difficult. The questions of how much power the king should retain led to another deadlock. Once again the decisive answer came from the poor—in this instance, the poor women of Paris.

Women customarily bought the food and managed the poor family's slender resources. In Paris great numbers of women also worked for wages. In the general economic crisis, increasing unemployment and hunger put tremendous pressure on household managers, and the result was another popular explosion.

On October 5 some seven thousand desperate women marched the twelve miles from Paris to Versailles to demand action. This great crowd invaded the National Assembly, "armed with scythes, sticks and pikes." One tough old woman directing a large group of younger women defiantly shouted into the debate, "Who's that talking down there? Make the chatterbox shut up. That's not the point: the point is that we want bread."[4] Hers was the genuine voice of the people, essential to any understanding of the French Revolution.

"To Versailles"   This print is one of many commemorating the women's march on Versailles. Notice on the left that the artist has depicted—and criticized—the fashionable lady from the well-to-do as a most reluctant revolutionary. *(Source: Giraudon/Art Resource, NY)*

The women invaded the royal apartments, slaughtered some of the royal bodyguards, and furiously searched for the queen, Marie Antoinette, who was widely despised for her lavish spending and supposedly immoral behavior. "We are going to cut off her head, tear out her heart, fry her liver, and that won't be the end of it," they shouted, surging through the palace in a frenzy. It seems likely that only the intervention of Lafayette and the National Guard saved the royal family. But the only way to calm the disorder was for the king to go and live in Paris, as the crowd demanded. With this victory, the women clearly emerged as a major and enduring element in the Parisian revolutionary crowd.[5]

The National Assembly followed the king to Paris, and the next two years, until September 1791, saw the consolidation of the liberal Revolution. Under middle-class leadership, the National Assembly abolished the French nobility as a legal order and pushed forward with the creation of a constitutional monarchy, which Louis XVI reluctantly agreed to accept in July 1790. In the final constitution, the king remained the head of state, but all lawmaking power was placed in the hands of the National Assembly, elected by the economic upper half of French males.

New laws broadened women's rights to seek divorce, to inherit property, and to obtain financial support from fathers for illegitimate children. But women were not allowed to vote or hold political office. The great majority of comfortable, well-educated males in the National Assembly believed that women should be limited to child raising and domestic duties and should leave politics and most public activities to men. The delegates to the National Assembly also believed that excluding women from politics would free the political system from the harmful effects of the sexual intrigue common at court; and pure, home-focused wives would raise the high-minded sons needed to govern and defend the nation.

The National Assembly replaced the complicated patchwork of historic provinces with eighty-three departments of approximately equal size. It replaced the jumble of weights and measures that varied from province to province with the simple, rational metric system in 1793. It prohibited monopolies, guilds, and workers' combinations, and it abolished barriers to trade within France in the name of economic liberty. Thus the National Assembly applied the critical spirit of the Enlightenment to reform France's laws and institutions completely.

The National Assembly also nationalized the Catholic church's property and abolished monasteries as useless relics of a distant past. The government sold all former church property in an attempt to put the state's finances on a solid footing. Peasants eventually purchased much of this land when it was subdivided. The purchases strengthened their attachment to the revolutionary state. These actions, however, brought the new government into conflict with the Catholic church and with many sincere Christians, especially in the countryside.

Many delegates to the National Assembly, imbued with the rationalism and skepticism of the eighteenth-century philosophes, harbored a deep distrust of popular piety and "superstitious religion." They were interested in the church only to the extent that they could seize its land and use the church to strengthen the new state. Thus they established a national church, with priests chosen by voters. In the face of widespread resistance, the National Assembly then required the clergy to take a loyalty oath to the new government. The Catholic clergy became just so many more employees of the state. The pope formally condemned this attempt to subjugate the church. Only half of the priests of France took the oath of allegiance, and confusion and hostility among French Catholics were pervasive. The attempt to remake the Catholic church, like the National Assembly's abolition of guilds and workers' combinations, sharpened the division between the educated classes and the common people that had been emerging in the eighteenth century. This policy toward the church was the revolutionary government's first important failure.

❋ WORLD WAR AND REPUBLICAN FRANCE (1791–1799)

When Louis XVI accepted the final version of the completed constitution in September 1791, a young and still obscure provincial lawyer and member of the National Assembly named Maximilien Robespierre (1758–1794) evaluated the work of two years and concluded, "The Revolution is over." Robespierre was both right and wrong. He

was right in the sense that the most constructive and lasting reforms were in place. Nothing substantial in the way of liberty and equality would be gained in the next generation. He was wrong in the sense that a much more radical stage lay ahead. New heroes and new ideologies were to emerge in revolutionary wars and international conflict.

Foreign Reactions and the Beginning of War

The outbreak and progress of revolution in France produced great excitement and a sharp division of opinion in Europe and the United States. Liberals and radicals saw a mighty triumph of liberty over despotism. In Great Britain especially, they hoped that the French example would lead to a fundamental reordering of the political system that had placed Parliament in the hands of the aristocracy and a few wealthy merchants, with the great majority of people having very little say in the government. Conservative leaders such as Edmund Burke (1729–1797) were deeply troubled by the aroused spirit of reform. In 1790 Burke published *Reflections on the Revolution in France,* one of the great intellectual defenses of European conservatism. Defending inherited privileges, he glorified the unrepresentative Parliament and predicted that thoroughgoing reform like that occurring in France would lead only to chaos and tyranny. Burke's work sparked vigorous debate.

One passionate rebuttal came from a young writer in London, Mary Wollstonecraft (1759–1797). Born into the middle class, Wollstonecraft was schooled in adversity by a mean-spirited father who beat his wife and squandered his inherited fortune. Determined to be independent in a society that generally expected women of her class to become homebodies and obedient wives, she struggled for years to earn her living as a governess and teacher—practically the only acceptable careers for single, educated women—before attaining success as a translator and author. Interested in politics and believing that "a desperate disease requires a powerful remedy" in Great Britain as well as France, Wollstonecraft was incensed by Burke's book. She immediately wrote a blistering, widely read attack, *A Vindication of the Rights of Man* (1790).

Then, fired up on controversy and commitment, she made a daring intellectual leap. She developed for the first time the logical implications of natural-law philosophy in her masterpiece, *A Vindication of the Rights of Woman* (1792). To fulfill the still-unrealized potential of the French Revolution and to eliminate the many-sided sexual inequality she had felt so keenly, she demanded that

the Rights of Women be respected . . . [and] JUSTICE for one-half of the human race. . . . It is time to effect a revolution in female manners, time to restore to them their lost dignity, and make them, as part of the human species, labor, by reforming themselves, to reform the world.

Setting high standards for women, Wollstonecraft advocated rigorous coeducation, which would make women better wives and mothers, good citizens, and even economically independent people. Women could manage businesses and enter politics if only men would give them the chance. Men themselves would benefit from women's rights, for Wollstonecraft believed that "the two sexes mutually corrupt and improve each other."[6] Wollstonecraft's analysis testified to the power of the Revolution to excite and inspire outside France. Paralleling ideas put forth independently in France by Olympe de Gouges (1748–1793), a self-taught writer and woman of the people (see Listening to the Past), Wollstonecraft's work marked the birth of the modern women's movement for equal rights, and it was ultimately very influential.

The kings and nobles of continental Europe, who had at first welcomed the revolution in France as weakening a competing power, began to feel no less threatened than Burke and his supporters. At their courts they listened to the diatribes of great court nobles who had fled France and were urging intervention in France's affairs. When Louis XVI and Marie Antoinette were arrested and returned to Paris after trying unsuccessfully to slip out of France in June 1791, the monarchs of Austria and Prussia, in the Declaration of Pillnitz, declared their willingness to intervene in France in certain circumstances.

But the crowned heads of Europe did not deter the revolutionary spirit in France. When the National Assembly disbanded, it sought popular support by decreeing that none of its members would be eligible for election to the new Legislative Assembly. This meant that when the new representative body convened in October 1791, it had a different character. The great majority of the legislators were still prosperous, well-educated, middle-class men, but they were younger and less cautious

Mary Wollstonecraft   Painted by an unknown artist when Mary Wollstonecraft was thirty-two and writing her revolutionary *Vindication of the Rights of Woman,* this portrait highlights the remarkable strength of character that energized Wollstonecraft's brilliant intellect. *(Source: The Board of Trustees of the National Museums and Galleries on Merseyside, Walker Art Gallery)*

than their predecessors. Loosely allied and known as Jacobins, after the name of their political club, the representatives to the Legislative Assembly were passionately committed to liberal revolution.

The Jacobins increasingly lumped "useless aristocrats" and "despotic monarchs" together and easily whipped themselves into a patriotic fury with bombastic oratory. If the courts of Europe were attempting to incite a war of kings against France, then "we will incite a war of people against kings. . . . Ten million Frenchmen, kindled by the fire of liberty, armed with the sword, with reason, with eloquence would be able to change the face of the world and make the tyrants tremble on their thrones."[7] Only Robespierre and a very few others argued that people would not welcome liberation at the point of a gun. Such warnings were brushed aside. France would "rise to the full height of her mission," as one deputy urged. In April 1792 France declared war on Francis II, the Habsburg monarch.

France's crusade against tyranny went poorly at first. Prussia joined Austria in the Austrian Netherlands (present-day Belgium), and French forces broke and fled at their first encounter with armies of this First Coalition. The road to Paris lay open, and it is possible that only conflict between the eastern monarchs over the division of Poland saved France from defeat.

Military reversals and Austro-Prussian threats caused a wave of patriotic fervor to sweep France. In this supercharged wartime atmosphere, rumors of treason by the king and queen spread in Paris. Once again, the common people of Paris acted decisively. On August 10, 1792, a revolutionary crowd captured the royal palace at the Tuileries after heavy fighting. The king and his family fled for their lives to the nearby Legislative Assembly, which suspended the king from all his functions, imprisoned him, and called for a new National Convention to be elected by universal male suffrage. Monarchy in France was on its deathbed, mortally wounded by war and popular upheaval.

The Second Revolution

The fall of the monarchy marked a rapid radicalization of the Revolution, a phase that historians often call the "second revolution." Louis's imprisonment was followed by the September Massacres. Wild stories seized the city that imprisoned counter-revolutionary aristocrats and priests were plotting with the allied invaders. As a result, angry crowds invaded the prisons of Paris and summarily slaughtered half of the men and women they found. In late September 1792, the new, popularly elected National Convention proclaimed France a republic.

The republic sought to create a new popular culture to assure its future and fashioned compelling symbols that broke with the past and glorified the new order. It adopted a brand-new revolutionary calendar, which eliminated saints' days and renamed the days and the months after the seasons of the year. Citizens were expected to address each other with the friendly "thou" of the people rather than with the formal "you" of the rich and powerful. The republic energetically promoted broad, open-air, democratic festivals that sought to redi-rect the people's traditional enthusiasm for Catholic religious celebrations to secular holidays. Instilling republican virtue and a love of nation, these spectacles were less successful in villages than in cities, where popular interest in politics was greater and Catholicism was weaker.

All of the members of the National Convention were Jacobins and republicans, and the great majority continued to come from the well-educated middle class. But the Convention was increasingly divided into two bitterly competitive groups—the Girondists, named after a department in southwestern France, and the Mountain, led by Robespierre and another young lawyer, Georges Jacques Danton. The Mountain was so called because its members sat on the uppermost left-hand benches of the assembly hall.

This division was clearly apparent after the National Convention overwhelmingly convicted Louis XVI of treason. By a single vote, 361 of the 720 members of the Convention then unconditionally sentenced him to death in January 1793. Louis died with tranquil dignity on the newly invented guillotine. One of his last statements was "I am innocent and shall die without fear. I would that my death might bring happiness to the French, and ward off the dangers which I foresee."[8]

Both the Girondists and the Mountain were determined to continue the "war against tyranny." After stopping the Prussians at the indecisive Battle of Valmy on September 20, 1792, Republican armies successfully invaded Savoy and the German Rhineland. To the north, the revolutionary armies won their first major battle at Jemappes and by November 1792 were occupying the entire Austrian Netherlands. Everywhere they went, French armies of occupation chased the princes, "abolished feudalism," and found support among some peasants and middle-class people.

But the French armies also lived off the land, requisitioning food and supplies and plundering local treasures. The liberators looked increasingly like foreign invaders. International tensions mounted. In February 1793 the National Convention, at war with Austria and Prussia, declared war on Britain, Holland, and Spain as well. Republican France was now at war with almost all of Europe, a great war that would last almost without interruption until 1815.

As the forces of the First Coalition drove the French from the Austrian Netherlands, peasants in western France revolted against being drafted into the army. They were supported and encouraged in their resistance by devout Catholics, royalists, and foreign agents.

In Paris the quarrelsome National Convention found itself locked in a life-and-death political struggle between the Girondists and the Mountain. Both groups hated privilege and wanted to temper economic liberalism with social concern. Yet personal hatreds ran deep. The Girondists feared a bloody dictatorship by the Mountain, and the Mountain was no less convinced that the more moderate Girondists would turn to conservatives and even royalists in order to retain power. With the middle-class delegates so bitterly divided, the laboring poor of Paris emerged as the decisive political factor.

The laboring men and women of Paris always constituted—along with the peasantry in the summer of 1789—the elemental force that drove the Revolution forward. It was they who had stormed the Bastille, marched on Versailles, driven the king from the Tuileries, and carried out the September Massacres. The petty traders and laboring poor were often known as the *sans-culottes,* "without breeches," because the men wore trousers instead of the knee breeches of the aristocracy and the solid middle class. The immediate interests of the sans-culottes were mainly economic, and in the spring of 1793 the economic situation was as bad as the military situation. Rapid inflation, unemployment, and food shortages were again weighing heavily on poor families.

By the spring of 1793, sans-culottes men and women, encouraged by the so-called angry men, were demanding radical political action to guarantee them their daily bread. At first the Mountain joined the Girondists in violently rejecting these demands. But in the face of military defeat, peasant revolt, and hatred of the Girondists, Robespierre's group joined with sans-culottes activists in the city government to engineer a popular uprising, which forced the Convention to arrest thirty-one Girondist deputies for treason on June 2. All power passed to the Mountain.

The End of Louis XVI   Some cheered and some wept when the executioner showed the crowd the condemned monarch's severed head. The execution of the king was a victory for the radicals in Paris, but it horrified Europe's monarchs and conservatives, and it strengthened their opposition to the French Revolution. *(Source: Musée Carnavalet/Laurie Platt Winfrey, Inc.)*

Robespierre and others from the Mountain joined the recently formed Committee of Public Safety, to which the Convention had given dictatorial power to deal with the national emergency. These developments in Paris triggered revolt in leading provincial cities, such as Lyons and Marseilles, where moderates denounced Paris and demanded a decentralized government. The peasant revolt spread, and the republic's armies were driven back on all fronts. By July 1793 defeat appeared imminent.

Total War and the Terror

A year later, in July 1794, the Austrian Netherlands and the Rhineland were once again in the hands of conquering French armies, and the First Coalition was falling apart. This remarkable change of fortune was due to the revolutionary government's success in harnessing, for perhaps the first time in history, the explosive forces of a planned economy, revolutionary terror, and modern nationalism in a total war effort.

Robespierre and the Committee of Public Safety advanced with implacable resolution on several fronts in 1793 and 1794. First, in an effort to save revolutionary France, they continued to collaborate with the fiercely patriotic and democratic sans-culottes, who retained the common people's traditional faith in fair prices and a moral economic order and who distrusted most wealthy capitalists and all aristocrats. Thus Robespierre and his co-workers established, as best they could, a planned economy with egalitarian social overtones. Rather than let supply and demand determine prices, the government decreed the maximum allowable prices for a host of key products. Though the state was too weak to enforce all its price regulations, it did fix the price of bread in Paris at levels the poor could afford. Bakers were permitted to make only the "bread of equality"—a brown bread made of a mixture of all available flours. White bread and pastries were outlawed as frivolous luxuries. The poor of Paris may not have eaten well, but at least they ate.

They also worked, mainly to produce arms and munitions for the war effort. Craftsmen and small manufacturers were told what to produce and when to deliver. The government nationalized many small workshops and requisitioned raw

The Last Roll Call   Prisoners sentenced to death by revolutionary courts listen to an official solemnly reading the names of those selected for immediate execution. After being bound, the prisoners will ride standing up in a small cart through the streets of Paris to the nearby guillotine. As this painting highlights, both women and men were executed for political crimes under the Terror. *(Source: Mansell Collection)*

THE FRENCH REVOLUTION

May 5, 1789	Estates General convenes at Versailles
June 17, 1789	Third estate declares itself the National Assembly
June 20, 1789	Oath of the Tennis Court
July 14, 1789	Storming of the Bastille
July–Aug. 1789	The Great Fear in the countryside
August 4, 1789	National Assembly abolishes feudal privileges
August 27, 1789	National Assembly issues Declaration of the Rights of Man
October 5, 1789	Women march on Versailles and force royal family to return to Paris
November 1789	National Assembly confiscates lands held by the Catholic church
July 1790	Civil Constitution of the Clergy establishes a national church Louis XVI reluctantly agrees to accept a constitutional monarchy
June 1791	Arrest of the royal family while attempting to flee France
August 1791	Declaration of Pillnitz by Austria and Prussia
April 1792	France declares war on Austria
August 1792	Parisian mob attacks palace and takes Louis XVI prisoner
September 1792	September Massacres National Convention declares France a republic and abolishes monarchy
January 1793	Execution of Louis XVI
February 1793	France declares war on Britain, Holland, and Spain
March 1793	Bitter struggle in the National Convention between Girondists and the Mountain
April–June 1793	Robespierre and the Mountain organize the Committee of Public Safety Revolts in provincial cities
September 1793	Price controls to aid the sans-culottes and mobilize war effort
1793–1794	Reign of Terror in Paris and the provinces
Spring 1794	French armies victorious on all fronts
July 1794	Execution of Robespierre Thermidorian Reaction begins
1795–1799	The Directory
1795	End of economic controls and suppression of the sans-culottes
1797	Napoleon defeats Austrian armies in Italy and returns triumphant to Paris
1798	Austria, Great Britain, and Russia form the Second Coalition against France
1799	Napoleon overthrows the Directory and seizes power

materials and grain from the peasants. Failures to control and coordinate were failures of means and not of desire: seldom if ever before had a government attempted to manage an economy so thoroughly. The second revolution and the ascendancy of the sans-culottes had produced an embryonic emergency socialism, which thoroughly frightened Europe's propertied classes and had great influence on the subsequent development of socialist ideology.

Second, while radical economic measures supplied the poor with bread and the armies with weapons, the Reign of Terror (1793–1794) was solidifying the home front. Special revolutionary courts responsible only to Robespierre's Committee of Public Safety tried rebels and "enemies of the nation" for political crimes. Drawing on popular, sans-culottes support, these local courts ignored normal legal procedures and judged severely. Some 40,000 French men and women were executed or died in prison. Another 300,000 suspects crowded the prisons.

Robespierre's Reign of Terror was one of the most controversial phases of the French Revolution. Most historians now believe that the Reign of Terror was not directed against any single class but was a political weapon directed impartially against all who might oppose the revolutionary government. For many Europeans of the time, however, the Reign of Terror represented a terrifying perversion of the generous ideals that had existed in 1789.

The third and perhaps most decisive element in the French republic's victory over the First Coalition was its ability to continue drawing on the explosive power of patriotic dedication to a national state and a national mission. This is the essence of modern nationalism, and it was something new in history. With a common language and a common tradition newly reinforced by the ideas of popular sovereignty and democracy, the French people were stirred by a common loyalty. The shared danger of foreign foes and internal rebels unified all classes in a heroic defense of the nation. Everyone had to participate in the national effort. According to a famous decree of August 23, 1793:

The young men shall go to battle and the married men shall forge arms. The women shall make tents and clothes, and shall serve in the hospitals; children shall tear rags into lint. The old men will be guided to the public places of the cities to kindle the courage of the young warriors and to preach the unity of the Republic and the hatred of kings.

Like the wars of religion, war in 1793 was a crusade, a life-and-death struggle between good and evil. This war, however, was fought for a secular, rather than a religious, ideology.

Because all unmarried young men were subject to the draft, the French armed forces swelled to a million men in fourteen armies. A force of this size was unprecedented in the history of European warfare. The soldiers were led by young, impetuous generals who had often risen rapidly from the ranks and personified the opportunities the Revolution seemed to offer gifted sons of the people. These generals used mass attacks at bayonet point by their highly motivated forces to overwhelm the enemy. By the spring of 1794, French armies were victorious on all fronts. The republic was saved.

The Thermidorian Reaction and the Directory (1794–1799)

The success of the French armies led Robespierre and the Committee of Public Safety to relax the emergency economic controls, but they extended the political Reign of Terror. Their lofty goal was increasingly an ideal democratic republic where justice would reign and there would be neither rich nor poor. Their lowly means were unrestrained despotism and the guillotine, which struck down any who might seriously question the new order. In March 1794, to the horror of many sans-culottes, Robespierre's Terror wiped out many of the angry men, who had been criticizing Robespierre for being soft on the wealthy. Two weeks later, several of Robespierre's long-standing collaborators, led by the famous orator Danton, marched up the steps to the guillotine. A strange assortment of radicals and moderates in the Convention, knowing that they might be next, organized a conspiracy. They howled down Robespierre when he tried to speak to the National Convention on 9 Thermidor (July 27, 1794). On the following day, it was Robespierre's turn to be shaved by the revolutionary razor.

As Robespierre's closest supporters followed their leader, France unexpectedly experienced a thorough reaction to the despotism of the Reign of Terror. In a general way, this "Thermidorian reaction" recalled the early days of the Revolution.

The respectable middle-class lawyers and professionals who had led the liberal revolution of 1789 reasserted their authority, drawing support from their own class, the provincial cities, and the better-off peasants. The National Convention abolished many economic controls, printed more paper currency, and let prices rise sharply. And all the while, wealthy bankers and newly rich speculators celebrated the sudden end of the Terror with an orgy of self-indulgence and ostentatious luxury, an orgy symbolized by the shockingly low-cut gowns that quickly became the rage among their wives and mistresses.

The collapse of economic controls, coupled with runaway inflation, hit the working poor very hard. The gaudy extravagance of the rich wounded their pride. The sans-culottes accepted private property, but they believed passionately in small business, decent wages, and economic justice. Increasingly disorganized after Robespierre purged radical leaders, the common people of Paris finally revolted against the emerging new order in early 1795. The Convention quickly used the army to suppress these insurrections. For the first time since the fall of the Bastille, bread riots and uprisings by Parisians living on the edge of starvation were effectively put down by a government that made no concessions to the poor. In the face of all these catastrophes, the revolutionary fervor of the laboring poor in Paris finally subsided.

In villages and small towns there arose a great cry for peace and a turning toward religion, especially from women, who had seldom experienced the political radicalization of sans-culottes women in the big cities. Instead, these women had frequently and tenaciously defended their culture and religious beliefs. As the frustrated government began to retreat on the religious question from 1796 to 1801, the women of rural France brought back the Catholic church and the open worship of God. In the words of a leading historian, these women worked constructively and effectively for a return to a normal and structured lifestyle:

Peacefully but purposefully, they sought to re-establish a pattern of life punctuated by a peeling bell and one in which the rites of passage—birth, marriage, and death—were respected and hallowed. The state had intruded too far and women entered the public arena to push it back and won. It was one of the most resounding political statements made by the populace in the entire history of the Revolution.[9]

As for the middle-class members of the National Convention, in 1795 they wrote yet another constitution, which they believed would guarantee their economic position and political supremacy. The mass of the population voted only for electors, who were men of means. Electors then elected the members of a reorganized Legislative Assembly, as well as key officials throughout France. The new assembly also chose a five-man executive—the Directory.

The Directory continued to support French military expansion abroad. War was no longer so much a crusade as a means to meet ever-present, ever-unsolved economic problems. Large, victorious French armies reduced unemployment at home and were able to live off the territories they conquered and plundered.

The unprincipled action of the Directory reinforced widespread disgust with war and starvation, and the national elections of 1797 returned a large number of conservative and even monarchist deputies who favored peace at almost any price. The members of the Directory, fearing for their skins, used the army to nullify the elections and began to govern dictatorially. Two years later, Napoleon Bonaparte ended the Directory in a coup d'état and substituted a strong dictatorship for a weak one. The effort to establish stable representative government had failed.

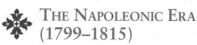

THE NAPOLEONIC ERA (1799–1815)

For almost fifteen years, from 1799 to 1814, France was in the hands of a keen-minded military dictator of exceptional ability. One of history's most fascinating leaders, Napoleon Bonaparte (1769–1821) realized the need to put an end to civil strife in France in order to create unity and consolidate his rule. And he did. But Napoleon saw himself as a man of destiny, and the glory of war and the dream of universal empire proved irresistible.

Napoleon's Rule of France

In 1799 when he seized power, young General Napoleon Bonaparte was a national hero. Born in Corsica into an impoverished noble family in 1769, Napoleon left home and became a lieutenant in the French artillery in 1785. After a brief and unsuccessful adventure fighting for Corsican independence in 1789, he returned to France as a French patriot and a dedicated revolutionary. Rising rapidly in the new army, Napoleon was placed in command of French forces in Italy and won brilliant victories there in 1796 and 1797. His next campaign, in Egypt, was a failure, but Napoleon made his way back to France before the fiasco was generally known. His reputation remained intact.

Napoleon soon learned that some prominent members of the Legislative Assembly were plotting against the Directory. The dissatisfaction of these plotters stemmed not so much from the fact that the Directory was a dictatorship as from the fact that it was a weak dictatorship. Ten years of upheaval and uncertainty had made firm rule much more appealing than liberty and popular politics to these disillusioned revolutionaries. They wanted a strong military ruler, and the flamboyant thirty-year-old Napoleon was ideal. Thus the conspirators and Napoleon organized a takeover. On November 9, 1799, they ousted the Directors, and the following day soldiers disbanded the Legislative Assembly at bayonet point. Napoleon was named first consul of the republic, and a new constitution consolidating his position was overwhelmingly approved in a plebiscite in December 1799. Republican appearances were maintained, but Napoleon was already the real ruler of France.

The essence of Napoleon's domestic policy was to use his great and highly personal powers to maintain order and put an end to civil strife. He did so by working out unwritten agreements with powerful groups in France. Napoleon's bargain with the solid middle class was codified in the Civil Code of 1804, which reasserted two of the fundamental principles of the liberal and essentially moderate revolution of 1789: equality of all male citizens before the law and absolute security of wealth and private property. Napoleon and the leading bankers of Paris established the privately owned Bank of France, which loyally served the interests of both the state and the financial oligarchy. Napoleon's defense of the new economic order also appealed successfully to the peasants, who had gained both land and status from the revolutionary changes.

At the same time, Napoleon accepted and strengthened the position of the French bureaucracy. Building on the solid foundations that revolutionary governments had inherited from the Old Regime, he perfected a thoroughly centralized state. A network of prefects, subprefects, and centrally appointed mayors depended on Napoleon and served him well. Nor were members of the old nobility slighted. Napoleon granted amnesty to émigrés on the condition that they return to France and take a loyalty oath. Members of this returning elite soon ably occupied many high posts in the expanding centralized state. Napoleon also created a new imperial nobility in order to reward his most talented generals and officials.

Napoleon's great skill in gaining support from important and potentially hostile groups is illustrated by his treatment of the Catholic church in France. Personally uninterested in religion, Napoleon wanted to heal the religious division remaining from the Revolution so that a united Catholic church in France could serve as a bulwark of order and social peace. After long and arduous negotiations, Napoleon and Pope Pius VII (r. 1800–1823) signed the Concordat of 1801. The pope gained for French Catholics the precious right to practice their religion freely, but Napoleon gained political power: his government now nominated bishops, paid the clergy, and exerted great influence over the church in France.

The domestic reforms of Napoleon's early years were his greatest achievement. Much of his legal and administrative reorganization has survived in France to this day. More generally, Napoleon's domestic initiatives gave the great majority of French people a welcome sense of order and stability. And when Napoleon added the glory of military victory, he rekindled a spirit of national unity.

Order and unity had their price: Napoleon's authoritarian rule. Women, who had often participated in revolutionary politics without having legal equality, lost many of the gains they had made in the 1790s under the new Napoleonic Code. Under the law, women were dependents of either their fathers or their husbands, and they could not make contracts or even have bank accounts in their own names. Indeed, Napoleon and his advisers aimed at re-establishing a "family monarch," where the power of the husband and father was as absolute over the wife and the children as that of Napoleon was over his subjects.

Free speech and freedom of the press—fundamental rights of the liberal revolution enshrined in the Declaration of the Rights of Man—were continually violated. Napoleon constantly reduced the number of newspapers in Paris. By 1811 only four were left, and they were little more than organs of government propaganda. The occasional elections were a farce. Later laws prescribed harsh penalties for political offenses.

These changes in the law were part of the creation of a police state in France. Since Napoleon was usually busy making war, this task was largely left to Joseph Fouché, an unscrupulous opportunist who had earned a reputation for brutality during the Reign of Terror. As minister of police, Fouché organized a ruthlessly efficient spy system, which kept thousands of citizens under continual police surveillance. People suspected of subversive activities were arbitrarily detained, placed under house arrest, or even consigned to insane asylums. After 1810 political suspects were held in state prisons, as they had been during the Terror. There were about twenty-five hundred such political prisoners in 1814.

Napoleon's Wars and Foreign Policy

Napoleon was above all a military man, and a great one. After coming to power in 1799, he sent peace feelers to Austria and Great Britain, the two remaining members of the Second Coalition, which had been formed against France in 1798. When these overtures were rejected, French armies led by Napoleon decisively defeated the Austrians. Once more, as in 1797, the British were alone—and war-weary, like the French. Still seeking to consolidate his regime domestically, Napoleon concluded the Treaty of Amiens with Great Britain in 1802. France remained in control of Holland, the Austrian Netherlands, the west bank of the Rhine, and most of the Italian peninsula. The Treaty of Amiens was clearly a diplomatic triumph for Napoleon, and peace with honor and profit increased his popularity at home.

In 1802 Napoleon was secure but unsatisfied. Ever a romantic gambler as well as a brilliant administrator, he could not contain his power drive. Thus he aggressively threatened British interests in the eastern Mediterranean and tried to restrict British trade with all of Europe. Deciding to renew war with Britain in May 1803, Napoleon began making preparations to invade England. But Great Britain remained dominant on the seas. When Napoleon tried to bring his Mediterranean fleet around Gibraltar to northern France, a combined French and Spanish fleet was, after a series of mishaps, virtually annihilated by Lord Nelson at the Battle of Trafalgar on October 21, 1805. A cross-Channel invasion of England was henceforth impossible. Renewed fighting had its advantages, however, for the first consul used the wartime atmosphere to have himself proclaimed emperor in late 1804.

Austria, Russia, and Sweden joined with Britain to form the Third Coalition against France shortly before the Battle of Trafalgar. Actions such as Napoleon's assumption of the Italian crown had convinced both Alexander I of Russia and Francis II of Austria that Napoleon was a threat to their interests and to the European balance of power. Yet the Austrians and the Russians were no match for Napoleon, who scored a brilliant victory over them at the Battle of Austerlitz in December 1805. Alexander I decided to pull back, and Austria accepted large territorial losses in return for peace as the Third Coalition collapsed.

David: Napoleon Crossing the Alps   Bold and commanding, with flowing cape and surging stallion, the daring young Napoleon Bonaparte leads his army across the Alps from Italy to battle the Austrians in 1797. This painting by the great Jacques-Louis David (1748–1825) is a stirring glorification of Napoleon, a brilliant exercise in mythmaking. *(Source: Louvre © Photo R.M.N.)*

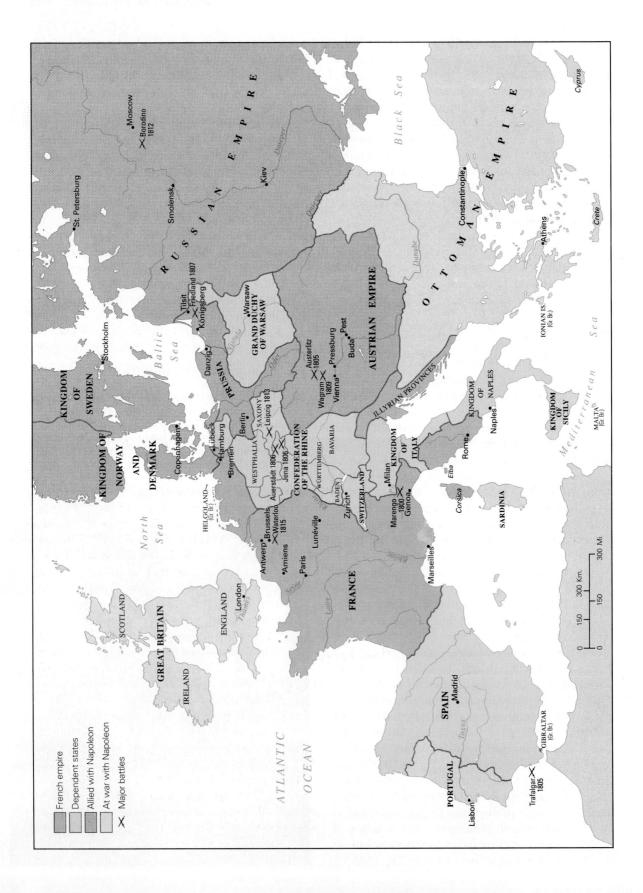

French empire
Dependent states
Allied with Napoleon
At war with Napoleon
✕ Major battles

ATLANTIC OCEAN

GREAT BRITAIN
SCOTLAND
IRELAND
ENGLAND
London
Thames

North Sea

KINGDOM OF NORWAY AND DENMARK
Copenhagen
Stockholm
KINGDOM OF SWEDEN
Baltic Sea

St. Petersburg

R U S S I A N   E M P I R E

Moscow
Borodino 1812
Smolensk
Kiev
Dnieper
Dniester

Tilsit
Friedland 1807
Königsberg
Danzig
Vistula
GRAND DUCHY OF WARSAW
Warsaw
PRUSSIA

Berlin
Lübeck
Hamburg
Bremen
Leipzig 1813
SAXONY
WESTPHALIA
Auerstädt 1806
Jena 1806
CONFEDERATION OF THE RHINE
WÜRTTEMBERG
BAVARIA
BADEN

Brussels
Antwerp
Waterloo 1815
Amiens
Paris
Lunéville
Zürich
SWITZERLAND

FRANCE
Seine
Loire
Rhône
Marseilles

Austerlitz 1805
Pressburg
Buda
Pest
AUSTRIAN EMPIRE
Wagram 1809
Vienna
Danube
ILLYRIAN PROVINCES

Black Sea

O T T O M A N   E M P I R E
Constantinople

Athens
IONIAN IS. (Gr. Br.)
Crete
Cyprus

Mediterranean Sea

KINGDOM OF ITALY
Milan
Marengo 1800
Genoa
Elba
Corsica
Rome
KINGDOM OF NAPLES
Naples
SARDINIA
KINGDOM OF SICILY
MALTA (Gr. Br.)

SPAIN
Madrid
Tagus
GIBRALTAR (Gr. Br.)
Trafalgar 1805
PORTUGAL
Lisbon

HELGOLAND (Gr. Br.)

0   150   300 Km.
0   150   300 Mi.

Victorious at Austerlitz, Napoleon proceeded to reorganize the German states to his liking. He established by decree the German Confederation of the Rhine, a union of fifteen German states minus Austria, Prussia, and Saxony. Naming himself "protector" of the confederation, Napoleon firmly controlled western Germany. His intervention in German affairs alarmed the Prussians, who mobilized their armies after more than a decade of peace with France. Napoleon attacked and won two more brilliant victories in October 1806, at Jena and Auerstädt. The war with Prussia, now joined by Russia, continued into the spring. After Napoleon's larger armies won another victory, Alexander I of Russia wanted peace. In the subsequent treaties of Tilsit, Prussia lost half of its population, while Russia accepted Napoleon's reorganization of western and central Europe. Alexander also promised to enforce Napoleon's recently decreed economic blockade against British goods.

After the victory of Austerlitz and even more after the treaties of Tilsit, Napoleon saw himself as the emperor of Europe and not just of France. The so-called Grand Empire he built had three parts. The core, or first part, was an ever-expanding France, which by 1810 included Belgium, Holland, parts of northern Italy, and much German territory on the east bank of the Rhine. Beyond French borders Napoleon established the second part: a number of dependent satellite kingdoms, on the thrones of which he placed (and replaced) the members of his large family. The third part comprised the independent but allied states of Austria, Prussia, and Russia. Both satellites and allies were expected after 1806 to support Napoleon's continental system and cease trade with Britain.

The impact of the Grand Empire on the peoples of Europe was considerable. In the areas incorporated into France and in the satellites (Map 23.1), Napoleon introduced many French laws, abolishing feudal dues and serfdom where French revolutionary armies had not already done so. Some of the peasants and middle class benefited from these reforms. Yet while he extended progressive measures to his cosmopolitan empire, Napoleon had to put the prosperity and special interests of France first in order to safeguard his power base. Levying heavy taxes in money and men for his armies, Napoleon came to be regarded more as a conquering tyrant than as an enlightened liberator.

The first great revolt occurred in Spain. In 1808 a coalition of Catholics, monarchists, and patriots rebelled against Napoleon's attempts to make Spain a French satellite with a Bonaparte as its king. French armies occupied Madrid, but the foes of Napoleon fled to the hills and waged uncompromising guerrilla warfare. Spain was a clear warning: resistance to French imperialism was growing. Yet Napoleon pushed on, determined to hold his complex and far-flung empire together.

In 1810 when the Grand Empire was at its height, Britain still remained at war with France, helping the guerrillas in Spain and Portugal. Napoleon's continental system, organized to exclude British goods from the European continent and force that "nation of shopkeepers" to its knees, was a failure. Instead, it was France that suffered from Britain's counter-blockade, which created hard times for French artisans and the middle class. Perhaps looking for a scapegoat, Napoleon turned on Alexander I of Russia, who had been giving only lukewarm support to Napoleon's war of prohibitions against British goods.

Napoleon's invasion of Russia began in June 1812 with a force that eventually numbered 600,000, probably the largest force yet assembled in a single army. Only one-third of this force was French, however; nationals of all the satellites and allies were drafted into the operation. After the great battle of Borodino, a draw from which the Russians retreated in good order, Alexander ordered the evacuation of Moscow, which then burned, and he refused to negotiate. Finally, after five weeks in the burned-out city, Napoleon ordered a retreat. That retreat was one of the great military disasters in history. The Russian army and the Russian winter cut Napoleon's army to pieces. Only 30,000 men returned to their homelands.

Leaving his troops to their fate, Napoleon raced to Paris to raise yet another army. When he refused to accept a France reduced to its historical size—the proposal offered by Austria's foreign minister, Prince Klemens von Metternich—Austria and Prussia deserted Napoleon and joined Russia and Great Britain in the Fourth Coalition. All across Europe patriots called for a "war of liberation"

Map 23.1 Napoleonic Europe in 1810   Only Great Britain remained at war with Napoleon at the height of the Grand Empire. Many British goods were smuggled through Helgoland, a tiny but strategic British possession off the German coast.

Goya: The Third of May, 1808 This famous painting screams in outrage at the horrors of war, which Goya witnessed in Spain. Spanish rebels, focused around the Christ-like figure at the center, are gunned down by anonymous French soldiers, grim forerunners of modern death squads and their atrocities. *(Source: Museo del Prado, Madrid)*

against Napoleon's oppression, and the well-disciplined regular armies of Napoleon's enemies closed in for the kill. Less than a month later, on April 4, 1814, a defeated, abandoned Napoleon abdicated his throne. After this unconditional abdication, the victorious allies granted Napoleon the island of Elba off the coast of Italy as his own tiny state.

The allies also agreed to the restoration of the Bourbon dynasty. The new monarch, Louis XVIII (r. 1814–1824), issued the Constitutional Charter, which accepted many of France's revolutionary changes and guaranteed civil liberties. Indeed, the Charter gave France a constitutional monarchy roughly similar to that established in 1791, al-

though far fewer people had the right to vote for representatives to the resurrected Chamber of Deputies. Moreover, in an attempt to strengthen popular support for Louis XVIII's new government, France was treated leniently by the allies, who agreed to meet in Vienna to work out a general peace settlement (see pages 805–807).

Louis XVIII—old, ugly, and crippled by gout—totally lacked the glory and magic of Napoleon. Hearing of political unrest in France and diplomatic tensions in Vienna, Napoleon staged a daring escape from Elba in February 1815. Landing in France, he issued appeals for support and marched on Paris with a small band of followers. French officers and soldiers who had fought so

THE NAPOLEONIC ERA

November 1799	Napoleon overthrows the Directory
December 1799	French voters overwhelmingly approve Napoleon's new constitution
1800	Napoleon founds the Bank of France
1801	France defeats Austria and acquires Italian and German territories in the Treaty of Lunéville Napoleon signs a concordat with the pope
1802	Treaty of Amiens with Britain
December 1804	Napoleon crowns himself emperor
October 1805	Battle of Trafalgar: Britain defeats the French and Spanish fleets
December 1805	Battle of Austerlitz: Napoleon defeats Austria and Prussia
1807	Treaties of Tilsit: Napoleon redraws the map of Europe
1810	Height of the Grand Empire
June 1812	Napoleon invades Russia with 600,000 men
Winter 1812	Disastrous retreat from Russia
March 1814	Russia, Prussia, Austria, and Britain form the Quadruple Alliance to defeat France
April 1814	Napoleon abdicates and is exiled to Elba
Feb.–June 1815	Napoleon escapes from Elba and rules France until suffering defeat at Battle of Waterloo

long for their emperor responded to the call. Louis XVIII fled, and once more Napoleon took command. But Napoleon's gamble was a desperate long shot, for the allies were united against him. At the end of a frantic period known as the Hundred Days, they crushed his forces at Waterloo on June 18, 1815, and imprisoned him on the rocky island of St. Helena, far off the western coast of Africa. Old Louis XVIII returned again—this time "in the baggage of the allies," as his detractors scornfully put it—and recommenced his reign. The allies now dealt more harshly with the apparently incorrigible French (see page 807). And Napoleon, doomed to suffer crude insults at the hands of sadistic English jailers on distant St. Helena, could take revenge only by writing his memoirs, skillfully nurturing the myth that he had been Europe's revolutionary liberator, a romantic hero whose lofty work had been undone by oppressive reactionaries. An era had ended.

SUMMARY

The French Revolution left a compelling and many-sided political legacy. This legacy included, most notably, liberalism, assertive nationalism, radical democratic republicanism, embryonic socialism, and self-conscious conservatism. It also left a rich and turbulent history of electoral competition, legislative assemblies, and even mass politics. Thus the French Revolution and conflicting interpretations of its significance presented a whole range of political options and alternative visions of the future. For this reason it was truly *the* revolution in modern European politics.

The revolution that began in America and spread to France was a liberal revolution. Revolutionaries on both sides of the Atlantic wanted to establish civil liberties and equality before the law within the framework of representative government, and they succeeded. In France liberal nobles and an increasingly class-conscious middle class overwhelmed declining monarchial absolutism and feudal privilege, thanks to the intervention of the common people—the sans-culottes and the peasants. France's new political system reflected a social structure based increasingly on wealth and achievement rather than on tradition and legal privileges.

After the establishment of the Republic, the radical phase of the revolution during the Terror, and the fall of Robespierre, the educated elites and the solid middle class reasserted themselves under the Directory. And though Napoleon sharply curtailed representative institutions and individual rights, he effectively promoted the reconciliation of old and new, of centralized bureaucracy and careers open to talent, of noble and bourgeois in a restructured property-owning elite. Louis XVIII had to accept the commanding position of this restructured elite, and in granting representative government and civil liberties to facilitate his restoration to the throne in 1814, he submitted to the rest of the liberal triumph of 1789 to 1791. The liberal core of the French Revolution had successfully survived a generation of war and dictatorship.

The lived experience of the French Revolution and the wars that went with it exercised a pervasive influence on politics and the political imagination in the nineteenth century, not only in France but throughout Europe and even the rest of the world. The radical legacy of the embattled republic of 1793 and 1794, with its sans-culottes democratic republicanism and its egalitarian ideology and embryonic socialism, would inspire republicans, democrats, and early socialists. Indeed, revolutionary upheaval encouraged generations of radicals to believe that political revolution might remake society and even create a new humanity. At the same time, there was a legacy of a powerful and continuing reaction to the French Revolution and to aggressive French nationalism. Monarchists and traditionalists believed that 1789 had been a tragic mistake. They concluded that democratic republicanism and sans-culottes activism led only to war, class conflict, and savage dictatorship. Conservatives and many com-

fortable moderates were profoundly disillusioned by the revolutionary era. They looked with nostalgia toward the supposedly ordered world of benevolent monarchy, firm government, and respectful common people.

NOTES

1. Quoted in R. R. Palmer, *The Age of the Democratic Revolution,* vol. 1 (Princeton, N.J.: Princeton University Press, 1959), p. 239.
2. G. Lefebvre, *The Coming of the French Revolution* (New York: Vintage Books, 1947), p. 81.
3. P. H. Beik, ed., *The French Revolution* (New York: Walker, 1970), p. 89.
4. G. Pernoud and S. Flaisser, eds., *The French Revolution* (Greenwich, Conn.: Fawcett, 1960), p. 61.
5. O. Hufton, *Women and the Limits of Citizenship in the French Revolution* (Toronto: University of Toronto Press, 1992), pp. 3–22.
6. Quotations from Wollstonecraft are drawn from E. W. Sunstein, *A Different Face: The Life of Mary Wollstonecraft* (New York: Harper & Row, 1975), pp. 208, 211; and H. R . James, *Mary Wollstonecraft: A Sketch* (London: Oxford University Press, 1932), pp. 60, 62, 69.
7. L. Gershoy, *The Era of the French Revolution, 1789–1799* (New York: Van Nostrand, 1957), p. 150.
8. Pernoud and Flaisser, *The French Revolution,* pp. 193–194.
9. Hufton, *Women and the Limits of Citizenship in the French Revolution,* p. 130.

SUGGESTED READING

For fascinating eyewitness reports on the French Revolution, see the edited works by Beik and by Pernoud and Flaisser mentioned in the Notes. In addition, A. Young's *Travels in France During the Years 1787, 1788 and 1789* (1969) offers an engrossing contemporary description of France and Paris on the eve of revolution. E. Burke, *Reflections on the Revolution in France,* first published in 1790, is the classic conservative indictment. The intense passions the French Revolution has generated may be seen in nineteenth-century French historians, notably the enthusiastic J. Michelet, *History of the French Revolution;* the hostile H. Taine; and the judicious A. de Tocqueville, whose masterpiece, *The Old Regime and the French Revolution,* was first published in 1856. Important general studies on the entire period include the work of R. R. Palmer, cited in the Notes, which paints a comparative international picture; E. J. Hobsbawm, *The Age of Revolution, 1789–1848* (1962); C. Breunig, *The Age of Revolution and Reaction, 1789–1850* (1970); O. Connelly, *French Revolution—Napoleonic Era* (1979); and L. Dehio, *The Precarious Balance: Four Centuries of the European Power Struggle* (1962).

Recent years have seen a wealth of new scholarship and interpretation. A. Cobban, *The Social Interpretation of the French Revolution* (1964), and F. Furet, *Interpreting the French Revolution* (1981), are major reassessments of long-dominant ideas, which are admirably presented in N. Hampson, *A Social History of the French Revolution* (1963), and in the volume by Lefebvre listed in the Notes. E. Kennedy, *A Cultural History of the French Revolution* (1989), beautifully written and handsomely illustrated, and W. Doyle, *Origins of the French Revolution,* 3d ed. (1988), are excellent on long-term developments. Among recent studies, which generally are often quite critical of revolutionary developments, several are noteworthy: J. Bosher, *The French Revolution* (1988); S. Schama, *Citizens: A Chronicle of the French Revolution* (1989); W. Doyle, *The Oxford History of the French Revolution* (1989); and D. Sutherland, *France, 1789–1815: Revolution and Counterrevolution* (1986).

Two valuable anthologies concisely presenting a range of interpretations are F. Kafker and J. Laux, eds., *The French Revolutions: Conflicting Interpretations,* 4th ed. (1989), and G. Best, ed., *The Permanent Revolution: The French Revolution and Its Legacy, 1789–1989* (1988). G. Rude makes the men and women of the great days of upheaval come alive in his *The Crowd in the French Revolution* (1959), whereas R. R. Palmer studies sympathetically the leaders of the Terror in *Twelve Who Ruled* (1941). Four other particularly interesting, detailed works are D. Jordan, *The Revolutionary Career of Maximilien Robespierre* (1985); J. P. Bertaud, *The Army of the French Revolution: From Citizen-Soldier to Instrument of Power* (1988); C. L. R. James, *The Black Jacobins* (1938, 1980), on black slave revolt in Haiti; and J. C. Herold, *Mistress to an Age* (1955), on the remarkable writer Madame de Staël. Other significant studies on aspects of revolutionary France include P. Jones's pathbreaking *The Peasantry in the French Revolution*

(1979); W. Sewell, Jr.'s imaginative *Work and Revolution in France: The Language of Labor from the Old Regime to 1848* (1980); and L. Hunt's innovative *Politics, Culture, and Class in the French Revolution* (1984).

An ongoing explosion of studies on women in the French Revolution is increasing knowledge and also raising conflicting interpretations. These developments may be seen by comparing two particularly important works: J. Landes, *Women and the Public Sphere in the Age of the French Revolution* (1988), and O. Hufton, listed in the Notes. D. Outram, *The Body and the French Revolution: Sex, Class and Political Culture* (1989), and L. Hunt, *The Family Romance of the French Revolution* (1992), also provide innovative analyses of the gender-related aspects of revolutionary politics and are highly recommended. D. Levy, H. Applewhite, and M. Johnson, eds., *Women in Revolutionary Paris, 1789–1795* (1979), is a valuable collection of contemporary documents with helpful commentaries. Mary Wollstonecraft's dramatic life is the subject of several good biographies, including those by Sunstein and James cited in the Notes.

Two important works placing political developments in a comparative perspective are P. Higonnet, *Sister Republics: The Origins of French and American Republicanism* (1988), and E. Morgan, *Inventing the People: The Rise of Popular Sovereignty in England and America* (1988). B. Bailyn, *The Ideological Origins of the American Revolution* (1967), is also noteworthy.

The best synthesis on Napoleonic France is L. Bergeron, *France Under Napoleon* (1981). P. Geyl, *Napoleon: For and Against* (1949), is a delightful discussion of changing political interpretations of Napoleon, which may be compared with a more recent treatment by R. Jones, *Napoleon: Man and Myth* (1977). Good biographies are J. Thompson, *Napoleon Bonaparte: His Rise and Fall* (1952); F. Markham, *Napoleon* (1964); and V. Cronin, *Napoleon Bonaparte* (1972). Wonderful novels inspired by the period include Raphael Sabatini's *Scaramouche,* a swashbuckler of revolutionary intrigue with accurate historical details; Charles Dickens's fanciful *Tale of Two Cities;* and Leo Tolstoy's monumental saga of Napoleon's invasion of Russia (and much more), *War and Peace.*

LISTENING TO THE
PAST

Revolution and Women's Rights

The 1789 Declaration of the Rights of Man was a revolutionary call for legal equality, representative government, and individual freedom. But the new rights were strictly limited to men; Napoleon tightened further the subordination of French women.

Among those who saw the contradiction in granting supposedly universal rights to only half of the population was Marie Gouze (1748–1793), known to history as Olympe de Gouges. The daughter of a provincial butcher and peddler, she pursued a literary career in Paris after the death of her husband. Between 1790 and 1793 she wrote more than two dozen political pamphlets under her new name. De Gouges's great work was her "Declaration of the Rights of Women" (1791). Excerpted here, de Gouges's manifesto went beyond the 1789 Rights of Man. It called on males to end their oppression of women and give women equal rights. A radical on women's issues, de Gouges sympathized with the monarchy and criticized Robespierre in print. Convicted of sedition, she was guillotined in November 1793.

. . . Man, are you capable of being just? . . . Tell me, what gives you sovereign empire to oppress my sex? Your strength? Your talents? Observe the Creator in his wisdom . . . and give me, if you dare, an example of this tyrannical empire. Go back to animals, consult the elements, study plants . . . and distinguish, if you can, the sexes in the administration of nature. Everywhere you will find them mingled; everywhere they cooperate in harmonious togetherness in this immortal masterpiece.

Man alone has raised his exceptional circumstances to a principle. . . . He wants to command as a despot a sex which is in full possession of its intellectual faculties; he pretends to enjoy the Revolution and to claim his rights to equality in order to say nothing more about it.

DECLARATION OF THE RIGHTS OF WOMAN AND THE FEMALE CITIZEN

For the National Assembly to decree in its last session, or in those of the next legislature:

PREAMBLE

Mothers, daughters, sisters and representatives of the nation demand to be constituted into a national assembly. Believing that ignorance, omission, or scorn for the rights of woman are the only causes of public misfortunes and of the corruption of governments, [the women] have resolved to set forth in a solemn declaration the natural, inalienable, and sacred rights of woman. . . .

. . . the sex that is as superior in beauty as it is in courage during the sufferings of maternity recognizes and declares in the presence and under the auspices of the Supreme Being, the following Rights of Woman and of Female Citizens:

I. Woman is born free and lives equal to man in her rights. Social distinctions can be based only on the common utility.

II. The purpose of any political association is the conservation of the natural and imprescriptible rights of woman and man; these rights are liberty, property, security, and especially resistance to oppression.

III. The principle of all sovereignty rests essentially with the nation, which is nothing but the union of woman and man. . . .

IV. Liberty and justice consist of restoring all that belongs to others; thus, the only limits on the exercise of the natural rights of woman are perpetual male tyranny; these limits are to be reformed by the laws of nature and reason.

V. Laws of nature and reason proscribe all acts harmful to society. . . .

VI. The law must be the expression of the general will; all female and male citizens must send representatives to its formation; it must be the same for all: male and female citizens, being equal in the eyes of the law, must be equally admitted to all honors, positions, and public employment according to their capacity and without other distinctions besides those of their virtues and talents.

VII. No woman is an exception; she is accused, arrested, and detained in cases determined by law. Women, like men, obey this rigorous law.

VIII. The law must establish only those penalties that are strictly and obviously necessary. . . .

IX. Once any woman is declared guilty, complete rigor is [to be] exercised by the law.

X. No one is to be disquieted for his very basic opinions; woman has the right to mount the scaffold; she must equally have the right to mount the rostrum, provided that her demonstrations do not disturb the legally established public order.

XI. The free communication of thoughts and opinions is one of the most precious rights of woman, since that liberty assures the recognition of children by their fathers. Any female citizen thus may say freely, I am the mother of a child which belongs to you, without being forced by a barbarous prejudice to hide the truth. . . .

XIII. For the support of the public force and the expenses of administration, the contributions of woman and man are equal; she shares all the duties . . . and all the painful tasks; therefore, she must have the same share in the distribution of positions, employment, offices, honors, and jobs. . . .

XIV. Female and male citizens have the right to verify, either by themselves or through their representatives, the necessity of the public contribution. This can only apply to women if they are granted an equal share, not only of wealth, but also of public administration. . . .

XV. The collectivity of women, joined for tax purposes to the aggregate of men, has the right to demand an accounting of his administration from any public agent.

XVI. No society has a constitution without the guarantee of rights and the separation of powers; the constitution is null if the majority of individuals comprising the nation have not cooperated in drafting it.

XVII. Property belongs to both sexes whether united or separate; for each it is an inviolable and sacred right. . . .

Late-eighteenth-century French painting, *La Liberté.* (Source: *Bibliothèque Nationale/Giraudon/Art Resource, NY*)

POSTSCRIPT

Women, wake up. . . . Discover your rights. . . . Oh women, women! When will you cease to be blind? What advantage have you received from the Revolution? A more pronounced scorn, a more marked disdain. . . . [If men persist in contradicting their revolutionary principles,] courageously oppose the force of reason to the empty pretensions of superiority . . . and you will soon see these haughty men, not groveling at your feet as servile adorers, but proud to share with you the treasure of the Supreme Being. Regardless of what barriers confront you; it is in your power to free yourselves; you have only to want to. . . .

Questions for Analysis

1. On what basis did de Gouges argue for gender equality? Did she believe in natural law?

2. What consequences did "scorn for the rights of women" have for France, according to de Gouges?

3. Did de Gouges stress political rights at the expense of social and economic rights? If so, why?

Source: Olympe de Gouges, "Declaration of the Rights of Woman" in Darline G. Levy, Harriet B. Applewhite, and Mary D. Johnson, eds., *Women in Revolutionary Paris, 1789–1795* (Urbana: University of Illinois Press, 1979), pp. 87–96. Copyright © 1979 by the Board of Trustees, University of Illinois. Used with permission.

24

The Industrial Revolution
in Europe

❈

A colored engraving by
J. C. Bourne of the
Great Western Railway
emerging from a tunnel.
*(Source: Science and Pic-
ture Library, London)*

While the Revolution in France was opening a new political era, another revolution was transforming economic and social life. The Industrial Revolution, which began in England around the 1780s, started to influence continental Europe and the rest of the world after 1815. Because the Industrial Revolution was less dramatic than the French Revolution, some historians see industrial development as basically moderate and evolutionary. From a long perspective, however, it was rapid and brought about radical changes. Perhaps only the development of agriculture during Neolithic times had a similar impact and significance.

The Industrial Revolution profoundly modified much of human experience. It changed patterns of work, transformed the social class structure, and even altered the international balance of political and military power, giving added impetus to ongoing Western expansion into non-Western lands. The Industrial Revolution also helped ordinary people gain a higher standard of living as the widespread poverty of the preindustrial world was gradually reduced.

Unfortunately, improvement in the European standard of living was quite limited until about 1850, for at least two reasons. First, even in England only a few key industries experienced a technological revolution. Many more industries continued to use old methods, especially on the European continent, and this held down the increase in total production. Second, the increase in total population, which began in the eighteenth century, continued all across Europe as the era of the Industrial Revolution unfolded. As a result, the rapid growth in population threatened—quite literally—to eat up the growth in production and to leave individuals poorer than ever. Thus rapid population growth formed a somber background for European industrialization and made the wrenching transformation even more difficult.

- What was the Industrial Revolution?
- What were the origins of the Industrial Revolution, and how did it develop?
- How did the changes brought by the Industrial Revolution affect people and society in an era of continued rapid population growth?

These are the questions that this chapter seeks to answer. Chapter 26 examines in detail the emergence of accompanying changes in urban civilization, and Chapter 27 probes the consequences of industrialization in Europe for non-Western peoples.

THE INITIAL BREAKTHROUGH IN ENGLAND

The Industrial Revolution began in England. It was something new in history, and it was quite unplanned. With no models to copy and no idea of what to expect, England had to pioneer not only in industrial technology but also in social relations and urban living. Between 1793 and 1815, almost constant war with France complicated these formidable tasks. The trailblazer in economic development, as France was in political change, England must command special attention.

Eighteenth-Century Origins

Although many aspects of the Industrial Revolution are still matters for scholarly debate, it is generally agreed that the industrial changes that did occur grew out of a complex combination of factors. These factors came together in eighteenth-century England and initiated a decisive breakthrough that many place in the 1780s—after the American war for independence and just before the French Revolution.

In analyzing the causes of the late-eighteenth-century acceleration in the English economy, historians have paid particular attention to dramatic changes in agriculture, foreign trade, technology, energy supplies, and transportation. Although this chapter focuses on those issues, one must first understand that England had other, less conspicuous, assets that favored the long process of development that culminated in industrial breakthrough.

Relatively good government was one such asset. The monarchy and the aristocratic oligarchy, which jointly ruled the country after the constitutional settlement of 1688, provided stable and predictable government. Neither civil strife nor invading armies threatened the peace of the realm. Thus the government let the domestic economy operate fairly freely and with few controls, encouraging personal initiative, technological change, and a free market.

A related asset was an experienced business class with very modern characteristics. This business class, which traced its origins to the High Middle Ages, eagerly sought to make profits and to accumulate capital. England also had a large class of hired agricultural laborers. These rural wage earners were relatively mobile—compared with village-bound peasants in France and western Germany, for example—and along with cottage workers they formed a potential labor force for capitalist entrepreneurs.

Several other assets supporting English economic growth stand out. First, unlike France and most other countries, England had an effective central bank and well-developed credit institutions. Second, although England may seem a rather small country today, it undoubtedly enjoyed the largest effective domestic market in eighteenth-century Europe. In an age when shipping goods by water was much cheaper than shipping goods by land, no part of England was more than twenty miles from navigable water. Beginning in the 1770s, a canal-building boom greatly enhanced this natural advantage (Map 24.1). Nor were there any tariffs within the country to hinder trade, as there were in France before 1789 and in politically fragmented Germany and Italy. Finally, only in Holland did the lower classes appear to live as well as in England. The ordinary English family did not have to spend almost everything it earned just to buy bread. It could spend more on other items, thereby adding significantly to the growing demand for manufactured goods that was a critical factor in initiating England's industrial breakthrough.

All these factors combined to bring about the Industrial Revolution, a term that awed contemporaries coined in the 1830s to describe the burst of major inventions and technical changes that they had witnessed in certain industries. This technical revolution went hand in hand with an impressive quickening in the annual rate of industrial growth in England. Thus industry grew at only 0.7 percent per year between 1700 and 1760—before the Industrial Revolution—but it grew at the much higher rate of 3 percent between 1801 and 1831, when industrial transformation was in full swing.[1] The decisive quickening of growth probably came in the 1780s, after the American war of independence and just before the French Revolution.

The great economic and political revolutions that shaped the modern world occurred almost simultaneously. The Industrial Revolution, however, was a longer process. It was not complete in England until 1830 at the earliest, and it had no real impact on continental European countries until after the Congress of Vienna (see page 805) ended the era of revolutionary wars in 1815.

The Agricultural Revolution

Although scholars no longer believe, as did an older generation of historians, that radical agricultural change was a necessary precondition for the industrial breakthrough, a gradual but profound revolution in agricultural methods did promote accelerated economic growth. That revolution mirrored the general economic leadership underpinning England's epoch-making industrial surge. In essence, the agricultural revolution eliminated the traditional pattern of village agriculture found in northern and central Europe. It replaced the medieval open-field system with a new system of continuous rotation that resulted in more food for humans and their animals. The new agricultural system had profound implications, for it eliminated long-standing common rights as well as the fallow. But whereas peasants and rural laborers checked the spread of the new system on the continent of Europe in the eighteenth century, large landowners and powerful market forces overcame such opposition in England.

The new methods of agriculture originated in the Low Countries. The vibrant, dynamic middle-class society of seventeenth-century republican Holland was the most advanced in Europe in many areas of human endeavor, including agriculture. By 1650 intensive farming was well established throughout much of the Low Countries. Enclosed fields, continuous rotation, heavy manuring, and a wide variety of crops—all these innovations were present. Agriculture was highly specialized and commercialized. The same skills that grew turnips produced flax to be spun into linen for clothes, as well as tulip bulbs to lighten the heart with beautiful flowers. The fat cattle of Holland, so beloved by Dutch painters, gave the most milk in Europe. The Low Countries became "the Mecca of foreign agricultural experts who came . . . to see Flemish agriculture with their own eyes, to write about it and to propagate its methods in their home lands."[2]

The English were the best students. They learned about water control from the Dutch, the world's leaders after centuries of effort in the skills of drainage. In the seventeenth century, Dutch experts made a great contribution to draining the extensive marshes, or fens, of wet and rainy England.

On such new land, where traditions and common rights were not established, farmers introduced new crops and new rotations fairly easily.

Dutch experience was also important to Viscount Charles Townsend (1674–1738), one of the pioneers of English agricultural improvement. This lord from the upper reaches of the English aristocracy learned about turnips and clover while serving as English ambassador to Holland. When Lord Charles retired from politics in 1730 and returned to his large estates in Norfolk in eastern England, it was said that he spoke of turnips, turnips, and nothing but turnips. This led some wit to nickname his lordship "Turnip" Townsend. But Townsend had the last laugh. Draining extensively, manuring heavily, and sowing crops in regular rotation without fallowing, the farmers who leased Townsend's lands produced larger crops. They and he earned higher incomes. Those who had scoffed reconsidered. By 1740 agricultural improvement had become a craze among the English aristocracy.

There were also improvements in livestock, inspired in part by the earlier successes of English country gentlemen in breeding ever-faster horses for the races and fox hunts that were their passions. Selective breeding of ordinary livestock was a marked improvement over the old pattern, which has been graphically described as little more than "the haphazard union of nobody's son with everybody's daughter."

By the mid-eighteenth century, English agriculture was in the process of a radical and technologically desirable transformation. The eventual result was that by 1870 English farmers produced 300 percent more food than they had produced in 1700, although the number of people working the land had increased by only 14 percent. This great surge of agricultural production provided food for England's rapidly growing urban population. It was a tremendous achievement.

The Cost of Enclosure

What was the cost of technical progress in England, and to what extent did its payment result in social injustice? Scholars agree that the impetus for enclosing the fields came mainly from the powerful ruling class—the English landowning aristocracy, who benefited directly from higher yields that could support higher rents. Beyond these certainties, there are important differences of interpretation among historians.

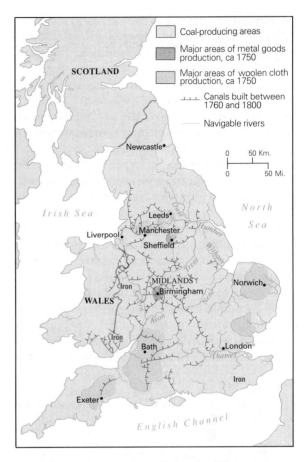

MAP 24.1 Cottage Industry and Transportation in Eighteenth-Century England   England had an unusually good system of navigable waterways even before river-linking canals made it better.

Many historians assert that the open fields were enclosed fairly and that both large and small owners received their fair share after the strips were surveyed and consolidated. Other historians argue that fairness was more apparent than real. These historians point out that the large landowners controlled Parliament, which made the laws. They had Parliament pass hundreds of "enclosure acts," each of which authorized the fencing of open fields in a given village and the division of the common in proportion to one's property in the open fields. The division of the heavy legal and surveying costs of enclosure among the landowners meant that many peasants who had small holdings had to sell out to pay their share of the expenses. Similarly, landless cottagers lost their age-old access to the common pasture but received no compensation. Landless families were dealt a serious blow, for women were deprived of the means to raise animals for market and to earn vital income. In the spirited words of one critical historian, "Enclosure (when all the sophistications are allowed for) was a plain enough case of class robbery, played according to the fair rules of property and law laid down by a Parliament of property-owners and lawyers."[3]

In assessing these conflicting interpretations, one needs to put eighteenth-century developments in a longer historical perspective. In the first place, as much as half of English farmland was already enclosed by 1750. A great wave of enclosure of English open fields into sheep pastures had occurred in the sixteenth and early seventeenth centuries, a wave that had dispossessed many English peasants in order to produce wool for the thriving textile industry. In the later seventeenth and early eighteenth centuries, many open fields were enclosed fairly harmoniously by mutual agreement among all classes of landowners in English villages. Thus parliamentary enclosure, the great bulk of which occurred after 1760 and particularly during the

Napoleonic wars, only completed a process that was in full swing.

Indeed, by 1700 a highly distinctive pattern of landownership and production existed in England. At one extreme were a few large landowners, at the other a large mass of landless cottagers who labored mainly for wages and who could graze only a pig or a cow on the village common. In between stood two other groups: small, independent peasant farmers who owned their own land, and substantial tenant farmers who rented land from the big landowners, hired wage laborers, and sold their output on a cash market. Yet the small, independent English farmers had been declining in numbers since the sixteenth-century enclosures (and even before). They could not compete with the profit-minded, market-oriented tenant farmers.

These tenant farmers, many of whom had formerly been independent owners, were the key to mastering the new methods of farming. Well financed by the large landowners, the tenant farmers fenced fields, built drains, and improved the

Enclosing the Fields   This remarkable aerial photograph illustrates key aspects of the agricultural revolution. Though the long ridges and furrows of the old open-field system still stretch across the whole picture, hedgerows now cut through the long strips to divide the land into several enclosed fields. *(Source: Cambridge University Collection)*

soil with fertilizers. Such improvements and new methods of farming actually increased employment opportunities for wage workers. Thus enclosure did not force people off the land by eliminating jobs.

At the same time, by eliminating common rights and greatly reducing the access of poor men and women to the land, the eighteenth-century enclosure movement marked the completion of two major historical developments in England: the rise of market-oriented estate agriculture and the emergence of a landless proletariat. By 1815 a tiny minority of wealthy English (and Scottish) landowners held most of the land and pursued profits aggressively, leasing their holdings through agents at competitive prices to middle-size farmers. These farmers produced mainly for cash markets and relied on landless laborers for their work force. In strictly economic terms, these landless laborers may have lived as well in 1800 as in 1700, but they had lost that bit of independence and self-respect that common rights had provided. They had become completely dependent on cash wages. In no other European country had this proletarianization—this transformation of large numbers of small peasant farmers into landless rural wage earners—gone so far as it had in England by the late eighteenth century. And, as in the earlier English enclosure movement, the village poor found the cost of economic change and technical progress heavy and unjust.

The Growth of Foreign Trade

In addition to leading Europe in agricultural improvement, Great Britain (formed in 1707 by the union of England and Scotland into a single kingdom) gradually became the leading maritime power. In the eighteenth century, British ships and merchants succeeded in dominating long-distance trade, particularly intercontinental trade across the Atlantic. This foreign trade stimulated the economy.

Britain's commercial leadership in the eighteenth century had its origins in the mercantilism of the seventeenth century. European mercantilism was a system of economic regulations aimed at increasing the power of the state. What distinguished English mercantilism was the unusual idea that government economic regulations could and should serve the private interest of individuals and groups as well as the public needs of the state.

The seventeenth-century Navigation Acts reflected the desire of Great Britain to increase both its military power and its private wealth. The initial target of these instruments of economic warfare was the Dutch, who were far ahead of the English in shipping and foreign trade in the mid-seventeenth century. By the later seventeenth century, after three Anglo-Dutch wars, the Netherlands was falling behind England in shipping, trade, and colonies. France then stood clearly as England's most serious rival in the competition for overseas empire. Rich in natural resources and endowed with a population three or four times that of England, continental Europe's leading military power was already building a powerful fleet and a worldwide system of rigidly monopolized colonial trade. Thus from 1701 to 1763, Britain and France were locked in a series of wars to decide, in part, which nation would become the leading maritime power and claim the lion's share of the profits of Europe's overseas expansion (Map 24.2).

The first round was the War of the Spanish Succession, which resulted in major gains for Great Britain in the Peace of Utrecht (1713). France ceded Newfoundland, Nova Scotia, and the Hudson Bay territory to Britain. Spain was compelled to give Britain control of the lucrative West African slave trade—the so-called *asiento*—and to let Britain send one ship of merchandise into the Spanish colonies annually.

The Seven Years' War (1756–1763) was the decisive round in the Franco-British competition for colonial empire. Led by William Pitt, whose grandfather had made a fortune as a trader in India, the British concentrated on using superior sea power to destroy the French fleet and choke off French commerce around the world. With the Treaty of Paris (1763), France lost all its possessions on the mainland of North America and gave up most of its holdings in India as well. By 1763, Britain had realized its goal of monopolizing a vast trade and colonial empire for its benefit.

This interconnected expansion of trade and empire marked a major step toward the Industrial Revolution, although people could not know it at the time. Protected colonial markets provided a great stimulus for many branches of English manufacturing. The value of the sales of manufactured products to the Atlantic economy—primarily the mainland colonies of North America and the West Indian sugar islands, with an important assist from West Africa and Latin America—soared from

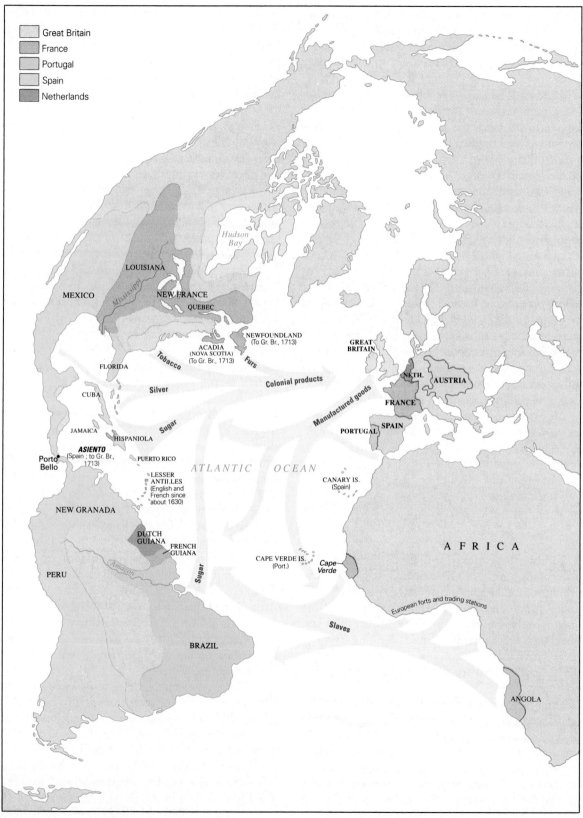

Great Britain
France
Portugal
Spain
Netherlands

Hudson Bay

LOUISIANA

MEXICO   NEW FRANCE

QUEBEC

NEWFOUNDLAND
(To Gr. Br., 1713)

ACADIA
(NOVA SCOTIA)
(To Gr. Br., 1713)

GREAT
BRITAIN

FLORIDA   NETH.   AUSTRIA

Tobacco   Furs

Colonial products   FRANCE

Silver   PORTUGAL   SPAIN

CUBA

Sugar

JAMAICA

HISPANIOLA

ASIENTO
(Spain ; to Gr. Br.,
1713)   PUERTO RICO

Porto
Bello   *ATLANTIC   OCEAN*   CANARY IS.
                                                                      (Spain)

LESSER
ANTILLES
(English and
French since
about 1630)

NEW GRANADA

DUTCH
GUIANA

FRENCH
GUIANA   A F R I C A

Amazon   CAPE VERDE IS.   *Cape
                                        (Port.)   Verde*

PERU   Sugar

European forts and trading stations

Slaves

BRAZIL

Manufactured goods

ANGOLA

The East India Dock, London
This painting by Samuel Scott captures the spirit and excitement of British maritime expansion. Great sailing ships line the quay, bringing profit and romance from far-off India. London grew in population from 350,000 in 1650 to 900,000 in 1800, when it was twice as big as Paris, its nearest rival. *(Source: Courtesy of Board of Trustees of the Victoria & Albert Museum)*

£475,000 in 1700 to £3.9 million in 1773 (Figure 24.1). English exports of manufactured goods to continental Europe grew hardly at all in these years, as states there adopted protectionist policies to help develop their own industries.

English exports became much more balanced and diversified. To America and Africa went large quantities of metal items—axes to frontiersmen, firearms, chains for slaveowners. Also exported were clocks and coaches, buttons and saddles, china and furniture, musical instruments and scientific equipment, and a host of other things. Thus the mercantile system established in the seventeenth century continued to shape trade in the eighteenth century, and the English concentrated in their hands much of the demand for manufactured goods from the growing Atlantic economy. Sales to other "colonies"—Ireland and India—also

MAP 24.2 Economy of the Atlantic Basin in 1701 The growth of trade encouraged both economic development and military conflict in the Atlantic basin.

rose substantially in the eighteenth century. Nor was this all. Demand from the well-integrated home market was also rising. The English were relatively well-off, and their population was growing. Moreover, new methods of farming and good weather brought a period of bountiful crops and low food prices, especially before 1760. Ordinary people could buy more manufactured goods. Rising demand from home and abroad put intense pressure on the whole system of production.

Land and Wealth in North America

Britain's colonies on the North American mainland proved particularly valuable in the long run (Map 24.3). Because the settlements along the Atlantic coast provided an important outlet for surplus population, migration abroad limited poverty in England, Scotland, and northern Ireland. The settlers benefited because for most of the eighteenth century they had privileged access to virtually free and unlimited land. The abundance of almost-free land resulted in a rapid increase in the

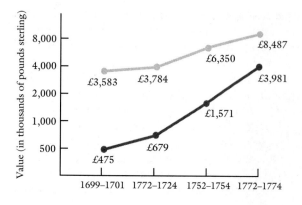

FIGURE 24.1 Exports of English Manufactured Goods, 1700–1774 Trade between England and Europe stagnated after 1700, but English exports to Africa and the Americas boomed and greatly stimulated English economic development. *(Source: Based on information from R. Davis, "English Foreign Trade, 1700–1774,"* Economic History Review, *2d series, 15 (1962): 302–303. Used with permission of Basil Blackwell Ltd.)*

white population, which multiplied a staggering ten times between 1700 and 1774 as immigrants arrived and colonial couples raised large families. In 1774, 2.2 million whites and 330,000 blacks inhabited what would soon become the independent United States.

Rapid population growth did not reduce the settlers to poverty. On the contrary, agricultural development resulted in fairly high standards of living. It has been estimated that between 1715 and 1775 the real income of the average American was increasing about 1 percent per year per person, almost two-thirds as fast as it increased with massive industrialization between 1840 and 1959.[4] There was also an unusual degree of economic equality, by European standards. Few people were extremely rich, and few were extremely poor. On the eve of the American Revolution, the average white man or woman in the mainland British colonies probably had the highest income and standard of living in the world.

The availability of land made labor expensive. This encouraged the growth of black slavery in the southern colonies and created a wealthy planter class with a taste for luxuries from the home country.

The First Factories

The pressure to produce more goods for a growing market was directly related to the first decisive breakthrough of the Industrial Revolution—the creation of the world's first large factories in the English cotton textile industry. Technological innovations in the manufacture of cloth led to a whole new pattern of production and social relationships. No other industry experienced such a rapid or complete transformation before 1830.

Although the putting-out system of merchant capitalism was expanding all across Europe in the eighteenth century, this pattern of rural industry was most fully developed in England. Thus it was in England, under the pressure of growing demand, that the system's shortcomings first began to outweigh its advantages—especially in the cottage textile industry after about 1760.

There was always a serious imbalance in this family enterprise: the work of four or five spinners was needed to keep one weaver steadily employed. The wife and the husband had constantly to try to find more thread and more spinners. Widows and unmarried women—"spinsters" who spun for their living—were recruited by the wife. Or perhaps the weaver's son went off on horseback to seek thread.

Deep-seated conflict between workers and employers complicated increased production. In "The Clothier's Delight, or the Rich Men's Joy and the Poor Men's Sorrow," an English popular song written about 1700, a merchant boasts of his countless tricks used to "beat down wages":

We heapeth up riches and treasure great store
Which we get by griping and grinding the poor.
And this is a way for to fill up our purse
Although we do get it with many a curse.[5]

There were constant disputes over the weights of materials and the quality of the cloth. Merchants accused workers of stealing raw materials, and weavers complained that merchants delivered underweight bales. Both were right; each tried to cheat the other, even if only in self-defense.

There was another problem, at least from the merchant-capitalist's point of view. Scattered rural labor was cheap, but hard to control. Cottage workers tended to work in spurts. After they got paid on Saturday afternoon, the men in particular tended to drink and carouse for two or three days. By the end of the week the weaver was probably working feverishly to make his quota. But if he did not succeed, there was little the merchant could do. Thus, in spite of its early virtues, the putting-out system in the textile industry revealed growing limitations, and the merchant-capitalist's search for more efficient methods of production intensified.

Attention focused on ways of improving spinning. Many a tinkering worker knew that a better spinning wheel promised rich rewards. It proved hard to spin the traditional raw materials—wool and flax—with improved machines, but cotton was different. Cotton textiles had first been imported into England from India by the East India Company, and by 1760 there was a tiny domestic industry in northern England. After many experiments over a generation, a gifted carpenter and jack-of-all-trades, James Hargreaves, invented his cotton-spinning jenny about 1765. At almost the same moment, a barber-turned-manufacturer named Richard Arkwright invented (or possibly pirated) another kind of spinning machine, the water frame. These breakthroughs produced an explosion in the infant cotton textile industry in the

MAP 24.3 European Claims in North America Before and After the Seven Year's War, 1756–1763 France lost its vast claims in North America, though the British government then prohibited colonists from settling west of a line drawn in 1763. The British wanted to avoid costly wars with native Americans living in the newly conquered territory.

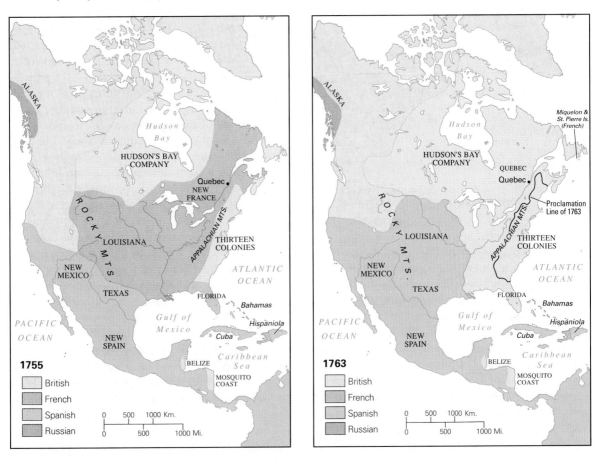

❋ **Hargreave's Spinning Jenny**   The loose cotton strands on the bobbins to the right passed to the sliding carriage and then on to the spindles on the left for fine spinning. The worker, almost always a woman, regulated the sliding carriage with one hand and with the other hand turned the crank on the wheel to supply power. By 1783 one woman could spin by hand a hundred threads at a time on an improved model. (*Source: Science Museum, London/Michael Holford*)

1780s. By 1790 the new machines were producing ten times as much cotton yarn as had been made in 1770.

Hargreaves's jenny was simple and inexpensive. It was also hand operated. In early models, from six to twenty-four spindles were mounted on a sliding carriage, and each spindle spun a fine, slender thread. The woman moved the carriage back and forth with one hand and turned a wheel to supply power with the other. Now it was the male weaver who could not keep up with the vastly more efficient female spinner.

Arkwright's water frame employed a different principle. It quickly acquired a capacity of several hundred spindles and demanded much more power—waterpower. The water frame thus required large specialized mills, factories that employed as many as one thousand workers from the very beginning. The water frame could spin only coarse, strong thread, which was then put out for respinning on hand-powered cottage jennies. After Samuel Crompton invented an alternative technique around 1790, all cotton spinning was gradually concentrated in factories.

The first consequences of these revolutionary developments were more beneficial than is generally believed. Cotton goods became much cheaper, and they were bought and treasured by all classes. In the past, only the wealthy could afford the comfort and cleanliness of underwear, which was called "body linen" because it was made from expensive linen cloth. Now millions of poor people, who had earlier worn nothing underneath their coarse, filthy outer garments, could afford to wear cotton slips and underpants as well as cotton dresses and shirts.

Families using cotton in cottage industry were freed from their constant search for adequate yarn from scattered, part-time spinners, for all the thread needed could be spun in the cottage on the jenny or obtained from a nearby factory. The wages of weavers, now hard pressed to keep up with the spinners, rose markedly until about 1792. Weavers were among the best-paid workers in England. They were known to walk proudly through the streets with £5 notes stuck in their hatbands, and they dressed like the middle class.

One result of this unprecedented prosperity was that large numbers of agricultural laborers became handloom weavers. The growth of handloom cotton weaving was an outstanding example of how breakthroughs in factory production normally stimulated complementary increases in handicraft output. It was also an example of how further mechanization threatened certain groups of handicraft workers, for mechanics and capitalists soon sought to invent a power loom to save on labor costs. This Edmund Cartwright achieved in 1785. But the power looms of the factories worked poorly at first, and handloom weavers continued to receive good wages until at least 1800.

Until the late 1780s, most English factories were in rural areas, where they had access to waterpower. These factories employed a relatively small percentage of all cotton textile workers. Working conditions in the early factories were less satisfactory than the conditions of cottage weavers and spinners, and people were reluctant to work in them. Therefore, factory owners turned to young children who had been abandoned by their parents and put in the care of local parishes. Parish officers often "apprenticed" such unfortunate orphans to factory owners, who gained over them almost the authority of slaveowners.

The creation of the world's first modern factories in the English cotton textile industry in the 1770s and 1780s, which grew out of the putting-out system of cottage production, was a major historical development. Both symbolically and substantially, the big new cotton mills marked the beginning of the Industrial Revolution in England. By 1831 the largely mechanized cotton textile industry towered above all others, accounting for fully 22 percent of the country's entire industrial production.

❖ ENERGY AND TRANSPORTATION

The growth of the cotton textile industry might have been stunted or cut short if water from rivers and streams had remained the primary source of power for the new factories. But this did not occur. Instead, an epoch-making solution was found to the age-old problem of energy and power. It was this solution to the energy problem (a problem that reappeared in recent times) that permitted continued rapid development in cotton textiles, the gradual generalization of the factory system, and the triumph of the Industrial Revolution in England and Scotland.

The Problem of Energy

Human beings, like all living organisms, require energy. Adult men and women need from 2,000 to 4,000 calories (units of energy) daily simply to fuel their bodies, work, and survive. Prehistoric people relied on plants and plant-eating animals as their sources of energy. With the development of agriculture, early civilizations were able to increase the number of useful plants and thus the supply of energy. Some plants could be fed to domesticated animals, such as the horse. Stronger than human beings, these animals converted the energy in the plants into work.

Human beings have used their toolmaking abilities to construct machines that convert one form of energy into another for their own benefit. In the

medieval period, people began to develop water mills to grind their grain and windmills to pump water and drain swamps. More efficient use of water and wind in the sixteenth and seventeenth centuries enabled human beings, especially Europeans, to accomplish more; intercontinental sailing ships were a prime example. Nevertheless, even into the eighteenth century, European society continued to rely for energy mainly on plants, and human beings and animals continued to perform most work. This dependence meant that Western civilization remained poor in energy and power.

Lack of power lay at the heart of the poverty that afflicted the large majority of people. The man behind the plow and the woman at the spinning wheel could employ only horsepower and human muscle in their labor. No matter how hard they worked, they could not produce very much. To produce more and live better, people needed new sources of energy and more power at their disposal.

Where was more energy to be found? Almost all energy came directly or indirectly from plants and therefore from the land: grain for people, hay for animals, and wood for heat. The land was also the principal source of raw materials needed for industrial production: wool and flax for clothing; leather for shoes; wood for housing, tools, and ironmaking. And though land could be reclaimed from swamps and marshes and its yield could be increased, as by the elimination of fallow, there were definite limits to such improvements.

The shortage of energy had become particularly severe in England by the eighteenth century. Because of the growth of population, most of the great forests of medieval England had long ago been replaced by fields of grain and hay. Wood was in ever-shorter supply, yet it remained tremendously important. In addition to serving as the primary source of heat for homes and industries and as a basic raw material, processed wood (charcoal) was the fuel that was mixed with iron ore in the blast furnace to produce pig iron. The iron industry's appetite for wood was enormous, and by 1740 the English iron industry was stagnating. Vast forests enabled Russia in the eighteenth century to become the world's leading producer of iron, much of which was exported to England. But Russia's potential for growth was limited, too, and in a few decades Russia would reach the barrier of inadequate energy that was already holding England back.

The Steam Engine Breakthrough

As this early energy crisis grew worse, England looked toward its abundant and widely scattered reserves of coal as an alternative to its vanishing wood. Coal was first used in England in the late Middle Ages as a source of heat. By 1640 most homes in London were heated with it, and it also provided heat for making beer, glass, soap, and other products. Coal, however, was not used to make iron, to produce mechanical energy, or to power machinery. It was there that coal's potential was enormous, as a simple example shows.

A hard-working miner can dig out 500 pounds of coal a day using hand tools. Even an extremely inefficient converter, which transforms only 1 percent of the heat energy in coal into mechanical energy, will produce 27 horsepower-hours of work from that 500 pounds of coal. The miner, by contrast, produces only about 1 horsepower-hour in the course of a day. Early steam engines were just such inefficient converters.

As more coal was produced, mines were dug deeper and deeper and were constantly filling with water. Mechanical pumps, usually powered by animals walking in circles at the surface, had to be installed. At one mine, fully five hundred horses were used in pumping. Such power was expensive and bothersome. In an attempt to overcome these disadvantages, Thomas Savery in 1698 and Thomas Newcomen in 1705 invented the first primitive steam engines. Both engines burned coal to produce steam, which was then used to operate a pump. Both engines were extremely inefficient, but by the early 1770s many of the Savery engines and hundreds of the Newcomen engines were operating successfully in English and Scottish mines.

In the early 1760s, a gifted young Scot named James Watt (1736–1819) was drawn to a critical study of the steam engine. Watt was employed at the time by the University of Glasgow as a skilled craftsman making scientific instruments. The Scottish universities were pioneers in practical technical education, and in 1763 Watt was called on to repair a Newcomen engine being used in a physics course. After a series of observations, Watt saw that the Newcomen engine's great waste of energy could be reduced by adding a separate condenser.

The Newcomen Engine The huge steam-filled cylinder [C] was cooled by injecting water from the tank above [G] through a pipe [M]. Atmospheric pressure then pushed down the piston, raised the beam, and pumped water from the mine. *(Source: Science Museum, London)*

This splendid invention greatly increased the efficiency of the steam engine.

To invent something in a laboratory is one thing; to make it a practical success is quite another. Watt needed skilled workers, precision parts, and capital, and the relatively advanced nature of the English economy proved essential. A partnership with a wealthy, progressive toymaker provided risk capital and a manufacturing plant. In the craft tradition of locksmiths, tinsmiths, and millwrights, Watt found skilled mechanics who could install, regulate, and repair his sophisticated engines. From ingenious manufacturers such as the cannonmaker John Wilkinson, Watt was gradually able to purchase precision parts. This support and more than twenty years of constant effort allowed him to create and regulate a complex engine. By the late 1780s, the steam engine had become a practical and commercial success in England.

The steam engine of Watt and his followers was the Industrial Revolution's most fundamental advance in technology. For the first time in history, humanity had, at least for a few generations, almost unlimited power at its disposal. For the first time, inventors and engineers could devise and implement all kinds of power equipment to aid people in their work. For the first time, abundance was at least a possibility for ordinary men and women.

The steam engine was quickly put to use in several industries in England. It drained mines and made possible the production of ever-more coal to feed steam engines elsewhere. The steampower plant began to replace waterpower in the cotton-spinning mills during the 1780s, contributing greatly to that industry's phenomenal rise. Steam also took the place of waterpower in flour mills, in the malt mills used in breweries, in the flint mills supplying the china industry, and in the mills exported by England to the West Indies to crush sugar cane.

Steampower promoted important breakthroughs in other industries. The English iron industry was radically transformed. The use of powerful, steam-driven bellows in blast furnaces helped ironmakers switch over rapidly from limited charcoal to unlimited coke (which is made from coal) in the smelting of pig iron after 1770. In the 1780s Henry Cort developed the puddling furnace, which allowed pig iron to be refined in turn with coke. Strong, skilled ironworkers—the puddlers— "cooked" molten pig iron in a great vat, raking off globs of refined iron for further processing. Cort also developed heavy-duty, steam-powered rolling mills, which were capable of spewing out finished iron in every shape and form.

The economic consequence of these technical innovations was a great boom in the English iron industry. In 1740 annual British iron production was only 17,000 tons. With the spread of coke smelting and the first impact of Cort's inventions, production reached 68,000 tons in 1788, 125,000 tons in 1796, and 260,000 tons in 1806. In 1844 Britain produced 3 million tons of iron. This was a truly amazing expansion. Once scarce and expensive, iron became the cheap, basic, indispensable building block of the economy.

The Coming of the Railroads

The second half of the eighteenth century saw extensive construction of hard and relatively smooth roads, particularly in France before the Revolution. Yet it was passenger traffic that benefited most from this construction. Overland shipment of freight, relying solely on horsepower, was still quite limited and frightfully expensive. Shippers used rivers and canals for heavy freight whenever possible. It was logical, therefore, that inventors would try to apply steampower to transportation.

As early as 1800, an American ran a "steamer on wheels" through city streets. Other experiments followed. In the 1820s, English engineers created steam cars capable of carrying fourteen passengers at 10 miles an hour—as fast as the mail coach. But the noisy, heavy steam automobiles frightened passing horses and damaged themselves as well as the roads with their vibrations. For the rest of the century, horses continued to reign on highways and city streets.

The coal industry had long been using plank roads and rails to move coal wagons within mines and at the surface. Rails reduced friction and allowed a horse or a human being to pull a heavier load. Thus once a rail capable of supporting a heavy locomotive was developed in 1816, all sorts of experiments with steam engines on rails went forward. In 1825 after ten years of work, George Stephenson built an effective locomotive. In 1830 his *Rocket* sped down the track of the just-completed Liverpool and Manchester Railway at 16 miles per hour. This was the world's first important railroad, fittingly steaming in the heart of industrial England. The line from Liverpool to Manchester was a financial as well as a technical success, and many private

The Third-Class Carriage French artist Honoré Daumier (1808–1879) was fascinated by the railroad and its human significance. This great painting focuses on the peasant grandmother, absorbed in memories. The nursing mother represents love and creativity; the sleeping boy, innocence. *(Source: The Metropolitan Museum of Art. Bequest of Mrs. H. O. Havemeyer, 1929. The H. O. Havemeyer Collection (29.100.129))*

companies were quickly organized to build more rail lines. Within twenty years, these companies had completed the main trunk lines of Great Britain. Other countries were quick to follow.

The significance of the railroad was tremendous. The railroad dramatically reduced the cost and uncertainty of shipping freight overland. This advance had many economic consequences. Previously, markets had tended to be small and local. As the barrier of high transportation costs was lowered, they became larger and even nationwide. Larger markets encouraged larger factories with more sophisticated machinery in a growing number of industries. Such factories could make goods more cheaply, and they gradually subjected most

cottage workers and many urban artisans to severe competitive pressures.

In all countries, the construction of railroads contributed to the growth of a class of urban workers. Cottage workers, farm laborers, and small peasants did not generally leave their jobs and homes to go directly to work in factories. However, the building of railroads created a strong demand for labor, especially unskilled labor, throughout a country. Many landless farm laborers and poor peasants, long accustomed to leaving their villages for temporary employment, went to work on railroad construction gangs. By the time the work was finished, life back home in the village often seemed dull and unappealing, and many men drifted to towns in search of work—with the railroad companies, in construction, in factories. By the time they sent for their wives and sweethearts to join them, they had become urban workers.

The railroad changed the outlook and values of the entire society. The last and culminating invention of the Industrial Revolution, the railroad dramatically revealed the power and increased the speed of the new age. Racing down a track at 16 miles per hour or, by 1850, at a phenomenal 50 miles per hour was a new and awesome experience. As a French economist put it after a ride on the Liverpool and Manchester in 1833, "There are certain impressions that one cannot put into words!"

Some great painters, notably Joseph M. W. Turner (1775–1851) and Claude Monet (1840–1926), succeeded in expressing this sense of power and awe. So did the massive new train stations, the cathedrals of the industrial age. Leading railway engineers such as Isambard Kingdom Brunel and Thomas Brassey, whose tunnels pierced mountains and whose bridges spanned valleys, became public idols—the astronauts of their day. Everyday speech absorbed the images of railroading. After you got up a "full head of steam," you "highballed" along. And if you didn't "go off the track," you might "toot your own whistle." The railroad fired the imagination.

Industry and Population

In 1851 London was the site of a famous industrial fair. This Great Exposition was held in the newly built Crystal Palace, an architectural masterpiece made entirely of glass and iron, both of which were now cheap and abundant. For the millions who visited, one fact stood out: the little island of Britain—England, Wales, and Scotland—was the "workshop of the world." It alone produced two-thirds of the world's coal and more than one-half of its iron and cotton cloth. More generally, it has been carefully estimated that in 1860 Britain produced a truly remarkable 20 percent of the entire world's output of industrial goods, whereas it had produced only about 2 percent of the world total in 1750.[6] Experiencing revolutionary industrial change, Britain became the first industrial nation (Map 24.4).

As the British economy significantly increased its production of manufactured goods, the gross national product (GNP) rose roughly fourfold at constant prices between 1780 and 1851. In other words, the British people as a whole increased their wealth and their national income dramatically. At the same time, the population of Great Britain boomed, growing from about 9 million in 1780 to almost 21 million in 1851. Thus growing numbers consumed much of the increase in total production. According to one important study, average consumption per person increased by only 75 percent between 1780 and 1851, as the growth in the total population ate up a large part of the fourfold increase in GNP in those years.[7]

Although the question is still debated, many economic historians now believe that rapid population growth in Great Britain was not harmful because it facilitated industrial expansion. More people meant a more mobile labor force, with a wealth of young workers in need of employment and

MAP 24.4 The Industrial Revolution in England, ca 1850 Industry concentrated in the rapidly growing cities of the north and the Midlands, where rich coal and iron deposits were in close proximity.

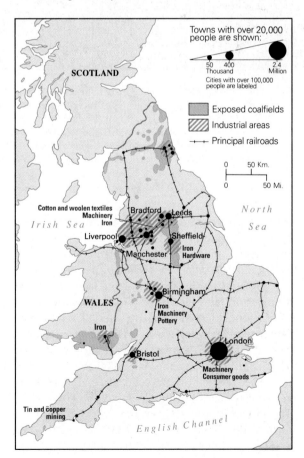

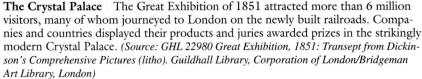 **The Crystal Palace**   The Great Exhibition of 1851 attracted more than 6 million visitors, many of whom journeyed to London on the newly built railroads. Companies and countries displayed their products and juries awarded prizes in the strikingly modern Crystal Palace. *(Source: GHL 22980 Great Exhibition, 1851: Transept from Dickinson's Comprehensive Pictures (litho). Guildhall Library, Corporation of London/Bridgeman Art Library, London)*

ready to go where the jobs were. Contemporaries were much less optimistic. In his famous and influential *Essay on the Principle of Population* (1798), Thomas Malthus (1766–1834) argued that population would always tend to grow faster than the food supply. In Malthus's opinion, the only hope of warding off such "positive checks" to population growth as war, famine, and disease was "prudential restraint": young men and women had to limit the growth of population by the old tried-and-true means of marrying late in life. But Malthus was not optimistic about this possibility. The powerful attraction of the sexes would cause most people to marry early and have many children.

Wealthy English stockbroker and leading economist David Ricardo (1772–1823) coldly spelled out the pessimistic implications of Malthus's thought. Ricardo's depressing "iron law of wages" posited that because of the pressure of population growth, wages would always sink to subsistence level—that is, wages would be just high enough to keep workers from starving. With Malthus and Ricardo setting the tone, economics was soon dubbed "the dismal science."

Malthus, Ricardo, and their many followers were proved wrong—in the long run. However, as the great economist John Maynard Keynes quipped during the Great Depression of the 1930s, "we are all dead in the long run." Those who lived through the Industrial Revolution could not see the long run in advance. As modern quantitative studies show, until the 1820s, or even the 1840s, contemporary observers might reasonably have concluded that the economy and the total population were racing neck and neck, with the outcome very much in doubt. The closeness of the race added to the difficulties inherent in the unprecedented journey toward industrial civilization.

There was another problem as well. Perhaps workers, farmers, and ordinary people did not get their rightful share of the new wealth. Perhaps only the rich got richer while the poor got poorer or made no progress. We will turn to this great issue after looking at the process of industrialization in continental European countries in the nineteenth century.

INDUSTRIALIZATION IN CONTINENTAL EUROPE

The new technologies developed in the British Industrial Revolution were adopted rather slowly by businesses in continental Europe. Indeed, the process of Western industrialization proceeded gradually, with uneven jerks and national (and regional) variations. Scholars are still struggling to explain these variations, especially since good answers may offer valuable lessons in our own time for poor countries seeking to improve their material condition through industrialization and economic development. The latest findings on the Western experience are encouraging. They suggest that there were alternative paths to the industrial world in the nineteenth century and that there was (and is) no need to follow a rigid, predetermined British model.

National Variations

European industrialization, like most economic developments, requires some statistical analysis as part of the effort to understand it. One set of data, the work of a Swiss scholar, compares the level of industrialization on a per capita basis in several countries from 1750 to 1913. These data are far from perfect because there are gaps in the underlying records. But they reflect basic trends and are presented in Table 24.1 for closer study.

The table is a comparison of how much industrial product was available, on average, to each person in a given country in a given year. Therefore,

all the numbers in Table 24.1 are expressed in terms of a single index number of 100, which equals the per capita level of industrial goods in Great Britain (and Ireland) in 1900. Every number is thus a percentage of the 1900 level in Great Britain and is directly comparable. The countries are listed in roughly the order that they began to use large-scale, power-driven technology.

What does this sophisticated quantitative overview of European industrialization tell us? First, it confirms the primacy and relative rapidity of Britain's Industrial Revolution. In 1750 all countries were fairly close together. But by 1800 Britain had opened up a noticeable lead, and that gap progressively widened as the British Industrial Revolution accelerated to full maturity by 1860. The British level of per capita industrialization was twice the French level in 1830, for example, and more than three times the French level in 1860. All other large countries (except the United States) had fallen even farther behind Britain than France had at both dates.

Second, variations in the timing and in the extent of industrialization in the continental powers and the United States are also apparent. Belgium, independent in 1831 and rich in iron and coal, led in adopting Britain's new technology. France developed factory production more gradually, and most historians now detect no burst in French mechanization and industrial output that may accurately be called revolutionary. They stress instead France's relatively good pattern of early industrial growth, which was unjustly tarnished by the spectacular rise of Germany and the United States after 1860. By 1913 Germany was rapidly closing in on Britain, and the United States had already passed Britain in per capita production.

Finally, all European states (as well as the United States, Canada, and Japan) managed to raise per capita industrial levels in the nineteenth century. These continent-wide increases stood in stark contrast to the large and tragic decreases that occurred at the same time in most non-Western countries, most notably in China and India. European countries industrialized to a greater or lesser extent even as most of the non-Western world de-industrialized. Thus differential rates of wealth- and power-creating industrial development, which heightened disparities within Europe, also greatly magnified existing inequalities between Europe and the rest of the world. We shall return to this momentous change in Chapter 27.

TABLE 24.1 PER CAPITA LEVELS OF INDUSTRIALIZATION, 1750–1913

	1750	1800	1830	1860	1880	1900	1913
Great Britain	10	16	25	64	87	100	115
Belgium	9	10	14	28	43	56	88
United States	4	9	14	21	38	69	126
France	9	9	12	20	28	39	59
Germany	8	8	9	15	25	52	85
Austria-Hungary	7	7	8	11	15	23	32
Italy	8	8	8	10	12	17	26
Russia	6	6	7	8	10	15	20
China	8	6	6	4	4	3	3
India	7	6	6	3	2	1	2

Note: All entries are based on an index value of 100, equal to the per capita level of industrialization in Great Britain in 1900.
Source: P. Bairoch, "International Industrialization Levels from 1750 to 1980," Journal of European Economic History 11 (Fall 1982): 294. Data for Great Britain are actually for the United Kingdom, thereby including Ireland with England, Wales, and Scotland.

The Challenge of Industrialization

The different patterns of industrial development suggest that the process of industrialization was far from automatic. Indeed, building modern industry was an awesome challenge. When the pace of English industry began to accelerate in the 1780s, continental businesses began to adopt the new methods as they proved their profitability. English industry enjoyed clear superiority, but at first continental Europe was close behind. By 1815, however, the situation was quite different. In spite of wartime difficulties, English industry maintained the momentum of the 1780s and continued to grow and improve between 1789 and 1815. On the continent, the unending political and economic upheavals that began with the French Revolution had another effect: they disrupted trade, created runaway inflation, and fostered social anxiety. War severed normal communications between England and the continent, severely handicapping continental efforts to use new British machinery and technology. Moreover, the years from 1789 to 1815 were, even for the privileged French economy, a time of "national catastrophe"—in the graphic words of a leading French scholar.[8] Thus whatever the French Revolution and the Napoleonic era meant politically, economically and industrially they meant that France and the rest of Europe were farther behind Britain in 1815 than in 1789.

This widening gap made it more difficult, if not impossible, for other countries to follow the British pattern in energy and industry after peace was restored in 1815. Above all, in the newly mechanized industries British goods were being produced very economically, and these goods had come to dominate world markets completely while the continental states were absorbed in war between 1792 and 1815. Continental European firms had little hope of competing with mass-produced British goods in foreign markets for a long time. In addition, British technology had become so advanced and complicated that very few engineers or skilled technicians outside England understood it. Moreover, the technology of steampower had grown much more expensive. It involved large investments in the iron and coal industries and, after 1830, required the existence of railroads, which were very costly. Continental business people had great difficulty finding the large sums of money the new methods demanded, and there was a shortage of laborers accustomed to working in factories. Landowners and government officials were often so suspicious of the new form of industry and the changes it brought that they did little

at first to encourage it. All these disadvantages slowed the spread of modern industry (Map 24.5).

After 1815, however, continental countries also had at least three important advantages. First, most had a rich tradition of putting-out enterprise, merchant capitalists, and skilled urban artisans. Such a tradition gave continental firms the ability to adapt and survive in the face of new market conditions. Second, continental capitalists could simply "borrow" the advanced technology already developed in Great Britain, as well as engineers and some of the financial resources these countries lacked. European countries such as France and Russia also had a third asset that many non-Western areas

MAP 24.5 Continental European Industrialization, ca 1850   Although continental European countries were beginning to make progress by 1850, they still lagged far behind England. For example, continental railroad building was still in an early stage, whereas the English rail system was essentially complete.

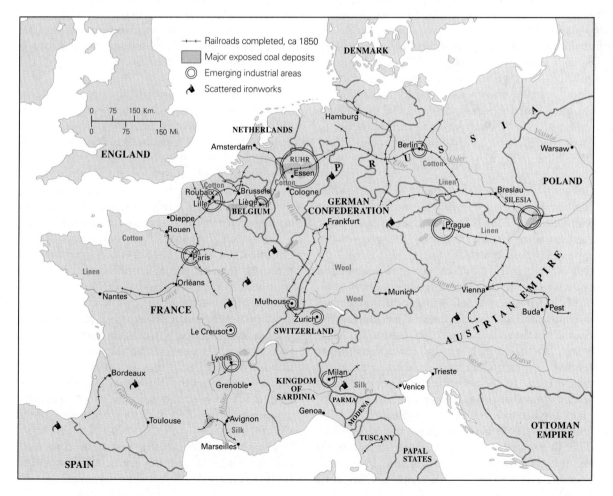

lacked in the nineteenth century. They had strong independent governments, which did not fall under foreign political control. These governments could fashion economic policies to serve their own interests, and they proceeded to do so. They would eventually use the power of the state to promote the growth of industry and catch up with Britain.

Agents of Industrialization

The British realized the great value of their technical discoveries and tried to keep their secrets to themselves. Until 1825 it was illegal for artisans and skilled mechanics to leave Britain; until 1843 the export of textile machinery and other equipment was forbidden. Many talented, ambitious workers, however, slipped out of the country illegally and introduced the new methods abroad.

One such man was William Cockerill, a Lancashire carpenter. He and his sons began building cotton-spinning equipment in French-occupied Belgium in 1799. In 1817 the most famous son, John Cockerill, purchased the old summer palace of the deposed bishops of Liège in southern Belgium. Cockerill converted the palace into a large industrial enterprise, which produced machinery, steam engines, and then railway locomotives. He also established modern ironworks and coal mines.

Many skilled British workers came illegally to work for Cockerill, and some went on to found their own companies throughout Europe. Newcomers brought the latest plans and secrets, so Cockerill could boast that ten days after an industrial advance occurred in Britain, he knew all about it in Belgium. Thus British technicians and skilled workers were a powerful force in the spread of early industrialization.

A second agent of industrialization was talented entrepreneurs such as Fritz Harkort, a business pioneer in the German machinery industry. Serving in England as a Prussian army officer during the Napoleonic wars, Harkort concluded that Germany had to match English achievements as quickly as possible. Setting up shop in an abandoned castle in the still-tranquil Ruhr Valley, he felt an almost religious calling to build steam engines and become the "Watt of Germany."

Harkort's basic idea was simple but enormously difficult to carry out. Lacking skilled laborers to do the job, Harkort turned to England for experienced, though expensive, mechanics. He had to import from England and at great cost the thick iron boilers that he needed. Moreover, German roads were so bad that steam engines had to be built at the works, completely dismantled, shipped piece by piece to the buyer, and then reassembled by Harkort's technicians. In spite of these problems, Harkort built and sold engines, winning fame and praise. His ambitious efforts over sixteen years also resulted in large financial losses for himself and his partners, and in 1832 his financial backers forced him out of his company and cut back operations to reduce losses. Harkort's career illustrates both the great efforts of a few important business leaders to duplicate the British achievement and the difficulty of the task.

Entrepreneurs like Harkort were obviously exceptional. Most continental businesses adopted factory technology slowly, and handicraft methods lived on. Indeed, as recent research on France has shown, industrialization in continental Europe usually brought substantial but uneven expansion of handicraft industry in both rural and urban areas for a time. Artisan production of luxury items grew in France as the rising income of the international middle class created foreign demand for silk scarfs, embroidered needlework, perfumes, and fine wines.

A third force for industrialization was government, which often helped business people in European countries to overcome some of their difficulties. Tariff protection was one such support. And after 1815 continental governments bore the cost of building roads and canals to improve transportation. They also bore to a significant extent the cost of building railroads, the all-important leading sector in continental industrialization.

The career of German journalist and thinker Friedrich List (1789–1846) reflects government's greater role in industrialization on the European continent than in England. List considered the growth of modern industry of the utmost importance because manufacturing was a primary means of increasing people's well-being and relieving their poverty. Moreover, List was a dedicated nationalist who believed that an agricultural nation was not only poor but also weak, increasingly unable to defend itself and maintain its political independence. To promote industry was to defend the nation.

The practical policies that List focused on were railroad building and the tariff. List supported the formation of a customs union, or *Zollverein,*

❄ **A Silesian Ironworks**   This plant is using the new British method of smelting iron with coke. Silesia and the Ruhr region emerged as the main centers of German heavy industry in the nineteenth century, but that development was only beginning in 1841, when this picture was painted. *(Source: Deutsches Museum Munich)*

among the separate German states. Such a tariff union came into being in 1834. It allowed goods to move without tariffs between the German member states. A single uniform tariff was erected against all other nations to help infant industries to develop and eventually hold their own against their more advanced British counterparts. List denounced the English doctrine of free trade as little more than England's attempt "to make the rest of the world, like the Hindus, its serfs in all industrial and commercial relations." By the 1840s List's economic nationalism had become increasingly popular in Germany and elsewhere.

Banks, like governments, also played a larger and more creative role in Europe than in England. Previously, almost all banks in Europe had been private, organized as secretive partnerships. All the active partners were liable for all the debts of the firm. This unlimited liability meant that in the event of a disastrous bankruptcy each partner could lose all of his or her personal wealth. Such banks were content to deal with a few rich clients

and a few big merchants. They generally avoided industrial investment as being too risky.

In the 1830s two important Belgian banks pioneered in a new direction, establishing themselves as corporations enjoying limited liability. A stockholder in these two banks could lose only his or her original investment in the bank's common stock. Able to attract many shareholders, large and small, because of the reduced risk, these Belgian banks mobilized impressive resources for investment in big industrial companies. They became industrial banks and successfully promoted industrial development.

Similar corporate banks became important in France and Germany in the 1850s and 1860s. Usually working in collaboration with governments, they established and developed many railroads and many companies working in heavy industry, which were increasingly organized as limited-liability corporations. The most famous such bank was the Crédit Mobilier of Paris, founded by Isaac and Émile Pereire, two young

Jewish journalists from Bordeaux. Using the savings of thousands of small investors as well as the resources of big ones, the Crédit Mobilier built railroads all over France and elsewhere in Europe. As Émile Pereire had said in 1835, "It is not enough to outline gigantic programs on paper. I must write my ideas on the earth."

The combined efforts of skilled workers, entrepreneurs, governments, and industrial banks meshed successfully between 1850 and the financial crash of 1873. In Belgium, Germany, and France, key indicators of modern industrial development—railway mileage, iron and coal production, and steam-engine capacity—increased at average annual rates ranging from 5 to 10 percent compounded. In the early 1870s, Britain was still Europe's most industrial nation, but a select handful of countries was closing the gap that had been opened up by the Industrial Revolution.

 CAPITAL AND LABOR

Industrial development brought new social relations and intensified long-standing problems between capital and labor. A new group of factory owners and industrial capitalists arose. These men and women and their families strengthened the wealth and size of the middle class, which had previously been made up mainly of merchants and professional people. The nineteenth century became the golden age of the middle class. Modern industry also created a much larger group: the factory workers. For the first time, large numbers of men, women, and children came together under one roof to work with complicated machinery for a single owner or a few partners in large companies.

The growth of new occupational groups in industry stimulated new thinking about social relations. It was argued, with considerable success, that individuals were members of economically determined classes that had conflicting interests. Accordingly, the comfortable, well-educated "public" of the eighteenth century came increasingly to see itself as the backbone of the middle class (or the middle classes), and the "people" gradually transformed themselves into the modern working class (or working classes). The new class interpretation appealed to many because it seemed to explain what was happening. Thus conflicting classes came

into being, in part, because many individuals came to believe that they existed and developed an appropriate sense of class feeling—what Marxists call "class consciousness."

What, then, was the relationship between capital and labor in the early Industrial Revolution? Did the new industrial middle class ruthlessly exploit the workers, as Karl Marx and others have charged?

The New Class of Factory Owners

Early industrialists operated in a highly competitive economic system in which success and large profits were by no means certain. Manufacturers waged a constant battle to cut their production costs and stay afloat. Much of the profit had to go back into the business for new and better machinery. "Dragged on by the frenzy of this terrible life," according to one of the dismayed critics, the struggling manufacturer had "no time for niceties. He must conquer or die, make a fortune or drown himself."[9]

The early industrialists came from a variety of backgrounds. Many, such as Harkort, were from well-established merchant families, but artisans and skilled workers of exceptional ability had unparalleled opportunities. The ethnic and religious groups that had been discriminated against in the traditional occupations controlled by the landed aristocracy jumped at the new chances. Quakers and Scots were tremendously important in England; Protestants and Jews dominated banking in Catholic France. Many of the industrialists were newly rich and, not surprisingly, very proud and self-satisfied.

As factories grew larger, opportunities declined, at least in well-developed industries. It became considerably harder for a gifted but poor young mechanic to end up as a wealthy manufacturer. Formal education became more important as a means of advancement, and formal education at the advanced level was expensive. In England by 1830 and in France and Germany by 1860, leading industrialists were more likely to have inherited their well-established enterprises, and they were financially much more secure than their fathers and grandfathers had been. They also had a greater sense of class consciousness, fully aware that ongoing industrial development had widened the gap between themselves and their workers.

The New Factory Workers

The social consequences of the Industrial Revolution have long been hotly debated. The condition of English workers during the transformation has always generated the most controversy among historians because England was the first country to industrialize and because the social consequences seemed harshest there. Before 1850 other countries had not proceeded very far with industrialization, and almost everyone agrees that the economic conditions of European workers improved after 1850. The countries that followed England were able to benefit from English experience in social as well as technical matters. Thus the experience of English workers to about 1850 deserves special attention. (Industrial growth also promoted rapid urbanization, with its own awesome problems, as will be shown in Chapter 26.)

From the beginning, the Industrial Revolution in England had its critics. Among the first were the romantic poets. William Blake (1757–1827) called the early factories "satanic mills" and protested against the hard life of the London poor. William Wordsworth (1770–1850) lamented the destruction of the rural way of life and the pollution of the land and water. Some handicraft workers—notably the Luddites, who attacked whole factories in northern England in 1812 and after—smashed the new machines, which they believed were putting them out of work. Doctors and reformers wrote eloquently of problems in the factories and new towns, and Malthus and Ricardo concluded that workers would earn only enough to stay alive.

Friedrich Engels (1820–1895), the future revolutionary and colleague of Karl Marx, accepted and reinforced this pessimistic view. After studying conditions in northern England, this young middle-class German published in 1844 *The Condition of the Working Class in England.* "At the bar of world opinion," he wrote, "I charge the English middle classes with mass murder, wholesale robbery, and all the other crimes in the calendar."[10] The new poverty of industrial workers was worse than the old poverty of cottage workers and agricultural laborers, according to Engels. The culprit was industrial capitalism, with its relentless competition and constant technical change. Engels's extremely influential charge of middle-class exploitation and increasing worker poverty was embellished by Marx and later socialists.

Meanwhile, other observers believed that conditions were improving for the working people. Edwin Chadwick, a great and conscientious government official well acquainted with the problems of the working population, concluded that the "whole mass of the laboring community" was increasingly able "to buy more of the necessities and minor luxuries of life."[11] Nevertheless, if all the contemporary assessments had been counted up, those who thought conditions were getting worse for working people would probably have been the majority.

In an attempt to go beyond the contradictory judgments of contemporaries, some historians have looked at different kinds of sources. Scholarly statistical studies, which continue to multiply rapidly in an age of easy calculations with computer technology, have weakened the idea that the condition of the working class got much worse with industrialization. But the most recent studies also confirm the view that the early years of the Industrial Revolution were hard ones for English and Scottish workers. From about 1780 to about 1820 there was little or no increase in the purchasing power of the average British worker's wages. The years from 1792 to 1815, a period of almost constant warfare with France, were particularly difficult. Food prices rose faster than wages, and the living conditions of the laboring poor declined. Only after 1820, and especially after 1840, did real wages rise substantially. The average worker earned and consumed roughly 50 percent more in real terms in 1850 than in 1770.[12] In short, there was considerable economic improvement for workers throughout Great Britain by 1850, but that improvement was hard won and slow in coming.

This important conclusion must be qualified, however. Increased purchasing power meant more goods but not necessarily greater happiness. More goods may have provided meager compensation for work that was dangerous and monotonous, for example. Also, statistical studies do not say anything about how the level of unemployment may have risen, for the simple reason that there are no good unemployment statistics from this period. Furthermore, the hours in the average workweek increased; to an unknown extent, workers earned more simply because they worked more. Finally, notwithstanding what came afterward, the wartime decline colored the early experience of modern industrial life in somber tones.

Another way to consider the workers' standard of living is to look at the goods they purchased. Again the evidence is somewhat contradictory. Speaking generally, workers ate somewhat more food of higher nutritional quality as the Industrial Revolution progressed, except during wartime, and diets became more varied. Clothing improved, but housing for working people probably deteriorated somewhat. In short, per capita use of specific goods supports the position that the standard of living of the working classes rose, at least moderately, after the long wars with France.

Conditions of Work

What about working conditions? Did workers eventually earn more only at the cost of working longer and harder? Were workers exploited harshly by the new factory owners?

The first factories were cotton mills, which began functioning along rivers and streams in the 1770s. Cottage workers, accustomed to the putting-out system, were reluctant to work in factories even when they received relatively good wages. In the factory, workers had to keep up with the machine and follow its tempo. They had to show up every day and work long, monotonous hours, adjusting their daily lives to the shrill call of the factory whistle.

Cottage workers were not used to that kind of life and discipline. All members of the family worked hard and long, but in spurts, setting their own pace. They could interrupt their work when they wanted to. Women and children could break up their long hours of spinning with other tasks. On Saturday afternoon the head of the family delivered the week's work to the merchant manufacturer and got paid. Saturday night began a time of

A Woolen Mill in 1800 This drawing of a mill near Birmingham highlights the complexity, discipline, and family character of the early factory system. To the right on the top floor, workers turn raw wool into long ropes, which are then drawn out into slivers (lower left) prior to power spinning (center right) and handloom weaving (upper left). The pace and noise are unrelenting. Men, women, and children (often under the supervision of their parents) labor throughout the mill. A giant water wheel provides power to the entire factory by a system of belts and shafts. *(Source: Warwickshire County, Record Office, Warwick, Courtesy of Lord Daventry)*

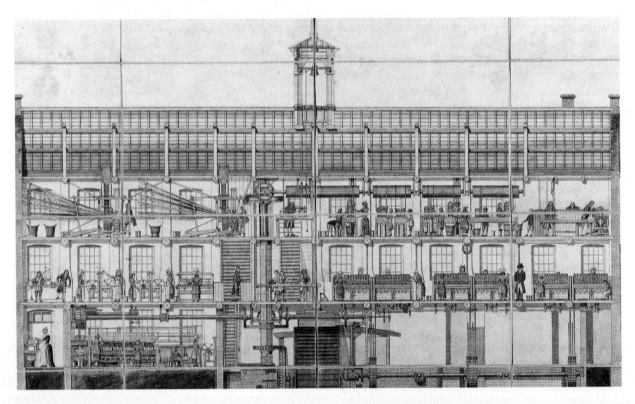

relaxation and drinking, especially for the men. Recovering from his hangover on Tuesday, the weaver bent to his task on Wednesday and then worked frantically to meet his deadline on Saturday. Like some students today, he might "pull an all-nighter" on Thursday or Friday in order to get his work in.

Also, early factories resembled English poorhouses, where totally destitute people went to live on welfare. Some poorhouses were industrial prisons where the inmates had to work in order to receive their food and lodging. The similarity between large brick factories and large stone poorhouses increased the cottage workers' fear of factories and their hatred of factory discipline.

It was cottage workers' reluctance to work in factories that prompted the early cotton mill owners to turn to abandoned and pauper children for their labor. As we have seen, these owners contracted with local officials to employ large numbers of these children, who had no say in the matter. Apprenticed as young as five or six years of age, boy and girl workers were forced by law to labor for their "master" for as many as fourteen years. Housed, fed, and locked up nightly in factory dormitories, the young workers received little or no pay. Hours were appalling—commonly thirteen or fourteen hours a day, six days a week. Harsh physical punishment maintained brutal discipline. To be sure, poor children typically worked long hours from an early age in the eighteenth century and frequently outside the home for a brutal master. In the eighteenth century, semiforced child labor seemed necessary and was socially accepted. But the wholesale coercion of orphans as factory apprentices constituted exploitation on a truly unprecedented scale. This exploitation ultimately stirred the conscience of reformers and reinforced humanitarian attitudes toward children and their labor.

By 1790 the early pattern was rapidly changing. The use of pauper apprentices was in decline, and in 1802 it was forbidden by Parliament. Many more factories were being built, mainly in urban areas, where they could use steampower rather than waterpower and attract a work force more easily than in the countryside. People came from near and far to work in the cities, both as factory workers and as laborers, builders, and domestic servants. Yet as they took these new jobs, working people did not simply give in to a system of labor that had formerly repelled them. Rather, they

helped modify the system by carrying over old, familiar working traditions.

For one thing, they often came to the mills and the mines as family units. This was how they had worked on farms and in the putting-out system. The mill or mine owner paid the head of the family for the work of the whole family. In the cotton mills, children worked for their mothers or fathers, collecting wastes and "piecing" broken threads together. In the mines, children sorted coal and worked the ventilation equipment. Their mothers hauled coal in the narrow tunnels below the surface, while their fathers hewed with pick and shovel at the face of the seam.

The preservation of the family as an economic unit in the factories from the 1790s on made the new surroundings more tolerable, both in Great Britain and in other countries. Parents disciplined their children and directed their upbringing. The presence of the whole family meant that children and adults worked the same long hours (twelve-hour shifts were normal in cotton mills in 1800). In the early years, some very young children were employed solely to keep the family together. Jedediah Strutt, for example, believed children should be at least ten years old to work in his mills, but he reluctantly employed seven-year-olds to satisfy their parents. Only when technical changes threatened to place control and discipline in the hands of impersonal managers and foremen did adult workers protest against inhuman conditions in the name of their children.

Some enlightened employers and social reformers in Parliament definitely felt otherwise. They argued that more humane standards were necessary, and they used widely circulated parliamentary reports to influence public opinion (see Listening to the Past). For example, Robert Owen (1771–1858), a very successful manufacturer in Scotland, testified in 1816 before an investigating committee on the basis of his experience. He stated that "very strong facts" demonstrated that employing children under ten years of age as factory workers was "injurious to the children, and not beneficial to the proprietors." The parliamentary committee asked him to explain, and the testimony proceeded as follows:

Seventeen years ago, a number of individuals, with myself, purchased the New Lanark establishment from the late Mr Dale, of Glasgow. At that period I find that there were 500 children, who had been taken from poor-houses, chiefly in Edinburgh. . . . The hours of work at that time were thirteen, inclusive of meal times, and an hour and a half was allowed for meals. I very soon discovered that although those children were very well fed, well clothed, well lodged, and very great care taken of them when out of the mills, their growth and their minds were materially injured by being employed at those ages within the cotton mills for eleven and a half hours per day. . . . Their limbs were generally deformed, their growth was stunted, and although one of the best school-masters upon the old plan was engaged to instruct those children every night, in general they made but a very slow progress, even in learning the common alphabet.[13]

Owen had already raised the age of employment in his mills and was promoting education for young children. Workers also provided graphic testimony at such hearings as the reformers pressed Parliament to pass corrective laws. They scored some important successes.

Their first major accomplishment was the Factory Act of 1833. It limited the factory workday for children between nine and thirteen to eight hours and that of adolescents between fourteen and eighteen to twelve hours, although the act made no effort to regulate the hours of work for children at home or in small businesses. The law also prohibited the factory employment of children under nine; they were to be enrolled in the elementary schools that factory owners were required to establish. The employment of children declined rapidly. Thus the Factory Act broke the pattern of whole families working together in the factory.

The Sexual Division of Labor

The era of the Industrial Revolution witnessed major changes in the sexual division of labor. In preindustrial Europe most people generally worked in family units. By tradition, certain jobs were defined by sex—women and girls for milking and spinning, men and boys for plowing and weaving. But many tasks might go to either sex because particular circumstances dictated a family's response in its battle for economic survival. This pattern of family employment carried over into early factories and subcontracting, but it collapsed as child labor was restricted and new attitudes emerged. A different sexual division of labor gradually arose to take its place. The man emerged as the family's primary wage earner, and the woman found only limited job opportunities. Generally denied good jobs at good wages in the growing urban economy, women were expected to concentrate on unpaid housework, child care, and craftwork at home.

This new pattern of "separate spheres" had several aspects. First, all studies agree that married women were much less likely to work full-time for wages outside the house after the first child arrived, although they often earned small amounts doing putting-out handicrafts at home and taking in boarders. Second, married women who did work for wages outside the house usually came from the poorest, most desperate families, where the husbands were poorly paid, sick, unemployed, or missing. Third, these poor married (or widowed) women were joined by legions of young unmarried women, who worked full-time but only in certain jobs. Fourth, all women were generally confined to low-paying, dead-end jobs. Virtually no occupation open to women paid a wage sufficient for a person to live independently. Evolving gradually as family labor declined, but largely in place in the urban sector of the British economy by 1850, the new sexual division of labor constituted a major development in the history of women and of the family.

Although the reorganization of paid work along gender lines is widely recognized, there is as yet no agreement on its causes. One school of scholars sees little connection with industrialization and finds the answer in the deeply ingrained sexist attitudes of a "patriarchal tradition," which predated the economic transformation. These scholars stress the role of male-dominated craft unions in denying women access to good jobs and in reducing them to unpaid maids dependent on their husbands. Other scholars, believing that the gender roles of women and men can vary enormously with time and culture, look more to a combination of economic and biological factors in order to explain the emergence of a sex-segregated division of labor.

Three ideas stand out in this more recent interpretation. First, the new and unfamiliar discipline of the clock and the machine was especially hard on married women. Above all, relentless factory discipline conflicted with child care in a way that labor on the farm or in the cottage had not done. A woman operating ear-splitting spinning machinery could mind a child of seven or eight working beside her (until such work was outlawed), but she could no longer pace herself through pregnancy, even though overwork during pregnancy heightened the already high risks of childbirth. Nor could a woman breast-feed her baby on the job, although breast-feeding saved lives. Thus a working-class woman had strong incentives to concentrate on child care within her home if her family could afford for her to do so.

Second, running a household in conditions of primitive urban poverty was an extremely demanding job in its own right. There were no supermarkets or discount department stores, no running water or public transportation. Everything had to be done on foot. As in the poor sections of many inner cities today, shopping and feeding the family constituted a never-ending challenge. The woman marched from one tiny shop to another, dragging her tired children (for who was to watch them?) and struggling valiantly with heavy sacks, tricky shopkeepers, and walk-up apartments. Yet another brutal job outside the house—a "second shift"—had limited appeal for the average married woman. Thus women might well accept the emerging division of labor as the best available strategy for family survival in the industrializing society.[14]

Third, why were the women who did work for wages outside the home segregated and confined to certain "women's jobs"? No doubt the desire of men to monopolize the best opportunities and hold women down provides part of the answer. But as some feminist scholars have argued, sex-segregated employment was also a collective response to the new industrial system. The growth of factories and mines brought unheard-of opportunities for girls and boys to mix on the job, free of familial supervision. Continuing to mix after work, they were "more likely to form liaisons, initiate courtships, and respond to advances."[15] Such intimacy also led to more unplanned pregnancies and fueled the illegitimacy explosion that had begun in the late eighteenth century and that gathered force until at least 1850. Thus segregation of jobs by gender was partly an effort by older people to help control the sexuality of working-class youths.

Investigations into the British coal industry before 1842 provide a graphic example of this concern (see Listening to the Past). The middle-class men leading the inquiry often failed to appreciate the physical effort of the girls and women who dragged the carts of coal along narrow underground passages. But they professed horror at the sight of girls and women working without shirts, which was a common practice because of the heat, and they quickly assumed the prevalence of licentious sex with the male miners, who also wore very little clothing. In fact, most girls and married

Girl Dragging a Coal Wagon   Published by reformers in Parliament as part of a multivolume investigation into child labor in coal mines (see Listening to the Past), this picture was one of several that shocked public opinion and contributed to the Mines Act of 1842. Stripped to the waist and harnessed to the wagon with belt and chain, this underground worker is "hurrying" coal from the face of the seam to the mine shaft. *(Source: The British Library)*

women worked for related males in a family unit that provided considerable protection and restraint. Yet many witnesses from the working class believed that "blackguardism and debauchery" were common and that "they are best out of the pits, the lasses." Some miners stressed particularly the sexual danger of letting girls work past puberty. As one explained: "I consider it a scandal for girls to work in the pits. Till they are 12 or 14 they may work very well but after that it's an abomination. . . . The work of the pit does not hurt them, it is

the effect on their morals that I complain of."[16] The Mines Act of 1842 prohibited underground work for all women as well as for boys under ten.

Some women who had to support themselves protested against being excluded from coal mining, which paid higher wages than most other jobs open to women. But the girls and the women who had worked underground were generally pleased with the law, if they were part of families that could manage economically. In explaining her satisfaction in 1844, one mother of four provided a real insight into why many women accepted the emerging sexual division of labor:

While working in the pit I was worth to my [miner] husband seven shillings a week, out of which we had to pay 2 1/2 shillings to a woman for looking after the younger children. I used to take them to her house at 4 o'clock in the morning, out of their own beds, to put them into hers. Then there was one shilling a week for washing; besides, there was mending to pay for, and other things. The house was not guided. The other children broke things; they did not go to school when they were sent; they would be playing about, and get ill-used by other children, and their clothes torn. Then when I came home in the evening, everything was to do after the day's labor, and I was so tired I had no heart for it; no fire lit, nothing cooked, no water fetched, the house dirty, and nothing comfortable for my husband. It is all far better now, and I wouldn't go down again.[17]

The Early Labor Movement

Many kinds of employment changed slowly during and after the Industrial Revolution in Great Britain. In 1850 more British people still worked on farms than in any other occupation. The second largest occupation was domestic service, with more than a million household servants, 90 percent of whom were women. Thus many old, familiar jobs outside industry lived on and provided alternatives for individual workers. This helped ease the transition to industrial civilization.

Within industry itself, the pattern of small-scale production with handicraft skills remained unchanged in many trades even as technological change revolutionized some others. For example, as in the case of cotton and coal, large-scale capitalist firms completely dominated the British iron industry by 1850, employing more than one thousand people. Yet the firms that fashioned iron into

Union Membership Issued in Glasgow in 1833, this card testifies that the bearer is a member of the West of Scotland Power Loom Female Workers. Unions were legalized in Great Britain in 1824 and 1825, and they played an important part in British industrial life. *(Source: Mansell Collection)*

small metal goods—such as tools, tableware, and toys—employed on average fewer than ten wage workers, who used time-honored handicraft skills. The survival of small workshops in some handicraft industries gave many workers an alternative to factory employment.

In Great Britain and in other countries later on, workers gradually built a labor movement to improve working conditions and to serve their needs. In 1799, partly in panicked reaction to the French Revolution, Parliament had passed the Combination Acts outlawing unions and strikes. These acts were widely disregarded by workers. Societies of skilled factory workers organized unions, as printers, papermakers, carpenters, and other such craftsmen had long since done. The unions sought to control the number of skilled workers, limit apprenticeship to members' own children, and bargain with owners over wages. They were not afraid to strike; there was, for example, a general strike of adult cotton spinners in Manchester in 1810. In the face of widespread union activity, Parliament repealed the Combination Acts in 1824, and unions were tolerated though not fully accepted after 1825.

The next stage in the development of the British trade-union movement was the attempt to create a single large national union. This effort was led not so much by working people as by social reformers such as Robert Owen. Owen, the self-made cotton manufacturer quoted earlier, had pioneered in industrial relations by combining firm discipline with concern for the health, safety, and hours of his workers. After 1815 he experimented with cooperative and socialist communities, including one at New Harmony, Indiana. Then in 1834 Owen organized one of the largest and most visionary of the early national unions, the Grand National Consolidated Trades Union. When this and other gradiose schemes collapsed, the British labor movement moved once again after 1851 in the direction of craft unions. The most famous of these "new model unions" was the Amalgamated Society of Engineers. These unions won real benefits for members by fairly conservative means and thus became an accepted part of the industrial scene.

British workers also engaged in direct political activity in defense of their own interests. After the collapse of Owen's national trade union, a great deal of the energy of working people went into the Chartist movement, whose goal was political democracy. The key Chartist demand—that all men be given the right to vote—became the great hope of millions of aroused people. Workers were also active in campaigns to limit the workday in factories to ten hours and to permit duty-free importation of wheat into Great Britain to secure cheap bread. Thus working people developed a sense of their own identity and played an active role in shaping the new industrial system. Clearly, they were neither helpless victims nor passive beneficiaries.

SUMMARY

Western society's industrial breakthrough grew out of a long process of economic and social change in which the rise of capitalism, overseas expansion, and the growth of rural industry stood out as critical preparatory developments. Eventually taking the lead in all of these developments, and also profiting from stable government, abundant natural resources, and a flexible labor force, England experienced between the 1780s and the 1850s an epoch-making transformation, one that is still aptly termed the Industrial Revolution. Building on technical breakthroughs, power-driven equipment, and large-scale enterprise, Great Britain became the first industrial nation. By 1850 the level of British per capita industrial production was surpassing levels on the European continent by a growing margin, and Britain savored a near monopoly in world markets for mass-produced goods.

Continental European countries inevitably took rather different paths to the urban industrial society. They relied more on handicraft production in both towns and villages. Only in the 1840s did railroad construction begin to create the strong demand for iron, coal, and railway equipment that speeded up the process of industrialization in the 1850s and 1860s.

The rise of modern industry had a profound impact on people and their lives. In the early stages Britain again led the way, experiencing in a striking manner the long-term social changes accompanying the economic transformation. Factory discipline and Britain's stern capitalist economy weighed heavily on working people, who, however, actively fashioned their destinies and refused to be passive victims. Improvements in the standard of living came slowly, although they were substantial by 1850. The era of industrialization fostered new attitudes toward child labor, encouraged protective factory legislation, and called forth a new sense of class feeling and an assertive labor movement. It also promoted within the family a more rigid division of roles and responsibilities that severely restricted women socially and economically, another gradual but profound change of revolutionary proportions.

NOTES

1. N. F. R. Crafts, *British Economic Growth During the Industrial Revolution* (Oxford: Oxford University Press, 1985), p. 32. These estimates are for Great Britain as a whole.

2. B. H. Slicher van Bath, *The Agrarian History of Western Europe, A.D. 500–1850* (New York: St. Martin's Press, 1963), p. 240.

3. E. P. Thompson, *The Making of the English Working Class* (New York: Vintage Books, 1966), p. 218.

4. G. Taylor, "America's Growth Before 1840," *Journal of Economic History* 24 (December 1970): 427–444.

5. Quoted in P. Mantoux, *The Industrial Revolution in the Eighteenth Century* (New York: Harper & Row, 1961), p. 75.

6. P. Bairoch, "International Industrialization Levels from 1750 to 1980," *Journal of European Economic History* 11 (Spring 1982): 269–333.

7. Crafts, *British Economic Growth During the Industrial Revolution,* pp. 45, 95–102.

8. M. Lévy-Leboyer, *Les banques européennes et l'industrialisation dans la première moitié du XIXe siècle* (Paris: Presses Universitaires de France, 1964), p. 29.

9. J. Michelet, *The People,* trans. with an introduction by J. P. McKay (Urbana: University of Illinois Press, 1973; original publication, 1846), p. 64.

10. F. Engels, *The Condition of the Working Class in England,* trans. and ed. W. O. Henderson and W. H. Chaloner (Stanford, Calif.: Stanford University Press, 1968), p. xxiii.

11. Quoted in W. A. Hayek, ed., *Capitalism and the Historians* (Chicago: University of Chicago Press, 1954), p. 126.

12. Crafts, *British Economic Growth During the Industrial Revolution,* p. 95.

13. Quoted in E. R. Pike, *"Hard Times": Human Documents of the Industrial Revolution* (New York: Praeger, 1966), p. 109.

14. See especially J. Brenner and M. Rama, "Rethinking Women's Oppression," *New Left Review* 144 (March–April 1984): 33–71, and sources cited there.

15. J. Humphries, ". . . 'The Most Free from Objection' . . . : The Sexual Division of Labor and Women's Work in Nineteenth-Century England," *Journal of Economic History* 47 (December 1987): 948.

16. Ibid., p. 941; Pike, *"Hard Times,"* p. 266.

17. Quoted in Pike, *"Hard Times,"* p. 208.

SUGGESTED READING

There is a vast and exciting literature on the Industrial Revolution. R. Cameron, *A Concise Economic History of the World* (1989), provides an introduction to the issues and has a carefully annotated bibliography. J. Goodman and K. Honeyman, *Gainful Pursuits: The Making of Industrial Europe, 1600–1914* (1988); D. S. Landes, *The Unbound Prometheus: Technological Change and Industrial Development in Western Europe from 1750 to the Present* (1969); and S. Pollard, *Peaceful Conquest: The Industrialization of Europe* (1981), are excellent general treatments of European industrial growth. These studies also suggest the range of issues and interpretations. T. Kemp, *Industrialization in Europe,* 2d ed. (1985), is also useful. M. Berg, *The Age of Manufactures: Industry, Innovation and Work in Britain, 1700–1820* (1985); P. Mathias, *The First Industrial Nation: An Economic History of Britain, 1700–1914* (1969); and P. Mantoux, *The Industrial Revolution in the Eighteenth Century* (1961), admirably discuss the various aspects of the English breakthrough and offer good bibliographies, as does the work by Crafts mentioned in the Notes. W. Rostow, *The Stages of Economic Growth: A Non-Communist Manifesto* (1960), is a popular, provocative study.

H. Kirsh, *From Domestic Manufacturing to Industrial Revolution: The Case of the Rhineland Textile Districts* (1989), and M. Neufield, *The Skilled Metalworkers of Nuremberg: Craft and Class in the Industrial Revolution* (1985), examine the persistence and gradual transformation of handicraft techniques. R. Cameron traces the spread of railroads and industry across Europe in *France and the Economic Development of Europe, 1800–1914* (1961). The works of A. S. Milward and S. B. Saul, *The Economic Development of Continental Europe, 1780–1870* (1973), and *The Development of the Economies of Continental Europe, 1850–1914* (1977), may be compared with J. Clapham's old-fashioned classic, *Economic Development of France and Germany* (1963). C. Kindleberger,

Economic Growth in France and Britain, 1851–1950 (1964), is a stimulating study, especially for those with some background in economics. Other important works in recent years on industrial developments are C. Tilly and E. Shorter, *Strikes in France, 1830–1848* (1974); D. Ringrose, *Transportation and Economic Stagnation in Spain, 1750–1850* (1970); and W. Blackwell, *The Industrialization of Russia,* 2d ed. (1982). L. Moch, *Paths to the City: Regional Migration in Nineteenth-Century France* (1983), and W. Schivelbusch, *Disenchanted Night: The Industrialization of Light in the Nineteenth Century* (1983), imaginatively analyze quite different aspects of industrialization's many consequences.

The debate between "optimists" and "pessimists" about the consequences of industrialization in England goes on. P. Taylor, ed., *The Industrial Revolution: Triumph or Disaster?* (1970), is a useful introduction to different viewpoints; Hayek's collection of essays, cited in the Notes, stresses positive aspects. It is also fascinating to compare F. Engels's classic condemnation, cited in the Notes, with Andrew Ure's optimistic defense, *The Philosophy of Manufactures,* first published in 1835 and reprinted recently. J. Rule, *The Labouring Classes in Early Industrial England, 1750–1850* (1987), is a recommended synthesis, whereas E. P. Thompson continues and enriches the Engels tradition in *The Making of the English Working Class* (1963), an exciting book rich in detail and early working-class lore. E. R. Pike's documentary collection, cited in the Notes, provides fascinating insights into the lives of working people. An unorthodox but moving account of a doomed group is D. Bythell, *The Handloom Weavers* (1969). F. Klingender, *Art and the Industrial Revolution,* rev. ed. (1968), is justly famous, and M. Ignatieff, *A Just Measure of Pain* (1980), is an engrossing study of prisons during English industrialization. D. S. Landes, *Revolution in Time: Clocks and the Making of the Modern World* (1983), is a brilliant integration of industrial and cultural history.

Among general studies, G. S. R. Kitson Clark, *The Making of Victorian England* (1967), is particularly imaginative. A. Briggs, *Victorian People* (1955), provides an engrossing series of brief biographies. H. Ausubel discusses a major reformer in *John Bright* (1966), and B. Harrison skillfully illuminates the problem of heavy drinking in *Drink and the Victorians* (1971). The most famous contemporary novel dealing with the new industrial society is Charles Dickens's *Hard Times,* an entertaining but exaggerated story. *Mary Barton* and *North and South* by Elizabeth Gaskell are more realistic portrayals, and both are highly recommended.

LISTENING TO THE
PAST

The Testimony of Young Mining Workers

The use of child labor in British industrialization quickly attracted the attention of humanitarians and social reformers. This interest led to investigations by parliamentary commissions, which resulted in laws limiting the hours and the ages of children working in large factories. Designed to build a case for remedial legislation, parliamentary inquiries gave large numbers of workers a rare chance to speak directly to contemporaries and to historians.

The moving passages that follow are taken from testimony gathered in 1841 and 1842 by the Ashley Mines Commission. Interviewing employers and many male and female workers, the commissioners focused on the physical condition of the youth and on the sexual behavior of workers far underground. The subsequent Mines Act of 1842 sought to reduce immoral behavior and sexual bullying by prohibiting underground work for all women (and for boys younger than ten).

Mr. Payne, coal master:

That children are employed generally at nine years old in the coal pits and sometimes at eight. In fact, the smaller the vein of coal is in height, the younger and smaller are the children required; the work occupies from six to seven hours per day in the pits; they are not ill-used or worked beyond their strength; a good deal of depravity exists but they are certainly not worse in morals than in other branches of the Sheffield trade, but upon the whole superior; the morals of this district are materially improving; Mr. Bruce, the clergyman, has been zealous and active in endeavoring to ameliorate their moral and religious education. . . .

Ann Eggley, hurrier, 18 years old:

I'm sure I don't know how to spell my name. We go at four in the morning, and sometimes at half-past four. We begin to work as soon as we get down. We get out after four,

sometimes at five, in the evening. We work the whole time except an hour for dinner, and sometimes we haven't time to eat. I hurry [move coal wagons underground] by myself, and have done so for long. I know the corves [small coal wagons] are very heavy, they are the biggest corves anywhere about. The work is far too hard for me; the sweat runs off me all over sometimes. I am very tired at night. Sometimes when we get home at night we have not power to wash us, and then we go to bed. Sometimes we fall asleep in the chair. Father said last night it was both a shame and a disgrace for girls to work as we do, but there was naught else for us to do. I began to hurry when I was seven and I have been hurrying ever since. I have been 11 years in the pits. The girls are always tired. I was poorly twice this winter; it was with headache. I hurry for Robert Wiggins; he is not akin to me. . . . We don't always get enough to eat and drink, but we get a good supper. I have known my father go at two in the morning to work . . . and he didn't come out till four. I am quite sure that we work constantly 12 hours except on Saturdays. We wear trousers and our shifts in the pit and great big shoes clinkered and nailed. The girls never work naked to the waist in our pit. The men don't insult us in the pit. The conduct of the girls in the pit is good enough sometimes and sometimes bad enough. I never went to a day-school. I went a little to a Sunday-school, but I soon gave it over. I thought it too bad to be confined both Sundays and week-days. I walk about and get the fresh air on Sundays. I have not learnt to read. I don't know my letters. I never learnt naught. I never go to church or chapel; there is no church or chapel at Gawber, there is none nearer than a mile. . . . I have never heard that a good man came into the world who was God's son to save sinners. I never heard of Christ at all. Nobody has ever told me about him, nor have my father and mother ever taught me to pray. I know no prayer; I never pray.

Patience Kershaw, aged 17:

My father has been dead about a year; my mother is living and has ten children, five lads and five lasses; the oldest is about thirty, the youngest is four; three lasses go to mill; all the lads are colliers, two getters and three hurriers; one lives at home and does nothing; mother does nought but look after home.

All my sisters have been hurriers, but three went to the mill. Alice went because her legs swelled from hurrying in cold water when she was hot. I never went to day-school; I go to Sunday-school, but I cannot read or write; I go to pit at five o'clock in the morning and come out at five in the evening; I get my breakfast of porridge and milk first; I take my dinner with me, a cake, and eat it as I go; I do not stop or rest any time for the purpose; I get nothing else until I get home, and then have potatoes and meat, not every day meat. I hurry in the clothes I have now got on, trousers and ragged jacked; the bald place upon my head is made by thrusting the corves; my legs have never swelled, but sisters' did when they went to mill; I hurry the corves a mile and more under ground and back; they weigh 300; I hurry 11 a day; I wear a belt and chain at the workings to get the corves out; the putters [miners] that I work for are *naked* except their caps; they pull off all their clothes; I see them at work when I go up; sometimes they beat me, if I am not quick enough, with their hands; they strike me upon my back; the boys take liberties with me, sometimes, they pull me about; I am the only girl in the pit; there are about 20 boys and 15 men; all the men are naked; I would rather work in mill than in coal-pit.

Isabel Wilson, 38 years old, coal putter:

When women have children thick [fast] they are compelled to take them down early. I have been married 19 years and have had 10 bairns [children]; seven are in life. When on Sir John's work was a carrier of coals, which caused me to miscarry five times from the strains, and was gai [very] ill after each. Putting is no so oppressive; last child was born on Saturday morning, and I was at work on the Friday night.

Female mine worker, from a parliamentary report, 1842. *(Source: Mary Evans Picture Library/Photo Researchers, Inc.)*

Once met with an accident; a coal brake my cheek-bone, which kept me idle some weeks.

I have wrought below 30 years, and so has the guid man; he is getting touched in the breath now.

None of the children read, as the work is no regular. I did read once, but no able to attend to it now; when I go below lassie 10 years of age keeps house and makes the broth or stir-about.

Questions for Analysis

1. To what extent are the testimonies of Ann Eggley and Patience Kershaw in harmony with that of Mr. Payne?

2. Describe the work of Eggley and Kershaw. What do you think of their work? Why?

3. What strikes you most about the lives of these workers?

4. The witnesses were responding to questions from middle-class commissioners. What did the commissioners seem interested in? Why?

Source: J. Bowditch and C. Ramsland, eds., *Voices of the Industrial Revolution.* Copyright © 1961, 1989 by the University of Michigan. Reprinted by permission.

25

Ideologies and Upheavals, 1815–1871

❋

A painting by Champin of revolutionary upheaval in Paris in 1848. *(Source: Ville de Paris/Photographie Bulloz)*

The momentous economic and political transformation of modern times began in the late eighteenth century with the Industrial Revolution in England and then the French Revolution. Until about 1815, these economic and political revolutions were separate, involving different countries and activities and proceeding at very different paces. The Industrial Revolution created the factory system and new groups of capitalists and industrial workers in northern England, but almost continual warfare with France checked the spread of that revolution to continental Europe. Meanwhile, England's ruling aristocracy suppressed all forms of political radicalism at home and joined with crowned heads abroad to oppose and eventually defeat revolutionary and Napoleonic France. The economic and political revolutions worked at cross-purposes and even neutralized each other.

After peace returned in 1815, the situation changed. Economic and political changes tended to fuse, reinforcing each other and bringing about what historian Eric Hobsbawm has incisively called the "dual revolution." For instance, the growth of the industrial middle class encouraged the drive for representative government, and the demands of the French sans-culottes in 1793 and 1794 inspired many socialist thinkers. Gathering strength, the dual revolution rushed on to alter completely first Europe and then the rest of the world. Much of world history in the last two centuries can be seen as the progressive unfolding of the dual revolution.

In Europe in the nineteenth century, as in Asia and Africa in more recent times, the interrelated economic and political transformation was built on complicated histories, strong traditions, and highly diverse cultures. Radical change was eventually a constant, but the particular results varied enormously. In central and eastern Europe especially, the traditional elites—the monarchs, noble landowners, and bureaucrats—proved capable of defending their privileges and eventually using the nationalism of the dual revolution to serve their interests.

The dual revolution posed a tremendous intellectual challenge. The meanings of the economic, political, and social changes that were occurring as well as the ways they would be shaped by human action were anything but clear. These changes fascinated observers and stimulated the growth of new ideas and powerful ideologies. The most important of these were conservatism, liberalism, nationalism, and socialism.

- How did thinkers develop these ideas to describe and shape the transformation going on before their eyes?
- How did the artists and writers of the romantic movement reflect and influence changes in this era?
- How after 1815 did popular political revolution well up again against established governments, and why did the revolutionary surge fail almost completely in 1848 after a fleeting moment of victory?
- How did strong leaders and the power of nationalism combine to redraw the map of Europe in the 1860s and provide a fateful answer to the challenge of the dual revolution?

These are the questions this chapter will explore.

THE PEACE SETTLEMENT

The eventual triumph of revolutionary economic and political forces was by no means certain as the Napoleonic era ended. Quite the contrary. The conservative, aristocratic monarchies of Russia, Prussia, Austria, and Great Britain had finally defeated France and reaffirmed their determination to hold France in line. But many other international questions were outstanding, and the allies agreed to meet at the Congress of Vienna to fashion a general peace settlement.

Most people felt a profound longing for peace. The great challenge for political leaders in 1814 was to construct a settlement that would last and not sow the seeds of another war. Their efforts were largely successful and contributed to a century unmarred by destructive, generalized war (Map 25.1).

The European Balance of Power

The allied powers were concerned first and foremost with the defeated enemy, France. Agreeing to the restoration of the Bourbon dynasty (see page 764), the allies were quite lenient toward France after Napoleon's abdication. France was given the boundaries it possessed in 1792, which were larger

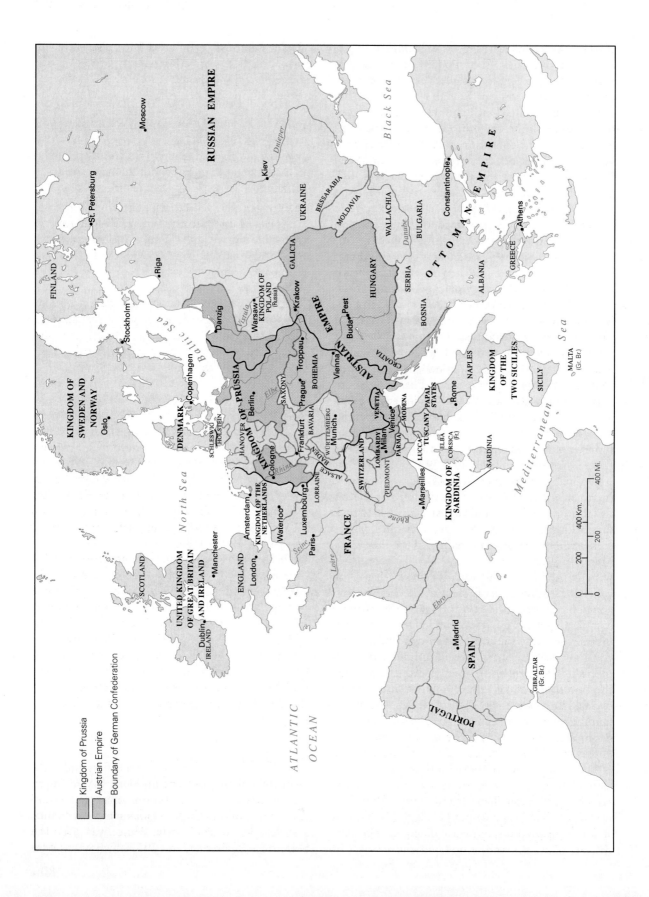

Kingdom of Prussia

Austrian Empire

Boundary of German Confederation

RUSSIAN EMPIRE

Moscow

St. Petersburg

Kiev

Dnieper

Black Sea

FINLAND

Riga

OTTOMAN EMPIRE

BESSARABIA

UKRAINE

GALICIA

MOLDAVIA

WALLACHIA

Danube

BULGARIA

Constantinople

Athens

GREECE

Stockholm

Danzig

Vistula

Warsaw

KINGDOM OF POLAND
(Russia)

Krakow

AUSTRIAN EMPIRE

HUNGARY

Buda Pest

SERBIA

BOSNIA

CROATIA

ALBANIA

Baltic Sea

KINGDOM OF SWEDEN AND NORWAY

Oslo

Copenhagen

DENMARK

SCHLESWIG HOLSTEIN

HANOVER OF PRUSSIA

Berlin

SAXONY

Prague

BOHEMIA

Troppau

Vienna

VENETIA

Venice

MODENA

PARMA

Rome

PAPAL STATES

TUSCANY

LUCCA

NAPLES

KINGDOM OF THE TWO SICILIES

SICILY

MALTA
(Gr. Br.)

Elbe

North Sea

Amsterdam

KINGDOM OF THE NETHERLANDS

Cologne

Rhine

Frankfurt

BAVARIA

Munich

WÜRTTEMBERG

BADEN

SWITZERLAND

LOMBARDY

Milan

PIEDMONT

KINGDOM OF SARDINIA

SARDINIA

CORSICA
(Fr.)

ELBA

Mediterranean Sea

SCOTLAND

Manchester

UNITED KINGDOM OF GREAT BRITAIN AND IRELAND

ENGLAND

London

Dublin

IRELAND

Waterloo

Luxembourg

LORRAINE

ALSACE

Paris

Seine

FRANCE

Loire

Marseilles

Rhône

ATLANTIC OCEAN

Ebro

Madrid

SPAIN

GIBRALTAR
(Gr. Br.)

PORTUGAL

0   200   400 Mi.

0   200   400 Km.

than those of 1789, and France did not have to pay any war reparations. Thus the victorious powers did not foment a spirit of injustice and revenge in the defeated country.

When the four allies of the Quadruple Alliance met together at the Congress of Vienna, assisted in a minor way by a host of delegates from the smaller European states, they also agreed to raise a number of formidable barriers against renewed French aggression. The Low Countries—Belgium and Holland—were united under an enlarged Dutch monarchy capable of opposing France more effectively. Moreover, Prussia received considerably more territory on France's eastern border so as to stand as the "sentinel on the Rhine" against France. In these ways the Quadruple Alliance combined leniency toward France with strong defensive measures.

In their moderation toward France, the allies were motivated by self-interest and traditional ideas about the balance of power. To Klemens von Metternich and Robert Castlereagh, the foreign ministers of Austria and Great Britain, respectively, as well as their French counterpart, Charles Talleyrand, the balance of power meant an international equilibrium of political and military forces that would discourage aggression by any combination of states or, worse, the domination of Europe by any single state.

The Great Powers—Austria, Britain, Prussia, Russia, and France—used the balance of power to settle their own dangerous disputes at the Congress of Vienna. There was general agreement among the victors that each of them should receive compensation in the form of territory for their successful struggle against the French. Great Britain had already won colonies and strategic outposts during the long wars. Metternich's Austria gave up territories in Belgium and southern Germany but expanded greatly elsewhere, taking the rich provinces of Venetia and Lombardy in northern Italy as well as former Polish possessions and new lands on the eastern coast of the Adriatic (see Map 25.1). There was also agreement that Prussia and Russia should be compensated. But where and to

what extent? That was the ticklish question that almost led to renewed war in January 1815.

The vaguely progressive, impetuous Tsar Alexander I of Russia wanted to restore the ancient kingdom of Poland, on which he expected to bestow the benefits of his rule. The Prussians agreed, provided they could swallow up the large and wealthy kingdom of Saxony, their German neighbor to the south. These demands were too much for Castlereagh and Metternich, who feared an unbalancing of forces in central Europe. In an astonishing about-face, they turned for diplomatic support to the wily Talleyrand and the defeated France he represented, signing a secret alliance directed against Russia and Prussia. War seemed imminent.

But the threat of war caused the rulers of Russia and Prussia to moderate their demands. Russia accepted a small Polish kingdom, and Prussia took only part of Saxony (see Map 25.1). This compromise was very much within the framework of balance-of-power ideology. And it enabled France to regain its Great Power status and end its diplomatic isolation.

Unfortunately for France, Napoleon suddenly escaped from his "comic kingdom" on the island of Elba. Yet the peace concluded after Napoleon's final defeat at Waterloo was still relatively moderate toward France. Fat old Louis XVIII was restored to his throne for a second time. France lost some territory, had to pay an indemnity of 700 million francs, and had to support a large army of occupation for five years.

The rest of the settlement already concluded at the Congress of Vienna was left intact. The members of the Quadruple Alliance, however, did agree to meet periodically to discuss their common interests and to consider appropriate measures for the maintenance of peace in Europe. This agreement marked the beginning of the European "congress system," which lasted long into the nineteenth century and settled many international crises through international conferences and balance-of-power diplomacy.

Intervention and Repression

There was also a domestic political side to the re-establishment of peace. Within their own countries, the leaders of the victorious states were much less flexible. In 1815 under Metternich's leadership, Austria, Prussia, and Russia embarked on a

✳ **MAP 25.1 Europe in 1815** Europe's leaders re-established a balance of political power after the defeat of Napoleon. Prussia gained territory on the Rhine and in Saxony and consolidated its power as a Great Power.

crusade against the ideas and politics of the dual revolution. This crusade lasted until 1848. The first step was the Holy Alliance, formed by Austria, Prussia, and Russia in September 1815. First proposed by Russia's Alexander I, the alliance soon became a symbol of the repression of liberal and revolutionary movements all over Europe.

In 1820 revolutionaries succeeded in forcing the monarchs of Spain and the southern Italian kingdom of the Two Sicilies to grant liberal constitutions against their wills. Metternich was horrified: revolution was rising once again. Calling a conference at Troppau in Austria under the provisions of the Quadruple Alliance, he and Alexander I proclaimed the principle of active intervention to maintain all autocratic regimes whenever they were threatened. Austrian forces then marched into Naples in 1821 and restored Ferdinand I to the

Metternich This portrait by Sir Thomas Lawrence (1769–1830) reveals much about Metternich the man. Handsome, refined, and intelligent, Metternich was a great aristocrat who was passionately devoted to his class and the defense of its interests. *(Source: Copyright reserved to Her Majesty Queen Elizabeth II)*

throne of the Two Sicilies, while French armies likewise restored the Spanish regime.

In the following years Metternich continued to battle against liberal political change. Sometimes he could do little, as in the case of the new Latin American republics that broke away from Spain. Nor could he undo the dynastic changes of 1830 and 1831 in France and Belgium. Nonetheless, until 1848 Metternich's system proved quite effective in central Europe, where his power was the greatest.

Metternich's policies dominated not only Austria and the Italian peninsula but also the entire German Confederation, which the peace settlement of Vienna had called into being. The confederation was composed of thirty-eight independent German states, including Prussia and Austria. These states met in complicated assemblies dominated by Austria, with Prussia a willing junior partner in the planning and execution of repressive measures.

It was through the German Confederation that Metternich had the infamous Carlsbad Decrees issued in 1819. These decrees required the thirty-eight German member states to root out subversive ideas in their universities and newspapers. The decrees also established a permanent committee with spies and informers to investigate and punish any liberal or radical organizations. Metternich's ruthless imposition of repressive internal policies on the governments of central Europe contrasted with the intelligent moderation he had displayed in the general peace settlement of 1815.

Metternich and Conservatism

Metternich's determined defense of the status quo made him a villain in the eyes of most progressive, optimistic historians of the nineteenth century. Yet rather than denounce the man, we can try to understand him and the general conservatism he represented.

Born into the middle ranks of the landed nobility of the Rhineland, Prince Klemens von Metternich (1773–1859) was an internationally oriented aristocrat who made a brilliant diplomatic career in Austria. Austrian foreign minister from 1809 to 1848, the cosmopolitan Metternich always remained loyal to his class and jealously defended its rights and privileges to the day he died. Like most other conservatives of his time, he did so with a clear conscience. The nobility was one of Europe's most ancient institutions, and conservatives regarded tradition as the basic source of human institutions. In their view, the proper state and society remained those of pre-1789 Europe, which rested on a judicious blend of monarchy, bureaucracy, aristocracy, and respectful commoners.

Metternich firmly believed that liberalism, as embodied in revolutionary America and France, had been responsible for a generation of war with untold bloodshed and suffering. Liberal demands for representative government and civil liberties had unfortunately captured the imaginations of some middle-class lawyers, business people, and intellectuals, who were engaged in a vast conspiracy to impose their beliefs on society and destroy the existing order. Like many other conservatives then and since, Metternich blamed liberal revolutionaries for stirring up the lower classes, which he believed desired nothing more than peace and quiet.

The threat of liberalism appeared doubly dangerous to Metternich because it generally went with national aspirations. Liberals believed that each people, each national group, had a right to establish its own independent government and seek to fulfill its own destiny. The idea of national self-determination was repellent to Metternich. It not only threatened the existence of the aristocracy but also threatened to destroy the Austrian Empire and revolutionize central Europe.

The vast Austrian Empire of the Habsburgs was a great dynastic state. Formed over centuries by war, marriage, and luck, it was made up of many peoples (Map 25.2). The Germans had long dominated the empire, yet they accounted for only one-fourth of the population. The Magyars (Hungarians), a substantially smaller group, dominated the kingdom of Hungary though even they did not account for a majority of the population in that part of the Austrian Empire.

The Czechs, the third major group, were concentrated in Bohemia and Moravia. There were also large numbers of Italians, Poles, and Ukrainians as well as smaller groups of Slovenes, Croats, Serbs, Ruthenians, and Rumanians. The various Slavic peoples, together with the Italians and the Rumanians, represented a widely scattered and completely divided majority in an empire dominated by Germans and Hungarians. Different ethnic groups often lived in the same provinces and even in the same villages. Thus the different parts and provinces of the empire differed in languages, customs, and institutions.

The multinational state that Metternich served was both strong and weak. It was strong because of its large population and vast territories; it was weak because of its many and potentially dissatisfied nationalities. In these circumstances, Metternich virtually had to oppose liberalism and nationalism, for Austria was simply unable to accommodate those ideologies of the dual revolution. Other conservatives supported Austria because they could imagine no better fate for the jumble of small nationalities wedged precariously between masses of Germans and hordes of Russians in east-central Europe. Metternich's repressive conservatism had understandable roots in the dilemma of a multinational state in an age of rising nationalism.

RADICAL IDEAS AND EARLY SOCIALISM

The years following the peace settlement of 1815 were years of profound intellectual activity. Intellectuals and social observers were seeking to understand the revolutionary changes that were taking place. These efforts led to ideas that still motivate the world.

Almost all of these basic ideas were radical. In one way or another they rejected the old, deeply felt conservatism, with its stress on tradition, a hereditary monarchy, a strong and privileged landowning aristocracy, and an official church. Instead, radicals developed and refined alternative visions—alternative ideologies—and tried to convince society to act on them. With time, they were very successful.

Liberalism

The principal ideas of liberalism—liberty and equality—were by no means defeated in 1815. First realized successfully in the American Revolution and then achieved in part in the French Revolution, liberalism demanded representative government as opposed to autocratic monarchy, equality before the law as opposed to legally separate classes. The idea of liberty also continued to mean specific individual freedoms: freedom of the press, freedom of speech, freedom of assembly, and freedom from arbitrary arrest. In Europe only France with Louis XVIII's Constitutional Charter and Great Britain with its Parliament and historic rights of English men and women had realized much of

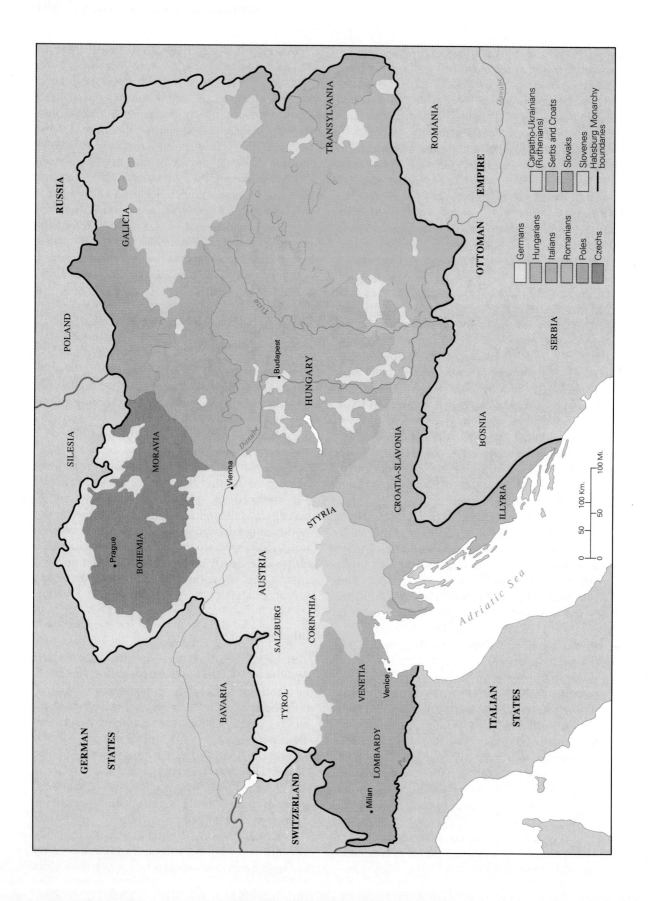

GERMAN
STATES

RUSSIA

POLAND

SILESIA

GALICIA

MORAVIA

BOHEMIA

• Prague

BAVARIA

AUSTRIA

• Vienna

SALZBURG

TYROL

CORINTHIA

STYRIA

SWITZERLAND

VENETIA

• Venice

LOMBARDY

• Milan

Danube

Tisza

HUNGARY

Budapest •

TRANSYLVANIA

ROMANIA

OTTOMAN EMPIRE

CROATIA-SLAVONIA

SERBIA

BOSNIA

ILLYRIA

Adriatic Sea

ITALIAN
STATES

Po

Germans

Hungarians

Italians

Romanians

Poles

Czechs

Carpatho-Ukrainians
(Ruthenians)

Serbs and Croats

Slovaks

Slovenes

Habsburg Monarchy
boundaries

0   50   100 Km.

0   50   100 Mi.

the liberal program in 1815. Even in those countries, liberalism had not fully succeeded.

Although liberalism retained its cutting edge, many considered it a somewhat duller tool than it had been. The reasons for this opinion were that liberalism faced more radical ideological competitors in the early nineteenth century. Opponents of classical liberalism especially criticized its economic principles, which called for unrestricted private enterprise and no government interference in the economy. This philosophy was popularly known as the doctrine of *laissez faire*. (This form of liberalism is often called "classical" liberalism in the United States to distinguish it sharply from modern American liberalism, which usually favors more government programs to meet social needs and to regulate the economy.)

The idea of a free economy had first been persuasively formulated by Scottish philosophy professor Adam Smith, whose *Inquiry into the Nature and Causes of the Wealth of Nations* (1776) founded modern economics. Smith was highly critical of eighteenth-century mercantilism and its attempt to regulate trade and economic activity. Far preferable, he believed, were free competition and the "invisible hand" of the self-regulating market, which would give all citizens a fair and equal opportunity to do what they did best. Smith argued effectively that freely competitive private enterprise would result in greater income for everyone, not just the rich.

In the early nineteenth century in Britain, this economic liberalism, which promoted economic growth in the Industrial Revolution, was embraced most enthusiastically by business groups and became a doctrine associated with business interests. Businessmen used the doctrine to defend their right to do as they wished in their factories. Labor unions were outlawed because they supposedly restricted free competition and the individual's "right to work."

In the early nineteenth century, liberal political ideals also became more closely associated with narrow class interests. Early-nineteenth-century liberals favored representative government, but

they generally wanted property qualifications attached to the right to vote. In practice, this meant limiting the vote to well-to-do aristocratic landowners, substantial businessmen, and successful members of the professions. Workers and peasants as well as the lower middle class of shopkeepers, clerks, and artisans did not own the necessary property and so could not vote.

Thus liberalism became increasingly identified with the middle class after 1815, and some intellectuals and foes of conservatism felt that liberalism did not go nearly far enough. Inspired by memories of the French Revolution and the young American republic, they called for universal voting rights, at least for males, and for democracy. These democrats and republicans were more radical than the liberals. They detested the power of the monarchy, the privileges of the aristocracy, and the great wealth of the upper middle class. Democrats and republicans were also more willing than most liberals to endorse violent upheaval to achieve goals. All of this meant that liberals and radical, democratic republicans could join forces against conservatives only up to a point.

Nationalism

Nationalism was a second radical idea in the years after 1815, an idea destined to have an enormous influence in the modern world. Nationalism has normally evolved from a real or imagined *cultural* unity, manifesting itself especially in a common language, history, and territory. And nationalists have usually sought to turn this cultural unity into *political* reality so that the territory of each people coincides with its state boundaries. It was this goal that made nationalism so potentially explosive in central and eastern Europe after 1815, when there were either too few states (Austria, Russia, and the Ottoman Empire) or too many (the Italian peninsula and the German Confederation) and when different peoples overlapped and intermingled. First harnessed by the French republic, nationalism had been preached by some patriots in the war against Napoleon. By 1815 there were already hints of nationalism's remarkable ability to spread and develop.

Between 1815 and 1850, most people who believed in nationalism also believed in either liberalism or radical, democratic republicanism. In more recent times, however, many governments have

✳ **MAP 25.2 Peoples of the Habsburg Monarchy, 1815** The old dynastic state was a patchwork of nationalities. Notice the widely scattered pockets of Germans and Hungarians.

been very nationalistic without favoring liberty and democracy. Why, then, was love of liberty almost synonymous with love of nation in the early nineteenth century?

A common faith in the creativity and nobility of the people was perhaps the single most important reason for the linking of these two concepts. Liberals and especially democrats saw the people as the ultimate source of all good government. Yet the benefits of self-government were possible only if the people were united by common traditions, loyalties, and language that transcended local interests and even class differences.

Early nationalists usually believed that every nation, like every citizen, had the right to exist in freedom and to develop its character and spirit. They were confident that a symphony of free nations would promote the harmony and ultimate unity of all peoples. As French historian Jules Michelet put it in *The People* in 1846, each citizen "learns to recognize his country . . . as a note in the grand concert; through it he himself participates and loves the world." Similarly, the great Italian patriot Giuseppe Mazzini (see Listening to the Past) believed that "in laboring according to the true principles of our country we are laboring for Humanity." Thus the liberty of the individual and the love of a free nation overlapped greatly in the early nineteenth century.

Yet even as early nationalists talked of serving the cause of humanity, they stressed the differences among peoples. German pastor and philosopher Johann Herder (1744–1803) had argued that every people has its own particular spirit and genius, which it expresses through culture and language. Herder (and others after him), however, could not define the uniqueness of the French, German, and Slavic peoples without comparing and contrasting one people with another. Thus even early nationalism developed a strong sense of "we" and "they."

To this "we-they" outlook, it was all too easy for nationalists to add two other highly volatile ingredients: a sense of national mission and a sense of national superiority. As Mazzini characteristically wrote, "Peoples never stop before they have achieved the ultimate aim of their existence, before having fulfilled their mission." In 1845 American journalist and strident nationalist John Louis O'Sullivan wrote that taking land from an "imbecile and distracted Mexico" was a laudable step in the "fulfillment of our manifest destiny to over-

spread the continent."[1] Even Michelet, so alive to the aspirations of other peoples, could not help speaking in 1846 of the "superiority of France"; the principles espoused in the French Revolution had made France the "salvation of mankind."

German and Spanish nationalists had a very different opinion of France. To them, the French often seemed oppressive, as the Germans did to the Czechs, as the Russians did to the Poles. Thus "they" were often the enemy.

Early nationalism was ambiguous. Its main thrust was liberal and democratic. But below the surface lurked ideas of national superiority and national mission that could lead to aggression and conflict.

French Utopian Socialism

Socialism was the new radical doctrine after 1815, and to understand it one must begin with France. Despite the fact that France trailed Great Britain in developing modern industry, most early socialists were French. These French thinkers were acutely aware that the political revolution in France, the rise of laissez faire, and the emergence of factory industry in England were transforming society. They were disturbed by what they saw. Liberal practices in politics, such as competition for votes, and in economics, such as free markets and the end of guild regulation, appeared to be fomenting selfish individualism and splitting the community into isolated fragments. There was, they believed, an urgent need for a further reorganization of society to establish cooperation and a new sense of community. Starting from this shared outlook, individual French thinkers searched the past, analyzed existing conditions, and fashioned luxurious utopias.

Early French socialists believed in economic planning. Inspired by the emergency measures of 1793 and 1794 in France, they argued that the government should rationally organize the economy and not depend on destructive competition to do the job. Early socialists also shared an intense desire to help the poor, and they preached that the rich and the poor should be more nearly equal economically. Finally, socialists believed that private property should be strictly regulated by the government or that it should be abolished and replaced by state or community ownership. Planning, greater economic equality, and state control of property—these were the key ideas of early French socialism and of all socialism since.

Fourier's Utopia   The vision of a harmonious planned community freed from capitalism and selfish individualism radiates from this 1847 illustration of Charles Fourier's principles. *(Source: Mary Evans Picture Library/Photo Researchers)*

One of the most influential early socialist thinkers was a nobleman, Count Henri de Saint-Simon (1760–1825). Saint-Simon optimistically proclaimed the tremendous possibilities of industrial development: "The age of gold is before us!" The key to progress was proper social organization. Such an arrangement of society required the "parasites"—the court, the aristocracy, lawyers, churchmen—to give way, once and for all, to the "doers"—the leading scientists, engineers, and industrialists. The doers would carefully plan the economy and guide it forward by undertaking vast public works projects and establishing investment banks. Saint-Simon also stressed in highly moralistic terms that every social institution ought to have as its main goal improved conditions for the poor.

After 1830 the socialist critique of capitalism became sharper. Charles Fourier (1772–1837), a lonely, saintly man with a tenuous hold on reality, envisaged a socialist utopia of mathematically pre-cise, self-sufficient communities, each made up of 1,620 people. Each day at noon Fourier stayed in his apartment, expecting a wealthy philanthropist who would endow his visionary schemes. He waited in vain, but several Fourier communities were founded, mainly in the United States.

Fourier was also an early proponent of the total emancipation of women. Extremely critical of middle-class family life, Fourier believed that most marriages were only another kind of prostitution. According to Fourier, young single women were shamelessly "sold" to their future husbands for dowries and other financial considerations. Fourier called for the abolition of marriage, free unions based only on love, and sexual freedom. To many middle-class men and women, these ideas were shocking and immoral. The suggested liberation of women as well as workers made the socialist program appear to them as doubly dangerous and revolutionary.

Louis Blanc (1811–1882), an intelligent journalist, was much more practical. In his *Organization of Work* (1839), he urged workers to agitate for universal voting rights and to take control of the state peacefully. Blanc believed that the state should guarantee full employment. The right to work had to become as sacred as any other right.

Finally, there was Pierre Joseph Proudhon (1809– 1865), a self-educated printer who wrote a pamphlet in 1840 entitled *What Is Property?* His answer was that it was nothing but theft. Property was profit that was stolen from the worker, who was the source of all wealth. Unlike most socialists, Proudhon feared the power of the state and was often considered an anarchist.

Of great importance, the message of French utopian socialists interacted with the experiences of French urban workers. In Paris especially, workers cherished the memory of the radical phase of the French Revolution and its efforts to regulate economic life and protect the poor. Skilled artisans, with a long tradition of exercising some control of their trades and conditions of work through guilds, became violently opposed to laissez-faire laws that denied workers the right to organize and instead promoted brutal, unrestrained competition. Developing a sense of class in the process, workers favored collective action and government intervention in economic life. Thus the aspirations of workers and utopian theorists reinforced each other, and a genuine socialist movement emerged in Paris in the 1830s and 1840s.

The French utopians had some influence outside France, but their specific programs often seemed too fanciful to be taken seriously. To Karl Marx was left the task of establishing firm foundations for modern socialism.

The Birth of Marxian Socialism

In 1848 the thirty-year-old Karl Marx (1818–1883) and the twenty-eight-year-old Friedrich Engels (1820–1895) published the *Communist Manifesto,* which became the bible of socialism. The son of a Jewish lawyer who had converted to Christianity, the atheistic young Marx had studied philosophy at the University of Berlin before turning to journalism and economics. He read widely in French socialist thought and like Fourier looked forward to the emancipation of women and the abolition of the family. By the time Marx was twenty-five, he was developing his own socialist ideas.

Early French socialists often appealed to the middle class and the state to help the poor. Marx ridiculed such appeals as naive. He argued that the interests of the middle class and those of the industrial working class were inevitably opposed to each other. Indeed, according to the *Manifesto,* the "history of all previously existing society is the history of class struggles." In Marx's view, one class had always exploited the other, and with the advent of modern industry, society was split more clearly than ever before: between the middle class (the bourgeoisie) and the modern working class (the proletariat). Moreover, the bourgeoisie had reduced everything to a matter of money and "naked self-interest." "In a word, for exploitation, veiled by religious and political illusions, the bourgeoisie had substituted naked, shameless, direct brutal exploitation."

Just as the bourgeoisie had triumphed over the feudal aristocracy, the proletariat, Marx predicted, would conquer the bourgeoisie in a violent revolution. While a tiny minority owned the means of production and grew richer, the ever-poorer proletariat was constantly growing in size and in class consciousness. The critical moment, Marx thought, was very near. "Let the ruling classes tremble at a Communist revolution. The proletarians have nothing to lose but their chains. They have a world to win. WORKING MEN OF ALL COUNTRIES, UNITE!" So ends the *Communist Manifesto.*

Marx's ideas united sociology, economics, and all human history in a vast and imposing edifice. He synthesized in his socialism not only French utopian schemes but also English classical economics and German philosophy—the major intellectual currents of his day.

Marx's debt to England was great. He was the last of the classical economists. Following David Ricardo, who had taught that labor was the source of all value, Marx went on to argue that profits were really wages stolen from the workers. Moreover, Marx incorporated Engels's account of the terrible oppression of the new class of factory workers in England; thus Marx's doctrines seemed to be based on hard facts.

Marx's theory of historical evolution was built on the philosophy of the German Georg Hegel (1770–1831). Hegel believed that each age in history is characterized by a dominant set of ideas, which produces opposing ideas and eventually a new synthesis. Thus history has pattern and purpose. Marx retained Hegel's view of history as a dialectic process of change but made economic relationships between classes the driving force. This dialectic explained the decline of agrarian feudalism and the rise of industrial capitalism. And Marx stressed again and again that the "bourgeoisie, historically, has played a most revolutionary part. . . . During its rule of scarcely one hundred years the bourgeoisie has created more massive and more colossal productive forces than have all preceding generations together." Marx's next idea, that it was now the bourgeoisie's turn to give way to the socialism of revolutionary workers, appeared to many the irrefutable capstone of a brilliant interpretation of humanity's long development. Thus Marx pulled together powerful insights to create one of the great secular religions of modern times.

THE ROMANTIC MOVEMENT

Radical concepts of politics and society were accompanied by comparable changes in literature and other arts during the dual revolution. The early nineteenth century marked the acme of the romantic movement, which profoundly influenced the arts and enriched European culture immeasurably.

The romantic movement was in part a revolt against classicism and the Enlightenment. The classicists believed that the ancient Greeks and Romans had discovered eternally valid aesthetic rules, that these rules fit with the Enlightenment's belief in rationality, order, and restraint, and that playwrights and painters should continue to follow them. Classicists could enforce these rules in the eighteenth century because they dominated the courts and academies for which artists worked.

Forerunners of the romantic movement appeared from about 1750 on. Of these, Rousseau—the passionate advocate of feeling, freedom, and natural goodness—was the most influential. Romanticism then crystallized fully in the 1790s, primarily in England and Germany. The French Revolution kindled the belief that radical reconstruction was also possible in cultural and artistic life (even though many early English and German romantics became disillusioned with events in France and turned from liberalism to conservatism in politics). Romanticism gained strength until the 1840s.

Karl Marx Active in the revolution of 1848, Marx fled from Germany in 1849 and settled in London. There he wrote *Capital,* the weighty exposition of his socialist theories, and worked to organize the working class. Marx earned a modest living as a journalist, supplemented by financial support from his coauthor, Friedrich Engels. *(Source: Istar-Tass/Sovfoto)*

Romanticism's Tenets

Romanticism was characterized by a belief in emotional exuberance, unrestrained imagination, and spontaneity in both art and personal life. In Germany early romantics of the 1770s and 1780s called themselves the "Storm and Stress" (*Sturm und Drang*) group, and many romantic artists of the early nineteenth century lived lives of tremendous emotional intensity. Suicide, duels to the death, madness, and strange illnesses were not uncommon among leading romantics. Romantics rejected materialism and sought to escape to lofty spiritual heights through their art. Great individualists, they believed the full development of one's unique human potential to be the supreme purpose in life. The romantics were driven by a sense of an unlimited universe and by a yearning for the unattained, the unknown, the unknowable.

Nowhere was the break with classicism more apparent than in romanticism's general conception of nature. Classicism was not particularly interested in nature. In the words of eighteenth-century English author Samuel Johnson, "A blade of grass is always a blade of grass; men and women are my subjects of inquiry." The romantics, in contrast, were enchanted by nature. Sometimes fascinated by its awesome and tempestuous side, at other times they saw nature as a source of spiritual inspiration. As the great English landscape artist John Constable declared, "Nature is Spirit visible."

Most romantics saw the growth of modern industry as an ugly, brutal attack on their beloved nature and on the human personality. They sought escape—in the unspoiled Lake District of northern England, in exotic North Africa, in an idealized Middle Ages. Yet some romantics found a vast, awesome, terribly moving power in the new industrial landscape. One of John Martin's greatest paintings, vividly depicting the Last Judgment foretold in Revelation 6, was inspired directly by a journey through the "Black country" of the industrial Midlands in the dead of night. According to Martin's son: "The glow of the furnaces, the red blaze of light, together with the liquid fire, seemed to him truly sublime and awful. He could not imagine anything more terrible even in the regions of everlasting punishment."[2]

Fascinated by color and diversity, the romantic imagination turned toward history with a passion. For romantics, history was beautiful and exciting. And it was the art of change over time—the key to a universe that was now perceived to be organic and dynamic. Historical studies supported the development of national aspirations and encouraged entire peoples to seek in the past their special destinies. This trend was especially strong in Germany and other eastern European countries.

Literature

Britain was the first country where romanticism flowered fully in poetry and prose, and the British romantic writers were among the most prominent in Europe. Wordsworth, Coleridge, and Scott were all active by 1800, to be followed shortly by Byron, Shelley, and Keats. All were poets: romanticism found its distinctive voice in poetry, as the Enlightenment had in prose.

A towering leader of English romanticism, William Wordsworth (1770–1850) traveled in France after his graduation from Cambridge University. There he fell passionately in love with a French woman, who bore him a daughter. He was deeply influenced by the philosophy of Rousseau and the spirit of the early French Revolution. Back in England, prevented by war and the Terror from returning to France, Wordsworth settled in the countryside with his sister, Dorothy, and Samuel Taylor Coleridge (1772–1834).

In 1798 the two poets published their *Lyrical Ballads,* one of the most influential literary works in the history of the English language. In defiance of classical rules, Wordsworth and Coleridge abandoned flowery poetic conventions for the language of ordinary speech, simultaneously endowing simple subjects with the loftiest majesty. One of Wordsworth's poems gracefully celebrates "a crowd,/A host, of golden daffodils; . . . /Fluttering and dancing in the breeze," and confides that "A poet could not but be gay,/In such a jocund company." Sharing the romantic conviction that nature has the power to elevate and instruct, Wordsworth also believed that nature could be appreciated, very democratically, by everyone and not just by an intellectual elite.

Born in Edinburgh, Walter Scott (1771–1832) personified the romantic movement's fascination with history. Raised on his grandfather's farm, Scott fell under the spell of the old ballads and tales of the Scottish border. He was also deeply influenced by German romanticism, particularly by the immortal poet and dramatist Johann Wolfgang von Goethe (1749–1832). A natural storyteller, Scott composed long narrative poems and a series of historical novels. He excelled in faithfully recreating the spirit of bygone ages and great historical events, especially those of Scotland.

At first, the strength of classicism in France inhibited the growth of romanticism there. Then between 1820 and 1850, the romantic impulse broke through in the poetry and prose of Lamartine, de Vigny, Hugo, Dumas, and Sand. Of these, Victor Hugo (1802–1885) was the greatest in both poetry and prose.

Son of a Napoleonic general, Hugo achieved an amazing range of rhythm, language, and image in his lyric poetry. His powerful novels exemplified the romantic fascination with fantastic characters,

John Martin: The Great Day of His Wrath   The combination of the terrible and the sublime fascinated English romantic artist John Martin (1789–1854). He painted wild visions of hell for a popular illustrated edition of John Milton's great epic poem *Paradise Lost*. But the reality of ironworks blazing in the night seemed to him even more awesome, and it inspired this image of the Last Judgment and the end of human history. *(Source: Tate Gallery, London/Art Resource, NY)*

strange settings, and human emotions. The hero of Hugo's famous *Hunchback of Notre Dame* (1831) is the great cathedral's deformed bellringer, a "human gargoyle" overlooking the teeming life of fifteenth-century Paris. Hugo also championed romanticism in drama. His play *Hernani* (1830) consciously broke all the old rules as Hugo renounced his early conservatism and equated freedom in literature with liberty in politics and society. Hugo's political evolution was thus exactly the opposite of Wordsworth's. In the English poet youthful radicalism gave way to middle-aged caution. As the contrast between the two artists suggests, romanticism was a cultural movement compatible with many political beliefs.

Amandine Aurore Lucie Dupin (1804–1876), a strong-willed and gifted woman generally known by her pen name, George Sand, defied the narrow conventions of her time in an unending search for self-fulfillment. After eight years of unhappy marriage in the provinces, she abandoned her dullard of a husband and took her two children to Paris to pursue a career as a writer. There Sand soon achieved fame and wealth, eventually writing over eighty novels on a variety of romantic and social themes. Her striking individualism went far beyond her flamboyant preference for men's clothing and cigars and her notorious love affairs. Her semi-autobiographical novel *Lélia* was shockingly modern, delving deeply into her tortuous quest for sexual and personal freedom.

In central and eastern Europe, literary romanticism and early nationalism often reinforced each other. Seeking a unique greatness in every people, well-educated romantics plumbed their own histories and cultures. Like modern anthropologists, they turned their attention to peasant life and transcribed the folk songs, tales, and proverbs that the cosmopolitan Enlightenment had disdained. The brothers Jacob and Wilhelm Grimm were particularly successful at rescuing German fairy tales from oblivion. In the Slavic lands, romantics played a decisive role in converting spoken peasant languages into modern written languages. The greatest of all Russian poets, Aleksander Pushkin (1799–1837), used his lyric genius to mold the modern literary language of Russia.

Art and Music

The greatest and most moving romantic painter in France was Eugène Delacroix (1798–1863), probably the illegitimate son of French foreign minister Talleyrand. Delacroix was a master of dramatic, colorful scenes that stirred the emotions. He was fascinated with remote and exotic subjects, whether lion hunts in Morocco or the languishing, sensuous women of a sultan's harem. He was also a passionate spokesman for freedom. His master-

Heroes of Romanticism   Observed by a portrait of Byron and a bust of Beethoven, Franz Liszt plays for friends in this painting by Josef Danhauser (1805–1845). From left to right sit Alexandre Dumas, George Sand (characteristically wearing men's garb), and Marie d'Agoult, Liszt's mistress. Standing are Victor Hugo, Nicolo Paganini, and Gioacchino Rossini. This gathering of geniuses was purely imaginary, part of an advertising campaign by a German piano manufacturer to sell pianos to the comfortable middle class. *(Source: Bildarchiv Preussischer Kulturbesitz)*

piece, *Liberty Leading the People,* celebrated the nobility of popular revolution in general and revolution in France in particular.

In England the most notable romantic painters were Joseph M. W. Turner (1775–1851) and John Constable (1776–1837). Both were fascinated by nature, but their interpretations of it contrasted sharply, aptly symbolizing the tremendous emotional range of the romantic movement. Turner depicted nature's power and terror; wild storms and sinking ships were favorite subjects. Constable painted gentle Wordsworthian landscapes in which human beings were at one with their environment, the comforting countryside of unspoiled rural England.

It was in music that romanticism realized most fully and permanently its goals of free expression and emotional intensity. Whereas the composers of the eighteenth century had remained true to well-defined structures, such as the classical symphony, the great romantics used a great range of forms. Romantic composers also transformed the small classical orchestra, tripling its size by adding wind instruments, percussion, and more brass and strings. The crashing chords evoking the surge of the masses in Frédéric Chopin's "Revolutionary" etude, the bottomless despair of the funeral march in Beethoven's Third Symphony—such were the musical paintings that plumbed the depths of human feeling.

This range and intensity gave music and musicians much greater prestige than in the past. Music no longer simply complemented a church service or helped a nobleman digest his dinner. It became for many the greatest of the arts, worthy of great concert halls and the most dedicated sacrifice. The one-in-a-million performer—the great virtuoso who could transport the listener to ecstasy and hysteria—became a cultural hero. People swooned for the composer Franz Liszt (1811–1886), lionized as the greatest pianist of his age, as they scream for rock stars today.

Though romanticism dominated music until late in the nineteenth century, no composer ever surpassed its first great master, Ludwig van Beethoven (1770–1827). As the contemporary German novelist Ernst Hoffmann (1776–1822) wrote, "Beethoven's music sets in motion the lever of fear, of awe, of horror, of suffering, and awakens just that infinite longing which is the essence of Romanticism." Beethoven's range was tremendous. He continued to pour out immortal music—

symphonies, chamber music, sonatas for violin and piano, masses, an opera, and a great many songs—until his death. But he never heard much of his later work, including the unforgettable choral finale to the Ninth Symphony, for his last years were spent in total deafness.

❊ REFORMS AND REVOLUTIONS (1815–1850)

While the romantic movement was developing, liberal, national, and socialist forces battered against the conservatism of 1815. In a few countries, change occurred gradually and peacefully. Elsewhere, pressure built up like steam in a pressure cooker without a safety valve. Then in 1848 revolutionary political and social ideologies combined with economic crisis and the romantic impulse to produce a vast upheaval. National independence, liberal-democratic constitutions, and social reform: the lofty aspirations of a generation seemed at hand. Yet in the end the revolutions failed, and the lofty aspirations were shattered.

National Liberation in Greece

National, liberal revolution, frustrated in Italy and Spain by conservative statesmen, succeeded first after 1815 in Greece. Since the fifteenth century, the Greeks had been living under the domination of the Ottoman Turks. In spite of centuries of foreign rule, the Greeks had survived as a people, united by their language and the Greek Orthodox religion. It was perfectly natural that the general growth of national aspirations and a desire for independence would inspire some Greeks in the early nineteenth century. This rising national movement led to revolt in 1821.

The Great Powers, particularly Metternich, were opposed to all revolution, even revolution against the Islamic Turks, and they supported the Ottoman Empire. Yet for many Europeans, the Greek cause became a holy one. Educated Americans and Europeans were in love with the culture of classical Greece; Russians were stirred by the piety of their Orthodox brethren. Writers and artists, moved by the romantic impulse, responded enthusiastically to the Greek struggle. The flamboyant, radical poet Lord Byron went to Greece and died there in the struggle "that Greece might still be free."

Turkish atrocities toward the rebels fanned the fires of European outrage and Greek determination. One of Delacroix's romantic masterpieces memorialized the massacre at Chios, where the Turks had slaughtered nearly a hundred thousand Greeks.

In 1827 Great Britain, France, and Russia responded to popular demands at home and directed Turkey to accept an armistice. When the Turks refused, the navies of these three powers trapped the Turkish fleet at Navarino and destroyed it. Russia then declared another of its periodic wars of expansion against the Turks. This led to the establishment of a Russian protectorate over much of present-day Rumania, which had also been under Turkish rule. Great Britain, France, and Russia finally declared Greece independent in 1830. In the end the Greeks had won: a small nation had gained its independence in a heroic war against a foreign empire.

Liberal Reform in Great Britain

Eighteenth-century British society had been both flexible and remarkably stable. It was dominated by the landowning aristocracy, but that class was neither closed nor rigidly defined. Successful business and professional people could buy land and become gentlefolk, while the common people had more than the usual opportunities of the preindustrial world. Basic civil rights for all were balanced by a tradition of deference to one's social superiors. Parliament was manipulated by the king and was thoroughly undemocratic. Only about 6 percent of the population could vote for representatives to Parliament, and by the 1780s there was growing interest in some kind of political reform. But the French Revolution threw the British aristocracy into a panic for a generation. The Tory party, completely controlled by the landed aristocracy, was particularly fearful of radical movements at home and abroad. After 1815 the aristocracy energetically defended its ruling position.

The first step in this direction began in 1815 with revival of the Corn Laws restricting foreign grain imports. During a generation of war with France the British had been unable to import cheap grain from eastern Europe. As shortages occurred and agricultural prices skyrocketed, a great deal of marginal land had been brought under cultivation, fattening the landed aristocracy's rent rolls. Peace meant that grain could be imported

again and that the price of wheat and bread would go down, benefiting almost everyone except the aristocracy. The aristocracy, however, rammed through Parliament a new law that prohibited the importation of foreign grain unless the price at home rose to improbable levels. Seldom has a class legislated more selfishly for its own narrow economic advantage or done more to promote a class-based interpretation of political action.

The change in the Corn Laws, coming at a time of widespread unemployment and postwar adjustment, led to protests and demonstrations by urban laborers, supported by radical intellectuals. In 1817 the Tory government responded by temporarily suspending the traditional rights of peaceable assembly and habeas corpus. Two years later, an enormous but orderly protest, at Saint Peter's Fields in Manchester, was savagely broken up by armed cavalry. Nicknamed the "Battle of Peterloo," in scornful reference to the British victory at Waterloo, this incident expressed the government's determination to repress and stand fast.

Strengthened by ongoing industrial development, the new manufacturing and commercial groups insisted on a place for their new wealth alongside the landed wealth of the aristocracy in the framework of political power and social prestige. They called for many kinds of liberal reform and pressed especially for reform of Parliament. The Whig party, though led like the Tories by great aristocrats, had by tradition been more responsive to commercial and manufacturing interests. In 1830 a Whig ministry introduced "an act to amend the representation of the people of England and Wales." The House of Lords successfully blocked this reform bill until 1832, when a mighty surge of popular protest helped convince the king and lords to give in.

The Reform Bill of 1832 had profound significance. First, the House of Commons had emerged as the all-important legislative body. Second, the new industrial areas of the country gained representation in the Commons, and many old "rotten boroughs"—electoral districts with very few voters that the landed aristocracy had bought and sold—were eliminated so that representation better reflected the shift in population to the northern manufacturing counties. Third, the number of voters increased by about 50 percent. Comfortable middle-class groups in the urban population, as well as some substantial farmers who leased their land, received the vote. Thus the pressures build-

Evictions of Irish Peasants   Surrounded by their few meager possessions, this family was turned out of their cottage in the 1880s. The door was nailed shut to prevent their return. The eviction of peasants who could not pay their rent continued for decades after the Great Famine. *(Source: Lawrence Collection, National Library of Ireland, Dublin)*

ing in Great Britain were temporarily released without revolution or civil war. More radical reforms within the system appeared difficult but not impossible.

The principal radical program was embodied in the "People's Charter" of 1838 and the Chartist movement (see page 799), with its core demand for universal male (but not female) suffrage. In three separate campaigns hundreds of thousands of people signed gigantic petitions calling on Parliament to grant all men the right to vote. Parliament rejected the petitions, but the working poor learned a valuable lesson in mass politics.

While calling for universal male suffrage, many working-class people joined with middle-class manufacturers in the Anti–Corn Law League, founded in Manchester in 1839. Mass participation made possible a popular crusade led by fighting liberals who argued that lower food prices and

more jobs in industry depended on repeal of the Corn Laws, which in the 1820s had been revised to allow grain imports subject to high tariffs. When Ireland's potato crop failed in 1845, famine prices for food and even famine itself also seemed likely in England. To avert the impending catastrophe, Tory prime minister Robert Peel joined with the Whigs and a minority of his own party to repeal the Corn Laws in 1846 and allow free imports of grain. England escaped famine. Thereafter, the liberal doctrine of free trade became almost sacred dogma in Great Britain.

The following year, the Tories passed a bill designed to help the working classes, but in a different way. The Ten Hours Act of 1847 limited the workday for women and young people in factories to ten hours. Tory aristocrats continued to champion legislation regulating factory conditions. They were competing vigorously with the middle class for the support of the working class. This healthy competition between a still-vigorous aristocracy and a strong middle class was a crucial factor in Great Britain's peaceful evolution. The working classes could make temporary alliances with either competitor to better their own conditions.

The people of Ireland did not benefit from this political competition. Long ruled as a conquered people, the great mass of the population (outside the northern counties of Ulster, which were partly Presbyterian) were Irish Catholic peasants who rented their land from a tiny minority of Church of England Protestants, many of whom lived in England. Ruthlessly exploited and growing rapidly in numbers, Irish peasants had come to depend on the potato crop.

The potato crop failed in 1845, 1846, 1848, and 1851 in Ireland and throughout much of Europe. Blight attacked the young plants, and the tubers rotted. The general result was high food prices, widespread suffering, and, frequently, social upheaval. In Ireland the result was unmitigated disaster—the Great Famine. Widespread starvation and mass fever epidemics occurred. Total losses of population were staggering. Fully 1 million emigrants fled the famine between 1845 and 1851, going primarily to the United States and Great Britain, and at least 1.5 million people died or went unborn because of the disaster. At the same time, the British government energetically supported heartless landowner demands with armed force. Tenants who could not pay their rents were evicted and their homes broken up or burned. Famine or not, Ireland remained a conquered province.

Revolutions in France

Louis XVIII's Constitutional Charter of 1814—theoretically a gift from the king but actually a response to political pressures—was basically a liberal constitution (see page 764). The economic and social gains made by sections of the middle class and the peasantry in the French Revolution were fully protected, great intellectual and artistic freedom was permitted, and a real parliament with upper and lower houses was created. The worldly and politically expedient Louis appointed as his ministers moderate royalists. These ministers obtained the support of a majority of the representatives elected to the lower Chamber of Deputies between 1816 and Louis's death in 1824.

Louis XVIII's charter was anything but democratic. Only about 100,000 of the wealthiest people out of a total population of 30 million had the right to vote for the deputies who, with the king and his ministers, made the laws of the nation. Nonetheless, the "notable people" who did vote came from very different backgrounds. There were wealthy businessmen, war profiteers, successful professionals, former revolutionaries, large landowners from the old aristocracy and the middle class, Bourbons, and Bonapartists.

The old aristocracy, with its pre-1789 mentality, was a minority within the voting population. It was this situation that Louis's successor, his brother Charles X (r. 1824–1830), could not abide. Crowned in a lavish, utterly medieval ceremony in 1824, Charles was a true reactionary who wanted to re-establish the old order in France. Finally repudiating the Constitutional Charter in an attempted coup in July 1830, Charles issued decrees stripping much of the wealthy middle class of its voting rights, and he censored the press. The immediate reaction, encouraged by journalists and lawyers, was an insurrection in the capital by printers, other artisans, and small traders. In "three glorious days" the revolution of 1830 brought down the government. Charles fled. Then the upper middle class, which had encouraged the revolt, skillfully seated Charles's cousin, Louis Philippe, duke of Orléans, on the vacant throne.

Louis Philippe (r. 1830–1848) accepted the Constitutional Charter of 1814; adopted the red, white, and blue flag of the French Revolution; and admitted that he was merely the "king of the French people." In spite of such symbolic actions, the situation in France remained fundamentally unchanged. The vote was extended only from 100,000 to 170,000 citizens. The wealthy notable elite actually tightened its control as the old aristocracy retreated to the provinces to sulk harmlessly. For the upper middle class, there had been a change in dynasty in order to protect the status quo and the narrowly liberal institutions of 1815. Republicans, democrats, social reformers, and the poor of Paris were bitterly disappointed.

These disappointments in France grew in the 1840s, which were economically hard and politically tense throughout Europe. Echoes of the potato famine in Ireland, bad harvests in France and other countries jacked up food prices and caused misery and unemployment in the cities. "Prerevolutionary" outbreaks occurred all across

Europe. Revolution was widely expected, but it took revolution in Paris—once again—to turn expectations into realities.

Louis Philippe's "bourgeois monarchy" had been characterized by stubborn inaction and complacency. There was a glaring lack of social legislation, and politics was dominated by corruption and selfish special interests. With only the rich voting for deputies, many of the deputies were docile government bureaucrats.

The government's stubborn refusal to consider electoral reform heightened a sense of class injus-

tice among shopkeepers and urban working people, and it eventually touched off a popular revolt in Paris. Barricades went up on the night of February 22, 1848, and by February 24 Louis Philippe had abdicated in favor of his grandson. But the common people in arms would tolerate no more monarchy. This refusal led to the proclamation of a provisional republic, headed by a ten-man executive committee and certified by cries of approval from the revolutionary crowd.

A generation of historians and journalists had praised the First French Republic, and their work

Delacroix: Liberty Leading the People   This romantic painting glorifies the July revolution in Paris in 1830. Raising high the revolutionary tricolor, Liberty unites the worker, the bourgeois, and the street child in a righteous crusade against privilege and oppression. The revolution of 1848 began as a similar crusade, but class warfare in Paris soon shattered the hope of rich and poor joining together for freedom. *(Source: Louvre © Photo R.M.N)*

had borne fruit: the revolutionaries were firmly committed to a republic (as opposed to any form of constitutional monarchy), and they immediately set about drafting a constitution for France's Second Republic. Moreover, they wanted a truly popular and democratic republic so that the healthy, life-giving forces of the common people—the peasants and the workers—could reform society with wise legislation. In practice, building such a republic meant giving the right to vote to every adult male, and this was quickly done. Revolutionary compassion and sympathy for freedom were expressed in the freeing of all slaves in French colonies, the abolition of the death penalty, and the establishment of a ten-hour workday for Paris.

Yet there were profound differences within the revolutionary coalition in Paris. On the one hand, there were the moderate, liberal republicans of the middle class. They viewed universal male suffrage as the ultimate concession to be made to popular forces, and they strongly opposed any further radical social measures. On the other hand, there were the radical republicans. Influenced by a generation of utopian socialists, and appalled by the poverty and misery of the urban poor, the radical republicans were committed to some kind of socialism.

Worsening depression and rising unemployment brought these conflicting goals to the fore. Louis Blanc, who along with a worker named Albert represented the republican socialists in the provisional government, pressed for recognition of a socialist right to work. Blanc asserted that permanent government-sponsored cooperative workshops should be established for workers. Such workshops would be an alternative to capitalist employment and a decisive step toward a new, noncompetitive social order.

The moderate republicans wanted no such thing. They were willing to provide only temporary relief. The resulting compromise set up national workshops—soon to become little more than a vast program of pick-and-shovel public works—and established a special commission under Blanc to "study the question." This satisfied no one. The national workshops were, however, better than nothing. An army of desperate poor from the French provinces and even from foreign countries streamed into Paris to sign up. The number enrolled in the workshops soared from 10,000 in March to 120,000 by June, and another 80,000 were trying unsuccessfully to join.

While the workshops in Paris grew, the French masses went to the election polls in late April. Voting in most cases for the first time, the people elected a majority of moderate republicans to the new Constituent Assembly. The socialism that seemed the most characteristic aspect of the revolution in Paris was evoking a violent reaction not only among the frightened middle and upper classes but also among the bulk of the population—the peasants. Many French peasants owned land and they had been seized with a universal hatred of radical Paris. A majority of the Constituent Assembly members were thus firmly committed to the republic and strongly opposed to the socialists.

This clash of ideologies—of liberal capitalism and socialism—became a clash of classes and arms after the elections. As the workshops continued to fill and grow more radical, the fearful but powerful propertied classes in the Assembly took the offensive. On June 22 the government dissolved the national workshops in Paris, giving the workers the choice of joining the army or going to workshops in the provinces.

The result was a spontaneous and violent uprising. Frustrated in attempts to create a socialist society, masses of desperate people were now losing even their life-sustaining relief. When the famous astronomer François Arago counseled patience, a voice from the crowd cried out, "Ah, Monsieur Arago, you have never been hungry!"[3] Barricades sprang up in the narrow streets of Paris, and a terrible class war began. Working people fought with the courage of utter desperation, but the government had the army and the support of peasant France. After three terrible "June Days" and the death or injury of more than ten thousand people, the republican army under General Louis Cavaignac stood triumphant in a sea of working-class blood and hatred.

The revolution in France thus ended in spectacular failure. The February coalition of the middle and working classes had in four short months become locked in mortal combat. In place of a generous democratic republic, the Constituent Assembly completed a constitution featuring a strong executive. This allowed Louis Napoleon, nephew of Napoleon Bonaparte, to win a landslide victory in the election of December 1848.

The Austrian Empire in 1848

Throughout central Europe, news of the upheaval in France evoked feverish excitement and eventually revolution. Liberals demanded written consti-

THE REVOLUTIONS OF 1848

February	Revolt in Paris against Louis Philippe's "bourgeois monarchy" Louis Philippe abdicates Proclamation of a provisional republic
February–June	Establishment and rapid growth of government-sponsored workshops in France
March 3	Nationalistic Hungarians demand autonomy from Austrian Empire
March 13	Uprising of students and workers in Vienna; Metternich flees to London
March 20	Ferdinand I of Austria abolishes serfdom and promises reforms
March 21	Frederick William IV of Prussia agrees to a liberal constitution and to the merger of Prussia into a new German state
March 26	Workers in Berlin issue a series of democratic and vaguely socialist demands
April 22	French voters favor moderate republicans over radicals
May 18	Frankfurt Assembly begins writing a new German constitution
June 17	Austrian army crushes working-class revolt in Prague
June 22–26	French government abolishes the national workshops, provoking an uprising June Days: republican army defeats rebellious Parisian working class
October	Austrian army besieges and retakes Vienna from students and working-class radicals
December	Conservatives force Ferdinand I of Austria to abdicate in favor of young Francis Joseph Frederick William IV disbands Prussian Constituent Assembly and grants Prussia a conservative constitution Louis Napoleon wins a landslide victory in French presidential elections
March 1849	Frankfurt Assembly elects Frederick William IV of Prussia emperor of the new German state; Frederick William refuses and reasserts royal authority in Prussia
June–August 1849	Habsburg and Russian forces defeat the Hungarian independence movement

tutions, representative government, and greater civil liberties from authoritarian regimes. When governments hesitated, popular revolts followed. Urban workers and students served as the shock troops, but they were allied with middle-class lib-

erals and peasants. In the face of this united front, monarchs collapsed and granted almost everything. The popular revolutionary coalition, having secured great and easy victories, then broke down as it had in France. The traditional forces—the monarchy, the aristocracy, and the regular army—recovered their nerve, reasserted their authority, and took back many, though not all, of the concessions. Reaction was everywhere victorious.

The revolution in the Austrian Empire began in Hungary, where nationalistic Hungarians demanded national autonomy, full civil liberties, and universal suffrage. When the monarchy in Vienna hesitated, Viennese students and workers took to the streets, and peasant disorders broke out in parts of the empire. The Habsburg emperor Ferdinand I (r. 1835–1848) capitulated and promised reforms and a liberal constitution. Metternich fled in disguise toward London. The old absolutist order seemed to be collapsing with unbelievable rapidity.

The coalition of revolutionaries was not stable, however. The Austrian Empire was overwhelmingly agricultural, and serfdom still existed. On March 20, as part of its capitulation before upheaval, the monarchy abolished serfdom, with its degrading forced labor and feudal services. Feeling they had won a victory reminiscent of that in France in 1789, newly free men and women of the land then lost interest in the political and social questions agitating the cities. Meanwhile, the coalition of urban revolutionaries also broke down. When the urban poor rose in arms and presented its own demands for socialist workshops and universal voting rights for men, the prosperous middle classes recoiled in alarm.

The coalition of March was also weakened, and ultimately destroyed, by conflicting national aspirations. In March the Hungarian revolutionary leaders pushed through an extremely liberal, almost democratic, constitution. But the Hungarian revolutionaries also sought to transform the mosaic of provinces and peoples that was the kingdom of Hungary into a unified, centralized, Hungarian nation. To the minority groups that formed half of the population—the Croats, Serbs, and Rumanians—such unification was completely unacceptable. Each felt entitled to political autonomy and cultural independence. The Habsburg monarchy in Vienna exploited the fears of the minority groups, and they were soon locked in armed combat with the new Hungarian government. In a somewhat similar way, Czech nationalists based in Bohemia and the city of Prague came into conflict with German nationalists. Thus the national aspirations within the Austrian Empire enabled the monarchy to play off one group against the other.

Finally, the conservative aristocratic forces gathered around Emperor Ferdinand I regained their nerve and reasserted their great strength. The archduchess Sophia, a conservative but intelligent and courageous Bavarian princess married to the emperor's brother, provided a rallying point. Deeply ashamed of the emperor's collapse before a "mess of students," she insisted that Ferdinand, who had no heir, abdicate in favor of her son, Francis Joseph.[4] Powerful nobles who held high positions in the government, the army, and the church agreed completely. They organized around Sophia in a secret conspiracy to reverse and crush the revolution.

Their first breakthrough came when the army bombarded Prague and savagely crushed a working-class revolt there on June 17. Other Austrian officials and nobles began to lead the minority nationalities of Hungary against the revolutionary government proclaimed by the Hungarian patriots. At the end of October, the well-equipped, predominantly peasant troops of the regular Austrian army attacked the student and working-class radicals in Vienna and retook the city at the cost of more than four thousand casualties. Thus the determination of the Austrian aristocracy and the loyalty of its army were the final ingredients in the triumph of reaction and the defeat of revolution.

When Francis Joseph (r. 1848–1916) was crowned emperor of Austria immediately after his eighteenth birthday in December 1848, only Hungary had yet to be brought under control. But another determined conservative, Nicholas I of Russia (r. 1825–1855), obligingly lent his iron hand. On June 6, 1849, 130,000 Russian troops poured into Hungary and subdued the country after bitter fighting. For a number of years, the Habsburgs ruled Hungary as a conquered territory.

Prussia and the Frankfurt Assembly

After Austria, Prussia was the largest and most influential German kingdom. Prior to 1848, the goal of middle-class Prussian liberals had been to transform absolutist Prussia into a liberal constitutional monarchy, which would lead the thirty-eight states of the German Confederation into the liberal, unified nation desired by liberals throughout the German states. The agitation following the fall of Louis Philippe encouraged Prussian liberals to press their demands. When the artisans and factory

Revolutionary Justice in Vienna   As part of the conservative resurgence, in October 1848 the Austrian minister of war ordered up reinforcements for an army that was marching on Hungary. In a last defiant gesture the outraged revolutionaries in Vienna seized the minister and hung him from a lamppost for treason. The army then reconquered the city in a week of bitter fighting. *(Source: Mary Evans Picture Library/Photo Researchers)*

workers in Berlin exploded in March and joined temporarily with the middle-class liberals in the struggle against the monarchy, the autocratic yet paternalistic Frederick William IV (r. 1840–1861) vacillated and finally caved in. On March 21 he promised to grant Prussia a liberal constitution and to merge Prussia into a new national German state that was to be created. But urban workers wanted much more and the Prussian aristocracy wanted

much less than the moderate constitutional liberalism the king conceded. The workers issued a series of democratic and vaguely socialist demands that troubled their middle-class allies, and the conservative clique gathered around the king to urge counter-revolution.

As an elected Prussian Constituent Assembly met in Berlin to write a constitution for the Prussian state, a self-appointed committee of liberals from various German states successfully called for a national assembly to begin writing a federal constitution for a unified German state. Meeting in Frankfurt in May, the National Assembly was a curious revolutionary body. It was really a serious middle-class body of lawyers, professors, doctors, officials, and businessmen.

Convened to write a constitution, the learned body was soon absorbed in a battle with Denmark over the provinces of Schleswig and Holstein, an extremely complicated issue from a legal point of view. The provinces were inhabited primarily by Germans but were ruled by the king of Denmark, although Holstein was a member of the German Confederation. When Frederick VII, the new nationalistic king of Denmark, tried to integrate both provinces into the rest of his state, the Germans in these provinces revolted. Hypnotized by this conflict, the National Assembly at Frankfurt debated ponderously and finally called on the Prussian army to oppose Denmark in the name of the German nation. Prussia responded and began war with Denmark. As the Schleswig-Holstein issue demonstrated, the national ideal was a crucial factor motivating the German middle classes in 1848.

In March 1849 the National Assembly finally completed its drafting of a liberal constitution and elected King Frederick William of Prussia emperor of the new German national state (minus Austria and Schleswig-Holstein). By early 1849, however, reaction had been successful almost everywhere. Frederick William had reasserted his royal authority, disbanded the Prussian Constituent Assembly, and granted his subjects a limited, essentially conservative constitution. Reasserting that he ruled by divine right, Frederick William contemptuously refused to accept the "crown from the gutter." Bogged down by their preoccupation with nationalist issues, the reluctant revolutionaries in Frankfurt had waited too long and acted too timidly.

When Frederick William, who really wanted to be emperor but only on his own authoritarian terms, tried to get the small monarchs of Germany to elect him emperor, Austria balked. Supported by Russia, Austria forced Prussia to renounce all its schemes of unification in late 1850. The German Confederation was re-established. Attempts to unite the Germans—first in a liberal national state and then in a conservative Prussian empire—had failed completely.

NATION BUILDING IN FRANCE, ITALY, AND GERMANY

Political, economic, and social pressures building up after 1815 exploded dramatically in 1848. But the upheavals were abortive, and very few revolutionary goals were realized. The moderate, nationalistic middle classes were unable to consolidate their initial victories in France or elsewhere in Europe. Instead, they drew back when artisans, factory workers, and radical socialists rose up to present their own much more revolutionary demands. This retreat made possible the crushing of Parisian workers by a coalition of solid bourgeoisie and landowning peasantry in France, and it facilitated the efforts of dedicated aristocrats in central Europe. A sea of blood and disillusion had washed away the lofty ideals and utopian visions of a generation. Thus the revolutions of 1848 closed one era in the West and opened another.

In thought and culture, exuberant romanticism gave way to hardheaded realism. In the Atlantic economy, the hard years of the 1840s were followed by good times and prosperity throughout most of the 1850s and 1860s. In international politics, the repressive peace and diplomatic stability of Metternich's time were replaced by a period of war and rapid change. Perhaps most important of all, Western society progressively found, for better or worse, a new and effective organizing principle capable of coping with the many-sided challenges of the dual revolution and the emerging urban civilization. That principle was nationalism—dedication to and identification with the nation-state.

The triumph of modern nationalism was an enormously significant historical development. A powerful force since at least 1789, after 1850 nationalism became an almost universal faith in Western society, evolving away from a narrow appeal to predominately middle-class liberals to an intoxicating creed moving the broad masses. Leaders of the entire world eventually embraced large parts of the doctrine of nationalism and the nation-state.

Louis Napoleon in France

France was representative of the general trend. Early nationalism in France was at least liberal and idealistic and often democratic and radical as well. The ideas of nationhood and popular sovereignty, so seductive in France, posed an awesome threat to conservatives like Metternich. Yet from the vantage point of the twentieth century, it is clear that nationalism can flourish in dictatorial states that are conservative, fascist, or communist. In France, Napoleon I had already combined national devotion with authoritarian rule. Significantly, it was Napoleon's nephew, Louis Napoleon, who revived and extended this merger. He showed how governments could reconcile popular and conservative forces in an authoritarian nationalism. In doing so, he provided a model for political leaders elsewhere.

Although Louis Napoleon Bonaparte had played no part in French politics before 1848, universal male suffrage gave him three times as many votes as the four other presidential candidates combined in the French presidential election of December 1848. This outcome occurred for several reasons. First, Louis Napoleon had the great name of his uncle, whom romantics had transformed from a dictator into a demigod as they created a Napoleonic legend after 1820. Second, as Karl Marx stressed at the time, middle-class and peasant property owners feared the socialist challenge of urban workers, and they wanted a tough ruler to provide protection. Third, in late 1848 Louis Napoleon had a positive "program" for France, which was to guide him throughout most of his long reign. This program had been elaborated earlier in pamphlets he had written while imprisoned for an attempt to overthrow Louis Philippe's government. Prior to the presidential election, these pamphlets had been widely circulated.

Above all, Louis Napoleon believed that the government should represent the people and that it should try hard to help them economically. But how were these tasks to be done? Parliaments and political parties were not the answer, according to Louis Napoleon. French politicians represented special-interest groups, particularly middle-class ones. When they ran a parliamentary government, they stirred up class hatred because they were not interested in helping the poor. The answer was a strong, even authoritarian, national leader, like the first Napoleon, who would serve all the people, rich and poor. This leader would be linked to the people by direct democracy, his sovereignty uncorrupted by politicians and legislative bodies. These political ideas went hand in hand with Louis Napoleon's vision of national unity and social progress. Rather than doing nothing or providing only temporary relief for the awful poverty of the poor, the state and its leader had a sacred duty to provide jobs and stimulate the economy. All classes would benefit by such action.

Louis Napoleon's political and social ideas were at least vaguely understood by large numbers of French peasants and workers in December 1848. To many common people he appeared to be a strong man *and* a forward-looking champion of their interests, and that is why they voted for him.

Elected to a four-year term, President Louis Napoleon at first shared power with a conservative National Assembly. But in 1851, after the Assembly failed to change the constitution so he could run for a second term, Louis Napoleon began to organize a conspiracy with key army officers. On December 2, 1851, he illegally dismissed the Assembly and seized power in a coup d'état. Armed resistance in Paris and widespread insurrection in the countryside in southern France were quickly crushed by the army. Louis Napoleon called on the French, as his uncle had done, to legalize his actions. They did: 92 percent voted to make him a strong president for ten years. A year later, 97 percent agreed in a national plebiscite to make him hereditary emperor; for the third time, and by the greatest margin yet, the authoritarian Louis Napoleon was overwhelmingly elected to lead France.

Louis Napoleon—now proclaimed Emperor Napoleon III—experienced both success and failure between 1852 and 1870. His greatest success was with the economy, particularly in the 1850s. His government encouraged the new investment banks and massive railroad construction that were at the heart of the Industrial Revolution in Europe. The government also fostered general economic expansion through an ambitious program of public works, which included the rebuilding of Paris to improve the urban environment. The profits of business people soared with prosperity, and unemployment declined greatly.

Louis Napoleon always hoped that economic progress would reduce social and political tensions. This hope was at least partially realized. Until the mid-1860s, there was considerable support for his government from France's most dissatisfied group, the urban workers. In the 1860s, Napoleon III granted workers the right to form unions and the right to strike—important economic rights denied by earlier governments.

At first, political power remained in the hands of the emperor. He alone chose his ministers, and they had great freedom of action. At the same time, Napoleon III restricted but did not abolish the Assembly. Members were elected by universal male suffrage every six years, and Louis Napoleon and his government took the parliamentary elections very seriously. They tried to entice notable people, even those who had opposed the regime, to stand as government candidates in order to expand the government's base of support. Moreover, the government used its officials and appointed mayors to spread the word that the election of the government's candidates—and the defeat of the opposition—were the key to roads, schools, tax rebates, and a thousand other local concerns.

In 1857 and again in 1863, Louis Napoleon's system worked brilliantly and produced overwhelming electoral victories. Yet in the 1860s, Napoleon III's electoral system gradually disintegrated. France's problems in Italy and the rising power of Prussia led to increasing criticism at home from his Catholic and nationalist supporters. With growing effectiveness, the middle-class liberals who had always wanted a less authoritarian regime continued to denounce his rule.

Napoleon was always sensitive to the public mood. Public opinion, he once said, always wins the last victory. Thus in the 1860s, he progressively liberalized his empire. He gave the Assembly greater powers and the opposition candidates greater freedom, which they used to good advantage. In 1869 the opposition, consisting of republicans, monarchists, and liberals, polled almost 45 percent of the vote.

The next year, a sick and weary Louis Napoleon again granted France a new constitution, which combined a basically parliamentary regime with a hereditary emperor as chief of state. In a final great plebiscite on the eve of a disastrous war with Prussia, 7.5 million Frenchmen voted in favor of the new constitution, and only 1.5 million opposed it. Napoleon III's attempt to reconcile a strong national state with universal male suffrage was still evolving and was doing so in a democratic direction.

Cavour, Garibaldi, and the Unification of Italy

Italy had never been a united nation prior to 1860. Part of Rome's great empire in ancient times, the Italian peninsula was divided in the Middle Ages into competing city-states, and it became a battleground for great powers after 1494. Italy was reorganized in 1815 at the Congress of Vienna. The rich northern provinces of Lombardy and Venetia were taken by Metternich's Austria. Sardinia and Piedmont were under the rule of an Italian monarch, and Tuscany, with its famous capital of Florence, shared north-central Italy with several smaller states. Central Italy and Rome were ruled by the papacy. Naples and Sicily were ruled by a branch of the Bourbons. Metternich was not wrong in dismissing Italy as "a geographical expression" (Map 25.3).

Between 1815 and 1848, the goal of a unified Italian nation captured the imaginations of increasing numbers of Italians. There were three basic approaches. The first was the radical program of the idealistic patriot Giuseppe Mazzini, who preached a centralized democratic republic based on universal suffrage and the will of the people (see pages 840–841). The second was that of Vincenzo Gioberti, a Catholic priest who called for a federation of existing states under the presidency of a progressive pope. The third was the program of those who looked for leadership toward the autocratic kingdom of Sardinia-Piedmont, much as many Germans looked toward Prussia.

The third alternative was strengthened by the failures of 1848, when an Austrian army smashed Italian revolutionaries in Austria's possessions in northern Italy and discredited Mazzini's republicanism. Almost by accident, independent Sardinia's monarch, Victor Emmanuel, retained the moderate liberal constitution granted under duress in March 1848. To the Italian middle classes, Sardinia appeared to be a liberal, progressive state ideally suited to achieve the goal of national unification. By contrast, Mazzini's brand of democratic republicanism seemed quixotic and too radical. As for the papacy, the initial cautious support by Pope Pius IX (r. 1846–1878) for unification had given way to fear and hostility after he was temporarily driven from Rome during the upheavals of 1848. For a long generation, the papacy would stand resolutely opposed not only to national unification but also to most modern trends. In 1864 in the *Syllabus of Errors,* Pius IX strongly denounced rationalism, socialism, separation of church and state, and religious liberty, denying that "the Roman pontiff can and ought to reconcile and align himself with progress, liberalism, and modern civilization."

Sardinia had the good fortune of being led by a brilliant statesman, Count Camillo Benso di

MAP 25.3 Unification of Italy, 1859–1870   The leadership of Sardinia-
Piedmont and nationalist fervor were decisive factors in the unification of Italy.

Cavour, the dominant figure in the Sardinian government from 1850 until his death in 1861. Indicative of the coming tacit alliance between the
aristocracy and the solid middle class under the
banner of the strong nation-state, Cavour came

from a noble family and embraced the economic
doctrines and business activities associated with the
prosperous middle class. Before entering politics,
he made a substantial fortune in sugar mills,
steamships, banks, and railroads. Cavour's national

goals were limited and realistic. Until 1859 he sought unity only for the states of northern and perhaps central Italy in a greatly expanded kingdom of Sardinia. He did not seek to incorporate the Papal States or the kingdom of the Two Sicilies, with their very different cultures and governments, into an Italy of all the Italians.

In the 1850s, Cavour worked to consolidate Sardinia as a liberal constitutional state capable of leading northern Italy. His program of highways and railroads, of civil liberties and opposition to clerical privilege, increased support for Sardinia throughout northern Italy. Yet Cavour realized that Sardinia could not drive Austria out of Lombardy and Venetia and unify northern Italy under Victor Emmanuel without the help of a powerful ally. Accordingly, he worked for a secret diplomatic alliance with Napoleon III against Austria. Finally, in July 1858 he succeeded and goaded Austria into attacking Sardinia. Napoleon III came to Sardinia's defense. Then after the victory of the combined Franco-Sardinian forces, Napoleon III did a complete about-face. Nauseated by the gore of war and criticized by French Catholics for supporting the pope's declared enemy, Napoleon III abandoned Cavour. He made a compromise peace with the Austrians in July 1859. Sardinia would receive only Lombardy, the area around Milan. The rest of the

Garibaldi and Victor Emmanuel   The historic meeting in Naples between the leader of Italy's revolutionary nationalists and the king of Sardinia sealed the unification of northern and southern Italy in a unitary state. With only the sleeve of his red shirt showing, Garibaldi offers his hand—and his conquests—to the uniformed king and his moderate monarchial government. (*Source: Fabio Lensini/Madeline Grimoldi*)

map of Italy would remain essentially unchanged. Cavour resigned in a rage.

Popular revolts and Italian nationalism salvaged Cavour's plans. While the war against Austria had raged in the north, dedicated nationalists in central Italy had risen and driven out their rulers. Nationalist fervor seized the urban masses, and the leaders of the nationalist movement called for fusion with Sardinia. This was not at all what France and the other Great Powers wanted, but the nationalists held firm and eventually had their way. Cavour returned to power in early 1860, and the people of central Italy voted overwhelmingly to join a greatly enlarged kingdom of Sardinia. Cavour had achieved his original goal of a north Italian state (see Map 25.3).

For superpatriots such as Giuseppe Garibaldi (1807–1882), the job of unification was still only half done. The son of a poor sailor, Garibaldi personified the romantic, revolutionary nationalism of Mazzini and 1848. Sentenced to death in 1834 for his part in an uprising in Genoa, Garibaldi escaped to South America. For twelve years, he led a guerrilla band in Uruguay's struggle for independence. Along the way, he found in a tough young woman, Anna da Silva, a mate and companion-in-arms. Their first children nearly starved in the jungle while Garibaldi, clad in his long red shirt, fashioned a revolutionary legend for himself. Returning to Italy to fight in 1848 and leading a corps of volunteers against Austria in 1859, Garibaldi emerged in 1860 as a powerful independent force in Italian politics.

Partly to use him and partly to get rid of him, Cavour secretly supported Garibaldi's bold plan to "liberate" the kingdom of the Two Sicilies. Landing on the shores of Sicily in May 1860, Garibaldi's guerrilla band of a thousand "Red Shirts" captured the imagination of the Sicilian peasantry. Outwitting the twenty-thousand-man royal army, the guerrilla leader took Palermo. Then he and his men crossed to the mainland, marched triumphantly toward Naples, and prepared to attack Rome and the pope. But the wily Cavour quickly sent Sardinian forces to occupy most of the Papal States (but not Rome) and to intercept Garibaldi.

Cavour realized that an attack on Rome would bring about war with France, and he also feared Garibaldi's popular appeal. Thus he immediately organized a plebiscite in the conquered territories.

Despite the urging of some more radical supporters, the patriotic Garibaldi did not oppose Cavour, and the people of the south voted to join Sardinia. When Garibaldi and Victor Emmanuel rode through Naples to cheering crowds, they symbolically sealed the union of north and south, of monarch and people.

Cavour had succeeded. He had controlled Garibaldi and had turned popular nationalism in a conservative direction. The new kingdom of Italy, which did not include Venice until 1866 or Rome until 1870, was a parliamentary monarchy under Victor Emmanuel, neither radical nor democratic. Only a small minority of Italian males had the right to vote. Despite political unity, the propertied classes and the common people were divided. A great and growing social and cultural gap separated the progressive, industrializing north from the stagnant, agrarian south.

Bismarck and German Unification

In the aftermath of 1848 the German states were locked in a political stalemate. After Austria and Russia had blocked Frederick William's attempt to unify Germany "from above," tension grew between Austria and Prussia as each power sought to block the other within the German Confederation. Stalemate and reaction also prevailed in the domestic politics of the individual German states in the 1850s.

At the same time, powerful economic forces were undermining the political status quo. Modern industry grew rapidly within the German customs union (*Zollverein*), founded officially in 1834 to stimulate trade and increase the revenues of member states. By the end of 1853 all the German states except Austria had joined the customs union, and a new Germany excluding Austria was becoming an economic reality. Prussia's leading role in the Zollverein gave it a valuable advantage in its struggle against Austria's supremacy in German political affairs.

The national uprising in Italy in 1859 made a profound impression in Prussia. Great political change and war—perhaps with Austria, perhaps with France—seemed quite possible. Along with his top military advisers, the tough-minded William I of Prussia (r. 1861–1888), who had replaced the unstable Frederick William IV as regent in

Otto von Bismarck The commanding presence and the fierce pride of the Prussian statesman are evident in this photo taken shortly before he came to power. Dressed in formal diplomatic attire as Prussia's ambassador in Paris, Bismarck is perhaps on his way to see Emperor Louis Napoleon and size up his future adversary. *(Source: Archiv für Kunst und Geschichte, Berlin)*

parliament, not the king, had the ultimate political power. They also wanted to ensure that the army was responsible to Prussia's elected representatives and was not a "state within a state." These demands were popular. The parliament rejected the military budget in 1862, and the liberals triumphed completely. King William then called on Count Otto von Bismarck to head a new ministry and defy the parliament. This was a momentous choice.

The most important figure in German history between Luther and Hitler, Otto von Bismarck (1815–1898) has been the object of enormous interest and debate. A great hero to some, a great villain to others, Bismarck was above all a master of politics. Born into the Prussian landowning aristocracy, the young Bismarck was a wild and tempestuous student given to duels and drinking. Proud of his Junker heritage and always devoted to his Prussian sovereign, Bismarck had a strong personality and an unbounded desire for power. Yet in his drive to secure power for himself and for Prussia, Bismarck was extraordinarily flexible and pragmatic. "One must always have two irons in the fire," he once said. He kept his options open, pursuing one policy and then another as he moved with skill and cunning toward his goal.

Bismarck first honed his political skills as a diplomat. Acquiring a reputation as an ultraconservative in the Prussian Assembly in 1848, he fought against Austria as the Prussian ambassador to the German Confederation from 1851 to 1859. Transferred next to St. Petersburg and then to Paris, he worked to build up Prussia's strength and consolidate Prussia's precarious Great Power status.

When Bismarck took office as chief minister in 1862, his appointment made a strong but unfavorable impression. His speeches were a sensation and a scandal. Declaring that the government would rule without parliamentary consent, Bismarck lashed out at the middle-class opposition: "The great questions of the day will not be decided by speeches and resolutions—that was the blunder of 1848 and 1849—but by blood and iron." Denounced for this view that "might makes right," Bismarck had the Prussian bureaucracy go right on collecting taxes even though the parliament refused to approve the budget. Bismarck reorganized the army. And for four years, from 1862 to 1866, the voters of Prussia continued to express their opposition by sending large liberal majorities to the parliament.

1858 and become king himself in 1861, was convinced of the need for major army reforms and wanted to double the size of the regular army. Army reforms meant a bigger defense budget and higher taxes.

Prussia had emerged from 1848 with a parliament of sorts, the Prussian Assembly, which was in the hands of the liberal middle class by 1859. The wealthy middle class wanted society to be less, not more, militaristic. Above all, middle-class representatives wanted to establish once and for all that the

THE ERA OF NATION BUILDING IN EUROPE, 1850–1871

1851	Louis Napoleon dismisses French National Assembly in coup d'état
1852–1870	Second Empire in France
1853–1856	Crimean War
1859–1870	Unification of Italy
1861	Abolition of serfdom in Russia
1862–1890	Bismarck's reign of power in German affairs
1864–1871	First Socialist International
1866	Prussia wins decisive victory in Austro-Prussian War
1866–1871	Unification of the German Empire
1867	Magyar nobility increases its power by restoring the constitution of 1848 in Hungary, thereby further dividing the Austro-Hungarian Empire Marx, *Capital* Second Reform Bill passed by British Parliament
1870–1871	Prussia wins decisive victory in Franco-Prussian War; William I proclaimed emperor of a united Germany
1871	Paris Commune

Opposition at home spurred the search for success abroad. The ever-knotty question of Schleswig-Holstein provided a welcome opportunity. When the Danish king tried again, as in 1848, to bring the provinces into a centralized Danish state, Prussia joined Austria in a short and successful war against Denmark in 1864. However, Bismarck was convinced that Prussia had to control completely the northern, predominantly Protestant part of the German Confederation, which meant expelling Austria from German affairs. After the victory over Denmark, Bismarck's skillful maneuvering had Prussia in position to force Austria out by war, if necessary. Bismarck knew that a war with Austria would have to be a localized one that would not provoke a mighty alliance against Prussia. Russia was no problem because Bismarck had gained Alexander II's gratitude by supporting Russia's repression of a Polish uprising in 1863. Napoleon III—the "sphinx without a riddle," according to Bismarck—was charmed into neutrality with vague promises of more territory along the Rhine. Thus when Austria proved unwilling to give up its his-

toric role in German affairs, Bismarck was in a position to engage in a war of his own making.

The Austro-Prussian War of 1866 lasted only seven weeks. Utilizing railroads to mass troops and the new breechloading needle gun to achieve maximum firepower, the reorganized Prussian army overran northern Germany and defeated Austria decisively at the Battle of Sadowa in Bohemia. Anticipating Prussia's future needs, Bismarck offered Austria realistic, even generous, peace terms. Austria paid no reparations and lost no territory to Prussia, although Venice was ceded to Italy. But the German Confederation was dissolved, and Austria agreed to withdraw from German affairs. The states north of the Main River were grouped in the new North German Confederation, led by an expanded Prussia. The mainly Catholic states of the south remained independent while forming alliances with Prussia. Bismarck's fundamental goal of Prussian expansion was being realized (Map 25.4).

Bismarck had long been convinced that the old order he so ardently defended should make peace,

MAP 25.4 Unification of Germany, 1866–1871   Prussian expansion, Austrian expulsion from the old German Confederation, and the creation of a new German Empire went hand in hand. Austria lost no territory, but Prussia's neighbors in the north suffered grievously or simply disappeared. The annexation of Alsace-Lorraine turned France into an enemy of Germany before 1914.

on its own conservative terms, with the liberal middle class and the nationalist movement. Moreover, Bismarck believed that because of the events of 1848, the German middle class could eventually be led to prefer the reality of national unity under conservative leadership to a long, uncertain battle for truly liberal institutions. Thus during the attack on Austria in 1866, he increasingly identified Prussia's fate with the "national development of Germany."

In the aftermath of victory, Bismarck fashioned a federal constitution for the new North German Confederation. Each state retained its own local government, but the king of Prussia became president of the Confederation and the chancellor—Bismarck—was responsible only to the president. The federal government—William I and Bismarck—controlled the army and foreign affairs. There was also a legislature consisting of two houses that shared equally in the making of laws. Delegates to the upper house were appointed by the different states, but members of the lower house were elected by universal, single category, male suffrage. With this radical innovation, Bismarck opened the door to popular participation and the possibility of going over the head of the middle class directly to the people, much as Napoleon III had done in France. All the while, however, ultimate power rested as securely as ever in the hands of Prussia and its king and army.

In Prussia itself Bismarck held out an olive branch to the parliamentary opposition. Marshaling all his diplomatic skill, he asked the parliament to pass a special indemnity bill to approve after the fact all of the government's spending between 1862 and 1866. Most of the liberals snatched at the chance to cooperate. For four long years, they had opposed and criticized Bismarck's "illegal" measures. Yet Bismarck, the king, and the army with its aristocratic leadership had in the end succeeded beyond the wildest dreams of the liberal middle class. In 1866 German unity was in sight, and the people were going to be allowed to participate actively in the new state.

Many liberals repented their "sins," and none more ardently than Hermann Baumgarten, a thoroughly decent history professor and member of the liberal opposition. In his essay "A Self-Criticism of German Liberalism," he confessed in 1866: "We thought by agitation we could transform Germany. . . . Yet we have experienced a miracle almost without parallel. The victory of our principles would have brought us misery, whereas the defeat of our principles has brought boundless salvation."[5] The constitutional struggle was over. The German middle class was bowing respectfully before Bismarck and the monarchial authority and aristocratic superiority he represented.

The final act in the drama of German unification followed quickly. Bismarck realized that a patriotic war with France would drive the south German states into his arms. The French obligingly played their part. The apparent issue—whether a distant relative of Prussia's William I (and France's Napoleon III) might become king of Spain—was only a diplomatic pretext. By 1870 the French leaders of the Second Empire, alarmed by their powerful new neighbor on the Rhine, had decided on a war to teach Prussia a lesson.

As soon as war against France began in 1870, Bismarck had the wholehearted support of the south German states. With other governments standing still—Bismarck's generosity to Austria in 1866 was paying big dividends—German forces under Prussian leadership decisively defeated Louis Napoleon's armies at Sedan on September 1, 1870. Three days later, French patriots in Paris proclaimed yet another French republic (the third) and vowed to continue fighting. But after five months, in January 1871, a starving Paris surrendered, and France went on to accept Bismarck's harsh peace terms. By this time, the south German states had agreed to join a new German empire. The victorious William I was proclaimed emperor of Germany in the Hall of Mirrors in the palace of Versailles. Europe had a nineteenth-century German "sun king." As in the 1866 constitution, the king of Prussia and his ministers had ultimate power in the new German Empire, and the lower house of the legislature was elected by universal male suffrage.

The Franco-Prussian War, which Europeans generally saw as a test of nations in a pitiless Darwinian struggle for existence, released an enormous surge of patriotic feeling in Germany. Bismarck's genius, the invincible Prussian army, the solidarity of king and people in a unified nation—these and similar themes were trumpeted endlessly during and after the war. The weakest of the Great Powers in 1862 (after Austria, Britain, France, and Russia), Prussia had become the most powerful state in Europe in less than a decade. Most

Germans were enormously proud, blissfully imagining themselves the fittest and best of the European species. Semi-authoritarian nationalism and a "new conservatism," which was based on an alliance of the properties classes and sought the active support of the working classes, had triumphed in Germany.

SUMMARY

In 1814 the victorious allied powers sought to restore peace and stability in Europe. Dealing moderately with France and wisely settling their own differences, the allies laid the foundations for beneficial international cooperation throughout much of the nineteenth century. Led by Metternich, the conservative powers also sought to prevent the spread of subversive ideas and radical changes in domestic politics. Yet European thought has seldom been more powerfully creative than after 1815, and ideologies of liberalism, nationalism, and socialism all developed to challenge the existing order. The romantic movement, breaking decisively with the dictates of classicism, reinforced the spirit of change and revolutionary anticipation.

All of these forces culminated in the liberal and nationalistic revolutions of 1848. Political, economic, and social pressures that had been building since 1815 exploded dramatically. Yet the failed upheavals of 1848 realized very few revolutionary goals. The moderate middle classes were unable to consolidate their initial victories. Instead, they drew back in fear when artisans, factory workers, and radical socialists rose up to present their own much more revolutionary demands.

This retreat facilitated a resurgence of conservative forces that crushed revolution all across Europe. These conservative forces then took the lead in refashioning politics after 1850, relying on strong rule that was fortified by popular nationalism at critical moments. Thus larger, more unified, and more popular states emerged in the West, and support for the nation appeared to provide the basis for a stabilizing response to the profoundly unsettling challenges of the dual revolution.

NOTES

1. Quoted in H. Kohn, *Nationalism* (New York: Van Nostrand, 1955), pp. 141–142.

2. Quoted in F. D. Klingender, *Art and the Industrial Revolution* (St. Albans, Eng.: Paladin, 1972), p. 117.
3. M. Agulhon, *1848* (Paris: Éditions du Seuil, 1973), pp. 68–69.
4. Quoted in W. L. Langer, *Political and Social Upheaval, 1832–1852* (New York: Harper & Row, 1969), p. 361.
5. Quoted in H. Kohn, *The Mind of Germany: The Education of a Nation* (New York: Charles Scribner's Sons/Macmillan, 1960), p. 159.

SUGGESTED READING

All of the works cited in the Notes are highly recommended. Kohn has written perceptively on nationalism in many books, and Langer's book is a balanced synthesis with an excellent bibliography. Among general studies, C. Morazé, *The Triumph of the Middle Classes* (1968), a wide-ranging procapitalist interpretation, may be compared with E. J. Hobsbawm's flexible Marxism in *The Age of Revolution, 1789–1848* (1962). Two important reconsiderations of nationalism are B. Anderson, *Imagined Communities,* 2d ed. (1991), and E. Hobsbawm and T. Ranger, *The Invention of Tradition* (1990). E. Kedourie, *Nationalism* (1960), is an influential historical critique of the new faith. H. Kissinger, *A World Restored* (1957), offers not only a provocative interpretation of the Congress of Vienna but also insights into the mind of Richard Nixon's famous secretary of state. Compare that volume with H. Nicolson's entertaining *The Congress of Vienna* (1946). On 1848, P. Robertson, *Revolutions of 1848: A Social History* (1960), is outstanding, and I. Deak, *The Lawful Revolution: Louis Kossuth and the Hungarians, 1848–49* (1979), is a noteworthy study of an interesting figure.

On early socialism and Marxism, there are A. Lindemann's stimulating survey, *A History of European Socialism* (1983), and W. Sewell, Jr.'s *Work and Revolution in France: The Language of Labor from the Old Regime to 1848* (1980) as well as G. Lichtheim's high-powered *Marxism* (1961) and his *Short History of Socialism* (1970). J. Seigel, *Marx's Fate: The Shape of a Life* (1978), is an outstanding biography. Fourier is treated sympathetically in J. Beecher, *Charles Fourier* (1986). J. Schumpeter, *Capitalism, Socialism and Democracy* (1947), is important but challenging, a real mind-stretcher. Also highly recommended is B. Taylor, *Eve and the New Jerusalem: Socialism and Feminism in the Nineteenth Century* (1983), which explores fascinating English attempts to emancipate workers and women at the same time. On liberalism, there are R. Heilbroner's entertaining *The Worldly Philosophers* (1967) and G. de Ruggiero's classic *History of Euro-*

pean Liberalism (1959). J. Barzun, *Classic, Romantic and Modern* (1961), skillfully discusses the emergence of romanticism, and J. Seigel, *Bohemian Paris: Culture, Politics, and the Boundaries of Bourgeois Life* (1986), imaginatively places romantic aspirations in a broad cultural framework. R. Stromberg, *An Intellectual History of Modern Europe,* 3d ed. (1981), is a valuable survey. The important place of religion in nineteenth-century thought is considered from different perspectives in H. McLeod, *Religion and the People of Western Europe* (1981), and O. Chadwick, *The Secularization of the European Mind in the Nineteenth Century* (1976). Two good church histories with useful bibliographies are J. Altholz, *The Churches in the Nineteenth Century* (1967), and A. Vidler, *The Church in an Age of Revolution: 1789 to the Present Day* (1961).

For English history, A. Briggs's socially oriented *The Making of Modern England, 1784 -1867* (1967) and D. Thomson's *England in the Nineteenth Century, 1815–1914* (1951), are excellent. Restoration France is sympathetically portrayed by G. de Bertier de Sauvigny in *The Bourbon Restoration* (1967), whereas R. Price, *A Social History of Nineteenth-Century France* (1987), is a fine synthesis incorporating recent research. D. Harvey, *Napoleon III and His Comic Empire* (1988), brings the world of Napoleon III vibrantly alive. Émile Zola's novel *The Debacle* treats the Franco-Prussian War realistically. D. M. Smith has written widely on Italy, and his *Garibaldi* (1956) and *Italy: A Modern History,* rev. ed. (1969), are recommended. Two stimulating general histories of Germany that skillfully incorporate recent research are H. James, *A German Identity, 1770–1990* (1989), and J. Sheehan, *Germany, 1770–1866* (1989), which may be compared with H. Treitschke's bombastic, pro-Prussian *History of Germany in the Nineteenth Century* (1915–1919), a classic of nationalistic history. O.

Pflanze, *Bismarck and the Development of Germany,* (1963), and E. Eyck, *Bismarck and the German Empire* (1964), are excellent biographies. H. Glasser, ed., *The German Mind in the Nineteenth Century* (1981), is an outstanding anthology, as are R. E. Joeres and M. Maynes, eds., *German Women in the Eighteenth and Nineteenth Centuries* (1986), and P. Mendes-Flohr, ed., *The Jew in the Modern World: A Documentary History* (1980). A. Sked, *The Decline and Fall of the Habsburg Empire, 1815–1918* (1989), and R. Kann, *The Multinational Empire,* 2 vols. (1950, 1964), probe the intricacies of the nationality problem in Austria-Hungary.

The thoughtful reader is strongly advised to delve into the rich writing of contemporaries. J. Bowditch and C. Ramsland, eds., *Voices of the Industrial Revolution* (1961), is an excellent starting point, with well-chosen selections from leading economic thinkers and early socialists. H. Hugo, ed., *The Romantic Reader,* is another fine anthology. Mary Shelley's *Frankenstein,* a great romantic novel, draws an almost lovable picture of the famous monster and is highly recommended. Jules Michelet's compassionate masterpiece *The People* is a famous historian's anguished examination of French social divisions on the eve of 1848. Alexis de Tocqueville covers some of the same ground less romantically in his *Recollections,* which may be compared with Karl Marx's white-hot "instant history," *Class Struggles in France, 1848–1850* (1850). Great novels that accurately portray aspects of the times are Victor Hugo, *Les Misérables,* an exciting story of crime and passion among France's poor; Honoré de Balzac, *La Cousine Bette* and *Le Père Goriot*; and Thomas Mann, *Buddenbrooks,* a wonderful historical novel that traces the rise and fall of a prosperous German family over three generations during the nineteenth century.

Faith in Democratic Nationalism

Early advocates of the national ideal usually believed that progress for one people would contribute to the progress of all humanity. They believed that a Europe of independent nation-states would provide the proper framework for securing freedom, democracy, social justice, and even international peace.

This optimistic faith guided Giuseppe Mazzini (1805–1872), the leading prophet of Italian nationalism and unification. Banished from Italy in 1830, the exiled Mazzini founded a secret society called Young Italy to fight for Italian unification and a democratic republic. Mazzini's group inspired numerous local insurrections and then led Italy's radicals in the unsuccessful revolutions of 1848. Italy was united a decade later, but by other means.

Mazzini's best known work was The Duties of Man, *a collection of essays. The following selection, entitled "Duties Towards Your Country," was written in 1858 and addressed to Italian working men.*

Your first Duties . . . are to Humanity. . . . But what can each of you, with his isolated powers, do for the moral improvement, for the progress of Humanity? . . .

God gave you the means of multiplying your forces and your powers of action indefinitely when he gave you a Country, when, like a wise overseer of labor, who distributes the different parts of the work according to the capacity of the workmen, he divided Humanity into distinct groups upon the face of our globe, and thus planted the seeds of nations. Evil governments have disfigured the design of God, which you may see clearly marked out, as far, at least, as regards Europe, by the courses of the great rivers, by the lines of the lofty mountains, and by other geographical conditions; they have disfigured it by conquest, by greed, by jealousy of the just sovereignty of others; disfigured it so much that today there is perhaps no nation except England and France whose confines correspond to this design.

[These evil governments] did not, and they do not, recognize any country except their own families and dynasties, the egoism of caste. But the divine design will infallibly be fulfilled. Natural divisions, the innate spontaneous tendencies of the peoples will replace the arbitrary divisions sanctioned by evil governments. The map of Europe will be remade. The Countries of the People will rise, defined by the voice of the free, upon the ruins of the Countries of Kings and privileged castes. Between these Countries there will be harmony and brotherhood. And then the work of Humanity for the general amelioration, for the discovery and application of the real law of life, carried on in association and distributed according to local capacities, will be accomplished by peaceful and progressive development.

Then each of you, strong in the affections and in the aid of many millions of men speaking the same language, endowed with the same tendencies, and educated by the same historic tradition, may hope by your personal effort to benefit the whole of Humanity.

Without Country you have neither name, voice, nor rights, no admission as brothers into the fellowship of the Peoples. You are the bastards of Humanity. Soldiers without a banner, . . . you will find neither faith nor protection. . . . Do not beguile yourselves with the hope of emancipation from unjust social conditions if you do not first conquer a Country for yourselves; where there is no Country there is no common agreement to which you can appeal; the egoism of self-interest rules alone, and he who has the upper hand keeps it, since there is no common safeguard for the interests of all. . . .

O my Brothers! love your Country. Our Country is our home, the home which God has given us, placing therein a numerous family which we love and are loved by.... In labouring according to true principles for our Country we are labouring for Humanity; our Country is the fulcrum of the lever which we have to wield for the common good. If we give up this fulcrum we run the risk of becoming useless to our Country and to Humanity.
...

There is no true Country without a uniform law. There is no true Country where the uniformity of that law is violated by the existence of caste, privilege, and inequality, where the powers and faculties of a large number of individuals arc suppressed or dormant, where there is no common principle accepted, recognized, and developed by all. In such a state of things there can be no Nation, no People, but only a multitude, a fortuitous agglomeration of men whom circumstances have brought together and different circumstances will separate. In the name of your love for your Country you must combat without truce the existence of every privilege, every inequality, upon the soil which has given you birth....

Your Country should be your Temple. God at the summit, a People of equals at the base. Do not accept any other formula, any other moral law, if you do not want to dishonour your Country and yourselves. Let the secondary laws for the gradual regulation of your existence be the progressive application of this supreme law.

And in order that they should be so, it is necessary that *all* should contribute to the making of them. The laws made by one fraction of the citizens only can never by the nature of things and men do otherwise than reflect the thoughts and aspirations and desires of that fraction; they represent, not the whole country, but a third, a fourth part, a class, a zone of the country. The law must express the general aspiration, promote the good of all, respond to a beat of the nation's heart. The whole nation therefore should be, directly or indirectly, the legislator. By yielding this mission to a few men, you put the egoism of one class in the place of the Country, which is the union of *all* the classes.

A Country is not a mere territory; the particular territory is only its foundation. The Country is the idea which rises upon that

Portrait of Giuseppe Mazzini *(Source: Museo del Risorgimento, Scala/Art Resource, NY)*

foundation; it is the sentiment of love, the sense of fellowship which binds together all the sons of that territory.

So long as a single one of your brothers is not represented by his own vote in the development of the national life—so long as a single one vegetates uneducated among the educated—so long as a single one able and willing to work languishes in poverty for want of work—you have not got a Country such as it ought to be, the Country of all and for all.

Votes, education, work are the three main pillars of the nation; do not rest until your hands have solidly erected them.

Questions for Analysis

1. What did Mazzini mean by "evil governments"? Why are they evil?

2. What are the characteristics of "the true country"?

3. What form of government is best? Why?

4. Why, according to Mazzini, should poor working men have been interested in the political unification of Italy?

5. How might a woman today criticize Mazzini's program? Debate how Mazzini might respond to such criticism.

Source: Slightly adapted from J. Mazzini, *The Duties of Man and Other Essays* (London: J. M. Dent and Sons, 1907), pp. 51–57.

26

European Life in the Age of Nationalism

A painting by Gustav Klimt (1862–1918) of the old Burgtheater in Vienna. *(Source: Museen der Stadt Wien)*

After 1848, as identification with the nation-state was becoming one of the basic organizing principles of Western society, the growth of towns and cities rushed forward with undiminished force. In 1900 Western society was urban and industrial as surely as it had been rural and agrarian in 1800. This rapid urbanization, both a result of the Industrial Revolution and a key element in its enormous long-term impact, posed pressing practical problems that governments had to deal with. Eventual success with urban problems encouraged people to look to government as a problem solver and put their faith in a responsive national state. Even socialists forming international alliances were not exempt from the trend.

- How did life in cities change?
- What did the emergence of urban industrial society mean for rich and poor and those in between?
- How did families change as they coped with the developing urban civilization?
- What changes in science and culture reflected and influenced this new civilization?
- How did governments respond to problems and try to win the support of politically active citizens?

These are the questions this chapter will investigate.

CITIES AND SOCIAL CLASSES

The growth of industry posed enormous challenges for all elements of Western society, from young factory workers confronting relentless discipline to aristocratic elites maneuvering to retain political power. As we saw in Chapter 23, the early consequences of economic transformation were mixed and far-reaching and by no means wholly negative. By 1850 at the latest, working conditions were improving and real wages were rising for the mass of the population, and they continued to do so until 1914. Given the poverty and uncertainty of preindustrial life, some historians maintain that the history of European industrialization in the nineteenth century is probably better written in terms of increasing opportunities than of greater

hardships. Critics of this relatively optimistic view of industrialization claim that it neglects the quality of life in urban areas, where poor people especially suffered from bad housing, lack of sanitation, and a sense of hopelessness. Did not these drawbacks more than cancel out higher wages and greater opportunity? An examination of cities in the nineteenth century provides some answers to this complex question.

Industry and the Growth of Cities

Since the Middle Ages, European cities had been centers of government, culture, and large-scale commerce. They had also been congested, dirty, and unhealthy. People were packed together almost as tightly as possible within the city limits. The typical city was a "walking city": for all but the wealthiest classes, walking was the only available form of transportation. Infectious disease spread with deadly speed in cities, and people were always more likely to die in the city than in the countryside.

Clearly, deplorable urban conditions did not originate with the Industrial Revolution. What the Industrial Revolution did was to reveal those conditions more nakedly than ever before. The steam engine freed industrialists from dependence on the energy of fast-flowing streams and rivers, so by 1800 there was every incentive to build new factories in urban areas. Cities had better shipping facilities than the countryside and thus better supplies of coal and raw materials. There were also many hands wanting work in the cities, for cities drew people like a magnet. Therefore, as industry grew, there was also a rapid expansion of already overcrowded and unhealthy cities.

The challenge of the urban environment was felt first and most acutely in Great Britain. The number of people living in cities of 20,000 or more in England and Wales jumped from 1.5 million in 1801 to 6.3 million in 1851 and reached 15.6 million in 1891. Such cities accounted for 17 percent of the total English population in 1801, 35 percent as early as 1851, and fully 54 percent in 1891. Other countries duplicated the English pattern as they industrialized. An American observer was hardly exaggerating when he wrote in 1899 that "the most remarkable social phenomenon of the present century is the concentration of population in cities" (Map 26.1).[1]

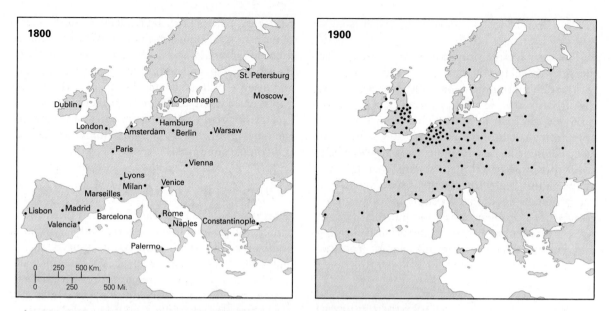

MAP 26.1 European Cities of 100,000 or More in 1800 and 1900   There were more large cities in Great Britain in 1900 than in all of Europe in 1800. Northwestern Europe was the most urbanized area.

In the 1820s and 1830s, people in Britain and France began to worry about the condition of their cities. With urban areas expanding at such previously undreamed-of rates, people's fatalistic acceptance of overcrowded, unsanitary urban living conditions began to give way to active concern.

On one point everyone could agree: except on the outskirts, each town or city was using every scrap of land to the fullest extent. Parks and open areas for exercise and recreation were almost nonexistent. Buildings were erected on the smallest possible lots in order to pack the maximum number of people into a given space. Narrow houses were built wall to wall in long rows. These row houses had neither front nor back yards, and only a narrow alley in back separated one row from the next. Or buildings were built around tiny courtyards completely enclosed on all four sides. Many people lived in extremely small, often overcrowded cellars or attics. "Six, eight, and even ten occupying one room is anything but uncommon," wrote a doctor from Aberdeen in Scotland for a government investigation in 1842.

These highly concentrated urban populations lived in extremely unsanitary and unhealthy conditions. Open drains and sewers flowed alongside or down the middle of unpaved streets. Toilet facilities were primitive in the extreme. In parts of Man-chester, as many as two hundred people shared a single outhouse. Such privies filled up rapidly, and sewage often overflowed and seeped into cellar dwellings. Moreover, some courtyards in the poorest neighborhoods became dunghills, collecting excrement that was sometimes sold as fertilizer. By the 1840s there was among the better-off classes a growing, shocking "realization that, to put it as mildly as possible, millions of English men, women, and children were living in shit."[2]

Who or what was responsible for these awful conditions? The crucial factors were the tremendous pressure of more people and the total absence of public transportation. People simply had to jam themselves together if they were to be able to walk to shops and factories. Another factor was that government, often uncertain how best to approach the problems, was slow to provide sanitary facilities and establish adequate building codes. Even many continental cities with strong traditions of municipal regulation were beset by overcrowded and unhealthy conditions. Also responsible was the sad legacy of rural housing conditions in preindustrial society. As one authority concludes, "the decent cottage was the exception, the hovel the rule."[3] Thus housing was far down on the newcomer's list of priorities, and ordinary people generally took dirt and dung for granted.

Public Health and the Bacterial Revolution

Although cleanliness was not next to godliness in most people's eyes, it was becoming so for some reformers. The most famous of these was Edwin Chadwick, one of the commissioners charged with the administration of relief to paupers under Britain's revised Poor Law of 1834. Chadwick was a good *Benthamite*—that is, a follower of radical philosopher Jeremy Bentham (1748–1832). Bentham had taught that public problems ought to be dealt with on a rational, scientific basis and according to the "greatest good for the greatest number." Applying these principles, Chadwick soon became convinced that disease and death actually caused poverty simply because a sick worker was an unemployed worker and orphaned children were poor children. Most important, Chadwick believed that disease could be prevented by cleaning up the urban environment. That was his "sanitary idea."

Building on a growing number of medical and sociological studies, Chadwick collected detailed reports from local Poor Law officials on the "sanitary conditions of the laboring population" and published his hard-hitting findings in 1842. This mass of widely publicized evidence proved that disease was related to filthy environmental conditions, which were in turn caused largely by lack of drainage, sewers, and garbage collection. Putrefying, smelly excrement was worse than just revolting. It polluted the atmosphere and caused disease.

Chadwick correctly believed that the stinking excrement of communal outhouses could be dependably carried off by water through sewers at less than one-twentieth the cost of removing it by hand. The cheap iron pipes and tile drains of the industrial age would provide running water and sewerage for all sections of town, not just the wealthy ones. In 1848, with the cause strengthened by the cholera epidemic of 1846, Chadwick's

Filth and Disease   This 1852 drawing from *Punch* tells volumes about the unhealthy living conditions of the urban poor. In the foreground, children play with a dead rat, and a woman scavenges a dungheap. Cheap rooming houses provide shelter for the frightfully overcrowded population. *(Source: The British Library)*

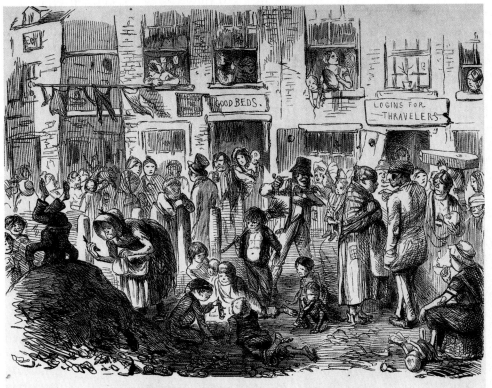

A COURT FOR KING CHOLERA.

report became the basis of Great Britain's first public health law, which created a national health board and gave cities broad authority to build modern sanitary systems.

The public health movement won dedicated supporters in the United States, France, and Germany from the 1840s on. Governments accepted at least limited responsibility for the health of all citizens, and their programs broke decisively with the age-old fatalism of urban populations in the face of shockingly high mortality. By the 1860s and 1870s European cities were making real progress toward adequate water supplies and sewerage systems, and city dwellers were beginning to reap the reward of better health.

Still, effective control of communicable disease required a great leap forward in medical knowledge and biological theory. Early reformers such as Chadwick were seriously handicapped by the prevailing *miasmatic theory* of disease—the belief that people contract disease when they breathe the bad

Louis Pasteur Shown here working in his laboratory, Pasteur made fundamental discoveries in biology and chemistry. A symbol of scientific achievement, he was—and is—greatly revered by all classes in France. *(Source: Institut Pasteur)*

odors of decay and putrefying excrement—in short, the theory that smells cause disease. The miasmatic theory was a reasonable deduction from empirical observations: cleaning up filth did produce laudable results. Yet the theory was very incomplete. Keen observation by doctors and public health officials in the 1840s and 1850s pinpointed the role of bad drinking water in the transmission of disease and suggested that contagion was *spread through* filth and not caused by it, thus weakening the miasmatic idea.

The breakthrough was the development of the *germ theory* of disease by Louis Pasteur (1822–1895), a French chemist who began studying fermentation in 1854 at the request of brewers. Using his microscope to develop a simple test that brewers could use to monitor the fermentation process and avoid spoilage, Pasteur found that fermentation depended on the growth of living organisms and that the activity of these organisms could be suppressed by heating the beverage—by "pasteurizing" it. The breathtaking implication was that specific diseases were caused by specific living organisms—germs—and that those organisms could be controlled in people as well as in beer, wine, and milk.

By 1870 the work of Pasteur and others had demonstrated the general connection between germs and disease. When, in the middle of the 1870s, German country doctor Robert Koch and his coworkers developed pure cultures of harmful bacteria and described their life cycles, the dam broke. Over the next twenty years, researchers—mainly Germans—identified the organisms responsible for disease after disease. These discoveries led to the development of a number of effective vaccines.

Acceptance of the germ theory brought about dramatic improvements in the deadly environment of hospitals and surgery. In 1865 when Pasteur showed that the air was full of bacteria, English surgeon Joseph Lister (1827–1912) immediately grasped the connection between aerial bacteria and the problem of wound infection. He reasoned that a chemical disinfectant applied to a wound dressing would "destroy the life of the floating particles." Lister's "antiseptic principle" worked wonders. In the 1880s, German surgeons developed the more sophisticated practice of sterilizing not only the wound but also everything—hands, instruments, clothing—that entered the operating room.

The achievements of the bacterial revolution coupled with the ever-more-sophisticated public health movement saved millions of lives, particularly after about 1890. Mortality rates began to decline dramatically in European countries (Figure 26.1) as the awful death sentences of the past—diphtheria, typhoid, typhus, cholera, yellow fever—became vanishing diseases. City dwellers benefited especially from these developments. By 1910 a great silent revolution had occurred: the death rates for people of all ages in urban areas were generally no greater than in rural areas, and sometimes they were less.

Urban Planning and Public Transportation

More effective urban planning also improved the quality of urban life. Urban planning was in decline by the early nineteenth century, but after 1850 its practice was revived and extended. France took the lead during the rule of Napoleon III (r. 1848–1870), who sought to stand above class conflict and believed that rebuilding much of Paris would provide employment, improve living conditions, and glorify his empire. In the baron Georges Haussmann (1809–1884), an aggressive, impatient Alsatian whom he placed in charge of Paris, Napoleon III found an authoritarian planner capable of bulldozing both buildings and opposition. In twenty years Paris was transformed (Map 26.2).

The Paris of 1850 was a labyrinth of narrow, dark streets, the results of desperate overcrowding. Terrible slum conditions and extremely high death rates were facts of life. There were few open spaces and only two public parks for the entire metropolis of 1 million. Public transportation played a very small role in this enormous walking city.

Haussmann and his fellow planners proceeded on many interrelated fronts. With a bold energy that often shocked their contemporaries, they razed old buildings in order to cut broad, straight, tree-lined boulevards through the center of the city as well as in new quarters on the outskirts. These boulevards, designed in part to prevent the easy construction and defense of barricades by revolutionary crowds, permitted traffic to flow freely and also afforded impressive vistas. Their creation also demolished some of the worst slums. New streets stimulated the construction of better housing, especially for the middle classes. Small neighborhood parks and open spaces were created

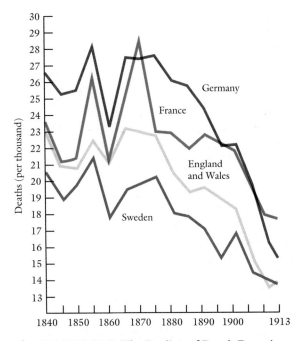

FIGURE 26.1 The Decline of Death Rates in England and Wales, Germany, France, and Sweden, 1840–1913 A rising standard of living, improvements in public health, and better medical knowledge all contributed to the dramatic decline of death rates in the nineteenth century.

throughout the city, and two very large parks suitable for all kinds of holiday activities were developed—one on the wealthy west side and one on the poor east side of the city. The city also improved its sewers and doubled the supply of good fresh water.

Rebuilding Paris provided a new model for urban planning and stimulated modern urbanism throughout Europe, particularly after 1870. In city after city, public authorities mounted a coordinated attack on many of the interrelated problems of the urban environment. As in Paris, improvements in public health through better water supply and waste disposal often went hand in hand with new boulevard construction, as did office buildings, town halls, theaters, opera houses, and museums. New boulevards also radiated out toward the outskirts, easing movement and encouraging urban expansion (see Map 26.2).

The development of mass public transportation was also of great importance in the improvement of urban living conditions. In the 1870s, many European cities authorized private companies to operate horse-drawn streetcars, which had been

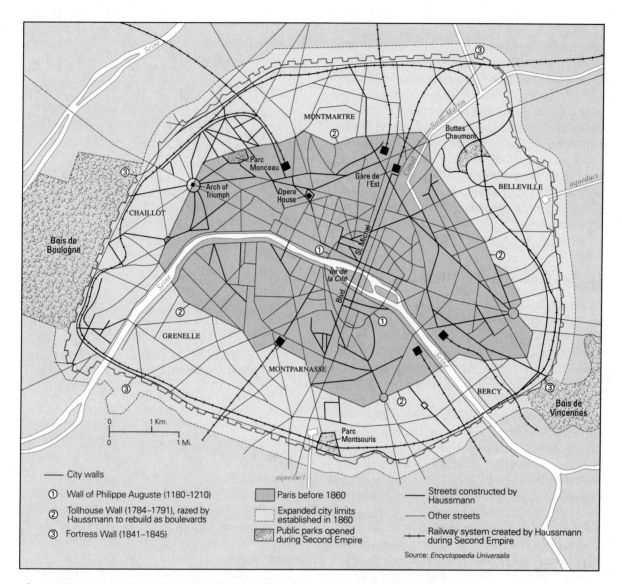

MAP 26.2 Modernization of Paris, ca 1850–1870   Broad boulevards, large parks, and grandiose train stations transformed Paris. The cutting of the new north-south axis—known as the Boulevard Saint-Michel—was one of Haussmann's most controversial projects. It razed much of Paris's medieval core and filled the Île de la Cité with massive government buildings.

developed in the United States. Then in the 1890s the real revolution occurred: European countries adopted another American transit innovation, the electric streetcar.

Electric streetcars were cheaper, faster, more dependable, and more comfortable than their horse-drawn counterparts. Service improved dramatically. Millions of Europeans—workers, shoppers, school-children—hopped on board during the workweek. And on weekends and holidays, streetcars carried millions on happy outings to parks and the countryside, racetracks and music halls. In 1886 the horse-drawn streetcars of Austria-Hungary, France, Germany, and Great Britain were carrying about 900 million riders. By 1910 electric streetcars in the four countries were carrying 6.7 billion riders.[4] Each person was using public transportation four times as often in 1910 as in 1886.

Good mass transit helped greatly in the struggle for decent housing. The new boulevards and horse-drawn streetcars had facilitated a middle-class move to better housing in the 1860s and 1870s; similarly, after 1890 electric streetcars gave people of modest means access to new, improved housing. The still-crowded city was able to expand and become less congested. In England in 1901, only 9 percent of the urban population was "overcrowded" in terms of the official definition of more than two persons per room. On the European continent, many city governments in the early twentieth century were building electric streetcar systems that provided transportation for the working classes to new public and private housing developments in outlying areas of the city. Poor, overcrowded housing, long one of the blackest blots on the urban landscape, was in retreat—another example of the gradual taming of the urban environment.

Urbanization and Social Structure

With general improvements in health and in the urban environment, the almost-completed journey to an urban industrialized world was bringing beneficial consequences for all kinds of people. The first great change was a substantial and undeniable increase in the standard of living for the average person. The real wages of British workers, for example, which had already risen by 1850, almost doubled between 1850 and 1906. Similar increases occurred in continental European countries as industrial development quickened after 1850. Ordinary people took a major step forward in the centuries-old battle against poverty, reinforcing efforts to improve many aspects of human existence.

There is another side to the income coin, however. Greater economic rewards for the average person did *not* eliminate hardship and poverty, nor did they make the wealth and income of the rich and the poor significantly more equal. In almost every advanced country around 1900, the richest 20 percent of households received anywhere from 50 to 60 percent of all national income, and the bottom 30 percent of households received 10 percent or less of all income (Figure 26.2). The middle classes, which were smaller than they are today, accounted for less than 20 percent of the population; thus the statistics show that the upper and middle classes alone received more than 50 percent of all income. The poorest 80 percent—the working classes, including peasants and agricultural laborers—received less altogether than the two rich-

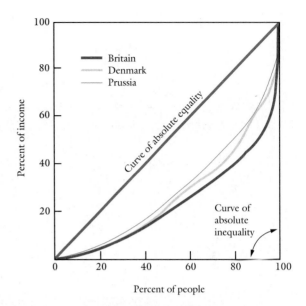

Percent of people

DISTRIBUTION OF INCOME

Country	Richest 5%	Richest 10%	Richest 20%	Poorest 60%
Britain	43%		59%	
Denmark	30	39%	55	31%
Prussia	30		50	33

FIGURE 26.2 The Distribution of Income in Britain, Denmark, and Prussia in 1913 The Lorenz curve is useful for showing the degree of economic inequality in a given society. The closer the actual distribution of income lies to the (theoretical) curve of absolute equality, where each 20 percent of the population receives 20 percent of all income, the more nearly equal are incomes. European society was very far from any such equality before the First World War. Notice that incomes in Prussia were somewhat more equal than those in Britain. *(Source: Based on information from S. Kuznets,* Modern Economic Growth, *Yale University Press, New Haven, 1966, pp. 208–209. Copyright © 1966 by Yale University Press. Used with permission.)*

est classes. Moreover, income taxes on the wealthy were light or nonexistent. Thus the gap between rich and poor remained enormous. It was probably almost as great in 1900 as it had been in the age of agriculture and aristocracy before the Industrial Revolution.

The great gap between rich and poor endured, in part, because industrial and urban development

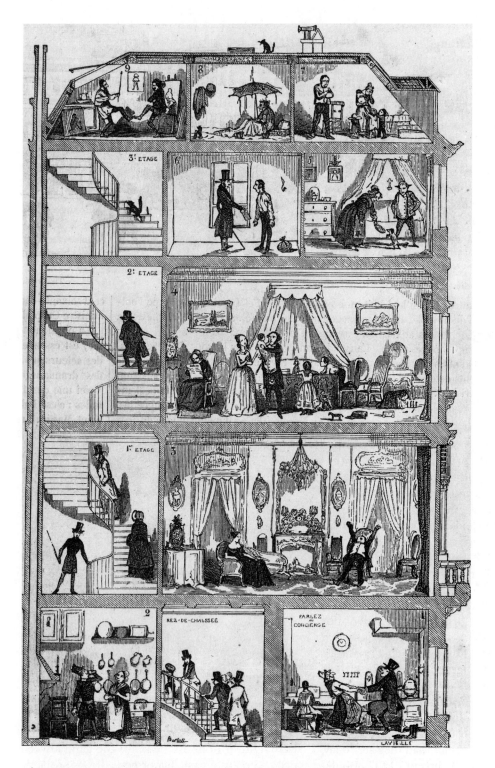

Apartment Living in Paris   As this drawing shows, different social classes lived close together in European cities about 1850. A middle-class family lives on the first (American second) floor, and the economic condition of the tenants declines at each higher floor. Residents of the garret live in abject poverty. *(Source: Bibliothèque Nationale, Paris)*

made society more diverse and less unified. By no means did society split into two sharply defined opposing classes, as Marx had predicted. Instead, economic specialization created more new social groups than it destroyed. There developed an almost unlimited range of jobs, skills, and earnings; one group or subclass shaded off into another in a complex, confusing hierarchy. The tiny elite of the very rich and the sizable mass of the dreadfully poor were separated from each other by a range of subclasses, each filled with individuals struggling to rise or at least to hold their own in the social order. In this atmosphere of competition and hierarchy, neither the middle classes nor the working classes acted as a unified force. This social and occupational hierarchy developed enormous variations, but the age-old pattern of great economic inequality remained firmly intact.

The Middle Classes

By the beginning of the twentieth century, the diversity and range within the urban middle class were striking. Indeed, it is more meaningful to think of a confederation of middle classes loosely united by occupations requiring primarily mental, rather than physical, skill. At the top stood the upper middle class, composed mainly of the most successful business families from banking, industry, and large-scale commerce. These families were the prime beneficiaries of modern industry and scientific progress. As people in the upper middle class gained in income and progressively lost all traces of radicalism after the trauma of 1848, they were almost irresistibly drawn toward the aristocratic lifestyle. And although the genuine hereditary aristocracy constituted only a tiny minority in every European country, it retained imposing wealth, unrivaled social prestige, and substantial political influence. This was especially true in central and eastern Europe, where the monarch—the highest-ranking noble of them all—continued to hold great political power.

As the aristocracy had long divided the year between palatial country estates and lavish town-houses during "the season," so the upper middle class purchased country places or built beach houses for weekend and summer use. The number of servants was an important indicator of wealth and standing for the middle class, as it had always been for the aristocracy. Private coaches and carriages, ever expensive items in the city, were also

signs of rising social status. More generally, the rich businessman and certainly his son devoted less time to business and more to "culture" and easy living than was the case in less wealthy or well-established commercial families.

The topmost reaches of the upper middle class tended to shade off into the old aristocracy to form a new upper class of at most 5 percent of the population. Much of the aristocracy welcomed this development. Having experienced a sharp decline in its relative income in the course of industrialization, the landed aristocracy had met big business coming up the staircase and was often delighted to trade titles, country homes, and snobbish elegance for good hard cash. Some of the best bargains were made through marriages to American heiresses. Correspondingly, wealthy aristocrats tended increasingly to exploit their agricultural and mineral resources as if they were business people. Bismarck was not the only proud nobleman to make a fortune distilling brandy on his estates.

Below the wealthy upper middle class were much larger, much less wealthy, and increasingly diversified middle-class groups. Here one found the moderately successful industrialists and merchants as well as professionals in law and medicine. This was the middle middle class, solid and quite comfortable but lacking great wealth. Below it were independent shopkeepers, small traders, and tiny manufacturers—the lower middle class. Both of these traditional elements of the middle class expanded modestly in size with economic development.

Meanwhile, the traditional middle class was gaining two particularly important additions. The expansion of industry and technology created a growing demand for experts with specialized knowledge. The most valuable of the specialties became solid middle-class professions. Engineering, for example, emerged from the world of skilled labor as a full-fledged profession of great importance, considerable prestige, and many branches. Architects, chemists, accountants, and surveyors, to name only a few, first achieved professional standing in this period. They established criteria for advanced training and certification and banded together in organizations to promote and defend their interests.

Management of large public and private institutions also emerged as a kind of profession as governments provided more services and as very large corporations such as railroads came into being.

Government officials and many private executives were not capitalists in the sense that they owned business enterprises. But public and private managers had specialized knowledge and good salaries. And they shared most of the values of the business-owning entrepreneurs and the older professionals.

Industrialization and urbanization also expanded and diversified the lower middle class. The number of shopkeepers and small business people grew, and so did the number of white-collar employees—a mixed group of traveling salesmen, bookkeepers, store managers, and clerks who staffed the offices and branch stores of large corporations. White-collar employees were propertyless and often earned no more than the better-paid workers. Yet white-collar workers were fiercely committed to the middle class and to the ideal of moving up in society. In the Balkans, for example, clerks let their fingernails grow very long to distinguish themselves from people who worked with their hands. The tie, the suit, and soft, clean hands were no-less-subtle marks of class distinction than wages.

Relatively well educated but without complex technical skills, many white-collar groups aimed at achieving professional standing and the accompanying middle-class status. Elementary school teachers largely succeeded in this effort. From being miserably paid part-time workers in the early nineteenth century, teachers rode the wave of mass education to respectable middle-class status and income.

In spite of growing occupational diversity and conflicting interests, the middle classes were loosely united by a certain style of life. Food was the largest item in the household budget, for middle-class people liked to eat very well. In France and Italy, the middle classes' love of good eating meant that even in large cities, activity ground almost to a halt between half past twelve and half past two on weekdays as husbands and schoolchildren returned home for the midday meal. The European middle classes consumed meat in abundance, and a well-off family might spend 10 percent of its substantial earnings on meat and fully 25 percent of its income on food and drink.

Spending on food was also great because the dinner party was this class's favored social occasion. A wealthy family might give a lavish party for eight to twelve almost every week, whereas more modest households would settle for once a month. Throughout middle-class Europe, such dinners were served in the "French manner": eight or nine separate courses, from appetizers at the beginning to coffee and liqueurs at the end. An ordinary family meal normally consisted of only four courses—soup, fish, meat, and dessert.

The middle-class wife could cope with this endless procession of meals, courses, and dishes because she had both servants and money at her disposal. Indeed, the employment of at least one enormously helpful full-time maid to cook and clean was the best single sign that a family had crossed the cultural divide separating the working classes from what some contemporary observers called the "servant-keeping classes." The greater a family's income, the greater the number of servants it employed. A really prosperous English family in 1900 might employ a hierarchy of ten servants: a manservant, a cook, a kitchen maid, two housemaids, a serving maid, a governess, a gardener, a coachman, and a stable boy. Food and servants together absorbed about 50 percent of income at all levels of the middle classes.

Well fed and well served, the middle classes were also well housed by 1900. Many quite prosperous families rented, rather than owned, their homes. Apartment living, complete with tiny rooms for servants under the eaves of the top floor, was commonplace, and wealthy investors and speculative builders found good profits in middle-class housing. By 1900 the middle classes were also quite clothes conscious. The factory, the sewing machine, and the department store had all helped reduce the cost and expand the variety of clothing. Middle-class women were particularly attentive to the fickle dictates of fashion.

Education was another growing expense, as middle-class parents tried to provide their children with ever-more-crucial advanced education. The keystones of culture and leisure were books, music, and travel. The long realistic novel, the heroics of composers Wagner and Verdi, the diligent striving of the dutiful daughter at the piano, and the packaged tour to a foreign country were all sources of middle-class pleasure.

Finally, the middle classes were loosely united by a shared code of expected behavior and morality. This code was strict and demanding. It laid great stress on hard work, self-discipline, and personal achievement. Men and women who fell into crime or poverty were generally assumed to be responsible for their own circumstances. Traditional Christian morality was reaffirmed by this code and was

Chabas: A Corner of the Table (1904)   In this oil painting French academic artist Paul-Émile Chabas (1867–1937) skillfully idealizes the elegance and intimacy of a sumptuous dinner party with photographic precision. *(Source: Bibliothèque des Arts Décoratifs/Jean-Loup Charmet)*

preached tirelessly by middle-class people. Drinking and gambling were denounced as vices; sexual purity and fidelity were celebrated as virtues. In short, the middle-class person was supposed to know right from wrong and was expected to act accordingly.

The Working Classes

About four out of five people belonged to the working classes at the turn of the century. Many members of the working classes—that is, people whose livelihoods depended on physical labor and who did not employ domestic servants—were still small landowning peasants and hired farm hands. This was especially true in eastern Europe. In western and central Europe, however, the typical worker had left the land. In Great Britain, less than 8 percent of the people worked in agriculture, and in rapidly industrializing Germany only 25 percent were employed in agriculture and forestry. Even in less industrialized France, less than 50 percent of the people depended on the land in 1900.

The urban working classes were even less unified and homogeneous than the middle classes. In the first place, economic development and increased specialization expanded the traditional range of working-class skills, earnings, and experiences. Meanwhile, the old sharp distinction between highly skilled artisans and unskilled manual workers gradually broke down. To be sure, highly skilled printers and masons as well as unskilled dockworkers and common laborers continued to exist. But between these extremes there appeared ever-more semiskilled groups, many of which were

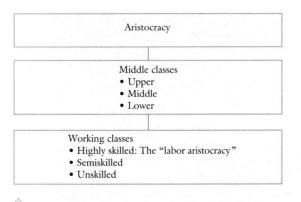

FIGURE 26.3 The Urban Social Hierarchy

composed of factory workers and machine tenders (Figure 26.3).

In the second place, skilled, semiskilled, and unskilled workers developed widely divergent lifestyles and cultural values, and their differences contributed to a keen sense of social status and hierarchy within the working classes. The result was great variety and limited class unity.

Highly skilled workers, who made up about 15 percent of the working classes, became a real "labor aristocracy." These workers earned only about two-thirds of the income of the bottom ranks of the servant-keeping classes, but that was fully twice as much as the earnings of unskilled workers. The most "aristocratic" of the highly skilled workers were construction bosses and factory foremen, men who had often risen from the ranks and were fiercely proud of their achievement. The labor aristocracy also included members of the traditional highly skilled handicraft trades that had not been mechanized or placed in factories, like cabinetmakers, jewelers, and printers. This group as a whole was under constant long-term pressure. Irregularly but inexorably, factory methods were being extended to more crafts, and many skilled artisans were being replaced by lower-paid semiskilled factory workers. In the later nineteenth century, traditional woodcarvers and watchmakers virtually disappeared, for example, as the making of furniture and timepieces was put into the factory.

At the same time, the labor aristocracy was consistently being enlarged by new kinds of skilled workers such as shipbuilders and railway locomotive engineers. Thus the labor elite remained in a state of flux as individuals and whole crafts moved in and out of it.

To maintain this precarious standing, the upper working class adopted distinctive values and straitlaced, almost puritanical behavior. Like the middle classes, the labor aristocracy was strongly committed to the family and to economic improvement. Families in the upper working class saved money regularly, worried about their children's education, and valued good housing. Yet skilled workers viewed themselves primarily not as aspirants to the middle class but as the pacesetters and natural leaders of all the working classes. Well aware of the degradation not so far below them, they practiced self-discipline and generally frowned on heavy drinking and sexual permissiveness.

Men and women of the labor aristocracy were quick to find fault with those below them who failed to meet their standards. In 1868 William Lovett, an English labor aristocrat if ever there was one, denounced "this ignorant recklessness and improvidence that produce the swarms of half-starved, neglected, and ignorant children we see in all directions; who mostly grow up to become the burdens and often the pests of society, which the industrious and frugal have to support."[5] Finally, many members of the labor aristocracy had definite political and philosophical beliefs, whether Christian or socialist or both. Such beliefs further strengthened the firm moral code of the upper working class.

Below the labor aristocracy stood semiskilled and unskilled urban workers. The enormous complexity of this sector of the world of labor is not easily summarized. Workers in the established crafts—carpenters, bricklayers, pipefitters—stood near the top of the semiskilled hierarchy, often flirting with (or sliding back from) the labor elite. A large number of the semiskilled were factory workers who earned highly variable but relatively good wages and whose relative importance in the labor force was increasing.

Below the semiskilled workers was a larger group of unskilled workers that included day laborers such as longshoremen, wagon-driving teamsters, teenagers, and every kind of "helper." Many of these people had real skills and performed valuable services, but they were unorganized and divided, united only by the common fate of meager earnings. The same lack of unity characterized street vendors and market people—self-employed workers who competed savagely with each other and with the established shopkeepers of the lower middle class.

One of the largest components of the unskilled group was domestic servants, whose numbers grew steadily in the nineteenth century. In advanced Great Britain, for example, one out of every seven employed persons was a domestic servant in 1911. The great majority were women; indeed, one out of every three girls in Britain between the ages of fifteen and twenty was a domestic servant. Throughout Europe and America, a great many female domestics in the cities were recent migrants from rural areas. As in earlier times, domestic service was still hard work at low pay with limited personal independence. For the full-time general maid in a lower-middle-class family, there was an unending routine of baby-sitting, shopping, cooking, and cleaning. In the great households, the girl was at the bottom of a rigid hierarchy of status-conscious butlers and housekeepers.

Nonetheless, domestic service had real attractions for "rough country girls" with strong hands and few specialized skills. Marriage prospects were better, or at least more varied, in the city. And though wages were low, they were higher and more regular than in hard agricultural work. Finally, as one London observer noted, young girls and other migrants were drawn to the city by

the contagion of numbers, the sense of something going on, the theaters and the music halls, the brightly lighted streets and busy crowds—all, in short, that makes the difference between the Mile End fair on a Saturday night, and a dark and muddy country lane, with no glimmer of gas and with nothing to do.[6]

Many young domestics from the countryside made a successful transition to working-class wife and mother. Yet with an unskilled or unemployed husband and a growing family, such a woman often had to join the broad ranks of working women in the "sweated industries." These industries flowered after 1850 and resembled the old putting-out and cottage industries of earlier times. The women

A School for Servants   Although domestic service was poorly paid, there was always plenty of competition for the available jobs. Schools sprang up to teach young women the manners and the household skills that employers in the servant-keeping classes demanded. *(Source: Greater London Council Photograph Library)*

normally worked at home, paid by the piece and not by the hour. They and their young daughters, for whom organization and collective action were virtually impossible, earned pitiful wages and lacked any job security.

Some women did hand-decorating of every conceivable kind of object; the majority, however, made clothing, especially after the advent of the foot-powered sewing machine. By 1900 only a few highly skilled male tailors lingered on in high-priced "tailor-made" shops. An army of poor women accounted for the bulk of the inexpensive "ready-made" clothes displayed on department store racks and in tiny shops.

Notwithstanding the rise and fall of groups and individuals, the urban working classes sought fun and recreation, and they found both. Across the face of Europe, drinking remained unquestionably the favorite leisure-time activity of working people. For many middle-class moralists as well as moralizing historians since, love of drink has been a curse of the modern age—a sign of social dislocation and popular suffering. Certainly, drinking was deadly serious business. One English slum dweller recalled that "drunkenness was by far the commonest cause of dispute and misery in working class homes. On account of it one saw many a decent family drift down through poverty into total want."[7]

Generally, however, heavy "problem" drinking declined in the late nineteenth century as it became less and less socially acceptable. This decline reflected in part the moral leadership of the upper working class. At the same time, drinking became more public and social. Cafés and pubs became increasingly bright, friendly places. Working-class political activities, both moderate and radical, were also concentrated in taverns and pubs. Moreover, social drinking in public places by married couples and sweethearts became an accepted and widespread practice for the first time. This greater participation by women undoubtedly helped civilize the world of drink and hard liquor.

The two other leisure-time passions of the working classes were sports and music halls. A great decline in "cruel sports," such as bullbaiting and cockfighting, had occurred throughout Europe by the late nineteenth century. Their place was filled by modern spectator sports, of which racing and soccer were the most popular. There was a great deal of gambling on sports events, and for many a working person a desire to decipher racing forms

provided a powerful incentive toward literacy. Music halls and vaudeville theaters, the working-class counterparts of middle-class opera and classical theater, were enormously popular throughout Europe. In 1900 there were more than fifty such halls and theaters in London alone. Music hall audiences were thoroughly mixed, which may account for the fact that drunkenness, sexual intercourse and pregnancy before marriage, marital difficulties, and problems with mothers-in-law were favorite themes of broad jokes and bittersweet songs.

Did religion and Christian churches continue to provide working people with solace and meaning? Although many historians see the early nineteenth century as an age of religious revival, historians also recognize that in the late nineteenth century a considerable decline in both church attendance and church donations was occurring in most European countries. And it seems clear that this decline was greater for the urban working classes than for their rural counterparts or for the middle classes. Yet most working-class families still baptized their children and considered themselves Christians.

Although more research is necessary, it appears that the urban working classes in Europe did become more secular and less religious in the late nineteenth and early twentieth centuries. They rarely repudiated the Christian religion, but it tended to play a diminishing role in their daily lives. Part of the reason for this change was that the construction of churches failed to keep up with the rapid growth of urban population, especially in new working-class neighborhoods. Thus in the vibrant, materialistic urban environment, popular religious impulses were poorly served.

Equally important, however, was the fact that throughout the nineteenth century both Catholic and Protestant churches were normally seen as they saw themselves—as conservative institutions defending social order and custom. Therefore, as the European working classes became more politically conscious, they tended to see the established (or quasi-established) "territorial church" as the defender of what they wished to change and as the ally of their political opponents. Especially the men of the urban working classes developed vaguely antichurch attitudes, even though they remained neutral or positive toward religion. They tended to regard regular church attendance as "not our kind of thing"—not part of urban working-class culture.

 **Renoir: Le Moulin de la Galette à Montmartre**   In this 1876 masterpiece impressionist painter Auguste Renoir (1841–1919) has transformed a popular outdoor dance hall enjoyed by the Parisian masses into an enchanted fairyland. Renoir was a joyous artist, and his work optimistically affirmed the beauty and value of modern life. *(Source: Musée d'Orsay © Photo R.M.N)*

The pattern was different in the United States. There, most churches also preached social conservatism in the nineteenth century. But church and state had always been separate, and there was always a host of competing denominations and even different religions. So working people in the United States identified churches much less with the political and social status quo and more often with an ethnic group, and churches thrived, in part, as an assertion of ethnic identity. This same process occurred in Europe if the church or synagogue had never been linked to the state and served as a focus for ethnic cohesion. Irish Catholic churches in Protestant Britain and Jewish synagogues in Russia were outstanding examples.

✤ THE CHANGING FAMILY

Urban life wrought many fundamental changes in the family. Although much is still unknown, it seems clear that in the second half of the nineteenth century the family had stabilized considerably after the disruption of the late eighteenth and early nineteenth centuries. The home became more important for both men and women. The role of women and attitudes toward children underwent substantial change, and the concept of adolescence as a distinct stage of life emerged. These are but a few of the transformations that affected all social classes in varying degrees.

Premarital Sex and Marriage

By 1850 the preindustrial pattern of lengthy courtship and mercenary marriage was pretty well dead among the working classes. In its place, the ideal of romantic love had triumphed. Couples were ever-more likely to come from different, even distant, towns and to be more nearly the same age, as romantic sentiment replaced tradition and financial considerations.

Economic considerations in marriage remained more important to the middle classes after 1850. In France dowries and elaborate legal marriage contracts were common practice among the middle classes in the later nineteenth century, and marriage was for many families one of life's most crucial financial transactions. A popular author advised young Frenchmen that "marriage is in general a means of increasing one's credit and one's fortune and of insuring one's success in the world."[8] This preoccupation with money led many middle-class men in France and elsewhere to marry late, after they had become established economically, and to choose women considerably younger and less sexually experienced than themselves. These differences between husband and wife became a source of tension in many middle-class marriages.

A young woman of the middle class found her romantic life carefully supervised by her well-meaning mother, who schemed for a proper marriage and guarded her daughter's virginity like the family's credit. After marriage, middle-class morality sternly demanded fidelity.

Middle-class boys were watched too, but not as vigilantly. By the time they reached late adolescence, they had usually attained considerable sexual experience with maids or prostitutes. With marriage a distant, uncertain possibility, it was all too easy for the young man of the middle classes to turn to the urban underworld of prostitution and sexual exploitation to satisfy his desires.

In the early nineteenth century among the working classes, sexual experimentation before marriage also triumphed, as did illegitimacy. By the 1840s, as many as one birth in three was occurring outside of wedlock in many large cities. In the second half of the century, however, the rising rate of illegitimacy was reversed: more babies were born to married mothers. Some have argued that this shift reflected the growth of puritanism and a lessening of sexual permissiveness among the unmarried. This explanation, however, is unconvincing.

The percentage of brides who were pregnant continued to be high and showed little or no tendency to decline after 1850. In many parts of urban Europe around 1900, as many as one woman in three was going to the altar an expectant mother. Moreover, unmarried people almost certainly used the cheap condoms and diaphragms the industrial age had made available to prevent pregnancy, at least in predominately Protestant countries. Unmarried young people were probably engaging in just as much sexual activity as their parents and grandparents who had created the illegitimacy explosion of 1750 to 1850. But in the later nineteenth century, pregnancy for a young single woman led increasingly to marriage and the establishment of a two-parent household. This important development reflected the growing respectability of the working classes as well as their gradual economic improvement. Skipping out was less acceptable, and marriage was less of an economic challenge. Thus the urban working-class couple became more stable, and that stability strengthened the family as an institution.

Prostitution

In Paris alone, 155,000 women were registered as prostitutes between 1871 and 1903, and 750,000 others were suspected of prostitution in the same years. Men of all classes visited prostitutes, but the middle and upper classes supplied much of the motivating cash. Although many middle-class men abided by the publicly professed code of stern puritanical morality, others indulged their appetites for prostitutes and sexual promiscuity.

My Secret Life, the anonymous eleven-volume autobiography of an English sexual adventurer from the servant-keeping classes, provides a remarkable picture of such a man. Beginning at an early age with a maid, the author becomes progressively obsessed with sex and devotes his life to living his sexual fantasies. In almost every one of his innumerable encounters all across Europe, this man of wealth simply buys his pleasure. Usually meetings are arranged in a businesslike manner: regular and part-time prostitutes quote their prices; working-class girls are corrupted by hot meals and baths.

At one point, he offers a young girl a sixpence for a kiss and gets it. Learning that the pretty, unskilled working girl earns nine pence a day, he offers her the equivalent of a week's salary for a few moments of fondling. When she finally agrees, he savagely exults that "*her* want was my opportunity." Later he offers more money for more gratification, and when she refuses, he tries unsuccessfully to rape her in a hackney cab. On another occasion he takes a farm worker by force: "Her tears ran down. If I had not committed a rape, it looked uncommonly like one." He then forces his victim to take money to prevent a threatened lawsuit, while the foreman advises the girl to keep quiet and realize that "you be in luck if he likes you."[9]

Obviously atypical in its excesses, *My Secret Life,* in its encyclopedic thoroughness, does reveal the dark side of sex and class in urban society. Frequently thinking of their wives largely in terms of money, family, and social position, the men of the comfortable classes often purchased sex and even affection from poor girls both before and after marriage. Moreover, the great continuing differences between rich and poor made for every kind of debauchery and sexual exploitation, including the brisk trade in poor virgins that the author of *My Secret Life* particularly relishes. Brutal sexist behavior was part of life—a part the sternly moral women (and men) of the upper working class detested and tried to shield their daughters from. For many poor young women, prostitution, like domestic service, was a stage of life and not a permanent employment. Having chosen it for two or three years in their twenties, they went on to marry (or live with) men of their own class and establish homes and families.

Sex Roles and Family Life

Industrialization and the growth of modern cities brought great changes to the lives of European women. These changes were particularly consequential for married women, and most women did marry in the nineteenth century.

After 1850 the work of most wives continued to become increasingly distinct and separate from that of their husbands (see pages 796–798). Husbands became wage earners in factories and offices; wives tended to stay home and manage households and care for children. As economic conditions improved, only married women in poor families tended more and more to work outside the home. One old English worker recalled that "the boy wanted to get into a position that would enable him to keep a wife and family, as it was considered

a thoroughly unsatisfactory state of affairs if the wife had to work to help maintain the home."[10] The ideal became a strict division of labor by sex: the wife as mother and homemaker, the husband as wage earner.

This rigid division of labor meant that married women faced great injustice if they tried to move into the man's world of employment outside the home. Husbands were unsympathetic or hostile. Well-paying jobs were off-limits to women, and a woman's wage was almost always less than a man's, even for the same work. Moreover, married women were subordinated to their husbands by law and lacked many basic legal rights. In France, for example, the Napoleonic Code enshrined the principle of female subordination and gave the wife few legal rights regarding property, divorce, and custody of the children.

With middle-class women suffering, sometimes severely, from a lack of legal rights and with all women facing discrimination in education and employment, there is little wonder that some women rebelled and began the long-continuing fight for equality of the sexes and the rights of women. Their struggle proceeded on two main fronts. First, following in the steps of women such as Mary Wollstonecraft (see page 752), organizations founded by middle-class feminists campaigned for equal legal rights for women as well as access to higher education and professional employment. In the later nineteenth century, these organizations scored some significant victories, such as the 1882 law giving English married women full property rights. In the years before 1914, middle-class feminists increasingly shifted their attention to securing the right to vote for women.

Women inspired by utopian and especially Marxian socialism blazed a second path. Often scorning the programs of middle-class feminists, socialist women leaders argued that the liberation of (working-class) women would come only with the liberation of the entire working class through revolution. In the meantime, they championed the cause of working women and won some practical improvements, especially in Germany, where the socialist movement was most effectively organized. In a general way, these different approaches to women's issues reflected the diversity of classes in urban society.

If the ideology and practice of rigidly separate roles undoubtedly narrowed women's horizons and caused some women to rebel, there was a brighter side to the same coin. As home and children became the typical wife's main concerns in the later nineteenth century, her control and influence there apparently became increasingly strong throughout Europe. Among the English working classes, it was the wife who generally determined how the family's money was spent. In many families the husband gave all his earnings to his wife to manage, whatever the law might read. She returned to him only a small allowance for carfare, beer, tobacco, and union dues. All the major domestic decisions, from the children's schooling and religious instruction to the selection of new furniture or a new apartment, were hers. In France women had even greater power in their assigned domain. One English feminist noted in 1908 that "though legally women occupy a much inferior status than men [in France], in practice they constitute the superior sex. They are the power behind the throne."[11]

Women ruled at home partly because running the urban household was a complicated, demanding, and valuable task. Twice-a-day food shopping, penny-pinching, economizing, and the growing crusade against dirt—not to mention child rearing—were a full-time occupation. Nor were there any laborsaving appliances to help. Working yet another job for wages outside the home had limited appeal for most married women unless such earnings were essential for family survival. Many married women in the working classes did make a monetary contribution to family income by taking in boarders or doing piecework at home in the sweated industries (see page 855).

The woman's guidance of the household went hand in hand with the increased emotional importance of home and family. The home she ran was idealized as a warm shelter in a hard and impersonal urban world. For a child of the English slums in the early 1900s, home, however poor, was the focus of all love and interests, a sure fortress against a hostile world. Songs about its beauties were ever on people's lips. "Home, Sweet Home," first heard in the 1870s, had become "almost a second national anthem." Wall hangings like "HOME IS THE NEST WHERE ALL IS BEST" attested to domestic joys.[12] By 1900 home and family were what life was all about for millions of people of all classes.

Married couples also developed stronger emotional ties to each other. Even in the comfortable classes, marriages in the late nineteenth century

A Working-Class Home, 1875 Emotional ties within ordinary families grew stronger in the nineteenth century. Parents gave their children more love and better care. *(Source: Illustrated London News, LXVI, 1875. Photo courtesy of Boston Public Library)*

were increasingly based on sentiment and sexual attraction as money and financial calculation gradually declined in importance. Affection and eroticism became more central to the couple after marriage. Gustave Droz, whose bestseller *Mr., Mrs., and Baby* went through 121 editions between 1866 and 1884, saw love within marriage as the key to human happiness. He urged women to follow their hearts and marry a man of nearly their own age:

A husband who is stately and a little bald is all right, but a young husband who loves you and who drinks out of your glass without ceremony, is better. Let him, if he ruffles your dress a little and places a kiss on your neck as he passes. Let him, if he undresses you after the ball, laughing like a fool. You have fine spiritual qualities, it is true, but your little body is not bad either and when one loves, one loves completely. Behind these follies lies happiness.[13]

Many French marriage manuals of the late 1800s stressed that women had legitimate sexual needs, such as the "right to orgasm." The rise of public socializing by couples in cafés and music halls as well as franker affection within the family suggests a more erotic, pleasurable intimate life for women throughout Western society. This, too, helped make the woman's role as mother and homemaker acceptable and even satisfying.

Child Rearing

One of the most striking signs of deepening emotional ties within the family was the growing love and concern that mothers gave their tiny infants. This was a sharp break with the past. Although it may seem hard to believe today, the typical mother in preindustrial Western society was frequently indifferent toward her baby. This indifference—an unwillingness to make real sacrifices for the welfare of the infant—was beginning to give way among the comfortable classes by the end of the eighteenth century, but the ordinary mother of modest means adopted new attitudes only as the nineteenth century progressed. The baby became more important, and women became better mothers.

Mothers increasingly breast-fed their infants, for example, rather than paying wet nurses to do so. Breast-feeding involved sacrifice—a temporary loss of freedom, if nothing else. Yet in an age when there was no good alternative to mother's milk, it saved lives. The surge of maternal feeling also gave rise to a wave of specialized books on child rearing and infant hygiene. Swaddling disappeared completely, as ordinary mothers allowed their babies freedom of movement and delighted in their spontaneity.

The loving care lavished on infants was matched by greater concern for older children and adolescents. They, too, were wrapped in the strong emotional ties of a more intimate and protective family. For one thing, European women began to limit the number of children they bore in order to care adequately for those they had. By the end of the century the birthrate was declining across Europe, and it continued to do so until after World War II (Figure 26.4). The Englishwoman who married in the 1860s, for example, had an average of about

FIGURE 26.4 The Decline of Birthrates in England and Wales, France, Germany, and Sweden, 1840–1913 Women had fewer babies for a variety of reasons, including the fact that their children were increasingly less likely to die before reaching adulthood. Compare with Figure 26.1.

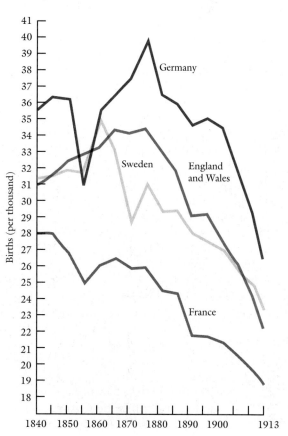

six children; her daughter marrying in the 1890s had only four; and her granddaughter marrying in the 1920s had only two or possibly three.

The most important reason for this revolutionary reduction in family size, in which the comfortable and well-educated classes took the lead, was parents' desire to improve their economic and social position and that of their children by having fewer youngsters. Thus the growing tendency of couples in the late nineteenth century to use a variety of contraceptive methods—rhythm, withdrawal, and mechanical devices—certainly reflected increased concern for children. Indeed, many parents, especially in the middle classes, probably became *too* concerned about their children, unwittingly subjecting them to an emotional pressure cooker of almost unbearable intensity. The result was that many children and especially adolescents came to feel trapped and in desperate need of greater independence.

Prevailing biological and medical theories led parents to believe in the possibility that their own emotional characteristics were passed on to their offspring and that they were thus directly responsible for any abnormality in a child. The rigid determinism of such views left little scope for the child's individual development. Another area of excessive parental concern was the sexual behavior of the child. Masturbation was viewed with horror, for it represented an act of independence and even defiance. Diet, clothing, games, and sleeping were carefully regulated. Girls were discouraged from riding horses and bicycling because rhythmic friction simulated masturbation. Boys were dressed in trousers with shallow and widely separated pockets. Between 1850 and 1880, there were surgical operations for children who persisted in masturbating. These and less blatant attempts to repress the child's sexuality were a source of unhealthy tension, often made worse by the rigid division of sexual roles within the family.

Sigmund Freud (1856–1939), the Viennese founder of psychoanalysis, formulated the most striking analysis of the explosive dynamics of the family, particularly the middle-class family in the late nineteenth century. A physician by training, Freud began his career treating mentally ill patients. He noted that the hysteria of his patients appeared to originate in bitter early childhood experiences wherein the child had been obliged to repress strong feelings. When these painful experiences were recalled and reproduced under hypno-

sis or through the patient's free association of ideas, the patient could be brought to understand his or her unhappiness and eventually deal with it.

One of Freud's most influential ideas concerned the Oedipal tensions resulting from the son's instinctive competition with the father for the mother's love and affection. More generally, Freud postulated that much of human behavior is motivated by unconscious emotional needs whose nature and origins are kept from conscious awareness by various mental devices he called "defense mechanisms." Freud concluded that much unconscious psychological energy is sexual energy, which is repressed and precariously controlled by rational thinking and moral rules. If Freud exaggerated the sexual and familial roots of adult behavior, that exaggeration was itself a reflection of the tremendous emotional intensity of family life in the late nineteenth century.

The working classes probably had more avenues of escape from such tensions than did the middle classes. Unlike their middle-class counterparts, who remained economically dependent on their families until a long education was finished or a proper marriage secured, working-class boys and girls went to work when they reached adolescence. Earning wages on their own, they could bargain with their parents for greater independence within the household by the time they were sixteen or seventeen. If they were unsuccessful, they could and did leave home to live cheaply as paying lodgers in other working-class homes. Thus the young person from the working classes broke away from the family more easily when emotional ties became oppressive. In the twentieth century, middle-class youths would follow this lead.

 ## SCIENCE AND CULTURE

Major changes in Western thought and culture accompanied the emergence of urban society. Two aspects of these complex developments stand out as especially significant. Scientific knowledge expanded rapidly and came to influence the Western world-view even more profoundly than it had since the scientific revolution and the early Enlightenment. And between about the 1840s and the 1890s, European literature underwent a shift from soaring romanticism to tough-minded realism.

The Triumph of Science

The intellectual achievements of the scientific revolution had resulted in few practical benefits, and theoretical knowledge had also played a relatively small role in the Industrial Revolution in England. But breakthroughs in industrial technology enormously stimulated basic scientific inquiry, as researchers sought to explain theoretically how such things as steam engines and blast furnaces actually worked. The result was an explosive growth of fundamental scientific discoveries from the 1830s onward, which were increasingly transformed into material improvements for the general population.

A perfect example of the translation of better scientific knowledge into practical human benefits was the work of Pasteur and his followers in biology and the medical sciences. Another was the development of the branch of physics known as *thermodynamics*. Building on Isaac Newton's laws of mechanics and on studies of steam engines, thermodynamics investigated the relationship between heat and mechanical energy. By midcentury, physicists had formulated the fundamental laws of thermodynamics, which were then applied to mechanical engineering, chemical processes, and many other fields.

Chemistry and electricity were two other fields characterized by extremely rapid scientific progress. Chemists devised ways of measuring the atomic weight of different elements, and in 1869 the Russian chemist Dmitri Mendeleev (1834–1907) codified the rules of chemistry in the periodic law and the periodic table. Chemistry was subdivided into many specialized branches, such as *organic chemistry*—the study of the compounds of carbon. Applying theoretical insights gleaned from this new field, researchers in large German chemical companies discovered ways of transforming the dirty, useless coal tar that accumulated in coke ovens into beautiful, expensive synthetic dyes for the world of fashion. The basic discoveries of Michael Faraday (1791–1867) on electromagnetism in the 1830s and 1840s resulted in the first dynamo (generator) and opened the way for the subsequent development of electric motors, electric lights, and electric streetcars. The rapid development of the electrical and organic chemical industries spurred European economic growth between 1880 and 1913.

The triumph of science and technology had at least three significant consequences. First, though ordinary citizens continued to lack detailed scientific knowledge, everyday experience and innumerable popularizers impressed the importance of science on the popular mind.

Second, as science became more prominent in popular thinking, the philosophical implications of science formulated in the Enlightenment spread to broad sections of the population. Natural processes appeared to be determined by rigid laws, leaving little room for either divine intervention or human will. Yet scientific and technical advances had also fed the Enlightenment's optimistic faith in human progress.

Third, the methods of science acquired unrivaled prestige after 1850. For many, the union of careful experiment and abstract theory was the only reliable route to truth and objective reality. Thus many thinkers tried to apply the objective methods of science to the study of society from the 1830s onward.

The new "social scientists" had access to the massive sets of numerical data that governments had begun to collect on everything from children to crime, from population to prostitution. In response, social scientists developed new statistical methods to analyze these facts "scientifically" and supposedly to test their theories. Leading nineteenth-century social scientists resembled the eighteenth-century philosophes, but their systems were more all-encompassing and dogmatic. Marx was a prime example (see pages 814–815).

Another extremely influential system builder was French philosopher Auguste Comte (1798–1857). Initially a disciple of the utopian socialist Saint-Simon (see page 813), Comte wrote the six-volume *System of Positive Philosophy* (1830–1842), which came into its own after 1850. Comte postulated that all intellectual activity progresses through predictable stages:

The great fundamental law . . . is this:—that each of our leading conceptions—each branch of our knowledge—passes successively through three different theoretical conditions: the Theological, or fictitious; the Metaphysical, or abstract; and the Scientific, or positive. . . . The first is the necessary point of departure of human understanding, and the third is the fixed and definitive state. The second is merely a transition.[14]

By way of example, Comte noted that the prevailing explanation of cosmic patterns had shifted, as knowledge of astronomy developed, from the will of God (the theological) to the will of an orderly nature (the metaphysical) to the rule of unchanging laws (the scientific). Later, this same intellectual progression took place in increasingly complex fields—physics, chemistry, and, finally, the study of society. By applying the scientific or *positivist* method, Comte believed, his new discipline of sociology would soon discover the eternal laws of human relations, which would enable expert social scientists to impose a disciplined harmony and well-being on less enlightened citizens.

Comte's stages of knowledge exemplify the nineteenth-century fascination with the idea of evolution and dynamic development. Thinkers in many fields, such as the romantic historians and "scientific" Marxists, shared and applied this basic

concept. In geology, Charles Lyell (1797–1875) effectively discredited the long-standing view that the earth's surface had been formed by short-lived cataclysms, such as biblical floods and earthquakes. Instead, according to Lyell's principle of uniformitarianism, the same geological processes that are at work today slowly formed the earth's surface over an immensely long time.

The most influential of all nineteenth-century evolutionary thinkers was Charles Darwin (1809–1882). As the official naturalist on a five-year scientific cruise to Latin America and the South Pacific beginning in 1831, Darwin carefully collected specimens of the different animal species he encountered on the voyage. Back in England, from fossil evidence, Darwin came to doubt the general belief in a special divine creation of each species of animals. Instead, he concluded, all life had gradually evolved from a common ancestral origin in an unending "struggle for survival." After long hesitation, Darwin published his research, which immediately attracted wide attention.

Darwin's theory is summarized in the title of his work *On the Origin of Species by the Means of Natural Selection* (1859). Darwin argued that chance differences among the members of a given species help some survive while others die. Thus the variations that prove useful in the struggle for survival are selected naturally and spread gradually to the entire species through reproduction.

As the capstone of already widespread evolutionary thinking, Darwin's theory had a powerful and many-sided influence on European thought and the European middle classes. Darwin was hailed as the great scientist par excellence, the "Newton of biology," who had revealed once again the powers of objective science. Darwin's findings also reinforced the teachings of secularists such as Comte and Marx, who scornfully dismissed religious belief in favor of agnostic or atheistic materialism. In the great cities especially, religion was on the defensive. Finally, many writers applied the theory of biological evolution to human affairs. Herbert Spencer (1820–1903), an English disciple of Auguste Comte, saw the human race as driven forward to ever-greater specialization and progress by the brutal economic struggle that efficiently determined the "survival of the fittest." The poor were the ill-fated weak; the prosperous, the chosen strong. Understandably, Spencer and other Social Darwinists were especially popular with the upper middle class.

Attracting Females Darwin theorized that those males who were most attractive to females would have the most offspring, like this type of monkey, which had developed ornamental hair, giving him devastating sex appeal. Darwin used this illustration in *The Descent of Man* (1871). *(Source: Library of Congress)*

Realism in Literature

In 1868 Émile Zola (1840–1902), the giant of the realist movement in literature, defended his violently criticized first novel against charges of pornography and corruption of morals. Such accusations were meaningless, Zola claimed: he was only a purely objective scientist using

the modern method, the universal instrument of inquiry of which this age makes such ardent use to open up the future. . . . I chose characters completely dominated by their nerves and their blood, deprived of free-will, pushed to each action of their lives by the fatality of their flesh. . . . I have simply done on living bodies the work of analysis which surgeons perform on corpses.[15]

Zola's literary manifesto articulated the key themes of realism, which had emerged in the 1840s and continued to dominate Western culture and style until the 1890s. Realist writers believed that literature should depict life exactly as it was. Forsaking poetry for prose and the personal, emotional viewpoint of the romantics for strict, scientific objectivity, the realists simply observed and recorded—content to let the facts speak for themselves.

The major realist writers focused their extraordinary powers of observation on contemporary everyday life. Emphatically rejecting the romantic search for the exotic and the sublime, they energetically pursued the typical and the commonplace. Beginning with a dissection of the middle classes, from which most of them sprang, many realists eventually focused on the working classes, especially the urban working classes, which had been neglected in imaginative literature before this time. The realists put a microscope to many unexplored and taboo subjects—sex, strikes, violence, alcoholism—and hastened to report that slums and factories teemed with savage behavior. Many shocked middle-class critics denounced realism as ugly sensationalism wrapped provocatively in pseudoscientific declarations and crude language.

The realists' claims of objectivity did not prevent the elaboration of a definite world-view. Unlike the romantics, who had gloried in individual freedom and an unlimited universe, realists such as Zola were strict determinists. Human beings, like atoms, were components of the physical world, and all human actions were caused by unalterable natural laws. Heredity and environment determined human behavior; good and evil were merely social conventions.

The realist movement began in France, where romanticism had never been completely dominant, and three of its greatest practitioners—Balzac, Flaubert, and Zola—were French. Honoré de Balzac (1799–1850) spent thirty years writing a vastly ambitious panorama of postrevolutionary French life. Known collectively as *The Human Comedy,* this series of nearly one hundred books vividly portrays more than two thousand characters from virtually all sectors of French society. Balzac pictures urban society as grasping, amoral, and brutal, characterized by a Darwinian struggle for wealth and power.

Madame Bovary (1857), the masterpiece of Gustave Flaubert (1821–1880), strove for depth and accuracy of psychological insight. Unsuccessfully prosecuted as an outrage against public morality and religion, Flaubert's carefully crafted novel tells the ordinary story of a frustrated middle-class housewife who has an adulterous love affair and is betrayed by her lover. Without moralizing, Flaubert portrays the provincial middle class as petty, smug, and hypocritical.

Zola was most famous for his seamy, animalistic view of working-class life. But he also wrote gripping, carefully researched stories featuring the stock exchange, the big department store, and the army as well as urban slums and bloody coal strikes. Like many later realists, Zola sympathized with socialism, a sympathy evident in his overpowering *Germinal* (1885).

Realism quickly spread beyond France. In England, Mary Ann Evans (1819–1880), who wrote under the pen name George Eliot, brilliantly achieved a more deeply felt, less sensational kind of realism. "It is the habit of my imagination," George Eliot wrote, "to strive after as full a vision of the medium in which a character moves" as of the character itself. Her great novel *Middlemarch: A Study of Provincial Life* examines the ways in which people are shaped by their social medium as well as their own inner strivings, conflicts, and moral choices. Thomas Hardy (1840–1928) was more in the Zola tradition. His novels, such as *Tess of the D'Urbervilles* and *Return of the Native,* depict men and women frustrated and crushed by fate and bad luck.

The greatest Russian realist, Count Leo Tolstoy (1828–1910), combined realism in description and character development with an atypical moralizing, which came to dominate his later work. Tolstoy's greatest work was *War and Peace,* a monumental novel set against the historical background of Napoleon's invasion of Russia in 1812. Tolstoy went to great pains to develop his fatalistic theory of history, which regards free will as an illusion and the achievements of even the greatest leaders as only the channeling of historical necessity. Yet Tolstoy's central message was one that most of the people discussed in this chapter would have readily accepted: human love, trust, and everyday family ties are life's enduring values.

✤ THE RESPONSIVE NATIONAL STATE (1871–1914)

After 1871 the heartland of Europe was organized into strong national states, and the common themes within that framework were the emergence of mass politics and growing mass loyalty toward the national state. On the borders of Europe—in Ireland and Russia, in Austria-Hungary and the Balkans—the dynamics were different. Subject peoples there were still striving for political unity and independence. National aspirations created tensions, and mass politics often undermined existing states.

There were good reasons why ordinary people—the masses of an industrializing, urbanizing society—felt increasing loyalty to their governments in central and western Europe. More people could vote. By 1914 universal male suffrage had become the rule rather than the exception. This development had as much psychological as political significance. Ordinary men were no longer denied the right to vote because they lacked wealth or education. They felt that they were becoming "part of the system."

Women also began to demand the right to vote. The women's suffrage movement achieved its first success in the western United States, and by 1913 women could vote in twelve states. Europe, too, moved slowly in this direction. In 1914 Norway gave the vote to most women. Elsewhere, women such as the English Emmeline Pankhurst were militant in their demands. They heckled politicians and held public demonstrations. These efforts generally failed before 1914, but they prepared the way for the triumph of the women's suffrage movement in many countries immediately after World War I.

As the right to vote spread, politicians and parties in national parliaments represented the people more responsively. The multiparty system prevailing in most countries meant that parliamentary majorities were built on shifting coalitions, which gave parties leverage to obtain benefits for their supporters. Governments also passed laws to alleviate general problems, thereby acquiring greater legitimacy and appearing more worthy of support.

Less positively, governments found that they could manipulate national feeling to create a sense of unity and to divert attention away from underlying class conflicts. For example, in Germany conservative and moderate leaders who despised socialism found that workers who voted socialist would still rally around the flag in a diplomatic crisis or that they would cheer enthusiastically when distant territory of doubtful value was seized in Africa or Asia (see Chapter 27). In Austria-Hungary and Russia conflicting ethnic groups would also close ranks when faced with a foreign foe. Therefore, governing elites frequently channeled national sentiment in an antiliberal and militaristic direction after 1871. This policy helped manage domestic conflicts, but only at the expense of increasing the international tensions that erupted in 1914 in cataclysmic war and revolution (see Chapter 29).

The German Empire

Politics in Germany after 1871 reflected many of the general developments. The new German Empire was a federal union of Prussia and twenty-four smaller states. Much of the everyday business of government was conducted by the separate states, but there was a strong national government with a chancellor—until 1890, Bismarck—and a popularly elected parliament, called the *Reichstag.* Although Bismarck refused to be bound by a parliamentary majority, he tried nonetheless to maintain one. This situation gave the political parties opportunities. Until 1878 Bismarck relied mainly on the National Liberals, who had rallied to him after 1866. They supported legislation useful for further economic and legal unification of the country.

Less wisely, they backed Bismarck's attack on the Catholic church, the so-called *Kulturkampf,* or "struggle for civilization." Like Bismarck, the middle-class National Liberals were particularly alarmed by Pius IX's declaration of papal infallibility in 1870. That dogma seemed to ask German

Catholics to put loyalty to their church above loyalty to their nation. Only in Protestant Prussia did the Kulturkampf have even limited success. Catholics throughout the country generally voted for the Catholic Center party, which blocked passage of national laws hostile to the church. Finally, in 1878 Bismarck abandoned his attack. Indeed, he and the Catholic Center party entered into an uneasy but mutually advantageous alliance. Their reasons for doing so were largely economic.

As cheap grain poured in from new lands in the United States, Canada, and Russia, European peasants, with their smaller, less efficient farms, could not compete in cereal production. In western and southern Germany, the peasantry was largely Catholic, and the Catholic Center party was thus converted to higher tariffs to protect the economic interests of its supporters.

The same competitive pressures caused the Protestant Junkers, who owned large estates in eastern Germany, to embrace the cause of higher tariffs. They were joined by some iron and steel magnates. Thus in going along with a new protective tariff in 1879, Bismarck won new Catholic and conservative supporters in the Reichstag, and he held on to most of the National Liberals.

Many other governments turned to higher tariffs in the 1880s and 1890s to protect agriculture and industry from foreign competition. Thus the German government and other governments responded to a major economic problem and won greater loyalty. The general rise of protectionism in the late nineteenth century was also an outstanding example of the dangers of self-centered nationalism: high tariffs led to international name calling and nasty trade wars.

As for socialism, Bismarck tried to stop its growth in Germany because he genuinely feared its revolutionary language and allegiance to a movement transcending the nation-state. In 1878, after two attempts on the life of William I by radicals (though not socialists), Bismarck used a carefully orchestrated national outcry to ram through the Reichstag a law that strictly controlled socialist meetings and publications and outlawed the Social Democratic party, which was thereby driven underground. German socialists, however, displayed a discipline and organization worthy of the Prussian army itself, so Bismarck decided to try another tack.

Bismarck's essentially conservative nation-state pioneered with social measures designed to win the support of working-class people. In 1883 he pushed through the Reichstag the first of several modern social security laws to help wage earners. Henceforth sick, injured, and retired workers could look forward to some regular benefits from the state. This national social security system, paid for through compulsory contributions by wage earners and employers as well as grants from the state, was the first of its kind anywhere. (The United States would not take similar measures for fifty years.) This enormously significant development was a product of political competition and government efforts to win popular support.

Increasingly, the great issues in German domestic politics were socialism and the Marxian Social Democratic party. In 1890 the new emperor, the young, idealistic, and unstable William II (r. 1888–1918), opposed Bismarck's attempt to renew the law outlawing the Social Democratic party. Eager to rule in his own right and to earn the support of the workers, William II forced Bismarck to resign. After this "dropping of the pilot," German foreign policy changed profoundly and mostly for the worse, but the government did pass new laws to aid workers and to legalize socialist political activity.

Yet William II was no more successful than Bismarck in getting workers to renounce socialism. Indeed, socialist ideas spread rapidly, and more and more Social Democrats were elected to the Reichstag in the 1890s. In the elections of 1912 the German Social Democratic party became the largest single party in the Reichstag. This victory shocked aristocrats and their wealthy conservative middle-class allies, heightening their fears of an impending socialist upheaval. Yet the "revolutionary" socialists were actually becoming less and less revolutionary in Germany. In the years before World War I, as the Social Democratic party broadened its base and adopted a more patriotic tone, German socialists identified increasingly with the German state, and they concentrated on gradual social and political reform.

Republican France

Although Napoleon III's reign made some progress in reducing antagonisms between classes, the war with Prussia undid these efforts, and in 1871 France seemed hopelessly divided once again. The patriotic republicans who proclaimed the Third Republic in Paris after the military disaster at

Sedan refused to admit defeat. They defended Paris with great heroism for weeks, living off rats and zoo animals until they were starved into submission by German armies in January 1871. When national elections then sent a large majority of conservatives and monarchists to the National Assembly, the traumatized Parisians exploded in patriotic frustration and proclaimed the Paris Commune in March 1871. Vaguely radical, the leaders of the Commune wanted to govern Paris without interference by the conservative French countryside. The National Assembly, led by aging politician Adolphe Thiers, would hear none of it. The Assembly ordered the French army into Paris and brutally crushed the Commune. Twenty thousand people died in the fighting. As in June 1848, it was Paris against the provinces, French against French.

Out of this tragedy France slowly formed a new national unity, achieving considerable stability before 1914. How is one to account for this? Luck played a part. Until 1875 the monarchists in the "republican" National Assembly had a majority but could not agree about who should be king. The compromise Bourbon candidate refused to rule except under the white flag of his ancestors—a completely unacceptable condition. In the meantime, Thiers's destruction of the radical Commune and his other firm measures showed the fearful provinces and the middle class that the Third Republic might be moderate and socially conservative. France therefore retained the republic, though reluctantly. As President Thiers cautiously said, this was "the government which divides us least."

Another stabilizing factor was the skill and determination of the moderate republican leaders in the early years. The most famous of these was Léon Gambetta, the son of an Italian grocer, a warm, easygoing lawyer who had turned professional politician. A master of emerging mass politics, Gambetta combined eloquence with the personal touch as he preached a republic of truly equal opportunity. Gambetta was also instrumental in establishing absolute parliamentary supremacy between 1877 and 1879, when the deputies forced the somewhat autocratic president of the republic to resign. By 1879 the great majority of members of both the upper and the lower houses of the National Assembly were republicans, and the Third Republic had firm foundations after almost a decade.

The moderate republicans sought to preserve their creation by winning the hearts and minds of the next generation. Trade unions were fully legalized, and France acquired a colonial empire. More important, a series of laws between 1879 and 1886 established free compulsory elementary education for both girls and boys. At the same time, the state system of public tax-supported schools was expanded. In France and elsewhere the general expansion of public education served as a critical nation-building tool in the late nineteenth century.

In France most elementary and much secondary education had traditionally been in the parochial schools of the Catholic church, which had long been hostile to republics and to much of secular life. Free compulsory elementary education in France became secular republican education. The pledge of allegiance and the national anthem replaced the catechism and the "Ave Maria." Militant young male and female teachers carried the ideology of patriotic republicanism into every corner of France. In their classes, these women and men sought to win the loyalty of the young citizens to the republic so that France would never again vote en masse for dictators like the two Napoleons.

Unlike most Western countries (including the United States), which insisted on the total "purity" of their female elementary teachers and would not hire a married woman, the Third Republic actively encouraged young teachers to marry and guaranteed that both partners would teach in the same location. There were three main reasons for this unusual policy. First, married female (and male) teachers with their own children provided a vivid contrast to celibate nuns (and priests), who had for generations stood for most primary education in the popular mind. Second, the republican leaders believed that married women (and men) would better cope with the potential loneliness and social isolation of unfamiliar towns and villages, especially where the local Catholic school was strong. Third, French politicians and opinion leaders worried continually about France's very low birthrate after 1870, and they believed that women combining teaching careers and motherhood would provide the country with a good example. The hiring of married schoolteachers was part of an effort to create a whole new culture of universal, secular, and republican education. This illustrates a larger truth—that truly lasting political change must usually be supported by changes in the underlying culture.

Although the educational reforms of the 1880s disturbed French Catholics, many of them rallied to the republic in the 1890s, and tensions between church and state eased. Unfortunately, the Dreyfus affair changed all that. Alfred Dreyfus, a Jewish captain in the French army, was falsely accused and convicted of treason. His family never doubted his innocence and fought to reopen the case, enlisting the support of prominent republicans and intellectuals such as novelist Émile Zola. In 1898 and 1899, the case split France apart. On one side was the army, which had manufactured evidence against Dreyfus, joined by anti-Semites and most of the Catholic establishment. On the other side stood the civil libertarians and most of the more radical republicans.

This battle, which eventually led to Dreyfus's being declared innocent, revived republican feeling against the church. Between 1901 and 1905, the government severed all ties between the state and the Catholic church after centuries of close relations. The salaries of priests and bishops were no longer paid by the government. Catholic schools were put completely on their own financially, and in a short time they lost a third of their students. The state school system's power of indoctrination was greatly strengthened. In France only the growing socialist movement, with its very different but thoroughly secular ideology, stood in opposition to patriotic, republican nationalism.

Captain Alfred Dreyfus   Leaving an 1899 reconsideration of his original court-martial, Dreyfus receives an insulting "guard of dishonor" from soldiers who turn their backs to him. Top army leaders were determined to brand Dreyfus as a traitor. *(Source: Bibliothèque Nationale, Paris)*

Great Britain and Ireland

Britain in the late nineteenth century has often been seen as a shining example of peaceful and successful political evolution, where an effective two-party parliament skillfully guided the country from classical liberalism to full-fledged democracy with hardly a misstep. This view of Great Britain is not so much wrong as incomplete. After the right to vote was granted to males of the solid middle class in 1832, opinion leaders and politicians wrestled with the uncertainties of a further extension of the franchise. In 1867 Benjamin Disraeli and the Conservatives extended the vote to all middle-class males and the best-paid workers in the Second Reform bill. The son of a Jewish stockbroker and himself a novelist and urban dandy, the ever-fascinating Disraeli (1804–1881) was willing to risk

this "leap in the dark" in order to broaden the Conservative party's traditional base of aristocratic and landed support. After 1867 English political parties and electoral campaigns became more modern, and the "lower orders" appeared to vote as responsibly as their "betters." Hence the Third Reform Bill of 1884 gave the vote to almost every adult male.

While the House of Commons was drifting toward democracy, the House of Lords, between 1901 and 1910, tried and ultimately failed to reassert itself. Aristocratic conservatism yielded to popular democracy once and for all. The result was that extensive social welfare measures, slow to come to Great Britain, were passed in a spectacular rush between 1906 and 1914. During those years, the Liberal party, inspired by the fiery Welshman David Lloyd George (1863–1945), substantially raised taxes on the rich as part of the so-called People's Budget. This income helped the government pay for national health insurance, unemployment benefits, old-age pensions, and a host of other social measures. The state was integrating the urban masses socially as well as politically.

This record of accomplishment was only part of the story, however. On the eve of World War I, the question of Ireland brought Great Britain to the brink of civil war. The Irish famine in the 1840s (see page 822) fueled an Irish revolutionary movement. Thereafter, the English slowly granted concessions, such as the abolition of the privileges of the Anglican church and rights for Irish peasants. Liberal prime minister William Gladstone (1809–1898) introduced bills to give Ireland self-government in 1886 and in 1893, but they failed to pass. After two decades of relative quiet, Irish nationalists in the British Parliament saw their chance. They supported the Liberals in their battle for the People's Budget and in 1913 received a home-rule bill for Ireland in return.

Ireland, however, was composed of two peoples. As much as the Irish Catholic majority in the southern counties wanted home rule, precisely that much did the Irish Protestants in the northern counties of Ulster come to oppose it. Motivated by the accumulated fears and hostilities of generations, the Ulsterites vowed to resist home rule in northern Ireland. By December 1913 they had raised a hundred thousand armed volunteers, and they were supported by much of English public opinion. Thus in 1914 the Liberals in the House of Lords introduced a compromise home-rule bill that did not apply to the northern counties. This bill, which openly betrayed promises made to Irish nationalists, was rejected, and in September the original home-rule bill was passed but simultaneously suspended for the duration of the hostilities. The momentous Irish question was overtaken by an earth-shattering world war in August 1914.

Irish developments illustrated once again that governments could not elicit greater loyalty unless they could capture and control that elemental current of national feeling. Though Great Britain had much going for it—power, Parliament, prosperity—none of these availed in the face of the conflicting nationalisms espoused by Catholics and Protestants in northern Ireland. Similarly, progressive Sweden was powerless to stop the growth of the Norwegian national movement, which culminated in Norway's breaking away from Sweden

and becoming a fully independent nation in 1905. In this light, one can also see how hopeless was the case of the Ottoman Empire in Europe in the later nineteenth century. It was only a matter of time before the Serbs, Bulgarians, and Rumanians would break away, and they did.

The Austro-Hungarian Empire

The dilemma of conflicting nationalisms in Ireland also helps one appreciate how desperate the situation in the Austro-Hungarian Empire had become by the early twentieth century. In 1849 Magyar nationalism had driven Hungarian patriots to declare an independent Hungarian republic, which was savagely crushed by Russian and Austrian armies (see pages 824–826). Throughout the 1850s, Hungary was ruled as a conquered territory, and Emperor Francis Joseph and his bureaucracy tried hard to centralize the state and Germanize the language and culture of the different nationalities.

Then in the wake of defeat by Prussia in 1866, a weakened Austria was forced to strike a compromise and establish the so-called dual monarchy. The empire was divided in two, and the nationalistic Magyars gained virtual independence for Hungary. The two states were joined only by a shared monarch and common ministries for finance, defense, and foreign affairs. After 1867 the disintegrating force of competing nationalisms continued unabated, for both Austria and Hungary had several "Irelands" within their borders.

In Austria ethnic Germans were only one-third of the population, and by 1895 many Germans saw their traditional dominance threatened by Czechs, Poles, and other Slavs. A particularly emotional issue in the Austrian parliament was the language used in government and elementary education at the local level. From 1900 to 1914, the parliament was so divided that ministries generally could not obtain a majority and ruled instead by decree. Efforts by both conservatives and socialists to defuse national antagonisms by stressing economic issues that cut across ethnic lines—endeavors that led to the introduction of universal male suffrage in 1907—proved largely unsuccessful.

One aspect of such national antagonisms was anti-Semitism, which was particularly virulent in Austria. The Jewish populations of Austrian cities grew very rapidly after Jews obtained full legal equality in 1867, and by 1900 Jews constituted 10 percent of the population of Vienna. Many Jewish

THE AGE OF NATIONALISM IN EUROPE, 1871–1914

1871–1914	Third Republic in France
1878	Suppression of Social Democrats in Germany
1881	Assassination of Tsar Alexander II
1883–1889	Enactment of social security laws in Germany
1884	Third Reform Bill passed by British Parliament
1889–1914	Second Socialist International
1890	Repeal of anti–Social Democrat law in Germany
1892–1903	Witte directs modernization of Russian economy
1904–1905	Japan wins decisive victory in Russo-Japanese War
1905	Revolution in Russia: Tsar Nicholas II forced to issue the October Manifesto promising a popularly elected Duma
1906–1914	Liberal reform in Great Britain
1907–1912	Stolypin's agrarian reforms in Russia
1912	German Social Democratic party becomes largest party in the German Reichstag
1914	Irish Home Rule bill passed by British Parliament but immediately suspended with outbreak of First World War

business people were quite successful in banking and retail trade, and Jewish artists, intellectuals, and scientists, such as the world-famous Sigmund Freud, played a major role in making Vienna a leading center of European culture and modern thought. When extremists charged the Jews with controlling the economy and corrupting German culture with alien ideas and ultramodern art, anxious Germans of all classes tended to listen—including an unsuccessful young artist named Adolf Hitler.

In Hungary the Magyar nobility in 1867 restored the constitution of 1848 and used it to dominate both the Magyar peasantry and the minority populations until 1914. Only the wealthiest one-fourth of adult males had the right to vote, making the parliament the creature of the Magyar elite. Laws promoting use of the Magyar (Hungarian) language in schools and government were rammed through and bitterly resented, especially by the Croatians and Rumanians. While Magyar extremists campaigned loudly for total separation from Austria, the radical leaders of the subject nationalities dreamed in turn of independence from Hungary. Unlike most major countries, which harnessed nationalism to strengthen the state after 1871, the Austro-Hungarian Empire was progressively weakened and destroyed by nationalism.

The Modernization of Russia

The Russian Empire was also an enormous multinational state, containing all the ethnic Russians and many other nationalities as well. Thus Russia's rulers saw national self-determination as a subversive ideology in the early nineteenth century, and they tried with some success to limit its development among their non-Russian subjects. Then after 1853 old autocratic Russia found itself in serious trouble. It became clear to Russia's leaders that the country had to embrace the process of modernization. A vague and often overworked term, *modernization* can be a useful concept if it is defined narrowly as the changes that enable a country to compete effectively with the leading countries at a given time. This concept of modernization fits Russia after the Crimean War particularly well.

In the 1850s Russia was a poor agrarian society. Industry was little developed, and almost 90 percent of the population lived on the land. Agricultural techniques were backward: the ancient open-field system reigned supreme. Serfdom was still the basic social institution, but it had become the great moral and political issue for the government by the 1840s. Then the Crimean War of 1853 to 1856, arising out of a dispute with France over who should protect certain Christian shrines in the Ottoman Empire, brought crisis. Because the fighting was concentrated in the Crimean peninsula on the Black Sea, Russia's transportation network of rivers and wagons failed to supply the distant Russian armies adequately. France and Great Britain, aided by Sardinia and the Ottoman Empire, inflicted a humiliating defeat on Russia.

Military defeat marked a turning point in Russian history because it clearly demonstrated that Russia had fallen behind the rapidly industrializing nations of western Europe in many areas. At the very least, Russia needed railroads, better armaments, and reorganization of the army if it was to maintain its international position. Moreover, the disastrous war had caused hardship and raised the specter of massive peasant rebellion. Reform of serfdom was imperative. Military disaster thus forced the new tsar, Alexander II (r. 1855–1881), and his ministers along the path of rapid social change and general modernization.

The first and greatest of the reforms was the freeing of the serfs in 1861. Human bondage was abolished forever, and the emancipated peasants received, on average, about half of the land. Yet they had to pay fairly high prices for their land, and because the land was owned collectively, each peasant village was jointly responsible for the payments of all the families in the village. The government hoped that collective responsibility would strengthen the peasant village as a social unit and prevent the development of a class of landless peasants. In practice, collective ownership and responsibility made it very difficult for individual peasants

to improve agricultural methods or leave their villages. Thus the effects of the reform were limited.

Most of the later reforms were also halfway measures. In 1864 the government established a new institution of local government, the *zemstvo,* but the local zemstvo remained subordinate to the traditional bureaucracy and the local nobility. More successful was reform of the legal system, which established independent courts and equality before the law. Education was also liberalized somewhat, and censorship was relaxed but not removed.

Until 1905 Russia's greatest strides toward modernization were economic rather than political. Industry and transport, both so vital to the military, were transformed in two industrial surges. After 1860 the government subsidized private railway companies, and construction boomed. In 1860 the empire had only about 1,250 miles of railroads; by 1880 it had about 15,500 miles. The railroads enabled agricultural Russia to export grain and thus earn money for further industrialization. Industrial suburbs grew up around Moscow and St. Petersburg, and a class of modern factory workers began to take shape.

Industrial development strengthened Russia's military forces and gave rise to territorial expansion to the south and east. Imperial expansion greatly excited many ardent Russian nationalists and superpatriots, who became some of the government's most enthusiastic supporters. Industrial development also contributed mightily to the spread of Marxian thought and the transformation of the Russian revolutionary movement after 1890.

In 1881 a small group of terrorists assassinated Alexander II. The era of reform came to an abrupt end, for the new tsar, Alexander III (r. 1881–1894), was a determined reactionary. Political modernization remained frozen until 1905, but economic modernization sped forward in the massive industrial surge of the 1890s. Nationalism played a decisive role, as it had after the Crimean War. The key leader was Sergei Witte, the tough, competent minister of finance from 1892 to 1903. Inspired by the writings of Friedrich List (see page 790), Witte believed that industrial backwardness was threatening Russia's power and greatness. Therefore, under Witte's leadership the government built state-owned railroads rapidly, doubling the network to 35,000 miles by the end of the century. The gigantic trans-Siberian line connecting Moscow with Vladivostok on the Pacific Ocean

5,000 miles away was Witte's pride. Following List's advice, Witte established high protective tariffs to build Russian industry, and he put the country on the gold standard of the "civilized world" to strengthen Russian finances.

Witte's greatest innovation, however, was to use the West to catch up with the West. He aggressively encouraged foreigners to use their abundant capital and advanced technology to build great factories in backward Russia. As he told the tsar, "The inflow of foreign capital is . . . the only way by which our industry will be able to supply our country quickly with abundant and cheap products."[16] This policy was brilliantly successful, especially in southern Russia. There, in eastern Ukraine, foreign capitalists and their engineers built an enormous and very modern steel and coal industry almost from scratch in little more than a decade. By 1900 only the United States, Germany, and Great Britain were producing more steel than Russia. The Russian petroleum industry had even pulled up alongside that of the United States and was producing and refining half of the world's output of oil. A fiercely autocratic and independent Russia was catching up with the advanced nations of the West.

Catching up partly meant vigorous territorial expansion, for this was the age of Western imperialism. By 1903 Russia had established a sphere of influence in Chinese Manchuria and was casting greedy eyes on northern Korea. When the diplomatic protests of equally imperialistic Japan were ignored, the Japanese launched a surprise attack in February 1904. To the amazement of self-confident Europeans, Asian Japan scored repeated victories, and Russia was forced in August 1905 to accept a humiliating defeat.

As is often the case, military disaster abroad brought political upheaval at home. The business and professional classes had long wanted to match economic with political modernization and a representative regime. Factory workers, strategically concentrated in the large cities, had all the grievances of early industrialization and were organized in a radical and still illegal labor movement. Peasants suffered from poverty and overpopulation. At the same time, nationalist sentiment was emerging among the empire's minorities. The politically and culturally dominant ethnic Russians were only about 45 percent of the population, and by 1900 some intellectuals among the subject nationalities,

especially the Poles and Ukrainians, were calling for self-rule and autonomy. With the army pinned down in Manchuria, all these currents of discontent converged in the revolution of 1905.

The beginning of the revolution pointed up the incompetence of the government. On a Sunday in January 1905, a massive crowd of workers and their families converged peacefully on the Winter Palace in St. Petersburg to present a petition to the tsar. Led by a trade-unionist priest, carrying icons, and respectfully singing, "God save the tsar," the workers did not know that Tsar Nicholas II (r. 1894–1917) had fled the city. Suddenly troops opened fire, killing and wounding hundreds. The "Bloody Sunday" massacre turned ordinary workers against the tsar and produced a wave of general indignation.

The Limits of Russian Modernization The business and professional classes grew stronger and became more prosperous in the era of reform, but the hard life of Russian peasants changed slowly. The striking contrast between the rugged old peasant and the elegant middle-class women in this photo aptly symbolizes the widening gap between the two sections of the population. *(Source: Sovfoto/Eastfoto)*

Outlawed political parties came out into the open, and by the summer of 1905 strikes, peasant uprisings, revolts among minority nationalities, and troop mutinies were sweeping the country. The revolutionary surge culminated in October 1905 in a great paralyzing general strike, which forced the government to capitulate. The tsar issued the October Manifesto, which granted full civil rights and promised a popularly elected *Duma* (parliament) with real legislative power.

On the eve of the opening of the first Duma in May 1906, the government issued the new constitution, the Fundamental Laws. The tsar retained great powers. The Duma, elected indirectly by universal male suffrage, and a largely appointive upper house could debate and pass laws, but the tsar had an absolute veto. As in Bismarck's Germany, the emperor appointed his ministers, who did not need to command a majority in the Duma.

The disappointed, predominately middle-class liberals, the largest group in the newly elected Duma, saw the Fundamental Laws as a step backward. Efforts to cooperate with the tsar's ministers soon broke down. The tsar then dismissed the Duma, only to see a more hostile and radical opposition elected in 1907. After three months of deadlock, the tsar dismissed the second Duma. Thereupon he and his reactionary advisers unilaterally rewrote the electoral law to increase greatly the weight of the propertied classes at the expense of workers, peasants, and national minorities.

The new law had the intended effect. With landowners assured half of the seats in the Duma, the government secured a loyal majority in 1907. Thus armed, the tough, energetic chief minister, Peter Stolypin, pursued a policy seeking to broaden support for the state. He pushed through important agrarian reforms designed to break down collective village ownership of land and to encourage the more enterprising peasants—a strategy known as the "wager on the strong." On the eve of World War I, Russia was partially modernized, a conservative constitutional monarchy with a peasant-based but industrializing economy.

❖ MARXISM AND THE SOCIALIST MOVEMENT

Nationalism served, for better or worse, as a new unifying principle. But what about socialism? Did the rapid growth of socialist parties, which were generally Marxian parties dedicated to an international proletarian revolution, mean that national states had failed to gain the support of workers? This question requires close examination.

The Socialist International

Certainly socialism appealed to large numbers of working men and women in the late nineteenth century (see Listening to the Past), and the growth of socialist parties after 1871 was phenomenal. Neither Bismarck's antisocialist laws nor his extensive social security system checked the growth of the German Social Democratic party, which espoused the Marxian ideology. By 1912 it had millions of followers and was the largest party in the Reichstag. Socialist parties also grew in other countries, though nowhere else with such success. In France various socialist parties were unified in 1905 in an increasingly powerful Marxian party called the French Section of the Workers International.

As the name of the French party suggests, Marxian socialist parties were eventually linked together in an international organization. As early as 1848, Marx had laid out his intellectual system in the *Communist Manifesto* (see pages 814–815). He had declared that "the working men have no country," and he had urged proletarians of all nations to unite against their governments. Joining the flood of radicals and republicans who fled continental Europe for England and America after the unsuccessful revolutions of 1848, Marx settled in London. Poor and depressed, he lived on his meager earnings as a journalist and on the gifts of his friend Engels. Marx never stopped thinking of revolution. Digging deeply into economics and history, he concluded that revolution follows economic crisis and tried to prove this position in *Critique of Political Economy* (1859) and in his greatest theoretical work, *Capital* (1867).

The bookish Marx also showed a rare flair for combining theorization with both lively popular writing and organizational ability. In 1864 he played an important role in founding the First International of socialists—the International Working Men's Association. In the following years, he battled successfully to control the organization, and he used its annual meetings as a means of spreading his realistic, "scientific" doctrines of inevitable socialist revolution. Then Marx enthusiastically embraced the passionate, vaguely radical patriotism of the Paris Commune and its terrible conflict with the French National Assembly as a giant step toward socialist revolution. This impetuous action frightened many of his early supporters, especially the more moderate British labor leaders. The First International collapsed.

Yet international proletarian solidarity remained an important objective for Marxists. In 1889, as the individual parties in different countries grew stronger, socialist leaders came together to form the Second International, which lasted until 1914. The International was only a federation of national socialist parties, but it had great psychological impact. Every three years, delegates from the different parties met to interpret Marxian doctrines and plan coordinated action. May 1 (May Day) was declared an annual international one-day strike, a day of marches and demonstrations. A permanent executive for the International was established. Many feared and many others rejoiced in the growing power of socialism and the Second International.

Unions and Revisionism

Was socialism really radical and revolutionary in these years? On the whole, it was not. Indeed, as socialist parties grew and attracted large numbers of members, they looked more and more toward gradual change and steady improvement for the working class and less and less toward revolution.

Workers themselves were progressively less inclined to follow radical programs. There were several reasons for this. As workers gained the right to vote and won real, tangible benefits, their attention focused more on elections than on revolutions. Workers were also not immune to patriotic education and indoctrination during military service, and many responded positively to drum-beating parades and aggressive foreign policy as they loyally voted for socialists. Nor were workers a unified social group.

Perhaps most important of all, workers' standard of living rose gradually but substantially after 1850 as the promise of the Industrial Revolution was at least partially realized. In Great Britain, for example, workers could buy almost twice as much with their wages in 1906 as in 1850, and most of the increase came after 1870. The quality of life also improved dramatically in urban areas. For all these reasons, workers tended more and more to become militantly moderate: they demanded gains, but they were less likely to take to the barricades in pursuit of them.

The growth of labor unions reinforced this trend toward moderation. In the early stages of industrialization, modern unions were considered subversive bodies and were generally prohibited by law. From this sad position workers struggled to escape. Great Britain led the way in 1824 and 1825 when unions won the right to exist but (generally) not the right to strike. After the collapse of Robert Owen's attempt to form one big union in the 1830s (see page 799), new and more practical kinds of unions appeared. Limited primarily to highly skilled workers such as machinists and carpenters, the "new model unions" avoided both radical politics and costly strikes. Instead, their sober, respectable leaders concentrated on winning better wages and hours for their members through collective bargaining and compromise. This approach helped pave the way to full acceptance in Britain in the 1870s, when unions won the right to strike without being held legally liable for the financial damage inflicted on employers. After 1890 unions for unskilled workers developed, and between 1901 and 1906 the legal position of British unions was further strengthened.

Germany was the most industrialized, socialized, and unionized country in continental Europe by 1914. German unions were not granted important rights until 1869, and until the antisocialist law was repealed in 1890, the government frequently harassed them as socialist fronts. The result was that as late as 1895, there were only about 270,000 union members in a male industrial work force of nearly 8 million. Then with German industrialization still storming ahead and almost all legal harassment eliminated, union membership skyrocketed, reaching roughly 3 million in 1912. Genuine collective bargaining, long opposed by socialist intellectuals as a "sellout," was officially recognized as desirable by the German Trade Union Congress in 1899. When employers proved unwilling to bargain, a series of strikes forced them to change their minds. Between 1906 and 1913, successful collective bargaining gained a prominent place in German industrial relations. Gradual improvement, not revolution, was becoming the primary goal of the German trade-union movement.

The German trade unions and their leaders were in fact, if not in name, thoroughgoing revisionists. *Revisionism* was an effort by various socialists to update Marxian doctrines to reflect the realities of the time. The socialist Edward Bernstein (1850–1932) argued in 1899 in his *Evolutionary Socialism*

May Day in Dresden, 1890   As this print from a German newspaper suggests, workers participated enthusiastically in the one-day strike honoring international socialist solidarity. But May Day was also a happy holiday, a celebration of working-class respectability and an independent working-class culture. *(Source: Archiv für Kunst und Geschichte, Berlin)*

that Marx's predictions of ever-greater poverty for workers had been proved false. Therefore, Bernstein suggested, socialists should reform their doctrines and tactics. They should combine with other progressive forces to win gradual evolutionary gains for workers through legislation, unions, and further economic development. The German Social Democratic party and later the entire Second International denounced these views as heresy. Yet the revisionist, gradualist approach continued to gain the tacit acceptance of many German socialists, particularly in the trade unions.

Moderation found followers elsewhere. In France the great socialist leader Jean Jaurès (1859–1914) formally repudiated revisionist doctrines in order to establish a unified socialist party, but he

remained at heart a gradualist. Questions of revolutionary versus gradualist policies split Russian Marxists.

Socialist parties before 1914 had clear-cut national characteristics. Russians and socialists in the Austro-Hungarian Empire tended to be the most radical. The German party talked revolution and practiced reformism, greatly influenced by its enormous trade-union movement. The French party talked revolution and tried to practice it, unrestrained by a trade-union movement that was both very weak and very radical. In England the socialist but non-Marxian Labour party, reflecting the well-established union movement, was formally committed to gradual reform. In Spain and Italy Marxian socialism was very weak. There anarchism, seeking to smash the state rather than the bourgeoisie, dominated radical thought and action.

In short, socialist policies and doctrines varied from country to country. Socialism itself was to a large extent "nationalized" behind the imposing façade of international unity. This helps explain why almost all socialist leaders supported their governments when war came in 1914.

SUMMARY

The Industrial Revolution had a decisive influence on the urban environment. As the populations of towns and cities grew rapidly, long-standing overcrowding and unhealthy living conditions worsened alarmingly. Eventually government leaders, city planners, reformers, scientists, and ordinary citizens responded to this frightening challenge. They took effective action in public health, developed badly needed urban services, and gradually tamed the savagery of the traditional city.

As urban civilization came to prevail, there were major changes in family life. Especially among the working classes, family life became more stable, more loving, and less mercenary. These improvements exacted a price, however. Sex roles for men and women became sharply defined and rigidly separate. Women tended to be locked into a subordinate and stereotypical role. Nonetheless, on balance, the quality of family life improved. Better, more stable family relations reinforced the benefits for the masses of higher real wages, increased social security, political participation, and education.

While the quality of urban and family life improved, the class structure became more complex and diversified than before. Urban society featured many distinct social groups, and the gap between rich and poor remained enormous. Large numbers of poor women in particular continued to labor as workers in sweated industries and as domestic servants and prostitutes, meeting the demands of the servant-keeping classes. Small wonder then that inequality was a favorite theme of realist novelists such as Balzac and Zola. More generally, literary realism reflected Western society's growing faith in science, material progress, and evolutionary thinking. The emergence of urban, industrial civilization accelerated the secularization of the Western world-view.

Finally, Western society became increasingly nationalistic as well as urban and industrial. Nation-states enlisted widespread support and gave men and women a greater sense of belonging. Even socialism became increasingly national in orientation, gathering strength as a champion of working-class interests in domestic politics. Yet even though nationalism served to unite peoples, it also drove them apart—not only in Austria-Hungary and Ireland but throughout Europe and the rest of the world. The national faith, which reduced social tensions within states, promoted a bitter, almost Darwinian competition between states and thus threatened the progress and unity it had helped to build, as we shall see in Chapter 32.

NOTES

1. A. Weber, *The Growth of Cities in the Nineteenth Century* (New York: Columbia University Press, 1899), p. 1.
2. S. Marcus, "Reading the Illegible," in *The Victorian City: Images and Realities,* ed. H. J. Dyos and Michael Wolff, vol. 1 (London: Routledge & Kegan Paul, 1973), p. 266.
3. E. Gauldie, *Cruel Habitations: A History of Working-Class Housing, 1780–1918* (London: George Allen & Unwin, 1974), p. 21.
4. J. P. McKay, *Tramways and Trolleys: The Rise of Urban Mass Transport in Europe* (Princeton, N.J.: Princeton University Press, 1976), p. 81.
5. Quoted in B. Harrison, "Underneath the Victorians," *Victorian Studies* 10 (March 1967): 260.
6. Quoted in J. A. Banks, "The Contagion of Numbers," in Dyos and Wolff, *The Victorian City,* p. 112.
7. Quoted in R. Roberts, *The Classic Slum: Salford Life in the First Quarter of the Century* (Manchester, Eng.: University of Manchester Press, 1971), p. 95.
8. Quoted in T. Zeldin, *France, 1848–1945,* vol. 1 (Oxford: Clarendon Press, 1973), p. 288.
9. Quoted in S. Marcus, *The Other Victorians: A Study of Sexuality and Pornography in Mid-Nineteenth-Century England* (New York: Basic Books, 1966), p. 142.
10. Quoted in G. S. Jones, "Working-Class Culture and Working-Class Politics in London, 1870–1900: Notes on the Remaking of a Working Class," *Journal of Social History* 7 (Summer 1974): 486.
11. Quoted in Zeldin, *France, 1848–1945,* p. 346.

12. Roberts, *The Classic Slum,* p. 35.

13. Quoted in Zeldin, *France, 1848–1945,* p. 295.

14. A. Comte, *The Positive Philosophy of Auguste Comte,* trans. H. Martineau, vol. 1 (London: J. Chapman, 1853), pp. 1–2.

15. Quoted in G. J. Becker, ed., *Documents of Modern Literary Realism* (Princeton, N.J.: Princeton University Press, 1963), p. 159.

16. Quoted in J. P. McKay, *Pioneers for Profit: Foreign Entrepreneurship and Russian Industrialization, 1885–1913* (Chicago: University of Chicago Press, 1970), p. 11.

Suggested Reading

All of the books and articles cited in the Notes are highly recommended. T. Zeldin, *France, 1848–1945,* is a pioneering social history. T. Hamerow, *The Birth of a New Europe: State and Society in the Nineteenth Century* (1983) is an ambitious synthesis, and P. Pillbeam, *The Middle Classes in Europe, 1789–1914: France, Germany, Italy, and Russia* (1990), is a stimulating introduction. Aristocratic strength and survival is the theme of A. Mayer's *Persistence of the Old Regime: Europe to the Great War* (1981).

On the European city, D. Harvey, *Consciousness and the Urban Experience* (1985), is provocative. D. Silverman's, *Art Nouveau in Fin-de-Siècle France: Politics, Psychology, and Style* (1989) and N. Evenson's beautifully illustrated *Paris: A Century of Change, 1878–1978* (1979), are fascinating, as are G. Masur's, *Imperial Berlin* (1970), M. Hamm, ed., *The City in Russian History* (1976), and D. Grew's authoritative *Town in the Ruhr: A Social History of Bochum, 1860–1914* (1979). J. Merriman, *Margins of City Life: Explorations on the French Urban Frontier* (1991), is an important work on France. The outstanding study by J. Schmiechen, *Sweated Industries and Sweated Labor: The London Clothing Trades* (1984), complements H. Mayhew's wonderful contemporary study, *London Labour and the Labouring Poor* (1861), reprinted recently. Michael Crichton's realistic historical novel on organized crime, *The Great Train Robbery* (1976), is excellent. J. P. Goubert, *The Conquest of Water: The Advent of Health in the Industrial Age* (1989), and G. Rosen, *History of Public Health* (1958), offer a fine introduction to sanitary and medical developments.

For society as a whole, J. Burnett, *History of the Cost of Living* (1969), cleverly shows how different classes spent their money, and B. Tuchman, *The Proud Tower* (1966), draws an unforgettable portrait of people and classes before 1914. J. Laver's handsomely illustrated *Manners and Morals in the Age of Optimism, 1848–1914* (1966) investigates the urban underworld and relations between the sexes. Sexual attitudes are also examined by J. Walkowitz, *Prostitution and Victorian Society: Women, Class and State* (1890); J. Phayer, *Sexual Liberation and Religion in Nineteenth-Century Europe* (1977); and L. Engelstein, *The Key to Happiness: Sex and the Search for Modernity in Fin-de-Siècle Russia* (1992). G. Alter, *Family and Female Life Course: The Women of Verviers, Belgium, 1849–1880* (1988), and A. McLaren, *Sexuality and Social Order: Birth Control in Nineteenth-Century France* (1982), explore attitudes toward family planning.

Women have come into their own in historical studies. Among general works L. Tilly and J. Scott, *Women, Work and Family* (1978), is especially recommended. There are a growing number of eye-opening specialized investigations. These include L. Davidoff, *The Best Circles* (1973), and P. Jalland, *Women, Marriage and Politics, 1860–1914* (1986), on upper-class society types; and P. Branca, *Women in Europe Since 1750* (1978). M. J. Peterson, *Love and Work in the Lives of Victorian Gentlewomen* (1989), L. Holcombe, *Victorian Ladies at Work* (1973), and M. Vicinus, *Independent Women: Work and Community for Single Women, 1850–1920* (1985), examine women at work. M. Vicinus, ed., *Suffer and Be Still* (1972), and *A Widening Sphere* (1981), are far-ranging collections of essays on women's history, as is R. Bridenthal, C. Koonz, and S. Stuard, eds., *Becoming Visible: Women in European History,* 2d ed. (1987). Feminism is treated perceptively in R. Evans, *The Feminists: Women's Emancipation in Europe, America, and Australia* (1979), and in C. Moses, *French Feminism in the Nineteenth Century* (1984). L. Tickner, *The Spectacle of Women: Imagery of the Suffrage Campaign, 1907–1914* (1988), perceptively discusses Britain. J. Gillis, *Youth and History* (1974), is a good introduction. D. Ransel, ed., *The Family in Imperial Russia* (1978), is an important work on the subject.

Among studies of special groups, J. R. Wegs, *Growing Up Working Class: Continuity and Change Among Viennese Youth, 1890–1938* (1989), is recommended. Two fine studies on universities and their professors are S. Rothblatt, *Revolution of the Dons: Cambridge and Society in Victorian England* (1968), and F. Ringer, *The Decline of the German Mandarins* (1969). Servants and their employers receive excellent treatment in T. McBride, *The Domestic Revolution: The Modernization of Household Service in England and France, 1820–1920* (1976), and B. Smith, *Ladies of the Leisure Class: The Bourgeoises of Northern France in the Nineteenth Century* (1981), which may be compared with the innovative study by M. Miller, *The Bon Marché: Bourgeois Culture and the Department Store, 1869–1920* (1981).

On Darwin, M. Ruse, *The Darwinian Revolution* (1979), and P. Bowler, *Evolution: The History of an Idea,* rev. ed. (1989), are good starting points. O. Chadwick, *The Secularization of the European Mind in the Nineteenth Century* (1976), analyzes the impact of science (and other factors) on religious belief. The masterpieces of the great realist social novelists remain one of the best and most memorable introductions to nineteenth-century culture and thought. In addition to the novels discussed in this chapter and those cited in the Suggested Reading for Chapters 24 and 25, Ivan Turgenev's *Fathers and Sons* and Émile Zola's *The Dram-Shop* are especially recommended.

For individual countries, in addition to the general works mentioned in the Suggested Reading for Chapter 25, G. Craig, *Germany, 1866–1945* (1980), and B. Moore, *Social Origins of Dictatorship and Democracy* (1966), are outstanding. R. Anderson, *France, 1870–1914* (1977), provides a good introduction and has a useful bibliography. E. Weber, *France, Fin de Siècle* (1986), captures the spirit of Paris at the end of the century. G. Chapman, *The Dreyfus Case: A Reassessment* (1955), and D. Johnson, *France and the Dreyfus Affair* (1967), are careful examinations of the famous case. In *Jean Barois,* Nobel Prize winner Roger Du Gard accurately recreates in novel form the Dreyfus affair. D. M. Smith has written widely on Italy, and his *Garibaldi* (1956) and *Italy: A Modern History,* rev. ed. (1969), are recommended.

H. Wehler, *The German Empire, 1871–1918* (1985), stresses the strength of the landed nobility and the weakness of the middle class in an influential synthesis, which is challenged by D. Blackbourn and G. Eley, *The Peculiarities of German History: Bourgeois Society and Politics in 19th-Century Germany* (1984). F. Stern, *Gold and Iron* (1977), is a fascinating examination of relations between Bismarck and his financial adviser, the Jewish banker Bleichröder. L. Cecil, *Wilhelm II: Prince and Emperor, 1859–1900* (1989), probes the character and politics of Germany's ruler. G. Iggers, *The German Conception of History* (1968), and E. Spencer, *Management and Labor in Imperial Germany: Ruhr Industrialists as Employers* (1984), are valuable in-depth investigations. C. Schorske, *Fin de Siècle Vienna: Politics and Culture* (1980), is brilliant on aspects of modern culture.

On Russia, in addition to McKay cited in the Notes, see T. von Laue, *Sergei Witte and the Industrialization of Russia* (1970); A. Rieber, *Merchants and Entrepreneurs in Imperial Russia* (1982); and H. Rogger, *Russia in the Age of Modernization and Revolution, 1881–1917* (1983), which has an excellent bibliography. H. Troyat, *Daily Life in Russia Under the Last Tsar* (1962), is lively and recommended. T. Friedgut, *Iuzovka and Revolution: Life and Work in Russia's Donbass, 1869–1924* (1989); R. Zelnik, *Labor and Society in Tsarist Russia, 1855–1870* (1971); and R. Johnson, *Peasant and Proletarian: The Working Class of Moscow at the End of the Nineteenth Century* (1979), skillfully treat different aspects of working-class life and politics. W. E. Mosse, *Alexander II and the Modernization of Russia* (1958), discusses midcentury reforms, whereas C. Black, ed., *The Transformation of Russian Society* (1960), offers a collection of essays on Russian modernization.

G. Dangerfield, *The Strange Death of Liberal England* (1961), brilliantly examines social tensions in Ireland as well as English women's struggle for the vote before 1914. D. Boyce, *Nationalism in Ireland,* 2d ed. (1991), provides an excellent account of the Irish struggle for nationhood.

J. Seigel, *Marx's Fate: The Shape of a Life* (1978), is an outstanding biography. C. Schorske, *German Social Democracy, 1905–1917* (1955), is a modern classic. V. Lidtke, *The Alternative Culture: Socialist Labor in Imperial Germany* (1985), and J. Quataert, *Reluctant Feminists in German Social Democracy, 1885–1917* (1979), are also recommended for the study of the German socialists. H. Goldberg, *The Life of Jean Jaurès* (1962), is a sympathetic account of the great French socialist leader. D. Geary, ed., *Labour and Socialist Movements in Europe Before 1914* (1989), contains excellent studies on different countries and has up-to-date references.

LISTENING TO THE
PAST

The Making of a Socialist

Nationalism and socialism appeared locked in bitter competition in Europe before 1914, but they actually complemented each other in many ways. Both faiths were secular as opposed to religious, and both fostered political awareness. A working person who became interested in politics and developed nationalist beliefs might well convert to socialism at a later date.

This was the case for Adelheid Popp (1869–1939), a self-taught working woman who became an influential socialist leader. Born into a desperately poor working-class family in Vienna and remembering only a "hard and gloomy childhood," she was forced by her parents to quit school at age ten to begin full-time work. She struggled with low-paying piecework for years before she landed a solid factory job, as she recounts in the following selection from her widely read autobiography.

Always an avid reader, Popp became the editor of a major socialist newspaper for German working women. She then told her life story so that all working women might share her truth: "Socialism could change and strengthen others, at it did me."

[Finally] I found work again; I took everything that was offered me in order to show my willingness to work, and I passed through much. But at last things became better. [At age fifteen] I was recommended to a great factory which stood in the best repute. Three hundred girls and about fifty men were employed. I was put in a big room where sixty women and girls were at work. Against the windows stood twelve tables, and at each sat four girls. We had to sort the goods which had been manufactured, others had to count them, and a third set had to brand on them the mark of the firm. We worked from 7 A.M. to 7 P.M. We had an hour's rest at noon, half-an-hour in the afternoon. . . . I had never yet been paid so much. . . .

I seemed to myself to be almost rich. . . . [Yet] from the women of this factory one can judge how sad and full of deprivation is the lot of a factory worker. In none of the neighbouring factories were the wages so high; we were envied everywhere. Parents considered themselves fortunate if they could get their daughters of fourteen in there on leaving school. . . . And even here, in this paradise, all were badly nourished. Those who stayed at the factory for the dinner hour would buy themselves for a few pennies a sausage or the leavings of a cheese shop. . . . In spite of all the diligence and economy, every one was poor, and trembled at the thought of losing her work. All humbled themselves, and suffered the worst injustice from the foremen, not to risk losing this good work, not to be without food. . . .

I did not only read novels and tales; I had begun . . . to read the classics and other good books. I also began to take an interest in public events. . . . I was not democratically inclined. I was full of enthusiasm then for emperors, and kings and highly placed personages played no small part in my fancies. . . . I bought myself a strict Catholic paper, that criticized very adversely the workers' movement, which was attracting notice. Its aim was to educate in a patriotic and religious direction. . . . I took the warmest interest in the events that occurred in the royal families, and I took the death of the Crown Prince of Austria so much to heart that I wept a whole day. . . . Political events [also] held me in suspense. The possibility of a war with Russia roused my patriotic enthusiasm. I saw my brother already returning from the battlefield covered with glory. . . .

When a particularly strong anti-Semitic feeling was noticeable in political life, I sympathised with it for a time. A broad sheet, "How Israel Attained Power and Sovereignty over all the Nations of the Earth," fascinated me. . . .

About this time an Anarchist group was active. Some mysterious murders which had taken place were ascribed to the Anarchists, and the police made use of them to oppress the rising workmen's movement. . . . I followed the trial of the Anarchists with passionate sympathy. I read all the speeches, and because, as always happens, Social Democrats, whom the authorities really wanted to attack, were among the accused, I learned their views. I became full of enthusiasm. Every single Social Democrat . . . seemed to me a hero. . . .

There was unrest among the workers . . . and demonstrations of protest followed. When these were repeated the military entered the "threatened" streets. . . . In the evenings I rushed in the greatest excitement from the factory to the scene of the disturbance. The military did not frighten me; I only left the place when it was "cleared."

Later on my mother and I lived with one of my brothers who had married. Friends came to him, among them some intelligent workmen. One of these workmen was particularly intelligent, and . . . could talk on many subjects. He was the first Social Democrat I knew. He brought me many books, and explained to me the difference between Anarchism and Socialism. I heard from him, also for the first time, what a republic was, and in spite of my former enthusiasm for royal dynasties, I also declared myself in favour of a republican form of government. I saw everything so near and so clearly, that I actually counted the weeks which must still elapse before the revolution of state and society would take place.

From this workman I received the first Social Democratic party organ. . . . I first learned from it to understand and judge of my own lot. I learned to see that all I had suffered was the result not of a divine ordinance, but of an unjust organization of society. . . .

In the factory I became another woman. . . . I told my [female] comrades all that I had read of the workers' movement. Formerly I had often told stories when they had begged me for them. But instead of narrating . . . the fate of some queen, I now held forth on oppression and exploitation. I told of accumu-

Engraving (1890) of a meeting of workers in Berlin. *(Source: Bildarchiv Preussischer Kulturbesitz)*

lated wealth in the hands of a few, and introduced as a contrast the shoemakers who had no shoes and the tailors who had no clothes. On breaks I read aloud the articles in the Social Democratic paper and explained what Socialism was as far as I understood it. . . . [While I was reading] it often happened that one of the clerks passing by shook his head and said to another clerk: "The girl speaks like a man."

Questions for Analysis

1. How did Popp describe and interpret work in the factory?

2. To what extent did Popp's socialist interpretation of factory life fit the facts she described?

3. What were Popp's political interests before she became a socialist?

4. How and why did Popp become a Social Democrat?

5. Was this account likely to lead other working women to socialism? Why or why not?

Source: Slightly adapted from A. Popp, *The Autobiography of a Working Woman*, trans. E. C. Harvey (Chicago: F. G. Browne, 1913), pp. 29, 34–35, 39, 66–69, 71, 74, 82–90.

27

The World and the West

The Emigrant Ship
(1898) by British painter
Charles J. Staniland.
*(Source: Bridgeman Art
Library, London)*

While industrialization and nationalism were transforming urban life and Western society, Western society itself was reshaping the world. At the peak of its power and pride, the West entered the third and most dynamic phase of the aggressive expansion that had begun with the Crusades and continued with the great discoveries and the rise of seaborne colonial empires. An ever-growing stream of products, people, and ideas flowed out of Europe in the nineteenth century. Hardly any corner of the globe was left untouched. The most spectacular manifestations of Western expansion came in the late nineteenth century when the leading European nations established or enlarged their far-flung political empires. The political annexation of territory in the 1880s—the "new imperialism," as it is often called by historians—was the capstone of a profound underlying economic and technological process.

- How and why did this many-sided, epoch-making expansion occur in the nineteenth century?
- What were some of its consequences for the West and the rest of the world?

These are the questions this chapter will examine.

✤ INDUSTRIALIZATION AND THE WORLD ECONOMY

The Industrial Revolution created, first in Great Britain and then in continental Europe and North America, a growing and tremendously dynamic economic system. In the course of the nineteenth century, that system was extended across the face of the earth. Some of this extension into non-Western areas was peaceful and beneficial for all concerned, for the West had many products and techniques that the rest of the world desired. If peaceful methods failed, however, Europeans used their superior military power to force non-Western nations to open their doors to Western economic interests. In general, Westerners fashioned the global economic system so that the largest share of the ever-increasing gains from trade, technology, and migration flowed to the West and its propertied classes.

The Rise of Global Inequality

The Industrial Revolution in Europe marked a momentous turning point in human history. Indeed, only by placing Europe's economic breakthrough in a global perspective can one truly appreciate its revolutionary implications and consequences.

From such a global perspective, the ultimate significance of the Industrial Revolution was that it allowed those regions of the world that industrialized in the nineteenth century to increase their wealth and power enormously in comparison to those that did not. As a result, a gap between the industrializing regions (mainly Europe and North America) and the nonindustrializing ones (mainly Africa, Asia, and Latin America) opened up and grew steadily throughout the nineteenth century. Moreover, this pattern of uneven global development became institutionalized, or built into the structure of the world economy, and the "lopsided world"—a world of rich lands and poor—evolved.

Historians have long been aware of this gap, but only recently have historical economists begun to chart its long-term evolution with some precision. Their findings are extremely revealing, although they contain a margin of error and other limitations as well. Figure 27.1 summarizes the findings of one such study. It compares the long-term evolution of average income per person in today's "developed" (or industrialized) regions with average income per person in the "Third World" (or developing regions) (see page 1173). To get these individual income figures, researchers estimate a country's gross national product (GNP) at different points in time, convert those estimates to some common currency, and divide by the total population.

Figure 27.1 highlights three main points. First, in 1750 the average standard of living was no higher in Europe as a whole than in the rest of the world. In 1750 Europe as a whole was still a poor agricultural society. By 1970, however, the average person in the wealthiest countries had an income fully twenty-five times as great as the income received by the average person in the poorest Third World countries of Africa and Asia.

Second, it was industrialization that opened the gaps in average wealth and well-being among countries and regions. Great Britain had jumped

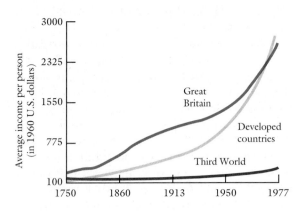

Note: The Third World includes Africa, Asia, Latin America, and Oceania. Developed countries include all European countries, Canada, the United States, and Japan.

❋ **FIGURE 27.1 The Growth of Average Income per Person in the Third World, Developed Countries, and Great Britain, 1750–1970** (*Source: Data from P. Bairoch and M. Lévy-Leboyer, eds.,* Disparities in Economic Development Since the Industrial Revolution. *St. Martin's Press, New York, 1981, pp. 7–8, 10)*

well above the developed countries' average by 1830. But as the developed countries successfully industrialized in the course of the nineteenth century, Great Britain's lead gradually narrowed.

Third, income per person stagnated in the Third World before 1913, in striking contrast to the industrializing regions. Only after 1945, in the era of political independence and decolonization, did Third World countries finally make some real economic progress, beginning the critical process of industrialization.

The rise of these enormous income disparities, which are poignant indicators of disparities in food and clothing, health and education, life expectancy and general material well-being, has generated a great deal of debate. One school of interpretation stresses that the West used science, technology, capitalist organization, and even its critical worldview to create its wealth and greater physical well-being. Another school argues that the West used its political and economic power to steal much of its riches, continuing in the nineteenth (and twentieth) century the rapacious colonialism born of the era of expansion.

These issues are complex, and there are few simple answers. As noted in Chapter 24, the wealth-creating potential of technological improvement

and more intensive capitalist organization was indeed great. At the same time, those breakthroughs rested, in part, on Great Britain's having already used political force to dominate the world economy in the nineteenth century. Wealth—unprecedented wealth—was indeed created, but the lion's share of that new wealth flowed to the West and its propertied classes and to a tiny non-Western elite of cooperative rulers, landowners, and merchants.

The World Market

Commerce between nations has always been a powerful stimulus to economic development. Never was this more true than in the nineteenth century. World trade grew modestly until about 1840 and then took off. After a slowdown in the last years of the century, another surge lasted until World War I. In 1913 the value of world trade was roughly $38 billion, or about *twenty-five* times what it had been in 1800, even though prices of manufactured goods and raw materials were lower in 1913 than in 1800. In a general way, the enormous increase in international commerce summed up the growth of an interlocking world economy centered in and directed by Europe.

Great Britain played a key role in using trade to tie the world together economically. In 1815 Britain already had a colonial empire, for India, Canada, Australia, and other scattered areas remained British possessions after American independence. The technological breakthroughs of the Industrial Revolution allowed Britain to manufacture cotton textiles, iron, and other goods more cheaply and to far outstrip domestic demand for such products. Thus British manufacturers sought export markets first in Europe and then around the world.

Take the case of cotton textiles. By 1820 Britain was exporting 50 percent of its production. Europe bought 50 percent of these cotton textile exports, and India, the world's largest producer of cotton textiles in the seventeenth century, bought 6 percent. When European nations and the United States erected protective tariff barriers and promoted domestic industry, British cotton textile manufacturers aggressively sought and found new foreign markets in non-Western areas. By 1850 India was buying 25 percent and Europe only 16 percent of a much larger total of exported British cotton textiles. As a British colony, India could not raise tariffs to protect its ancient cotton textile industry, so thousands of Indian weavers lost their livelihoods.

After the repeal of the Corn Laws in 1846 (see page 820), Britain became the world's single best market, and it remained the world's emporium until 1914. Free access to Britain's enormous market stimulated the development of mines and plantations in many non-Western areas.

The growth of trade was facilitated by the conquest of distance. The earliest railroad construction occurred in Europe (including Russia) and in America north of the Rio Grande; other parts of the globe saw the building of rail lines after 1860. By 1920 more than a quarter of the world's railroads were in Latin America, Asia, Africa, and Australia. Wherever railroads were built, they drastically reduced transportation costs, opened new economic opportunities, and called forth new skills and attitudes.

The power of steam revolutionized transportation by sea as well as by land. Steampower, long used to drive paddle-wheelers on rivers, particularly in Russia and North America, finally began to supplant sails on the oceans of the world in the late 1860s. Lighter, stronger, cheaper steel replaced iron, which had replaced wood. Screw propellers superseded paddle wheels, and mighty compound steam engines cut fuel consumption by half. Passenger and freight rates tumbled, and the shipment of low-priced raw materials from one continent to another became feasible.

An account of an actual voyage by a typical tramp freighter highlights nineteenth-century developments in global trade. The ship left England in 1910 carrying rails and general freight to western Australia. From there it carried lumber to Melbourne in southeastern Australia, where it took on harvester combines for Argentina. In Buenos Aires it loaded wheat for Calcutta, and in Calcutta it took on jute for New York. From New York it carried a variety of industrial products to Australia before returning to England with lead, wool, and wheat after a voyage of approximately 72,000 miles to six continents in seventeen months.

The revolution in land and sea transportation helped European pioneers open vast new territories and produce agricultural products and raw materials there for sale in Europe. Moreover, the development of refrigerated railway cars and, from the 1880s, refrigerator ships enabled first Argentina and then the United States, Australia, and New Zealand to ship mountains of chilled or frozen beef and mutton to European (mainly British) consumers. From Asia, Africa, and Latin America came not only the traditional tropical products—spices, tea, sugar, coffee—but also new raw materials for industry, such as jute, rubber, cotton, and coconut oil.

Intercontinental trade was enormously facilitated by the Suez and Panama canals. Of great importance, too, was large and continual investment in modern port facilities, which made loading and unloading cheaper, faster, and more dependable. Finally, transoceanic telegraph cables inaugurated rapid communications among the financial centers of the world. While a British tramp freighter steamed from Calcutta to New York, a broker in London was arranging by telegram for it to carry an American cargo to Australia. World commodity prices were also instantaneously conveyed by the same network of communications.

The growth of trade and the conquest of distance encouraged the expanding European economy to make massive foreign investments, beginning about 1840. By the outbreak of the First World War in 1914, Europeans had invested more than $40 billion abroad. Great Britain, France, and Germany were the principal investing countries, although by 1913 the United States was emerging as a substantial foreign investor. The sums involved were enormous. In the decade before 1914, Great Britain was investing 7 percent of its annual national income abroad, or slightly more than it was investing in its entire domestic economy. The great gap between rich and poor within Europe meant that the wealthy and moderately well-to-do could and did send great sums abroad in search of interest and dividends.

Most of the capital exported did not go to European colonies or protectorates in Asia and Africa. About three-quarters of total European investment went to other European countries, the United States and Canada, Australia and New Zealand, and Latin America. Europe found its most profitable opportunities for investment in construction of the railroads, ports, and utilities that were necessary to settle and develop the almost-vacant lands. Much of this investment was peaceful and mutually beneficial for lenders and borrowers. The victims were native American Indians and Australian aborigines, who were displaced and decimated by the diseases, liquor, and weapons of an aggressively expanding Western society.

The Opening of China and Japan

Europe's relatively peaceful development of robust offshoots in sparsely populated North America, Australia, and much of Latin America absorbed huge quantities of goods, investments, and migrants. From a Western point of view, that was the most important aspect of Europe's global thrust. Yet Europe's economic and cultural penetration of old, densely populated civilizations was also profoundly significant, especially for the non-European peoples affected by it. With such civilizations Europeans also increased their trade and profit. Moreover, as had been the case ever since Vasco da Gama and Christopher Columbus, the expanding Western society was prepared to use force, if necessary, to attain its desires. This was what happened in China and Japan, two crucial examples of the general pattern of intrusion into non-Western lands.

Traditional Chinese civilization was self-sufficient. For centuries China had sent more goods and inventions to Europe than it had received, and this was still the case in the eighteenth century. Europeans and the English in particular had developed a taste for Chinese tea, but they had to pay for it with hard silver since China was supremely uninterested in European wares. Trade with Europe was carefully regulated by the Chinese imperial government—the Manchu Dynasty—which was more interested in isolating and controlling the strange "sea barbarians" than in pursuing commercial exchange. The imperial government refused to establish diplomatic relations with the "inferior" European states, and it required all foreign merchants to live in the southern city of Gwangzhou (Canton) and to buy from and sell to only the local merchant monopoly. Practices considered harmful to Chinese interests, such as the sale of opium and the export of silver from China, were strictly forbidden.

For years the little community of foreign merchants in Gwangzhou had to accept the Chinese system. By the 1820s, however, the dominant group, the British, were flexing their muscles. Moreover, in the smoking of opium—that "destructive and ensnaring vice" denounced by patriotic Chinese decrees—they had found something the Chinese really wanted. Grown legally in British-occupied India, opium was smuggled into China by means of fast ships and bribed officials. The more this rich trade developed, the greedier

British merchants became. By 1836 the aggressive goal of the British merchants in Gwangzhou was an independent British colony in China and "safe and unrestricted liberty" in trade. Spurred on by economic motives, they pressured the British government to take decisive action and enlisted the support of British manufacturers with visions of vast Chinese markets to be opened.

At the same time, the Manchu government decided that the opium trade had to be stamped out. The tide of drug addiction was ruining the people and stripping the empire of its silver, which was going to British merchants to pay for the opium. The government began to prosecute Chinese drug dealers vigorously and in 1839 sent special envoy Lin Tse-hsü to Gwangzhou. Lin Tse-hsü ordered the foreign merchants to obey China's laws, "for our great unified Manchu Empire regards itself as responsible for the habits and morals of its subjects and cannot rest content to see any of them become victims of a deadly poison."[1] The British merchants refused and were expelled, whereupon war soon broke out.

Using troops from India and being in control of the seas, the British occupied several coastal cities and forced China to surrender. In the Treaty of Nanjing (Nanking) in 1842, the imperial government was forced to cede the island of Hong Kong to Britain forever, pay an indemnity of $100 million, and open four large cities to foreign trade with low tariffs.

Thereafter the opium trade flourished, and Hong Kong developed rapidly as an Anglo-Chinese enclave. China continued, however, to refuse to accept foreign diplomats in Beijing (Peking), the imperial capital. Finally, there was a second round of foreign attack between 1856 and 1860, culminating in the occupation of Beijing by seventeen thousand British and French troops and the intentional burning of the emperor's summer palace. Another round of harsh treaties gave European merchants and missionaries greater privileges and protection and forced the Chinese to accept trade and investment on unfavorable terms for the foreseeable future. Thus did Europeans use military aggression to blow a hole in the wall of Chinese seclusion and sovereignty.

China's neighbor Japan had its own highly distinctive civilization and even less use for Westerners. European traders and missionaries first arrived in Japan in the sixteenth century. By 1640 Japan had reacted quite negatively to their presence. The

Britain and China at War, 1841   Britain capitalized on its overwhelming naval superiority, and this British aquatint celebrates a dramatic moment in a crucial battle near Gwangzhou. Having received a direct hit from a steam-powered British ironclad, a Chinese sailing ship explodes into a wall of flame. The Chinese lost eleven ships and 500 men in the two-hour engagement; the British suffered only minor damage. *(Source: National Maritime Museum, London)*

government decided to seal off the country from all European influences in order to preserve traditional Japanese culture and society. When American and British whaling ships began to appear off Japanese coasts almost two hundred years later, the policy of exclusion was still in effect. An order of 1825 commanded Japanese officials to "drive away foreign vessels without second thought."[2]

Japan's unbending isolation seemed hostile and barbaric to the West, particularly to the United States. Americans shared the self-confidence and dynamism of expanding Western society and felt destined to play a great role in the Pacific. To Americans, therefore, it seemed their duty to force the Japanese to share their ports and behave as a "civilized" nation.

After several unsuccessful American attempts to establish commercial relations with Japan, Commodore Matthew Perry steamed into Edo (now Tokyo) Bay in 1853 and demanded diplomatic negotiations with the emperor. Japan entered a grave crisis. Some Japanese warriors urged resistance, but

senior officials realized how defenseless their cities were against naval bombardment. Shocked and humiliated, they reluctantly signed a treaty with the United States that opened two ports and permitted trade. Japan was "opened." What the British had done in China with war, the Americans had done in Japan with the threat of war.

Western Penetration of Egypt

Egypt's experience illustrates not only the explosive power of the expanding European economy and society but also their seductive appeal in non-Western lands. European involvement in Egypt also led to a new model of formal political control, which European powers applied widely in Africa and Asia after 1882.

Of great importance in African and Middle Eastern history, since 525 B.C. the ancient land of the pharaohs had been ruled by a succession of foreigners, most recently by the Ottoman Turks. In

1798 French armies under young General Napoleon Bonaparte invaded the Egyptian part of the Ottoman Empire and occupied the territory for three years. Into the power vacuum left by the French withdrawal stepped an extraordinary Albanian-born Turkish general, Muhammad Ali (1769–1849).

First appointed governor of Egypt by the Turkish sultan, Muhammad Ali soon disposed of his political rivals and set out to build his own state on the strength of a large, powerful army organized along European lines and trained by hired French and Italian army officers. The government was also reformed, new lands were cultivated, and communications were improved. By the time of his death in 1849, Muhammad Ali had established a strong and virtually independent Egyptian state, to be ruled by his family on a hereditary basis within the Turkish empire.

Muhammad Ali's policies of modernization attracted large numbers of Europeans to the banks of the Nile. As one Arab sheik of the Ottoman Empire remarked in the 1830s, "Englishmen are like ants; if one finds a bit of meat, hundreds follow."[3] The port city of Alexandria had more than fifty thousand Europeans by 1864. Europeans served not only as army officers but also as engineers, doctors, high government officials, and police officers. Others found their "meat" in trade, finance, and shipping.

To pay for a modern army as well as for European services and manufactured goods, Muhammad Ali encouraged the development of commercial agriculture geared to the European market. This development had profound implications. Egyptian peasants had been poor but largely self-sufficient, growing food for their own consumption on state-owned lands allotted to them by tradition. Faced with the possibility of export agriculture, high-ranking officials and members of Muhammad Ali's family began carving large private landholdings out of the state domain. The new landlords made the peasants their tenants and forced them to grow cash crops for European markets. Borrowing money from European lenders at high rates and still making good profits, Egyptian landowners "modernized" agriculture, but to the detriment of peasant well-being.

These trends continued under Muhammad Ali's grandson Ismail, who in 1863 began his sixteen-

East Meets West   This painting gives a Japanese view of the first audience of the American consul and his staff with the shogun, Japan's hereditary military governor, in 1859. The Americans appear strange and ill at ease. (*Source: Laurie Platt Winfrey, Inc.*)

127 Ancien Veranda de l' Hotel Shepeard   J.O.Zebah

❋ **A Western Hotel in Cairo**   This photo suggests both the reality and the limits of modernization in Ismail's Egypt. An expensive hotel, complete with terrace café and gas lighting, adorns the Egyptian capital. But the hotel is for foreigners, and the native Egyptians are servants and outsiders. *(Source: Popperfoto)*

year rule as Egypt's khedive, or prince. Educated at France's leading military academy, Ismail was a westernizing autocrat. He dreamed of using European technology and capital to modernize Egypt quickly and build a vast empire in northeast Africa. The large irrigation networks he promoted caused cotton production and exports to Europe to boom. Ismail also borrowed large sums to install modern communications, and with his support the Suez Canal was completed by a French company in 1869. The Arabic of the masses, rather than the Turkish of the conquerors, became the official language, and young Egyptians educated in Europe helped spread new skills and new ideas in the bureaucracy. Cairo acquired modern boulevards, Western hotels, and an opera house. As Ismail proudly declared, "My country is no longer in Africa, we now form part of Europe."[4]

But Ismail was impatient and reckless. His projects were enormously expensive, and by 1876

Egypt owed foreign bondholders a colossal $450 million and could not pay the interest on its debt. Rather than let Egypt go bankrupt and repudiate its loans, as some Latin American countries and U.S. state governments had done in the early nineteenth century, the governments of France and Great Britain intervened politically to protect the European bankers who held the Egyptian bonds. They forced Ismail to appoint French and British commissioners to oversee Egyptian finances so that the Egyptian debt would be paid in full. This was a momentous decision. It implied direct European political control: Europeans were going to determine the state budget and in effect rule Egypt.

Foreign financial control evoked a violent nationalistic reaction among Egyptian religious leaders, young intellectuals, and army officers. In 1879, under the leadership of Colonel Ahmed Arabi, they formed the Egyptian Nationalist party. Continuing diplomatic pressure, which forced

Ismail to abdicate in favor of his weak son, Tewfiq (r. 1879–1892), resulted in bloody anti-European riots in Alexandria in 1882. A number of Europeans were killed, and Tewfiq and his court had to flee to British ships for safety. When the British fleet bombarded Alexandria, more riots swept the country, and Colonel Arabi declared that "an irreconcilable war existed between the Egyptians and the English." But a British expeditionary force decimated Arabi's forces and occupied all of Egypt.

The British said their occupation was temporary, but British armies remained in Egypt until 1956. They maintained the façade of the khedive's government as an autonomous province of the Ottoman Empire, but the khedive was a mere puppet. The able British consul, General Evelyn Baring, later Lord Cromer, ruled the country after 1883. Once a vocal opponent of involvement in Egypt, Baring was a paternalistic reformer who had come to believe that "without European interference and initiative reform is impossible here." Baring's rule did result in tax reforms and better conditions for peasants, while foreign bondholders tranquilly clipped their coupons and Egyptian nationalists nursed their injured pride.

In Egypt Baring and the British reluctantly but spectacularly provided a new model for European expansion in densely populated lands. Such expansion was based on military force, political domination, and a self-justifying ideology of beneficial reform. This model was to predominate until 1914. Thus did Europe's Industrial Revolution lead to tremendous political as well as economic expansion throughout the world.

THE GREAT MIGRATION

A poignant human drama was interwoven with economic expansion: millions of people pulled up stakes and left their ancestral lands in the course of history's greatest migration. To millions of ordinary people, for whom the opening of China and the interest on the Egyptian debt had not the slightest significance, this great movement was the central experience in the saga of Western expansion.

The Pressure of Population

In the early eighteenth century, the growth of European population entered its third and decisive stage, which continued unabated until the twentieth century. Birthrates eventually declined in the nineteenth century, but so did death rates, mainly because of the rising standard of living and secondarily because of the medical revolution. Thus the population of Europe (including Asiatic Russia) more than doubled, from approximately 188 million in 1800 to roughly 432 million in 1900.

These figures actually understate Europe's population explosion, for between 1815 and 1932 more than 60 million people left Europe. These migrants went primarily to "areas of European settlement"—North and South America, Australia, New Zealand, and Siberia—where they contributed to a rapid growth in numbers. The population of North America (the United States and Canada) alone grew from 6 million to 81 million between 1800 and 1900 because of continual immigration and high fertility rates. Since population grew more slowly in Africa and Asia than in Europe, Europeans and people of European origin

FIGURE 27.2 The Increase of European and World Populations, 1750–1980   (Source: Data from W. Woodruff, Impact of Western Man: A Study of Europe's Role in the World Economy. St. Martin's Press, New York, 1967, p. 103; United Nations, Statistical Yearbook, 1982, 1985, pp. 2–3)

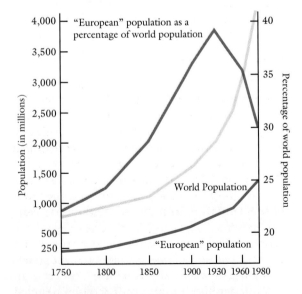

Note: "European" population includes Europe and also areas of predominately European settlement—Asiatic Russia, North America, South America, and Australia/New Zealand.

jumped from about 22 percent of the world's total to about 38 percent on the eve of World War I, as Figure 27.2 shows.

The growing number of Europeans was a driving force behind emigration and Western expansion. As in the eighteenth century, the rapid increase in numbers led to relative overpopulation in area after area. Children of these baby booms grew up, saw little available land and few opportunities, and migrated, especially where rapid population increase predated extensive industrial development. Thus millions of country folk went abroad as well as to nearby cities in search of work and economic opportunity.

Before looking at the people who migrated, let us consider three facts. First, as Figure 27.3 shows, more than 11 million men and women left Europe in the first decade of the twentieth century, over five times the number departing in the 1850s. The outflow of migrants was clearly an enduring characteristic of European society for the entire period.

Second, different countries had very different patterns of movement. As Figure 27.3 also shows, people left Britain and Ireland (which are not distinguished in the British figures) in large numbers from the 1840s on. This emigration reflected not only rural poverty but also the movement of skilled, industrial technicians and the preferences shown to British migrants in the British Empire. Ultimately, about one-third of all European migrants between 1840 and 1920 came from the British Isles. German migration was quite different. It grew irregularly after about 1830, reaching a first peak in the early 1850s and another in the early 1880s. Thereafter it declined rapidly, for Germany's rapid industrialization was providing adequate jobs at home. This pattern contrasted sharply with that of Italy. More and more Italians left the country right up to 1914, reflecting severe problems in Italian villages and relatively slow industrial growth. Thus migration patterns mirrored social and economic conditions in the various European countries and provinces.

Third, although the United States absorbed the largest number of European migrants, less than half of all migrants went to the United States. Asiatic Russia, Canada, Argentina, Brazil, and Australia also attracted large numbers, as Figure 27.4 shows. Moreover, migrants accounted for a larger proportion of the total population in Argentina, Brazil, and Canada than in the United States. The common American assumption that European mi-

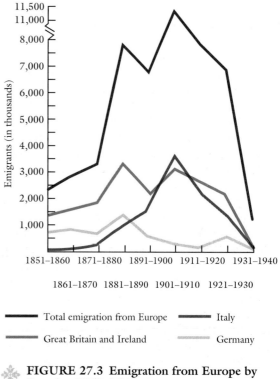

FIGURE 27.3 Emigration from Europe by Decades, 1851–1940 *(Source: Data from W. Woodruff,* Impact of Western Man: A Study of Europe's Role in the World Economy. *St. Martin's Press, New York, 1967, pp. 106–107 and references cited therein)*

gration meant migration to the United States is quite inaccurate.

European Migrants

What kind of people left Europe, and what were their reasons for leaving? The European migrant was most often a small peasant landowner or a village craftsman whose traditional way of life was threatened by too little land, estate agriculture, and cheap, factory-made goods. German peasants who left the Rhineland and southwestern Germany between 1830 and 1854, for example, felt trapped by what Friedrich List called the "dwarf economy," with its tiny landholdings and declining craft industries. Selling out and moving to buy much cheaper land in the American Midwest became a common response.

Contrary to what is often said, the European migrant was generally an energetic small farmer or skilled artisan trying hard to stay ahead of poverty,

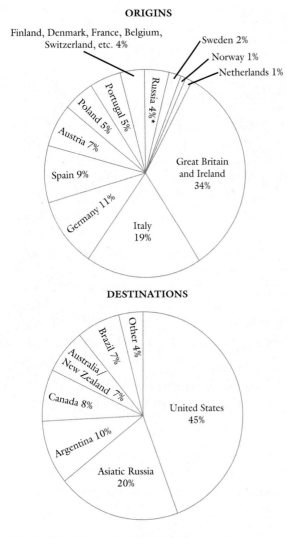

ORIGINS

Finland, Denmark, France, Belgium,
Switzerland, etc. 4%

Sweden 2%
Norway 1%
Netherlands 1%

Portugal 5%
Poland 5%
Austria 7%
Spain 9%
Germany 11%
Russia 4% *

Great Britain
and Ireland
34%

Italy
19%

DESTINATIONS

Other 4%
Brazil 7%
Australia/
New Zealand 7%
Canada 8%
Argentina 10%

United States
45%

Asiatic Russia
20%

* Not including migrants to Asiatic Russia.

FIGURE 27.4 Origin and Destination of European Emigrants, 1851–1960 *(Source: Data from W. Woodruff,* Impact of Western Man: A Study of Europe's Role in the World Economy. *St. Martin's Press, New York, 1967, pp. 108–109 and references cited therein)*

not a desperately impoverished landless peasant or urban proletarian. Determined to maintain or improve their status, migrants were a great asset to the countries that received them. This was doubly so because the vast majority were young and very often unmarried. Fully 67 percent of those admitted to the United States were under thirty-one years of age, and 90 percent were under forty. They came in the prime of life and were ready to

work hard in the new land, at least for a time. Many Europeans, especially by the end of the nineteenth century, were truly migrants as opposed to immigrants—that is, they returned home after some time abroad. One in two migrants to Argentina and probably one in three to the United States eventually returned to their native land.

The likelihood of repatriation varied greatly by nationality. People who migrated from the Balkans, for instance, were far more likely to return to their countries than were people from Ireland and eastern European Jews. Once again, the possibility of buying land in the old country was of central importance. In Ireland (as well as in England and Scotland) land was tightly held by large, often absentee landowners, and little land was available for purchase. In Russia most land was held by non-Jews. Russia's 5 million Jews were already confined to the market towns and small cities of the so-called Pale of Settlement, where they worked as artisans and petty traders. They lived in relative peace until the assassination of Alexander II by non-Jewish terrorists in 1881 brought a new tsar and an official policy of pogroms and savage discrimination. Therefore, when Russian Jewish artisans began in the 1880s to escape both oppression and factory competition by migrating—a migration that eventually totaled 2 million people—this was basically a once-and-for-all departure.

In contrast, most Italian migrants were not landless laborers from areas dominated by large estates; such people tended to stay in Italy and turned increasingly toward radical politics. Instead, most Italian migrants were small landowning peasants whose standard of living was falling because of rural overpopulation and agricultural depression. Migration provided them with an escape valve and possible income to buy more land. Many Italians had no intention of settling abroad permanently. Some called themselves "swallows." After harvesting their own wheat and flax in Italy, they "flew" to Argentina to harvest wheat between December and April. Returning to Italy for the spring planting, they repeated this exhausting process. This was a very hard life, but a frugal worker could save from $250 to $300 in the course of a season.

Ties of family and friendship played a crucial role in the movement of peoples. Many people from a given province or village settled together in rural enclaves or tightly knit urban neighborhoods thousands of miles away. Very often a strong individual—a businessman, a religious leader—would

The Drama of Migration   These Italian migrants are passing through the port of Naples around 1900, heading for temporary work and permanent settlement in North and South America. Naples was the principal outlet for large-scale migration from southern Italy. It handled more passengers than all other Italian ports combined. *(Source: Touring Club Italiano, Milan)*

blaze the way and others would follow, forming a "migration chain."

Many landless young European men and women were spurred to leave by a spirit of revolt and independence. In Sweden and in Norway, in Jewish Russia and in Italy, these young people felt frustrated by the small privileged classes, which often controlled both church and government and resisted demands for change and greater opportunity. Many a young Norwegian seconded the passionate cry of Norway's national poet, Bjørnstjerne Bjørnson (1832–1910): "Forth will I! Forth! I will be crushed and consumed if I stay."[5]

Many young Jews wholeheartedly agreed with a spokesman of Kiev's Jewish community who declared in 1882, "Our human dignity is being trampled upon, our wives and daughters are being dishonored, we are looted and pillaged: either we get decent human rights or else let us go wherever our eyes may lead us."[6] Thus for many, migration was a radical way to "get out from under." Migration slowed when the people won basic political and social reforms, such as the right to vote and social security.

Asian Migrants

Not all migration was from Europe. A substantial number of Chinese, Japanese, Indians, and Filipinos—to name only four key groups—responded to rural hardship with temporary or permanent migration. At least 3 million Asians (as opposed to more than 60 million Europeans) moved abroad before 1920. Most went as indentured laborers to work under incredibly difficult conditions on the plantations or in the gold mines of Latin America, southern Asia, Africa, California, Hawaii, and Australia.

The Jewish Market Located on New York's Lower East Side, this market was a bustling center of economic and social life in 1900. Jewish immigrants could usually find work with Jewish employers, and New York's Jewish population soared from 73,000 in 1880 to 1.1 million in 1910. *(Source: The Granger Collection)*

White estate owners very often used Asians to replace or supplement blacks after the suppression of the slave trade. In the 1840s, for example, there was a strong demand for field hands in Cuba, and the Spanish government actively recruited Chinese laborers. They came under eight-year contracts, were paid about 25 cents a day, and were fed potatoes and salted beef. Between 1853 and 1873, more than 130,000 Chinese laborers went to Cuba. The majority spent their lives as virtual slaves. Such migration was stopped in 1873. The great landlords of Peru also brought in more than 100,000 workers from China in the nineteenth century, and there were similar movements of Asians elsewhere.

Such migration from Asia would undoubtedly have grown to much greater proportions if planters and mine owners in search of cheap labor had had their way. But they did not. Asians fled the plantations and gold mines as soon as possible, seeking greater opportunities in trade and towns, where they came into conflict with brown-skinned peoples—as in Malaya and East Africa—and with white settlers in areas of European settlement. These settlers demanded a halt to Asian migration. One Australian brutally summed up the typical view: "The Chinaman knows nothing about Caucasian civilization. . . . It would be less objectionable to drive a flock of sheep to the poll than to allow Chinamen to vote. The sheep at all events would be harmless."[7] By the 1880s Americans and Australians were building "great white walls"—discriminatory laws designed to keep Asians out. Thus a final, crucial factor in the migrations before

1914 was the general policy of "whites only" in the open lands of possible permanent settlement. This, too, was part of Western dominance in the increasingly lopsided world.

Largely successful in monopolizing the best overseas opportunities, Europeans and people of European ancestry reaped the main benefits from the great migration. By 1913 people in Australia, Canada, and the United States all had higher average incomes than people in Great Britain, still Europe's wealthiest nation.

WESTERN IMPERIALISM

The expansion of Western society reached its apex between about 1880 and 1914. In those years, the leading European nations continued to send massive streams of migrants, money, and manufactured goods around the world, and they rushed to create or enlarge vast *political* empires abroad. This fran-tic political empire building contrasted sharply with the economic penetration of non-Western territories between 1816 and 1880, which, albeit by naked military force, had left a China or a Japan "opened" but politically independent. By contrast, the empires of the late nineteenth century recalled the old European colonial empires of the seventeenth and eighteenth centuries and led contemporaries to speak of the "new imperialism."

The new imperialism had momentous consequences. It resulted in new tensions among competing European states, and it led to wars and rumors of war with non-European powers. The new imperialism was aimed primarily at Africa and Asia. It put millions of black, brown, and yellow peoples directly under the rule of whites. How and why did whites come to rule these peoples?

The Scramble for Africa

The most spectacular manifestation of the new imperialism was the seizure of Africa, which broke

"Is She Hardworking?"   Entering the United States in their colorful kimonos, these Japanese women are "picture brides." Their marriages to Japanese men in the United States have already been arranged by friends and marriage brokers, who have used pictures and references to strike bargains with prospective husbands. About six hundred Japanese picture brides entered annually until the U.S. government outlawed the practice in 1921. *(Source: California Department of Parks and Recreation)*

sharply with previous patterns and fascinated contemporary Europeans and Americans. As late as 1880, European nations controlled only 10 percent of the African continent, and their possessions were hardly increasing.

The French had begun conquering Algeria in 1830, and within fifty years substantial numbers of French, Italian, and Spanish colonists had settled among the overwhelming Arab majority. At the other end of the continent, in South Africa, the British had taken possession of the Dutch settlements at Cape Town during the wars with Napoleon I. This takeover had led disgruntled Dutch cattle ranchers and farmers in 1835 to make their so-called Great Trek into the interior, where they fought the Zulu and Xhosa peoples for land. After 1853, the Boers, or Afrikaners (as the descendants of the Dutch in the Cape Colony were beginning to call themselves), proclaimed their political independence and defended it against British armies. By 1880 Afrikaner and British settlers, who detested each other, had wrested control of much of South Africa from the Zulu, Xhosa, and other African peoples.

European trading posts and forts dating back to the Age of Discovery and the slave trade dotted the coast of West Africa. The Portuguese proudly but ineffectively held their old possessions in Angola and Mozambique. Elsewhere over the great mass of the continent, Europeans did not rule.

Between 1880 and 1900, the situation changed drastically. Britain, France, Germany, and Italy scrambled for African possessions as if their national livelihoods were at stake. By 1900 nearly the whole continent had been carved up and placed under European rule. Only Ethiopia in northeast Africa and Liberia on the West African coast remained independent. Even the Dutch settler republics of southern Africa were conquered by the British in the bloody Boer War (1899–1902). In the years before 1914, the European powers tightened their control and established colonial governments to rule their gigantic empires (Map 27.1).

In the complexity of the European seizure of Africa, certain events and individuals stand out. Of enormous importance was the British occupation of Egypt, which established the new model of formal political control. There was also the role of Leopold II of Belgium (r. 1865–1909), an energetic, strong-willed monarch with a lust for distant territory. "The sea bathes our coast, the world lies

before us," he had exclaimed in 1861. "Steam and electricity have annihilated distance, and all the non-appropriated lands on the surface of the globe can become the field of our operations and of our success."[8] By 1876 Leopold was focusing on central Africa. Subsequently, he formed a financial syndicate under his personal control to send Henry M. Stanley, a sensation-seeking journalist and part-time explorer, to the Congo basin. Stanley was able to establish trading stations, sign "treaties" with African chiefs, and plant Leopold's flag. Leopold's actions alarmed the French, who quickly sent out an expedition under Pierre de Brazza. In 1880 de Brazza signed a treaty of protection with the chief of the large Teke tribe and began to establish a French protectorate on the north bank of the Congo River.

Leopold's buccaneering intrusion into the Congo area raised the question of the political fate of black Africa—Africa south of the Sahara. By 1882 when the British successfully invaded and occupied Egypt, Europe had caught "African fever." There was a gold-rush mentality, and the race for territory was on.

To lay down some basic rules for this new and dangerous game of imperialist competition, Premier Jules Ferry of France and Chancellor Otto von Bismarck of Germany arranged an international conference on Africa in Berlin in 1884 and 1885. The conference established the principle that European claims to African territory had to rest on "effective occupation" in order to be recognized by other states. This principle was very important. It meant that Europeans would push relentlessly into interior regions from all sides and that no single European power would be able to claim the entire continent. The conference recognized Leopold's personal rule over a neutral Congo free state and declared all of the Congo basin a free-trade zone. The conference also agreed to work to stop slavery and the slave trade in Africa.

The Berlin conference coincided with Germany's sudden emergence as an imperial power. Prior to about 1880, Bismarck, like many other

MAP 27.1 The Partition of Africa European nations carved up Africa after 1880 and built vast political empires. What African states remained independent?

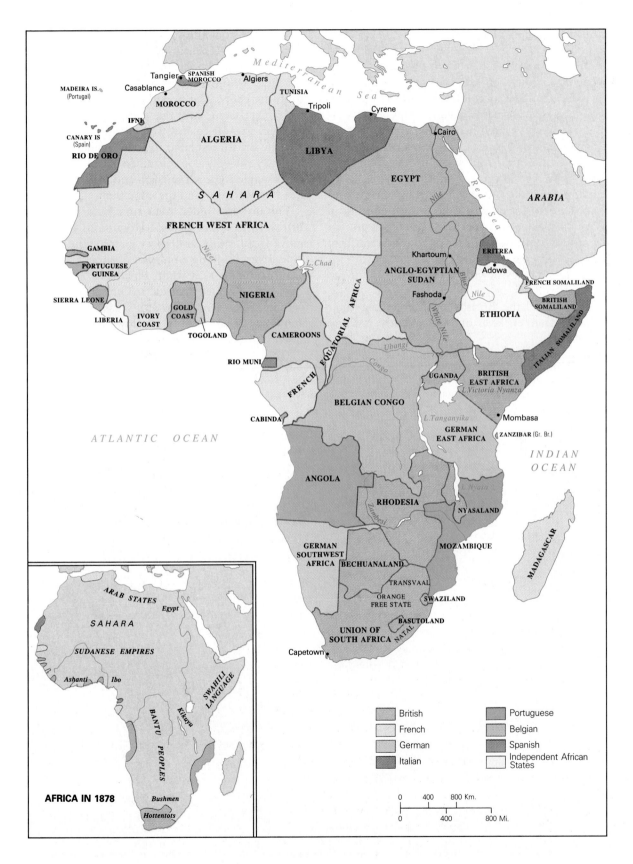

Mediterranean Sea

Tangier
SPANISH
MOROCCO
Algiers
MADEIRA IS.
(Portugal)
Casablanca
TUNISIA
MOROCCO
Tripoli
Cyrene
IFNI
Cairo
CANARY IS
(Spain)
ALGERIA
LIBYA
RIO DE ORO
EGYPT
Nile
ARABIA
S A H A R A
Red Sea
FRENCH WEST AFRICA
GAMBIA
Niger
L. Chad
Khartoum
ERITREA
PORTUGUESE
GUINEA
ANGLO-EGYPTIAN
SUDAN
Adowa
FRENCH SOMALILAND
Blue Nile
NIGERIA
Nile
BRITISH
SOMALILAND
SIERRA LEONE
Fashoda
White Nile
LIBERIA
IVORY
COAST
GOLD
COAST
ETHIOPIA
TOGOLAND
CAMEROONS
ITALIAN SOMALILAND
RIO MUNI
Ubangi
FRENCH EQUATORIAL AFRICA
UGANDA
BRITISH
EAST AFRICA
Congo
L.Victoria Nyanza
BELGIAN CONGO
CABINDA
L.Tanganyika
Mombasa
GERMAN
EAST AFRICA
ZANZIBAR (Gr. Br.)
ATLANTIC OCEAN
INDIAN
OCEAN
L.Nyasa
ANGOLA
RHODESIA
NYASALAND
Zambesi
MADAGASCAR
GERMAN
SOUTHWEST
AFRICA
MOZAMBIQUE
BECHUANALAND
TRANSVAAL
SWAZILAND
ORANGE
FREE STATE
BASUTOLAND
UNION OF
SOUTH AFRICA
NATAL
Capetown

ARAB STATES
Egypt
SAHARA
SUDANESE EMPIRES
Ashanti
Ibo
SWAHILI LANGUAGE
BANTU PEOPLES
Kikuyu
Bushmen
Hottentots
AFRICA IN 1878

British
French
German
Italian
Portuguese
Belgian
Spanish
Independent African
States

0   400   800 Km.
0   400   800 Mi.

European leaders at the time, had seen little value in colonies. Colonies reminded him, he said, of a poor but proud nobleman who wore a fur coat when he could not afford a shirt underneath. Then in 1884 and 1885 as political agitation for expansion increased, Bismarck did an abrupt about-face, and Germany established protectorates over a number of small African kingdoms and tribes in Togo, Cameroon, Southwest Africa, and, later, East Africa. In acquiring colonies, Bismarck cooperated against the British with France's Ferry, who was as ardent for empire as he was for education. With Bismarck's tacit approval, the French pressed vigorously southward from Algeria, eastward from their old forts on the Senegal coast, and northward from de Brazza's newly formed protectorate on the Congo River.

Meanwhile, the British began enlarging their West African enclaves and impatiently pushing northward from the Cape Colony and westward from Zanzibar. Their thrust southward from Egypt was blocked in the Sudan by fiercely independent Muslims, who massacred a British force at Khartoum in 1885. The peoples of the Sudan maintained the Islamic state that they had established in 1881 in a revolt against foreign control of Egypt, and the British retreated to Cairo. Sudanese Muslims were deeply committed to Islam. For them the struggle to preserve Islam and the struggle for freedom were one and the same thing.

The invaders bided their time, and in 1896 a British force under General Horatio H. Kitchener moved cautiously and more successfully up the Nile River, building a railroad to supply arms and reinforcements as it went. Finally, in 1898 these British troops met their foe at Omdurman, where Muslim tribesmen armed with spears charged time and time again only to be cut down by the recently

Omdurman, 1898 European machine guns cut down the charging Muslim tribesmen again and again. "It was not a battle but an execution," said one witness. Thus the Sudan was conquered, and a million square miles were added to the British Empire. *(Source: E. T. Archive)*

invented machine gun. For one smug participant, the young British officer Winston Churchill, it was "like a pantomime scene" in a play. "These extraordinary foreign figures . . . march up one by one from the darkness of Barbarism to the footlights of civilization . . . and their conquerors, taking their possessions, forget even their names. Nor will history record such trash." For another, more somber English observer, "It was not a battle but an execution. The bodies were not in heaps . . . but they spread evenly over acres and acres."[9] In the end, eleven thousand brave but poorly armed Muslim tribesmen lay dead. Only twenty-eight Britons had been killed.

The British conquest of the Sudan exemplifies the general process of empire building in Africa. The fate of the Muslim force at Omdurman was eventually inflicted on all native peoples who resisted European rule: they were blown away by vastly superior military force. But however much the European powers squabbled for territory and privilege around the world, they always had the sense to stop short of actually fighting each other. Imperial ambitions were not worth a great European war.

Imperialism in Asia

Although the sudden division of Africa was more spectacular, Europeans also extended their political control in Asia. In 1815 the Dutch ruled little more than the island of Java in the East Indies. Thereafter they gradually brought almost all of the 3,000-mile archipelago under their political authority, though—in good imperialist fashion—they had to share some of the spoils with Britain and Germany. In the critical decade of the 1880s, the French under the leadership of Ferry took Indochina. India, Japan, and China also experienced a profound imperialist impact (Map 27.2).

Two other great imperialist powers, Russia and the United States, also acquired rich territories in Asia. Russia, whose history since the later Middle Ages had been marked by almost continual expansion, moved steadily forward on two fronts throughout the nineteenth century. Russians conquered Muslim areas to the south in the Caucasus and in central Asia and also proceeded to nibble greedily on China's outlying provinces in the Far East, especially in the 1890s.

The United States' great conquest was the Philippines, taken from Spain in 1898 after the Spanish-American War. When it quickly became clear that the United States had no intention of granting independence, Philippine patriots rose in revolt and were suppressed only after long, bitter fighting.

Causes of the New Imperialism

Many factors contributed to the late-nineteenth-century rush for territory and empire, which was in turn one aspect of Western society's generalized expansion in the age of industry and nationalism. It is little wonder that controversies have raged over interpretation of the new imperialism. But despite complexity and controversy, basic causes are clearly identifiable.

Economic motives played an important role in the extension of political empires, especially the British Empire. By the late 1870s, France, Germany, and the United States were industrializing rapidly behind rising tariff barriers. Great Britain was losing its early lead and facing increasingly tough competition in foreign markets. In this new economic situation, Britain came to value old possessions, such as India and Canada, more highly. But when European continental powers began to grab any and all unclaimed territory in the 1880s, the British followed suit immediately. They feared that France and Germany would seal off their empires with high tariffs and restrictions and that future economic opportunities would be lost forever.

Actually, the overall economic gains of the new imperialism proved quite limited before 1914. The new colonies were simply too poor to buy much, and they offered few immediately profitable investments. Nonetheless, even the poorest, most barren desert was jealously prized, and no territory was ever abandoned. Colonies became important for political and diplomatic reasons. Each leading country saw colonies as crucial to national security, military power, and international prestige. For instance, safeguarding the Suez Canal played a key role in the British occupation of Egypt, and protecting Egypt in turn led to the bloody conquest of the Sudan. National security was a major factor in the U.S. decision to establish firm control over the Panama Canal Zone in 1903. Far-flung possessions guaranteed ever-growing navies the safe havens and the dependable coaling stations they needed in time of crisis or war.

Many people were convinced that colonies were essential to great nations. "There has never been a

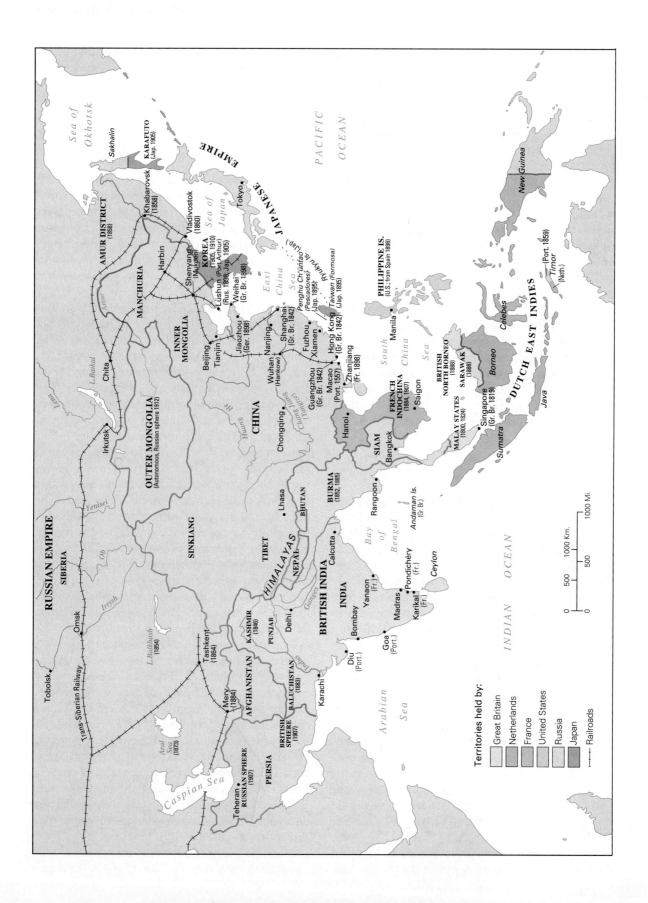

Sea of Okhotsk

Sakhalin

KARAFUTO
(Jap. 1905)

JAPANESE EMPIRE

PACIFIC

OCEAN

AMUR DISTRICT
(1858)

Khabarovsk
(1858)

Vladivostok
(1860)

Harbin

MANCHURIA

Shenyang
(Mukden)

KOREA
(1905, 1910)

Lüshun (Port Arthur)
(Rus. 1898; Jap. 1905)

Weihai
(Gr. Br. 1898)

Sea of Japan

Tokyo

New Guinea

(Port. 1859)
Timor
(Neth.)

Penghu Ch'üntao
(Pescadores)
(Jap. 1895)

Taiwan (Formosa)
(Jap. 1895)

Ryukyu Is. (Jap.)

East China Sea

PHILIPPINE IS.
(U.S. from Spain 1898)

INNER MONGOLIA

Beijing

Tianjin

Jiaozhou
(Ger. 1898)

Nanjing

Shanghai
(Gr. Br. 1842)

Fuzhou

Xiamen

Hong Kong
(Gr. Br. 1842)

Manila

South China Sea

DUTCH EAST INDIES

Celebes

Borneo

RUSSIAN EMPIRE

SIBERIA

OUTER MONGOLIA
(Autonomous, Russian sphere 1912)

SINKIANG

CHINA

Wuhan
(Hankow)

Chongqing

Huang He

Chang Jiang (Yangtze)

Guangzhou
(Gr. Br. 1842)

Macao
(Port. 1557)

Zhanjiang
(Fr. 1898)

Hanoi

FRENCH INDOCHINA
(1884, 1907)

Saigon

SIAM

Bangkok

MALAY STATES
(1800, 1824)

BRITISH NORTH BORNEO
(1888)

SARAWAK
(1888)

Singapore
(Gr. Br. 1819)

Sumatra

Java

L. Baikal

Chita

Irkutsk

Lena

Yenisei

Ob

Irtysh

L. Balkhash

Omsk

Tobolsk

Trans-Siberian Railway

Tashkent
(1864)

Merv
(1884)

Aral Sea
(1873)

AFGHANISTAN

BALUCHISTAN
(1883)

BRITISH SPHERE
(1907)

PERSIA

RUSSIAN SPHERE
(1907)

Teheran

Caspian Sea

Arabian Sea

Karachi

Diu
(Port.)

Bombay

Goa
(Port.)

KASHMIR
(1846)

PUNJAB

Delhi

Indus

Ganges

HIMALAYAS

NEPAL

BHUTAN

TIBET

Lhasa

BRITISH INDIA

INDIA

Madras

Karikal
(Fr.)

Pondichéry
(Fr.)

Yanaon
(Fr.)

Calcutta

BURMA
(1852, 1885)

Rangoon

Bay of Bengal

Andaman Is.
(Gr. Br.)

Ceylon

INDIAN OCEAN

Territories held by:

Great Britain

Netherlands

France

United States

Russia

Japan

Railroads

0   500   1000 Mi.

0   500   1000 Km.

great power without great colonies," wrote one French publicist in 1877. "Every virile people has established colonial power," echoed the famous nationalist historian of Germany, Heinrich von Treitschke. "All great nations in the fullness of their strength have desired to set their mark upon barbarian lands and those who fail to participate in this great rivalry will play a pitiable role in time to come."[10]

Treitschke's harsh statement reflects not only the increasing aggressiveness of European nationalism after Bismarck's wars of German unification but also Social Darwinian theories of brutal competition among races. Thus European nations, which were seen as racially distinct parts of the dominant white race, had to seize colonies to show they were strong and virile. Moreover, the conquest of inferior peoples was just. "The path of progress is strewn with the wreck . . . of inferior races," wrote one professor in 1900. "Yet these dead peoples are, in very truth, the stepping stones on which mankind has risen to the higher intellectual and deeper emotional life of today."[11] Social Darwinism and harsh racial doctrines fostered imperialist expansion.

So did the industrial world's unprecedented technological and military superiority. Three aspects were crucial. First, the rapidly firing machine gun, so lethal at Omdurman in the Sudan, was an ultimate weapon in many another unequal battle. Second, newly discovered quinine proved effective in controlling attacks of malaria, which had previously decimated whites in the tropics whenever they left breezy coastal enclaves and dared to venture into mosquito-infested interiors. Third, the combination of the steamship and the international telegraph permitted Western powers to quickly concentrate their firepower in a given area when it was needed. Never before—and never again after 1914—would the technological gap between the West and non-Western regions of the world be so great.

Social tensions and domestic political conflicts also contributed mightily to overseas expansion,

according to a prominent interpretation of recent years. In Germany, in Russia, and in other countries to a lesser extent, conservative political leaders were charged with manipulating colonial issues in order to divert popular attention from the class struggle at home and to create a false sense of national unity. Therefore, imperial propagandists relentlessly stressed that colonies benefited workers as well as capitalists, providing jobs and cheap raw materials that raised workers' standard of living. Government leaders and their allies in the tabloid press successfully encouraged the masses to savor foreign triumphs and glory in the supposed increase in national prestige.

Finally, certain special-interest groups in each country were powerful agents of expansion. Shipping companies wanted lucrative subsidies. White settlers on dangerous, turbulent frontiers constantly demanded more land and greater protection. Missionaries and humanitarians wanted to spread religion and stop the slave trade. Explorers and adventurers sought knowledge and excitement. Military men and colonial officials, whose role has often been overlooked by those who write on imperialism, foresaw rapid advancement and high-paid positions in growing empires. The actions of such groups and the determined individuals who led them thrust the course of empire forward.

Western society did not rest the case for empire solely on naked conquest and a Darwinian racial struggle or on power politics and the need for naval bases on every ocean. Imperialists developed additional arguments in order to satisfy their consciences and answer their critics. A favorite idea was that Europeans and Americans could and should "civilize" supposedly primitive, nonwhite peoples (see Listening to the Past). According to this view, nonwhites would receive the benefits of modern economies, cities, advanced medicine, and higher standards of living and eventually might be ready for self-government and Western democracy.

Another argument was that imperial government protected natives from tribal warfare as well as from cruder forms of exploitation by white settlers and business people. Thus the French spoke of their sacred "civilizing mission." Rudyard Kipling (1865–1936), who wrote masterfully of Anglo-Indian life and was perhaps the most influential British writer of the 1890s, exhorted Europeans to unselfish service in distant lands:

MAP 27.2 Asia in 1914 India remained under British rule while China precariously preserved its political independence. The Dutch empire in modern-day Indonesia was old, but French control of Indochina was a product of the new imperialism.

✿ **A Missionary School** A Swahili schoolboy leads his classmates in a reading lesson in Dar es Salaam in German East Africa before 1914, as portraits of Emperor William II and his wife look down on the classroom. Europeans argued that they were spreading the benefits of a superior civilization with schools like this one, which is unusually solid because of its strategic location in the capital city. *(Source: Ullstein Bilderdienst)*

Take up the White Man's Burden—
Send forth the best ye breed—
Go bind your sons to exile
To serve your captives' need,
To wait in heavy harness,
On fluttered folk and wild—
Your new-caught, sullen peoples
Half-devil and half-child.[12]

Another rationalization for the new imperialism was that peace and stability under European control would permit the spread of Christianity. In Africa Catholic and Protestant missionaries competed with Islam south of the Sahara, seeking converts and building schools to spread the Gospel. Many Africans' first real contact with whites was in mission schools. Some peoples, such as the Ibo in Nigeria, became highly Christianized.

Such occasional successes in black Africa contrasted with the general failure of missionary efforts in India, China, and the Islamic world. There Christians often preached in vain to peoples with ancient, complex religious beliefs. Yet the number of Christian believers around the world did increase substantially in the nineteenth century, and missionary groups kept trying. Unfortunately, "many missionaries had drunk at the well of European racism," and this probably prevented them from doing better.[13]

Critics of Imperialism

The expansion of empire aroused sharp, even bitter, critics. A forceful attack was delivered in 1902, after the unpopular Boer War, by radical English economist J. A. Hobson (1858–1940) in his *Imperialism,* a work that influenced Lenin and others. Hobson contended that the rush to acquire colonies was due to the economic needs of unregulated capitalism, particularly the need of the rich to find outlets for their surplus capital. Yet, Hobson argued, imperial possessions did not pay off economically for the home country as a whole. Only unscrupulous special-interest groups profited from them, at the expense of both the European taxpayer and the natives. Moreover, Hobson argued that the quest for empire diverted popular attention away from domestic reform and the need to reduce the great gap between rich and poor. These and similar arguments were not very persuasive, however. Most people then (and now) were sold on the idea that imperialism was economically profitable for the homeland, and a broad and genuine enthusiasm for empire developed among the masses.

Hobson and many other critics struck home, however, with their moral condemnation of whites imperiously ruling nonwhites. They rebelled against crude Social Darwinian thought. "O Evolution, what crimes are committed in thy name!" cried one foe. Another sardonically coined a new beatitude: "Blessed are the strong, for they shall prey on the weak."[14] Kipling and his kind were lampooned as racist bullies whose rule rested on brutality, racial contempt, and the Maxim machine gun. Polish-born novelist Joseph Conrad (1857–1924), in *Heart of Darkness,* castigated the "pure selfishness" of Europeans in "civilizing" Africa. The main character in the novel, once a liberal scholar, turns into a savage brute.

Critics charged Europeans with applying a degrading double standard and failing to live up to their own noble ideals. At home Europeans had won or were winning representative government, individual liberties, and a certain equality of opportunity. In their empires Europeans imposed military dictatorships on Africans and Asians; forced them to work involuntarily, almost like slaves; and discriminated against them shamelessly. Only by renouncing imperialism, critics insisted, and giving captive peoples the freedoms idealized in Western society would Europeans be worthy of their traditions. Europeans who denounced the imperialist tide provided colonial peoples with a Western ideology of liberation.

❧ RESPONSES TO WESTERN IMPERIALISM

To peoples in Africa and Asia, Western expansion represented a profoundly disruptive assault. Everywhere it threatened traditional ruling classes, economies, and ways of life. Christian missionaries and European secular ideologies challenged established beliefs and values. Non-Western peoples ex-

perienced a crisis of identity, one made all the more painful by the power and arrogance of the white intruders.

Often the initial response of African and Asian rulers was to try driving the unwelcome foreigners away, as in China, Japan, and the upper Sudan. Violent antiforeign reactions exploded elsewhere again and again, but the superior military technology of the industrialized West almost invariably prevailed. Beaten in battle, many Africans and Asians concentrated on preserving their cultural traditions at all costs. Others found themselves forced to reconsider their initial hostility. Some (such as Ismail of Egypt) concluded that the West was indeed superior in some ways and that it was therefore necessary to reform their societies and copy European achievements. Thus it is possible to think of responses to the Western impact as a spectrum, with "traditionalists" at one end, "westernizers" or "modernizers" at the other, and many shades of opinion in between. The struggle among these groups was often intense. With time, however, the modernizers tended to gain the upper hand.

When resistance to European domination was thoroughly shattered by superior force, the great majority of Asians and Africans accepted imperial rule. Political participation in non-Western lands was historically limited to small elites, and the masses were used to doing what their rulers told them. In these circumstances Europeans, clothed in power and convinced of their righteousness, governed smoothly and effectively. They received considerable support from both traditionalists (local chiefs, landowners, religious leaders) and modernizers (Western-educated professional classes and civil servants).

Nevertheless, imperial rule was in many ways an imposing edifice built on sand. Support for European rule among the conforming and accepting millions was shallow and weak. Thus the conforming masses followed with greater or lesser enthusiasm a few determined personalities who came to oppose the Europeans. Such leaders always arose, both when Europeans ruled directly and when they manipulated native governments, for at least two basic reasons.

First, the nonconformists—the eventual anti-imperialist leaders—developed a burning desire for human dignity. They came to feel that such dignity was incompatible with foreign rule, with its smirks and smiles, its paternalism and condescension.

Second, potential leaders found in the Western world the ideologies and justification for their protest. They discovered liberalism, with its credo of civil liberty and political self-determination. They echoed the demands of anti-imperialists in Europe and America that the West live up to its own ideals.

More important, they found themselves attracted to modern nationalism, which asserted that every people had the right to control its own destiny. After 1917 anti-imperialist revolt would find another weapon in Lenin's version of Marxian socialism. Thus the anti-imperialist search for dignity drew strength from Western culture, as is apparent in the development of three major Asian countries—India, Japan, and China.

Empire in India

India was the jewel of the British Empire, and no colonial area experienced a more profound British impact. Unlike Japan and China, which maintained a real or precarious independence, and unlike African territories, which were annexed by Europeans only at the end of the nineteenth century, India was ruled more or less absolutely by Britain for a very long time.

Arriving in India on the heels of the Portuguese in the seventeenth century, the British East India Company had conquered the last independent native state by 1848. The last "traditional" response to European rule—the attempt by the established ruling classes to drive the white man out by military force—was broken in India in 1857 and 1858. Those were the years of the Great Rebellion (which the British called a "mutiny"), when an insurrection by Muslim and Hindu mercenaries in the British army spread throughout northern and central India before it was finally crushed, primarily by loyal native troops from southern India. Thereafter Britain ruled India directly. India illustrates, therefore, for better and for worse, what generations of European domination might produce.

The British in India This photo suggests not only the power and luxury of the British ruling class in India but also its confidence and self-satisfaction. As one British viceroy said, "We are all British gentlemen engaged in the magnificent work of governing an inferior race." *(Source: Hulton Deutsch Collection)*

After 1858 India was ruled by the British Parliament in London and administered by a tiny, all-white civil service in India. In 1900 this elite consisted of fewer than 3,500 top officials, for a population of 300 million. The white elite, backed by white officers and native troops, was competent and generally well disposed toward the welfare of the Indian peasant masses. Yet it practiced strict job discrimination and social segregation, and most of its members quite frankly considered the jumble of Indian peoples and castes to be racially inferior. As Lord Kitchener, one of the most distinguished top military commanders of India, stated:

It is this consciousness of the inherent superiority of the European which has won for us India. However well educated and clever a native may be, and however brave he may prove himself, I believe that no rank we can bestow on him would cause him to be considered an equal of the British officer.[15]

When, for example, the British Parliament in 1883 was considering a major bill to allow Indian judges to try white Europeans in India, the British community rose in protest and defeated the measure. The idea of being judged by Indians was inconceivable to the Europeans, for it was clear to them that the empire in India rested squarely on racial inequality.

In spite of (or perhaps even because of) their strong feelings of racial and cultural superiority, the British acted energetically and introduced many desirable changes to India. Realizing that they needed well-educated Indians to serve as skilled subordinates in the government and army, the British established a modern system of progressive secondary education in which all instruction was in English. Thus through education and government service, the British offered some Indians excellent opportunities for both economic and social advancement. High-caste Hindus formed a new elite profoundly influenced by Western thought and culture.

This new bureaucratic elite played a crucial role in modern economic development, which was a second result of British rule. Irrigation projects for agriculture, the world's third largest railroad network for good communications, and large tea and jute plantations geared to the world economy were all developed. Unfortunately, the lot of the Indian masses improved little, for the increase in production was eaten up by an increase in population.

Finally, with a well-educated, English-speaking Indian bureaucracy and modern communications, the British created a unified, powerful state. They placed under the same general system of law and administration the different Hindu and Muslim peoples of the subcontinent that had fought each other for centuries during the Middle Ages and had been repeatedly conquered by Muslim and Mongol invaders. It was as if Europe, with its many states and varieties of Christianity, had been conquered and united in a single great empire.

In spite of these achievements, the decisive reaction to European rule was the rise of nationalism among the Indian elite. No matter how anglicized and necessary a member of the educated classes became, he or she could never become the white ruler's equal. The top jobs, the best clubs, the modern hotels, and even certain railroad compartments were sealed off to brown-skinned men and women. The peasant masses might accept such inequality as the latest version of age-old oppression, but the well-educated, English-speaking elite eventually could not. For the elite, racial discrimination meant not only injured pride but also bitter injustice. And it was based on dictatorship, no matter how benign.

By 1885 when educated Indians came together to found the predominately Hindu Indian National Congress, demands were increasing for the equality and self-government that Britain enjoyed and had already granted white-settler colonies, such as Canada and Australia. By 1907, emboldened in part by Japan's success (see the next section), the radicals in the Indian National Congress were calling for complete independence. Even the moderates were demanding home rule for India through an elected parliament. Although there were sharp divisions between Hindus and Muslims, the common heritage of British rule and Western ideals, along with the reform and revitalization of the Hindu religion, had created a genuine movement for national independence.

The Example of Japan

When Commodore Perry arrived in Japan in 1853 with his crude but effective gunboat diplomacy, Japan was a complex feudal society. At the top stood a figurehead emperor, but for more than two hundred years real power had been in the hands of the *shogun,* general-in-chief. With the help of the warrior nobility *samurai,* the shogun governed a country of hard-working, productive peasants and city dwellers. Often poor and restless, the intensely proud samurai were humiliated by the sudden American intrusion and the unequal treaties with Western countries.

When foreign diplomats and merchants began to settle in Yokohama, radical samurai reacted with a wave of antiforeign terrorism and antigovernment assassinations between 1858 and 1863. The

A Japanese View of America Japanese publishers memorialized the opening of Japan to foreign trade with popular woodblock prints. An 1860 American newspaper illustration showing the visit of the Japanese embassy to the sewing and laundry rooms of the Willard Hotel in Washington, D.C., inspired this print. The Americans hold symbols of their technology—a pocket watch and a sewing machine. The Japanese text celebrates American wealth, power, and technological superiority, which the Japanese admired and soon imitated. *(Source: Private Collection)*

imperialist response was swift and unambiguous. An allied fleet of American, British, Dutch, and French warships demolished key forts, further weakening the power and prestige of the shogun's government. Then in 1867, a coalition led by patriotic samurai seized control of the government with hardly any bloodshed and restored the political power of the emperor. This was the Meiji Restoration, a great turning point in Japanese development.

The immediate, all-important goal of the new government was to meet the foreign threat. The battle cry of the Meiji reformers was "Enrich the state and strengthen the armed forces." But how were these tasks to be done? In an about-face that was one of history's most remarkable chapters, the young but well-trained, idealistic but flexible leaders of Meiji Japan dropped their antiforeign attacks. Convinced that Western civilization was indeed superior in its military and industrial aspects, they initiated from above a series of measures to reform Japan along modern, Western lines. They were convinced that "Japan must be reborn with America its mother and France its father."[16]

In 1871 the new leaders abolished the old feudal structure of aristocratic, decentralized government and formed a strong unified state. Following the example of the French Revolution, they dismantled the four-class legal system and declared social equality. They decreed freedom of movement in a country where traveling abroad had been a most serious crime. They created a free, competitive, government-stimulated economy. Japan began to build railroads and modern factories. Thus the new generation adopted many principles of a free, liberal society. As in Europe, such freedom resulted in a tremendously creative release of human energy.

The overriding concern of Japan's political leadership, however, was always a powerful state, and to achieve this, the new leaders borrowed more than liberalism from the West. A powerful modern navy was created, and the army was completely reorganized along French and German lines, with three-year military service for all males and a professional officer corps. In 1877, this army of draftees crushed a major rebellion by feudal elements protesting the loss of their privileges. Japan also borrowed rapidly and adapted skillfully the West's science and modern technology, particularly in industry, medicine, and education. Many Japanese were encouraged to study abroad, and the

THE SPREAD OF WESTERN IMPERIALISM

1800–1913	World trade increases 25-fold
1816–1880	European economic penetration of non-Western countries
1835	Great Trek: Boers proclaim independence from Great Britain in the South African hinterland
1840s	European capitalists begin large-scale foreign investment
1842	Treaty of Nanjing: Manchu government of China cedes Hong Kong to Great Britain
1846	Repeal of Corn Laws: Great Britain declares its strong support of free trade
1848	British defeat of last independent native state in India
1853	Perry's arrival in Tokyo: Japan opened to European influence
1857–1858	Great Rebellion in India
1858–1863	Anti-foreign reaction in Japan
1867	Meiji Restoration in Japan: adoption of Western reforms
1869	Completion of Suez Canal
1871	Abolition of feudal domains in Japan
1876	Ismail, khedive of Egypt, appoints British and French commissioners to oversee government finances
1880	Establishment of French protectorate on the northern bank of the Congo
1880–1900	European powers intensify their "scramble for Africa"
1882	British occupation of Egypt
1884–1885	International conference on Africa in Berlin: European powers require "effective occupation"; Germany acquires protectorates in Togo, Cameroon, Southwest Africa, and East Africa; Belgium acquires the Congo free state
1885	Formation of the Indian National Congress
1890	Establishment of an authoritarian constitution in Japan
1893	France completes its acquisition of Indochina
1894	Sino-Japanese War: Japan acquires Formosa
1898	Battle of Omdurman: under Kitchener, British forces reconquer the Sudan Spanish-American War: United States acquires the Philippines "Hundred Days of Reform" in China
1899–1902	Boer War: British defeat Dutch settlers in South Africa
1900	The Boxer Rebellion in China
1903	American occupation of the Panama Canal Zone
1904–1905	Russo-Japanese War: Japan wins protectorate over Port Arthur in China
1910	Japanese annexation of Korea
1912	Fall of Manchu Dynasty in China

government paid large salaries to attract foreign experts. These experts were always carefully controlled, however, and were replaced by trained Japanese as soon as possible.

By 1890, when the new state was firmly established, the wholesale borrowing of the early restoration had given way to more selective emphasis on those things foreign that were in keeping with Japanese tradition. Following the model of the German Empire, Japan established an authoritarian constitution and rejected democracy. The power of the emperor and his ministers was vast; that of the legislature, limited.

Japan successfully copied the imperialism of Western society. Expansion not only proved that Japan was strong; it also cemented the nation together in a great mission. Having "opened" Korea with the gunboat diplomacy of imperialism in 1876, Japan decisively defeated China in a war over Korea in 1894 to 1895 and took Formosa (modern-day Taiwan). In the next years, Japan competed aggressively with the leading European powers for influence and territory in China, particularly Manchuria. There Japanese and Russian imperialism met and collided. In 1904 Japan attacked Russia without warning, and after a bloody war Japan emerged with a valuable foothold in China—Russia's former protectorate over Port Arthur (see Map 27.2). By 1910, with the annexation of Korea, Japan had become a major imperialist power.

Japan became the first non-Western country to use an ancient love of country to transform itself and thereby meet the many-sided challenge of Western expansion. Moreover, Japan demonstrated convincingly that a modern Asian nation could defeat and humble a great Western power. Japan provided patriots in Asia and Africa with an inspiring example of national recovery and liberation.

Toward Revolution in China

In 1860 the two-hundred-year-old Manchu Dynasty in China appeared on the verge of collapse. Efforts to repel foreigners had failed, and rebellion and chaos wracked the country. Yet two factors helped the government achieve a surprising comeback that lasted more than thirty years. First, the traditional ruling groups temporarily produced new and effective leadership. Loyal scholar-statesmen and generals quelled disturbances such as the great Tai Ping Rebellion. The empress dowager Tzu Hsi, a truly remarkable woman, governed in the name of her young son and combined shrewd insight with vigorous action to revitalize the bureaucracy. Second, destructive foreign aggression lessened, for the Europeans had obtained their primary goal of commercial and diplomatic relations. Indeed, some Europeans assisted in the dynasty's efforts to adopt some aspects of Western government and technology while maintaining traditional Chinese values and beliefs.

The parallel movement toward domestic reform and limited cooperation with the West collapsed under the blows of Japanese imperialism. The Sino-Japanese War of 1894 to 1895 and the subsequent harsh peace treaty revealed China's helplessness in the face of aggression, triggering a rush for foreign concessions and protectorates in China. At the high point of this rush in 1898, it appeared that the European powers might actually divide China among themselves, as they had recently divided Africa. Probably only the jealousy each nation felt toward its imperialist competitors saved China from partition, although the U.S. Open Door policy, which opposed formal annexation of Chinese territory, may have helped tip the balance. In any event, the tempo and impact of foreign penetration greatly accelerated after 1894.

So, too, did the intensity and radicalism of the Chinese reaction. Like the leaders of the Meiji Restoration, some modernizers saw salvation in Western institutions. In 1898 the government launched a desperate "hundred days of reform" in an attempt to meet the foreign challenge. Radical reformers, such as the revolutionary Sun Yat-sen (1866–1925), who came from the peasantry and was educated in Hawaii by Christian missionaries, sought to overthrow the Manchu Dynasty altogether and establish a republic.

On the other side, some traditionalists turned back toward ancient practices, political conservatism, and fanatical hatred of the "foreign devils." "Protect the country, destroy the foreigner" was their simple motto. Such conservative, antiforeign patriots had often clashed with foreign missionaries, whom they charged with undermining reverence for ancestors and thereby threatening the Chinese family and the entire society. In the agony of defeat and unwanted reforms, secret societies such as the Boxers rebelled. In northeastern China, more than two hundred foreign missionaries and several thousand Chinese Christians were killed.

The Empress Dowager Tzu Hsi   To maintain her power, the empress drew on conservative forces such as the court eunuchs surrounding her here. Three years after her death in 1908, a revolution broke out and forced the last Chinese emperor, a boy of six, to abdicate. *(Source: Courtesy of the Freer Gallery of Art, Smithsonian Institution, Washington, D.C.)*

Once again the imperialist response was swift and harsh. Foreign armies occupied and plundered Beijing. A heavy indemnity was imposed.

The years after the Boxer Rebellion in 1900 were ever more troubled. Anarchy and foreign influence spread as the power and prestige of the Manchu Dynasty declined still further. Antiforeign, antigovernment revolutionary groups agitated and plotted. Finally in 1912, a spontaneous uprising toppled the Manchu Dynasty. After thousands of years of emperors and empires, a loose coalition of revolutionaries proclaimed a Western-style republic and called for an elected parliament. The transformation of China under the impact of expanding Western society entered a new phase, and the end was not in sight.

SUMMARY

In the nineteenth century, the industrializing West entered the third and most dynamic phase of its centuries-old expansion into non-Western lands. In so doing, Western nations profitably subordinated those lands to their economic interests, sent forth millions of emigrants, and established political influence in Asia and vast political empires in Africa. The reasons for this culminating surge were many, but the economic thrust of robust industrial capitalism, an ever-growing lead in technology, and the competitive pressures of European nationalism were particularly important.

Western expansion had far-reaching consequences. For the first time in human history, the world became in many ways a single unit. Moreover, European expansion diffused the ideas and techniques of a highly developed civilization. Yet the West relied on force to conquer and rule, and it treated non-Western peoples as racial inferiors. Thus non-Western elites, often armed with Western doctrines, gradually responded to the Western challenge. They launched a national, anti-imperialist struggle for dignity, genuine independence, and modernization. This struggle would emerge as a central drama of world history after the great European civil war of 1914 to 1918, which reduced the West's technological advantage and shattered its self-confidence and complacent moral superiority.

NOTES

1. Quoted in A. Waley, *The Opium War Through Chinese Eyes* (New York: Macmillan, 1958), p. 29.
2. Quoted in J. W. Hall, *Japan, from Prehistory to Modern Times* (New York: Delacorte Press, 1970), p. 250.
3. Quoted in R. Hallett, *Africa to 1875* (Ann Arbor: University of Michigan Press, 1970), p. 109.
4. Quoted in Earl of Cromer, *Modern Egypt* (London, 1911), p. 48.
5. Quoted in T. Blegen, *Norwegian Migration to America,* vol. 2 (Northfield, Minn.: Norwegian-American Historical Association, 1940), p. 468.
6. Quoted in I. Howe, *World of Our Fathers* (New York: Harcourt Brace Jovanovich, 1976), p. 25.
7. Quoted in C. A. Price, *The Great White Walls Are Built: Restrictive Immigration to North America and Australia, 1836–1888* (Canberra: Australian National University Press, 1974), p. 175.
8. Quoted in W. L. Langer, *European Alliances and Alignments, 1871–1890* (New York: Vintage Books, 1931), p. 290.
9. Quoted in J. Ellis, *The Social History of the Machine Gun* (New York: Pantheon Books, 1975), pp. 86, 101.
10. Quoted in G. H. Nadel and P. Curtis, eds., *Imperialism and Colonialism* (New York: Macmillan, 1964), p. 94.
11. Quoted in W. L. Langer, *The Diplomacy of Imperialism,* 2d ed. (New York: Knopf, 1951), pp. 86, 88.
12. Rudyard Kipling, *The Five Nations* (London, 1903), quoted by the permission of Mrs. George Bambridge, Methuen & Company, and Doubleday & Company, Inc.

13. E. H. Berman, "African Responses to Christian Mission Education," *African Studies Review* 17 (1974): 530.
14. Quoted in Langer, *The Diplomacy of Imperialism,* p. 88.
15. Quoted in K. M. Panikkar, *Asia and Western Dominance: A Survey of the Vasco da Gama Epoch of Asian History* (London: George Allen & Unwin, 1959), p. 116.
16. Quoted in Hall, *Japan, from Prehistory to Modern Times,* p. 289.

SUGGESTED READING

General surveys of European expansion in a broad perspective include R. Betts, *Europe Overseas* (1968); A. Thornton, *Imperialism in the Twentieth Century* (1977); T. Smith, *The Patterns of Imperialism* (1981); and W. Woodruff, *Impact of Western Man* (1967), which has an extensive bibliography. D. K. Fieldhouse has written two fine surveys, *Economics and Empire, 1830–1914* (1970), and *Colonialism, 1870–1945* (1981). G. Barraclough, *An Introduction to Contemporary History* (1964), argues powerfully that Western imperialism and the non-Western reaction to it have been crucial in world history since about 1890. J. A. Hobson's classic *Imperialism* (1902) is readily available, and the Marxist-Leninist case is effectively presented in V. G. Kieran, *Marxism and Imperialism* (1975). Two excellent anthologies on the problem of European expansion are the volume by Nadel and Curtis cited in the Notes, and H. Wright, ed., *The "New Imperialism,"* rev. ed. (1975).

Britain's leading position in European imperialism is examined in a lively way by B. Porter, *The Lion's Share* (1976); J. Morris, *Pax Britannica* (1968); and D. Judd, *The Victorian Empire* (1970), a stunning pictorial history. G. Stocking, *Victorian Anthropology* (1987), is a brilliant analysis of the cultural and racial implications of Western expansion. B. Semmel has written widely on the intellectual foundations of English expansion, as in *The Rise of Free Trade Imperialism* (1970). J. Gallagher and R. Robinson, *Africa and the Victorians: The Climax of Imperialism* (1961), is an influential reassessment. H. Brunschwig, *French Colonialism, 1871–1914* (1966), and W. Baumgart, *Imperialism: The Idea and Reality of British and French Colonial Expansion* (1982), are well-balanced studies. A. Moorehead, *The White Nile* (1971), tells the fascinating story of the European exploration of the mysterious Upper Nile. Volumes 5 and 6 of K. Latourette, *History of the Expansion of Christianity,* 7 vols. (1937–1945), examine the powerful impulse for missionary work in non-European areas. D. Headrick stresses Western technological superiority in *Tools of Empire* (1981). C. Erikson, *Emigration from Europe, 1815–1914* (1976), and R. Vecoli and S. Sinke, eds., *A Century of European Migrations, 1830–1930* (1991), are valuable general studies.

Howe and Blegen, cited in the Notes, provide dramatic accounts of Jewish and Norwegian migration to the United States. Most other migrant groups have also found their historians: M. Walker, *Germany and the Emigration, 1816–1885* (1964), and W. Adams, *Ireland and Irish Emigration to the New World* (reissued 1967), are outstanding. Langer's volumes consider the diplomatic aspects of imperialism in exhaustive detail. Ellis's well-illustrated study of the machine gun is fascinating, as is Price on the restriction of Asian migration to Australia. All these works are cited in the Notes.

E. Wolf, *Europe and the People Without History* (1982), considers, with skill and compassion, the impact of imperialism on non-Western peoples. Two unusual and provocative studies on personal relations between European rulers and non-European subjects are D. Mannoni, *Prospero and Caliban: The Psychology of Colonialization* (1964), and F. Fanon, *Wretched of the Earth* (1965), a bitter attack on white racism by a black psychologist active in the Algerian revolution. V. Ware, *Beyond the Pale: White Women, Racism and History* (1992), examines the complex role of European women in imperialism. Novels also bring the psychological and human dimensions of imperialism alive. H. Rider Haggard, *King Solomon's Mines,* portrays the powerful appeal of adventure in exotic lands; Rudyard Kipling, the greatest writer of European expansion, is at his stirring best in *Kim* and *Soldiers Three.* Joseph Conrad unforgettably probes European motives in *Heart of Darkness,* and André Gide, *The Immoralist,* closely examines European moral corruption in North Africa. William Boyd, *An Ice-Cream War,* a good story of British and Germans fighting each other in Africa during the First World War, is a favorite with students.

Hall, cited in the Notes, is an excellent introduction to the history of Japan. Waley, also cited in the Notes, has written extensively and well on China. I. Hsü, *The Rise of Modern China,* 2d ed. (1975), and K. Latourette, *The Chinese: Their History and Culture,* rev. ed. (1964), are fine histories with many suggestions for further reading. E. Reischauer's topical survey, *Japan: The Story of a Nation* (1981), is recommended, as are T. Huber, *The Revolutionary Origins of Modern Japan* (1981), and Y. Fukuzawa, *Autobiography* (1966), the personal account of a leading intellectual who witnessed the emergence of modern Japan.

G. Perry, *The Middle East: Fourteen Islamic Centuries* (1983), concisely surveys nineteenth-century developments and provides an up-to-date bibliography. B. Lewis, *The Middle East and the West* (1963), is a penetrating analysis of the impact of Western ideas on Middle Eastern thought. Hallett, cited in the Notes, and R. July, *A History of the African People* (1970), contain excellent introductions to Africa in the age of imperialism. J. D. Fage, *A History of Africa* (1978), is also recommended. A classic study of Western expansion from an Indian viewpoint is Panikkar's volume mentioned in the Notes. S. Wolpert, *A New History of India,* 2d ed. (1982), incorporates recent scholarship in a wide-ranging study that is highly recommended.

LISTENING TO THE
PAST

A Scholar's Defense of Imperialism

Western expansion in the nineteenth century offered opportunities not only to soldiers and foreign investors but also to those spurred by non-economic motives. For example, some scholars plunged into the study of the different non-Western cultures and became experts on their languages and customs. Such scholars also provided general interpretations that usually supported at least some aspects of Western imperialism.

One such scholar was Arminius Vambery (1832–1913), an influential professor of Asian languages at the University of Budapest in Hungary. Living in Constantinople in his twenties and learning several Asian languages and dialects, Vambery wrote many books on his travels and on the peoples and languages of central and western Asia. The following defense of Western expansion is taken from his introductory overview to Western Culture in Eastern Lands *(1906), a comparison on English and Russian imperialism in action.*

There are, perhaps, no subjects of human knowledge and research in which such progress has been made during the past century as in those of the geography and ethnography of Asia. . . . For instance, on the subject of Central Asia . . . we now have elaborate and exhaustive narratives and descriptions upon all possible subjects connected with those countries. In the regions where some decades ago the traveller's life was in constant danger, and where the struggle with the elements and with the natives made his progress necessarily slow and tedious, we now find a well-organised railway system, and in the place of the grunting camel the fiery steam-horse ploughs its way through endless vistas of sandy steppes. . . .

And great changes similar to those which have taken place in Central Asia may also be noticed in greater or less degree in other parts and regions of the Eastern world, [where] . . . we now find that the supreme power of the Western world is gradually making itself felt. The walls of seclusion are ruthlessly pulled down, and the resistance caused by the favoured superstitions, prejudices, and the ignorance of the sleepy and apathetic man in the East, is slowly being overcome. . . . Our present-day Europe, in its restless, bustling activity will take good care not to let the East relapse again into its former indolence. We forcibly tear its eyes open; we push, jolt, toss, and shake it, and we compel it to exchange its world-worn, hereditary ideas and customs for our modern views of life; nay, we have even succeeded to some extent in convincing our Eastern neighbours that our civilisation, our faith, our customs, our philosophy, are the only means whereby the well-being, the progress, and the happiness, of the human race can be secured.

For well-nigh 300 years we have been carrying on this struggle with the Eastern world, and persist in our unsolicited interference, following in the wake of ancient Rome, which began the work with marked perseverance, but naturally never met with much success because of the inadequate means at its disposal. . . . Compared with the real earnest work done in our days by Western Powers, the efforts of Rome are as the flickering of an oil-lamp in comparison with the radiance of the sun in its full glory. It may be said without exaggeration that never in the world's history has any one continent exercised such influence over another as has the Europe of our days over Asia: never were two such diametrically opposed elements engaged in so deadly a strife as is now to be seen in all parts of the Old World. This being so, it appears to me most important that we should realise what is the extent and the purpose of our civilising influence over Asia. We have to consider not only its historical growth and the means employed in its development, but also the results so far obtained, and the ultimate ends to be accomplished. . . . In the first place, then, we must ask ourselves the question: Have we a right thus to interfere in the concerns of the ancient world; and in the second place, What do the Asiatics think of it?

If we start with the assumption that every man has a right to his own opinion and to the views which best correspond with his ideas of morality and material comfort, our pretended crusade in the name of civilisation must look like an unwarrantable interference. But the correctness of this assumption has so far been contradicted by historical events, for no community can remain in absolute isolation. Even China, the prototype of a seclusion extending over thousands of years, has before now migrated far into neighbouring lands. . . . If Western nations had checked their passion for migration the aspect of things in Asia would now be even worse than it actually is. Of course the Asiatics themselves do not view the matter in this light. Many of them look upon our enforced reforms as hostile attacks upon their liberty, and as means to bring their people under our yoke. But the better-informed amongst them, who know what the East now is and what it used to be, will hardly share this view. Humanity in Asia has never known culture and liberty in the sense in which we understand it, and has therefore never known true happiness, which is unavoidably dependent upon these two chief factors of mental and physical well-being.

During the much-extolled golden era of the history of Asia, tyranny and despotism were the ruling elements, justice a vain chimera, everything depended on the arbitrary will of the Sovereign, and a prolonged period of rest and peace was quite the exception. Asiatics, from motives of vanity or inborn laziness, may condone these abnormal conditions, but still it remains our duty to recognise the true state of affairs, and to take pity upon our oppressed fellow-men. Without our help Asia will never rise above its low level, and even granted that

Oil painting (on glass) of Western factories in Canton. *(Source: Courtesy Peabody Essex Museum, Salem, Mass.)*

the politics of European Powers are not purely unselfish, we must nevertheless, keeping the ultimate object in view, approve of the interference of Europe in the affairs of the East, and give the undertaking our hearty support.

Viewed in this light, we may be thankful that the Christian West for 300 years has been unceasing in its interference in Asiatic affairs.

Questions for Analysis

1. What changes did Vambery see occurring in Asia?

2. Why, according to Vambery, did Western nations have a right to "interfere" in Asia?

3. How did Asians react to Western interference? Did all Asians react the same way? Why or why not?

4. Did Vambery believe in progress? What lessons did he draw from history?

Source: A. Vambery, *Western Culture in Eastern Lands: A Comparison of the Methods Adopted by England and Russia in the Middle East* (New York: E. P. Dutton, 1906), pp. 1–6.

28

Nation Building in the Western Hemisphere and in Australia

An allegorical painting of 1825 honoring Simón Bolívar, center, as the Liberator of Peru. Other portraits on the shield include that of Antonio Sucre, Bolívar's favorite general, top right, and William Miller, a British general who volunteered to serve under Bolívar, bottom right. *(Source: Instituto Nacional De Cultura Tesoreria General, Peru. Courtesy the Haywood Gallery, London)*

In the Western Hemisphere and in Australia, as in Europe, the nineteenth century was a period of nation building, geographic expansion, and industrial and commercial growth. Waves of emigrants moved from Europe and Asia to the Americas and to Australia. The millions who braved the oceans populated and built new nations and linked the Western Hemisphere and Australia with the rest of the globe.

The countries of North and South America became highly diverse ethnically and culturally, and the issue of race created serious tensions throughout the hemisphere. In the United States it helped to bring on the Civil War. In the late nineteenth and early twentieth centuries, European immigration directly affected the ways with which the United States and the Latin American nations coped with racial situations.

At the end of the eighteenth century, Canada and the countries of South America remained colonies. Their European mother countries looked on the democratic experiment of the infant United States with suspicion and scorn. The island continent of Australia, remote from Europe and economically undeveloped, served as a dumping ground for English criminals. By 1914 the Latin American states, Canada, and Australia were enjoying political independence and playing a crucial role in the world economy. The United States had become a colossus on which the Old World depended in the First World War.

- Why and how did the Spanish colonies of Latin America shake off European domination and develop into national states?

- What role did the concept of manifest destiny play in the evolution of the United States?

- How did slavery affect blacks in the United States?

- How did the Americas and Australia absorb new peoples, and what was the social impact of the immigrants?

- What geographical, economic, and political conditions shaped the development of Canada?

- What factors aided the economic growth of Australia?

These are among the questions that this chapter addresses.

❋ LATIN AMERICA (1800–1929)

In 1800 the Spanish Empire in the Western Hemisphere stretched from the headwaters of the Mississippi River in present-day Minnesota to the tip of Cape Horn in the Antarctic (see Map 28.1). According to the Kentucky statesman Henry Clay (1777–1852), "Within this vast region, we behold the most sublime and interesting objects of creation: the loftiest mountains, the most majestic rivers in the world; the richest mines of precious metals, the choicest productions of the earth."[1] Spain believed that this great wealth existed for its benefit, and Spanish policies fostered bitterness and the desire for independence in the colonies. Between 1806 and 1825 the Spanish colonies in Latin America were convulsed by upheavals that ultimately resulted in their separation from Spain.

The Latin American wars were *revolutions* because the colonists were revolting against the domination of Spain and fighting for direct self-government. They were *wars of independence* because the colonies were seeking economic liberation and management of their own commercial affairs. They were *civil wars* because social and racial groups were fighting one another. The *Creoles*—people of Spanish descent born in America—resented the economic and political dominance of the *peninsulares,* as natives of Spain or Portugal were called. Peninsulares controlled the rich export-import trade, intercolonial trade, and the mining industries. At the same time, *mestizos* of mixed Spanish and Indian background and *mulattos* of mixed Spanish and African heritage sought an end to their systematic subordination.

Between 1850 and the worldwide depression of 1929, the countries of Latin America developed into national states. The predominant factors in this evolution were the heritage of colonial exploitation, a neocolonial economic structure, massive immigration from Europe and Asia, and the fusion of Amerindian, Caucasian, African, and Asian peoples.

The Origins of the Revolutions

Because of regional, geographic, and racial differences, the Latin American movements for independence took different forms in different places. Everywhere, however, they grew out of recent colonial economic grievances. By the late seventeenth century the Spanish colonies had achieved a high degree of economic diversity and independence. The mercantilist imperialism of the days of Hernando Cortés (1485–1547) and Francisco Pizarro (1470–1541), which held that the colonies existed for Spain's financial benefit and should be economically dependent on Spain, had faded away. The colonies had become self-sufficient producers of foodstuffs, wine, textiles, and consumer goods. What was not produced domestically was secured through a healthy intercolonial trade that had developed independently of Spain, despite formidable geographic obstacles and colonial policies designed to restrict it.

In Peru, for example, domestic agriculture supported the large mining settlements, and the colony did not have to import food. Craft workshops owned by the state or by private individuals produced consumer goods for the working class; what was not manufactured locally was bought from Mexico and transported by the Peruvian merchant marine. By 1700 Mexico and Peru were sending shrinking percentages of their revenues to Spain and retaining more for public works, defense, and administration. The colonies lived for themselves, not for Spain.

The reforms of the Spanish Bourbons radically reversed this economic independence. Spain's humiliating defeat in the War of the Spanish Succession (1701–1713) prompted demands for sweeping reform of all of Spain's institutions, including colonial policies and practices. To improve administrative efficiency, the enlightened monarch Charles III (r. 1759–1788) carved the region of modern Colombia, Venezuela, and Ecuador out of the vast viceroyalty of Peru; it became the new viceroyalty of New Granada with its capital at Bogotá. The Crown also created the viceroyalty of Rio de la Plata (present-day Argentina) with its capital at Buenos Aires (Map 28.1).

Far more momentous was Charles III's radical overhaul of colonial trade policies, to enable Spain to compete with Great Britain and Holland in the great eighteenth-century struggle for empire. The Spanish crown intended the colonies to serve as sources of raw materials and as markets for Spanish manufactured goods. Charles III's free-trade policies cut duties and restrictions drastically for Spanish merchants. In Latin America these actions stimulated the production of crops in demand in Europe: coffee in Venezuela; sugar in Cuba and throughout the Caribbean; hides, leather, and salted beef in the Rio de la Plata viceroyalty. In Mexico and Peru, production of silver climbed steadily in the last quarter of the century. The volume of Spain's trade with the colonies soared, possibly as much as 700 percent between 1778 and 1788.[2]

Colonial manufacturing, which had been growing steadily, suffered severely. Better-made and cheaper European goods drove colonial goods out of the marketplace. Colonial textiles, china, and wine, for example, could not compete with cheap Spanish products. For one thing, Latin American free laborers were paid more than European workers in the eighteenth century; this disparity helps explain the great numbers of immigrants to the colonies. Also, intercolonial transportation costs were higher than transatlantic costs. In the Rio de la Plata region, for example, heavy export taxes and light import duties shattered the wine industry. Geographic obstacles—mountains, deserts, jungles, and inadequate natural harbors—also frustrated colonial efforts to promote economic integration.

Having made the colonies dependent on essential Spanish goods, however, Spain found that it could not keep the sea routes open. After 1789 the French Revolution and Napoleonic wars isolated Spain from Latin America. Foreign traders, especially from the United States, swarmed into Spanish-American ports. In 1796 the Madrid government lifted the restrictions against neutrals trading with the colonies, thus acknowledging Spain's inability to supply the colonies with needed goods and markets.[3] All these difficulties spelled disaster for colonial trade and industry.

At the end of the eighteenth century colonists also complained bitterly that only peninsulares were appointed to the *audiencias*—the colonies' highest judicial bodies, which also served as councils to the viceroys—and to other positions in the colonial governments. According to the nineteenth-century Mexican statesman and historian Lucas Alamán (1792–1853),

MAP 28.1 Latin America Before Independence Consider the factors that led to the boundaries of the various Spanish and Portuguese colonies in North and South America.

ATLANTIC
OCEAN

Disputed by Great Britain,
Spain, and Russia

Effective frontier of
Spanish settlement

COAHUILA

**VICEROYALTY
OF
NEW SPAIN**

BAJIO LEÓN

Mexico City• •Veracruz

Havana•

CUBA

JAMAICA

SAINT DOMINGUE (HAITI)

SANTO
DOMINGO

PUERTO
RICO

•Guatemala

Caribbean Sea

Caracas•

Suarez

•Bogotá

**VICEROYALTY OF
NEW GRANADA**

GUIANA

Magdalena

Amazon

PACIFIC

OCEAN

A
N
D
E
S

Lima•

**VICEROYALTY
OF PERU**

VICEROYALTY OF BRAZIL

•Bahia

A
N
D
E
S

Parana

São Paulo• •Rio de Janeiro

**VICEROYALTY OF
RIO DE LA PLATA**

Santiago•

Buenos Aires• •Montevideo

**AUDIENCIA
OF CHILE**

Spanish colonies

Viceroyalty of New Spain

Viceroyalty of New Granada

Viceroyalty of Peru

Audiencia of Chile

Viceroyalty of Rio de la Plata

Portuguese colony

Viceroyalty of Brazil

Disputed territory

Disputed by Great Britain, Spain, and Russia

0   500   1000 Km.

0   500   1000 Mi.

ISLAS MALVINAS
(FALKLAND ISLANDS)

Cape Horn

this preference shown to Spaniards in political offices and ecclesiastical benefices has been the principal cause of the rivalry between the two classes; add to this the fact that Europeans possessed great wealth, which although it may have been the just reward of effort and industry, excited the envy of Americans and was considered as so much usurpation from them; consider that for all these reasons the Spaniards had obtained a decided preponderance over those born in the country; and it will not be difficult to explain the increasing jealousy and rivalry between the two groups which culminated in hatred and enmity.[4]

From 1751 to 1775, only 13 percent of appointees to the audiencias were Creoles.[5] To the Creole elite of Spanish America, the world seemed "upside down."[6] Creoles hungered for political office and resented their successful Spanish rivals.

Madrid's tax reforms also aggravated discontent. In the 1770s and 1780s the Spanish crown needed income to finance imperial defense. Colonial ports had to be fortified and standing armies built. Like Great Britain, Spain believed its colonies should bear some of the costs of their own defense. Accordingly, Madrid raised the prices of tobacco and liquor and increased the *alcabala* (a sales tax of Arabic origin) on many items. Improved government administration made tax collection more efficient. Creole business and agricultural interests resented the Crown's monopoly of the tobacco industry and opposed new taxes.

As in the thirteen North American colonies a decade earlier, protest movements in Latin America claimed that the colonies were being taxed unconstitutionally. Merchants in Boston and Philadelphia had protested taxation without representation; the Spanish colonies, however, had no tradition of legislative approval of taxes. Creole mercantile leaders argued instead that relations between imperial authorities and colonial interests stayed on an even keel through consultation and compromise and that when the Crown imposed taxes without consultation, it violated ancient constitutional practice.

The imperial government recognized the potential danger of the North American example. Although Spain had joined France on the side of the rebel colonies against Great Britain during the American Revolution, the Madrid government refused in 1783 to grant diplomatic recognition to the new United States. North American ships calling at South American ports had introduced the subversive writings of Thomas Paine and Thomas Jefferson. For decades the ideas of Voltaire, Rousseau, and Montesquieu had been trickling into Latin America. In 1794 the Colombian Antonio Nariño translated and published the French *Declaration of the Rights of Man and the Citizen* (Spanish authorities sentenced him to ten years in an African prison, but he lived to become the father of Colombian independence). By 1800 the Creole elite throughout Latin America was familiar with liberal Enlightenment political thought.[7] The Creoles assumed, however, that the "rights of man" were limited, and they did not share such rights with Indians and blacks.

Race in the Colonial Period

The racial complexion of Latin American societies is one of the most complicated in the world. Because few European women emigrated to the colonies, Spanish men had relations with Indian and African women. African men deprived of black women sought Indian women. The result was a population composed of every possible combination of Indian, Spanish, and African blood.

Spanish theories of racial purity rejected people of mixed blood, particularly those of African descent. A person's social status depended on the degree of European blood he or she possessed or appeared to possess. Peninsulares and Creoles reinforced their privileged status by showing contempt for people who were not white. As the great nineteenth-century German scientist Alexander von Humboldt put it, having spent five years traveling throughout South America, "Any white person, although he rides his horse barefoot, imagines himself to be of the nobility of the country."[8] Coupled with the Spaniard's aristocratic disdain for manual labor, a three-hundred-year tradition had instilled in the minds of Latin Americans the notion that dark skin and manual labor went together. Owners of mines, plantations, and factories had a vested interest in keeping blacks and Indians in servile positions. Racism and discrimination pervaded all the Latin American colonies.

Demographers estimate that Indians still accounted for between three-fifths and three-fourths of the total population of Latin America at the end of the colonial period, in spite of the tremendous population losses caused by the introduction of diseases in the sixteenth and seventeenth centuries. The colonies that became Peru and Bolivia had Indian majorities; the regions that became Argentina and Chile had European majorities. Indians and black slaves toiled in the silver and gold mines of Mexico, Colombia, and Peru, in the wheat fields of Chile, in the humid, mosquito-ridden cane brakes of Mexico and the Caribbean, and in the diamond mines and coffee and sugar plantations of Brazil.

Nevertheless, nonwhites in Latin America did experience some social mobility in the colonial period, certainly more than nonwhites in North America experienced. In Mexico, decreasing reliance on slaves led to a great increase in manumissions. Once freed, however, Negroes (the Spanish term for "black persons" coined in 1555) immediately became subject to the payment of a money tribute, as were the Indians. Freedmen also incurred the obligation of military service. A few mulattos rose in the army, some as high as the rank of colonel. The army and the church seem to have offered the greatest opportunities for social mobility. Many black slaves gained their freedom by fleeing to the jungles or mountains, where they established self-governing communities. Around the year 1800 Venezuela counted 24,000 fugitive slaves in a total population of 87,000.

Many Indians were still subject to the mita and repartimiento. The *mita,* a system of forced labor requiring all adult Indian males to work for part of each year in the silver mines, was thinly disguised slave labor; the silver mines were deathtraps. The law of *repartimiento* required Indians to buy goods solely from local *corregidores,* officials who collected taxes. The new taxes of the 1770s and 1780s fell particularly heavily on the Indians. When Indian opposition to these taxes and to oppressive conditions exploded into violence, Creoles organized the protest movements and assumed leadership of them.

The Comunero Revolution

In Peru in November 1779 the wealthy, well-educated mestizo Tupac Amaru (1742–1781), a descendant of the Inca kings, captured, tried, and executed the local corregidor. Tupac Amaru and his mostly Indian followers demanded the abolition of both the alcabala tax and the mita and replacement of the corregidores with Indian governors. Proclaiming himself liberator of the people, Tupac Amaru waged a costly war of blood and fire against the Spanish governors. Poor communication among the rebel forces and the superior organiza-

Diamond Mining in Brazil   The discovery of gold and diamonds in Brazil in the seventeenth century increased the demand for slave labor. The English geologist John Mawe made this dramatic engraving of slaves washing for diamonds in the early nineteenth century. *(Source: Courtesy, Oliveira Lima Library, The Catholic University of America. Photo: Paul McKane, OSB)*

tion of the imperial armies enabled the Spanish to crush the revolt. Tupac Amaru, his family, and his captains were captured and savagely executed. Frightened colonial administrators did grant some reforms. The Crown repealed the repartimiento, reduced the mita, and replaced the corregidores with a lighter system of intendants. The condition of the Indians temporarily improved.

News of the rebellion of Tupac Amaru trickled northward, where it helped stimulate revolution in the New Granada viceroyalty. Disorders occurred first at Socorro in modern Colombia (Map 28.2). Throughout the eighteenth century Socorro had prospered. Sugar cane, corn, and cattle flourished because of its exceptionally fertile soil. Large cotton crops stimulated the production of textiles,

mostly in a primitive cottage industry worked by women. Socorro's location on the Suarez River made it an agricultural and manufacturing center and an entrepôt for trade with the hinterland. Hard-working Spanish immigrants had prospered and often intermarried with the Indians.

When the viceroy published new taxes on tobacco and liquor and reorganized the alcabala, riots broke out in Socorro in March 1781 and spread to other towns. Representatives of peasants and artisan groups from many towns elected a *comun,* or central committee, to lead the insurrection. Each town elected its local comun and the captain of its militia. Known as the Comunero Revolution, the insurrection in New Granada enjoyed broad-based support and good organization and appeared far more threatening to government authorities than had the uprising in Peru.

An Indian peasant army commanded by Creole captains marched on Bogotá. Government officials, lacking adequate military resources, sent a commission to play for time by negotiating with the comuneros. On June 4 the commission agreed to the rebels' terms: reduction of the alcabala and of the Indians' forced tribute, abolition of the new taxes on tobacco, and preference for Creoles over peninsulares in government positions. The joyful Indian army disbanded and went home. What the Indians did not know was that the commission had already secretly disclaimed the agreement with the rebels on the grounds that it had been achieved by force. Having succeeded in dispersing the Indians, the government at Bogotá won over the Creole leaders with promise of pardons and then moved in reserve troops who captured large numbers of rebels. When the last rebel base—that of José Antonio Galan—had been captured, a kangaroo court tried Galan and condemned him

to be taken out of jail, dragged and taken to the place of execution where he will be hung until dead, that his head be removed from his dead body, that the rest of his body be quartered, that his torso be committed to flames for which purpose a fire shall be lit in front of the platform. . . . All his descendants shall be declared infamous, all his property shall be confiscated by the

royal treasury, his home shall be burnt, and the ground salted, so that in this fashion his infamous name may be forgotten.[9]

Thus ended the revolt of the comuneros in New Granada. They failed to win self-rule, but they forced the authorities to act in accordance with the spirit of the "unwritten constitution," whose guiding principle was consultation and compromise.

Independence

In 1808, as part of his effort to rule Europe, Napoleon Bonaparte deposed the Spanish king Ferdinand VII and placed his own brother on the Spanish throne (see page 763). In Latin America the Creoles subsequently seized the opportunity. Since everything in Spanish America was done in the name of the king, the Creoles argued that the removal of the legitimate king shifted sovereignty to the people—that is, to themselves. In 1810 the small, wealthy Creole aristocracy used the removal of the Spanish king as justification for their seizure of political power and their preservation of that power.

The Creoles who led the various movements for independence did not intend a radical redistribution of property or reconstruction of society. They merely rejected the authority of the Spanish crown. An able scholar has described the war for independence as

a prolonged, confused, and in many ways contradictory movement. In Mexico it began as a popular social movement and ended many years later as a conservative uprising against a liberal Spanish constitution. In Venezuela it came to be a war unto the death; in other places it was a war between a small Creole minority and the Spanish authorities. It was not an organized movement with a central revolutionary directorate. It had no Continental Congress. . . . If there was no central direction, no centrally recognized leadership, likewise there was no formally accepted political doctrine. . . .

In Latin America each separate area went its own way. Central America broke way from Mexico and then splintered into five separate nations. Uruguay, Paraguay, and Bolivia separated themselves from Argentina, Chile from Peru, and [Simón] Bolívar's attempt to federate the state of Greater Colombia (Venezuela, Colombia, and Ecuador) with Peru and Bolivia under a centralized government broke down.[10]

✿ **MAP 28.2 Latin America in 1830** What geographical factors have led to the relative political power of the United States and the Latin American nations?

✳ **Fernando Leal: Epic of Bolívar** Often hated in his lifetime, Simón Bolívar is today revered as the greatest Latin American hero, and a rich body of legend surrounds him. This huge three-paneled watercolor mural showing "Bolívar as a Child," "Bolívar as Liberator," and "The Death of Bolívar" contributes to the Bolívar legend. *(Source: ARCHIVO CENIDIAP-INBA, Mexico City. Collection Fernando Leal Audirac)*

The great hero of the movement for independence was Simón Bolívar (1783–1830), a very able general who is considered the Latin American George Washington. Bolívar's victories over the royalist armies won him the presidency of Greater Colombia in 1819. He dreamed of a continental union and in 1826 summoned a conference of the American republics at Panama. The meeting achieved little. Bolívar organized the government of Bolivia and became the head of the new state of Peru. The territories of Greater Colombia splintered apart, however, and a sadly disillusioned Bolívar went into exile, saying, "America is ungovernable. Those who served the revolution plowed the seas." The failure of Pan-Americanism isolated individual countries, prevented collective action, and later paved the way for the political and economic intrusion of the United States and other powers.

Brazil's quest for independence from Portugal was unique: Brazil won its independence without violent upheaval. When Napoleon's troops entered Portugal, the royal family fled to Brazil and made Rio de Janeiro the capital of the Portuguese Empire. The new government immediately lifted the old mercantilist restrictions and opened Brazilian ports to the ships of all friendly nations. Under popular pressure, King Pedro I (r. 1822–1831)

proclaimed Brazil's independence in 1822 and published a constitution. Pedro's administration was wracked by factional disputes between Portuguese courtiers and Brazilian Creoles, a separatist movement in the Rio Grande do Sul region, and provincial revolts. His successor, Pedro II (r. 1831–1889), restored order and laid the foundations of the modern Brazilian state. The reign of Pedro II witnessed the expansion of the coffee industry, the beginnings of the rubber industry, and massive immigration.

The Consequences of Independence

The wars of independence ended around 1825. What effects did they have on Latin American societies, governments, and national development? Because the movements for independence differed in character and course in different regions and countries, generalizations are likely to be misleading. Significant changes did occur, however, throughout Latin America.

The newly independent nations did not achieve immediate political stability when the wars of independence ended. The Spanish crown had served as a unifying symbol, and its disappearance left a power vacuum. Civil disorder typically followed. The Creole leaders of the revolutions had no experience in government, and the wars left a legacy of military, not civilian, leadership. Throughout the continent, idealistic but impractical leaders proclaimed republics governed by representative assemblies. In practice, the generals ruled.

In Argentina, Juan Manuel de Rosas (r. 1835–1852) assumed power amid widespread public disorder and ruled as dictator. In Mexico, liberals declared a federal republic, but incessant civil strife led to the rise of the dictator Antonio López de Santa Anna in the mid-nineteenth century. Likewise in Venezuela, strongmen, dictators, and petty aristocratic oligarchs governed from 1830 to 1892. Some countries suffered constant revolutions. In the course of the century Bolivia had sixty and Venezuela fifty-two. The rule of force prevailed almost everywhere. Enlightened dictatorship was the typical form of government.

Although isolated territories such as Paraguay and much of Central America suffered little damage, the wars of liberation disrupted the economic life of most Latin American countries. The prosperity that many areas had achieved toward the end of the colonial period was destroyed. Mexico and Venezuela in particular lost large percentages of their populations and suffered great destruction of farmland and animals. Even areas that saw relatively little violence, such as Chile and New Granada, experienced a weakening of economic life. Armies were frequently recruited by force; and when the men were demobilized, many did not return home. The consequent population dislocation hurt agriculture and mining. Guerrilla warfare disrupted trade and communications. Forced loans and the seizure of private property for military use ruined many people.

Brazil, which had a large slave population, did not free the slaves until 1888. Spain abolished slavery in its Cuban colony in a series of measures between 1870 and 1886; Cuba itself became independent in 1903, a consequence of the Spanish-American War. Elsewhere, however, independence accelerated the abolition of slavery. The destruction of agriculture in countries such as Mexico and Venezuela caused the collapse of the plantation system, and fugitive slaves could not be recaptured. Also, the royalists and patriot generals such as Bolívar offered slaves their freedom in exchange for military service. Most of the new independent states adopted republican constitutions declaring the legal equality of all men. For Indians and blacks, however, these noble words were meaning-

less, for the revolution brought about no redistribution of property. Nor could long-standing racist attitudes be eliminated by the stroke of a pen.

Although the edifice of racism persisted in the nineteenth century, Latin America experienced much more assimilation and offered Negroes greater economic and social mobility than did the United States. As a direct result of their heroic military service in the wars of independence, a substantial number of Negroes improved their social

Diego Rivera: Orgy Night of the Rich   Depicting upper-class Mexican society as rife with drunkenness, bribery, and corruption and backed by the military, while the church feigns shock, Rivera (1886–1957) painted this enormous fresco, part of a series, as a condemnation of capitalism and a glorification of ordinary people. Although the artist was familiar with artistic movements in Europe, his work paintings are rooted in the Mexican tradition. *(Source: ARCHIVO CENIDIAP-INBA, Mexico City)*

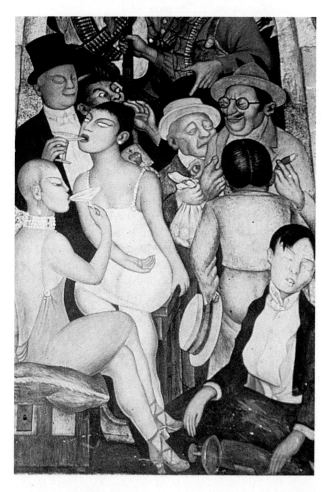

status. Some even attained the political heights: the Mexican revolutionary Vicente Guerrero, served as president of his country in 1829; Antonio Guzmán governed Venezuela as a benevolent dictator (r. 1870–1888); Ramón Castilla served as president of Peru (r. 1845–1851 and 1855–1862) and made great improvements in state financing.

What accounts for the relative racial permeability of Latin America in contrast with the severe segregation in the United States? As the Dutch scholar H. Hoetink points out, Latin American countries evolved a three-tiered sociracial structure, in contrast to the two-tiered racial edifice in the United States. Legally and socially, Latin American societies classified people as white, colored, or black, and marriages between whites and light-skinned colored people were commonly accepted. Legislative discrimination against colored people proved unenforceable. Thus light skin allowed for gradual assimilation into the middle and upper social echelons. In the United States, by contrast, anyone who was not "pure" white was classified as black (see page 940).

Hoetink explains the problem partly in terms of the large population of poor whites in the United States: "Nowhere, but in the North American mainland, did the number of extremely poor whites always exceed the number of slaves. Nowhere, but in the U.S. South, were special police forces predominantly manned by poor whites."[11] Also, Latin American elites' definition of *whiteness* and perception of physical beauty seem to have been broader than the definition and perception of the white majority in the United States.

Nevertheless, the advantages of assimilation did not (and do not) apply to dark-skinned people in Latin America. Substantial numbers of light-skinned colored people rose economically and socially, but the great mass of dark-skinned blacks continued to experience all the consequences of systematic and insistent racism.

Neocolonialism

At first, political instability and the preoccupation of European and North American financiers with industrial expansion in their own countries discouraged foreign investment in Latin America's newly independent nations. The advent of stable dictatorships, however, eventually paved the way for economic growth. After 1870 capital began to flow south and across the Atlantic. In Mexico,

North American capital supported the production of hemp (used in the United States for grain harvesting), sugar, bananas, and rubber, frequently on American-owned plantations. British and American interests backed the development of tin, copper, and gold mining in Mexico. By 1911 Mexico had taken third place among the world's oil producers. British financiers built Argentina's railroads, meatpacking industry, and utilities. British businessmen in Chile developed the copper and nitrate industries (nitrate is used in the production of pharmaceuticals and fertilizers). Likewise in Brazil, foreign capital—primarily British—flowed into coffee, cotton, and sugar production and manufacturing. By 1904, Brazil produced 76 percent of the world's coffee. When massive overproduction of coffee led to a sharp drop in prices in 1906, a commission of British, American, German, and French bankers rescued the Brazilian government from near disaster.

The price that Latin America paid for economic development at the end of the nineteenth century was a new form of economic domination. Foreign investors acquired control of the railroads, mineral resources, and banking, and they made heavy inroads into real estate. British investments led all others. But beginning in 1898, the United States flexed its imperialistic muscles and sent gunboats and troops to defend its dollars in the Caribbean and Central America. By the turn of the century the Latin American nations were active participants in the international economic order, but foreigners controlled most of their industries. Between 1904 and 1929, for example, the United States intervened in Latin American affairs whenever it felt its economic interests threatened. Americans secured control of the Panama Canal in 1904 on their own terms; in 1912 and 1926 U.S. Marines interfered in Nicaragua to bolster conservative governments; and the Marines that were sent to Haiti in 1915 to protect American property stayed until 1934. The result has been a bitter legacy of anti-American feeling throughout Latin America. Only with the launching of President Franklin Roosevelt's Good Neighbor Policy did relations between the United States and Latin America begin to improve.

Another distinctive feature of the neocolonial order was that each country's economy revolved around only one or two products: sugar in Cuba, nitrates and copper in Chile, meat in Argentina, coffee in Brazil. A sharp drop in the world market demand for a product could destroy the industry

LATIN AMERICA, CA 1760–1900

1764–1780	Charles III of Spain's administrative and economic reforms
1781	Comunero Revolution in New Granada
1810–1825	Latin American wars of independence against Spain
1822	Proclamation by Portugal of Brazil's independence
1826	Call by Simón Bolívar for Panama Conference on Latin American union
1825–ca 1870	Political instability in most Latin American nations
ca 1870–1919	Latin American neocolonialism
1876–1911	Porfirio Díaz's control of Mexico
1888	Emancipation of slaves in Brazil Final abolition of slavery in Western Hemisphere
1880–1914	Massive immigration from Europe and Asia to Latin America
1898	Spanish American War End of Spanish control over Cuba Transfer of Puerto Rico and the Philippines to United States

and with it the nation's economic structure. The outbreak of the First World War in 1914 drastically reduced exports of Latin American raw materials and imports of European manufactured goods, provoking general economic crisis.[12]

Throughout the eighteenth century the Spanish-owned *haciendas*—large landed estates—and plantations had continued to expand to meet the needs of commercial agriculture: wheat for the cities, corn for the Indians' consumption, sugar for export to Europe and North America. By means of purchase, forced removal of Indians, and outright seizure, the Spanish continued to take Indian land, as they had done in the seventeenth century. Some land was acquired merely to eliminate competition by depriving Indians of their fields, which were then left fallow.

The late nineteenth century witnessed ever greater concentrations of land in ever fewer hands. In places like the Valley of Mexico in southern Mexico, a few large haciendas controlled all the land. Under the dictatorship of General Porfirio Díaz, the Mexican government in 1883 passed a law allowing real estate companies (controlled by Díaz's political cronies) to survey public and "vacant" lands and to retain one-third of the land they surveyed. An 1894 law provided that land could be declared vacant if legal title to it could not be produced. Since few Indians had deeds to the land that their ancestors had worked for centuries, the door swung open to wholesale expropriation of small landowners and entire villages. Shrewd speculators tricked illiterate Indians into selling their lands for trifling sums. Thousands of litigants clogged the courts. Indians who dared armed resistance were crushed by government troops and carried off to virtual slave labor. Vast stretches of land came into the hands of private individuals—in one case, 12 million acres. Stripped of their lands, the Indians were a ready labor supply. They were mercilessly exploited. Debt peonage became common: landowners paid their laborers not in cash but in vouchers redeemable only at the company store, whose high prices and tricky bookkeeping kept the peons permanently in debt.

Some scholars maintain that the hacienda owners usually let their land lie fallow until it rose in value or attracted American investors. The lack of cultivation, they assert, kept the prices of corn and other crops artificially high. The owners themselves, supported by rents, passed indolent lives in extravagant luxury in Mexico City and other cities.

Other scholars argue that the haciendas were efficient enterprises whose owners sought to maximize profits on invested capital. The Sanchez Navarro family of northwestern Mexico, for instance, engaged in a wide variety of agricultural and commercial pursuits, exploiting their lands and resources as fully as possible. Ultimately, their *latifundio*—a large landed estate—was about the size of West Virginia. Along with vast cattle ranches and sheep runs containing as many as 250,000 sheep, the Sanchez Navarros cultivated maize, wheat, and cotton. They invested heavily and profitably in silver mining and manufacturing and lent sizable sums at high interest. Although they brutally exploited their peons and practiced debt peonage, the Sanchez Navarros lived very modestly on their own estates rather than luxuriating in Mexico City.[13] A final determination of whether the Sanchez Navarros were unique or representative of Mexican agricultural and business communities must await further investigation.

The Impact of Immigration

In 1852 the Argentine political philosopher Juan Bautista Alberdi published *Bases and Points of Departure for Argentine Political Organization,* arguing that "to govern is to populate." Alberdi meant that the development of his country—and, by extension, all of Latin America—depended on immigration. Argentina had an adequate labor supply, but it was unevenly distributed throughout the country. Moreover, Alberdi maintained, Indians and blacks lacked basic skills, and it would take too long to train them. Thus he pressed for massive immigration from the "advanced" countries of northern Europe and the United States. Alberdi's ideas won immediate acceptance and were even incorporated into the Argentine constitution, which declared that "the Federal government will encourage European immigration." Other Latin American countries adopted similar policies promoting immigration.[14]

European needs coincided perfectly with those of Latin America. After 1880, Ireland, Great Britain, Germany, Italy, Spain, and the central European nations experienced greater population growth than their labor markets could absorb.

Meanwhile, the growing industries of Europe needed South American raw materials and markets for their finished goods, and South American countries wanted European markets for their minerals, coffee, sugar, beef, and manufactured goods. Italian, Spanish, and Portuguese peoples poured into Latin America.

Immigration led to rapid urbanization, which meant Europeanization and industrialization. By 1900, Buenos Aires and Rio de Janeiro had populations of more than 500,000 people; Mexico City, Montevideo, Santiago, and Havana also experienced spectacular growth. Portuguese, Italian, French, Chinese, and Japanese immigrants gave an international flavor to the cities, and a more vigorous tempo replaced the somnolent Spanish atmosphere.

By 1914 Buenos Aires had emerged as one of the most cosmopolitan cities in the world. In less than a half-century, the population of the city and its province had grown from 500,000 to 3.6 million. As Argentina's political capital, the city housed all its government bureaucracies and agencies. The meatpacking, food-processing, flourmilling, and wool industries were concentrated in Buenos Aires. Half of all overseas tonnage passed through the city, which was also the heart of the nation's railroad network. The University of Buenos Aires was the intellectual hub of the nation. Elegant shops near the Plaza de Mayo catered to the expensive tastes of the elite upper classes, who constituted about 5 percent of the population. But the thousands of immigrants who toiled twelve hours a day, six days a week, on docks and construction sites and in meatpacking plants crowded into the city's *conventillos,* or tenements:

The one-room dwelling . . . served a family with two to five children or a group of four or five single men. At the door to each room stood a pile of wooden boxes. One generally held a basin for washing; another a charcoal brazier on which to cook the daily watery stew, or puchero; and garbage accumulated in a third. Two or three iron cots, a pine table, a few wooden chairs, an old trunk, perhaps a sewing machine, and more boxes completed the furnishings. Light came from the open door and one window, from an oil or gas lamp, or occasionally from a bare electric light bulb. On the once-whitewashed walls were tacked pictures of popular heroes, generals, or kings torn from magazines, an image of the Madonna and a couple of saints, perhaps a faded photograph of fam-

ily members in Europe. The women often eked out miserable incomes by taking in laundry and washing and drying it in the patios. Others ironed or sewed on a piecework basis. Some men worked here: in one corner a shoemaker might ply his trade, in another a man might bend over a small table repairing watches.[15]

Immigrants dreamed of rapid economic success in the New World, and there was in fact plenty of upward social mobility. The first generation almost always did manual labor, but its sons often advanced to upper blue-collar or to white-collar jobs. The rare Genoese or Neapolitan immigrant whose labor and thrift made his son a millionaire quickly learned the meaning of assimilation: the son typically imitated the dress, style, and values of the Spanish elite. Hispanic attitudes toward class, manual labor, and egalitarianism prevailed.[16]

Europeans gave an enormous boost to the development of industry and commerce. Italian and Spanish settlers in Argentina stimulated the expansion of the cattle industry and the development of the wheat and shoe industries. In Brazil, Swiss immigrants built the cheese business; Italians gained a leading role in the coffee industry; and the Japanese pioneered the development of the cotton industry. In Peru, the British controlled railroad construction, Italians became influential in banking and the restaurant business, and the French dominated jewelry, dressmaking, and pharmaceuticals. The arrival of millions of migrants changed the entire commercial structure of South America.

Immigration promoted further ethnic integration. The vast majority of migrants were unmarried males; seven out of ten people who landed in Argentina between 1857 and 1924 were single males between thirteen and forty years old. There, as in other South American countries, many of those who stayed sought out Indian or other low-status women. Male settlers from eastern Europe and women of all nationalities preferred to marry within their own ethnic groups. But men greatly outnumbered women, and a man who chose to marry usually had to marry an Indian.[17] Immigration, then, furthered the racial mixture of Europeans, Asians, and native South Americans.

For Latin America's sizable black population, immigration proved a calamity. The abolition of slavery in Spanish America had scarcely changed the economic and social status of the Negro population. Accustomed to working the rural coffee plantations and the mines, blacks sometimes had little preparation for urban living. Many former slaves had skills, even for factory work, but racism explains the greater presence of white immigrants in factories. In 1893, 71.2 percent of the working population of São Paulo was foreign-born. Anxious to adapt to America and to climb the economic ladder, immigrants quickly learned the traditional racial prejudices. Negro women usually found work as domestics, but employers excluded black males from good jobs. Racial prejudice kept the vast bulk of the South American black population in a wretched socioeconomic position until the Second World War.

Independence did little to change the basic social, economic, and political structure of Latin American countries. Although republican constitutions declared all men (but not women) equal under law, the elite continued to control status, wealth, and power almost everywhere as Creoles moved into positions formerly held by peninsulares. Neocolonialism's modernizing influence on commerce and industry strengthened the position of the elite and allowed it to use capitalistic values and ideals as a shield against demands for fundamental socioeconomic reforms. European styles in art, clothing, housing, and literature became highly popular, particularly among members of the elite as they sought acceptance and approval by their economic masters. Meaningful structural change would await the revolutions and violent confrontations of the twentieth century.

THE UNITED STATES (1789–1929)

The victory of the North American colonies and the founding of the United States seemed to validate the Enlightenment idea that a better life on earth was possible. Americans carried over into the nineteenth and twentieth centuries an unbounded optimism about the future. Although most eastern states retained a property or tax-paying qualification for the vote down to 1860, the suffrage was gradually expanded to include most adult white males; New Jersey alone gave (propertied) women the vote for a time. The movement toward popular democracy accelerated as the young nation, confident of its "manifest destiny," pushed relentlessly across the continent. Westward movement, however, threatened to extend black slavery, which

Christian Mayr, Kitchen Ball at White Sulphur Springs, 1838   The German artist who painted this picture shortly after his arrival in the U.S. apparently had no preconceived racial views; he portrayed blacks without the insulting caricatures, marginalized situations, or political formulas typical of many mid-century representations. Rather, African Americans are shown here as graceful, dignified, and in a social scene of their own creation. Light-skinned and dark-skinned, old and young, plain and beautiful celebrate and reveal an individual and a group dignity. White Sulphur Springs was (and is) a fashionable resort. *(Source: North Carolina Museum of Art, Raleigh. Purchased with funds from the state of North Carolina)*

generated increasing disagreement between the industrialized North and the agricultural South. The ensuing Civil War cost more American lives than any other war the nation was to fight. The victory of the North did not resolve the racial issue that had led to war, but it did preserve the federal system.

The years between 1865 and 1917 witnessed the building of a new industrialized nation. Immigrants settled much of the West, provided the labor to exploit the country's mineral resources, turned small provincial towns into sophisticated centers of ethnic and cultural diversity, and built the railroads that tied the country together. The ideology of manifest destiny lived on after the frontier closed and considerably affected relations between the United States and Latin America. In the First World War, American aid and American troops were the deciding factor in the Allied victory. After the war, "normalcy" and the façade of prosperity supported a persistent optimism.

Manifest Destiny

In an 1845 issue of the *United States Magazine and Democratic Review,* editor John L. O'Sullivan boldly declared that foreign powers were trying to prevent American annexation of Texas in order to impede "the fulfillment of our manifest destiny to overspread the continent allotted by Providence for the free development of our yearly multiplying millions." O'Sullivan was articulating a sentiment prevalent in the United States since early in its history: that God had foreordained the nation to cover the entire continent. After a large-circulation newspaper picked up the phrase "manifest destiny," it was used on the floor of Congress and soon entered the language as a catchword for and justification of expansion. The concept of manifest destiny played an important role in some basic developments in American history: the settlement of peoples of diverse nationalities, the issue of slavery, the conflict over whether the United States was to remain agrarian or become a commercial and industrial society.

Two other concepts also played a powerful role in the formation of the young republic: social equality, by which was meant equality of opportunity, and optimism about the future. After a visit to the United States in 1831, the French nobleman Alexis de Tocqueville wrote in *Democracy in America,* a classic analysis of American civilization, "No novelty in the United States struck me more visibly during my stay there than the equality of conditions." By equality Tocqueville meant the relative fluidity of American society, and he attributed this to Americans' mobility. Unlike Europe, where family and inherited wealth meant a great deal and people typically lived all their lives in the regions where they were born, geographic mobility in America provided enormous opportunity. A deeply rooted work ethic taught that everyone could advance through thrift and hard work. Americans also had an unbounded faith in the future. This belief that America offered golden and limitless opportunities is epitomized in the letter an immigrant Englishman wrote home to his wife:

I do not repent coming, for you know that there was nothing but poverty before me, and to see you and the dear children want was more than I could bear. I would rather cross the Atlantic ten times than hear my children cry for victuals. . . . There is plenty of room yet, and will be for a thousand years to come.[18]

When George Washington took office in 1789, fewer than 4 million people inhabited the thirteen states on the eastern seaboard. By the time Abraham Lincoln became the sixteenth president in 1861, the United States stretched across the continent and had 31 million inhabitants.

During the colonial period, pioneers had pushed westward to the Appalachian Mountains. After independence, westward movement accelerated. The eastern states claimed all the land from the Atlantic Ocean to the Mississippi River, but two forces blocked immediate expansion. The Indians, trying to save their lands, allied with the British in Canada to prevent further American encroachment. In 1794, however, Britain agreed to evacuate border forts in the Northwest Territory, roughly the area north of the Ohio River and east of the Mississippi, and thereby end British support for the Indians. A similar treaty with Spain paved the way for southeastern expansion (Map 28.3).

Events in Europe and the Caribbean led to a massive increase in American territory. In 1800 Spain ceded the Louisiana Territory—the land between the Mississippi River and the Rocky Mountains—to France. Napoleon intended to use the Louisiana Territory to make France an imperial power in America, but a black revolution on the island of Hispaniola (present-day Haiti and Dominican Republic) upset his plans. Led by Toussaint L'Ouverture, Haiti's 500,000 slaves revolted against their 40,000 white owners. Napoleon quickly dispatched troops with orders to crush the revolt, seize New Orleans, and take possession of the Louisiana Territory. Alarmed, President Thomas Jefferson ordered the American minister in Paris, Robert Livingston, to negotiate to buy the Louisiana Territory.

When yellow fever and Haitian bullets carried off most of the French troops in Haiti, Napoleon relinquished his grandiose plans. He was planning war with Great Britain, and on the day he opened hostilities with England, his foreign minister Talleyrand casually asked Livingston, "What would you give us for the whole of Louisiana?" The astonished American proposed $4 million. "Too low!" said Talleyrand. "Reflect and see me tomorrow." Less than three weeks later the deed of sale was signed. The United States paid only $12 million for millions of acres of some of the world's richest farmland.

Scarcely was the ink dry on the agreement when pressure rose for war with England. Repeated British attacks on American vessels on the high seas and British interference in American trade provided diplomatic justification for the War of 1812. Western "war hawks" wanted further expansion and believed that a war with Britain would yield Canada, permanently end Indian troubles, and open up vast forest lands for settlement. The Treaty of Ghent (1814) ended the conflict but left the prewar boundaries unchanged.

After the restoration of peace, settlers poured into the Northwest Territory and the Gulf Plains (the region of Georgia, Alabama, and Mississippi). Congress sold land in lots of 160 acres at $2 an acre; only $80 was needed as down payment. Irish and German immigrants rapidly put the black earth of Indiana and Illinois under cultivation. Pioneers of American stock planted cotton in the lush delta of the Gulf Plains. Scandinavian and German settlers found the softly rolling hills of the Wisconsin country ideal for cattle.

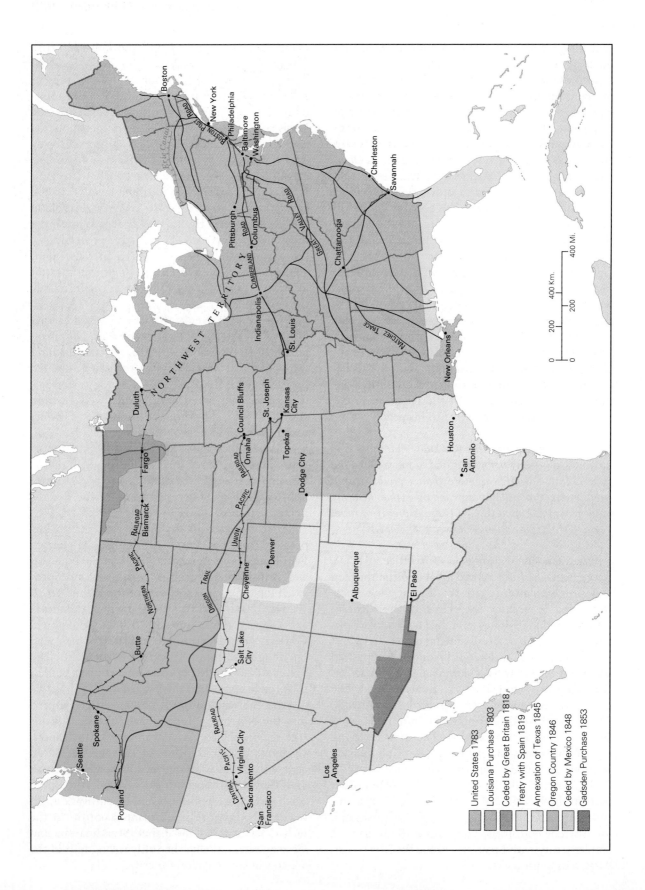

United States 1783
Louisiana Purchase 1803
Ceded by Great Britain 1818
Treaty with Spain 1819
Annexation of Texas 1845
Oregon Country 1846
Ceded by Mexico 1848
Gadsden Purchase 1853

NORTHWEST TERRITORY

Boston
New York
Philadelphia
Baltimore
Washington
Charleston
Savannah
Pittsburgh
Columbus
Indianapolis
St. Louis
New Orleans
Chattanooga

BOSTON POST ROAD
Erie Canal
CUMBERLAND ROAD
GREAT VALLEY ROAD
NATCHEZ TRACE

Duluth
Fargo
Bismarck
Butte
Spokane
Seattle
Portland
Council Bluffs
Omaha
St. Joseph
Kansas City
Topeka
Dodge City
Denver
Cheyenne
Salt Lake City
Virginia City
Sacramento
San Francisco
Los Angeles
Albuquerque
El Paso
Houston
San Antonio

NORTHERN PACIFIC RAILROAD
UNION PACIFIC RAILROAD
CENTRAL PACIFIC RAILROAD
OREGON TRAIL

400 Mi.
400 Km.
200
200
0
0

Spain, preoccupied with rebellions in South America, sold the Florida Territory to the U.S. government; and beginning in 1821, American settlers poured into the Mexican territory of Texas, whose soil proved excellent for the production of cotton and sugar. Contemptuous of the government of the Mexican president Santa Anna, Texans rebelled and proclaimed Texas an independent republic in 1836. Southern politicians, fearing that Texas would become a refuge for fugitive slaves, pressured President John Tyler to admit Texas to the United States. A joint resolution of Congress, hastily signed by Tyler, did so in 1845.

The absorption of Texas's 267,339 square miles (France, by comparison, covers 211,200 square miles) whetted American appetites for the rest of the old Spanish Empire in North America. Some expansionists even dreamed of taking Cuba and Central America.

Exploiting Mexico's political instability, President James Polk goaded Mexico into war. Mexico suffered total defeat and in the Treaty of Guadalupe Hidalgo (1848) surrendered its remaining claims to Texas, yielded New Mexico and California, and recognized the Rio Grande as the international border. A treaty with Great Britain in 1846 had already recognized the American settlement in the Oregon Territory. The continent had been acquired. Then, in 1898, a revolt in Cuba against incompetent Spanish administration had consequences beyond "manifest destiny." Inflamed by press reports of Spanish atrocities, public opinion swept the United States into war. The Spanish-American War—the "splendid little war," as Secretary of State John Hay called it—lasted just ten weeks and brought U.S. control over Cuba, the Philippine Islands, and Puerto Rico. Denying imperialistic ambitions, President William McKinley justified the U.S. acquisition of Cuba and the Philippines with a classic imperialistic argument: the nation wanted only "to take them all and educate the Filipinos and uplift and civilize and Chris-

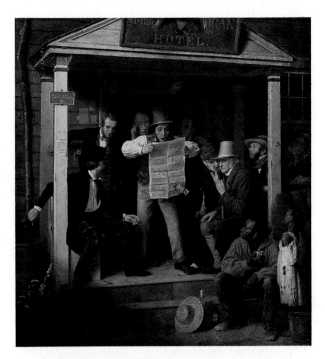

Richard Caton Woodville: War News from Mexico (1848)   In this scene of everyday life, the front porch of the "American Hotel" represents a microcosm of American society. The man reading the newspaper bursts with excitement, as the well-dressed white men (and woman, partly hidden) eagerly listen to the news from the front. In showing the black child in a tattered dress while the seated black man drinks whiskey (a jug is half hidden under his hat) from a silver cup, Woodville makes a stereotypically racist statement. The American artist, however, did not witness such a scene: he painted this in Dusseldorf, Germany. (*Source: Manoogian Foundation*)

tianize them." McKinley, like most other Americans, did not know that the Filipinos had an old, sophisticated culture and that they had been Christians for three centuries. The nation's "manifest destiny" had evolved into worldwide imperialism.

The Fate of the Indians

How did the only people who were native to this vast continent fare under manifest destiny? The Indians faithfully observed their treaties with the United States, but "white pioneers in the Northwest committed the most wanton and cruel murders of them, for which it was almost impossible to

MAP 28.3 Territorial Growth of the United States   The Cumberland Road between Cumberland, Maryland, and—by 1833—Columbus, Ohio, and the Erie Canal, which linked New York City and the Great Lakes region, carried thousands of easterners and immigrants to the Old Northwest and the frontier beyond. Transcontinental railroads subsequently made all the difference.

obtain a conviction from a pioneer jury."[19] Government officials sometimes manipulated the Indians by gathering a few chiefs, plying them with cheap whiskey, then inducing them to hand over the tribes' hunting grounds. Sometimes officials exploited rivlaries among tribes, or used bribes. By these methods, William Henry Harrison, superintendent of the Indians of the Northwest Territory and a future president, got some native Americans to cede 48 million acres. He had the full backing of President Jefferson.

The policy of pushing the Indians westward across the Mississippi, which President James Monroe's administration had adopted early in the century, accelerated during Andrew Jackson's presidency (1829–1837). Thousands of Delawares, Shawnees, and Wyandots, tricked into moving from the Northwest Territory to reservations west of Missouri, died of cholera and measles during the journey. The survivors found themselves hopelessly in debt for supplies and farming equipment. The state of Georgia, meanwhile, was nibbling away at Cherokee lands, which were theoretically protected by treaty with the U.S. government. Then gold was discovered on the Cherokee lands, and a gold rush took place. A Vermont missionary, the Reverend Samuel C. Worcester, carried the Indians' case to the Supreme Court. Chief Justice John Marshall ruled that the laws of Georgia had no force within the Cherokee territory and that white settlers and gold rustlers had to leave. President Jackson retorted, "John Marshall has made his decision. Now let him enforce it." The Creek, Cherokee, and other tribes were rounded up, expelled, and sent beyond the western boundaries of Missouri and Arkansas.[20] Later in the century, Indians in the West were forced onto government-designated reservations. The shameful price of westward expansion was the dislocation and extermination of millions of native Americans (Map 28.4).

❄ **Jackson as the "Great Father"** This cartoon satirizes Andrew Jackson, who as president (1829–1837) pushed a policy forcing the relocation of eastern Indian tribes to the west of the Mississippi. The cartoon also insults native Americans by depicting them as diminutive, doll-like, and dependent on the "Great Father," who stands for the power of the federal government. *(Source: William L. Clements Library, The University of Michigan, Ann Arbor)*

Black Slavery in the South

Dutch traders brought the first black people as prisoners to Virginia in 1619 as one solution to the chronic shortage of labor in North America (white indentured servants who worked for a term of years was another solution). The first black arrivals, however, were not slaves. In the seventeenth century, a system of racial servitude and discrimination did not exist. Some blacks themselves acquired property and indentured servants.

In the early eighteenth century, as rice cultivation expanded in the Carolinas and tobacco in the Chesapeake Bay colonies of Virginia and Maryland, planters demanded more laborers. Between 1720 and 1770, black prisoners poured into the southern colonies. In South Carolina they came to outnumber whites by almost two to one. In the decades 1730 through 1760 white fears of black revolts pushed colonial legislatures to pass laws that established tight white control and blacks' legal position as slaves, enshrining the slave system in law. Economic demands led to the legal and social institutionalization of black slavery in North Amer-

John Antrobus: Plantation Burial   Apart from the detached figure (far left) and the couple strolling under the trees—presumably the plantation owner and his wife (far right)—all the figures in this painting are black. English art historian Hugh Honour described the painting as a "rare surviving visual record of the independent culture of Afro-Americans under slavery." The preacher raises his hands in blessing and consigns the dead to the grave. Some listen; some mourn; some seem indifferent or preoccupied. (*Source: The Historic New Orleans Collection, Accession no. 1760.46*)

ica. Racist arguments of blacks' supposed inferiority were used to justify that institutionalization.

Slavery and race relations have posed a serious dilemma for the American majority for more than two centuries. Powerful moral, legal, political, and sociological arguments have characterized slavery as a great evil, a violation of the central principle of the Declaration of Independence that all men are created equal. Eighteenth- and nineteenth-century Americans, however, could not decide whether the ringing words of the Declaration applied to blacks. One scholar posed the question in this way:

How did the slave-holding class, which was molded by the same forces that shaped the nation, which fought America's wars and helped inspire its Revolution, a class which boasted of its patriotism, its devotion to freedom, its adherence to the major tenets of liberalism—how did such a class justify its continuing commitment to slavery?[21]

The answer can be given in two words: *profit* and *status*.

The system of slavery involved many factors—the size of a plantation or farm and the number of slaves working it, the arability of the soil and the quantity of rainfall, the efficiency of plantation management, and individual initiative. Many slaveowners realized reasonable, sometimes handsome, profits in the decades before the Civil War. For white planters and farmers, slavery proved lucrative, and ownership of slaves was a status symbol as well as a means of social control. Slavery "was at the center of a well-established way of life to which

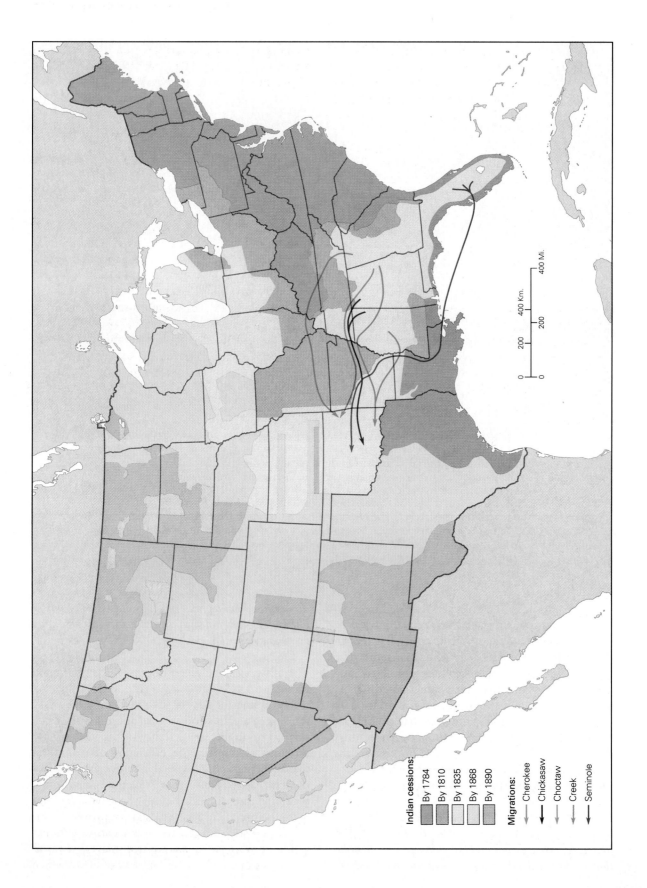

Indian cessions:

By 1784
By 1810
By 1835
By 1868
By 1890

Migrations:

Cherokee
Chickasaw
Choctaw
Creek
Seminole

400 Mi.
400 Km.
200
200
0
0

[slaveowners] were accustomed and attached, and the disruption or demise of which they feared above all else."[22] Millions of whites, whether or not they owned many slaves, would have agreed with the South Carolina planter who wrote, "Slavery informs all our modes of life, all our habits of thought, lies at the basis of our social existence, and of our political faith." Since the possession of slaves brought financial profit *and* conferred social status and prestige, struggling small farmers had a material and psychological interest in maintaining black bondage. Slavery provided the means by which they might rise, and the floor beneath which they could not fall.

American society subsequently paid a high price in guilt and psychological conflict. Some slaveholders, like President George Washington, found the subject of slavery too uncomfortable even to talk about: "I shall frankly declare to you that I do not like even to think, much less talk of it."[23] In the half-century before the Civil War, most slaveowners were deeply religious. On the one hand, they taught their children to get rich by the accumulation of land and slaves; on the other hand, they taught that God would punish the greedy with eternal damnation. Slaveholders justified slavery by dismissing blacks as inferior, but religion preached that in the eyes of God black and white were equal and would ultimately be judged on that basis.

Some slaveowners felt completely trapped by the system. One master wrote, "I cannot just take them up and sell them though that would be clearly the best I could do for myself. I cannot free them. I cannot keep them with comfort. . . . What would I not give to be freed from responsibility for these poor creatures." Perhaps to an even greater extent than men, women of the planter class felt troubled by slavery. The South Carolina aristocrat Mary Boykin Chesnut confided to her diary in 1861:

I wonder if it be a sin to think slavery a curse to any land. . . . God forgive us, but ours is a monstrous sys-tem and wrong and iniquity. Perhaps the rest of the world is as bad—this only I see. Like the patriarchs of old our men live all in one house with their wives and their concubines, and the mulattoes one sees in every family exactly resemble the white children—and every lady tells you who is the father of all the mulatto children in everybody's household, but those in her own she seems to think drop from the clouds, or pretends so to think.[24]

Mary Chesnut believed that most white women of the South were abolitionists in their hearts. She enjoyed the attentions and services of her slaves, but when Lincoln issued the Emancipation Proclamation, she welcomed it with "an unholy joy."[25]

What impact did slavery have on the black family? Herbert G. Gutman's authoritative *The Black Family in Slavery and Freedom, 1750–1925,* has demonstrated that, in spite of the destructive effects of slavery, African-Americans established strong family units.[26] Most slave couples had long marriages. A study of the entire adult slave population of North Carolina in 1860 has shown that 25 percent of slave marriages lasted between ten and nineteen years, 20 percent lasted at least twenty years, and almost 10 percent endured thirty years or more. Most slave women spent their entire adult lives in settled unions with the same husband. Planters encouraged slave marriages, because, as one owner put it, "marriage adds to the comfort, happiness, and health of those entering upon it, besides insuring a greater increase."[27] Large slave families advanced owners' economic interests, and planters rewarded slave women who had many children. Forcible separation due to the sale of one partner proved the greatest threat to the permanence of slave marriages. Evidence from all parts of the South reveals that, in spite of illiteracy, separated spouses tried to remain in touch with one another and, once slavery had been abolished, went to enormous lengths to reunite their families.

Women often had to resist the attentions of the slaveowners. In addition, owners not infrequently supplied slave women with black men who had reputations for sexual prowess. Slave women, however, made choices: they tried to select their own husbands, rejecting—up to the point of risking being sold—mates chosen by their owners.

Typically, slave women had their first child around the age of nineteen. On the Good Hope

MAP 28.4 **Indian Cession of Lands to the United States**   Forced removal of the Creek, Cherokee, and Chickasaw Indians led to the deaths of thousands on the Trail of Tears to reservations in Oklahoma, and to the destruction of their cultures.

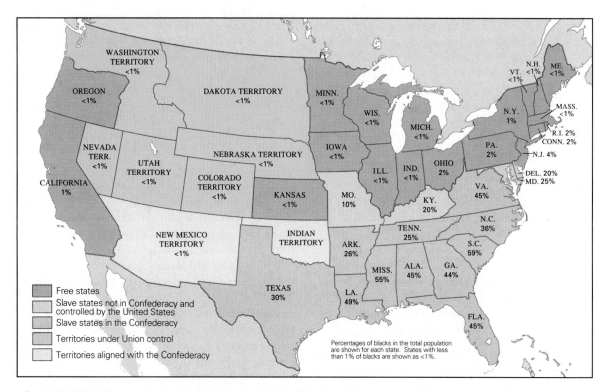

MAP 28.5 Slavery in the United States, 1860 The Confederacy waged a heroic struggle, but the North's industrial might and the waves of immigrants who fought in the Union army decided the outcome of the war. Note the slave populations of such states as South Carolina and Mississippi, and consider how they influenced the later social and economic history of those regions.

plantation in South Carolina, 80 percent of slave couples had at least four children. Almost all women had all their children by one husband, and most children grew to their teens in households with both parents present. Although premarital intercourse was common among slaves—though not as common as among young American adults during the 1970s—the weight of the evidence shows that women rarely engaged in extramarital sexual activity. The pattern of stable black marriages lasted into the present century.

Westward Expansion and Civil War

Cotton was king in the mid-nineteenth century, and cotton carried slavery westward. It was westward expansion, not moral outrage, that brought the controversy over slavery to a head. As Congress created new territories, the question of whether slavery would be extended arose again and again (Map 28.5). For years elaborate com-

promises were worked out, but the North increasingly feared that the South was intent on controlling the nation. The South was afraid that free territories would harbor fugitive slaves. Issues of sectional political power became more and more heated.

In the 1850s the question of the further expansion of slavery agitated the nation. Perhaps no statesman better summarized the dilemma than Abraham Lincoln in a speech in 1854:

Slavery is founded in the selfishness of man's nature—opposition to it, in his love of justice. These principles are in eternal antagonism; and when brought into collision so fiercely, as slavery extension brings them, shocks, and throes, and convulsions must ceaselessly follow.[28]

Accepting the Republican party nomination for a seat in the U.S. Senate in 1858, Lincoln predicted the tragic events ahead:

A house divided against itself cannot stand.

I believe this government cannot endure, permanently half slave *and half* free.

I do not expect the Union to be dissolved—*I do not expect the house to fall—but I* do *expect it will cease to be divided.*

It will become all one thing, or all the other.

Either the opponents of slavery will arrest the further spread of it, and place it where the public mind shall rest in the belief that it is in the course of ultimate extinction; or its advocates will push it forward, till it shall become alike lawful in all *the States, old as well as new—North as well as South.*[29]

In this and every other speech that Lincoln made between 1854 and his election to the presidency in 1860, he argued against slavery less on moral or legal grounds and more in terms of free labor's self-interest.

If slavery continued to expand, Lincoln insisted, it would become a nationwide institution. He appealed to both immigrants and native-born whites when he declared that slavery should be excluded from new territories so that they could be "an outlet for free white people everywhere, the world over—in which Hans, and Baptiste, and Patrick, and all other men from all the world, may find new homes and better their condition in life."[30] Free white workers, in other words, could not compete in the labor market against blacks; therefore, the territories should be kept open.

To protest Lincoln's victory in the election of 1860, South Carolina seceded from the Union in December 1860. Ten southern states soon followed South Carolina's example and formed the Confederacy. Its capital was at Richmond, Virginia.

The Civil War began in 1861. Lincoln fought it to preserve the Union and to maintain the free labor system; the abolition of slavery was a secondary outcome, which he in fact tried to avoid. When a Union general in the field declared the slaves of South Carolina and Georgia free, Lincoln overruled the order. He wanted to bring the seceding states back into the Union with their institutions intact. To many people it seemed absurd to fight the Confederacy, which depended on slavery to wage the war, without abolishing slavery. In the words of one historian, Lincoln wanted "to conduct the war for the preservation of *status quo,* which had produced the war."[31] Only after the war had dragged on and the slaughter had become frightful on both sides, and only when it had been proved that the southern war effort benefited considerably from slave labor, did Lincoln, reluctantly, resolve on emancipation.

The Emancipation Proclamation became effective on January 1, 1863. It expressed no moral indignation. It freed slaves only in states and areas that were in rebellion against the United States. It preserved slavery in states that were loyal to the United States or under military jurisdiction. The London *Spectator* sneered, "The principle is not that a human being cannot justly own another, but that he cannot own him unless he is loyal to the United States."[32] The Emancipation Proclamation nevertheless spelled the doom of North American slavery. It transformed the Civil War from a political struggle to preserve the Union into a moral crusade for the liberty of more Americans.

European and English liberals greeted the proclamation with joy. A gathering of working people in Manchester, England, wrote President Lincoln: "The erasure of that foul blot upon civilization and Christianity—chattel slavery—during your Presidency will cause the name of Abraham Lincoln to be honoured and revered by posterity."[33] As Lincoln acknowledged, this was a magnanimous statement, for the Civil War hurt working people in Manchester. In fact, it had a worldwide impact socially and economically.

By 1862, deprived of cotton from the American South because of the Union blockade of Confederate ports, the mills of Lancashire in England had closed. Tens of thousands of workers were thrown out of work and nearly starved. Many emigrated to the United States. Between 1862 and 1864, efforts to alleviate the terrible suffering severely taxed the resources of the British government. English manufacturers looked for new suppliers and found them in Egypt, India, and Brazil, where cotton production had been stimulated by the Union blockade. The demands of English industry for Egyptian and Indian cotton played a significant role in the expansion of the English merchant marine fleet. Although England initially opposed construction of the Suez Canal, it later became a major shareholder. The canal was the swiftest route to Indian cotton.

The war also had important political consequences in Europe. In 1861 British and European opinion had divided along class lines. The upper classes sympathized with the American South; the commercial classes and working people sided with the North. The English people interpreted the northern victory as a triumph of the democratic experiment over aristocratic oligarchy. Thus the United States gave a powerful stimulus to those in Britain and elsewhere who supported the cause of political democracy. When parliaments debated the extension of suffrage, the American example was frequently cited.

Military historians describe the American Civil War as the first modern war:

It was the first conflict in which the massive productive capacities of the Industrial Revolution were placed at the disposal of the military machine. It witnessed the first prominent use of mass production of goods to sustain mass armies, mass transportation on railroads, and telegraphic communication between different theaters and on the battlefield. It saw also the first use of such devices of the future as armored warships, breech-loading and repeating rifles, rifled artillery, land and sea mines, submarines, balloons, precursors of the machine gun, and trench warfare. . . . In its material manifestations alone, in its application of the resources of technology to the business of killing, the Civil War presaged the later world wars.[34]

In April 1865, the Confederate general Robert E. Lee surrendered his army at Appomattox Court House in Virginia, ending the war. Lincoln had called for "malice toward none and charity for all" in his second inaugural address in 1864 and

The Battle of Gettysburg, July 1–3, 1863 This battle marked the high point of the Confederate advance and was the greatest battle of the American Civil War. This painting commemorates the climax on the third day, when Confederate General Robert E. Lee commanded Pickett's division to charge the Union center. Coming toward the viewer in the face of terrible fire, the brave southerners have reached the first Union line. But General Hancock, shown with arm extended in the left foreground, is ordering the northern counterattack that will decimate Pickett's troops and force the Confederates back into Virginia. (*Source: Photograph by Al Freni © 1985 Time-Life Books, Inc. Courtesy, The Seventh Regiment Fund, Inc.*)

planned a generous policy toward the defeated South. The bullet that killed him brought on a different kind of reconstruction, the central figure in which was the Negro.

During the period called Reconstruction (1865–1877), the vanquished South adjusted to a new social and economic order without slavery, and the eleven Confederate states rejoined the Union. For former slaves, Reconstruction meant the reunion of black families separated before emancipation. Reconstruction also represented an opportunity for blacks to exercise their new freedom, though southerners detested the very notion of social equality and northerners were ambivalent on the subject.

Blacks wanted land to farm; but, lacking cash, they soon accepted the sharecropping system: farmers paid landowners about half of a year's crops at harvest time in return for a cabin, food, mules, seed, and tools the rest of the year. Believing that education was the key to economic advancement, blacks flocked to country schools and to colleges supported by northern religious groups. Although the Fifteenth Amendment to the U.S. Constitution forbade states to deny anyone the vote "on account of race, color, or previous condition of servitude," whites used violence, terror, and, between 1880 and 1920, so-called Jim Crow laws to prevent blacks from voting and to enforce rigid racial segregation. Lacking strong northern support, blacks did not gain legal equality or suffrage in many parts of the old Confederacy until the 1960s. Racist assumptions and attitudes thwarted their legal, social, and economic advance.

In the construction of a black community, no institution played a larger role than the black Protestant churches. Local black churches provided hope, education, and a forum for the spread of political ideas and platforms. During Reconstruction, black preachers esteemed for their oratorical skill, organizational ability, and practical judgment held important positions in black politics. In a racist and exploitative society, the black church gave support, security, and a sense of solidarity.

Who Is Black? The Racial Debate

In the summer of 1925, Abraham Lincoln's aging son, Robert Todd Lincoln, visited a resort in Manchester, Vermont. Lincoln hated blacks and refused to allow them to wait on him, and if a black man touched his luggage, car, or possessions, he whacked him with his cane. Lincoln selected the fair, blue-eyed, blond-haired Adam Clayton Powell (1908–1972) as his servant. Powell was an undergraduate at Colgate University working as a bellhop for the summer. The other bellhops were very amused because Powell, by the peculiarity of American society, was "black." Powell went on to represent Harlem in the U.S. Congress, 1945–1970.

Millions of other biracial Americans could tell a similar tale. From the seventeenth century to the present, the issue of race has permeated virtually every aspect of American life and culture. Although Americans rarely explore the terms they use when discussing race, a critical analysis of racial concepts is as important to the study of U.S. history as analyses of concept of gender and class.[35] Who is black? How have Americans come to make racial classifications? Why are millions of people whose genetic origins are more European than African defined by custom, by law, and by even themselves as black? Why is there a tremendous disparity between the scientific definition of who is black and the socio-cultural one?

Words can mean anything a community wants them to mean. The use of "black" as a racial category in the United States is actually of recent origin. Until the 1960s, persons with some African ancestry were described in the United States as "negro" or sometimes "colored"; neither the federal government nor people of some African ancestry described themselves as "black." In the late 1960s, leaders of the Black Power movement (see page 1117), which emphasized racial pride and insisted on self-definition, demanded the substitution of the Old English word *black* for the traditional Spanish or Portuguese term *negro*. The broader American society accepted the word. The recent adoption of the expression *African American* suggests blacks' conscious desire to preserve a link with Africa. Some research shows that in the nineteenth century, however, no one tried to preserve an African culture in the United States and free people of color strongly rejected any hint of an African connection.

Since the arrival of the first Africans in Jamestown, Virginia, in 1619, sexual contacts have taken place between whites and blacks. The colonists and later the young American republic, with some hesitations and variation, defined all children born of such unions, regardless of their personal appearances, as negro. In the American South this manner of definition became known as the "one drop rule," meaning a single drop of "African blood" made a person "black." Anthropologists call this the "hypo descent rule": racially mixed persons are arbitrarily assigned the status of the subordinate group.

During the long period of slavery (1619–1865), when white planters sexually exploited slave women and when some free blacks and whites intermingled, the number of mixed-race children multiplied. The U.S. census of 1850 showed that 11.2 percent of the population classed as negro were of mixed race; the 1910 census put the figure at 20.9 percent. Because these counts were based solely on the census taker's perception of racial visibility, the estimates were probably gross undercounts of all Negroes with some white ancestry. Today, according to reliable estimates, between 75 and 90 percent of all American blacks have some white ancestry, and millions of white Americans have at least small amounts of black genetic heritage. A central theme in *Light in August* and other novels by Mississippi writer William Faulkner is the anxiety that thousands of white southerners have felt about their racial purity.

Before the Civil War many parts of the South, but especially Charleston and New Orleans, had sizable populations of mulattos (persons with one negro parent), quadroons (one negro grandparent), and octoroons (one negro great-grandparent). These persons were the results of liaisons (some of long, sometimes lifelong duration) between whites and women of some African ancestry. Louisiana and South Carolina did not apply the "one drop rule" to these mixed-race people, and in 1835 Judge William Harper of South Carolina ruled that a person's acceptance as white, not the proportion of white and black "blood," determined a person's race. In short, the local community determined an individual's race. But as the South came under increasing abolitionist pressure to defend slavery, and as fears of slave revolts increased, attitudes hardened. Custom became law that defined as negro all persons with any perceptible African ancestry (see Listening to the Past).

Southerners encouraged the "one drop rule" as a way of enlarging the slave population. Likewise, after 1865 when native-born whites feared and resented blacks' economic and political potential; and when, between 1880 and 1910 floods of poor immigrants from southern and eastern Europe competed with former slaves for jobs, the physical contrast between blacks and whites (skin pigmentation) proved useful to whites in justifying and legitimating their economic interests. After 1920, because there were so many mixed-race persons, and because so many Americans with some black ancestry appeared white, the U.S. census stopped counting mixed-race peoples, and the "one drop rule" became the national legal standard. Scorned and rejected by whites, biracial persons allied with "pure" blacks and in the twentieth century began to lead the struggle for racial equality.[36] The great advocate of nonviolent social action and perhaps the greatest leader of the civil rights movement, Martin Luther King, Jr. (see page 1117), had an Irish grandmother.

Racial categories rest on socially constructed beliefs and on custom backed by law, not on any biological or anthropological classification. Race and culture are not the same thing. Anthropologists define *race* as a grouping of human beings on the basis of average differences in biological characteristics; biological characteristics of race cannot be equated with mental characteristics, such as intelligence, personality, character. *Culture,* in contrast, is patterns of behavior, life, and beliefs. Peoples of the same race often have vastly different cultures, as, for example, Chinese culture differs from Japanese culture though both the Chinese and the Japanese are Asian, or as Italian culture differs from Russian culture though both peoples are Caucasian. So with African-Americans among whom different cultures also exist.

The accelerated immigration of huge numbers of Latin Americans and Asians to the United States since 1975 has complicated these issues. In preparation for the federal census of the year 2000, government agencies are considering modifications of customary racial categories and questioning whether it is even proper for the national government to classify people according to the arbitrary and nonscientific criteria of race. The federal Office of Management and Budget, which sets racial and ethnic standards on all governmental forms on the basis of census results, will provide rules that will influence the size and shape of congressional districts, college and business affirmative action programs, university scholarships, loans and mortgages. As one congressman puts it, "The numbers drive the dollars."

More native Americans marry outside their group than within it. In the 1980s black men mar-

✳ **Harlem Hellfighters**   Returning to New York in 1919 aboard the U.S.S. *Stockholm*, these black men of the famed U.S. 369th Division had fought in the bloody battle of the Meuse-Argonne during the First World War. The French government awarded 150 of them the coveted Croix de Guerre. *(Source: Springer/ Bettmann Film Archive)*

ried white women at the rate of 10 percent (black women married whites at half that rate). Immigration also means cultural change. Large numbers of Asian women are today marrying white, Hispanic, and black men. Hispanic people pose the greatest complexity. According to the Latin American concept of race, skin color is an individual variable, not a group marker; thus within a given family, one child might be considered white, another black.

The 1960 census listed all people from Latin America as white—blacks from the Dominican Republic, European whites from Argentina, and Mexicans who resembled native Americans (Indians). In neither the State of Hawaii nor the Commonwealth of Puerto Rico does the term *race* carry the connotation it has on the U.S. mainland.

As the millennial year 2000 approaches, three broad currents of opinion about racial classification are emerging. One group urges doing away with all racial classifications because they are meaningless and unscientific and have been the historical means of exploiting persons perceived as "inferior." Other thinkers, primarily African-American scholars, agree that the notion of race is a cruel hoax but insist that the racial idea of "black" makes an important political statement. They argue that racial categories are needed to correct injustices and that the U.S. relinquishing of the racial idea of "black" would amount to the abandonment of a poor underclass. These writers have not so far addressed the situations of Hispanics, Asians, and native Americans. The third group consists of increasing numbers of biracial and multiracial persons who resent being assigned to any single category—persons who feel strong ethnic and cultural ties to two or more groups.[37] Should their feelings and pain be ignored? What do racial categories mean, anyway? Should people be discriminated against, or rewarded, on the basis of others' perceptions of who they are? Should the federal government continue its pattern of defining race in order to support the dominant race's economic goals? What if the dominant race is Hispanic? Should "the numbers drive the dollars"?

Industrialization and Immigration

After the Civil War the United States underwent an industrial boom powered by exploitation of the country's natural resources. The federal government turned over vast amounts of land and mineral resources to industry for development. In particular, the railroads—the foundation of industrial expansion—received 130 million acres. By 1900 the American railroad system was 193,000 miles long, connected every part of the nation, and represented 40 percent of the railroad mileage of the entire world. Immigrant workers built it.

The late nineteenth and early twentieth centuries witnessed the immigration of unprecedented numbers of Europeans and Asians to the United States (see page 892). Between 1860 and 1900, 14 million immigrants came, and during the peak years between 1900 and 1914, another 14 million passed through the U.S. customs inspection station at Ellis Island in New York City. All sought a better life and higher standard of living.

The immigrants' ambitions precisely matched the labor needs of the times. Chinese, Scandinavian, and Irish immigrants laid 30,000 miles of railroad tracks between 1867 and 1873 and another 73,000 miles in the 1880s. Poles, Hungarians, Bohemians, and Italians poured into the coal and iron mines of western Pennsylvania and Appalachia. At the Carnegie Steel Corporation (later USX), Slavs and Italians produced one-third of the world's total steel supply in 1900. Thousands of Czechs, Poles, and other Slavs worked in oil fields around the country. Lithuanians, Poles, Croats, Scandinavians, Irish, and Negroes entered the Chicago stockyards and built the meatpacking industry. Irish immigrants continued to operate the spinning frames and knitting machines of New England's textile mills. Industrial America devel-

oped on the sweat and brawn—the cheap labor—of its immigrant millions.

As industrial expansion transformed the eastern half of the United States, thousands of land-hungry farmers moved westward, where land was still only $1.25 an acre. In the final third of the nineteenth century, pioneers put 225 million acres under cultivation.

The West also held precious metals. The discovery of gold and silver in California, Colorado, Arizona, and Montana, and on the reservations of the Sioux Indians of South Dakota, precipitated huge rushes. Even before 1900, miners had extracted $1.24 billion in gold and $901 million in silver from western mines. Many miners settled down to farm and help their territories toward statehood. By 1912 the West had been won.

Generally speaking, the settler's life blurred sex roles. Women commonly did the same dawn-to-dusk backbreaking agricultural work as men.[38] In addition, it fell to women to make a home out of crude log cabins that had no windows or doors or out of tarpaper shacks that had mud floors. One "gently reared" bride of seventeen took one look at her mud roof and dirt floor and indignantly announced, "My father had a much better house for his hogs!" Lacking cookstoves, they prepared food over open fireplaces, using all kinds of substitutes for ingredients easily available back east. Before they could wash clothes, women had to make soap out of lye and carefully saved household ashes.

Considered the carriers of "high culture," women organized whatever educational, religious, musical, and recreational activities the settlers' society possessed. Women also had to defend their homes against prairie fires and Indian attacks. These burdens were accompanied by frequent pregnancies and, often, the need to give birth without medical help or even the support of other women. Many women settlers used such contraceptive devices as spermicides, condoms, and, after 1864, vaginal diaphragms. The death rate for infants and young children ran as high as 30 percent in the mid-nineteenth century. Even so, these women had large families.

As in South America, immigration led to rapid urbanization. In 1790 only 5.1 percent of Americans were living in centers of 2,500 or more people. By 1860 this figure had risen to 19.9 percent, and by 1900 almost 40 percent were living in cities. The overwhelming majority of the southern and eastern Europeans who came to North America at the turn of the century became urban industrial workers, their entire existence framed by the factory and the tenement. Newly uprooted from rural Europe, Italians, Greeks, Croats, Hungarians, Czechs, Poles, Russians, and Jews contrasted sharply with their urban neighbors and with each other. Older residents saw only "a sea of strange faces, babbling in alien tongues and framed by freakish clothes. Walking through these multitudes now was really like a voyage round the globe."[39]

Between 1880 and 1920 industrial production soared. New inventions such as the steam engine, the dynamo (generator), and the electric light were given industrial and agricultural applications. Large factories replaced small ones. Large factories could buy large machines, operate them at full capacity, and take advantage of railroad discount rates. In the automobile industry, Henry Ford of Detroit set up assembly lines. Each worker working on the line performed only one task instead of assembling an entire car. In 1910 Ford sold 10,000 cars; in 1914, a year after he inaugurated the first moving assembly line, he sold 248,000 cars. Such developments changed the face of American society. Sewing machines made cheap, varied, mass-produced clothing available to city people in department stores and to country people through mail-order catalogues. The automobile increased opportunities for travel, general mobility, and change.

As elsewhere, by the 1890s U.S. factory managers were stressing industrial efficiency and the importance of time. Management engineers wanted to produce more at lower cost. They aimed to reduce labor costs by eliminating unnecessary workers. As quantity rather than quality became the measure of acceptability, workers' skills were less valued. Assembly-line workers more and more performed only monotonous and time-determined work; in effect they became interchangeable parts of the machines they operated.

Chinese Laborers   Chinese immigrant laborers, who laid thousands of miles of railroad track across the United States in the nineteenth century, played a major role in industrial expansion. *(Source: California State Railroad Museum, Southern Pacific Collection)*

Despite accelerated production, and perhaps because of overproduction, the national economy experienced repeated cycles of boom and bust in the late nineteenth century. Serious depressions in 1873, 1884, and 1893 slashed prices and threw many people out of work. Leading industrialists responded by establishing larger corporations and consolidated companies into huge conglomerates. As a result of the merger of several small oil companies, John D. Rockefeller's Standard Oil Company controlled 84 percent of the nation's oil and most American pipelines in 1898. J. P. Morgan's United States Steel monopolized the iron and steel industries; and Swift & Co. of Chicago, the meat-processing industry.

Industrialization led to the creation of a vast class of wage workers who depended totally on their employers for work. Corporate managers, however, were always preoccupied with cutting labor costs. Thus employers paid workers piecemeal for the number of articles produced, to encourage the use of the new machines; and managers hired more women and children and paid them much less than they paid men. Most women worked in the textile industry. Some earned as little as $1.56 for seventy hours of work, while men received from $7 to $9 for the same work. Employers reduced wages, forcing workers to toil longer and harder to maintain a certain level of income. Owners fought in legislatures and courts against the installation of safety devices, so working conditions in mines and mills were frightful. In 1913, even after some safety measures had been taken, 25,000 people died in industrial accidents. Between 1900 and 1917, 72,000 railroad worker deaths occurred. Workers responded with strikes, violence, and, gradually, unionization.

Urbanization brought serious problems. In *How the Other Half Lives* (1890), Jacob Riis, a newspaper reporter and recent immigrant from Denmark, drew national attention to what he called "the foul core of New York's slums." Riis estimated that 300,000 people inhabited a single square mile on New York's Lower East Side. Overcrowding, poor sanitation, and lack of health services caused frequent epidemics. The blight of slums increased crime, prostitution, alcoholism, and other drug-related addictions. Riis attacked the vicious economic exploitation of the poor.

New York City was not unique; slums and the social problems resulting from them existed in all large American cities. Reformers fought for slum clearance, but public apathy and vested economic interests delayed massive urban renewal until after the Second World War. In spite of all these industrial and urban difficulties, immigrants continued to come: the United States offered opportunity, upward social mobility, and a better life.

European and Asian immigrants aroused nativist sentiments—that is, intense hostility to foreign and "un-American" looks, behavior, and loyalties—in native-born Americans. Some of this antagonism sprang from the deep-rooted Anglo-Saxon racism of many Americans. Some grew out of old Protestant suspicions of Roman Catholicism, the faith of most of the new arrivals. A great deal of the dislike of the foreign-born sprang from fear of economic competition. To most Americans, the Chinese with their exotic looks and willingness to work for very little seemed the most dangerous. Increasingly violent agitation against Asians led to race riots in California and finally culminated in the Chinese Exclusion Act of 1882, which denied Chinese laborers entrance to the country.

Immigrants from Europe seized on white racism as a way to compensate for their immigrant status by claiming superiority to former slaves and their descendants. The arrival of thousands of Irish immigrants in the 1850s, followed by millions of Italians and Slavs between 1880 and 1914, aggravated an already bad situation. What the German scientist Alexander von Humboldt wrote about the attitude of peninsulares toward Creoles in Latin America in the early nineteenth century—"the lowest, least educated, and uncultivated European believes himself superior to the white born in the New World"[40]—precisely applies to the outlook of Irish, Italian, or Slavic immigrants to the United States at the turn of this century if one merely substitutes *black* for *white*. In the eyes of all ethnic groups, the social status of blacks remained the lowest, while that of immigrants rose. As the United States underwent expansion and industrialization during the nineteenth century, blacks remained the worst off *because of immigration.*[41]

In the 1890s the nation experienced a severe economic depression. Faced with overproduction, the rich and politically powerful owners of mines, mills, and factories fought the organization of labor unions, laid off thousands, slashed wages, and ruthlessly exploited their workers. Workers in turn feared that immigrant labor would drive salaries lower. The frustrations provoked during the depression boiled over into savage attacks on the foreign-born. One of the bloodiest incidents took place in western Pennsylvania in 1897, when about 150 unarmed Polish and Hungarian coal miners tried to persuade others to join their walkout. The mine owners convinced the local sheriff that the strike was illegal. As the strikers approached, the sheriff panicked and ordered his deputies to shoot. Twenty-one immigrants died, and forty were wounded. The sheriff declared that the miners were only "infuriated foreigners . . . like wild beasts." Local people agreed that if the strikers had been American-born, no blood would have been shed.[42]

After the First World War, labor leaders lobbied Congress for restrictions because they feared losing the wage gains achieved during the war. Some intellectuals argued that immigrants from southern and eastern Europe, with their unfamiliar cultural traditions, threatened to destroy American society. Italians were feared because of possible Cosa Nostra connections. Eastern Europeans were thought to have communist connections. In the 1920s Congress responded with laws that set severe quotas—2 percent of resident nationals as of the 1890 census—on immigration from southern and eastern Europe. The Japanese were completely excluded. These racist laws remained on the books until 1965.

CANADA, FROM FRENCH COLONY TO NATION

In 1608 the French explorer Samuel de Champlain (1567–1635) sailed down the St. Lawrence River and established a trading post on the site of present-day Quebec. Thus began the permanent colony of New France. The fur-trading monopolies subsequently granted to Champlain by the French crown attracted settlers, and Jesuit missionaries to the Indians further increased the French population. The British, however, vigorously challenged French control of the lucrative fur trade, and the long mid-eighteenth-century global struggle for empire between the British and the French, known in North America as the French and Indian Wars because of Indian border warfare, tested French control. In 1759, on the Plains of Abraham, a field next to the city of Quebec, the English under General James Wolfe defeated the French under General Louis Montcalm. This battle ended the French Empire in North America. By the Treaty of Paris of 1763, France ceded Canada to Great Britain.

British Colony (1763–1839)

For the French Canadians, who in 1763 numbered about 90,000, the British conquest was a tragedy and the central event in their history. British governors replaced the French; English-speaking merchants from Britain and the thirteen American colonies to the south took over the colony's economic affairs. The Roman Catholic church remained and until about 1960 played a powerful role in the political and cultural, as well as religious, life of French Canadians. Most of the French Canadians engaged in agriculture, though a small merchant class sold furs and imported manufactured goods.

Intending to establish a permanent administration for Canada, in 1774 the British Parliament passed the Quebec Act. This law granted religious freedom to French Canadians and recognized French law in civil matters, but it denied Canadians a legislative assembly, a traditional feature of British colonial government. Parliament placed power in the hands of an appointed governor and an appointed council; the latter, however, was composed of French Canadians as well as English-speaking members. English Canadian businessmen protested that they were being denied a basic right of Englishmen—representation.

During the American Revolution, about forty thousand Americans demonstrated their loyalty to Great Britain and its empire by emigrating to Canada. These "loyalists" not only altered the French-English ratio in the population but also pressed for a representative assembly. In 1791 Parliament responded with the Constitution Act, which divided the province of Quebec at the Ottawa River into Lower Canada (present-day Quebec, predominantly French and Catholic) and Upper Canada (present-day Ontario, primarily English and Protestant). The act also provided for an elective assembly in each of the two provinces. Because the assemblies' decisions could be vetoed by an appointed upper house or by the governor and his council, general discontent continued. Finally, in 1837, disputes over control of revenue, the judiciary, and the established churches erupted into open rebellion in both Upper and Lower Canada. The British government, fearful of a repetition of the American events of 1776, decided on a full investigation and appointed Lord Durham, a prominent liberal reformer, to make recommendations for reform. Lord Durham published his

Report on the Affairs of British North America, later called the "Magna Carta" of British colonial administration, in 1839.

The Age of Confederation (1840–1905)

Acting on Lord Durham's recommendations, Parliament in 1840 passed the Union Act, which united Ontario and Quebec under one government composed of a governor, an appointed legislative council, and an elective assembly in which the two provinces had equal representation. The imperial government in London was to retain control over trade, foreign affairs, public lands, and the colonial constitution. The Union Act marks an important milestone toward confederation. When Lord Durham's son-in-law, Lord Elgin, was appointed governor in 1847, he made it clear that his cabinet (council) would be chosen from the party with the majority in the elected assembly; and, following the British model, the cabinet had to retain the support of that majority in order to stay in office.

The idea of a union or confederation of the other Canadian provinces persisted in the 1860s. During the American Civil War, English-American relations were severely strained, and according to one historian, "Canada found herself in the centre of the storm. The resulting fear of American aggression was a powerful factor in bringing confederation to completion."[43] Parliament's passage of the British North America Act in 1867 brought the Canadian constitution to its modern form. By the act the traditional British parliamentary system was adapted to the needs of the new North American nation. The provinces of New Brunswick and Nova Scotia joined Ontario and Quebec to form the Dominion of Canada. A governor general, who represented the British crown and fulfilled ceremonial functions, governed through the Dominion Cabinet, which, like the British Cabinet, was composed of members selected from the lower house of the legislature, to which it was responsible.

Legislative power rested in a Parliament of two houses: a Senate, whose members were appointed for life by the governor general, and a House of Commons, whose members were elected by adult males. (Canadian women won the right to vote in national elections in 1917, shortly before women in the United States and Great Britain but after women in Australia.) In theory, the two houses had equal power, though money bills had to originate in the House of Commons; in practice, the Senate came to serve only as a deliberative check on hasty legislation and as a means of rewarding elder statesmen for their party services.

The Dominion Cabinet received complete jurisdiction over internal affairs. Britain retained control over foreign policy. (In 1931 the British Statute of Westminster officially recognized Canadian autonomy in foreign affairs.)

Believing that the American system of the division of powers between the states and the federal government left the states too strong and helped to bring on the Civil War, the framers of the Canadian constitution intended to create a powerful central government. Thus provincial legislatures were assigned powers explicitly stated and applicable only to local conditions. With the implementation of the British North America Act, John A. Macdonald (1815–1891), the strongest advocate of confederation, became the Dominion's first prime minister.

Macdonald vigorously pushed Canada's "manifest destiny" to absorb all the northern part of the continent. In 1869 his government purchased for $1,500,000 the vast Northwest Territories of the Hudson Bay Company. From this territory the province of Manitoba emerged to become part of the Dominion in 1870. Fearful that the sparsely settled colony of British Columbia would join the United States, Macdonald lured British Columbia into the confederation with a subsidy to pay its debts and the promise of a transcontinental railroad. Likewise, the debt-ridden little maritime province of Prince Edward Island was drawn into confederation with a large subsidy. In five short years, between 1868 and 1873, through Macdonald's imagination and drive, Canadian sovereignty stretched from coast to coast.

Believing that a transcontinental railroad was essential to Canada's survival as a nation, Macdonald declared that "until this great work is completed our Dominion is little more than a 'geographical expression.' We have as much interest in British Columbia as in Australia, and no more. The railroad, once finished, we become a great united country with a large interprovincial trade and a common interest."[44] On November 7, 1885, Macdonald received a telegram announcing that the first train from Montreal in Quebec was approaching the Pacific; traveling at 24 miles per hour, the train had made the coast-to-coast trip in a little

✳ **Russian Immigrant Women in Saskatchewan**   These women were Duokhobors, a religious sect that came to Canada seeking religious freedom from tsarist persecution. Because most of the men took railroad jobs, the women planted the vast plains with rye, wheat, oats, and flax. Their farms and orchards flourished, and the Duokhobors played an important part in the development of western Canada. *(Source: Saskatchewan Archives, University of Saskatchewan)*

over five days. The completion of the railroad led to the formation of two new prairie provinces, Alberta and Saskatchewan, which in 1905 entered the Dominion. (Only in 1949 did the island of Newfoundland renounce colonial status and join the Dominion.) The Canadian Pacific Railroad was Macdonald's greatest achievement.

Growth, Development, and National Maturity

Macdonald's hopes for large numbers of immigrants to people the thinly populated country did not immediately materialize. Between 1897 and 1912, however, 961,000 entered Canada from the British Isles, 594,000 from Europe, and 784,000 from the United States. Some immigrants went to work in the urban factories of Hamilton, Toronto, and Montreal. Most immigrants from continental Europe—Poles, Germans, Scandinavians, and Russians—flooded the midwestern plains and soon

transformed the prairies into one of the world's greatest grain-growing regions.

Because of Canada's small population, most of which in the early twentieth century was concentrated in Ontario and Quebec, the assimilation of the immigrants to the older English-Canadian culture occurred more slowly than in the "melting pot" of the United States. French Canadians remained the largest minority in the population. Distinctively different in language, law, and religion, and fiercely proud of their culture, they resisted assimilation. Since the 1950s, Italian and Hungarian immigration has contributed to the evolution of a more cosmopolitan culture.

Supported by population growth, Canada experienced an agricultural and industrial boom between 1891 and 1914. In those years wheat production rocketed from 2 million bushels per year to 150 million bushels. The discovery of gold, silver, copper, and nickel in northern Ontario led to the full exploitation of those mineral resources.

British Columbia, Ontario, and Quebec produced large quantities of wood pulp, much of it sold to the United States. Canada's great rivers were harnessed to supply hydroelectric power for industrial and domestic use. Meanwhile, the government erected tariffs to protect industry, established a national civil service, and built a sound banking system.

Canada's powerful support of the Allied cause in the First World War demonstrated its full maturity as a nation. In 1914 the British government still controlled the foreign policy of all parts of the empire. When Britain declared war on Germany, Canada unhesitatingly followed. More than 600,000 Canadian soldiers served with distinction in the army, some of them in the bloodiest battles in France. The 60,661 Canadians killed represent a greater loss than that experienced by the more populous United States. Canadian grain and foodstuffs supplied much of the food of the Allied troops, and Canadian metals were in demand for guns and shells. Canadian resentment, therefore, over lack of voice in the formulation of Allied war policies was understandable.

In 1917 the British government established the Imperial War Cabinet, a body composed of the chief British ministers and the prime ministers of the Dominions (Australia, Canada, New Zealand, and South Africa) to set policy. In 1918 Canada demanded and received—over the initial opposition of Britain, France, and the United States—the right to participate in the Versailles Peace Conference and in the League of Nations. Canada had become a respected and independent nation. Since 1939, Canada has been a member of the British Commonwealth of Nations. The constitution of 1982 abolished the power of the London Parliament to amend Canada's constitution and ended all appeals from the provinces to London. Quebec did not sign the 1982 document, and the strong separatist movement within Quebec continues to articulate the desire of French-speaking Canadians for independence from English Canada and sovereignty as a separate nation.

AUSTRALIA, FROM PENAL COLONY TO NATION

In April 1770, James Cook, the English explorer, navigator, and captain of H.M.S. *Endeavor*, dropped anchor in a wide bay about ten miles south of the present city of Sydney on the coast of eastern Australia. Because the young botanist on board the ship, Joseph Banks, subsequently discovered 30,000 specimens of plant life in the bay, 1,600 of them unknown to European science, Captain Cook called the place Botany Bay. Totally unimpressed by the flat landscape and its few naked inhabitants—the Aborigines, or native people—Cook sailed north along the coast. Finally, the ship rounded Cape York Peninsula, the northernmost point of Australia (Map 28.6). On August 21, on a rock later named Possession Island, Cook formally claimed the entire land south of where he stood for King George III, 16,000 miles away. Cook called the land "New South Wales." In accepting possession, the British crown acted on the legal fiction that Australia was *Terra Nullius,* completely unoccupied, thus entirely ignoring the native people.

The world's smallest continent, Australia is located southeast of Asia between the Pacific and Indian Oceans. It is about half the size of Europe and almost as large as the United States (excluding Alaska and Hawaii). Three topographical zones roughly divide the continent. The Western Plateau, a vast desert and semidesert region, covers almost two-thirds. The Central Eastern Lowlands extend from the Gulf of Carpentaria in the north to western Victoria in the south. The Eastern Highlands are a complex belt of tablelands. Australia is one of the world's driest continents. It has a temperate climate and little intense cold.

When Cook arrived in Australia, about 300,000 Aborigines inhabited the continent. A peaceful and nomadic people who had emigrated from southern Asia millennia before, the Aborigines lived entirely by food gathering, fishing, and hunting. They had no domestic agriculture. Tribal customs governed their lives. Although they used spears and bows and arrows in hunting, they never practiced warfare as it was understood by more technologically advanced peoples such as the Aztecs of Mexico or the Mandinke of West Africa. When white settlers arrived, they occupied the Aborigines' lands unopposed. According to one Australian scholar, from 1788 to the present "Australian governments have been much more concerned with protecting the Aborigines than with fighting them."[45] Nevertheless, like the Indians of Central and South America, the Aborigines fell victim to the white peoples' diseases and to a spiritual malaise caused by the breakdown of their tribal life. Today, only about 45,000 pureblood Aborigines survive.

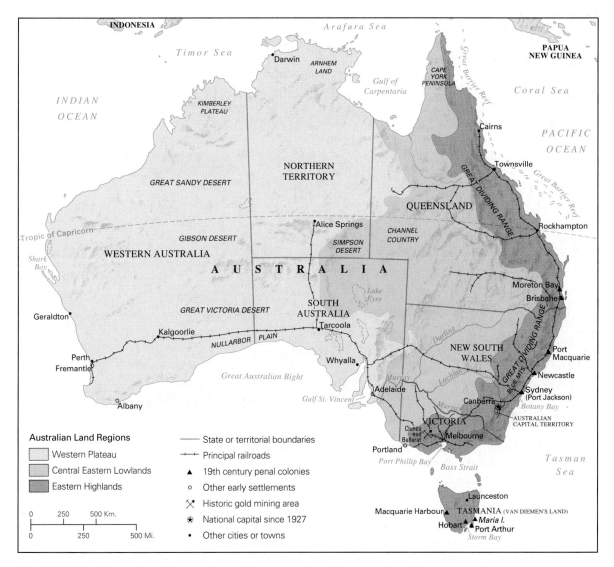

MAP 28.6 Australia   The vast deserts in western Australia meant that cities and industries would develop mainly in the east. Australia's early geographical and cultural isolation bred a sense of inferiority. Air travel, the communications revolution, and the massive importation of Japanese products and American popular culture have changed that.

Penal Colony

The victory of the thirteen North American colonies in 1783 inadvertently contributed to the establishment of a colony in Australia five years later. Before 1775, the British government had shipped about one thousand convicts annually to Georgia. Crime in England was increasing in the 1770s and 1780s, and the transportation of felons "beyond the seas" seemed the answer to the problem of overcrowded prisons. Moreover, the estab-

lishment of a colony in Australia would provide a home for dispossessed loyalists who had fled America during the American Revolution.

In England, the prisons were so full that old transport ships in southern naval ports were being used to house criminals, and pressure on the government to do something was intense. Finally, in August 1786, the British Cabinet approved the establishment of a penal colony at Botany Bay to serve as "a remedy for the evils likely to result from the late alarming and numerous increase of felons

Convicts Embarking for Botany Bay The English printmaker and caricaturist Thomas Rowlandson (1756–1827) sketched this scene with ink and watercolor wash. In the background the gibbet with hanging felons shows the legal alternative to transportation to Australia. *(Source: National Library of Australia)*

in this country, and more particularly in the metropolis (London)."[46] The name "Botany Bay" became a byword for the forced and permanent exile of criminals. In May 1787 a fleet of eleven ships packed with one thousand felons and their jailers sailed for Australia. After an eight-month voyage it landed in Sydney Cove on January 28, 1788.

Mere survival in an alien world was the first challenge. Because the land at Botany Bay proved completely unsuited for agriculture and lacked decent water, the first governor, Arthur Phillip, moved the colony ten miles north to Port Jackson, later called Sydney. Announcing that those who did not work would not eat, Phillip set the prisoners to planting seeds. Coming from the slums of London, the convicts knew nothing of agriculture, and some were too ill or old to work. The colony lacked draft animals and plows. The troop detachments sent to guard the prisoners considered it below their dignity to work the land. For years the

colony of New South Wales tottered on the brink of starvation.

For the first thirty years, men far outnumbered women. Because the British government refused to allow wives to accompany their convict-husbands, prostitution flourished. Many women convicts, if not professional prostitutes when they left England, became such during the long voyage south. Army officers, government officials, and free immigrants chose favorite convicts as mistresses.

Recent research provides useful information about the official attitude toward women. On May 3, 1791, Lieutenant Ralph Clark recorded in his diary that he had ordered three women convicts flogged. Catherine White fainted after the first 15 lashes, Mary Teut after 22. When Mary Higgins had received 26 lashes, Lieutenant Clark "forgave her the remainder [he had ordered 50] because she was an old woman." From other sources we know that another woman convict was six months pregnant at the time with Clark's child.[47] This incident shows the brutality of power and the hypocrisy of an administration that simultaneously savagely punished and sexually exploited women. The vast majority of children born in the colony were illegitimate.

Officers and jailers, though descended from the middle and lower middle classes, tried to establish a colonial gentry and to impose the rigid class distinctions that they had known in England. Known as *exclusionists,* this self-appointed colonial gentry tried to exclude from polite society all freed or emancipated persons, called *emancipists.* Deep and bitter class feeling took root.

Economic Development

For eighty long years after 1787, Britain continued to transport convicts to New South Wales. Transportation rested on two premises: that criminals should be punished and that they should not be a financial burden on the state. Convicts became free when their sentences expired or were remitted. Few returned to England.

Governor Phillip and his successors urged the Colonial Office to send free settlers. The Napoleonic war slowed emigration before 1815, but thereafter a steady stream of people relocated. The end of the European wars also released capital for potential investment. But investment in what? What commodity could be developed and exported to England?

Immigrants explored several economic enterprises. In the last decade of the eighteenth century, for example, sealing seemed a likely possibility. Sealing merchants hired Aborigine women to swim out to the seal rocks, lie down among the seals until their suspicions were dulled, and then at a signal rise up and club the seals to death. In 1815, a single ship carried 60,000 seal skins to London (a normal cargo contained at least 10,000 skins). Such destruction rapidly depleted the seals.

Credit for the development of the product that was to be Australia's staple commodity for export—wool—goes to John Macarthur (1767–1834). Granted a large tract of crown lands and assigned thirty convicts to work for him, Macarthur conducted experiments in the production of fine merino wool. In 1800 he sent sample fleeces to England to determine their quality. He also worked to change the government's penal view of New South Wales to a commercial one and to attract the financial support of British manufacturers.

The report of J. T. Bigge, an able lawyer sent out in 1819 to evaluate the colony, proved decisive. Persuaded by large landowners like Macarthur, Bigge reported that wool was the country's future staple. He recommended that convicts be removed from the temptations of towns and seaports and dispersed to work on the estates of men of capital. He also urged that British duties on colonial wool be suspended. The Colonial Office accepted this advice, and the pastoral economy of Australia, as the continent was beginning to be called, began.

Australia's temperate though capricious climate is ideally suited to sheep farming. Moreover, wool production requires much land and little labor—precisely the situation in Australia. In 1820 the sheep population was 120,000; by 1830 it reached a half-million. After 1820 the commercial importance of Australia exceeded its significance as a penal colony, and wool export steadily increased: from 75,400 pounds in 1821, to 2 million pounds in 1830, to 24 million pounds in 1845.

Settlers also experimented with wheat farming. Soil deficiencies and the dry climate slowed early production, but farmers eventually developed a successful white-grained winter variety. By 1900 wheat proved Australia's second most valuable crop.

Population shortage remained a problem. In this area, the development of Australia owes something to the vision of Edward Gibbon Wakefield (1769–1862), a theorist of colonization. Between 1825 and 1850, 3 million people emigrated from Great Britain. In the quest for immigrants, Australia could not really compete with North America. The 12,000-mile journey to Australia cost between £20 and £25 and could take five weary months. By contrast, the trip to Canada or the United States cost only £5 and lasted just ten weeks. Wakefield proposed that Australian land be sold relatively cheaply and that proceeds from the sale be used to pay the passages of free laborers and mechanics. That eliminated the disadvantage of cost. Although over 2,500,000 British immigrants went to North America, 223,000 industrious English and Irish people chose Australia.

Population in the early nineteenth century concentrated on the eastern coast of the continent. The growth of sheep farming stimulated exploration and led to the opening of the interior. In 1813 explorers discovered a route over the Blue Mountains. New settlements were made in Hobart, Tasmania, in 1813; in Queensland on the

Brisbane River in 1824; and on the Swan River in Western Australia in 1829. Melbourne was established on Port Phillip Bay in 1835 and Adelaide on Gulf St. Vincent in 1836. These settlements served as the bases for further exploration and settlement. Population continued to grow with the arrival of more convicts (a total of 161,000 when the system was finally abolished in 1868). The Ripon Land Regulation Act of 1831, which provided land grants, attracted free settlers. By 1850 Australia had 500,000 inhabitants. The discovery of gold in Victoria in 1851 quadrupled that number in a few years.

From Colony to Nation

On February 12, 1851, Edward Hargraves, an Australian-born prospector who had returned to Australia after unsuccessful digging in the California gold rush of 1849, discovered gold in a creek on the western slopes of the Blue Mountains. Hargraves gave the district the biblical name Ophir (Job 22:24), and the newspapers said the region was "one vast gold field." In July a miner found gold at Clunes, 100 miles west of Melbourne, and in September gold was found in what proved to be the richest field of all, Ballarat, just 75 miles west of Melbourne. Gold fever convulsed Australia. Although the government charged prospectors a very high license fee, men and women from all parts of the globe flocked to Australia to share in the fabulous wealth.

Contemporaries agreed with explorer and politician W. C. Wentworth, who said that the gold rush opened in Australia a new era "which must in a very few years precipitate us from a colony to a nation."[48] Although recent scholars have disputed Wentworth, there is much truth to his viewpoint. The gold rush led to an enormous improvement in transportation within Australia. People customarily traveled by horseback or on foot and used two-wheel ox-drawn carts to bring wool from inland ranches to coastal cities. Then two newly arrived Americans, Freeman Cobb and James Rutherford, built sturdy four-wheel coaches capable of carrying heavy cargo and of negotiating the bush tracks. Carrying passengers and mail up to 80 miles a day, a week's work for ox-drawn vehicles, by 1870 Cobb and Co. coaches covered 28,000 miles per week. Railroad construction began in the 1870s, and by 1890 9,000 miles of track were laid. Rail-

road construction, financed by British investors, stimulated agricultural growth.

The gold rush also provided the financial means for the promotion of education and culture. The 1850s witnessed the establishment of universities at Sydney and Melbourne and later at Adelaide and Hobart. Public libraries, museums, art galleries, and schools opened in the thirty years after 1851. In keeping with the overwhelmingly British ethnic origin of most immigrants to Australia, these institutions dispensed a distinctly British culture, though a remote and provincial version.

On the negative side, the large numbers of Asians in the gold fields—in Victoria in 1857 one adult male in seven was Chinese—sparked bitter racial prejudice. Scholars date the "white Australia policy" to the hostility, resentment, and fear that whites showed the Chinese.

Although Americans numbered only about 5,000 in Victoria and Asians 40,000, Americans with their California gold-rush experience, aggressive ways, and "democratic" frontier outlook, exercised an influence on Australian society far out of proportion to their numbers. "There was evidence to suggest that some Americans, bringing with them their pre–Civil War racist attitudes, had an appreciable influence on the growth of color prejudice in Australia."[49] On the Fourth of July in 1852, 1854, and 1857 (anniversaries of the American Declaration of Independence), anti-Chinese riots occurred in the gold fields of Victoria. After the gold-rush decade, public pressure for the exclusion of all colored peoples increased. Nevertheless, Asian peoples continued to arrive. Chinese and Japanese built the railroads and ran the market gardens near, and the shops in, the towns. Filipinos and Pacific Islanders did the hard work in the sugar-cane fields. Afghanis and their camels controlled the carrying trade in some areas.

"Colored peoples" (as all nonwhites were called in Australia) adapted more easily than the British to the warm climate and worked for lower wages. Thus they proved essential to the country's economic development in the nineteenth century. But fear that colored labor would lower living standards and undermine Australia's distinctly British culture triumphed. The Commonwealth Immigration Restriction Act of 1901 closed immigration to Asians and established the "white Australia policy." Australia achieved racial and cultural unity only at the price of Asian resentment at discrimination and

Ladies Embarking for Australia   When the blockade of southern ports during the American Civil War halted the flow of cotton to England, the mills of Lancashire were forced to lay off thousands who emigrated to the United States, Canada, and Australia. *The Illustrated London News* referred to these emigrants as "Distressed Needlewomen." *(Source: The Illustrated London News Picture Library)*

retarded economic development in the northern colonies, which desperately needed labor. The laws of 1901 remained on the books until the 1970s.

The gold rush had a considerable political impact. In 1850 the British Parliament had passed the Australian Colonies Government Act, which allowed the four most populous colonies—New South Wales, Tasmania, Victoria, and South Australia—to establish colonial legislatures, determine the franchise, and frame their own constitutions. The gold rush, vastly increasing population, accelerated the movement for self-government. Acknowledging this demand, the Colonial Secretary in London wrote that the gold discoveries "imparted new and unforeseen features to (Australia's) political and social condition." Western Australia's

decision to remain a penal colony delayed responsible government there, but by 1859 all other colonies were self-governing. The provincial parliament of South Australia was probably the most democratic in the world, since it was elected by universal manhood suffrage and by secret ballot. Other colonies soon adopted the secret ballot. In 1909 Australia became the first country in the world to adopt woman suffrage.

The government of Australia combines features of the British and American systems. In the later nineteenth century, pressure for continental federation culminated in meetings of the premiers (governors) of the colonies. They drafted a constitution that the British Parliament approved in 1900. The Commonwealth of Australia came into existence on January 1, 1901. From the British model, Australia adopted the parliamentary form of government in which a cabinet is responsible to the House of Commons. From the American system, Australia took the concept of decentralized government whereby the states and the federal government share power. The states in Australia, as in the United States, retain considerable power, especially in local or domestic affairs.

Deep loyalty to the mother country led Australia to send 329,000 men and vast economic aid to Britain in the First World War. The issue of conscription, however, bitterly divided the country, partly along religious lines. About one-fourth of Australia's population was (and is) Irish and Roman Catholic. Although the Catholic population, like the dominant Anglican one, split over conscription, the powerful, influential, and long-lived Catholic archbishop of Melbourne, Daniel Mannix (r. 1917–1963) publicly supported the Sinn Fein, the Irish nationalist (and later terrorist) movement. Mannix also denounced the English and the European war.

Twice submitted to public referendum, conscription twice failed. When the Australian poet Frank Wilmot (1881–1942) wrote, "The fumes of ancient hells have invaded your spirit," he meant that English wrongs in Ireland had become part of Australian culture.

Australian troops fought valiantly in the Dardanelles campaign, where more than 10,000 died. During the long nightmare of trench warfare on the western front, Australian soldiers were brilliantly led by Sir John Monash, a Jewish Australian whose planning led to the Allied breakthrough and the ultimate defeat of Germany. Australia's staggering 213,850 casualties, however, exerted a traumatic effect on Australian life and society. With the young men died the illusion that remote Australia could escape the problems and sins of the Old World. But the experience of the Great War forged a sense of national identity among the states of Australia.

At the Paris Peace Conference in 1919, Australian delegates succeeded in excluding recognition of the principle of racial equality in the League of Nations Covenant. Australians did not want Asian immigrants. The treaties that followed the war allowed Australia a mandate over German New Guinea and the equatorial island of Nauru. Nauru had vast quantities of phosphates that Australian wheatfields needed as fertilizer. The former penal colony had become a colonial power.

Summary

Between 1788 and 1931, the United States, Canada, and Australia developed from weak, agricultural colonies of Great Britain into powerful industrial and commercial nations, and the countries of Latin America first secured independence from Spain and then began the process of nation building. Inspired by notions of social equality and manifest destiny, galvanized by the optimism of millions of immigrants who came seeking a better life, Americans subdued the continent, linked it with railroads, and built gigantic steel, oil, textile, food-processing, and automobile industries. The North's victory in the bloody Civil War, fought largely over the issue of black slavery, proved the permanence of the Union, but the unresolved ideal of equality remains the American dilemma. Industrialization and the assimilation of foreign peoples also preoccupied the nations of Latin America, but political instability and economies often dominated by the United States or Great Britain slowed growth.

Canada and Australia followed the path of the United States, though at a slower pace. Adopting the British model of cabinet government under John A. Macdonald, and utilizing rich natural resources, the provinces of Canada formed a strong federation with close economic ties to the United States; each is the other's major trading partner. French separatism, centered in Quebec, remains the Canadian dilemma. Australia utilized political features of both the British and the American systems. Immigrant production of wool, wheat, and now wine has transformed Australia from a remote penal colony into the great democratic nation of the Pacific.

Notes

1. Quoted in W. S. Robertson, *Rise of the Spanish American Republics* (New York: Free Press, 1965), p. 19.
2. See B. Keen and M. Wasserman, *A Short History of Latin America* (Boston: Houghton Mifflin, 1980), pp. 109–115.

3. J. Lynch, *The Spanish-American Revolutions, 1808–1826* (New York: Norton, 1973), pp. 13–14; Keen and Wasserman, *A Short History of Latin America,* pp. 145–146.

4. Quoted in Lynch, *The Spanish-American Revolutions, 1808–1826,* p. 18.

5. M. Burkholder and D. S. Chandler, *From Impotence to Authority: The Spanish Crown and the American Audiencias, 1687–1808* (Columbia: University of Missouri Press, 1977), p. 145.

6. Ibid., p. 141.

7. Keen and Wasserman, *A Short History of Latin America,* p. 146.

8. Quoted in J. L. Phelan, *The People and the King: The Comunero Revolution in Colombia, 1781* (Madison: University of Wisconsin Press, 1978), p. 62; see also L. B. Rout, *The African Experience in Spanish America* (New York: Cambridge University Press, 1977), p. 165.

9. Quoted in Phelan, *The People and the King,* pp. 206–207.

10. F. Tannenbaum, *Ten Keys to Latin America* (New York: Random House, 1962), pp. 69–71.

11. H. Hoetink, *Slavery and Race Relations in the Americas* (New York: Harper & Row, 1973), p. 14.

12. Keen and Wasserman, *A Short History of Latin America,* pp. 201–204.

13. See C. H. Harris, *A Mexican Family Empire: The Latifundio of the Sanchez Navarros, 1765–1867* (Austin: University of Texas Press, 1975).

14. N. Sanchez-Albornoz, *The Population of Latin America: A History,* trans. W. A. R. Richardson (Berkeley: University of California Press, 1974), pp. 151–152.

15. J. R. Scobie, "Buenos Aires as a Commercial-Bureaucratic City, 1880–1910: Characteristics of a City's Orientation," *American Historical Review* 77 (October 1972): 1046.

16. Ibid., p. 1064.

17. See M. Morner, ed., *Race and Class in Latin America. Part II: Immigration, Stratification, and Race Relations* (New York: Columbia University Press, 1971), pp. 73–122; Sanchez-Albornoz, *The Population of Latin America,* pp. 160–167.

18. Quoted in M. B. Norton et al., *A People and a Nation: A History of the United States,* 4th ed. (Boston: Houghton Mifflin, 1994), p. 351.

19. S. E. Morison, *The Oxford History of the American People* (New York: Oxford University Press, 1965), pp. 380–381.

20. Ibid., pp. 446–452.

21. J. Oakes, *The Ruling Race: A History of American Slaveholders* (New York: Knopf, 1982), pp. x–xi.

22. See P. J. Parish, *Slavery: History and Historians* (New York: Harper & Row, 1989), pp. 45–46.

23. Quoted in Oakes, *The Ruling Race,* p. 120.

24. C. V. Woodward, ed., *Mary Chesnut's Civil War* (New Haven, Conn.: Yale University Press, 1981), p. 29.

25. Ibid., pp. xlix–l.

26. H. G. Gutman, *The Black Family in Slavery and Freedom, 1750–1925* (New York: Random House, 1977).

27. Quoted in R. W. Fogel and S. L. Engerman, *Time on the Cross: The Economics of American Negro Slavery* (Boston: Little, Brown, 1974), p. 84.

28. R. P. Basler, ed., *The Collected Works of Abraham Lincoln,* vol. 2 (New Brunswick, N.J.: Rutgers University Press, 1953), pp. 255–256, 271.

29. Ibid., pp. 461–462.

30. Quoted in R. Hofstadter, *The American Political Tradition* (New York: Random House, 1948), p. 114.

31. T. H. Williams, quoted ibid., pp. 128–129.

32. Quoted in ibid., p. 132.

33. Quoted in Morison, *The Oxford History of the American People,* p. 654.

34. T. H. Williams, *The History of American Wars: From Colonial Times to World War I* (New York: Knopf, 1981), p. 202.

35. Report of the University Committee on Diversity and Liberal Education to President Harold Shapiro of Princeton University as cited in *Princeton Today,* vol. 7, no. 2 (Summer 1994): 7.

36. F. James Davis, *Who Is Black? One Nation's Definition* (University Park: Pennsylvania State University Press, 1991), passim, but esp. Chs. 2 and 3, pp. 31–80.

37. See Lawrence Wright, "One Drop of Blood," *The New Yorker,* July 25, 1994, pp. 46–55.

38. S. L. Myres, *Westering Women and the Frontier Experience, 1800–1915* (Albuquerque: University of New Mexico Press, 1982), Chs. 6 and 7.

39. G. Barth, *City People: The Rise of Modern City Culture in the Nineteenth Century* (New York: Oxford University Press, 1980), p. 15.

40. Quoted in Lynch, *The Spanish-American Revolutions, 1808–1826,* p. 18.

41. Hoetink, *Slavery and Race Relations in the Americas,* p. 18.

42. Quoted in J. Higham, *Strangers in the Land: Patterns of American Nativism, 1860–1925* (New York: Atheneum, 1971), pp. 89–90.

43. Quoted in R. Cook, *Canada: A Modern Study* (Toronto: Clarke, Irwin, 1971), p. 89.

44. Quoted ibid., p. 127.

45. R. Ward, *Australia* (Englewood Cliffs, N.J.: Prentice-Hall, 1965), p. 21.

46. Quoted in R. Hughes, *The Fatal Shore* (New York: Knopf, 1987), p. 66.

47. J. Kociumbas, *The Oxford History of Australia,* Vol. 2, *Colonial Australia, 1770–1860* (New York: Oxford University Press, 1992), p. 1.

48. Quoted in Ward, *Australia,* p. 60.

49. Ibid., p. 59.

SUGGESTED READING

Perhaps the best introduction to the independence movements in Latin America is J. Lynch, *The Spanish-American Revolutions, 1808–1826* (1973), which is soundly researched and includes a good bibliography. The most useful biographies of Simón Bolívar are those of G. Masur, *Simón Bolívar,* 2d ed. (1969), and J. J. Johnson and D. M. Ladd, *Simón Bolívar and Spanish American Independence, 1783–1830* (1968); the latter contains good selections of Bolívar's writings. For Brazil, see K. R. Maxwell, *Conflicts and Conspiracies: Brazil and Portugal, 1750–1808* (1973), and A. J. R. Russell-Wood, ed., *From Colony to Nation: Essays in the Independence of Brazil* (1975). A. P. Whitaker, *The United States and the Independence of Latin America, 1800–1830* (1941), remains the standard study of the role of the United States. The essays in E. Viotti da Costa, *The Brazilian Empire: Myths and Histories* (1985), are sound and penetrating.

J. Bazant, *A Concise History of Mexico* (1978), is a good starting point for the study of Mexican history, but M. C. Meyer and W. L. Sherman, *The Course of Mexican History* (1979), is the most thorough treatment. T. Halperin-Donghi, *The Aftermath of Revolution in Latin America* (1973), and C. C. Griffin, "Economic and Social Aspects of the Era of Spanish-American Independence," *Hispanic American Historical Review* 29 (1949), provide important interpretations of the consequences of the revolutions.

The following studies offer good treatments of society and politics in Latin America in the nineteenth century: R. Graham and P. H. Smith, eds., *New Approaches to Latin American History* (1974); R. Roeder, *Juarez and His Mexico,* 2 vols. (1947), perhaps the best available work in English; H. S. Ferns, *Argentina* (1969); J. Kinsbruner, *Chile: A Historical Interpretation* (1973); A. J. Bauer, *Chilean Rural Society from the Spanish Conquest to 1930* (1975); E. B. Burns, *A History of Brazil* (1970); Robert Conrad, *The Destruction of Brazilian Slavery, 1850–1888* (1973).

J. C. Miller, *Slavery and Slaving in World History: A Bibliography, 1900–1901* (1993) is a useful reference tool with material comparing slavery in North and in South America. Some important comparative studies are I. Berlin and P. Morgan, eds. *Cultivation and Culture: Labor and the Shaping of Slave Life in the Americas* (1991); H. Klein, *Slavery in the Americas: A Comparative Study of Virginia and Cuba* (1967); C. Degler, *Neither Black Nor White: Slavery and Race Relations in Brazil and the United States* (1971). For South American labor and conditions of slavery, see S. Schwartz, *Sugar Plantations in the Formation of Brazilian Society* (1985) and the same author's *Slaves, Peasants, and Rebels: Reconsidering Brazilian Society* (1992); F. P. Bowser, *African Slavery in Colonial Peru* (1974); C. E. Martin, *Rural Society in Colonial Morelos* (1985); P. J. Carroll, *Blacks in Colonial Veracruz* (1991); and for North America, see S. Innes, *Work and Labor in Early America* (1988); J. F. Smith, *Slavery and Rice Culture in Colonial Georgia, 1750–1860* (1985); R. L. Lewis, *Coal, Iron, and Slaves: Industrial Slavery in Maryland and Virginia, 1715–1865* (1979) and S. Mintz, *Sweetness and Power: The Place of Sugar in Modern History* (1985). The elegant study by P. J. Parish cited in the Notes surveys a large body of scholarship. W. Jordan, *White Over Black: American Attitudes Towards the Negro, 1550–1812* (1969) remains a solid treatment of the relationship of racism to slavery. E. D. Genovese, *Roll, Jordan, Roll: The World the Slaves Made* (1974) gives a Marxist interpretation.

For social and economic developments and the triumph of neocolonialism, the following titles are useful: R. C. Conde, *The First Stages of Modernization in Spanish America* (1967); J. Bazant, *A Concise History of Mexico from Hidalgo to Cardenas, 1805–1940* (1978); R. Knowlton, *Church Property and the Mexican Reform, 1856–1910* (1976); R. D. Anderson, *Outcasts in Their Own Land: Mexican Industrial Workers, 1906–1911* (1976); J. Scobie, *Argentina: A City and a Nation,* 2d ed. (1971); M. J. Mamalakis, *The Growth and Structure of the Chilean Economy from Independence to Allende* (1976), which provides an excellent economic overview; A. G. Frank, *Capitalism and Underdevelopment in Latin America: Historical Studies of Chile and Brazil* (1969); D. Rock, *Politics in Argentina, 1890–1930: The Rise and Fall of Radicalism* (1975); and R. Graham, *Britain and the Onset of Modernization in Brazil, 1850–1914* (1968).

The major themes in U.S. history have been extensively treated by many able scholars, and students will have no difficulty finding a wealth of material. J. M. Burns, *The Vineyard of Liberty* (1982), traces the origins and development of American society, politics, and culture, from the 1780s to 1863, emphasizing the growth of liberty; this work is a classic achievement. The standard study of manifest destiny remains F. Merk, *Manifest Destiny and Mission in American History: A Reinterpretation* (1963), but see also K.

Jack Bauer, *The Mexican-American War, 1846–1848* (1976). In *The Only Land They Knew: The Tragic Story of the American Indians in the Old South* (1981), J. Leitch Wright recounts the interaction of native Americans, Africans, and Europeans in the American South.

On black culture and black women and the family, see, in addition to Gutman's work cited in the Notes, J. Jones, *Labor of Love, Labor of Sorrow: Black Women, Work, and the Family from Slavery to the Present* (1985); C. Neverdon-Morton, *Afro-American Women of the South and the Advancement of the Race, 1895–1925* (1989); and M. R. Malson et al., *Black Women in America: Social Science Perspectives* (1988), which offers useful essays for classroom discussion. See also W. S. McFeely, *Frederick Douglass* (1991), and I. Berlin et al., eds., *Freedom: A Documentary History of Emancipation* (1990). For the powerful influence of the black church see E. Lincoln and C. H. Mamiya, *The Black Church in the African American Experience* (1990).

The literature on the Civil War and Reconstruction is mammoth. The best comprehensive treatment of the pre-Civil War years is K. M. Stampp, *America in 1857: A Nation on the Brink* (1990). The following titles should also prove useful to students: J. M. McPherson, *Battle Cry of Freedom: The Era of the Civil War* (1988); D. M. Potter, *The Impending Crisis, 1848–1861* (1976); D. Donald, ed., *Why the North Won the Civil War* (1977); and E. Foner, *Reconstruction: America's Unfinished Revolution, 1863–1877* (1988).

T. C. Cochrane, *Business in American Life* (1977); A. D. Chandler, *Strategy and Structure: Chapters in the History of American Industrial Enterprise* (1966); H. C. Livesay, *Andrew Carnegie and the Rise of Big Business* (1975); and D. F. Hawkes, *John D.: The Founding Father of the Rockefellers* (1980), are fine studies of industrialism and corporate growth in the late nineteenth century.

On the lives of Jews and other immigrants in American cities, see I. Howe's brilliant achievement, *World of Our Fathers* (1976), which is splendidly illustrated and contains a good bibliography, and S. S. Weinberg, *The World of Our Mothers: The Lives of Jewish Immigrant Women* (1988).

For developments in Canada, see, in addition to the highly readable sketch by R. Cook cited in the Notes, K. McNaught, *The Pelican History of Canada* (1976), a sound survey that emphasizes those cultural traits that are distinctly Canadian. For the Age of Confederation, J. M. S. Careless, *The Union of the Canadas, 1841–1857* (1967), offers a solid treatment by a distinguished scholar. D. G. Creighton, *John A. Macdonald,* 2 vols. (1952, 1955), is probably the best study of the great prime minister. The critical years of expansion and development are discussed in the full accounts of R. C. Brown and G. R. Cook, *Canada, 1896–1921* (1974), and R. Graham, *Canada, 1922–1939* (1979).

Perhaps the best starting point for the study of Australian history is the title by R. Hughes, cited in the Notes. M. Clark, *A Short History of Australia* (1987), is a highly readable general sketch. C. M. H. Clark, *A History of Australia,* 6 vols. (1962–1987), is the standard political history. R. Terrill, *The Australians* (1987), offers an attractive appreciation of the Australian people and the society they made, from the first settlers to the present.

LISTENING TO THE
PAST

Separate but Equal

"We hold these truths to be self-evident that all men are created equal," Thomas Jefferson wrote in the Declaration of Independence. But how could the rich merchants and slaveholders of the Second Continental Congress believe in equality? Jefferson recognized the contradiction and laid the blame on George III: the draft of the Declaration charged that the English king had "waged a cruel war . . . by assaulting distant people and captivating and carrying them into slavery in another hemisphere." Southern delegates rejected the notion that slavery violated "the most sacred rights of life and liberty" and, as a condition for endorsing the entire document, insisted that the slavery passage be deleted. Jefferson acquiesced, but the term equality *remained. So did the contradiction.*

The Thirteenth Amendment to the U.S. Constitution abolished slavery (1865), the Fourteenth granted civil rights to freed persons (1868), and the Fifteenth gave blacks the right to vote (1869). Between 1880 and 1910, southern legislatures responded with a flood of legislation designed to reduce blacks to a servile position and to create a system of rigid racial segregation. Laws required separate schools; separate public accommodations on trains and buses and in libraries, restaurants, parks, prisons, and institutions for the blind and deaf; separate telephone booths, water fountains, rest rooms, and even cemeteries. The State of Louisiana in 1890 adopted a law providing for "equal but separate" accommodations for the white and colored races on its railroads, with the interesting proviso that "nothing in this act shall be construed as applying to (black) nurses attending children of the other race." In 1892, Homer Plessy, seven of whose eight great-grandparents had been white, a passenger between two train stations in Louisiana, refused to sit in the railcar marked for blacks only. He was taken before Judge John H. Ferguson of the New Orleans Criminal Court. Ferguson upheld the Louisiana law, and the case was appealed to the U.S. Supreme Court. Refusing to rule on who is a Negro, the Court took "judicial notice" of Mr. Plessy's background, based its decision on sociocultural, not genetic, factors, and held that being known in the community as Negro is evidence of Negro ancestry.

The object of the Fourteenth Amendment was undoubtedly to enforce the absolute equality of the two races before the law, but in the nature of things it could not have been intended to abolish distinctions based upon color or to enforce social, as distinguished from political, equality or a commingling of the races upon terms unsatisfactory to either. . . . The case reduces itself to the question whether the statute of Louisiana is a reasonable regulation, and . . . it is at liberty to act with reference to established usages, customs, and traditions of the people, and with a view to the promotion of their comfort, and the preservation of public peace and good order. Gauged by this standard, we cannot say that a law which authorizes or even requires the separation of the two races in public conveyances is unreasonable or more obnoxious to the Fourteenth Amendment than the acts of Congress requiring separate schools for colored children in the District of Columbia, the constitutionality of which does not seem to have been questioned. . . . If the two races are to meet on terms of social equality, it must be the result of natural affinities, a mutual appreciation of each other's merits. . . . If one race be inferior to the other socially, the Constitution of the United States cannot put them upon the same plane.

Mr. Justice John Marshall Harlan dissented:

Our Constitution is color blind, and neither knows nor tolerates classes among citizens. In respect of civil rights, all citizens are equal before the law. . . . The arbitrary separation of citizens, on the basis of race, while they are on a public highway, is a badge of servitude wholly inconsistent with the civil freedom and the equality before the law established by the Constitution. It cannot be justified upon any legal grounds.

Harlan was the sole dissenter. The majority opinion in Plessy v. Ferguson *(1896) remained the law of the land until the 1950s, when a school girl in Topeka, Kansas, appealed to the courts claiming that separate schools were unequal. The case that came before the U.S. Supreme Court in 1954,* Brown v. Board of Education of Topeka *combined a series of cases designed to challenge segregation in Kansas, Delaware, South Carolina, and Virginia. Delivering the unanimous opinion of the Court, Chief Justice Earl Warren declared:*

We come to the question presented: Does segregation of children in public schools solely on the basis of race, even though the facilities may be equal and other "tangible" factors may be equal, deprive the children of the minority group of equal educational opportunities? We believe that it does. . . . To separate them from others of similar age and qualifications solely because of their race generates a feeling of inferiority as to their status in the community that may affect their hearts and minds in a way unlikely ever to be undone. . . . We conclude that in the field of public education the doctrine of "separate but equal" has no place. Separate educational facilities are inherently unequal. . . . We have now announced that segregation is a denial of the equal protection of the laws.

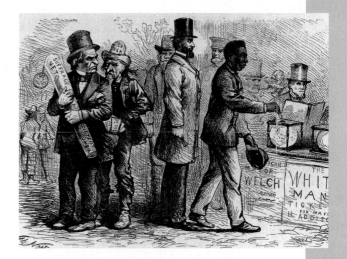

The Georgetown Election. In 1866, as the United States Congress prepared to enfranchise negroes in D.C., the city's mayor took a vote to ascertain public opinion. The results: 6,591 against black suffrage, 35 in favor; in Georgetown the vote was 712 against, 1 in favor. President Johnson vetoed the enfranchisement bill and Congress immediately overrode it. The strongly Republican cartoonist Thomas Nast drew this scene prior to Congress's passage of the XVth Amendment (1867) granting blacks the right to vote. *(Source: Private Collection)*

Questions for Analysis

1. What was Homer Plessy's race? Why?

2. How would you evaluate the Supreme Court's comments in *Plessy v. Ferguson* on general race relations?

3. How does the decision in the *Brown* case sound the death knell for all segregation?

4. The 1954 Supreme Court has been accused of "social engineering." What does that phrase mean? Is it proper for the Supreme Court to attempt to reform society?

29

The Great Break:
War and Revolution

Gassed, a World War I painting by John Singer Sargent (1856–1925). *(Source: By courtesy of the Trustees of the Imperial War Museum)*

In the summer of 1914 the nations of Europe went willingly to war. They believed they had no other choice. Moreover, both peoples and governments confidently expected a short war leading to a decisive victory. Such a war, they believed, would "clear the air," and then European society would be able to go on as before.

These expectations were almost totally mistaken. The First World War was long, indecisive, and tremendously destructive. To the shell-shocked generation of survivors, it was known simply as the Great War: the war of unprecedented scope and intensity. From today's perspective it is clear that the First World War marked a great break in the course of world historical development. The war accelerated the growth of nationalism in Asia (see Chapter 30), and it consolidated the position of the United States as a global power. Yet the war's greatest impact was on Europe, the focus of this chapter. A noted British political scientist has gone so far as to say that even in victorious and relatively fortunate Great Britain, the First World War was *the* great turning point in government and society "as in everything else in modern British history. . . . There's a much greater difference between the Britain of 1914 and, say, 1920, than between the Britain of 1920 and today."[1] This strong statement contains a great amount of truth, for all Europe as well as for Britain.

- What caused the Great War?
- How did the war lead to revolution and the fall of empires?
- How and why did war and revolution have such enormous and destructive consequences?
- How did the years of trauma and bloodshed form elements of today's world, many of which people now accept and even cherish?

These are the questions this chapter will try to answer.

 THE FIRST WORLD WAR

The First World War was so long and destructive because it involved all the Great Powers and because it quickly degenerated into a senseless military stalemate. Like evenly matched boxers in a championship bout, the two sides tried to wear each other down. But there was no referee to call a draw, only the blind hammering of a life-or-death struggle.

The Bismarckian System of Alliances

The defeat of France in 1871 (see page 868) and the founding of the German Empire opened a new era in international relations. In ten short years, from 1862 to 1871, Bismarck had made Prussia-Germany—traditionally the weakest of the Great Powers—the most powerful nation in Europe. Yet, as Bismarck never tired of repeating after 1871, Germany was a "satisfied" power. Within Europe, Germany had no territorial ambitions and wanted only peace.

But how was peace to be preserved? Bismarck's first concern was to keep an embittered France diplomatically isolated and without military allies. His second concern was the threat to peace posed by Austria-Hungary and Russia. Those two enormous multinational empires had many conflicting interests, particularly in the Balkans, where the Ottoman Empire—the "sick man of Europe"—was ebbing fast. There was a real threat that Germany might be dragged into a great war between the two rival empires. Bismarck's solution was a system of alliances (Figure 29.1) to restrain both Russia and Austria-Hungary, to prevent conflict between them, and to isolate a hostile France.

A first step was the creation in 1873 of the conservative Three Emperors' League, which linked the monarchs of Austria-Hungary, Germany, and Russia in an alliance against radical movements. In 1877 and 1878, when Russia's victories over the Ottoman Empire threatened the balance of Austrian and Russian interests in the Balkans and the balance of British and Russian interests in the Middle East, Bismarck played the role of sincere peacemaker at the Congress of Berlin in 1878 (see page 965). But his balancing efforts at the congress infuriated Russian nationalists, and their anger led Bismarck to conclude a defensive military alliance with Austria against Russia in 1879. Motivated by tensions with France, Italy joined Germany and Austria in 1882, thereby forming what became known as the Triple Alliance.

Bismarck continued to work for peace in eastern Europe, seeking to neutralize tensions between Austria-Hungary and Russia. In 1881 he cajoled them both into a secret alliance with Germany.

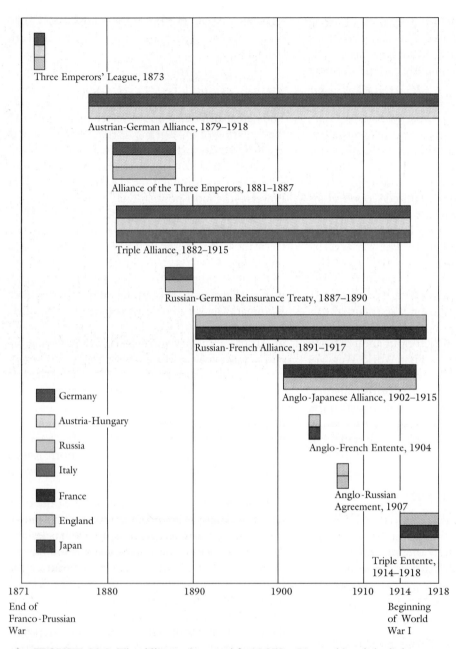

FIGURE 29.1 The Alliance System After 1871 Bismarck's subtle diplomacy maintained reasonably good relations among the eastern monarchies—Germany, Russia, and Austria-Hungary—and kept France isolated. The situation changed dramatically in 1891, when the Russian-French Alliance divided the Great Powers into two fairly equal military blocs.

This Alliance of the Three Emperors lasted until 1887.

Bismarck also maintained good relations with Britain and Italy while encouraging France in Africa but keeping France isolated in Europe. In 1887 Russia declined to renew the Alliance of the Three Emperors because of new tensions in the Balkans. Bismarck craftily substituted the Russian-German Reinsurance Treaty, by which both states promised neutrality if the other was attacked.

The Congress of Berlin, 1878   With the Austrian representative on his right and with other participants looking on, Bismarck the mediator symbolically seals the hard-won agreement by shaking hands with the chief Russian negotiator. In the nineteenth century the Great Powers often relied on such special conferences to settle their international disputes. *(Source: The Bettmann Archive)*

Bismarck's accomplishments in foreign policy after 1871 were great. For almost a generation, he maintained German leadership in international affairs, and he worked successfully for peace by managing conflicts and by restraining Austria-Hungary and Russia with defensive alliances.

The Rival Blocs

In 1890 the young, impetuous German emperor William II dismissed Bismarck, in part because of the chancellor's friendly policy toward Russia since the 1870s. William then adamantly refused to renew the Russian-German Reinsurance Treaty, in spite of Russian willingness to do so. This fateful departure in foreign affairs prompted long-isolated republican France to court absolutist Russia, offering loans, arms, and friendship. In both countries there were enthusiastic public demonstrations, and

in St. Petersburg Harbor the autocratic tsar Alexander III stood bareheaded on a French battleship while a band played the "Marseillaise," the hymn of the French Revolution. After a preliminary agreement was reached in 1891, France and Russia became military allies in 1894, pledging to remain so as long as the Triple Alliance of Austria, Germany, and Italy existed (see Figure 29.1). As a result, continental Europe was dangerously divided into two rival blocs.

Great Britain's foreign policy became increasingly crucial. Long content with "splendid isolation" and no permanent alliances, Britain after 1891 was the only uncommitted Great Power. Could Britain afford to remain isolated, or would it feel compelled to take sides? Alliance with France or Russia certainly seemed highly unlikely. With a vast and rapidly expanding empire, Britain was often in serious conflict with these countries around the world.

Britain also squabbled with Germany, but many Germans and some Britons felt that a "natural alliance" united the advanced, racially related Germanic and Anglo-Saxon peoples. However, the generally good relations that had prevailed between Prussia and Great Britain ever since the mid-eighteenth century, and certainly under Bismarck, gave way to a bitter Anglo-German rivalry.

There were several reasons for this tragic development. Commercial rivalry in world markets between Germany and Great Britain increased sharply in the 1890s. Above all, Germany's decision in 1900 to expand greatly its battle fleet posed a challenge to Britain's long-standing naval supremacy. This decision coincided with the hard-fought Boer War (1899–1902) between the British and the tiny Dutch republics of South Africa, a conflict that had a major impact on British policy. British political leaders saw that Britain was overextended around the world. The Boer War also brought into the open widespread anti-British feeling as editorial writers in many nations denounced this latest manifestation of British imperialism. There was even talk of Germany, Austria, France, and Russia forming a grand alliance against the bloated but insatiable British Empire. Thus British leaders prudently set about shoring up their exposed position with alliances and agreements.

Britain improved its often-strained relations with the United States and in 1902 concluded a formal alliance with Japan (see Figure 29.1). Britain then responded favorably to the advances of France's skillful foreign minister Théophile Delcassé, who wanted better relations with Britain and was willing to accept British rule in Egypt in return for British support of French plans to dominate Morocco. The resulting Anglo-French Entente of 1904 settled all outstanding colonial disputes between Britain and France.

Frustrated by Britain's turn toward France in 1904 and wanting a diplomatic victory to gain greater popularity at home, Germany's leaders decided to test the strength of the entente. Rather than accept the typical territorial payoff of imperial competition—a slice of French jungle somewhere in Africa or a port in Morocco—in return for French primacy in Morocco, the Germans foolishly rattled their swords by insisting in 1905 on an international conference on the whole Moroccan question; nor did the Germans present precise or reasonable demands. Germany's crude bullying forced France and Britain closer together, and Ger-

many left the resulting Algeciras Conference of 1906 empty-handed and isolated (except for Austria-Hungary).

The result of the Moroccan crisis and the Algeciras Conference was something of a diplomatic revolution. Britain, France, Russia, and even the United States began to see Germany as a potential threat, a would-be intimidator that might seek to dominate all Europe. At the same time, German leaders began to see sinister plots to "encircle" Germany and block its development as a world power. In 1907 Russia, battered by its disastrous war with Japan and the revolution of 1905, agreed to settle its quarrels with Great Britain in Persia and central Asia with a special Anglo-Russian Agreement (see Figure 29.1). As a result of that agreement, Germany's blustering paranoia increased, as did Britain's thinly disguised hostility.

Germany's decision to add a large, enormously expensive fleet of big-gun battleships to its already expanding navy also heightened tensions after 1907. German nationalists saw a large navy as the legitimate mark of a great world power and as a source of pride and patriotic unity. But British leaders such as David Lloyd George saw it as a detestable military challenge that forced them to spend the "People's Budget" on battleships rather than social welfare. Ongoing economic rivalry also contributed to distrust and hostility between the two nations, while proud nationalists in both countries simultaneously admired and feared the power and accomplishments of their nearly equal rival. In 1909 the mass-circulation London *Daily Mail* hysterically informed its readers in a series of reports that "Germany is deliberately preparing to destroy the British Empire."[2] By then Britain was psychologically, if not officially, in the Franco-Russian camp. The leading nations of Europe were divided into two hostile blocs, both ill prepared to deal with upheaval on Europe's southeastern frontier.

The Outbreak of War

In the early years of the twentieth century, war in the Balkans was as inevitable as anything can be in human history. The reason was simple: nationalism was destroying the Ottoman Empire and threatening to break up the Austro-Hungarian Empire. The only questions were what kinds of wars would occur and where would they lead.

German Warships Under Full Steam   As these impressive ships engaged in battle exercises in 1907 suggest, Germany did succeed in building a large modern navy. But Britain was determined to maintain its naval superiority, and the spiraling arms race helped poison relations between the two countries. *(Source: Bibliothèque des Arts Décoratifs/Jean-Loup Charmet)*

Greece had long before led the struggle for national liberation, winning its independence in 1832. In 1875 widespread nationalist rebellion in the Ottoman Empire had resulted in Turkish repression, Russian intervention, and Great Power tensions. Bismarck had helped resolve this crisis at the 1878 Congress of Berlin, which worked out the partial division of Turkish possessions in Europe. Austria-Hungary obtained the right to "occupy and administer" Bosnia and Herzegovina. Serbia and Romania won independence, and a part of Bulgaria won local autonomy. The Ottoman Empire retained important Balkan holdings, for Austria-Hungary and Russia each feared the other's domination of totally independent states in the area (Map 29.1).

By 1903 Balkan nationalism was asserting itself once again. Serbia led the way, becoming openly hostile toward both Austria-Hungary and the Ottoman Empire. The Serbs, a Slavic people, looked to Slavic Russia for support of their national aspirations. To block Serbian expansion and to take advantage of Russia's weakness after the revolution of 1905, Austria in 1908 formally annexed Bosnia and Herzegovina, with their large Serbian, Croatian, and Muslim populations. The kingdom of Serbia erupted in rage but could do nothing without Russian support.

Then in 1912, in the First Balkan War, Serbia turned southward. With Greece and Bulgaria it took Macedonia from the Ottoman Empire and then quarreled with Bulgaria over the spoils of victory—a dispute that led in 1913 to the Second Balkan War. Austria intervened in 1913 and forced Serbia to give up Albania. After centuries, nationalism had finally destroyed the Ottoman Empire in Europe (Map 29.2). This sudden but long-awaited event elated the Balkan nationalists and dismayed

MAP 29.1 The Balkans After the Congress of Berlin, 1878 The Ottoman Empire suffered large territorial losses but remained a power in the Balkans.

MAP 29.2 The Balkans in 1914 Ethnic boundaries did not follow political boundaries, and Serbian national aspirations threatened Austria-Hungry.

the leaders of multinational Austria-Hungary. The former hoped and the latter feared that Austria might be next to be broken apart.

Within this tense context, Archduke Francis Ferdinand, heir to the Austrian and Hungarian thrones, and his wife, Sophie, were assassinated by ultranationalist Serbian revolutionaries on June 28, 1914, during a state visit to the Bosnian capital of Sarajevo. Although the leaders of Austria-Hungary did not and could not know all the details of Serbia's involvement in the assassination plot, they concluded after some hesitation that Serbia had to be severely punished once and for all. On July 23 Austria-Hungary presented Serbia with an unconditional ultimatum. The Serbian government had just forty-eight hours in which to agree to de-

mands that would amount to Austrian control of the Serbian state. When Serbia replied moderately but evasively, Austria began to mobilize and then declared war on Serbia on July 28. Thus a desperate multinational Austria-Hungary deliberately chose war in a last-ditch attempt to stem the rising tide of hostile nationalism within its borders and save the existing state. The "Third Balkan War" had begun.

Of prime importance in Austria-Hungary's fateful decision was Germany's unconditional support. Emperor William II and his chancellor, Theobald von Bethmann-Hollweg, gave Austria-Hungary a "blank check" and urged aggressive measures in early July, even though they realized that war between Austria and Russia was the most probable result. A resurgent Russia could not stand by, as in the Bosnian crisis, and simply watch the Serbs be crushed. Yet Bethmann-Hollweg apparently hoped that while Russia (and therefore France) would go to war, Great Britain would remain neutral, unwilling to fight for "Russian aggression" in the distant Balkans.

In fact, the diplomatic situation was already out of control. Military plans and timetables began to dictate policy. On July 28 as Austrian armies bombarded Belgrade, Tsar Nicholas II ordered a partial mobilization against Austria-Hungary. Almost immediately he found that this was impossible. All the complicated mobilization plans of the Russian general staff had assumed a war with both Austria and Germany: Russia could not mobilize against one without mobilizing against the other. Therefore, on July 29 Russia ordered full mobilization and in effect declared general war.

The same tragic subordination of political considerations to military strategy shaped events in Germany. The German general staff had also thought only in terms of a two-front war. The staff's plan for war called for knocking out France first with a lightning attack through neutral Belgium before turning on Russia. So on August 2, 1914, General Helmuth von Moltke, "acting under a dictate of self-preservation," demanded that Belgium permit German armies to pass through its territory. Belgium, whose neutrality had been solemnly guaranteed in 1839 by all the great states including Prussia, refused. Germany attacked. Thus Germany's terrible, politically disastrous response to a war in the Balkans was an all-out invasion of France by way of the plains of neutral Belgium on August 3. In the face of this act of aggression, Great Britain joined France and declared war on Germany the following day. The First World War had begun.

In reflecting on the origins of the First World War, it seems clear that Austria-Hungary deliberately started the conflict. A war for the right to survive was Austria-Hungary's desperate response to the aggressive, revolutionary drive of Serbian nationalists to unify their people in a single state. Moreover, in spite of Russian intervention in the quarrel, it is also clear that Germany was most responsible for turning a third war in the Balkans into the Great War by means of a sledgehammer attack on Belgium and France. Why Germany was so aggressive in 1914 is less certain.

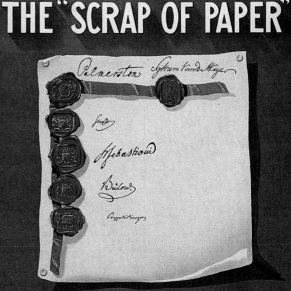

Anti-German Propaganda This British poster shows the signature page of the 1839 treaty guaranteeing the neutrality of Belgium. When German armies invaded Belgium in 1914, Chancellor Bethmann-Hollweg cynically dismissed the treaty as a "scrap of paper"—a perfect line for anti-German propaganda. *(Source: By courtesy of the Trustees of the Imperial War Museum)*

Diplomatic historians stress that German leaders lost control of the international system after Bismarck's resignation in 1890. They felt increasingly that Germany's status as a world power was declining while the status of Britain, France, Russia, and the United States was growing. Indeed, the powers of what officially became in August 1914 the Triple Entente—Great Britain, France, and Russia—were checking Germany's vague but real aspirations as well as working to strangle Austria-Hungary, Germany's only real ally. Germany's

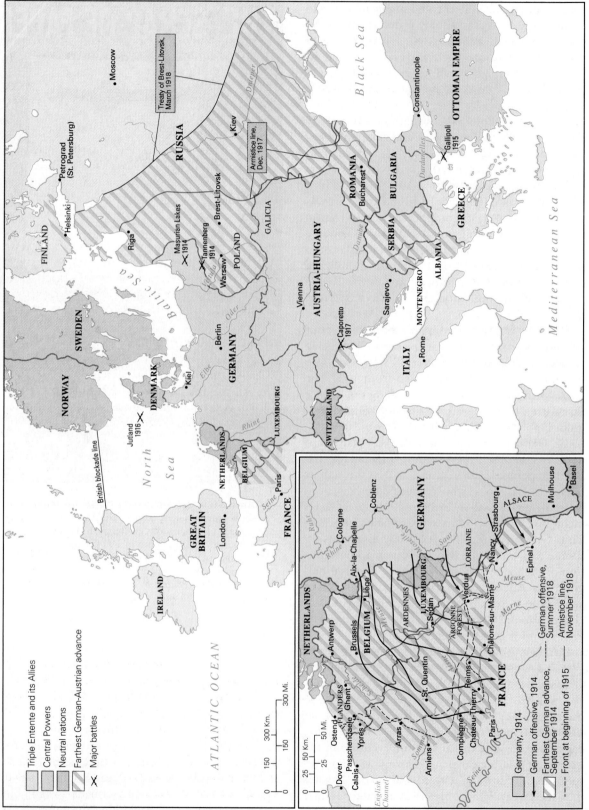

Legend (main map):

Triple Entente and its Allies
Central Powers
Neutral nations
Farthest German-Austrian advance
X Major battles

Main map labels:

ATLANTIC OCEAN

North Sea

Baltic Sea

Black Sea

Mediterranean Sea

NORWAY

SWEDEN

FINLAND
Helsinki

Petrograd
(St. Petersburg)

Moscow

RUSSIA

Treaty of Brest-Litovsk,
March 1918

Armistice line,
Dec. 1917

Riga

Kiev
Dnieper

Brest-Litovsk

Masurian Lakes
1914
Tannenberg
1914
Warsaw
POLAND
Vistula

GALICIA

IRELAND

GREAT
BRITAIN
London

British blockade line

Jutland
1916

DENMARK
Kiel

GERMANY
Berlin
Elbe
Oder

NETHERLANDS
BELGIUM

LUXEMBOURG

Rhine

Paris
Seine

FRANCE

SWITZERLAND

AUSTRIA-HUNGARY
Vienna
Danube

Caporetto
1917

ITALY
Rome

MONTENEGRO
Sarajevo
SERBIA

ALBANIA

ROMANIA
Bucharest

BULGARIA

GREECE

Dardanelles

Gallipoli
1915

Constantinople

OTTOMAN EMPIRE

Scale (main map):

0 150 300 Km.
0 150 300 Mi.

Inset map (France/Belgium):

Legend (inset):

Germany, 1914
→ German offensive, 1914
Farthest German advance,
September 1914
Front at beginning of 1915
German offensive,
Summer 1918
Armistice line,
November 1918

English Channel

Dover
Calais
Ostend
Passchendaele
Ghent
FLANDERS
Ypres
Yser

Antwerp
NETHERLANDS
Brussels
BELGIUM
Liège
Aix-la-Chapelle
Cologne
Rhine
Ruhr
GERMANY
Coblenz

Meuse
ARDENNES
LUXEMBOURG
Sedan

Arras
St. Quentin
Somme
Scheldt

Amiens
Compiègne
Reims
Château-Thierry
Châlons-sur-Marne
Marne
Seine
Paris

ARGONNE
FOREST
Verdun
Meuse

LORRAINE
Moselle
Saar

Nancy
Strasbourg
ALSACE
Épinal

Mulhouse
Basel

Scale (inset):

0 25 50 Km.
0 25 50 Mi.

aggression in 1914 reflected the failure of all European leaders, not just those in Germany, to incorporate Bismarck's mighty empire permanently and peacefully into the international system.

Growing tensions between European states correctly suggest that the triumph of nationalism was a crucial underlying precondition of the Great War. Nationalism was at the heart of the Balkan wars, and it drove the spiraling international arms race. Broad popular commitment to "my country right or wrong" weakened groups that thought in terms of international communities and consequences. Thus the big international bankers, who were frightened by the prospect of war in July 1914, and the extreme-left socialists, who believed that the enemy was at home and not abroad, were equally out of step with national feeling. In each country the great majority of the population enthusiastically embraced the outbreak of war in August 1914. They rallied to defend the nation, and patriotic nationalism brought unity in the short run.

In all of this, Europe's governing classes underestimated the risk of war to themselves in 1914. They had forgotten that great wars and great social revolutions very often go hand in hand. Metternich's alliance of conservative forces in support of international peace and the social status quo had become a distant memory.

Stalemate and Slaughter

When the Germans invaded Belgium in August 1914, they and everyone else believed that the war would be short, for urban society rested on the food and raw materials of the world economy: "The boys will be home by Christmas." The Belgian army heroically defended its homeland, however, and fell back in good order to join a rapidly landed British army corps near the Franco-Belgian border. Instead of quickly capturing Paris in a vast encircling movement, by the end of August deadtired German soldiers were advancing along an enormous front in the scorching summer heat. On September 6, the French attacked a gap in the German line at the Battle of the Marne. For three days, France threw everything into the attack. At one point, the French government desperately requisitioned all the taxis of Paris to rush reserves to the troops at the front. Finally, the Germans fell back. Paris and France had been miraculously saved (Map 29.3).

Soon, with the armies stalled, both sides began to dig trenches to protect themselves from machine-gun fire. By November 1914 an unbroken line of trenches extended from the Belgian ports through northern France past the fortress of Verdun and on to the Swiss frontier. In the face of this unexpected stalemate, slaughter on the western front began in earnest. The defenders on both sides dug in behind rows of trenches, mines, and barbed wire. For days and even weeks, ceaseless shelling by heavy artillery supposedly "softened up" the enemy in a given area (and also signaled the coming attack). Then young draftees and their junior officers went "over the top" of the trenches in frontal attacks on the enemy's line.

The cost in lives was staggering; the gains in territory, minuscule. The massive French and British offensives during 1915 never gained more than three miles of blood-soaked earth from the enemy. In the Battle of the Somme in the summer of 1916, the British and French gained an insignificant 125 square miles at the cost of 600,000 dead or wounded, and the Germans lost 500,000 men. In that same year, the unsuccessful German campaign against Verdun cost 700,000 lives on both sides. British poet Siegfried Sassoon (1886–1967) wrote of the Somme offensive, "I am staring at a sunlit picture of Hell."

The year 1917 was equally terrible. The hero of Erich Remarque's great novel *All Quiet on the Western Front* (1929) describes a typical attack:

We see men living with their skulls blown open; we see soldiers run with their two feet cut off. . . . Still the little piece of convulsed earth in which we lie is held. We have yielded no more than a few hundred yards of it as a prize to the enemy. But on every yard there lies a dead man.

Such was war on the western front.

The war of the trenches shattered an entire generation of young men. Millions who could have provided political creativity and leadership after the

❀ **MAP 29.3 The First World War in Europe**
Trench warfare on the western front was concentrated in Belgium and northern France. The war in the east encompassed an enormous territory.

The Fruits of War   The extent of the carnage, the emotional damage, and the physical destruction on the western front were all unprecedented. Once-great cathedrals standing in ruin symbolized the disaster. *(Source: UPI/Bettmann Newsphotos)*

war were forever missing. Moreover, those who lived through the holocaust were maimed, shell-shocked, embittered, and profoundly disillusioned. The young soldiers went to war believing in the world of their leaders and elders—the pre-1914 world of order, progress, and patriotism. Then, in Remarque's words, the "first bombardment showed us our mistake, and under it the world as they had taught it to us broke in pieces."

The Widening War

On the eastern front, slaughter did not degenerate into suicidal trench warfare. With the outbreak of

the war, the "Russian steamroller" immediately moved into eastern Germany. Very badly damaged by the Germans under General Paul von Hindenburg and General Erich Ludendorff at the Battle of Tannenberg and the Battle of the Masurian Lakes in August and September 1914, Russia never threatened Germany again (see Map 29.3). On the Austrian front, enormous armies seesawed back and forth, suffering enormous losses. Austro-Hungarian armies were repulsed twice by little Serbia in bitter fighting. But with the help of German forces, they reversed the Russian advances of 1914 and forced the Russians to retreat deep into their own territory in the eastern campaign of 1915.

A staggering 2.5 million Russians were killed, wounded, or taken prisoner that year.

These changing tides of victory and hopes of territorial gains brought neutral countries into the war. Italy, a member of the Triple Alliance since 1882, had declared its neutrality in 1914 on the grounds that Austria had launched a war of aggression. Then, in May 1915, Italy joined the Triple Entente of Great Britain, France, and Russia in return for promises of Austrian territory. Bulgaria also declared its neutrality in 1914. But after the Ottoman Empire joined in October 1914 with Austria and Germany, by then known as the Central Powers, Bulgaria weighed enticing promises from all sides. In September 1915 it decided to follow the Ottoman Empire's lead in order to settle old scores with Serbia. Bulgarian and German armies were successful, and the Central Powers occupied all of the Balkans, with the exception of Greece (see Map 29.3).

The entry of the Ottoman Turks carried the war into the Middle East, a momentous development. Heavy fighting with Russia saw bloody battle lines seesawing back and forth. In 1915 British forces tried to take the Dardanelles and Constantinople from Turkey but were badly defeated. The British were more successful at inciting Arab nationalists against their Turkish overlords. An enigmatic British colonel, soon known to millions as Lawrence of Arabia, helped lead the Arab revolt in early 1917. In 1918 British armies totally smashed the old Ottoman state, drawing primarily on imperial forces from Egypt, India, Australia, and New Zealand. Thus war brought revolutionary change to the Middle East (see pages 996, 999).

War also spread to some parts of East Asia and Africa. Instead of revolting as the Germans hoped, the colonial subjects of the British and French supported their foreign masters, providing critical supplies and fighting in armies in Europe and in the Ottoman Empire. They also helped local British and French commanders seize Germany's colonies around the globe. The Japanese, allied in Asia with the British since 1902, similarly used the war to grab German outposts in the Pacific Ocean and on the Chinese mainland, infuriating Chinese patriots and heightening long-standing tensions between China and Japan.

Another crucial development in the expanding conflict came in April 1917 when the United States declared war on Germany. American intervention grew out of the war at sea, sympathy for the Triple Entente, and the increasing desperation of total war. At the beginning of the war, Britain and France had established a total naval blockade to strangle the Central Powers. No neutral ship was permitted to sail to Germany with any cargo. The blockade annoyed Americans, but effective propaganda about German atrocities in occupied Belgium as well as lush profits from selling war supplies to Britain and France blunted American indignation.

Moreover, in early 1915 Germany launched a counter-blockade using the murderously effective submarine, a new weapon that sank ships without traditional niceties of fair warning under international law. In May 1915, a German submarine sank the British passenger liner *Lusitania,* which was also carrying arms and munitions. More than a thousand lives, among them 139 Americans, were lost. President Woodrow Wilson protested vigorously. Germany was forced to relax its submarine warfare for almost two years; the alternative was almost certain war with the United States.

Early in 1917, the German military command—confident that improved submarines could starve Britain into submission before the United States could come to its rescue—resumed unrestricted submarine warfare. Like the invasion of Belgium, this was a reckless gamble. "German submarine warfare against commerce," President Wilson told a sympathetic Congress and people, "is a warfare against mankind." Thus the last uncommitted great nation, as fresh and enthusiastic as Europe had been in 1914, entered the world war in April 1917, almost three years after it began. Eventually the United States was to tip the balance in favor of the Triple Entente and its allies.

 THE HOME FRONT

Before looking at the last year of the Great War, let us turn our attention to the people on the home front. They were tremendously involved in the titanic struggle. War's impact on them was no less massive than on the men crouched in the trenches.

Mobilizing for Total War

In August 1914 most people had greeted the outbreak of hostilities enthusiastically. In every country the masses believed that their nation was in the right and was defending itself from aggression. With the exception of a few extreme left-wingers, even socialists supported the war. A German socialist volunteered for the front, explaining to fellow members of the Reichstag that "to shed one's blood for the fatherland is not difficult: it is enveloped in romantic heroism."[3] Everywhere the support of the masses and working class contributed to national unity and an energetic war effort.

By mid-October generals and politicians had begun to realize that more than patriotism would be needed to win the war, whose end was not in sight. Each country experienced a relentless, desperate demand for men and weapons. And each quickly faced countless shortages, for prewar Europe had depended on foreign trade and a great international division of labor. In each country economic life and organization had to change and change fast to keep the war machine from sputtering to a stop. And change they did.

In each country a government of national unity began to plan and control economic and social life in order to wage "total war." Free-market capitalism was abandoned, at least "for the duration." Instead, government planning boards established priorities and decided what was to be produced and consumed. Rationing, price and wage controls, and even restrictions on workers' freedom of movement were imposed by government. Only through such regimentation could a country make the greatest possible military effort. Thus, though there were national variations, the great nations all moved toward planned economies commanded by the established political leadership.

The economy of total war blurred the old distinction between soldiers on the battlefield and civilians at home. The war was a war of whole peoples and entire populations. Based on tremendously productive industrial economies not confined to a single nation, total war yielded an effective—and therefore destructive—war effort on all sides.

However awful the war was, the ability of governments to manage and control highly complicated economies strengthened the cause of socialism. With the First World War, socialism became for the first time a realistic economic blueprint rather than a utopian program. Germany illustrates the general trend. It also went furthest in developing a planned economy to wage total war.

As soon as war began, the talented, foresighted, Jewish industrialist Walter Rathenau convinced the German government to set up the War Raw Materials Board to ration and distribute raw materials. Under Rathenau's direction, every useful material from foreign oil to barnyard manure was inventoried and rationed. Moreover, the board launched successful attempts to produce substitutes, such as synthetic rubber and synthetic nitrates, needed to make explosives and essential to the blockaded German war machine. Food was also rationed in accordance with physical need. Men and women doing hard manual work were given extra rations. During the last two years of the war, only children and expectant mothers received milk rations. At the same time, Germany failed to tax the war profits of private firms heavily enough. This failure contributed to massive deficit financing, inflation, the growth of a black market, and the eventual reemergence of class conflict.

Following the terrible battles of Verdun and the Somme in 1916, Chancellor Bethmann-Hollweg was driven from office in 1917 by military leaders Hindenburg and Ludendorff, who became the real rulers of Germany. They decreed the ultimate mobilization for total war: all agriculture, industry, and labor must be "used exclusively for the conduct of War."[4] Thus in December 1916, military leaders rammed through the Reichstag the Auxiliary Service Law, which required all males between seventeen and sixty to work only at jobs considered critical to the war effort.

Although women and children were not specifically mentioned, this forced-labor law was also aimed at them. Many women already worked in war factories, mines, and steel mills, where they labored, like men, at the heaviest and most dangerous jobs. With the passage of the Auxiliary Service Law, many more women followed. Children were organized by their teachers into garbage brigades to collect every scrap of useful materials: grease strained from dishwater, coffee grounds, waste paper, tin cans, metal door knockers, bottles, rags, hair, bones, and so forth, as well as acorns, chestnuts, pine cones, and rotting leaves. Potatoes gave way to turnips, and people averaged little more than 1,000 calories a day. Thus in Germany total war led to the establishment of history's first "totalitarian" society, and war production increased while some people starved to death.

Waging Total War   A British war plant strains to meet the insatiable demand for trench-smashing heavy artillery shells. Quite typically, many of these defense workers are women. *(Source: By courtesy of the Trustees of the Imperial War Museum)*

Great Britain mobilized for total war less rapidly and less completely than Germany, for it could import materials from its empire and from the United States. By 1915, however, a serious shortage of shells had led to the establishment of the Ministry of Munitions under David Lloyd George. The ministry organized private industry to produce for the war, controlled profits, allocated labor, fixed wage rates, and settled labor disputes. By December 1916 the British economy was largely planned and regulated directly by the state. Subsequently, even food was strictly rationed, while war production continued to soar. Great Britain had followed successfully in Germany's footsteps.

The Social Impact

The social impact of total war was no less profound than the economic impact, though again there were important national variations. The insatiable needs of the military created a tremendous de-

mand for workers. Jobs were available for everyone. This situation—seldom, if ever, seen before 1914, when unemployment and poverty had been facts of urban life—brought about momentous changes.

One such change was greater power and prestige for labor unions. Having proved their loyalty in August 1914, labor unions cooperated with war governments on work rules, wages, and production schedules in return for real participation in important decisions. This entry of labor leaders into policy-making councils paralleled the entry of socialist leaders into the war governments.

The role of women changed dramatically. In every country large numbers of women left home and domestic service to work in industry, transportation, and offices. Moreover, women became highly visible—not only as munitions workers but as bank tellers, mail carriers, even police officers. Women also served as nurses and doctors at the front. In general, the war greatly expanded the range of women's activities and changed attitudes toward women. As a direct result of women's many-sided war effort, Britain, Germany, and Austria granted women the right to vote immediately after the war. Women also showed a growing spirit of independence during the war, as they started to bob their hair, shorten their skirts, and smoke in public.

War promoted greater social equality, blurring class distinctions and lessening the gap between rich and poor. This blurring was most apparent in Great Britain, where wartime hardship was never extreme. In fact, the bottom third of the population generally lived better than they ever had, for the poorest gained most from the severe shortage of labor. English writer Robert Roberts recalled how his parents' tiny grocery store in the slums of Manchester thrived during the war as never before when people who had scrimped to buy bread and soup bones were able to afford fancy cakes and thick steaks. In continental European countries greater equality was reflected in full employment, rationing according to physical needs, and a sharing of hardships. There, too, society became more uniform and more egalitarian, in spite of some war profiteering.

Finally, death itself had no respect for traditional social distinctions. It savagely decimated both the young aristocratic officers who led the charge and the mass of drafted peasants and unskilled workers who followed. Death, however, often spared the aristocrats of labor—the skilled workers and fore-

Wartime Propaganda   The poster on the left celebrates African Army Day and tells French civilians that loyal troops from Africa and the colonies will help turn the tide against Germany. The German poster on the right draws upon a rich historical image, linking the brave German knight who slew the dragon with an appeal to patriotic citizens to buy yet another series of war bonds. *(Source: By courtesy of the Trustees of the Imperial War Museum)*

men. Their lives were too valuable to squander at the front, for they were needed to train the newly recruited women and older unskilled men laboring valiantly in war plants at home.

Growing Political Tensions

During the first two years of war, most soldiers and civilians supported their governments. Even in Austria-Hungary—the most vulnerable of the belligerents, with its competing nationalities—loyalty to the state and monarchy remained astonishingly strong through 1916. Belief in a just cause, patriotic nationalism, the planned economy, and a sharing of burdens united peoples behind their various national leaders.

Each government employed rigorous censorship to control public opinion and to bolster morale. And each used both crude and subtle propaganda to maintain popular support. German propaganda hysterically pictured black soldiers from France's African empire raping German women. The French and British ceaselessly recounted and exaggerated German atrocities in Belgium and elsewhere. Patriotic posters and slogans, slanted news, and biased editorials inflamed national hatreds and helped sustain superhuman efforts.

By the spring of 1916, however, people were beginning to crack under the strain of total war. In April 1916 Irish nationalists in Dublin tried to take advantage of this situation and rose up against British rule in their great Easter Rebellion. A week of bitter fighting passed before the rebels were crushed and their leaders executed. Strikes and protest marches over inadequate food began to flare up on every home front. Soldiers' morale began to decline. Italian troops mutinied. Numerous French units refused to fight for a time after General Robert Nivelle's disastrous offensive of May 1917. A rising tide of war-weariness and defeatism also swept France's civilian population before Georges Clemenceau emerged as a ruthless and effective wartime leader in November 1917. Clemenceau (1841–1929) established a virtual dictatorship, pouncing on strikers and jailing without trial journalists and politicians who dared to suggest a compromise peace with Germany.

The strains were worse for the Central Powers. In October 1916 the chief minister of Austria was assassinated by a young socialist crying, "Down with Absolutism! We want peace!"[5] The following month, when feeble old Emperor Francis Joseph

died, a symbol of unity disappeared. In spite of absolute censorship, political dissatisfaction and conflicts among nationalities grew. Both Czech and Yugoslav leaders demanded autonomous democratic states for their peoples. In April 1917 Austria's chief minister summed up the situation in the gloomiest possible terms. The country and army were exhausted. Another winter of war would bring revolution and disintegration.

The strain of total war and of the Auxiliary Service Law was also evident in Germany. By 1917 the national political unity of the first two years of war was collapsing as the social conflict of prewar Germany re-emerged. A growing minority of socialists in the Reichstag began to vote against war credits. In July 1917 a coalition of socialists and Catholics passed a resolution in the Reichstag calling for a compromise "peace without annexations or reparations." Such a peace was unthinkable for conservatives and military leaders. So also was the surge in revolutionary agitation and strikes by war-weary workers that occurred in early 1917. When the bread ration was further reduced in April, more than 200,000 workers struck and demonstrated for a week in Berlin, returning to work only under the threat of prison and military discipline. Thus militaristic Germany, like its ally Austria-Hungary (and its enemy France), was beginning to crack in 1917. But it was Russia that collapsed first and saved the Central Powers—for a time.

❖ THE RUSSIAN REVOLUTION

The Russian Revolution of 1917, directly related to the growing tensions of World War I, had a significance far beyond the wartime agonies of a single European nation. The Russian Revolution opened a new era. For some, it was Marx's socialist vision come true; for others, it was the triumph of dictatorship. To all, it presented a radically new prototype of state and society.

The Fall of Imperial Russia

Like its allies and its enemies, Russia embraced war with patriotic enthusiasm in 1914. At the Winter Palace, while throngs of people knelt and sang "God Save the Tsar," Tsar Nicholas II (r. 1894–1917) repeated the oath Alexander I had sworn in 1812 and vowed never to make peace as long as the enemy stood on Russian soil. Russia's lower

Family Portrait   With husband Nicholas II standing behind, the beautiful but tense Alexandra shows one of her daughters, who could not inherit the throne, to her grandmother, Queen Victoria of Britain, and Victoria's son, the future Edward VII. European monarchs were closely related by blood and breeding before 1914. *(Source: Nicholas A. de Basily Collection, Hoover Institution)*

house, the Duma, voted war credits. Conservatives anticipated expansion in the Balkans. Liberals and most socialists believed alliance with Britain and France would bring democratic reforms. For a moment, Russia was united. But soon the strains of war began to take their toll.

Unprecedented artillery barrages used up Russia's supplies of shells and ammunition, and better-equipped German armies inflicted terrible losses. In 1915, substantial numbers of Russian soldiers were sent to the front without rifles; they were told to find their arms among the dead. There were 2 million Russian casualties in 1915 alone. Nevertheless, Russia's battered peasant army continued to fight courageously, and Russia moved toward full mobilization on the home front. The Duma and organs of local government took the lead, setting

up special committees to coordinate defense, industry, transportation, and agriculture. These efforts improved the military situation, and Russian factories produced more than twice as many shells in 1916 as in 1915. Yet there were many failures, and Russia mobilized less effectively for total war than the other warring nations.

The great problem was leadership. Under the constitution resulting from the revolution of 1905 (see pages 873–874), the tsar had retained complete control over the bureaucracy and the army. Legislation proposed by the Duma, which was weighted in favor of the wealthy and conservative classes, was subject to the tsar's veto. Moreover, Nicholas II fervently wished to maintain the sacred inheritance of supreme royal power, which, with the Orthodox church, was for him the key to Russia's greatness. A kindly, slightly stupid man, of whom a friend said he "would have been an ideal country gentleman, devoting his life to wife and children, his farms and his sport," Nicholas failed to form a close partnership with his citizens in order to fight the war more effectively. He relied instead on the old bureaucratic apparatus, distrusting the moderate Duma, rejecting popular involvement, and resisting calls to share power.

As a result, the Duma, the educated middle classes, and the masses became increasingly critical of the tsar's leadership. Following Nicholas's belated dismissal of the incompetent minister of war, demands for more democratic and responsive government exploded in the Duma in the summer of 1915. In September parties ranging from conservative to moderate socialist formed the Progressive Bloc, which called for a completely new government responsible to the Duma instead of to the tsar. In answer, Nicholas temporarily adjourned the Duma and announced that he was traveling to the front in order to lead and rally Russia's armies.

His departure was a fatal turning point. With the tsar in the field with the troops, control of the government was taken over by the hysterical empress, Tsarina Alexandra, and a debauched adventurer, the monk Rasputin. A minor German princess and granddaughter of England's Queen Victoria, Nicholas's wife was a devoted mother with a sick child, a strong-willed woman with a hatred of parliaments. Having constantly urged her husband to rule absolutely, Alexandra herself tried to do so in his absence. She seated and unseated the top ministers. Her most trusted adviser was "our Friend Grigori," an uneducated Siberian preacher who was appropriately nicknamed "Rasputin"—the "Degenerate."

Rasputin began his career with a sect noted for mixing sexual orgies with religious ecstasies, and his influence rested on mysterious healing powers. Alexis, Alexandra's fifth child and heir to the throne, suffered from a rare disease, hemophilia. The tiniest cut meant uncontrollable bleeding, terrible pain, and possible death. Medical science could do nothing. Only Rasputin could miraculously stop the bleeding, perhaps through hypnosis. The empress's faith in Rasputin was limitless. "Believe more in our Friend," she wrote her husband in 1916. "He lives for you and Russia." In this atmosphere of unreality, the government slid steadily toward revolution.

In a desperate attempt to right the situation and end unfounded rumors that Rasputin was the empress's lover, three members of the high aristocracy murdered Rasputin in December 1916. The empress went into semipermanent shock, her mind haunted by the dead man's prophecy: "If I die or you desert me, in six months you will lose your son and your throne."[6] Food shortages in the cities worsened; morale declined. On March 8 women calling for bread in Petrograd (formerly St. Petersburg) started riots, which spontaneously spread throughout the city. From the front the tsar ordered troops to restore order, but discipline broke down, and the soldiers joined the revolutionary crowd. The Duma responded by declaring a provisional government on March 12, 1917. Three days later, Nicholas abdicated.

The Provisional Government

The March revolution was joyfully accepted throughout the country. The patriotic upper and middle classes rejoiced at the prospect of a more determined and effective war effort. Workers happily anticipated better wages and more food. All classes and political parties called for liberty and democracy. They were not disappointed. After generations of arbitrary authoritarianism, the provisional government quickly established equality before the law; freedom of religion, speech, and assembly; the right of unions to organize and strike; and the rest of the classic liberal program.

But both the liberal and the moderate socialist leaders of the provisional government rejected social revolution. The reorganized government formed in May 1917, which included the fiery agrarian socialist Alexander Kerensky, who became prime minister in July, refused to confiscate large landholdings and give them to peasants, fearing that such drastic action in the countryside would only complete the disintegration of Russia's peasant army. For the patriotic Kerensky as for other moderate socialists, the continuation of war was still the all-important national duty. There would be plenty of time for land reform later, and thus all the government's efforts were directed toward a last offensive in July. Human suffering and war-weariness grew, sapping the limited strength of the provisional government.

From its first day, the provisional government had to share power with a formidable rival—the Petrograd Soviet (or council) of Workers' and Soldiers' Deputies. Modeled on the revolutionary soviets of 1905, the Petrograd Soviet was a huge, fluctuating mass meeting of from two to three thousand workers, soldiers, and socialist intellectuals. This counter- or half-government issued its own radical orders, further weakening the provisional government. Most famous of these was Army Order No. 1, which stripped officers of their authority and placed power in the hands of elected committees of common soldiers.

Army Order No. 1 led to a total collapse of army discipline. Many an officer was hanged for his sins. Meanwhile, following the foolhardy summer offensive, masses of peasant soldiers began "voting with their feet," to use Lenin's graphic phrase. They began returning to their villages to help their families get a share of the land, which peasants were simply seizing as they settled old scores in a great agrarian upheaval. All across the country, liberty was turning into anarchy in the summer of 1917. It was an unparalleled opportunity for the most radical and most talented of Russia's many socialist leaders, Vladimir Ilyich Lenin (1870–1924).

Lenin and the Bolshevik Revolution

From his youth, Lenin's whole life had been dedicated to the cause of revolution. Born into the middle class, Lenin became an implacable enemy of imperial Russia when his older brother was executed for plotting to kill the tsar in 1887. As a law student Lenin began searching for a revolutionary faith. He found it in Marxian socialism. Exiled to Siberia for three years because of socialist agitation, Lenin studied Marxian doctrines with religious intensity. After his release, this young priest of socialism joined fellow believers in western Europe. There he lived for seventeen years and developed his own revolutionary interpretations of the body of Marxian thought.

Three interrelated ideas were central for Lenin. First, turning to the early fire-breathing Marx of 1848 and the *Communist Manifesto* for inspiration, Lenin stressed that capitalism could be destroyed only by violent revolution. He tirelessly denounced all revisionist theories of a peaceful evolution to socialism as betraying Marx's message of unending class conflict. Lenin's second, more original, idea was that a socialist revolution was possible even in a country like Russia, where capitalism was not fully developed. There the industrial working class was small, but the peasants were poor and thus potential revolutionaries.

Lenin believed that at a given moment revolution was determined more by human leadership than by vast historical laws. Thus was born his third basic idea: the necessity of a highly disciplined workers' party, strictly controlled by a dedicated elite of intellectuals and full-time revolutionaries like Lenin himself. Unlike ordinary workers and trade-union officials, this elite would never be seduced by short-term gains. It would not stop until revolution brought it to power.

Lenin's theories and methods did not go unchallenged by other Russian Marxists. At meetings of the Russian Social Democratic Labor party in London in 1903, matters came to a head. Lenin demanded a small, disciplined, elitist party; his opponents wanted a more democratic party with mass membership. The Russian party of Marxian socialism promptly split into two rival factions.

Mass Demonstrations in Petrograd in June 1917   In this surge of working-class support for the Bolsheviks, the few banners of the Mensheviks and other moderate socialists are drowned in a sea of Bolshevik slogans. *(Source: Sovfoto)*

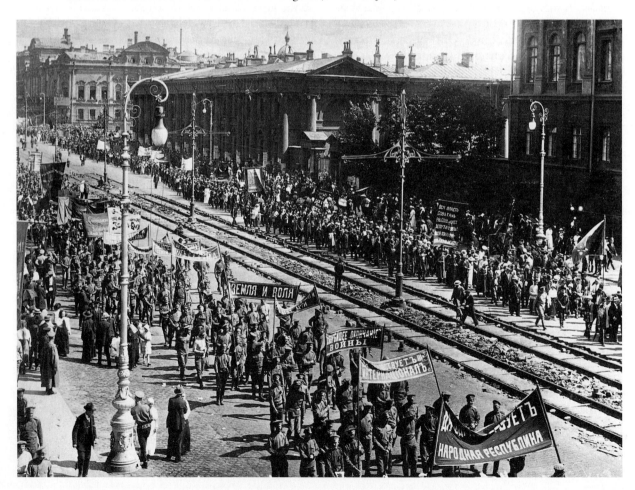

THE RUSSIAN REVOLUTION 979

Lenin's camp was called *Bolsheviks,* or "majority group"; his opponents were *Mensheviks,* or "minority group." Lenin's majority did not last, but Lenin did not care. He kept the fine-sounding name Bolshevik and developed the party he wanted: tough, disciplined, revolutionary.

Lenin, from neutral Switzerland, saw the war as a product of imperialistic rivalries and as a marvelous opportunity for class war and socialist upheaval. After the March revolution, the German government provided the impatient Lenin, his wife, and about twenty trusted colleagues with safe passage across Germany and back into Russia in April 1917. The Germans hoped that Lenin would undermine Russia's sagging war effort. They were not disappointed.

Arriving triumphantly at Petrograd's Finland Station on April 3, Lenin attacked at once. To the great astonishment of the local Bolsheviks, he rejected all cooperation with the "bourgeois" provisional government of the liberals and moderate socialists. His slogans were radical in the extreme: "All power to the soviets"; "All land to the peasants"; "Stop the war now." Never a slave to Marxian determinism, the brilliant but not unduly intellectual Lenin was a superb tactician. The moment was now.

Yet Lenin almost overplayed his hand. An attempt by the Bolsheviks to seize power in July collapsed, and Lenin fled and went into hiding. He was charged with being a German agent, and indeed he and the Bolsheviks were getting money from Germany.[7] But no matter. In September commander-in-chief General Lavr Kornilov, a popular war hero "with the heart of a lion and the brains of a sheep," led a feeble attack against the provisional government. In the face of this rightist "counter-revolutionary" threat, the Bolsheviks were rearmed and redeemed. Kornilov's forces disintegrated, but Kerensky lost all credit with the army, the only force that might have saved him and democratic government in Russia.

Throughout the summer, the Bolsheviks markedly increased their popular support, and in October they gained a fragile majority in the Petrograd Soviet. It was now Lenin's supporter Leon Trotsky (1879–1940), a spellbinding revolutionary orator and independent radical Marxist, who brilliantly executed the Bolshevik seizure of power.

Painting a vivid but untruthful picture of German and counter-revolutionary plots, Trotsky first convinced the Petrograd Soviet to form a special military-revolutionary committee in October and make him its leader. Military power in the capital passed into Bolshevik hands. Trotsky then insisted that the Bolsheviks take power in the name not of the Bolsheviks but of the more popular and democratic soviets, which were meeting in Petrograd from all over Russia in early November. On the night of November 6, militants from Trotsky's committee joined with trusty Bolshevik soldiers to seize government buildings and pounce on members of the provisional government. Then they went on to the congress of soviets. There a Bolshevik majority—roughly 390 of 650 turbulent delegates—declared that all power had passed to the soviets and named Lenin head of the new government, which was soon named the Union of Soviet Socialist Republics, or Soviet Union for short.

The Bolsheviks came to power for three key reasons. First, by late 1917 democracy had given way to anarchy: power was there for those who would take it. Second, in Lenin and Trotsky the Bolsheviks had an utterly determined and truly superior leadership. Third, in 1917 the Bolsheviks succeeded in appealing to many soldiers and urban workers, people who were exhausted by war and eager for socialism. With time, many workers would become bitterly disappointed, but for the moment they had good reason to believe that they had won what they wanted.

Dictatorship and Civil War

History is full of short-lived coups and unsuccessful revolutions. The truly monumental accomplishment of Lenin, Trotsky, and the rest of the Bolsheviks was not taking power but keeping it and conquering the chaos they had helped create. How was this done?

Lenin had the genius to profit from developments over which he and the Bolsheviks had no control. Since summer, a peasant revolution had been sweeping across Russia as the tillers of the soil invaded and divided among themselves the estates of the landlords and the church. Peasant seizure of the land was not very Marxian, but it was unstoppable in 1917. Thus Lenin's first law, which supposedly gave land to the peasants, actually merely approved what peasants were already doing. Urban workers' great demand in November was direct control of individual factories by local workers' committees. This, too, Lenin rectified with a decree in November.

Vladimir Lenin Displaying his determination and skill as a revolutionary orator, Lenin in 1920 exhorts soldiers in the Red Army to defend the revolution in the last stage of the civil war. These units departing from Moscow will help retake Kiev and establish unshakable Bolshevik power in Ukraine and Belorussia. *(Source: Novosti)*

Lenin also acknowledged that Russia had lost the war with Germany and that the only realistic goal was peace at any price. That price was very high. Germany demanded in December 1917 that the Soviet government give up all its western territories. These areas were inhabited by Poles, Finns, Lithuanians, and other non-Russians—all those people who had been conquered by the tsars over three centuries and put into the "prisonhouse of nationalities," as Lenin had earlier called the Russian Empire.

At first, Lenin's fellow Bolsheviks would not accept such great territorial losses. But when German armies resumed their unopposed march into Russia in February 1918, Lenin had his way in a very close vote in the Central Committee of the party. A third of old Russia's population was sliced away by the German meat ax in the Treaty of Brest-Litovsk in March 1918. With peace, Lenin had escaped the certain disaster of continued war and could pursue his goal of absolute political power for the Bolsheviks—now renamed Communists—within Russia.

In November 1917 the Bolsheviks had cleverly proclaimed their regime only a "provisional workers' and peasants' government," promising that a freely elected Constituent Assembly would draw up a new constitution. But after the Bolsheviks won less than one-fourth of the elected delegates, the Constituent Assembly met for only one day, on January 18, 1918. It was then permanently disbanded by Bolshevik soldiers acting under Lenin's orders.

With the destruction of the democratically elected Constituent Assembly, people who had risen up for self-rule in November saw that once again they were getting dictatorship from the capital. For the next three years, "Long live the [democratic] soviets; down with the Bolsheviks" was to be a popular slogan. The officers of the old army took the lead in organizing the so-called White opposition to the Bolsheviks in southern Russia, Ukraine, Siberia, and west of Petrograd. The Whites came from many social groups and were united only by their hatred of the Bolsheviks—the Reds. By the end of 1918, White armies were on the attack. In October 1919 it appeared they might triumph, as they closed in on Lenin's government from three sides. Yet they did not. By the spring of 1920, the White armies had been almost completely defeated, and by the following year the civil war was over. Lenin had won.

Lenin and the Bolsheviks won for several reasons. Strategically, they controlled the center, while the Whites were always on the fringes and disunited. Moreover, the poorly defined political program of the Whites was vaguely conservative, and it did not unite all the foes of the Bolsheviks under a progressive, democratic banner. Most important, the Communists quickly developed a better army, an army for which the divided Whites were no match.

Once again, Trotsky's leadership was decisive. As war commissar Trotsky re-established the draft and the most drastic discipline for the newly formed Red Army. Soldiers deserting or disobeying an or-

der were summarily shot. Moreover, Trotsky effectively recruited former tsarist army officers. In short, he formed a disciplined and effective fighting force.

The Bolsheviks also mobilized the home front. Establishing "war communism"—the application of the total-war concept to a civil conflict—they seized grain from peasants, introduced rationing, nationalized all banks and industry, and required everyone to work. Although these measures contributed to a breakdown of normal economic activity, they also served to maintain labor discipline and to keep the Red Army supplied.

"Revolutionary terror" also contributed to the Communist victory. The old tsarist secret police was re-established as the Cheka, which hunted down and executed thousands of real or supposed foes, such as the tsar and his family and other "class enemies." Moreover, people were shot or threatened with being shot for minor nonpolitical failures. The terror caused by the secret police became a tool of the government. The Cheka sowed fear, and fear silenced opposition.

Finally, foreign military intervention in the civil war ended up helping the Communists. The Allies (the Americans, British, and Japanese) sent troops to Archangel and Vladivostok to prevent war material that they had sent to the provisional government from being captured by the Germans. After the Soviet government nationalized all foreign-owned factories without compensation and refused to pay all of Russia's foreign debts, Western governments, particularly that of France, began to support White armies. Yet these efforts were small and halfhearted. Allied intervention in the civil war did not aid the Whites effectively, though it did permit the Communists to appeal to the patriotic nationalism of ethnic Russians, in particular former tsarist army officers.

Together, the Russian Revolution and the Bolshevik triumph were one of the reasons why the First World War was such a great turning point in modern history. A radically new government, based on socialism and one-party dictatorship, came to power in a great European state, maintained power, and eagerly encouraged worldwide revolution. Although Russia was undoubtedly headed for some kind of political crisis before 1914, it is hard to imagine the triumph of the most radical proponents of change and reform except in a situation of total collapse. That was precisely what happened to Russia in the First World War.

THE RUSSIAN REVOLUTION

1914	Russia enthusiastically enters the First World War
1915	Two million Russian casualties Progressive Bloc calls for a new government responsible to the Duma rather than to the tsar Tsar Nicholas adjourns the Duma and departs for the front Strong influence of Alexandra and Rasputin on the government
December 1916	Murder of Rasputin
March 8, 1917	Bread riots in Petrograd (St. Petersburg)
March 12, 1917	Duma declares a provisional government
March 15, 1917	Tsar Nicholas abdicates without protest
April 3, 1917	Lenin returns from exile and denounces the provisional government
May 1917	Reorganized provisional government, including Kerensky, continues the war Petrograd Soviet issues Army Order no. 1, granting military power to committees of common soldiers
Summer 1917	Agrarian upheavals: peasants seize estates, peasant soldiers desert the army to participate
October 1917	Bolsheviks gain a majority in the Petrograd Soviet
November 6, 1917	Bolsheviks seize power Lenin heads the new "provisional workers' and peasants' government"
November 1917	Lenin accepts peasant seizure of land and worker control of factories All banks nationalized
January 1918	Lenin permanently disbands the Constituent Assembly
February 1918	Lenin convinces the Bolshevik Central Committee to accept a humiliating peace with Germany in order to safeguard the revolution
March 1918	Treaty of Brest-Litovsk: Russia loses one-third of its population Trotsky as war commissioner begins to rebuild the Russian army
1918–1920	Civil war between the Whites and the Reds
1919	White armies on the offensive but divided politically They receive little benefit from Allied intervention
1920	Lenin and Red armies victorious

 THE PEACE SETTLEMENT

Victory over revolutionary Russia boosted sagging German morale, and in the spring of 1918 the Germans launched their last major attack against France. This offensive, just like those before it, failed. With breathtaking rapidity, the United States, Great Britain, and France decisively defeated Germany militarily. Austria-Hungary and the Ottoman Empire broke apart and ceased to exist. The guns of world war finally fell silent. Then as civil war spread in Russia and as chaos engulfed much of eastern Europe, the victorious Western Allies came together in Paris to establish a lasting peace.

Expectations were high; optimism was almost unlimited. The Allies labored intensively and soon worked out terms for peace with Germany and for the creation of the peacekeeping League of Nations. Nevertheless, the hopes of peoples and politicians were soon disappointed, for the peace settlement of 1919 turned out to be a failure. Rather than creating conditions for peace, it sowed the seeds of another war. Surely this was the ultimate tragedy of the Great War, a war that directly and indirectly cost $332 billion and left 10 million people dead and another 20 million wounded. How did this tragedy happen? Why was the peace settlement unsuccessful?

The End of the War

In early 1917 the strain of total war was showing everywhere. After the Russian Revolution in March, there were major strikes in Germany. In July a coalition of moderates passed a "peace resolution" in the Reichstag, calling for peace without territorial annexations. To counter this moderation born of war-weariness, the German military established a virtual dictatorship. The military also aggressively exploited the collapse of Russian armies, winning great concessions in the Treaty of Brest-Litovsk.

With victory in the east quieting German moderates, General Ludendorff and company fell on France once more in the great spring offensive of 1918. For a time, German armies pushed forward, coming within thirty-five miles of Paris. But Ludendorff's exhausted, overextended forces never broke through. They were decisively stopped in July at the second Battle of the Marne, where

140,000 fresh American soldiers saw action. Adding 2 million men in arms to the war effort by August, the late but massive American intervention decisively tipped the scales in favor of Allied victory.

By September, British, French, and American armies were advancing steadily on all fronts, and on October 4 the emperor formed a new, more liberal German government to sue for peace. As negotiations over an armistice dragged on, an angry and frustrated German people finally rose up. On November 3 sailors in Kiel mutinied, and throughout northern Germany soldiers and workers began to establish revolutionary councils on the Russian soviet model. The same day Austria-Hungary surrendered to the Allies and began breaking apart. With army discipline collapsing, the German emperor abdicated and fled to Holland. Socialist leaders in Berlin proclaimed a German republic on November 9 and simultaneously agreed to tough Allied terms of surrender. The armistice went into effect on November 11, 1918. The war was over.

Military defeat brought political revolution to Austria-Hungary, as it had to Germany, Russia, and the Ottoman Empire (see pages 999–1000). In Austria-Hungary the revolution was primarily nationalistic and republican in character. Independent Austrian, Hungarian, and Czechoslovak republics were proclaimed, and a greatly expanded Serbian monarchy united the south Slavs and took the name Yugoslavia. The prospect of firmly establishing the new national states overrode class considerations for most people in east-central Europe.

The Treaty of Versailles

The peace conference opened in Paris in January 1919 with seventy delegates representing twenty-seven victorious nations. There were great expectations. A young British diplomat later wrote that the victors "believed in nationalism, we believed in the self-determination of peoples." Indeed, "we were journeying to Paris . . . to found a new order in Europe. We were preparing not Peace only, but Eternal Peace."[8] This general optimism and idealism had been greatly strengthened by President Wilson's January 1918 peace proposal, the Fourteen Points, which stressed national self-determination and the rights of small countries.

The real powers at the conference were the United States, Great Britain, and France, for Germany was not allowed to participate and Russia was locked in civil war and did not attend. Italy was considered one of the Big Four, but its role was quite limited. Almost immediately the three great Allies began to quarrel. President Wilson, who was wildly cheered by European crowds as the spokesman for a new idealistic and democratic international cooperation, was almost obsessed with creating the League of Nations. Wilson insisted that this question come first, for he passionately believed that only a permanent international organization could protect member states from aggression and avert future wars. Wilson had his way, although Lloyd George of Great Britain and especially Clemenceau of France were unenthusiastic. They were primarily concerned with punishing Germany.

Playing on British nationalism, Lloyd George had already won a smashing electoral victory in December on the popular platform of making Germany pay for the war. "We shall," the British prime minister promised, "squeeze the orange until the pips squeak." Personally inclined to make a somewhat moderate peace with Germany, Lloyd George was to a considerable extent a captive of demands for a total victory worthy of the sacrifices of total war against a totally depraved enemy. As Rudyard Kipling summed up the general British feeling at the end of the war, the Germans were "a people with the heart of beasts."[9]

France's Georges Clemenceau, "the Tiger" who had broken wartime defeatism and led his country to victory, wholeheartedly agreed. Like most French people, Clemenceau wanted old-fashioned revenge. He also wanted lasting security for France. This, he believed, required the creation of a buffer state between France and Germany, the permanent demilitarization of Germany, and vast German reparations. He feared that sooner or later Germany with its 60 million people would attack France with its 40 million, unless the Germans were permanently weakened. Moreover, France had no English Channel (or Atlantic Ocean) as a reassuring barrier against German aggression. Wilson, supported by Lloyd George, would hear none of this. Clemenceau's demands seemed vindictive, violating morality and the principle of national self-determination. By April the conference was deadlocked on the German question, and Wilson packed his bags to go home.

In the end, convinced that France should not break with its allies because France could not af-

ford to face Germany alone in the future, Clemenceau agreed to a compromise. He gave up the French demand for a Rhineland buffer state in return for a formal defensive alliance with the United States and Great Britain. Under the terms of this alliance, both Wilson and Lloyd George promised that their countries would come to France's aid in the event of a German attack. Thus Clemenceau appeared to win his goal of French security, as Wilson had won his of a permanent international organization. The Allies moved quickly to finish the settlement, believing that any adjustments would later be possible within the dual framework of a strong Western alliance and the League of Nations (Map 29.4).

The Treaty of Versailles between the Allies and Germany was the key to the settlement, and the terms were not unreasonable as a first step toward re-establishing international order (see Listening to the Past). (Had Germany won, it seems certain that France and Belgium would have been treated with greater severity, as Russia had been at Brest-Litovsk.) Germany's colonies were given to France, Britain, and Japan as League of Nations mandates. Germany's territorial losses within Europe were minor, thanks to Wilson. Alsace-Lorraine was returned to France. Parts of Germany inhabited primarily by Poles were ceded to the new Polish state, in keeping with the principle of national self-determination. Germany had to limit its army to 100,000 men and agree to build no military fortifications in the Rhineland.

More harshly, the Allies declared that Germany (with Austria) was responsible for the war and had therefore to pay reparations equal to all civilian damages caused by the war. This unfortunate and much-criticized clause expressed inescapable popular demands for German blood, but the actual figure was not set, and there was the clear possibility that reparations might be set at a reasonable level in the future when tempers had cooled.

When presented with the treaty, the German government protested vigorously. But there was no alternative, especially considering that Germany was still starving because the Allies had not yet lifted their naval blockade. On June 28, 1919, German representatives of the ruling moderate Social Democrats and the Catholic party signed the treaty in the Sun King's Hall of Mirrors at Versailles, where Bismarck's empire had been joyously proclaimed almost fifty years before.

**MAP 29.4 Shattered Empires and Territorial Changes After the First World
War**   The Great War brought tremendous changes in eastern Europe. New nations
were established, and a dangerous power vacuum was created between Germany and
Soviet Russia.

Separate peace treaties were concluded with the
other defeated powers—Austria, Hungary, Bulgaria, and Turkey. For the most part, these treaties
merely ratified the existing situation in east-central

Europe following the breakup of the Austro-
Hungarian Empire. Like Austria, Hungary was a
particularly big loser, as its "captive" nationalities
(and some interspersed Hungarians) were ceded to

Versailles, June 28, 1919   This group portrait by William Orpen features the three principal Allied leaders, seated in the center, who have finally reached an agreement. The scholarly Wilson is third from the left, next to the old tiger, Clemenceau of France, who is turned toward the strong-willed Lloyd George of Britain. *(Source: By courtesy of the Trustees of the Imperial War Museum)*

Romania, Czechoslovakia, Poland, and Yugoslavia. Italy got some Austrian territory. The Turkish empire was broken up. France received Lebanon and Syria. Britain took Iraq and Palestine, which was to include a Jewish national homeland first promised by Britain in 1917. Officially League of Nations mandates, these acquisitions of the Western powers were one of the most imperialistic elements of the peace settlement. Another was mandating Germany's holdings in China to Japan (see pages

1010–1012). The age of Western imperialism lived on. National self-determination remained a reality only for Europeans and their offspring.

American Rejection of the Versailles Treaty

The rapidly concluded peace settlement of early 1919 was not perfect, but within the context of war-shattered Europe it was an acceptable beginning. The principle of national self-determination, which had played such a large role in starting the war, was accepted and served as an organizing framework. Germany had been punished but not dismembered. A new world organization complemented a traditional defensive alliance of satisfied powers. The serious remaining problems could be worked out in the future. Moreover, Allied leaders had seen speed as essential for another reason: they detested Lenin and feared that his Bolshevik Revolution might spread. They realized that their best answer to Lenin's unending calls for worldwide upheaval was peace and tranquility for war-weary peoples.

There were, however, two great interrelated obstacles to such peace: Germany and the United States. Plagued by communist uprisings, reactionary plots, and popular disillusionment with losing the war at the last minute, Germany's moderate socialists and their liberal and Catholic supporters faced an enormous challenge. Like French republicans after 1871, they needed time (and luck) if they were to establish firmly a peaceful and democratic republic. Progress in this direction required understanding yet firm treatment of Germany by the victorious Western Allies, particularly by the United States.

However, the U.S. Senate and, to a lesser extent, the American people rejected Wilson's handiwork. Republican senators led by Henry Cabot Lodge refused to ratify the Treaty of Versailles without changes in the articles creating the League of Nations. The key issue was the League's power— more apparent than real—to require member states to take collective action against aggression. Lodge and others believed that this requirement gave away Congress's constitutional right to declare war. In failing health, Wilson, with narrow-minded self-righteousness, rejected all attempts at compromise. In doing so, he assured that the treaty would never be ratified by the United States in any form and that the United States would never join the League of Nations. Moreover, the Senate refused to ratify Wilson's defensive alliance with France and Great Britain. America turned its back on Europe.

The Wilson-Lodge fiasco and the new-found gospel of isolationism represented a tragic and cowardly renunciation of America's responsibility. Using America's action as an excuse, Great Britain, too, refused to ratify its defensive alliance with France. Bitterly betrayed by its allies, France stood alone. Very shortly France was to take actions against Germany that would feed the fires of German resentment and seriously undermine democratic forces in the new German republic. The great hopes of early 1919 had turned to ashes by the end of the year. The Western alliance had collapsed, and a grandiose plan for permanent peace had given way to a fragile truce. For this and for what came later, the United States must share a large part of the guilt.

SUMMARY

Why did World War I have such revolutionary consequences? Why was it such a great break with the past? World War I was, first of all, a war of committed peoples. In France, Britain, and Germany in particular, governments drew on genuine popular support. This support reflected not only the diplomatic origins of the war but also the way western European society had been unified under the nationalist banner in the later nineteenth century, despite the fears that the growing socialist movement aroused in conservatives. The relentlessness of total war helps explain why so many died, why so many were crippled physically and psychologically, and why Western civilization would in so many ways never be the same again. More concretely, the war swept away monarchs and multinational empires. National self-determination apparently triumphed, not only in Austria-Hungary but also in many of Russia's western borderlands. Except in Ireland and parts of Soviet Russia, the revolutionary dream of national unity, born of the French Revolution, had finally come true.

Two other revolutions were products of the war. In Russia the Bolsheviks established a radical regime, smashed existing capitalist institutions, and stayed in power with a new kind of authoritarian rule. Whether the new Russian regime was truly rule. Whether the new Russian regime was truly Marxian or socialist was questionable, but it indisputably posed a powerful, ongoing revolutionary challenge to Europe and its colonial empires.

More subtle but quite universal in its impact was an administrative revolution. This revolution, born of the need to mobilize entire societies and economies for total war, greatly increased the power of government in the West. And after the guns grew still, government planning and wholesale involvement in economic and social life did not disappear in Europe. Liberal market capitalism and a well-integrated world economy were among the many casualties of the administrative revolution, and greater social equality was everywhere one of its results. Thus even in European countries where a communist takeover never came close to occurring, society still experienced a great revolution.

Finally, the "war to end war" brought not peace but only a fragile truce. In the West the Allies failed to maintain their wartime solidarity. Germany remained unrepentant and would soon have more grievances to nurse. Moreover, the victory of national self-determination in eastern Europe created a power vacuum between a still-powerful Germany and a potentially mighty communist Russia. A vast area lay open to military aggression from two sides.

NOTES

1. M. Beloff, quoted in *U.S. News & World Report,* March 8, 1976, p. 53.
2. Quoted in J. Remak, *The Origins of World War I* (New York: Holt, Rinehart and Winston, 1967), p. 84.
3. Quoted in J. E. Rodes, *The Quest for Unity: Modern Germany, 1848–1970* (New York: Holt, Rinehart and Winston, 1971), p. 178.
4. Quoted in F. P. Chambers, *The War Behind the War, 1914–1918* (London: Faber & Faber, 1939), p. 168.
5. Quoted in R. O. Paxton, *Europe in the Twentieth Century* (New York: Harcourt Brace Jovanovich, 1975), p. 109.
6. Quoted in Chambers, *The War Behind the War, 1914–1918,* pp. 302, 304.
7. A. B. Ulam, *The Bolsheviks* (New York: Collier Books, 1968), p. 349.
8. H. Nicolson, *Peacemaking 1919* (New York: Grosset & Dunlap Universal Library, 1965), pp. 8, 31–32.
9. Quoted ibid., p. 24.

SUGGESTED READING

O. Hale, *The Great Illusion, 1900–1914* (1971), is a thorough account of the prewar era. Remak's volume cited in the Notes; J. Joll, *The Origins of the First World War* (1992); and L. Lafore, *The Long Fuse* (1971), are recommended studies of the causes of the First World War. A. J. P. Taylor, *The Struggle for Mastery in Europe, 1848–1919* (1954), is an outstanding survey of diplomatic developments, with an exhaustive bibliography. V. Steiner, *Britain and the Origins of the First World War* (1978), and G. Kennan, *The Decline of Bismarck's European Order: Franco-Russian Relations, 1875–1890* (1979), are also major contributions. K. Jarausch's *The Enigmatic Chancellor* (1973) is an important recent study on Bethmann-Hollweg and German policy in 1914. C. Falls, *The Great War* (1961), is the best brief introduction to military aspects of the war. B. Tuchman, *The Guns of August* (1962), is a marvelous account of the dramatic first month of the war and the beginning of military stalemate. G. Ritter provides an able study in *The Schlieffen Plan* (1958). J. Winter, *The Experience of World War I* (1988), is a strikingly illustrated history of the war, and A. Horne, *The Price of Glory: Verdun 1916* (1979), is a moving account of the famous siege. J. Ellis, *Eye-Deep in Hell* (1976), is a vivid account of trench warfare, whereas J. Keegan's fascinating *Face of Battle* (1976) examines soldiers and warfare in a long-term perspective. V. Brittain's *Testament of Youth,* the moving autobiography of an English nurse in wartime, shows lives buffeted by new ideas and personal tragedies. A. Marwick, *War and Change in Twentieth-Century Europe* (1990), is a useful synthesis.

F. L. Carsten, *War Against War* (1982), considers radical movements in Britain and Germany. The best single volume on the home fronts is still the one by Chambers mentioned in the Notes. Chambers draws heavily on the many fine books on the social and economic impact of the war in different countries published by the Carnegie Endowment for International Peace under the general editorship of J. T. Shotwell. M. Higonnet, J. Jensen, and M. Weitz, eds., *Behind the Lines: Gender and the Two World Wars* (1987), examines the changes that the war brought for women and for relations between the sexes. A. Marwick, *The Deluge* (1970), is a lively account of war and society in Britain; G. Feldman, *Army, Industry, and Labor in Germany, 1914–1918* (1966), shows the impact of total war and military dictatorship on Germany. Three excellent collections of essays—R. Wall and J. Winter, eds., *The Upheaval of War: Family, Work, and Welfare in Europe, 1914–1918* (1988); J. Roth, ed., *World War I* (1967); and R. Albrecht-Carrié, ed., *The Meaning of the First World War* (1965)—probe the enormous consequences of the war for people and society. The debate over Germany's guilt and aggression, which has been reopened in recent years, may be best approached through G. Feldman, ed., *German Imperialism, 1914–1918* (1972), and A. Hillgruber, *Germany and the Two World Wars* (1981). M. Fainsod, *International Socialism and the World War* (1935), ably discusses the splits between radical and moderate socialists during the conflict. In addition to Erich Maria Remarque's great novel *All Quiet on the Western Front,* Henri Barbusse, *Under Fire* (1917), and Jules Romains, *Verdun* (1939), are highly recommended for their fictional yet realistic re-creations of the war. P. Fussell, *The Great War and Modern Memory* (1975), probes all the powerful literature inspired by the war. M. Ecksteins, *Rites of Spring: The Great War and the Birth of the Modern Age* (1989), is an imaginative cultural investigation that has won critical acclaim.

R. Suny and A. Adams, eds., *The Russian Revolution and Bolshevik Victory* (1990), presents a wide range of old and new interpretations. A. Ulam's work cited in the Notes, which focuses on Lenin, is a masterful introduction to the Russian Revolution, whereas S. Fitzpatrick, *The Russian Revolution* (1982), provides a provocative reconsideration. B. Wolfe, *Three Who Made a Revolution* (1955), a collective biography of Lenin, Trotsky, and Stalin, and R. Conquest, *V. I. Lenin* (1972), are recommended. L. Trotsky himself wrote the colorful and exciting *History of the Russian Revolution* (1932), which may be compared with the classic eyewitness account of the young, pro-Bolshevik American J. Reed, *Ten Days That Shook the World* (1919). R. Daniels, *Red October* (1969), provides a clear account of the Bolshevik seizure of power, and R. Pipes, *The Formation of the Soviet Union* (1968), is recommended for its excellent treatment of the nationality problem during the revolution. D. Koenker, W. Rosenberg, and R. Suny, eds., *Party, State and Society in the Russian Civil War* (1989), probes the social foundations of Bolshevik victory. A. Wildman, *The End of the Russian Imperial Army* (1980), is a fine account of the soldiers' revolt, and G. Leggett, *The Cheka: Lenin's Secret Police* (1981), shows revolutionary terror in action. Boris Pasternak's justly celebrated *Doctor Zhivago* is a great historical novel of the revolutionary era. R. Massie, *Nicholas and Alexandra* (1971), is a moving popular biography of Russia's last royal family and the terrible health problem of the heir to the throne. H. Nicolson's study listed in the Notes captures the spirit of the Versailles settlement. T. Bailey, *Woodrow Wilson and the Lost Peace* (1963), and W. Widenor, *Henry Cabot Lodge and the Search for an American Foreign Policy* (1981), are also highly recommended. A. Mayer provocatively stresses the influence of domestic social tensions and widespread

German War Aims and the Treaty of Versailles

Was Germany treated too harshly by the Allies in the Treaty of Versailles? Or before and during the First World War, was Germany pursuing reckless and aggressive policies that justified the victors' attempt to restrain Germany in 1919? Politicians and historians have long debated these questions.

Fresh controversies arose in the 1960s when young German historians argued that Germany not only was especially responsible for the outbreak of the First World War but also planned to impose brutal terms on its foes after they were defeated. A newly discovered memorandum, which was prepared on September 9, 1914, by German chancellor Bethmann-Hollweg after consulting with powerful business leaders, supported the young historians and attracted great interest. Bethmann-Hollweg's memorandum, which follows first (1), may be compared with key provisions from the June 28, 1919, Treaty of Versailles, excerpted second (2).

(1)

[The general aim is security] for the German Reich in west and east for all imaginable time. For this purpose France must be so weakened as to make her revival as a great power impossible for all time. Russia must be thrust back as far as possible from Germany's eastern frontier and her domination over the non-Russian vassal peoples [of the Russian empire] broken. . . .

1. *France.* . . . The [French iron] ore-field of Briey, which is necessary for the supply of ore for our industry, to be ceded [to Germany].

Further, a war indemnity, to be paid in installments; it must be high enough to prevent France from spending any considerable sums on armaments in the next 15–20 years.

Furthermore: a commercial treaty which makes France economically dependent on Germany, secures the French market for our exports and makes it possible to exclude British commerce from France. . . .

2. *Belgium.* . . . At any rate Belgium, even if allowed to continue to exist as a state, must be reduced to a vassal state, must allow us to occupy any militarily important ports, must place her coast at our disposal in military aspects, must become economically a German province. . . .

3. *Luxemburg.* [This country] will become a German federal state and will receive a strip of the present Belgian province of Luxemburg and perhaps the corner of Longwy [in France]. . . .

4. We must create a *central European economic association* through common custom treaties, to include France, Belgium, Holland, Denmark, Austria-Hungary, Poland, and perhaps Italy, Sweden and Norway. This association will not have any common constitutional supreme authority and all its members will be formally equal, but in practice will be under German leadership and must stabilize Germany's economic dominance over Mitteleuropa [central Europe].

5. *The question of colonial acquisitions,* where the first aim is the creation of a continuous Central African colonial empire, will be considered later . . . .

7. *Holland.* . . . [This country] must be left independent in externals, but be made internally dependent on us.

(2)

ARTICLE 42. Germany is forbidden to maintain or construct any fortifications either on the left bank of the Rhine or on the right bank to the west of a line drawn 50 kilometers to the East of the Rhine. . . .

ARTICLE 45. As compensation for the destruction of the coal mines in the north of France and as part payment towards the total reparation due from Germany for the damage resulting from the war, Germany cedes to France in full and absolute possession, with exclusive right of exploitation, unencumbered and free from all debts and charges of any kind, the coal mines situated in the Saar Basin. . . .

ARTICLE 49. Germany renounces in favor of the League of Nations, in the capacity of trustee, the government of the territory defined above [Saar Basin].

At the end of fifteen years . . . the inhabitants of the said territory shall be called upon to indicate the sovereignty under which they desire to be placed. . . .

ARTICLE 51. The territories [of Alsace and Lorraine] which were ceded to Germany [in 1871] . . . are restored to French sovereignty. . . .

ARTICLES 80, 81, AND 87. Germany acknowledges and will strictly respect the independence of Austria . . . [and] recognizes the complete independence of the Czecho-Slovak state . . . and of Poland. . . .

ARTICLE 116. Germany acknowledges and agrees to respect as permanent and inalienable the independence of all the territories which were part of the former Russian empire on August 1, 1914. . . .

ARTICLE 159. The German military forces shall be demobilized and reduced as prescribed hereinafter.

ARTICLE 160. . . . After that date [March 31, 1920] the total number of effectives in the Army of the States constituting Germany must not exceed 100,000 men, including officers and establishments of depots. The Army shall be devoted exclusively to the maintenance of order within the territory and to the control of the frontiers. . . .

ARTICLE 231. The Allied and Associated Governments affirm and Germany accepts the responsibility of Germany and her allies for causing all the loss and damage to which the Allied and Associated Governments and their nationals have been subjected as a consequence of the war imposed upon them by the aggression of Germany and her allies.

ARTICLE 232. The Allied and Associated Governments recognize that the resources of Germany are not adequate . . . to make complete reparation for all such loss and damage.

The Allied and Associated Governments, however, require, and Germany undertakes, that she will make compensation for all damage done to the civilian population of the Allied and Associated Power and to their property. . . .

ARTICLE 233. The amount of the above damage for which compensation is to be made

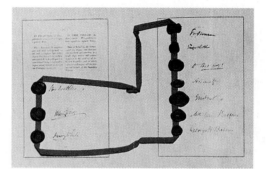

The last two pages of the Treaty of Versailles, with seals and signatures of participants. *(Source: Courtesy of the Trustees of the Imperial War Museum)*

by Germany shall be determined by an Inter-Allied Commission. . . . The findings of the commission as to the amount of damage defined as above shall be concluded and notified to the German Government on or before May 1, 1921. . . .

ARTICLE 428. As a guarantee for the execution of the present Treaty by Germany, the German territory situated to the west of the Rhine, together with the bridgeheads, will be occupied by Allied and Associated troops for a period of fifteen years from the coming into force of the present Treaty.

Questions for Analysis

1. How did Bethmann-Hollweg believe Germany should treat a defeated France? A defeated Belgium?

2. How would you characterize Bethmann-Hollweg's proposals in general?

3. Locate on Map 29.4 the territories discussed in the Treaty of Versailles. (The Saar is on Map 32.1.) Were the territorial changes imposed on Germany harsh or fair? Why or why not?

4. What measures were the Allies taking to enforce the treaty?

5. Imagine you are a lawyer. Prepare a defense of Germany's actions before and during World War I.

Source: F. Fischer, *Germany's Aims in the First World War* (New York: Norton, 1967) pp. 103–104; United States, Foreign Relations, *Treaty of Versailles, Paris Peace Conference, 1919* (Washington, D.C.: Government Printing Office, 1947).

Turks celebrating victory at Smyrna, October 1922. *(Source: Bettmann/Hulton)*

From Asia's perspective the First World War was largely a European civil war that shattered the united front of Western imperialism and convulsed prewar relationships throughout Asia. Most crucially, the war speeded the development of modern nationalism in Asia. Before 1914, the nationalist gospel of anti-imperialist political freedom and racial equality had already won converts among Asia's westernized, educated elites. In the 1920s and 1930s it increasingly won the allegiance of the masses. As in Europe in the nineteenth century, nationalism in Asia between 1914 and 1939 became a mass movement with potentially awesome power.

There were at least three reasons for the upsurge of nationalism in Asia. First and foremost, nationalism provided the most effective means of organizing the anti-imperialist resistance both to direct foreign rule and to indirect Western domination. Second, nationalism called for fundamental changes and challenged old political and social practices and beliefs. Thus modernizers used it as a weapon in their ongoing contest for influence and power with conservative traditionalists. Third, nationalism spread because it gave both leaders and followers a vision of a shining future for a rejuvenated people. Thus nationalism provided an ideology to ennoble the sacrifices that the struggle for rejuvenation would require.

The spread of nationalism also had its dark side. As in Europe (see page 812), nationalists in Asia developed a strong sense of "we" and "they." "They" were often the enemy—the oppressor. White-skinned European imperialists were just such a "they," and nationalist feeling generated the power to destroy European empires and challenge foreign economic domination. But, as in Europe, nationalism in Asia also stimulated bitter conflicts and wars between peoples, in two different ways.

First, it stimulated conflicts between relatively homogeneous peoples in large states, rallying, for example, Chinese against Japanese and vice versa. Second, nationalism often heightened tensions between ethnic (or religious) groups within states, especially states with a variety of peoples, like British India or the Ottoman Empire. Such states had been formed by authoritarian rulers and their armies and bureaucracies, very much like the Austrian or Russian empires before 1914. When their rigid rule declined or snapped, increasingly self-conscious and nationalistic peoples might easily quarrel, seeking to divide the existing state or to dominate the enemy "they" within its borders.

Although modern nationalism has everywhere exhibited certain shared characteristics, it has never been monolithic. In Asia especially, the range of historical experience has been enormous, and the new and often narrow ideology of nationalism was grafted onto old, rich, and complex civilizations. Between the outbreak of the First and Second World Wars each Asian country developed a distinctive national movement, rooted in its unique culture and history. Each nation's people created its own national reawakening, which renovated thought and culture as well as politics and economics.

- How did modern nationalism—the dominant force in most of the world in the twentieth century—develop in Asia between the First and Second World Wars?

- How did national movements arise in different countries, and how did some of these parallel movements come into brutal conflict?

These are the questions that this chapter seeks to answer.

❀ THE FIRST WORLD WAR AND WESTERN IMPERIALISM

Every Asian national movement shared in a burning desire for genuine freedom from foreign imperialism. The First World War had a profound effect on these aspirations by altering relations between Asia and Europe.

In the words of a distinguished Indian historian, "the Great War of 1914–1918 was from the Asian point of view a civil war within the European community of nations."[1] For four years Asians watched the haughty bearers of what Kipling had called "the White Man's Burden" (see page 901) vilifying and destroying each other. Far from standing united and supremely self-confident, the Western nations were clawing at each other in total disarray. The impact of this spectacle was enormous. Japan's defeat of imperial Russia in 1904 (see page 908) had shown that an Asian power could beat a European Great Power; now for the first time Asians saw the entire West as divided and vulnerable.

In the East Asian countries of China and Japan few people particularly cared who won the vicious family quarrel in distant Europe. In India and French Indochina enthusiasm was also limited, but the impact of the war was unavoidably greater. The British and the French were driven by the harsh logic of total war to draft their colonial subjects into the conflict. They uprooted hundreds of thousands of Asians to fight the Germans and the Ottoman Turks. This too had major consequences. An Indian or Vietnamese soldier who fought in France and came in contact there with democratic and republican ideas was likely to be less willing to accept foreign rule when he returned home.

The British and the French also made rash promises to gain the support of colonial peoples during the war. British leaders promised Jewish nationalists in Europe a homeland in Palestine even as they promised Arab nationalists independence from the Ottoman Empire. In India the British were forced in 1917 to announce a new policy of self-governing institutions in order to counteract Indian popular unrest fanned by wartime inflation and heavy taxation. After the war the nationalist genie that the colonial powers had called on refused to slip meekly back into the bottle.

The war aims of President Wilson also raised the hopes of peoples under imperial rule. In January 1918 Wilson proposed to make peace on the basis of his Fourteen Points (see page 983), whose key idea was national self-determination for the peoples of Europe and of the Ottoman Empire. Wilson also proposed that in all colonial questions "the interests of native populations be given equal weight with the desires of European governments," and he seemed to call for national self-rule. This subversive message had enormous appeal for educated Asians, fueling their hopes of freedom and dignity.

Military service and Wilsonian self-determination also fired the hopes of some Africans and some visionary American black supporters of African freedom. The First World War, however, had less impact on European imperialism in sub-Saharan Africa than in Asia and the Arab world. For sub-Saharan Africa, the Great Depression and the Second World War were to prove much more influential in the growth of nationalist movements (see pages 1156, 1157).

Once the Allies had won the war, they tried to shift gears and re-establish or increase their politi-cal and economic domination in Asia and Africa. Although fatally weakened, Western imperialism remained very much alive in 1918. Part of the reason for its survival was that President Wilson was certainly no revolutionary. At the Versailles Peace Conference he proved willing to compromise on colonial questions in order to achieve some of his European goals and the creation of the League of Nations. Also, Allied statesmen and ordinary French and British citizens quite rightly believed that their colonial empires had contributed to their ultimate victory over the Central Powers. They were in no mood to give up such valuable possessions voluntarily. Finally, the victors remained convinced of the superiority of their civilization. They believed that their rule was best for colonial peoples. A few "discontented" Asian or African intellectuals might agitate for self-rule, but Europeans generally believed that the "humble masses" were grateful for the law and order brought by the white man's administration. If pressed, Europeans said that such administration was preparing colonial subjects for eventual self-rule, but only in the distant future.

The compromise at Versailles between Wilson's vague, moralistic idealism and the European preoccupation with "good administration" was the establishment of a system of League of Nations mandates over Germany's former colonies and the old Ottoman Empire. Article 22 of the League of Nations Covenant, which was part of the Treaty of Versailles, assigned territories "inhabited by peoples incapable of governing themselves" to various "developed nations." "The well-being and development of such peoples" was declared "a sacred trust of civilization." A Permanent Mandates Commission was created to oversee the developed nations' fulfillment of their international responsibility; most of the members of the Permanent Mandates Commission came from European countries that had colonies. Thus the League elaborated a new principle—development toward the eventual goal of self-government—but left its implementation to the colonial powers themselves.

The mandates system demonstrated that Europe was determined to maintain its imperial power and influence. It is no wonder that patriots throughout Asia were bitterly disappointed after the First World War. They saw France, Great Britain, and other nations—industrialized Japan was the only Asian state to obtain mandates—grabbing Ger-

Delegates to the Peace Conference of 1919   Standing in the foreground is Prince Faisal, third son of King Hussein of Hejaz and frustrated spokesman for the Arab cause at Versailles. The British officer T. E. Lawrence—popularly known as Lawrence of Arabia because of his daring campaign against the Turks in World War I—is second from the right in the middle row. *(Source: By courtesy of the Trustees of the Imperial War Museum)*

many's colonies as spoils of war and extending the existing system of colonial protectorates in Muslim North Africa into the territories of the old Ottoman Empire. Yet Asian patriots were not about to give up. They preached national self-determination and struggled to build mass movements capable of achieving freedom and independence.

In this struggle they were encouraged and sometimes inspired by Soviet communism. Immediately after seizing power in 1917, Lenin and his fellow Bolsheviks declared that the Asian peoples conquered by the tsars, now inhabitants of the new Soviet Union, were complete equals of the Russians with a right to their own development. (In actuality this equality hardly existed, but the propaganda was effective nonetheless.) The Communists also denounced European and American imperialism and pledged to support revolutionary movements in all colonial countries, even when they were primarily movements of national independence led by "middle-class" intellectuals instead of by revolutionary workers. Foreign political and economic exploitation was the immediate enemy, they said, and socialist revolution could wait until after Western imperialism had been defeated.

The example, ideology, and support of Russian Communists exerted a powerful influence in the

1920s and 1930s, particularly in China and French Indochina. A nationalistic young Vietnamese man who had pleaded the cause of Vietnamese independence unsuccessfully at the Versailles Peace Conference described his feelings when he read Lenin's statement on national self-determination for colonial peoples, adopted by the Communist Third International in 1920:

These resolutions filled me with great emotion, enthusiasm, and faith. They helped me see the problem clearly. My joy was so great I began to cry. Alone in my room I wrote the following words, as if I were addressing a great crowd: "My dear compatriots, so miserable and oppressed, here is what we need. Here is the path to our liberation."[2]

The young nationalist was Ho Chi Minh (1890–1969), who was to fight a lifetime to create an independent, communist Vietnam.

The appeal of nationalism in Asia was not confined to territories under direct European rule. The extraordinary growth of international trade after 1850 had drawn millions of peasants and shopkeepers throughout Asia into the Western-dominated world economy, disrupting local markets and often creating hostility toward European businessmen. Moreover, Europe and the United States had forced even the most solid Asian states, China and Japan, to accept unequal treaties and humiliating limitations on their sovereignty. Thus the nationalist promise of genuine economic independence and true political equality with the West appealed as powerfully in old but weak states like China as in colonial territories like British India.

Finally, as in Russia after the Crimean War or in Japan after the Meiji Restoration, the nationalist creed went hand in hand with acceptance of modernization by the educated elites. Modernization promised changes that would enable old societies to compete effectively with the world's leading nations.

 THE MIDDLE EAST

The most flagrant attempt to expand the scope of Western imperialism occurred in what is usually called the Middle East but is perhaps more accurately termed West Asia—that vast expanse that

stretches eastward from the Suez Canal and Turkey's Mediterranean shores across the Tigris-Euphrates Valley and the Iranian Plateau to the Arabian Sea and the Indus Valley. There the British and the French successfully encouraged an Arab revolt in 1916 and destroyed the Ottoman Empire. The conquering Europeans then sought to replace the Turks as principal rulers throughout the region, even in Turkey itself. Turkish, Arab, and Iranian nationalists, as well as Jewish nationalists arriving from Europe, reacted violently. They struggled to win dignity and nationhood, and as the Europeans were forced to make concessions, they sometimes came into sharp conflict with each other, most notably in Palestine.

The First World War and the Arab Revolt

The Ottoman Empire, like neighboring Egypt (see pages 887–880), had long been subject to European pressure and had also adopted European military and educational reforms in the 1820s and 1830s. In the late nineteenth century, however, the Ottoman Empire became increasingly weak and autocratic. The combination of declining international stature and domestic tyranny eventually led to an upsurge of revolutionary activity among idealistic exiles and young army officers who wanted to seize power and save the Ottoman state. These fervent patriots, the so-called Young Turks, succeeded in the revolution of 1908, and subsequently they were determined to hold together the remnants of the vast multiethnic empire. Defeated by Bulgaria, Serbia, and Greece in the Balkan War of 1912, stripped of practically all territory in Europe, the Young Turks redoubled their efforts in Asia. The most important of their Asian possessions were Syria—consisting of modern-day Lebanon, Syria, Israel, and Jordan—and Iraq. The Ottoman Turks also claimed the Arabian peninsula but exercised only a loose control there.

For centuries the largely Arabic populations of Syria and Iraq had been tied to their Ottoman rulers by their common faith in Islam (though there were Christian Arabs as well). Yet beneath the surface, ethnic and linguistic tensions simmered between Turks and Arabs, who were as different as Chinese and Japanese or French and Germans. As early as 1883, a Frenchman who had traveled widely in the Arab provinces claimed:

Everywhere I came upon the same abiding and universal sentiment: hatred of the Turks. The notion of concerted action to throw off the detested yoke is gradually shaping itself. . . . An Arab movement, newly-risen, is looming in the distance; a race hitherto downtrodden will presently claim its due place in the destinies of Islam.[3]

The actions of the Young Turks after 1908 made the embryonic "Arab movement" a reality. Although some Turkish reformers argued for an Ottoman federalism that would give equal political rights to all ethnic and religious groups within the empire, the majority successfully insisted on a narrow Turkish nationalism. They further centralized the Ottoman Empire and extended the sway of the Turkish language, culture, and race. In 1909 the Turkish government brutally slaughtered thousands of Armenian Christians, a prelude to the wholesale destruction of more than a million Armenians during the heavy fighting with Russia in the First World War. Meanwhile, the Arab revolt gathered strength. By 1914 a large majority of Arab leaders believed that armed conflict with their Turkish masters was inevitable.

In close contact with Europeans for centuries, the Turks willingly joined forces with Germany and Austria-Hungary in late 1914. The Young Turks were pro-German because Germans had helped reform Ottoman armies before the war and had built important railroads, like the one to Baghdad. Alliance with Germany permitted the Turks to renounce immediately the limitations on Ottoman sovereignty that the Europeans had imposed in the nineteenth century, and it offered the prospect of settling old scores with Russia, the historic enemy.

The Young Turks' fatal decision to side with the Central Powers pulled the entire Middle East into the European civil war and made it truly a world conflict. While Russia attacked the Ottomans in the Caucasus, the British had to protect Egypt and the Suez Canal, the life line to India. Thus Arab leaders opposed to Ottoman rule suddenly found an unexpected ally in Great Britain. The foremost Arab leader was Hussein ibn-Ali (1856–1931), a direct descendant of the prophet Muhammad through the house of Quraysh. As the *sharif,* or chief magistrate of Mecca, the most holy city in the Muslim world, Hussein governed much of the Ottoman Empire's territory along the Red Sea, an area known as the Hejaz (Map 30.1). Basically anti-Turkish, Hussein refused to second the Turkish sultan's call for a holy war against the Triple Entente. His refusal pleased the British, who feared that such calls would trigger a Muslim revolt in India.

In 1915 Hussein managed to win vague British commitments for an independent Arab kingdom. The British attempt to take the Dardanelles and capture Constantinople in 1915 failed miserably, and Britain (and Russia) badly needed a new ally on the Ottoman front. Thus in 1916 Hussein revolted against the Turks, proclaiming himself king of the Arabs. Hussein joined forces with the British under T. E. Lawrence, who in 1917 led Arab tribesmen and Indian soldiers in a highly successful guerrilla war against the Turks on the Arabian peninsula. In September 1918, British armies and their Arab allies smashed into Syria. This offensive culminated in the triumphal entry of Hussein's son Faisal into Damascus.

Similar victories were eventually scored in the Ottoman province of Iraq. Britain occupied the southern Iraqi city of Basra in 1914 and captured Baghdad in 1917. Throughout Syria and Iraq there was wild Arab rejoicing. Many patriots expected a large, unified Arab state to rise from the dust of the Ottoman collapse. Within two years, however, many Arab nationalists felt bitterly betrayed by Great Britain and its allies. The issues involved are complex and controversial, but it is undeniable that this bitterness left a legacy of hatred toward the West.

Part of the reason for the Arabs' bitterness was that Britain and France had signed secret wartime treaties to divide and rule the old Ottoman Empire. In the Sykes-Picot Agreement of 1916, Britain and France had secretly agreed that France would receive modern-day Lebanon, Syria, and much of southern Turkey, and Britain would receive Palestine, Jordan, and Iraq. The Sykes-Picot treaties contradicted British (and later Wilsonian) promises concerning Arab independence after the war. When Britain and France set about implementing these secret plans, Arab nationalists felt cheated and betrayed.

A related source of Arab bitterness was Britain's wartime commitment to a Jewish homeland in Palestine. The Balfour Declaration of November

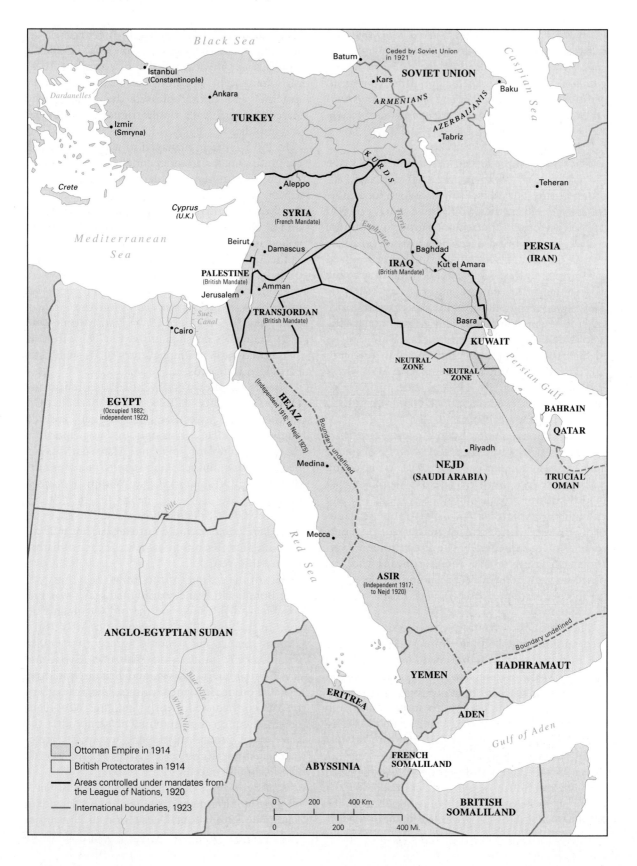

Black Sea

Batum

Ceded by Soviet Union
in 1921

Kars

SOVIET UNION

Baku

Caspian Sea

Istanbul
(Constantinople)

Dardanelles

Ankara

ARMENIANS

AZERBAIJANIS

Tabriz

TURKEY

Izmir
(Smryna)

K U R D S

Teheran

Crete

Aleppo

Cyprus
(U.K.)

SYRIA
(French Mandate)

Euphrates

Tigris

*Mediterranean
Sea*

Beirut

Damascus

Baghdad

IRAQ
(British Mandate)

Kut el Amara

**PERSIA
(IRAN)**

PALESTINE
(British Mandate)

Amman

Jerusalem

*Suez
Canal*

TRANSJORDAN
(British Mandate)

Basra

KUWAIT

Persian Gulf

Cairo

NEUTRAL
ZONE

NEUTRAL
ZONE

BAHRAIN

EGYPT
(Occupied 1882;
independent 1922)

HEJAZ
(Independent 1916; to Nejd 1925)

Boundary undefined

QATAR

Riyadh

**NEJD
(SAUDI ARABIA)**

**TRUCIAL
OMAN**

Nile

Medina

ANGLO-EGYPTIAN SUDAN

Red Sea

Mecca

ASIR
(Independent 1917;
to Nejd 1920)

Boundary undefined

Blue Nile

White Nile

YEMEN

HADHRAMAUT

ERITREA

ADEN

Gulf of Aden

**FRENCH
SOMALILAND**

ABYSSINIA

**BRITISH
SOMALILAND**

Ottoman Empire in 1914

British Protectorates in 1914

Areas controlled under mandates from
the League of Nations, 1920

International boundaries, 1923

| 0 | 200 | 400 Km. |

| 0 | 200 | 400 Mi. |

1917, made by the Britsh foreign secretary Arthur Balfour, declared:

His Majesty's Government views with favor the establishment in Palestine of a National Home for the Jewish People, and will use their best endeavors to facilitate the achievement of this object, it being clearly understood that nothing shall be done which may prejudice the civil and religious rights of existing non-Jewish communities in Palestine, or the rights and political status enjoyed by Jews in any other country.

As careful reading reveals, the Balfour Declaration made contradictory promises to European Jews and Middle Eastern Arabs. It has been a subject of passionate debate ever since 1917.

Some British Cabinet members apparently believed such a declaration would appeal to German, Austrian, and American Jews and thus help the British war effort. Others sincerely supported the Zionist vision of a Jewish homeland. These supporters also believed that such a homeland would be grateful to Britain and help maintain British control of the Suez Canal. In any event, Arabs were dismayed.

In 1914 Jews accounted for about 11 percent of the predominantly Arab population in the three Ottoman administrative units that would subsequently be lumped together by the British to form Palestine. The "National Home for the Jewish People" mentioned in the Balfour Declaration implied to the Arabs—and to the Zionist Jews as well—the establishment of some kind of Jewish state that would be incompatible with majority rule. But a state founded on religious and ethnic exclusivity was out of keeping with both Islamic and Ottoman tradition, which had historically been more tolerant of religious diversity and minorities than had the Christian monarchs or nation-states in Europe.

Despite strong French objections, Hussein's son Faisal (1885–1933) was allowed to attend the Paris Peace Conference, but his effort to secure an independent state embracing all Arabs came to nothing. The independence of the kingdom of Hejaz was confirmed, but in return Faisal was forced to accept Franco-British demands for mandates in Syria, Iraq, and Palestine. (The Saudis had attacked Hussein in 1916, and they conquered his kingdom of Hejaz in 1924–1925, incorporating it with the Nejd in 1932 to form Saudi Arabia.) The British mandate in Palestine formally incorporated the Balfour Declaration and its commitment to a Jewish national home. On his return to Syria, Faisal's followers repudiated the agreement he had reluctantly accepted. In March 1920 they met as the Syrian National Congress and proclaimed Syria independent with Faisal as king. A similar congress declared Iraq an independent kingdom.

Western reaction to events in Syria and Iraq was swift and decisive. A French army stationed in Lebanon attacked Syria, taking Damascus in July 1920. Faisal fled and the French took over. Meanwhile, the British put down an uprising in Iraq with bloody fighting and established military rule there. Western imperialism appeared to have replaced Turkish rule in the Middle East (see Map 30.1).

The Turkish Revolution

In November 1918 the Allied fleet entered Constantinople, the Ottoman capital. A young English official vividly described the strange and pathetic situation he encountered:

I found the Ottoman Empire utterly smashed, her vast territories stripped into pieces, and her conquered populations blinded and bewildered by their sudden release. The Turks were worn out, dead-tired, and without bitterness awaited their fate. . . . The debris of the old order waited to be constructed into a new system.[4]

The Allies' "new system" was blatant imperialism, and it proved harsher for the defeated Turks than for the "liberated" Arabs. A treaty forced on

✿ MAP 30.1 The Partition of the Ottoman Empire, 1914–1923 The decline of the mighty Ottoman Empire began in 1699, when the Habsburgs conquered Hungary, and it accelerated after 1805, when Egypt became virtually independent. By 1914 the Ottoman Turks had been pushed out of the Balkans, and their Arab provinces were on the edge of revolt; that revolt erupted in the First World War and contributed greatly to the Ottomans' defeat. When the Allies then attempted to implement their plans, including independence for the Armenian people, Mustafa Kemal arose to forge in battle the modern Turkish state.

the helpless sultan dismembered Turkey and reduced it to a puppet state. Great Britain and France occupied parts of Turkey, and Italy and Greece claimed shares as well. There was a sizable Greek minority in western Turkey, and Greek nationalists cherished the "Great Idea" of incorporating this territory into a modern Greek empire modeled on long-dead Christian Byzantium. In 1919 Greek armies carried by British ships landed on the Turkish coast at Smyrna. The sultan ordered his exhausted troops not to resist, and Greek armies advanced into the interior. Turkey seemed finished.

But Turkey produced a great leader and revived to become an inspiration to the entire Middle East. Mustafa Kemal (1881–1938), the father of modern Turkey, was a military man. The son of a petty government official and sympathetic to the Young Turk movement, Kemal had distinguished himself in the Great War by directing the successful defense of the Dardanelles against British attack. After the armistice, Mustafa Kemal watched with anguish the Allies' aggression and the sultan's cowardice. In early 1919 he moved from Constantinople to central Turkey and began working to unify the Turkish resistance.

Greek Exodus   In the port city of Smyrna in 1922, Greeks are evacuated after Turkish victory over the Greek and British invaders. After three years of fighting, Mustafa Kemal ended the Greek idea of establishing a modern empire that would include part of Turkey. *(Source: Hulton Deutsch Collection Ltd.)*

The sultan, bowing to Allied pressure, initially denounced Kemal, but the cause of national liberation proved more powerful. The catalyst was the Greek invasion and attempted annexation of much of western Turkey. A young woman who was to play a major role in the Turkish revolution described feelings she shared with countless others:

After I learned about the details of the Smyrna occupation by Greek armies, I hardly opened my mouth on any subject except when it concerned the sacred struggle. . . . I suddenly ceased to exist as an individual. I worked, wrote and lived as a unit of that magnificent national madness.[5]

Refusing to acknowledge the Allied dismemberment of their country, the Turks battled on through 1920 despite staggering defeats. The next year the Greeks, egged on by the British, advanced almost to Ankara, the nationalist stronghold in central Turkey. There Mustafa Kemal's forces took the offensive and won a great victory. The Greeks and their British allies sued for peace. After long negotiations, the resulting Treaty of Lausanne (1923) solemnly abolished the hated Capitulations, which the European powers had imposed in the nineteenth century to give their citizens special privileges in the Ottoman Empire, and recognized the territorial integrity of a truly independent Turkey. Turkey lost only its former Arab provinces.

Mustafa Kemal, a nationalist without religious faith, believed that Turkey should modernize and secularize along Western lines. His first moves were political. Drawing on his prestige as a war hero, Kemal called on the somewhat reluctant National Assembly to depose the sultan and establish a republic. He had himself elected president and moved the capital from cosmopolitan Constantinople (soon to be renamed Istanbul) to Ankara in the Turkish heartland. Kemal savagely crushed the demands for independence of ethnic minorities like the Armenians and the Kurds, but he realistically abandoned all thought of winning back lost Arab territories. He focused instead on internal affairs, creating a one-party system—partly inspired by the Bolshevik example—in order to work his will.

The most radical of Kemal's changes pertained to religion and culture. For centuries, most of the intellectual and social activities of believers had been sternly regulated by Islamic religious authori-

Mustafa Kemal   The father of modern Turkey explains his radical reform of the written Turkish language. Impeccably elegant European dress symbolizes Kemal's conception of a modernized Turkey. *(Source: Stock Montage)*

ties, in keeping with the Sacred Law. Profoundly influenced by the example of western Europe, Mustafa Kemal set out, like the philosophes of the Enlightenment, to limit the place of religion and religious leaders in daily affairs. Like Russia's Peter the Great, he employed dictatorial measures rather than reason to reach his goal. Kemal and his followers simply decreed a revolutionary separation of church and state. Religious courts were abolished, replaced by a completely new legal system based on European law codes. Religious schools gave way to state schools that taught such secular subjects as science, mathematics, and social sciences.

To dramatize the break with the past, Mustafa Kemal struck down many entrenched patterns of behavior. Women, traditionally secluded and inferior to males in Islamic society, received the right to vote. Marriage was now governed by civil law on a European model, rather than by the Islamic code. Women were allowed to seek divorces, and no man could have more than one wife at a time. Men were forbidden to wear the tall red fez as headgear; government employees were ordered to wear business suits and felt hats, erasing the visible differences between Muslims and "infidel" Europeans. The old Arabic script was replaced with a new Turkish alphabet based on Roman letters, which moved the written language closer to the spoken vernacular and facilitated massive government efforts to spread literacy after 1928. Finally, in 1935, family names on the European model were introduced. The National Assembly granted Mustafa Kemal the surname Atatürk, which means "father of the Turks."

By the time of his death in 1938, Atatürk and his supporters had consolidated their revolution. Government-sponsored industrialization was fostering urban growth and new attitudes, encouraging Turks to embrace business and science. Poverty persisted in rural areas, as did some religious discontent among devout Muslims. But like the Japanese after the Meiji Restoration, the Turkish people had rallied around the nationalist banner to repulse European imperialism and were building a modern secular nation-state.

Iran and Afghanistan

In Persia (renamed Iran in 1935), strong-arm efforts to build a unified modern nation ultimately proved less successful than in Turkey.

The late nineteenth century had been a sorry period in Iran's long and sometimes glorious history. Iran was subject to extreme foreign pressure: the Russians were pressing relentlessly from the north, and the British were pushing upward from India and the Persian Gulf. Like China in a similar predicament at the same time, Iran managed to play the Great Powers against each other to maintain a precarious independence. However, the spectacle of the shah granting economic privileges to foreigners alienated native merchants. An inspired religious leader, Jamal al-Din al-Afghani (1838–

1897), began to preach government reform as a means of reviving Islamic civilization. In 1906 a nationalistic coalition of merchants, religious leaders, and intellectuals revolted. The despotic shah was forced to grant a constitution and establish a national assembly, the *Majlis*. Nationalist hopes ran high.

Yet the Iranian revolution of 1906 was doomed to failure, largely because of European imperialism. Without consulting Iran, Britain and Russia in 1907 simply divided the country into spheres of influence. Britain's sphere ran along the Persian Gulf; the Russian sphere encompassed the whole northern half of Iran (see Map 30.1). Thereafter Russia intervened constantly. It blocked reforms, occupied cities, and completely dominated the country by 1912. When Russian power temporarily collapsed in the Bolshevik Revolution, British armies rushed into the power vacuum. By bribing corrupt Iranians liberally, Great Britain in 1919 negotiated a treaty allowing the installation of British "advisers" in every department of the government.

The Majlis refused to ratify the treaty, and the blatant attempt to make Iran a British satellite aroused the national spirit. In 1921 reaction against the British brought to power a military dictator, Reza Shah Pahlavi (1877–1944), who proclaimed himself shah in 1925 and ruled until 1941.

Inspired throughout his reign by the example of Turkey's Mustafa Kemal, the patriotic, religiously indifferent Reza Shah had three basic goals: to build a modern nation, to free Iran from foreign domination, and to rule with an iron fist. The challenge was enormous. Iran was a vast, backward country of deserts, mountain barriers, and rudimentary communications. Most of the rural population was poor and illiterate, and among the Persian majority were sizable ethnic minorities with their own aspirations. Furthermore, Iran's powerful religious leaders hated Western (Christian) domination but were no less opposed to a more secular, less Islamic society.

To realize his vision of a strong Iran, the energetic shah created a modern army, built railroads, and encouraged commerce and industry. He won control over ethnic minorities such as the Kurds in the north and Arab tribesmen on the border with Iraq. He withdrew many of the privileges granted to foreigners and raised taxes on the powerful Anglo-Persian Oil Company, which had been founded in 1909 to exploit the first great oil strike in the Middle East. Yet Reza Shah was less successful than Atatürk.

Because the European-educated elite in Iran was smaller than the comparable group in Turkey, the idea of re-creating Persian greatness on the basis of a secularized society attracted relatively few determined supporters. Many powerful religious leaders turned against Reza Shah, and he became increasingly brutal, greedy, and tyrannical, murdering his enemies and lining his pockets. His support of Hitler's Nazi Germany also exposed Iran's tenuous and fragile independence to the impact of European conflicts.

Afghanistan, meanwhile, was nominally independent in the nineteenth century, but the British imposed political restrictions and constantly meddled in the country. In 1919 the new, violently anti-British amir Amanullah (1892–1960) declared a holy war on the British government in India and won complete independence for the first time. Amanullah then decreed revolutionary reforms designed to hurl his primitive country into the twentieth century. The result was tribal and religious revolt, civil war, and retreat from reform. Islam remained both religion and law. A powerful but primitive patriotism had enabled Afghanistan to win political independence from the West, but modest efforts to build a modern society met with little success.

The Arab States and Palestine

The establishment of French and British mandates at gunpoint forced Arab nationalists to seek independence by gradual means after 1920. Arab nationalists were indirectly aided by Western taxpayers, who wanted cheap—that is, peaceful—empires. As a result, Arabs won considerable control over local affairs in the mandated states, except Palestine, though the mandates remained European satellites in international and economic affairs.

The wily British chose Faisal, whom the French had so recently deposed in Syria, as king of Iraq. Faisal obligingly signed an alliance giving British advisers broad behind-the-scenes control. The king also accepted British ownership of Iraq's oil fields, thereby giving the West a stranglehold on the Iraqi economy. Given the limitations imposed on him, Faisal (r. 1921–1933) proved an able ruler, gaining the support of his people and encouraging moderate reforms. In 1932 he secured Iraqi independence at the price of a long-term military alliance with Great Britain.

Egypt, occupied by Great Britain ever since 1882 (see page 890) and a British protectorate since 1914, pursued a similar path. Following intense nationalist agitation after the Great War, Great Britain in 1922 proclaimed Egypt formally independent but continued to occupy the country militarily. In 1936, the British agreed to a treaty restricting their troops to their big bases in the Suez Canal Zone.

The French were less compromising in Syria. They practiced a policy of divide-and-rule, carving out a second mandate in Lebanon and generally playing off ethnic and religious minorities against each other. Lebanon eventually became a republic, dominated by a very slender Christian majority and under French protection. Arab nationalists in Syria finally won promises of Syrian independence in 1936 in return for a treaty of friendship with France.

In short, the Arab states gradually freed themselves from Western political mandates but not from the Western military threat or from pervasive Western influence. Of great importance, large Arab landowners and urban merchants increased their wealth and political power after 1918, and they often supported the Western hegemony, from which they benefited greatly. Western control over the newly discovered oil fields by foreign companies helped to convince radical nationalists that economic independence and genuine freedom had not yet been achieved.

Relations between the Arabs and the West were complicated by the tense situation in the British mandate of Palestine, and that situation deteriorated in the interwar years. Both Arabs and Jews denounced the British, who tried unsuccessfully to compromise with both sides. The anger of Arab nationalists, however, was aimed primarily at Jewish settlers. The key issue was Jewish migration from Europe to Palestine.

A small Jewish community had survived in Palestine ever since the destruction of Jerusalem and the dispersal of the Jews in Roman times. But Jewish nationalism, known as Zionism, was a recent phenomenon of European origin. The Dreyfus affair (see page 869) and anti-Jewish riots in Russia had convinced a cultured Austrian

✶ **Home to Zion**   Chaim Weizmann carries sacred Torahs of the Jewish people toward a synagogue in Tel-Aviv, a new city founded in 1909. Born in Russia and educated as a chemist in Berlin, Weizmann became a British citizen and in 1917 helped secure the Balfour Declaration. In the 1920s Weizmann led the Zionist movement. In 1948 he became the first president of Israel. *(Source: Central Zionist Archives, Jerusalem)*

journalist named Theodore Herzl (1860–1904) that even nonreligious Jews would never be fully accepted in Europe. He believed that only the re-creation of a Jewish state could guarantee Jews dignity and security. Under Herzl's leadership, the Zionist movement encouraged Jews from all over the world to settle in the Palestine region, but until 1921 the great majority of Jewish emigrants preferred the United States.

After 1921 the situation changed radically. An isolationist United States drastically limited immigration from eastern Europe, where war and revolution had caused chaos and kindled anti-Semitism. Moreover, the British began honoring the Balfour Declaration despite Arab protests. Thus the number of Jewish immigrants to Palestine from turbulent Europe grew rapidly. In the 1930s German and Polish persecution created a mass of Jewish refugees. By 1939 the Jewish population of Palestine had increased almost fivefold since 1914 and accounted for about 30 percent of all inhabitants.

Jewish settlers in Palestine faced formidable economic and political difficulties. Much of the land purchased by the Jewish National Fund was productive. But many of the sellers of such land were wealthy absentee Arab landowners who had little interest in the welfare of their Arab tenants (see page 888). When the new Jewish owners subsequently replaced those age-old Arab tenants with Jewish settlers, Arab farmers and intellectuals burned with a sense of injustice. Moreover, most Jewish immigrants came from urban backgrounds and preferred to establish new cities like Tel Aviv

THE MIDDLE EAST, 1914–1939

1914	Ottoman Empire enters First World War on Germany's side
1916	Allies agree secretly to partition Ottoman Empire
1916–1917	Arab revolt against Turkish rule grows
November 1917	Balfour Declaration pledges British support for a Jewish homeland in Palestine
October 1918	Arabs and British triumph as Ottoman Empire collapses
1919	Treaty of Versailles divides old Ottoman Empire into League of Nations mandates
1919	Mustafa Kemal mounts nationalist struggle against foreign occupation
1920	Faisal proclaimed king of Syria but quickly deposed by the French, who establish their mandate in Syria
Early 1920s	Tide of Jewish immigration surges into British mandate of Palestine
1923	Treaty of Lausanne recognizes independent Turkey Mustafa Kemal begins to secularize Turkish society
1925	Reza Shah takes power in Iran and rules to 1941
1932	Iraq gains independence in return for military alliance with Great Britain
1936	Syrian nationalists sign treaty with France in return for promises of independence
late 1930s	Tensions mount between Arabs and Jews in Palestine

or to live in existing towns, where they competed with the Arabs. The land issue combined with economic and cultural friction to harden Arab protest into hatred. Anti-Jewish riots and even massacres ensued.

The British gradually responded to Arab pressure and tried to slow Jewish immigration. This effort satisfied neither Jews nor Arabs, and by 1938 the two communities were engaged in an undeclared civil war. On the eve of the Second World War, the frustrated British proposed an independent Palestine as well as a cap of seventy-five thousand additional Jewish immigrants. The reason for this low number was to permanently limit the Jews to being only about one-third of Palestine's total population. Zionists felt themselves in grave danger.

In the face of adversity, Jewish settlers from many different countries gradually succeeded in forging a cohesive community. Hebrew, which for centuries had been used only in religious worship, was revived as a living language to bind the Jews in Palestine together. Despite its slow beginnings, rural development achieved often spectacular results. The key unit of agricultural organization was the *kibbutz,* a collective farm on which each member shared equally in the work, rewards, and defense of the farm. Men and women labored side by side; a nursery cared for the children, and a common dining hall served meals. Some cooperative farms turned arid grazing land into citrus groves and irrigated gardens. An egalitarian socialist ideology also characterized industry, which grew rapidly and was owned largely by the Jewish trade unions. By 1939 a new but old nation was emerging in the Middle East.

❧ TOWARD SELF-RULE IN INDIA

The national movement in British India grew out of two interconnected cultures, Hindu and Muslim, which came to see themselves as fundamentally different in rising to challenge British rule. Nowhere has the power of modern nationalism, both to unify and to divide, been more strikingly demonstrated than in India.

Promises and Repression (1914–1919)

Indian nationalism had emerged in the late nineteenth century (see page 905), and when the First World War began, the British feared revolt. Instead, somewhat like Europe's equally mistrusted socialist workers, Indians supported the war effort. About 1.2 million Indian soldiers and laborers volunteered for duty and served in Europe, Africa, and the Middle East. The British government in India and the native Indian princes sent large supplies of food, money, and ammunition. In return, the British opened more good government jobs to Indians and made other minor concessions.

As the war in distant Europe ground on, however, inflation, high taxes, food shortages, and a terrible influenza epidemic created widespread suffering and discontent. The prewar nationalist movement revived, stronger than ever, and the moderate and radical wings of the Indian National Congress joined forces. Moreover, in 1916 the Hindus leading the Congress party hammered out an alliance—the Lucknow Pact—with India's Muslim League. Founded in 1906 to uphold Muslim interests, the league had grown out of fears arising from the fact that under British rule the once-dominant Muslim minority had fallen behind the Hindu majority, especially in the Western education necessary to secure good jobs in the government. The Lucknow Pact forged a powerful united front of Hindus and Muslims and called for putting India on equal footing with self-governing white British dominions like Canada, Australia, and New Zealand.

The British response was contradictory. On the one hand, the secretary of state for India made the unprecedented announcement in August 1917 that British policy in India called for the "gradual development of self-governing institutions and the progressive realization of responsible government." The means of achieving this great step forward were spelled out in late 1919 in the Government of India Act, which established a dual administration: part Indian and elected, part British and authoritarian. Such noncontroversial activities as agriculture, health, and education were transferred from British to Indian officials who were accountable to elected provincial assemblies. More sensitive matters like taxes, police, and the courts remained solely in British hands.

The positive impact of this reform, so typical of the British tradition of gradual political change, was seriously undermined by old-fashioned authoritarian rule. Despite the unanimous opposition of the elected Indian members, the British in 1919 rammed the repressive Rowlatt Acts through India's Imperial Legislative Council. These acts indefinitely extended wartime "emergency measures" designed to curb unrest and root out "conspiracy." The result was a wave of rioting across India.

Under these tense conditions an unsuspecting crowd of some ten thousand gathered to celebrate a Hindu religious festival in an enclosed square in Amritsar, a city in the northern province of Punjab. Without the knowledge of the crowd, the local English commander, General Reginald Dyer, had banned all public meetings that very day. Dyer marched his native Gurkha troops onto the field and, without warning, ordered them to fire into the unarmed mass at point-blank range until the ammunition ran out. The Amritsar Massacre, killing 379 and wounding 1,137, shattered wartime hopes in a frenzy of postwar reaction. India seemed to stand on the verge of more violence and repression and, sooner or later, terrorism and guerrilla war. That India took a different path to national liberation was due largely to Mohandas "Mahatma" Gandhi (1869–1948), who became the most fascinating and influential Indian of modern times.

Hindu Society and Mahatma Gandhi

By the time of Gandhi's birth in 1869, the Indian subcontinent was firmly controlled by the British. Part of the country was directly ruled by British (and subordinate Indian) officials, ultimately answerable to the British Parliament in London. These areas included Bengal and its teeming capital Calcutta in eastern India, Bombay and its hinterland in western India, the Punjab in the northwest, and Madras on the southeast coast (see Map 34.1, page 1142). So-called protected states were more sheltered from European ideas and from the world economy. There many of the old ways remained intact. The native prince—usually known as the *maharaja*—remained the titular ruler, though he was bound to the British by unequal treaties and had to accept the "advice" of the British resident assigned to his court.

It was in just such a tiny backwater protected state that Gandhi grew up. His father was a member of the merchant caste. But the Indian caste system has always been more flexible and dynamic than unsympathetic Westerners have wanted to believe, and for six generations the heads of Gandhi's family had served as hereditary prime ministers in various minuscule realms on the Kathiawar peninsula, north of Bombay on the Arabian Sea.

British Repression   After the Amritsar massacre of 1919 British repression in northern India was harsh and sadistic. Assisted by obedient native policemen wielding heavy clubs, these British officers are inflicting the kind of pain and humiliation that would soon fuel Gandhi's nationalist movement. *(Source: J. C. Allen)*

The extended (or joint) family, which had for generations been the most important unit of Indian society, powerfully influenced young Gandhi. Gandhi's father was the well-to-do head of the clan, which included five brothers and their wives, children, and children's children. The big three-story ancestral home swarmed with relatives. A whole community crowded into the labyrinth of tiny rooms and spilled out into the open courtyards. In such a communal atmosphere, patience, kindness, and a good-natured love of people were essential virtues. The aggressive, solitary individualism so prized in Europe and North America would have threatened group harmony. So it was for Gandhi.

In the Hindu family the woman was subordinate but respected. She was "worshipped as a mother, venerated as a wife, loved as a sister, but not much regarded as a woman." Her duty was "to worship her husband, to bear and rear his children."[6] Every Hindu girl married young, often before puberty; her husband was chosen by her parents. The young bride moved into her father-in-law's house. Marriage was a sacrament that could not be dissolved by divorce or even by death. Widows were forbidden by custom to remarry. More generally, a woman's fate was linked to that of the family, in which she was the trusted guardian of orthodox Hindu values.

Gandhi's mother was the ideal Hindu housewife. Married as a young illiterate girl to a forty-two-year-old man whose first wives had died without male children, Putali Ba bore three boys and a girl. According to Gandhi, his ever-cheerful mother was "the first to rise and the last to go to bed . . . and she never made any distinction between her own children and other children in the family."[7] Very devoted but undogmatic in religious matters, Putali Ba fasted regularly and exercised a strong influence on her precocious son. Gandhi was married at thirteen to a local girl who became his lifelong companion.

After his father's death, Gandhi decided to study law in England. No member of his subcaste had ever done so, and the local elders declared Gandhi an outcaste, claiming that Hindu practices would not be possible in alien England. Gandhi disagreed. To win over his wife and anxious mother, he swore that he would not touch meat, women, or wine in the foreign land. Gandhi kept his word.

After passing the English bar, he returned to India. But his practice in Bombay failed, and in 1893 he decided to try his luck as a lawyer for wealthy Indian merchants in South Africa. It was a momentous decision.

The Roots of Militant Nonviolence

Soon after arriving in South Africa, the elegant young lawyer in Western dress took a business trip by train. A white man entered the first-class compartment in which Gandhi was riding, took one look at him, and called the conductor. Gandhi was ordered to ride in the baggage car. When he protested, a policeman threw him off the train. Years later Gandhi recalled this experience as a critical turning point in his life. He had refused to bow to naked racial injustice.

As Gandhi's law practice flourished, he began to examine the plight of Indians in South Africa. After the British abolished black slavery in the empire, plantation owners in South Africa and elsewhere had developed a "new system of slavery."[8] They imported desperately poor Indians as indentured laborers on five-year renewable contracts. When some thrifty, hard-working Indians completed their terms and remained in South Africa as free persons and economic competitors, the Dutch and British settlers passed brutally discriminatory laws. Poor Indians had to work on white-owned plantations or return to India; rich Indians lost the vote. Gandhi undertook the legal defense of his countrymen, infuriating the whites. In 1896 a hysterical mob almost lynched the "coolie lawyer."

Meanwhile, Gandhi was searching for a spiritual theory of social action. Identifying with South Africa's black majority as well as with his own countrymen, he meditated on the Hindu pursuit of spiritual strength through fasting, sexual abstinence, devotion to duty, and reincarnation. He also studied Christian teachings. Gradually Gandhi developed and articulated a weapon for the weak that he called *Satyagraha*. Gandhi conceived of Satyagraha, loosely translated as "Soul Force," as a means of striving for truth and social justice through love, suffering, and conversion of the oppressor. Its tactic is courageous nonviolent resistance. Satyagraha owed a good deal to the Christian Gospels, for Christ's call to "love your enemies" touched Gandhi to the core.

As the undisputed leader of South Africa's Indians before the First World War, Gandhi put his philosophy into action. When the white government of South Africa severely restricted Asians' immigration and internal freedom of movement, he led a campaign of mass resistance. Thousands of Indian men and women marched across forbidden borders and peacefully withstood beatings, arrest, and imprisonment.

In 1914, South Africa's exasperated whites agreed to many of the Indians' demands. A law was passed abolishing discriminatory taxes on Indian traders, recognizing the legality of non-Christian marriages, and permitting the continued immigration of free Indians. Satyagraha—militant nonviolence in pursuit of social justice—had proved itself a powerful force in Gandhi's hands.

Gandhi Leads the Way

In 1915 Gandhi returned to India. His reputation had preceded him: the masses hailed him as a *Mahatma,* or "Great Soul"—a Hindu title of veneration for a man of great knowledge and humanity—and the name stuck. Feeling his way into Indian affairs, Gandhi, dressed in peasant garb, crisscrossed India on third-class trains, listening to common folk and talking to Congress party leaders. Moved by the wretched misery of the very poor, he led some sharecroppers against British landowners and organized a strike of textile workers in his native Gujarat. But it was the aftermath of the Amritsar Massacre that catapulted Gandhi to leadership of the national movement in India.

Drawing on his South African experience, Gandhi in 1920 launched a national campaign of nonviolent resistance to British rule. Denouncing British injustice, he urged his countrymen to boycott British goods and jobs and honors. He told peasants not to pay taxes or buy heavily taxed liquor. Gandhi electrified the people. The result was nothing less than a revolution in Indian politics.

The nationalist movement had previously touched only the tiny, prosperous, Western-educated elite. Now both the illiterate masses of village India and the educated classes heard a voice that seemed to be in harmony with their profoundest values. Even Gandhi's renunciation of sex—with his wife's consent—accorded with a popular

Hindu belief attributing special power to those who do not squander their life force in sexual intercourse. Gandhi's call for militant nonviolence was particularly appealing to the masses of Hindus who were not members of the warrior caste or the so-called military races and who were traditionally passive and nonviolent. The British had regarded ordinary Hindus as cowards. Gandhi told them that they could be courageous and even morally superior:

What do you think? Wherein is courage required—in blowing others to pieces from behind a cannon, or with a smiling face to approach a cannon and be blown to pieces? Who is the true warrior—he who keeps death always as a bosom-friend, or he who controls the death of others? Believe me that a man devoid of courage and manhood can never be a passive resister.[9]

Gandhi made Congress into a mass political party, welcoming members from every ethnic group and cooperating closely with the Muslim minority.

In 1922, some Indian resisters turned to violence. A mob murdered twenty-two policemen, and savage riots broke out. Gandhi abruptly called off his campaign. Arrested for fomenting rebellion, Gandhi told the British judge that he had committed "a Himalayan blunder to believe that India had accepted nonviolence."[10] Released from prison after two years, Gandhi set up a commune, established a national newspaper, and set out to reform Indian society and improve the lot of the poor. He welcomed the outcaste untouchables into his fellowship. He worked to help child widows, promote cottage industry, and end the use of alcohol. For Gandhi, moral improvement, social progress, and the national movement went hand in hand.

The resistance campaign of 1920–1922 left the British severely shaken. Although moderate Indians had participated effectively in the system of dual government, the commission formed by the British in 1927 to consider further steps toward self-rule included no Indian members. Indian resentment was intense. In 1929, the radical nationalists, led by the able and aristocratic Jawaharlal Nehru (1889–1964), pushed through the National Congress a resolution calling for virtual independence within a year. The British stiffened, and Indian radicals talked of a bloody showdown.

The March to the Sea   Gandhi repeatedly used nonviolent confrontation to challenge British rule and mobilize the Indian masses. These marchers are picking up salt-encrusted sand in defiance of British law. Gandhi is on the left and wearing eyeglasses. He was arrested but the march continued (see Listening to the Past). *(Source: The Bettmann Archive)*

In this tense situation Gandhi masterfully reasserted his leadership. To satisfy the extremists, he took a hard line toward the British, but he controlled the extremists by insisting on nonviolent methods. He then organized another massive resistance campaign, this time against the hated salt tax, which affected every Indian family. Gandhi himself led fifty thousand people in a spectacular march to the sea to make salt without paying a tax, in defiance of the law. Gandhi was arrested but his followers continued the march to the sea. Demonstrating peacefully at the salt pans and disregarding orders to disperse, they were then beaten senseless by policemen in a brutal and well-publicized encounter (see Listening to the Past). The marchers

did not even raise their arms to protect themselves. "They went down like ten-pins. . . . The survivors, without breaking ranks, silently and doggedly marched on until struck down."[11]

Over the next few months sixty thousand protesters followed Gandhi to jail. But this time there was very little rioting. Finally, in 1931, the frustrated, unnerved British released Gandhi from jail and sat down to negotiate with him, as an equal, over self-rule for India. There were many complications, including the determined opposition of diehard imperialists like Winston Churchill. But in 1935 the negotiations resulted in a new constitution, which greatly strengthened India's parliamentary representative institutions. It was virtually a blueprint for independence, which would come quickly after World War Two.

Gandhi inspired people far beyond India's borders. Martin Luther King, Jr., was later to be deeply influenced by his tactic and philosophy of nonviolent social action. Gandhi did much to transform the elitist nationalism of Indian intellectuals into a mighty mass movement with social as well as political concerns. Above all, Gandhi nurtured national identity and self-respect. As Nehru summed it up, Gandhi "instilled courage and man-hood in India's people; . . . courage is the one sure foundation of character, he had said; without courage there is no morality, no religion, no love."[12]

Despite his best efforts, Gandhi failed to heal a widening split between Hindus and Muslims. The development of an Indian nationalism based largely on Hindu symbols and customs increasingly disturbed the Muslim minority. Tempers mounted, and atrocities were committed by both sides. By the late 1930s the leaders of the Muslim

Textile Workers in Lancashire When Gandhi came to Britain for negotiations in 1931, these textile workers cheered him. The Great Depression had sent unemployment soaring, but many British workers told Gandhi that they could understand why he had organized an effective boycott against the sale of British cloth in India. *(Source: The Bettman Archive)*

League were calling for the creation of a Muslim nation in British India, a "Pakistan" or "land of the pure." As in Palestine, the rise of conflicting nationalisms in India was to lead to tragedy (see page 0000).

TURMOIL IN EAST ASIA

Because of the efforts of the Meiji reformers, nationalism and modernization were well developed in Japan by 1914. Not only was Japan capable of competing politically and economically with the world's leading nations, but it had already begun building its own empire and proclaiming its special mission in Asia. China lagged far behind, but after 1912 the pace of nationalist development there began to quicken.

In the 1920s the Chinese nationalist movement managed to win a large measure of political independence from the imperialist West and promoted extensive modernization. But these achievements were soon undermined by internal conflict and war with an expanding Japan. Nationalism also flourished elsewhere in Asia, scoring a major victory in the Philippine Islands.

The Rise of Nationalist China

The revolution of 1911–1912, which overthrew the Manchu Dynasty (see page 909), opened an era of unprecedented change for Chinese society. Before the revolution, many progressive Chinese had realized that fundamental technological and political reforms were necessary to save the Chinese state and to meet the many-sided Western challenge. Most had hoped, however, to preserve the traditional core of Chinese civilization and culture. The fall of the two-thousand-year-old dynastic system shattered such hopes. If the emperor himself was no longer sacred, what was? Everything was open to question and to alteration.

The central figure in the revolution was a crafty old military man, Yuan Shigai (Yüan Shih-k'ai). Called out of retirement to save the dynasty, Yuan (1859–1916) betrayed the Manchus and convinced the revolutionaries that he was a strong man who could unite the country peacefully and prevent foreign intervention. Once elected president of the republic, however, Yuan concentrated on building his own power. In 1913, he used military force to dissolve China's parliament and ruled as a dictator. China's first modern revolution had failed.

The extent of the failure became apparent only after Yuan's death in 1916. The central government in Beijing (Peking) almost disintegrated. For more than a decade power resided in a multitude of local military leaders, the so-called warlords. Most warlords were men of strong, flamboyant personality, capable of building armies by preying on the peasantry and of winning legal recognition from Beijing. None of them proved able to establish either a new dynasty or a modern state. Their wars, taxes, and corruption created only terrible suffering.

Foreign imperialism intensified the agony of warlordism. Although China declared its neutrality in 1914, Japan used the Great War in Europe as an opportunity to seize Germany's holdings on the Shandong (Shantung) Peninsula and in 1915 forced China to accept Japanese control of Shandong and southern Manchuria (see Map 29.4, page 000). Japan's expansion angered China's growing middle class and enraged China's young patriots. On May 4, 1919, five thousand students in Beijing exploded against the decision of the Versailles Peace Conference to leave the Shandong Peninsula in Japanese hands. This famous incident launched the May Fourth Movement, which opposed both foreign domination and warlord government.

The May Fourth Movement and the anti-imperialism of Bolshevik Russia renewed the hopes of Chinese nationalists. Struggling for a foothold in southern China, Sun Yat-sen (1866–1925) decided in 1923 to ally his Nationalist party, or Guomindang (Kuomintang), with the Communist Third International and the newly formed Chinese Communist party. The result was the first of many so-called national liberation fronts, in keeping with Lenin's blueprint for (temporarily) uniting all anti-conservative, anti-imperialist forces in a common revolutionary struggle. In an effort to develop a disciplined party apparatus and a well-indoctrinated party army, Sun reorganized the Nationalist party along Bolshevik lines.

Sun, however, was no Communist. In his *Three Principles of the People,* elaborating on the official Nationalist party ideology—nationalism, democ-

EAST ASIA, 1911–1939

1911–1912	Revolution in China overthrows Manchu Dynasty and establishes republic
1915	Japan seizes German holdings in China and expands into southern Manchuria
May 4, 1919	Demonstration by Chinese students against Versailles Peace Conference and Japan sparks broad nationalist movement
1920s	New Cultural Movement challenges traditional Chinese values
1922	Japan signs naval agreement with Western powers
1923	Sun Yat-sen allies the Nationalist party with Chinese Communists Kita Ikki advocates ultranationalism in Japan
1925–1928	Chiang Kai-shek, leader of the Nationalist Party, attacks warlord government and seeks to unify China
1927	Chiang Kai-shek purges his Communist allies Mao Tse-tung recognizes the revolutionary potential of the Chinese peasantry
1930–1934	Nationalists campaign continually against the Chinese Communists
1931	Mukden Incident leads to Japanese occupation of Manchuria
1932	Japan proclaims Manchuria an independent state
1934	Mao leads Communists on Long March to new base in northwestern China The Philippines gain self-governing commonwealth status from United States
1936	Japan allies with Germany in anti-Communist pact
1937	Japanese militarists launch general attack on China

racy, and people's livelihood—nationalism remained of prime importance:

Compared to the other peoples of the world we have the greatest population and our civilization is four thousand years old; we should be advancing in the front rank with the nations of Europe and America. But the Chinese people have only family and clan solidarity, they do not have national spirit. Therefore even though we have four hundred million people gathered together in one China, in reality they are just a heap of loose sand. Today we are the poorest and weakest nation in the world, and occupy the lowest position in international affairs. . . . If we do not earnestly espouse nationalism and weld together our four hundred million people into a strong nation, there is a danger of China's being lost and our people being destroyed. If we wish to avert this catastrophe, we must espouse nationalism and bring this national spirit to the salvation of the country.[13]

Democracy, in contrast, had a less exalted meaning. Sun equated it with firm rule by the Nationalists, who would promote the people's livelihood through land reform and welfare measures. Sun was in some ways a traditional Chinese rebel and reformer who wanted to re-establish order and protect the peasants.

Sun's plan was to use the Nationalist party's revolutionary army to crush the warlords and reunite China under a strong central government. When Sun unexpectedly died in 1925, this task was assumed by Jiang Jieshi (Chiang Kai-shek), the young Japanese-educated director of the party's army training school. In 1926 and 1927, Jiang (1887–1975) led enthusiastic Nationalist armies in a highly successful attack on warlord governments in central and northern China. Preceded by teams of party propagandists, the well-disciplined Nationalist armies were welcomed by the people. In a series of complicated moves, the Nationalists consolidated their rule in 1928 and established a new capital at Nanjing (Nanking). Foreign states recognized the Nanjing government, and superficial observers believed China to be truly reunified.

In fact, national unification was only skin deep. China remained a vast agricultural country plagued by foreign concessions, regional differences, and a lack of modern communications. Moreover, Japan was opposed to a China strong enough to challenge Japan's stranglehold on Manchuria. And the uneasy alliance between the Nationalist party and the Chinese Communist party had turned into a bitter, deadly rivalry. Justifiably fearful of Communist subversion of the Nationalist government and encouraged by his military success and by wealthy Chinese capitalists, Jiang decided in April 1927 to liquidate his left-wing "allies" in a bloody purge. Secret agents raided Communist cells without warning, and soldiers gunned down suspects on sight. Chinese Communists went into hiding and vowed revenge.

China's Intellectual Revolution

Nationalism was the most powerful idea in China between 1911 and 1929, but it was only one aspect of a complex intellectual revolution that hammered at traditional Chinese thought and custom, advocated cultural renaissance, and pushed China into the modern world. Two other currents in that intellectual revolution, generally known as the New Culture Movement, were significant.

The New Culture Movement was founded by young Western-oriented intellectuals in Beijing during the May Fourth era. These intellectuals fiercely attacked China's ancient Confucian ethics, which subordinated subjects to rulers, sons to fathers, and wives to husbands. Confucius had lived in a distant feudal age, they said; his teachings were totally inappropriate to modern life. In such widely read magazines as *New Youth* and *New Tide,* the modernists provocatively advocated new and anti-Confucian virtues: individualism, democratic equality, and the critical scientific method. They also promoted the use of simple, understandable written language, a language freed from classical scholarship and literary conventions, as a means to clear thinking and mass education. China, they said, needed a whole new culture, a radically different world-view.

The most influential of these intellectuals championing liberalism was Hu Shi (1891–1962). Educated on a scholarship in the United States, the mature Hu Shi envisioned a vague and uninspiring future. The liberation and reconstruction of China was possible, he said, but it would have to occur gradually, "bit by bit, drop by drop." Hu personified the limitations of the Western liberal tradition in China.

The other major current growing out of the New Culture Movement was Marxian socialism. It too was Western in origin, "scientific" in approach, and materialist in its denial of religious belief and Confucian family ethics. But while liberalism and individualism reflected the bewildering range of Western thought since the Enlightenment, Marxian socialism offered Chinese intellectuals the certainty of a single all-encompassing creed. As one young Communist exclaimed: "I am now able to impose order on all the ideas which I could not reconcile; I have found the key to all the problems which appeared to me self-contradictory and insoluble."[14]

Marxism was undeniably Western and therefore modern. But it also provided a means of criticizing Western dominance, thereby salving Chinese pride. Chinese Communists could blame China's pitiful weakness on rapacious foreign capitalistic imperialism. Thus Marxism, as modified by Lenin and applied by the Bolsheviks in the Soviet Union, appeared as a means of catching up with the hated but envied West. For Chinese believers, it promised salvation soon.

Chinese Communists could and did interpret Marxism-Leninism to appeal to the masses—the peasants. Mao Zedong (Mao Tse-tung) in particular recognized quickly the enormous revolutionary potential of the Chinese peasantry, impoverished and oppressed by parasitic landlords. A member of a prosperous, hard-working peasant family, Mao (1893–1976) converted to Marxian socialism in 1918 while employed as an assistant librarian at Beijing University. He began his revolutionary career as an urban labor organizer. In 1925 protest strikes by Chinese textile workers against their Japanese employers unexpectedly spread from the big coastal cities to rural China, prompting Mao to reconsider the peasants. Investigating the rapid growth of radical peasant associations in Hunan province, Mao argued passionately in a 1927 report that

the force of the peasantry is like that of the raging winds and driving rain. It is rapidly increasing in violence. No force can stand in its way. The peasantry will tear apart all nets which bind it and hasten along the road to liberation. They will bury beneath them all forces of imperialism, militarism, corrupt officialdom, village bosses and evil gentry. Every revolutionary party, every revolutionary comrade will be subjected to their scrutiny and be accepted or rejected by them.[15]

The task of Communists was to harness the peasant hurricane and use its elemental force to destroy the existing order and take power. Mao's first experiment in peasant revolt—the Autumn Harvest Uprising of September 1927—was no more successful than the abortive insurrections of urban workers launched by his more orthodox comrades. But Mao learned quickly. He advocated equal distribution of land and broke up his forces into small guerrilla groups. After 1928 he and his supporters built up a self-governing Communist soviet, centered at Ruijin (Juichin) in southeastern China, and dug in against Nationalist attacks.

The Changing Chinese Family

For many generations, Confucian reverence for the family and family ties had helped to stabilize traditional Chinese society and had given life meaning. The Confucian principle of subordination had suffused family life—subordination of the individual to the group, of the young to the old, of the wife to the husband.

A Daughter of Han, a rare autobiography of a Chinese woman, as told to an American friend, of-

Mao Zedong Adapting Marxian theory to Chinese reality, Mao concentrated on the revolutionary potential of the peasantry. Here the forty-year-old Mao is preaching his gospel to representatives of poor peasants in southern China in 1933. *(Source: Wide World Photos)*

fers an unforgettable glimpse of traditional Chinese family life. Born in 1867 to poor parents in a northern city, Lao Tai Tai lived it all. Her foot-binding was delayed to age nine, "since I loved so much to run and play." When the bandages were finally drawn tight, "my feet hurt so much that for two years I had to crawl on my knees."[16] Her arranged marriage at fourteen was a disaster: her husband was a drug addict—"in those days everyone took opium to some extent"—who grabbed everything to pay for his habit. "There was no freedom then for women," and she endured her situation until her husband sold their four-year-old daughter to buy opium. Taking her remaining baby daughter, Lao Tai Tai fled. She became a beggar, a cook in wealthy households, and a peddler of luxury goods to wealthy cooped-up women.

The two unshakable values that buoyed her were a tough, fatalistic acceptance—"Only fortune that comes of itself will come. There is no use to seek for it"—and devotion to her family. Lao Tai Tai eventually returned home to her husband, who was "good" in those years, "but I did not miss him when he died. I had my newborn son and I was happy. My house was established. . . . Truly all my life I spent thinking of my family." Her lifelong devotion was reciprocated by her faithful son and granddaughter, who cared for her well in old age.

Lao Tai Tai's remarkable life history encompasses both old and new Chinese attitudes toward the family. Her son moved to the city, prospered, and had only one wife. Her granddaughter eventually became a college teacher, an anti-Japanese patriot, and a determined foe of arranged marriages, admirably personifying the trend toward greater freedom and equality for Chinese women after 1911. Foot-binding was outlawed and gradually died out unlamented. Marriage for love became increasingly common, and unprecedented educational and economic opportunities opened up for women. Polygamy declined. In the short space of three generations, rising nationalism and the intellectual revolution accomplished monumental changes in Chinese family life.

From Liberalism to Ultranationalism in Japan

The efforts of the Meiji reformers (see page 906) to build a powerful nationalistic state and resist Western imperialism were spectacularly successful and deeply impressive to Japan's fellow Asians. The Japanese, alone among the peoples of Asia, had mastered modern industrial technology by 1910 and fought victorious wars against both China and Russia. The First World War brought more triumphs. Japan easily seized Germany's Asian holdings and held on to most of them as League of Nations mandates. The Japanese economy expanded

Lao Tai Tai   Seated beside her American friend Ida Pruitt, a tough and resilient Lao Tai Tai shares her remarkable story and reflects on the meaning of her life. *(Source: From Ida Pruitt,* A Daughter of Han, *Yale University Press. Reproduced with permission)*

Japanese Suffragettes In the 1920s Japanese women pressed for political emancipation in demonstrations like this one, but they did not receive the right to vote until 1946. Like these suffragettes, some young women adopted Western fashions. Most workers in modern Japanese textile factories were also women. *(Source: Mansell Collection)*

enormously. Profits soared as Japan won new markets that wartime Europe could no longer supply.

In the early 1920s Japan seemed to make further progress on all fronts. Most Japanese nationalists believed that Japan had a semidivine mission to enlighten and protect Asia, but some were convinced that they could achieve their goal peacefully. In 1922, Japan signed a naval arms limitation treaty with the Western powers and returned some of its control over the Shandong Peninsula to China. These conciliatory moves reduced tensions in East Asia. At home, Japan seemed headed toward genuine democracy. The electorate expanded twelvefold between 1918 and 1925 as all males over twenty-five won the vote. Two-party competition was intense, and cabinet ministers were made responsible to the lower house. Japanese living standards were the highest in Asia. Literacy was universal.

Japan's remarkable rise, however, was accompanied by serious problems. Japan had a rapidly growing population, but natural resources were scarce. As early as the 1920s Japan was exporting manufactured goods in order to pay for imports of food and essential raw materials. Deeply enmeshed in world trade, Japan was vulnerable to every boom and bust. These conditions reinforced the widespread belief that colonies and foreign expansion were matters of life and death for Japan.

Also, rapid industrial development had created an imbalanced "dualistic" economy. The modern sector consisted of a handful of giant conglomerate firms, the *zaibatsu,* or "financial combine." A zai-batsu firm like Mitsubishi employed thousands of workers and owned banks, mines, steel mills, cotton factories, shipyards, and trading companies, all of which were closely interrelated. Zaibatsu firms had enormous economic power and dominated the other sector of the economy, which consisted of an unorganized multitude of peasant farmers and craftsmen. The result was financial oligarchy, corruption of government officials, and a weak middle class.

Behind the façade of party politics, the old and new elites—the emperor, high government officials, big businessmen, and military leaders—were jockeying savagely for the real power. Cohesive leadership, which had played such an important role in Japan's modernization by the Meiji reformers, had ceased to exist. By far the most serious challenge to peaceful progress, however, was fanatical nationalism. As in Europe, ultranationalism first emerged in Japan in the late nineteenth century but did not flower fully until the First World War and the 1930s.

Though often vague, Japan's ultranationalists shared several fundamental beliefs. They were violently anti-Western. They rejected democracy, big business, and Marxian socialism, which they blamed for destroying the older, superior Japanese practices that they wanted to restore. Reviving old myths, they stressed the emperor's godlike qualities and the samurai warrior's code of honor and obedience. Despising party politics, they assassinated moderate leaders and plotted armed uprisings to achieve their goals. Above all else, the ultranationalists preached foreign expansion. Like Western imperialists shouldering "the White Man's Burden," Japanese ultranationalists thought their mission was a noble one. "Asia for the Asians" was their self-satisfied rallying cry. As the famous ultranationalist Kita Ikki wrote in 1923:

Our seven hundred million brothers in China and India have no other path to independence than that offered by our guidance and protection. . . . The noble Greece of Asian culture [Japan] must complete her national reorganization on the basis of her own national polity. At the same time, let her lift the virtuous banner of an Asian league and take the leadership in a world federation which must come.[17]

The ultranationalists were noisy and violent in the 1920s, but it took the Great Depression of the 1930s to tip the scales decisively in their favor. The worldwide depression hit Japan like a tidal wave in 1930. Exports and wages collapsed; unemployment and raw suffering soared. Starving peasants ate the bark off trees and sold their daughters to brothels. The ultranationalists blamed the system, and people listened.

Japan Against China

Among those who listened with particular care were young Japanese army officers in Manchuria, the underpopulated, resource-rich province of northeastern China, controlled by the Japanese army since its victory over Russia in 1905. Many junior Japanese officers in Manchuria came from the peasantry and were distressed by the stories of rural suffering they heard from home. They also knew that the budget and prestige of the Japanese army had declined in the prosperous 1920s.

Most worrisome of all to the young officers was the rise of Chinese nationalism. This new political force challenged the control that Japan exercised over Manchuria through Chinese warlords that they controlled. In response, junior Japanese officers in Manchuria, in cooperation with top generals in Tokyo, secretly manufactured an excuse for aggression in late 1931. They blew up some tracks on a Japanese-owned railroad near the city of Mukden and then quickly occupied all of Manchuria in "self-defense."

In 1932 Japan proclaimed Manchuria an independent state and installed a member of the old Manchu dynasty as puppet emperor. When the League of Nations condemned its aggression in Manchuria, Japan resigned in protest. Politics in Japan became increasingly chaotic. The army, though reporting directly to the emperor of Japan, was clearly an independent force subject to no outside control.

For China, the Japanese conquest of Manchuria was disastrous. Japanese aggression in Manchuria drew attention away from modernizing efforts, which in any event had been none too vigorous. The Nationalist government promoted a massive boycott of Japanese goods but lost interest in social reform. Above all, the Nationalist government after 1931 completely neglected land reform and the grinding poverty of the Chinese peasants. As in many poor agricultural societies throughout history, Chinese peasants paid roughly half of their crops to their landlords as rent. Ownership of land was very unequal. One careful study estimated that fully half of the land was owned by a mere 4 percent of the families, usually absentee landlords living in cities. Poor peasants and farm laborers—70 percent of the rural population—owned only one-sixth of the land.

As a result, peasants were heavily in debt and chronically underfed. Eggs and meat accounted for only 2 percent of the food consumed by poor and middle-income peasants. A contemporary Chinese economist spelled out the revolutionary implications: "It seems clear that the land problem in China today is as acute as that of eighteenth-century France or nineteenth-century Russia."[18] Mao Zedong certainly agreed.

Having abandoned land reform, partly because they themselves were often landowners, the Nationalists under Jiang Jieshi devoted their energies between 1930 and 1934 to five great campaigns of encirclement and extermination against the Communists' rural power base in southeastern China. In 1934 they closed in for the kill, only to miss again. In one of the most incredible sagas of modern times, the main Communist army broke out of the Nationalist encirclement, beat off attacks, and marched 6,000 miles in twelve months to a remote region on the northwestern border (Map 30.2). Of the estimated 100,000 men and women who began the Long March, only from 8,000 to 10,000 reached the final destination. There Mao built up his forces once again, established a new territorial base, and won the support of local peasants by undertaking land reform.

In 1937, the Japanese military and the ultranationalists were in command and decided to use a minor incident near Beijing as a pretext for a general attack. The Nationalist government, which had just formed a united front with the Communists in response to the demands of Chinese patriots, fought hard but could not halt the Japanese. By late 1938, Japanese armies occupied sizable portions of coastal China (see Map 30.2). The Nationalists and the Communists had retreated to the interior, both refusing to accept defeat. The determination of the Communist guerrillas equaled that of the Nationalists, and their political skill proved superior. In 1939, as Europe (and the United States) edged toward another great war, the undeclared war between China and Japan bogged down in a savage stalemate. The bloody clash on the mainland provided a spectacular example of conflicting nationalisms, convulsing China and preparing for Communist victory (see pages 1133, 1134).

The Fall of Nanjing In December 1937 Japanese armies crossed into the fallen Chinese city and disgraced themselves in a frenzy of destruction known as the Rape of Nanjing. Japanese soldiers' reputation for brutality lasted until the end of World War II. *(Source: Robert Hunt Library)*

Southeast Asia

The tide of nationalism was also rising in Southeast Asia. Like their counterparts in India, China, and Japan, nationalists in Southeast Asia urgently

U.S.S.R.

Amur

MANCHURIA

• Qiqihar

• Jiamusi

Ussuri

OUTER MONGOLIA
(Independent 1924)

• Harbin

• Jinzhou

Zhangjiakou
(Kalgan) •

• Shenyang
(Mukden)

KOREA
(Japanese 1910–1945)

Baotou •

• Beijing

• Tianjin

Lüshun •
(Port Arthur)

• Taiyuan

Yan'an •

Lanzhou •

Huang He

(Yellow)

• Jinan

• Qingdao

SHAANXI
Xi'an •

Luoyang • Zhengzhou
•

CHINA

• Xuzhou

• Nanjing

Chengdu •

Chang Jiang
(Yangtze)

• Shanghai

SICHUAN
Chongqing •

Wuhan •

• Hangzhou

Zunyi •

Nanchang •

Changsha •

HUNAN

Kiangsi Soviet under
Mao Zedong and
Chu Teh, 1929–1934

Guiyang •

• Ji'an

Kunming •

PACIFIC
OCEAN

Canton uprising
Dec. 1927

Shantou •

Xiamen •
(Amoy)

TAIWAN
(Japanese
1895–1945)

BURMA

Guangzhou •
(Canton)

Hailufeng Soviet,
1927–1928

FRENCH
INDO-CHINA

Hong Kong
(British)

◤◤ Areas under Communist control before Nov. 1934

▓ Areas under Communist control, 1929–1938

▒ Areas occupied by Japan by end of 1938

⟵ Route of the Long March, Oct. 1934–Oct. 1935: Main forces from Ji'an

⟵ Other forces

0 — 250 — 500 Km.

0 — 250 — 500 Mi.

wanted genuine political independence and freedom from foreign rule. In both French Indochina and the Dutch East Indies, local nationalists, inspired by events elsewhere in Asia, pressed their own demands. In both cases they ran up against an imperialist stone wall.

In the words of one historian, "Indochina was governed by Frenchmen for Frenchmen, and the great liberal slogans of liberty, equality, and fraternity were not considered to be export goods for overseas dominions."[19] This uncompromising attitude stimulated the growth of an equally stubborn Communist opposition, which despite ruthless repression emerged as the dominant anti-French force.

In the East Indies—modern Indonesia—the Dutch made some concessions after the First World War, establishing a people's council with very limited lawmaking power. But in the 1930s the Dutch cracked down hard, jailing all the important nationalist leaders. Like the French, the Dutch were determined to hold on.

In the Philippines, however, a well-established nationalist movement achieved greater success. As in colonial Latin America, the Spanish in the Philippines had been indefatigable missionaries. By the late nineteenth century 80 percent of the Filipino population was Catholic. Filipinos shared a common cultural heritage as well as a common racial origin. Education, especially for girls, was quite advanced for Southeast Asia, and in 1843 a higher percentage of people could read in the Philippines than in Spain itself. Economic development helped to create a westernized elite, which turned first to reform and then to revolution in the 1890s. As in Egypt or Turkey, long-standing intimate contact with Western civilization created a strong nationalist movement at an early date.

Filipino nationalists were bitterly disillusioned when the United States, having taken the Philippines from Spain in the Spanish-American War of 1898, ruthlessly beat down a patriotic revolt and denied the universal Filipino desire for independence. The Americans claimed that the Philippines were not ready and might be seized by Germany or Britain. As the imperialist power in the Philippines, the United States encouraged education and promoted capitalistic economic development. As in British India, an elected legislature was given some real powers. In 1919 President Wilson even promised eventual independence, though subsequent Republican administrations saw it as a distant goal.

As in India and French Indochina, demands for independence grew. One important contributing factor was American racial attitudes. Americans treated Filipinos as inferiors and introduced segregationist practices borrowed from the American South. American racism made passionate nationalists of many Filipinos. However, it was the Great Depression that had the most radical impact on the Philippines.

As the United States collapsed economically, the Philippines suddenly appeared to be a liability rather than an asset. American farm groups lobbied for protection from cheap Filipino sugar. To protect American jobs, labor unions demanded an end to Filipino immigration. In 1934 Congress made the Philippines a self-governing commonwealth and scheduled independence for 1944. Sugar imports were reduced, and immigration was limited to only fifty Filipinos per year.

Like Britain and France in the Middle East, the United States was determined to hold on to its big military bases in the Philippines as it permitted increased local self-government and promised eventual political independence. Some Filipino nationalists denounced the continued presence of U.S. fleets and armies. Others were less certain that the American presence was the immediate problem. Japan was fighting in China and expanding economically into the Philippines and throughout Southeast Asia. By 1939, a new threat to Filipino independence appeared to come from Asia itself.

MAP 30.2 The Chinese Communist Movement and the War with Japan, 1927–1938 After urban uprisings ordered by Stalin failed in 1927, Mao Zedong succeeded in forming a self-governing Communist soviet in mountainous southern China. Relentless Nationalist attacks between 1930 and 1934 finally forced the Long March to Yenan, where the Communists were well positioned for guerrilla war against the Japanese.

Summary

The Asian revolt against the West began before the First World War. But only after 1914 did Asian nationalist movements broaden their bases and become capable of challenging Western domination effectively. These mass movements sought human dignity as well as political freedom. Generally speaking, Asian nationalists favored modernization and adopted Western techniques and ideas even as they rejected Western rule. Everywhere Asian nationalists had to fight long and hard, though their struggle gained momentum from growing popular support and the encouragement of the Soviet Union.

Asia's nationalist movements arose out of separate historical experiences and distinct cultures. Variations on the common theme of nationalism were evident in Turkey, the Arab world, India, China, Japan, and the Philippines. This diversity helps explain why Asian peoples became defensive in their relations with one another while rising against Western rule. Like earlier nationalists in Europe, Asian nationalists developed a strong sense of "we" and "they"; "they" included other Asians as well as Europeans. Nationalism meant freedom, modernization, and cultural renaissance, but it nonetheless proved a mixed blessing.

NOTES

1. K. M. Panikkar, *Asia and Western Dominance: A Survey of the Vasco da Gama Epoch of Asian History* (London: George Allen & Unwin, 1959), p. 197.
2. Quoted in H. Grimal, *La Décolonisation, 1919–1965* (Paris: Armand Colin, 1965), p. 100.
3. Quoted in P. Mansfield, *The Ottoman Empire and Its Successors* (New York: St. Martin's Press, 1973), p. 18.
4. H. Armstrong, *Turkey in Travail: The Birth of a New Nation* (London: John Lane, 1925), p. 75.
5. Quoted in Lord Kinross, *Atatürk: A Biography of Mustafa Kemal, Father of Modern Turkey* (New York: Morrow, 1965), p. 181.
6. P. Spear, *India, Pakistan, and the West,* 3d ed. (Oxford: Oxford University Press, 1958), p. 67.
7. Quoted in E. Erikson, *Gandhi's Truth: On the Origins of Militant Nonviolence* (New York: Norton, 1969), p. 105.
8. H. Tinker, *A New System of Slavery: The Export of Indian Labour Overseas, 1830–1920* (London: Oxford University Press, 1974).
9. Quoted in Erikson, *Gandhi's Truth,* p. 225.
10. Quoted in W. Bingham, H. Conroy, and F. Iklé, *A History of Asia,* vol. 1, 2d ed. (Boston: Allyn and Bacon, 1974), p. 447.
11. W. Miller, *I Found No Peace: The Journal of a Foreign Correspondent* (New York: Simon and Schuster, 1936), p. 193.
12. Quoted in L. Rudolph and S. Rudolph, *The Modernity of Tradition: Political Development in India* (Chicago: University of Chicago Press, 1967), p. 248.
13. Quoted in W. T. deBary, W. Chan, and B. Watson, *Sources of Chinese Tradition* (New York: Columbia University Press, 1964), pp. 768–769.
14. Quoted in J. F. Fairbank, E. O. Reischauer, and A. M. Craig, *East Asia: Tradition and Transformation* (Boston: Houghton Mifflin, 1973), p. 774.
15. Quoted in B. I. Schwartz, *Chinese Communism and the Rise of Mao* (Cambridge, Mass.: Harvard University Press, 1951), p. 74.
16. I. Pruitt, *A Daughter of Han: The Autobiography of a Chinese Working Woman* (New Haven, Conn.: Yale University Press, 1945), p. 22. Other quotations are taken, in order, from pages 83, 71, 182, 166, and 235.
17. Quoted in W. T. deBary, R. Tsunoda, and D. Keene, *Sources of Japanese Tradition,* vol. 2 (New York: Columbia University Press, 1958), p. 269.
18. Quoted in O. Lang, *Chinese Family and Society* (New Haven, Conn.: Yale University Press, 1946), p. 70.
19. Quoted in W. Bingham, H. Conroy, and F. Iklé, *A History of Asia,* vol. 2, 2d ed. (Boston: Allyn and Bacon, 1974), p. 480.

SUGGESTED READING

All of the works cited in the Notes are highly recommended. Two important general interpretations of nationalism and independence movements are P. Chatterjee, *Nationalist Thought and the Colonial World: A Derivative Discourse* (1986), and R. Emerson, *From Empire to Nation: The Rise to Self-Assertion of Asian and African Peoples* (1960). These may be compared with the provocative works of E. Kedourie, including *Nationalism in Asia and Africa* (1970), and with an influential global history of the twentieth century by G. Barraclough, *An Introduction to Contemporary History* (1975). B. Lewis, *The Shaping of the Modern Middle East* (1993), is a reflective work by a leading historian, which complements A. Hourani,

History of the Arab Peoples (1991). On Turkey, in addition to Lord Kinross's *Atatürk* (1965), see B. Lewis, *The Emergence of Modern Turkey* (1961), and D. Kushner, *The Rise of Turkish Nationalism, 1876–1908* (1977). Peter Mansfield, *The Arab World: A Comprehensive History* (1976), and S. G. Haim, ed., *Arab Nationalism: An Anthology* (1964), provide engaging general coverage and important source materials. W. Lacqueur, *A History of Zionism* (1972), and A. Eban, *My People* (1968), discuss the Jewish homeland in Palestine. The Arab viewpoint is presented by G. Antonius, *The Arab Awakening: The Story of the Arab National Movement* (1946). R. Cottam, *Nationalism in Iran,* rev. ed. (1979), complements the classic study of D. Wilbur, *Iran: Past and Present,* 9th ed. (1981).

The historical literature on modern India is very rich. S. Wolpert, *A New History of India,* 4th ed. (1993), is an excellent introduction, with up-to-date scholarship and detailed suggestions for further reading. Also see the handsomely illustrated volume by F. Watson, *A Concise History of India* (1975). In addition to the biography by Erikson cited in the Notes, L. Fischer, *Gandhi: His Life and Message for the World* (1954), is fascinating. J. Brown, *Gandhi's Rise to Power: Indian Politics, 1915–1922* (1972), and V. Mehta, *Mahatma Gandhi and His Apostles* (1977), are major studies. Developments in the Muslim community are considered by P. Hardy, *The Muslims of British India* (1972); B. Metcalf, *Islamic Revival in British India: Deoband, 1860–1900* (1982); and F. Robinson, *Atlas of the Islamic World Since 1500* (1982), a beautifully illustrated survey encompassing far more than India.

Studies of China in the twentieth century are also very numerous. J. Spence, *The Search for Modern China* (1990), and I. Hsü, *The Rise of Modern China,* 4th ed. (1990), are comprehensive studies with extensive bibliographies, which may be supplemented by the documentary collection of F. Schurmann and O. Schell, eds., *Republican China: Nationalism, War and the Rise of Communism, 1911–1949* (1967). J. Spence, *The Gate of Heavenly Peace: The Chinese and Their Revolution, 1895–1980* (1981), skillfully focuses on leading literary figures. T. Chow, *The May Fourth Movement: Intellectual Revolution in Modern China* (1960), examines a critical time period. Other important studies of China in this period include R. Hofheinz, Jr., *The Broken Wave: The Chinese Communist Peasant Movement, 1922–1928* (1977); S. Schram, *Mao Tse-tung* (1966); and H. Schriffrin, *Sun Yat-sen and the Origins of the Chinese Revolution* (1970). L. Eastman, *Family, Consistency and Change in China's Social and Economic History, 1550–1949* (1974), is a masterful synthesis. P. Ebrey, ed., *Chinese Civilization and Society: A Sourcebook* (1981), complements the classic studies of the Chinese family by Lang and Pruitt, which may be compared with M. J. Levy, *The Family Revolution in Modern China* (1949).

E. Reischauer, *Japan: The Story of a Nation,* rev. ed. (1970), and P. Duus, *The Rise of Modern Japan* (1976), are excellent interpretations of the recent history of the island nation. W. Lockwood, *The Economic Development of Japan, 1868–1938* (1954), and R. Storry, *The Double Patriots: A Story of Japanese Nationalism* (1973), are valuable specialized works. M. Hane, *Peasants, Rebels, and Outcasts: The Underside of Modern Japan* (1982), sees few benefits for the poor before 1945. S. Garon, *The State and Labor in Modern Japan* (1988), skillfully analyzes the history of Japanese labor relations. Two edited collections, J. Morley, *The China Quagmire* (1983), and R. Myers and M. Peattie, *The Japanese Colonial Expansion, 1895–1945* (1984), probe Japan's imperial expansion.

For Southeast Asia, see D. G. E. Hall, *A History of South-East Asia,* 4th ed. (1981); J. Pluvier, *South-East Asia from Colonialism to Independence* (1974); and the Suggested Reading for Chapter 34. Two more recommended works are M. Osborne, *Southeast Asia: An Illustrated History,* expanded ed. (1988), and D. R. Sardesa, *Southeast Past and Present,* 2d ed. (1989).

Nonviolent Resistance in India

Mahatma Gandhi developed a powerful spiritual theory of social action. Drawing on both Hindu and Christian morality, Gandhi taught that the weak and unarmed could combine love and courage to overcome oppression and injustice. Gandhi's chosen tactic was nonviolent resistance, which challenged British rule in India with illegal protest marches and mass civil disobedience. Nonviolent resistance demanded tremendous self-discipline from protesters because they had to "turn the other cheek" and accept great pain and suffering.

The first protest campaign, in 1920–1922, ended in violence, and Gandhi felt compelled to call it off. In 1930 Gandhi launched a new round of nonviolent disobedience, which focused on the hated salt tax. Gandhi was jailed, but his army of peaceful resisters continued the struggle and did not give in to violence.

One eyewitness was Webb Miller, an American correspondent dispatched from London to cover the story in India. Arriving in India by air on the weekly passenger service after fifteen days and 16,000 miles, Miller met with Congress party leaders and caught up with the protesters near the sea. There he saw the dramatic climax of the salt-tax demonstrations, foiled the British censorship, and got the story out to the world's newspapers. The following account comes from Webb's 1936 autobiography.

After plodding about six miles across country [from the nearest railroad station] . . . I reached the assembling place of the Gandhi followers. Several long, open, thatched sheds . . . buzzed like a beehive with some 2,500 Congress or Gandhi men dressed in the regulation uniform of rough homespun cotton dhotis and triangular Gandhi caps. . . . I was warmly welcomed by young college-educated, English-speaking men and escorted to Mme. Naidu. The famous Indian poetess . . . explained that she was busy martialing her forces for the demonstration against the salt pans.

. . . She was educated in England and spoke English fluently.

Mme. Naidu called for prayer before the march started and the entire assemblage knelt. She exhorted them: "Gandhi's body is in jail but his soul is with you. India's prestige is in your hands. You must not use any violence under any circumstances. You will be beaten but you must not resist; you must not even raise a hand to ward off blows." Wild, shrill cheers terminated her speech.

Slowly and in silence the throng commenced the half-mile march to the salt deposits. . . .

The salt deposits were surrounded by ditches filled with water and guarded by four hundred native Surat police in khaki shorts and brown turbans. Half a dozen British officials commanded them. The police carried *lathis*—five-foot clubs tipped with steel. Inside the stockade twenty-five native riflemen were drawn up.

In complete silence the Gandhi men drew up and halted a hundred yards from the stockade. A picked column advanced from the crowd, waded the ditches, and approached the barbed-wire stockade, which the Surat police surrounded, holding their clubs at the ready. Police officials ordered the marchers to disperse. . . . The column silently ignored the warning and slowly walked forward.

Suddenly, at a word of command, scores of native policemen rushed upon the advancing marchers and rained blows on their heads with their steel-shod *lathis*. Not one of the marchers even raised an arm to fend off the blows. They went down like ten-pins. From where I stood I heard the sickening whacks of the clubs on unprotected skulls. The waiting crowd of watchers groaned and sucked in their breaths in sympathetic pain at every blow.

Those struck down fell sprawling, unconscious or writhing in pain with fractured skulls or broken shoulders. In two or three minutes the ground was quilted with bodies. Great patches of blood widened on their white clothes. The survivors, without breaking ranks, silently and doggedly marched on until struck down. When every one of the first column had been knocked down stretcher-bearers rushed up unmolested by the police and carried off the injured to a thatched hut which had been arranged as a temporary hospital.

Then another column formed while the leaders pleaded with them to retain their self-control. They marched slowly toward the police. Although every one knew that within a few minutes he would be beaten, perhaps killed, I could detect no signs of wavering or fear. They marched steadily with heads up, without the encouragement of music or cheering or any possibility that they might escape serious injury or death. The police rushed out and methodically and mechanically beat down the second column. There was no fight, no struggle; the marchers simply walked forward until struck down. There were no outcries, only groans after they fell. . . .

At times the spectacle of unresisting men being methodically bashed into a bloody pulp sickened me so much that I had to turn away. The Western mind finds it difficult to grasp the idea of nonresistance. I felt an indefinable sense of helpless rage and loathing, almost as much against the men who were submitting unresistingly to being beaten as against the police wielding the clubs, and this despite the fact that when I came to India I sympathized with the Gandhi cause.

Several times the leaders nearly lost control of the waiting crowd. They rushed up and down, frantically pleading with and exhorting the intensely excited men to remember Gandhi's instructions. It seemed that the unarmed throng was on the verge of launching a mass attack upon the police. . . . [But this did not happen.] Group after group walked forward, sat down, and submitted to being beaten into insensibility without raising an arm to fend off the blows. . . .

Hour after hour stretcher-bearers carried back a stream of inert, bleeding bodies . . . back to the temporary hospital. . . . I counted 320 injured, many still insensible with fractured skulls, others writing in agony from kicks in the testicles and stomach. . . .

I was the only foreign correspondent who had witnessed the amazing scene—a classic example of "Satyagraha" or nonviolent civil disobedience. . . . My story of the beatings at Dharasana caused a sensation when it appeared in the 1,350 newspapers served by the United Press throughout the world. . . . Representatives of the Gandhi movement in the United States printed it as a leaflet and distributed more than a quarter of a million copies.

Gandhi chose the Indian spinning wheel as a symbol of national rejuvenation. *(Source: Wide World Photos)*

Questions for Analysis

1. What happened at this demonstration against the salt tax in India? What seems most important to you?
2. How did Miller react to what he saw? Do you share his reaction? Why or why not?
3. Gandhi believed that nonviolent resistance required great courage. Do you agree or disagree? Why?
4. What are the strengths and weaknesses of nonviolent resistance as a strategy of social action?

Source: Webb Miller, *I Found No Peace: The Journal of a Foreign Correspondent* (New York: Simon and Schuster, 1925), pp. 192–96, 198–99.

The Age of Anxiety in the West

Dust, a painting of the Great Depression by the Russian-born American painter Ben Shahn (1898–1969). *(Source: Courtesy, Kennedy Galleries, New York)*

When Allied diplomats met in Paris in early 1919 with their optimistic plans for building a lasting peace, most looked forward to happier times. They hoped that life would return to normal after the terrible trauma of total war. They hoped that once again life would make sense in the familiar prewar terms of peace, prosperity, and progress. These hopes were in vain. The Great Break—the First World War and the Russian Revolution—had mangled too many things beyond repair. Life would no longer fit neatly into the old molds.

Instead, great numbers of men and women in the West felt themselves increasingly adrift in a strange, uncertain, and uncontrollable world. They saw themselves living in an age of anxiety, an age of continual crisis (this age lasted until at least the early 1950s). In almost every area of human experience, people went searching for ways to put meaning back into life.

- What did such doubts and searching mean for Western thought, art, and culture?
- How did leaders deal with the political dimensions of uncertainty and try to re-establish real peace and prosperity between 1919 and 1939?
- Why did those leaders fail?

These are the questions this chapter will explore.

❖ UNCERTAINTY IN MODERN THOUGHT

A complex revolution in thought and ideas was under way in Western society before the First World War, but only small, unusual groups were aware of it. After the war, new and upsetting ideas began to spread through the entire population. Western society began to question and even abandon many cherished values and beliefs that had guided it since the eighteenth-century Enlightenment and the nineteenth-century triumph of industrial development, scientific advances, and evolutionary thought.

Before 1914 most people in the West still believed in progress, reason, and the rights of the individual. Progress was a daily reality, apparent in the rising standard of living, the taming of the city, and the steady increase in popular education. Such developments also encouraged the comforting be-

lief in the logical universe of Newtonian physics as well as faith in the ability of a rational human mind to understand that universe through intellectual investigation. And just as there were laws of science, so were there laws of society that rational human beings could discover and then wisely act on. At the same time, the rights of the individual were not just taken for granted; they were actually increasing. Well-established rights were gradually spreading to women and workers, and new "social rights," such as old-age pensions, were emerging. In short, before World War I most Europeans and North Americans had a moderately optimistic view of the world, and with good reason.

Nevertheless, since the 1880s, a small band of serious thinkers and creative writers had been attacking these well-worn optimistic ideas. These critics rejected the general faith in progress and the power of the rational human mind. An expanding chorus of thinkers echoed and enlarged their views after the experience of history's most destructive war—a war that suggested to many that human beings were a pack of violent, irrational animals quite capable of tearing the individual and his or her rights to shreds. Disorientation and pessimism were particularly acute in the 1930s, when the rapid rise of harsh dictatorships and the Great Depression transformed old certainties into bitter illusions.

No one expressed this state of uncertainty better than French poet and critic Paul Valéry (1871–1945) in the early 1920s. Speaking of the "crisis of the mind," Valéry noted that Europe was looking at its future with dark foreboding:

The storm has died away, and still we are restless, uneasy, as if the storm were about to break. Almost all the affairs of men remain in a terrible uncertainty. We think of what has disappeared, and we are almost destroyed by what has been destroyed; we do not know what will be born, and we fear the future, not without reason. . . . Doubt and disorder are in us and with us. There is no thinking man, however shrewd or learned he may be, who can hope to dominate this anxiety, to escape from this impression of darkness.[1]

In the midst of economic, political, and social disruptions, Valéry saw the "cruelly injured mind," besieged by doubts and suffering from anxieties. In this general intellectual crisis of the twentieth

"The War, as I Saw It"
This was the title of a series of grotesque drawings that appeared in 1920 in *Simplicissimus,* Germany's leading satirical magazine. Nothing shows better the terrible impact of the First World War than this profoundly disturbing example of expressionist art. *(Source: Caroline Buckler)*

century, the implications of new ideas and discoveries in philosophy, physics, psychology, and literature played a central role.

Modern Philosophy

Among those thinkers in the late nineteenth century who challenged the belief in progress and the general faith in the rational human mind, German philosopher Friedrich Nietzsche (1844–1900) was particularly influential. The son of a Lutheran minister, Nietzsche utterly rejected Christianity. In

1872 in his first great work he argued that ever since classical Athens the West had overemphasized rationality and stifled the passion and animal instinct that drive human activity and true creativity. Nietzsche went on to question all values. He claimed that Christianity embodied a "slave morality" that glorified weakness, envy, and mediocrity. In Nietzsche's most famous line, a wise fool proclaims that "God is dead," murdered by lackadaisical modern Christians who no longer really believe in Him. Nietzsche viewed the pillars of conventional morality—reason, democracy, progress, respectability—as outworn social and psychological constructs whose influence was suffocating self-realization and excellence.

Nietzsche painted a dark world, foreshadowing perhaps his loss of sanity in 1889. The West was in decline; false values had triumphed. The only hope for the individual was to accept the meaninglessness of human existence and then make that very meaninglessness a source of self-defined personal integrity and hence liberation. This would at least be possible for a few superior individuals, who could free themselves from the humdrum thinking of the masses and become true heroes. Little read during his active years, Nietzsche attracted growing attention in the early twentieth century, and his influence remains enormous to this day.

Growing dissatisfaction with established ideas before 1914 was apparent in other important thinkers. In the 1890s, French philosophy professor Henri Bergson (1859–1941) convinced many young people through his writing that immediate experience and intuition were as important as rational and scientific thinking for understanding reality. Indeed, according to Bergson, a religious experience or a mystical poem was often more accessible to human comprehension than was a scientific law or a mathematical equation.

Another thinker who agreed about the limits of rational thinking was French socialist Georges Sorel (1847–1922). Sorel frankly characterized Marxian socialism as an inspiring but unprovable religion rather than a rational scientific truth. Socialism would come to power, he believed, through a great, violent strike of all working people, which would miraculously shatter capitalist society. Sorel rejected democracy and believed that the masses of the new socialist society would have to be tightly controlled by a small revolutionary elite.

The First World War accelerated the revolt against established certainties in philosophy, but that revolt went in two very different directions. In English-speaking countries, the main development was the acceptance of logical empiricism (or logical positivism) in university circles. In continental Europe, where esoteric and remote logical empiricism did not win many converts, the primary development in philosophy was existentialism.

Logical empiricism was truly revolutionary. It rejected most of the concerns of traditional philosophy, from the existence of God to the meaning of happiness, as nonsense and hot air. This outlook began primarily with Austrian philosopher Ludwig Wittgenstein (1889–1951), who later emigrated to England, where he trained numerous disciples.

Wittgenstein argued in his pugnacious *Tractatus Logico-Philosophicus* (*Essay on Logical Philosophy*) in 1922 that philosophy is only the logical clarification of thoughts and that it therefore becomes the study of language, which expresses thoughts. In Wittgenstein's opinion, the great philosophical issues of the ages—God, freedom, morality, and so on—are quite literally senseless, a great waste of time, for statements about them can neither be

Friedrich Nietzsche   This colored photograph of the German philosopher was taken in 1882, when he was at the height of his creative powers. A brilliant iconoclast, Nietzsche debunked European values and challenged the optimistic faith in human rationality before the World War I. *(Source: Archiv für Kunst and Geschichte, Berlin)*

tested by scientific experiments nor demonstrated by the logic of mathematics. Instead, statements about such matters reflect only the personal preferences of a given individual. As Wittgenstein put it in the famous last sentence of his work, "Of what one cannot speak, of that one must keep silent." Logical empiricism drastically reduced the scope of philosophical inquiry. Anxious people could find few, if any, answers in this direction.

Some looked for answers in *existentialism.* Highly diverse and even contradictory, existential thinkers were loosely united in a courageous search for moral values in a world of terror and uncertainty. Theirs were true voices of the age of anxiety.

Most existential thinkers in the twentieth century were atheists. Often inspired by Nietzsche, they did not believe a supreme being had established humanity's fundamental nature and given life its meaning. In the words of the famous French existentialist Jean-Paul Sartre (1905–1980), human beings simply exist: "They turn up, appear on the scene." Only after they "turn up" do they seek to define themselves. Honest human beings are terribly alone, for there is no God to help them. They are hounded by despair and the meaninglessness of life. The crisis of the existential thinker epitomized the modern intellectual crisis—the shattering of traditional beliefs in God, reason, and progress.

Existentialists did recognize that human beings, unless they kill themselves, must act. Indeed, in the words of Sartre, "man is condemned to be free." There is therefore the possibility—indeed, the necessity—of giving meaning to life through actions, of defining oneself through choices. To do so, individuals must become "engaged" and choose their own actions courageously and consistently and in full awareness of their inescapable responsibility for their own behavior. In the end, existentialists argued, human beings can overcome life's absurdity.

It was in France during and immediately after World War II that existentialism came of age. The terrible conditions of the war reinforced the existential view of and approach to life. With the German dictator Hitler's hideous reign of barbarism, men and women had more than ever to define themselves by their actions. Specifically, each individual had to choose whether to join the resistance against Hitler or accept and even abet tyranny. Sartre himself was active in the French Resistance, and he and his colleagues offered a powerful answer to profound moral issues and the contemporary crisis.

The Revival of Christianity

The loss of faith in human reason and in continual progress also led to a renewed interest in the Christian view of the world. Christianity and religion in general had been on the defensive in intellectual circles since the Enlightenment. In the years before 1914, some theologians, especially Protestant ones, had felt the need to interpret Christian doctrine and the Bible so that they did not seem to contradict science, evolution, and common sense. Christ was therefore seen primarily as the greatest moral teacher, and the "supernatural" aspects of his divinity were strenuously played down. Indeed, some modern theologians were embarrassed by the miraculous, unscientific aspects of Christianity and turned away from them.

Especially after World War I, a number of thinkers and theologians began to revitalize the fundamentals of Christianity. Sometimes described as Christian existentialists because they shared the loneliness and despair of atheistic existentialists, they stressed human beings' sinful nature, the need for faith, and the mystery of God's forgiveness. The revival of fundamental Christian belief after World War I was fed by rediscovery of the work of nineteenth-century Danish religious philosopher Søren Kierkegaard (1813–1855), whose ideas became extremely influential. Having rejected formalistic religion, Kierkegaard had eventually resolved his personal anguish over his imperfect nature by making a total religious commitment to a remote and majestic God.

Similar ideas were brilliantly developed by Swiss Protestant theologian Karl Barth (1886–1968). Barth maintained that religious truth is made known to human beings only through God's grace. Sinful creatures whose reason and will are hopelessly flawed, people have to accept God's word and the supernatural revelation of Jesus Christ with awe, trust, and obedience. Lowly mortals should not expect to "reason out" God and his ways.

Among Catholics, the leading existential Christian thinker was Gabriel Marcel (1887–1973), who found in the Catholic church an answer to what he called the postwar "broken world." Catholicism and religious belief provided the hope, humanity, honesty, and piety for which he hungered. Flexible and gentle, Marcel and his countryman Jacques Maritain (1882–1973) denounced anti-Semitism and supported closer ties with non-Catholics.

After 1914 religion became much more relevant and meaningful to thinking people than it had been before the Great War. In addition to Marcel and Maritain, many other illustrious individuals turned to religion between about 1920 and 1950. Poets T. S. Eliot and W. H. Auden, novelists Evelyn Waugh and Aldous Huxley, historian Arnold Toynbee, Oxford professor C. S. Lewis, psychoanalyst Karl Stern, physicist Max Planck, and philosopher Cyril Joad were all either converted to religion or attracted to it for the first time (see Listening to the Past). Religion, often of a despairing, existential variety, was one meaningful answer to terror and anxiety. In the words of another famous Roman Catholic convert, English novelist Graham Greene, "One began to believe in heaven because one believed in hell."[2]

The New Physics

Ever since the scientific revolution of the seventeenth century, scientific advances and their implications had greatly influenced the beliefs of thinking people. By the late nineteenth century, science was one of the main pillars supporting Western society's optimistic and rationalistic view of the world. Progressive minds believed that science, unlike religion and philosophical speculation, was based on hard facts and controlled experiments. Science seemed to have achieved an unerring and almost completed picture of reality. Unchanging natural laws seemed to determine physical processes and permit useful solutions to more and more problems. All this was comforting, especially to people who were no longer committed to traditional religious beliefs. And all this was challenged by the new physics.

An important first step toward the new physics was the discovery at the end of the nineteenth century that atoms were not like hard, permanent little billiard balls. They were actually composed of many far-smaller, fast-moving particles, such as electrons and protons. Polish-born physicist Marie Curie (1867–1934) and her French husband discovered that radium constantly emits subatomic particles and thus does not have a constant atomic weight. Building on this and other work in radiation, German physicist Max Planck (1858–1947) showed in 1900 that subatomic energy is emit-

ted in uneven little spurts, which Planck called "quanta," and not in a steady stream, as previously believed. Planck's discovery called into question the old sharp distinction between matter and energy and challenged the old view of atoms as the stable, basic building blocks of nature.

In 1905 German-born Jewish genius Albert Einstein (1879–1955) went further than the Curies and Planck in challenging Newtonian physics. His famous theory of special relativity postulated that time and space are relative to the viewpoint of the observer and that only the speed of light is constant for all frames of reference in the universe. In order to make his revolutionary and paradoxical idea somewhat comprehensible to the nonmathematical lay person, Einstein later used analogies involving moving trains. For example, if a woman in the middle of a moving car gets up and walks forward to the door, she has gone, relative to the train, a half car length. But relative to an observer on the embankment, she has gone farther. The closed framework of Newtonian physics was quite limited compared to that of Einsteinian physics, which unified an apparently infinite universe with the incredibly small, fast-moving subatomic world. Moreover, Einstein's theory stated clearly that matter and energy are interchangeable and that even a particle of matter contains enormous levels of potential energy.

The 1920s opened the "heroic age of physics," in the apt words of one of its leading pioneers, Ernest Rutherford (1871–1937). Breakthrough followed breakthrough. In 1919 Rutherford showed that the atom could be split. By 1944 seven subatomic particles had been identified, of which the most important was the neutron. The neutron's capacity to pass through other atoms allowed for even more intense experimental bombardment of matter, leading to chain reactions of unbelievable force. This was the road to the atomic bomb.

Although few nonscientists understood this revolution in physics, the implications of the new theories and discoveries, as presented by newspapers and popular writers, were disturbing to millions of men and women in the 1920s and 1930s. The new universe was strange and troubling. It seemed to lack any absolute objective reality. Everything was said to be "relative"—that is, dependent on the observer's frame of reference. Moreover, in 1927 German physicist Werner Heisenberg (1901–1976) formulated the "principle of uncertainty," which postulates that because it is impossible to know the position and speed of an individual electron, it is therefore impossible to predict its behavior. Instead of Newton's dependable, rational laws, there seemed to be only tendencies and probabilities in an extraordinarily complex and uncertain universe that was described by abstract mathemati-cal symbols and seemed to have little to do with human experience and human problems. When, for example, Planck was asked what science could contribute to resolving conflicts of values, his response was simple: "Science is not qualified to speak to this question."

Freudian Psychology

With physics presenting an uncertain universe so unrelated to ordinary human experience, questions about the power and potential of the human mind assumed special significance. The findings and speculations of leading psychologist Sigmund Freud (see page 862) were particularly disturbing.

Before Freud, poets and mystics had probed the unconscious and irrational aspects of human behavior. But most professional, "scientific" psychologists assumed that human behavior was the result of rational calculation—of "thinking"—by the single, unified conscious mind. Basing his insights on the analysis of dreams and of hysteria, Freud developed a very different view of the human psyche, beginning in the late 1880s.

According to Freud, human behavior is basically irrational. The key to understanding the mind is the primitive, irrational unconscious, which he called the *id*. The unconscious is driven by sexual, aggressive, and pleasure-seeking desires and is locked in a constant battle with the other parts of the mind: the rationalizing conscious (the *ego*), which mediates what a person *can* do, and ingrained moral values (the *superego*), which specify what a person *should* do. Human behavior is a product of a fragile compromise between instinctual drives and the controls of rational thinking and moral values. Since the instinctual drives are extremely powerful, the ever-present danger for individuals and whole societies is that unacknowledged drives will overwhelm the control mechanisms in a violent, distorted way. Yet Freud also agreed with Nietzsche that the mechanisms of rational thinking and traditional moral values can be too strong. They can repress sexual desires too effectively, crippling individuals and entire peoples with guilt and neurotic fears.

Freudian psychology and clinical psychiatry had become an international movement by 1910, but only after 1918 did they receive popular attention, especially in the Protestant countries of northern Europe and in the United States. Many interpreted

Lord Rutherford The great physicist Ernest Rutherford split the atom in 1919 with a small device that he could hold in his hands. Here he stands with a colleague in Cambridge University's renowned Cavendish Laboratory in 1932, when scientific laboratories engaging in pure research were still relatively small. *(Source: Cavendish Laboratory, Cambridge University/C. E. Wynn-Williams)*

Edvard Munch: The Dance of Life (1899–1900)   Like his contemporary Sigmund Freud, the expressionist Norwegian painter Edvard Munch (1863–1944) studied the turmoil and fragility of human thought and action. Solitary figures struggling with fear and uncertainty dominate his work. Here the girl in white represents innocence, the tense woman in black stands for mourning and rejection, and the woman in red evokes the joy of passing pleasure. *(Source: Nasjonalgalleriet, Oslo. Photo: Jacques Lathion)*

Freud as saying that the first requirement for mental health is an uninhibited sex life. This popular interpretation reflected and encouraged growing sexual experimentation, particularly among middle-class women. For more serious students, the psychology of Freud and his followers drastically undermined the old, easy optimism about the rational and progressive nature of the human mind.

Twentieth-Century Literature

The general intellectual climate of pessimism, relativism, and alienation was also articulated in literature. Novelists developed new techniques to express new realities. The great nineteenth-century novelists had typically written as all-knowing narrators, describing realistic characters and their relationship to an understandable, if sometimes harsh, society. In the twentieth century, most major writers adopted the limited, often confused viewpoint of a single individual. Like Freud, these novelists focused their attention on the complexity and irrationality of the human mind, where feelings, memories, and desires are forever scrambled. The great French novelist Marcel Proust (1871–1922), in his semiautobiographical *Remembrance of Things Past* (1913–1927), recalled bittersweet memories of childhood and youthful love and tried to discover their innermost meaning. To do so, Proust lived like a hermit in a soundproof Paris apartment for ten years, withdrawing from the present to dwell on the past.

Virginia Woolf Her novels captured sensations like impressionist paintings, and her home attracted a circle of artists and writers known as the Bloomsbury Group. Many of Woolf's essays dealt with women's issues and urged greater opportunity for women's creativity. *(Source: Gisèle Freund/Photo Researchers)*

Serious novelists also used the stream-of-consciousness technique to explore the psyche. In *Jacob's Room* (1922), Virginia Woolf (1882–1941) created a novel made up of a series of internal monologues, in which ideas and emotions from different periods of time bubble up as randomly as from a patient on a psychoanalyst's couch. William Faulkner (1897–1962), perhaps America's greatest twentieth-century novelist, used the same technique in *The Sound and the Fury* (1922), much of whose intense drama is confusedly seen through the eyes of an idiot. The most famous stream-of-consciousness novel—and surely the most disturbing novel of its generation—is *Ulysses,* which Irish novelist James Joyce (1882–1941) published in 1922. Into an account of an ordinary day in the life of an ordinary man, Joyce weaves an extended ironic parallel between his hero's aimless wanderings through the streets and pubs of Dublin and the adventures of Homer's hero Ulysses on his way home from Troy. Abandoning conventional grammar and blending foreign words, puns, bits of knowledge, and scraps of memory together in bewildering confusion, the language of *Ulysses* is intended to mirror modern life itself: a gigantic riddle waiting to be unraveled.

As creative writers turned their attention from society to the individual and from realism to psychological relativity, they rejected the idea of progress. Some even described "anti-utopias," nightmare visions of things to come. In 1918 an obscure German high school teacher named Oswald Spengler (1880–1936) published *The Decline of the West,* which quickly became an international sensation. According to Spengler, every culture experiences a life cycle of growth and decline. Western civilization, in Spengler's opinion, was in its old age, and death was approaching in the form of conquest by the yellow race. T. S. Eliot (1888–1965), in his famous poem *The Waste Land* (1922), depicted a world of growing desolation, although after his conversion to Anglo-Catholicism in 1927, Eliot came to hope cautiously for humanity's salvation. No such hope appeared in the work of Franz Kafka (1883–1924), whose novels *The Trial* (1925) and *The Castle* (1926) as well as several of his greatest short stories portray helpless individuals crushed by inexplicably hostile forces.

Englishman George Orwell (1903–1950) had seen the nightmarish reality of the Nazi state and its Stalinist counterpart by 1949 when he wrote perhaps the ultimate in anti-utopian literature: *1984.* Orwell set the action in the future, in 1984. Big Brother—the dictator—and his totalitarian state use a new kind of language, sophisticated technology, and psychological terror to strip a weak individual of his last shred of human dignity. The supremely self-confident chief of the Thought Police tells the tortured, broken, and framed Winston Smith, "If you want a picture of the future, imagine a boot stamping on a human face—forever."[3] A phenomenal bestseller, *1984* spoke to millions of people in the closing years of the age of anxiety.

MODERN ART AND MUSIC

Throughout the twentieth century, there has been considerable unity in the arts. The "modernism" of the immediate prewar years and the 1920s is still strikingly modern. Like the scientists and creative artists who were partaking of the same culture, creative artists rejected old forms and old values. Modernism in art and music meant constant experimentation and a search for new kinds of expression. And though many people find the many and varied modern visions of the arts strange, disturbing, and even ugly, the twentieth century, so dismal in many respects, will probably stand as one of Western civilization's great artistic eras.

Architecture and Design

Modernism in the arts was loosely unified by a revolution in architecture. This revolution intended nothing less than a transformation of the physical framework of urban society according to a new principle: *functionalism.* Buildings, like industrial products, should be useful and "functional"—that is, they should serve, as well as possible, the purpose for which they were made. Thus architects and designers had to work with engineers, town planners, and even sanitation experts. Moreover, they had to throw away useless ornamentation and find beauty and aesthetic pleasure in the clean lines of practical constructions and efficient machinery. Franco-Swiss genius Le Corbusier (1887–1965) insisted that "a house is a machine for living in."[4]

The United States, with its rapid urban growth and lack of rigid building traditions, pioneered in the new architecture. In the 1890s the Chicago school of architects, led by Louis H. Sullivan (1856–1924), used cheap steel, reinforced concrete, and electric elevators to build skyscrapers and office buildings lacking almost any exterior ornamentation. In the first decade of the twentieth century, Sullivan's student Frank Lloyd Wright (1869–1959) built a series of radically new and truly modern houses featuring low lines, open interiors, and mass-produced building materials. Europeans were inspired by these and other American examples of functional construction, like the massive, unadorned grain elevators of the Midwest.

In Europe, architectural leadership centered in German-speaking countries until Hitler took power in 1933. In 1911 twenty-eight-year-old Walter Gropius (1883–1969) broke sharply with the past in his design of the Fagus shoe factory at Alfeld, Germany, a clean, light, elegant building of glass and iron. After the First World War, Gropius merged the schools of fine and applied arts at Weimar into a single, interdisciplinary school, the Bauhaus. The Bauhaus brought together many leading modern architects, artists, designers, and theatrical innovators. Working as an effective, inspired team, they combined the study of fine art, such as painting and sculpture, with the study of applied art in the crafts of printing, weaving, and furniture making. Throughout the 1920s, the Bauhaus, with its stress on functionalism and good design for everyday life, attracted enthusiastic students from all over the world. It had a great and continuing impact.

Another leader in the "international" style, Ludwig Mies van der Rohe (1886–1969), followed Gropius as director of the Bauhaus in 1930 and immigrated to the United States in 1937. His classic Lake Shore Apartments in Chicago, built between 1948 and 1951, symbolized the triumph of steel-frame and glass-wall modern architecture in the great building boom after the Second World War.

Modern Painting and Music

Modern painting grew out of a revolt against French impressionism. The *impressionism* of such French painters as Claude Monet (1840–1926), Pierre Auguste Renoir (1841–1919), and Camille Pissarro (1830–1903) was, in part, a kind of "superrealism." Leaving exact copying of objects to photography, these artists sought to capture the momentary overall feeling, or impression, of light falling on a real-life scene before their eyes. By 1890, when impressionism was finally established, a few artists known as *postimpressionists,* or sometimes as *expressionists,* were already striking out in new directions. After 1905 art increasingly took on a nonrepresentational, abstract character, a development that reached its high point after World War II.

Though individualistic in their styles, postimpressionists were united in their desire to know and depict unseen, inner worlds of emotion and imagination. Like modern novelists, they wanted to express a complicated psychological view of

Frank Lloyd Wright: The "Falling Water" House   Often considered Wright's masterpiece, Falling Water combines modern architectural concepts with close attention to a spectacular site. Anchored to a high rock ledge by means of reinforced concrete, the house soars out over a cascading waterfall at Bear Run in western Pennsylvania. Built in 1937 for a Pittsburgh businessman, Falling Water is now open to the public and attracts seventy thousand visitors each year. *(Source: Western Pennsylvania Conservancy/Art Resource, NY)*

reality as well as an overwhelming emotional intensity. In *The Starry Night* (1889), for example, the great Dutch expressionist Vincent van Gogh (1853–1890) painted the vision of his mind's eye. Flaming cypress trees, exploding stars, and a cometlike Milky Way swirl together in one great cosmic rhythm. Paul Gauguin (1848–1903), the French stockbroker-turned-painter, pioneered in expressionist techniques, though he used them to infuse his work with tranquillity and mysticism. In 1891 he fled to the South Pacific in search of unspoiled beauty and a primitive way of life. Gauguin believed that the form and design of a picture were important in themselves and that the painter need not try to represent objects on canvas as the eye actually saw them.

Fascination with form, as opposed to light, was characteristic of postimpressionism and expressionism. Paul Cézanne (1839–1906), who had a profound influence on twentieth-century painting, was particularly committed to form and ordered design. He told a young painter, "You must see in nature the cylinder, the sphere, and the cone."[5] As Cézanne's later work became increasingly abstract and nonrepresentational, it also moved away from the traditional three-dimensional perspective toward the two-dimensional plane, which has characterized much of modern art. The expressionism of a group of painters led by Henri Matisse (1869–1954) was so extreme that an exhibition of their work in Paris in 1905 prompted shocked critics to call them *les fauves*—"the wild beasts." Matisse and his followers still painted real objects, but their primary concern was the arrangement of color, line, and form as an end in itself.

In 1907 a young Spaniard in Paris, Pablo Picasso (1881–1973), founded another movement—*cubism.* Cubism concentrated on a complex geometry of zigzagging lines and sharply angled, overlapping planes. About three years later came the ultimate stage in the development of abstract, nonrepresentational art. Artists such as the Russian-born Wassily Kandinsky (1866–1944) turned away from nature completely. "The observer," said Kandinsky, "must learn to look at [my] pictures . . . as form and color combinations . . . as a representation of mood and not as a representation of *objects.*"[6]

In the 1920s and 1930s, the artistic movements of the prewar years were extended and consolidated. The most notable new developments were *dadaism* and *surrealism.* Dadaism attacked all accepted standards of art and behavior, delighting in outrageous conduct. Its name, from the French word *dada,* meaning "hobbyhorse," is deliberately nonsensical. A famous example of dadaism was a reproduction of Leonardo da Vinci's *Mona Lisa* in which the famous woman with the mysterious smile sports a mustache and is ridiculed with an obscene inscription. After 1924 many dadaists were attracted to surrealism, which became very influential in art in the late 1920s and 1930s. Surrealists painted a fantastic world of wild dreams and complex symbols, where watches melted and giant metronomes beat time in precisely drawn but impossible alien landscapes.

Refusing to depict ordinary visual reality, surrealist painters made powerful statements about the age of anxiety. Picasso's 26-foot-long mural *Guernica* (1937) masterfully unites several powerful

Picasso: Guernica (1937) In this rich, complex work a shrieking woman falls from a burning house on the far right. On the left a woman holds a dead child. Toward the center are fragments of a warrior and a screaming horse pierced by a spear. Picasso used only the mournful colors of black, white, and gray. *(Source: Museo del Prado, Madrid. Pablo Picasso, Guernica [1937, May–early June]. Oil on canvas. © SPADEM, Paris/VAGA, New York, 1982)*

strands in twentieth-century art. Inspired by the Spanish civil war (see page 1076), the painting commemorates the bombing of the ancient Spanish town of Guernica by fascist planes, an attack that took the lives of a thousand people—one out of every eight inhabitants—in a single night of terror. Combining the free distortion of expressionism, the overlapping planes of cubism, and the surrealist fascination with grotesque subject matter, *Guernica* is what Picasso meant it to be: an unforgettable attack on "brutality and darkness."

Developments in modern music were strikingly parallel to those in painting. Composers, too, were attracted by the emotional intensity of expressionism. The ballet *The Rite of Spring* by composer Igor Stravinsky (1882–1971) practically caused a riot when it was first performed in Paris in 1913 by Sergei Diaghilev's famous Russian dance company. The combination of pulsating, dissonant rhythms from the orchestra pit and an earthy representation of lovemaking by the dancers on the stage seemed a shocking, almost pornographic enactment of a primitive fertility rite.

After the experience of the First World War, when irrationality and violence seemed to pervade the human experience, expressionism in opera and ballet flourished. Some composers turned their backs on long-established musical conventions. As abstract painters arranged lines and color but did not draw identifiable objects, so modern composers arranged sounds without creating recognizable harmonies. Led by Viennese composer Arnold Schönberg (1874–1951), they abandoned traditional harmony and tonality. The musical notes in a given piece were no longer united and organized by a key; instead they were independent and unrelated. Schönberg's twelve-tone music of the 1920s arranged all twelve notes of the scale in an abstract, mathematical pattern, or "tone row." This pattern sounded like no pattern at all to the ordinary listener. Accustomed to the harmonies of classical and romantic music, audiences generally resisted modern atonal music.

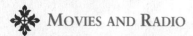

MOVIES AND RADIO

Until after World War II at the earliest, these revolutionary changes in art and music appealed mainly to a minority of "highbrows" and not to the general public. That public was primarily and enthusiastically wrapped up in movies and radio. The long-declining traditional arts and amusements of people in villages and small towns almost vanished, replaced by standardized, commercial entertainment.

Moving pictures were first shown as a popular novelty in naughty peepshows—"What the Butler Saw"—and penny arcades in the 1890s, especially in Paris. The first movie houses date from an experiment in Los Angeles in 1902. They quickly attracted large audiences and led to the production of short, silent action films such as the eight-minute *Great Train Robbery* of 1903. American directors and business people then set up "movie factories," at first in the New York area and then after 1910 in Los Angeles. These factories churned out two short films each week. On the eve of the First World War, full-length feature films such as the Italian *Quo Vadis* and the American *Birth of a Nation,* coupled with improvements in the quality of pictures, suggested the screen's vast possibilities.

During the First World War, the United States became the dominant force in the rapidly expanding silent-film industry. In the 1920s, Mack Sennett (1884–1960) and his zany Keystone Cops specialized in short, slapstick comedies noted for frantic automobile chases, custard-pie battles, and gorgeous bathing beauties. Screen stars such as Mary Pickford and Lillian Gish, Douglas Fairbanks and Rudolph Valentino, had their own "fan clubs" and became household names. But in the 1920s Charlie Chaplin (1889–1978), a funny little Englishman working in Hollywood, was unquestionably the king of the "silver screen." In his enormously popular role as a lonely tramp, complete with baggy trousers, battered derby, and an awkward, shuffling walk, Chaplin symbolized the "gay spirit of laughter in a cruel, crazy world."[7] Chaplin also demonstrated that in the hands of a genius the new medium could combine mass entertainment and artistic accomplishment.

The early 1920s was also the great age of German films. Protected and developed during the war, the large German studios excelled in bizarre expressionist dramas, beginning with *The Cabinet of Dr. Caligari* in 1919. Unfortunately, their period of creativity was short-lived. By 1926 American money was drawing the leading German talents to Hollywood and consolidating America's international domination. Film making was big business, and European theater owners were forced to book whole blocks of American films to get the few pictures they really wanted. This system put European producers at a great disadvantage until "talkies" permitted a revival of national film industries in the 1930s, particularly in France.

Whether foreign or domestic, motion pictures became the main entertainment of the masses until after the Second World War. In Great Britain one in every four adults went to the movies twice a week in the late 1930s, and two in five went at least once a week. Continental European countries had similar figures. The greatest appeal of motion pictures was that they offered ordinary people a temporary escape from the hard realities of international tensions, uncertainty, unemployment, and personal frustrations. The appeal of escapist entertainment was especially strong during the Great Depression. Millions flocked to musical comedies featuring glittering stars such as Ginger Rogers and Fred Astaire and to the fanciful cartoons of Mickey Mouse and his friends.

Radio became possible with the transatlantic "wireless" communication of Guglielmo Marconi (1874–1937) in 1901 and the development of the vacuum tube in 1904, which permitted the transmission of speech and music. But only in 1920 were the first major public broadcasts of special events made in Great Britain and the United States. Singing from London in English, Italian, and French, "the world's very best, the soprano Nellie Melba,"[8] was heard simultaneously all over Europe on June 16, 1920. This historic event captured the public's imagination. The meteoric career of radio was launched.

Every major country quickly established national broadcasting networks. In the United States, such networks were privately owned and were financed by advertising. In Great Britain, Parliament set up an independent, public corporation, the British Broadcasting Corporation (BBC), supported by licensing fees. Elsewhere in Europe, the typical pattern was direct control by the government. Whatever the institutional framework, radio became popular and influential. By the late 1930s, more than three out of every four households in both democratic Great Britain and dictatorial Germany had at least one cheap, mass-produced radio. In other European countries, radio ownership was not quite so widespread, but the new medium was no less important.

Radio was particularly well suited for political propaganda. Dictators such as Mussolini and Hitler controlled the airwaves and could reach enormous national audiences with their frequent, dramatic speeches. In democratic countries, politicians such as President Franklin Roosevelt and Prime Minister Stanley Baldwin effectively used informal "fireside chats" to bolster their support.

Motion pictures also became powerful tools of indoctrination, especially in countries with dictatorial regimes. Lenin himself encouraged the development of Soviet film making, believing that the new medium was essential to the social and ideological transformation of the country. Beginning in the mid-1920s, a series of epic films, the most famous of which were directed by Sergei Eisenstein (1898–1948), brilliantly dramatized the communist view of Russian history.

In Germany Hitler turned to a young and immensely talented woman film maker, Leni

The Great Dictator   In 1940 Charlie Chaplin, the renowned actor and director, abandoned his popular characterization of little tramp to satirize the great dictator, Adolf Hitler. Chaplin (1889–1977) had strong political views and made a number of films with political themes as the escapist fare of the Great Depression gave way to the reality of the Second World War. (*Source: The Museum of Modern Art/Still Film Archives*)

Riefenstahl (b. 1902), for a masterpiece of documentary propaganda, *The Triumph of the Will,* based on the Nazi party rally at Nuremberg in 1934. Riefenstahl combined stunning aerial photography, joyful crowds welcoming Hitler, and mass processions of young Nazi fanatics. Her film was a brilliant and all-too-powerful documentary of Germany's "Nazi rebirth." The new media of mass culture were potentially dangerous instruments of political manipulation.

THE SEARCH FOR PEACE AND POLITICAL STABILITY

As established patterns of thought and culture were challenged and mangled by the ferocious impact of World War I, so also was the political fabric stretched and torn by the consequences of the great conflict. The Versailles settlement had established a shaky truce, not a solid peace. Thus national leaders faced a gigantic task as they struggled with uncertainty and sought to create a stable international order within the general context of intellectual crisis and revolutionary artistic experimentation.

The pursuit of real and lasting peace proved difficult for many reasons. Germany hated the Treaty of Versailles. France was fearful and isolated. Britain was undependable, and the United States had turned its back on European problems. Eastern Europe was in ferment, and no one could predict the future of communist Russia. In addition, the international economic situation was poor and greatly complicated by war debts and disrupted patterns of trade. Yet for a time, from 1925 to late 1929, it appeared that peace and stability were within reach. When the subsequent collapse of the 1930s mocked these hopes, the disillusionment of liberals in the democracies was intensified.

Germany and the Western Powers

Germany was the key to lasting peace. Yet to Germans of all political parties, the Treaty of Versailles represented a harsh, dictated peace, to be revised or repudiated as soon as possible. The treaty had neither broken nor reduced Germany, which was potentially still the strongest country in Europe. Thus the treaty had fallen between two stools: too harsh for a peace of reconciliation, too soft for a peace of conquest.

Moreover, with ominous implications for the future, France and Great Britain did not see eye to eye on Germany. By the end of 1919, France wanted to stress the harsh elements in the Treaty of Versailles. Most of the war in the West had been fought on French soil, and the expected costs of reconstruction, as well as repaying war debts to the United States, were staggering. Thus French politicians believed that massive reparations from Germany were a vital economic necessity. Also, having compromised with President Wilson only to be betrayed by America's failure to ratify the treaty, many French leaders saw strict implementation of all provisions of the Treaty of Versailles as France's last best hope. Large reparation payments could hold Germany down indefinitely, and France would realize its goal of security.

The British soon felt differently. Prewar Germany had been Great Britain's second-best market in the entire world, and after the war a healthy, prosperous Germany appeared to be essential to the British economy. Indeed, many English people agreed with the analysis of the young English economist John Maynard Keynes (1883–1946). In his famous *Economic Consequences of the Peace* (1919), Keynes argued that astronomical reparations and harsh economic measures would indeed reduce Germany to the position of an impoverished second-rate power but such impoverishment would increase economic hardship in all countries. Only a complete revision of the foolish treaty could save Germany—and Europe. Keynes's attack stirred deep guilt feelings about Germany in the English-speaking world, feelings that often paralyzed English and American leaders in their relations with Germany and its leaders between the First and the Second World Wars.

The British were also suspicious of France's army—momentarily the largest in Europe—and France's foreign policy. Ever since 1890, France had looked to Russia as a powerful ally against Germany. But with Russia hostile and socialist, and with Britain and the United States unwilling to make any firm commitments, France associated itself closely with the newly formed states of eastern Europe and their alliance against defeated and bitter Hungary. The British and the French were also on cool terms because of conflicts relating to their League of Nations mandates in the Middle East (see page 994).

While French and British leaders drifted in different directions, the Allied reparations commission completed its work. In April 1921 it announced that Germany had to pay the enormous sum of 132 billion gold marks ($33 billion) in annual installments of 2.5 billion gold marks. Facing possible occupation of more of its territory, the young German republic, which had been founded in Weimar but moved back to Berlin, made its first payment in 1921. Then in 1922, wracked by rapid inflation and political assassinations and motivated by hostility and arrogance as well, the Weimar Republic announced its inability to pay more. It proposed a moratorium on reparations for three years, and the implication was that thereafter reparations would either be drastically reduced or eliminated entirely.

The British were willing to accept a moratorium on reparations, but the French were not. Led by their tough-minded, legalistic prime minister, Raymond Poincaré (1860–1934), they decided they either had to call Germany's bluff or see the entire peace settlement dissolve to France's great disadvantage. So, despite strong British protests, in early January 1923, armies of France and its ally Belgium began to occupy the Ruhr district, the heartland of industrial Germany, creating the most serious international crisis of the 1920s. If forcible collection proved impossible, France would use occupation to paralyze Germany and force it to accept the Treaty of Versailles.

Strengthened by a wave of patriotism, the German government ordered the people of the Ruhr to stop working and start passively resisting the French occupation. The coal mines and steel mills of the Ruhr grew silent, leaving 10 percent of Germany's total population in need of relief. The French answer to passive resistance was to seal off not only the Ruhr but also the entire Rhineland from the rest of Germany, letting in only enough food to prevent starvation. The French also revived plans for a separate state in the Rhineland.

By the summer of 1923, France and Germany were engaged in a great test of wills. French armies could not collect reparations from striking workers at gunpoint. But French occupation was indeed paralyzing Germany and its economy and had turned rapid German inflation into runaway inflation. Faced with the need to support the striking Ruhr workers and their employers, the German government began to print money to pay its bills. Prices soared. People went to the store with a big bag of paper money; they returned home with a handful of groceries. German money rapidly lost

"Hands Off the Ruhr"   The French occupation of the Ruhr to collect reparations payments raised a storm of patriotic protest in Germany. This anti-French poster of 1923 turns Marianne, the symbol of French republican virtue, into a vicious harpy. *(Source: Internationaal Instituut voor Sociale Geschiedenis)*

all value, and so did anything else with a stated fixed value.

Runaway inflation brought about a social revolution. The accumulated savings of many retired and middle-class people were wiped out. Catastrophic inflation cruelly mocked the old middle-class virtues of thrift, caution, and self-reliance. Many Germans felt betrayed. They hated and blamed the Western governments, their own government, big business, the Jews, the workers, and the communists for their misfortune. They were psychologically prepared to follow radical leaders in a crisis.

In August 1923, as the mark fell and political unrest grew throughout Germany, Gustav Stresemann (1878–1929) assumed leadership of the government. Stresemann adopted a compromising attitude. He called off passive resistance in the Ruhr and in October agreed in principle to pay reparations but asked for a re-examination of Germany's ability to pay. Poincaré accepted. His hard line was becoming increasingly unpopular with French citizens, and it was hated in Britain and the United States.

More generally, in both Germany and France power was finally passing to the moderates, who realized that continued confrontation was a destructive, no-win situation. Thus after five long years of hostility and tension, culminating in a kind of undeclared war in the Ruhr in 1923, Germany and France decided to give compromise and cooperation a try. The British, and even the Americans, were willing to help. The first step was a reasonable compromise on the reparations question.

Hope in Foreign Affairs (1924–1929)

The reparations commission appointed an international committee of financial experts headed by American banker Charles G. Dawes to re-examine reparations from a broad perspective. The resulting Dawes Plan (1924) was accepted by France, Germany, and Britain. Germany's yearly reparations were reduced and depended on the level of German economic prosperity. Germany would also receive large loans from the United States to promote German recovery. In short, Germany would get private loans from the United States and pay reparations to France and Britain, thus enabling those countries to repay the large sums they owed the United States.

This circular flow of international payments was complicated and risky. But for a while it worked. The German republic experienced a spectacular economic recovery. By 1929 Germany's wealth and income were 50 percent greater than in 1913. With prosperity and large, continual inflows of American capital, Germany easily paid about $1.3 billion in reparations in 1927 and 1928, enabling France and Britain to pay the United States. In this way the Americans, who did not have armies but who did have money, belatedly played a part in the

general economic settlement that, though far from ideal, facilitated the worldwide recovery of the late 1920s.

This economic settlement was matched by a political settlement. In 1925 the leaders of Europe signed a number of agreements at Locarno, Switzerland. Germany and France solemnly pledged to accept their common border, and both Britain and Italy agreed to fight either France or Germany if one invaded the other. Stresemann also agreed to settle boundary disputes with Poland and Czechoslovakia by peaceful means, and France promised those countries military aid if Germany attacked them. For years, a "spirit of Locarno" gave Europeans a sense of growing security and stability in international affairs.

Other developments also strengthened hopes. In 1926 Germany joined the League of Nations, where Stresemann continued his "peace offensive." In 1928 fifteen countries signed the Kellogg-Briand Pact, initiated by French Prime Minister Aristide Briand and U.S. Secretary of State Frank B. Kellogg. This multinational pact "condemned and renounced war as an instrument of national policy." The signing states agreed to settle international disputes peacefully. Often seen as idealistic nonsense because it made no provisions for action in case war actually occurred, the pact was still a positive step. It fostered the cautious optimism of the late 1920s and also encouraged the hope that the United States would accept its responsibilities as a great world power and contribute to European stability.

Domestic politics also offered reason to hope. During the occupation of the Ruhr and the great inflation, republican government in Germany had appeared on the verge of collapse. In 1923 communists momentarily entered provincial governments, and in November an obscure nobody named Adolf Hitler leaped on to a table in a beer hall in Munich and proclaimed a "national socialist revolution." But Hitler's plot to seize control of the government was poorly organized and easily crushed, and Hitler was sentenced to prison, where he outlined his theories and program in his book *Mein Kampf* (*My Struggle*). Throughout the 1920s, Hitler's National Socialist party attracted support only from a few fanatical anti-Semites, ultranationalists, and disgruntled former servicemen.

The moderate businessmen who tended to dominate the various German coalition governments believed that economic prosperity demanded good relations with the Western powers, and they supported parliamentary government at home. Stresemann himself was a man of this class, and he was the key figure in every government until his death in 1929. Elections were held regularly, and as the economy boomed, republican democracy appeared to have growing support among a majority of the Germans.

There were, however, sharp political divisions in the country. Many unrepentant nationalists and monarchists populated the right and the army. Germany's Communists were noisy and active on the left. The Communists, directed from Moscow, reserved their greatest hatred and sharpest barbs for their cousins the Social Democrats, whom they endlessly accused of betraying the revolution. The working classes were divided politically, but most supported the nonrevolutionary but socialist Social Democrats.

The situation in France had numerous similarities to that in Germany. Communists and Socialists battled for the support of the workers. After 1924 the democratically elected government rested mainly in the hands of coalitions of moderates, and business interests were well represented. France's great accomplishment was rapid rebuilding of its war-torn northern region. The expense of this undertaking, however, led to a large deficit and substantial inflation by 1926. The government proceeded to slash spending and raise taxes, restoring confidence in the economy. Good times prevailed until 1930.

Despite political shortcomings, France attracted artists and writers from all over the world in the

An American in Paris The young Josephine Baker (1906–1975) suddenly became a star when she brought an exotic African eroticism to French music halls in 1925. American blacks and Africans had a powerful impact on entertainment in Europe in the 1920s and 1930s. *(Source: Hulton Deutsch Collection)*

1920s. Much of the intellectual and artistic ferment of the times flourished in Paris. As writer Gertrude Stein (1874–1946), a leader of the large colony of American expatriates living in Paris, later recalled, "Paris was where the twentieth century was."9 More generally, France appealed to foreigners and to the French as a harmonious combination of small businesses and family farms, of bold innovation and solid traditions.

Britain, too, faced challenges after 1920. The wartime trend toward greater social equality continued, however, helping maintain social harmony. The great problem was unemployment. Many of Britain's best markets had been lost during the war, and throughout the 1920s unemployment hovered around 12 percent. The state provided unemployment benefits of equal size to all those without jobs and supplemented those payments with subsidized housing, medical aid, and increased old-age pensions. These and other measures kept living standards from seriously declining, defused class tensions, and pointed the way toward the welfare state that Britain established after World War II.

Relative social harmony was accompanied by the rise of the Labour party as a determined champion of the working classes and of greater social equality. Committed to the kind of moderate, "revisionist" socialism that had emerged before World War I (see page 878), the Labour party replaced the Liberal party as the main opposition to the Conservatives. The new prominence of the Labour party reflected the decline of old liberal ideals of competitive capitalism, limited government control, and individual responsibility. In 1924 and 1929, the Labour party under Ramsay MacDonald (1866–1937) governed the country with the support of the smaller Liberal party. Yet Labour moved toward socialism gradually and democratically, so that the middle classes were not overly frightened as the working classes won new benefits.

The Conservatives under Stanley Baldwin (1867–1947) showed the same compromising spirit on social issues. The last line of Baldwin's greatest speech in March 1925 summarized his international and domestic programs: "Give us peace in our time, O Lord." In spite of such conflicts as the 1926 strike by hard-pressed coal miners, which ended in an unsuccessful general strike, social unrest in Britain was limited in the 1920s and in the 1930s as well. In 1922 Britain granted southern,

Catholic Ireland full autonomy after a bitter guerrilla war, thereby removing another source of prewar friction. Thus developments in both international relations and in the domestic politics of the leading democracies gave cause for cautious optimism in the late 1920s.

THE GREAT DEPRESSION (1929–1939)

Like the Great War, the Great Depression must be spelled with capital letters. Economic depression was nothing new. Depressions occurred throughout the nineteenth century with predictable regularity, as they recur in the form of recessions and slumps to this day. What was new about this depression was its severity and duration. It struck the entire world with ever-greater intensity from 1929 to 1933, and recovery was uneven and slow. Only with the Second World War did the depression disappear in much of the world.

The social and political consequences of prolonged economic collapse were enormous all around the world. Subsequent military expansion in Japan has already been described (see page 908), and later chapters examine a similarly powerful impact on Latin America and Africa. In Europe and the United States the depression shattered the fragile optimism of political leaders in the late 1920s. Mass unemployment made insecurity a reality for millions of ordinary people, who had paid little attention to the intellectual crisis or to new directions in art and ideas. In desperation, people looked for leaders who would "do something." They were willing to support radical attempts to deal with the crisis by both democratic leaders and dictators.

The Economic Crisis

Though economic activity was already declining moderately in many countries by early 1929, the crash of the stock market in the United States in October of that year really started the Great Depression. The American stock market boom, which had seen stock prices double between early 1928 and September 1929, was built on borrowed money. Many wealthy investors, speculators, and people of modest means had bought stocks by paying only a small fraction of the total purchase price and borrowing the remainder from their stockbrokers. Such buying "on margin" was extremely dangerous. When prices started falling, the hard-pressed margin buyers started selling all at once. The result was a financial panic. Countless investors and speculators were wiped out in a matter of days or weeks.

The general economic consequences were swift and severe. Stripped of wealth and confidence, battered investors and their fellow citizens reduced their purchases of goods. Production began to slow down, and unemployment began to rise. Soon the entire American economy was caught in a vicious, spiraling decline.

The financial panic in the United States triggered a worldwide financial crisis, and that crisis resulted in a drastic decline in production in country after country. Throughout the 1920s, American bankers and investors had lent large amounts of capital not only to Germany but also to many other countries. Many of these loans were short-term, and once panic broke, New York bankers began recalling them. It became very hard for European business people to borrow money, and the panicky public began to withdraw its savings from the banks. These banking problems eventually led to the crash of the largest bank in Austria in 1931 and then to general financial chaos. The recall of private loans by American bankers also accelerated the collapse in world prices, as business people around the world dumped industrial goods and agricultural commodities in a frantic attempt to get cash to pay what they owed.

The financial crisis led to a general crisis of production. Between 1929 and 1933, world output of goods fell by an estimated 38 percent. As this happened, each country turned inward and tried to go it alone. Country after country followed the example of the United States when it raised protective tariffs to their highest levels ever in 1930 and tried to seal off shrinking national markets for American producers only. Within this context of fragmented and destructive economic nationalism, recovery finally began in 1933.

Although opinions differ, two factors probably best explain the relentless slide to the bottom from 1929 to early 1933. First, the international economy lacked a leadership able to maintain stability when the crisis came. Specifically, as a noted American economic historian concludes, the seriously weakened British, the traditional leaders of the world economy, "couldn't and the United States

wouldn't" stabilize the international economic system in 1929.[10] The United States, which had momentarily played a positive role after the occupation of the Ruhr, cut back its international lending and erected high tariffs.

The second factor was poor national economic policy in almost every country. Governments generally cut their budgets and reduced spending when they should have run large deficits in an attempt to stimulate their economies. Since World War II, such a "counter-cyclical policy," advocated by John Maynard Keynes, has become a well-established weapon against depression. But in the 1930s, orthodox economists generally regarded Keynes's prescription with horror.

Mass Unemployment

The need for large-scale government spending was tied to mass unemployment (Map 31.1). As the financial crisis led to cuts in production, workers lost their jobs and had little money to buy goods. This led to still more cuts in production and still more unemployment, until millions were out of work. In Britain unemployment had averaged 12 percent in the 1920s; between 1930 and 1935, it averaged more than 18 percent. Far worse was the case of the United States. In the 1920s, unemployment there had averaged only 5 percent; in 1932, unemployment soared to about 33 percent of the entire labor force: 14 million people were out of work. Only by pumping new money into the economy could the government increase demand and break the vicious cycle of decline.

Along with economic effects, mass unemployment posed a great social problem that mere numbers cannot adequately express. Millions of people lost their spirit and dignity in an apparently hopeless search for work. Homes and ways of life were disrupted in millions of personal tragedies. In 1932 the workers of Manchester, England, appealed to their city officials—a typical appeal echoed throughout the Western world:

We tell you that thousands of people . . . are in desperate straits. We tell you that men, women, and children are going hungry. . . . We tell you that great numbers are being rendered distraught through the stress and worry of trying to exist without work. . . .

If you do not do this—if you do not provide useful work for the unemployed—what, we ask, is your alternative? Do not imagine that this colossal tragedy of

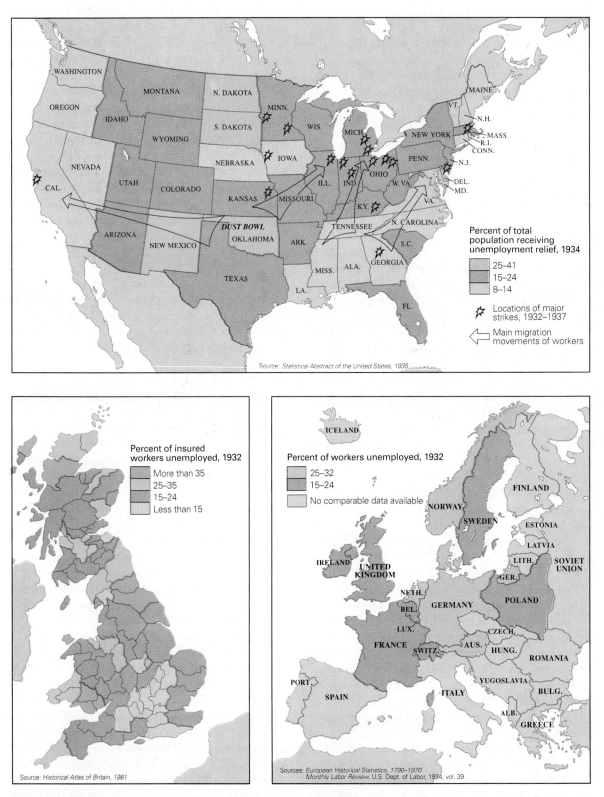

Percent of total population receiving unemployment relief, 1934
- 25–41
- 15–24
- 8–14

⭐ Locations of major strikes, 1932–1937

⬅ Main migration movements of workers

Source: *Statistical Abstract of the United States, 1935*

Percent of insured workers unemployed, 1932
- More than 35
- 25–35
- 15–24
- Less than 15

Source: *Historical Atlas of Britain, 1981*

Percent of workers unemployed, 1932
- 25–32
- 15–24
- No comparable data available

Sources: *European Historical Statistics, 1790–1970*
Monthly Labor Review, U.S. Dept. of Labor, 1934, vol. 39

✳ MAP 31.1 The Great Depression in the United States, Britain, and Europe
National and regional differences were substantial. Germany, industrial northern Britain, and the American Middle West were particularly hard hit.

Isaac Soyer: Employment Agency (1937)   The frustration and agony of looking for work against long odds are painfully evident in this American masterpiece. The time-killing, the resignation, and the dejection seen in the four figures are only aspects of the larger problem. One of three talented brothers born in Russia and trained as artists in New York, Isaac Soyer worked in the tradition of American realism and concentrated on people and the influence of their environment. *(Source: Collection of Whitney Museum of American Art)*

unemployment is going on endlessly without some fateful catastrophe. Hungry men are angry men.[11]

Mass unemployment was a terrible time bomb preparing to explode.

The New Deal in the United States

Of all the major industrial countries, only Germany was harder hit by the Great Depression, or reacted more radically to it, than the United States. Depression was so traumatic in the United States because the 1920s had been a period of complacent prosperity. The Great Depression and the response

to it marked a major turning point in American history.

President Herbert Hoover (1895–1972) and his administration initially reacted to the stock market crash and economic decline with dogged optimism and limited action. But when the full force of the financial crisis struck Europe in the summer of 1931 and boomeranged back to the United States, people's worst fears became reality. Banks failed; unemployment soared. In 1932 industrial production fell to about 50 percent of its 1929 level. In these tragic circumstances Franklin Delano Roosevelt (1882–1945), an inspiring wheelchair-bound aristocrat previously crippled by polio, won a landslide electoral victory with grand but vague promises of a "New Deal for the forgotten man."

Roosevelt's basic goal was to reform capitalism in order to preserve it. In his words, "A frank examination of the profit system in the spring of 1933 showed it to be in collapse; but substantially everybody in the United States, in public office and out of public office, from the very rich to the very poor, was as determined as was my Administration to save it."[12] Roosevelt rejected socialism and government ownership of industry in 1933. To right the situation, he chose forceful government intervention in the economy.

In this choice, Roosevelt was flexible, pragmatic, and willing to experiment. Roosevelt and his "brain trust" of advisers adopted policies echoing the American experience in World War I, when the American economy had been thoroughly planned and regulated.

The first and most ambitious attempt to control and plan the economy was the National Recovery Administration (NRA). Intended to reduce competition and fix prices and wages for everyone's benefit, the NRA broke with the cherished American tradition of free competition and aroused conflicts among business people, consumers, and bureaucrats. It did not work well and was declared unconstitutional in 1935.

Roosevelt and his advisers then attacked the key problem of mass unemployment directly. The federal government accepted the responsibility of employing directly as many people as financially possible. New agencies were created to undertake a vast range of public works projects. The most famous of these was the Works Progress Administration (WPA), set up in 1935. One-fifth of the entire labor force worked for the WPA at some point in the 1930s, building public buildings, bridges, and highways. The WPA was enormously popular, and the hope of a job with the government helped check the threat of social revolution in the United States.

Other social measures aimed in the same direction. Following the path blazed by Germany's Bismarck in the 1880s (see page 867), the U.S. government in 1935 established a national social security system, with old-age pensions and unemployment benefits, to protect many workers against some of life's uncertainties. The National Labor Relations Act of 1935 gave union organizers the green light by declaring collective bargaining to be the policy of the United States. Follow-

ing some bitter strikes, such as a sit-down strike at General Motors in early 1937, union membership more than doubled, from 4 million in 1935 to 9 million in 1940. In general, between 1935 and 1938, government rulings and social reforms chipped away at the privileges of the wealthy and tried to help ordinary people.

Yet despite undeniable accomplishments in social reform, the New Deal was only partly successful as a response to the Great Depression. At the height of the recovery in May 1937, 7 million workers were still unemployed. The economic situation then worsened seriously in the recession of 1937 and 1938. Production fell sharply, and although unemployment never again reached the 15 million mark of 1933, it hit 11 million in 1938 and was still a staggering 10 million when war broke out in Europe in September 1939. The New Deal brought fundamental reform, but it never did pull the United States out of the depression.

The Scandinavian Response to the Depression

Of all the Western democracies, the Scandinavian countries under Socialist leadership responded most successfully to the challenge of the Great Depression. Having grown steadily in number in the late nineteenth century, the Socialists became the largest political party in Sweden and then in Norway after the First World War. In the 1920s they passed important social reform legislation for both peasants and workers, gained practical administrative experience, and developed a unique kind of socialism. Flexible and nonrevolutionary, Scandinavian socialism grew out of a strong tradition of cooperative community action. Even before 1900, Scandinavian agricultural cooperatives had shown how individual peasant families could join together for everyone's benefit. Labor leaders and capitalists were also inclined to work together.

When the economic crisis struck in 1929, Socialist governments in Scandinavia built on this pattern of cooperative social action. Sweden in particular pioneered in the use of large-scale deficits to finance public works and thereby maintain production and employment. Scandinavian governments also increased social welfare benefits, from old-age pensions and unemployment insurance to subsidized housing and maternity allowances. All this spending required a large bureaucracy and high taxes, first on the rich and then on practically everyone. Yet both private and cooperative enterprise thrived, as did democracy. Some observers saw Scandinavia's welfare socialism as an appealing "middle way" between sick capitalism and cruel communism or fascism.

Recovery and Reform in Britain and France

In Britain MacDonald's Labour government and then, after 1931, the Conservative-dominated coalition government followed orthodox economic theory. The budget was balanced, but unemployed workers received barely enough welfare to live. Despite government lethargy, the economy recovered considerably after 1932. By 1937 total production was about 20 percent higher than in 1929. In fact, for Britain the years after 1932 were actually somewhat better than the 1920s had been, quite the opposite of the situation in the United States and France.

This good but by no means brilliant performance reflected the gradual reorientation of the British economy. After going off the gold standard in 1931 and establishing protective tariffs in 1932, Britain concentrated increasingly on the national, rather than the international, market. The old export industries of the Industrial Revolution, such as textiles and coal, continued to decline, but new industries, such as automobiles and electrical appliances, grew in response to British home demand. Moreover, low interest rates encouraged a housing boom. These developments encouraged Britain to look inward and avoid unpleasant foreign questions.

Because France was relatively less industrialized and more isolated from the world economy, the Great Depression came there late. But once the depression hit France, it stayed and stayed. Decline was steady until 1935, and a short-lived recovery never brought production or employment back up to predepression levels. Economic stagnation both reflected and heightened an ongoing political crisis. There was no stability in government. As before 1914, the French parliament was made up of many political parties, which could never cooperate for very long. In 1933, for example, five coalition cabinets formed and fell in rapid succession.

The French lost the underlying unity that had made government instability bearable before 1914. Fascist-type organizations agitated against parliamentary democracy and looked to Mussolini's Italy and Hitler's Germany for inspiration. In Feb-ruary 1934 French fascists and semifascists rioted and threatened to overturn the republic. At the same time, the Communist party and many workers opposed to the existing system were looking to Stalin's Russia for guidance. The vital center of moderate republicanism was sapped from both sides.

Frightened by the growing strength of the fascists at home and abroad, the Communists, the Socialists, and the Radicals formed an alliance—the Popular Front—for the national elections of May 1936. Their clear victory reflected the trend toward polarization. The number of Communists in the parliament jumped dramatically from 10 to 72, and the Socialists, led by Léon Blum, became the strongest party in France, with 146 seats. The really quite moderate Radicals slipped badly, and the conservatives lost ground to the semifascists.

In the next few months, Blum's Popular Front government made the first and only real attempt to deal with the social and economic problems of the 1930s in France. Inspired by Roosevelt's New Deal, the Popular Front encouraged the union movement and launched a far-reaching program of social reform, complete with paid vacations and a forty-hour workweek. Popular with workers and the lower middle class, these measures were quickly sabotaged by rapid inflation and cries of revolution from fascists and frightened conservatives. Wealthy people sneaked their money out of the country, labor unrest grew, and France entered a severe financial crisis. Blum was forced to announce a "breathing spell" in social reform.

The fires of political dissension were also fanned by civil war in Spain. Communists demanded that France support the Spanish republicans, while many French conservatives would gladly have joined Hitler and Mussolini in aiding the attack of Spanish fascists. Extremism grew, and France itself was within sight of civil war. Blum was forced to resign in June 1937, and the Popular Front quickly collapsed. An anxious and divided France drifted aimlessly once again, preoccupied by Hitler and German rearmament.

SUMMARY

After the First World War, Western society entered a complex and difficult era—truly an age of anxiety. Intellectual life underwent a crisis marked by pessimism, uncertainty, and fascination with irrational forces. Ceaseless experimentation and rejection of old forms characterized art and music, while motion pictures and radio provided a new, standardized entertainment for the masses. Intellectual and artistic developments that before 1914 had been confined to small avant-garde groups gained wider currency, as did the insecure state of mind they expressed.

Politics and economics were similarly disrupted. In the 1920s political leaders groped to create an enduring peace and rebuild the prewar prosperity, and for a brief period late in the decade they seemed to have succeeded. Then the Great Depression shattered that fragile stability. Uncertainty returned with redoubled force in the 1930s. The international economy collapsed, and unemployment struck millions worldwide. The democracies turned inward as they sought to cope with massive domestic problems and widespread disillusionment. Generally speaking, they were not very successful. The old liberal ideals of individual rights and responsibilities, elected government, and economic freedom, even when they managed to survive, seemed ineffective and outmoded to many. And in many countries these ideals were abandoned completely.

NOTES

1. P. Valéry, *Variety*, trans. M. Cowley (New York: Harcourt Brace, 1927), pp. 27–28.
2. G. Greene, *Another Mexico* (New York: Viking Press, 1939), p. 3.
3. G. Orwell, *1984* (New York: New American Library, 1950), p. 220.
4. C. E. Jeanneret-Gris (Le Corbusier), *Towards a New Architecture* (London: J. Rodker, 1931), p. 15.
5. Quoted in A. H. Barr, Jr., *What Is Modern Painting?* 9th ed. (New York: Museum of Modern Art, 1966), p. 27.
6. Quoted ibid., p. 25.
7. R. Graves and A. Hodge, *The Long Week End: A Social History of Great Britain, 1918–1939* (New York: Macmillan, 1941), p. 131.
8. Quoted in A. Briggs, *The Birth of Broadcasting,* vol. 1 (London: Oxford University Press, 1961), p. 47.
9. Quoted in R. J. Sontag, *A Broken World, 1919–1939* (New York: Harper & Row, 1971), p. 129.
10. C. P. Kindleberger, *The World in Depression, 1929–1939* (Berkeley: University of California Press, 1973), p. 292.
11. Quoted in S. B. Clough et al., eds., *Economic History of Europe: Twentieth Century* (New York: Harper & Row, 1968), pp. 243–245.
12. Quoted in D. Dillard, *Economic Development of the North Atlantic Community* (Englewood Cliffs, N.J.: Prentice-Hall, 1967), p. 591.

SUGGESTED READING

Among general works, E. Wiskemann's *Europe of the Dictators, 1919–1945* (1966), and Sontag's study cited in the Notes are particularly recommended. The latter has an excellent bibliography. A. Bullock, ed., *The Twentieth Century* (1971), is a lavish visual feast combined with penetrating essays on major developments since 1900. Two excellent accounts of contemporary history—one with a liberal and the other with a conservative point of view—are R. Paxton, *Europe in the Twentieth Century* (1975), and P. Johnson, *Modern Times: The World from the Twenties to the Eighties* (1983). Crucial changes in thought before and after World War I are discussed in three rewarding intellectual histories: G. Masur, *Prophets of Yesterday* (1961); H. S. Hughes, *Consciousness and Society* (1956); and M. Biddiss, *Age of the Masses: Ideas and Society Since 1870* (1977). R. Stromberg, *European Intellectual History Since 1789* (1986), and F. Baumer, *Modern European Thought: Continuity and Change in Ideas, 1600–1950* (1970), are recommended general surveys. W. Kaufmann, *Nietzsche* (1974), is a sympathetic and justly famous study, and S. Aschheim, *The Nietzsche Legacy in Germany, 1890–1990* (1992), considers the range of responses to the pioneering philosopher. W. Barrett, *Irrational Man: A Study in Existential Philosophy* (1958), is still useful.

N. Cantor, *Twentieth-Century Culture: Modernism to Deconstruction* (1988), is a pugnacious and stimulating survey. J. Rewald's *The History of Impressionism* (1961) and *Post-Impressionism* (1956) are excellent, as is the work by Barr cited in the Notes. P. Collaer, *A History of Modern Music* (1961), and H. R. Hitchcock, *Architecture: Nineteenth and Twentieth Centuries* (1958), are good introductions. T. Wolfe, *From Bauhaus to My House* (1981), is a lively critique of modern architecture. L. Barnett, *The Universe and Dr. Einstein* (1952), is a fascinating study of the new physics. A. Storr, *Freud* (1989), and P. Rieff, *Freud* (1956), consider the man and how his theories have stood the test of time. In *Civilization and Its Discontents* (1930), which is highly recommended, S. Freud explores his theory of instinct and repression, arguing that society's necessary repression of instinctual drives will always leave people unhappy. M. White, ed., *The Age of Analysis* (1955), opens up basic questions of twentieth-century psychology and philosophy. H. Liebersohn, *Fate and Utopia in German Sociology* (1988), analyzes developments in German social science. J. Willett, *The New Sobriety: Art and Politics in the Weimar Period, 1917–1933* (1978), and P. Gay, *Weimar Culture* (1970), consider the artistic renaissance and the political culture in Germany in the 1920s. M. Marrus, ed., *Emergence of Leisure* (1974), is a pioneering inquiry into an important aspect of mass culture. H. Daniels-Rops, *A Fight for God,* 2 vols. (1966), is a sympathetic history of the Catholic church between 1870 and 1939.

G. Ambrosius and W. Hibbard, *A Social and Economic History of Twentieth-Century Europe* (1989), provides a good survey; C. Maier, *Recasting Bourgeois Europe* (1975), is an ambitious comparative study of social classes and conflicts in France, Germany, and Italy after World War I. P. Fritzsche, *Rehearsals for Fascism: Populism and Political Mobilization in Weimar Germany* (1990); R. Wohl, *The Generation of 1914* (1979); R. Kuisel, *Capital and State in Modern France: Renovation and Economic Management* (1982); and W. McDougall, *France's Rhineland Diplomacy, 1914–1924* (1978), are four more important studies on aspects of the postwar challenge. H. James, *The German Slump: Politics and Economics, 1924–1936* (1986), is an excellent analysis of economic recovery and subsequent collapse. M. Childs, *Sweden: The Middle Way* (1961), applauds Sweden's efforts at social reform. W. Neuman, *The Balance of Power in the Interwar Years, 1919–1939* (1968), perceptively examines international politics after the Locarno treaties of 1925. In addition to the contemporary works discussed in the text, the crisis of the interwar period comes alive in R. Crossman, ed., *The God That Failed* (1950), in which famous Western writers tell why they were attracted to and later repelled by communism; J. Ortega y Gasset's renowned *The Revolt of the Masses* (1932); and F. A. Hayek's *The Road to Serfdom* (1944), a famous warning of the dangers to democratic freedoms.

In addition to Kindleberger's excellent study of the Great Depression cited in the Notes, there is J. Galbraith's very lively and understandable account of the stock market collapse, *The Great Crash* (1955). J. Garraty, *Unemployment in History* (1978), is noteworthy, though novels best portray the human tragedy of economic decline. Winifred Holtby, *South Riding* (1936), and Walter Greenwood, *Love on the Dole* (1933), are moving stories of the Great Depression in England; Hans Fallada, *Little Man, What Now?* (1932), is the classic counterpart for Germany. Also highly recommended as commentaries on English life between the wars are Robert Graves, *Goodbye to All That* (1957), and George Orwell, *The Road to Wigan Pier* (1972). Among French novelists, André Gide painstakingly examines the French middle class and its values in *The Counterfeiters;* and the great existentialist Albert Camus is at his unforgettable best in *The Stranger* (1942) and *The Plague* (1947).

A Christian View of Evil

The English philosopher C. E. M. Joad (1891–1953) stands out among intellectuals who turned toward religion in the age of anxiety. As a university student he shed his faith and became a militant rationalist who was "frequently in demand for lectures and articles which adopted an attitude hostile to revealed religion in general, and to the Christian Church in particular." Only after intense reflection did Joad retrace his steps and come to reaccept Christianity. Ever the serious intellectual, he described and analyzed his "spiritual odyssey" in closely reasoned and influential writings.

The following selection is taken from God and Evil, *published in 1942 when Hitler's empire posed the problem of human depravity in the starkest terms. Reconsidering the modern secular faith in the primacy of environmental influences and in the perfectibility of humankind, Joad found these beliefs wanting. He reaffirmed the Christian focus on sin and the need for God's grace to escape from evil and find salvation.*

There is, we are told, a revival of interest in religious matters. . . . In this revival of interest I have shared. . . . As a young man at Oxford, I participated, as was natural to my age and generation, in prolonged and frequent discussions of religion which, finding me a Christian, left me as they did many of my generation, an agnostic, an agnostic who entertained a deep-seated suspicion of all dogmatic creeds. . . .

As an agnostic, I felt convinced of two things: first, . . . within the sphere of religion that we did not and probably could not know the truth; secondly, in regard to the so-called religious truths that I had been taught, as, for example, that God created the world as stated in Genesis [and] . . . sent His Son into it to redeem mankind, that it was improbable that they were true and certain that they could not

be *known* to be true. In the confidence of this conviction I proceeded, to all intents and purposes, to turn my back upon the whole subject. . . .

It was only after the coming of the Nazis that my mind began again to turn in the direction of religion. . . . [With] the outbreak of [the Second World] war the subject leapt straight into the forefront of my consciousness where it has remained ever since. . . .

I take it [my spiritual odyssey] to be not untypical. From conversations and discussions, especially with students, I surmise that the revival of interest in religion is widespread. . . . This topical relevance of religion derives from two sources. [First, there is] the relation between religion and politics. This connection . . . subsists at all times, but in quiet times of peace it usually remains implicit. The peculiar circumstances of the last twenty-five years have, however, combined to thrust it into the foreground of men's consciousness. . . . Thus times of revolutionary political change are also times of religious questioning and discussion.

The other source of the specifically topical interest in religion is . . . the obtrusiveness of evil. [Perhaps] there is no more evil abroad in Western civilization than there was at the end of the last century, but it cannot be denied that what there is of it is more obtrusive. I am not referring to evils arising from the relation between the sexes upon which the Church has laid such exclusive stress. . . . I mean the evils of cruelty, savagery, oppression, violence, egotism, aggrandisement, and lust for power. So pervasive and insistent have these evils become that it is at times difficult to avoid concluding that the Devil has been given a longer rope than usual, . . . [and] it becomes correspondingly more difficult to explain it away by the various methods which have been fashionable during the last twenty years.

There was, for example, the explanation of evil in terms of economic inequality and injustice. Socialist writers had taught my generation that bad conditions were the cause of human wretchedness . . . and also of human wickedness. Poverty . . . was the supreme sin; supreme if only because it was the source of all the others. . . .

And the moral [of this teaching]? That evil is due to bad social conditions. Now you can reform bad social conditions by Act of Parliament, substituting comfort, cleanliness, security, and financial competence for discomfort, dirt, insecurity, and want. Therefore, presumably, you can make men virtuous . . . by Act of Parliament.

There was a later explanation of evil in terms of early psychological maltreatment and consequent psychological maladjustment. Evil, then, according to this view, was the result not of bad social, but of bad psychological conditions; not so much of an imperfect society, as of an imperfect family, an ill-directed nursery, and a wrongly run school. Reform society, said the Socialist, and evil will disappear. Reform the school and the family, the psychoanalysts added, and society will reform itself and, once again, evil will disappear. . . .

The contemporary view of evil is untenable. . . . Evil is not *merely* a by-product of unfavourable circumstances; it is too widespread and too deep-seated to admit of any such explanation; so widespread, so deep-seated that one can only conclude that what the religions have always taught is true, and that evil is endemic in the heart of man. . . . The intellectual blunder [of the comfortable and secure late-nineteenth century was] . . . denying what we had traditionally been taught, the doctrine of original sin. . . .

For the simple truth is that one cannot help oneself. . . . For one cannot help but know that one's character is *not* strong enough, one's efforts *not* efficacious, at least, that they are not, if unaided. . . . There are two alternatives [to giving in to evil].

The first, since the world is evil, is to escape from it and to find, first in withdrawal, and, as an ultimate hope, in Nirvana, the true way of life. The second is to face evil and to seek to overcome it. . . . The first is the way of the East, the second of Christianity. My temperament and disposition incline me to the second, but the second I know to be impossible

The British philosopher Cyril Edwin Mitchinson Joad (1891–1953). *(Source: Hulton-Deutsch Collection)*

unless I am assisted from without. By the grace of God we are assured, such assistance may be obtained and evil may be overcome; otherwise, there is no resource and no resistance.

Questions for Analysis

1. How did Joad account for a renewed interest in religious matters?

2. Joad concentrated on the problem of evil in human affairs. What did he mean by "evil"? Was it becoming more powerful in his time?

3. What, according to Joad, were the usual explanations for the existence of evil? What was his view of these explanations?

4. In Joad's view, how did the Christian doctrine of original sin relate to the problem of evil? How could the Christian overcome sin and evil?

Source: C. E. M. Joad, *God and Evil* (New York: Harper and Brothers, 1943), pp. 9–20, 103–104.

32

Dictatorships and the Second World War

Hugo Jager's photograph of a crowd of enthusiastic Hitler supporters *(Source: Hugo Jager,* Life Magazine, © *Time Warner, Inc.)*

The era of anxiety and economic depression was also a time of growing strength for political dictatorship. In Europe, as in Japan and China in the 1930s, popularly elected governments and basic civil liberties declined drastically. On the eve of the Second World War, liberal democratic governments were surviving only in Great Britain, France, the Low Countries, the Scandinavian nations, and neutral Switzerland. Elsewhere in Europe, various kinds of strongmen ruled. Dictatorship seemed the wave of the future. Thus the decline in liberal political institutions and the intellectual crisis were related elements in the general crisis of European civilization.

The West's era of dictatorship is a highly disturbing chapter in the history of civilization. The key development was not only the resurgence of authoritarian rule but also the rise of a particularly ruthless and dynamic tyranny. This new kind of tyranny reached its fullest realization in the Soviet Union and Nazi Germany in the 1930s. Stalin and Hitler mobilized their peoples for enormous undertakings and ruled with unprecedented severity. Hitler's mobilization was ultimately directed toward racial aggression and territorial expansion, and his sudden attack on Poland in 1939 started World War II.

Nazi armies were defeated by a great coalition, and today we want to believe that the era of totalitarian dictatorship was a terrible accident, that Stalin's slave labor camps and Hitler's gas chambers "can't happen again." But the cruel truth is that horrible atrocities continue to plague the world in our time. The Khmer Rouge inflicted genocide on its people in Kampuchea (Cambodia), and civil war in Bosnia led to ethnically motivated atrocities recalling the horrors of the Second World War. And there are other examples. Thus it is vital that we understand Europe's era of brutal dictatorship in order to guard against the possibility of its recurrence.

- What was the nature of twentieth-century dictatorship and authoritarian rule?
- How did people live in the most extreme states: the Soviet Union and Nazi Germany?
- How did the rise of aggressive dictatorships result in another world war?

These are the questions this chapter will seek to answer.

AUTHORITARIAN STATES

Both conservative and radical dictatorships swept through Europe in the 1920s and the 1930s. Although these two types of dictatorship shared some characteristics and sometimes overlapped in practice, they were in essence profoundly different. Conservative authoritarian regimes were an old story in Europe. Radical dictatorships were a new and frightening development.

Conservative Authoritarianism

The traditional form of antidemocratic government in European history was conservative authoritarianism. Like Catherine the Great in Russia and Metternich in Austria, the leaders of such governments tried to prevent major changes that would undermine the existing social order. To do so, they relied on obedient bureaucracies, vigilant police departments, and trustworthy armies. They forbade popular participation in government or else severely limited it to natural allies such as landlords, bureaucrats, and high church officials. They persecuted liberals, democrats, and socialists as subversive radicals, often consigning them to jail or exile.

Yet old-fashioned authoritarian governments were limited in their power and in their objectives. They had neither the ability nor the desire to control many aspects of their subjects' lives. Preoccupied with the goal of mere survival, these governments largely limited their demands to taxes, army recruits, and passive acceptance. As long as the people did not try to change the system, they often had considerable personal independence.

After the First World War, this kind of authoritarian government revived, especially in the less developed eastern part of Europe. There the parliamentary regimes that had been founded on the wreckage of empires in 1918 fell one by one. There were several reasons for this development. These lands lacked a strong tradition of self-government, with its necessary restraint and compromise, and many of these new states, such as Yugoslavia, were torn by ethnic conflicts. Dictatorship appealed to nationalists and military leaders as a way to repress such tensions and preserve national unity. Large landowners and the church were still powerful forces in these largely agrarian areas, and they often looked to dictators to save them from progressive land reform or communist agrarian upheaval. So did some members of the middle class, which was small and weak in eastern Europe. Finally, though some kind of democracy managed to stagger through the 1920s in Austria, Bulgaria, Romania, Greece, Estonia, and Latvia, the Great Depression delivered the final blow to those countries in 1936. By early 1938 in eastern Europe only economically and socially advanced Czechoslovakia remained true to liberal political ideals. Conservative dictators also took over in Spain and Portugal.

Although some of the conservative authoritarian regimes adopted certain Hitlerian and fascist characteristics in the 1930s, their general aims were limited. They were concerned more with maintaining the status quo than with mobilizing the masses or forcing society into rapid change or war. This tradition continued into our own time, especially in some of the military dictatorships that ruled in Latin America until quite recently.

Hungary was a good example of conservative authoritarianism. In the chaos of collapse in 1919, Béla Kun formed a Lenin-style government, but foreign troops, large landowners, and hostile peasants soon crushed communism in Hungary. Thereafter, a combination of great and medium-size landowners instituted a semi-authoritarian regime, which maintained the status quo in the 1920s. Hungary had a parliament, but elections were carefully controlled. The peasants did not have the right to vote, and an upper house representing the landed aristocracy was re-established. There was no land reform or major social change. The Hungarian government remained conservative and nationalistic throughout the 1930s.

Radical Dictatorships

While conservative authoritarianism predominated in the smaller states of central and eastern Europe by the mid-1930s, radical dictatorships emerged in the Soviet Union, in Germany, and to a lesser extent in Italy. Almost all scholars agree that the leaders of these radical dictatorships violently rejected parliamentary restraint and liberal values. Scholars also agree that these dictatorships exercised unprecedented control over the masses and sought to mobilize them for constant action. But beyond these certainties, there has always been controversy and debate over how best to interpret and explain these regimes.

Three leading interpretations of radical dictatorships will concern us here. The first interpretation relates the radical dictatorships to the rise of modern totalitarianism. The second interpretation focuses on the idea of fascism as the unifying impulse. The third stresses the limitations of such broad generalizations and the uniqueness of each regime. Each school of interpretation has strengths and weaknesses.

The concept of *totalitarianism* as an explanation of radical twentieth-century dictatorships emerged in the 1920s and the 1930s, although it is frequently and mistakenly seen as developing only after 1945 during the cold war.[1] In 1924 Mussolini spoke of the "fierce totalitarian will" of his movement in Italy. In the 1930s many British, American, and German writers-in-exile used the concept of totalitarianism to link Italian and German fascism with Soviet communism under a common antiliberal umbrella. The alliance between Hitler and Stalin in 1939 reinforced this explanation.

Early writers believed that modern totalitarianism burst on the scene with the revolutionary total-war effort of 1914 to 1918. The war called forth a tendency to subordinate all institutions and all classes to one supreme objective: victory. As French thinker Elie Halévy put it in 1936, the varieties of modern totalitarian tyranny—fascism, Nazism, and communism—could be thought of as "feuding brothers" with a common father: the nature of modern war.[2]

Writers such as Halévy believed that the crucial experience of World War I was carried further by Lenin and the Bolsheviks during the Russian civil war. Lenin showed that a dedicated minority could make a total effort and achieve victory over a less determined majority. Lenin also demonstrated how institutions and human rights might be subordinated to the needs of a single group—the Communist party—and its leader, Lenin. Thus he provided a model for single-party dictatorship, and he inspired imitators, including Adolf Hitler. According to this school of interpretation, modern totalitarianism reached maturity in the 1930s in the Stalinist Soviet Union and in Nazi Germany.

As numerous Western political scientists and historians argued in the 1950s and the 1960s, the totalitarian state used modern technology and communications to exercise complete political power. But it did not stop there. Increasingly, the state took over and tried to control just as completely the economic, social, intellectual, and cultural aspects of people's lives. Deviation from the norm even in art or family behavior could become a crime. In theory, nothing was politically neutral; nothing was outside the scope of the state.

This grandiose vision of total state control broke decisively not only with conservative authoritarianism but also with nineteenth-century liberalism and democracy. Indeed, totalitarianism was a radical revolt against liberalism. Classical liberalism (see page 811) sought to limit the power of the state and protect the sacred rights of the individual. Liberals stood for rationality, peaceful prog-

ress, economic freedom, and a strong middle class. All of that disgusted totalitarians as sentimental slop. They believed in willpower, preached conflict, and worshiped violence. They believed that the individual was infinitely less valuable than the state and that there were no lasting rights, only temporary rewards for loyal and effective service. Only a single powerful leader and a single party, both unrestrained by law or tradition, determined the destiny of the totalitarian state.

Unlike old-fashioned authoritarianism, modern totalitarianism was based not on an elite but on mass movements led by committed individuals. Totalitarian societies were fully mobilized societies moving toward some goal and possessing boundless dynamism. As soon as one goal was achieved at

Nazi Mass Rally in 1936 This picture captures the essence of the totalitarian interpretation of dynamic modern dictatorship. The uniformed members of the Nazi party have willingly merged themselves into a single force and await the command of the godlike leader. *(Source: Wide World Photos)*

the cost of enormous sacrifice, another arose at the leader's command to take its place. Thus totalitarianism was in the end a *permanent* revolution, an *unfinished* revolution, in which rapid, profound change imposed from on high went on forever.

A second group of writers developed the concept of *fascism* to explain the rise of radical dictatorships outside the Soviet Union. A term of pride for Mussolini and Hitler, who used it to describe the supposedly "total" and revolutionary character of their movements, fascism was severely criticized by these writers. They linked it to reactionary forces, decaying capitalism, and domestic class conflict. Orthodox Marxists first argued that fascism was the way powerful capitalists sought to create a mass nationalist movement capable of destroying the revolutionary working class, thereby protecting the enormous profits that capitalists reaped through war and territorial expansion. Both orthodox Marxists and less doctrinaire socialists usually rejected the totalitarian interpretation, discerning in communist regimes such as that of Stalin at least some elements of the genuine socialism they desired.

Recent comparative studies of fascist movements all across Europe have shown that they shared many characteristics, including extreme, often expansionist nationalism; antipathy to socialism and a desire to destroy working-class movements; alliances with powerful capitalists and landowners; mass parties that appealed especially to the middle class and the peasantry; a dynamic and violent leader; and glorification of war and the military. European fascism remains a product of class conflict, capitalist crisis, and postwar upheaval in these recent studies, but the basic interpretation has become less dogmatic and more convincing.

Historians today often adopt a third interpretive approach, which emphasizes the uniqueness of developments in each country. This approach has been both reflected and encouraged in recent years by an outpouring of specialized historical studies that challenge parts of the overarching totalitarian and fascist interpretations. This is especially true for Hitler's Germany, and a similar re-evaluation of Stalin's Soviet Union may be expected now that the fall of communism has opened Soviet archives to new research. To this third school of historians, differences in historical patterns are often more important than striking but frequently superficial similarities.

Four tentative judgments concerning these debates about radical dictatorships in the twentieth century seem appropriate. First, as is often the case in history, the leading interpretations are rather closely linked to the political passions and the ideological commitments of the age. Thus in the 1930s and in the early cold war, modern Western "bourgeois-liberal" observers, worried by the dual challenge of the Nazi and Soviet dictatorships, often found the totalitarian explanation convincing. At the same time, Marxist, socialist, and New Left writers easily saw profound structural differences between the continued capitalism in fascist countries and the socialism established in the Soviet Union.

Second, as a noted scholar has recently concluded, the concept of totalitarianism retains real value. It correctly highlights that both Hitler's Germany and Stalin's Soviet Union made an unprecedented "total claim" on the belief and behavior of their respective citizens.[3] Third, antidemocratic, antisocialist movements sprang up all over Europe, but only in Italy and Germany (and some would say Spain) were they able to take power. Studies of fascist movements seeking power locate common elements, but they do not explain what fascist governments actually did. Fourth, the problem of Europe's radical dictatorships is complex, and there are few easy answers.

STALIN'S SOVIET UNION

Lenin's harshest critics claim that he established the basic outlines of a modern totalitarian dictatorship after the Bolshevik Revolution and during the Russian civil war. If this is so, then Joseph Stalin (1879–1953) certainly finished the job. A master of political infighting, Stalin cautiously consolidated his power and eliminated his enemies in the mid-1920s. Then in 1928, as undisputed leader of the ruling Communist party, he launched the first five-year plan—the "revolution from above," as he so aptly termed it.

The five-year plans were extremely ambitious. Often incorrectly considered a mere set of economic measures to speed the Soviet Union's industrial development, the five-year plans marked the beginning of a renewed attempt to mobilize and transform Soviet society along socialist lines.

Their ultimate goal was to generate new attitudes, new loyalties, and a new socialist humanity. The means Stalin and the small Communist party elite chose in order to do so were constant propaganda, enormous sacrifice, and unlimited violence and state control. Thus many historians argue that the Soviet Union in the 1930s became a dynamic, modern totalitarian state.

From Lenin to Stalin

By spring 1921 Lenin and the Bolsheviks had won the civil war, but they ruled a shattered and devastated land. Many farms were in ruins, and food supplies were exhausted. In southern Russia drought combined with the ravages of war to produce the worst famine in generations. By 1920, according to the government, from 50 to 90 percent of the population in seventeen provinces was starving. Industrial production also broke down completely. In 1921, for example, output of steel and cotton textiles was only about 4 percent of what it had been in 1913. Leon Trotsky later wrote that the "collapse of the productive forces surpassed anything of the kind history had ever seen. The country, and the government with it, were at the very edge of the abyss."[4] The Bolsheviks had destroyed the economy as well as their foes.

In the face of economic disintegration, riots by peasants and workers, and an open rebellion by

Lenin and Stalin in 1922   Lenin re-established limited economic freedom throughout Russia in 1921, but he ran the country and the Communist party in an increasingly authoritarian way. Stalin carried the process much further and eventually built a regime based on harsh dictatorship. *(Source: Sovfoto)*

previously pro-Bolshevik sailors at Kronstadt, the tough but ever-flexible Lenin changed course. In March 1921 he announced the New Economic Policy (NEP), which re-established limited economic freedom in an attempt to rebuild agriculture and industry. During the civil war, the communists had simply seized grain without payment. With the NEP, Lenin substituted a grain tax on the country's peasant producers, who were permitted to sell their surpluses in free markets. Peasants were also encouraged to buy as many goods as they could afford from private traders and small handicraft manufacturers, groups that were now allowed to reappear. Heavy industry, railroads, and banks, however, remained wholly nationalized.

The NEP was shrewd and successful both politically and economically. Politically, it was a necessary but temporary compromise with the Soviet Union's overwhelming peasant majority. Flushed with victory after the revolutionary gains of 1917, the peasants would have fought to hold onto their land. Realizing that his government was not strong enough to take land from the peasants, Lenin made a deal with the only force capable of overturning his government. Economically, the NEP brought rapid recovery. In 1926 industrial output surpassed the level of 1913, and Soviet peasants were producing almost as much grain as before the war. Counting shorter hours and increased social benefits, workers were living somewhat better than they had in the past.

As the economy recovered and the government partially relaxed its censorship and repression, an intense struggle for power began in the inner circles of the Communist party, for Lenin had left no chosen successor when he died in 1924. The principal contenders were the stolid Stalin and the flamboyant Trotsky.

The son of a shoemaker, Joseph Dzhugashvili—later known as Stalin—studied for the priesthood but was expelled from his theological seminary, probably for rude rebelliousness. By 1903 he had joined the Bolsheviks. In the years before the First World War, he engaged in many revolutionary activities in the southern Transcaucasian area of the multinational Russian Empire, including a daring bank robbery to get money for the Bolsheviks. This raid gained Lenin's attention and approval.

Stalin was a good organizer but a poor speaker and writer, with no experience outside Russia. Trotsky, a great and inspiring leader who had planned the 1917 takeover (see page 000) and then created the victorious Red Army, appeared to have all the advantages. Yet it was Stalin who succeeded Lenin. Stalin won because he was more effective at gaining the all-important support of the party, the only genuine source of power in the one-party state. Rising to general secretary of the party's Central Committee just before Lenin's first stroke in 1922, Stalin used his office to win friends and allies with jobs and promises.

The practical Stalin also won because he appeared better able than the brilliant Trotsky to relate Marxian teaching to Soviet realities in the 1920s. Stalin developed a theory of "socialism in one country" that was more appealing to the majority of communists than Trotsky's doctrine of "permanent revolution." Stalin argued that the Russian-dominated Soviet Union had the ability to build socialism on its own. Trotsky maintained that socialism in the Soviet Union could succeed only if revolution occurred quickly throughout Europe. To many communists, especially Soviet communists, Trotsky's views seemed to sell their country short and to promise risky conflicts with capitalist countries by recklessly encouraging revolutionary movements around the world. Stalin's willingness to break with the NEP and push socialism at home appealed to many in the party who had come to detest the capitalist-appearing NEP.

With cunning skill Stalin gradually achieved absolute power between 1922 and 1927. First, he allied with Trotsky's personal enemies to crush Trotsky, who was expelled from the Soviet Union in 1929 and eventually was murdered in Mexico in 1940, undoubtedly on Stalin's order. Second, Stalin aligned with the moderates, who wanted to go slow at home, to suppress Trotsky's radical followers. Third, having defeated all the radicals, he turned against his allies, the moderates, and destroyed them as well. Stalin's final triumph came at the party congress of December 1927, which condemned all "deviation from the general party line" formulated by Stalin. The dictator was then ready to launch his revolution from above—the real revolution for millions of ordinary citizens.

The Five-Year Plans

The party congress of 1927, which ratified Stalin's seizure of power, marked the end of the NEP and the beginning of the era of socialist five-year plans.

The first five-year plan had staggering economic objectives. In just five years, total industrial output was to increase by 250 percent. Heavy industry, the preferred sector, was to grow even faster; steel production, for example, was to jump almost 300 percent. Agricultural production was slated to increase by 150 percent, and one-fifth of the peasants in the Soviet Union were scheduled to give up their private plots and join socialist collective farms. In spite of warnings from moderate communists that these goals were unrealistic, Stalin raised them higher as the plan got under way. By 1930 economic and social change was sweeping the country.

Stalin unleashed his "second revolution" for a variety of interrelated reasons. There were, first of all, ideological considerations. Like Lenin, Stalin and his militant supporters were deeply committed to socialism as they understood it. Purely economic motivations were also important. Although the economy had recovered, it seemed to have stalled in 1927 and 1928. A new socialist offensive seemed necessary if industry and agriculture were to grow rapidly.

Political considerations were most important. Internationally, there was the old problem, remaining from prerevolutionary times, of catching up with the advanced and presumably hostile capitalist nations of the West. Stalin said in 1931, when he pressed for ever-greater speed and sacrifice, "We are fifty or a hundred years behind the advanced countries. We must make good this distance in ten years. Either we do it, or we shall go under."[5]

Domestically, there was what communist writers of the 1920s called the "cursed problem"—the problem of the peasants. For centuries, the peasants had wanted to own the land, and finally they had it. Sooner or later, the communists reasoned, the peasants would become conservative little capitalists and pose a threat to the regime. Therefore, Stalin decided on a preventive war against the peasantry in order to bring it under the absolute control of the state.

That war was *collectivization*—the forcible consolidation of individual peasant farms into large, state-controlled enterprises. Beginning in 1929, peasants all over the Soviet Union were ordered to give up their land and animals and become members of collective farms, although they continued to live in their own homes. As for the *kulaks,* the better-off peasants, Stalin instructed party workers to "liquidate them as a class." Stripped of land and livestock, the kulaks were generally not even permitted to join the collective farms. Many starved or were deported to forced-labor camps for "reeducation."

Since almost all peasants were in fact poor, the term *kulak* soon meant any peasant who opposed the new system. Whole villages were often attacked. One conscience-stricken colonel in the secret police confessed to a foreign journalist, "I am an old Bolshevik. I worked in the underground against the Tsar and then I fought in the Civil War. Did I do all that in order that I should now surround villages with machine guns and order my men to fire indiscriminately into crowds of peasants? Oh, no, no!"[6]

Forced collectivization of the peasants led to economic and human disaster. Large numbers of peasants slaughtered their animals and burned their crops in sullen, hopeless protest. Between 1929 and 1933, the number of horses, cattle, sheep, and goats in the Soviet Union fell by at least half. Nor were the state-controlled collective farms more productive. The output of grain barely increased between 1928 and 1938, when it was almost identical to the output of 1913. Collectivized agriculture was unable to make any substantial financial contribution to Soviet industrial development during the first five-year plan. And the human dimension of the tragedy was shocking. Collectivization created human-made famine in 1932 and 1933, and many perished. Indeed, Stalin confided to British prime minister Winston Churchill at Yalta in 1945 (see page 1092) that 10 million people had died in the course of collectivization.

Nevertheless, collectivization was a political victory of sorts. By the end of 1932, fully 60 percent of peasant families had been herded onto collective farms; by 1938, 93 percent. Regimented and indoctrinated as employees of an all-powerful state, the peasants were no longer even a potential political threat to Stalin and the Communist party. Moreover, the state was assured of grain for bread for urban workers, who were much more important politically than the peasants. Collective farmers had to meet their grain quotas first and worry about feeding themselves second. Many collectivized peasants drew much of their own food from tiny, grudgingly tolerated garden plots that they worked in their off hours.

Decorative Art in Soviet Russia Russia had a rich tradition of icon-painting and decorative religious art, which was expected to glorify Soviet life and socialist achievements after the Russian Revolution. This beautiful lacquered lid of a wooden box was produced in the old icon-painting center of Palekh, 200 miles east of Moscow. The painter skillfully combines modern motifs, such as tractors and factories, with traditional themes of peasant life. Historians usually find considerable continuity in the midst of revolutionary change. *(Source: Novosti)*

The industrial side of the five-year plans was more successful—indeed, quite spectacular. Soviet industry produced about four times as much in 1937 as it had in 1928. No other major country had ever achieved such rapid industrial growth. Heavy industry led the way; consumer industry grew quite slowly. Steel production—a near-obsession with Stalin, whose name fittingly meant "man of steel" in Russian—increased roughly 500 percent between 1928 and 1937. A new heavy industrial complex was built almost from scratch in western Siberia. Industrial growth also went hand in hand with urban development. Cities rose where nomadic tribes had grazed their flocks. More than 25 million people migrated to cities during the 1930s.

The great industrialization drive, concentrated between 1928 and 1937, was an awe-inspiring achievement purchased at enormous sacrifice. The sudden creation of dozens of new factories (*and* the increasingly voracious military) demanded tremendous resources. The money was collected from the people by means of heavy, hidden sales taxes. There was therefore no improvement in the average standard of living. Indeed, the most careful studies show that the average nonfarm wage apparently purchased only about *half* as many goods in 1932 as in 1928. After 1932 real wages rose slowly, so that in 1937 workers could buy about 60 percent of what they had bought in 1928.

Two other factors contributed importantly to rapid industrialization: firm labor discipline and foreign engineers. Between 1930 and 1932, trade unions lost most of their power. The government could assign workers to any job anywhere in the country, and individuals could not move without the permission of the police. When factory managers needed more hands, they called on their counterparts on the collective farms, who sent them millions of "unneeded" peasants over the years.

Foreign engineers were hired to plan and construct many of the new factories. Highly skilled American engineers, hungry for work in the depression years, were particularly important until newly trained Soviet experts began to replace them after 1932. The gigantic mills of the new Siberian steel industry were modeled on America's best.

Stalin's planners harnessed even the skill and technology of capitalist countries to promote the surge of socialist industry.

Life in Stalinist Society

The aim of Stalin's five-year plans was to create a new kind of society and human personality as well as a strong industrial economy and a powerful army. Stalin and his helpers were Marxian economic determinists. Once everything was owned by the state, they believed, a socialist society and a new kind of human being would inevitably emerge. They were by no means totally successful, but they did build a new society, whose broad outlines existed through the early 1980s. For the people, life in Stalinist society had both good and bad aspects.

The most frightening aspect of Stalinist society was brutal, unrestrained police terrorism. First directed primarily against the peasants after 1929, terror was increasingly turned on leading Communists, powerful administrators, and ordinary people for no apparent reason. As one Soviet woman later recalled, "We all trembled because there was no way of getting out of it. Even a Communist himself can be caught. To avoid trouble became an exception."[7] A climate of fear swept over the land.

In the early 1930s, the top members of the party and government were Stalin's obedient servants, but there was some grumbling in the party. At a small gathering in November 1932, even Stalin's wife complained bitterly about the misery of the people. Stalin showered her with insults, and she died that same night, apparently by her own hand. In late 1934 Stalin's number-two man, Sergei Kirov, was suddenly and mysteriously murdered. Although Stalin himself probably ordered Kirov's murder, he used the incident to launch a reign of terror.

In August 1936 sixteen prominent old Bolsheviks confessed to all manner of plots against Stalin in spectacular public trials in Moscow. Then in 1937 lesser party officials and newer henchmen were arrested. Some prisoners were cruelly tortured and warned that their loved ones would also die if they did not confess. In addition to party members, union officials, managers, intellectuals, army officers, and countless ordinary citizens were struck down. Local units of the secret police were even ordered to arrest a certain percentage of the people in their districts. In all, at least 8 million people were probably arrested, and millions never returned from prisons and forced-labor camps.

Stalin's mass purges were truly baffling, and many explanations have been given for them. Possibly Stalin believed that the old Communists, like the peasants under NEP, were a potential threat to be wiped out in a preventive attack. There are many other interpretations. Some scholars argue that the purges demonstrated that Stalin was sadistic or insane, for his bloodbath greatly weakened the government and the army. Others see the terror as an aspect of the fully developed totalitarian state, which must by its nature always be fighting real or imaginary enemies. At the least, the mass purges were a message to the people: no one was secure; everyone had to serve the party and its leader with redoubled devotion.

Another aspect of life in the 1930s was constant propaganda and indoctrination. Party activists lectured workers in factories and peasants on collective farms. Newspapers, films, and radio broadcasts endlessly recounted socialist achievements and capitalist plots. Art and literature became highly political. Intellectuals were ordered by Stalin to become "engineers of human minds." Writers and artists who could effectively combine genuine creativity and political propaganda became the darlings of the regime. They often lived better than top members of the political elite. It became increasingly important for the successful writer and artist to glorify Russian nationalism. Russian history was rewritten so that early tsars such as Ivan the Terrible and Peter the Great became worthy forerunners of the greatest Russian leader of all—Stalin.

Stalin seldom appeared in public, but his presence was everywhere—in portraits, statues, books, and quotations from his "sacred" writings. Although the government persecuted religion and turned churches into "museums of atheism," the state had both an earthly religion and a high priest—Marxism-Leninism and Joseph Stalin.

Life was hard in Stalin's Soviet Union. The masses of people lived primarily on black bread and wore old, shabby clothing. There were constant shortages in the stores, although very heavily taxed vodka was always readily available. A shortage of housing was a particularly serious problem. Millions were moving into the cities, but the government built few new apartments. In 1940 there were approximately 4 people per room in every urban dwelling, as opposed to 2.7 per room in 1926. A relatively lucky family received one room for all its members and shared both a kitchen and a toilet with others on the floor. Less fortunate workers, kulaks, and class enemies built scrap-lumber shacks or underground dugouts in shantytowns.

Life was hard but by no means hopeless. Idealism and ideology had real appeal for many communists, who saw themselves heroically building the world's first socialist society while capitalism crumbled and degenerated into fascism in the West. This optimistic belief in the future of the Soviet Union also attracted many disillusioned Westerners to communism in the 1930s.

On a more practical level, Soviet workers did receive some important social benefits, such as old-age pensions, free medical services, free education, and day-care centers for children. Unemployment was almost unknown. And there was the possibility of personal advancement.

The keys to improving one's position were specialized skills and technical education. Rapid industrialization required massive numbers of trained experts, such as skilled workers, engineers, and plant managers. Thus the state provided tremendous incentives to those who could serve its needs. It paid the mass of unskilled workers and collective farmers very low wages, but it dangled high salaries and many special privileges before its growing technical and managerial elite. This elite joined with the political and artistic elites in a new upper class, whose members were rich, powerful, and insecure, especially during the purges. Yet the possible gains of moving up outweighed the risks. Millions struggled bravely in universities, institutes, and night schools for the all-important spe-

Adult Education Illiteracy, especially among women, was a serious problem after the Russian Revolution. This early photo shows how adults successfully learned to read and write throughout the Soviet Union. *(Source: Sovfoto)*

cialized education. One young man summed it up: "In Soviet Russia there is no capital except education. If a person does not want to become a collective farmer or just a cleaning woman, the only means you have to get something is through education."[8]

Mobilizing Women in the Soviet Union

The radical transformation of Soviet society had a profound impact on women's lives. Marxists had traditionally believed that both capitalism and the middle-class husband exploited women. The Russian Revolution of 1917 immediately proclaimed complete equality of rights for women. In the 1920s divorce and abortion were made easily available, and women were urged to work outside the home and liberate themselves sexually. After Stalin came to power, sexual and familial liberation was played down, and the most lasting changes for women involved work and education.

These changes were truly revolutionary. Young women were constantly told that they had to be fully equal to men, that they could and should do anything men could do. Peasant women in Russia had long experienced the equality of backbreaking physical labor in the countryside, and they continued to enjoy that equality on collective farms. With the advent of the five-year plans, millions of women also began to toil in factories and in heavy construction, building dams, roads, and steel mills in summer heat and winter frost. Most of the opportunities open to men through education were also open to women. Determined women pursued their studies and entered the ranks of the better-paid specialists in industry and science. Medicine practically became a woman's profession. By 1950, 75 percent of all doctors in the Soviet Union were women.

Thus Stalinist society gave women great opportunities but demanded great sacrifices as well. The vast majority of women simply *had* to work outside the home. Wages were so low that it was almost impossible for a family or couple to live only on the husband's earnings. Moreover, the full-time working woman had a heavy burden of household tasks in her off hours, for most Soviet men in the 1930s still considered the home and the children the woman's responsibility. Men continued to monopolize the best jobs. Finally, rapid change and economic hardship led to many broken families, creat-

ing further physical, emotional, and mental strains for women. In any event, the often-neglected human resource of women was ruthlessly mobilized in Stalinist society. This, too, was an aspect of the Soviet totalitarian state.

MUSSOLINI AND FASCISM IN ITALY

Mussolini's movement and his seizure of power in 1922 were important steps in the rise of dictatorships in Europe between the two world wars. Like all the future dictators, the young Mussolini hated liberalism and wanted to destroy it in Italy. At the same time, he and his supporters were the first to call themselves "fascists"—revolutionaries determined to create a certain kind of totalitarian state. Few scholars today would argue that Mussolini succeeded. His dictatorship was brutal and theatrical, but it remained a halfway house between conservative authoritarianism and modern totalitarianism.

The Seizure of Power

In the early twentieth century Italy was a liberal state with civil rights and a constitutional monarchy. On the eve of the First World War, the parliamentary regime finally granted universal male suffrage. But there were serious problems. Much of the Italian population was still poor, and many peasants were more attached to their villages and local interests than to the national state. Moreover, the papacy, many devout Catholics, conservatives, and landowners remained strongly opposed to the middle-class lawyers and politicians who ran the country largely for their own benefit. Relations between church and state were often tense. Class differences were also extreme, and a powerful revolutionary socialist movement had developed. The radical left wing of the Socialist party gained the leadership as early as 1912, and the party unanimously opposed the war from the very beginning.[9]

The war worsened the political situation. Having fought on the side of the Allies almost exclusively for purposes of territorial expansion, the parliamentary government bitterly disappointed Italian nationalists with Italy's modest gains at Versailles. Workers and peasants also felt cheated: to win their support during the war, the government had promised social and land reform, which it did not deliver after the war.

The Russian Revolution inspired and energized Italy's revolutionary socialist movement, and radical workers and peasants began occupying factories and seizing land in 1920. These actions scared and mobilized the property-owning classes. Moreover, after the war the pope lifted his ban on participation by Catholics in Italian politics, and a strong Catholic party quickly emerged. Thus by 1921 revolutionary socialists, antiliberal conservatives, and frightened property owners were all opposed—though for different reasons—to the liberal parliamentary government.

Into these crosscurrents of unrest and fear stepped the blustering, bullying Benito Mussolini (1883–1945). Son of a village schoolteacher and a poor blacksmith, Mussolini began his political career as a Socialist leader and radical newspaper editor before World War I. In 1914, powerfully influenced by antidemocratic cults of violent action, the young Mussolini urged that Italy join the Allies, a stand for which he was expelled from the Italian Socialist party. Later Mussolini fought at the front and was wounded in 1917. Returning home, he began organizing bitter war veterans like himself into a band of fascists—from the Italian word for "a union of forces."

At first Mussolini's program was a radical combination of nationalist and socialist demands, including territorial expansion, benefits for workers, and land reform for peasants. It competed directly with the well-organized Socialist party and failed to get off the ground. When Mussolini saw that his violent verbal assaults on rival Socialists won him growing support from conservatives and the frightened middle classes, he shifted gears in 1920. In thought and action, Mussolini was a striking example of the turbulent uncertainty of the age of anxiety.

Mussolini and his growing private army of Black Shirts began to grow violent. Typically, a band of fascist toughs would roar off in trucks at night and swoop down on a few isolated Socialist organizers, beating them up and force-feeding them almost deadly doses of castor oil. Few people were killed, but socialist newspapers, union halls, and local Socialist party headquarters were destroyed. Mussolini's toughs pushed Socialists out of the city governments of northern Italy.

A skillful politician, Mussolini allowed his followers to convince themselves that they were not just opposing the "Reds" but also making a real revolution of their own, forging a strong, dynamic movement that would help the little people against the established interests. With the government breaking down in 1922, largely because of the chaos created by his direct-action bands, Mussolini stepped forward as the savior of order and property. Striking a conservative note in his speeches and gaining the sympathetic neutrality of army leaders, Mussolini demanded the resignation of the existing government and his own appointment by the king. In October 1922, to force matters, a large group of Fascists marched on Rome to threaten the king and force him to call on Mussolini. The threat worked. Victor Emmanuel III (r. 1900–1946), who had no love for the old liberal politicians, asked Mussolini to form a new cabinet. Thus after widespread violence and a threat of armed uprising, Mussolini seized power "legally." He was immediately granted dictatorial authority for one year by the king and the parliament.

The Regime in Action

Mussolini became dictator on the strength of Italians' rejection of parliamentary government coupled with fears of Soviet-style revolution. Yet what he intended to do with his power was by no means clear until 1924. Some of his dedicated supporters pressed for a "second revolution." Mussolini's ministers, however, included old conservatives, moderates, and even two reform-minded Socialists. A new electoral law was passed giving two-thirds of the representatives in the parliament to the party that won the most votes. That change allowed the Fascists and their allies to win an overwhelming majority in 1924. Shortly thereafter five of Mussolini's fascist thugs kidnapped and murdered Giacomo Matteotti, the leader of the Socialists in the parliament. In the face of this outrage, the opposition demanded that Mussolini's armed squads be dissolved and all violence be banned.

Although Mussolini may or may not have ordered Matteotti's murder, he stood at the crossroads of a severe political crisis. After some hesitation, he charged forward. Declaring his desire to "make the nation Fascist," he imposed a series of repressive measures. Freedom of the press was abolished, elections were fixed, and the government ruled by decree. Mussolini arrested his political opponents, disbanded all independent labor unions, and put dedicated fascists in control of Italy's schools. He created a fascist youth movement, fascist labor unions, and many other fascist organizations. He trumpeted his goal in a famous slogan of 1926, "Everything in the state, nothing outside the state, nothing against the state." By the end of that year, Italy was a one-party dictatorship under Mussolini's unquestioned leadership.

Mussolini, however, did not complete the establishment of a modern totalitarian state. His Fascist party never became all-powerful. It never destroyed the old power structure, as the communists did in the Soviet Union; nor did it succeed in dominating the old power structure, as the Nazis did in Germany. Membership in the Fascist party was more a sign of an Italian's respectability than a commitment to radical change. Interested primarily in personal power, Mussolini was content to compromise with the old conservative classes that controlled the army, the economy, and the state. He never tried to purge these classes or even move very vigorously against them. He controlled and propagandized labor but left big business to regulate itself, profitably and securely. There was no land reform.

Mussolini also drew increasing support from the Catholic church. In the Lateran Agreement of 1929, he recognized the Vatican as a tiny independent state, and he agreed to give the church heavy financial support. The pope expressed his satisfaction and urged Italians to support Mussolini's government.

Nothing better illustrates Mussolini's unwillingness to harness everyone and everything for dynamic action than his treatment of women. He abolished divorce and told women to stay at home and produce children. To promote that goal, he decreed a special tax on bachelors in 1934. In 1938 women were limited by law to a maximum of 10 percent of the better-paying jobs in industry and government. Italian women appear not to have changed their attitudes or behavior in any important way under fascist rule.

Mussolini's government did not pass racial laws until 1938 and did not persecute Jews savagely until late in the Second World War, when Italy was under Nazi control. Nor did Mussolini establish a truly ruthless police state. Only twenty-three political prisoners were condemned to death between

Mussolini A charismatic orator with a sure touch for emotional propaganda, Mussolini loved settings that linked fascist Italy to the glories of imperial Rome. Poised to address a mass rally in Rome at the time of Matteotti's murder, Mussolini then called for ninety thousand more volunteers to join his gun-toting fascist militia. Members of the militia stand as an honor guard in front of the podium. *(Source: Popperfoto)*

1926 and 1944. In spite of much pompous posing by the chauvinist leader and in spite of mass meetings, salutes, and a certain copying of Hitler's aggression in foreign policy after 1933, Mussolini's fascist Italy, though repressive and undemocratic, was never really totalitarian.

✤ HITLER AND NAZISM IN GERMANY

The most frightening dictatorship developed in Nazi Germany. A product of Hitler's evil genius as well as of Germany's social and political situation and the general attack on liberalism and rationality in the age of anxiety, the Nazi movement shared some of the characteristics of Mussolini's Italian model and was a form of fascism. The Nazi dictatorship smashed or took over most independent organizations, mobilized the economy, and began brutally persecuting the Jewish population. Thus Nazism asserted an unlimited claim over German society and put all final power in the hands of its endlessly aggressive leader—Adolf Hitler. In this regard Nazism was truly totalitarian.

The Roots of Nazism

Nazism grew out of many complex developments, of which the most influential were extreme nationalism and racism. These two ideas captured the mind of the young Hitler, and it was he who dominated Nazism for as long as it lasted.

Born the fourth child of a successful Austrian customs official and an indulgent mother, Adolf Hitler (1889–1945) spent his childhood in small towns in Austria. A good student in grade school, Hitler did poorly in high school and dropped out at age fourteen after the death of his father. After four years of unfocused loafing, Hitler finally left for Vienna to become an artist. Denied admission to the Imperial Academy of Fine Arts because he lacked talent, the dejected Hitler stayed in Vienna. There he lived a comfortable, lazy life on his generous orphan's pension and found most of the perverted beliefs that guided his life.

In Vienna Hitler soaked up extreme German nationalism, which was particularly strong there. Austro-German nationalists, as if to compensate for their declining position in the Austro-Hungarian Empire, believed Germans to be a superior people and the natural rulers of central Europe. They often advocated union with Germany and violent expulsion of "inferior" peoples as the means of maintaining German domination of the Austro-Hungarian Empire.

Hitler was deeply impressed by Vienna's mayor, Karl Lueger (1844–1910). With the help of the Catholic trade unions, Lueger had succeeded in winning the support of the little people of Vienna for an attack on capitalism and liberalism. A master of mass politics in the urban world, Lueger showed Hitler the enormous potential of anticapitalist and antiliberal propaganda.

From Lueger and others, Hitler eagerly absorbed virulent anti-Semitism, racism, and hatred of Slavs, along with an unshakable belief in the crudest, most exaggerated distortions of the Darwinian theory of survival, the superiority of Germanic races, and the inevitability of racial conflict. Anti-Semitism and racism became Hitler's most passionate convictions, his explanation for everything. The Jews, he claimed, directed an international conspiracy of finance capitalism and Marxian socialism against German culture, German unity, and the German race. Hitler's belief was totally irrational, but he never doubted it.

Although he moved to Munich in 1913 to avoid being drafted into the Austrian army, the lonely Hitler greeted the outbreak of the First World War as a salvation. He later wrote in his autobiography, *Mein Kampf,* that, "overcome by passionate enthusiasm, I fell to my knees and thanked heaven out of an overflowing heart." The struggle and discipline of war gave life meaning, and Hitler served bravely as a dispatch carrier on the western front.

When Germany was suddenly defeated in 1918, Hitler's world was shattered. Not only was he a fanatical nationalist, but war was his reason for living. Convinced that Jews and Marxists had "stabbed Germany in the back," he vowed to fight on. And in the bitterness and uncertainty of postwar Germany, his wild speeches began to attract attention.

In late 1919 Hitler joined a tiny extremist group in Munich called the German Workers' party. In addition to denouncing Jews, Marxists, and democrats, the German Workers' party promised unity under a uniquely German "national socialism," which would abolish the injustices of capitalism and create a mighty "people's community." By 1921 Hitler had gained absolute control of this small but growing party. He was already a master of mass propaganda and political showmanship. His most effective tool was the mass rally, a kind of political revival meeting, where he often worked his audience into a frenzy with wild, demagogic attacks on the Versailles treaty, the Jews, war profiteers, and Germany's Weimar Republic.

Party membership multiplied tenfold after early 1922. In late 1923, when the Weimar Republic seemed on the verge of collapse, Hitler decided on an armed uprising in Munich, inspired by Mussolini's recent easy victory. Despite the failure of the poorly organized plot and the arrest of Hitler, Nazism had been born.

Hitler's Road to Power

At his trial, Hitler violently denounced the Weimar Republic and skillfully presented his own program. In doing so, he gained enormous publicity and attention. Moreover, he learned from his unsuccessful revolt. Hitler concluded that he had to undermine, rather than overthrow, the government, that he had to use its tolerant democratic framework to intimidate the opposition and come to power through electoral competition. He forced his more violent supporters to accept his new strategy. He also used his brief prison term—he was released in less than a year—to dictate *Mein Kampf* (1924). There he expounded on his basic themes: "race," with a stress on anti-Semitism; "living space," with a sweeping vision of war and conquered territory; and the leader-dictator (*Führer*), with unlimited, arbitrary power. Hitler's followers had their bible.

In the years of prosperity and relative stability between 1924 and 1929, Hitler concentrated on building his National Socialist German Workers' party, or Nazi party. By 1928 the party had a hundred thousand highly disciplined members under Hitler's absolute control. To appeal to the middle classes, Hitler de-emphasized the anticapitalist elements of national socialism and vowed to fight Bolshevism.

The Nazis were still a small splinter group in 1928, when they received only 2.6 percent of the vote in the general elections and twelve seats in the Reichstag. There the Nazi deputies pursued the legal strategy of using democracy to destroy democracy. As Hitler's talented future minister of propaganda, Joseph Goebbels (1897–1945), explained in 1928 in the party newspaper, "We become Reichstag deputies in order to paralyze the spirit of Weimar with its own aid. . . . We come as enemies! As the wolf breaks into the sheepfold, so we come."[10]

In 1929 the Great Depression began striking down economic prosperity, one of the barriers that had kept the wolf at bay. In 1930 Germany had almost as many unemployed as all the other countries of Europe combined. By the end of 1932, an incredible 43 percent of the labor force was unemployed, and it was estimated that only one in every three union members was working full-time. No factor contributed more to Hitler's success than the economic crisis. Never very interested in economics before, Hitler began promising German

Hitler in Opposition Hitler returns the salute of his Brown Shirts in this photograph from the third party day rally in Nuremberg in 1927. The Brown Shirts formed a private army within the Nazi movement, and their uniforms, marches, salutes, and vandalism helped keep Hitler in the public eye in the 1920s. *(Source: Courtesy, Bison Books, London)*

voters economic as well as political and military salvation. He pitched his speeches especially to the middle and lower middle classes—small business people, office workers, artisans, and peasants. Already disillusioned by the great inflation of 1923, these people were seized by panic as bankruptcies increased, unemployment soared, and the dreaded Communists made dramatic election gains. The middle and lower middle classes deserted the conservative and moderate parties for the Nazis in great numbers.

Simultaneously, Hitler worked hard behind the scenes to win the support of two key elite groups. First, he promised big business leaders that he would restore their depression-shattered profits, by breaking Germany's strong labor movement and reducing workers' wages if need be. Second, he assured top army leaders that the Nazis would overturn the Versailles settlement and rearm Germany. Thus Hitler successfully followed Mussolini's fascist recipe. He won at least the tacit approval of powerful conservatives who could have blocked his bid for power.

The Nazis also appealed strongly to German youth. Indeed, in some ways the Nazi movement was a mass movement of young Germans. "National Socialism is the organized will of the youth," proclaimed the official Nazi slogan, and the battle cry of Gregor Strasser, a leading Nazi organizer, was "Make way, you old ones."[11] In 1931 almost 40 percent of Nazi party members were under thirty, compared with 20 percent of Social Democrats. National recovery, exciting and rapid change, and personal advancement: these were the appeals of Nazism to millions of German youths.

As the economic and political situation continued to deteriorate, Hitler and the Nazis kept promising that they would bring economic recovery and national unity. In the election of 1932 the Nazis won 14.5 million votes and became the largest party in the Reichstag.

Another reason why Hitler came to power was the breakdown of democratic government as early as May 1930. Unable to gain the support of a majority in the Reichstag, Chancellor Heinrich Brüning convinced the president, the aging war hero General Hindenburg, to authorize rule by decree, which the Weimar Republic's constitution permitted in emergency situations. Brüning was determined to overcome the economic crisis by cutting back government spending and ruthlessly forcing down prices and wages. These failed policies convinced the lower middle classes that the country's republican leaders were stupid and corrupt. These classes were pleased, rather than dismayed, by Hitler's attacks on the republican system. After President Hindenburg forced Brüning to resign in May 1932, the new government continued to rule by decree.

Meanwhile, the struggle between the Social Democrats and Communists persisted right up until the moment Hitler took power. Even after the elections of 1932, the Communists refused to cooperate with the Social Democrats, despite the fact that the two parties together outnumbered the Nazis in the Reichstag. German Communists (and the still-complacent Stalin) were blinded by hatred of Socialists and by ideology. Socialist leaders pleaded, even at the Soviet Embassy, for at least a temporary alliance with the Communists to block Hitler, but to no avail.

Finally, there was Hitler's skill as a politician. A master of mass propaganda and psychology, he had written in *Mein Kampf* that the masses were the "driving force of the most important changes in this world" and were themselves driven by hysterical fanaticism and not by knowledge. To arouse such hysterical fanaticism, he believed, all propaganda had to be limited to a few simple, endlessly repeated slogans. Thus in the terrible economic and political crisis, he harangued vast audiences with passionate, irrational oratory. Men moaned and women cried, seized by emotion. And many uncertain individuals, surrounded by thousands of entranced listeners, found security and a sense of belonging.

At the same time, Hitler continued to excel at dirty, back-room politics. That, in fact, brought him to power. Through complicated infighting in 1932 he cleverly succeeded in gaining additional support from key people in the army and big business. These people thought they could use Hitler for their own advantage to get increased military spending, fat contracts, and tough measures against workers. Many conservative and nationalistic politicians thought similarly. They thus accepted Hitler's demand to join the government only if he became chancellor. There would be only two other National Socialists and nine staunch conservatives as ministers, and in such a coalition government, they reasoned, Hitler could be used and controlled. On January 30, 1933, Hitler was legally appointed chancellor by President Hindenburg.

The Nazi State and Society

Hitler moved rapidly and skillfully to establish an unshakable dictatorship. Continuing to maintain legal appearances, he immediately called for new elections. In the midst of a violent electoral campaign, the Reichstag building was partly destroyed by fire. Although the Nazis themselves may have set the fire, Hitler screamed that the Communist party was responsible. On the strength of this accusation, he convinced President Hindenburg to sign dictatorial emergency acts that practically abolished freedom of speech and assembly as well as most personal liberties.

When the Nazis won only 44 percent of the vote in the elections, Hitler immediately outlawed the Communist party and arrested its parliamentary representatives. Then on March 23, 1933, the Nazis used threats and blackmail to help push through the Reichstag the so-called Enabling Act, which gave Hitler absolute dictatorial power for four years. Armed with the Enabling Act, Hitler and the Nazis moved to smash or control all independent organizations. Their deceitful stress on legality, coupled with divide-and-conquer techniques, disarmed the opposition until it was too late for effective resistance. Germany soon became a one-party state. Only the Nazi party was legal. Elections were farces. The Reichstag was jokingly referred to as the most expensive glee club in the country, for its only function was to sing hymns of praise to the Führer. Hitler and the Nazis took over the government bureaucracy intact, installing many Nazis in top positions. At the same time, they created a series of overlapping Nazi party organizations responsible solely to Hitler.

As recent research shows, the resulting system of dual government was riddled with rivalries, contradictions, and inefficiencies. The Nazi state lacked the all-compassing unity that its propagandists claimed and was sloppy and often disorganized, but this fractured system suited Hitler and his purposes. He could play the established bureaucracy against his private, personal "party government" and maintain his freedom of action. Hitler could concentrate on general principles and the big decisions, which he always made.

In the economic sphere, one big decision outlawed strikes and abolished independent labor unions, which were replaced by the Nazi Labor Front. Professional people—doctors and lawyers, teachers and engineers—also saw their previously

The Mobilization of Young People A prime objective of the Nazi leadership was to appeal to young Germans. Here boys in a Nazi youth group—some of them are only children—are disciplined and conditioned to devote themselves to the regime. *(Source: Hulton Deutsch Collection)*

independent organizations swallowed up in Nazi associations. Nor did the Nazis neglect cultural and intellectual life. Publishing houses and universities were put under Nazi control. Democratic, socialist, and Jewish literature was put on ever-growing blacklists. Passionate students and pitiful professors burned forbidden books in public squares. Modern art and architecture were ruthlessly prohibited. Life became violently anti-intellectual. As the cynical Goebbels put it, "When I hear the word 'culture' I reach for my gun."[12] By 1934 a brutal dictatorship characterized by frightening dynamism and obedience to Hitler was already largely in place.

Only the army retained independence, and Hitler moved ruthlessly and skillfully to establish his control there, too. The Nazi storm troopers (the SA), the quasi-military band of 3 million toughs in brown shirts who had fought communists and beaten up Jews before the Nazis took power, expected top positions in the army and even talked of a "second revolution" against capitalism. Needing to preserve good relations with the army and with big business, Hitler decided that the SA leaders had to be eliminated. On the night of June 30, 1934, he struck. Hitler's elite personal guard—the SS—arrested and shot without trial roughly a thousand SA leaders and assorted political enemies. Shortly thereafter army leaders swore a binding oath of "unquestioning obedience . . . to the Leader of the German State and People, Adolf Hitler." The SS grew rapidly. Under its methodical, inhuman leader, Heinrich Himmler (1900–1945), the SS joined with the political police, the Gestapo, to expand its network of special courts and concentration camps. Nobody was safe.

From the beginning, Jews were a special object of Nazi persecution. By the end of 1934, most Jewish lawyers, doctors, professors, civil servants, and musicians had lost their jobs and the right to practice their professions. In 1935 the infamous Nuremberg Laws classified as Jewish anyone having one or more Jewish grandparents and deprived Jews of all rights of citizenship. By 1938 roughly one-quarter of Germany's half-million Jews had emigrated, sacrificing almost all their property in order to leave Germany.

In late 1938 the attack on the Jews accelerated. A well-organized wave of violence destroyed homes, synagogues, and businesses, after which German Jews were rounded up and made to pay for the damage. It became very difficult for Jews to leave Germany. Some Germans privately opposed these outrages, but most went along or looked the other way. Although this lack of response reflected the individual's helplessness in a totalitarian state, it was more certainly a sign of the strong popular support Hitler's government enjoyed.

Hitler's Popularity

Hitler had promised the masses economic recovery—"work and bread"—and he delivered. Breaking with Brüning's do-nothing policies, Hitler immediately launched a large public works program to pull Germany out of the depression. Work began on superhighways, offices, gigantic sports stadiums, and public housing. In 1936 Germany turned decisively toward rearmament, and government spending began to concentrate on the military. The result was that unemployment dropped steadily, from 6 million in January 1933 to about 1 million in late 1936. By 1938 there was a shortage of workers, and women eventually took many jobs previously denied them by the antifeminist Nazis. Thus everyone had work, and between 1932 and 1938 the standard of living for the average employed worker increased moderately. The profits of business rose sharply. For millions of people, economic recovery was tangible evidence that Nazi promises were more than show and propaganda.

For the masses of ordinary German citizens who were not Jews, Slavs, Gypsies, Jehovah's Witnesses, communists, or homosexuals, Hitler's government meant greater equality and more opportunities. In 1933 barriers between classes in Germany were generally high. Hitler's rule introduced changes that lowered these barriers. For example, stiff educational requirements, which favored the well-to-do, were relaxed. The new Nazi elite included many young and poorly educated dropouts, rootless lower-middle-class people like Hitler who rose to the top with breathtaking speed. More generally, the Nazis tolerated privilege and wealth only as long as they served the needs of the party. Even big business was constantly ordered around.

Yet few historians today believe that Hitler and the Nazis brought about a real social revolution, as an earlier generation of scholars often argued. Quantitative studies show that the well-educated classes held on to most of their advantages and that only a modest social leveling occurred in the Nazi years. It is significant that the Nazis shared with

EVENTS LEADING TO WORLD WAR II

1919	Treaty of Versailles; J. M. Keynes, *Economic Consequences of the Peace*
1919–1920	U.S. Senate rejects the Treaty of Versailles
1922	Mussolini seizes power in Italy; Germany stops paying reparations
January 1923	France and Belgium occupy the Ruhr; Germany orders passive resistance
October 1923	Stresemann agrees to reparations with re-examination of Germany's ability to pay
1924	Dawes Plan: German reparations reduced; occupation of the Ruhr ends Adolf Hitler, *Mein Kampf*
1924–1929	Spectacular German economic recovery; international flow of capital
1925	Treaties of Locarno promote European security and stability
1928	Kellogg-Briand Pact renounces war as an instrument of international policy
1929	Crash of U.S. stock market
1930–1933	Depths of the Great Depression
1931	Japan invades Manchuria
1932	Nazis become the largest party in the Reichstag
January 1933	Hitler appointed chancellor
March 1933	Reichstag passes the Enabling Act, granting Hitler absolute dictatorial power
March 1935	Hitler establishes military draft and begins German rearmament
June 1935	Anglo-German naval agreement
September 1935	Nuremberg Laws deprive Jews of all rights of citizenship
October 1935	Mussolini invades Ethiopia and receives Hitler's support
March 1936	German armies move unopposed into the demilitarized Rhineland
July 1936	Outbreak of civil war in Spain
October 1936	Rome-Berlin Axis
1937	Japan invades China
March 1938	Germany annexes Austria
September 1938	Munich Conference: Britain and France agree to German seizure of the Sudetenland from Czechoslovakia
March 1939	Germany occupies the rest of Czechoslovakia; the end of appeasement in Britain
August 1939	Nazi-Soviet nonaggression pact
September 1939	Germany invades Poland; Britain and France then declare war on Germany

the Italian fascists the stereotypic view of women as housewives and mothers. Only under the relentless pressure of war did they reluctantly mobilize large numbers of German women for work in offices and factories.

Hitler's rabid nationalism, which had helped him gain power, continued to appeal to Germans after 1933. Thus in later years when Hitler went from one foreign triumph to another and a great German empire seemed within reach, the majority of the population was delighted and kept praising the Führer's actions well into the war.

Not all Germans supported Hitler, however, and a number of German groups actively resisted him after 1933. Tens of thousands of political enemies were imprisoned, and thousands were executed. In the first years of Hitler's rule, the principal resisters were the communists and the social democrats in the trade unions. But the expansion of the SS sys-

tem of terror after 1935 smashed most of these leftists. A second group of opponents arose in the Catholic and Protestant churches. However, their efforts were directed primarily at preserving genuine religious life, not at overthrowing Hitler. Finally in 1938 (and again from 1942 to 1944), some high-ranking army officers, who feared the consequences of Hitler's reckless aggression, plotted against him, unsuccessfully.

NAZI EXPANSION AND THE SECOND WORLD WAR

Although economic recovery and somewhat greater opportunity for social advancement won Hitler support, they were only byproducts of the Nazi regime. The guiding and unique concepts of Nazism remained space and race—the territorial

"Spineless Leaders of Democracy"   Cartoonist David Low's biting criticism of appeasing leaders appeared shortly after Hitler remilitarized the Rhineland. Appeasement also appealed to millions of ordinary citizens, who wanted to avoid at any cost another great war. *(Source: Cartoon by David Low. Reproduced by permission of London Evening/Soho Standard)*

expansion of the superior German race. As Germany regained its economic strength and as independent organizations were brought under control, Hitler formed alliances with other dictators and began expanding. German expansion was facilitated by the uncertain, divided, pacific Western democracies, which tried to buy off Hitler to avoid war.

Yet war inevitably broke out, in both the West and the East, for Hitler's ambitions were essentially unlimited. On both war fronts Nazi soldiers scored enormous successes until late 1942, establishing a horrifyingly vast empire of death and destruction. Hitler's reckless aggression also raised a mighty coalition determined to smash the Nazi order. Led by Britain, the United States, and the Soviet Union, the Grand Alliance—to use Winston Churchill's favorite term—functioned quite effectively in military terms. Thus the terrible Nazi empire proved short-lived.

Aggression and Appeasement (1933–1939)

Hitler realized that his aggressive policies had to be carefully camouflaged at first, for Germany's army was limited by the Treaty of Versailles to only a hundred thousand men. As he told a group of army commanders in February 1933, the early stages of his policy of "conquest of new living space in the East and its ruthless Germanization" had serious dangers. If France had real leaders, Hitler said, it would "not give us time but attack us, presumably with its eastern satellites."[13] To avoid such threats to his plans, Hitler loudly proclaimed his peaceful intentions to all the world. Nevertheless, he felt strong enough to walk out of a sixty-nation disarmament conference and withdraw from the League of Nations in October 1933. The Nazi determination to rearm was out in the open.

Following this action, which met with widespread approval at home, Hitler moved to incorporate independent Austria into a greater Germany. Austrian Nazis climaxed an attempted overthrow by murdering the Austrian chancellor in July 1934. They were unable to take power, however, because a worried Mussolini, who had initially greeted Hitler as a fascist little brother, massed his troops on the Brenner Pass and threatened to fight. When in March 1935 Hitler established a general military draft and declared the "unequal" disarmament

clauses of the Treaty of Versailles null and void, other countries appeared to understand the danger. With France taking the lead, Italy and Great Britain protested strongly and warned against future aggressive actions.

But the emerging united front against Hitler quickly collapsed. Britain adopted a policy of appeasement, granting Hitler everything he could reasonably want (and more) in order to avoid war. The first step was an Anglo-German naval agreement in June 1935 that broke Germany's isolation. The second step came in March 1936 when Hitler suddenly marched his armies into the demilitarized Rhineland, brazenly violating the treaties of Versailles and Locarno. This was the last good chance to stop the Nazis, for Hitler had ordered his troops to retreat if France resisted militarily. But an uncertain France would not move without British support, and the occupation of German soil by German armies seemed right and just to Britain (Map 32.1). With a greatly improved strategic position, Germany handed France a tremendous psychological defeat.

British appeasement, which practically dictated French policy, lasted far into 1939. It was motivated by British feelings of guilt toward Germany and the pacifism of a population still horrified by the memory of the First World War. As in Germany, many powerful conservatives in Britain underestimated Hitler. They also believed that Soviet communism was the real danger and that Hitler could be used to stop it. A leading member of Britain's government personally told Hitler in November 1937 that it was his conviction that Hitler "not only had accomplished great things in Germany itself, but that through the total destruction of Communism in his own country . . . Germany rightly had to be considered as a Western bulwark against Communism."[14] Such rigid anticommunist feelings made an alliance between the Western powers and Stalin unlikely.

As Britain and France opted for appeasement and the Soviet Union watched all developments suspiciously, Hitler found powerful allies. In 1935 the bombastic Mussolini decided that imperial expansion was needed to revitalize Italian fascism. From Italian colonies on the east coast of Africa, he attacked the independent African kingdom of Ethiopia. The Western powers and the League of Nations piously condemned Italian aggression—a posture that angered Mussolini—without saving

MAP 32.1 The Growth of Nazi Germany, 1933–1939   Until March 1939
Hitler brought ethnic Germans into the Nazi state; then he turned on the Slavic peoples, whom he had always hated. He stripped Czechoslovakia of its independence
and prepared for an attack on Poland in September 1939.

Ethiopia from defeat. Hitler, who had secretly supplied Ethiopia with arms to heat up the conflict,
supported Italy energetically and thereby overcame
Mussolini's lingering doubts about the Nazis. The
result in 1936 was an agreement on close cooperation between Italy and Germany, the so-called
Rome-Berlin Axis. Japan, which had been expand-

ing into Manchuria since 1931, soon joined the
Axis alliance.

At the same time, Germany and Italy intervened
in the Spanish civil war (1936–1939). Their support eventually helped General Francisco Franco's
fascist movement defeat republican Spain. Spain's
only official aid came from the Soviet Union, for

public opinion in Britain and especially in France was hopelessly divided on the Spanish question.

In late 1937, while proclaiming peaceful intentions to the British and their gullible prime minister Neville Chamberlain, Hitler moved forward with his plans to crush Austria and Czechoslovakia as the first step in his long-contemplated drive to the east for living space. By threatening Austria with invasion, Hitler forced the Austrian chancellor in March 1938 to put local Nazis in control of the government. The next day German armies moved in unopposed, and Austria became two provinces of Greater Germany (see Map 32.1).

Simultaneously, Hitler began demanding that the pro-Nazi, German-speaking minority of western Czechoslovakia—the Sudetenland—be turned over to Germany. Democratic Czechoslovakia, however, was prepared to defend itself. Moreover, France had been Czechoslovakia's ally since 1924; and if France fought, the Soviet Union was pledged to help. War appeared inevitable, for Hitler had already told the leader of the Sudeten Germans that "we must always ask so much we cannot be satisfied." But appeasement triumphed again. In September 1938 Prime Minister Chamberlain flew to Germany three times in fourteen days. In these negotiations, to which the Soviet Union was deliberately not invited, Chamberlain and the French agreed with Hitler that the Sudetenland should be ceded to Germany immediately. Returning to London from the Munich Conference, Chamberlain told cheering crowds that he had secured "peace with honor . . . peace for our time." Sold out by the Western powers, Czechoslovakia gave in.

Confirmed once again in his opinion of the Western democracies as weak and racially degenerate, Hitler accelerated his aggression. In a shocking violation of his solemn assurances that the Sudetenland was his last territorial demand, Hitler sent his armies to occupy the remainder of Czechoslovakia in March 1939. The effect on Western public opinion was electrifying. For the first time, there was no possible rationale of self-determination for Nazi aggression, because Hitler was treating the Czechs and Slovaks as captive peoples. Thus when Hitler used the question of German minorities in Danzig as a pretext to confront Poland, a suddenly militant Chamberlain declared that Britain and France would fight if Hitler attacked his eastern neighbor.

Hitler did not take these warnings seriously and decided to press on.

In an about-face that stunned the world, Hitler offered and Stalin signed a ten-year Nazi-Soviet nonaggression pact in August 1939. Each dictator promised to remain neutral if the other became involved in war. An attached secret protocol, which became known only after the war, ruthlessly divided eastern Europe into German and Soviet zones "in the event of a political territorial reorganization." The nonaggression pact itself was enough to make Britain and France cry treachery, for they, too, had been negotiating with Stalin. But Stalin had remained distrustful of Western intentions, and Hitler had offered territorial gain.

For Hitler, everything was set. He told his generals on the day of the nonaggression pact, "My only fear is that at the last moment some dirty dog will come up with a mediation plan." On September 1, 1939, German armies and warplanes smashed into Poland from three sides. Two days later Britain and France, finally true to their word, declared war on Germany. The Second World War had begun.

Hitler's Empire (1939–1942)

Using planes, tanks, and trucks in the first example of a *blitzkrieg,* or "lightning war," Hitler's armies crushed Poland in four weeks. The Soviet Union quickly took its part of the booty—the eastern half of Poland and the Baltic states of Lithuania, Estonia, and Latvia. French and British armies dug in in the west; they expected another war of attrition and economic blockade.

In spring 1940 the lightning war struck again. After occupying Denmark, Norway, and Holland, German motorized columns broke through southern Belgium, split the Franco-British forces, and trapped the entire British army on the beaches of Dunkirk. By heroic efforts the British were able to withdraw their troops but not their equipment.

France was taken by the Nazis. Aging marshal Henri-Philippe Pétain formed a new French government—the so-called Vichy government—to accept defeat, and German armies occupied most of France. By July 1940 Hitler ruled practically all of western continental Europe; Italy was an ally, the Soviet Union a friendly neutral (Map 32.2). Only Britain, led by the uncompromising Winston Churchill (1874–1965), remained unconquered.

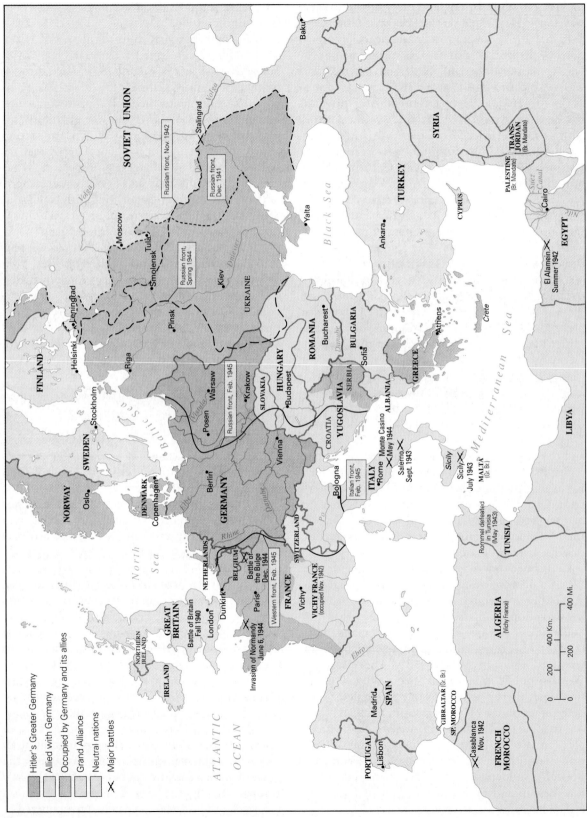

SOVIET UNION

Russian front, Nov. 1942

Stalingrad ✕

Russian front, Dec. 1941

Russian front, Spring 1944

Moscow

Smolensk
Tula

Leningrad
Helsinki

FINLAND

Kiev

UKRAINE

Pinsk

Riga

Stockholm

SWEDEN

Baltic Sea

NORWAY

Oslo

DENMARK
Copenhagen

Elbe

Berlin

GERMANY

Rhine

Danube

Vienna

Posen

Krakow

Warsaw

Russian front, Feb. 1945

Vistula

Dnieper

SLOVAKIA

HUNGARY
Budapest

ROMANIA
Bucharest

BULGARIA
Sofia

Danube

CROATIA

YUGOSLAVIA

SERBIA

ALBANIA

GREECE
Athens

Black Sea

TURKEY
Ankara

CYPRUS

SYRIA

TRANS-
JORDAN
(Br. Mandate)

PALESTINE
(Br. Mandate)

Suez Canal

Cairo

EGYPT

Nile

El Alamein ✕
Summer 1942

Mediterranean Sea

Crete

LIBYA

Volga
Don

Baku

Yalta

SWITZERLAND

Po

Bologna

Italian front,
Feb. 1945

ITALY
Rome

Monte Casino
May 1944 ✕

Salerno ✕
Sept. 1943

Sicily ✕
July 1943

Sicily

MALTA
(Gr. Br.)

Rommel defeated
in Tunisia
(May 1943)

TUNISIA

ALGERIA
(Vichy France)

FRENCH
MOROCCO

SP. MOROCCO

GIBRALTAR (Gr. Br.)

Casablanca
Nov. 1942 ✕

SPAIN
Madrid

PORTUGAL
Lisbon

Ebro

ATLANTIC
OCEAN

NETHERLANDS

BELGIUM ✕
Battle of
the Bulge
Dec. 1944

Western front, Feb. 1945

FRANCE

VICHY FRANCE
(occupied Nov. 1942)

Vichy

Paris

Dunkirk

Invasion of Normandy
June 6, 1944 ✕

Battle of Britain
Fall 1940

London

GREAT
BRITAIN

NORTHERN
IRELAND

IRELAND

North
Sea

Legend:
Hitler's Greater Germany
Allied with Germany
Occupied by Germany and its allies
Grand Alliance
Neutral nations
✕ Major battles

400 Mi.
400 Km.
200
0

Prelude to Murder   This photo conveys the inhumanity of Nazi racism. Frightened and bewildered families from the soon-to-be-destroyed Warsaw ghetto are being forced out of their homes by German soldiers for deportation to concentration camps. There they face murder in the gas chambers. *(Source: Roger-Viollet)*

Germany sought to gain control of the air, the necessary first step for an amphibious invasion of Britain. In the Battle of Britain, up to a thousand German planes attacked British airfields and key factories in a single day, dueling with British defenders high in the skies. Losses were heavy on both sides. Then in September Hitler angrily and foolishly changed his strategy, turning from military objectives to indiscriminate bombing of British cities in an attempt to break British morale.

MAP 32.2 The Second World War in Europe
This map shows the extent of Hitler's empire at its height, before the Battle of Stalingrad in late 1942, and the subsequent advances of the Allies until Germany surrendered on May 7, 1945.

British factories increased production of their excellent fighter planes, anti-aircraft defense improved with the help of radar, and the heavily bombed people of London defiantly dug in. In September and October 1940, Britain was beating Germany three to one in the air war. There was no possibility of immediate German invasion of Britain.

In these circumstances, the most reasonable German strategy would have been to attack Britain through the eastern Mediterranean, taking Egypt and the Suez Canal and pinching off Britain's supply of oil. By April 1941 Germany had already moved to the southeast, conquering Greece and Yugoslavia and forcing Hungary, Romania, and Bulgaria into alliances. But Hitler was not a reasonable person. His lifetime obsession with a vast eastern European empire for the "master race" dictated policy. So in June 1941 German armies suddenly attacked the Soviet Union along a vast front. By October Leningrad was practically surrounded, Moscow was besieged, and most of Ukraine had been conquered. But with Britain still unconquered, Hitler's decision to strike at Stalin was a wild, irrational gamble epitomizing the violent, unlimited, and ultimately self-destructive ambitions of Nazism. The Soviets did not collapse, and when a severe winter struck German armies that were outfitted in summer uniforms, the invaders were stopped.

While Hitler's armies dramatically expanded the war in Europe, his Japanese allies did the same in Asia. Engaged in an undeclared war against China since 1937, Japan's rulers had increasingly come into diplomatic conflict with the Pacific basin's other great power, the United States. When the Japanese occupied French Indochina in July 1941, the United States retaliated by cutting off sales of vital rubber, scrap iron, oil, and aviation fuel. Tension mounted, and on December 7, 1941, Japan attacked the U.S. naval base at Pearl Harbor in Hawaii. Hitler immediately declared war on the United States, and Japanese forces advanced swiftly into Southeast Asia (Map 32.3).

Meanwhile, though stalled in Russia, Hitler had come to rule a vast European empire stretching from the outskirts of Moscow to the English Channel. He and the top Nazi leadership began building their "New Order," and they continued their efforts until their final collapse in 1945. In doing so, they showed what Nazi victory would have meant.

Hitler's New Order was based firmly on the guiding principle of Nazi totalitarianism: racial imperialism. Within this New Order, the Nordic peoples—the Dutch, Norwegians, and Danes—received preferential treatment, for they were racially related to the Germans. The French, an "inferior" Latin people, occupied the middle position. They were heavily taxed to support the Nazi war effort but were tolerated as a race. All the occupied territories of western and northern Europe, however, were to be exploited with increasing intensity. Material shortages and both mental and physical suffering afflicted millions of people.

Slavs in the conquered territories to the east were treated with harsh hatred as "subhumans."

Hitler painted for his intimate circle the fantastic details of a vast eastern colonial empire where Poles, Ukrainians, and Russians would be enslaved and forced to die out while Germanic peasants resettled the resulting abandoned lands. Himmler and the elite corps of SS volunteers struggled loyally, sometimes against the German army, to implement part of this general program. In parts of Poland, the SS arrested and evacuated Polish peasants to create a German "mass settlement space." Polish workers and Soviet prisoners of war were transported to Germany, where they did most of the heavy labor and were systematically worked to death. The conditions of Soviet slave labor in Germany were so harsh that four out of five Soviet prisoners did not survive the war.

Jews were condemned to extermination, along with Gypsies, Jehovah's Witnesses, and captured communists. By 1939 German Jews had lost all their civil rights, and after the fall of Warsaw the Nazis began deporting them to Poland. There they and Jews from all over Europe were concentrated in ghettos, compelled to wear the Jewish star, and turned into slave laborers. But by late 1941 Himmler's SS was beginning to carry out the "final solution of the Jewish question"—the murder of every Jew. All over Hitler's empire, Jews were systematically arrested, packed like cattle onto freight trains, and dispatched to extermination camps. Many Jews in small towns could hardly imagine the enormity of the crime that lay before them (see Listening to the Past).

At the camps the victims were taken by force or deception to "shower rooms," which were actually gas chambers. These gas chambers, first perfected in the quiet, efficient execution of seventy thousand mentally ill Germans between 1938 and 1941, permitted rapid, hideous, and thoroughly bureaucratized mass murder. For fifteen to twenty minutes came the terrible screams and gasping sobs of men, women, and children choking to death on poison gas. Then, only silence. Special camp workers quickly yanked the victims' gold teeth from their jaws and cut off their hair for use as chair stuffing. The bodies were then cremated or sometimes boiled for oil to make soap. The bones were crushed to produce fertilizer. At Auschwitz-Birkenau, the most infamous of the Nazi death factories, as many as twelve thousand human beings were slaughtered each day. On the

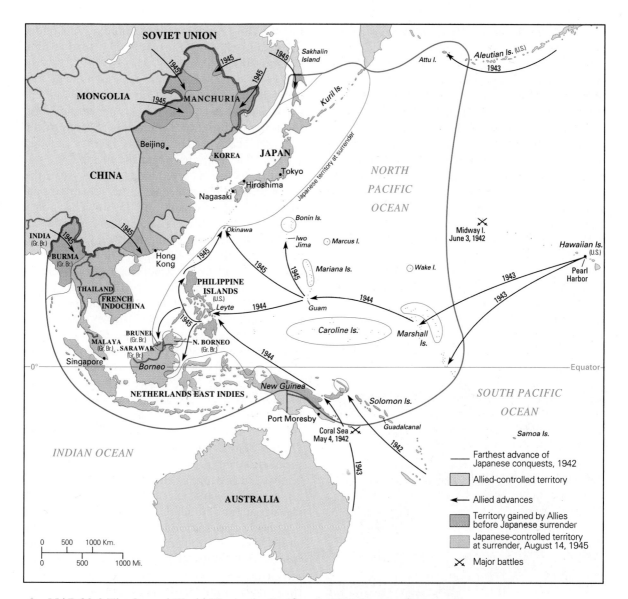

MAP 32.3 The Second World War in the Pacific   In 1942 Japanese forces overran an enormous territory, which the Allies slowly recaptured in a long, bitter struggle. As this map shows, Japan still held a large Asian empire in August 1945, when the unprecedented devastation of atomic warfare suddenly forced it to surrender.

turbulent Russian front, the SS death squads forced the Jewish population to dig giant pits, which became mass graves when the victims were lined up on the edge and cut down by machine guns. The extermination of European Jews was the ultimate monstrosity of Nazi racism and racial imperialism. By 1945 6 million Jews had been murdered.

The Grand Alliance

While the Nazis built their savage empire, the Allies faced the hard fact that chance, rather than choice, had brought them together. Stalin had been cooperating fully with Hitler between August 1939 and June 1941, and only the Japanese attack on Pearl Harbor in December 1941 and Hitler's immediate declaration of war had overwhelmed powerful isolationism in the United States. The Allies' first task was to overcome their mutual suspicions and build an unshakable alliance on the quicksand of accident. By means of three interrelated policies they succeeded.

First, U.S. president Franklin D. Roosevelt accepted the contention of Winston Churchill (Chamberlain's successor as British prime minister) that the United States should concentrate first on defeating Hitler. Only after victory in Europe was achieved would the United States turn toward the Pacific for an all-out attack on Japan, the lesser

✴ **"For the Motherland's Sake, Go Forward, Heroes"** Joining the historic Russian warrior and the young Soviet soldier in the common cause, this poster portrays the defense of the nation as a sacred mission and illustrates the way Soviet leaders successfully appealed to Russian nationalism during the war. *(Source: Library of Congress)*

threat. The promise of huge military aid under America's policy of "Europe first" helped solidify the anti-Hitler coalition.

Second, within the European framework the Americans and the British put immediate military needs first. They consistently postponed until after the war tough political questions relating to the eventual peace settlement and thereby avoided conflicts that might have split the alliance.

Third, to further encourage mutual trust, the Allies adopted the principle of the "unconditional surrender" of Germany and Japan. This policy cemented the Grand Alliance because it denied Hitler any hope of dividing his foes. Of great importance for the postwar shape of Europe, it meant that Soviet and Anglo-American armies would almost certainly come together to divide all of Germany, and most of the European continent, among the victorious allies.

The military resources of the Grand Alliance were awesome. The strengths of the United States were its mighty industry, its large population, and its national unity. Even before the attack on Pearl Harbor, President Roosevelt had called America the "arsenal of democracy" and had given military aid to Britain and the Soviet Union. Now the United States geared up rapidly for all-out war production and drew heavily on a generally cooperative Latin America for resources. It not only equipped its own armies but also eventually gave its allies about $50 billion in arms and equipment.

Too strong to lose and too weak to win standing alone, Britain continued to make a great contribution as well. The British economy was totally and effectively mobilized, and the sharing of burdens through rationing and heavy taxes on war profits maintained social harmony. Moreover, by early 1943 the Americans and the British were combining small aircraft carriers with radar-guided bombers to rid the Atlantic of German submarines. Britain, the impregnable floating fortress, became a gigantic front-line staging area for the decisive blow to the heart of Germany.

As for the Soviet Union, so great was its strength that it might well have defeated Germany without Western help. In the face of the German advance, whole factories and populations were successfully evacuated to eastern Russia and Siberia. There war production was reorganized and expanded, and the Red Army was increasingly well supplied. The Red Army was also well led, for a new generation of talented military leaders quickly arose to replace those so recently purged. Most important of all, Stalin drew on the massive support and heroic determination of the Soviet people, especially those in the central Russian heartland. Broad-based Russian nationalism, as opposed to narrow communist ideology, became the powerful unifying force in what the Soviet people appropriately called the "Great Patriotic War of the Fatherland."

Finally, the United States, Britain, and the Soviet Union were not alone. They had the resources of much of the world at their command. And, to a greater or lesser extent, they were aided by a growing resistance movement against the Nazis throughout Europe, even in Germany. Thus although Ukrainian peasants often welcomed the Germans as liberators, the barbaric occupation policies of the Nazis quickly drove them to join and support behind-the-lines guerrilla forces. More generally, after the Soviet Union was invaded in June 1941, communists throughout Europe took the lead in the underground resistance, joined by a growing number of patriots and Christians. Anti-Nazi leaders from occupied countries established governments-in-exile in London, like that of the Free French under the intensely proud General Charles de Gaulle. These governments gathered valuable secret information from resistance fighters and even organized armies to help defeat Hitler.

The Tide of Battle

Barely halted at the gates of Moscow and Leningrad in 1941, the Germans renewed their offensive against the Soviet Union in July 1942, driving toward the southern city of Stalingrad and occupying most of the city in a month of incredibly savage house-to-house fighting.

Then in November 1942, Soviet armies counterattacked. They quickly rolled over Romanian and Italian troops to close a trap surrounding the entire German Sixth Army of 300,000 men. The surrounded Germans were systematically destroyed, until by the end of January 1943 only 123,000 soldiers were left to surrender. Hitler, who had refused to allow a retreat, had suffered a catastrophic defeat. In the summer of 1943, the larger, better-equipped Soviet armies took the offensive and began moving forward (see Map 32.2).

In late 1942 the tide also turned in the Pacific and in North Africa. By late spring 1942, Japan had established a great empire in East Asia (Map 32.3). Unlike the Nazis, the Japanese made clever appeals to local nationalists, who hated European imperial domination and preferred Japan's so-called Greater Asian Co-prosperity Sphere.

Then in the Battle of the Coral Sea in May 1942, Allied naval and air power stopped the Japanese advance and also relieved Australia from the threat of invasion. This victory was followed by the Battle of Midway Island, in which American pilots sank all four of the attacking Japanese aircraft carriers and established American naval superiority in the Pacific. In August 1942 American marines attacked Guadalcanal in the Solomon Islands. Badly hampered by the policy of "Europe first"— only 15 percent of Allied resources were going to fight the war in the Pacific in early 1943—the Americans and the Australians nevertheless began "island hopping" toward Japan. Japanese forces were on the defensive.

In North Africa the war had been seesawing back and forth since 1940 (see Map 32.2). In the summer of 1942 combined German and Italian armies were finally defeated by British forces at the Battle of El Alamein, only seventy miles from Alexandria. In October the British counterattacked in Egypt, and almost immediately thereafter an Anglo-American force landed in Morocco and Algeria. These French possessions, which were under the control of Pétain's Vichy French government, quickly went over to the side of the Allies.

Having driven the Axis powers from North Africa by the spring of 1943, Allied forces maintained the initiative by invading Sicily and then mainland Italy. Mussolini was deposed by a war-weary people, and the new Italian government publicly accepted unconditional surrender in September 1943. Italy, it seemed, was liberated. But then German commandos in a daring raid rescued Mussolini and put him at the head of a puppet government. German armies seized Rome and all of northern Italy. Fighting continued in Italy.

Indeed, bitter fighting continued in Europe for almost two years. Germany, less fully mobilized for war than Britain in 1941, applied itself to total war in 1942 and enlisted millions of German women and millions of prisoners of war and slave laborers from all across occupied Europe in that effort. Between early 1942 and July 1944, German war production actually tripled. Although British and American bombing raids killed many German civilians, these raids were surprisingly ineffective from a military point of view. Also, German resistance against Hitler failed. After an unsuccessful attempt on Hitler's life in July 1944, SS fanatics brutally liquidated thousands of Germans. Terrorized at home and frightened by the prospect of unconditional surrender, the Germans fought on with suicidal stoicism.

On June 6, 1944, American and British forces under General Dwight Eisenhower landed on the beaches of Normandy, France, in history's greatest naval invasion. In a hundred dramatic days, more than 2 million men and almost a half-million vehicles pushed inland and broke through German lines. Rejecting proposals to strike straight at Berlin in a massive attack, Eisenhower moved forward cautiously on a broad front. Not until March 1945 did American troops cross the Rhine and enter Germany.

The Soviets, who had been advancing steadily since July 1943, reached the outskirts of Warsaw by August 1944. For the next six months they moved southward into Romania, Hungary, and Yugoslavia. In January 1945 Red armies again moved westward through Poland, and on April 26 they met American forces on the Elbe River. The Allies had closed their vise on Nazi Germany and overrun Europe. As Soviet forces fought their way into Berlin, Hitler committed suicide in his bunker, and on May 7 the remaining German commanders capitulated.

Three months later, the United States dropped atomic bombs on Hiroshima and Nagasaki in Japan. Mass bombing of cities and civilians, one of

The City of Nagasaki   An atomic bomb struck Nagasaki on August 9, 1945, three days after an atomic blast incinerated Hiroshima. Approximately seventy-five thousand Japanese were killed or injured at Nagasaki. In this grim photo, taken about a month after the attack, a Japanese survivor pushes his bicycle along a path cleared through the ruins. *(Source: UPI/Bettmann Newsphotos)*

the terrible new practices of World War II, had ended in the final nightmare—unprecedented human destruction in a single blinding flash. On August 14, 1945, the Japanese announced their surrender. The Second World War, which had claimed the lives of more than 50 million soldiers and civilians, was over.

SUMMARY

The Second World War marked the climax of the tremendous practical and spiritual maladies of the age of anxiety, maladies which led in many lands to the rise of dictatorships. Many of these dictatorships were variations on conservative authoritarianism, but there was also a fateful innovation—a new kind of radical dictatorship that was exceptionally dynamic and theoretically unlimited in its actions.

When apprehensive middle-class liberals in the West faced the rise of these new dictatorships, they often focused on their perceived similarities. Liberals fastened on the violent, profoundly antiliberal, and apparently totalitarian character of these brutal challengers, linking the one-party socialism of Lenin and Stalin with the one-party fascism of Mussolini and Hitler. In contrast, the political left usually insisted on the differences between the revolutionary socialist tradition—triumphing, however imperfectly, in the Bolsheviks' Soviet Union —and the reactionary and capitalist nature of European fascist movements and fascist governments in Italy and Germany. As the dramatic struggles of the 1930s and the Second World War (and early cold war) fall into a longer historical perspective and as more research adds new insights, a growing number of historians are stressing the limitations of both the totalitarian and the fascist interpretations and are concentrating instead on the uniqueness of developments in each regime.

Hitler's Nazism appears increasingly as a uniquely evil and nihilistic system. Nazism had fascist origins, but German fascism in power ultimately presented only superficial similarities with fascism in Italy. As for Hitler's Germany and Stalin's Soviet Union, both asserted a total claim on the lives of their citizens, posed ambitious goals, and demanded popular support. This combination gave both dictatorships their awesome power and dynamism. That dynamism, however, was channeled in quite different directions. Stalin and the Communist party aimed at building their kind of socialism and the new socialist personality at home. Hitler and the Nazi elite aimed at unlimited territorial and racial aggression on behalf of a "master race"; domestic recovery was only a means to that end.

Nazi racism and unlimited aggression made war inevitable, first with the western European democracies, then with hated eastern neighbors, and finally with the United States. Plunging Europe into the ultimate nightmare, unlimited aggression unwittingly forged a mighty coalition that smashed the racist Nazi empire and its leader. In the words of the ancient Greeks, he whom the gods would destroy, they first make mad.

NOTES

1. I. Kershaw, *The Nazi Dictatorship: Problems and Perspectives of Interpretation,* 2d ed. (London: Edward Arnold, 1989), pp. 20–23.
2. E. Halévy, *The Era of Tyrannies* (Garden City, N.Y.: Doubleday, 1965), pp. 265–316, esp. p. 300.
3. Kershaw, *The Nazi Dictatorship,* p. 34.
4. Quoted in P. C. Roberts, "'War Communism': A Re-examination," *Slavic Review* 29 (June 1970): 257.
5. Quoted in A. G. Mazour, *Soviet Economic Development: Operation Outstrip, 1921–1965* (Princeton, N.J.: Van Nostrand, 1967), p. 130.
6. Quoted in I. Deutscher, *Stalin: A Political Biography,* 2d ed. (New York: Oxford University Press, 1967), p. 325.
7. Quoted in H. K. Geiger, *The Family in Soviet Russia* (Cambridge, Mass.: Harvard University Press, 1968), p. 123.
8. Quoted ibid., p. 156.
9. R. Vivarelli, "Interpretations on the Origins of Fascism," *Journal of Modern History* 63 (March 1991): 41.
10. Quoted in K. D. Bracher, "The Technique of the National Socialist Seizure of Power," in *The Path to Dictatorship, 1918–1933,* ed. T. Eschenburg et al. (Garden City, N.Y.: Doubleday, 1966), p. 117.
11. Quoted in K. D. Bracher, *The German Dictatorship: The Origins, Structure and Effects of National Socialism* (New York: Praeger, 1970), pp. 146–147.
12. Quoted in R. Stromberg, *An Intellectual History of Modern Europe* (New York: Appleton-Century-Crofts, 1966), p. 393.

13. Quoted in Bracher, *The German Dictatorship,* p. 289.
14. Quoted ibid., p. 306.

SUGGESTED READING

The historical literature on fascist and totalitarian dictatorships is rich and fascinating. Kershaw's work cited in the Notes provides an excellent recent survey of this literature, includes extensive bibliographical references, and is highly recommended. H. Arendt, *The Origins of Totalitarianism* (1951), and D. Schoenbaum, *Hitler's Social Revolution: Class and Status in Nazi Germany, 1933–1939* (1967), are classic, influential interpretations. E. Weber, *Varieties of Fascism* (1964), stresses the radical social aspirations of fascist movements all across Europe. F. L. Carsten, *The Rise of Fascism* (1982), and W. Laqueur, ed., *Fascism* (1976), are also recommended. Z. Sternhell, *Neither Right nor Left: Fascist Ideology in France* (1986), is important and stimulating, stressing the antiliberal and antisocialist origins of fascist thinking in France.

R. Stites, *The Women's Liberation Movement in Russia: Feminism, Nihilism, and Bolshevism, 1860–1930* (1978); S. Fitzpatrick, *Cultural Revolution in Russia, 1928–1931* (1978); and the works by Geiger and Deutscher cited in the Notes are all highly recommended, as is Deutscher's sympathetic three-volume study of Trotsky. R. McNeal, *Stalin: Man and Ruler* (1988), is useful. S. Cohen, *Bukharin and the Bolshevik Revolution* (1973), examines the leading spokesman of moderate communism, who was destroyed by Stalin. R. Conquest, *The Great Terror* (1968), is an excellent account of Stalin's purges of the 1930s. A. Solzhenitsyn, *The Gulag Archipelago* (1964), passionately condemns Soviet police terror, which Solzhenitsyn tracks back to Lenin. Arthur Koestler, *Darkness at Noon* (1956), is a famous fictional account of Stalin's trials of the Old Bolsheviks. R. Medvedev, *Let History Judge* (1972), is a penetrating and highly recommended history of Stalinism by a Russian dissident. It may be compared with the excellent synthesis by M. Lewin, *The Making of the Soviet System* (1985). R. Conquest, *The Harvest of Sorrow* (1986), authoritatively recounts Soviet collectivization and the human-made famine. Three other remarkable books are J. Scott, *Behind the Urals* (1973), an eyewitness account of an American steelworker in the Soviet Union in the 1930s; S. Alliluyeva, *Twenty Letters to a Friend* (1967), the amazing reflections of Stalin's daughter, who chose twice to live in the United States before returning home; and M. Fainsod, *Smolensk Under Soviet Rule* (1958), a unique study based on communist records captured first by the Germans and then by the Americans.

A. De Grand, *Italian Fascism: Its Origins and Development* (1989); A. Lyttelton, *The Seizure of Power* (1987); and E. R. Tannebaum, *The Fascist Experience* (1972), are excellent studies of Italy under Mussolini. D. Mack Smith, *Mussolini* (1982), is authoritative. Ignazio Silone, *Bread and Wine* (1937), is a moving novel by a famous opponent of dictatorship in Italy. Elsa Morante, *History: A Novel* (1978), a fictional account of one family's divergent reactions to Mussolini's rule, is recommended. Two excellent books on Spain are H. Thomas, *The Spanish Civil War* (1977), and E. Malefakis, *Agrarian Reform and Peasant Revolution in Spain* (1970).

In the area of foreign relations, G. Kennan, *Russia and the West Under Lenin and Stalin* (1961), is justly famous; A. L. Rowse, *Appeasement* (1961), powerfully denounces the policies of the appeasers. R. Paxton, *Vichy France* (1973), tells a controversial story extremely well, and J. Lukac, *The Last European War* (1976), argues provocatively that victory by Hitler could have saved Europe from both Soviet and American domination.

On Germany, F. Stern, *The Politics of Cultural Despair* (1963), and W. Smith, *The Ideological Origins of Nazi Imperialism* (1986), are fine complementary studies on the origins of Nazism. Bracher's *The German Dictatorship,* cited in the Notes, remains the best single work on Hitler's Germany. It may be compared with the important work by M. Brozat, *The Nazi State* (1981), and with W. Shirer, *The Rise and Fall of the Third Reich* (1960), a gripping account of an American journalist who experienced Nazi Germany firsthand. J. Fest, *Hitler* (1974), and A. Bullock, *Hitler: A Study in Tyranny* (1964), are engrossing biographies of the Führer. In addition to *Mein Kampf, Hitler's Secret Conversations, 1941–1944* (1953) reveals the dictator's wild dreams and beliefs. I. Kershaw, *The "Hitler Myth": Image and Reality in the Third Reich* (1987), is a provocative reassessment of the limits of Hitler's power. M. Mayer, *They Thought They Were Free* (1955), probes the minds of ten ordinary Nazis and why they believed Hitler was their liberator. A. Speer, *Inside the Third Reich* (1970), contains the fascinating recollections of Hitler's wizard of the armaments industry. C. Koonz, *Mothers in the Fatherland: Women, the Family, and Nazi Politics* (1987), and D. Peukert, *Inside Nazi Germany: Conformity, Opposition, and Racism in Everyday Life* (1987), are pioneering forays into the social history of the Nazi era. G. Mosse, *Toward the Final Solution* (1978), is a powerful history of European racism.

Moving accounts of the Holocaust include A. Mayer, *Why Did the Heavens Not Darken? The "Final*

Solution" in History (1989); M. Gilbert, *The Holocaust: The History of the Jews During the Second World War* (1985); and L. Dawidowicz, *The War Against the Jews, 1933–1945* (1975). M. Marrus, *The Holocaust in History* (1987), is an excellent interpretive survey by a leading authority. Especially recommended is E. Weisel, *Night* (1961), a brief and very compelling autobiographical account of a young Jew in a Nazi concentration camp. J. Haestrup, *Europe Ablaze* (1978), is a monumental account of wartime resistance movements throughout Europe, and A. Frank, *The Diary of a Young Girl* (1947, reissued 1995) is a remarkable personal account of a young Jewish girl in hiding during the Nazi occupation of Holland.

J. Campbell's *The Experience of World War II* (1989) is attractively illustrated and captures the drama of global conflict, as does G. Keegan, *The Second World War* (1990). G. Wright, *The Ordeal of Total War, 1939–1945* (1990), and C. Emsley, *World War II and Its Consequences* (1990), are also recommended. B. H. Liddell Hart, *The History of the Second World War* (1971), is an overview of military developments. G. Weinberg, *The Foreign Policy of Hitler,* 2 vols. (1970, 1980), is an excellent detailed account of the diplomatic origins and course of World War II from the German perspective. Three dramatic studies of special aspects of the war are A. Dallin, *German Rule in Russia, 1941–1945* (1981), which analyzes the effects of Nazi occupation policies on the Soviet population; L. Collins and D. La Pierre, *Is Paris Burning?* (1965), a best-selling account of the liberation of Paris and Hitler's plans to destroy the city; and J. Toland, *The Last Hundred Days* (1966), a lively account of the end of the war.

LISTENING TO THE
PAST

Witness to the Holocaust

The Second World War brought mass murder to the innocent. The Nazis and their allies slaughtered 6 million Jews in addition to about 5 million Slavs, Gypsies, Jehovah's Witnesses, homosexuals, and mentally ill. On the Russian front some Jews were simply mowed down with machine guns, but most Jews were arrested in their homelands and taken in freight cars to unknown destinations, which were in fact extermination camps. The most infamous camp—really two camps on different sides of a railroad track—was Auschwitz-Birkenau in eastern Poland. There 2 million people were murdered in gas chambers.

The testimony of camp survivors helps us comprehend the unspeakable crime known to history as the Holocaust. One eyewitness was Marco Nahon, a Greek Jew and physician who escaped extermination at Auschwitz-Birkenau along with several thousand other slave laborers in the camp. The following passage is taken from Birkenau: The Camp of Death, *which Nahon wrote in 1945 after his liberation. Conquered by Germany in 1941, Greece was divided into German, Italian, and Bulgarian zones of occupation. The Nahon family lived in Dimotika in the Bulgarian zone.*

Early in March 1943, disturbing news arrives from Salonika [in the German occupation zone]: the Germans are deporting the Jews [of Salonika]. They lock them up in railway cattlecars . . . and send them to an unknown destination—to Poland, it is said. . . . Relatives and friends deliberate. What can be done in the face of this imminent threat? . . . My friend Vitalis Djivré speaks with conviction: "We must flee, cross over into Turkey at once, go to Palestine, Egypt—anywhere at all—but leave immediately." . . . A few friends and I held a completely different opinion. . . . [I say that] I am not going to emigrate. They are going to take us away to Germany or Poland

[to work]? If so, I'll work. . . . It is certain that the Allies will be the victors, and once the war is over, we'll go back home. . . .

Until the end we were deaf to all the warnings. . . . [None of the warnings] would be regarded as indicating the seriousness of the drama in preparation. But does not the human mind find inconceivable the total extermination of an innocent population? In this tragic error lay the main cause, the sole cause, of our perdition. . . .

On Monday May 10, 1943, the bugles awaken us at a very early hour. We [have already been arrested and] today we are leaving for Poland. . . . As soon as a freight car has been packed to capacity with people, it is quickly locked up, and immediately the remaining passengers are pushed into the next one. . . .

Every two days the train stops in some meadow in open country. The car doors are flung open, and the whole transport spreads out in the fields. Men and women attend to their natural needs, side by side, without any embarrassment. Necessity and common misfortune have made them part of one and the same family. . . .

We are now in a small station in Austria. Our car door half opens; a Schupo [German police officer] is asking for the doctor. . . . He leads me to the rear of the convoy and shuts me inside the car where the woman is in labor. She is very young; this is her first child. The car, like all the others, is overcrowded. The delivery takes place in deplorable conditions, in front of everybody—men, women, and children. Fortunately, everything turns out well, and a few hours later a baby boy comes into the world. The new mother's family is very happy and passes candy around. Surely no one realizes that two days later the mother and her baby and more than half of the company will pass through the chimney of a crematorium at Birkenau.

It is May 16, 1943. We have reached the end of our journey [and arrived at Auschwitz-Birkenau]. The train stops along a wooden platform. Through the openings of the cars we can see people wearing strange costumes of blue and white stripes [the prisoners who work in the camp]. We immediately notice that they are doing nothing voluntarily but are moving and acting on command. . . . The people in stripes . . . line us up five by five, the women on one side, the men on the other. I lose sight of my wife and little girl in the crowd. I will never see them again.

They make us march, swiftly as always, before a group of [German] officers. One of them, without uttering a word and with the tip of his forefinger, makes a rapid selection. He is, as we know later on, the Lagerarzt, the SS medical doctor of the camp [the notorious Dr. Mengele]. They call him here the "Angel of Death." [Mengele divides the men into two groups; those who are young and sturdy for work in the camp, and those who are old, sick, and children. The women are also divided and only healthy young women without children are assigned to work. All those not selected for work] are immediately loaded on trucks and driven off somewhere. Where? Nobody knows yet. . . .

[After being assigned to a crude windowless barrack,] we must file before the . . . scribes, who are responsible for receiving and registering the transport. Each prisoner must fill out a form in which he relinquishes his identity and becomes a mere number. . . . I am given the number 122274. My son, who is next, gets 122275. This tattoo alarms us terribly. . . . Each one of us now comes to realize in the deepest part of his conscious being, and with a bitter sense of affliction, that from this moment on he is no more than an animal. . . .

After our meal [of watery soup] Léon Yahiel, a veteran among the Lager inmates, . . . gives us this little speech: "My friends, here you must . . . forget your families, your wives, your children. You must live only for yourselves and try to last as long as possible." At these words our spirits plunge into grief and despair. Forget about our families? The hint is

Deportees getting off the coaches at Auschwitz. *(Source: Hulton Deutsch Collection Limited)*

unmistakable. Our minds are confused. . . . Our families taken away from us forever? No, it is humanly not conceivable that we should pay such a penalty without having done anything to deserve it, without any provocation.

What miserable wretches we prisoners are! We have no idea that while we entertain these thoughts, our wives, our children, our mothers and our fathers have already ceased to exist. They have arrived at Auschwitz this morning, healthy and full of life. They have now been reduced to smoke and ashes.

Questions for Analysis

1. How did the Jews of Dimotika react in early 1943 to the news of Jews being deported? Why?

2. Describe the journey to Auschwitz-Birkenau. Did those on the train know what was awaiting them there?

3. How did the Nazis divide the Jews at Auschwitz-Birkenau? Why?

4. What did you learn from Nahon's account? What parts of his testimony made the greatest impression on you?

Source: Slightly adapted from M. Nahon, *Birkenau: The Camp of Death,* trans. J. Bowers (Tuscaloosa: University of Alabama Press, 1989), pp. 21, 23, 33–39.

33

Recovery and Crisis in Europe and the Americas

The reality of the Berlin Wall, grim symbol of postwar division in Europe. *(Source: Sahm Doherty/Liaison)*

The total defeat of the Nazis and their allies laid the basis for one of Western civilization's most remarkable recoveries. A battered western Europe dug itself out from under the rubble and fashioned a great renaissance. The Western Hemisphere, with its strong European heritage, also made exemplary progress. And the Soviet Union became more humane and less totalitarian after Stalin's death. Yet there was also a tragic setback. Dictatorship settled over eastern Europe, and the Grand Alliance against Hitler gave way to an apparently endless cold war, in which tension between East and West threatened world peace.

As cold war competition originating in Europe became a factor in the lives of peoples the world over, the global economic boom of the 1950s and 1960s finally came to an end in the early 1970s. In Europe and the Americas postwar certainties like domestic political stability and social harmony evaporated, and several countries experienced major crises. Subsequently, serious economic difficulties returned with distressing regularity to Europe and the Americas in the 1980s and 1990s, and these difficulties encompassed much of the globe, as the next two chapters will show. This similarity of world economic trends accelerated the knitting together of the world's peoples and regions in recent times. The spectacular collapse of communism in eastern Europe in 1989 and the end of the cold war reinforced the trend toward global integration.

- What were the causes of the cold war?
- How and why, in spite of the cold war, did western Europe recover so successfully from the ravages of war and Nazism?
- To what extent did communist eastern Europe and the Americas experience a similar recovery?
- Why, after a generation, did the economy shift into reverse gear, and what were some of the social consequences of the reversal?
- How did political crisis strike many countries from the late 1960s onward?
- Why did a reform movement eventually triumph in eastern Europe in 1989 and bring an end to the cold war?

These are the questions that this chapter seeks to answer.

THE COLD WAR (1942–1953)

In 1945 triumphant American and Russian soldiers came together and embraced on the banks of the Elbe River in the heart of vanquished Germany. At home, in the United States and in the Soviet Union, the soldiers' loved ones erupted in joyous celebration. Yet victory was flawed. The Allies could not cooperate politically in peacemaking. Motivated by different goals and hounded by misunderstandings, the United States and the Soviet Union soon found themselves at loggerheads. By the end of 1947, Europe was rigidly divided. It was West versus East in a cold war that eventually was waged around the world.

The Origins of the Cold War

The most powerful allies in the wartime coalition—the Soviet Union and the United States—began to quarrel almost as soon as the unifying threat of Nazi Germany disappeared. A tragic disappointment for millions of people, the hostility between the Eastern and Western superpowers was the sad but logical outgrowth of military developments, wartime agreements, and long-standing political and ideological differences.

In the early phases of the Second World War, the Americans and the British made military victory their highest priority. They consistently avoided discussion of Stalin's war aims and the shape of the eventual peace settlement. For example, when Stalin asked the United States and Britain to agree to the Soviet Union's moving its western border of 1938 farther west at the expense of Poland, in effect ratifying the gains that Stalin had made from his deal with Hitler in 1939, the British and Americans declined. Stalin received only a military alliance and no postwar commitments. Yet the United States and Britain did not try to take advantage of the Soviet Union's precarious position in 1942, because they feared that hard bargaining would encourage Stalin to consider making a separate peace with Hitler. They focused instead on the policy of unconditional surrender to solidify the alliance.

By late 1943 decisions that would affect the shape of the postwar world could no longer be postponed. The conference that Stalin, Roosevelt, and Churchill held in the Iranian capital of

Teheran in November 1943 thus proved of crucial importance in determining subsequent events. There, the "Big Three" jovially reaffirmed their determination to crush Germany and searched for the appropriate military strategy. Churchill, fearful of the military dangers of a direct attack, argued that American and British forces should follow up their Italian campaign with an indirect attack on Germany through the Balkans. Roosevelt, however, agreed with Stalin that an American-British frontal assault through France would be better. This agreement was part of Roosevelt's general effort to meet Stalin's wartime demands whenever possible, and it had momentous political implications. It meant that Soviet armies, on their own, would liberate eastern Europe.

When the Big Three met again in February 1945 at Yalta on the Black Sea in southern Russia, advancing Soviet armies were within a hundred miles of Berlin. The Red Army had occupied not only Poland but also Bulgaria, Romania, Hungary, part of Yugoslavia, and much of Czechoslovakia. The temporarily stalled American-British forces had yet to cross the Rhine into Germany. Moreover, the United States was far from defeating Japan. In short, the Soviet Union's position was strong and America's weak.

There was little the increasingly sick and apprehensive Roosevelt could do but double his bet on Stalin's peaceful intentions. It was agreed at Yalta that Germany would be divided into zones of occupation and would pay heavy reparations to the Soviet Union. At American insistence, Stalin agreed to declare war on Japan after Germany was defeated. As for Poland and eastern Europe—"that Pandora's Box of infinite troubles," according to American Secretary of State Cordell Hull—the Big Three struggled to reach an ambiguous compromise at Yalta: eastern European governments were to be freely elected but pro-Russian. As Churchill put it at the time, "The Poles will have their future in their own hands, with the single limitation that they must honestly follow, in harmony with their allies, a policy friendly to Russia."[1]

The Yalta compromise over eastern Europe broke down almost immediately. Even before the Yalta Conference, Bulgaria and Poland were controlled by communists who arrived home with the Red Army. Elsewhere in eastern Europe, pro-Soviet "coalition" governments of several parties were formed, but the key ministerial posts were reserved for Moscow-trained communists.

At the postwar Potsdam Conference of July 1945, the long-avoided differences over eastern Europe finally surged to the fore. The compromising Roosevelt had died and been succeeded by the more determined President Harry Truman, who demanded immediate free elections throughout eastern Europe. Stalin refused point-blank. "A freely elected government in any of these East European countries would be anti-Soviet," he admitted simply, "and that we cannot allow."[2]

Here, then, is the key to the much-debated origins of the cold war. American ideals, pumped up by the crusade against Hitler, and American politics, heavily influenced by millions of U.S. voters of eastern European heritage, demanded free elections in Soviet-occupied eastern Europe. Stalin, who had lived through two enormously destructive German invasions, wanted absolute military security from Germany and its potential eastern European allies, once and for all. Suspicious by nature, he believed that only communist states could be truly dependable allies, and he realized that free elections would result in independent and possibly hostile governments on his western border. Moreover, by the middle of 1945 there was no way short of war that the United States could determine political developments in eastern Europe, and war was out of the question. Stalin was bound to have his way.

West Versus East

The American response to Stalin's exaggerated conception of security was to "get tough." In May 1945 Truman abruptly cut off all aid to Russia. In October he declared that the United States would never recognize any government established by force against the free will of its people. In March 1946 former British prime minister Churchill ominously informed an American audience that an "iron curtain" had fallen across the European continent, dividing Germany and all of Europe into two antagonistic camps. Emotional, moralistic denunciations of Stalin and communist Russia emerged as part of American political life. Yet the United States also responded to the popular desire to "bring the boys home" and demobilized with great speed. When the war against Japan ended in

The Big Three   In 1945 a triumphant Winston Churchill, an ailing Franklin Roosevelt, and a determined Joseph Stalin met at Yalta in southern Russia to plan for peace. Cooperation soon gave way to bitter hostility. *(Source: F. D. R. Library)*

September 1945, there were 12 million Americans in the armed forces; by 1947 there were only 1.5 million, as opposed to 6 million for the Soviet Union. Some historians have argued that American leaders believed that the atomic bomb gave the United States all the power it needed, but "getting tough" really meant "talking tough."

Stalin's agents quickly reheated what they viewed as the "ideological struggle against capitalist imperialism." The large, well-organized Communist parties of France and Italy obediently started to uncover American plots to take over Europe and challenged their own governments with violent criticisms and large strikes. The Soviet Union also put pressure on Iran, Turkey, and Greece, while a bitter civil war raged in China. By

the spring of 1947, it appeared to many Americans that Stalin was determined to export communism by subversion throughout Europe and around the world.

The United States responded to this challenge with the Truman Doctrine, which was aimed at "containing" communism in areas already occupied by the Red Army. Truman told Congress in March 1947: "I believe it must be the policy of the United States to support free people who are resisting attempted subjugation by armed minorities or by outside pressure." To begin, Truman asked Congress for military aid to Greece and Turkey. Then, in June, Secretary of State George C. Marshall offered Europe economic aid—the Marshall Plan—to help it rebuild (see Listening to the Past).

Stalin refused Marshall Plan assistance for all of eastern Europe. He purged the last remaining noncommunist elements from the coalition governments of eastern Europe and established Soviet-style, one-party communist dictatorships. The seizure of power in Czechoslovakia in February 1948 was particularly brutal and antidemocratic, and it greatly strengthened Western fears of limitless communist expansion, beginning with Germany. Thus, when Stalin blocked all traffic through the Soviet zone of Germany to Berlin, the former capital, which the occupying powers had also divided into sectors at the end of the war, the Western Allies acted firmly but not provocatively.

Hundreds of planes began flying over the Soviet roadblocks around the clock, supplying provisions to thwart Soviet efforts to swallow up the West Berliners. After 324 days the Soviets backed down: containment seemed to work. In 1949, therefore, the United States formed an anti-Soviet military alliance of Western governments: the North Atlantic Treaty Organization (NATO). Stalin countered by tightening his hold on his satellites, later united in the Warsaw Pact. Europe was divided into two hostile blocs.

In late 1949 the communists triumphed in China (see page 1133), frightening and angering many Americans, who saw new evidence of a pow-

The Berlin Airlift Standing in the rubble of their bombed-out city, Germans in the American sector await the arrival of a U.S. transport plane flying in over the Soviet blockade in 1948. The crisis over Berlin was a dramatic indication of growing tensions among the Allies, which resulted in the division of Europe into two hostile camps. (*Source: Walter Sanders,* Life Magazine, © *Time Warner, Inc.*)

erful worldwide communist conspiracy. When the Russian-backed communist forces of northern Korea invaded southern Korea in 1950, President Truman acted swiftly. American-led United Nations armies intervened. The cold war had spread around the world and had become very hot.

The rapid descent from victorious Grand Alliance to bitter cold war was intimately connected with the tragic fate of eastern Europe. After having appeased Nazi racist imperialism in eastern Europe, the Western democracies during the war chose to ignore the question of Stalin's aims on his western borders and hope for the best. But when Stalin later began to claim the spoils of victory, the United States began to protest and professed outrage. This belated opposition quite possibly encouraged even more aggressive measures by the always-suspicious Stalin, and it helped explode the quarrel over eastern Europe into a global confrontation. This Soviet-American confrontation became institutionalized, and it lasted until the Soviet Union's policy toward eastern Europe changed dramatically in the 1980s (see pages 1114, 1115).

THE WESTERN EUROPEAN RENAISSANCE

As the cold war divided Europe into two blocs, the future appeared bleak on both sides of the iron curtain. Economic conditions were the worst in generations. Politically, Europe was weak and divided, a battleground for cold war ambitions. Moreover, European empires were crumbling in the face of nationalism in Asia and Africa. Yet Europe recovered, and the Western nations led the way. In less than a generation, western Europe achieved unprecedented economic prosperity and peaceful social transformation. It was an amazing rebirth—a true renaissance.

The Postwar Challenge

After the war, economic conditions in western Europe were terrible. Runaway inflation and black markets testified to severe shortages and hardship. Many believed that Europe was simply finished.

Suffering was most intense in defeated Germany. The major territorial change of the war had moved the Soviet Union's border far to the west. Poland was in turn compensated for this loss to the Soviets with land taken from Germany (Map 33.1). To solidify these changes in boundaries, 13 million people were driven from their homes in eastern Germany (and other countries in eastern Europe) and forced to resettle in a greatly reduced Germany. The Russians were also seizing factories and equipment as reparations, even tearing up railroad tracks and sending the rails to the Soviet Union.

In 1945 and 1946, conditions were not much better in the Western zones, for the Western Allies also treated the German population with great severity at first. Countless Germans sold prized possessions to American soldiers to buy food. By the spring of 1947, refugee-clogged, hungry, prostrate Germany was on the verge of total collapse and threatening to drag down the rest of Europe. Yet western Europe was not finished. The Nazi occupation and the war had discredited old ideas and old leaders. All over Europe, many people were willing to change and experiment, and new groups and new leaders were coming to the fore to guide these aspirations. Progressive Catholics and revitalized Catholic political parties—the Christian Democrats—were particularly influential.

In Italy, the Christian Democrats emerged as the leading party, and in early 1948 they won an absolute majority in the parliament in a landslide victory. Their very able leader was Alcide De Gasperi, a courageous antifascist firmly committed to political democracy, economic reconstruction, and moderate social reform. In France, too, the Catholic party also provided some of the best postwar leaders after January 1946, when General Charles de Gaulle, the inspiring wartime leader of the Free French, resigned after having re-established the free and democratic Fourth Republic. As Germany was partitioned by the cold war, a radically purified Federal Republic of Germany (as West Germany was officially known) found new and able leadership among its Catholics. In 1949 Konrad Adenauer, the former mayor of Cologne and a longtime anti-Nazi, began his long, highly successful democratic rule; the Christian Democrats became West Germany's majority party for a generation. In providing effective leadership for their respective countries, the Christian Democrats were inspired and united by a common Christian and European heritage. They steadfastly rejected totalitarianism

MAP 33.1 Europe After the Second World War Both the Soviet Union and Poland took land from Germany, which the Allies partitioned into four occupation zones. Those zones subsequently formed the basis of the east and the west German states, as the iron curtain fell to divide both Germany and Europe. Austria was detached from Germany and also divided into four occupation zones, but the Soviets later permitted Austria to be unified as a neutral state.

and narrow nationalism and placed their faith in democracy and cooperation.

The Socialists and the Communists, active in the Resistance against Hitler, also emerged from the war with increased power and prestige, especially in France and Italy. They, too, provided fresh leadership and pushed for social change and economic reform with considerable success. In the immediate postwar years, welfare measures such as family allowances, health insurance, and increased public housing were enacted throughout much of continental Europe. Britain followed the same trend. The voters threw out Churchill and the Conservatives in 1945, and the victorious socialist Labour party moved toward establishment of a "welfare state." Many industries were nationalized, and the government provided free medical service. Thus all across Europe, social reform complemented political transformation, creating solid foundations for a great European renaissance.

The United States also supplied strong and creative leadership, providing western Europe with both massive economic aid and ongoing military protection. Economic aid was channeled through the Marshall Plan and military security was provided through NATO, which featured American troops stationed permanently in Europe and the American nuclear umbrella. Thus the United States assumed its international responsibilities after the Second World War, exercising the leadership it had shunned after 1919.

As Marshall Plan aid poured in, the battered economies of western Europe began to turn the corner in 1948, and Europe entered a period of unprecedented economic progress that lasted into the late 1960s. There were many reasons for this brilliant economic performance. American aid helped the process get off to a fast start. Moreover, economic growth became a basic objective of all western European governments, for leaders and voters were determined to avoid a return to the dangerous and demoralizing stagnation of the 1930s. Thus governments generally accepted Keynesian economics (see page 1045) and sought to stimulate their economies. They also adopted a variety of imaginative and successful strategies.

In postwar West Germany, Minister of Economy Ludwig Erhard, a roly-poly, cigar-smoking former professor, broke decisively with the straitjacketed Nazi economy. Erhard bet on the free-market economy while maintaining the extensive social welfare network inherited from the Hitler era. He and his teachers believed not only that capitalism was more efficient but also that political and social freedom could thrive only if there were real economic freedom. Erhard's first step was to reform the currency and abolish rationing and price controls in 1948. He boldly declared, "The only ration coupon is the Mark."[3] West German success renewed respect for free-market capitalism.

The French innovation was a new kind of planning. A planning commission set ambitious but flexible goals for the French economy and used the nationalized banks to funnel money into key industries. Thus France combined flexible planning and a "mixed" state and private economy to achieve the most rapid economic development in its long history.

In most countries there were many people ready to work hard for low wages and the hope of a better future. Moreover, although many consumer products had been invented or perfected since the late 1920s, during the Great Depression and war few Europeans had been able to buy them. In 1945 the electric refrigerator, the washing machine, and the automobile were rare luxuries. There was great potential demand, which the economic system moved to satisfy. Finally, West European nations abandoned protectionism and gradually created a large, unified market known as the Common Market. This historic action, which certainly stimulated the economy, was part of a larger search for European unity.

Toward European Unity

Western Europe's political recovery was spectacular in the generation after 1945. Republics were reestablished in France, West Germany, and Italy. Constitutional monarchs were restored in Belgium, the Netherlands, and Norway. Democratic governments, often within the framework of multiparty politics and shifting parliamentary coalitions, took root again and thrived in an atmosphere of civil liberties and individual freedom.

A similarly extraordinary achievement was the march toward a united Europe. The Christian Democrats with their common Catholic heritage were particularly committed to "building Europe," and other groups shared their dedication. Many Europeans believed that only unity could forestall European conflict in the future and that only a new

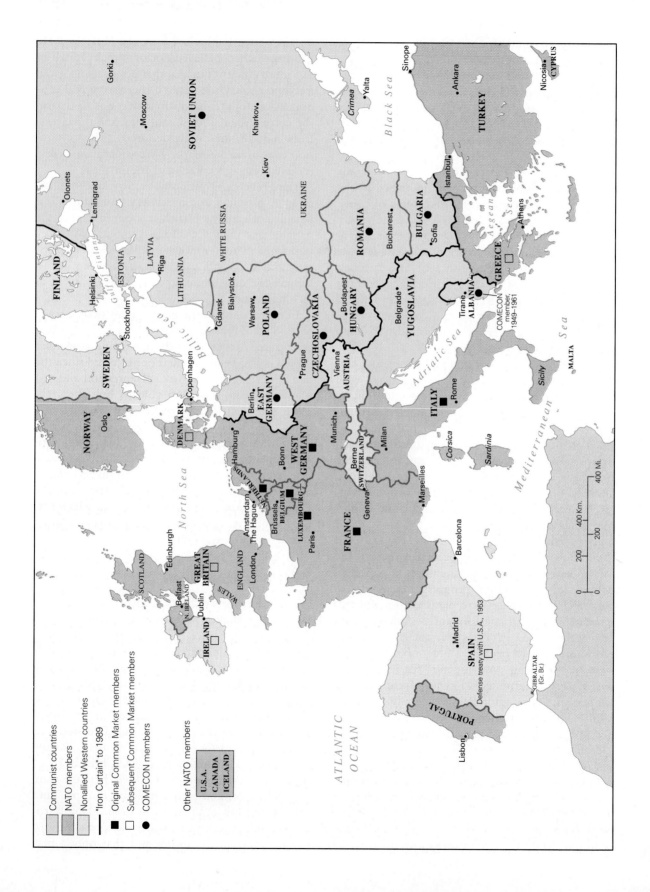

"European nation" could reassert western Europe's influence in world affairs dominated by the United States and the Soviet Union.

The close cooperation among European states required by the Americans for Marshall Plan aid led to the creation of both the Organization of European Economic Cooperation (OEEC) and the Council of Europe in 1948. European federalists hoped that the Council of Europe would quickly evolve into a true European parliament with sovereign rights, but this did not happen. Britain, with its empire and its "special relationship" with the United States, consistently opposed giving any real political power—any sovereignty—to the council. Many old-fashioned continental nationalists and communists felt similarly.

Frustrated in the direct political approach, European federalists turned toward economics as a way of working toward genuine unity. French statesmen took the lead in 1950 and called for a special international organization to control and integrate all European steel and coal production. West Germany, Italy, Belgium, the Netherlands, and Luxembourg accepted the French idea in 1952; the British would have none of it. The immediate economic goal—a single steel and coal market without national tariffs or quotas—was rapidly realized. The more far-reaching political goal was to bind the six member nations so closely together economically that war among them would become unthinkable and virtually impossible.

In 1957 the six nations of the Coal and Steel Community signed the Treaty of Rome, which created the European Economic Community, generally known as the Common Market (Map 33.2). The first goal of the treaty was a gradual reduction of all tariffs among the Six in order to create a single market almost as large as that of the United States. Other goals included the free movement of capital and labor and common economic policies and institutions. The Common Market was a great success, encouraging companies and regions to specialize in what they did best.

❄ **MAP 33.2 European Alliance Systems** After the cold war divided Europe into two hostile military alliances, six western European countries formed the Common Market in 1957. The Common Market grew later to include most of western Europe. The Communist states organized their own economic association—COMECON.

The development of the Common Market fired imaginations and encouraged hopes of rapid progress toward political as well as economic union. In the 1960s, however, these hopes were frustrated by a resurgence of more traditional nationalism. France took the lead. Mired in a bitter colonial war in Algeria, the French turned in 1958 to General de Gaulle, who established the Fifth French Republic and ruled as its president until 1969. De Gaulle was at heart a romantic nationalist, and he labored to re-create a powerful, truly independent France. Viewing the United States as the main threat to genuine French (and European) independence, he withdrew all French military forces from the "American-controlled" NATO command as France developed its own nuclear weapons. Within the Common Market, de Gaulle refused to permit the scheduled advent of majority rule. Thus throughout the 1960s the Common Market thrived economically but remained a union of sovereign states.

Decolonization

In the postwar era Europe's long overseas expansion was dramatically reversed. Between 1947 and 1962 almost every colonial territory gained formal independence. Future generations will almost certainly see this rolling back of Western expansion as one of world history's truly great turning points (Map 33.3).

The basic cause of imperial collapse—what Europeans called *decolonization*—was the rising demand of Asian and African peoples for national self-determination, racial equality, and personal dignity. This demand spread from intellectuals to the masses in virtually every colonial territory after the First World War. As a result, colonial empires had already been shaken by 1939, and the way was prepared for the eventual triumph of independence movements (see pages 1040–1058). Yet decolonization also involved the imperial powers, and looking at the process from their perspective helps explain why independence came so quickly and why a kind of neocolonialism subsequently took its place in some areas.

European empires had been based on an enormous power differential between the rulers and the ruled, a difference that had declined almost to the vanishing point by 1945. Not only was western

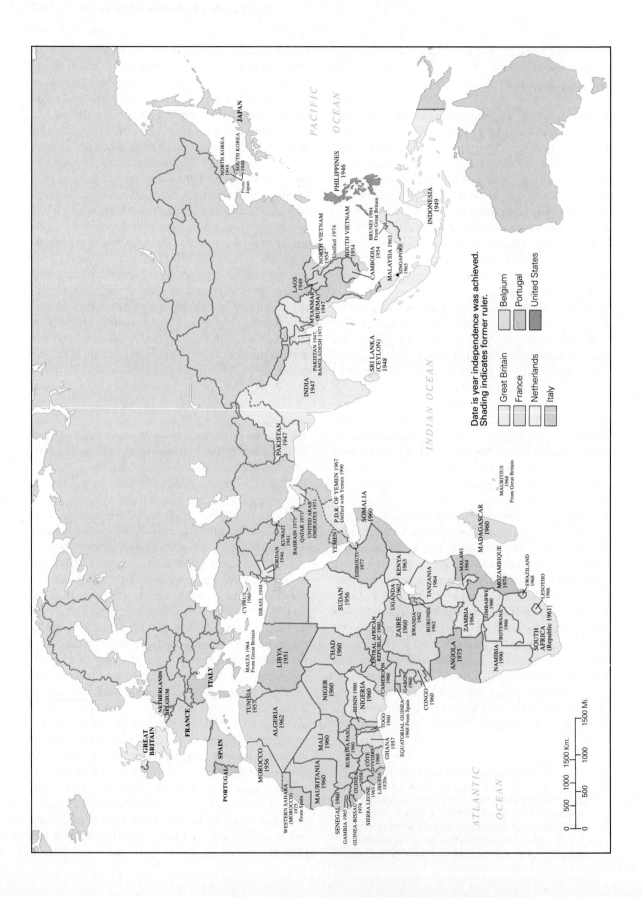

Europe poor and battered, but most Europeans regarded their empires very differently after 1945 than before 1914, or even before 1939. Empire had rested on self-confidence and self-righteousness; Europeans had believed their superiority to be not only technical and military but spiritual and moral as well. The horrors of the Second World War destroyed such complacent arrogance and gave opponents of imperialism much greater influence in Europe. With its political power and moral authority in tatters, Europe could either submit to decolonization or enter into risky wars of reconquest. After 1945 many Europeans were willing to let go of their colonies more or less voluntarily and to concentrate on rebuilding at home.

Indian independence played a key role in decolonization. When the Labour party came to power in Great Britain in 1945, it was determined to leave India. British socialists had always opposed imperialism, and the heavy cost of governing India had become an intolerable burden. Empire in India ended in 1947, and most Asian colonies achieved independence shortly thereafter. Although the French obstinately tried to re-establish colonial rule in Indochina, they were defeated in 1954, and two independent Vietnamese states came into being. The French also fought a long, dirty war to keep Algeria French, but Algeria won its independence in 1962 (see Map 33.3).

In much of Africa south of the Sahara, decolonization proceeded much more smoothly. Beginning in 1957, Britain's colonies achieved independence with little or no bloodshed and then entered a very loose association with Britain as members of the British Commonwealth of Nations. In 1958 the clever de Gaulle offered the leaders of French black Africa the choice of a total break with France or immediate independence within a kind of French commonwealth. All but one of the new states chose association with France (see page 1160). As in the past, the French and their Common Market partners saw themselves as continuing their civilizing mission in black Africa. More im-

portant, they saw in Africa untapped markets for their industrial goods, raw materials for their factories, outlets for profitable investment, and good temporary jobs for their engineers and teachers. The British acted somewhat similarly.

As a result, western European countries actually managed to increase their economic and cultural ties with their former African colonies in the 1960s and 1970s. Above all, they used the lure of special trading privileges with the Common Market and heavy investment in French- and English-language education to enhance a powerful Western presence in the new African states. This situation led a variety of leaders and scholars to charge that western Europe (and the United States) had imposed a system of neocolonialism on the former colonies. According to this view, *neocolonialism* was a system designed to perpetuate Western economic domination and undermine the promise of political independence, thereby extending to Africa (and much of Asia) the neocolonial subordination that the United States had established in Latin America after the political revolutions of the early nineteenth century. At the very least, enduring influence in black Africa testified to western Europe's resurgent economic and political power in international relations.

The Changing Class Structure

Rapid economic growth went a long way toward creating a new society in Europe after the Second World War. European society became more mobile and more democratic. Old class barriers relaxed, and class distinctions became fuzzier.

Changes in the structure of the middle class were particularly influential in the general drift toward a less rigid class structure. In the nineteenth and early twentieth centuries, the model for the middle class had been the independent, self-employed property owner who owned a business or practiced a liberal profession like law or medicine. After 1945, a new breed of managers and experts replaced traditional property owners as the leaders of the middle class. Ability to serve the needs of a big organization largely replaced inherited property and family connections in determining an individual's social position in the middle and upper middle class. At the same time, the middle class grew massively and became harder to define.

✳ **MAP 33.3 New States in Africa and Asia**
Divided primarily along religious lines into two states, British India led the way to political independence in 1947. Most African territories achieved statehood by the mid-1960s, as European empires passed away, unlamented.

There were several reasons for these developments. Rapid industrial and technological expansion created in large corporations and government agencies a powerful demand for technologists and managers. Moreover, the old propertied middle class lost control of many family-owned businesses (including family farms) and joined the ranks of salaried employees.

Top managers and ranking civil servants therefore represented the model for a new middle class of salaried specialists. Well paid and highly trained, pragmatic and realistic, these experts increasingly came from all social classes, even the working class. Everywhere successful managers and technocrats passed on the opportunity for all-important advanced education to their children, but only in rare instances could they pass on the positions they had attained. Thus the new middle class, which was based largely on specialized skills and high levels of education, was more open, democratic, and insecure than the old propertied middle class.

The structure of the lower classes also became more flexible and open. There was a mass exodus from farms and the countryside, as one of the most traditional and least mobile groups in European society drastically declined. Meanwhile, because of rapid technological change, the industrial working class ceased to expand, and job opportunities for white-collar and service employees grew rapidly. Such employees bore a greater resemblance to the new middle class of salaried specialists than to industrial workers, who were also better educated and more specialized.

European governments were reducing class tensions with a series of social security reforms. Many of these reforms—like increased unemployment benefits and more extensive old-age pensions—simply strengthened social security measures first pioneered in Bismarck's Germany before the First World War. Other programs were new, like comprehensive national health systems directed by the state. Most countries also introduced family allowances—direct government grants to parents to help them raise their children. These allowances helped many poor families make ends meet. Most European governments also gave maternity grants and built inexpensive public housing for low-income families and individuals. These and other social reforms provided a humane floor of well-being. Reforms also promoted greater equality be-

cause they were expensive and were paid for in part by higher taxes on the rich.

The rising standard of living and the spread of standardized consumer goods also worked to level Western society, as the percentage of income spent on food and drink declined substantially. For example, in 1948 there were only 5 million cars in western Europe, but in 1965 there were 44 million. Car ownership was democratized and came within the range of better-paid workers.

Europeans took great pleasure in the products of the "gadget revolution" as well. Like Americans, Europeans filled their houses and apartments with washing machines, vacuum cleaners, refrigerators, dishwashers, radios, TVs, and stereos. The purchase of consumer goods was greatly facilitated by installment purchasing. Before the Second World War, Europeans had rarely bought on credit. But with the expansion of social security safeguards, reducing the need to accumulate savings for hard times, ordinary people were increasingly willing to take on debt. This change had far-reaching consequences.

The most astonishing leisure-time development in the consumer society was the blossoming of mass travel and tourism. With month-long paid vacations required by law in most European countries, and widespread automobile ownership, beaches and ski resorts came within the reach of the middle class and many workers. By the late 1960s packaged tours with cheap group flights and bargain hotel accommodations had made even distant lands easily accessible. A French company grew rich building imitation Tahitian paradises around the world. At Swedish nudist colonies on secluded West African beaches, office workers from Stockholm fleetingly worshiped the sun in the middle of the long northern winter. Truly, consumerism had come of age.

The Troubled Economy in Recent Times

For twenty years after 1945, most Europeans were preoccupied with the possibilities of economic progress and consumerism. The more democratic class structure also helped to reduce social tension, and ideological conflict went out of style. In the late 1960s, however, sharp criticism and social conflicts re-emerged, heralding a new era of uncertainty and crisis.

A Modern Manager   Despite considerable discrimination, women were increasingly found in the expanding middle class of salaried experts after World War II, working in business, science, and technology. *(Source: Niépce-Rapho/Photo Researchers)*

Much of the criticism in western Europe came from radical students, who formed part of an international counterculture that came to oppose the Vietnam War as immoral and imperialistic (see pages 1120–1121). But student protests in western Europe also highlighted more general problems of education in a society of specialists. Higher education expanded rapidly in western Europe after World War II, and this expansion created problems as well as opportunities for students. Classes were badly overcrowded, and competition for grades was intense. "Practical" areas of study were added to the curriculum, but they were added less quickly than some students wanted. Thus many students felt that Western governments were evil and imperialistic or that governments were not providing the kind of education that young people needed for jobs in the modern economy. They concluded that universities as well as society needed fundamental, even revolutionary reforms.

Tensions came to a head in the late 1960s and early 1970s. Following in the footsteps of their American counterparts, European university students rose to challenge their university administrations and even their governments. The most far-reaching of these revolts occurred in France in 1968. Students occupied university buildings, clashed violently with police, and appealed to France's industrial workers for help. A general strike then spread across France in May 1968, and it seemed certain that President de Gaulle's Fifth Republic would collapse. De Gaulle, however, stiffened, moving troops toward Paris and calling for new elections. Thoroughly frightened and fearful that a successful revolution could lead only to an eventual communist takeover, the masses of France voted for a return to law and order. De Gaulle and his party scored the biggest electoral victory in modern French history, and the mini-revolution collapsed. But the proud de Gaulle and the confident though old-fashioned nationalism that he represented had been cruelly mocked. In 1969, tired and discouraged, he resigned over a minor issue, and within a year he was dead.

The international student revolution of the late 1960s announced the passing of postwar social

Student Rebellion in Paris   These rock-throwing students in the Latin Quarter of Paris are trying to force education reforms and even to topple de Gaulle's government. Throughout May 1968 students clashed repeatedly with France's tough riot police in bloody street fighting. De Gaulle remained in power, but a major reform of French education did follow. *(Source: Bruno Barbey/Magnum)*

stability, but it was the reappearance of economic crisis in the 1970s that brought the most serious challenges for the average person. The postwar international monetary system was based on the American dollar. Foreign governments could exchange dollars for gold at $35 an ounce and considered dollars "as good as gold." Giving foreign aid and fighting foreign wars, the United States sent billions of dollars abroad. By early 1971, it had only $11 billion in gold left, and Europe had accumulated 50 billion American dollars. Foreigners then panicked and raced to exchange their dollars for gold. President Richard Nixon responded

by stopping the sale of American gold; the value of the dollar fell sharply, and inflation accelerated worldwide. Fixed rates of exchange were abandoned, and great uncertainty replaced postwar predictability in international trade and finance.

Even more damaging was the dramatic reversal in the price and availability of energy. The great postwar boom was fueled by cheap oil, especially in western Europe. By 1971, the Arab-led Organization of Petroleum Exporting Countries (OPEC) had watched the price of crude oil decline consistently compared with the rising price of manufactured goods. OPEC decided to reverse that trend by presenting a united front against the oil companies. After the fourth Arab-Israeli war in October 1973 (see page 0000), crude oil prices quadrupled in the course of a year. It was widely realized that the rapid price rise was economically destructive, but the world's big powers did nothing. The Soviet Union was a great oil exporter and benefited directly; the United States was immobilized, its attention absorbed by the Watergate crisis in politics (see page 0000). Thus governments, companies, and individuals had no choice other than to deal piecemeal with the so-called oil shock—a "shock" that really turned out to be an earthquake.

Coming on the heels of upheaval in the international monetary system, the revolution in energy prices plunged the world into its worst economic decline since the 1930s. Unemployment rose. Productivity and living standards declined. By 1976 a modest recovery was in progress, but when Iranian oil production collapsed during Iran's fundamentalist Islamic revolution (see page 1152), the price of crude oil doubled again in 1979, and the world economy succumbed to its second oil shock. Unemployment and inflation rose dramatically before another uneven recovery began in 1982. But in the summer of 1985 the unemployment rate in western Europe rose again, to its highest levels since the Great Depression. Although unemployment declined somewhat in the late 1980s, the 1990s opened with renewed recession in the United States and in Europe, where it was especially severe. Global recovery was painfully slow until late 1993.

One telling measure of the troubled economy was the "misery index," first used with considerable effect by candidate Jimmy Carter in the 1976 U.S. presidential debates. The misery index combined rates of inflation and unemployment in a single, powerfully emotional number. Figure 33.1 presents a comparison of misery indexes for the United States, Japan, and the European Economic Community (the Common Market) between 1970 and 1986. "Misery" increased on both sides of the Atlantic, but the increase was substantially greater in western Europe—where these hard times are often referred to simply as "the crisis"—and it remained so in the early 1990s.

Throughout the 1970s and 1980s anxious observers, recalling the disastrous consequences of the Great Depression, worried that the Common Market might disintegrate in the face of severe

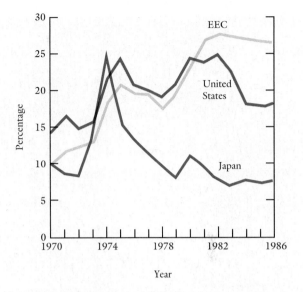

FIGURE 33.1 The Misery Index, 1970–1986 Combining rates of unemployment and inflation provided a simple but effective measure of economic hardship. This particular index represents the sum of two times the unemployment rate plus the inflation rate, reflecting the widespread belief that joblessness causes more suffering than higher prices. EEC = European Economic Community, or Common Market countries. *(Source: OECD data, as given in* The Economist, *June 15, 1985, p. 69.)*

economic dislocation and that economic nationalism would halt steps toward European unity. Yet the Common Market continued to exert a powerful attraction on nonmembers. In 1973, Denmark and Iceland, in addition to Britain, finally joined. Greece joined in 1981, and Portugal and Spain entered in 1986.

After de Gaulle's death, the nations of the Common Market cooperated more closely in many international undertakings, and the movement toward European unity stayed alive. The Common Market countries eventually set 1992 as the year for the attainment of total economic and social integration, which was achieved, at least on paper, in the Maastricht treaty of 1992. The European Community was renamed the European Union, and 1997 was ambitiously set as the date for full monetary union with a single European currency. Western Europe had weathered the storms of the 1970s and 1980s, which contrasted so sharply with the clear sailing of the 1950s and 1960s.

Saudi Riches   Enormous oil reserves make Saudi Arabia one of the most influential members of the Organization of Petroleum Exporting Countries (OPEC) and give it one of the world's highest per capita incomes. Oil has also made rich men of Prince Fahd and King Khalid, shown here considering plans for a new urban development. *(Source: Robert Azzi/Woodfin Camp & Associates)*

Society in a Time of Economic Uncertainty

The most pervasive consequences of this recent economic stagnation were probably psychological and attitudinal. Optimism gave way to pessimism; romantic utopianism yielded to sober realism. This drastic change in mood—a complete surprise only to those who had never studied history—affected states, institutions, and individuals in countless ways.

To be sure, there were heartbreaking human tragedies—lost jobs, bankruptcies, homelessness, and mental breakdowns. But on the whole, the welfare system fashioned in the postwar era prevented mass suffering and degradation through extended benefits for the unemployed, free medical care and special allowances for the needy, and a host of lesser supports. The responsive, socially concerned national state undoubtedly contributed to the preservation of political stability and democracy in the face of economic difficulties that might have brought revolution and dictatorship in earlier times.

The energetic response of governments to social needs helps explain the sharp increase in total government spending in most countries during the 1970s and 1980s. In 1982 western European governments spent an average of more than 50 percent of gross national income, as compared to only 37 percent fifteen years earlier. In all countries, people were much more willing to see their governments increase spending than raise taxes. This imbalance contributed to the rapid growth of budget deficits, national debts, and inflation. By the late 1970s, a powerful reaction against government's ever-increasing role had set in, however, and Western governments were gradually forced to introduce austerity measures to slow the seemingly inexorable growth of public spending and the welfare state.

Part of a broad cultural shift toward greater conservatism, growing voter dissatisfaction with government and government spending helped bring Margaret Thatcher (b. 1925) to power in Britain in 1979. Thatcher had some success in slowing government spending and in privatizing industry—that is, in selling off state-owned companies to private investors. Of great social significance, Thatcher's Conservative government encouraged low- and moderate-income renters in state-owned housing projects to buy their apartments at rock-bottom prices. This privatization initiative created a whole new class of property owners, thereby eroding the electoral base of Britain's socialist Labour party.

The striking but temporary exception to the trend toward greater frugality was François Mitterrand (b. 1916) of France. After his election as president in 1981, Mitterrand led his Socialist party and Communist allies on a lurch to the left, launching a vast program of nationalization and public investment designed to spend France out of economic stagnation. By 1983 this attempt had clearly failed. Mitterrand's Socialist government was then compelled to impose a wide variety of austerity measures, but the French economy continued to limp and sputter through the decade.

In early 1993 frustrated French voters gave a coalition of conservatives and moderates an overwhelming victory, as the Socialist party suffered total defeat and the once-powerful Communists were reduced almost to fringe party status. With industrial production and national income declining in France (and in Germany, Italy, and Spain, among others), and with unemployment climbing to a new high of 10.7 percent in the European Union in October 1993, the hard times that began in the West in 1973 were continuing.

When governments were forced to restrain spending, large scientific projects were often singled out for cuts. These reductions reinforced the ongoing computer revolution. That revolution thrived on the diffusion of ever-cheaper computa-

tional and informational capacity to small research groups and private businesses, which were both cause and effect of the revolution itself. Big organizations lost some of their advantages as small firms and even individuals became able to link electronically with their region and most of the world. By the 1990s a student with an inexpensive personal computer had the power of a 1950s mainframe that had filled a room and cost hundreds of thousands of dollars. From fax machines to new cars, computer technology was everywhere.

Despite the advantages offered by electronic gadgetry, individuals felt the impact of austerity at an early date, for, unlike governments, they could not pay their bills by printing money and going ever further into debt. The energy crisis of the 1970s forced them to re-examine not only their fuel bills but also the whole pattern of self-indulgent materialism in the postwar era. The result in both Europe and North America was a leaner, tougher lifestyle, featuring more attention to nutrition and a passion for exercise. Correspondingly, there was less blind reliance on medical science for good health and a growing awareness that individuals had to accept a large portion of the responsibility for illness and disease. More people began to realize that they could substantially increase their life spans simply by eating regular meals, sleeping seven or eight hours each night, exercising two or three times a week, maintaining moderate weight, foregoing smoking, and using alcohol only in moderation. For example, a forty-five-year-old American male who practiced three or fewer of these habits in the late 1970s could expect to live to be sixty-seven, but one who adhered to five or six could expect to live eleven more years, to age seventy-eight.

Economic troubles also strengthened existing trends within the family. Men and women were encouraged to postpone marriage until they had put their careers on a firm foundation, so the age of marriage rose sharply for both sexes in many Western countries. Indeed, the very real threat of unemployment—or "underemployment" in a dead-end job—seemed to shape the outlook of a whole generation. The students of the 1980s were serious, practical, and often conservative. As one young woman at a French university told a reporter in 1985, "Jobs are the big worry now, so everyone wants to learn something practical."[4] In France as elsewhere, the shift away from the romantic visions and the political activism of the late 1960s was astonishing.

Harder times also meant that ever-more women entered or remained in the work force after they married. Although attitudes related to personal fulfillment were one reason for the continuing increase—especially for well-educated, upper-middle-class women—many wives in poor and middle-class families simply had to work outside the home because of economic necessity. As in preindustrial Europe, the wife's earnings provided the margin of survival for millions of hard-pressed families.

 **SOVIET EASTERN EUROPE**

While western Europe surged ahead economically after the Second World War and regained political independence as American influence gradually waned, eastern Europe followed a different path. The Soviet Union under Stalin first tightened its grip on the "liberated" nations of eastern Europe and then refused to let go. Thus postwar economic recovery in eastern Europe proceeded along Soviet lines, and changes in the Soviet Union strongly influenced political and social developments. These changes went forward at a slow and uneven pace, and they appeared to almost halt after Leonid Brezhnev came to power and crushed a socialist reform movement in Czechoslovakia in 1968.

Yet beneath the apparent stagnation of the Brezhnev years Soviet society experienced a major transformation. This transformation encouraged new political thinking in the Soviet Union and in turn enabled the long-frustrated reform movement to triumph spectacularly in eastern Europe in the unexpected revolution of 1989. Thus one must look primarily at the Soviet Union in order to understand the history of eastern European peoples since 1945.

Stalin's Last Years

Americans were not the only ones who felt betrayed by Stalin's postwar actions. The Great Patriotic War of the Fatherland had fostered Russian nationalism and a relaxation of totalitarian terror. It also produced a rare but real unity between Soviet rulers and most Russian people. Having made a heroic war effort, the vast majority of the Soviet people hoped in 1945 that a grateful party and government would grant greater freedom and democracy. Such hopes were soon crushed.

Even before the war ended, Stalin was moving his country back toward rigid dictatorship. As early as 1944, the leading members of the Communist party were being given a new motivating slogan: "The war on Fascism ends, the war on capitalism begins."[5] By early 1946, Stalin was publicly singing the old tune that war was inevitable as long as capitalism existed. Stalin's new foreign foe in the West provided an excuse for re-establishing a harsh dictatorship. Thousands of returning soldiers and ordinary civilians were purged in 1945 and 1946, as Stalin revived the terrible forced-labor camps of the 1930s.

Culture and art were also purged in violent campaigns that reimposed rigid anti-Western ideological conformity. Many artists were denounced, including the composers Sergei Prokofiev and Dimitri Shostakovich and the outstanding film director Sergei Eisenstein. In 1949 Stalin launched a savage verbal attack on Soviet Jews, accusing them of being pro-Western and antisocialist.

In the political realm, Stalin reasserted the Communist party's complete control of the government and his absolute mastery of the party. Five-year plans were reintroduced to cope with the enormous task of economic reconstruction. Once again, heavy and military industry were given top priority, and consumer goods, housing, and collectivized agriculture were neglected. Everyday life was very hard. In short, it was the 1930s all over again in the Soviet Union, although police terror was less intense.

Stalin's prime postwar innovation was to export the Stalinist system to the countries of eastern Europe. The Communist parties of eastern Europe had established one-party states by 1948, thanks to the help of the Red Army and the Russian secret police. Rigid ideological indoctrination, attacks on religion, and a lack of civil liberties were soon facts of life. Industry was nationalized, and the middle class was stripped of its possessions. Economic life was then faithfully recast in the Stalinist mold. Forced industrialization, with five-year plans and a stress on heavy industry, lurched forward without regard for human costs. The collectivization of agriculture began.

Only Josip Tito (1892–1980), the popular resistance leader and Communist chief of Yugoslavia, was able to resist Soviet domination successfully. Tito openly broke with Stalin in 1948, and since

Frenz: Pink Snow   This lighthearted rendition of traditional Russian themes hardly seems a threat to the Stalinist state. Yet it failed to conform to the official style of socialist realism and thus was suppressed along with a host of other works during Zhdanov's brutal cultural purge. *(Source: Sovfoto)*

there was no Russian army in Yugoslavia, he got away with it. Yugoslavia thrived until it began to break apart in the late 1980s (see pages 1209–1210). Tito's successful proclamation of Communist independence led the infuriated and humiliated Stalin to re-enact the great show trials of the 1930s (see page 1063). Popular Communist leaders in eastern Europe who, like Tito, had led the resistance against Germany were thus purged as Stalin sought to create absolutely obedient instruments of domination in eastern Europe.

Reform and De-Stalinization

In 1953 the aging Stalin finally died, and the dictatorship that he had built began to change. Even as Stalin's heirs struggled for power, they realized that reforms were necessary because of the widespread fear and hatred of Stalin's political terrorism. The power of the secret police was curbed, and gradually many of the forced-labor camps were closed. Change was also necessary for economic reasons. Agriculture was in bad shape, and shortages of consumer goods were discouraging hard work and initiative. Moreover, Stalin's belligerent foreign policy had led directly to a strong Western alliance, which isolated the Soviet Union.

On the question of just how much change should be permitted, the Communist leadership was badly split. Conservatives wanted to make as few changes as possible. Reformers, who were led by Nikita Khrushchev, argued for major innovations. Khrushchev (1894–1971) had joined the party as an uneducated coal miner in 1918 at twenty-four and had risen steadily to a high-level position in the 1930s. By 1955 he was emerging as the new ruler.

To strengthen his position and that of his fellow reformers within the party, Khrushchev launched an all-out attack on Stalin and his crimes at a closed session of the Twentieth Party Congress in 1956. In gory detail he described to the startled Communist delegates how Stalin had tortured and murdered thousands of loyal Communists, how he had trusted Hitler completely and bungled the country's defense, and how he had "supported the glorification of his own person with all conceivable methods." Khrushchev's "secret speech" was read to Communist party meetings throughout the country, and it strengthened the reform movement.

The liberalization—or *de-Stalinization,* as it was called in the West—of the Soviet Union was genuine. The Communist party jealously maintained its monopoly on political power, but Khrushchev shook up the party and brought in new members. Some resources were shifted from heavy industry and the military toward consumer goods and agriculture, and Stalinist controls over workers were relaxed. The Soviet Union's very low standard of living finally began to improve and continued to rise substantially throughout the booming 1960s.

De-Stalinization created great ferment among writers and intellectuals who hungered for cultural freedom. The poet Boris Pasternak (1890–1960) finished his great novel *Doctor Zhivago* in 1956. Published in the West but not in Russia, *Doctor Zhivago* is both a literary masterpiece and a powerful challenge to communism. It tells the story of a prerevolutionary intellectual who rejects the violence and brutality of the revolution of 1917 and the Stalinist years. Even as he is destroyed, he triumphs because of his humanity and Christian spirit. Pasternak was denounced—but he was not shot. Other talented writers followed Pasternak's lead, and courageous editors let the sparks fly.

The writer Alexander Solzhenitsyn (b. 1918) created a sensation when his *One Day in the Life of Ivan Denisovich* was published in the Soviet Union in 1962. Solzhenitsyn's novel portrays in grim detail life in a Stalinist concentration camp—a life to which Solzhenitsyn himself had been unjustly condemned—and is a damning indictment of the Stalinist past.

Khrushchev also de-Stalinized Soviet foreign policy. "Peaceful coexistence" with capitalism was possible, he argued, and great wars were not inevitable. Khrushchev even made concessions, agreeing in 1955 to real independence for a neutral Austria after ten long years of Allied occupation. Thus there was considerable relaxation of cold war tensions between 1955 and 1957. At the same time, Khrushchev began wooing the new nations of Asia and Africa—even if they were not communist—with promises and aid.

De-Stalinization stimulated rebelliousness in the eastern European satellites. Having suffered in silence under Stalin, Communist reformers and the masses were quickly emboldened to seek much greater liberty and national independence. Poland took the lead in 1956, when extensive rioting brought a new government that managed to win greater autonomy.

Hungary experienced a real and tragic revolution. Led by students and workers—the classic urban revolutionaries—the people of Budapest installed a liberal Communist reformer as their new chief in October 1956. Soviet troops were forced to leave the country. But after the new government promised free elections and renounced Hungary's military alliance with Moscow, the Russian leaders ordered an invasion and crushed the national and democratic revolution. Fighting was bitter until the end, for the Hungarians hoped that the United States would come to their aid. When this did not occur, most people in eastern Europe concluded that their only hope was to strive for small domestic gains while following Russia obediently in foreign affairs.

Brezhnev and Stagnation

By late 1962, opposition in party circles to Khrushchev's policies was strong, and within two years Khrushchev fell in a bloodless palace revolution. Under Leonid Brezhnev (1906–1982), the Soviet Union began a period of stagnation and limited *re-Stalinization.* The basic reason for this development was that Khrushchev's Communist colleagues saw de-Stalinization as a dangerous, two-sided threat. How could Khrushchev denounce the dead dictator without eventually denouncing and perhaps even arresting his still-powerful henchmen? Moreover, the widening campaign of de-Stalinization posed a clear threat to the dictatorial authority of the party. It was producing growing, perhaps uncontrollable, criticism of the whole communist system. The party had to tighten up while there was still time. Khrushchev had to go.

Another reason for conservative opposition was that Khrushchev's policy toward the West was erratic and ultimately unsuccessful. In 1958 he ordered the Western allies to evacuate West Berlin within six months. In response, the allies reaffirmed their unity, and Khrushchev backed down. Then in 1961, as relations with communist China deteriorated dramatically, Khrushchev ordered the East Germans to build a wall between East and West Berlin. After the recently elected U.S. president, John F. Kennedy, acquiesced to the construction of the Berlin Wall, an emboldened Khrushchev ordered missiles with nuclear warheads installed in Fidel Castro's communist Cuba in 1962. President Kennedy countered with a naval blockade of Cuba. After a tense diplomatic crisis, Khrushchev agreed to remove the Soviet missiles in return for American pledges not to disturb Castro's regime. Khrushchev looked like a bumbling buffoon; his influence, already slipping, declined rapidly after the Cuban fiasco.

After Brezhnev and his supporters took over in 1964, they started talking quietly of Stalin's "good points" and ignoring his crimes. This change informed Soviet citizens that further liberalization could not be expected at home. Soviet leaders, determined never to suffer Khrushchev's humiliation in the face of American nuclear superiority, also launched a massive arms buildup. Yet Brezhnev and company proceeded cautiously in the mid-1960s.

In the wake of Khrushchev's reforms, the 1960s brought modest liberalization and more consumer goods to eastern Europe, as well as somewhat greater national autonomy, especially in Poland and Romania. In January 1968, the reform elements in the Czechoslovak Communist party gained a majority and voted out the long-time Stalinist leader in favor of Alexander Dubček (b. 1921), whose new government launched dramatic reforms.

Educated in Moscow, Dubček was a dedicated Communist. But he and his allies believed that they could reconcile genuine socialism with personal freedom and internal party democracy. Thus local decision making by trade unions, managers, and consumers replaced rigid bureaucratic planning. Censorship was relaxed, and the reform program proved enormously popular.

Although Dubček remembered the lesson of the Hungarian revolution and constantly proclaimed his loyalty to the Warsaw Pact, the determination of the Czech reformers to build what they called "socialism with a human face" frightened hard-line Communists. These fears were particularly strong in Poland and East Germany, where leaders knew full well that they lacked popular support. Moreover, the Soviet Union feared that a liberalized Czechoslovakia would eventually be drawn to neutralism or even to the democratic West. Thus in August 1968, 500,000 Russian and allied eastern European troops suddenly occupied Czechoslovakia. The Czechs made no attempt to resist militarily, and the arrested Czech leaders surrendered to Soviet demands. The reform program was abandoned, and the Czechoslovak experiment in humanizing communism came to an end. Shortly afterward, Brezhnev declared the so-called Brezhnev Doctrine, according to which the Soviet Union and its allies had the right to intervene in any socialist country whenever they saw the need.

The 1968 invasion of Czechoslovakia was the crucial event of the Brezhnev era, which really lasted beyond the aging leader's death in 1982 until the emergence in 1985 of Mikhail Gorbachev. The invasion demonstrated the determination of the Soviet Union's ruling elite to maintain the status quo in the Soviet bloc. In the U.S.S.R. that determination resulted in further repression, but the Soviet Union appeared quite stable in the 1970s and early 1980s.

A rising standard of living for ordinary people contributed to stability, although the economic crisis of the 1970s greatly slowed the rate of improvement, and long lines and innumerable shortages persisted. The enduring advantages of the elite also reinforced the system. Ambitious individuals still had tremendous incentive to do as the state wished in order to gain access to special, well-stocked stores, attend superior schools, and travel abroad.

Another source of stability was the enduring nationalism of ordinary Russians. Party leaders successfully identified themselves with Russian patriotism, stressing their role in saving the motherland during the Second World War and protecting it now from foreign foes, including eastern European "counter-revolutionaries." Moreover, the politically dominant Great Russians, who constituted only half of the total Soviet population, held through the Communist party the commanding leadership positions in the Soviet Union's non-Russian republics. The Great Russian leaders generally feared that greater freedom might result in demands for autonomy and even independence by non-Russian nationalities. Thus liberalism and democracy appeared as alien and divisive political philosophies that would undermine the U.S.S.R.'s power and achievements.

The strength of the government was expressed in the re-Stalinization of culture and art. Free expression and open protest disappeared. Modest acts of open nonconformity and protest were severely punished—but sophisticated, cunning methods of coercion replaced the uncontrolled terror of the Stalin era. Most frequently, dissidents were blacklisted and thus rendered unable to find a decent job. The most determined but least well known protesters were quietly imprisoned in jails or mental institutions. Celebrated nonconformists such as Solzhenitsyn were permanently expelled from the country. Overall, rule by a self-perpetuating Communist elite apeared to be quite solid in the 1970s and early 1980s.

Beneath the immobility of political life in the Brezhnev era, however, the Soviet Union was experiencing profound changes. As a perceptive British journalist put it in 1986, "The country went through a social revolution while Brezhnev slept."[6] Three aspects of this revolution, which was appreciated by few Western observers at the time, were particularly significant.

First, the growth of the urban population continued rapidly in the 1960s and 1970s. In 1985 two-thirds of all Soviet citizens lived in cities, and one-fourth lived in big cities. This expanding urban population lost its old peasant ways, exchanging them for more education, better job skills, and greater sophistication.

Second, the number of highly trained scientists, managers, and specialists expanded prodigiously, jumping fourfold between 1960 and 1985. Thus the class of well-educated, pragmatic, and self-confident experts, which played such an important role in restructuring industrial societies after the Second World War (see pages 1101–1102), developed rapidly in the Soviet Union.

Third, the education that created expertise also helped foster the growth of Soviet public opinion. Educated people read, discussed, and formed definite ideas about social questions, from environmental pollution to urban transportation. Thus educated urban people increasingly saw themselves as worthy of having a voice in society's decisions, even its political decisions. This change was also part of the quiet transformation that set the stage for the dramatic reforms of the Gorbachev era.

The Gorbachev Era

Fundamental change in Russian history has often come in short, intensive spurts, which contrast vividly with long periods of immobility. So it was with the era of fundamental reforms launched by Mikhail Gorbachev in 1985. Gorbachev's initiatives brought liberalization in the Soviet Union, and they then permitted democracy and national self-determination to triumph spectacularly in the old satellite empire and eventually in the Soviet Union itself.

The Soviet Union's Communist elite seemed safe in the early 1980s from any challenge from below. The Communist party's long-established system of centralized administrative controls stretched downward to provincial cities and from there to factories, neighborhoods, and villages. The party hierarchy continued to manipulate every aspect of national life. Organized opposition was impossible, and average people simply left politics to the bosses.

The massive state and party bureaucracy safeguarded the elite, but it discouraged personal initiative and promoted economic inefficiency and apathy among the masses and the rapidly growing class of well-educated urban experts. Therefore, when the ailing Brezhnev finally died in 1982, efforts were made to improve economic performance and to combat worker absenteeism and high-level corruption. These efforts set the stage for the emergence in 1985 of Mikhail Gorbachev (b. 1931), the most vigorous Soviet leader since Stalin.

Smart, charming, and tough, Gorbachev was also an idealist who believed in communism, though he realized it was failing. He (and his intelligent, influential wife, Raisa, a dedicated professor of Marxist-Leninist thought) wanted to save the Soviet system by improving it with fundamental reforms. And Gorbachev realized full well that success at home required better relations with the West, for the endless waste of the arms race had had a disastrous impact on living standards in the Soviet Union.

In his first year in office, Gorbachev attacked corruption and incompetence in the upper reaches of the bureaucracy, and he consolidated his power by packing the top level of the party with his supporters. He also attacked alcoholism and drunkenness, which were deadly scourges of Soviet society. More basically, he elaborated a series of reform policies designed to revive and even remake the vast Soviet Union.

The first set of reform policies was designed to transform and restructure the economy, which was falling ever further behind the economy of the West and failing to provide for the very real needs of the Soviet population. To accomplish this economic restructuring—this *perestroika*—Gorbachev and his supporters permitted freer prices, more independence for state enterprises, and the setting up of some profit-seeking private cooperatives. But the reforms were rather timid and left the economy stalled between central planning and free-market mechanisms. This lack of success gradually eroded Gorbachev's popular support and that of the Communist party.

Gorbachev's bold and far-reaching campaign "to tell it like it is" was much more successful. Very popular in a country where censorship, dull uniformity, and outright lies had long characterized public discourse, the newfound openness—the *glasnost*—of the government and the media marked an astonishing break with the past. A disaster like the Chernobyl nuclear-reactor accident, which devastated part of the Ukraine and showered Europe with radioactive fallout, was investigated and reported with honesty and painstaking thoroughness. The works of long-banned and vilified Russian émigré writers sold millions of copies in new editions, and denunciations of Stalin and his terror became standard fare in plays and movies. Openness in government pronouncements led rather quickly to something approaching free speech and free expression, a veritable cultural revolution.

Democratization was the third element of Gorbachev's reform. Beginning as an attack on corruption in the Communist party and as an attempt to bring the class of educated experts into the decision-making process, it led to the first free elections in the Soviet Union since 1917. Gorbachev and the party remained in control, but a minority of critical independents were elected in April 1989 to a revitalized Congress of People's Deputies. Many top-ranking Communists who ran unopposed saw themselves defeated as a majority of angry voters struck their names from the ballot.

Democratization also encouraged demands for greater autonomy by non-Russian minorities, especially in the Baltic region and in the Caucasus.

Newly Elected President Mikhail Gorbachev In his acceptance speech before the Supreme Soviet, Gorbachev vowed to assume "all responsibility" for the success or failure of *perestroika*. Previous Soviet parliaments were no more than tools of the Communist party, but this one actively debated and even opposed government programs. (*Source: Vlastimir Shone/Liaison*)

These demands certainly went beyond what Gorbachev had envisaged. In April 1989 troops with sharpened shovels charged into a rally of Georgian separatists in Tbilisi and left twenty dead. But whereas China's Communist leaders brutally massacred similar prodemocracy demonstrators in Beijing (Peking) in June 1989 (see page 1136), Gorbachev drew back from repression. Thus nationalist demands continued to grow in the non-Russian Soviet republics.

Finally, the Soviet leader brought "new political thinking" to the field of foreign affairs—and he acted on it. He withdrew Soviet troops from Afghanistan, encouraged reform movements in Poland and Hungary, and sought to reduce East-West tensions. Of enormous historical importance, Gorbachev pledged to respect the political choices of the peoples of eastern Europe, and he thereby repudiated the Brezhnev Doctrine. By 1989 it seemed that if Gorbachev held to his word, the tragic Soviet occupation of eastern Europe might gradually wither away, taking the long cold war with it.

The Revolutions of 1989

Instead, history accelerated, and 1989 brought a series of largely peaceful revolutions throughout eastern Europe. These revolutions overturned existing communist regimes and led to the formation of provisional governments dedicated to democratic elections, human rights, and national rejuvenation. The face of eastern Europe changed dramatically, almost overnight.

The Polish people led the way. Poland had been an unruly satellite from the beginning, and Stalin said that introducing communism to Poland was like putting a saddle on a cow. Efforts to saddle the cow—really a spirited stallion—had led to widespread riots in 1956. As a result, the Polish Communists dropped efforts to impose Soviet-style collectivization on the peasants and to break the Roman Catholic church. With an independent agriculture and a vigorous church, the Communists failed to monopolize society.

They also failed to manage the economy effectively, and bureaucratic incompetence coupled with worldwide recession had put the economy of Poland into a nosedive by the mid-1970s. Then the "Polish miracle" occurred: Cardinal Karol Wojtyla, archbishop of Cracow, was elected pope, and in June 1979 he returned to his native land to preach the love of Christ and country and the "inalienable rights of man." Pope John Paul II electrified the Polish nation, and the economic crisis became a spiritual crisis as well.

In August 1980, scattered strikes snowballed into a working-class revolt. Led by a feisty electrician and devout Catholic named Lech Walesa, the workers organized a free and democratic trade union that they called "Solidarity." Solidarity became the union of the nation, and cultural and intellectual freedom blossomed in Poland. As economic hardship increased, grassroots radicalism and frustration mounted: a hunger-march banner proclaimed that "A hungry nation can eat its rulers."[7] In response the Communist leader General Wojciech Jaruzelski proclaimed martial law in December 1981 and arrested Solidarity's leaders.

Although outlawed and driven underground, Solidarity maintained its organization, and popular support remained strong and deep under martial law in the 1980s. By 1988 widespread labor unrest, raging inflation, and the refusal of outlawed Solidarity to cooperate with the military government had brought Poland to the brink of economic collapse. Profiting from Gorbachev's tolerant attitude and skillfully mobilizing its forces, Solidarity pressured Poland's frustrated Communist leaders into another round of negotiations that might work out a sharing of power. The subsequent agreement legalized Solidarity again and announced free elections for some seats in the Polish parliament for June 1989. Solidarity won every single contested seat in an overwhelming victory. A month later the editor of Solidarity's weekly newspaper was sworn in as the first noncommunist leader in eastern Europe in a generation. Communism also died in Czechoslovakia in 1989. In December an almost good-humored ousting of Communist bosses occurred in ten short days.

Hungary followed Poland and Czechoslovakia when growing popular resistance forced the Hungarian Communist party to renounce one-party rule and schedule free elections for early 1990. Hungarians gleefully tore down the barbed-wire "iron curtain" that separated Hungary and Austria and opened their border to refugees from East Germany.

As thousands of dissatisfied East Germans began pouring through Hungary on their way to thriving West Germany, growing economic dislocation and huge candlelight demonstrations brought revolution in East Berlin. The Berlin Wall was opened, and people danced for joy atop that grim symbol of the prison state. East Germany's aging Communist leaders were swept aside and in some cases arrested. In general elections in March 1990, a conservative-liberal "Alliance for Germany" defeated the East German Social Democrats and quickly negotiated an economic union on favorable terms with West Germany. In July 1990 a historic agreement between West German Chancellor Helmut Kohl and Gorbachev removed the last obstacles to German unification, which came in October 1990.

Only in Romania was revolution violent and bloody. There the iron-fisted Communist dictator Nicolae Ceausescu, alone among eastern European bosses, ordered his ruthless security forces to slaughter thousands, thereby sparking a classic armed uprising. After Ceausescu's forces were defeated, the tyrant and his wife were captured and executed by a military court. A coalition government emerged to govern the troubled country.

As the 1990s began, the great question then became whether the Soviet Union would follow its former satellites in a popular anticommunist revolution. Near civil war between Armenians and Azerbaijanis in the Caucasus, assertions of independence in the Baltic states, and growing dissatisfaction among the Great Russian masses were all parts of a fluid, unstable political situation. Increasingly, the reform-minded Gorbachev stood as a moderate, besieged by those who wanted revolutionary changes and by hard-line Communists who longed to reverse course and clamp down.

East Germans Escaping to the West   After Hungary allowed more than thirty thousand "vacationing" East Germans to pass into Austria and on to a tumultuous welcome in West Germany, Czechoslovakia followed suit. Hordes of East Germans, like those shown here, converged on the West German embassy in Prague. Then the East German government gave up, opening the Berlin Wall and scheduling free elections. *(Source: BUU/Saussier/Liaison)*

MAP 33.4 The End of the Soviet Union After the attempt in August 1991 to depose Gorbachev failed, an anticommunist revolution swept the Soviet Union. Led by Russia and Boris Yeltsin, the republics that formed the Soviet Union declared their sovereignty and independence. Most of the fifteen republics then formed a loose confederation with an uncertain future, the Commonwealth of Independent States.

In August 1991 a gang of hard-liners kidnapped Gorbachev and his family and tried to seize the Soviet government. The attempted coup collapsed in the face of massive popular resistance, which rallied in Moscow around Boris Yeltsin, the popularly elected president of the Russian Federation. Gorbachev was rescued and returned to power as head of the Soviet Union.

The leaders of the coup wanted to preserve communist power and the multinational Soviet Union, but they succeeded only in destroying both. An anticommunist revolution swept the Russian Federation as the Communist party was outlawed and its property confiscated. Locked in a personal and political duel with Gorbachev, Yeltsin and his liberal allies declared Russia independent

and withdrew from the Soviet Union. All the other Soviet republics followed suit; the Soviet Union—and Gorbachev's job—ceased to exist on December 25, 1991 (Map 33.4). A loose but indispensable confederation of former Soviet republics, named the Commonwealth of Independent States, was established in 1992.

The early 1990s remained turbulent, for three reasons. First, ethnic tensions abounded in the Commonwealth of Independent States. Localized civil war broke out in newly independent Georgia and Armenia. In 1995 civil war spread to Russia itself as Yeltsin ordered the Russian army to attack secessionist Chechnya and destroy the city of Grosny. Second, the Russian economy continued to decline. The result was rapid inflation and intense hardship for millions of ordinary people. Third, ethnic conflict, economic collapse, and political stalemate encouraged millions of dissatisfied Russians to vote against the democratic reforms in the general elections of December 1993. The old communists made a strong comeback, and a flamboyant ultranationalist named Vladimir Zhirinovsky captured a surprisingly large share of the vote. Communist dictatorship was gone, but the ultimate fate of Russia and the states of the old Soviet Union remained uncertain.

THE WESTERN HEMISPHERE

One way to think of what historians used to call the "New World" is as a vigorous offshoot of Western civilization, an offshoot that has gradually developed its own characteristics while retaining European roots. From this perspective can be seen many illuminating parallels and divergences in the histories of Europe and the Americas. After the Second World War, the Western Hemisphere experienced a many-faceted recovery, somewhat similar to that of Europe though it began earlier, especially in Latin America. And after a generation the countries of the New World experienced their own period of turbulence and crisis.

America's Civil Rights Revolution

The Second World War ended the Great Depression in the United States and brought about a great economic boom. Unemployment practically vanished, and the well-being of Americans increased dramatically. Despite fears that peace would bring renewed depression, conversion to a peacetime economy went smoothly. Then, as in western Europe, the U.S. economy proceeded to advance fairly steadily for a long generation.

Prosperity helps explain why postwar domestic politics consisted largely of modest adjustments to the status quo until the 1960s. Truman's upset victory in 1948 demonstrated that Americans had no interest in undoing Roosevelt's social and economic reforms. The Congress proceeded to increase social security benefits, subsidize middle- and lower-class housing, and raise the minimum wage. These and other liberal measures consoli-

dated the New Deal. In 1952 the Republican party and the voters turned to General Dwight D. Eisenhower (1890–1969), a national hero and self-described moderate.

The federal government's only major new undertaking during the Eisenhower years (1952–1960) was the interstate highway system, a suitable symbol of the basic satisfaction of the vast majority. Some Americans feared that the United States was becoming a "blocked society," obsessed with stability and incapable of wholesome change. This feeling contributed in 1960 to the election of the young John F. Kennedy (1917–1963), who promised to "get the country moving again." President Kennedy captured the popular imagination, revitalized the old Roosevelt coalition, and modestly expanded existing liberal legislation before he was struck down by an assassin's bullet in 1963.

Belatedly and reluctantly, complacent postwar America did experience a genuine social revolution: after a long struggle, African Americans (and their white supporters) threw off a deeply entrenched system of segregation, discrimination, and repression. This civil rights movement advanced on several fronts. Eloquent lawyers from the National Association for the Advancement of Colored People (NAACP) challenged school segregation in the courts. In 1954 they won a landmark decision in the Supreme Court, which ruled in *Brown v. Board of Education* that "separate educational facilities are inherently unequal." Blacks effectively challenged institutionalized inequality with bus boycotts, sit-ins, and demonstrations. As civil rights leader Martin Luther King, Jr. (1929–1968), told the white power structure, "We will not hate you, but we will not obey your evil laws."[8]

In key northern states African Americans used their growing political power to gain the support of the liberal wing of the Democratic party. In a liberal landslide, Lyndon Johnson (1908–1973) won the presidential election in 1964. The Civil Rights Act of 1964 categorically prohibited discrimination in public services and on the job. In the follow-up Voting Rights Act of 1965, the federal government firmly guaranteed all blacks the right to vote. By the 1970s, substantial numbers of blacks had been elected to public and private office throughout the southern states, proof positive that dramatic changes had occurred in American race relations.

African Americans enthusiastically supported new social legislation in the mid-1960s. President Johnson solemnly declared "unconditional war on poverty." Congress and the administration created a host of antipoverty projects, such as a domestic peace corps, free preschools for poor children, and community-action programs. Although these programs were directed to all poor Americans—the majority of whom were white—they were also intended to increase economic equality for blacks. Thus the United States promoted in the mid-1960s the kind of fundamental social reform that western Europe had embraced immediately after the Second World War. The United States became more of a welfare state, as government spending for social benefits rose dramatically and approached European levels.

Youth and the Counterculture

Economic prosperity and a more democratic class structure had a powerful impact on youth throughout the Western world. The bulging cohort of youth born after World War II developed a distinctive and very international youth culture. Self-consciously different in the late 1950s, this youth culture became increasingly oppositional in the 1960s, interacting with a revival of leftist thought to create a counterculture that rebelled against parents, authority figures, and the status quo.

Young people in the United States took the lead. American college students in the 1950s were docile and often dismissed as the "Silent Generation," but some young people did revolt against

"I Have a Dream"   August 1963 marked a dramatic climax in the civil rights struggle in the United States. More than 200,000 people gathered at the Lincoln Memorial in Washington, D.C., to hear Martin Luther King, Jr., deliver his greatest address. *(Source: Francis Miller,* Life Magazine, © *Time Warner, Inc.)*

✿ **The Beatles in Concert**   The older generation often saw sexual license and immorality in the group's frank lyrics and suggestive style. But in comparison with all that came after them in the world of pop music, the Beatles were sentimental and wholesome, as this concert scene suggests. *(Source: Fred Ward/Black Star)*

the conformity and boredom of middle-class suburbs. These "young rebels" wore tightly pegged pants and idolized singer Elvis Presley and actor James Dean. The "beat" movement of the late 1950s expanded on the theme of revolt, and Jack Kerouac vividly captured the restless motion of the beatniks in his autobiographical novel *On the Road.* People like Kerouac clustered together in certain urban areas, such as the Haight-Ashbury district of San Francisco or the Near North Side of Chicago. There the young (and the not-so-young) fashioned a highly publicized subculture that blended radical politics, unbridled personal experimentation (with drugs and communal living, for example), and new artistic styles. This subculture quickly spread to major American and western European cities.

Rock music helped tie this international subculture together. Rock grew out of the black music culture of rhythm and blues, which was flavored with country and western to make it more accessible to white teenagers. The mid-1950s signaled a breakthrough: Bill Haley called on record buyers to "Rock Around the Clock," and Elvis Presley

warned them not to step on his "Blue Suede Shoes." In the 1960s the Beatles thrilled millions of young people, often to their parents' dismay. Like Elvis, the Beatles suggested personal and sexual freedom that many older people found disturbing.

It was Bob Dylan, a young folk singer turned rock poet with an electric guitar, who best expressed the radical political as well as cultural aspirations of the "younger generation." In a song that became a rallying cry, Dylan sang that "the times they are a'changing."[9] The song captured the spirit of growing alienation between the generation whose defining experience had been World War II and the generation ready to reject the complacency of the 1950s. Increasing discontent with middle-class conformity and the injustices of racism and imperialism fueled the young leaders of social protest and reflected a growing spirit of rebellion.

Certainly the sexual behavior of young people, or at least some young people, appeared to change dramatically in the 1960s and into the 1970s. More young people engaged in intercourse, and they did so at an earlier age. Perhaps even more significant was the growing tendency of young unmarried people to live together in a separate household on a semipermanent basis, with little thought of getting married or having children. Thus many youths, especially middle-class youths, defied social custom, claiming in effect that the long-standing monopoly of married couples on legitimate sexual unions was dead.

Several factors contributed to the emergence of the international youth culture in the 1960s. First, mass communications and youth travel linked countries and continents together. Second, the postwar baby boom meant that young people became an unusually large part of the population and could therefore exercise exceptional influence on society as a whole. Third, postwar prosperity and greater equality gave young people more purchasing power than ever before. This enabled them to set their own trends and fads in everything from music to chemical stimulants. Common patterns of consumption and behavior fostered generational loyalty. Finally, prosperity meant that good jobs were readily available. Students and young job seekers had little need to fear punishment from strait-laced employers for unconventional behavior.

The youth culture practically fused with the counterculture in opposition to the established order in the late 1960s. Student protesters embraced romanticism and revolutionary idealism, dreaming of complete freedom and simpler, purer societies. The materialistic West was hopelessly rotten, but better societies were being built in the newly independent countries of Asia and Africa, or so many young radicals believed. Thus the Vietnam War took on special significance. Many politically active students in the United States and Europe believed that the older generation in general and American leaders in particular were fighting an immoral and imperialistic war against a small and heroic people that wanted only national unity and human dignity. As the war in Vietnam intensified, so did worldwide student opposition to it.

The Vietnam Trauma and Beyond

President Johnson wanted to go down in history as a master reformer and a healer of old wounds. Instead he opened new ones with the Vietnam War.

Although many student radicals believed that imperialism was the main cause, American involvement in Vietnam was more clearly a product of the cold war and the ideology of containment (see page 0000). From the late 1940s on, most Americans and their leaders viewed the world in terms of a constant struggle to stop the spread of communism. As Europe began to revive and China established a communist government in 1949, efforts to contain communism shifted to Asia. The bloody Korean War (1950–1953) ended in stalemate, but the United States did succeed in preventing a communist government in South Korea. After the defeat of the French in Indochina in 1954 (see page 1148), the Eisenhower administration refused to sign the Geneva accords that temporarily divided the country into two zones pending national unification by means of free elections. President Eisenhower then acquiesced in the refusal of the anticommunist South Vietnamese government to accept the verdict of elections and provided it with military aid. President Kennedy greatly increased the number of American "military advisers" to sixteen thousand.

After successfully depicting his opponent, Barry Goldwater, as a trigger-happy extremist in a nuclear age and resoundingly winning the 1964 election in large part on a peace platform, President Johnson greatly expanded the American role in the Vietnam conflict. As Johnson explained to his ambassador in Saigon, "I am not going to lose Vietnam. I am not going to be the President who saw Southeast Asia go the way China went."[10] American strategy was to "escalate" the war sufficiently to break the will of the North Vietnamese and their southern allies without resorting to "overkill" that might risk war with the entire communist bloc. Thus South Vietnam received massive military aid; American forces in the South gradually grew to a half-million men; and the United States bombed North Vietnam with ever-greater intensity. But there was no invasion of the North or naval blockade. In the end, the American strategy of limited warfare backfired. It was the Americans themselves who grew weary and the American leadership that cracked.

The undeclared war in Vietnam, fought nightly on American television, eventually divided the nation. Initial support was strong. The politicians, the media, and the population as a whole saw the war as part of a legitimate defense against communist totalitarianism in all poor countries. But an antiwar movement quickly emerged on college campuses, where the prospect of being drafted to fight savage battles in Asian jungles made male stomachs churn. In October 1965 student protesters joined forces with old-line socialists, New Left intellectuals, and pacifists in antiwar demonstrations in fifty American cities. By 1967 a growing number of critics denounced the war as a criminal intrusion into a complex and distant civil war.

Criticism reached a crescendo after the Vietcong Tet Offensive against major cities in South Vietnam in January 1968. The attack was a military failure, but it resulted in heavy losses on both sides, and it belied Washington's claims that victory in South Vietnam was in sight. The U.S. critics of the Vietnam War quickly interpreted the bloody combat as a decisive American defeat. America's leaders lost heart, and in 1968 President Johnson called for negotiations with North Vietnam and announced that he would not stand for re-election.

Elected by a razor-slim margin in 1968, Richard Nixon (1913–1994) sought to disengage America gradually from Vietnam and the accompanying national crisis. Intensifying the continuous bombardment of the enemy while simultaneously pursuing peace talks with the North Vietnamese, President Nixon suspended the draft, so hated on college campuses, and cut American forces in Vietnam from 550,000 to 24,000 in four years. Moreover, he launched a flank attack in diplomacy. He journeyed to China in 1972 and reached a spectacular if limited reconciliation with the People's Republic of China. In doing so, Nixon took advantage of China's growing fears of the Soviet Union and undermined North Vietnam's position.

Fortified by the overwhelming endorsement of the voters in his 1972 electoral triumph, President Nixon and Secretary of State Henry Kissinger finally reached a peace agreement with North Vietnam in 1973. The agreement allowed remaining American forces to complete their withdrawal, and the United States reserved the right to resume bombing if the accords were broken. Fighting declined markedly in South Vietnam. The storm of crisis in the United States seemed past.

On the contrary, the country reaped the Watergate whirlwind. Like some other recent American presidents, Nixon authorized domestic spying activities that went beyond the law. Going further than his predecessors, Nixon authorized special units to use various illegal means to stop the leaking of government documents to the press. One such group broke into the Democratic party headquarters in Washington's Watergate complex in June 1972 and was promptly arrested. Nixon and many of his assistants then tried to hush up the bungled job, but the media and the machinery of congressional investigation eventually exposed the administration's web of lies and lawbreaking. In 1974 a beleaguered Nixon was forced to resign in disgrace.

The consequences of renewed political crisis flowing from the Watergate affair were profound. First, Watergate resulted in a major shift of power away from the presidency toward Congress, especially in foreign affairs. Therefore, as American aid to South Vietnam diminished in 1973 and as an emboldened North Vietnam launched a general invasion against South Vietnamese armies in early 1974, Congress refused to permit any American military response. After more than thirty-five years of battle, the Vietnamese communists unified their country in 1975 as a harsh dictatorial state—a second consequence of the U.S. crisis. Third, the belated fall of South Vietnam in the wake of Watergate shook America's postwar confidence and left the country divided and uncertain about its proper role in world affairs.

One alternative to the badly damaged policy of containing communism was the policy of *détente,* or progressive relaxation of cold war tensions. Nixon's phased withdrawal from Vietnam was sold as part of détente. Détente reached its high point when all European nations (except isolationist Albania), the United States, and Canada signed the Final Act of the Helsinki Conference in 1975. Thirty-five nations agreed that Europe's existing political frontiers could not be changed by force, and they solemnly accepted numerous provisions guaranteeing the human rights and political freedoms of their citizens.

Optimistic hopes for détente in international relations gradually faded in the later 1970s. Brezhnev's Soviet Union ignored the human rights provisions of the Helsinki agreement, and East-West political competition remained very much alive outside Europe. Many Americans became convinced that the Soviet Union was taking advantage of détente, steadily building up its military might and pushing for political gains and revolutions in Africa, Asia, and Latin America. The Soviet invasion of Afghanistan in December 1979, which was designed to save an increasingly unpopular Marxist regime, was especially alarming. Many Americans feared that the oil-rich states of the Persian Gulf would be next, and once again they looked to the

✳ **Margaret Thatcher and Ronald Reagan**   The British prime minister and American president, seen here in the White House garden, worked well together, united by a fierce determination to oppose communism abroad and to reduce spending on social programs at home. *(Source: Brad Markel/Liaison)*

Atlantic alliance and military might to thwart communist expansion.

Jimmy Carter (b. 1924), elected president in 1976, tried to lead the Atlantic alliance beyond verbal condemnation, but among the European allies only Great Britain supported the American policy of economic sanctions. The alliance showed the same lack of concerted action when Solidarity rose in Poland. Some observers concluded that the alliance had lost the will to think and act decisively in dealings with the Soviet bloc.

The Atlantic alliance endured, however. The U.S. military buildup launched by Jimmy Carter in his last years in office was greatly accelerated by Ronald Reagan (b. 1911), who was swept into office in 1980 by a wave of patriotism and economic discontent. The new American leadership acted as if the military balance had tipped in favor of the Soviet Union, which President Reagan anathema-

tized as the "evil empire." Increasing defense spending enormously, the Reagan administration concentrated especially on nuclear arms and an expanded navy as keys to American power in the post-Vietnam age.

The broad swing of the historical pendulum toward greater conservatism in the 1980s gave Reagan invaluable allies in western Europe. In Great Britain a strong-willed Margaret Thatcher (see page 1109) worked well with Reagan and was a strong advocate for a revitalized Atlantic alliance. After a distinctly pro-American Helmut Kohl (b. 1930) came to power with the conservative Christian Democrats in 1982, West Germany and the United States once again effectively coordinated military and political policy toward the Soviet bloc.

Passing from détente to confusion to regeneration, the Atlantic alliance bent but did not break. In maintaining the alliance, the Western nations gave indirect support to ongoing efforts to liberalize authoritarian communist eastern Europe and probably helped convince Mikhail Gorbachev that endless cold war conflict was foolish and dangerous.

Economic Nationalism in Latin America

Although the countries of Latin America exhibit striking differences, the growth of economic nationalism has been a major development throughout the region in the twentieth century. As the early nineteenth century saw Spanish and Portuguese colonies win wars of political independence, so has much of recent history been a quest for genuine economic independence through local control and industrialization.

To understand the rise of economic nationalism, one must remember that Latin American countries developed as producers of foodstuffs and raw materials that were exported to Europe and the United States in return for manufactured goods and capital investment. This exchange brought considerable economic development but exacted a heavy price: neocolonialism (see pages 924–926). Latin America became very dependent on foreign markets, products, and investments. Industry did not develop, and large landowners tied to production for the world market profited most from economic development and thus enhanced their social and political power.

The old international division of labor, badly shaken by World War I, was destroyed by the Great Depression. Prices and exports of Latin American commodities collapsed as Europe and the United States drastically reduced their purchases and raised tariffs to protect domestic products. With their foreign sales plummeting, Latin American countries could not buy the industrial goods that they needed from abroad.

Latin America suffered the full force of the global depression. Especially in the largest Latin American countries—Argentina, Brazil, Chile, and Mexico—the result was a profound shift toward economic nationalism after 1930. The most popularly based governments worked to reduce foreign influence and gain control of their own economies and natural resources. They energetically promoted national industry by means of high tariffs, government grants, and even state enterprise. They favored the lower middle and urban working classes with social benefits and higher wages in order to increase their purchasing power and gain their support. These efforts at recovery gathered speed during the Second World War and were fairly successful. By the late 1940s, the factories of Argentina, Brazil, and Chile could generally satisfy domestic consumer demand for the products of light industry. In the 1950s, some countries began moving into heavy industry.

Economic nationalism and the rise of industry are particularly striking in the two largest and most influential countries, Mexico and Brazil. These countries account for half of the population of Latin America.

The spasmodic, often-chaotic Mexican Revolution of 1910 overthrew the elitist, upper-class rule of the tyrant Porfirio Díaz and culminated in 1917 in a new constitution. This radical nationalistic document called for universal suffrage, massive land reform, benefits for labor, and strict control of foreign capital. Actual progress was quite modest until 1934, when a charismatic young Indian from a poor family, Lázaro Cárdenas, became president and dramatically revived the languishing revolution. Under Cárdenas, many large estates were divided up among small farmers or returned undivided to Indian communities.

Meanwhile, state-supported Mexican businessmen built many small factories to meet domestic needs. The government also championed the cause of industrial workers. In 1938, when Mexican workers became locked in a bitter dispute with British and American oil companies, Cárdenas nationalized the petroleum industry—to the amazement of a world unaccustomed to such bold action. Finally, the 1930s saw the flowering of a distinctive Mexican culture, which proudly embraced its long-despised Indian past and gloried in the modern national revolution.

In 1940 the official, semi-authoritarian party that has governed Mexico continuously since the revolution selected the first of a series of more moderate presidents. These presidents used the full power of the state to promote industrialization through a judicious mixture of public, private, and even foreign enterprise. Following the postwar trend in Europe and the United States, the Mexican economy grew rapidly, at about 6 percent per year from the early 1940s to the late 1960s. However, in Mexico, unlike Europe and the United States, the upper and middle classes reaped the lion's share of the benefits.

In Brazil, politics was dominated by the coffee barons and by regional rivalries after the fall of Brazil's monarchy in 1889 (see page 922). Regional rivalries and deteriorating economic conditions allowed a military revolt led by Getúlio Vargas to seize control of the federal government in 1930. Vargas, who proved to be a consummate politician, fragmented the opposition and established a mild dictatorship that lasted until 1945. His rule was generally popular, combining effective economic nationalism and moderate social reform.

Vargas and his allies set out to industrialize Brazil and gain economic independence. While the national coffee board used mountains of surplus coffee beans to fire railroad locomotives, the government supported Brazilian manufacturers with high tariffs, generous loans, and labor peace encouraged by new social legislation: workers received shorter hours, pensions, health and accident insurance, paid vacations, and other benefits. Finally, Vargas shrewdly upheld the nationalist cause in his relations with the giant to the north. Brazil was modernizing rapidly.

Modernization continued for the next fifteen years. The economy boomed. Presidential politics was re-established, though the military kept a watchful eye for extremism among the civilian politicians. Economic nationalism was especially vigorous under the flamboyant President Juscelino Kubitschek. Between 1956 and 1960, the government borrowed heavily from international bankers to promote industry and built the new capital of Brasília in the midst of a wilderness. Kubitschek's slogan was "Fifty Years' Progress in Five," and he meant it.

The Brazilian and Mexican formula of national economic development, varying degrees of electoral competition, and social reform was shared by some other Latin American countries, notably Argentina and Chile. By the late 1950s, optimism was widespread though cautious. Economic and social progress seemed to be bringing less violent, more democratic politics to the region. These expectations were shaken by the Cuban Revolution.

The Cuban Revolution

Achieving nominal independence in 1898 as a result of the Spanish-American War, Cuba was for many years virtually an American protectorate. The Cuban constitution gave the United States the le-

gal right to intervene in Cuban affairs, a right that was frequently exercised until President Franklin Roosevelt renounced it in 1934. Partly because the American army had often been the real power on the island, Cuba's political institutions were weak and Cuban politicians were corrupt. Nevertheless, Cuba was one of Latin America's most prosperous countries by the 1950s, although its sugar-and-tourist economy was completely dependent on the United States and it displayed the enormous differences between rich and poor that were typical of Latin America.

Fidel Castro (b. 1927), a magnetic leader with the gift of oratory, managed to unify all opposition elements in a revolutionary front, and his guerrilla forces triumphed in late 1958. Castro had promised a "real" revolution, and it soon became clear that "real" meant "communist." Wealthy Cubans fled to Miami, and the middle class began to follow. Cuban relations with the Eisenhower administration deteriorated rapidly. Thus in April 1961 the newly elected U.S. president, John Kennedy, went ahead with a pre-existing CIA plan to use Cuban exiles to topple Castro. But the Kennedy administration abandoned the exiles as soon as they were put ashore at the Bay of Pigs, and the invaders were quickly captured.

The Bay of Pigs invasion—a triumph for Castro and a humiliating fiasco for the United States—freed Castro to build his version of a communist society. Political life in Cuba featured "anti-imperialism," an alliance with the Soviet bloc, the dictatorship of the party, and a Castro cult. Revolutionary enthusiasm was genuine among party activists, much of Cuba's youth, and some of the masses some of the time. Prisons and emigration silenced opposition. The economy was characterized by state ownership, collective farms, and Soviet trade and aid. Early efforts to industrialize ran aground, and sugar production continued to dominate the economy. Socially, the Castro regime pursued equality and the creation of a new socialist personality. In short, the communism of eastern Europe came to the Americas.

The failure of the United States to derail Castro probably encouraged Khrushchev to start putting nuclear missiles in Cuba and in turn led directly to the most serious East-West crisis since the Korean War. The Soviets backed down (see page 0000), but Castro's survival heightened both hopes and fears that similar revolutions could spread throughout Latin America. In the United States, such cold war fears led in 1961 to a pledge of $10 billion in aid over ten years to a new hemispheric "Alliance for Progress." The Alliance was intended to promote long-term economic development and social reform, which American liberals assumed would immunize the rest of Latin America from the Cuban disease.

Authoritarianism and Democracy in Latin America

U.S. aid contributed modestly to continued Latin American economic development in the 1960s, although population growth canceled out two-thirds of the increase on a per capita basis. Democratic social reforms—the other half of the Alliance for Progress formula—proceeded slowly, however. Instead, the era following the Cuban Revolution saw increasing conflict between leftist movements and ruling elites contending for power. In most countries the elites and their military allies won the struggle, but at the cost of imposing a new kind of conservative authoritarianism as their collective response to the social and economic crisis. By the late 1970s, only four Latin American countries—Costa Rica, Venezuela, Colombia, and Mexico—retained some measure of democratic government. Brazil, Argentina, and Chile represented the general trend.

Influential Brazil led the way. Intense political competition in the early 1960s prompted President João Goulart to swing to the left to gain fresh support. Castroism appeared to spread in the impoverished northeast, and mass meetings of leftists were answered by huge demonstrations of conservatives. Meanwhile, Goulart called for radical change, proposing that the great landed estates be broken up and that Brazil's many illiterates receive the right to vote. When Goulart and his followers appeared ready to use force to implement their program, army leaders took over in 1964. The right-wing military government banned political parties and ruled by decree. Industrialization and urbanization went forward under military rule, but the gap between rich and poor widened as well.

In Argentina, the military had intervened in 1955 to oust the dictatorial populist and economic nationalist Juan Perón, but it had restored elected government. Then, worried by a Peronist revival and heartened by the Brazilian example, the army took control in 1966 and again in 1976 after a brief civilian interlude. Each military takeover was followed by an escalation of repression. Culturally and economically advanced Argentina became a brutal military dictatorship.

Events in Chile were truly tragic. Chile has a population of predominantly European origin and a long tradition of democracy and moderate reform. Thus when Salvador Allende, a doctor and the Marxist head of a coalition of Communists, Socialists, and Radicals, won a plurality of 36 percent of the vote in fair elections in 1970, he was duly elected president by the Congress. Allende completed the nationalization of the American-owned copper companies—the great majority of Chileans had already embraced economic nationalism—and proceeded to socialize private industry, accelerate the breakup of landed estates, and radicalize the poor.

Marxism in action evoked a powerful backlash in Chile. The middle class struck back, and by 1973 Chile seemed headed for civil war. Then, with widespread conservative support and strong U.S. backing, the traditionally impartial army struck in a well-organized coup. Allende died, probably murdered, and thousands of his supporters were arrested, or worse. As in Argentina, the military imposed a harsh despotism.

The military governments that revived antidemocratic authoritarianism in Latin America, with Washington's support, blocked not only the Marxist and socialist program but most liberal and moderate reform as well. Yet the new military governments grew out of political crises that threatened national unity as well as the upper classes and big business. In such circumstances, the politically conscious officer corps saw the military as the only institution capable of preventing chaos. Moreover, the new authoritarians were determined modernizers. Eager to catch up with the more advanced countries, they were often deeply committed to nationalism, industrialization, technology, and some modest social progress. They even promised free elections in the future.

That time came in the 1980s, when another democratic wave gained momentum throughout Latin America. The three Andean nations—Peru, Bolivia, and Ecuador—led the way with the reestablishment of elected governments, all of which were committed in varying degrees to genuine social reform. In Argentina, the military government gradually lost almost all popular support because of its "dirty war" against its own citizens, in which it imprisoned, tortured, and murdered thousands whom it arbitrarily accused of opposing the regime. In 1982, in a desperate gamble to rally the people around the nationalist flag, Argentina's military rulers sent nine thousand troops to seize the Falkland (or Malvinas) Islands (see Map 28.2, page 920) from Great Britain. But the British retook the islands in a brief war, routing Argentina's poorly led troops and forcing its humiliated generals to schedule national elections. The democratically elected government prosecuted the former military rulers for their crimes, reformed the currency, and laid solid foundations for liberty and political democracy.

In 1985, the Brazilian military also turned over power to an elected government. Relatively successful in its industrialization effort, Brazil's military government had proved unable (or unwilling) to improve the social and economic position of the masses. After twenty-one years of rule the military leaders were ready to let civilian politicians have a try. Chile also turned from right-wing military dictatorship to elected government. Thus by the second half of the 1980s 94 percent of Latin America's population lived under regimes that guaranteed elections and civil liberties.

The most dramatic developments in Central America occurred in Nicaragua. In 1979, a broad coalition of liberals, socialists, and Marxist revolutionaries drove long-time dictator Anastasio So-

Return to Democracy in Argentina Elected president in 1983 after seven years of brutal military rule, Raul Alfonsín stands with sash and rod—the symbols of authority—to swear the presidential oath of office in Buenos Aires. Alfonsín's inauguration gave rise to great popular rejoicing. *(Source: Urraca/Sygma)*

moza from power. The Somoza family had relied on solid U.S. support in its four-decade dictatorship. The new leaders, known as the Sandinistas, wanted genuine political and economic independence from the United States, as well as thoroughgoing land reform, some state ownership of industry, and friendly ties with communist countries. These policies infuriated the Reagan administration, which tried to undermine the Sandinista government. The Nicaraguan economy collapsed, and the popularity of the Sandinista government eventually declined. Then, after a decade of rule, the Sandinistas accepted free elections and stepped down when they were defeated by a coalition of opposition parties. In 1994 Haiti, one of the last repressive dictatorships in the Americas, also established democratic rule, with the help of U.S. military intervention.

As the 1990s progressed, Latin America's popularly elected governments boldly extended greater liberty from the political to the economic sphere. Beginning with Argentina in 1989 and followed by Chile, Mexico, and Brazil, governments moved from tariff protection and economic nationalism toward free markets and international trade, revitalizing their economies and registering solid gains. Mexico, for example, turned from high tariffs to free trade with its powerful northern neighbors, as in 1994 it joined with the United States and Canada in the North American Free Trade Agreement, commonly known as NAFTA. Building on NAFTA and the Southern Common Market, which already linked Brazil, Argentina, Paraguay, and Uruguay, a summit meeting of thirty-four governments agreed in Miami in December 1994 to forge a vast free-trade area incorporating every country of the Americas by 2005. Latin Americans were eager to trade freely with the United States, confident they could prosper by competing successfully with the hemisphere's largest economic power.

SUMMARY

The postwar recovery of western Europe and the Americas was a memorable achievement in the long, uneven course of Western civilization. The transition from imperialism to decolonization proceeded rapidly and without serious damage to western Europe. Genuine political democracy gained unprecedented strength in the West, and economic progress and social reforms improved the lives of ordinary citizens.

Postwar developments in eastern Europe displayed both similarities to and differences from developments in western Europe and the Americas. Perhaps the biggest difference was that Stalin imposed harsh one-party rule in the lands occupied by his armies, which led to the long and bitter cold war. Nevertheless, the Soviet Union became more liberal and less dictatorial under Khrushchev, and in the 1950s and 1960s the standard of living in the Soviet Union improved markedly.

In the late 1960s and early 1970s, Europe and the Americas entered a new and turbulent time of crisis. Many nations, from France to Czechoslovakia and from Argentina to the United States, experienced major political difficulties, as social conflicts and ideological battles divided peoples and shook governments. Beginning with the oil shocks of the 1970s, severe economic problems added to the turmoil. Yet in western Europe and North America the welfare system held firm, and both democracy and the movement toward European unity successfully passed through the storm.

Elsewhere the response to political and economic crisis sent many countries veering off toward repression. The communist system in eastern Europe was tightened up in the Brezhnev years, and a new kind of conservative authoritarianism arose in most of Latin America. Then, in the 1980s, both regions turned toward free elections and civil liberties, most spectacularly so in the east European revolutions of 1989. Like eastern Europe, Latin America also moved toward freer markets and embraced international trade and foreign investment, thereby abandoning its long-standing commitment to economic nationalism. The remarkable result of all these parallel developments was that differences in political organization, human rights, and economic philosophy were less pronounced in the reuniting Western civilization of the 1990s than at any time since the guns of 1914 had opened a new era.

NOTES

1. Quoted in N. Graebner, *Cold War Diplomacy, 1945–1960* (Princeton, N.J.: Van Nostrand, 1962), p. 17.
2. Ibid.

3. Quoted in J. Hennessy, *Economic "Miracles"* (London: André Deutsch, 1964), p. 5.

4. *Wall Street Journal,* June 25, 1985, p. 1.

5. Quoted in D. Treadgold, *Twentieth Century Russia,* 5th ed. (Boston: Houghton Mifflin, 1981), p. 442.

6. M. Walker, *The Waking Giant: Gorbachev's Russia* (New York: Pantheon Books, 1987), p. 175.

7. T. G. Ash, *The Polish Revolution: Solidarity* (New York: Scribner's, 1983), p. 186.

8. Quoted in S. E. Morison et al., *A Concise History of the American Republic* (New York: Oxford University Press, 1977), p. 697.

9. Quoted in N. Cantor, *Twentieth Century Culture: Modernism to Deconstruction* (New York: Peter Lang, 1988), p. 252.

10. Quoted in Morison et al., *A Concise History of the American Republic,* p. 735.

Suggested Reading

A good introduction to international politics is provided by W. Keylor, *The Twentieth Century: An International History* (1984), which has extensive, up-to-date bibliographies. An excellent way to approach wartime diplomacy is through the accounts of the statesmen involved. Great leaders and matchless stylists, both Winston Churchill and Charles de Gaulle have written histories of the war in the form of memoirs. Other interesting memoirs are those of Harry Truman (1958); Dwight Eisenhower, *Crusade in Europe* (1948); and Dean Acheson, *Present at the Creation* (1969), a beautifully written defense of American foreign policy in the early cold war. W. A. Williams, *The Tragedy of American Diplomacy* (1962), and W. La Feber, *America, Russia, and the Cold War* (1967), claim, on the contrary, that the United States was primarily responsible for the conflict with the Soviet Union. Two other important studies focusing on American policy are J. Gaddis, *The United States and the Origins of the Cold War* (1972), and D. Yergin, *Shattered Peace: The Origins of the Cold War and the National Security Council* (1977). V. Mastny's thorough investigation of Stalin's war aims, *Russia's Road to the Cold War* (1979), is recommended.

Three important general studies with extensive bibliographies are W. Laqueur, *Europe in Our Time: A History, 1945–1992* (1992); P. Johnson, *Modern Times: The World from the Twenties to the Eighties* (1983); and C. Black, *Rebirth: A History of Europe Since World War II* (1992). P. Lane, *Europe Since 1945: An Introduction* (1985), is an interesting combination of text and political documents. I. Unger and D. Unger, *Postwar America: The United States Since 1945*

(1989), and W. Leuchtenberg, *In the Shadow of FDR: From Harry Truman to Ronald Reagan* (1989), ably discuss developments in the United States. Postwar economic and social developments are analyzed in G. Ambrosius and W. Hibbard, *A Social and Economic History of Twentieth-Century Europe* (1989), and F. Tipton and R. Aldrich, *An Economic and Social History of Europe from 1939 to the Present* (1986).

The culture and politics of protest are provocatively analyzed in H. Hughes, *Sophisticated Rebels: The Political Culture of European Dissent, 1968–1987* (1988), and W. Hampton, *Guerrilla Minstrels: John Lennon, Joe Hill, Woody Guthrie, Bob Dylan* (1986). The work by N. Cantor, cited in the Notes is stimulating general cultural history. Two outstanding works on France are J. Ardagh, *The New French Revolution* (1969), which puts the momentous social changes after 1945 in human terms, and S. Bernstein, *The Republic of de Gaulle, 1958–1969* (1993). On Germany, H. Turner, *The Two Germanies Since 1945: East and West* (1987), and R. Dahrendorf, *Society and Democracy in Germany* (1971), are recommended. The spiritual dimension of West German recovery is probed by Gunter Grass in his world-famous novel *The Tin Drum* (1963). W. Laqueur, *The Germans* (1985), is a recent journalistic report by a well-known historian. A. Marwick, *British Society Since 1945* (1982), is good on postwar developments; P. Jenkins, *Mrs. Thatcher's Revolution: The End of the Socialist Era* (1988), is a provocative critique. Two outstanding books on the Vietnam War are N. Sheehan, *A Bright and Shining Lie: John Paul Vann and America in Vietnam* (1988), and A. Short, *The Origins of the Vietnam War* (1989). On feminism and the women's movement, see N. Cott, *The Grounding of Modern Feminism* (1987). J. Lovenduski, *Women and European Politics: Contemporary Feminism and Public Policy* (1986), provides an extremely useful comparative study of similar developments in different countries.

Z. Brzezinski, *The Grand Failure: The Birth and Death of Communism in the Twentieth Century* (1989), is a readable overview by a leading American scholar. H. Seton-Watson, *The East European Revolution* (1965), is a good history of the communization of eastern Europe, and S. Fischer-Galati, ed., *Eastern Europe in the Sixties* (1963), discusses early developments. P. Zinner, *Revolution in Hungary* (1962), is excellent on the tragic events of 1956. I. Svitak, *The Czechoslovak Experiment, 1968–1969* (1971), and Z. Zeman, *Prague Spring* (1969), are good on Czechoslovakia. T. Ash, cited in the Notes, is the best book on Solidarity, and M. Kaufman, *Mad Dreams, Saving Graces: Poland, a Nation in Conspiracy* (1989), is recommended. J. Hough and M. Fainsod, *How the Soviet Union Is Governed* (1978), is an important general study. A. Amalrik, *Will the Soviet Union Survive*

Until 1984? (1970), is a fascinating interpretation of Soviet society and politics in the 1960s by a Russian who paid for his criticism with prison and exile. A. Lee, *Russian Journal* (1981), is a moving personal account of a young American woman. H. Smith has written two outstanding journalistic reports on the Soviet Union under Brezhnev and Gorbachev, *The Russians* (1976) and *The New Russians* (1990). Gorbachev's reforms are perceptively examined by M. Walker, cited in the Notes, and M. Lewin, *The Gorbachev Phenomenon: A Historical Interpretation* (1988). G. Stokes, *The Walls Came Tumbling Down: The Collapse of Communism in Eastern Europe* (1993), is wide ranging and recommended.

R. von Albertini, *Decolonialization* (1971), is a good history of the decline and fall of European empires; T. von Laue, *The World Revolution of Westernization: The Twentieth Century in Global Perspective* (1987), is a stimulating interpretation. Related economic developments are considered in T. Vadney, *The World Since 1945* (1988), and H. van der Wee, *Prosperity and Upheaval: The World Economy, 1945–1980* (1986). Two excellent general studies on Latin America are J. E. Fagg, *Latin America: A General History,* 3d ed. (1977), and R. J. Shafer, *A History of Latin America* (1978). Both contain detailed suggestions for further reading. A. Lowenthal and G. Treverton, eds., *Latin America in a New World* (1994), analyzes the move toward regional cooperation and market economies. E. Burns, *A History of Brazil* (1970); M. Meyer and W. Sherman, *The Course of Mexican History* (1979); and B. Loveman, *Chile: The Legacy of Hispanic Capitalism* (1979), are recommended studies of developments in three leading nations. W. La Feber, *Inevitable Revolutions: The United States in Central America* (1983), is an important, quite critical assessment of U.S. support of neocolonial patterns in Central America. F. Fukuyama, *The End of History and the Last Man* (1992), sees the collapse of communism as the victory of democratic capitalism over all its competitors.

LISTENING TO THE
PAST

George Marshall's Plan for European Recovery, 1947

Although commencement speeches are usually quickly forgotten, the following address by Secretary of State George C. Marshall at the Harvard University graduation ceremonies on June 5, 1947, was a famous exception. Signaling a historic U.S. initiative, Marshall analyzed Europe's desperate economic conditions and proposed a program of American aid—the Marshall Plan.

Marshall offered U.S. aid to all European governments willing to cooperate, and the Soviet Union joined in early European efforts to draw up a collective response to the American proposal. But Joseph Stalin, probably fearing American domination and wanting to conceal the Soviet Union's terrible economic position, refused to provide the detailed data that western Europeans (and Americans) deemed essential for effective coordination. Marshall Plan aid went only to western Europe, accelerating the division of Europe and the onset of the cold war.

I need not tell you gentlemen that the world situation is very serious. That must be apparent to all intelligent people. . . .

In considering the requirements for the rehabilitation of Europe, the physical loss of life, the visible destruction of cities, factories, mines, and railroads was correctly estimated, but it has become obvious during recent months that this visible destruction was probably less serious than the dislocation of the entire fabric of the European economy. For the past ten years conditions have been highly abnormal. The feverish preparation for war and more feverish maintenance of the war effort engulfed all aspects of national economies. Machinery has fallen into disrepair or is entirely obsolete. . . . In many countries, confidence in the local currency has been severely shaken. The breakdown of the business structure of Europe during the war was complete. Recovery has been seriously retarded by the fact that two years after the close of hostilities a peace settlement with Germany and Austria has not been agreed upon. But even given a more prompt solution of these difficult problems, the rehabilitation of the economic structure of Europe quite evidently will require a much longer time and a greater effort than had been foreseen.

[One aspect of the situation in Europe is that] the farmer has always produced the foodstuffs to exchange with the city dweller for the other necessities of life. [But now] the town and city industries are not producing adequate goods to exchange with the food-producing farmer. [Thus farmers and peasants keep the food they produce, and] meanwhile people in the cities are short of food and fuel. So the governments are forced to use their foreign money and [dollar] credits to procure these necessities abroad. This process exhausts the funds which are urgently needed for reconstruction. [Thus a very serious situation is rapidly developing, and the modern exchange economy is in danger of breaking down.]

The truth of the matter is that Europe's requirements for the next three or four years of foreign food and other essential products —principally from America—are so much greater than her present ability to pay that she must have substantial additional help or face economic, social, and political deterioration of a very grave character.

The remedy lies in breaking the vicious circle and restoring the confidence of the European people in the economic future of their own countries and of Europe as a whole. The manufacturer and the farmer throughout wide areas must be able and willing to exchange their products for currencies the continuing value of which is not open to question.

Aside from the demoralizing effect on the world at large and possibilities of disturbances arising as a result of the desperation of the people concerned, the consequences to the economy of the United States should be apparent to all. It is logical that the United States should do whatever it is able to do to assist in the return of normal economic health in the world, without which there can be no political stability and no assured peace. Our policy is directed not against any country or doctrine but against hunger, poverty, desperation, and chaos. Its purpose should be the revival of a working economy in the world so as to permit the emergence of political and social conditions in which free institutions can exist. Such assistance, I am convinced, must not be on a piecemeal basis as various crises develop. Any assistance that this Government may render in the future should provide a cure rather than a mere palliative. Any government that is willing to assist in the task of recovery will find full cooperation, I am sure, on the part of the United States Government. Any government which maneuvers to block the recovery of other countries cannot expect help from us. Furthermore, governments, political parties, or groups which seek to perpetuate human misery in order to profit therefrom politically or otherwise will encounter the opposition of the United States.

It is already evident that, before the United States Government can proceed much further in its efforts to alleviate the situation and help start the European world on its way to recovery, there must be some agreement among the countries of Europe as to the requirements of the situation and the part those countries will take in order to give proper effect to whatever action might be taken by this Government. It would be neither fitting nor efficacious for this Government to undertake to draw up unilaterally a program designed to place Europe on its feet economically. This is the business of the Europeans. The initiative, I think, must come from Europe. The role of this country should consist of friendly aid in the drafting of a European program and of later support of such a program so far as it may be practical for us to do so. The program should be a joint one, agreed by a number of, if not all, European nations.

An essential part of any successful action on the part of the United States is an understanding on the part of the people of America of the character of the problem and remedies to be applied. Political passion and prejudice should have no part. With foresight, and a

German poster promoting Marshall Plan aid. (*Source: Bundesarchiv, Koblenz*)

willingness on the part of our people to face up to the vast responsibility which history has clearly placed upon our country, the difficulties I have outlined can and will be overcome.

Questions for Analysis

1. Why, according to Marshall, was the European economy on the verge of a breakdown? What was the specific financial problem?

2. What kind of responses did Marshall want Americans and Europeans to make? Why?

3. Do you find any evidence of tensions between the United States and the Soviet Union in Marshall's speech? What evidence?

4. What assumptions did Marshall make about the relationship between economics and politics? What caused upheaval and instability, according to Marshall?

Source: Slightly adapted from G. Marshall, "Address at Harvard University, June 5, 1947," *A Decade of American Foreign Policy: Basic Documents, 1941–1949*, U.S. Senate Document 123, 81st Cong., 1st sess., (Washington, D.C.: Government Printing Office, 1950), pp. 1268–1270.

34

Asia and Africa in the Contemporary World

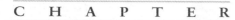

Shinto priests perform a ceremony of purification in front of a reactor pressure chamber, Japan. *(Source: Yoshitaka Nakatani/PLUS ONE, Inc., Tokyo)*

When future historians look back at our era, they are likely to be particularly struck by the epoch-making resurgence of Asia and Africa after the Second World War. They will try to explain the astonishingly rapid rise of new or radically reorganized Asian and African countries and their increasingly prominent role in world affairs. And they will try to understand the continued development of these countries as they sought to realize the promise of independence and build strong nations and societies.

- How did Asian and African countries reassert or establish their political independence in the postwar era?
- How in the postindependence world did leading states face up to the enormous challenges of nation building, challenges that were all the more difficult after the 1960s?

These are the questions that this chapter seeks to answer.

 THE RESURGENCE OF EAST ASIA

In 1945 Japan and China, the two great powers of East Asia, lay exhausted and devastated. Japanese aggression had sown extreme misery in China and reaped an atomic whirlwind at Hiroshima and Nagasaki. The future looked bleak. Yet both nations recovered even more spectacularly than western Europe. In the course of recovery the two countries, closely linked since the 1890s, went their separate ways. China under Mao Zedong (Mao Tsetung) transformed itself into a strong, one-party communist state. Japan under American occupation turned from military expansion to democracy and extraordinarily successful economic development. Not until the 1970s did the reborn giants begin moving somewhat closer together.

The Communist Victory in China

There were many reasons for the triumph of communism in China. As a noted historian has forcefully argued, however, "Japanese aggression was . . . the most important single factor in Mao's rise to power."[1] When Japanese armies advanced rapidly in 1938, the Nationalist government of Jiang Jieshi (Chiang Kai-shek) moved its capital to Chongqing (Chungking), deep in the Chinese interior (see page 1019). As the Communists, aided by their uneasy "united front" alliance with the Nationalists, built up their strength in guerrilla bases in the countryside behind Japanese lines, Mao, at the peak of his creative powers, avoided pitched battles and concentrated on winning peasant support and forming a broad anti-Japanese coalition. By reducing rents, promising land redistribution, enticing intellectuals, and spreading propaganda, Mao and the Communists emerged in peasant eyes as the true patriots, the genuine nationalists.

Meanwhile, the long war with Japan was exhausting the established government and its supporters. Half of Japan's overseas armies were pinned down in China in 1945. Jiang Jieshi's Nationalists had mobilized 14 million men, and a staggering 3 million Chinese soldiers had been killed or wounded. The war created massive Chinese deficits and runaway inflation, hurting morale and ruining lives.

When Japan suddenly collapsed in August 1945, Communists and Nationalists both rushed to seize evacuated territory. Heavy fighting broke out in Manchuria. The United States, which had steadfastly supported the Nationalists during the Second World War, tried unsuccessfully to work out a political compromise, but civil war resumed in earnest in April 1946. At first Jiang Jieshi's more numerous Nationalists had the upper hand. Soon the better-led, more determined Communists rallied, and by 1948 the demoralized Nationalist forces were disintegrating. The following year Jiang Jieshi and a million mainland Chinese fled to the island of Taiwan, and in October 1949 Mao Zedong proclaimed the People's Republic of China.

Within three years the Communists had succeeded in consolidating their rule. The Communist government seized the holdings of landlords and rich peasants—10 percent of the farm population had owned between 70 and 80 percent of the land—and distributed it to 300 million poor peasants and landless laborers. This revolutionary land reform was extremely popular. Although the Chinese Communists soon began pushing the development of socialist collectives, they did so less brutally than had the Soviets in the 1930s, and they retained genuine support in the countryside.

Meanwhile, the Communists were dealing harshly with their foes. Mao admitted in 1957 that 800,000 "class enemies" had been summarily liquidated between 1949 and 1954; the true figure is probably much higher. By means of mass arrests, forced-labor camps, and re-education through relentless propaganda and self-criticism sessions, all visible opposition from the old ruling groups was destroyed.

Finally, Mao and the Communists reunited China's 550 million inhabitants in a strong centralized state. They laid claim to a new Mandate of Heaven and demonstrated that China was once again a great power. This was the real significance of China's participation in the Korean War. In 1950, when the American-led United Nations forces in Korea crossed the 38th parallel and appeared to threaten China's industrial base in Manchuria, the Chinese attacked, advanced swiftly, and fought the Americans to a bloody standstill on the Korean peninsula. This struggle against "American imperialism" mobilized the masses, and military success increased Chinese self-confidence.

Mao's China

Asserting Chinese power and prestige in world affairs, Mao and the party looked to the Soviet Union for inspiration in the early 1950s. Along with the gradual collectivization of agriculture, China adopted a typical Soviet five-year plan to develop large factories and heavy industry rapidly. Russian specialists built many Chinese plants. Soviet economic aid was also considerable. The first five-year plan was successful, as were associated efforts to redirect higher education away from the liberal arts toward science and engineering. People were very poor, but undeniable economic growth followed the Communists' social revolution.

In the cultural and intellectual realms too, the Chinese followed the Soviet example. Basic civil and political rights, which had been seriously cur-

A People's Court   The man on his knees is accused in a people's court of selling a young girl living in his household, an old practice that became a serious crime in revolutionary China. Local villagers follow the proceedings intently. *(Source: Popperfoto/ Archive Photos)*

tailed by the Nationalists, were simply abolished. Temples and churches were closed; all religion was persecuted. Freedom of the press died, and the government went to incredible lengths to control information. A Soviet-style puritanism took hold. To the astonishment of "old China hands," the Communists quickly eradicated the long-standing scourges of prostitution and drug abuse, which they had long regarded as humiliating marks of exploitation and national decline. The Communists enthusiastically promoted Soviet-Marxian ideas concerning women and the family. Full equality, work outside the home, and state-supported child care became primary goals.

By the mid-1950s, the People's Republic of China seemed to be firmly set on the Marxist-Leninist course of development previously perfected in the Soviet Union. In 1958, however, China began to go its own way. Mao had always stressed revolutionary free will and peasant equality. Now he proclaimed a spectacular acceleration of development, a "Great Leap Forward" in which soaring industrial growth was to be based on small-scale backyard workshops run by peasants living in gigantic self-contained communes. Creating an authentic new socialist personality that rejected individualism and traditional family values was a second goal. In extreme cases, commune members ate in common dining halls, nurseries cared for children, and fiery crusaders preached the evils of family ties.

The intended great leap past the Soviets to socialist utopia—true communism—produced an economic disaster in the countryside, for frantic efforts with primitive technology often resulted only in chaos. By 1960, only China's efficient rationing system was preventing starvation. But when Soviet premier Nikita Khrushchev criticized Chinese policy, Mao condemned Khrushchev and his Russian colleagues as detestable "modern revisionists"— capitalists and cowards unwilling to risk a world war that would bring communist revolution in the United States. The Russians abruptly cut off economic and military aid. A mood of fear and hostility developed in both China and the Soviet Union in the 1960s as the communist world split apart.

Mao lost influence in the party after the fiasco of the Great Leap Forward and the Sino-Soviet split, but in 1965 the old revolutionary staged a dramatic comeback. Fearing that China was becoming bureaucratic, capitalistic, and "revisionist" like the

Soviet Union, Mao launched what he called the "Great Proletarian Cultural Revolution." Its objective was to purge the party of time-serving bureaucrats and to recapture the revolutionary fervor of his guerrilla struggle (see page 1019). The army and the nation's young people, especially students, responded enthusiastically. Encouraged by Mao to organize themselves into radical cadres called Red Guards, young people denounced their teachers and practiced rebellion in the name of revolution. One Red Guard manifesto, "Long Live the Revolutionary Rebel Spirit of the Proletariat," exulted:

Revolution is rebellion, and rebellion is the soul of Mao Tse-tung's thought. Daring to think, to speak, to act, to break through, and to make revolution—in a word, daring to rebel—is the most fundamental and most precious quality of proletarian revolutionaries; it is fundamental to the Party spirit of the Party of the proletariat! . . .

You say we are too arrogant? "Arrogant" is just what we want to be. Chairman Mao says, "And those in high positions we counted as no more than the dust." We are bent on striking down not only the reactionaries in our school, but the reactionaries all over the world. Revolutionaries take it as their task to transform the world. How can we not be "arrogant"?[2]

The Red Guards sought to purge China of all traces of "feudal" and "bourgeois" culture and thought. Some ancient monuments and works of art were destroyed. Party officials, professors, and intellectuals were exiled to remote villages to purify themselves with heavy labor. The Red Guards attracted enormous worldwide attention and served as an extreme model for the student rebellions in the West in the late 1960s (see page 1120).

The Limits of Reform

Mao and the Red Guards succeeded in mobilizing the masses, shaking up the party, and creating greater social equality. But the Cultural Revolution also created growing chaos and a general crisis of confidence, especially in the cities. Persecuted intellectuals, technicians, and purged party officials launched a counterattack on the radicals and regained much of their influence by 1969. Thus China shifted to the right at the same time that Europe and the United States did. This shift in

China, coupled with actual fighting between China and the Soviet Union on the northern border in 1969, opened the door to a limited but lasting reconciliation between China and the United States in 1972.

The moderates were led by Deng Xiaoping (b. 1904), a long-time member of the Communist elite who had been branded a dangerous agent of capitalism during the Cultural Revolution. After Mao's death in 1976, Deng and his supporters initiated a series of new policies, embodied in the ongoing campaign of the "Four Modernizations"—agriculture, industry, science and technology, and national defense. The campaign to modernize had a profound effect on China's people, and Deng proudly called it China's "second revolution."

China's 800 million peasants experienced the greatest and most beneficial change from this "second revolution"—a fact that at first glance may seem surprising. The support of the peasantry had played a major role in the Communist victory. After 1949, land reform and rationing undoubtedly improved the diet of poor peasants. Subsequently, literacy campaigns taught rural people how to read, and "barefoot doctors"—local peasants trained to do simple diagnosis and treatment—brought modern medicine to the countryside. Handicraft industries grew to provide rural employment. But rigid collectivized agriculture failed to provide either the peasants or the country with adequate food, as Chinese documents published in the 1980s made clear. Levels of agricultural production and per capita food consumption were no higher in the mid-1970s than in the mid-1950s, and only slightly higher than in 1937, before the war with Japan.

Determined to prevent a return to Maoist extremism as well as to modernize the economy, Deng and the reformers looked to the peasants as natural allies. Their answer to the stalemate in agricultural production was to let China's peasants farm the land in small family units rather than in large collectives. Peasants were encouraged to produce what they could produce best and "dare to be rich." Peasants responded enthusiastically, increasing food production by more than 50 percent in just six years after 1978. Thus most Chinese finally gained enough calories and protein for normal life and growth.

The successful use of free markets and family responsibility in agriculture encouraged further economic experimentation. Foreign capitalists were allowed to open factories in southern China, and they successfully exported Chinese products around the world. The private enterprise of Chinese citizens was also permitted in cities. Snack shops, beauty parlors, and a host of small businesses sprang up. As signs of liberalization abounded, the Chinese economy bucked the world trend and grew rapidly between 1978 and 1987. The level of per capita income doubled in these years.

Change, however, was also circumscribed. As in the Soviet Union under Mikhail Gorbachev (see page 1113), most large-scale industry remained state owned and state subsidized. Cultural change proceeded slowly, and the party maintained its strict control of the media. Above all, under Deng's leadership the Communist party zealously preserved its monopoly of political power.

When the worldwide movement for greater democracy and political freedom in the late 1980s also took root in China, the government responded by banning all demonstrations and slowing the trend toward a freer economy. Inflation then soared to more than 30 percent a year, and in 1988 consumers cleared the shelves in a buying panic. The economic reversal, the continued lack of political freedom, and the conviction that Chinese society was becoming more corrupt led China's idealistic university students to spearhead demonstrations in April 1989.

The students evoked tremendous popular support, and more than a million people streamed into Beijing's central Tiananmen Square on May 17 in support of their demands. The government then declared martial law and ordered the army to clear the students. Incredibly, masses of courageous Chinese citizens using only their bodies and voices as weapons peacefully blocked the soldiers' entry into the city for two weeks. But the hesitant army finally struck. In the early hours of June 4, 1989, tanks rolled into Tiananmen Square. At least seven hundred students died as a wave of repression, arrests, and executions descended on China. China's Communist leaders claimed that they had saved the country from plots to destroy socialism and national unity. Advocates of democracy were outraged around the world.

In the months after Tiananmen Square, communism fell in eastern Europe, the Soviet Union broke apart, and China's rulers felt vindicated.

✳ **Chinese Students in 1989**   These exuberant demonstrators in Tiananmen Square personify the idealism and the optimism of China's pro-democracy movement. After some hesitation the Communist government crushed the student leaders and their supporters with tanks and executions, reaffirming its harsh, authoritarian character. *(Source: Erika Lansner/Black Star)*

They believed that their strong action had preserved Communist power, prevented chaos, and showed the limits of permissible reform. After some hesitation Deng reaffirmed economic liberalization. Private enterprise and foreign investment boomed. Consumerism was encouraged, and the regime permitted ever more products. But the rulers tortured and jailed critics of Communist rule, and they made every effort to ensure that the People's Army would again crush the people if called to do so. Thus the 1990s coupled growing economic freedom with rigid political repression, a contradictory and unstable combination in the eyes of many foreign observers.

Japan's American Revolution

After Japan's surrender in August 1945, American occupation forces began landing in the Tokyo-Yokohama area. Riding through what had been the heart of industrial Japan, where mighty mills and factories had once hummed with activity, they found only smokestacks and giant steel safes standing amid miles of rubble and debris. The bleak landscape manifested Japan's state of mind as the nation lay helpless before its conqueror.

Japan, like Nazi Germany, was formally occupied by all the Allies, but real power resided in American hands. The commander was General Douglas MacArthur (1880–1964), the five-star hero of the Pacific, who with his advisers exercised almost absolute authority.

MacArthur and the Americans had a revolutionary plan for defeated Japan. Convinced that militaristic, antidemocratic forces were responsible for Japanese aggression and had to be destroyed, they introduced fundamental reforms designed to make Japan a free, democratic society along American lines. The exhausted, demoralized Japanese, who had feared a worse fate, accepted passively. Long-suppressed liberal leaders emerged to offer crucial support and help carry the reforms forward.

Japan's sweeping American revolution began with demilitarization and a systematic purge. A special international tribunal tried and convicted as war criminals twenty-five top government leaders and army officers. Other courts sentenced hundreds to death and sent thousands to prison. Over 220,000 politicians, businessmen, and army officers were declared ineligible for office.

Although the American-dictated constitution of 1946 allowed the emperor to remain "the symbol of the State," the new constitution made the government fully responsible to the Diet, whose members were popularly elected by all adults. A bill of rights granted basic civil liberties and freed all political prisoners, including Communists. The constitution also abolished all Japanese armed forces. Japan's resurrected liberals enthusiastically supported this American move to destroy militarism.

The American occupation left Japan's powerful bureaucracy largely intact and used it to implement the fundamental social and economic reforms that were rammed through the Japanese Diet. Many had a New Deal flavor. The occupation promoted the Japanese labor movement and introduced American-style antitrust laws. The gigantic zaibatsu firms were broken up into many separate companies in order to encourage competition and economic democracy. The American reformers proudly "emancipated" Japanese women, granting them equality before the law.

The occupation also imposed revolutionary land reform. MacArthur pressured the Japanese Diet into buying up the land owned by absentee landlords and selling it to peasants on very generous terms. This reform strengthened the small, independent peasant, who became a staunch defender of postwar democracy.

The United States' efforts to remake Japan in its own image were powerful but short-lived. By 1948, when the United States began to look at the world through a cold war lens, occupation policy shifted gears. The Japanese later referred to this about-face as "the reverse course." As China went decisively communist, American leaders began to see Japan as a potential ally, not as an object of social reform. The American command began purging leftists and rehabilitating prewar nationalists, many of whom joined the Liberal Democratic party, which became increasingly conservative and emerged as the dominant political organization in postwar Japan. The United States ended the occupation in 1952. Under the treaty terms, Japan regained independence, and the United States retained its vast military complex in Japan.

"Japan, Inc."

Restricted to satellite status in world politics, the Japanese people applied their exceptional creative powers to rebuilding their country. Japan's economic recovery, like Germany's, proceeded painfully slowly immediately after the war. At the time of the Korean War, however, the economy took off and grew with spectacular speed for a whole generation. Between 1950 and 1970 the real growth rate of Japan's economy—adjusted for inflation—averaged a breathtaking 10 percent a year—almost three times that of the United States. Even after the shock of much higher energy prices in 1973, the petroleum-poor Japanese did considerably better than most other peoples. In 1986 average per capita income in Japan exceeded that in the United States for the first time. As recently as 1965, the average Japanese had earned only one-fourth of the average American's income.

Japan's emergence as an economic superpower fascinated some outsiders and troubled others. Many Asians and Africans looked to Japan for the secrets of successful modernization, but some of Japan's Asian neighbors again feared Japanese exploitation. And in the 1970s and 1980s, some Americans and Europeans bitterly accused "Japan, Inc.," of an unholy alliance between government and business and urged their governments to retaliate.

Many of the ingredients in western Europe's recovery also operated in Japan. American aid, cheap labor, and freer international trade all helped spark

the process. Japan's astonishing economic surge also seems to have had deep roots in Japanese history, culture, and national character. By the time American and European pressure forced open its gates in the mid-nineteenth century, Japanese agriculture, education, and material well-being were advanced even by European standards. Moreover, a culturally homogeneous Japanese society put the needs of the group before those of the individual. When the Meiji reformers redefined Japan's primary task as catching up with the West, they had the support of a sophisticated and disciplined people (see pages 906–908). Japan's modernization, even including a full share of aggressive imperialism, was extremely rapid.

Building Team Spirit   Shouting company slogans in unison, these young managers and salespeople are hiking near snowcapped Mount Fuji as part of a two-week training course teaching business skills and company loyalty. Many customs encourage group solidarity in Japan, where the success of the group is placed above the success of the individual. *(Source: M. MacIntyre/The Hutchinson Library)*

By the end of the American occupation, this tight-knit, group-centered society had reassessed its future and worked out a new national consensus. Japan's new task was to build its economy and compete efficiently in world markets. Improved living standards emerged as a related goal after the initial successes of the 1950s. The ambitious "double-your-income" target for the 1960s was ultimately surpassed by 50 percent.

Government and big business shared leading roles in the drama of economic growth. As during the Meiji Restoration, capable, respected bureaucrats directed and aided the efforts of cooperative business leaders. The government decided which industries were important, then made loans and encouraged mergers to create powerful firms in those industries. The antitrust policy introduced by the American occupation was scrapped, and the home market was protected from foreign competition by various measures.

Big business was valued and respected because it served the national goal and mirrored Japanese society. Big companies, and to a lesser extent small ones, traditionally hired workers for life immediately after they finished school, and in return workers were loyal and obedient. The business firm in Japan was a big, well-disciplined family. The workday began with the company song. Employees' social lives revolved around the company. Wages were based on age. (Discrimination against women remained severe: their wages and job security were strikingly inferior to men's.) Most unions became moderate, agreeable company unions. The social and economic distance between salaried managers and workers was slight and often breached. *Efficiency, quality,* and *quantity* were the watchwords. Management was quick to retrain employees, who would not take their valuable new skills elsewhere. These factors were most important in accounting for Japan's economic success. Japan's stubborn protection of its home market, which foreigners frequently decried as "unfair" competition, played only a supporting role.

Japanese society, with its inescapable stress on discipline, cooperation, and national self-interest, has proved well adapted to the unending challenges of modern industrial urban civilization. Japan alone among industrial nations has experienced a marked decrease in crime over the last generation. In the 1970s and 1980s the Japanese ad-

dressed themselves effectively to such previously neglected problems as serious industrial pollution and their limited energy resources. Highly dependent on imported resources and foreign sales, Japan groped for a new role in world politics. Closer relations with China, increased loans to Southeast Asia, and tough trade negotiations with the United States were all features of that ongoing effort.

NEW NATIONS IN SOUTH ASIA AND THE MUSLIM WORLD

South Asia and the Muslim world have transformed themselves no less spectacularly than China and Japan. The national independence movements, which had been powerful mass campaigns since the 1930s, triumphed decisively over weakened and demoralized European imperialism after the Second World War. Between 1947 and 1962, as decolonization gathered irresistible strength, virtually every colonial territory won its political freedom. The complete reversal of the long process of European expansion was a turning point in world history.

The newly independent nations of South Asia and the revitalized states of the Muslim world exhibited many variations on the dominant themes of national renaissance and modernization, especially as the struggle for political independence receded into the past. Both ethnic rivalries and cold war conflict complicated the process of renewal and development.

The Indian Subcontinent

After the First World War, Mahatma Gandhi and the Indian Congress party developed the philosophy of militant nonviolence to oppose British rule of India and to lessen oppression of the Indian poor by the Indian rich (see pages 1009–1011). By 1929 Gandhi had succeeded in transforming the Congress party from a narrow, middle-class party into a mass independence movement. Gradually and grudgingly, Britain's rulers introduced reforms culminating in limited self-government in 1937.

The Second World War accelerated the drive toward independence but also pointed it in a new direction. Congress party leaders, humiliated that

Great Britain had declared war against Germany on India's behalf without consulting them, resigned their posts in the Indian government and demanded self-rule as the immediate price of political cooperation. In 1942, Gandhi called on the British to "Quit India" and threatened another civil disobedience campaign. He and the other Congress leaders were quickly arrested and jailed for most of the war. As a result, India's wartime support for hard-pressed Britain was substantial but not always enthusiastic. Meanwhile, the Congress party's prime political rival skillfully seized the opportunity to increase its influence.

That rival was the Muslim League, led by the brilliant, elegant, English-educated lawyer Muhammad Ali Jinnah (1876–1948). Jinnah and the other leaders of the Muslim League feared Hindu domination of an independent Indian state led by the Congress party. Asserting in nationalist terms the right of Muslim areas to separate from the Hindu majority, Jinnah described the Muslims of India as "a nation with our distinct culture and civilization, . . . our own distinctive outlook on life and of life."[3] Thus Jinnah told a hundred thousand listeners at the Muslim League's Lahore Conference in March 1940,

If the British Government is really in earnest and sincere to secure the peace and happiness of the people of the subcontinent, the only course open to us all is to allow the major nations separate homelands by dividing India into autonomous national states.[4]

The Muslim League's insistence on the division of India appalled Gandhi. He regarded Jinnah's two-nation theory as simply untrue and as promising the victory of hate over love. The passionate debate continued unabated during the war as millions argued whether India was one nation or two. By 1945 the subcontinent was intellectually and emotionally divided, though still momentarily held together by British rule.

When Britain's Labour government agreed to speedy independence for India after 1945, conflicting Hindu and Muslim nationalisms and religious hatred became obstacles leading to murderous clashes between the two communities in 1946. In a last attempt to preserve the subcontinent's political unity, the British proposed a federal constitution providing for extensive provincial—and thus religious and cultural—autonomy. When after some hesitation Jinnah and the Muslim League would accept nothing less than an independent Pakistan, India's last viceroy—war hero Lord Louis Mountbatten (1900–1979), Queen Victoria's great-grandson—proposed partition. Both sides accepted. At the stroke of midnight on August 14, 1947, one-fifth of humanity gained political independence.

Yet independence through partition also brought tragedy. In the weeks after independence, communal strife exploded into an orgy of massacres and mass expulsions. Perhaps a hundred thousand Hindus and Muslims were slaughtered, and an estimated 5 million refugees from both communities fled in opposite directions to escape being hacked to death by frenzied mobs.

This wave of violence was a bitter potion for Congress leaders, who were completely powerless to stop it. "What is there to celebrate?" exclaimed Gandhi. "I see nothing but rivers of blood."[5]

In January 1948, announcing yet another fast to protest Hindu persecution of Muslims in the Indian capital of New Delhi and to restore "heart friendship" between the two communities, Gandhi was gunned down by a Hindu fanatic. As the Mahatma's death tragically testifies, the constructive and liberating forces of modern nationalism have frequently deteriorated into blind hatred.

After the ordeal of independence, relations between India and Pakistan—both members of the British Commonwealth—remained tense. Fighting over the disputed area of Kashmir continued until 1949 and broke out again in 1965–1966 and 1971. Mutual hostility remains deeply ingrained to this day (Map 34.1).

Pakistan   Like many newly independent states, Pakistan eventually adopted an authoritarian government in 1958. Unlike most, Pakistan failed to preserve its exceptionally fragile unity, which proved to be the unworkable dream of the intellectuals leading the Muslim League.

Pakistan's western and eastern provinces were separated by more than a thousand miles of Indian territory, as well as by language, ethnic background, and social custom. They shared only the Muslim faith that had temporarily brought them together against the Hindus. The Bengalis of East Pakistan constituted a majority of the population

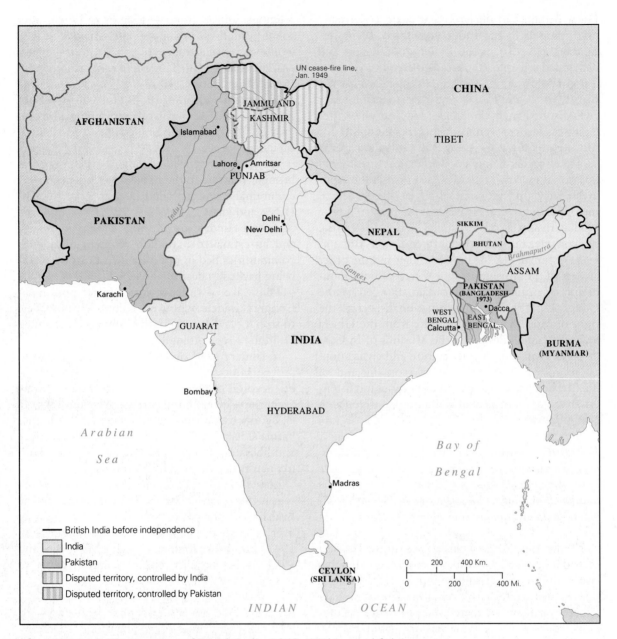

MAP 34.1 The Partition of British India, 1947 Violence and fighting were most intense where there were large Hindu and Muslim minorities—in Kashmir, Punjab, and Bengal. The tragic result of partition, which has occurred repeatedly throughout the world in the twentieth century, was a forced exchange of populations and greater homogeneity on both sides of the border.

of Pakistan as a whole but were neglected by the central government, which remained in the hands of West Pakistan's elite after Jinnah's death. In essence, East Pakistan remained a colony of West Pakistan.

Tensions gradually came to a head in the late 1960s. Bengali leaders calling for virtual independence were charged with treason, and martial law was proclaimed in East Pakistan. In 1971 the Bengalis revolted. Despite savage repression—10 million Muslim Bengalis fled temporarily to India, which provided some military aid—the Bengalis won their independence as the new nation of Bangladesh in 1973. The world's eighth most populous country, Bangladesh was also one of its poorest.

India India was ruled for a generation after 1947 by Jawaharlal Nehru (1889–1964) and the Con-

gress party, which introduced major social reforms. Hindu women and even young girls were granted legal equality, which included the right to vote, to seek a divorce, and to marry outside their caste. The constitution abolished the untouchable caste and, in an effort to compensate for centuries of the most profound discrimination, established "ex-untouchable" quotas for university scholarships and government jobs. In practice, attitudes toward

Indian Refugees Independence and partition brought a wave of bloodshed that sent millions of Hindus and Muslims fleeing for their lives in opposite directions. Here desperate Muslims seek precious space atop a train that will carry them to safety in Pakistan. (*Source: Wide World Photos*)

women and untouchables evolved slowly—especially in the villages, where 85 percent of the people lived.

The Congress leadership tried with modest success to develop the country economically by means of democratic socialism. But population growth of about 2.4 percent per year ate up much of the increase in output, and halfhearted government efforts to promote birth control met with in difference or hostility. Intense poverty remained the lot of most people and encouraged widespread corruption within the bureaucracy.

The Congress party maintained a moralizing neutrality in the cold war and sought to group India and other newly independent states in Asia and Africa into a "third force" of "nonaligned" nations. This effort culminated in the Afro-Asian Conference in Bandung, Indonesia, in 1955.

Nehru's daughter, Indira Gandhi (1917–1984), became prime minister in 1966. Mrs. Gandhi (whose deceased husband was no relation to Mahatma Gandhi) dominated Indian political life for a generation with a combination of charm, tact, and toughness. As it became clear that population growth was frustrating efforts to improve living standards, Mrs. Gandhi's government stepped up measures to promote family planning and birth control measures, including vasectomy for both psychological and religious reasons. As a doctor in a market town explained to a Western journalist:

They have mostly heard of family planning around here by now, but they are afraid. They are afraid that the sterilizing operation will destroy their male power and make them docile, like castrated animals. Mostly, they are afraid of interfering with God's will.[6]

In the face of such reluctance—and in an effort to clamp down on widespread corruption at all levels of government—Mrs. Gandhi in 1975 subverted parliamentary democracy and proclaimed a state of emergency. Attacking dishonest officials, blackmarketeers, and tax evaders, she also threw the weight of the government behind a heavy-handed campaign of mass sterilization to reduce population growth. In some areas, poor men with large families were made to accept a few cents' payment to submit to a simple, almost painless irreversible vasectomy. More than 7 million men were sterilized in 1976.

Many Indian and foreign observers believed that Mrs. Gandhi's emergency measures marked the end of the parliamentary democracy and Western liberties introduced in the last phase of British rule. But Mrs. Gandhi—true to the British tradition—called for free elections. She suffered a spectacular electoral defeat, largely because of the vastly unpopular sterilization campaign and her subversion of democracy. Her successors, however, fell to fighting among themselves, and in 1980 Mrs. Gandhi won an equally stunning electoral victory. Her defeat and re-election undoubtedly strengthened India's democratic tradition.

Mrs. Gandhi's last years in office were plagued by another old political problem, one that cost her her life. Democratic India remained a patchwork of religions, languages, and peoples. This enduring diversity threatened to further divide the country along ethnic or religious lines, as several peoples began to make political demands—most notably the 15 million Sikhs of the Punjab in northern India (see Map 34.1).

The Sikhs have their own religion—a blend of Islam and Hinduism—and a distinctive culture, including a warrior tradition and the wearing of elegantly coiled turbans. Industrious and cohesive, most Sikhs wanted greater autonomy for the Punjab. By 1984, some radicals were fighting for an independent homeland—a Sikh national state. In retaliation, Mrs. Gandhi tightened control in the Punjab and ordered the army to storm the Sikhs' sacred Golden Temple at Amritsar. Six hundred died in the assault. Five months later, two of Mrs. Gandhi's Sikh bodyguards—she prided herself on their loyalty—cut her down with machine-gun fire in her own garden. Violence followed as Hindu mobs slaughtered over a thousand Sikhs throughout India.

Elected prime minister by a landslide sympathy vote, one of Mrs. Gandhi's sons, Rajiv Gandhi (1944–1991), showed considerable skill at effecting a limited reconciliation with a majority of the Sikh population. But slow economic growth, government corruption, and Rajiv Gandhi's lack of warmth gradually undermined his support. In 1989, he was voted out of office, and a fragile coalition of opposition took power. Despite poverty and ethnic tensions, India remained committed to free elections and representative government.

Sikh Patriots   With the domes of the majestic Golden Temple rising behind them, a mass of Sikhs gather to protest the Indian army's bloody assault on their most holy shrine. The vast majority of Sikhs want greater autonomy at the least. Sikh radicals seek an independent state. *(Source: Bartholomew/Liaison)*

Southeast Asia

The rest of southeast Asia gained independence quickly after 1945, but the attainment of stable political democracy proved a more difficult goal. Ethnic conflicts and cold war battles could easily divide countries. Thus leaders frequently turned to authoritarian rule and military power in an effort to impose order and unity.

Malaysia and Singapore   Malaya encountered serious problems not unlike those of British India. The native Malays, an Islamic agricultural people, feared and disliked the Chinese, who had come to the Malay Peninsula as poor migrant workers in the nineteenth century and stayed on to dominate

the urban economy. The Malays pressured the British into giving them the dominant voice in a multiethnic federation of Malayan territories. In 1948 local Chinese communists launched an all-out guerrilla war. They were eventually defeated by the British and the Malays, and Malaya became self-governing in 1957 and independent in 1961. Yet two peoples soon meant two nations. In 1965, the largely Chinese city of Singapore was pushed out of the Malayan-dominated Federation of Malaysia. The independent city-state of Singapore prospered on the hard work and inventiveness of its largely Chinese population.

The Philippine Islands   The Philippine Islands suffered greatly under Japanese occupation during the

ASIA SINCE 1945

1945	Japan surrenders Civil war begins in China
1946	Japan receives democratic constitution Philippines gain independence
1947	Communal strife follows independence for India and Pakistan
1948	Civil war between Arabs and Jews in Palestine
1949	Mao Zedong proclaims the People's Republic of China Indonesia under Sukarno wins independence from the Dutch
1950	Korean War begins Japan begins long period of rapid economic growth
1952	U.S. occupation of Japan officially ends
1954	Vietnamese nationalists defeat the French at Dien Bien Phu
1955	First Afro-Asian Conference of nonaligned nations meets at Bandung, Indonesia
1958	Mao announces the "Great Leap Forward"
1960	Open split between China and the Soviet Union emerges
1965	The "Great Proletarian Cultural Revolution" begins in China Growing U.S. involvement in the Vietnamese civil war
1966	Indira Gandhi becomes prime minister of India
1967	Arab-Israeli conflict: Six-Day War
1972	President Nixon's visit to China signals improved Sino-American relations
1973	Arab-Israeli conflict: Yom Kippur War
1975	War in Vietnam ends with Communist victory
1976	China pursues modernization after Mao's death
1979	Revolution topples the shah of Iran
1980–1988	War between Iran and Iraq
1984	Growth of Sikh nationalism in India
1986	Democratic movement in the Philippines brings Corazón Aquino to power
1989	Chinese government uses the army to crush student demonstrations
1991	U.S.-led United Nations–sanctioned military coalition forces Iraq out of Kuwait
1993	Unexpected agreement between Israel and the Palestinian Liberation Organization

Second World War. After the war the United States retained its large military bases but followed through on its earlier promises by granting the Philippines independence in 1946. As in Malaya, communist guerrillas tried unsuccessfully to seize power. The Philippines pursued American-style two-party competition until 1965, when President Ferdinand Marcos (1917–1989) subverted the constitution and ruled as a dictator. Abolishing martial law in 1981 but retaining most of his power, Marcos faced growing opposition as the economy crumbled and land-hungry communist guerrillas made striking gains in the countryside. Led by a courageous Corazón Aquino (b. 1933), whose politician husband had been murdered, probably by Marcos supporters, the opposition won a spectacular electoral victory in 1986 and forced Marcos to take refuge in Hawaii, where he subsequently died.

As president, Mrs. Aquino negotiated a cease-fire with the communist rebels, beat off several attempted takeovers by dissident army officers, and pursued a policy of national reconciliation. She

eventually sided with nationalists who argued that U.S. military bases in the Philippines should be closed in order for the nation to achieve complete independence. When the lease on the bases was not renewed in 1991, the American military left. Yet a tiny elite continued to dominate the country, and years of mismanagement had led to decline in the standard of living. The Filipino people still faced an enormous challenge.

Indonesia   The Netherlands East Indies emerged in 1949 as independent Indonesia under the nationalist leader Achmed Sukarno (1901–1970),

President Corazón Aquino   Shown here with her infectious smile and dignity, Corazón Aquino led the democratic movement to power in the Philippines and enjoyed tremendous popular support. For millions of Filipinos she was simply "Cory"—their trusted friend. *(Source: Wide World Photos)*

after successfully resisting stubborn Dutch efforts at reconquest. Like the Philippines, the populous new nation encompassed a variety of peoples, islands, and religions (Islam was predominant; see Map 34.2). Beginning in 1957, Sukarno tried to forge unity by means of his so-called guided democracy. He rejected parliamentary democracy as politically divisive and claimed to replicate at the national level the traditional deliberation and consensus of the Indonesian village. For a time the authoritarian, anti-Western Sukarno seemed to be under the sway of well-organized Indonesian communists, who murdered and mutilated seven leading army generals as part of an unsuccessful uprising in 1965. The army immediately retaliated, systematically slaughtering a half-million or more Indonesian communists, radicals, and noncommunist Chinese. Sukarno was forced to resign.

The Muslim military leaders, led by General Suharto, established their own form of authoritarian rule and concentrated on economic development. Blessed with large oil revenues, Suharto's New Order welcomed foreign capital, expanded the Indonesian middle classes, and achieved solid economic growth in the 1970s and 1980s. Combining controlled elections with government-party majorities, the government promoted an official ideology stressing belief in one God, nationalism, humanitarianism, democracy, and social justice. Largely secular in inspiration, this ideology appeared to strengthen the modernizing effort, although it was questioned by some devout Muslims.

Vietnam, Laos, and Cambodia The most bitter struggle for independence in Southeast Asia occurred in French Indochina. The French tried to reimpose imperial rule there after the communist and nationalist guerrilla leader Ho Chi Minh (1890–1969) declared an independent republic in 1945, but they were decisively defeated in 1954 in the Battle of Dien Bien Phu. At the subsequent international peace conference, French Indochina gained independence. Laos and Cambodia (later known as Kampuchea) became separate states; Vietnam was "temporarily" divided into two hostile sections at the 17th parallel pending elections to select a single unified government within two years (see Map 33.3, page 000).

The elections were never held, and the civil war that soon broke out between the two Vietnamese governments, one communist and one anticommunist, became the hottest cold war conflict in the 1960s. The United States invested tremendous military effort but fought its Vietnam War as a deeply divided country (see pages 0000–0000). The tough, dedicated communists eventually proved victorious in 1975. Thus events in Vietnam roughly recapitulated those in China, but in a long, drawn-out fashion: after a bitter civil war worsened by cold war hatreds, the communists succeeded in creating a unified Marxist nation. And after another generation the Vietnamese communists also began to turn from central planning toward freer markets and private initiative, even as they zealously guarded their political power.

The Muslim World

Throughout the vast arc of predominantly Islamic lands that stretches from Indonesia in Southeast Asia to Senegal in West Africa (Map 34.2), nationalism remained the predominant political force after 1945. Anti-Western and anticommunist in most instances, nationalism in the Muslim world generally combined a strong secular state with a basic loyalty to Islam. Cold war conflicts and enormous oil resources enhanced the region's global standing.

In the Arab countries of North Africa and the Middle East, with their shared but highly differentiated language and culture, nationalism wore two faces. The idealistic side focused on the Pan-Arab dream of uniting all Arabs in a single nation that would be strong enough to resist the West and achieve genuine independence. This Pan-Arab vision contributed to political and economic alliances like the Arab League; but no Arab Bismarck appeared, and the vision foundered on intense regional, ideological, and personal rivalries. Thus the practical, down-to-earth side of Arab nationalism focused largely on nation building within the particular states that supplanted former League of Nations mandates and European colonies.

This effort eventually seemed to some to result in one-party dictatorship, corruption, and continued daily hardship. Beginning in the 1970s, some Islamic preachers and devoted lay people charged that the model of modernizing, Western-inspired nationalism had failed. These critics, known in the West as fundamentalists, urged a return to Islamic principles and traditional morality. They evoked a

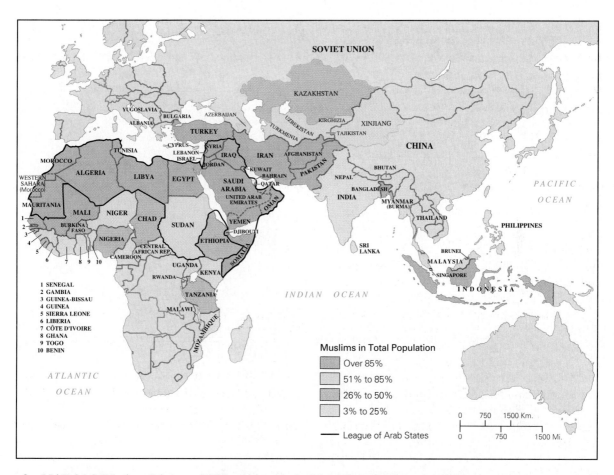

MAP 34.2 Modern Islam, ca 1990 Although the Islamic heartland remains the Middle East and North Africa, Islam is growing steadily in Africa south of the Sahara and is the faith of heavily populated Indonesia.

sympathetic response among many educated Muslims as well as among villagers and city dwellers.

Israel and the Palestinian Question Before the Second World War, Arab nationalists were loosely united in their opposition to the colonial powers and to Jewish migration to Palestine. The French gave up their League of Nations mandates in Syria and Lebanon in 1945, having been forced by popular uprisings to follow the British example. Attention then focused even more sharply on British-mandated Palestine. The situation was volatile. The Jews' demand that the British permit all survivors of Hitler's death camps to settle in Palestine was strenuously opposed by the Palestinian Arabs and the seven independent states of the newly founded Arab League (Egypt, Iraq, Jordan, Lebanon, Saudi

Arabia, Syria, and Yemen). Murder and terrorism flourished, nurtured by bitterly conflicting Arab and Jewish nationalisms.

The British—their occupation policies in Palestine condemned by Arabs and Jews, by Russians and Americans—announced in 1947 their intention to withdraw from Palestine in 1948. The insoluble problem was dumped in the lap of the United Nations. In November 1947 the United Nations General Assembly passed a nonbinding resolution supporting a plan to partition Palestine into two separate states—one Arab and one Jewish (Map 34.3). The Jews accepted, but the Arabs rejected partition of Palestine.

By early 1948 an undeclared civil war was raging in Palestine. When the British mandate officially ended on May 14, 1948, the Jews proclaimed the

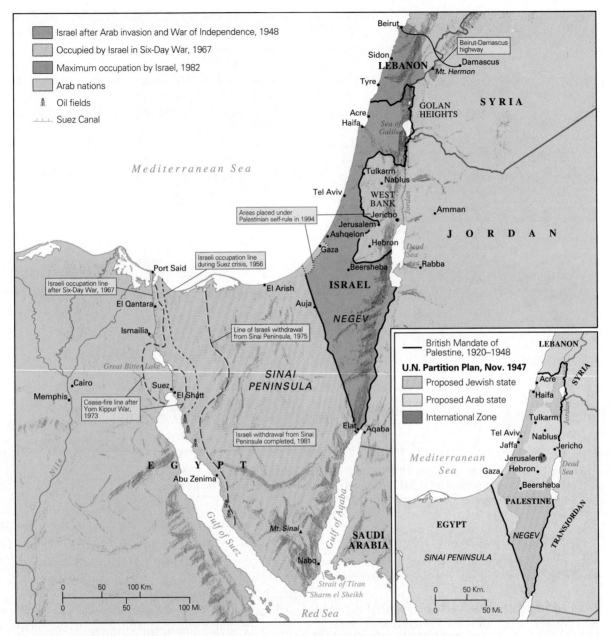

MAP 34.3 Palestine, Israel, and the Middle East, 1947–1993 Since the British mandate expired on May 14, 1948, there have been five major wars and innumerable armed clashes in what was formerly Palestine. After winning the War of Independence in 1948, Israel achieved spectacular victories in 1967 in the Six-Day War, occupying the Sinai Peninsula, the Golan Heights, and the West Bank. The Yom Kippur War of 1973 eventually led to the Israeli evacuation of the Sinai and peace with Egypt. In 1993 Israel and the Palestinian Liberation Organization agreed to self-rule for Palestinian Arabs in the West Bank in five years.

state of Israel. Arab countries immediately launched an attack on the new Jewish state. Fighting for their lives, the Israelis drove off the invaders and conquered more territory. Roughly 900,000 Arab refugees—the exact number is disputed—fled or were expelled from old Palestine. This war left an enormous legacy of Arab bitterness toward Israel and its political allies, Great Britain and the United States, and it led to the creation of the Palestine Liberation Organization, a loose union of Palestinian refugee groups opposed to Israel.

Egypt   In Egypt the humiliation of Arab defeat triggered a nationalist revolution. A young army colonel named Gamal Abdel Nasser (1918–1970)

drove out the corrupt and pro-Western king Farouk in 1952. A gifted politician and the unchallenged leader of the largest Arab state, Nasser enjoyed powerful influence in the Middle East and throughout Asia and Africa. Perhaps his most successful and widely imitated move was radical land reform: large estates along the Nile were nationalized and divided up among peasants without violence or drastic declines in production.

Nasser preached the gospel of neutralism in the cold war, jailed Egyptian communists, and turned for aid to the Soviet Union to demonstrate Egypt's independence of the West. Relations with Israel and the West worsened, and in 1956 the United States abruptly canceled its offer to finance a giant

Freedom for Palestinians   Jubilant friends and relatives embrace the first political prisoners released by Israel from the grim central prison in Gaza city. Israel freed a thousand Palestinian political prisoners to show its willingness to implement the interim peace agreement with the Palestinian Liberation Movement. *(Source: Larry Towell/Magnum Photos)*

new dam on the Nile, intended to promote economic development. Nasser retaliated by immediately nationalizing the European-owned Suez Canal Company, the last remaining vestige and symbol of European power in the Middle East. Outraged, the British and French joined forces with the Israelis and successfully invaded Egypt. The Americans, suddenly moralistic, reversed course and sided with the Soviets—who were at that very moment crushing the Hungarian revolution (see page 1110)—to force the British, French, and Israelis to withdraw from Egypt.

This great victory for Nasser encouraged anti-Western radicalism, hopes of Pan-Arab political unity, and a vague "Arab socialism." Yet the Arab world remained deeply divided. The only shared goals were bitter opposition to Israel—war recurred in 1967 and in 1973—and support for the right of Palestinian refugees to return to their homeland. In late 1977 President Anwar Sadat of Egypt tried another tack: a stunningly unexpected official visit to Israel.

Sadat's visit led to direct negotiations between Israel and Egypt, which were effectively mediated by U.S. president Jimmy Carter, and a historic though limited peace settlement. Each country gained: Egypt got back the Sinai Peninsula, which Israel had taken in the 1967 Six-Day War (see Map 34.3), and Israel obtained peace and normal relations with Egypt. Other Arab leaders denounced Sadat's initiative as treason and continued to support the Palestine Liberation Organization against Israel.

After Sadat's assassination by Islamic radicals in 1981, Egypt's relations with Israel deteriorated badly over the question of ever-increasing Israeli settlement on the West Bank—the area west of the Jordan River inhabited by Palestinian Arabs but taken by Israel from Jordan during the 1967 war. Yet Egypt and Israel maintained their fragile peace.

In 1988 young Palestinians in the occupied territories began a prolonged campaign of rock throwing and civil disobedience against Israeli soldiers. Inspired increasingly by Islamic fundamentalists, the Palestinian uprising eventually posed a serious challenge not only to Israel but to the secular Palestinian liberation movement, long led from abroad by Yasir Arafat. The result was a totally unexpected agreement in 1993 between Israel and the Palestinian Liberation Organization. The agreement granted Palestinian self-rule in Gaza and Jericho and called for self-rule throughout the West Bank in five years. Almost miraculously, peace between Israel and its neighbors seemed possible in the foreseeable future.

Nationalism, Fundamentalism, and Competition The recent history of the non-Arab states of Turkey and Iran and of the Arab states of Iraq and Algeria (see Map 34.2) testifies to the diversity of national development in the Muslim world. That history also dramatically illustrates the intense competition between rival states and the growing strength of Islamic revival.

Turkey remained basically true to Atatürk's vision of a thoroughly modernized, secularized, Europeanized state (see page 1001). Islam continued to exert less influence in daily life and thought there than it did in other Middle Eastern countries. Turkey still looked toward the West, joining NATO in 1952 and becoming an associate member of the European Community.

Iran tried again to follow Turkey's example, as it had before 1939 (see page 1002). Once again, its success was limited. The new shah—Muhammad Reza Pahlavi (r. 1941–1979), the son of Reza Shah Pahlavi—angered Iranian nationalists by courting Western powers and Western oil companies in the course of freeing his country from Soviet influence after the Second World War. In 1953, after leading the effort to nationalize the British-owned Anglo-Iranian Oil Company, the Iranian Majlis and the fiery Prime Minister Muhammad Mossaddeq forced the shah to flee to Europe. But Mossaddeq's victory was short-lived. Loyal army officers, with the help of the American CIA, quickly restored the shah to his throne.

The shah set out to build a powerful modern nation to ensure his rule. Iran's gigantic oil revenues provided the necessary cash. The shah undermined the power bases of the traditional politicians—large landowners and religious leaders—by means of land reform, secular education, and increased power for the central government. Modernization surged forward, but at the price of ancient values, widespread corruption, and harsh dictatorship. The result was a violent reaction against modernization and secular values: an Islamic revolution in 1978 that aimed at infusing strict Islamic principles into all aspects of personal and public life. Led by religious leaders grouped around the spellbinding Ayatollah Ruholla Khomeini, the radicals deposed the shah and tried to build their vision of a true Islamic state.

Iran's Islamic republic frightened its neighbors. Iraq, especially, feared that Iran—a nation of Shi'ite Muslims—would succeed in getting Iraq's Shi'ite majority to revolt against its Sunnite leaders. Thus in September 1980, Iraq's president Saddam Hussein (b. 1937) launched a surprise attack, expecting his well-equipped armies to defeat an increasingly chaotic Iran. Instead, Iraqi aggression galvanized the Iranian revolutionaries in a fanatical determination to defend their homeland and punish Iraq's leader. Iranians and Iraqis—Persians and Arabs—clashed in one of the bloodiest wars in modern times, a savage stalemate that killed hundreds of thousands of soldiers before finally grinding to a halt in 1988.

Emerging from the eight-year war with a big tough army equipped by Western countries and the Soviet bloc, Iraq's strongman set out to make himself the leader of the entire Arab world. Eyeing the great oil wealth of his tiny southern neighbor, Saddam Hussein suddenly ordered his forces to overrun Kuwait in August 1990, and he proclaimed its annexation to Iraq. To Saddam's surprise, his aggression brought a vigorous international response (see page 1205).

In early 1991 his troops were chased out of Kuwait by an American-led, United Nations–sanctioned military coalition, after American planes had first destroyed most of Iraq's infrastructure with the heaviest bombing since the Second World War. American troops, accompanied by small British, French, and Italian forces, were joined in ground operations against Iraq by some Arab forces from Egypt, Syria, and Saudia Arabia. Thus the Arab peoples, long wracked by bitter rivalries between nation-building states, came to fight a kind of bloody civil war. Disillusionment with existing Arab governments increased in the early 1990s.

The important north African country of Algeria highlighted the development of first nationalism and then fundamentalism. Nationalism in the French colony of Algeria was emboldened by Nasser's great triumph—and by the defeat of the French in Indochina. But Algeria's large European population of more than a million considered Algeria home and were determined to keep it an integral part of France. It was this determination that made the ensuing Algerian war so bitter and bloody.

In 1958 a military coup in Algeria, resulting from the fears of the European settlers that a disillusioned, anticolonial majority of French voters would sell them out, brought General Charles de Gaulle back to power in France. Contrary to expectations, de Gaulle accepted the principle of self-determination for Algeria in 1959, and French voters agreed in a national referendum. In 1962, after more than a century of French conquest, Algeria became an independent Arab state. The European population quickly fled.

The victorious anticolonial movement, known as the National Liberation Front, or FLN, used the revenues of Algeria's nationalized oil fields to promote state-owned industries, urban growth, and technical education. But the FLN also imposed a one-party state, which crushed dissent and favored a self-serving party elite. In the 1980s increasing numbers of dissatisfied Algerians looked toward Islam for moral and social revival, and in the early 1990s the Islamic opposition swept municipal and national elections. The FLN called on the army to preserve its power, claiming that the fundamentalists would "hijack" democracy and create an Islamic dictatorship. Military rule then led to growing violence and armed struggle between the government and the radical minority in the fundamentalist opposition, placing in bold relief the cultural and ideological divisions simmering just below the surface in the Muslim world.

✤ IMPERIALISM AND NATIONALISM IN BLACK AFRICA

Most of sub-Saharan Africa won political independence fairly rapidly after the Second World War. Only Portugal's old but relatively underdeveloped African territories and white-dominated southern Africa remained beyond the reach of African nationalists by 1964. The rise of independent states in black Africa—a major development in world history—resulted directly from both a reaction against Western imperialism and the growth of African nationalism.

The Imperial System (1900–1930)

After 1880 the Great Powers scrambled for territory and pushed into the interior, using overwhelming military force to mow down or intimidate

African opposition and establish firm rule (see pages 000–000). By 1900, most of black Africa had been conquered—or, as Europeans preferred to say, "pacified"—and a system of imperial administration was taking shape.

Gradually but relentlessly, this imperial system transformed Africa. Generally, its effect was to weaken or shatter the traditional social order and challenge accepted values. Yet this generalization must be qualified. For one thing, sub-Saharan Africa consisted of an astonishing diversity of peoples and cultures prior to the European invasion. There were, for example, over eight hundred distinct languages and literally thousands of independent political units, ranging from tiny kinship groups to large and powerful kingdoms like Ashanti of central Ghana and Ethiopia. The effects of imperialism varied accordingly.

European powers also took rather different approaches to colonial rule. The British tended to exercise indirect rule through existing chiefs. The French believed in direct rule by appointed officials, both black and white. Moreover, the number of white settlers varied greatly from region to region, and their presence had important consequences. In light of these qualifications, how did imperial systems generally operate in black Africa?

The self-proclaimed political goal of the French and the British—the principal foreign powers in black Africa—was to provide good government for their African subjects, especially after 1919. "Good government" meant, above all, law and order. It meant strong, authoritarian government, which maintained a small army, and building up an African police force to put down rebellion, suppress tribal warfare, and protect life and property. Good government required a modern bureaucracy capable of taxing and governing the population. Many African leaders and their peoples had chosen not to resist the invaders' superior force, and most others had stopped fighting after experiencing crushing military defeat. Thus the goal of law and order was widely achieved.

Colonial governments demonstrated much less interest in providing basic social services. Expenditures on education, public health, hospitals, and other social services increased after the First World War but still remained small. Europeans feared the political implications of mass education and typically relied instead on the modest efforts of state-subsidized mission schools. Moreover, they tried to make even their poorest colonies pay for themselves. Thus salaries for government workers normally absorbed nearly all tax revenues.

Economically, the imperialist goal was to draw the African interior into the world economy on terms favorable to the dominant Europeans. The key was railroads linking coastal trading centers to outposts hundreds of miles into the interior. Cheap, dependable transportation facilitated easy shipment of raw materials out and manufactured goods in. Most African railroads were built after 1900; fifty-two hundred miles were in operation by 1926, when attention turned to road building for trucks. Railroads and roads had two other important outcomes. They allowed the quick movement of troops to put down any local unrest, and they allowed many African peasants to earn wages for the first time.

Efforts to force Africa into the world economy on European terms went hand in hand with the advent of plantations and mines. The Europeans often imposed head taxes, payable in money or labor, to compel Africans to work for their white overlords. No aspect of imperialism was more disruptive and more despised by Africans than forced labor, widespread until about 1920. In some regions, however, particularly in West Africa, African peasants responded freely to the new economic opportunities by voluntarily shifting to export crops on their own farms. Overall, the result was increased production geared to the world market and a gradual decline in both traditional self-sufficient farming and nomadic herding.

In sum, the imposition of bureaucratic Western rule and the gradual growth of a world-oriented cash economy between 1900 and 1930 had a revolutionary impact on large parts of Africa. The experiences of Ghana and Kenya, two very different African countries, dramatically illustrate variations on the general pattern.

Present-day Ghana (see Map 34.4), which takes its name from one of West Africa's famous early kingdoms, had a fairly complex economy well before British armies smashed the powerful Ashanti kingdom in 1873 and established the Crown colony that they called the Gold Coast. Precolonial local trade was vigorous and varied. Into this sophisticated economy the British introduced production of cocoa beans for the world's chocolate bars. Output rose spectacularly, from a few hundred tons in the 1890s to 305,000 tons in 1936.

British imperialists loved to brag about the railroads to the interior, but recent studies clearly show that independent peasants and energetic African business people—many of the traders were women—were mainly responsible for the spectacular success of cocoa-bean production. Creative African entrepreneurs even went so far as to build their own roads, and they sometimes reaped big profits. During the boom of 1920, "motor cars were purchased right and left, champagne flowed freely, and expensive cigars scented the air."[7] As neighboring West African territories followed the Gold Coast's entrepreneurial example, West Africa took its place in the world economy.

The Gold Coast also showed the way politically and culturally. The westernized elite—relatively prosperous and well-educated lawyers, professionals, and journalists—and business people took full advantage of opportunities provided by the fairly enlightened colonial regime. The black elite was the main presence in the limited local elections permitted by the British, for few permanent white settlers had ventured to hot and densely populated West Africa.

Across the continent in the British East African colony of Kenya, events unfolded differently. The East African peoples were more self-sufficient, less numerous, and less advanced commercially and politically than Africans in the Gold Coast. Once the British had built a strategic railroad from the Indian Ocean coast across Kenya to Uganda, foreigners from Great Britain and India moved in to exploit the situation. Indian settlers became shopkeepers, clerks, and laborers in the towns. The British settlers dreamed of turning the cool, beautiful, and fertile Kenya highlands into a "white man's country" like Southern Rhodesia or the Union of South Africa. They dismissed the local population of peasant farmers as "barbarians," fit only to toil as cheap labor on their large estates and plantations. By 1929, two thousand white settlers were producing a variety of crops for export. The white settlers in Kenya manipulated the colonial government for their own interests and imposed rigorous segregation on the black and Indian populations. Kenya's Africans thus experienced much harsher colonial rule than did their fellow Africans in the Gold Coast.

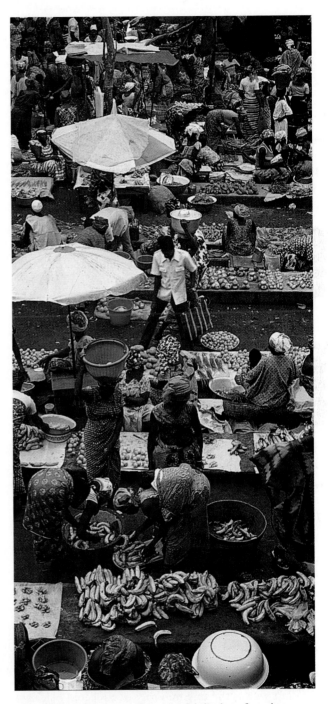

African Traders   This colorful display of produce suggests the competition and the dynamism of a West African market. African traders and peasants have played a key role in the economic development of West Africa since the 1920s. *(Source: Cynthia Johnson/Liaison)*

The Growth of African Nationalism

Western intrusion was the critical factor in the development of African nationalism, as it had been in Asia and the Middle East. But two things were different about Africa. Because the imperial system and Western education did not solidify in Africa until after 1900, national movements did not come of age there until after 1945. And, too, Africa's multiplicity of ethnic groups, coupled with imperial boundaries that often bore no resemblance to existing ethnic boundaries, greatly complicated the development of political—as distinct from cultural—nationalism. Was a modern national state to be based on ethnic tribal loyalties (as it had been in France and Germany, in China and Japan)? Was it to be founded on an all-African union of all black peoples? Or would such a state have to be built on the multitribal territories arbitrarily carved out by competing European empires? Only after 1945 did a tentative answer emerge.

A few educated West Africans in British colonies had articulated a kind of black nationalism before 1914. But the first real impetus came from the United States and the British West Indies. American blacks struggling for racial justice and black self-confidence took a keen interest in their African origins and in the common problems of all black people. Their influence on educated Africans was great.

Of the many persons who participated in this "black nationalism" and in the "Renaissance" of American black literature in the 1920s, the most renowned was W. E. B. Du Bois (1868–1963). The first black to receive a Ph.D. from Harvard, this brilliant writer and historian organized Pan-African congresses in Paris during the Versailles Peace Conference and in Brussels in 1921. The goals of Pan-Africanists were solidarity among blacks everywhere and, eventually, a vast self-governing union of all African peoples.

The European powers were hostile, of course, but so was the tiny minority of educated blacks in French Africa. As the influential Blaise Daigne, a black politician elected to the French parliament by the privileged African "citizens" of Senegal, told Du Bois:

We Frenchmen of Africa wish to remain French, for France has given us every liberty and accepted us without reservation along with her European chil- *dren. None of us aspire to see French Africa delivered exclusively to the Africans as is demanded, though without any authority, by the American Negroes.*[8]

Many educated French and British Africans, however, experienced a strong surge of pride and cultural nationalism in the 1920s and 1930s, inspired in part by American and West Indian blacks. The Senegalese poet and political leader Léopold Senghor (b. 1906) is an outstanding example. A gifted interpreter of Catholicism and of the French language in his native Senegal, Senghor discovered his African heritage in the cafés and lecture halls of Paris. He and other black and white students and intellectuals marveled at the accomplishments of American blacks in art, literature, African history, and anthropology. They listened to black musicians—jazz swept Europe by storm—and concluded that "in music American Negroes have acquired since the War a place which one can call pre-eminent; for they have impressed the entire world with their vibrating or melancholy rhythms."[9]

Senghor and his circle formulated and articulated the rich idea of *négritude,* or blackness: racial pride, self-confidence, and joy in black creativity and the black spirit. The powerful cultural nationalism that grew out of the cross-fertilization of African intellectuals and blacks from the United States and the West Indies was an unexpected byproduct of European imperialism.

Black consciousness also emerged in the British colonies between the world wars—especially in West Africa. The westernized elite pressed for more equal access to government jobs, modest steps toward self-government, and an end to humiliating discrimination. This elite began to claim the right to speak for ordinary Africans and to denounce the government-supported chiefs as "Uncle Toms." Yet the great majority of well-educated British and French Africans remained moderate in their demands.

The Great Depression was the decisive turning point in the development of African nationalism. For the first time, unemployment was widespread among educated Africans. Hostility toward well-paid white officials rose sharply. The Western-educated elite became more vocal, and some real radicals appeared.

Educated Africans ventured into new activities, often out of necessity. Especially in the towns, they supplied the leadership for many new organizations, including not only political parties and trade unions but also social clubs, native churches, and agricultural cooperatives. Radical journalists published uncompromising attacks on colonial governments in easy-to-read mass-circulation newspapers. The most spectacular of these journalists was the Nigerian Nnamdi Azikiwe, who had attended black colleges in the United States and learned his trade on an African-American weekly in Baltimore. The popular, flamboyant "Zik" was demanding independence for Nigeria as early as the late 1930s.

The Great Depression also produced extreme hardship and profound discontent among the African masses. African peasants and small business people who had been drawn into world trade, and who sometimes profited from booms, felt the agony of the decade-long bust, as did urban workers. In some areas the result was unprecedented mass protest. The Gold Coast "cocoa holdups" of 1930–1931 and 1937–1938 are the most famous example.

Cocoa completely dominated the Gold Coast's economy. As prices plummeted after 1929, cocoa farmers refused to sell their beans to the large British firms that fixed prices and monopolized the export trade. Instead, the farmers organized cooperatives to cut back production and sell their crops directly to European and American chocolate manufacturers. Small African traders and traditional tribal leaders largely supported the movement, which succeeded in mobilizing much of the population against the foreign companies. Many Africans saw the economic conflict in racial terms.

The holdups were only partially successful, but they did force the government to establish an independent cocoa marketing board. They also demonstrated that mass organization and mass protest had come to advanced West Africa. Powerful mass movements for national independence would not be far behind.

Achieving Independence with New Leaders

The repercussions of the Second World War in black Africa greatly accelerated the changes begun in the 1930s. Mines and plantations strained to meet wartime demands. Towns mushroomed into cities whose tin-can housing, inflation, and shortages of consumer goods created discontent and

hardship. Africans had such eye-opening experiences as the curious spectacle of the British denouncing the racism of the Germans. Many African soldiers who served in India were powerfully impressed by Indian nationalism.

The attitudes of Western imperialists changed also. Both the British and the French acknowledged the need for rapid social and economic improvement in their colonies; both began sending money and aid on a large scale for the first time. The French funneled more money into their West African colonies between 1947 and 1957 than during the entire previous half-century. The principle of self-government was written into the United Nations charter and was supported by Great Britain's postwar Labour government. As one top British official stated in 1948:

The central purpose of British colonial policy is simple. It is to guide the colonial territories to responsible government within the commonwealth in conditions that ensure to the people concerned both a fair standard of living and freedom from oppression from any quarter.[10]

Thus the key question for Great Britain's various African colonies was their rate of progress toward self-government. The British and the French were in no rush. But a new breed of African leader was emerging. Impatient and insistent, these spokesmen for modern African nationalism were remarkably successful: by 1964 almost all of western, eastern, and central Africa had achieved statehood, usually without much bloodshed.

The new postwar African leaders shared common characteristics. They formed an elite by virtue of advanced European or American education, and they were profoundly influenced by Western thought. But compared with the interwar generation of educated Africans, they were more radical and humbler in social origin. Among them were former schoolteachers, union leaders, government clerks, and unemployed students, as well as lawyers and prize-winning poets.

Furthermore, the postwar African leaders expressed their nationalism in terms of the existing territorial governments. They accepted prevailing boundaries to avoid border disputes and to achieve freedom as soon as possible. Sometimes tribal chiefs became their worst political enemies. Skillfully, the new leaders channeled postwar hope and

NATIONALISM IN BLACK AFRICA

1919	Du Bois organizes first Pan-African congress
1920s	Cultural nationalism grows among Africa's educated elites
1929	Great Depression brings economic hardship and discontent
1930–1931	Farmers in the Gold Coast organize first "cocoa holdups"
1939–1945	World War Two accelerates political and economic change
1951	Nkrumah and Convention People's Party win national elections in Ghana
1957	Nkrumah leads Ghana—former Gold Coast—to independence
1958	De Gaulle offers commonwealth status to France's African territories Guinea alone chooses independence
1960	Mali and Nigeria become independent states
1966	Ghana's Nkrumah deposed in military coup
1967	Eastern Region secedes from Nigeria to form state of Biafra
1979	Nigeria's military rulers permit elected civilian government
1980	Blacks rule Zimbabwe—formerly Southern Rhodesia—after long civil war with white settlers
1983	South Africa's whites maintain racial segregation and discrimination
1989–1990	South African government begins process of reform Black leader Nelson Mandela freed from prison
1994	Mandela elected president of South Africa

discontent into support for mass political organizations. These organizations staged gigantic protests and became political parties. Eventually they came to power by winning the general elections that the colonial government belatedly called to choose its successor.

Ghana Shows the Way

Perhaps the most charismatic of this generation of African leaders was Kwame Nkrumah (1909–1972). Under his leadership the Gold Coast—which he rechristened "Ghana"—became the first independent African state to emerge from colonialism. Having begun his career as a schoolteacher in the Gold Coast, Nkrumah spent ten years studying in the United States, where he was deeply influ-

enced by European socialists and by the Jamaican-born black leader Marcus Garvey (1887–1940). Convinced that blacks could never win justice in countries with white majorities, Garvey had organized a massive "Back to Africa" movement in the 1920s. He also preached "Africa for the Africans," calling for independence. Nkrumah returned to the Gold Coast immediately after the Second World War and entered politics.

The time was ripe. Economic discontent erupted in rioting in February 1948; angry crowds looted European and Lebanese stores. The British, embarking on their new course, invited African proposals for constitutional reform. These proposals became the basis of the new constitution, which gave more power to Africans within the framework of (eventual) parliamentary democracy. Mean-

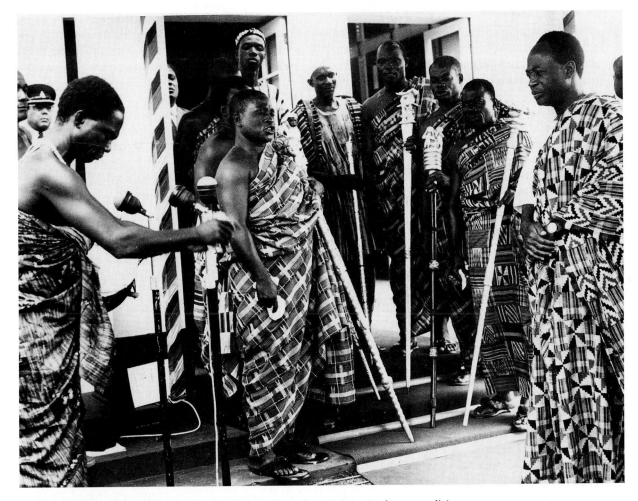

⁂ **The Opening of Parliament in Ghana**   As part of an ancient ritual, two medicine men pour out sacred oil and call on the gods to bless the work of the Second Parliament and President Kwame Nkrumah, standing on the right. The combination of time-honored customs and modern political institutions has been characteristic of African states since independence. *(Source: Wide World Photos)*

while, Nkrumah was building a radical mass party appealing particularly to modern elements—former servicemen, market women, union members, urban toughs, and cocoa farmers. He and his party injected the joy and enthusiasm of religious revivals into their rallies and propaganda: "Self-Government Now" was their credo, secular salvation the promise.

Rejecting halfway measures—"We prefer self-government with danger to servitude in tranquility"—Nkrumah and his Convention People's party staged strikes and riots. Arrested, the "Deliv-

erer of Ghana" campaigned from jail and saw his party win a smashing victory in the national elections of 1951. Called from prison to head the transitional government, Nkrumah and his nationalist party defeated both westernized moderates and more traditional "tribal" rivals in free elections. By 1957 Nkrumah had achieved worldwide fame and influence as Ghana became the first African state to emerge from colonial control.

After Ghana's breakthrough, independence for other African colonies followed rapidly. As in Algeria, the main problem was the permanent white settlers, as distinguished from the colonial officials. Wherever white settlers were at all numerous, as in Kenya, they sought to preserve their privileged position. But only in Southern Rhodesia were whites numerous enough to prevail long. Southern Rhodesian whites declared independence illegally in 1965 and held out until 1980, when black nationalists won a long guerrilla war and renamed the country Zimbabwe. In Zambia (formerly Northern Rhodesia) and East Africa, white settlers simply lacked the numbers to challenge black nationalists or the British colonial office for long.

French-speaking Regions

Decolonization took a somewhat different course in French-speaking Africa. France tried hard to hold on to Indochina and Algeria after 1945. Thus although France upped its aid to its African colonies, independence remained a dirty word until de Gaulle came to power in 1958. Seeking to head off radical nationalists, and receiving the crucial support of moderate black leaders, de Gaulle chose a divide-and-rule strategy. He divided the federations of French West Africa and French Equatorial Africa into thirteen separate governments, thus creating a "French commonwealth." Plebiscites were called in each territory to ratify the new arrangement. An affirmative vote meant continued ties with France; a negative vote signified immediate independence and a complete break with France.

De Gaulle's gamble was shrewd. The educated black elite—as personified by the poet Senghor, who now led the government of Senegal (see Map 34.4)—loved France and dreaded a sudden divorce. They also wanted French aid to continue. France, in keeping with its ideology of assimilation, had given the vote to the educated elite in its colonies after the Second World War, and about forty Africans held seats in the French parliament after 1946. Some of these impressive African politicians exercised real power and influence in metropolitan France. The Ivory Coast's Félix Houphouét-Boigny, for instance, served for a time as France's minister of health. For both cultural and practical reasons, therefore, French Africa's leaders tended to be moderate and in no rush for independence.

Yet political nationalism was not totally submerged. In Guinea, an inspiring young radical named Sekou Touré (1922–1984) led his people in overwhelming rejection of the new constitution in 1958. Inspired by Ghana's Nkrumah, Touré laid it out to de Gaulle, face to face:

We have to tell you bluntly, Mr. President, what the demands of the people are. . . . We have one prime and essential need: our dignity. But there is no dignity without freedom. . . . We prefer freedom in poverty to opulence in slavery.[11]

De Gaulle punished Guinea as best he could. French officials and equipment were withdrawn, literally overnight, down to the last man and pencil. Guinea's total collapse was widely predicted—and devoutly hoped for in France. But Guinea's new government survived. Following Guinea's lead, Mali asked for independence in 1960. The other French territories quickly followed suit, though the new states retained close ties with France.

Belgium tried belatedly to imitate de Gaulle in its enormous Congo colony, but without success. Long-time practitioners of paternalism, coupled with harsh, selfish rule, the Belgians had discouraged the development of an educated elite. In 1959, therefore, when after wild riots they suddenly decided to grant independence, the fabric of government simply broke down. Independence was soon followed by violent tribal conflict, civil war, and foreign intervention. The Belgian Congo was the great exception to black Africa's generally peaceful and successful transition to independence between 1957 and 1964.

BLACK AFRICA SINCE 1960

The facility with which most of black Africa achieved independence stimulated buoyant optimism in the early 1960s. As Europeans congratulated themselves on having fulfilled their "civilizing mission," Africans anticipated even more rapid progress. But in the course of a generation the outlook changed. In most former colonies, democratic government and civil liberties gave way to one-party rule or military dictatorship. In many countries it became common for the winners in a political power struggle to imprison, exile, or murder the losers. Corruption was widespread; politicians, army officers, and even lowly government clerks used their positions to line their pockets and reward their relatives.

Nevertheless, conditions should be viewed in historical perspective. Given the tremendous scope of their challenges, the new African countries did rather well after achieving political independence. Nationalism, first harnessed to throw off imperialism, served to promote some degree of unity and ongoing modernization. Divisive ethnic conflicts arose, but fragile states survived.

Striving for National Unity

The course of African history after independence was complex and often confusing, but the common legacy of imperialism resulted in certain basic patterns and problems. The legacy of imperialism in Africa was not all bad. One positive outcome was the creation of about forty well-defined states (see Map 33.3, page 1110). These new states inherited functioning bureaucracies, some elected political leaders, and some modern infrastructure—that is, transportation, schools, hospitals, and the like.

The new African states inherited relatively modern, diversified social structures. Traditional tribal and religious rulers had generally lost out to a dynamic westernized elite whose moderate and radical wings faithfully reproduced the twentieth-century political spectrum. Each new state had the beginnings of an industrial working class and a volatile urban poor. Each country inherited the cornerstone of imperial power—a tough, well-equipped army to maintain order.

Other features of the imperialist legacy, however, served to torment independent Africa. The disruption of traditional life caused real suffering and resulted in postindependence expectations that could not be met. The prevailing export economies were weak, lopsided, and concentrated in foreign hands. Technical, managerial, and medical skills were in acutely short supply. Above all, the legacy of political boundaries imposed by foreigners without regard to ethnic and cultural groupings weighed heavily on postindependence Africa. Almost all of the new states encompassed a variety of peoples, with different languages, religions, and cultures. As in the Austrian Empire in the nineteenth century or in British India before independence, different peoples might easily develop conflicting national aspirations.

Great Britain and France had granted their African colonies democratic government as they prepared to depart. Yet belated, Western-style democracy served the new multiethnic states poorly. After freedom from imperialism no longer provided a unifying common objective, political parties often coalesced along regional and ethnic lines. Open political competition often encouraged regional and ethnic conflict, complicated nation building, and promoted political crisis. Many African leaders concluded that democracy threatened to destroy the existing states, which they deemed essential for social and economic progress in spite of their less-than-perfect boundaries. Thus these leaders did not abandon the authoritarian tradition they inherited from the imperialists. They imposed tough measures to hold their countries together, and free elections often gave way to dictators and one-party rule.

After Ghana won its independence, for instance, Nkrumah jailed without trial his main opponents—chiefs, lawyers, and intellectuals—and outlawed opposition parties. Embracing the authoritarian model, Nkrumah worked to build a dynamic "revolutionary" one-party state. His personality, his calls for African unity, and his bitter attacks on "Western imperialists" aroused both strong support and growing opposition. By the mid-1960s Nkrumah's grandiose economic projects had almost bankrupted Ghana, and in 1966 the army suddenly seized power while Nkrumah was visiting China. Across the continent in East Africa, Kenya and Tanzania likewise became one-party states with strong leaders.

The French-speaking countries also shifted toward one-party government to promote state unity and develop distinctive characteristics that could serve as the basis for statewide nationalism. Mali followed Guinea into fiery radicalism. Senegal and the Ivory Coast stressed moderation and close economic and cultural ties with France.

Like Nkrumah, many of the politicians at the helm of one-party states were eventually overthrown by military leaders. Between 1952, when Egypt's King Farouk was overthrown by Colonel Nasser, and 1968, Africa experienced at least seventy attempted military takeovers. Twenty of them succeeded. The trend continued after 1968. The rise of would-be Napoleons was lamented by many

Western liberals and African intellectuals, who often failed to note that military rule was also widespread in Latin America, Asia, and the Near East.

As elsewhere, military rule in Africa was authoritarian and undemocratic. Sometimes it placed a terrible burden on Africans. In Uganda, for instance, Idi Amin (b. 1925?), a brutal former sergeant, seized power in 1971, packed the army with his tribal supporters, and terrorized the population for a decade. Yet military government often had redeeming qualities. African military leaders generally managed to hold their countries together, and they worked to build existing states into viable nations.

Equally important, many military regimes, like their counterparts in Latin America (see pages 1125–1126), were committed to social and economic modernization. Drawing on an educated, well-organized, and highly motivated elite, they sometimes accomplished a good deal. African military leaders often believed in the ultimate goal of free, representative civilian government, which they sometimes restored after surmounting a grave national crisis. It was a question of priorities: unity came first, democracy second.

Nigeria, Africa's Giant

The history of Nigeria illustrates just how difficult nation building could be when state and ethnic boundaries were at odds with each other. "Nigeria" was a name coined by the British to designate their conquests in the Niger River basin (Map 34.4). The peoples of Nigeria encompassed many ancient kingdoms and hundreds of smaller groupings. The northern region was part of a great open plain, devoted to grazing and intensive farming. The much smaller southern region was a combination of coastal swamp and inland forest belt. Most of the peoples of the north were Muslims; most southerners were Christians or animists. The south was dominated by two very different peoples: in the west the proud Yorubas, with a military tradition and strong, well-defined kingdom; in the east the Ibos, with a tradition of business enterprise and independent villages.

Modern Nigeria came into being in 1914, when the British arbitrarily consolidated the northern and southern territories for administrative convenience. At least one British governor, who described Nigeria in 1920 as a "collection of

self-contained and mutually independent Native States,"[12] believed such a land could never be welded into a single nation. However, in spite of its internal divisions, by 1945 Nigeria had spawned a powerful independence movement. The British responded receptively, and Nigeria entered into a period of intense but peaceful negotiation. In 1954, the third constitution in seven years set up the framework within which independence was achieved in 1960.

The key constitutional question was the relationship between the central government and the various regions. Some Nigerians, like the fiery Ibo journalist Azikiwe, wanted a strong centralized state, but the Yorubas in the west and the Muslim Hausa-Fulani leaders in the north wanted real power concentrated in large regions. Ultimately Nigeria adopted a federal system, whereby the national government at Lagos shared power with three regional or state governments in the north, west, and east. Each region had a dominant tribe and a corresponding political party. The parties were expected to cooperate in the national parliament, and the rights of minorities were protected by law.

With a population of 55 million in 1963, "Africa's Giant" towered over the other new African nations. But after independence, Nigerians' bright hopes gradually dimmed because of ethnic rivalries. In 1964, minorities in the Western Region began forming their own Midwestern Region in an attempt to escape Yoruba domination (see Map 34.4), and tribal battles followed in the Western Region. At this point a group of young army officers seized power in the capital city of Lagos, executing leading politicians and all officers above the rank of major. In an attempt to end the national crisis, the new military council imposed martial law and abolished the regional governments.

At first the young officers were popular, for the murdered politicians had been widely considered weak, corrupt, and too pro-Western. However,

MAP 34.4 Nationalism and Independence in West Africa   Most of West Africa achieved independence by 1960. Borders inherited from the colonial era were generally accepted, although the Ibo people tried unsuccessfully to break away from Nigeria in the bitter Nigerian civil war.

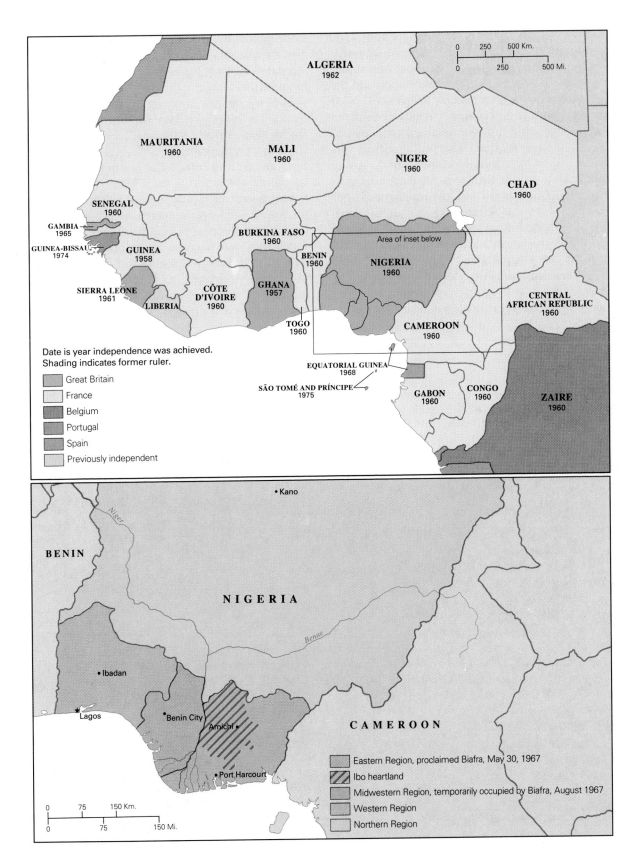

Date is year independence was achieved.
Shading indicates former ruler.

Great Britain
France
Belgium
Portugal
Spain
Previously independent

Eastern Region, proclaimed Biafra, May 30, 1967
Ibo heartland
Midwestern Region, temporarily occupied by Biafra, August 1967
Western Region
Northern Region

many of the new military leaders were Ibos. The Muslim northerners had long distrusted the hard-working, clannish, non-Muslim Ibos, who under the British had come to dominate business and the professions throughout Nigeria. When the Ibo-led military council proclaimed a highly centralized dictatorship, wild mobs in northern cities massacred thousands of Ibos. The panic-stricken survivors fled to their Ibo homeland. When a group of northern officers then seized the national government in a counter-coup, the traumatized Ibos revolted. Like the American South in the Civil War, the Eastern Region seceded from Nigeria in 1967 and proclaimed itself the independent state of Biafra (see Map 34.4).

The war in Biafra lasted three long years. The Ibos fought with heroic determination, believing that political independence was their only refuge from genocide. Heavily outnumbered, the Ibos were gradually surrounded. Perhaps millions starved to death as Biafra became another name for monumental human tragedy.

But Nigeria, like Abraham Lincoln's Union, endured. The bloody civil war in Nigeria showed the world that Africa's "artificial" boundaries and states were remarkably durable. Having preserved the state in the 1960s, Nigeria's military focused on building a nation in the 1970s. Although the federal government held the real power, the country was divided into nineteen small, manageable units to handle local and cultural matters. The defeated Ibos were generously pardoned, not slaughtered, and Iboland was rebuilt with federal money. Modernizing investments of this kind were made possible by soaring oil revenues; Nigeria became the world's seventh largest oil producer.

Mobilizing in Biafra A Biafran officer, himself only nine years old, drills a column of fresh recruits in 1969 during the Nigerian civil war. The boy soldiers were used for spying and sabotage, as Biafra struggled desperately against encirclement and starvation to win its independence. *(Source: Pictorial Parade)*

In 1979, after thirteen years of military rule, Nigeria's army leaders were confident enough to return power to an elected civilian government. But four years later the army again seized control, arresting the civilian politicians who had mismanaged the economy and demanded bribes and kickbacks. The military rulers soon imposed a harsh dictatorship, which was dominated by Hausa-Fulani Muslims. These northerners practiced a tribal favoritism that threatened to re-ignite regional and ethnic tensions that were never far beneath the surface. Thus a group of reforming officers engineered another coup in 1985, promising more liberty and less favoritism. The new generals did show greater respect for basic rights, but they repeatedly postponed or nullified national elections. Elected government remained an enduring goal in Nigeria, but military rule to preserve unity has been the reality.

The Struggle in Southern Africa

After the great rush toward political independence, decolonization stalled. Southern Africa remained under white rule, largely because of the numerical strength and determination of its white settlers. In Portuguese Angola and Mozambique, the white population actually increased from 70,000 to 380,000 between 1940 and the mid-1960s as white settlers using forced native labor established large coffee farms.

As economic exploitation grew, so did resentment. Nationalist liberation movements arose to wage unrelenting guerrilla warfare. After a coup overturned the long-established dictatorship in Portugal, African guerrillas managed to take control in Angola and Mozambique in 1975. Shortly thereafter, a coalition of nationalist groups also won in Zimbabwe after a long struggle.

This second round of decolonization in black Africa was bloodier than the first, and a third round in South Africa threatened to be still worse. The racial conflict in the white-ruled Republic of South Africa could be traced back in part to the outcome of the Boer War (see page 896). Although the British finally conquered the inland Afrikaner republics, they had to compromise to avoid a long guerrilla war. Specifically, the British agreed to grant all of South Africa self-government as soon as possible and to let its government decide which nonwhites, if any, should vote. It was to be a tragic compromise.

Defeated on the battlefield, the embittered Afrikaners elaborated a potently racist nationalism. Between 1910—when South Africa became basically a self-governing dominion, like Canada and Australia—and 1948, the Afrikaners gradually won political power from their English-speaking settler rivals. After their decisive electoral victory in 1948, Afrikaner nationalists spoke increasingly for a large majority of South African whites, who supported the political leadership with varying degrees of enthusiasm.

The goals of Afrikaner nationalism in the twentieth century were remarkably consistent: white supremacy and racial segregation. In 1913, the new South African legislature passed the Native Land Act, which limited black ownership of land to native reserves encompassing a mere one-seventh of the country. Poor, overpopulated, and too small to feed themselves, the native reserves in the countryside served as a pool of cheap, temporary black labor for white farms, gold mines, and urban factories. A black worker—typically a young single person—could leave the reserve only with special permission. In the eyes of the law, he or she was only a temporary migrant who could be returned at will by the employer or the government. The native reserves system, combining racial segregation and indirect forced labor, formed the foundation of white supremacy in South Africa.

After 1948, successive Afrikaner governments wove the somewhat haphazard early racist measures into an authoritarian fabric of racial discrimination and inequality. This system was officially known as *apartheid*, meaning "separation" or "segregation." The population was divided into four legally unequal racial groups: whites, blacks, Asians, and racially mixed "coloureds." Afrikaner propagandists claimed to serve the interests of all racial groups by preserving separate cultures and racial purity; marriage and sexual relations between races became criminal offenses. Most observers saw apartheid as a way of maintaining the lavish privileges of the white minority, which accounted for only one-sixth of the total population.

After 1940, South Africa's cities grew rapidly in conjunction with its emergence as the most highly industrialized country in Africa. Urbanization changed the face of the country, but good jobs in the cities were reserved for whites. Whites lived in luxurious modern central cities. Blacks, legally classified as temporary migrants, were restricted to outlying black townships plagued by poverty, crime, and white policemen. In spite of segregation, the growing cities produced a vibrant urban black culture, largely distinct from that of the tribal reserves. As a black journalist in Johannesburg explained in 1966:

I am supposed to be a Pondo, but I don't even know the language of that tribe. . . . I am just not a tribesman, whether I like it or not. I am, inescapably, a part of the city slums, the factory machines and our beloved shebeens [illegal bars].[13]

South Africa's harsh white supremacy elicited many black nationalist protests from the 1920s onward. Black nationalists began as moderates, seeking gradual reforms. By the 1950s, blacks—and their coloured, white, and Asian allies—were staging large-scale peaceful protests. A high point came in 1960, when police at Sharpeville fired into a crowd of demonstrators and killed sixty-nine blacks. The main black nationalist organization—the African National Congress (ANC)—was outlawed but sent some of its leaders abroad to establish new headquarters. Other members, led by a young black lawyer named Nelson Mandela (b. 1918), stayed in South Africa to set up an underground army to oppose the government. Captured after seventeen months, Mandela was tried for treason and sentenced to life imprisonment (see Listening to the Past). With harsh laws, a powerful police force, and an army of spies, the South African government defended and strengthened the apartheid system.

By the late 1970s, the white government had apparently destroyed the moderate black opposition within South Africa. Operating out of the sympathetic black states of Zimbabwe and Mozambique to the north, the militant ANC turned increasingly to armed struggle. South Africa struck back hard. It supported separatist movements that destabilized its neighbors, and it forced Marxist Mozambique in particular to curtail the ANC's guerrilla activities. Fortified by these successes, South Africa's white leaders launched in 1984 a program of "reforms"—changes designed to preserve white domination by means of a few strategic concessions.

For the first time, the 3 million coloureds and the 1 million South Africans of Asian descent were granted limited parliamentary representation. But no provision was made for any representation of the country's 22 million blacks. The government also made minor adjustments to apartheid, permitting marriage between races, for example. But laws controlling black movement and settlement were maintained.

The government's self-serving reforms provoked black indignation and triggered a massive reaction. In the segregated townships young black militants took to the streets, attacking in particular black civil servants and policemen as agents of white oppression. Heavily armed white security forces clashed repeatedly with black protesters, who turned funerals for fallen comrades into mass demonstrations. In 1985 the white government delared a state of emergency, and in 1986 it imposed unlimited press censorship and took a gigantic step toward dictatorship for all, regardless of race. Between 1985 and 1989, 5,000 died and 50,000 were jailed without charges because of the political unrest.

By 1989, the white government and the black opposition had reached an impasse. Black protesters had been bloodied but not beaten, and their movement for democracy had gathered worldwide support. The U.S. Congress had applied strong sanctions against South Africa in October 1986, and the Common Market had followed. The white government still held power, but the white population was increasingly divided. Being rejected as outcasts by the world community wounded the pride of some whites, and, more important, harsh repression of the black resistance had obviously failed.

A major step toward breaking the political stalemate came in September 1989 with the election of a new state president, Frederik W. de Klerk, an Afrikaner lawyer and politician. A late-blooming reformer, de Klerk moved cautiously toward reducing tensions and opening a dialogue with the ANC leaders. Negotiating with Nelson Mandela, whose reputation had soared among urban blacks during his long years in prison, de Klerk lifted the state of emergency in most of the country, legalized the ANC, and freed Mandela in February 1990. Emerging from prison as a proud and impressive leader, Mandela received a hero's welcome in South Africa and then in the United States and Europe.

In August 1990, Mandela showed again his courage and statesmanship. Overriding the doubts

Men of Destiny   Nelson Mandela shakes hands with Frederik de Klerk following a televised presidential debate in the 1994 electoral campaign. Mandela won and replaced de Klerk as president of South Africa after 350 years of white supremacy. De Klerk became vice president. Both leaders vowed to build a multiracial democratic society. *(Source: Mark Peters/Sipa Press)*

of some militant supporters, he suspended the ANC's armed struggle, thereby meeting de Klerk's condition for serious talks on South Africa's political future. Negotiations were long and difficult, greatly complicated by bitter opposition from right-wing whites and by violent clashes between some Zulus and some supporters of the ANC. But Mandela and de Klerk persevered. They reached an agreement calling for universal suffrage, which meant black majority rule, and they also guaranteed the civil rights of minorities.

Elected president of South Africa by an overwhelming majority in May 1994, Mandela told his jubilant supporters of his "deep pride and joy—pride in the ordinary, humble people of this country. . . . And joy that we can loudly proclaim from the roof tops—free at last!"[14] Heading the new "government of national unity," which included de Klerk as vice president, Mandela and the peoples of South Africa set about building a democratic, multiracial nation. It was a stunning climax to the long struggle for African liberation.

SUMMARY

Asian and African peoples experienced a remarkable resurgence after the Second World War, a resurgence that will almost certainly stand as a decisive turning point in world history. The long-developing nationalist movement in China culminated in a social revolution led by communists who went on to pursue innovative and fiercely independent policies that redeemed China as a great power in world affairs. Japan, defeated, demilitarized, and democratized, took a completely different path to the rank of economic superpower in a no less spectacular renaissance. Elsewhere—in India, Indonesia, and the Philippines—Asian peoples won their freedom and self-confidently charted independent courses. The Muslim world was also rejuvenated, most notably under Nasser in Egypt. In black Africa, a generation of nationalist leaders successfully guided colonial territories to self-rule by the middle of the 1960s, although liberation did not come in South Africa until the 1990s.

The resurgence and political self-assertion of Asian and African peoples in revitalized or developing nation-states did not proceed without conflict. Serious regional and ethnic confrontations erupted, notably between Hindus and Muslims in India and between Arabs and Israelis in the Middle East, and similar conflicts continued after independence was won. The vestiges of Western colonialism and cold war struggles resulted in atypical but highly destructive conflicts in Algeria, Vietnam, and Zimbabwe. The revitalized peoples of Asia and Africa continued to face tremendous economic and social challenges, which had to be met if the emerging nations were to realize fully the promise of self-assertion and independence.

Notes

1. S. Schram, *Mao Tse-tung* (New York: Simon and Schuster, 1966), p. 151.
2. Quoted in P. B. Ebrey, ed., *Chinese Civilization and Society: A Source Book* (New York: Free Press, 1981), p. 393.
3. Quoted in W. Bingham, H. Conroy, and F. Iklé, *A History of Asia,* vol. 2, 2d ed. (Boston: Allyn and Bacon, 1974), p. 459.
4. Quoted in S. Wolpert, *A New History of India,* 2d ed. (New York: Oxford University Press, 1982), p. 330.
5. Quoted in K. Bhata, *The Ordeal of Nationhood: A Social Study of India Since Independence, 1947–1970* (New York: Atheneum, 1971), p. 9.
6. Quoted in B. D. Nossiter, *Soft State: A Newspaperman's Chronicle of India* (New York: Harper & Row, 1970), p. 52.
7. G. B. Kay, ed., *The Political Economy of Colonialism in Ghana: A Collection of Documents and Statistics* (Cambridge: Cambridge University Press, 1972), p. 48.
8. Quoted in R. W. July, *A History of the African People,* 3d ed. (New York: Scribner's, 1980), pp. 519–520.
9. Quoted in J. L. Hymans, *Léopold Sédar Senghor: An Intellectual Biography* (Edinburgh: University of Edinburgh Press, 1971), p. 58.
10. Quoted in L. H. Gann and P. Duignan, *Colonialism in Africa,* vol. 2 (Cambridge: Cambridge University Press, 1970), p. 512.
11. Quoted in R. Hallett, *Africa Since 1875: A Modern History* (Ann Arbor: University of Michigan Press, 1974), pp. 378–379.
12. Ibid., p. 345.
13. Ibid., p. 657.
14. Quoted in *Chicago Tribune,* May 3, 1994, section 1, p. 5.

Suggested Reading

Many of the works mentioned in the Suggested Reading for Chapter 30 are also valuable for considering postwar developments in Asia and the Middle East. Three other important studies on developments in China are E. Friedman, *Chinese Village, Socialist State* (1991); C. Johnson, *Peasant Nationalism and Communist Power: The Emergence of Revolutionary China, 1937–1945* (1962); and W. L. Parish and M. K. Whyte, *Village and Family in Contemporary China* (1978). M. Meisner, *Mao's China: A History of the People's Republic* (1977), is an excellent comprehensive study, and C. P. FitzGerald, *Communism Takes China: How the Revolution Went Red* (1971), is a lively, illustrated account by a scholar who spent many years in China. Recent developments are ably analyzed by J. Spence, *The Search for Modern China* (1990), and Lin Binyan, *China's Crisis, China's Hope* (1990). T. Yueh and C. Wakeman, *To the Storm: The Odyssey of a Revolutionary Chinese Woman* (1985), is the poignant drama of a participant. R. Lardy, *Agriculture in China's Economic Development* (1983), carefully studies the poor performance that led to Deng's reforms, which are fully examined in R. Evans, *Deng Xiaoping and the Making of Modern China* (1994).

K. Kawai, *Japan's American Interlude* (1960), and R. P. Dore, *Land Reform in Japan* (1959), consider key problems of occupation policy. A. Gordon, ed., *Postwar Japan as History* (1993), contains essays by leading scholars and has an extensive bibliography. Three excellent and thought-provoking studies of contemporary Japanese society are E. Reischauer, *The Japanese Today, Change and Continuity* (1989); F. Gibney, *Japan, the Fragile Superpower* (1977); and E. Vogel, *Japan as Number One: Lessons for America* (1979). G. Bernstein, *Haruko's World: A Japanese Farm Woman and Her Community* (1983), probes changing patterns of rural life. Akira Iriye, *The Cold*

War in Asia: A Historical Introduction (1974), and M. Schaller, *The United States and China in the Twentieth Century* (1979), analyze international conflicts in the postwar Pacific basin.

S. Wolpert, *India* (1991), a wise and beautifully written introduction, is highly recommended. G. Hutchins, *India's Revolution: Gandhi and the Quit India Movement* (1973), is an excellent account of wartime developments in India, which may be compared with J. Nehru, *An Autobiography* (1962), the appealing testimony of a principal architect of Indian freedom. F. Frankel, *India's Political Economy, 1947–1977* (1978), intelligently discusses the economic policies of independent India. There is a good biography of Indira Gandhi by D. Moraes (1980). J. Novak, *Bangladesh: Reflections of the Water* (1993), is a moving introduction. H. Tinker, *South Asia: A Short History,* 2d ed. (1990), is a good guide to the states of the Indian subcontinent.

For Southeast Asia there are solid general accounts by C. Dubois, *Social Forces in Southeast Asia* (1967), and R. N. Kearney, *Politics and Modernization in South and Southeast Asia* (1974). C. Cooper, *The Lost Crusade: America in Vietnam* (1972), and F. FitzGerald, *Fire in the Lake* (1973), probe the tragic war in Vietnam. Two valuable works on other Asian countries are B. Dahm, *Sukarno and the Struggle for Indonesian Independence* (1969), and T. Friend, *Between Two Empires: The Ordeal of the Philippines, 1929–1946* (1965).

Recommended studies of the Middle East and Israel include a cultural investigation by R. Patai, *The Arab Mind* (1973); a balanced account by C. Smith, *Palestine and the Arab-Israeli Conflict* (1988); an excellent biography of Israel's inspiring leader during its war for independence by A. Avi-Hai, *Ben Gurion, State Builder* (1974); and B. Kimmerling and J. Migdal, *The Palestinians: The Making of a People* (1992). A. Goldschmidt, Jr., *Modern Egypt: The Formation of a Nation-State* (1988), treats the post-Nasser years extensively. Religious fundamentalism is sympathetically analyzed in J. Esposito, *The Islamic Threat: Myth or Reality?* (1992). H. Munson, Jr., *Islam and Revolution in the Middle East* (1988), is an earlier comparison of Iran and Arab countries.

The studies by July and Hallett cited in the Notes are outstanding interpretations of modern Africa's rich and complex history. Both have extensive bibliographies. Important works on the colonial era include A. Boahen, *African Perspectives on Colonialism* (1989); J. A. Langley, *Pan-Africanism and Nationalism in West Africa, 1900–1945: A Study in Ideology and Social Classes* (1973); and R. O. Collins, *Problems in the History of Colonial Africa, 1860–1960* (1970). B. Davidson, *The Black Man's Burden: Africa and the Curse of the Nation State* (1993), is a thought-provoking reconsideration by a noted historian. W. E. B. Du Bois, *The World and Africa* (1947), and J. Kenyatta, *Facing Mount Kenya* (1953), are powerful comments on African nationalism by, respectively, the distinguished American black thinker and Kenya's foremost revolutionary and political leader. R. July, *The African Voice: The Role of the Humanities in African Independence* (1987), focuses on intellectuals and artists struggling against cultural imperialism. A. Hopkins, *An Economic History of West Africa* (1973), is a pioneering synthesis. C. Dewey and A. Hopkins, eds., *The Imperial Impact: Studies in the Economic History of Africa and India* (1978), is an innovative comparative study. R. Olaniyan, ed., *African History and Culture* (1982), is a valuable recent collection. M. Crowder, ed., *The Cambridge History of Africa,* vol. 8, examines the struggle for independence and nationhood between 1940 and 1975 in broad perspective. Major works on specific countries include M. Crowder, *The Story of Nigeria,* 4th ed. (1978); P. Hill, *Migrant Cocoa Farmers in Ghana* (1963); and R. W. Johnson, *How Long Will South Africa Survive?* (1977). P. C. Lloyd, *Africa in Social Change* (1972), is a useful study on the contemporary era, and F. Willett, *African Art* (1971), is a good introduction. Nelson Mandela tells his story in his autobiography, *Long Walk to Freedom* (1994).

The Struggle for Freedom in South Africa

Many African territories won political freedom in the mid-1960s, but in South Africa the struggle was long and extremely difficult. Only in 1990 did the white government release Nelson Mandela from prison and begin negotiations with the famous black leader and the African National Congress (ANC). Only in 1994 did Mandela and the ANC finally come to power and establish a new system based on majority rule and racial equality.

Born in 1918 into the royal family of the Transkei, Nelson Mandela received an education befitting the son of a tribal chief. But he ran away to escape an arranged tribal marriage, experienced the harsh realities of black life in Johannesburg, studied law, and became an attorney. A born leader with a natural air of authority, Mandela was drawn to politics and the ANC. In the 1950s the white government responded to the growing popularity of Mandela and the ANC with tear gas and repression.

In 1960 the ANC called a general strike to protest the shooting of peaceful protesters at Sharpeville. Acts of sabotage then shook South Africa, and Mandela led the underground opposition. Betrayed by an informer, he was convicted of treason in 1964 and sentenced to life imprisonment. Mandela defended all of the accused in the 1964 treason trial. The following selection is taken from Mandela's opening statement.

At the outset, I want to say that the suggestion made by the State in its opening that the struggle in South Africa is under the influence of foreigners or communists is wholly incorrect. I have done whatever I did, both as an individual and as a leader of my people, because of my experience in South Africa and my own proudly felt African background, and not because of what any outsider might have said.

In my youth in the Transkei I listened to the elders of my tribe telling stories of the old days. Amongst the tales they related to me were those of wars fought by our ancestors in defence of the fatherland. . . . I hoped then that life might offer me the opportunity to serve my people and make my own humble contribution to their freedom struggle. . . .

It is true that there has often been close co-operation between the ANC [African National Congress] and the Communist Party. But cooperation is merely proof of a common goal—in this case the removal of White supremacy—and is not proof of a complete community of interests. . . . What is more, for many decades communists were the only political group in South Africa who were prepared to treat Africans as human beings and their equals; who were prepared to eat with us, talk with us, live with us, and work with us. . . . Because of this, there are many Africans who today tend to equate freedom with communism. . . .

I turn now to my own position. I have denied that I am a communist. . . . [But] I am attracted by the idea of a classless society, an attraction which springs in part from Marxist reading and, in part, from my admiration of the structure and organization of early African societies in this country. The land, then the main means of production, belonged to the tribe. There were no rich or poor and there was no exploitation. . . .

[Unlike communists] I am an admirer of the parliamentary system of the West. . . . [Thus] I have been influenced in my thinking by both West and East. . . . [I believe] I should be absolutely impartial and objective. I should tie myself to no particular system of society other than of socialism. I must leave myself free to borrow the best from the West and from the East. . . .

Our fight is against real, and not imaginary, hardships or, to use the language of the State

Prosecutor, "so-called hardships". . . . Basically, we fight against two features which are the hallmarks of African life in South Africa and which are entrenched by legislation which we seek to have repealed. These features are poverty and lack of human dignity, and we do not need communists or so-called "agitators" to teach us about these things.

South Africa is the richest country in Africa, and could be one of the richest countries in the world. But it is a land of extremes and remarkable contrasts. The Whites enjoy what may well be the highest standard of living in the world, while Africans live in poverty and misery. . . . Poverty goes hand in hand with malnutrition and disease. . . .

The lack of human dignity experienced by Africans is the direct result of the policy of White supremacy. White supremacy implies Black inferiority. Legislation designed to preserve White supremacy entrenches this notion. . . . Because of this sort of attitude, Whites tend to regard Africans as a separate breed. They do not look upon them as people with families of their own; they do not realize that they have emotions. . . .

Africans want to be paid a living wage. Africans want to perform work which they are capable of doing, and not work which the Government declares them to be capable of. . . . Africans want a just share in the whole of South Africa; they want security and a stake in society.

Above all, we want equal political rights, because without them our disabilities will be permanent. I know this sounds revolutionary to the Whites in this country, because the majority of voters will be Africans. This makes the White man fear democracy.

But this fear cannot be allowed to stand in the way of the only solution which will guarantee racial harmony and freedom for all. It is not true that the enfranchisement of all will result in racial domination. Political division, based on color, is entirely artificial and, when it disappears, so will the domination of one color group by another. The ANC has spent half a century fighting against racialism. When it triumphs it will not change that policy.

This then is what the ANC is fighting. Their struggle is a truly national one. It is a struggle of the African people, inspired by their own suffering and their own experience. It is a struggle for the right to live.

Nelson Mandela at the time of his imprisonment in 1964. (*Source: Mohamed Lounes/Liaison*)

During my lifetime I have dedicated myself to this struggle of the African people. I have fought against White domination, and I have fought against Black domination. I have cherished the ideal of a democratic and free society in which all persons live together in harmony and with equal opportunities. It is an ideal which I hope to live for and to achieve. But if needs be, it is an ideal for which I am prepared to die.

Questions for Analysis

1. How does Nelson Mandela respond to the charge that he and the ANC are controlled by communists?

2. What factors influenced Mandela's thinking? In what ways has he been influenced by "both East and West" and by his African background?

3. According to Mandela, what is wrong with South Africa? What needs to be done?

4. What are Mandela's goals for South Africa? Are his goals realistic or idealistic? Or both?

Source: Slightly adapted from Nelson Mandela, *No Easy Walk to Freedom: Articles, Speeches and Trial Addresses* (London: Heinemann, 1973), pp. 163, 179–185, 187–189.

CHAPTER

35

The Changing Lives of Third World Peoples

Women in the west African country of Burkina Faso handle industrial waste as part of their work. *(Source: Sipa Press)*

fter the Second World War everyday life in the emerging nations of Asia and Africa changed dramatically as many peoples struggled to overcome the legacy of imperialism and build effective nation-states. Some of the changes paralleled the experiences of Europe and North America: science and modern technology altered individuals' lives in countless ways, and efforts to raise the standard of living by means of industrialization profoundly affected relations among social classes. Most observers, however, stressed the differences in development between the emerging nations and the industrialized nations. The new nations—along with the older states of Latin America—suffered widespread poverty and had a heritage of foreign domination, and life there remained very hard. Many observers discerned a widening economic gap between the industrialized nations of Europe and North America on the one hand and most of the emerging nations on the other. Some writers even argued that the gap between North and South—that is, between rich nations and poor nations—had replaced the cold war between East and West and its immediate aftermath as humankind's most explosive division.

This chapter concentrates on shared problems of development and everyday life in Asia, Africa, and Latin America—a vast geographical expanse commonly known as the Third World.

- How have the emerging nations of the Third World sought to escape from poverty, and what have been the results of their efforts?

- What has caused the prodigious growth of cities in the Third World, and what does their growth mean for their inhabitants?

- How have thinkers and artists from the Third World interpreted the modern world and the experiences of their peoples before, during, and after foreign domination?

These three questions guide the investigation.

✵ DEFINING THE THIRD WORLD

Since the late 1950s many scholars, journalists, and politicians have viewed Africa, Asia, and Latin America as a single entity—the "Third World." Is this label valid and useful? Some experts prefer to speak of these regions as containing the "emerging nations" or the "less-developed countries"—deliberately vague terms suggesting a spectrum of conditions ranging from near-hopeless poverty to moderate well-being. Other experts increasingly add a "Fourth" and even a "Fifth World" in recognition of the growing diversity among the less-developed nations in recent years. Nevertheless, for a long generation the countries commonly termed "Third World" have shared characteristics that have joined them together and created a Third World consciousness and ideology. There are several reasons for this important development.

First, virtually all the countries of Africa, Asia, and even Latin America experienced political or economic domination, nationalist reaction, and a struggle for genuine independence. This shared past gave rise to a common consciousness and a widespread feeling of having been oppressed and victimized in dealings with Europe and North America. A variety of nationalists, Marxists, and anti-imperialist intellectuals has nurtured this outlook arguing forcibly that the Third World's problems are the result of past and present exploitation the wealthy capitalist nations. Precisely because of their shared sense of past injustice, many influential Latin Americans have identified with the Third World, despite their countries' greater affluence. The term also came into global use in the cold war era as a handy way of distinguishing Africa, Asia, and Latin America from the "First" and "Second Worlds"—the capitalist and communist industrialized nations, respectively.

Second, in the 1950s and 1960s a large majority of men and women in most Third World countries lived in the countryside and depended on agriculture for a living. Agricultural goods and raw materials are still the primary exports of many Third World countries. In Europe, North America, and Japan, by contrast, most people live in cities and depend mainly on industry and urban services for employment.

Finally, the agricultural countries of Asia, Africa, and most of Latin America were united by awareness of their common poverty. By no means was everyone in the Third World poor; some people were quite wealthy. The average standard of living, however, was low, especially compared with that of people in the wealthy industrial nations, and massive poverty was ever present.

 Coal Miner Families in India   With their tools and many of their possessions loaded on their rickety carts, these workers struggle with steep grades and grinding poverty. The hardships of life in the Third World weigh heavily on these people. *(Source: Sebastiao Salgado/Magnum Photos)*

ECONOMIC AND SOCIAL CHALLENGES IN THE THIRD WORLD

As the Third World confronted the tough postindependence task of preserving political unity and building cohesive nation-states, the enormous challenges of poverty, malnutrition, and disease weighed especially heavily on rural people. In the 1950s and 1960s most Third World leaders and their advisers saw rapid industrialization and "modernization" as the answer to rural poverty and disease. Industrialization and modernization also kindled popular enthusiasm and thus served nation building, which in turn promised economic self-sufficiency and cultural renewal. For these reasons, the leaders and peoples of the Third World in the 1950s and 1960s set themselves the massive task of building modern factories, roads, and public health services like those of Europe and North

America. Their considerable success fueled rapid economic progress.

Yet social problems, complicated by surging population growth, almost dwarfed the accomplishment. Disappointments multiplied. By and large, the poorest rural people in the poorest countries gained the least from industrialization, and industrial expansion provided jobs for only a small segment even of the urban population. By the late 1960s, widespread dissatisfaction with policies of all-out industrialization prompted a greater emphasis on rural development.

Poverty

It was easy to lose sight of the true dimensions of poverty in the Third World in a fog of economic statistics. In the 1950s and 1960s the United Nations and the emerging nations began collecting national income statistics. Dividing those estimates by total population yields a nation's average per capita income. These figures received enormous attention because they were stunningly low compared with those of wealthy nations. In 1960, for example, average annual income per person in all of Africa and Southeast Asia was about $100. In North America it was $2,500—twenty-five times more. Journalists, politicians, and scholars using such figures often concluded that Third World people were unspeakably poor and verging on mass starvation.

Such comparisons, however, exaggerated the economic gap between the North and the South because income data on poor countries were incomplete and usually did not include some productive activities. Simplistic comparisons also failed to adjust for the fact that basic necessities cost considerably less in poor countries than in rich countries. Still, the gap in *real income*—income adjusted for differences in prices—between the industrialized world and the former colonies and dependencies of Africa, Asia, and Latin America was truly enormous. According to a leading historian, in 1950, when war-scarred Europe was in the early phase of postwar reconstruction,

the real income per capita of the Third World was five or six times lower than that of the developed countries. . . . In the developed countries, a century and a half of Industrial Revolution had resulted in a multiplication by more than five of the average standard of living in 1950. . . . For the average Third World countries the 1950s level was practically that of 1800 or, at best, only 10–20 percent above.[1]

A deeper understanding arises from considering Third World poverty not just in statistical terms but also in human terms, as did the postwar generation of nationalist leaders. To them, poverty meant, above all, not having enough to eat. For millions, hunger and malnutrition were harsh facts of life. In India, Ethiopia, Bolivia, and other extremely poor countries, the average adult ate fewer than 2,000 calories a day—only 85 percent of the minimal requirement. Although many poor countries fared better, in the 1960s none but Argentina could match the 3,000 or more calories consumed in the more fortunate North. Even Third World people who consumed enough calories often suffered from the effects of unbalanced high-starch diets and inadequate protein. Severe protein deficiency stunts the brain as well as the body, and

many of the poorest children grew up mentally retarded.

Poor housing—crowded, often damp, and exposed to the elements—also contributed significantly to the less-developed world's high incidence of chronic ill health. So too did scanty education and lack of the fundamentals of modern public health: adequate and safe water, sewage disposal, immunizations, prenatal care, and control of communicable diseases. Village women around the world spent much of each day carrying water and searching for firewood or dung to use as fuel, as they must still do in many countries. Infant mortality was savage, and chronic illness weakened and demoralized many adults, making them unfit for the hard labor that their lives required.

Generally speaking, health status in Asia and Latin America was better than in the new states of sub-Saharan Africa. As one authority described the situation in the early 1960s:

In the African social drama, sickness has a strong claim to being archvillain. . . . In tropical Africa, most men, women, and children are habitually unwell. Many are unwell from the day of their birth to the day of their death. . . . Most of the sick are sick of more than one disease.[2]

The people of poor countries were overwhelmingly concentrated in the countryside as small farmers and landless laborers. Mass poverty represented an awesome challenge to the postwar leaders of the newly emerging nations. Having raised peoples' hopes in the struggle for freedom, they had to start delivering on their promises if they were to maintain trust and stay in power. A strong commitment to modern economic and social development, already present in parts of Latin America in the 1930s, took hold in Asia and Africa in the postwar era.

The Medical Revolution and the Population Explosion

The most thoroughgoing success achieved by the Third World after the Second World War was a spectacular medical revolution. Immediately after winning independence, the governments of emerging nations began adopting modern methods of immunology and public health. These methods were often simple and inexpensive but extremely effective. One famous measure was spraying DDT in Southeast Asia to control mosquitoes bearing malaria, one of the deadliest and most debilitating tropical diseases. In Sri Lanka (formerly Ceylon), DDT spraying halved the yearly toll of deaths in the very first postwar decade—at a modest cost of $2 per person. According to the United Nations' World Health Organization, which helped provide medical expertise to the new states, deaths from smallpox, cholera, and plague declined by more than 95 percent worldwide between 1951 and 1966.

Asian and African countries increased the small numbers of hospitals, doctors, and nurses that they had inherited from the colonial past. Sophisticated medical facilities became symbols of the commitment to a better life. Some critics, however, maintained that expensive medical technology was an indulgence that Third World countries could not afford, for it was ill suited to the pressing health problems of most of the population. Such criticism eventually prompted greater emphasis on delivering medical services to the countryside. Local people were successfully trained as paramedics to staff rural outpatient clinics that offered medical treatment, health education, and prenatal and postnatal care. Many paramedics were women: many health problems involved childbirth and infancy, and villagers the world over considered it improper for a male to examine a woman's body.

The medical revolution significantly lowered death rates and lengthened life expectancy. In particular, children became increasingly likely to survive their early years, though infant and juvenile mortality remained far higher in the Third World

The Medical Revolution   A woman doctor in Yemen on the Arabian peninsula makes house calls by motorcycle, thereby carrying modern medicine to women in isolated desert communities. The doctor wears the veil traditionally required of women in public throughout much of the Arab world. *(Source: Hans Bollinger for STERN magazine)*

Improving Public Health   This poster from the early 1970s urges Chinese children to kill as many flies as possible in order to help the authorities prevent the spread of infectious diseases. Mass campaigns to improve public health played a major role in reducing mortality in the Third World. *(Source: From Eileen Hsü-Balzer, Richard Balzer, Francis L. K. Hsü,* China Day by Day. *Reproduced with permission.)*

than in rich countries. By 1980 the average inhabitant of the Third World could expect at birth to live about 54 years; life expectancy varied from 40 to 64 years depending on the country. In developed countries, by contrast, life expectancy at birth averaged 71 years.

A less favorable consequence of the medical revolution was the acceleration of population growth. As in Europe during the nineteenth century, a rapid decline in the death rate was not immediately accompanied by a similar decline in the birthrate. Third World women continued to bear from five to seven children, as their mothers and grandmothers had done. The combined populations of Asia, Africa, and Latin America, which had grown relatively modestly from 1925 to 1950, increased between 1950 and 1975 from 1,750 million to 3,000 million (Map 35.1). Barring catastrophe, experts predicted that the population of the three continents would surge to 5,200 million in the year 2000—an unprecedented explosion.

The population explosion aroused fears of approaching famine and starvation. Thomas Malthus's gloomy late-eighteenth-century conclusion that population always tends to grow faster than the food supply (see page 786) was revived and updated by "neo-Malthusian" social scientists. Such fears were exaggerated, but they did produce uneasiness in the Third World, where leaders saw that their countries had to run fast just to maintain already low standards of living.

Some governments began pushing family planning and birth control to slow population growth. These measures were not very successful in the 1950s and 1960s. In many countries, Islamic and Catholic religious teachings were hostile to birth control. Moreover, widespread cultural attitudes dictated that a real man keep his wife pregnant. There were also economic reasons for preferring large families. Farmers needed the help of plenty of children at planting and harvest times. And sons and daughters were a sort of social security system for their elders; thus a prudent couple wanted several children because some would surely die young.

The Race to Industrialize (1950–1970)

Throughout the 1950s and most of the 1960s, many key Third World leaders, pressed on by their European, American, and Soviet advisers, were convinced that all-out industrialization was the only answer to poverty and population growth. The masses, they concluded, were poor because they were imprisoned in a primitive, inefficient agricultural economy. Only modern factory industry appeared capable of creating wealth quickly enough to outrace the growth of numbers.

The two-century experience of the West, Japan, and the Soviet Union seemed to validate this faith in industrialization. To Third World elites economic history taught the encouraging lesson that the wealthy countries had also been agricultural and "underdeveloped" until the Industrial Revolution had lifted them out of poverty, one by one. According to this view, the uneven progress of industrialization was primarily responsible for the great income gap that existed between the rich

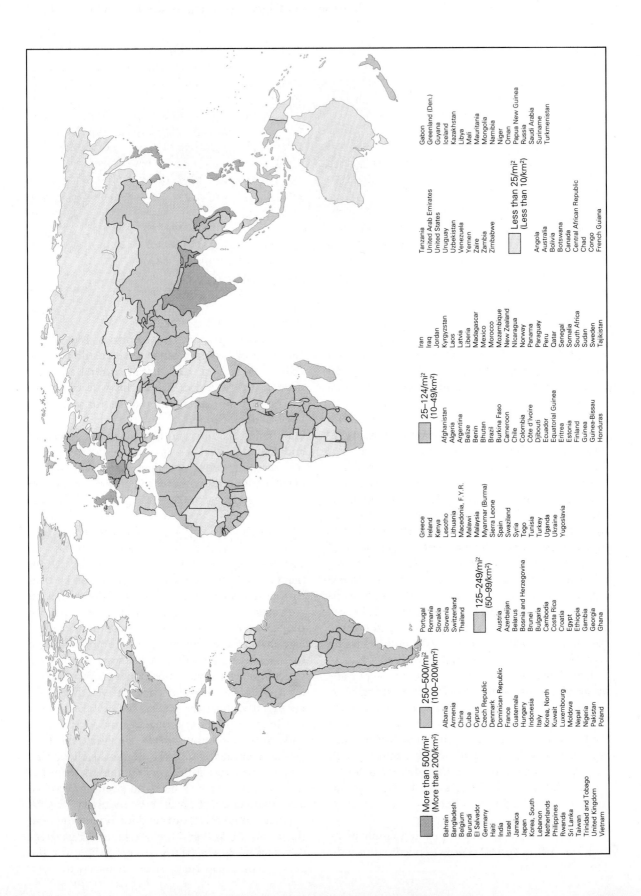

countries and the poor countries of the postindependence Third World.

Theories of modernization, which were particularly popular in the 1960s, also assumed that all countries were following the path already taken by the industrialized nations and that the task of the elite was to speed the trip. Marxism, with its industrial and urban bias, preached a similar gospel. These ideas reinforced the Third World's desire to industrialize.

Nationalist leaders believed that successful industrialization required state action and enterprise. Many were impressed by socialism in general and by Stalin's forced industrialization in particular, which they saw as having won the Soviet Union international power and prominence, whatever its social costs. In Asia and Africa, furthermore, capitalists and private enterprise were often equated with the old rulers and colonial servitude. The reasoning was practical as well as ideological: socialism meant an expansion of steady government jobs for political and ethnic allies, and modern industry meant ports, roads, schools, and hospitals, as well as factories. Only the state could afford such expensive investments. With the exception of the People's Republic of China, however, the new governments recognized private property and also tolerated native (and foreign) businessmen. The "mixed economy"—part socialist, part capitalist—became the general rule in the Third World.

Political leaders concentrated state investment in big, highly visible projects that proclaimed the country's independence and stimulated national pride. Enormous dams for irrigation and hydroelectric power were favored undertakings. Nasser's stupendous Aswan Dam harnessed the Nile, demonstrating that modern Egyptians could surpass even the pyramids of their ancient ancestors. The gigantic state-owned steel mill was another favorite project. These big projects testified to the prevailing faith in expensive advanced technology and modernization along European lines.

Nationalist leaders and their economic experts measured overall success by how fast national income grew, and they tended to assume that social problems and income distribution would take care of themselves. India, the world's most popu-

lous noncommunist country, exemplified the general trends. After India achieved independence in 1947, Mahatma Gandhi's special brand of nationalism was redirected toward economic and social rebirth through state enterprise and planning. Jawaharlal Nehru and many Congress party leaders believed that unregulated capitalism and free trade under British rule had deepened Indian poverty. Considering themselves democratic socialists, they introduced five-year plans, built state-owned factories and steel mills, and raised tariffs to protect Indian manufacturers. Quite typically, they neglected agriculture, land reform, and village life.

The Third World's first great industrialization drive was in many ways a success. Industry grew faster than ever before, though from an admittedly low base in Africa and most of Asia. According to the United Nations, industry in the noncommunist developing nations grew at more than 7 percent per year between 1950 and 1970, which meant a per capita rate of about 4.5 percent per year. This was very solid industrial growth by historical standards. It matched the fastest rates of industrialization in the United States before 1914 and was double the rate of Britain and France in the same years.

Industrial expansion stimulated the other sectors of Third World economies. National income per capita grew about 2.5 percent per year in the booming world economy of the 1950s and 1960s. This pace was far superior to the very modest increases that had occurred under colonial domination between 1900 and 1950. Future historians may well see the era after political emancipation as the era of industrial revolution in Asia and Africa. This was certainly the case for a few small Asian countries that downgraded government control and emphasized private enterprise and the export of manufactured goods. South Korea, Taiwan, the city-state of Singapore, and the British colony of Hong Kong were genuine "economic miracles," rapidly industrializing and remarkably improving the living standards of ordinary people.

Nevertheless, by the late 1960s, disillusionment with the Third World's relatively rapid industrialization was spreading, for several reasons. In the first place, the experience of a few small states like South Korea and Taiwan was the exception. The countries of Asia, Africa, and Latin America did not as a whole match the "miraculous" concurrent advances of western Europe and Japan, and the

❖ **MAP 35.1** World Population Density

Building the Aswan Dam Financed and engineered by the Soviet Union, the massive high dam at Aswan was Nasser's dream for Egypt's economic future. Here an army of workers lay the stones that will harness the Nile for irrigation and hydroelectric power. *(Source: Popperfoto)*

great economic gap between the rich and the poor nations continued to widen.

Also, most Third World leaders had genuinely believed that rapid industrial development would help the rural masses. Yet careful studies were showing that the main beneficiaries of industrialization were businessmen, bureaucrats, skilled workers, and urban professionals. Peasants and agricultural laborers gained little or nothing. It was estimated that about 40 percent of the population in fast-growing, dynamic Mexico, for instance, was completely excluded from the benefits of industrialization. Moreover, the very poorest countries—such as India and Indonesia in Asia, and Ethiopia

and the Sudan in Africa—were growing most slowly in per capita terms. The industrialization prescription appeared least effective where poverty was most intense. Economic dislocations after 1973, and especially the worldwide economic crisis of the early 1980s, accentuated this trend, visiting particularly devastating effects on the poorest countries.

Perhaps most serious, industrialization failed to provide the sheer number of jobs needed for the sons and daughters of the population explosion. Statisticians estimated that the growth of Third World manufacturing between 1950 and 1970 provided jobs for only about one-fifth of the 200 million young men and women who entered the exploding labor force in the same period. For the foreseeable future, most Third World people would have to remain on the farm or work in traditional handicrafts and service occupations. All-out modern industrialization had failed as a panacea.

Agriculture and Village Life

From the late 1960s onward, the limitations of industrial development forced Third World governments to take a renewed interest in rural people and village life. At best, this attention meant giving agriculture its due and coordinating rural development with industrialization and urbanization. At worst, especially in the very poorest countries, it

deflated the optimistic vision of living standards approaching those of the wealthy North and led to the pessimistic conclusion that it was possible to ease only modestly the great hardships.

Nationalist elites had neglected agriculture in the 1950s and the 1960s for various reasons. They regarded an agricultural economy as a mark of colonial servitude, which they were symbolically repudiating by embracing industrialization. They wanted to squeeze agriculture and peasant producers in order to provide capital for industry. Thus governments often established artificially low food prices, which also subsidized their volatile urban supporters at the expense of the farmers.

In addition, the obstacles to more productive farming seemed overwhelming to unsympathetic urban elites and condescending foreign experts:

Peasants Farming in Ecuador   Cultivating the land with simple hand tools, these peasant women in Latin America appear doomed to poverty despite backbreaking labor. In many cases, a high rent to an absentee landlord reduces the peasants' income still further. *(Source: Bernard Pierre Wolff/Photo Researchers)*

farms were too small and fragmented for mechanization, peasants were too stubborn and ignorant to change their ways, and so on. Little wonder that only big farmers and some plantations received much government support. Wherever large estates and absentee landlords predominated—in large parts of Asia and in most of Latin America, excluding Mexico, though not in sub-Saharan Africa—landless laborers and poor peasants who had no other choice than to rent land simply lacked the incentive to work harder. Any increased profits from larger crops went mainly to the absentee landowners.

Most honest observers were convinced that improved farm performance required land reform. Yet ever since the French Revolution, genuine land reform has been a profoundly radical measure, frequently bringing violence and civil war. Powerful landowners and their allies generally succeeded in blocking or subverting redistribution of land to benefit the poor. Land reform, unlike industrialization, was generally too hot for most politicians to handle.

Third World governments also neglected agriculture because feeding the masses was deceptively easy in the 1950s and early 1960s. Very poor countries received food from the United States at giveaway prices as part of a U.S. effort to dispose of enormous grain surpluses and help American farmers. Before 1939, the countries of Asia, Africa, and Latin America had collectively produced more grain than they consumed. But after 1945, as their populations soared, they began importing ever-increasing quantities.

Crops might fail in poor countries, but starvation seemed a thing of the past. In 1965, when India was urged to build up its food reserves, one top Indian official expressed a widespread attitude: "Why should we bother? Our reserves are the wheat fields of Kansas."[3] In the short run, the Indian official was right. In 1966 and again in 1967, when the monsoon failed to deliver its life-giving rains to the Indo-Pakistan subcontinent and famine gripped the land, the United States gave India one-fifth of the U.S. wheat crop. More than 60 million Indians lived exclusively on American grain. The effort required a food armada of six hundred ships, the largest fleet assembled since the Normandy invasion of 1944. The famine was ultimately contained, and instead of millions of deaths there were only a few thousand.

That close brush with mass starvation sent a shiver down the world's spine. Complacency dissolved in the Third World, and prophecies of disaster multiplied in wealthy nations. Paul Ehrlich, an American scientist, envisioned a grisly future in his polemical 1968 bestseller *The Population Bomb:*

The battle to feed all of humanity is over. In the 1970s the world will undergo famines—hundreds of millions of people are going to starve to death in spite of any crash programs embarked upon now. At this stage nothing can prevent a substantial increase in the world death rate.[4]

Other Western commentators outdid each other with nightmare visions. One portrayed the earth as a crowded lifeboat in a sea of hungry poor who would have to drown in order not to swamp the lifeboat. Another vision compared truly poor countries like Bangladesh, Ethiopia, and Haiti to hopelessly wounded soldiers on a gory battlefield. Such victims were best left to die so that scarce resources could be concentrated on the "walking wounded" who might yet be saved. Such crude and brutal Social Darwinism made it easy for Third World intellectuals to believe the worst about the rich industrialized nations and their economies.

Countering such visions was technology. Plant scientists and agricultural research stations had already set out to develop new hybrid seeds genetically engineered to suit the growing conditions of tropical agriculture. Their model was extraordinarily productive hybrid corn developed for the American Midwest in the 1940s. The first breakthrough came in Mexico in the 1950s, when an American-led team developed new high-yielding dwarf wheats. These varieties enabled farmers to double their yields, though they demanded greater amounts of fertilizer and water for irrigation. Mexican wheat production soared. Thus began the transformation of Third World agriculture—the so-called Green Revolution.

In the 1960s an American-backed team of scientists in the Philippines turned their attention to rice, the Asian staff of life; they quickly developed a "miracle rice." The new hybrid required more fertilizer and water but yielded more and grew much faster. It permitted the revolutionary advent of year-round farming on irrigated land, making possible two, three, or even four crops a year. The brutal tropical sun of the hot dry season became an

Old and New   A fetish statue designed to frighten off evil spirits stands by as the proud owner of a two-acre plot in southern India shows a visiting expert his crop of miracle rice. As this picture suggests, the acceptance of modern technology does not necessarily require the repudiation of cultural traditions. *(Source: Marc and Evelyne Bernheim/Woodfin Camp & Associates)*

agricultural blessing for the first time. Asian scientists, financed by their governments, developed similar hybrids to meet local conditions.

Increases in grain production were rapid and dramatic in some Asian countries. In gigantic India, for example, farmers upped production more than 60 percent in fifteen years. By 1980, thousands of new grain bins dotted the countryside, symbols of the agricultural revolution in India and the country's new-found ability to feed all its people. China followed with its own highly successful version of the Green Revolution under Deng Xiaoping.

The Green Revolution offered new hope to the Third World but was no cure-all. At first most of its benefits seemed to flow to large landowners and substantial peasant farmers who could afford the necessary investments in irrigation and fertilizer. Subsequent experience in China and other Asian countries showed, however, that even peasant fam-

ilies with tiny farms could gain substantially. Indeed, the Green Revolution's greatest successes occurred in Asian countries with broad-based peasant ownership of land.

The technical revolution shared relatively few of its benefits with the poorest classes—landless laborers, tenant farmers, and tiny landholders. Lacking even the two or three acres necessary to feed themselves with intensive effort, the very poorest groups gained only slightly more regular employment from the Green Revolution's demand for more labor. Pakistan, the Philippines, and other countries with large numbers of landless peasants and insecure tenant farmers experienced less improvement than did countries like South Korea and Taiwan, where land was generally owned by peasants. This helps to explain why the Green Revolution failed to spread from Mexico throughout Latin America: as long as 3 or 4 percent of the rural population owned 60 to 80 percent of the land, as was still the case in many Latin American countries, the Green Revolution usually remained stillborn.

The same fatal equation of property ownership has prevailed in Bangladesh. There an elite tenth of the population owned half of the land, and the poorest half owned nothing at all. People ate less in the 1970s and 1980s, yet land reform remained a political and social minefield. One member of a big (fifty-acre) landowning family in Bangladesh told an American reporter in 1981: "They talk of removing property markers. It cannot happen. I will kill you if you move my property markers one inch."[5]

Sub-Saharan Africa benefited little from the new agricultural techniques, even though land reform was a serious problem only in white-ruled South Africa. Poor transportation, inadequate storage facilities, and low government-imposed agricultural prices must bear much of the blame. More generally, the climatic conditions of black Africa encouraged continued adherence to dry farming and root crops, whereas the Green Revolution has been almost synonymous with intensive irrigation and grain production.

The Green Revolution, like the medical revolution and industrialization, represented a large but uneven step forward for the Third World. Relatively few of its benefits flowed to the poorest groups. These poor, who lacked political influence and had no clear idea about what needed to be done, increasingly longed to escape from ill-paid, irregular work in somebody else's fields. For many of the bravest and most enterprising, life in a nearby town or city seemed a way out.

 THE GROWTH OF CITIES

The changing lives of Third World people were marked by violent contrasts, which were most striking in urban areas. Shiny airports, international hotels, and massive government buildings were built next to tar-paper slums. Like their counterparts in the North, these rapidly growing cities were monuments to political independence and ongoing industrial development. They were also testimonials to increasing population, limited opportunities in the countryside, and neocolonial influence. Runaway urban growth became a distinctive feature of the Third World.

Urbanization in the Third World

The cities of the Third World expanded at an astonishing pace after the Second World War. Many doubled and some even tripled in size in a single decade. The Algerian city of Algiers jumped from 300,000 to 900,000 between 1950 and 1960; Accra in Ghana, Lima in Peru, and Nairobi in Kenya grew just as fast. Moreover, rapid urban growth continued. The less-developed countries became far more thoroughly urbanized in recent times than most people realize. In Latin America, three out of four people lived in towns and cities by 1975; in Asia and Africa, as Table 35.1 shows, one in four lived in an urban area by the same year.

The urban explosion continued in the 1980s, so that by 1990 fully 60 percent of the planet's city dwellers lived in the cities of the Third World, according to United Nations estimates. Rapid Third World urbanization represented a tremendous historical change. As recently as 1920, three out of every four of the world's urban inhabitants were concentrated in Europe and North America.

In most Third World countries the largest cities grew fastest. Gigantic "super cities" of from 2 million to 10 million persons arose. The capital typically emerged as the all-powerful urban center, encompassing all the important elite groups and dwarfing smaller cities as well as villages. Mexico City, for example, grew from 3 million to 12 million people between 1950 and 1975, and it will probably reach 20 million in the year 2000. The pattern of a dominant megalopolis has continued to spread from Latin America to Africa and Asia (though not to Asia's giants, China and India).

In the truly poor countries of Africa and Asia, the process of urbanization is still in the early stages. However populous the cities, the countryside still holds the majority of the people. But if present trends continue, a city like Jakarta, the capital of Indonesia, will have about 15 million people by the end of this century. Calcutta and Bombay will be equally large. In the year 2000, the world will have twenty-six megalopolises with more than 10 million people, and twenty of them will be in Asia, Latin America, and Africa, according to World Bank estimates. Such rapid urbanization has posed enormous challenges for peoples and governments.

What caused this urban explosion? First, the general growth of population in the Third World was critical. Urban residents gained substantially

TABLE 35.1 URBAN POPULATION AS A PERCENTAGE OF TOTAL POPULATION IN THE WORLD AND IN EIGHT MAJOR AREAS, 1925–2025

Area	1925	1950	1975	2000 (est.)	2025 (est.)
World total	21	28	39	50	63
North America	54	64	77	86	93
Europe	48	55	67	79	88
Soviet Union	18	39	61	76	87
East Asia	10	15	30	46	63
Latin America	25	41	60	74	85
Africa	8	13	24	37	54
South Asia	9	15	23	35	51
Oceania	54	65	71	77	87

Little more than one-fifth of the world's population was urban in 1925. In 1990 the urban proportion in the world total was about 45 percent and, according to United Nations experts, it should reach one-half by the century's end and two-thirds by about 2025. The most rapid urban growth will come in Africa and Asia, where the move to cities is still in its early stages. *(Source: United Nations,* Concise Report on the World Population Situation in 1970–1975 and Its Long-Range Implications, *New York, 1974, p. 63.)*

from the medical revolution but only gradually began to reduce the size of their families. At the same time, the pressure of numbers in the countryside encouraged millions to set out for the nearest city. More than half of all urban growth has been due to rural migration.

Second, in the less-developed countries even more than in Europe and North America in the nineteenth century, great cities became the undisputed centers of industry. Half of all the industrial jobs in Mexico were concentrated in Mexico City in 1980. The same kind of extreme concentration of industry occurred in many Third World countries. Yet careful study leads scholars to play down industrialization as a cause of urban explosion. In the words of a leading authority:

After about 1930 a new phenomenon which might be termed "urbanization without industrialization" be-gan to appear in the Third World. This phenomenon very rapidly acquired an inflationary character and in the early 1960s began to present most serious problems of urban employment and underemployment.[6]

In short, urban population grew much faster than industrial employment. It was a lucky migrant who found a real factory job.

Third, newcomers also streamed to the cities for nonindustrial employment. Many were pushed: they simply lacked enough land to survive. Large landowners found it more profitable to produce export crops, like sugar or coffee, for wealthy industrialized countries, and their increasingly mechanized operations provided few jobs for agricultural laborers. The push factor was particularly strong in Latin America, with its neocolonial pattern of large landowners and foreign companies exporting food and raw materials. More generally, much migration was seasonal or temporary. Many a young person left home for the city to work in construction or serve as a maid, expecting higher wages and steadier work in the city and planning to return shortly with a modest nest egg.

Finally, the magnetic attraction of Third World cities was more than economic. Their attraction rested on the services and opportunities they offered, as well as on changing attitudes and the urge to escape from the traditional restraints of village life. Most of the modern hospitals, secondary schools, and transportation systems in less-developed countries were in the cities. So were most banks, libraries, movie houses, and basic conveniences. Safe piped water and processed food were rare in rural areas, for instance, and village women by necessity spent much of their time carrying water and grinding grain.

The city held a special appeal for rural people who had been exposed to the seductive influence of modern education. In Africa, a European economist concluded that "the number of people who are prepared to go back to the land after more than three or four years in the classroom is infinitesimal."[7] One survey from the 1960s in the Ivory Coast found two out of three rural high school graduates planning to move to the city; only one in ten of the illiterates expressed the same intention. Africa was not unique in this. For the young and the ambitious, the allure of the city was the excitement and opportunity of modern life. The village took on the curse of boredom and failure.

Overcrowding and Shantytowns

Rapid population growth placed great pressure on existing urban social services, and in many Third World cities the local authorities could not keep up with demand. New neighborhoods often lacked running water, paved streets, electricity, and police and fire protection. As in the early days of Europe's industrialization, sanitation was minimal in poor sections of town. Outdoor toilets were shared by many. Raw sewage often ran in streets and streams.

Faced with a rising human tide, government officials and their well-to-do urban allies sometimes tried to restrict internal migration to preserve the cities. Particularly in Africa, politicians talked of sending newcomers "back to the land" in order to reduce urban unemployment, crime rates, conges-

tion, and environmental decline. In Africa as elsewhere, these antimigration efforts proved unsuccessful, and frustrated officials often threw up their hands in despair.

Surging population growth had particularly severe consequences for housing. As in western Europe in the early nineteenth century, overcrowding reached staggering proportions in a great many Third World cities. Old buildings were often divided and redivided until population density reached the absolute saturation point. Take, for example, this vivid description of an old inner-city area, Singapore's Chinatown, in the late 1950s:

Chinatown . . . consists almost entirely of two or three story shop-houses. These shop-houses, originally intended to house one or two families, have been divided by a maze of interior partitions into cubicles, the majority of which are without windows and in permanent semi-darkness. Most of these cubicles are about the size of two double beds, placed side by side. In one such cubicle—dark, confined, unsanitary, and without comfort—may live a family of seven or more persons. Many of them sleep on the floor, often under the bed. Their possessions are in boxes, placed on shelves to leave the floor free for sleeping. Their food . . . is kept in tiny cupboards, which hang from the rafters. Their clothes hang on the walls, or from racks.[8]

Makeshift squatter settlements were another manifestation of the urban housing problem. These shantytowns sprang up continuously, almost overnight, on the worst possible urban land—dismal mudflats, garbage dumps, railroad sidings, steep hills on the outskirts, even polluted waterfronts. Typically, a group of urban poor "invaded" unoccupied land and quickly threw up tents or huts. Often beaten off by the police, they invaded again and again until the authorities gave up and a new squatter beachhead had been secured.

Squatter shantytowns grew much faster than more conventional urban areas in most Third World cities. In the giant Brazilian city of Rio de Janeiro, for example, the population of the shantytowns grew four times faster than the population of the rest of the city in the 1950s and 1960s. As a result, the Third World's squatter settlements came to house up to two-fifths of the urban population. The proportion was particularly high in Asia. Such settlements had occasionally grown up in American

Shacks and Skyscrapers This striking view of Bombay, India, has many counterparts in the Third World. Makeshift dwellings coexist with luxurious high-rise apartments, and the urban landscape expands rapidly as newcomers pour into the swollen city from rural areas. *(Source: Camera Press London/Globe Photos; Photographer, Alan Whicker)*

mining towns and in Europe, but never to the same extent as in Latin America, Asia, and Africa. The Third World created a new urban form.

The meaning of squatter housing has been hotly debated. For a long time "pessimists" stressed the miseries of squatter settlements—the lack of the most basic services, the pitiful one-room shacks, the hopelessness of disoriented migrants in a strange environment, the revolutionary discontent. Recently, in detailed case studies, "optimists" have stressed the vitality of what are seen as real neighborhoods whose resourceful residents often share common ethnic origins and kinship ties.

Moreover, the shantytowns themselves evolved, most notably in Latin America, where they have existed longest. There poor but enterprising inhabitants relied on self-help to improve their living conditions. With much sweat labor and a little

hard-earned cash, a family replaced its mud walls with concrete blocks and gradually built a real home. Or the community pressured the city to install a central water pump or build a school. Low-paid office workers in search of cheap housing sometimes moved in and continued the upgrading process.

Few members of squatter communities were particularly attracted to revolutionary doctrines, despite widespread fears (and hopes) to the contrary. Indeed, one observer described squatters' beliefs as resembling those of the classic small businessman:

These beliefs can be summed up in the familiar and accepted maxims: Work hard, save your money, trust only family members (and them not too much), outwit the state, vote conservatively if possible, but always in your own economic self-interest; educate your children for their future and as old-age insurance for yourself.[9]

Thus the optimists counseled politicians to abandon their hostility to squatter settlements and help them to help themselves. The rush to the city could not be stopped, they said. However bad life in the city was, it appeared relatively desirable to the millions of rural people who "voted with their feet." Since hard-pressed Third World governments could provide only a fraction of the urban masses with subsidized housing, they were urged to support the creativity of the "spontaneous settlement." However squalid such settlements appear, they are preferable to sleeping on sidewalks.

Rich and Poor

After the less-developed countries achieved political independence, massive inequality continued, with few exceptions, to be the reality of life. A monumental gap separated rich and poor. In about 1975 in most developing countries, the top 20 percent took more than 50 percent of all national income. At the other end of the scale, the poorest 60 percent received on average less than 30 percent of all income, and the poorest fifth got about 5 percent. Thus the average household in the top fifth of the population received about ten times as much monetary income as the average household in the bottom fifth in the 1970s. This situation did not change significantly in the 1980s.

Such differences have been the rule in human history. The distribution of income in the Third World strongly resembled that of Europe prior to the First World War, before the movement toward greater equality accelerated sharply (see page 849). It is noteworthy that types of economy—rightist or leftist, capitalist or socialist—have had limited effect on shares of income. For example, in the 1970s income inequality was almost as pronounced in Mexico with its progressive, even revolutionary, tradition as in Brazil with its rightist military rule.

Differences in wealth and well-being were most pronounced in the exploding towns and cities of the Third World. Few rich or even middle-class people lived in the countryside. Urban squatters may have been better off than landless rural laborers, but they were light-years away from the luxury of the urban elite. In Asia and Africa, the rich often moved into the luxurious sections previously reserved for colonial administrators and white businessmen. Particularly in Latin America, upper-class and upper-middle-class people built fine mansions in exclusive suburbs, where they lived behind high walls, with many servants, protected from intruders by armed guards and fierce dogs.

A lifestyle in the "modern" mold was almost the byword of the Third World's urban elite. From French perfume and Scotch whiskey to electronic gadgets and the latest rock music, imported luxuries, especially automobiles, became the unmistakable signs of wealth and privilege. In Swahili-speaking East Africa, the common folk called the elite *wa Benzi,* "those who ride in a Mercedes-Benz." Even in Mao Zedong's relatively egalitarian China, the urban masses saved to buy bicycles while government officials rode in chauffeur-driven state-owned limousines.

Education also distinguished the wealthy from the masses. Young people from the elite often studied abroad at leading European and North American universities, or they monopolized openings in local universities. While absorbing the latest knowledge in a prestigious field like civil engineering or economics, they also absorbed foreign customs and values. They mastered the fluent English or French that is indispensable for many top-paying jobs, especially with international agencies and giant multinational corporations. Thus Third World elites often had more in common with the power brokers of the industrialized nations than with their own people, and they seemed willing tools of neocolonial penetration.

The middle classes of the Third World generally remained small relative to the total population. White-collar workers and government bureaucrats joined the traditional ranks of merchants and professionals in the urban middle class. Their salaries, though modest, were wonderfully secure and usually carried valuable fringe benefits. Unlike recent migrants and the rural poor, white-collar workers often received ration cards entitling them to cheap subsidized food.

An unexpected component of the urban middle classes was the modern factory proletariat, a privileged segment of the population in many poor countries. Few in number because sophisticated machines require few workers relative to agriculture or traditional crafts, they received high wages for their skilled work. On the Caribbean island of Jamaica in the late 1960s, for example, aluminum workers in big, modern American-owned plants earned from $60 to $65 a week. Meanwhile, cane cutters on sugar plantations earned $3 a week, and many laborers on small farms earned only $1 a week. Little wonder that modern factory workers tended to be self-satisfied in the Third World.

The great majority, the urban poor, earned precarious livings in a modern yet traditional "bazaar economy"—an economy of petty trades and unskilled labor. Here regular salaried jobs were rare and highly prized, and a complex world of tiny, unregulated businesses and service occupations predominated.

As in industrializing countries a century ago, irregular armies of peddlers and pushcart operators hawked their wares and squeezed a living from commerce. West African market women, with their colorful dresses and overflowing baskets, provided a classic example of this pattern. Sweatshops and home-based workers manufactured cheap goods for popular consumption. Maids, prostitutes, small-time crooks, and unemployed former students sold all kinds of services. This old-yet-new bazaar economy continued to grow prodigiously as migrants streamed to the cities, as modern industry provided few jobs, and as the wide gap between rich and poor persisted.

Migration and the Family

Large-scale urban migration had a massive impact on traditional family patterns in the Third World. Particularly in Africa and Asia, the great majority of migrants to the city were young men, married and unmarried; women tended to stay in the villages. The result was a sexual imbalance in both places. There were several reasons for this pattern. Much of the movement to cities (and mines) remained

A Sleek Automobile   The most ambitious of these four boys in an African village may already dream of acquiring power and wealth in the city. *(Source: Marc and Evelyne Bernheim/Woodfin Camp & Associates)*

temporary or seasonal. At least at first, young men left home to earn hard cash to bring back to their villages. Moreover, the cities were expensive, and prospects there were uncertain. Only after a man secured a genuine foothold did he become married or send for his wife and children.

Kinship and village ties helped ease the rigors of temporary migration. Often a young man could go to the city rather easily because his family had close ties with friends and relatives there. Many city neighborhoods were urban versions of their residents' original villages. Networks of friendship and mutual aid helped young men (and some women, especially brides) move back and forth without being overwhelmed.

For rural women, the consequences of male out-migration were mixed. Asian and African women had long been treated as subordinates, if not inferiors, by their fathers and husbands (see Listening to the Past). Rather suddenly, such women found themselves heads of households, faced with managing the farm, feeding the children, and running their own lives. In the east African country of Kenya, for instance, one-third of all rural households were headed by women in the late 1970s.

African and Asian village women had to become unprecedentedly self-reliant and independent. The real beginnings of more equal rights and opportunities, of women's liberation, became readily visible in Africa and Asia. But the price was high and progress uneven. Rural women often had only their children to help in the endless, backbreaking labor. And their husbands, when they returned, often expected their wives to revert to the old subordination.

In economically more advanced Latin America, the pattern of migration was different. Whole families migrated, very often to squatter settlements, much more commonly than in Asia and Africa. These families frequently belonged to the class of landless laborers, which was generally larger in Latin America than in Africa or even Asia. Migration was also more likely to be once-and-for-all. Another difference was that single women were as likely as single men to move to the city. The situation in Mexico in the late 1970s was typical:

They [women] leave the village seeking employment, often as domestic servants. When they do not find work in the cities, they have few alternatives. If they are young, they frequently turn to prostitution; if not, they often resort to begging in the streets. Homeless peasant women, often carrying small children, roam every quarter of Mexico City.[10]

Some women also left to escape the narrow, male-dominated villages. Even so, in Latin America urban migration seemed to have less impact on traditional family patterns and on women's attitudes than it did in Asia and Africa. This helps explain why the women's movement lagged in Latin America.

Developments Since 1980

The urban explosion promoted diversity within the Third World. This growing diversity had several aspects. First, in addition to the uneven impact of urban migration on women, the transformation of modest cities into gigantic agglomerations sharpened the contrast between life in urban and rural areas. This difference in life experiences made individual Third World countries and their citizens less homogeneous. Second, ongoing urbanization diversified further the class structure in those countries achieving solid economic growth, expanding especially the middle classes. Third, the growth of middle-income people was itself very uneven in the Third World. It depended primarily on economic performance, which has varied greatly by country and region since the world recession of the early 1980s.

Momentous economic changes occurred in East Asia. The breathtaking industrial progress that characterized first Japan and then the "Four Dragons"—Taiwan, Hong Kong, Singapore, and South Korea—was replicated in China in the 1980s and the early 1990s. After Deng Xiaoping took over in 1978 and launched economic reforms (see page 1136), the Chinese economy grew through 1993 at an average annual rate of about 9 percent. Per capita income in China was doubling every ten years, a rate three to five times faster than the rate in successfully industrializing countries like the United States and Britain before 1914. According to the World Bank, the number of very poor people in China declined by 60 percent after 1978. The spectacular economic surge of almost one-fourth of the human race helped to vitalize all of East Asia. Among big countries, first Indonesia and then India did fairly well; Malaysia and Thai-

The World's Largest McDonald's   The remarkable success of the Beijing McDonald's, shown here, illustrates how rapidly China has been urbanizing and industrializing since 1980. China is moving swiftly in the direction of a consumer society. *(Source: Mu Zhou/Sipa Press)*

land led the smaller countries. A vibrant, independent East Asia emerged as the world's economic pacesetter, an event of enormous significance in long-term historical perspective.

One key to China's success was the example of South Korea and Taiwan, which showed the way in the postwar years. Both South Korea and Taiwan were typical underdeveloped countries after the Second World War—poor, small, agricultural, densely populated, and lacking in natural resources. They had also suffered from Japanese imperialism, yet they managed to make good. How was this possible?

Radical land reform drew the mass of small farmers into a competitive market economy, which proved an excellent school of self-reliance and initiative. As in Japan, probusiness governments in South Korea and Taiwan cooperated with capitalists and helped keep wages low. These governments protected their own farmers and industrialists from foreign competition while also securing almost free access to the large American market.

And like Japan, both countries succeeded in preserving many fundamentals of their interrelated Korean and Chinese cultures even as they accepted and mastered Western technology. Tough nationalist leaders maintained political stability at the expense of genuine political democracy.

When China turned toward the market in 1979, it could also build on the national unity and radical land distribution inherited from Mao. Introducing economic reforms gradually, China also drew on the business talent of wealthy "overseas" Chinese in Hong Kong and Taiwan. They knew the world, needed cheap labor, and played a key role in the emerging "Greater China." Harsh authoritarian political rule encouraged China's people to focus on "daring to be rich," as Deng advised them.

No other region of the Third World (or Europe or North America) came close to matching East Asia after 1980. Latin America revealed some bright spots, most notably in Brazil and Argentina. But West Asia and North Africa, wracked by war, political instability, and low oil prices, experienced spiraling urbanization without much new industrialization or economic development. The situation in sub-Saharan Africa was particularly grave. Severe famines, bitter ethnic conflicts, and low prices for African exports weighed heavily on the vast region, vivid testimony to growing diversity in the Third World.

 ## MASS CULTURE AND CONTEMPORARY THOUGHT

Ideas and beliefs continued to change dramatically in the Third World after independence. Education fostered new attitudes, and mass communications relentlessly spread the sounds and viewpoints of modern life. Third World intellectuals, in their search for the meanings of their countries' experiences, articulated a wide spectrum of independent opinion in keeping with growing regional and national diversity.

Education and Mass Communications

In their efforts to modernize and better their societies, Third World leaders became increasingly convinced of the critical importance of education. They realized that "human capital"—skilled and educated workers, managers, and citizens—played a critical role in the development process. Faith in education and "book learning" spread surprisingly rapidly to the Third World's masses, for whom education principally meant jobs (see Listening to the Past). Thus young people in the Third World headed for schools and universities in unprecedented numbers. There still remained, however, a wide education gap with the rich countries, where more than 90 percent of both sexes attended school through age seventeen.

Moreover, the quality of education in the Third World was often mediocre. African and Asian universities tended to retain the old colonial values, stressing law and liberal arts at the expense of technical and vocational training. As a result, many poor countries found themselves with large numbers of unemployed or underemployed liberal-arts graduates. These "generalists" competed for scarce jobs in the already bloated government bureaucracies while less prestigious technical jobs went begging.

A related problem was the Third World's "brain drain": many gifted students in vital fields like engineering and medicine ended up pursuing their careers in the rich countries of the developed world. For example, in the early 1980s, as many Indian-trained doctors practiced abroad, mainly in advanced countries, as served India's entire rural population of 480 million. The threat represented by the brain drain helped explain why the Third World's professional elite received high salaries even in very poor countries.

In recent years many observers have concluded that the education drive, like its forerunner the industrialization drive, served the rural masses poorly. It sometimes seemed that its greatest beneficiaries were schoolteachers, who profited from the elite status provided by a permanent government job. Instruction was often impractical and mind numbing. The children of farmers generally learned little about agriculture, animal raising, or practical mechanics. Instead, students often memorized passages from ancient literary works and religious texts and spewed back cut-and-dried answers. No wonder children stayed away from school in droves. Village schools succeeded best at identifying the exceptional pupils, who were then siphoned off to the city for further study and were lost forever to the village.

Whatever its shortcomings, formal education spread with another influential agent of popular instruction: mass communications. The transistor radio penetrated the most isolated hamlets of the Third World. Governments universally embraced radio broadcasting as a means of power, propaganda, and education. Relentlessly, the transistor radio propagated the outlook and attitudes of urban elites and in the process challenged old values.

The second communications revolution—the visual one—is now in the process of reaching rural people everywhere. Television is bringing the whole planet into the bars and meetinghouses of the world's villages. Experience elsewhere—in remote French villages, in Eskimo communities above the Arctic Circle—shows that television is having a profound, even revolutionary impact. At the very least the lure of the city continues to grow.

Interpreting the Experiences of the Emerging World

Popular education and mass communications compounded the influence of the Third World's writers and thinkers—its purveyors of explanations.

Some intellectuals meekly obeyed their employers, whether the ministry of information or a large newspaper. Others simply embellished or reiterated some received ideology like Marxism or free-market capitalism. But some Third World intellectuals led in the search for meanings and direction that has accompanied rapid social change and economic struggle.

Having come of age during and after the struggle for political emancipation, some Third World intellectuals argued that genuine independence and freedom from outside control required a total break with the former colonial powers and a total rejection of Western values. This was the message of Frantz Fanon (1925–1961) in his powerful study of colonial peoples, *The Wretched of the Earth* (1968).

Fanon, a French-trained black psychiatrist from the Caribbean island of Martinique, was assigned to a hospital in Algeria during the bloody war for Algerian independence. He quickly came to sympathize with the guerrillas and probed deeply into the psychology of colonial revolt. According to Fanon, decolonization is always a violent and totally consuming process whereby one "species" of men, the colonizers, is completely replaced by an absolutely different species—the colonized, the wretched of the earth. During decolonization the colonized masses mock colonial values, "insult them, and vomit them up," in a psychic purge.

Fanon believed that the battle for formal independence was only the first step. The former imperialists and their local collaborators—the "white men with black faces"—remained the enemy:

Education in an African Village   An instructor at an open-air school in Kenya teaches blue-shirted children from the Masai tribe to tell time. Basic literacy has risen substantially in Third World countries since they achieved independence. *(Source: Peter Carmichael/Aspect Picture Library)*

During the colonial period the people are called upon to fight against oppression; after national liberation, they are called upon to fight against poverty, illiteracy, and underdevelopment. The struggle, they say, goes on. The people realize that life is an unending contest.

. . . The apotheosis of independence is transformed into the curse of independence, and the colonial power through its immense resources of coercion condemns the young nation to regression. In plain words, the colonial power says: "Since you want independence, take it and starve."

. . . We are not blinded by the moral reparation of national independence; nor are we fed by it. The wealth of the imperial countries is our wealth too. . . . Europe is literally the creation of the Third World. The wealth which smothers her is that which was stolen from the underdeveloped peoples.[11]

For Fanon, independence and national solidarity went hand in hand with outrage at the misdeeds

❀ **A Proud Warrior of the Samburu tribe**   This man personifies the precolonial values and dignified self-confidence that African writers like Chinua Achebe have celebrated in the postindependence era. One great political leader who was inspired by his African heritage was Nelson Mandela, the son of a chief. *(Source: From* Samburu: The Proud Warriors/*photo by Mohamed Amin. Reproduced by permission.)*

and moral posturings of the former colonial powers. Fanon's passionate, angry work became a sacred text for radicals attacking imperialism and struggling for liberation.

As independence was gained and nationalist governments were established, some later writers looked beyond wholesale rejection of the industrialized powers. They too were "anti-imperialist," but they saw colonial domination as only one chapter in the life of their people. Many of these writers were cultural nationalists who applied their talents to celebrating the rich histories and cultures of their people. At the same time, they did not hesitate to criticize their own leaders and fellow citizens, with whom they often disagreed.

The Nigerian writer Chinua Achebe (b. 1930) rendered these themes with acute insight and vivid specificity in his short, moving novels. Achebe wrote in English rather than his native Ibo tongue, but he wrote primarily for Africans, seeking to restore his people's self-confidence by reinterpreting the past. For Achebe, the "writer in a new nation" had first to embrace the "fundamental theme":

This theme—quite simply—is that the African people did not hear of culture for the first time from Europeans; that their societies were not mindless but frequently had a philosophy of great depth and volume and beauty, that they had poetry and above all, they had dignity. It is this dignity that many African peoples all but lost in the colonial period, and it is this that they must now regain. The worst thing that can happen to any people is the loss of their dignity and self-respect. The writer's duty is to help them regain it by showing what happened to them, what they lost.[12]

In *Things Fall Apart* (1959) Achebe achieves his goal by bringing vividly to life the men and women of an Ibo village at the beginning of the twentieth century, with all their virtues and frailties. The hero, Okonkwo, is a mighty wrestler and a hardworking, prosperous farmer, but he is stern and easily angered. Enraged at the failure of his people to reject newcomers, and especially at the white missionaries who convert his son to Christianity and provoke the slaying of the sacred python, Okonkwo kills a colonial messenger. When his act fails to spark a tribal revolt, he commits suicide. Okonkwo is destroyed by the general breakdown of tribal authority and his own intransigent recklessness. Woven into the story are the proverbs and

Nyassa Miners Going Home   Photographed in 1952 as they waited patiently at a railway station near Johannesburg, these migrant workers have completed a year's contract in a South African gold mine and are returning home. Laden with presents for their families, these Africans are living through an era of enormous change. *(Source: David Goldblatt)*

wisdom of a sophisticated people and the beauty of a vanishing world.

In later novels, especially *A Man of the People* (1966), Achebe portrays the postindependence disillusionment of many Third World intellectuals. The villain is Chief The Honorable Nanga, a politician with the popular touch. This "man of the people" lives in luxury, takes bribes to build expensive apartment buildings for foreigners, and flimflams the voters with celebrations and empty words. The hero, an idealistic young schoolteacher, tries to unseat Chief Nanga, with disastrous results. Beaten up and hospitalized, the hero broods that the people "had become even more cynical than their leaders and were apathetic into the bargain."[13] Achebe's harsh but considered judgment reflected trends in many Third World nations in the 1960s

and 1970s: the rulers seemed increasingly corrupted by Western luxury and estranged from the rural masses, and idealistic intellectuals could only gnash their teeth in frustration.

The celebrated novelist V. S. Naipaul, born in Trinidad in 1932 of Indian parents, has also castigated Third World governments for corruption, ineptitude, and self-deception. Another of Naipaul's recurring themes is the poignant loneliness and homelessness of uprooted people. In *The Mimic Men* (1967), the blacks and whites and the Hindus and Chinese who populate the tiny Caribbean islands are all aliens, thrown together by "shipwreck." As one of the characters says:

It was my hope in writing to give expression to the restlessness, the deep disorder, which the great exploration, the overthrow in three continents of established social organizations, the unnatural bringing together of peoples who could achieve fulfillment only within the security of their own societies and the landscapes hymned by their ancestors . . . has brought about. The empires of our time were short-lived, but they altered the world for ever; their passing away is their least significant feature.[14]

Naipaul and Achebe, like many other talented Third World writers and intellectuals, probed Third World experiences in pursuit of understanding and identity. A similar soul searching went on in other creative fields, from art and dance to architecture and social science, and seemed to reflect the intellectual maturity of genuine independence.

SUMMARY

As Third World leaders and peoples threw off foreign domination after 1945 and reasserted themselves in new or revitalized states, they turned increasingly inward to attack poverty and limited economic development. The collective response was an unparalleled medical revolution and the Third World's first great industrialization drive. Long-neglected agriculture also made progress, and some countries experienced a veritable Green Revolution. Moreover, rapid urbanization, expanding educational opportunities, and greater rights for women were striking evidence of modernization and fundamental human progress. The achievement was great.

But so was the challenge, and results fell far short of aspirations. Deep and enduring rural poverty, overcrowded cities, enormous class differences, and the sharp criticisms of leading Third World writers mocked early hopes of quick solutions. Since the late 1960s there has been growing dissatisfaction and frustration in Third World nations, lessened only slightly by the emergence of China and East Asia as an economic powerhouse. Thus, as the next chapter will examine, the belief has grown that the Third World can meet the challenge only by reordering the global system and dissolving the unequal ties that bind it to the rich nations.

NOTES

1. P. Bairoch, *Economics and World History: Myths and Paradoxes* (Chicago: University of Chicago Press, 1993), p. 95.
2. P. J. McEwan and R. B. Sutcliffe, eds., *Modern Africa* (New York: Thomas Y. Crowell, 1965), p. 349.
3. Quoted in L. R. Brown, *Seeds of Change: The Green Revolution and Development in the 1970s* (New York: Praeger, 1970), p. 16.
4. P. Ehrlich, *The Population Bomb* (New York: Ballantine, 1968), p. 11.
5. *Wall Street Journal,* April 16, 1981, p. 17.
6. P. Bairoch, *The Economic Development of the Third World Since 1900* (London: Methuen, 1975), p. 144.
7. R. Dumont, *False Start in Africa* (London: André Deutsch, 1966), p. 88.
8. B. Kaye, *Upper Nankin Street, Singapore: A Sociological Study of Households Living in a Densely Populated Area* (Singapore: University of Malaya Press, 1960), p. 2.
9. W. Mangin, "Latin American Squatter Settlements," *Latin American Research Review* 2 (1967): 84–85.
10. P. Hudson, *Third World Women Speak Out: Interviews in Six Countries on Change, Development, and Basic Needs* (New York: Praeger, 1979), p. 11.
11. F. Fanon, *The Wretched of the Earth* (New York: Grove Press, 1968), pp. 43, 93–94, 97, 102.
12. C. Achebe, *Morning Yet on Creation Day* (London: Heinemann, 1975), p. 81.
13. C. Achebe, *A Man of the People* (London: Heinemann, 1966), p. 161.
14. V. S. Naipaul, *The Mimic Men* (New York: Macmillan, 1967), p. 38.

SUGGESTED READING

Many of the suggested readings for Chapter 34 discuss themes considered in this chapter. P. Bairoch, *Economics and World History: Myths and Paradoxes* (1993), is a concise summatiom of a leading specialist's many valuable studies. T. von Laue, *The World Revolution of Westernization: The 20th Century in Global Perspective* (1988), and L. Harrison, *Who Prospers? How Cultural Values Shape Economic and Polical Success* (1992), are stimulating recent interpretations of development problems in the Third World. A. B. Mountjoy, ed., *The Third World: Problems and Perspectives* (1978), and A. MacBean and V.

N. Balasubramanyam, *Meeting the Third World Challenge* (1976), are reliable, evenhanded introductions to postindependence trends and policies. R. Gamer, *The Developing Nations: A Comparative Perspective,* 2d ed. (1986), is a useful synthesis. Two excellent works from a truly Third World perspective are especially recommended: E. Hermassi, *The Third World Reassessed* (1980), and M. ul-Haq, *The Poverty Curtain: Choices for the Third World* (1976). B. Ward, *The Lopsided World* (1968), and G. Myrdal: *Asian Drama: An Inquiry into the Poverty of Nations,* 3 vols. (1968), movingly convey the hopes and frustrations of sympathetic Western economists in the 1960s. Valuable introductions to world agriculture and population are found in various works by L. R. Brown, notably the work cited in the Notes and in *In the Human Interest: A Strategy to Stabilize World Population* (1974). R. King, *Land Reform: A World Survey* (1977), is a good introduction to key problems.

Three valuable studies on African questions are R. Austen, *African Economic History: Internal Development and External Dependency* (1987); B. Turner et al., eds., *Population Growth and Agricultural Change in Africa* (1993); and P. Lloyd, ed., *The New Elites of Tropical Africa* (1966). C. Turnbull, *The Lonely African* (1962), provides intimate portraits of Africans caught up in decolonization and rapid social change; J. Iliffe, *The African Poor: A History* (1987), is an original and important work that is highly recommended. Critical aspects of contemporary Indian economic development are carefully considered by M. Franda, *India's Rural Development: An Assessment of Alternatives* (1980), and A. G. Noble and A. K. Dutt, eds., *Indian Urbanization and Planning: Vehicles of Modernization* (1977). China's economic and social challenges in the early 1980s are skillfully placed in a broad and somewhat somber perspective by two Chinese-speaking journalists, F. Butterfield, *China: Alive in the Bitter Sea* (1982), and R. Bernstein, *From the Center of the Earth: The Search for the Truth About China* (1982). W. Overholt, *The Rise of China: How Economic Reform Is Creating a Modern Superpower* (1993), is an enthusiastic account of recent success.

For the prodigious growth of Third World cities, J. Abu-Lughod and R. Hay, Jr., eds., *Third World Urbanization* (1977); P. Bairoch, *Cities and Economic Development* (1988); and D. J. Dwyer, *People and Housing in Third World Cities: Perspectives on the Problem of Spontaneous Settlements* (1975), are highly recommended. Similarly recommended is a fascinating investigation of enduring urban-rural differences by M. Lipton, *Why Poor People Stay Poor: Urban Bias in World Development* (1977).

A good introduction to changes within families is Hudson, cited in the Notes, a truly remarkable study. C. Johnson-Odim and M. Stroebel, eds., *Expanding the Boundaries of Women's History: Essays on Women in the Third World* (1992), is an important recent study. Other useful works on Third World women and the changes they are experiencing include L. Iglitzen and R. Ross, *Women in the World: A Comparative Study* (1976); N. Keddie and B. Baron, eds., *Women in Middle Eastern History: Shifting Boundaries in Sex and Gender* (1992); A. de Souza, *Women in Contemporary India and South Asia* (1980); N. J. Hafkin and E. Bay, eds., *Women in Africa* (1977); and M. Wolf, *Revolution Postponed: Women in Contemporary China* (1985). K. Kakar, *The Inner World: A Psychoanalytic Study of Childhood and Society in India* (1978), is a stimulating interpretation of Indian dependence on family and personal relations, which is provocatively compared with the compulsive individualism of Western society.

The reader is especially encouraged to enter into the contemporary Third World with the aid of the gifted writers discussed in this chapter. F. Fanon, *The Wretched of the Earth* (1968), is a particularly strong indictment of colonialism from the 1960s. Chinua Achebe illuminates the proud search for a viable past in his classic novel of precolonial Africa, *Things Fall Apart* (1959), and the disillusionment with unprincipled postindependence leaders in *A Man of the People* (1966). G. Moore and U. Beier, eds., *Modern Poetry from Africa* (1963), is a recommended anthology. In addition to his rich and introspective novels like *The Mimic Men* (1967), V. S. Naipaul has reported extensively on life in Third World countries. His *India: A Wounded Civilization* (1978), impressions gleaned from a trip to his family's land of origin, and *A Bend in the River* (1980), an investigation of the high price that postcolonial Africa is paying for modernization, are especially original and thought provoking. E. Burke III, ed., *Struggle and Survival in the Modern Middle East, 1700 to the Present* (1993), contains colorful brief biographies of a wide variety of ordinary people and is outstanding. L. Heng and J. Shapiro, *Son of the Revolution* (1983), brilliantly captures the drama of Mao's China through the turbulent real-life story of a young Red Guard.

Voices from the Village

How has social and economic development been changing women's lives and family relations in the villages of the Third World? How have women and families been coping with enormous changes, and how can governments and international agencies better respond to the real needs of rural people? These questions have fascinated the American writer Perdita Huston ever since she worked as a medical-social worker in rural North Africa in the early 1960s. The only literate woman in the area, she served as "nurse, letter-writer, marriage counselor, and midwife." And she learned to respect the wisdom and courage of poor peasant women "who searched ceaselessly for food, firewood, dung, water, and hope."

In the mid-1970s, as the critical importance of women in both development and population control was increasingly recognized, Huston received a grant from the United Nations to study the needs of village women in Tunisia, Egypt, Sudan, Kenya, Sri Lanka, and Mexico. Assisted by interpreters and using unstructured interviews, Huston talked first with women in groups and then with volunteers in private, "heart-to-heart" exchanges. In each village she began with a simple but profound question: "How does your life differ from that of your mother or grandmother?" This question brought many answers and opened up further discussion of key issues, such as housing, education, jobs, male-female relationships, and children. The following women were representative.

A young, high-school educated woman in Sri Lanka, the eldest of nine children:

"My mother's generation did not have all the opportunities we have. They did not have education, health services, or the transportation systems that exist now. But economically, they were better off. The income they got was sufficient to meet all their needs. At the moment, the high cost of living makes life diffi-cult. They find it difficult to have a happy life.

Today young people have the opportunity to show their capabilities in sports and cultural activities—even in social and public affairs. Earlier generations did not allow girls to leave the home and attend public meetings. Now we have that opportunity. Even without the consent of our parents, we take part in social and public affairs or in political matters.

That is why I wanted to come and join this [agricultural] cooperative. When I live at home, I have no freedom. Wherever I go, I have to be accompanied by a brother and I have to return home early. I am questioned all the time. . . . But here I can earn my living and have some freedom to move about and make choices about participation in after-work activities.

Of course, my parents didn't want me to come here. They refused at first. They were concerned about letting a daughter come to a place like this, but the second time I asked—or rather, insisted—they gave their consent.

You see, my father is a farmer. My parents lived from the land, but when my grandfather died, the land was distributed among his sons. Now my parents' portion is very small. It is not sufficient for them to exist on. They continue to work the land and to search for other jobs.

I want my children to have a firmer footing—not to have this type of life. They must learn a profession and have a better job than mine. Women in Sri Lanka need employment. They should all have jobs. They must be taught skills so that they can earn a bit for their families.

I will have only two children: When you have more than two, you have all sorts of problems and expenses to worry about."

A nomadic Bedouin woman in Tunisia:

"I was given in marriage at age thirteen. I hadn't even reached puberty. My father was dead, so my uncle arranged the marriage with a neighbor. Now it is better; there is a law that says girls mustn't marry before the age of seventeen. That is good. You know, I hadn't had my period when I married. A month later it came—and a month after that I was pregnant. I had five children—three girls and two boys—but one daughter was stillborn.

My children go to school, and I want them, both sons and daughters, to go as far as their ability lets them. I want them to have a good future, a profession, a happy life. I don't want them working in the fields, picking up straws and leftovers as I do. I would like so much to have gone to school. I would like to have opened my mind. I would have taught other people about things. I want to know everything—everything you can learn if you have an education. I won't let my daughters marry earlier than seventeen.

Men are much better these days than they were before. They respect women more. . . . Before, a woman could be divorced, beaten, and poorly treated. That kind of thing doesn't exist anymore, thanks to President Bourguiba. Thanks to him and the laws, women are much better off today.

We have family planning now, and you can take better care of your children. That, too, is different. You can't imagine how many things I tried to swallow to prevent myself from having more children. I even used to eat mothballs, thinking that would help. I am only thirty-six years old, and I have planned my family now for five years. I have a loop. I don't want any more children. Life is too difficult." [She paused.] "Before the new laws, all women lived the lives of beasts."

A young Muslim woman in Sudan:

"Mother's life was, and is, very different from my own. She couldn't go out or talk to any men other than her husband. She never even went out into the street with him. She just stays home all the time; that is her life. But I go to market; I go out with my husband; we may even go to a movie. My husband does not mind. Sometimes I don't even put on my tow [veil]. Mother would never go outside without a full veil covering her face and hair.

These changes are all due to education. Before, women did not go to school. They did not know their husbands. They never saw them until the wedding night, once they were already married. But here in Sudan, women

❋ Village women and their daughters in a hut in southern Mexico. *(Source: Cindy Karp/ Black Star)*

don't have as much access to education as men. It is better for boys, much better. I want my children to have more education than I did; then they will be different from me, just as I am different from my mother. The main thing is education. Schools are very important for girls.

A girl and a boy must be equal. A woman must work in all areas—doctor, teacher, anything. Any work a man can do, a woman can do also."

Questions for Analysis

1. In what ways do these women think their lives are different from their mothers'?

2. What common themes emerge in these responses?

3. What do these women think about education and jobs? About marriage and children?

4. Huston found many women who spoke openly in private but who did not want their names used or their neighbors or husbands informed of their views. How do you explain this?

Source: Perdita Huston, *Third World Women Speak Out: Interviews in Six Countries on Change, Development, and Basic Needs* (New York: Praeger, 1979), pp. 25, 27–28.

36

One Small Planet

Thousands of women from various countries and cultures gathered in the Beijing Olympic Stadium for the United Nations Fourth World Conference on Women in September 1995. *(Source: Forrest Anderson/Gamma Liaison)*

The idea of visitors from elsewhere in the universe has kindled the modern imagination. Motorists swear that they have seen unidentified flying objects; the alchemy of imagination even lands the crew of the starship *Enterprise* on our earth in our era. A best-selling author spins preposterous theories about "ancient astronauts" who landed on earth and built everything from the pyramids at Giza to the temples of the Aztecs. It is as if we earthlings, believers in the power of technology but weighed down by apparently insoluble human conflicts, yearn for some superior intelligence to decipher our little world and set it straight.

Perhaps our yearning for enlightened interstellar guidance can be put to good use. We can imagine how superior intelligences, easily able to grasp our world and its complex history, would view the planet and its talented but quarrelsome human race. Surely interstellar observers would take a genuinely global perspective, free from our customary biases of creed and nation. If we try to do the same, perhaps we too can gain insight into our world's ongoing development and its prospects.

- How has the planet organized itself politically, and will competing nation-states continue to dominate world politics?

- How has the human race been using its resources to meet its material needs?

- What key ideas are guiding human behavior as our planet moves toward an uncertain future?

From a global perspective, these questions might seem particularly important.

 WORLD POLITICS

Although many earthlings are deeply impressed by our recent scientific and technological achievements, highly advanced space travelers might be less so. They might instead be astonished that accelerated technological achievement has not been matched by any corresponding change in the way the human race governs—or fails to govern—itself. Sovereign nation-states reign supreme, as assertive and as competitive as ever, and are reinforced by enormously destructive weapons. The embryonic growth of an effective global political organization, of a government that could protect the world's nations from themselves, appears permanently arrested. The tension generated by powerful, warlike states in a fragile and interdependent world remains one of the most striking—and dangerous— characteristics of this small planet.

Nation-States and the United Nations

The rise of the nation-state and the global triumph of nationalism have been a grand theme of modern world history. The independent territorial nation-state—sometimes containing separatist ethnic groups striving for nationhood in their own right—is clearly the fundamental principle of political organization in our times. Yet from a global perspective we must surely question what we take for granted.

Has the nation-state system, with its apparently inevitable conflicts, become a threat to life on the planet? Some have thought so. It is one of history's ironies that nationalism has been widely condemned in the twentieth century, especially in Europe, just as it has triumphed decisively in world politics. In *Mankind and Mother Earth* (1976), his last work, the renowned British historian Arnold Toynbee (1889–1975) poignantly expressed the post-1914 disillusionment of many European and American intellectuals. At the time of his birth, Toynbee wrote, his middle-class countrymen "supposed Earthly Paradise was just around the corner." They also assumed that the national state was "the natural, normal, rightful political unit." Toynbee's generation of Europeans, however, lived through an era of "self-inflicted tribulation," war and genocide, largely due to their "explosive, subversive" faith in national self-determination.

Toynbee borrowed a term from the ancient Greeks to explain that the spread of the western European political idea of the national state, first to eastern Europe and then to Asia and Africa, had created a fatal discrepancy—

the discrepancy between the political partition of the Oikoumené [the habitat of the human race] into local sovereign states and the global unification of the Oikoumené on technological and economic planes. This misfit is the crux of mankind's present plight. Some form of global government is now needed for keeping the peace . . . and for reestablishing the balance between Man and the rest of the biosphere.[1]

A small but articulate group of intellectuals and political scientists has continued to advocate similar views. Thus we should probably take the "unrealistic" question of world government seriously. Let us look more closely than usual at the United Nations for signs of the emergence of a global authority transcending sovereign states.

When the United Nations was founded in San Francisco in 1945, the United States was the driving force behind its creation. President Franklin D. Roosevelt and Democrats in the Wilsonian tradition believed that the failure of the United States to join the League of Nations had contributed to the tragic breakdown of "collective security" in the 1930s. A resurrected League, they believed, would facilitate Allied cooperation in the postwar era.

The prime purpose of the new organization was to be "to maintain international peace and security." Primary responsibility for this awesome task was assigned to the twelve-nation Security Council. According to the United Nations charter, the Security Council had the authority to examine any international conflict, impose economic and political penalties on an aggressor, and even "take such action by air, sea, or land forces as may be necessary to restore international peace and security." In short, the Security Council had the power to police the world.

In practice, however, this theoretical power was severely restricted. China, Great Britain, France, the Soviet Union, and the United States were all made permanent members of the Security Council,

The United Nations in Action   These soldiers are part of a French battalion serving in a United Nations peacekeeping operation in Cambodia (Kampuchea), a country wracked by war and civil conflict since 1970. United Nations forces usually provide humanitarian aid as they try to preserve fragile cease-fires after warring armies agree to stop fighting. *(Source: J. F. Roussier/Sipa Press)*

and all five had to agree on any peacekeeping action. The veto power of the Big Five has been criticized for preventing the United Nations from ever regulating its most powerful members. But that was precisely the point: none of the Big Five, and certainly not the United States, was willing to surrender sovereign power to a potential world government.

Indeed, a second principle of the United Nations affirmed and reinforced the primacy of the national state in world politics. The charter directed the United Nations to pursue "friendly relations between nations based on the principle of equal rights and self-determination of peoples." Every "peace-loving" state was eligible to join and to participate in the General Assembly, the United Nations' second main body. Founded with 50 members, the General Assembly reached 122 members in 1965 and 159 in 1990. Each member state, whatever its size, always had one voice and one vote on all resolutions, but the resolutions of the General Assembly became legally binding on states only if all five of the Security Council's permanent members agreed. The General Assembly was a world debating society for nation-states, not a lawmaking body for the peoples of the planet.

The third express purpose of the United Nations testified to the expanded scope of government tasks since the late nineteenth century, as well as to global interdependence. According to its charter, the United Nations was "to achieve international cooperation in solving international problems of an economic, social, cultural, or humanitarian character, and in promoting and encouraging respect for human rights and for fundamental freedom for all without distinction as to race, sex, language, or religion." This open-ended assignment was the province of a Social and Economic Council, whose eighteen members were to be elected periodically by the General Assembly. The council was also to work with specialized affiliated agencies such as the World Health Organization in Geneva and the Food and Agriculture Organization in Rome.

The scope of its original purposes helps explain the evolution of the United Nations. Hopes of effective Allied cooperation in the Security Council faded as cold war rhetoric and vetoes by the outnumbered Soviet Union began to paralyze that body. The Security Council proved somewhat more successful at quieting bloody conflicts between smaller states where the interests of the superpowers were not directly involved, such as the dispute between India and Pakistan over Kashmir and that between Greece and Turkey over Cyprus. In 1960, it even sent military forces to re-establish order in the former Belgian Congo. This ambitious undertaking, criticized from all sides and ultimately unsuccessful, marked an early high point of Security Council peacekeeping.

With the Security Council often deadlocked, the rapidly changing General Assembly claimed ever greater authority. As decolonization picked up speed and the number of member states more than doubled by the early 1960s, a nonaligned, anticolonial Afro-Asian bloc emerged. Reinforced by sympathetic Latin American countries, the bloc succeeded in organizing a coherent Third World majority in the General Assembly by the mid-1960s. This majority concentrated on economic and social issues, passing many fiery and fine-sounding resolutions often directed against the former colonial powers, the United States, Israel, imperialist Portugal, and the white government of South Africa.

The long-term significance of these developments at the United Nations was by no means clear. The Third World majority, predominantly composed of small and poor countries, clearly mistook the illusion of power at the United Nations for the substance of power in world affairs. By the late 1970s, many of the General Assembly's resolutions were simply ignored. Meanwhile, many critical international issues, such as the Arab-Israeli conflict, were increasingly resolved by resort to traditional diplomacy or war. From the mid-1980s onward, the United Nations experienced a serious financial crisis as the United States and other Western countries cut their contributions in order to retaliate against United Nations policies that they opposed.

Nor did the United Nations generate much popular support around the world. Most people continued to identify with their national states, which may even provide adults with a psychological substitute for the family bonds that nurtured them in childhood. Thus nation-states have continued to weave the powerful social bonds necessary for group action. As two American political scientists put it, "The nation-state may all too seldom speak the voice of reason. But it remains the only serious alternative to chaos."[2]

❖ ✦ **Famine Relief** These desperate Ethiopians, fleeing from drought and starvation in 1985, hope to find enough food to escape death in makeshift refugee camps. The recent arrivals in the foreground are completely exhausted by hunger, fatigue, and a cold night in the desert. The United Nations has coordinated most famine relief in recent years. *(Source: Sebastiao Salgado/Magnum Photos)*

Despite these limitations the United Nations also proved to be a remarkably hardy institution. Particularly significant was the Third World majority's successful expansion of the scope of the organization's economic, social, and cultural mission. By the 1970s, an alphabet soup of United Nations committees, specialized agencies, and affiliated international organizations was studying and promoting health, labor, agriculture, industrial development, and world trade, not to mention disarmament, control of narcotics, and preservation of the great whales. These agencies and affiliated organizations derived their initial authority from treaties and agreements between sovereign states, but once in operation they took on a life of their own.

Staffed by a talented international bureaucracy, United Nations agencies worked tenaciously to consolidate their power and to serve their main constituency—the overwhelming Third World majority in both the General Assembly and the world's total population. Without directly challenging national sovereignty, they exerted a steady pressure for more "international cooperation" in dealing with specific global issues, and the world's big powers sometimes went along. The United Nations also emerged as the central forum for the debate on the world economic order and the relations between rich and poor countries, issues of fundamental importance in the late twentieth century. Thus sharp-eyed observers detected a gradual, many-sided enlargement of United Nations involvement in the planet's social and economic affairs.

Throughout the 1970s and 1980s the United Nations also continued to play a role in establishing peace in conflicts that did not directly involve the superpowers. Typically, United Nations negotiators helped weary foes to work out a cease-fire agreement, which was then monitored by a United Nations command drawing its troops mainly from small neutral countries. Then, as the 1990s opened, the United Nations again acted on a grand scale to stop aggression and police the world. In response to Iraq's invasion and annexation of the small state of Kuwait, the five permanent members of the Security Council agreed in August 1990 to impose a strict naval blockade on Iraq. Naval forces, led by the United States but augmented by ships from several nations, then enforced the blockade and halted all trade between Saddam Hussein's country and the rest of the world. Receiving the support of ground units from some Arab states as well as from Great Britain and France, the United States also landed first 200,000 and then a total of 500,000 American soldiers in Saudia Arabia near the border of Kuwait. When a defiant Saddam Hussein refused to withdraw from Kuwait and pay reparations, the Security Council authorized the U.S.-led military coalition to attack Iraq.

The subsequent war (Map 36.1) and the defeat of Iraqi armies received saturation coverage in the world's media. It was clear that this spectacular military operation could not have occurred—at least under United Nations auspices—without the approval of China and the Soviet Union. Once before, in the Korean War, the United States and its Western allies had fought with United Nations authorization. But that was only because an angry Soviet Union had walked out of the Security Council and was not present to cast its veto—a tactical error that none of the five permanent members ever repeated when their far-flung interests appeared threatened or even challenged. In the flush of victory over Iraqi armies, some leaders and observers believed that a "new world order" might

be at hand. Perhaps Great Power cooperation on the Security Council would enable the United Nations to fulfill its original purpose and impose peace and security throughout the world.

One such attempt came in December 1992, when armed forces from the United States landed on the east African beaches of Somalia in order to stop a savage civil war and allow United Nations soldiers to maintain peace thereafter. But the operation failed, as some Somali fighters attacked, killed, and drove out their would-be benefactors. United Nations negotiators and miliary observers (as well as NATO) were also unable to stop the equally savage civil war in Bosnia. These setbacks discredited United Nations efforts to impose peace on unwilling warring factions and forced a scaling back of United Nations peacekeeping ambitions. As a result the United Nations again concentrated on helping warring factions that wanted peace and did not try to impose peace. Even this was an awesome task: in early 1995 more than sixty-seven thousand United Nations soldiers were stationed in hot spots—such as Cyprus, the Gaza strip, Kashmir, Lebanon, and Haiti—all around the world. United Nations peacekeeping efforts were imperfect, but they were also indispensable. These efforts, combined with the United Nations' ambitious range of social and economic activities, suggest that the first historic steps toward some kind of world government have been taken.

Complexity and Violence

In between territorial nation-states and international organizations that focus on specific problems stretches a vast middle ground of alliances, blocs, partnerships, and ongoing conflicts and rivalries. It is often difficult to make sense of this tangle of associations, for four fundamental developments have structured a complexity sometimes bordering on chaos.

First, East-West competition and the mutual hostility of the bloc leaders, the Soviet Union and the United States, was until recently one of the planet's most enduring realities. The cold war raged in the 1980s, when Soviet armies decimated Afghanistan and the United States modernized its military might. To be sure, neither bloc by then was as solid as it had been a generation earlier. China had long since broken with the Soviet

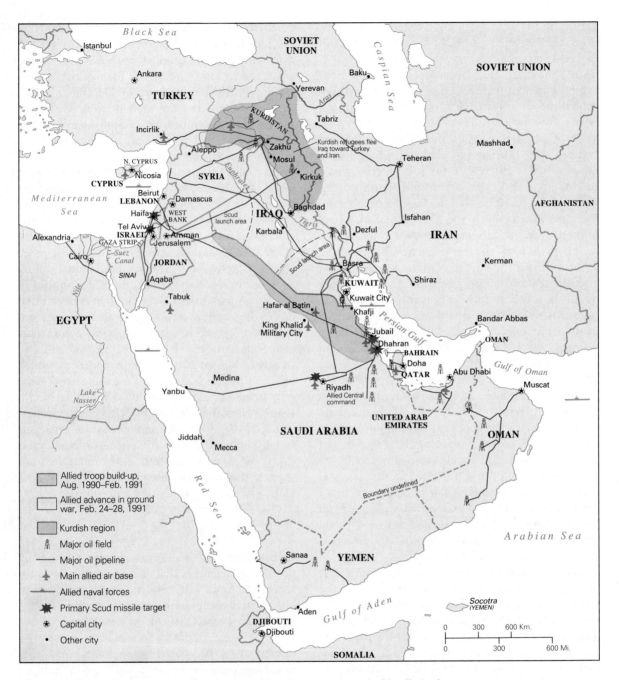

※ **MAP 36.1 The Persian Gulf War** The United States' most valuable ally in the Gulf War was the kingdom of Saudi Arabia, which feared it might be next on the list after Iraq suddenly seized Kuwait. Providing U.S. commanders with both bases and troops, Saudi Arabia emerged from the war with increased regional influence and unique superpower status in the world oil industry.

Union, and Poland's effort to chart its own course testified eloquently to tensions within the East bloc. As for the West, serious differences on military matters surfaced within NATO (which France had long since quit), and economic quarrels flared between the Common Market and the United States. In short, during the cold war the hostile superpowers both dominated their allies and were restrained by them. The sudden end of the cold war shattered these interlocking restraints, removing a basic principle of global organization and signaling a new era in world politics.

The long cold war contributed to the ideology of Third World solidarity, a second significant factor in planetary affairs. A critical step was taken in 1955, when Asian and African nations came together in Bandung, Indonesia, to form a "third force" of nonaligned nations. The neutralist leaders of Asia and Africa believed that genuine independence and social justice were the real challenges before them, and they considered the cold war a wasteful and irrelevant diversion. African, Asian, and Latin American countries learned to work together at the United Nations, and they called for a restructuring of the world economic system. These efforts brought mixed results (see below), but a loose majority of Third World countries did coalesce around some global issues.

A striking third development was the increasingly "multipolar" nature of world politics. Regional conflict and a fluid, complicated jockeying for regional influence were the keynotes. During the cold war, while the two superpowers struggled to control their allies and competed for global power and influence, a number of increasingly assertive "middle powers" arose around the world. Often showing by their actions only limited commitment to Third World solidarity, these middle powers strove to be capable of leading or dominating their neighbors and of standing up to the world's superpowers on regional questions. The rise of middle powers reflected the fact that most of the world's countries were small and weak, with fewer than 20 million people. Only a few countries had the large populations, natural resources, and industrial bases necessary for real power on a regional or global scale.

Latin America presented two striking examples of rising middle powers. Brazil, with more than 140 million people, vast territory and resources, and one of the world's most rapidly industrializing economies, emerged rather suddenly as South America's dominant nation-state. Equally impressive was the emergence of Mexico, with its population of over 80 million, its substantial industrial base and oil wealth, and its tradition of revolution and proud nationalism. By the early 1980s, Mexico clearly saw itself as the natural leader of the Spanish-speaking Americas.

Strong regional powers like France and West Germany had re-emerged in western Europe by the early 1960s. The unification of Germany in 1990 created a dominant economic power in Europe, with far-reaching implications for the Common Market and Europe's role in world affairs. Resurgent Nigeria was unquestionably the leading power in sub-Saharan Africa. Heavily populated Egypt and much smaller Israel were also regional powerhouses. Iran sought under the shah to dominate the Persian Gulf but came out of the long, bitter war with Iraq in the 1980s a bloodied loser. This defeat encouraged Saddam Hussein to launch his surprise attack on tiny Kuwait as part of Iraq's unsuccessful bid to become the dominant power in the region. China, India, and Japan were all leading regional powers, and several other Asian countries—notably Indonesia, Vietnam, Pakistan, and the Philippines—were determined to join them.

A fourth development is the high degree of conflict and violence that has characterized the emerging multipolar political system. Conflict in Europe remained mainly verbal during the cold war, but in Africa, Asia, and Central America blood flowed freely. Of the 145 wars that occurred worldwide between 1945 and 1979, 117 were in the Third World. Some countries were literally torn apart. Lebanon, which had long been considered the most advanced state in the Arab world, was practically destroyed by endless war, civil conflict, and foreign occupation. Cambodia (Kampuchea), invaded by American armies in 1970, then ravaged by the savage Pol Pot regime and finally occupied by Vietnamese armies, became another terrible tragedy.

The ongoing plague of local wars and civil conflicts caused great suffering. Millions of refugees, like Vietnam's "boat people," fled for their lives. The war for independence in Bangladesh temporarily created over 10 million refugees, who fled into India toward Calcutta. Hungry, homeless

✳ **Beirut: The Fruits of Civil War** Savage conflict between rival militias divided and decimated the Lebanese capitol in the 1980s. This Muslim family is walking along the previously fortified "green line," which separated the city's warring Muslim and Christian quarters for fifteen years before it was dismantled by a resurgent national government in 1990. *(Source: Wide World Photos)*

people overwhelmed the Indian relief centers, sleeping in trees, huddling in the rain, starving to death. After the Soviet invasion of Afghanistan, fully one-tenth of that country's population of 1.7 million people fled. In 1981, the United Nations' commission for emergency relief counted 10 million refugees in Asia and Africa. It was an appalling commentary on organized violence in our time.

Regional competition and local hot wars brought military questions once again to the forefront of world attention. During the cold war nearly every country in the world joined the superpowers in an ever-intensifying arms race. In garrison states like Israel, South Africa, and Vietnam, defense expenditures assumed truly fantastic proportions. For example, in the early 1980s Vietnam

was spending half of its national income on the military; its standing army of a million men was the world's third largest, after the Soviet Union and China, and one of the best.

The end of the cold war did not reduce the level of local strife and violence. In many African states local politicians and ethnic rivalries had sometimes been restrained by superpower patrons and their aid. Now Africans found themselves neglected by the superpowers and without much outside financial support. Competition for power and resources increased in Africa, leading to still more ethnic battles and civil wars.

The most brutal, destructive, and long-lasting conflict has been occurring not in the Third World but in supposedly advanced Europe, in Bosnia-

Herzegovina and Croatia in the former Yugoslavia. Long-standing tensions between the country's three main ethnic groups—the Catholic Croats, the Orthodox Serbs, and the Muslim Bosnians—was rekindled by civil war and Nazi occupation in the Second World War. After the liberation the communist war leader Tito, who broke with Stalin in 1948 (see page 1108), established a federated Yugoslavia consisting of six separate republics. Tito then ruled his independent communist state with a firm hand. After his death in 1980, economic difficulties and large foreign debts weakened Yugoslavia. In 1989 the complex ethnic quota system that Tito had established finally fell apart as communist power withered away. Ethnic conflicts reignited. Politicians and peoples could not agree on whether Yugoslavia should remain united, though under Serb domination, or whether the six republics should become independent sovereign states.

The Serbs insisted that Serbian minorities living in Croatia and Bosnia-Herzegovina had to be included in a new and expanded "Greater Serbia." When the Croats refused to accept this demand, Serbs in Croatia declared their autonomy. Fighting began in 1991, and Serbian forces occupied roughly one-third of Croatian territory. Fighting then spread to Bosnia-Herzegovina, where the Serbs seized about two-thirds of the territory and inflicted heavy losses on Croats and Bosnian Muslims. Serbian forces repeatedly expelled Croats and Bosnian Muslims from their homes and villages, terrorizing the women and imprisoning the men in concentration camps. These acts of barbarism,

A Victim in Bosnia This child lives in an orphanage in Sarajevo, the capital of Bosnia-Herzegovina. The orphanage has no food and has sent the orphans out to scavenge in dumpsters for scraps of garbage. For many Europeans the terrible Bosnian tragedy recalls the Nazi nightmare. *(Source: Roger Richards/Liaison)*

known as "ethnic cleansing," shocked world public opinion and led to many United Nations–sponsored cease-fires and efforts to restore peace. As of May 1995, all of these efforts had failed. The Serbs, the Croats, and the Bosnian Muslims were all rebuilding their armies, and renewed heavy fighting was much more likely than a negotiated peace.

In summary, regional competition, local hot wars, and brutal civil conflicts brought military matters once again to the forefront of the world's attention. In an effort to deal with insecurity and violence almost every country in the world joined the superpowers in a global arms race.

Nuclear Arms and Nuclear Proliferation

A particularly ominous aspect of the global arms race was the threat of nuclear war and nuclear proliferation. For a generation after 1945, nuclear weapons were concentrated mainly in the hands of the two superpowers, who learned a grudging respect for each other. But other states also developed nuclear weapons, and by the 1970s many more were capable of doing so. Some experts then feared that as many as twenty countries might have their own atomic bombs in a few brief years. By the early 1990s these fears had not come true. Moreover, the end of the cold war reduced the logic of superpower arsenals, encouraging widespread hopes that the nightmare vision of the mushroom cloud would be permanently lifted. In fact, the specter of nuclear proliferation still loomed, and the threat of nuclear war remained. How, a superior intelligence would surely ask, had this frightening situation arisen? And what was being done to find a solution?

Having let the atomic genie out of the bottle at Hiroshima and Nagasaki in 1945, a troubled United States immediately proposed that it be recaptured through effective international control of all atomic weapons. As American representative Bernard Baruch told the first meeting of the United Nations Atomic Energy Commission in 1946:

We are here to make a choice between the quick and the dead. . . . We must elect World Peace or World Destruction. . . . Therefore the United States proposes the creation of an International Atomic Development

Authority, to which should be entrusted all phases of the development and use of atomic energy.

The Soviets, suspicious that the United States was really trying to preserve its atomic monopoly through its proposal for international control and inspection, rejected the American idea and continued their crash program to catch up with the United States. The Soviet Union exploded its first atomic bomb in 1949. As the cold war raged on in the 1950s, the two superpowers pressed forward with nuclear development. The United States exploded its first hydrogen bomb in 1952; within ten months the Soviet Union did the same. Further American, Soviet, and then British tests aroused intense worldwide concern about nuclear fallout. There was well-founded fear that radioactive fallout entering the food chain would cause leukemia, bone cancer, and genetic damage. Concerned scientists called for an international agreement to stop all testing of atomic bombs.

Partly in response to worldwide public pressure, the United States, the Soviet Union, and Great Britain agreed in 1958 to stop testing for three years. In 1963 these three powers signed an agreement, later signed by more than one hundred countries, banning nuclear tests in the atmosphere. A second step toward control was the 1968 Treaty on the Non-Proliferation of Nuclear Weapons, designed to halt their spread to other states and to reduce stockpiles of existing bombs. It seemed that the nuclear arms race might yet be reversed.

This outcome did not come to pass. De Gaulle's France and Mao's China, seeing themselves as great world powers, simply disregarded the test ban and refused to sign the nonproliferation treaty. By 1968, they too had hydrogen bombs. Reversing its previous commitment to nuclear arms limitations, India also refused to sign the treaty. In 1974, India exploded an atomic device.

India's reversal was partly due to the failure of the Soviet Union and the United States to abide by the terms of the 1968 treaty on nuclear nonproliferation. According to the terms of the treaty, the nuclear powers agreed "to pursue negotiations in good faith on effective measures relating to cessation of the nuclear arms race at an early date and to nuclear disarmament, and on a treaty on general and complete disarmament under strict and effective international control." The non-nuclear states, which had seen serious efforts at disarmament by the superpowers as their payoff for promising not to go nuclear, had offered a series of proposals ranging from a complete test ban to a freeze or reduction on nuclear weapons before agreeing to sign the treaty.

In fact, the nuclear arms race between the Soviet Union and the United States surged ahead after 1968. According to American officials, the United States was capable in 1974 of dropping 36 bombs on each of the 218 Soviet cities with populations of 100,000 or more. The Soviet Union had 11 nuclear weapons for each American city of comparable size. The much-discussed SALT talks confined themselves to limiting the rate at which the Soviet Union and the United States produced more nuclear warheads. After 1980, when the second Strategic Arms Limitation Treaty failed to be ratified by the U.S. Senate, the superpowers appeared once again to be locked into a nuclear arms race.

Partly out of fear for their own security, many near-nuclear powers appeared poised to go nuclear in the 1980s. The worldwide energy crisis of the 1970s had played a part: peaceful use of the atom to generate electric power had created as a byproduct large quantities of plutonium, the raw material for bombs. Ominously, some countries began to regard nuclear bombs as just another weapon in the struggle for power and survival.

India developed its atomic capability partly out of fear of China, which had manhandled India in a savage border war in 1962. India's nuclear blast in 1974 in turn frightened Pakistan, which regarded India as a bitter enemy after 1947 and lost Bangladesh because of Indian armies. Pakistan's President Zulfikar Ali Bhutto (1928–1979) was reported to have said that Pakistan must have the bomb even if its people had to eat grass. In the 1980s, Pakistan was clearly on the verge of producing nuclear weapons.

It was also generally believed that both Israel and South Africa had arsenals of nuclear bombs. Israel's apparent nuclear superiority was profoundly distasteful to the Arabs. Hence Iraq pushed hard, with help from France, to develop nuclear capability. In June 1981, Israel responded suddenly, attacking and destroying the Iraqi nuclear reactor. When Iraq subsequently used deadly chemical weapons in its war against Iran and against its own dissatisfied minorities, the terrible

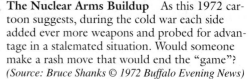

The Nuclear Arms Buildup As this 1972 cartoon suggests, during the cold war each side added ever more weapons and probed for advantage in a stalemated situation. Would someone make a rash move that would end the "game"? *(Source: Bruce Shanks © 1972 Buffalo Evening News)*

dangers of nuclear proliferation were driven home to all.

If countries like Iraq developed nuclear arms, and if regional conflicts remained so intense, would not some nation use the dreadful weapons sooner or later? And what about nuclear terrorism and blackmail? In a world full of nuclear weapons and nuclear potential, might not fanatical political groups and desperate states resort to nuclear blackmail to gain their demands? None of these menacing possibilities came to pass in the 1980s, but in a world of bitter political rivalries they made the hard-headed observer grimly apprehensive. Was the human race, as one expert on nuclear arms warned, "an endangered species"?[3]

The end of the cold war offered new hope. The likelihood of nuclear war between the United States and the Soviet Union declined greatly. In addition, effective Soviet-American cooperation presented the possibility of a great reduction in existing nuclear arsenals along with a continued renunciation of such weapons by non-nuclear countries, as already spelled out in the 1968 Treaty on the Non-Proliferation of Nuclear Weapons. One important step in this direction was taken in July 1990, when the Soviet Union, no doubt with U.S. support, required West Germany to renounce forever the manufacture of nuclear arms in return for Soviet agreement to German reunification. After the breakup of the Soviet Union, the United States and Russia agreed to big cuts in their respective nuclear arsenals, so that in a few years the United States would have thirty-five hundred nuclear warheads and Russia would have three thousand.

Apparently planning to maintain such enormous nuclear power, the United States and Russia, as well as the other nuclear powers, showed little interest in realizing the 1968 goal of *complete* nuclear disarmament. Thus when negotiations opened on a permanent extension of the 1968 Treaty on the Non-Proliferation of Nuclear Weapons, which was scheduled to expire in 1995, a large number of non-nuclear countries voiced objections. These countries charged that the treaty had created an exclusive club of nuclear powers and had condemned the non-nuclear powers signing the treaty to permanent inferiority. They pressed the five declared nuclear powers to move meaningfully toward total nuclear disarmament. Regional conflicts also undermined support for a permanent extension of the treaty. In particular, Arab nations wanted Israel to sign the treaty and renounce nuclear arms, which Israel was not prepared to do. The difficult negotiations over the renewal of the Non-Proliferation Treaty poignantly illustrated the tremendous difficulty of effective international cooperation in a world of proud and suspicious nation-states.

❖ GLOBAL INTERDEPENDENCE

Alongside political competition, war, and violence, a contradictory phenomenon unfolded: as Toynbee suggested, the nations of our small world became increasingly interdependent both economically and technologically. Even the great continental states with the largest landmasses and populations and the richest natural resources found that they could not depend only on themselves. The United States required foreign oil, and Russia needed foreign grain. All countries and peoples had need of each other.

Mutual dependence in economic affairs was often interpreted as a promising sign for the human race. Dependence promoted peaceful cooperation and limited the scope of violence. Yet the existing framework of global interdependence also came under intense attack. The poor countries of the South—the Third World—charged that the North continued to receive far more than its rightful share from existing economic relationships—relationships that had been forged to the South's disadvantage in the era of European expansion and political domination. The South demanded a new international economic order (see Listening to the Past). Critics also saw strong evidence of neocolonialism in the growing importance of the North's huge global business corporations—the so-called multinationals—in world economic development. Thus global interdependence was widely acknowledged in principle and hotly debated in practice.

Pressure on Vital Resources

During the postwar economic boom of the 1950s and the 1960s, the nations of the world became more dependent on each other for vital resources. Yet resources also seemed abundant, and rapid industrialization was a worldwide article of faith. Only those alarmed by the population explosion predicted grave shortages, and they spoke almost exclusively about food shortages in the Third World.

The situation changed suddenly in the early 1970s. Fear that the world was running out of resources was widely voiced. In a famous study aptly titled *The Limits to Growth* (1972), a group of American and European scholars argued that unlimited growth is impossible on a finite planet. By the early twenty-first century, they predicted, the ever-increasing demands of too many people and factories would exhaust the world's mineral resources and destroy the fragile biosphere with pollution.

Meanwhile, Japan was importing 99 percent of its petroleum, western Europe 96 percent. When the Organization of Petroleum Exporting Countries (OPEC) increased the price of crude oil fourfold in 1973 (see page 0000), there was panic in many industrial countries. Skyrocketing prices for oil and other raw materials seemed to confirm grim predictions that the world was exhausting its vital resources.

In much of the Third World, the pressure to grow more food for more people led to piecemeal destruction of forests and increased soil erosion. Much of the Third World suffered from what has been called "the other energy crisis"—a severe lack of firewood for cooking and heat. A striking case was the southern edge of the Sahara. Population growth caused the hard-pressed peoples of this region to overgraze the land and denude the forests. As a result, the sterile sand of the Sahara advanced southward as much as thirty miles a year along a 3,000-mile front. Thus land available for cultivation decreased, leaving Africa all the more exposed to terrible droughts. In the 1980s, crops shriveled up, and famine stalked the land; but an interdependent world mobilized, and international relief prevented mass starvation.

Recognition of interdependence was also reinforced by a common dependence on the air and the sea. Just as radioactive fallout has no respect for national boundaries, so pollution may sully the whole globe. Deadly chemicals, including mercury, lead, and arsenic, accumulated in the biosphere. Some feared that pollution of the oceans would lead to the contamination of fish, one of the world's main sources of protein. Others, worried that the oceans had been overfished, feared that the significant decline in the worldwide fish catch in the 1970s indicated abuse of the sea, the common heritage of humankind.

Of all the long-term pressures on global resources, many observers believed that the growth of population was the most serious. Here recent experience offered room for cautious optimism. Population growth in the industrialized countries slowed markedly or even stopped. Of much greater importance from a global perspective, the world's poor women began to bear fewer children. Small countries like Barbados, Chile, Costa Rica, South Korea, Taiwan, Tunisia, and the British colony of Hong Kong led the way. Between 1970 and 1975 China followed, registering the fastest five-year decline in the birthrate in recorded history. Then other big countries, especially in Latin America

and East Asia, also experienced large declines in fertility. In 1970, the average Brazilian woman had close to six children; by 1994, she had slightly more more than two. In 1970, the average woman in Bangladesh had more than seven children; in 1994, she had 4.5. Overall, the average Third World woman had 6.2 children in 1950 and 3.6 in 1994.

There were several reasons for the decline of fertility among Third World women. Fewer babies were dying of disease or malnutrition; thus couples needed fewer births to guarantee the survival of the number of children they wanted. As had happened earlier in the industrialized nations, better living conditions, urbanization, and more education encouraged women to have fewer children. No wonder that the most rapidly industrializing countries, like Taiwan or South Korea, led the way in birthrate declines. On the other hand, state-run birth control programs proved most successful in authoritarian China. The birth control pill, borrowed from the West but manufactured locally, was widely used in conjunction with heavy financial penalties for couples who exceeded the birth quota, increasingly fixed at one child per couple. As in most communist countries, abortion was free and available on demand.

Outside East Asia, contraception and especially abortion remained controversial. This helps explain why birthrates and population growth remained much higher in Africa and in the Muslim world than in East Asia. In 1985, Africa led the world with a population growth of 3.2 percent per year—enough to double the continent's numbers in only twenty-two years. Yet even in fast-growing Africa the rate of growth began to fall, with the average woman having about six children in 1994 as opposed to eight a few years earlier.

Indira Gandhi's fiasco with compulsory sterilization (see page 1144) and recent experience suggest that, barring catastrophe, worldwide population growth will continue to decline primarily as the result of billions of private decisions, decisions supplemented by government policies supporting contraception. These decisions are being made. Half of the world's couples now practice birth control, up from one in eight 40 years ago. Nonetheless, as the Third World's current huge population of young adults form their own families, the world's population will grow for a long time even if the use of contraception continues to increase.

The One-Child Family China's continued moderate rate of population increase resulted in the early 1980s in drastic laws that generally prohibit Chinese families from having more than one child. The happy grandmother and the government posters behind preach the joys of the one-child family, which is at odds with Chinese tradition. *(Source: Jin Xuqi/Picture Group)*

Thus the world's population—5.6 billion in 1994, as opposed to 1.6 billion in 1900—will probably not stabilize until the mid-twenty-first century at the earliest, when it is estimated to reach between 10 billion and 11 billion people. Such continued growth will put tremendous pressure on global resources.

Gloom, however, is not the proper perspective. Even with 11 billion people, the earth would be less densely populated than Europe is today, and only one-fourth as densely populated as small, prosperous countries like Belgium and the Netherlands, which largely feed themselves (see Map 35.1, page 1178). Such countries, often overlooked in world politics, are promising models for life on a crowded planet. Moreover, the human race has exhibited considerable skill throughout its history at finding new resources and inventing new technologies. A striking example was the way that conservation, alternative energy sources, and world recession in the early 1980s at least temporarily belied gloomy prophecies about dwindling energy resources. An optimist could conclude that, at least from a quantitative and technical point of view, the adequacy of resources is a serious but by no means insoluble problem.

North-South Relations

The real key to adequate resources is probably global cooperation. Will the world's peoples work together, or will they eventually fight over resources like wild dogs over meat?

After the late 1960s there was dissatisfaction in Asia, Africa, and Latin America not only with the fruits of the industrialization drive but also with the world's economic system. Scholars imbued with a Third World perspective and spokesmen for the United Nations majority declared that the international system was unjust and in need of radicals change. A brilliant Pakistani, World Bank official and member of the international bureaucratic elite, sympathetically articulated this position in 1976:

The vastly unequal relationship between the rich and the poor nations is fast becoming the central issue of our time. The poor nations are beginning to question the basic premises of an international order which leads to ever-widening disparities between the rich and the poor countries and to a persistent denial of equality of opportunity to many poor nations. They are, in fact, arguing that in international order—just as much as within national orders—all distribution of benefits, credit, services, and decision-making becomes warped in favor of a privileged minority and that this situation cannot be changed except through fundamental institutional reforms.[4]

The subsequent Third World demand for a "new international economic order" had many causes, both distant and immediate. Critics of imperialism like J. A. Hobson (see page 902) and Third World writers on decolonization like Frantz Fanon (see page 1193) had long charged that the colonial powers grew rich exploiting Asia, Africa, and Latin America. Beginning in the 1950s, a number of writers, many of them Latin American Marxists, breathed new life into these ideas with their "theory of dependency."

The poverty and so-called underdevelopment of the South, they argued, were not the starting points but the deliberate and permanent results of exploitation by the capitalist industrialized nations in the modern era. Third World countries produced cheap raw materials for wealthy, industrialized countries and were conditioned to buy their expensive manufactured goods. As in the case of Latin America since the nineteenth century, the industrialized nations perpetuated this neocolonial pattern after Third World countries gained political independence. Thus the prevailing economic interdependence was the unequal, unjust interdependence of dominant and subordinate, of master and peon. Declining economic aid, smug pro-nouncements about the overpopulation of the Third World, and the natural resentment of the poor toward the rich also fostered calls for radical restructuring of the international order.

It was the highly successful OPEC oil coup of 1973–1974 that ignited Third World hopes of actually achieving a new system of economic interdependence. From the industrialized North's point of view, OPEC's action in quadrupling the price of oil was a dangerous attack. It brought an end to the postwar economic boom and created serious social problems. From a global perspective, however, the sudden price rise brought a massive global transfer of wealth unprecedented since the looting of Mexico and Peru by the Spanish conquistadors. Perhaps 2 percent of all the income of the rich nations was suddenly forwarded to the OPEC countries (Map 36.2). Third World critics of dependence and neocolonialism were euphoric. For years the developed countries had gradually been reducing their economic aid. They had never seriously tried to meet the goal suggested by the United Nations General Assembly of earmarking 1 percent of their income each year for foreign aid. OPEC's success suggested that radical change was possible.

In 1974, a special session of the General Assembly rammed through two landmark resolutions calling for a "new international economic order" and a "program of action" to attain it. Among the specific demands were firm control by each country of its own natural resources, higher and more stable prices for raw materials, and equal tariff treatment for manufactured goods from the Third World. These demands were subject to "collective bargaining," but the Third World vigorously insisted on new terms. As one sympathetic scholar observed in 1980:

There has taken place a unionization of the Third World that has marked a profound shift in international relations. It looks as if the confrontation between unions and employers that stirred capitalist societies in the nineteenth century is being reenacted, but this time on a world scale between developed and developing nations. The question this time is whether the new nations command as many assets and opportunities as did the laboring classes of capitalist nations.[5]

That profound question remained unanswered in the late twentieth century. The developing

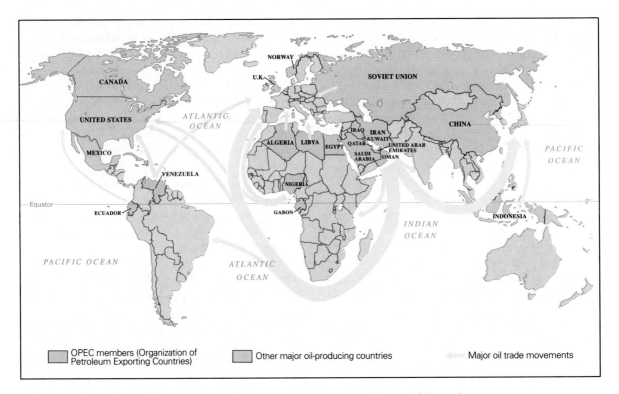

MAP 36.2 OPEC and the World Oil Trade   Though much of the world depends on imported oil, western Europe and Japan are OPEC's biggest customers. What major oil exporters remain outside of OPEC?

countries did negotiate some victories, notably a Common Fund under United Nations auspices to support the prices of raw materials and a scaling down of their enormous debts to the industrial nations (see below). Moderate socialists and some liberal economists in the North also supported some of the demands of the developing countries (see Listening to the Past). But generally the North, deeply troubled by inflation and by its own economic problems, proved a very tough bargainer when it came to basic changes.

For example, in the late 1970s the South laid great hopes on a long, complicated conference to formulate a new Law of the Sea. The proposed new law was based on the principle that the world's oceans are "a common heritage of mankind" and should be exploited only for the benefit of all nations. In practice, this was to mean that a United Nations–sponsored authority would regulate and tax use of the sea and that a global organization would even mine the ocean floor.

Some wealthy countries and their business firms were reluctant to accept such an infringement of their economic sovereignty and scope of action. The United States withdrew from the negotiations in 1981, and in 1982 the administration of U.S. president Ronald Reagan and the governments of several other developed nations refused to sign the final draft of the new Law of the Sea.

Increasingly frustrated in their desire to fashion a new international economic order quickly, some Third World leaders predicted more confrontation and perhaps military conflict between North and South. Some alarmists in the North voiced similar concerns. For example, these alarmists charged that many Third World governments secretly condoned the production of illegal drugs for sale in the industrialized nations, and they predicted that this behavior would dangerously increase the tensions existing between the rich and the poor countries (Map 36.3).

In considering these frightening predictions, an impartial observer was initially struck by the great gap between the richest and poorest nations. That gap was built on the coercive power of Western imperialism as well as on the wealth-creating achievements of continuous technological improvement since the Industrial Revolution. In the face of bitter poverty, unbalanced economies, and local elites that often cater to Western interests, Third World peoples had reason for anger.

But close examination of our small planet hardly suggested two sharply defined economic camps, a "North" and a "South." Rather, by the early 1980s there were several distinct classes of nations in terms of wealth and income, as may be seen in Map 36.4. The communist countries of eastern Europe formed something of a middle-income group, as did the major oil-exporting states, which still lagged behind the wealthier countries of western Europe and North America. Latin America was much better off than sub-Saharan Africa, having a number of middle-range countries to match their counterparts in highly diverse Asia.

When one added global differences in culture, religion, politics, and historical development, the supposed clear-cut split between the rich North and the poor South broke down further. Moreover, the solidarity of the Third World was fragile, resting largely on the ideas of some Third World intellectuals and their supporters. As one writer put it,

in the advocacy of growth and equalization at the international level . . . Third World states have astonished everybody, their enemies and their friends alike, for no one has ever believed that such a diverse congress of countries, separated by geography, geopolitics, cultural traditions, size, ideology, and a host of other factors, could ever manage to build a cohesive alliance.[6]

The oil cartel's achievement rested in large part on regional (and perhaps temporary) Arab solidarity, for example, and duplicating its success with less vital raw materials and more complicated issues proved impossible. Thus a continuation of the global collective bargaining that emerged in the 1970s seems more likely than an international class (and race) war. The poorer nations will press to reduce international economic differences through trade preferences, redistribution measures, and

special aid to the most unfortunate countries. And because global interdependence has become a reality, they will gradually win concessions, as the working classes have won gains within the wealthy nations since the late nineteenth century.

The international debt crisis of recent times illustrated the process of global bargaining. The economic dislocations of the 1970s and early 1980s worsened the problems of many Third World countries, especially those that had to import the oil they needed. Growing unemployment, unbalanced budgets, and large trade deficits forced many Third World countries to borrow rapidly from the wealthy industrialized nations. By the middle of 1982, Third World nations—led by Mexico, Brazil, and Argentina—owed foreign banks and governments about $600 billion. Much of this staggering debt was short-term and could not possibly be repaid as it fell due.

In 1982, when Mexico was unable to keep up with the payments on $80 billion of foreign debts, default and financial chaos in Mexico seemed at hand. Yet the Reagan administration, consistently opposed to Third World calls for a new international system, quickly organized a gigantic rescue operation to pump new money into Mexico and prevent default. The reason was simple: Mexico's failure to service its foreign debt would cripple large American banks that had lent Mexico money and possibly cause a financial panic that would plunge the whole world into depression and turmoil. Thus a series of international negotiations in the 1980s reduced the debts of Third World countries, granted desperately needed new loans, and encouraged economic liberalization. Lenders and borrowers, rich and poor, North and South, realized that they were bound together in mutual dependence by the international debt crisis. In 1995 Mexico again could not pay its debts, and the administration of U.S. president Bill Clinton granted another round of emergency loans, convinced that it was rescuing the United States as well as Mexico.

The Multinational Corporations

One of the most striking features of global economic interdependence since the early 1950s has been the rapid emergence of *multinational corporations,* business firms that operate in a number of different countries and tend to adopt a global rather than a national perspective. Multinational

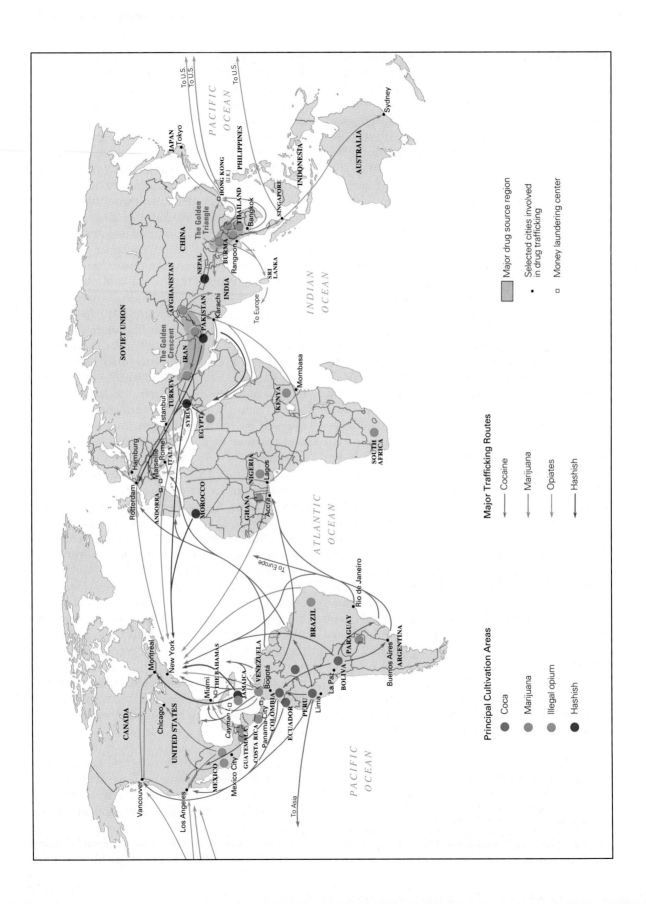

PACIFIC OCEAN

To U.S.
To U.S.
To U.S.

JAPAN
Tokyo

PHILIPPINES

HONG KONG
(U.K.)

The Golden
Triangle

CHINA

THAILAND
Bangkok

BURMA
Rangoon

SINGAPORE

INDONESIA

AUSTRALIA

Sydney

NEPAL

SOVIET UNION

AFGHANISTAN

PAKISTAN
Karachi

INDIA

SRI
LANKA

To Europe

INDIAN OCEAN

The Golden
Crescent

IRAN

TURKEY
Istanbul

SYRIA

EGYPT

KENYA
Mombasa

Hamburg
Rotterdam
Marseille
ITALY Rome

ANDORRA

MOROCCO

NIGERIA
Lagos

GHANA
Accra

SOUTH
AFRICA

ATLANTIC OCEAN

To Europe

To Europe

CANADA

Montreal

Vancouver

Chicago

UNITED STATES

New York

Miami
THE BAHAMAS

JAMAICA

Cayman I.

Los Angeles

Mexico City

MEXICO

GUATEMALA
COSTA RICA
Panama City

ECUADOR

VENEZUELA
Bogotá
COLOMBIA

PERU
Lima

BRAZIL

BOLIVIA
La Paz

PARAGUAY

Rio de Janeiro

ARGENTINA
Buenos Aires

PACIFIC OCEAN

To Asia

Principal Cultivation Areas

● Coca
● Marijuana
● Illegal opium
● Hashish

Major Trafficking Routes

→ Cocaine
→ Marijuana
→ Opiates
→ Hashish

[ ] Major drug source region

• Selected cities involved
  in drug trafficking

□ Money laundering center

corporations themselves were not new, but their great importance was. By 1971, each of the ten largest multinational corporations—the IBMs, the Royal Dutch Shells, the General Motors—was selling more than $3 billion worth of goods annually, more than the total national incomes of four-fifths of the world's countries. Multinational corporations accounted for fully a fifth of the noncommunist world's annual income, and they have grown even more important in the last two decades.

The rise of multinationals aroused a great deal of heated discussion around the world. Defenders saw the multinational corporations as building an efficient world economic system and transcending narrow national ties. In the words of a top manager of Royal Dutch Shell, the multinational corporation was

a new form of social architecture, matching the world-girding potential inherent in modern technology. . . .

In an age when modern technology has shrunk the world, and brought us all closer together, the multinational corporation and the nation state must get used to living with each other.[7]

Critics worried precisely that the nation-state was getting the worst of the new arrangement. Provocative book titles portrayed *Frightening Angels* holding *Sovereignty at Bay* while building *Invisible Empires* and extending their nefarious *Global Reach*. As usual whenever a major development attracted widespread attention, exaggerations and unreasonable predictions abounded on both sides.

The rise of the multinationals was partly due to the general revival of capitalism after the Second World War, relatively free international economic relations, and the worldwide drive for rapid industrialization. The multinationals also had three specific assets, which they used to their advantage.

First, "pure" scientific knowledge unrelated to the military was freely available, but its highly profitable industrial applications remained in the hands of the world's largest business firms. These firms held advanced, fast-changing technology as a kind of property and hurried to make profitable use of it wherever they could. Second, the multinationals knew how to sell, as well as how to innovate and produce. They used modern advertising and marketing skills to push their products relentlessly, especially the ever-expanding range of consumer products, around the world. Third, the multinationals developed new techniques to escape from political controls and national policies. Managers found ways to treat the world as one big market, coordinating complex activities across many political boundaries so as to reap the greatest profits.

Multinational industrial corporations began in the last quarter of the nineteenth century. U.S. businessmen took the lead, for reasons rooted in the nature of the American economy and society. Above all, the United States had a vast, unified market and the world's highest standard of living by 1890, so U.S. businessmen were positioned to pioneer in the mass production of standardized consumer goods. Many of the most famous examples—such as kerosene (John D. Rockefeller and Standard Oil), sewing machines (Singer), and farm machinery (Cyrus McCormick and International Harvester)—date from the 1880s. Others—like the cheap automobile (Henry Ford), the mass retailer (Sears), and standardized food (Coca-Cola, Wrigley's chewing gum)—were thriving by 1914.

Having developed mass-marketing techniques as well as new products, the biggest, most monopolistic American corporations quickly expanded abroad. Before 1914 they had created wholly owned subsidiaries to produce and sell American-style consumer goods in foreign lands, and they continued to do so between the world wars. With ever more products and the attractions of the European Common Market, there followed a mighty surge of American investment in Europe after 1945. Nor were other parts of the world neglected by the giant American manufacturing firms: there was continued multinational investment in raw-material production in Latin America (particularly copper, sugar, and bananas) as well as in the Middle East and Africa (primarily oil and gold). By 1967, American corporations—mainly the largest, most familiar household names—had sunk $60 billion into their foreign operations (Figure 36.1).

A few European companies, notably German chemical and electrical firms, also became

✳ **MAP 36.3 World Drug Trade**   As the drug trade has grown, the area of production has greatly expanded from the traditional Asian centers—the Golden Crescent and the Golden Triangle—to include many Third World countries. Poverty provides the drug lords with an army of drug runners.

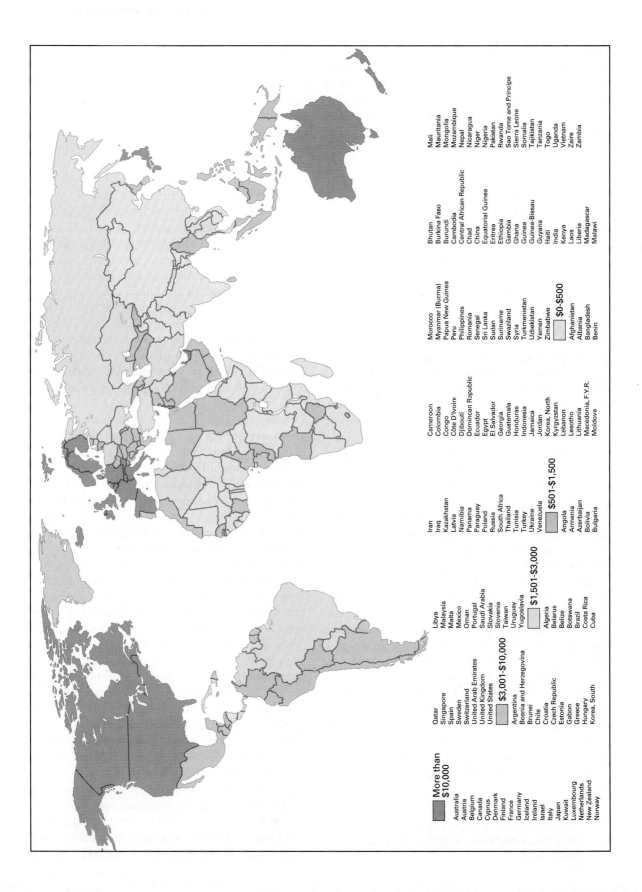

More than
$10,000

Australia
Austria
Belgium
Canada
Cyprus
Denmark
Finland
France
Germany
Iceland
Ireland
Israel
Italy
Japan
Kuwait
Luxembourg
Netherlands
New Zealand
Norway

Qatar
Singapore
Spain
Sweden
Switzerland
United Arab Emirates
United Kingdom
United States

$3,001–$10,000

Argentina
Bosnia and Herzegovina
Brunei
Chile
Croatia
Czech Republic
Estonia
Gabon
Greece
Hungary
Korea, South

Libya
Malaysia
Malta
Mexico
Oman
Portugal
Saudi Arabia
Slovakia
Slovenia
Taiwan
Uruguay
Yugoslavia

$1,501–$3,000

Algeria
Belarus
Belize
Botswana
Brazil
Costa Rica
Cuba

Iran
Iraq
Kazakhstan
Latvia
Namibia
Panama
Paraguay
Poland
Russia
South Africa
Thailand
Tunisia
Turkey
Venezuela

$501–$1,500

Angola
Armenia
Azerbaijan
Bolivia
Bulgaria

Cameroon
Colombia
Congo
Côte D'Ivoire
Djibouti
Dominican Republic
Ecuador
Egypt
El Salvador
Georgia
Guatemala
Honduras
Indonesia
Jamaica
Jordan
Korea, North
Kyrgyzstan
Lebanon
Lesotho
Lithuania
Macedonia, F.Y.R.
Moldova

Morocco
Myanmar (Burma)
Papua New Guinea
Peru
Philippines
Romania
Senegal
Sri Lanka
Sudan
Suriname
Swaziland
Syria
Turkmenistan
Uzbekistan
Yemen
Zimbabwe

$0–$500

Afghanistan
Albania
Bangladesh
Benin

Bhutan
Burkina Faso
Burundi
Cambodia
Central African Republic
Chad
China
Equatorial Guinea
Eritrea
Ethiopia
Gambia
Ghana
Guinea
Guinea-Bissau
Guyana
Haiti
India
Kenya
Laos
Liberia
Madagascar
Malawi

Mali
Mauritania
Mongolia
Mozambique
Nepal
Nicaragua
Niger
Nigeria
Pakistan
Rwanda
Sao Tome and Principe
Sierra Leone
Somalia
Tajikistan
Tanzania
Togo
Uganda
Vietnam
Zaire
Zambia

multinationals before 1900. Others emerged in the twentieth century. By the 1970s these European multinationals were in hot pursuit. Some, like Volkswagen, pushed directly into the American heartland and also into the Third World. Big Japanese firms like Sony also rushed to catch up and go multinational in the 1960s and 1970s. Whereas American investment had been heavily concentrated in Europe, Canada, and the Middle East, Japanese firms turned at first to Asia for raw materials and cheap, high-quality factory labor. By the 1970s Japanese subsidiaries in Taiwan, Thailand, Hong Kong, and Malaysia were pouring out a torrent of transistor radios, televisions, cameras, and pocket calculators.

Fearful of a growing protectionist reaction in their largest foreign market, the United States (where unemployed autoworkers symbolically demolished a Japanese automobile with sledgehammers in 1979), a host of Japanese firms followed Sony's example and began manufacturing in the United States in the 1980s. The Japanese inflow was so great that by 1989 Japanese multinationals had invested $70 billion in their subsidiaries in the United States, far surpassing the $19 billion that American multinationals had invested in Japan. In 1989 investment by European multinationals in the United States was also about 50 percent greater than American multinational investment in Europe. The emergence of European and Japanese multinational corporations alongside their American forerunners marked the coming of age of global business in an interdependent world.

The impact of multinational corporations, especially on Third World countries, has been heatedly debated. From an economic point of view, the effects were mixed. The giant firms provided advanced technology, but the technology was expensive and often inappropriate for poor countries with widespread unemployment.

The social consequences were quite striking. The multinationals helped spread the products and values of consumer society to the elites of the Third World. They fostered the creation of growing islands of Western wealth, management, and consumer culture around the world. After buying

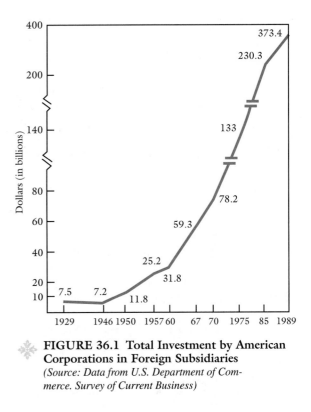

FIGURE 36.1 Total Investment by American Corporations in Foreign Subsidiaries *(Source: Data from U.S. Department of Commerce. Survey of Current Business)*

up local companies with offers that local business people did not dare to refuse, multinational corporations often hired Third World business leaders to manage their operations abroad. Critics considered this practice an integral part of the process of neo-colonialism, whereby local elites abandoned the national interest and made themselves willing tools of continued foreign domination.

Some global corporations used aggressive techniques of modern marketing to sell products that are not well suited to Third World conditions. For example, Third World mothers were urged to abandon "old-fashioned, primitive" breast-feeding (which was, ironically, making a strong comeback in rich countries) and to buy powdered milk formulas for their babies. But the use of unsanitary bottles and contaminated water and the dilution of the expensive formula to make it last longer resulted in additional infant deaths. On this and many other issues, the multinationals came into sharp conflict with host countries.

Far from acting helpless in such conflicts, some poor countries found ways to assert their sovereign rights over the foreign multinationals. Many foreign

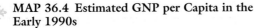

MAP 36.4 Estimated GNP per Capita in the Early 1990s

mining companies, like the fabulously profitable U.S. oil companies in the Middle East, were simply nationalized by the host countries. More important, Third World governments began to learn how to make foreign manufacturing companies conform to some of their plans and desires. Increasingly, multinationals had to share ownership with local investors, hire more local managers, provide technology on better terms, and accept a variety of controls.

Host governments learned to play Americans, Europeans, and Japanese off against each other. Frustrated by such treatment, one American managing director in Malaysia pounded his desk in 1979 and sputtered, "This little country and her little people need help, but they must be reasonable, otherwise we will get out of here." A Japanese manager in the same country expressed a more cooperative view: "We came here as guests, and our nation is small and needs natural resources, as well as foreign trade and investment to survive."[8] A growing proliferation of multinationals opened up new opportunities for Third World countries that wanted to use these powerful foreign corporations without being dominated by them.

❖ PATTERNS OF THOUGHT

The renowned economist John Maynard Keynes often said that we live by our ideas and by very little else. True or not, a global perspective surely requires keen attention to patterns of collective thinking. As Keynes saw, we need to be aware of the ideas that are shaping the uncertain destiny of this small, politically fragmented, economically interdependent planet.

To be sure, human thought can be baffling in its rich profusion. Nevertheless, in the late twentieth century, three distinct patterns on a global scale can be identified: the enduring strength of the modern world's secular ideologies, a vigorous revival of the world's great religions, and a search for mystical experience.

Secular Ideologies

Almost all of the modern world's great secular ideologies—liberalism, nationalism, Marxian socialism, as well as faith in scientific and technical progress, industrialism, and democratic republi-

canism—took form in Europe between the eighteenth-century Enlightenment and the revolutions of 1848. These ideologies continued to evolve with the coming of mass society in the late nineteenth century and were carried by imperialism to the highly diverse societies of Asia and Africa. There they won converts among the local elites, who eventually conquered their imperialist masters in the twentieth century. European ideologies became worldwide ideologies, gradually outgrowing their early, specifically European character.

All this can be seen as a fundamental aspect of global interdependence. The world came to live, in part, by shared ideas. These ideas continued to develop in a complex global dialogue, and champions of competing views arose from all regions. This was certainly true of nationalist ideology and also of Marxism. Europe, the birthplace of Marxism, made few original intellectual contributions to Marxism after Stalin transformed it into a totalitarian ideology of forced industrialization. After 1945, it was Marxists from the Third World who injected new meanings into the old ideology, notably with Mao's brand of peasant-based revolution and the Marxist theory of Third World dependency. Leftist intellectuals in Europe cheered and said "me too."

It was primarily as critics that Europeans contributed to world Marxism. Yugoslavs were particularly influential. After breaking with Stalin in 1948, they revived and expanded the ideas of Stalin's vanquished rival, Leon Trotsky. Trotsky claimed that Stalin perverted socialism by introducing "state capitalism" and reactionary bureaucratic dictatorship. According to the influential Yugoslav Milovan Djilas (b. 1911), Lenin's dedicated elite of full-time revolutionaries became Stalin's ruthless bureaucrats, "a new class" that was unprecedented in history. Djilas's powerful impact stemmed from his mastery of the Marxian theory of history and the Marxian dialectic:

The social origin of the new class lies in the proletariat just as the aristocracy arose in peasant society, and the bourgeoisie in a commercial and artisans' society. . . .

Former sons of the working class are the most steadfast members of the new class. It has always been the fate of slaves to provide for their masters the most clever and gifted representatives. In this case a new exploiting and governing class is born from the exploited class. . . .

The communists are . . . a new class.

As in other owning classes, the proof that it is a special class lies in its ownership and in its special relations to other classes. In the same way, the class to which a member belongs is indicated by the material and other privileges which ownership brings him. . . . The communist political bureaucracy uses, enjoys, and disposes of nationalized property.[9]

Non-Marxian criticism of communism also continued to develop, as in Jean François Revel's provocative *The Totalitarian Temptation* (1977). According to Revel, the application of the Marxist-Leninist-Maoist model brought about phony revolution. Under the guise of supposedly progressive socialism, it built reactionary totalitarian states of the Stalinist variety. Critics of Marxism-Leninism like Revel and Djilas undermined the intellectual appeal of communism and thereby contributed to its being overthrown in eastern Europe in 1989.

As the varieties of Marxism lost luster, old-fashioned, long-battered liberalism and democracy survived and flourished as a global ideology. In every communist country small, persecuted human rights movements bravely demanded the basic liberties first set into law in the American and French Revolutions, preparing the way against all odds for the renewed triumph of liberal revolution in eastern Europe in 1989. And there were always some African and Asian intellectuals, often in exile, calling for similar rights even in the most authoritarian states. The call for human rights and representative government coincided with a renewed faith in market forces and economic liberalism as effective tools of economic and social development. That countries as highly diverse as Brazil, China, Ghana, and the Soviet Union all moved in this direction in recent times was little short of astonishing.

Efforts to combine the best elements of socialism and liberalism in a superior hybrid were also important. The physicist Andrei Sakharov (1921–1990), the father of the Russian atomic bomb, who in the 1960s became a fearless leader of the human rights movement in the Soviet Union, was an eloquent spokesman for what might be called the "convergence school." According to Sakharov, humanity's best hope lay in the accelerated convergence of liberal capitalism and dictatorial communism on some middle ground of welfare capitalism and democratic socialism, like that which has flourished in the small, close-knit societies of Scandinavia, Iceland, and New Zealand. This outlook

Solzhenitsyn Returns to Russia In 1994, after living in exile in the United States for twenty years, the great novelist and implacable foe of communism moved back to Russia, taking a train trip home to Moscow across Siberia. Shown here with his son, Solzhenitsyn preached rebirth for Russia to crowds along the way. *(Source: Sichov/Sipa Press)*

waned somewhat in the 1980s, but it had deep historical roots in Western society and remained a potent force in world thought.

Finally, there was a many-sided global reaction to the dominant faith in industrialization, consumerism, and unrestrained "modernization." The disillusionment of the Third World was matched by disillusionment in the developed countries and a search for alternative secular visions of the future. The student revolt of the 1960s (see page 1120), with its vague ideology of broad participation in community decisions, coincided with widespread nostalgia for simple, close-knit rural societies. The great Russian novelist Alexander Solzhenitsyn, caught up in the vanishing-resources doctrine of the 1970s, called on Soviet leaders to renounce Western technology and return to the earth:

Herein lies Russia's hope for winning time and winning salvation: In our vast northeastern spaces, which over four centuries our sluggishness has prevented us from mutilating by our mistakes, we can build anew: not the senseless, voracious civilization of "progress"—no; we can set up a stable economy without pain or delay and settle people there for the first time

❋ **The Revolution in Communications** Although this young man must carry his motorbike up a rocky path to reach his home, he has gained access to speed and excitement, to roads and cities. The messages of the modern world easily reach remote villages by transistor radio. *(Source: S. Pern/The Hutchinson Library)*

according to the needs and principles of that economy. These spaces allow us to hope that we shall not destroy Russia in the general crisis of Western civilization.[10]

Communes sprang up in the United States and Europe in the late 1960s. There were many advocates of alternative lifestyles and technologies friendly to the environment. E. F. Schumacher, an English disciple of Mahatma Gandhi, in *Small Is Beautiful* (1973) urged the building of solar-heated houses to conserve nonrenewable oil. Africa and Asia increasingly stressed "appropriate technologies" tailored to village life rather than borrowed from large-scale urban industrialized society—such as small, rugged, three-wheeled motorized carts suited to existing country lanes, rather than large trucks requiring expensive modern highways and imported fuel.

A striking aspect of the worldwide reappraisal of industrialization was the heretical revival of Jean-Jacques Rousseau's belief in the superiority of the simple, frugal "noble savage." As Robert Heilbroner poignantly put it in 1974 in his otherwise gloomy *An Inquiry into the Human Prospect:*

One element [of hope] . . . is our knowledge that some human societies have existed for millennia, and that others can probably exist for future millennia, in a continuous rhythm of birth and coming of age and death, without pressing toward those dangerous ecological limits, or engendering those dangerous social tensions, that threaten present-day "advanced" societies. In our discovery of "primitive" cultures, living out their timeless histories, we may have found the single most important object lesson for future man.[11]

Other writers from the industrialized countries reassessed traditional cultures and found nobility and value similar to that championed by the Nigerian novelist Chinua Achebe (see page 1194). Opponents of modern industrial society and defenders of the environment remained only a vocal minority, but their worldwide presence was a vivid example of the globalization of intellectual life.

Religious Belief: Christianity and Islam

The reaction to industrialism and consumerism was part of a broader religious response to the dominance of secular ideologies in general. The revival of Christianity among intellectuals after the

Pope John Paul II   Nuns radiant with joy welcome the man of peace and goodwill in 1993 as he arrives in West Africa. John Paul, determined to minister to Catholics in all lands, has drawn large and enthusiastic crowds on repeated visits to Africa. (*Source: Paul Yao/Liaison*)

First World War (see pages 1030–1031) was matched in the 1970s and 1980s by a surge of popular, often fundamentalist, Christianity in many countries. Judaism and Islam also experienced resurgence, and Buddhism and Hinduism stopped losing ground. The continuing importance of religion in contemporary human thought—an importance that has often escaped those fascinated by secular ideology and secular history—must impress the unbiased observer.

Pope John Paul II (r. 1978–) exemplified several aspects of the worldwide Christian revival. A jet-age global evangelist, John Paul journeyed to Africa, Asia, and North and South America, inspiring enthusiatic multitudes with his warm sincerity and unfailing popular touch. John Paul's melding of a liberal social gospel with conservatism in doctrinal matters often seemed to reflect the spirit of the age. Thus the pope boldly urged a more equitable distribution of wealth in plutocratic Brazil

and more civil liberties in Marcos's authoritarian Philippines while reaffirming the church's long-standing opposition to mechanical contraception and women in the priesthood. Many of Christianity's most rapidly growing Protestant churches also espoused theological fundamentalism, based on a literal reading of the Bible.

It was also emblematic that the "Polish Pope" came from an officially atheist communist country. Yet after thirty-five years of communist rule, Poland was more intensely Catholic than ever before. Lech Walesa, the courageous leader of Poland's trade union Solidarity, said that he never could be a communist because he was a devout Roman Catholic. Poland illustrated the enduring strength of spiritual life in the face of materialistic culture and secular ideologies, of which communism was only the most openly hostile.

Islam, the religion of one-seventh of the earth's people, also experienced a powerful resurgence

Ayatollah Khomeini The apostle of Islamic regeneration and the unwavering critic of the shah returned in triumph to Teheran from exile in February 1979. The shah had visions of making Iran a major military power, but all his military might crumbled before the emotional appeal of Islamic revolution. *(Source: Setboun/Sipa Press)*

accelerated the impact of secularism on the Muslim world.

The generation of Muslim intellectual and political leaders born in the interwar years, who reached maturity after the Second World War, agreed that Islam required at least some modernizing. They accepted the attractively simple Muslim creed "There is no god but Allah, and Muhammad is his Prophet," but they did not think that the laws of the Qur'an should be taken literally. The prohibition on lending money at interest, the social inferiority of women, even cutting off the hands of thieves and public beheading of murderers, had made sense for the Arabian peninsula in the Middle Ages. But, they argued, such practices did not suit the modern age. It was necessary for Islam to adapt.

These views were still common among educated elites in the 1970s, and they remained dominant in Turkey and probably in Egypt. But throughout much of the Middle East they had to bow before a revival of Islamic fundamentalism, the critical development of recent years. Like some of their Christian and Jewish counterparts, orthodox Muslim believers wanted to return to unalterable fundamentals. In taking the Qur'an literally, they demanded that the modern world adapt to the Prophet's teachings, not vice versa. And because the masses remained deeply religious and profoundly disturbed by rapid change, Islamic fundamentalism aroused a heartfelt popular response.

Iran provided a spectacular manifestation of resurgent Islamic fundamentalism. In the 1970s, Iran's religious leaders, notably the charismatic Ayatollah Khomeini, catalyzed intense popular dissatisfaction with the shah's all-out industrialization and heavy-handed religious reform into a successful revolution. An "Islamic Republic" was established to govern according to the sacred laws of the Qur'an. State and church were tightly bound together. The holy men and their followers sanctioned the stoning to death of prostitutes and adulterers and revised the legal code along strictly Qur'anic lines.

Iran's fundamentalism was exceptionally rigid and antimodern, partly because the country adhered to the minority Shi'ite version of Islam. But similar movements developed in every Muslim country. In Algeria in the early 1990s only harsh military rule prevented the fundamentalists from forming a popularly elected government (see page

from the 1970s onward. Like orthodox Christianity, Islam had been challenged by the self-confident secular ideologies of the West since the early nineteenth century. And although the acids of modern thought did not eat as deeply as in Europe and North America, they etched a seductive alternative to Islam. Moderate Muslim intellectuals advocated religious reforms; radicals wanted drastic surgery. The most famous and successful of the radicals was the twentieth-century Turkish nationalist Kemal Atatürk (see pages 0000–0000), who reflected and

1153). Even where the fundamentalists seemed unlikely to take power, as in Indonesia or Pakistan, and where they were co-opted and neutralized, as in Saudi Arabia, they found enthusiastic support among the masses and revitalized the Muslim faith. Islamic missionary activity also remained extremely vigorous and continued to win converts, especially in black Africa.

Searching for Mystical Experience

Alongside secular ideologies and a revival of the world's great religions, the third powerful current of intellectual attraction was an enormous variety of religious sects, cults, and spiritual yearnings. Some of these new outpourings welled up within one or another of the great religions; many more did not. Though widely divergent, these movements seemed to share a common urge toward nonrational experiences such as meditation, spiritual mysteries, and direct communication with supernatural forces.

Not that this was new. So-called primitive peoples have always embraced myths, visions, and continuous revelation. So too have the world's main religions, especially those of the ancient East— Taoism, Hinduism, and the Zen form of Buddhism. What was new was the receptiveness of many people in the rationalistic, scientific industrialized countries (and their disciples, the Third World elite) to ancient modes of mystical experience. Some of this interest stems from the doubt about the power of the rational human mind that blossomed after the First World War. By the 1960s, it had struck deep roots in the mass culture of Europe and North America.

In this sense, the late twentieth century is reminiscent of the initial encounter of West and East in the Hellenistic Age. Then, the rationalistic, humanistic Greeks encountered the Eastern mystery religions and were profoundly influenced by them. Now, various strains of mystical thought are again appearing from the East and from "primitive" peoples. It can be said that the non-Western world is providing intellectual repayment for the powerful secular ideologies that it borrowed in the nineteenth century.

Reflecting on this ongoing encounter, the American social scientist Robert Heilbroner was not alone in suggesting startling implications for the future:

It is therefore possible that a post-industrial society would also turn in the direction of many preindustrial societies—toward the exploration of inner states of experience rather than the outer world of fact and material accomplishment. Tradition and ritual, the pillars of life in virtually all societies other than those of an industrial character, would probably once again assert their ancient claims as the guide to and solace for life.[12]

Some observers saw the onrush of science and technology as actually reinforcing the search for

Buddhism in the West Americans from different backgrounds come together for worship in this Buddhist temple in Santa Fe, New Mexico. This temple adheres to the Tibetan form of Buddhism, which combines mysticism and colorful ceremony. *(Source: Mimi Forsyth/Monkmeyer Press)*

spiritual experience. Electronic communications are demolishing time and distance; information itself is becoming the new global environment. According to the philosopher William Thompson:

Culture is full of many surprises, because culture is full of the play of opposites. And so there will be scientists and mystics in the New Age. . . . To look at the American counterculture today, one would guess . . . that the East was about to engulf the West. But in fact . . . America is swallowing up and absorbing the traditional Eastern techniques of transformation, because only these are strong enough to humanize its technology. In the days before planetization, when civilization was split between East and West, there were basically two cultural directions. The Westerner went outward to level forests, conquer nations, and walk on the moon; the Easterner went inward and away from the physical into the astral and causal planes. Now . . . we can glimpse the beginnings of a new level of religious experience, neither Eastern nor Western, but planetary.[13]

Many people may have doubts about the significance of such views. But it seems quite possible that the upsurge of mysticism and religious searching will exert a growing influence in the coming era, especially if political conflict and economic problems continue to undermine the old secular faith in endless progress.

SUMMARY

Whatever does or does not happen, the study of world history puts the future in perspective. Future developments on this small planet will surely build on the many-layered foundations hammered out in the past. Moreover, the study of world history, of mighty struggles and fearsome challenges, of shining achievements and tragic failures, imparts a strong sense of life's essence: the process of change over time. Again and again we have seen how peoples and societies evolve, influenced by ideas, human passions, and material conditions. Armed with the ability to think historically, students of history are prepared to comprehend this inexorable process of change in their own lifetimes, as the world races forward toward an uncertain destiny.

NOTES

1. A. Toynbee, *Mankind and Mother Earth* (New York: Oxford University Press, 1976), pp. 576–577.
2. D. Calleo and B. Rowland, *America and the World Political Economy* (Bloomington: Indiana University Press, 1973), p. 191.
3. W. Epstein, *The Last Chance: Nuclear Proliferation and Arms Control* (New York: Free Press, 1976), p. 274.
4. M. ul-Haq, *The Poverty Curtain: Choices for the Third World* (New York: Columbia University Press, 1976), p. 152.
5. E. Hermassi, *The Third World Reassessed* (Berkeley: University of California Press, 1980), p. 76.
6. Ibid., p. 185.
7. Quoted in H. Stephenson, *The Coming Clash: The Impact of Multinational Corporations on National States* (New York: Saturday Review Press, 1973), p. 60.
8. Quoted in A. R. Negandhi, *The Functioning of the Multinational Corporation: A Global Comparative Study* (New York: Pergamon Press, 1980), p. 142.
9. M. Djilas, *The New Class* (New York: Praeger, 1957), pp. 41–42, 44.
10. A. I. Solzhenitsyn, *Letter to the Soviet Leaders* (New York: Harper & Row, 1974), p. 33.
11. R. L. Heilbroner, *An Inquiry into the Human Prospect* (New York: Norton, 1974), p. 141.
12. Ibid., p. 140.
13. W. I. Thompson, *Evil and World Order* (New York: Harper & Row, 1980), p. 53.

SUGGESTED READING

Many of the books cited in the Suggested Reading for Chapter 35 pertain to the themes of this chapter. Three helpful and stimulating studies on global politics from different viewpoints are R. Barnet, *The Lean Years: The Politics of the Age of Scarcity* (1980); F. M. Lappé and J. Collins, *Food First: Beyond the Myth of Scarcity* (1977); and S. Hoffman, *Primacy or World Order: American Foreign Policy Since the Cold War* (1978). Two wide-ranging appraisals of current trends are found in Z. Brzezinski, *Out of Control: Global Turmoil on the Eve of the 21st Century* (1993), and D. Snow, *The Shape of the Future: The Post–Cold War World* (1991).

An excellent introduction to international negotiations for the control of nuclear arms is W. Epstein,

The Last Chance: Nuclear Proliferation and Arms Control (1976). Other recommended studies are D. Holloway, *The Soviet Union and the Arms Race* (1983), and L. Freedman, *The Evolution of Nuclear Strategy* (1982), a history of American thinking about nuclear weapons and nuclear war. Stimulating recent works include K. Bailey, *Doomsday in the Hands of Many: The Arms Control Challenge of the '90s* (1991), and M. van Creveld, *Nuclear Proliferation and the Future of Conflict* (1993).

M. ul Haq's book cited in the Notes is an excellent presentation of Third World demands for a new economic order. This position is expanded in J. Tinbergen and A. J. Dolman, eds., *RIO, Reshaping the International Order: A Report to the Club of Rome* (1977), and *North-South: A Program for Survival* (1980), a report calling for increased help for the South by the blue-ribbon Independent Commission on International Development Issues, under the chairmanship of Willy Brandt. Such views do not go unchallenged, and P. T. Bauer, *Equality, the Third World, and Economic Delusion* (1981), is a vigorous defense of the industrialized nations and their wealth. J. K. Galbraith, the witty economist and former U.S. ambassador to India, argues simply and effectively in *The Voice of the Poor* (1983) that poor countries have important lessons to teach rich countries. Common problems and aspirations are also the focus of E. Laszlo et al., *Goals for Mankind* (1977). The important study by R. Ayres, *Banking on the Poor: The World Bank and World Poverty* (1983), shows how this international financial organization has emerged as a standard-bearer for the poorest countries. *World Development Report,* which the World Bank publishes annually, is an outstanding source of information about current trends. Valuable studies on multinational corporations and global indebtedness include L. Solomon, *Multinational Corporations and the Emerging World Order* (1978); the work by A. R. Negandhi, cited in the Notes; R. Barnet and R. Muller, *Global Reach: The Power of the Multinational Corporations* (1975); and A. Sampson, *The Money Lenders: The People and Politics of the World Banking Crisis* (1983).

Contemporary thought is so rich and diverse that any selection must be highly arbitrary. Among works not mentioned elsewhere, G. Blainey, *The Great Seesaw: A New View of the Western World, 1750–2000* (1988), uncovers a cyclical pattern of optimism and pessimism and is recommended as an introduction to the history of ideas. E. Banfield, *The Unheavenly City Revisited* (1974), is a provocative and influential reassessment of urban problems and solutions in the United States. D. H. Meadows and D. L. Meadows, *The Limits of Growth* (1974), argue that the world will soon exhaust its natural resources. E. F. Schumacher, *Small Is Beautiful: Economics as If People Mattered* (1973), advocates conservation and a scaling-down of technology to avoid disaster. R. M. Pirsig, *Zen and the Art of Motorcycle Maintenance: An Inquiry into Values* (1976), is a stimulating exploration of the tie between modern technology and personal development.

E. Rice, *Wars of the Third Kind: Conflict in Underdeveloped Countries* (1988), is a thoughtful inquiry into the dynamics of guerrilla movements. T. R. Gurr, *Why Men Rebel* (1970), skillfully reworks the idea that revolutions occur when rising expectations are frustrated. M. Djilas, in the work cited in the Notes, criticizes the ruling Communist bureaucracies from a Marxist point of view. J. Revel, *The Totalitarian Temptation* (1977), claims that many Western intellectuals have been seduced into seeing Communist dictatorships as progressive socialist societies. A. Sakharov, *Progress, Coexistence, and Intellectual Freedom,* rev. ed. (1970), soberly assesses the prospects for improved relations between the Soviet Union and the United States.

The Islamic revival may be approached through the sympathetic work of E. Gellner, *Muslim Society* (1981); and the reservations of V. S. Naipaul, *Among the Believers: An Islamic Journey* (1981); H. Algar, ed., *Islam and Revolution: Writings and Declarations of Imam Khomeini* (1982); and J. Stempel, *Inside the Iranian Revolution* (1981). Muslim writers address issues in the Islamic world in J. Donohue and J. Esposito, eds., *Islam in Transition: Muslim Perspectives* (1982).

Studies of the future are so numerous that M. Marien, *Societal Directions and Alternatives: A Critical Guide to the Literature* (1977), is a useful aid with its annotated bibliography. P. Kennedy, *Preparing for the Twenty-first Century* (1993), is the work of a well-known historian. Also recommended is J. Lukacs, *The End of the Twentieth Century and the End of the Modern Age* (1993).

The many future-oriented works of the members of the Hudson Institute usually combine optimism and conservatism, as in H. Kahn et al., *The Next Two Hundred Years* (1976), and H. Kahn, *The Coming Boom* (1982). J. Lorraine's *Global Signposts to the 21st Century* (1979) and R. L. Heilbroner's work cited in the Notes are stimulating and intelligent studies.

One World and a Plan for Survival

In the 1970s Third World countries of the South called on the industrialized countries of the North to join with them in establishing a "new international order." Using the United Nations General Assembly as a platform, Third World countries argued that the world economy worked to their disadvantage and that the ominous gap between the wealthy North and the poor South was widening.

Third World countries found only limited support from politicians and voters in the North, which was wracked by a deep recession caused in part by an explosion in oil prices. Yet the South did find some sympathy in the North, especially among journalists, professors, and moderate west European socialists.

An outstanding example of such support came from the Brandt Commission, an independent, self-appointed international study group chaired by Willy Brandt, the former chancellor of West Germany, a moderate socialist and a renowned world leader. Brandt's blue-ribbon commission presented its findings and proposals in 1980 as North-South Relations: A Program for Survival. *The following selection is taken from this influential and widely publicized call to action.*

The crisis through which international relations and the world economy are now passing presents great dangers, and they appear to be growing more serious. We believe that the gap which separates rich and poor countries—a gap so wide that at the extremes people seem to live in different worlds—has not been sufficiently recognized as a major factor in this crisis. It is a great contradiction of our age that these disparities exist—and are in some respects widening—just when human society is beginning to have a clearer perception of how it is interrelated and of how North and South depend on each other in a single world economy. . . .

The nations of the South see themselves as sharing a common predicament. Their solidarity in global negotiations stems from the awareness of being dependent on the North, and unequal to it; and a great many of them are bound together by their common colonial experience. The North including Eastern Europe has a quarter of the world's population and four-fifths of its income; the South including China has three billion people— three-quarters of the world's population but living on one-fifth of the world's income. . . .

Behind these differences lies the fundamental inequality of economic strength. . . . Because of this economic power northern countries dominate the international economic system—its rules and regulations, and international institutions of trade, money and finance. Some developing nations have swum against this tide . . . but most of them find the currents too strong for them. In the world as in nations, economic forces left entirely to themselves tend to produce growing inequality. Within nations public policy has to protect the weaker partners. The time has come to apply this precept to relations between nations within the world community. . . .

The North-South debate is often described as if the rich were being asked to make sacrifices in response to the demands of the poor. We reject this view. The world is now a fragile and interlocking system, whether for its people, its ecology or its resources. Many individual societies have settled their inner conflicts by accommodation, to protect the weak and to promote principles of justice, becoming stronger as a result. The world too can become stronger by becoming a just and humane society. If it fails in this, it will move towards its own destruction. . . .

[In conclusion] mankind already faces basic problems which cannot be solved purely at the national or even regional levels, such as security, protection of the environment, energy, and the control of space and ocean resources. The international community has begun to tackle these problems, though inadequately.

At the beginning of the 1980s the world community faces much greater dangers than at any time since the Second World War. It is clear that the world economy is now functioning so badly that it damages both the immediate and the longer-run interests of all nations. . . . A new international order will take time to achieve. . . . But the present world crisis is so acute that we also feel compelled to draw up an emergency program . . . [and lay out the] tasks for the 80s and 90s. . . .

Priority must be given to the needs of the poorest countries and regions. We call for a major initiative in favor of the poverty belts of Africa and Asia. We recognize that the removal of poverty requires both substantial resource transfers from the developed countries and an increased determination of the developing countries to improve economic management and deal with social and economic inequalities.

The world must aim to abolish hunger and malnutrition by the end of the century through the elimination of absolute poverty. Greater food production, intensified agricultural development, and measures for international food security are essential. These too require both major additional external assistance and revised priorities in many developing countries. . . .

The North should reverse the present trend towards protecting its industries against competition from the Third World. . . .

The objectives we have defined . . . will call for a transfer of funds [from North to South] on a very considerable scale . . . [and] will require sums equal to more than a doubling of the current $20 billion of annual official development assistance, together with substantial additional lending on market terms. . . . The large-scale transfer of resources we call for should be organized in partnership between developed and developing countries. . . .

The global agreement we envisage, with the understanding that must lie behind it, will call for a joint effort of political will and a high degree of trust between the partners, with a common conviction in their mutual interest. . . . [And indeed] whatever their differences and however profound, there is a mutuality of in-

Earth Summit in Rio de Janeiro, 1992
(Source: Claus Meyer/Black Star)

terest between North and South. The fate of both is intimately connected. The search for solutions is not an act of benevolence but a condition of mutual survival. We believe it is dramatically urgent today to start taking concrete steps, without which the world situation can only deteriorate still further, even leading to conflict and catastrophe.

Questions for Analysis

1. Why do the nations of the South "see themselves sharing a common predicament"?

2. Why, according to the Brandt Commission, should the North aid the South?

3. What does the Brandt Commission propose. What are the most urgent priorities?

4. "Resolved: the North must help the South to avoid conflict and global catastrophe." What are the arguments for and against this proposition? Take sides, and debate this proposition.

5. Do you think the members of this commission would support steps toward world government? Why or why not?

Source: Independent Commission on International Development Issues [Brandt Commission], *North-South Relations: A Program for Survival* (Cambridge, Mass.: MIT Press, 1980), pp. 30–33, 267, 270–273, 280–282.

A History of World Societies: A Brief Overview

Period (CA 10,000–CA 400 B.C.)	Africa and the Middle East	The Americas
10,000 B.C.	New Stone Age culture, ca 10,000–3500	Migration into Americas begins, ca 11,000
5000 B.C.	"Agricultural revolution" originates in Tigris-Euphrates and Nile River Valleys, ca 6000 First writing in Sumeria; Sumerian city-states emerge, ca 3500 Egypt unified under Narmer, 3100–2660 Metalworking in Caucasus, 3000	Maize domesticated in Mexico, ca 5000
2500 B.C.	Old Kingdom in Egypt; construction of the pyramids, 2660–2180 Akkadian Empire, 2370–2150 Middle Kingdom in Egypt, 2080–1640 Hyksos "invade" Egypt, 1640–1570 Hammurabi, 1792–1750 Hebrew monotheism, ca 1700	First pottery in Americas, Ecuador, ca 3000 First metalworking in Peru, ca 2000
1500 B.C.	Hittite Empire, ca 1450–1200 Akhenaten institutes worship of Aton, ca 1360 New Kingdom in Egypt; creation of Egyptian Empire, ca 1570–1075 Moses leads Hebrews out of Egypt, ca 1300–1200	Olmec civilization, Mexico, ca 1500 B.C.–A.D. 300
1000 B.C.	Political fragmentation of Egypt; rise of small kingdoms, ca 1100–700 United Hebrew kingdom, 1020–922: Saul, David, Solomon Ironworking spreads throughout Africa, ca 1000 B.C.–A.D. 300 Divided Hebrew kingdom: Israel (922–721), Judah (922–586) Assyrian Empire, 745–612 Zoroaster, ca 600	Olmec center at San Lorenzo destroyed, ca 900; power passes to La Venta in Tabasco Chavin civilization in Andes, ca 1000–200 B.C.
500 B.C.	Babylonian captivity of the Hebrews, 586–539 Cyrus the Great founds Persian Empire, 550 Persians conquer Egypt, 525 Darius and Xerxes complete Persian conquest of Middle East, 521–464	Olmec civilization, ca 1500 B.C.–A.D. 300 Fall of La Venta; Tres Zapotes becomes leading Olmec site
400 B.C.	Spartan Hegemony in Greece 399–371 B.C. Theban Hegemony in Greece 371–362 B.C. Philip of Macedon's Conquest of Greece, 338 B.C.	

East Asia	India and Southeast Asia	Europe
"Agricultural revolution" originates in Yellow River Valley, ca 4000		
Horse domesticated in China, ca 2500	Indus River Valley civilization, ca 2500–1500; capitals at Mohenjo-daro and Harappa	Greek Bronze Age, 2000–1100 Arrival of Greeks in peninsular Greece
Shang Dynasty, first writing in China, ca 1523–ca 1027	Aryans arrive in India; Early Vedic Age, ca 1500–1000 Vedas, oldest Hindu sacred texts	Height of Minoan culture, 1700–1450 Mycenaeans conquer Minoan Crete, ca 1450 Mycenaean Age, 1450–1200
Zhou Dynasty, promulgation of the Mandate of Heaven, ca 1027–221	Later Vedic Age; solidification of caste system, ca 1000–500 Upanishads; foundation of Hinduism, 800–600	Trojan War, ca 1180 Fall of the Mycenaean kingdom, 1100 Greek Dark Age, ca 1100–800 Roman Republic founded, 509 Origin of Greek polis, ca 700 Greek Lyric Age; rise of Sparta and Athens, 800–500
Confucius, 551–479 First written reference to iron, ca 521	Siddhartha Gautama (Buddha), 563–483	Persian Wars, 499–479 Growth of Athenian Empire; flowering of Greek drama, philosophy, and history, 5th century Peloponnesian War, 431–404 Plato, 426–347

Period (CA 300 B.C.–AD 500)	Africa and the Middle East	The Americas
300 B.C.	Alexander the Great extends empire, 334–331 Death of Alexander (323): Ptolemy conquers Egypt, Seleucus rules Asia	
200 B.C.	Scipio Africanus defeats Hannibal at Zama, 202	
100 B.C.	Dead Sea Scrolls Pompey conquers Syria and Palestine, 63	
A.D 100	Jesus Christ, ca 4 B.C.–A.D. 30 Paul, d. ca 65 Bantu migrations begin Jews revolt from Rome, Romans destroy Hebrew temple in Jerusalem: end of the ancient Hebrew state, 70	
A.D 200	Camel first used for trans-Saharan transport, ca 200 Expansion of Bantu peoples, ca 200–900 Axum (Ethiopia) controls Red Sea trade, ca 250	Classic Age of the Maya, ca 300–900 Olmec civilization, ca 1500 B.C.–A.D. 300
A.D 300	Axum accepts Christianity, ca 4th century	Maya civilization in Central America, ca 300–1500 Classic period of Teotihuacán civilization in Mexico, ca 300–900
A.D 500	Political and commercial ascendancy of Axum, ca 6th–7th centuries Muhammad, 570–632; the *hijra,* 622 Extensive slave trade from sub-Saharan Africa to Mediterranean, ca 600–1500 Umayyad Dynasty, 661–750, with capital at Damascus; continued expansion of Islam	Tiahuanaco civilization in South America, ca 600–1000

East Asia	India and Southeast Asia	Europe
Lao-tzu and development of Taoism, 4th century Han Fei-tzu and Li Ssu and development of Legalism, ca 250–208	Alexander invades India, 327–326 Chandragupta founds Mauryan Dynasty, 322–ca 185 Ashoka, 273–232 King Arsaces of Parthia defeats Seleucid monarchy and begins conquest of Persia, ca 250–137	Peloponnesian War, 431–404 Plato, 426–347 Gauls sack Rome, ca 390 Roman expansion, 390–146 Sparton Hegemony in Greece, 399–371 B.C. Theban Hegemony in Greece, 371–362 B.C. Philip of Macedon's Conquest of Greece, 338 B.C. Conquests of Alexander the Great, 334–323 Punic Wars, destruction of Carthage, 264–146
Qin Dynasty and unification of China; construction of the Great Wall, destruction of Confucian literature, 221–210 Han Dynasty, 202 B.C.–A.D. 220	Greeks invade India, ca 183–145 Mithridates creates Parthian Empire, ca 171–131	Late Roman Republic, 133–27
Chinese expansion to South China Sea and Vietnam, ca 111 Silk Road opens to Parthian and Roman Empires; Buddhism enters China, ca 104	First Chinese ambassadors to India and Parthia, ca 140 Bhagavad Gita, ca 100 B.C.–A.D. 100	Formation of First Triumvirate (Caesar, Crassus, Pompey), 60 Julius Caesar killed, 44 Formation of Second Triumvirate, (Octavian, Antony, Lepidus), 43 Octavian seizes power, 31
First written reference (Chinese) to Japan, A.D. 45 Chinese invent paper, 105 Emperor Wu, 140–186	Shakas and Kushans invade eastern Parthia and India, 1st century A.D. Roman attacks on Parthian Empire, 115–211	Octavian rules imperial Rome as Augustus, 27 B.C.–A.D. 14 Roman Empire at greatest extent, 117
Creation of Yamato state in Japan, ca 3d century Buddhism gains popularity in China and Japan, ca 220–590 Fall of Han Dynasty, 220 Three Kingdoms era in China, 221–280	Kushan rule in northwestern India, A.D. 2d–3d centuries Fall of the Parthian Empire, rise of the Sassanids, ca 225	Breakdown of the pax Romana, ca 180–284; civil wars, economic decline, invasions Reforms by Diocletian, 284–305
Barbarian invasions, 4th–5th centuries	Chandragupta I founds Gupta Dynasty in India, ca 320–500 Chandragupta II conquers western India, establishes trade with Middle East and China, ca 400 Huns invade India, ca 450	Reign of Constantine, 306–337; Edict of Milan, 313; founding of Constantinople, 324; Council of Nicaea, 325 Theodosius recognizes Christianity as official state religion, 380 Germanic raids of western Europe, 5th century Clovis unites Franks and rules Gauls, 481–511
Sui Dynasty in China, 580–618; restoration of public order "Constitution" of Shotoku in Japan, 604 Tang Dynasty, 618–907; cultural flowering	Sanskrit drama, ca 600–1000 Muslim invasions of India, ca 636–1206	Saint Benedict publishes his *Rule,* 529 Law Code of Justinian, 529 Synod of Whitby, 664

Period (CA 700–1500)	Africa and the Middle East	The Americas
700	Abbasid Dynasty, 750–1258; Islamic capital moved to Baghdad Decline of Ethiopia, ca 9th century Golden age of Muslim learning, ca 900–1100 Kingdom of Ghana, ca 900–1100 Mahmud of Ghazna, 998–1030	"Time of Troubles" in Mesoamerica, 800–1000
1000	Islam penetrates sub-Saharan Africa, ca 11th century Kingdom of Benin, ca 1100–1897 Kingdom of Mali, middle Niger region, ca 1200–1450 Mongol invasion of Middle East, ca 1220	Inca civilization in South America, ca 1000–1500 Toltec hegemony, ca 1000–1300 Aztecs arrive in Valley of Mexica, ca 1325
1200	Kingdom of Mali, ca 1200–1450 Mongols conquer Baghdad, 1258; fall of Abbasid Dynasty	Maya civilization in Central America, ca 300–1500 Inca civilization in South America, ca 1000–1500 Toltec hegemony, ca 1000–1300
1300	Rise of Yoruba states, West Africa, ca 1300 Height of Swahili (East African) city-states, ca 1300–1500 Mansa Musa rules Mali, 1312–1337	Tenochtitlán (Mexico City) founded by Aztecs, 1325
1400	Zara Yakob rules Ethiopia, 1434–1468 Arrival of Portugese in Benin, ca 1440 Songhay Empire, West Africa, ca 1450–1591 Atlantic slave trade, ca 1450–1850 Ottoman Empire, 1453–1918 Vasco da Gama arrives on East African coast, 1498	Height of Inca Empire, 1438–1493 Reign of Montezuma I, 1440–1468; height of Aztec culture Columbus reaches the Americas, 1492
1500	Portugal dominates East Africa, ca 1500–1650 Safavid Empire in Persia, 1501–1722 Peak of Ottoman power under Suleiman the Magnificent, 1520–1566 Height of Kanem-Bornu under Idris Alooma, 1571–1603 Portuguese found Angola, 1571 Battle of Lepanto, 1571, signals Ottoman naval weakness in the eastern Mediterranean Height of Safavid power under Shah Abbas, 1587–1629	South American holocaust, ca 1500–1600 First African slaves, ca 1510 Cortés arrives in Mexico, 1519; Aztec Empire falls, 1521 Pizarro reaches Peru, 1531; conquers Incas Spanish conquer the Philippines, 1571

East Asia	India and Southeast Asia	Europe
Taika Reform Edict in Japan, 655 Nara era, creation of Japan's first capital, 710–784 Heian era in Japan, 794–1185; literary flowering Era of the Five Dynasties in China, 907–960; warfare, revolt Song Dynasty, 960–1279	Khmer Empire (Kampuchea) founded, 802	Charles Martel defeats Muslims at Tours, 733 Charles the Great (Charlemagne), 768–814 Invasions of Carolingian Empire, 9th–10th centuries Treaty of Verdun divides Carolingian Empire, 843 Cluny monastery founded, 910
Vietnam gains independence from China, ca 1000 China divided between empires of Song (south) and Jin (north), 1127 Kamakura Shogunate, 1185–1333 Mongol conquest of China, 1215–1368	Construction of Angkor Wat, ca 1100–1150 Muslim conquerors end Buddhism in India, 1192 Peak of Khmer Empire in southeast Asia, ca 1200 Turkish sultanate at Delhi, 1206–1526; Indian culture divided into Hindu and Muslim	Yaroslav the Wise, 1019–1054; peak of Kievan Russia Schism between Latin and Greek churches, 1054 Norman Conquest of England, 1066 Investiture struggle, 1073–1122 The Crusades, 1096–1270 Growth of trade and towns, 12th–13th centuries Frederick Barbarossa invades Italy, 1154–1158
Kamakura Shogunate, 1185–1333 Unsuccessful Mongol invasions of Japan, 1274, 1281 Yuan (Mongol) Dynasty, 1279–1368	Peak of Khmer Empire in southeast Asia, ca 1200 Turkish sultanate at Delhi, 1206–1526; Indian culture divided into Hindu and Muslim	Magna Carta, 1215 Thomas Aquinas, *Summa Theologica,* 1253 Prince Alexander Nevsky recognizes Mongol overlordship of Moscow, 1252
Marco Polo arrives at Kublai Khan's court, ca 1275 Ashikaga Shogunate, 1336–1408 Hung Wu drives Mongols from China, 1368; founds Ming Dynasty, 1368–1644	Mongol chieftain Timur the Lame (Tamerlane) conquers the Punjab, 1398	Babylonian Captivity of the papacy, 1309–1376 Tver revolt in Russia, 1327–1328 Hundred Years' War, 1337–1453 Bubonic plague, 1347–1700 Ottoman Turks invade Europe, 1356 Peasants' Revolt in England, 1381
Early Ming policy encourages foreign trade, ca 15th century Ming maritime expeditions to India, Middle East, Africa, 1405–1433	Sultan Mehmed II, 1451–1481 Pasha Sinon, Ottoman architect, 1491–1588 Vasco da Gama reaches India, 1498	Beginnings of representative government, ca 1350–1500 Italian Renaissance, ca 1400–1530 Voyages of discovery, ca 1450–1600 Ottomans capture Constantinople, 1453; end of Byzantine Empire War of the Roses in England, 1455–1485 Unification of Spain completed, 1492
Portuguese trade monopoly in East Asia, ca 16th century Christian missionaries active in China and Japan, ca 1550–1650 Unification of Japan, 1568–1600	Barbur defeats Delhi sultanate, 1526–1527; founds Mughal Empire Akbar expands Mughal Empire, 1556–1605	Martin Luther, Ninety-five Theses, 1517 Charles V elected Holy Roman emperor, 1519 Henry VIII leads English Reformation, 1534 Council of Trent, 1545–1563 Dutch United Provinces declare independence, 1581 Spanish Armada, 1588

Period (CA 1600–1900)	Africa and the Middle East	The Americas
1600	Dutch West India Co. supplants Portuguese in West Africa, ca 1630 Dutch settle Cape Town, 1651 Rise of Ashanti Empire, founded on Gold Coast trade, ca 1700–1750	British settle Jamestown, 1607 Champlain founds Quebec, 1608 Dutch found New Amsterdam, 1624 Black labor allows tenfold increase in production of Carolinian rice and Virginian tobacco, ca 1730–1760 Silver production quadruples in Mexico and Peru, ca 1700–1800
1700	Approximately 11 million slaves shipped from Africa, ca 1450–1850 Dutch found Cape Colony, 1657 Rise of the Ashanti, West Africa, ca 1700 Decline of the Safavid Empire under Nadir Shah, 1737–1747	Spain's defeat in War of the Spanish Succession, 1701–1714, prompts trade reform, leading to colonial dependence on Spanish goods, 18th century
1750	Sultan Selim III introduces administrative and military reforms, 1761–1808 British seize Cape Town, 1795 Napoleon's campaign in Egypt, 1798	"French and Indian Wars," 1756–1763 Quebec Act, 1774 American Revolution, 1775–1783 Comunero revolution, New Granada, 1781
1800	Muhammad Ali founds dynasty in Egypt, 1805–1848 Slavery abolished in British Empire, 1807 Peak year of African transatlantic slave trade, 1820	Latin American wars of independence from Spain, 1806–1825 Brazil wins independence from Portugal, 1822 Monroe Doctrine, 1823 Political instability in most Latin American countries, 1825–1870 Mexican War, 1846–1848
1850	Crimean War, 1853–1856 Suez Canal opens, 1869 Europeans intensify "scramble for Africa," 1880–1900 Battle of Omdurman, 1898 Boer War, 1899–1902	American Civil War, 1861–1865 British North America Act, 1867, for Canada Porfirio Diaz controls Mexico, 1876–1911 United States practices "dollar diplomacy" in Latin America, 1890–1920s Spanish-American War, 1898; United States gains Philippines
1900	Union of South Africa formed, 1910 French annex Morocco, 1912 Ottoman Empire enters World War One on Germany's side Treaty of Sèvres dissolves Ottoman Empire, 1919; Mustafa Kemal mounts nationalist struggle in Turkey	Massive immigration from Europe and Asia to the Americas, 1880–1914 Mexican Revolution, 1910 Panama Canal opens, 1914 United States enters World War One, 1917 Mexico adopts constitution, 1917

East Asia	India and Southeast Asia	Europe
Tokugawa Shogunate, 1600–1867 Japan expels all Europeans, 1637 Manchus establish Qing Dynasty, 1644 Height of Qing Dynasty under K'ang-hsi, 1662–1722 Height of Edo urban culture in Japan, ca 1700	Height of Mughal Empire under Shah Jahan, 1628–1658 British found Calcutta, 1690 Decline of Mughal Empire, ca 1700–1800 Persian invaders sack Delhi, 1739	Romanov Dynasty in Russia, 1613 Thirty Years' War, 1618–1648 Brandenburg-Prussia unified, 1640–1688 English Civil War, 1642–1646 Louis XIV, king of France, 1643–1715 Ottoman Turks besiege Vienna, 1683 Revocation of Edict of Nantes, 1685 The Glorious Revolution in England, 1688 War of Spanish Succession, 1701–1713 Treaty of Utrecht, 1713
Tokugawa regime in Japan, characterized by political stability and economic growth, 1600–1867 Manchus establish Qing Dynasty, 1644–1911 Height of Qing Dynasty under Emperor Ch'ien-lung, 1736–1799	Mughal power contested by Hindus and Muslims, 18th century Persian invaders defeat Mughal army, loot Delhi, 1739 French and British fight for control of India, 1740–1763	Growth of absolutism in central and eastern Europe, ca 1680–1790 The Enlightenment, ca 1680–1800 Development of Cabinet system in England, 1714–1742 Height of land enclosure in England, ca 1760–1810
Maximum extent of Qing Empire, 1759	Battle of Plassey, 1757 Treaty of Paris, 1763; French colonies to Britain Cook in Australia, 1768–1771; first British prisoners to Australia, 1788 East India Act, 1784	Englishman James Watt produces first steam engine, 1769 Louis XVI of France, 1774–1792 Outbreak of French Revolution, 1789 National Convention declares France a republic, 1792
Java War, 1825–1830 Anglo-Chinese Opium War, 1839–1842 Treaty of Nanjing, 1842: Manchus surrender Hong Kong to British	British found Singapore, 1819 British defeat last independent native state in India, 1848	Napoleonic Empire, 1804–1814 Congress of Vienna, 1814–1815 European economic penetration of non-Western countries, ca 1816–1880 Greece wins independence from Ottoman Empire, 1829 Revolutions in France, Prussia, Italy, and Austria, 1848–1849
Taiping Rebellion, 1850–1864 Perry's arrival opens Japan to United States and Europe, 1853 Meiji Restoration in Japan, 1867 Adoption of constitution in Japan, 1890 Sino-Japanese War, 1894–1895 "Hundred Days of Reform" in China, 1898	Great Rebellion in India, 1857–1858 French seize Saigon, 1859 Indian National Congress formed, 1885 French acquire Indochina, 1893	Second Empire and Third Republic in France, 1852–1914 Unification of Italy, 1859–1870 Otto von Bismarck's reign of power in German affairs, 1862–1890 Franco-Prussian War, 1870–1871; foundation of the German Empire Parliamentary Reform Bill, Great Britain, 1867 Second Socialist International, 1889–1914
Boxer Rebellion in China, 1900–1903 Russo-Japanese War, 1904–1905 Chinese Revolution; fall of Qing Dynasty, 1911 Chinese Republic, 1912–1949	Commonwealth of Australia, 1900 Muslim League formed, 1906 Radicals make first calls for Indian independence, 1907 Amritsar massacre in India, 1919 Intensification of Indian nationalism, 1919–1947	Revolution in Russia; Tsar Nicholas II forced to issue October Manifesto, 1905 Triple Entente (Britain, Russia, France), 1914–1918 World War One, 1914–1918 Treaty of Versailles, 1919

Period (CA 1920–1990)	Africa and the Middle East	The Americas
1920	Cultural nationalism in Africa, 1920s Treaty of Lausanne recognizes Turkish Republic, 1923 Reza Shah leads Iran, 1925–1941	U.S. "consumer revolution," 1920s Stock market crash in United States; Great Depression begins, 1929
1930	African farmers organize first "cocoa holdups," 1930–1931 Iraq gains independence, 1932 Syrian-French friendship treaty, 1936	Revolutions in six South American countries, 1930 New Deal begins in United States, 1933
1940	Civil war between Arabs and Jews in Palestine; state of Israel is created, 1948 Apartheid system in South Africa, 1948–1991 Libya gains independence, 1949	Surprise attack by Japan on Pearl Harbor, 1941 United Nations established, 1945 Perón regime in Argentina, 1946–1953
1950	Egypt declared a republic; Nasser named premier, 1954 Morocco, Tunisia, Sudan, and Ghana gain independence, 1956–1957 French-British Suez invasion, 1956	Fidel Castro takes power in Cuba, 1959
1960	Mali, Nigeria, and the Congo gain independence, 1960 Biafra declares independence from Nigeria, 1967 Arab-Israeli Six-Day War, 1967	Cuban missile crisis, 1962 Military dictatorship in Brazil, 1964–1985 United States escalates war in Vietnam, 1964
1970	"Yom Kippur War," 1973 Islamic revolution in Iran, 1979 Camp David Accords, 1979	Military coup in Chile, 1973 U.S. Watergate scandal, 1974 Revolutions in Nicaragua and El Salvador, 1979
1980	Iran-Iraq War, 1980–1988 Reforms in South Africa, 1989 to present	U.S. military buildup, 1980–1988 Argentina restores civilian rule, 1983
1990	Growth of Islamic fundamentalism, 1990 to present Iraq driven from Kuwait by United States and allies, 1991 Israel and Palestinians sign peace agreement, 1993 Nelson Mandela elected president of South Africa, 1994	Canada, Mexico, and United States form free-trade area (NAFTA), 1994 Haiti establishes democratic government, 1994 Permanent extension of Treaty on the Non-Proliferation of Nuclear Weapons, 1995

East Asia	India and Southeast Asia	Europe
Kita Ikki advocates ultranationalism in Japan, 1923 Jiang Jieshi unites China, 1928	Mohandas "Mahatma" Gandhi launches nonviolent resistance campaign, 1920	Mussolini seizes power in Italy, 1922 Stalin takes power in U.S.S.R., 1927 Depths of Great Depression, 1929–1933
Japan invades China, 1931 Mao Zedong's Long March, 1934 Sino-Japanese War, 1937–1945	Mahatma Gandhi's Salt March, 1930 Japanese conquer empire in southeast Asia, 1939–1942	Hitler gains dictatorial power, 1933 Civil War in Spain, 1936–1939 Germany invades Poland, 1939 World War Two, 1939–1945
United States drops atomic bombs on Hiroshima and Nagasaki, 1945 Chinese civil war, 1945–1949; Communists win	Philippines gain independence, 1946 India (Hindu) and Pakistan (Muslim) gain independence, 1947	Yalta Conference, 1945 Marshall Plan, 1947 NATO alliance, 1949 Soviet Union and Red China sign 30-year alliance treaty, 1949
Korean War, 1950–1953 Japan begins long period of rapid economic growth, 1950 Mao Zedong announces Great Leap Forward, 1958	Vietnamese nationalists defeat French; Vietnam divided, 1954 Islamic Republic of Pakistan declared, 1956	Death of Stalin, 1953 Warsaw Pact, 1955 Revolution in Hungary, 1956 Creation of the Common Market, 1957
Sino-Soviet split becomes apparent, 1960 Great Proletarian Cultural Revolution in China, 1965–1969	Indira Gandhi prime minister of India, 1966–1977, 1980–1984	Student revolution in France, 1968 Soviet invasion of Czechoslovakia, 1968
Communist victory in Vietnam War, 1975 China pursues modernization, 1976 to present	India-Pakistan war, 1971 Chinese invade Vietnam, 1979	German Chancellor Willy Brandt's Ostpolitik, 1969–1973 Soviet invasion of Afghanistan, 1979
Japanese foreign investment surge, 1980–1992 China crushes democracy movement, 1989	Sikh nationalism in India, 1984 to present Corazón Aquino takes power in Philippines, 1986	Soviet reform under Mikhail Gorbachev, 1985–1991 Anticommunist revolutions sweep eastern Europe, 1989
Birthrates keep falling Economic growth and political repression in China, 1990 to present Japan and United States reach auto agreement, 1995	Vietnam embraces foreign investment, 1990 to present U.S. military bases closed in Philippines, 1991	Continued high unemployment, 1990 to present Soviet Union ceases to exist, 1991 Civil war in Bosnia, 1991 to present

Index

Midway Island, Battle of, 1083

Mies van der Rohe, Ludwig, 1035

Migration(s), 890–895, 893 (illus.); population pressure and, 890–891; migrant characteristics, 891–893; from Europe, 891–893; chain of, 893; Asian, 893–895; in Third World, 1189–1190. *See also* Immigration

Militant nonviolence, Gandhi and, 1007–1012

Militarism: of Hitler, 1075–1077; of Japanese, 1138

Military: under Frederick William I, 573 (illus.), 573–574; Turkish, 681; under Suleiman I, 682; Safavid, 691; of Aurangzeb, 697–698; in China, 710; Japanese samurai and, 723; power, imperialism and, 901; in Japan, 906; U.S. Civil War and, 938; draft, in Red Army, 981; U.S., in Europe, 1097; African takeovers by, 1161–1162; in Nigeria, 1162

Military government, in England, 584–585

Milk, 640

Miller, Webb, 1024

Millet, François, 624 (illus.)

Mills, *see* Cotton mills; Textiles and textile industry

Mimic Men, The, (Naipaul), 1195–1196

Mines Act (1842), 798

Ming Dynasty (China), 707; spice trade and, 520; Hong Wu and, 707; agriculture and commerce under, 707–709; hereditary occupations under, 709; land reclamation by, 709 (illus.); government of Hong Wu, 709–711; absolute power of emperor in, 710; Great Wall and, 711; Asian power of, 711–712; maritime expansion of, 711–712; decline of, 712–715; Manchu threats to, 714; imperial court of, 714–715

Mining and mining industry: labor in, 795; girls in, 797 (illus.); child workers in, 802–803; female workers in, 803 (illus.); in Brazil, 919 (illus.); Latin American, 924; in U.S. West, 942; working conditions in, 944; labor strike in, 945; in Canada, 947–948

Minorca, surrender to England, 565

Minorities: in Canada, 947; in Nigeria, 1162

Mint, in Mughal Empire, 693

Misery index, 1105 and *illus.*

Missile crisis, *see* Cuba

Missionaries: contact with China and Japan, 529–531; in China, 718, 719, 886; and imperialism, 902; African school of, 902 (illus.); in Philippines, 1021

Mississippi River, expansion toward, 929

Mita, 919

Mitterand, François, 1107

Mixed economy, in postwar France, 1097

Mobilization: in First World War, 967; impact on home front, 971–973; of Russia, 976

Modernization, 1179, 1223; in Asia, 993; nationalism and, 996; in Brazil, 1124; in Japan, 1139; in Muslim world, 1148–1149; in Third World, 1174. *See also* Industrialization

Mogadishu (city-state), 664 and *map*

Mohács, Battle of, 680

Mohammed II (Ottoman Turk), 517; cannon of, 518

Molière, 563 and *illus.*

Moltke, Helmuth von, 967

Moluccan islands, Portuguese trade with, 517

Mombasa (city-state), 664, 665

Monarchies,

Monarchies: in 17th century Europe, 557; absolute, 557; in England, 582–586; restoration in England, 585–586; enlightened, 611; destruction of French, 754. *See also* Absolutism; French Revolution

Monash, John, 954

Monet, Claude, 785, 1035

Monetary system, gold standard and, 1104

Mongols: conquest of Russia by, 574–575; Catherine the Great and, 613; destruction of Persia, 689, 690 (map); Mughals and, 691; under Yuan Dynasty, 707; Great Wall and, 711; raids on China, 711; pressure on China by, 712; Chinese defeat of, 717

Monopolies, in U.S. business, 944

Monroe, James, Indians and, 932

Monserrate, Antonio: as Mughal tutor, 693; on Akbar, 704–705 and *illus.*

Montague, Mary Wortley, 684–685 and *illus.*

Montaigne, Michel de, 546–547, 531

Montcalm, Louis, 945

Montesquieu, baron de (Secondat, Charles-Louis de), 604–605, 740, 744

Montezuma II, conquest of, 522, 523

Moon, Galileo's paintings of, 598 (illus.)

Morality: of middle classes, 853; of upper working class, 854

Moravia, 809

Morgan, J. P., 944

Morison, Samuel Eliot, on Columbus, 520

Moroccan crisis, 964

Morocco, invasion of Songhay by, 661–662

Mortality rates, *see* Death rates

Moscow: rise of, 574–578; princes of, 575; principality of, 576 (map); invasions of, 578; in 17th century, 593 (illus.); Napoleon's attack on, 763; Trans-Siberian railway and, 872; Second World War and, 1083

Mosques: in Kanem-Bornu, 663; of Safavid Empire, 692 (illus.)

Mossaddeq, Muhammad, 1152

Mosul, Safavid capture of, 691

Mothers, child rearing and, 861–862. *See also* Family; Girls; Women

Motion: Aristotle and, 595–596; Galileo and, 597–598

Mountain (French Revolutionary faction), 754–756

Mountbatten, Louis, 1141

Movement, *see* Immigration; Migration

Movies, 1038–1040; counterculture and, 1119

Mozambique, 665, 896, 1165; ANC and, 1166

Mozart, Wolfgang Amadeus, 610 (illus.)

Mr., Mrs., and Baby (Droz), 861

Mughal Empire, 679, 691–701, 697 (map); wedding celebration in, 678 (illus.); Mongols and, 691; expansion of, 692; identification with Muslim saint, 693; Persian as language of, 693–694; succession in, 696, 698; Akbar's religious policies and, 704–705

Muhammad Ali (Egypt), 888

Muhammad Reza Pahlavi, 1152

Muhammad Rimfa of Kano (Hausa king), 663

Mulattos, 915

Multinational corporations, 1217–1222

Multipolar world politics, 1207

Mummies, cult of (Peru), 524

Munch, Edvard, 1033 (illus.)

Munich, Germany, Hitler in, 1068, 1069

Murad (Mughal Empire), 693

Muscovite princes, 575. *See also* Moscow; Russia

Music: baroque, 549–550; Bach, Johann Sebastian, 550; in France, 562–563; Mozart, Wolfgang Amadeus, and, 610 (illus.); romantic movement in, 819; 20th-century, 1038; Soviet, 1108; counterculture and, 1119

Muslim League, 1141; India and, 1006

Muslims: Ottoman Turk conquests and, 517; spice trade and, 517–518; defeat in Ethiopia, 663; Hausaland and, 663; as Ottoman ruling class, 682; Shi'ite, 689, 690 and *map*; India, 691; Akbar and, 693; British battle at Khartoum and, 898; defeat at Omdurman, 899; rebellion in India, 904;

split with Hindus, 1011–1012; in India, 1141; Pakistan and, 1141–1143; in Malaysia, 1145; in Indonesia, 1148; Hausa-Fulani, 1165; Bosnia, 1209–1210

Muslim world, 1148–1153; Israel and, 1149–1153

Mussolini, Benito, 1049, 1056, 1067 (illus.); seizure of power by, 1065–1066; and fascism in Italy, 1065–1067; as Nazi ally, 1075–1076; deposed by Allies, 1083

Mustafa, Kara (Ottoman Empire), 686

My Secret Life, prostitution and, 858–859

Mysore, India, 700

Mystery religions, 1227

Mysticism, searching for, 1227–1228

Mythology, *see* Religion

N

NAACP, *see* National Association for the Advancement of Colored People

Nadir Shah, invasion of India by, 698

NAFTA, *see* North American Free Trade Agreement

Nagasaki, 531, 1210; Nobunaga and, 725; Dutch in, 727–728; atomic bombing of, 1084 and *illus.*

Nahon, Marco, 1088–1089

Naima, Mustafa, 682

Naipual, V. S., 1195–1196

Nairobi, Kenya, 1184

Nanjing (Nanking) China, 1014; reforestation in, 708; as capital, 709; commerce in, 709; Treaty of, 886; Japanese conquest of, 1019 (illus.)

Naples, Austrian intervention in, 808

Napoleon I, 759–765; French economy and, 760; Roman Catholic Church and, 760; government by, 760–761; defeat at Trafalgar, 761; crossing Alps, 761 (illus.); wars and foreign policy of, 761–765; Grand Empire of, 762 (map); revolts against, 763–765; as Emperor, 763; German Confederation of, 763; invasion of Russia by, 763; war of liberation against, 763–764; exile at Elba, 764; defeat at Waterloo, 765; Hundred Days of, 765; abdication of, 805; Egyptian invasion by, 888; Spanish throne and, 921; Portuguese Empire and, 922; Louisiana Purchase and, 929. *See also* Louis Napoleon

Napoleonic Code, 760; women's roles and, 859

Napoleonic Era, 765; Congress of Vienna after, 805. *See also* Napoleon I

Napoleon III, *see* Louis Napoleon

Nariño, Antonio, 918

Nasser, Gamal Abdel, 1151, 1161

National Assembly: in France, 747–748; Declaration of the Rights of Man and, 750; abolition of nobility by, 751; national reorganization by, 751–752; in Prussia, 828; Louis Napoleon and, 829; Paris Commune and, 868

National Association for the Advancement of Colored People (NAACP), 1117

National Congress, in India, 1009

National Convention (France), 754; war declaration by, 754; Directory and, 759

National debts, 1107

Nationalism, 811–812; economic, 790–791; democratic, 840–841; in Europe, 843; organization of society during period of, 843–857; national state and, 866–874; in Europe, 871 (illus.); in Asia, 904; in India, 905; in Latin America, 915–927; in United States, 927–945; in Canada, 945–946; in Australia, 948–954; in Balkans, 964–967; First World War and, 969; in Asia, 992, 993; in Africa, 994; in Ottoman Empire, 996–997; Turkish, 997; in Middle East, 997–999; Turkish revolution and, 999–1002; in Afghanistan, 1002–1003; in Iran, 1002–1003; in India, 1006–1012; in China, 1012–1014; in Japan, 1016–1018; in Southeast Asia, 1019–1021; in Philippines, 1021; German, 1068; of Hitler, 1074; of Soviet citizens, 1111; economic, in Latin America, 1123–1124; in South Asia, 1140–1148; in Arab world, 1152–1153; in black Africa, 1153–1160; cultural, 1156; African, 1156–1160; in West Africa, 1163 (map); in Third World, 1173. *See also* National state; Nations

Nationalist China, 1012–1014, 1133

Nationalist party, in China, 1012–1014, 1019

National Labor Relations Act, 1048

National Liberal party, in Germany, 866, 867

National liberation: wars of, 743; in Greece, 819–820

National Liberation Front (FLN), 1153

National Recovery Administration (NRA), 1048

National self-determination, 984

National Socialism: Hitler and, 1042, 1068; youth movement of, 1070

National state, 866–874; loyalty to, 866–867

National unification: in Japan, 725; in Africa, 1161–1162

National workshops, in Paris, 824

Nations: France as, 828–830; in Europe (1850–1871), 835

Nation-states, and United Nations, 1201–1205

Native Americans: Columbus and, 522; South American slaughter by Europeans, 524–526; gold and, 525 (illus.); as slave labor, 545; in Latin America, 918–919; revolt by, 925; American expansion and, 929; fate of American, 931–932; cession of lands to U.S. by, 934 (map); race in U.S. and, 941; in Canada, 945; in Mexico, 1123

Native Land Act (South Africa), 1165

Nativism, in U.S., 944

NATO, *see* North Atlantic Treaty Organization

Natural resources, *see* Resources

Natural science, *see* Science

Natural selection, 864

Naval agreement, Anglo-German, 1075

Naval arms limitation treaty (1922), 1017

Naval battles, over Mediterranean, 682. *See also* Battles; battles by name

Navarino, Battle at, 820

Navarro, Sanchez, family of, 926

Navigation: developments in, 518–519; and scientific revolution, 600

Navigation Acts (England), 584; trade and, 775

Navy: Spanish vs. English, 537; German, 964, 964 (illus.)

Nazi Germany, 1054, 1055; propaganda of, 1039–1040; mass rally in, 1057 (illus.); roots of Nazism, 1068–1069; Hitler and, 1068–1074; consolidation of, 1071–1072; storm troopers in, 1072; expansion of, and Second World War, 1074–1085; growth of, 1076 (map); Soviet pact with, 1077; defeats of, 1083–1085; defeat of, 1091

Nazi Labor Front, 1071–1072

Nazi-Soviet nonaggression pact, 1077

Negroes: use of term, 919, 939. *See also* Africans; Blacks; Slaves and slavery

Nehru, Jawaharlal, 1009, 1143, 1179

Nejd, *see* Saudi Arabia

Nelson, Horatio (Lord), Battle of Trafalgar and, 761

Neocolonialism, 1101; in Latin America, 924–926, 1123

Neo-Malthusian social scientists, 1177

NEP, *see* New Economic Policy

Nepotism, civil service and, in China, 710–711

Netherlands, 537 (map); revolt of, 534–535; Spanish (Belgium), 536; religious division of, 536–537; in 17th century, 586–589; trade of, 775; constitutional monarch in, 1097. *See also* Austrian Netherlands. *See also* Dutch; Holland